Lecture Notes in Artificial Intelligence 2256

Subseries of Lecture Notes in Computer Science
Edited by J. G. Carbonell and J. Siekmann

Lecture Notes in Computer Science
Edited by G. Goos, J. Hartmanis, and J. van Leeuwen

Lecture Notes in Artificial Intelligence 2256

Subseries of Lecture Notes in Computer Science
Edited by J. G. Carbonell and J. Siekmann

Lecture Notes in Computer Science
Edited by G. Goos, J. Hartmanis, and J. van Leeuwen

Springer
Berlin
Heidelberg
New York
Barcelona
Hong Kong
London
Milan
Paris
Tokyo

Markus Stumptner Dan Corbett
Mike Brooks (Eds.)

AI 2001: Advances in Artificial Intelligence

14th Australian Joint Conference on Artificial Intelligence
Adelaide, Australia, December 10-14, 2001
Proceedings

Volume Editors

Markus Stumptner
Dan Corbett
University of South Australia, School of Computer and Information Science
Mawson Lakes, SA, Australia 5095
E-mail: {stumptner,corbett}@cs.unisa.edu.au

Mike Brooks
University of Adelaide, Department of Computer Science
Adelaide, SA, Australia 5001
E-mail: mjb@cs.adelaide.edu.au

Cataloging-in-Publication Data applied for

Die Deutsche Bibliothek - CIP-Einheitsaufnahme

Advances in artificial intelligence : proceedings / AI 2001, 14th Australian Joint Conference on Artificial Intelligence, Adelaide, Australia, December 10 - 14, 2001. Markus Stumptner ... (ed.). - Berlin ; Heidelberg ; New York ; Barcelona ; Hong Kong ; London ; Milan ; Paris ; Tokyo : Springer, 2001
(Lecture notes in computer science ; 2256 : Lecture notes in artificial intelligence)
ISBN 3-540-42960-3

CR Subject Classification (1998): I.2, F.1, F.4.1

ISBN 3-540-42960-3 Springer-Verlag Berlin Heidelberg New York

Springer-Verlag Berlin Heidelberg New York
a member of BertelsmannSpringer Science+Business Media GmbH

http://www.springer.de

Printed in Germany

Typesetting: Camera-ready by author
Printed on acid-free paper SPIN: 10846026 06/3142 5 4 3 2 1 0

Preface

This volume contains the proceedings of AI 2001, the 14th Australian Joint Conference on Artificial Intelligence. The aim of this conference series is to support the Australian artificial intelligence community with a forum for discussion and presentation. As before, this conference not only brought together a great deal of Australian AI research, but also attracted widespread international interest.

The conference this year saw an impressive array of about 110 submitted papers from no fewer than 16 countries. Full-length versions of all submitted papers were refereed by the international program committee. As a result, these proceedings contain 55 papers not just from Australia, but also Canada, France, Germany, The Netherlands, Japan, Korea, New Zealand, and the UK and USA.

The conference also comprised a tutorial program and several workshops, and featured five invited speakers on theoretical, philosophical, and applied topics: Didier Dubois of the Université Paul Sabatier, James Hendler of the University of Maryland, Liz Sonenberg of the University of Melbourne, Peter Struss of OCC'M Software and TU Munich, and Alex Zelinsky of the Australian National University.

We extend our thanks to the members of the program committee who processed a large review workload under tight time constraints. We especially thank our host, Professor Robin King, Pro Vice Chancellor of the Division of Information Technology, Engineering, and the Environment at UniSA, for providing infrastructure and financial support. We are also grateful to the US Air Force Office of Scientific Research, Asian Office of Aerospace Research and Development, and the Commonwealth Defence Science and Technology Organisation for their financial support. Finally we would like to thank all those who contributed to the conference organization, without their help the conference could not have taken place.

December 2001

Dan Corbett
Markus Stumptner

AI 2001 Organization

Conference Chair: Dan Corbett, University of South Australia

Program Committee Co-chairs:
Mike Brooks, University of Adelaide
David Powers, Flinders University
Markus Stumptner, University of South Australia

Tutorial Chair: Alex Farkas, Tenix

Workshop Chair: Sam Mosel, Tenix

Applied AI Symposium Chair: Brian Hanisch, i2Net

Organizing Committee:
Committee Chair: Alex Farkas, Tenix
Carolyn Bellamy, University of South Australia
Richi Nayak, Queensland University of Technology
Dale Perin, University of South Australia
Sponsorship Chair: Helen Mitchard, Defence Science and Technology Organisation, Adelaide
Web Site: Anton van den Hengel, University of Adelaide

Program Committee

Grigoris Antoniou, Brisbane
Robert Dale, Sydney
Peter Deer, Adelaide
Susan George, Adelaide
Greg Gibbon, Newcastle
Ray Jarvis, Melbourne
Michael Maher, Brisbane
Mehmet Orgun, Sydney
Jeff Pelletier, Edmonton
Eric Tsui, Sydney
Peter Wallis, Melbourne
Mary-Anne Williams
Chengqi Zhang, Melbourne
Paul Compton, Sydney
John Debenham, Sydney
Peter Eklund, Brisbane
John Gero, Sydney
Achim Hoffmann, Sydney
Cara MacNish, Perth
Phan Minh Dung, Bangkok
Maurice Pagnucco, Sydney
Geoff Sutcliffe, Miami
Anton van den Hengel, Adelaide
Geoff Webb, Melbourne
Vilas Wuwongse, Bangkok

Additional Reviewers

Ayman Ammoura	Luigi Barone
John Bastian	Damien Brain
Vadin Bulitko	Samir Chopra
Jirapun Daengdej	Marc Denecker
Renee Elio	Matthias Fuchs
Bernd Groh	Thomas Havelka
Robert Holte	Ryszard Kozera
Rex Kwok	Yuefeng Li
Dekang Lin	Xudong Luo
Martin Luerssen	Wolfgang Mayer
Chris McDonald	Andrew Myers
Pavlos Peppas	Yongyuth Permpoontanalarp
Daniel Pooley	Krishna Rao
Jochen Renz	Chiaki Sakama
Stephan Schulz	Tran Cao Son
Michael Thielscher	Bruce Thomas
Quoc Bao Vo	Dominik Wieland
Franz Wotawa	Li-Yan Yuan
Dongmo Zhang	Hong Zhang
Zili Zhang	Zhi-Hua Zhou

Table of Contents

Papers

Invited Contribution

A Memetic Pareto Evolutionary Approach to Artificial Neural Networks

H.A. Abbass

University of New South Wales, School of Computer Science, ADFA Campus, Canberra, ACT 2600, Australia, h.abbass@adfa.edu.au.

Abstract. *Evolutionary Artificial Neural Networks* (EANN) have been a focus of research in the areas of *Evolutionary Algorithms* (EA) and *Artificial Neural Networks* (ANN) for the last decade. In this paper, we present an EANN approach based on pareto multi-objective optimization and differential evolution augmented with local search. We call the approach *Memetic Pareto Artificial Neural Networks* (MPANN). We show empirically that MPANN is capable to overcome the slow training of traditional EANN with equivalent or better generalization.

Keywords: neural networks, genetic algorithms

1 Introduction

Evolutionary Artificial Neural Networks (EANNs) have been a key research area for the last decade. On the one hand, methods and techniques have been developed to find better approaches for evolving *Artificial Neural Networks* and more precisely - for the sake of our paper – Multi–layer feed–forward *Artificial Neural Networks* (ANNs). On the other hand, finding a good ANNs' architecture has been an issue as well in the field of ANNs. Methods for network growing (such as Cascade Correlation [4]) and for network pruning (such as Optimal Brain Damage [14]) have been used to overcome the long process for determining a good network architecture. However, all these methods still suffer from their slow convergence and long training time. In addition, they are based on gradient–based techniques and therefore can easily stuck in a local minimum. EANNs provide a better platform for optimizing both the network performance and architecture simultaneously. Unfortunately, all of the research undertaken in the EANN literature ignores the fact that there is always a trade–off between the architecture and the generalization ability of the network. A network with more hidden units may perform better on the training set, but may not generalize well on the test set. This trade–off is a well known problem in *Optimization* known as the Multi-objective Optimization Problem (MOP).

With the trade–off between the network architecture – taken in this paper to be the number of hidden units – and the generalization error, the EANN problem is in effect a MOP. It is, therefore, natural to raise the question of why not applying a multi–objective approach to EANN.

M. Brooks, D. Corbett, and M. Stumptner (Eds.): AI 2001, LNAI 2256, pp. 1–12, 2001.

The objective of this paper is to present a *Memetic* (*ie. evolutionary algorithms* (EAs) augmented with local search [18]) Pareto Artificial Neural Networks (MPANN). The rest of the paper is organized as follows: In Section 2, background materials are covered followed by an explanation of the methods in Section 3. Results are discussed in Section 4 and conclusions are drawn in Section 5.

2 Background Materials

In this section, we introduce necessary background materials for Multi-objective Optimization, ANNs, *Differential Evolution* (DEs), Evolutionary Multi-objective, and EANN.

2.1 Multi-objective Optimization

Consider a *Multi-Objective Optimization Problem* (MOP) model as presented below:-

$$\text{Optimize } F(\boldsymbol{x})$$
$$\text{subject to: } \Omega = \{\boldsymbol{x} \in R^n | G(\boldsymbol{x}) \leq 0\}$$

Where $\boldsymbol{x}$ is a vector of decision variables $(x_1, \ldots, x_n)$ and $F(\boldsymbol{x})$ is a vector of objective functions $(f_1(\boldsymbol{x}), \ldots, f_K(\boldsymbol{x}))$. Here $f_1(\boldsymbol{x}), \ldots, f_K(\boldsymbol{x})$, are functions on R^n and Ω is a nonempty set in R^n. The vector $G(\boldsymbol{x})$ represents a set of constraints.

In MOPs, the aim is to find the optimal solution $\boldsymbol{x}^* \in \Omega$ which optimize $F(\boldsymbol{x})$. Each objective function, $f_i(\boldsymbol{x})$, is either maximization or minimization. Without any loss of generality, we assume that all objectives are to be minimized for clarity purposes. We may note that any maximization objective can be transformed to a minimization one by multiplying the former by -1.

To define the concept of non-dominated solutions in MOPs, we need to define two operators, $\ncong$ and $\precsim$ and then assume two vectors, $\boldsymbol{x}$ and $\boldsymbol{y}$. We define the first operator as $\boldsymbol{x} \ncong \boldsymbol{y}$ iff $\exists\, x_i \in \boldsymbol{x}$ and $y_i \in \boldsymbol{y}$ such that $x_i \neq y_i$. And, $\boldsymbol{x} \precsim \boldsymbol{y}$ iff $\forall\, x_i \in \boldsymbol{x}$ and $y_i \in \boldsymbol{y}, x_i \leq y_i$, and $\boldsymbol{x} \ncong \boldsymbol{y}$. The operators $\ncong$ and $\precsim$ can be seen as the "not equal to" and "less than or equal to" operators respectively, between two vectors. We can now define the concepts of local and global optimality in MOPs.

Definition 1: Neighborhood or open ball The open ball (*ie.* a neighborhood centered on $\boldsymbol{x}^*$ and defined by the Euclidean distance) $B_\delta(\boldsymbol{x}^*) = \{\boldsymbol{x} \in R^n | \, ||\boldsymbol{x} - \boldsymbol{x}^*|| < \delta\}$.

Definition 2: Local efficient (non-inferior/ pareto-optimal) solution A vector $\boldsymbol{x}^* \in \Omega$ is said to be a local efficient solution of MOP iff $\nexists\, \boldsymbol{x} \in (B_\delta(\boldsymbol{x}^*) \cap \Omega)$ such that $F(\boldsymbol{x}) \precsim F(\boldsymbol{x}^*)$ for some positive δ.

Definition 3: Global efficient (non-inferior/ pareto-optimal) solution A vector $\boldsymbol{x}^* \in \Omega$ is said to be a global efficient solution of MOP iff $\nexists\, \boldsymbol{x} \in \Omega$ such that $F(\boldsymbol{x}) \precsim F(\boldsymbol{x}^*)$.

Definition 4: Local non-dominated solution A vector $\boldsymbol{y}^* \in F(\boldsymbol{x})$ is said to be local non-dominated solution of MOP iff its projection onto the decision space, $\boldsymbol{x}^*$, is a local efficient solution of MOP.

Definition 5: Global non-dominated solution A vector $\boldsymbol{y}^* \in F(\boldsymbol{x})$ is said to be global non-dominated solution of MOP iff its projection onto the decision space, $\boldsymbol{x}^*$, is a global efficient solution of MOP.

In this paper, the term "non-dominated solution" is used as a shortcut for the term "local non-dominated solution".

2.2 Artificial Neural Networks

We may define an ANN by a graph: $G(N, A, \psi)$, where N is a set of neurons (also called nodes), A denotes the connections (also called arcs or synapses) between the neurons, and ψ represents the learning rule whereby neurons are able to adjust the strengths of their interconnections. A neuron receives its inputs (also called activation) from an external source or from other neurons in the network. It then undertakes some processing on this input and sends the result as an output. The underlying function of a neuron is called the activation function. The activation, a, is calculated as a weighted sum of the inputs to the node in addition to a constant value called the bias. The bias can be easily augmented to the input set and considered as a constant input. From herein, the following notations will be used for a single hidden layer MLP:

- I and H are the number of input and hidden units respectively.
- $\mathbf{X}^p \in \mathbf{X} = (x_1^p, x_2^p, \ldots, x_I^p), p = 1, \ldots P$, is the pth pattern in the input feature space $\mathbf{X}$ of dimension I, and P is the total number of patterns. Without any loss of generality, $\mathbf{Y}_o^p \subset \mathbf{Y_o}$ is the corresponding scalar of pattern $\mathbf{X}^p$ in the hypothesis space $\mathbf{Y_o}$.
- w_{ih} and w_{ho}, are the weights connecting input unit i, $i = 1 \ldots I$, to hidden unit h, $h = 1 \ldots H$, and hidden unit h to the output unit o (where o is assumed to be 1 in this paper) respectively.
- $\Theta_h(\mathbf{X}^p) = \sigma(a_h)$; $a_h = \sum_{i=0}^{I} w_{ih} x_i^p$, $h = 1 \ldots H$, is the hth hidden unit's output corresponding to the input pattern $\mathbf{X}^p$, where a_h is the activation of hidden unit h, and $\sigma(.)$ is the activation function that is taken in this paper to be the logistic function $\sigma(z) = \frac{1}{1+e^{-Dz}}$, with D the function's sharpness or steepness and is taken to be 1 unless it is mentioned otherwise.
- $\hat{Y}_o^p = \sigma(a_o)$; $a_o = \sum_{h=0}^{H} w_{ho} \Theta_h(\mathbf{X}^p)$ is the network output and a_o is the activation of output unit o corresponding to the input pattern $\mathbf{X}^p$.

MLPs are in essence non-parametric regression methods which approximate underlying functionality in data by minimizing a risk function. The data are presented to the network and the risk function is approximated empirically R_{emp} by summing over all data instances as follows:

$$R_{emp}(\alpha) = \sum_{p=1}^{P} (Y_o^p - \hat{Y}_o^p)^2 \tag{1}$$

The *Back-propagation algorithm* (BP), developed initially by Werbos [25] and then independently by Rumelhart group [21], is commonly used for training the network. BP uses the gradient of the empirical risk function to alter the parameter set α until the empirical risk is minimum. BP in its simple form uses a single parameter, η representing the learning rate. For a complete description for the derivations of this algorithm, see for example [8]. The algorithm can be described in the following steps:-

1. Until termination conditions are satisfied, do
   a) for each input-output pairs, $(\mathbf{X}^p, Y_o^p)$, in the training set, apply the following steps
      i. Inject the input pattern $\mathbf{X}^p$ into the network
      ii. Calculate the output, $\Theta_h(\mathbf{X}^p)$, for each hidden unit h.
      iii. Calculate the output, $\hat{Y}_o^p$, for each output unit o.
      iv. for the output unit o, calculate $r_o = \hat{Y}_o^p(1 - \hat{Y}_o^p)(Y_o^p - \hat{Y}_o^p)$ where r_o is the rate of change in the error of the output unit o.
      v. for each hidden unit h, $r_h = \Theta_h^p(1 - \Theta_h^p)w_{ho}r_o$ where r_h is the rate of change in the error of hidden unit h.
      vi. update each weight in the network using the learning rate η as follows:

$$w_{ih} \leftarrow w_{ih} + \Delta w_{ih}, \qquad \Delta w_{ih} = \eta r_j a_{ih} \tag{2}$$

$$w_{ho} \leftarrow w_{ho} + \Delta w_{ho}, \qquad \Delta w_{ho} = \eta r_k a_{ho} \tag{3}$$

2.3 Differential Evolution

Evolutionary algorithms [5] is a kind of global optimization techniques that use selection and recombination as their primary operators to tackle optimization problems. *Differential evolution* (DE) is a branch of evolutionary algorithms developed by Rainer Storn and Kenneth Price [24] for optimization problems over continuous domains. In DE, each variable is represented in the chromosome by a real number. The approach works as follows:-

1. Create an initial population of potential solutions at random, where it is guaranteed, by some repair rules, that variables' values are within their boundaries.
2. Until termination conditions are satisfied
   a) Select at random a trail individual for replacement, an individual as the main parent, and two individuals as supporting parents.
   b) With some probability, called the *crossover probability*, each variable in the main parent is perturbed by adding to it a ratio, F, of the difference between the two values of this variable in the other two supporting parents. At least one variable must be changed. This process represents the crossover operator in DE.
   c) If the resultant vector is better than the trial solution, it replaces it; otherwise the trial solution is retained in the population.
   d) go to 2 above.

2.4 Evolutionary Multi-objective

EAs for MOPs [3] can be categorized into one of three categories: plain aggregating, population–based non–Pareto and Pareto–based approaches. The plain aggregating approach combines all the objectives into one using linear combination (such as in the weighted sum method, goal programming, and goal attainment). Therefore, each run results in a single solution and many runs are needed to generate the pareto frontier. In addition, the quantification of the importance of each objective (*eg.* by setting numerical weights) is needed, which is very difficult for most practical situations. Meanwhile, optimizing all the objectives simultaneously and generating a set of alternative solutions as in population-based approaches, offers more flexibility.

There has been a number of methods in the literature for population–based non–pareto [23] and pareto [9,32,13] approaches to MOPs. More recently, we developed the *Pareto Differential Evolution* (PDE) method using *Differential Evolution* (DE) for MOPs [1]. The PDE method outperformed all previous methods on five benchmark problems.

2.5 Evolutionary Artificial Neural Networks

Over the last two decades, research into EANN has witnessed a flourish period [28,27]. Yao [29] presents a thorough review to the field with over 300 references just in the area of EANN. This may indicate that there is an extensive need for finding better ways to evolve ANN.

A major advantage to the evolutionary approach over traditional learning algorithms such as *Back-propagation* (BP) is the ability to escape a local optima. More advantages include robustness and ability to adopt in a changing environment. In the literature, research into EANN has been taking one of three approaches; evolving the weights of the network, evolving the architecture, or evolving both simultaneously.

The EANN approach uses either binary representation to evolve the weight matrix [10,11] or real [6,7,16,19]. There is not an obvious advantage of binary encoding in EANN over the real. However, with real encoding, there are more advantages including compact and natural representation.

The key problem (other than being trapped in a local minimum) with BP and other traditional training algorithms is the choice of a correct architecture (number of hidden nodes and connections). This problem has been tackled by the evolutionary approach in many studies [12,15,20,30,31]. In some of these studies, weights and architectures were evolved simultaneously.

The major disadvantage to the EANN approach is it is computationally expensive, as the evolutionary approach is normally slow. To overcome the slow convergence of the evolutionary approach to ANN, hybrid techniques were used to speed up the convergence by augmenting evolutionary algorithms with a local search technique (*ie.* memetic approach), such as BP [26].

3 The MPANN Algorithm

3.1 Representation

In deciding on an appropriate representation, we tried to choose a representation that can be used for other architectures without further modifications. Our chromosome is a class that contains one matrix Ω and one vector ρ. The matrix Ω is of dimension $(I+O) \times (H+O)$. Each element $\omega_{ij} \in \Omega$, is the weight connecting unit i with unit j, where $i = 0, \ldots, (I-1)$ is the input unit i; $i = I, \ldots, (I+O-1)$ is the output unit $(i-I)$; $j = 0, \ldots, (H-1)$ is the hidden unit j; and $j = H, \ldots, (H+O-1)$ is the output unit $(j-H)$. This representation has the following two characteristics that we are not using in the current version but can easily be incorporated in the algorithm for future work:-

1. It allows direct connection from each input to each output units (we allow more than a single output unit in our representation).
2. It allows recurrent connections between the output units and themselves.

The vector ρ is of dimension H, where $\rho_h \in \rho$ is a binary value used to indicate if hidden unit h exists in the network or not; that is, it works as a switch to turn a hidden unit on or off. The sum, $\sum_{h=0}^{H} \rho_h$, represents the actual number of hidden units in a network, where H is the maximum number of hidden units. This representation allows simultaneous training of the weights in the network and selecting a subset of hidden units.

3.2 Methods

As the name indicates in our proposed method, we have a multi–objective problem with two objectives; one is to minimize the error and the other is to minimize the number of hidden units. The pareto–frontier of the tradeoff between the two objectives will have a set of networks with different number of hidden units (note the definition of pareto-optimal solutions). However, sometimes the algorithm will return two pareto-networks with the same number of hidden units. This will only take place when the actual number of pareto-optimal solutions in the population is less than 3. Because of the condition in DE of having at least 3 parents in each generation, if there are less than three parents, the pareto optimal solutions are removed from the population and the population is re-evaluated. For example, assume that we have only 1 pareto optimal solution in the population. In this case, we need another 2. The process simply starts by removing the pareto optimal solution from the population and finding the pareto optimal solutions in the remainder of the population. Those solutions dominating the rest of the population are added to the pareto list until the number of pareto solutions in the list is 3.

Our proposed method augments the original PDE [1,22] algorithm with local search (*ie.* BP) to form the memetic approach. In initial investigations, the algorithm was quite slow and the use of local search improved its performance. MPANN consists of the following steps:

1. Create a random initial population of potential solutions. The elements of the weight matrix Ω are assigned random values according to a Gaussian distribution $N(0,1)$. The elements of the binary vector ρ are assigned the value 1 with probability 0.5 based on a randomly generated number according to a uniform distribution between $[0,1]$; otherwise 0.
2. Repeat
   a) Evaluate the individuals in the population and label those who are non-dominated.
   b) If the number of non-dominated individuals is less than 3 repeat the following until the number of non-dominated individuals is greater than or equal to 3:-
      i. Find a non-dominated solution among those who are not labelled.
      ii. Label the solution as non-dominated.
   c) Delete all dominated solutions from the population.
   d) Mark 20% of the training set as a validation set for BP.
   e) Repeat
      i. Select at random an individual as the main parent α_1, and two individuals, α_2, α_3 as supporting parents.
      ii. With some crossover probability $Uniform(0,1)$, do

$$\omega_{ih}^{child} \leftarrow \omega_{ih}^{\alpha_1} + Gaussian(0,1)(\omega_{ih}^{\alpha_2} - \omega_{ih}^{\alpha_3}) \tag{4}$$

$$\rho_h^{child} \leftarrow \begin{cases} 1\, if(\rho_h^{\alpha_1} + Gaussian(0,1)(\rho_h^{\alpha_2} - \rho_h^{\alpha_3})) \geq 0.5 \\ 0\; otherwise \end{cases} \tag{5}$$

      otherwise

$$\omega_{ih}^{child} \leftarrow \omega_{ih}^{\alpha_1} \tag{6}$$

$$\rho_h^{child} \leftarrow \rho_h^{\alpha_1} \tag{7}$$

      and with some crossover probability $Uniform(0,1)$, do

$$\omega_{ho}^{child} \leftarrow \omega_{ho}^{\alpha_1} + Gaussian(0,1)(\omega_{ho}^{\alpha_2} - \omega_{ho}^{\alpha_3}) \tag{8}$$

      otherwise

$$\omega_{ho}^{child} \leftarrow \omega_{ho}^{\alpha_1} \tag{9}$$

      where each weight in the main parent is perturbed by adding to it a ratio, $F \in Gaussian(0,1)$, of the difference between the two values of this variable in the two supporting parents. At least one variable must be changed.
      iii. Apply BP to the child.
      iv. If the child dominates the main parent, place it into the population.
   f) Until the population size is M
3. Until termination conditions are satisfied, go to 2 above.

One may note that before each generation starts, 20% of the instances in the training set are marked as a validation set for the use of BP; that is, BP will use 80% of the original training set for training and 20% for validation. Also, the termination condition in our experiments is the maximum number of epochs is reached; where one epoch is equivalent to one pass through the training set. Therefore, one iteration of BP is equivalent to one epoch since 80% of the training set is used for training and the other 20% for validation; that is, one complete pass through the original training set. After the network is trained, the chromosome changes to reflect the new weight sets.

4 Experiments

4.1 Data Sets

We have tested MPANN on two benchmark data sets; the Australian credit card assessment problem and the diabetes problem. Both data sets are available by anonymous ftp from ice.uci.edu [2]. The following is a brief description of each data set.

- **The Australian Credit Card Assessment Data Set**
  This data set contains 690 patterns with 14 attributes; 6 of them are numeric and 8 discrete (with 2 to 14 possible values). The predicted class is binary - 1 for awarding the credit and 0 for not. The problem is to assess applications for credit cards [17].
- **The Diabetes Data Set**
  This data set has 768 patterns; 500 belonging to the first class and 268 to the second. It contains 8 attributes. The objective is to test if a patient has a diabetes or not. The classification problem is difficult as the class value is a binarized form of another attribute that is highly indicative of a certain type of diabetes without having a one-to-one correspondence with the medical condition of being diabetic [17].

4.2 Experimental Setup

To be consistent with the literature [17], the Australian credit card assessment data set is divided into 10 folds and the Diabetes data set into 12 folds where class distribution is maintained in each fold. One–leave–out cross–validation is used where we run the algorithm with 9 (11) out of the 10 (12) folds for each data set then we test with the remaining one. We vary the crossover probability between 0 to 1 with an increment of 0.1. The maximum number of epochs is set to 2000, the population size 25, the learning rate for BP 0.003, the maximum number of hidden units is set to 10, and the number of epochs for BP is set to 5.

4.3 Results

The average of the pareto networks with the best generalization and the corresponding number of hidden units in each fold are being calculated along with the standard deviations as shown in Table 1. It is interesting to see the small standard deviations for the test error in both data sets, which indicates consistency and stability of the method.

Table 1. The average and standard deviations of the pareto network with the best generalization (smallest test error) in each run

Data set	Error	Number of hidden units
Australian Credit Card	0.136 ± 0.045	5.000 ± 1.943
Diabetes	0.251 ± 0.062	6.6 ± 1.505

In Figure 1, the average test and training errors corresponding to the best generalized network in each fold is plotted against each of the eleventh crossover probabilities. In Figure 1 (left), with crossover 0.1 and upward, the test error is always smaller than the training error, which indicates better generalization. However, the degree of this generalization varied across the different crossover probabilities. The best performance occurs with crossover probability 0.3, which indicates that 30% of the weights, on the average, in each parent change. This is quite important as it entails that the building blocks in MPANN is effective; otherwise a better performance would have occurred with the maximum crossover probability. We may note here that crossover in DE is in effect a guided mutation operator. In Figure 1 (right), it is also apparent that an average crossover probability of 0.8 resulted in the best generalization ability. Very high or low crossover probabilities are not as good.

In summary, the best performances for the Australian credit card and Diabetes data sets are 0.136 ± 0.045 and 0.251 ± 0.062 respectively and occur with crossover probabilities 0.3 and 0.8 respectively.

4.4 Comparisons and Discussions

We compare our results against 23 algorithms tested by Michie *et al.* [17]. These algorithms can be categorized into decision trees (CART, IndCART, NewID, AC^2, Baytree, Cal5, and C4.5), rule–based methods (CN2, and ITrule), neural networks (Backprob, Kohonen, LVQ, RBF, and DIPOL92), and statistical algorithms (Discrim, Quadisc, Logdisc, SMART, ALLOC80, k-NN, CASTLE, NaiveBay, and Default). For a complete description of these algorithms, the reader may refer to [17].

In Tables 2 and 3, we find that MPANN is equivalent or better than BP and comparable to the others. However, we notice here that MPANN also optimized

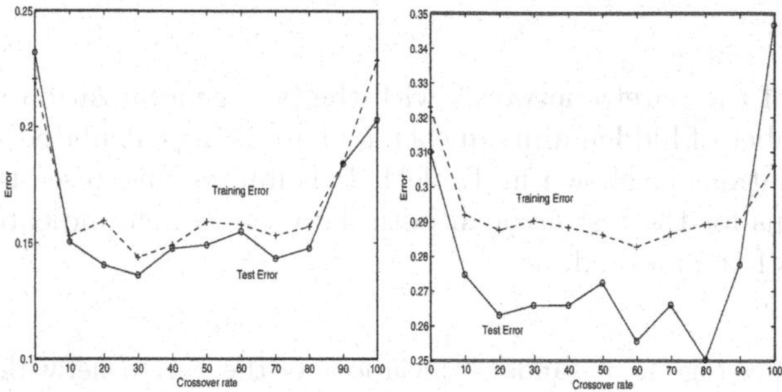

Fig. 1. *The average training and test error for the Australian Credit Card (on the left) and Diabetes data sets (on the right) obtained by each crossover probability.*

Table 2. Comparing MPANN against 23 traditional methods in terms of the average generalization error for the Australian Credit Card data set.

Algorithm	Error Rate	Algorithm	Error Rate	Algorithm	Error Rate	Algorithm	Error Rate
MPANN	0.136	CASTLE	0.148	NaiveBay	0.151	Default	0.440
CART	0.145	IndCART	0.152	NewID	0.181	AC^2	0.181
Baytree	0.171	Cal5	0.131	C4.5	0.155	CN2	0.204
ITrule	0.137	Backprob	0.154	Kohonen	Fail	LVQ	0.197
RBF	0.145	DIPOL92	0.141	Discrim	0.141	Quadisc	0.207
Logdisc	0.141	SMART	0.158	ALLOC80	0.201	k-NN	0.181

its architecture while optimizing its generalization ability. Therefore, in terms of the amount of computations, it is by far faster than BP as we simultaneously optimize the architecture and generalization error. In addition, the total number of epochs used is small compared to the corresponding number of epochs needed by BP.

5 Conclusion

In this paper, we presented a new evolutionary multi–objective approach to artificial neural networks. We showed empirically that the proposed approach outperformed traditional Back-propagation and had comparable results to 23 classification algorithms. For future work, we will evaluate the performance of the proposed method on regression problems and test the scalability of the evolutionary approach.

Acknowledgement. The author would like to thank Xin Yao, Bob Mckay, and Ruhul Sarker for their insightful comments while discussing an initial idea with

Table 3. Comparing MPANN against 23 traditional methods in terms of the average generalization error for the Diabetes data set.

Algorithm	Error Rate	Algorithm	Error Rate	Algorithm	Error Rate	Algorithm	Error Rate
MPANN	0.251	CASTLE	0.258	NaiveBay	0.262	Default	0.350
CART	0.255	IndCART	0.271	NewID	0.289	AC^2	0.276
Baytree	0.271	Cal5	0.250	C4.5	0.270	CN2	0.289
ITrule	0.245	Backprob	0.248	Kohonen	0.273	LVQ	0.272
RBF	0.243	DIPOL92	0.224	Discrim	0.225	Quadisc	0.262
Logdisc	0.223	SMART	0.232	ALLOC80	0.301	k-NN	0.324

them. This work is supported with ADFA Special Research Grants TERM6 2001 DOD02 ZCOM Z2844.

References

1. H.A. Abbass, R. Sarker, and C. Newton. A pareto differential evolution approach to vector optimisation problems. *Congress on Evolutionary Computation*, 2:971–978, 2001.
2. C.L. Blake and C.J. Merz. UCI repository of machine learning databases, http://www.ics.uci.edu/~mlearn/mlrepository.html. *University of California, Irvine, Dept. of Information and Computer Sciences*, 1998.
3. C.A. Coello. A comprehensive survey of evolutionary-based multiobjective optimization techniques. *Knowledge and Information Systems*, 1(3):269–308, 1999.
4. S. Fahlman and C. Lebiere. The cascade correlation learning architecture. Technical Report CMU-CW-90-100, Canegle Mellon University, Pittsburgh, PA, 1990.
5. D.B. Fogel. *Evolutionary Computation: towards a new philosophy of machine intelligence.* IEEE Press, New York, NY, 1995.
6. D.B. Fogel, E.C. Wasson, and E.M. Boughton. Evolving neural networks for detecting breast cancer. *Cancer letters*, 96(1):49–53, 1995.
7. D.B. Fogel, E.C. Wasson, and V.W. Porto. A step toward computer-assisted mammography using evolutionary programming and neural networks. *Cancer letters*, 119(1):93, 1997.
8. S. Haykin. *Neural networks - a comprehensive foundation.* Printice Hall, USA, 2 edition, 1999.
9. J. Horn, N. Nafpliotis, and D.E. Goldberg. A niched pareto genetic algorithm for multiobjective optimization. *Proceedings of the First IEEE Conference on Evolutionary Computation*, 1:82–87, 1994.
10. D.J. Janson and J.F. Frenzel. Application of genetic algorithms to the training of higher order neural networks. *Systems Engineering*, 2:272–276, 1992.
11. D.J. Janson and J.F. Frenzel. Training product unit neural networks with genetic algorithms. *IEEE Expert*, 8(5):26–33, 1993.
12. H. Kitano. Designing neural networks using genetic algorithms with graph generation system. *Complex Systems*, 4(4):461–476, 1990.
13. J. Knowles and D. Corne. Approximating the nondominated front using the pareto archived evolution strategy. *Evolutionary Computation*, 8(2):149–172, 2000.

14. Y. LeCun, J.J. Denker, and S.A. Solla. Optimal brain damage. In D. Touretzky, editor, *Advances in Neural Information Processing Systems*. Morgan Kaufmann, 1990.
15. V. Maniezzo. Genetic evolution of the topology and weight distribution of neural networks. *IEEE Transactions on Neural Networks*, 5(1):39–53, 1994.
16. F. Menczer and D. Parisi. Evidence of hyperplanes in the genetic learning of neural networks. *Biological Cybernetics*, 66:283–289, 1992.
17. D. Michie, D.J. Spiegelhalter, and C.C. Taylor. *Machine learning, neural and statistical classification*. Ellis Horwood, 1994.
18. P. Moscato. Memetic algorithms: a short introduction. In D. Corne, M. Dorigo, and F. Glover, editors, *New ideas in optimization*, pages 219–234. McGraw-Hill, 1999.
19. V.W. Porto, D.B. Fogel, and L.J. Fogel. Alternative neural network training methods. *IEEE Expert*, 10(3):16–22, 1995.
20. J.C.F. Pujol and R. Poli. Evolving the topology and the weights of neural networks using a dual representation. *Applied Intelligence*, 8(1):73–84, 1998.
21. D.E. Rumelhart, G.E. Hinton, and R.J. Williams. Learning internal representations by error propagation. In J.L. McClelland D.E. Rumelhart and the PDP Research Group Eds, editors, *Parallel Distributed Processing: Explorations in the Microstructure of Cognition., Foundations, 1, 318,*. MIT Press Cambridge, 1986.
22. R. Sarker, H.A. Abbass, and C. Newton. Solving multiobjective optimization problems using evolutionary algorithm. *The International Conference on Computational Intelligence for Modelling, Control and Automation (CIMCA'2001), Los Vegas, USA*, 2001.
23. J.D. Schaffer. Multiple objective optimization with vector evaluated genetic algorithms. *Genetic Algorithms and their Applications: Proceedings of the First International Conference on Genetic Algorithms*, pages 93–100, 1985.
24. R. Storn and K. Price. Differential evolution: a simple and efficient adaptive scheme for global optimization over continuous spaces. Technical Report TR-95-012, International Computer Science Institute, Berkeley, 1995.
25. P. Werbos. *Beyond regression: new tools for prediction and analysis in the behavioral sciences.* PhD thesis, Harvard University, 1974.
26. W. Yan, Z. Zhu, and R. Hu. Hybrid genetic/bp algorithm and its application for radar target classification. *Proceedings of the 1997 IEEE National Aerospace and Electronics Conference, NAECON*, pages 981–984, 1997.
27. X. Yao. Evolutionary artificial neural networks. *International Journal of Neural Systems*, 4(5):203–222, 1993.
28. X. Yao. A review of evolutionary artificial neural networks. *International Journal of Intelligent Systems*, 8(4):529–567, 1993.
29. X. Yao. Evolving artificial neural networks. *Proceedings of the IEEE*, 87(9):1423–1447, 1999.
30. X. Yao and Y. Liu. Making use of population information in evolutionary artificial neural networks. *IEEE Trans. on Systems, Man, and Cybernetics, Part B: Cybernetics*, 28(3):417–425, 1998.
31. X. Yao and Y. Liu. Towards designing artificial neural networks by evolution. *Applied Mathematics and Computation*, 91(1):83–90, 1998.
32. E. Zitzler and L. Thiele. Multiobjective evolutionary algorithms: A comparative case study and the strength pareto approach. *IEEE Transactions on Evolutionary Computation*, 3(4):257–271, 1999.

Relating Defeasible and Default Logic

Grigoris Antoniou [1] and David Billington [2]

[1] Dept of Computer Science, University of Bremen, P.O. Box 330440, D-28334, Germany
ga@tzi.de

[2] School of Computing and I.T., Griffith University, Nathan, QLD 4111, Australia
db@cit.gu.edu.au

Abstract. Defeasible reasoning is a simple but efficient approach to nonmonotonic reasoning that has recently attracted considerable interest and that has found various applications. Defeasible logic and its variants are an important family of defeasible reasoning methods. So far no relationship has been established between defeasible logic and mainstream nonmonotonic reasoning approaches.
In this paper we will compare an ambiguity propagating defeasible logic with default logic. In fact the two logics take rather contrary approaches: defeasible logic takes a directly deductive approach, whereas default logic is based on alternative possible world views, called extensions. Computational complexity results suggest that default logics are more expressive than defeasible logics. This paper answers the opposite direction: an ambiguity propagating defeasible logic can be directly embedded into default logic.

1 Introduction

Defeasible reasoning is a nonmonotonic reasoning [11] approach in which the gaps due to incomplete information are closed through the use of defeasible rules that are usually appropriate. Defeasible logics were introduced and developed by Nute over several years [13]. These logics perform defeasible reasoning, where a conclusion supported by a rule might be overturned by the effect of another rule. Roughly, a proposition p can be defeasibly proved only when a rule supports it, and it has been demonstrated that no rule supports $\neg p$. These logics also have a monotonic reasoning component, and a priority on rules. One advantage of Nute's design was that it was aimed at supporting efficient reasoning, and in our work we follow that philosophy.

This family of approaches has recently attracted considerable interest. Apart from implementability, its use in various application domains has been advocated, including the modelling of regulations and business rules [12, 8, 2], modelling of contracts [15], legal reasoning [14] and electronic commerce [7].

An interesting question is the relationship to more mainstream nonmonotonic approaches such as default logic [16]. [10] shows that defeasible logic has linear complexity. In contrast to that the complexity of default logic is known to be high even in simple cases [9, 6]. Therefore we cannot expect default logic to be naturally embedded in defeasible logics (under the natural representation of normal defaults as defeasible rules).

The opposite question, that is whether defeasible logics can be embedded into default logics, is answered in this paper. This result cannot be expected for the "standard"

M. Brooks, D. Corbett, and M. Stumptner (Eds.): AI 2001, LNAI 2256, pp. 13–24, 2001.

defeasible logic [4]. It is easily seen that defeasible logic is ambiguity blocking [17], while default logic propagates ambiguity.

Recently a family of defeasible logics [3] was introduced, among them an ambiguity propagating defeasible logic. In this paper we show that this logic can be fully embedded in default logic under the natural representation of defeasible rules as normal default rules, and strict rules as defaults without justifications. If D is a defeasible theory and $T(D)$ is its translation into a default theory, this paper shows that if a literal is defeasibly provable in D, then it is sceptically provable in $T(D)$ (that is, it is included in all extensions of $T(D)$).

The establishment of relationships between different approaches is important: each approach may benefit from work done on the other; the combination of strengths can lead to new, better approaches; and the assimilation of knowledge is supported. Based on the results of this paper, defeasible logic can be viewed as an efficient approximation of default logic for certain classes of default theories.

2 Defeasible Logic

2.1 A Language for Defeasible Reasoning

A defeasible theory (a knowledge base in defeasible logic) consists of three different kinds of knowledge: strict rules, defeasible rules, and a superiority relation. (Fuller versions of defeasible logic also have facts and defeaters, but [4] shows that they can be simulated by the other ingredients).

Strict rules are rules in the classical sense: whenever the premises are indisputable (e.g. facts) then so is the conclusion. An example of a strict rule is "Emus are birds". Written formally:

$$emu(X) \rightarrow bird(X).$$

Defeasible rules are rules that can be defeated by contrary evidence. An example of such a rule is "Birds typically fly"; written formally:

$$bird(X) \Rightarrow flies(X).$$

The idea is that if we know that something is a bird, then we may conclude that it flies, *unless there is other, not inferior, evidence suggesting that it may not fly.*

The *superiority relation* among rules is used to define priorities among rules, that is, where one rule may override the conclusion of another rule. For example, given the defeasible rules

$$\begin{aligned} r: &\quad bird(X) \Rightarrow flies(X) \\ r': &\ brokenWing(X) \Rightarrow \neg flies(X) \end{aligned}$$

which contradict one another, no conclusive decision can be made about whether a bird with broken wings can fly. But if we introduce a superiority relation $>$ with $r' > r$, with the intended meaning that r' is strictly stronger than r, then we can indeed conclude that the bird cannot fly.

It is worth noting that, in defeasible logic, priorities are *local* in the following sense: Two rules are considered to be competing with one another only if they have complementary heads. Thus, since the superiority relation is used to resolve conflicts among competing rules, it is only used to compare rules with complementary heads; the information $r > r'$ for rules r, r' without complementary heads may be part of the superiority relation, but has no effect on the proof theory.

2.2 Formal Definition

In this paper we restrict attention to essentially propositional defeasible logic. Rules with free variables are interpreted as rule schemas, that is, as the set of all ground instances; in such cases we assume that the Herbrand universe is finite. We assume that the reader is familiar with the notation and basic notions of propositional logic. If q is a literal, $\sim q$ denotes the complementary literal (if q is a positive literal p then $\sim q$ is $\neg p$; and if q is $\neg p$, then $\sim q$ is p).

Rules are defined over a *language* (or *signature*) Σ, the set of propositions (atoms) and labels that may be used in the rule.

A *rule* $r : A(r) \hookrightarrow C(r)$ consists of its unique *label* r, its *antecedent* $A(r)$ ($A(r)$ may be omitted if it is the empty set) which is a finite set of literals, an arrow $\hookrightarrow$ (which is a placeholder for concrete arrows to be introduced in a moment), and its *head* (or *consequent*) $C(r)$ which is a literal. In writing rules we omit set notation for antecedents and sometimes we omit the label when it is not relevant for the context. There are two kinds of rules, each represented by a different arrow. Strict rules use $\rightarrow$ and defeasible rules use $\Rightarrow$.

Given a set R of rules, we denote the set of all strict rules in R by R_s, and the set of defeasible rules in R by R_d. $R[q]$ denotes the set of rules in R with consequent q.

A *superiority relation on* R is a relation $>$ on R. When $r_1 > r_2$, then r_1 is called *superior* to r_2, and r_2 *inferior* to r_1. Intuitively, $r_1 > r_2$ expresses that r_1 overrules r_2, should both rules be applicable. $>$ must be acyclic (that is, its transitive closure must be irreflexive).

A *defeasible theory* D is a pair $(R, >)$ where R a finite set of rules, and $>$ a superiority relation on R.

2.3 An Ambiguity Propagating Defeasible Logic

Here we discuss a defeasible logic that was first introduced in [3]. It is a logic that propagates ambiguity. A preference for ambiguity blocking or ambiguity propagating behaviour is one of the properties of non-monotonic inheritance nets over which intuitions can clash [17]. Ambiguity propagation results in fewer conclusions being drawn, which might make it preferable when the cost of an incorrect conclusion is high.

A *conclusion* of a defeasible theory D is a tagged literal. A conclusion has one of the following six forms:

- $+\Delta q$, which is intended to mean that the literal q is definitely provable, using only strict rules.

- $-\Delta q$, which is intended to mean that q is provably not strictly provable (finite failure).
- $+\partial q$, which is intended to mean that q is defeasibly provable in D.
- $-\partial q$ which is intended to mean that we have proved that q is not defeasibly provable in D.
- $+\int q$, which is supposed to mean that q is supported (what this means will be explained soon).
- $-\int q$, which is supposed to mean that q is provably not supported.

Provability is defined below. It is based on the concept of a *derivation* (or *proof*) in $D = (R, >)$. A derivation is a finite sequence $P = P(1), \ldots, P(n)$ of tagged literals satisfying the following conditions. The conditions are essentially inference rules phrased as conditions on proofs. $P(1..i)$ denotes the initial part of the sequence P of length i.

$+\Delta$: If $P(i+1) = +\Delta q$ then
$\exists r \in R_s[q]\ \forall a \in A(r) : +\Delta a \in P(1..i)$

That means, to prove $+\Delta q$ we need to establish a proof for q using strict rules only. This is a deduction in the classical sense – no proofs for the negation of q need to be considered (in contrast to defeasible provability below, where opposing chains of reasoning must be taken into account, too).

$-\Delta$: If $P(i+1) = -\Delta q$ then
$\forall r \in R_s[q]\ \exists a \in A(r) : -\Delta a \in P(1..i)$

The definition of $-\Delta$ is the so-called *strong negation* of $+\Delta$. $-\Delta q$ $[-\partial q]$ means that we have a proof that $+\Delta q$ $[+\partial q]$ cannot be proved.

$+\partial$: If $P(i+1) = +\partial q$ then either
(1) $+\Delta q \in P(1..i)$ or
(2) (2.1) $\exists r \in R[q]\ \forall a \in A(r) : +\partial a \in P(1..i)$ and
(2.2) $-\Delta \sim q \in P(1..i)$ and
(2.3) $\forall s \in R[\sim q]$ either
(2.3.1) $\exists a \in A(s) : -\int a \in P(1..i)$ or
(2.3.2) $\exists t \in R[q]$ such that
$\forall a \in A(t) : +\partial a \in P(1..i)$ and $t > s$

$-\partial$: If $P(i+1) = -\partial q$ then
(1) $-\Delta q \in P(1..i)$ and
(2) (2.1) $\forall r \in R[q]\ \exists a \in A(r) : -\partial a \in P(1..i)$ or
(2.2) $+\Delta \sim q \in P(1..i)$ or
(2.3) $\exists s \in R[\sim q]$ such that
(2.3.1) $\forall a \in A(s) : +\int a \in P(1..i)$ and
(2.3.2) $\forall t \in R[q]$ either
$\exists a \in A(t) : -\partial a \in P(1..i)$ or
not $t > s$

Let us explain this definition. To show that q is provable defeasibly we have two choices: (1) We show that q is already definitely provable; or (2) we need to argue using the defeasible part of D as well. In particular, we require that there must be a strict or defeasible rule with head q which can be applied (2.1). But now we need to consider possible "counterattacks", that is, reasoning chains in support of $\sim q$. To be more specific: to prove q defeasibly we must show that $\sim q$ is not definitely provable (2.2). Also (2.3) we must consider the set of all rules which are not known to be inapplicable and which have head $\sim q$. Essentially each such rule s attacks the conclusion q. For q to be provable, each such rule s must be counterattacked by a rule t with head q with the following properties: (i) t must be applicable at this point, and (ii) t must be stronger than (i.e. superior to) s. Thus each attack on the conclusion q must be counterattacked by a stronger rule.

The only issue we did not discuss was when the attacking rules s should be disregarded because they are inapplicable. One way is to ignore a rule s if one of its antecedants is not defeasibly provable. However this approach leads to the blocking of ambiguity, as shown in [3]. To propagate ambiguity we make attacks on potential conclusions easier, or stated another way, we make it more difficult for attacking rules s to be ignored. This will only happen if at least one of the antecedents is not even *supported*.

Next we define the inference conditions for support.

$+\int$: If $P(i+1) = +\int q$ then either
    $+\Delta q \in P(1..i)$ or
    $\exists r \in R[q]$ such that
        $\forall a \in A(r) : +\int a \in P(1..i)$, and
        $\forall s \in R[\sim q]$ either
            $\exists a \in A(s) : -\partial a \in P(1..i)$ or
            not $s > r$

$-\int$: If $P(i+1) = -\int q$ then
    $-\Delta q \in P(1..i)$ and
    $\forall r \in R[q]$ either
        $\exists a \in A(r) : -\int a \in P(1..i)$, or
        $\exists s \in R[\sim q]$ such that
            $\forall a \in A(s) : +\partial a \in P(1..i)$ and
            $s > r$

The elements of a derivation are called *lines* of the derivation. We say that a tagged literal L is *provable* in $D = (R, >)$, denoted by $D \vdash L$, iff there is a derivation in D such that L is a line of P.

Example 1. Consider the defeasible theory

$\Rightarrow p$
$\Rightarrow \neg p$
$\Rightarrow q$
$p \Rightarrow \neg q$

Neither p nor $\neg p$ is defeasibly provable, however they are both supported. In an ambiguity blocking defeasible logic the last rule would be disregarded because we can prove $-\partial p$. However, in the definition we just gave, although the last rule is not applicable, its prerequisite is supported, thus the rule has to be counterattacked if we wish to derive $+\partial q$. However the superiority relation is empty, so no counterattack is possible and we can derive $-\partial q$. In this example no positive defeasible conclusions can be drawn.

3 Default Logic with Priorities

A *default* δ has the form $\frac{\varphi:\psi_1,\ldots,\psi_n}{\chi}$ with closed formulae $\varphi, \psi_1, \ldots, \psi_n, \chi$. φ is the *prerequisite* $pre(\delta)$, $\psi_1, \ldots, \psi_n$ the *justifications* $just(\delta)$, and χ the *consequent* $cons(\delta)$ of δ. A default is called *normal* if $just(\delta) = \{cons(\delta)\}$.

A *default theory* T is a pair (W, Def) consisting of a set of formulae W (the set of *facts*) and a countable set Def of defaults.

Let $\delta = \frac{\varphi:\psi_1,\ldots,\psi_n}{\chi}$ be a default, and E a deductively closed set of formulae. We say that δ *is applicable to* E iff $\varphi \in E$, and $\neg\psi_1, \ldots, \neg\psi_n \notin E$.

Let $\Pi = (\delta_0, \delta_1, \delta_2, \ldots)$ be a finite or infinite sequence of defaults from Def without multiple occurrences (modelling an application order of defaults from Def). We denote by $\Pi[k]$ the initial segment of Π of length k, provided the length of Π is at least k.

- $In(\Pi) = Th(W \cup \{cons(\delta) \mid \delta$ occurs in $\Pi\})$, where Th denotes the deductive closure.
- $Out(\Pi) = \{\neg\psi \mid \psi \in just(\delta), \delta$ occurs in $\Pi\}$.

Π is called a *process of* T iff δ_k is applicable to $In(\Pi[k])$, for every k such that δ_k occurs in Π. Π is *successful* iff $In(\Pi) \cap Out(\Pi) = \emptyset$, otherwise it is *failed*. Π is *closed* iff every default that is applicable to $In(\Pi)$ already occurs in Π. For normal default theories all processes are successful.

[1] shows that Reiter's original definition [16] of extensions is equivalent to the following one: A set of formulae E is an *extension* of a default theory T iff there is a closed and successful process Π of T such that $E = In(\Pi)$.

Now we consider the addition of priorities to default logic. We will concentrate on static priorities, and will adopt a presentation similar to that of [5].

A *prioritized default theory* is a triple $T = (W, Def, >)$ where W is a set of facts, Def a countable set of defaults, and $>$ an acyclic relation on Def.

Consider a total order $\gg$ on Def that expands $>$ (in the sense that it contains more pairs). We define a process $\Pi_{\gg} = (\delta_0, \delta_1, \ldots)$ as follows: δ_i is the $\gg$ largest default in $Def - \Pi[i]$ that is applicable to $In(\Pi[i])$ (slightly abusing notation we have used processes here as sets). Note that, by definition, $\Pi_{\gg}$ is a closed process because the selection of the next default is fair (see [1]).

A set of formulas E is called an *extension* of T iff $E = In(\Pi_{\gg})$, where $\gg$ is a total order on Def that extends $>$, and for which the process $\Pi_{\gg}$ is successful.

This definition extends definitions such as [5] which usually assume that all defaults are normal. The definition can be viewed as a two-step construction:

- Compute all extensions, disregarding priorities.
- Filter out those extensions that can only be obtained using a total order that violates $>$.

4 Connections

First we define the natural translation of a defeasible theory $D = (R, >)$ into default logic. We define a prioritized default theory $T(D) = (\emptyset, \bigcup_{r \in R} def(r), >_d)$ as follows.

A defeasible rule r

$$\{p_1, \ldots, p_n\} \Rightarrow p$$

is translated into the following default:

$$def_d(r) = \frac{p_1 \wedge \ldots \wedge p_n : p}{p}.$$

$def(r) = \{def_d(r)\}$. This is the natural translation of a defeasible rule into a normal default.

It would appear natural to represent a strict rule r

$$\{p_1, \ldots, p_n\} \rightarrow p$$

as the default

$$\frac{p_1 \wedge \ldots \wedge p_n :}{p}.$$

However this translation does not work as the following example demonstrates.

Example 2. Consider the defeasible theory consisting of the rules

$\Rightarrow p$
$p \rightarrow q$
$\Rightarrow \neg q$

Here p is defeasibly provable, but neither q nor $\neg q$. There is one rule to support each conclusion, but there are no priorities to resolve the conflict (and strict rules are not deemed to be superior to defeasible rules). However, in the translation into default logic

$$\frac{true : p}{p} \quad \frac{p :}{q} \quad \frac{true : \neg q}{\neg q}$$

there is only one extension, $Th(\{p, q\})$, so q is sceptically provable.

A close analysis of the inference conditions in defeasible logic reveals that strict rules play a dual role: on one hand they can be combined with other strict rules to prove literals strictly. On the other hand they may combined with other strict and at least one defeasible rule to prove literals defeasibly, but then strict rules are treated exactly like defeasible rules.

This point is analysed in [4]. There it is shown that every defeasible theory can be equivalently transformed into one where the two roles are separated. We could then apply the natural translation into default logic, as outlined above, and get the desired result. Instead, in this paper we take a slightly different path: We maintain the generality of defeasible theories, but make the translation slightly more complicated.

A strict rule r, as above, leads to three different defaults:

$$def_s(r) = \frac{p_1' \wedge \ldots \wedge p_n' :}{p'}$$

$$new(p) = \frac{p' :}{p}$$

$$def_d(r) = \frac{p_1 \wedge \ldots \wedge p_n : p}{p}$$

Hereby $'$ is an operator that generates new, pairwise distinct names. We have $def(r) = \{def_d(r), def_s(r), new(p)\}$.

Finally we define

$$def_d(r) >_d def_d(s) \Longleftrightarrow r > s.$$

There is no priority information regarding the $def_s(.)$ and $new(.)$ defaults.

Example 2 (continued) We reconsider the defeasible theory D

$\Rightarrow p$
$p \rightarrow q$
$\Rightarrow \neg q$

The translation into default logic $T(D)$ consists of the defaults:

$$\frac{true : p}{p} \quad \frac{p : q}{q} \quad \frac{p' :}{q'} \quad \frac{q' :}{q} \quad \frac{true : \neg q}{\neg q}$$

There are two extensions, $Th(\{p, q\})$ and $Th(\{p, \neg q\})$, so only p is sceptically provable in $T(D)$. This outcome corresponds to p being the only literal that is defeasibly provable in D.

Lemma 1.

(a) If $D \vdash +\Delta p$ then $p' \in E$ for all extensions E of $T(D)$.
(b) If $D \vdash -\Delta p$ then $p' \notin E$, for all extensions E of $T(D)$.

Proof: The proof goes by induction on the length of a derivation in defeasible logic. We only show (a) here, (b) can be proven in the same way.

Consider a proof P, and suppose $P(i+1) = +\Delta q$. Then, by definition, there is a rule $r \in R_s[q]$ such that for all $a \in A(r)$, $+\Delta a \in P(1..i)$.

By induction hypothesis, a' is included in all extensions E of $T(D)$, for all $a \in A(r)$. Consider an arbitrary $E = In(\Pi_\gg)$ for a total order $\gg$ that includes $>_d$ and generates a successful $\Pi_\gg$. Then a' is included in $In(\Pi_\gg)$, for all $a \in A(r)$. But then the prerequisite of $def_s(r)$ is in $In(\Pi_\gg)$, so $def_s(r)$ is applicable to $In(\Pi_\gg)$, and $def_s(r)$ occurs in $\Pi_\gg$ because $\Pi_\gg$ is closed. Thus the consequent of $def_s(r)$, p', is included in $In(\Pi_\gg)$. □

Lemma 2.

(a) If $D \vdash -\int p$ then $p \notin E$, for all extensions E of $T(D)$.
(b) If $D \vdash +\partial p$ then $p \in E$ for all extensions E of $T(D)$.

Proof: We use simultaneous induction for (a) and (b) on the length of a derivation P.

(a): Let $P(i+1) = -\int p$.

Suppose there is a total order $\gg$ on the defaults of $T(D)$ which extends $>_d$, generates a successful process $\Pi_\gg$, and $p \in In(\Pi_\gg)$. We will show that these assumptions lead to a contradiction.

First we note that $p \in In(\Pi_\gg)$ and that there are neither facts nor disjunctions in $T(D)$. Therefore there must be a default in $\Pi_\gg$ with consequent p.

One possibility is that a default $new(p)$ occurs in $\Pi_\gg$. However, by the $-\int$ condition, we have $-\Delta p \in P(1..i)$. Then, by Lemma 1, $p' \notin E$ for all extensions E of $T(D)$. So $p' \notin In(\Pi_\gg)$. But then $new(p)$ is not applicable to $In(\Pi_\gg)$, so it can't occur in $\Pi_\gg$, which gives us a contradiction.

The other possibility is that $def_d(r)$ occurs in $\Pi_\gg$, for some rule $r \in R[p]$. Consider the first such default that appears in $\Pi_\gg$, and suppose it occurs in the $k+1$st position (that is, $def_d(r)$ is applicable to $In(\Pi_\gg[k])$). Then $def_d(r) \gg \delta$ for all defaults δ that are applicable to $In(\Pi_\gg[k])$ and not yet in $\Pi_\gg[k]$. That means, because $\gg$ extends $>_d$, that

$$def_d(r) \not< def_d(s) \qquad (*)$$

for all rules $s \in R[\sim p]$ such that $def_d(s)$ is applicable to $In(\Pi_\gg[k])$.

However, from the condition $-\int$ and the assumption $P(i+1) = -\int p$, we know that either there is $a \in A(r)$ such that $-\int a \in P(1..i)$. Then, by induction hypothesis, $a \notin In(\Pi_\gg)$, so $pre(def_d(r)) \notin In(\Pi_\gg)$, which gives a contradiction to the assumption that $def_d(r)$ occurs in the process $\Pi_\gg$.

The other case of the $-\int$ condition is that there is a rule $s \in R[\sim p]$ such that $s > r$ and $+\partial a \in P(1..i)$, for all $a \in A(s)$. By definition, we have

$$def_d(s) > def_d(r).$$

Moreover, by induction hypothesis (part (b)), $a \in In(\Pi_\gg)$, for all $a \in A(s)$. Thus $pre(def_d(s)) \in In(\Pi_\gg)$.

By definition of a derivation in defeasible logic, the derivation of an antecedent a cannot depend on p (otherwise the derivation of a and p would fail due to looping). By construction of $T(D)$, that means that $pre(def_d(s)) \in In(\Pi_\gg[k])$. Moreover $In(\Pi_\gg[k])$ is consistent with the justification of $def_d(s)$, namely $\sim p$, because $def_d(r)$ was assumed to be the first default with consequent p that occurs in $\Pi_\gg$.

Thus $def_d(s)$ has been established to be applicable to $In(\Pi_\gg[k])$, and $def_d(s) > def_d(r)$. So either $def_d(s)$ already occurs in $\Pi_\gg[k]$, which contradicts the applicability of $def_d(r)$ $(pre(def_d(r)) =\sim just(def_d(s)))$; or $def_d(s)$ does not occur in $\Pi_\gg[k]$, which contradicts $(*)$.

Part (b) is proven in a similar way. □

It is worth noting that a similar result does not hold for $+\int$ and $-\partial$. For example, one might think that if $+\int p$ is provable then p is included in at least one extension. That is not the case.

Example 3. Consider the theory

$\Rightarrow p$
$\Rightarrow \neg p$
$\{p, \neg p\} \Rightarrow q$

Here q is supported because both p and $\neg p$ are supported, but q is not included in any extension of the corresponding default theory (the prerequisite $p \wedge \neg p$ of the third default cannot be proved).

The following theorem summarizes the main result.

Theorem 1. *If a literal p is defeasibly provable in D, then p is included in all extensions of* $T(D)$.

The converse is not true, as the following example shows.

Example 4. Consider the defeasible theory

$\Rightarrow p$
$\Rightarrow \neg p$
$p \Rightarrow q$
$\neg p \Rightarrow q$

In defeasible logic, q is not defeasibly provable because neither p nor $\neg p$ are defeasibly provable. However, the default logic translation

$$\frac{true : p}{p} \quad \frac{true : \neg p}{\neg p} \quad \frac{p : q}{q} \quad \frac{\neg p : q}{q}$$

has two extensions, $Th(\{p, q\})$ and $Th(\{\neg p, q\})$, so q is included in all extensions.

Example 5. Consider the defeasible theory

$r_1 : \Rightarrow p$
$r_2 : \Rightarrow p$
$r_3 : \Rightarrow \neg p$
$r_4 : \Rightarrow \neg p$
$r_1 > r_3$
$r_2 > r_4$

p is defeasibly provable. Now consider the translation into default logic.

$$def_d(r_1) = \frac{true : p}{p} \quad def_d(r_2) = \frac{true : p}{p}$$

$$def_d(r_3) = \frac{true : \neg p}{\neg p} \quad def_d(r_4) = \frac{true : \neg p}{\neg p}$$

$$def_d(r_1) >_d def_d(r_3) \quad def_d(r_2) >_d def_d(r_4)$$

Six total orders are possible which do not violate the relation $>_d$:

$$def_d(r_1) \gg def_d(r_2) \gg def_d(r_3) \gg def_d(r_4)$$
$$def_d(r_1) \gg def_d(r_3) \gg def_d(r_2) \gg def_d(r_4)$$
$$def_d(r_1) \gg def_d(r_3) \gg def_d(r_4) \gg def_d(r_2)$$
$$def_d(r_3) \gg def_d(r_4) \gg def_d(r_1) \gg def_d(r_2)$$
$$def_d(r_3) \gg def_d(r_1) \gg def_d(r_4) \gg def_d(r_2)$$
$$def_d(r_3) \gg def_d(r_1) \gg def_d(r_2) \gg def_d(r_4)$$

It is easy to see that each such arrangement leads to an extension $Th(\{p\})$.

Example 1 (continued)

The translation into default logic consists of the defaults

$$\frac{true : p}{p} \quad \frac{true : \neg p}{\neg p} \quad \frac{true : q}{q} \quad \frac{p : \neg q}{\neg q}$$

There are three extensions, $Th(\{p, q\})$, $Th(\{p, \neg q\})$ and $Th(\{\neg p, q\})$. Thus none of $p, \neg p, q, \neg q$ is included in all extensions. This outcome is consistent with our previous result that the original defeasible theory does not have any positive defeasible conclusion. This example demonstrates the ambiguity propagating nature of default logic, and justifies our selection of an ambiguity propagating defeasible logic to conduct the comparison.

5 Conclusions

This paper established for the first time a relationship between default logic and a defeasible logic. In particular, it showed how an ambiguity propagating defeasible logic can be embedded into default logic. Based on our results defeasible logic can be viewed as an efficient approximation of classes of default theories.

Acknowledgements

This research was supported by the Australian Research Council.

References

[1] G. Antoniou. *Nonmonotonic Reasoning*. MIT Press 1997.

[2] G. Antoniou, D. Billington and M.J. Maher. On the analysis of regulations using defeasible rules. In *Proc. 32nd Hawaii International Conference on Systems Science*, 1999.

[3] G. Antoniou, D. Billington, G. Governatori and M.J. Maher. A flexible framework for defeasible logics. In *Proc. 17th American National Conference on Artificial Intelligence (AAAI-2000)*, 405-41.

[4] G. Antoniou, D. Billington, G. Governatori and M.J. Maher. Representation results for defeasible logic. *ACM Transactions on Computational Logic* (in print)

[5] G. Brewka. Reasoning About Priorities in Default Logic. In *Proc. AAAI-94*, 940-945.

[6] G. Gottlob 1992. Complexity results for nonmonotonic logics. *Journal of Logic and Computation* 2: 397–425.

[7] G. Governatori, A. ter Hofstede and P. Oaks. Defeasible Logic for Automated Negotiation. In *Proc. Fifth CollECTeR Conference on Electronic Commerce*, Brisbane 2000.

[8] B.N. Grosof, Y. Labrou and H.Y. Chan. A Declarative Approach to Business Rules in Contracts: Courteous Logic Programs in XML. In *Proc. 1st ACM Conference on Electronic Commerce (EC-99)*, ACM Press 1999.

[9] H.A. Kautz and B. Selman. Hard problems for simple default theories. *Artificial Intelligence* 28 (1991): 243-279.

[10] M.J. Maher, A. Rock, G. Antoniou, D. Billington and T. Miller. Efficient Defeasible Reasoning Systems. In *Proc. 12th IEEE International Conference on Tools with Artificial Intelligence (ICTAI 2000)*, IEEE 2000, 384-392.

[11] V. Marek and M. Truszczynski. *Nonmonotonic Logic*, Springer 1993.

[12] L. Morgenstern. 1998. Inheritance Comes of Age: Applying Nonmonotonic Techniques to Problems in Industry. *Artificial Intelligence*, 103 (1998): 1–34.

[13] D. Nute. 1994. Defeasible Logic. In D.M. Gabbay, C.J. Hogger and J.A. Robinson (eds.): *Handbook of Logic in Artificial Intelligence and Logic Programming Vol. 3*, Oxford University Press, 353–395.

[14] H. Prakken. 1997. *Logical Tools for Modelling Legal Argument: A Study of Defeasible Reasoning in Law.* Kluwer Academic Publishers.

[15] D.M. Reeves, B.N. Grosof, M.P. Wellman, and H.Y. Chan. Towards a Declarative Language for Negotiating Executable Contracts, *Proceedings of the AAAI-99 Workshop on Artificial Intelligence in Electronic Commerce (AIEC-99)*, AAAI Press / MIT Press, 1999.

[16] R. Reiter. A Logic for Default Reasoning. *Artificial Intelligence* 13(1980): 81–132.

[17] D.D. Touretzky, J.F. Horty and R.H. Thomason. 1987. A Clash of Intuitions: The Current State of Nonmonotonic Multiple Inheritance Systems. In *Proc. IJCAI-87*, 476–482, Morgan Kaufmann, 1987.

Resolving Minsky's Paradox : The d-Dimensional Normal Distribution Case

Luis Rueda[1] and B. John Oommen[2]

[1] School of Computer Science, Carleton University, 1125 Colonel By Dr., Ottawa, ON, K1S 5B6, Canada. Partially supported by Departamento de Informática, Universidad Nacional de San Juan, Argentina.
lrueda@scs.carleton.ca

[2] Senior Member, IEEE. School of Computer Science, Carleton University, 1125 Colonel By Dr., Ottawa, ON, K1S 5B6, Canada. Partially supported by NSERC, the National Science and Engineering Research Council of Canada.
oommen@scs.carleton.ca

Abstract. We consider the well-studied Pattern Recognition (PR) problem of designing linear classifiers. When dealing with normally distributed classes, it is well known that the optimal Bayes classifier is linear only when the covariance matrices are equal. This was the only known condition for discriminant linearity. In a previous work, we presented the theoretical framework for optimal *pairwise* linear classifiers for two-dimensional normally distributed random vectors. We derived the necessary and sufficient conditions that the distributions have to satisfy so as to yield the *optimal* linear classifier as a pair of straight lines.
In this paper we extend the previous work to d-dimensional normally distributed random vectors. We provide the necessary and sufficient conditions needed so that the optimal Bayes classifier is a pair of hyperplanes. Various scenarios have been considered including one which resolves the multi-dimensional *Minsky's paradox* for the perceptron. We have also provided some three dimensional examples for all the cases, and tested the classification accuracy of the relevant pairwise linear classifier that we found. In all the cases, these linear classifiers achieve very good performance.

1 Introduction

The problem of finding linear classifiers has been the study of many researchers in the field of Pattern Recognition (PR). Linear classifiers are very important because of their simplicity when it concerns implementation, and their classification speed. Various schemes to yield linear classifiers are reported in the literature such as *Fisher's approach* [2,7,18], the *perceptron algorithm* (the basis of the back propagation *neural network* learning algorithms) [6,8,11,12], *piecewise recognition models* [9], *random search optimization* [10], and *removal classification structures* [1]. All of these approaches suffer from the lack of optimality, and thus, although they do determine linear discriminant functions, the classifier is not optimal.

M. Brooks, D. Corbett, and M. Stumptner (Eds.): AI 2001, LNAI 2256, pp. 25–36, 2001.

Apart from the results reported in [16, 17], in *statistical* PR, the Bayesian linear classification for normally distributed classes involves a single case. This traditional case is when the covariance matrices are equal [4, 13]. In this case, the classifier is a single straight line (or a hyperplane in the d-dimensional case) completely specified by a first-order equation.

In [16, 17], we showed that although the general classifier for two dimensional normally distributed random vectors is a second-degree polynomial, this polynomial degenerates to be either a single straight line or a pair of straight lines. Thus, as opposed to the traditional results, we showed that the classifier can be linear even when the covariance matrices are not equal. In this case, the discriminant function is a pair of first-order equations, which are factors of the second-order polynomial (i.e. the discriminant function). When the factors are equal, the discriminant function is given by a single straight line, which corresponds to the traditional case when the covariance matrices are equal.

In this paper, we extend these conditions for d-dimensional normal random vectors, where $d > 2$. We assume that the features of an object to be recognized are represented as a d-dimensional vector which is an ordered tuple $X = [x_1 \ldots x_d]^T$ characterized by a probability distribution function. We deal only with the case in which these random vectors have a jointly normal distribution, where class ω_i has a mean M_i and covariance matrix Σ_i, $i = 1, 2$.

Without loss of generality, we assume that the classes ω_1 and ω_2 have the same *a priori* probability, 0.5, in which case, the discriminant function is given by:

$$\log \frac{|\Sigma_2|}{|\Sigma_1|} - (X - M_1)^T \Sigma_1^{-1} (X - M_1) + (X - M_2)^T \Sigma_2^{-1} (X - M_2) = 0 \,. \quad (1)$$

When $\Sigma_1 = \Sigma_2$, the discriminant function is linear [3, 19]. For the case when Σ_1 and Σ_2 are arbitrary, the classifier results in a general equation of second degree which results in the discriminant being a hyperparaboloid, a hyperellipsoid, a hypersphere, a hyperboloid, or a pair of hyperplanes. This latter case is the focus of our present study.

The results presented here have been rigorously tested. In particular, we present some empirical results for the cases in which the optimal Bayes classifier is a pair of hyperplanes. It is worth mentioning that we tested the case of Minsky's paradox on randomly generated samples, and we have found that the accuracy is very high even though the classes are significantly overlapping.

The formal proof of a few theorems are omitted in the interest of brevity. They are found in the unabridged version of the paper [14] and in [15], and can be made available to the reader.

2 Linear Discriminants for Diagonalized Classes: The 2-D Case

The concept of *diagonalization* is quite fundamental to our study. Diagonalization is the process of transforming a space by performing linear and whitening transformations [3]. Consider a normally distributed random vector, $\mathbf{X}$, with any mean vector and covariance matrix. By performing diagonalization, $\mathbf{X}$ can be transformed into another normally distributed random vector, $\mathbf{Z}$, whose covariance is the identity matrix. This can be easily generalized to incorporate what is called "simultaneous diagonalization". By performing this process, two normally distributed random vectors, $\mathbf{X}_1$ and $\mathbf{X}_2$, can be transformed into two other normally distributed random vectors, $\mathbf{Z}_1$ and $\mathbf{Z}_2$, whose covariance matrices are the identity and a diagonal matrix, respectively. A more in-depth discussion of diagonalization can be found in [3, 18], and is omitted here as it is assumed to be fairly elementary. We discuss below the conditions for the mean vectors and covariance matrices of simultaneously diagonalized vectors in which the Bayes optimal classifier is pairwise linear.

In [16, 17], we presented the necessary and sufficient conditions required so that the optimal classifier is a pair of straight lines, for the two dimensional space. Using these results, we present here the cases for the d-dimensional case in which the optimal Bayes classifier is a pair of hyperplanes.

Since we repeatedly refer to the work of [16, 17], we state (without proof) the relevant results below.

One of the cases in which we evaluated the possibility of finding a pair of straight lines as the optimal classifier is when we have *inequality constraints.* This case is discussed below.

Theorem 1. *Let $\mathbf{X}_1 \sim N(M_1, \Sigma_1)$ and $\mathbf{X}_2 \sim N(M_2, \Sigma_2)$ be two normally distributed random vectors with parameters of the form:*

$$M_1 = \begin{bmatrix} r \\ s \end{bmatrix}, \; M_2 = \begin{bmatrix} -r \\ -s \end{bmatrix}, \; \Sigma_1 = \begin{bmatrix} 1 & 0 \\ 0 & 1 \end{bmatrix}, \; \text{and } \Sigma_2 = \begin{bmatrix} a^{-1} & 0 \\ 0 & b^{-1} \end{bmatrix}. \tag{2}$$

There exist real numbers, r and s, such that the optimal Bayes classifier is a pair of straight lines if one of the following conditions is satisfied:

(a) $0 < a < 1$ *and* $b > 1$,
(b) $a > 1$ *and* $0 < b < 1$.

Moreover, if

$$a(1-b)r^2 + b(1-a)s^2 - \frac{1}{4}(ab - a - b + 1)\log ab = 0\,, \tag{3}$$

the optimal Bayes classifier is a pair of straight lines. □

Another case evaluated in [16, 17] is when we have *equality constraints.* In this case, the optimal Bayes classifier is a pair of parallel straight lines. In particular, when $\Sigma_1 = \Sigma_2$, these lines are coincident.

Theorem 2. *Let $\mathbf{X}_1 \sim N(M_1, \Sigma_1)$ and $\mathbf{X}_2 \sim N(M_2, \Sigma_2)$ be two normally distributed random vectors with parameters of the form of (2). The optimal Bayes classifier is a pair of straight lines if one of the following conditions is satisfied:*

(a) $a = 1,\ b \neq 1$, *and* $r = 0$,
(b) $a \neq 1,\ b = 1$, *and* $s = 0$.
The classifier is a single straight line if:
(c) $a = 1$ *and* $b = 1$. □

3 Multi-dimensional Pairwise Hyperplane Discriminants

Let us consider now the more general case for $d > 2$. Using the results mentioned above, we derive the necessary and sufficient conditions for a pairwise-linear optimal Bayes classifier. From the inequality constraints (a) and (b) of Theorem 1, we state and prove that it is not possible to find the optimal Bayes classifier as a pair of hyperplanes for these conditions when $d > 2$. We modify the notation marginally. We use the symbols $(a_1^{-1}, a_2^{-1}, \ldots, a_d^{-1})$ to synonymously refer to the marginal variances $(\sigma_1^2, \sigma_2^2, \ldots, \sigma_d^2)$.

Theorem 3. *Let* $\mathbf{X}_1 \sim N(M_1, \Sigma_1)$ *and* $\mathbf{X}_2 \sim N(M_2, \Sigma_2)$ *be two normally distributed random vectors, such that*

$$M_1 = -M_2 = \begin{bmatrix} m_1 \\ m_2 \\ \vdots \\ m_d \end{bmatrix}, \Sigma_1 = I, \text{ and } \Sigma_2 = \begin{bmatrix} a_1^{-1} & 0 & \ldots & 0 \\ 0 & a_2^{-1} & \ldots & 0 \\ \vdots & \vdots & \ddots & \vdots \\ 0 & 0 & \ldots & a_d^{-1} \end{bmatrix}, \tag{4}$$

where $a_i \neq 1$, $i = 1, \ldots, d$. *There are no real numbers* m_i, $i = 1, \ldots, d$, *such that the optimal Bayes classifier is a pair of hyperplanes.*

The proof of Theorem 3 can be found in the unabridged version of this paper, [14], and in [15]. This proof is achieved by checking if there is an optimal pairwise linear classifier for all the pairs of axes. This is not possible since, if the condition has to be satisfied when the first element on the diagonal is less than unity, the second one must be greater than unity. Consequently, there is no chance for a third element to satisfy this condition in a pairwise manner, in conjunction with the first two elements. □

Using the results of Theorem 2, we now analyze the possibility of finding the optimal pairwise linear classifiers for the d-dimensional case when some of the entries in Σ_2 are unity.

Theorem 4. *Let* $\mathbf{X}_1 \sim N(M_1, \Sigma_1)$ *and* $\mathbf{X}_2 \sim N(M_2, \Sigma_2)$ *be two normally distributed random vectors with parameters of the form of (4). If there exists* i *such that* $a_i \neq 1$, *and* $a_j = 1$, $m_j = 0$, *for* $j = 1, \ldots, d$, $i \neq j$, *then the optimal Bayes classifier is a pair of hyperplanes.*

The proof of Theorem 4 can be found in [14,15]. □

We now combine the results of Theorems 1 and 2, and state more general necessary and sufficient conditions to find a pair of hyperplanes as the optimal

Bayes classifier. We achieve this using the inequality and equality constraints of these theorems

The main difference between Theorem 4 and the theorem given below is that in the former, all the elements but one of the diagonal of Σ_2 are equal to unity. In the theorem presented below, there are two elements of the diagonal of Σ_2 which are not equal to unity, and therefore they must satisfy (3) and either condition (a) or (b) of Theorem 1.

Theorem 5. *Let* $\mathbf{X}_1 \sim N(M_1, \Sigma_1)$ *and* $\mathbf{X}_2 \sim N(M_2, \Sigma_2)$ *be two normally distributed random vectors with parameters of the form of (4). The optimal Bayes classifier is a pair of hyperplanes if there exist* i *and* j *such that any of the following conditions are satisfied:*

(a) $0 < a_i < 1$, $a_j > 1$, $a_k = 1$, $m_k = 0$, *for all* $k = 1, \ldots, d$, $k \neq i$, $k \neq j$, *with*

$$a_i(1-a_j)m_i^2 + a_j(1-a_i)m_j^2 - \frac{1}{4}(a_ia_j - a_i - a_j + 1)\log a_ia_j = 0 \ . \quad (5)$$

(b) $a_i \neq 1$, $a_j = 1$, $m_j = 0$, *for all* $j \neq i$.
(c) $a_i = 1$, *for all* $i = 1, \ldots, d$.

The proof of Theorem 5 can be found in [14, 15]. □

Note that the final case considered in condition (c) corresponds to the traditional case in which the optimal Bayes classifier is a single hyperplane when both the covariance matrices are identical.

4 Linear Discriminants with Different Means

In [16], we have shown that given two normally distributed random vectors, $\mathbf{X}_1$ and $\mathbf{X}_2$, with mean vectors and covariance matrices of the form:

$$M_1 = \begin{bmatrix} r \\ s \end{bmatrix}, M_2 = \begin{bmatrix} -r \\ -s \end{bmatrix}, \Sigma_1 = \begin{bmatrix} a^{-1} & 0 \\ 0 & b^{-1} \end{bmatrix}, \text{ and } \Sigma_2 = \begin{bmatrix} b^{-1} & 0 \\ 0 & a^{-1} \end{bmatrix}, \quad (6)$$

the optimal Bayes classifier is a pair of straight lines when $r^2 = s^2$, where a and b are any positive real numbers. The discriminant function for this case is given by:

$$a(x-r)^2 + b(y-s)^2 - b(x+r)^2 - a(y+s)^2 = 0 \ . \quad (7)$$

We consider now the more general case for $d > 2$. We are interested in finding the conditions that guarantee a pairwise linear discriminant function. This is given in Theorem 6 below.

Theorem 6. *Let* $X_1 \sim N(M_1, \Sigma_1)$ *and* $X_2 \sim N(M_2, \Sigma_2)$ *be two normal random vectors such that*

$$M_1 = [m_1 \ldots m_i \ldots m_j \ldots m_d]^T \ , \ M_2 = [m_1 \ldots - m_i \ldots - m_j \ldots m_d]^T \ , \tag{8}$$

$$\Sigma_1 = \begin{bmatrix} a_1^{-1} & 0 & 0 & 0 & 0 & 0 & 0 \\ 0 & \ddots & 0 & 0 & 0 & 0 & 0 \\ 0 & 0 & a_i^{-1} & 0 & 0 & 0 & 0 \\ 0 & 0 & 0 & \ddots & 0 & 0 & 0 \\ 0 & 0 & 0 & 0 & a_j^{-1} & 0 & 0 \\ 0 & 0 & 0 & 0 & 0 & \ddots & 0 \\ 0 & 0 & 0 & 0 & 0 & 0 & a_d^{-1} \end{bmatrix} , \Sigma_2 = \begin{bmatrix} a_1^{-1} & 0 & 0 & 0 & 0 & 0 & 0 \\ 0 & \ddots & 0 & 0 & 0 & 0 & 0 \\ 0 & 0 & a_j^{-1} & 0 & 0 & 0 & 0 \\ 0 & 0 & 0 & \ddots & 0 & 0 & 0 \\ 0 & 0 & 0 & 0 & a_i^{-1} & 0 & 0 \\ 0 & 0 & 0 & 0 & 0 & \ddots & 0 \\ 0 & 0 & 0 & 0 & 0 & 0 & a_d^{-1} \end{bmatrix} , \tag{9}$$

The optimal classifier, obtained by Bayes classification, is a pair of hyperplanes when

$$m_i^2 = m_j^2 \ . \tag{10}$$

The proof of Theorem 6 is quite involved and can be found in [14, 15]. It is omitted here for the sake of brevity. □

Theorem 6 can be interpreted geometrically as follows. Whenever we have two covariance matrices that differ only in two elements of their diagonal; and whenever the two elements in the second covariance matrix are a permutation of the same rows in the first matrix, if the mean vectors differ only in these two elements, the resulting discriminant function is a pair of hyperplanes.

Indeed, by performing a projection of the space in the x_i and x_j axes, we observe that the discriminant takes on exactly the same shape as that which is obtained from the distribution given in (6). Thus effectively, we obtain a pair of straight lines in the two dimensional space from the projection of the pair of hyperplanes in the d-dimensional space.

5 Linear Discriminants with Equal Means

We consider now a particular instance of the problem discussed in Section 4, which leads to the resolution of the generalization of the d-dimensional Minsky's paradox. In this case, the covariance matrices have the form of (9), but the mean vectors are the same for both classes. We shall show now that, with these parameters, it is always possible to find a pair of hyperplanes, which resolves Minsky's paradox in the most general case.

Theorem 7. *Let* $\mathbf{X}_1 \sim N(M_1, \Sigma_1)$ *and* $\mathbf{X}_2 \sim N(M_2, \Sigma_2)$ *be two normal random vectors, where* $M_1 = M_2 = [m_1, \ldots, m_d]^T$, *and* Σ_1 *and* Σ_2 *have the form of (9). The optimal classifier, obtained by Bayes classification, is a pair of hyperplanes.*

Proof. From Theorem 6, we know that when the mean vectors and covariance matrices have the form of (8) and (9), respectively, then the optimal Bayes classifier is a pair of hyperplanes if $m_i^2 = m_j^2$. Since $M_1 = M_2$, then $m_i^2 = m_j^2$, for $j = 1, \ldots, d$, $i \neq j$. Hence the optimal Bayes classifier is a pair of hyperplanes. The theorem is thus proved. □

6 Simulation Results

In order to test the accuracy of the pairwise linear discriminants and to verify the results derived here, we have performed some simulations for the different cases discussed above. We have chosen the dimension $d = 3$, since it is easy to visualize and plot the corresponding hyperplanes. In all the simulations, we trained our classifier using 100 randomly generated training samples (which were three dimensional vectors from the corresponding classes). Using the *maximum likelihood* estimation method [18], we then approximated the mean vectors and covariance matrices for each of the three cases.

We considered two classes, ω_1 and ω_2, which are represented by two normal random vectors, $\mathbf{X}_1 \sim N(M_1, \Sigma_1)$ and $\mathbf{X}_2 \sim N(M_2, \Sigma_2)$, respectively. For each class, we used two sets of 100 normal random points to test the accuracy of the classifiers.

In all the cases, to display the distribution, we plotted the ellipsoid of equiprobable points instead of the training points. This was because the plot of the three dimensional points caused too much cluttering, making the shape of the classes and the discriminants indistinguishable.

6.1 Linear Discriminants for Two Diagonalized Classes

In the first test, DD-1, we considered the pairwise linear discriminant function for two diagonalized classes. These classes are normally distributed with covariance matrices being the identity matrix and another matrix in which two elements of the diagonal are not equal to unity and the remaining are unity. This is indeed, the case in which the optimal Bayes classifier is shown to be a pair of hyperplanes, stated and proven in Theorem 5. The following mean vectors and covariance matrices were estimated from 100 training samples to yield the respective classifier:

$$\textbf{DD-1:}\ M_1 = M_2 \approx \begin{bmatrix} 1.037 \\ 2.049 \\ 0 \end{bmatrix}, \Sigma_1 \approx I, \Sigma_2 \approx \begin{bmatrix} .481 & 0 & 0 \\ 0 & 3.131 & 0 \\ 0 & 0 & 1 \end{bmatrix}$$

The plot of the ellipsoid simulating the points and the linear discriminant hyperplanes in the three dimensional space are depicted in Fig. 1. The accuracy of the classifier was 96% for ω_1 and 97% for ω_2. The power of the scheme is obvious!

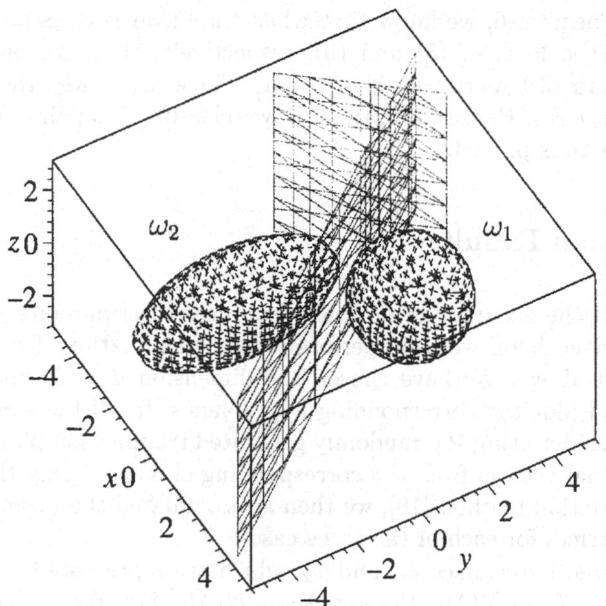

Fig. 1. Example of pairwise linear discriminant for diagonalized normally distributed classes. This example corresponds to the data set DD-1.

6.2 Pairwise Linear Discriminant with Different Means

To demonstrate the properties of the classifier satisfying the conditions of Theorem 6, we considered the pairwise linear discriminant with different means. In this case, the diagonal covariance matrices differ only in two elements. These two elements in the first matrix have switched positions in the second covariance matrix. The remaining elements are identical in both covariance matrices. The mean vectors and covariance matrices estimated from 100 training samples are given below.

$$\textbf{DM-1: } M_1 \approx \begin{bmatrix} 1.54 \\ 1.54 \\ 1.98 \end{bmatrix}, M_2 \approx \begin{bmatrix} -1.54 \\ -1.54 \\ 1.98 \end{bmatrix}, \Sigma_1 \approx \begin{bmatrix} .38 & 0 & 0 \\ 0 & 2.12 & 0 \\ 0 & 0 & .48 \end{bmatrix}, \Sigma_2 \approx \begin{bmatrix} 2.12 & 0 & 0 \\ 0 & .38 & 0 \\ 0 & 0 & .48 \end{bmatrix}$$

Using these parameters, the pairwise linear classifier was derived. The plot of the ellipsoid simulating the points and the linear discriminant hyperplanes are shown in Fig. 2. With this classifier, we obtained an accuracy of 94% for ω_1 and 97% for ω_2.

6.3 Pairwise Linear Discriminant with Equal Means

We also tested our scheme for the case of the pairwise linear classifier with equal means, EM-1, for the generalized multi-dimensional Minsky's Paradox. This is

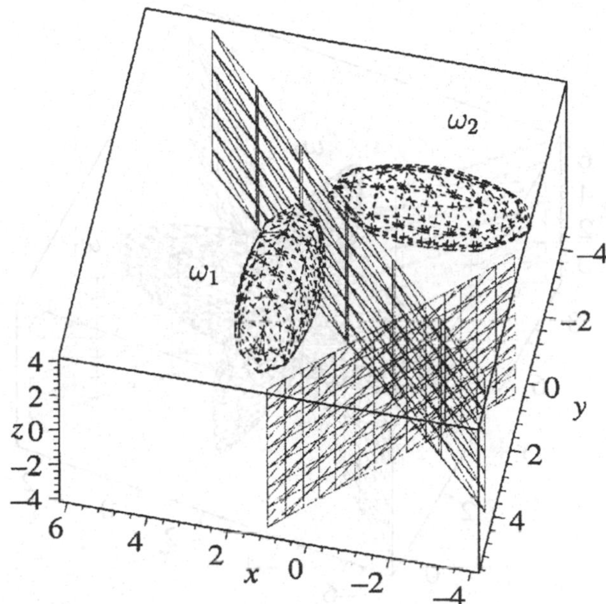

Fig. 2. Example of pairwise linear discriminant with different means for the case described in Section 4. These classes corresponds to the data set DM-1.

the case in which we have coincident mean vectors, but covariance matrices as in the the case of DM-1. Two classes having parameters like these are proven in Theorem 7 to be optimally classified by a pair of hyperplanes. We obtained the following estimated mean vectors and covariance matrices from 100 training samples:

$$\textbf{EM-1:}\ M_1 = M_2 \approx \begin{bmatrix} -1.95 \\ 4.067 \\ 1.988 \end{bmatrix}, \Sigma_1 \approx \begin{bmatrix} 5.327 & 0 & 0 \\ 0 & .171 & 0 \\ 0 & 0 & .238 \end{bmatrix}, \Sigma_2 \approx \begin{bmatrix} .171 & 0 & 0 \\ 0 & 5.327 & 0 \\ 0 & 0 & .238 \end{bmatrix}$$

The shape of the overlapping classes and the linear discriminant function from these estimates are given in Fig. 3. We evaluated the classifier with 100 randomly generated test points, and the accuracy was 82% for ω_1 and 85% for ω_2. Observe that such a linear classifier is not possible using any of the reported traditional methods.

6.4 Analysis of Accuracy

Finally, we analyze the accuracy of the classifiers for the different cases discussed above. The accuracy of classification for the three cases is given in Table 1. The first column corresponds to the test case. The second and third columns represent the percentage of correctly classified points belonging to ω_1 and ω_2, respectively. Observe that the accuracy of DD-1 is very high. This case corresponds to the

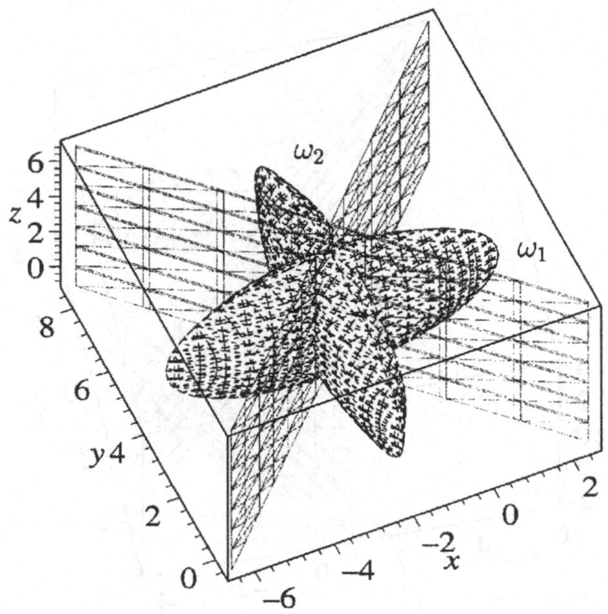

Fig. 3. Example of pairwise linear discriminant with equal means for the case described in Section 5. The data set is EM-1. This resolves the generalized multi-dimensional Minsky's paradox.

pairwise linear discriminant when dealing with covariance matrices being the identity and another diagonal matrix in which two elements are not equal to unity, as shown in Theorem 5. The accuracy of the case in which the means are different and the covariance matrices as given in (8) and (9) (third row) is still very high. The fourth row corresponds to the case where the means are identical, referred to as EM-1. The accuracy is lower than that of the other cases but still very high, even though the classes overlap and the discriminant function is pairwise linear. This demonstrates the power of our scheme to resolve Minsky's Paradox in three dimensions !

Table 1. Accuracy of classification of 100 three dimensional random test points generated with the parameters of the examples presented above. The accuracy is given in percentage of points correctly classified.

Example	Accuracy for ω_1	Accuracy for ω_2
DD-1	96 %	97 %
DM-1	94 %	97 %
EM-1	83 %	88 %

7 Conclusions

In this paper we have extended the theoretical framework of obtaining optimal pairwise linear classifiers for normally distributed classes. We have shown that it is still possible to find the optimal classifier as a pair of hyperplanes for more than two dimensions.

We have determined the necessary and sufficient conditions for an optimal pairwise linear classifier when the covariance matrices are the identity and a diagonal matrix. In this case, we have formally shown that it is possible to find the optimal linear classifier by satisfying certain conditions specified in the planar projections of the various components.

In the second case, we have dealt with normally distributed classes having different mean vectors and with some special forms of covariance matrices. When the covariance matrices differ only in two elements of the diagonal, and these elements are inverted in positions in the second covariance matrix, it has been shown that the optimal classifier is a pair of hyperplanes only if the mean vectors differ in the two elements of these positions. The conditions for this have been formalized too.

The last case that we have considered is the generalized Minsky's paradox for multi-dimensional normally distributed random vectors. By a formal procedure, we have found that when the classes are overlapping and the mean vectors are coincident, under certain conditions on the covariance matrices, the optimal classifier is a pair of hyperplanes. This resolves the multi-dimensional Minsky's paradox.

We have also provided some examples for each of the cases discussed above, and we have tested our classifier on some three dimensional normally distributed features. The classification accuracy obtained is very high, which is reasonable as the classifier is optimal in the Bayesian context. The degree of accuracy for the third case is not as high as that of the other cases, but is still impressive given the fact that we are dealing with significantly overlapping classes.

References

1. M. Aladjem. Linear Discriminant Analysis for Two Classes Via Removal of Classification Structure. *IEEE Trans. Pattern Analysis and Machine Intelligence*, 19(2):187–192, 1997.
2. R. Duda and P. Hart. *Pattern Classification and Scene Analysis.* John Wiley and Sons, Inc., 1973.
3. K. Fukunaga. *Introduction to Statistical Pattern Recognition.* Academic Press, 1990.
4. W. Krzanowski, P. Jonathan, W. McCarthy, and M. Thomas. Discriminant Analysis with Singular Covariance Matrices: Methods and Applications to Spectroscopic Data. *Applied Statistics*, 44:101–115, 1995.
5. C. Lau, editor. *Neural Networks: Theoretical Foundations and Analysis.* IEEE Press, 1992.
6. R. Lippman. An Introduction to Computing with Neural Nets. In Lau [5], pages 5–24.

7. W. Malina. On an Extended Fisher Criterion for Feature Selection. *IEEE Trans. Pattern Analysis and Machine Intelligence*, 3:611–614, 1981.
8. O. Murphy. Nearest Neighbor Pattern Classification Perceptrons. In Lau [5], pages 263–266.
9. A. Rao, D. Miller, K. Rose, , and A. Gersho. A Deterministic Annealing Approach for Parsimonious Design of Piecewise Regression Models. *IEEE Trans. Pattern Analysis and Machine Intelligence*, 21(2):159–173, 1999.
10. S. Raudys. On Dimensionality, Sample Size, and Classification Error of Nonparametric Linear Classification. *IEEE Trans. Pattern Analysis and Machine Intelligence*, 19(6):667–671, 1997.
11. S. Raudys. Evolution and Generalization of a Single Neurone: I. Single-layer Perception as Seven Statistical Classifiers. *Neural Networks*, 11(2):283–296, 1998.
12. S. Raudys. Evolution and Generalization of a Single Neurone: II. Complexity of Statistical Classifiers and Sample Size Considerations. *Neural Networks*, 11(2):297–313, 1998.
13. B. Ripley. *Pattern Recognition and Neural Networks.* Cambridge Univ. Press, 1996.
14. Luis G. Rueda and B. John Oommen. On Optimal Pairwise Linear Classifiers for Normal Distributions: The d-Dimensional Case. *Submitted for Publication.*
15. Luis G. Rueda and B. John Oommen. On Optimal Pairwise Linear Classifiers for Normal Distributions: The d-Dimensional Case. Technical report, School of Computer Science, Carleton University, Ottawa, Canada. In Preparation.
16. Luis G. Rueda and B. John Oommen. On Optimal Pairwise Linear Classifiers for Normal Distributions: The Two-Dimensional Case. Technical Report TR-00-03, School of Computer Science, Carleton University, Ottawa, Canada, May 2000.
17. Luis G. Rueda and B. John Oommen. The Foundational Theory of Optimal Bayesian Pairwise Linear Classifiers. In *Proceedings of the Joint IAPR International Workshops SSPR 2000 and SPR 2000*, pages 581–590, Alicante, Spain, August/September 2000. Springer.
18. R. Schalkoff. *Pattern Recognition: Statistical, Structural and Neural Approaches.* John Wiley and Sons, Inc., 1992.
19. A. Webb. *Statistical Pattern Recognition.* Oxford University Press Inc., New York, 1999.

Solving Overconstrained Temporal Reasoning Problems

Matthew Beaumont, Abdul Sattar, Michael Maher, and John Thornton

Knowledge Representation and Reasoning Unit (KRRU)
Faculty of Engineering and Information Technology
Griffith University,
QLD 4215, AUSTRALIA
email: {mbeaumon,sattar,mjm,easjohnt}@cit.gu.edu.au

Abstract. Representing and reasoning with temporal information is an essential part of many tasks in AI such as scheduling, planning and natural language processing. Two influential frameworks for representing temporal information are interval algebra and point algebra [1, 8]. Given a knowledge-base consisting of temporal relations, the main reasoning problem is to determine whether this knowledge-base is satisfiable, i.e., there is a scenario which is consistent with the information provided. However, when a given set of temporal relations is unsatisfiable, no further reasoning is performed. We argue that many real world problems are inherently overconstrained, and that these problems must also be addressed. This paper investigates approaches for handling overconstrainedness in temporal reasoning. We adapt a well studied notion of *partial satisfaction* to define *partial scenarios* or optimal partial solutions. We propose two reasoning procedures for computing an optimal partial solution to a problem (or a complete solution if it exists).

1 Introduction

Temporal reasoning is a vital task in many areas such as planning [2], scheduling [5] and natural language processing [6]. Currently the main focus of research has been on how to represent temporal information and how to gain a complete solution from a problem. How the information is represented depends on the type of temporal reasoning that is needed.

There are two ways in which we can reason about a temporal problem. The reasoning method chosen depends on the information available. If a problem is presented with only qualitative information (i.e. information about how events are ordered with other events) Qualitative Temporal Reasoning is performed. From the sentence "Fred drank his coffee while he ate his breakfast" we can only gather information about the relative timing of the two events. On the other hand, information can be presented as quantitative information, that is information about when certain events can or do happen. For example, Fred ate his breakfast at 7:35am and drank his coffee at 7:40am. For this paper we deal only with qualitative information.

M. Brooks, D. Corbett, and M. Stumptner (Eds.): AI 2001, LNAI 2256, pp. 37–49, 2001.

Current research has been aimed at finding a complete solution or determining that a problem has a solution [1,8,4]. If the problem is not solvable then only an error is provided. However in many situations simply determining that the problem has no solution is not enough. What is needed is a partial solution, where some of the constraints or variables have been weakened or removed to allow a solution to be found.

While there has been no research on finding a partial solution to an overconstrained temporal reasoning problem, there has been research on finding partial solutions to overconstrained constraint satisfaction problems (OCSP). One such approach is Partial Constraint Satisfaction [3]. Partial Constraint Satisfaction takes an overconstrained problem and obtains a partial solution by selectively choosing variables or constraints to either remove or weaken. This is done in such a way as to minimize the total number of variables or constraints that are removed or weakened and leads to an optimal partial solution.

In this paper we define two methods for finding a solution to an overconstrained Temporal Reasoning problem. The first method uses a standard brute force approach with forward checking/pruning capabilities. The second method also uses a brute force strategy but replaces forward checking/pruning with a cost function that can revise previous decisions at each step of the search. Both methods provide the ability to find an optimal partial solution or a complete solution if one exists.

In sections 2 and 3 we give the relevant background information for both Temporal Reasoning and Partial Constraint Satisfaction. Section 4 introduces both methods and explains in detail how they work. We also present some preliminary experimental results in Section 5.

2 Interval and Point Algebra

The way in which qualitative temporal information is represented plays a key role in efficiently finding a solution to a problem or determining that no solution exists. Two representation schemes are Allen's Interval Algebra [1] and Vilain and Kautz's Point Algebra [8].

Interval algebra (IA) represents events as intervals in time. Each interval has a start and an end point represented as an ordered pair (S, E) where S < E. The relation between two fixed intervals can consist of one of the 13 atomic interval relations. The set of these relations is represented by I and is shown in table 1.

Representing indefinite information about relations between non-fixed intervals can be achieved by allowing relations to be disjunctions of any of the atomic relations from the set I. By allowing disjuncts of the 13 atomic relations we can construct the set A containing all 2^{13} possible binary relations, including the empty relation $\emptyset$ and the no information relation I. The relation I is known as the no information relation because it contains all of the atomic relations, this implies that nothing is known about the relationship between two events that have this relation. To complete the algebra Allen also defined 4 interval operations over the set A: intersection, union, inverse and composition. The operations and their definitions are shown in table 2.

Table 1. The set I of all 13 atomic relations.

Relation	Symbol	Semantics	Symbol	Relation
X before Y	<		>	Y after X
X meets Y	m		mi	Y meet-by X
X overlaps Y	o		oi	Yoverlapped-by X
X during Y	d		di	Y contains X
X starts Y	s		si	Y started-by X
X finishes Y	f		fi	Y finished-by X
X equals Y	=		=	Y equals X

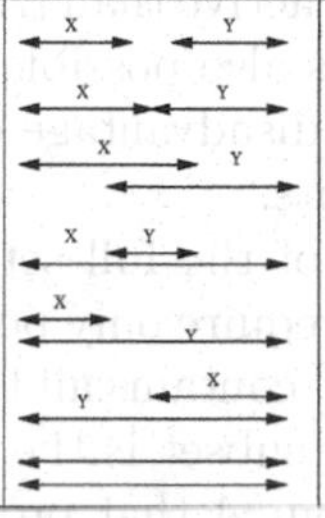

Table 2. The 4 interval operations and their definitions.

Operation	Symbol	Formal Definition
Intersection	$\bigcap$	$\forall x, y\ xA_1 \bigcap A_2 y$ iff $xA_1y \wedge xA_2y$
Union	$\bigcup$	$\forall x, y\ x(A_1 \bigcup A_2)y$ iff $xA_1y \vee xA_2y$
Inverse	$\smile$	$\forall x, y\ xA^{\smile}y$ iff yAx
Composition	$\circ$	$\forall x, y\ x(A_1 \circ A_2)y$ iff $\exists z\ xA_1z \wedge zA_2y$

A temporal problem expressed with IA can also be represented as a temporal constraint graph [4] . In a temporal constraint graph nodes represent intervals and the arcs between nodes are labeled with interval relations. Such a graph can be re-expressed as a matrix M of size $n * n$ where n is the number of intervals in the problem. Every element of the matrix contains an interval relation from the set A of all possible interval relations with two restrictions: for the elements M_{ii} the interval relation is always $=$ and $M_{ji} = M_{ij}^{\smile}$.

One of the key reasoning tasks in IA is to determine if a problem is satisfiable. A problem is satisfiable if we can assign a value to each interval's start and end point such that all the interval relations are satisfied. Satisfiability can be determined by the use of the path-consistency method [1]. The method simply computes the following for all a, b, c of the matrix M:

$$M_{ac} = M_{ac} \bigcap (M_{ab} \circ M_{bc})$$

until there is no change in M_{ac}. A matrix M is said to be path-consistent when no elements are the empty set $\emptyset$ and there is no further change possible in M. However, as shown by Allen [1], path-consistency does not imply satisfiability for interval algebra. In fact determining satisfiability for IA is NP-Hard [8] and a backtracking algorithm is required with path consistency to determine satisfiability.

Point Algebra (PA) differs from IA in that events in time are represented as points instead of intervals. By representing events as points the relations between events are reduced to three possibilities $\{<, =, >\}$. The set $P = \{\emptyset, <$

$, \leq, =, >, \geq, \neq, ?\}$ contains every possible relation between events. The relation $? = \{<, =, >\}$, means no information is known about that relation.

PA is more computationally attractive than IA in that for PA path-consistency alone ensures satisfiability [8]. It is also possible to encode some relations from IA into PA [8]. However a major disadvantage of PA is that expressive power is lost by representing time as points.

While computing satisfiability of the full set of interval relations A is NP-Hard there exist subsets of A that require only polynomial time. The SA_c subset defined by Van Beek and Cohen [7] contains all the relations from A that can be converted to PA. Another popular subset is the ORD-Horn maximal subset H which contains all the relations from A that provide satisfiability for the path-consistency method [4]. The ORD-Horn subset also includes all the relations in SA_c such that $SA_c \subset H$.

3 Partial Constraint Satisfaction

Partial Constraint Satisfaction (PCS) [3] is the process of finding values for a subset of the variables in a problem that satisfies a subset of the constraints. A partial solution is desirable in several cases:

- The problem is overconstrained and as such has no solution.
- The problem is computationally too large to find a solution in a reasonable amount of time.
- The problem has to be solved within fixed resource bounds.
- The problem is being solved in a real-time environment where it is necessary to report the current best solution found at anytime.

There are several methods that can be used to obtain a partial solution [3]:

1. Remove variables from the problem.
2. Remove constraints from the problem.
3. Weaken constraints in a problem.
4. Widen the domains of variables to include extra values.

Removing a variable from the problem is a very drastic approach to obtain a partial solution. By removing a variable, all the constraints associated with that variable are also removed. Conversely if, when removing constraints, a variable is left with no constraints, then this effectively removes that variable. Weakening a constraint to the point where that constraint no longer constrains the variable effectively removes that constraint from the problem. From this we can see that methods 1 and 2 are really special instances of method 3. The fourth method however has no relation to the other methods. If a variable's domain is widened to the extent that it includes all possible values, the constraints on that variable can still make it impossible to assign a value to that variable, and hence the variable is not removed from the problem.

No matter the method that is chosen to find a partial solution there is still the question of what constitutes an optimum partial solution. The simplest method is to count the number of variables/constraints removed or the number of domains/constraints weakened. The solution that provides the minimal count is then considered optimal (a solution with a count of 0 equates to a fully consistent solution) and the solution count can be used to represent the solution cost.

4 Temporal Constraint Partial Satisfaction

While current temporal reasoning algorithms are relatively fast and efficient they are unable to provide partial solutions to overconstrained problems. Many applications, such as scheduling, require a solution to the problem presented even when the problem is overconstrained. Applying the current temporal reasoning algorithms will only identify that the problem is indeed overconstrained and as such has no solution. To address this shortcoming we introduce two algorithms for finding partial solutions:

4.1 Method 1

The first method uses a standard branch and bound search with forward checking/pruning to gain an optimal partial solution. The algorithm starts by initializing a dummy network such that all relations in the network are the relation I. This dummy network is then passed to the branch and bound algorithm and the search begins.

First a relation is chosen, which is then divided into two sets: a consistent set CS and an inconsistent set IS. The set CS contains only relations that appear in both the original relation and in what remains in the dummy network's relation. For example, if the original had the relation {<, m, mi, s} and the dummy relation {<, mi, f, fi, >} then the set CS would be {<, mi}. The set IS contains those relations not in CS, which in our example would be {f, fi, >}. After this, a single relation is chosen first from the set CS and instantiated in the dummy network. The Path Consistency algorithm is then called to propagate the effects of this instantiation. In the event that the branch and bound algorithm backtracks to this point or the Path Consistency call fails, another atomic relation is chosen. If all relations from the set CS have been tried then atomic relations are chosen from the set IS. However when a relation from the set IS is chosen, a cost count is incremented to reflect that a relation was chosen in conflict with the originally desired relations.

If the Path Consistency call was successful then another relation is chosen and the process begins again. At anytime if the cost of the current path exceeds the current best cost then backtracking occurs to a point where the cost is lower than the best cost and processing is started again. When all relations are exhausted the best result is returned as the optimal solution.

```
Input:    Original: The original network
          Dummy: A dummy network
          Cost
Method1
Begin
  If Cost >= BestCost then backtrack
  If PathConsistent(Dummy) fails then backtrack
  If there are still relations to process in Dummy then
  begin
    get next relation (X, Y) from Dummy
    CS = Dummy[X, Y] ∩ Original[X, Y]
    IS = Dummy[X, Y] − CS
    for all i in CS do
    begin
      instantiate Dummy[X, Y] to i
      Method1(Original, Dummy, Cost)
    end
    for all i in IS do
    begin
      instantiate Dummy[X, Y] to i
      Method1(Original, Dummy, Cost + 1)
    end
  end
  else
  begin
    Record Dummy as the best solution found so far
    BestCost = Cost
  end
End
```

4.2 Method 2

The second method, as before, uses a branch and bound algorithm to control the search. However, unlike the first method, no forward checking/pruning is performed as the actual cost is only computed at the end of a search path. Instead at each step in the search an approximate cost is found based on how many relations need to potentially be changed to make the network consistent. With this approximate value a decision is made as to whether to proceed on this path or abandon it. This requires two additional calculations, a Real Cost function and an Approximate Cost function:

Approximate Cost Function. At each level of the search it is necessary to judge the cost of the partially explored solution. The ApproximateCost function finds an approximate cost that is always equal to or less than the real cost of the partially explored solution. The reason for using an approximate cost function (instead of finding the real cost) is that until all relations are atomic it is very costly to find an absolute cost (as finding every inconsistency at this point would require a separate NP-Hard search and an additional search to find the best cost).

To calculate the approximate cost we first determine a lower bound of the number of inconsistent triples. A triple is a set of any three nodes from the problem. A triple $T = (A,B,C)$ is inconsistent if: $M_{AC} \bigcap (M_{AB} \circ M_{BC}) \neq \emptyset$. Testing path (A,B,C) is enough to determine an inconsistency. Computing (B,C,A) and (B,A,C) is unnecessary due to the fact that if the path (A,B,C) is consistent then there is an atomic relation X in M_{AB} and Y in M_{BC} that make some or all atomic relations in M_{AC} consistent. Now if we take the composition of M_{AC} and the inverse of Y, the resulting allowed relations will include A. This is because given any three atomic relations N, P, Q that are path consistent then $Q \in (N \circ P)$, $N \in (Q \circ P^{\smile})$ and $P \in (N^{\smile} \circ Q)$.

When a triple is determined as inconsistent it is added to a list and a count for each relation in the triple is incremented. The counts for all relations are stored in an occurrence matrix O, with each element of O starting at 0. For example, if the triple (A, B, C), is inconsistent then O_{AB}, O_{BC} and O_{AC} are all incremented by 1 to represent that each relation occurred in an inconsistency.

```
Input:      Network M
Output:     A List containing all inconsistent triples
            A matrix O recording the occurrence count for each relation
DetermineInconsistencies
  Begin
    For A = 1 to size(M) − 2 do
      For B = A + 1 to size(M) − 1 do
        For C = B + 1 to size(M) do
        begin
          If (M_AC ⋂(M_AB ∘ M_BC)) = ∅ do
          begin
            add (A,B,C) to List
            increment O_AB, O_BC and O_AC by 1
          end
        end
    return (List, O)
  End
```

Once the list of inconsistencies is determined it is processed to find an approximate number of relations to weaken to remove all inconsistencies. In simplified terms the algorithm takes a triple from the inconsistency list and tries each relation one at a time, effectively performing a brute force search. However there are some special circumstances which allow the algorithm to be more efficient:

The first situation occurs when every relation in a triple occurs only once. Here it does not matter which relation is chosen, as no other triple will be removed from the list, hence the cost is incremented by 1 and processing continues. Lines 9-13 of the following code handle this case.

The second situation is when a triple is chosen that contains a relation that has already been selected. In this case the occurrence matrix is reduced by 1 for each relation in the triple and the cost remains the same. Lines 14-20 of the following code handle this situation.

The last case is when a triple contains certain relations that only occur once. These relations are ignored as choosing them will not affect other triples and therefore will provide no possibility of offering a lower approximate cost. Line 23 is used to check for and handle this case.

```
Input:      List of inconsistencies
            An occurrence matrix O
            Cost
            BestCost
ApproxCost
1.  Begin
2.    If Cost >= BestCost then backtrack
3.    If there are no more triples left in List then
4.    begin
5.      BestCost = Cost
6.      backtrack
7.    end
8.    get and remove the next triple (A,B,C) from List
9.    If O_AB and O_AC and O_BC all equal 1 then
10.   begin
11.     ApproxCost(List, O, Cost + 1, BestCost)
12.     backtrack
13.   end
14.   If O_AB or O_AC or O_BC <= 0 then
15.   begin
16.     decrement all three relations in the occurence matrix O by 1
17.     ApproxCost(List, O, Cost, BestCost)
18.     increment all three relations in the occurence matrix O by 1
19.     backtrack
```

```
    end
    For each relation R in {AB, AC, BC} do
    begin
      If O_R ≠ 1 then
      begin
        TVal = O_R
        decrement O_AB, O_AC, O_BC by 1
        set O_R to 0
        ApproxCost(List, O, Cost + 1, BestCost)
        increment O_AB, O_AC, O_BC by 1
        O_R = TVal
      end
    end
End
```

The ApproximateCost function is responsible for calling DetermineInconsistencies and then passing its results to ApproxCost.

```
Input:    Network M
          CurrentBestCost the current BestCost value
Output:   Cost
ApproximateCost
Begin
  (List, O) = DetermineInconsistencies(Network)
  BestCost = CurrentBestCost
  ApproxCost(List, O, 0, BestCost)
  return BestCost
End
```

Real Cost Function. At the end of a search, when all relations are atomic, the real cost of that solution can be determined. Unlike the ApproximateCost algorithm, RealCost returns not only a cost but also a consistent network. The question arises however of why it is not possible to use the ApproximateCost algorithm to determine the real cost when all relations are atomic? When presented with the network in Figure 1 it is possible for ApproximateCost to work out a minimal cost that does not provide a consistent network. In this network the cost of solving is 2, however if the relations chosen are R(A,D) and R(B,C) then this still does not provide a solution as no value can be assigned to those relations together to make them consistent.

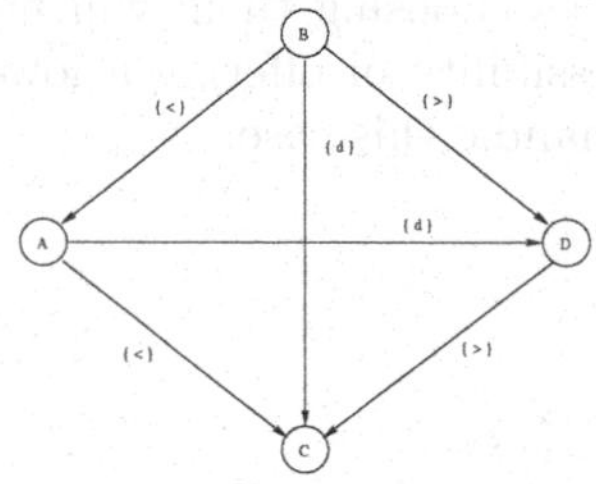

Fig. 1.

To handle this problem it is necessary to perform a full PathConsistency check at the end of a search. Furthermore it is also necessary to include relations with an occurrence of 1 in the search, which impacts the performance significantly. Another problem that can arise is illustrated by the network in figure 1 and occurs when relation R(A,D) and R(B,C) are both the relation *I*. In this case the real cost algorithm will never find a solution since no inconsistencies are reported by the DetermineInconsistencies algorithm. This problem is handled by allowing the search path to extend into these relations and thus allowing real cost to function properly. Unfortunately this also results in an large increase in the search space.

Finding the real cost of a network is similar to finding the approximate cost in that we process a list of inconsistencies to find the least number of relations to change to remove all inconsistencies. However we can no longer make use of all the special circumstances used in the approximate cost algorithm and some extra processing is also required to verify that the solution found is consistent.

The only special circumstance that can be kept is when one of the relations in a triple has an occurrence of 0 or less. As before these triples are ignored as they are already solved. However we must record any relation in that triple that has an occurrence greater than 0 in the Removed list. This is due to the possibility that we may remove a relation from consideration that needs to be weakened to gain the optimal cost. Lines 10-18 of the following code handle this circumstance.

All other triples are processed normally and relations that have an occurrence of 1 are treated the same as other relations. Since the solution found is required to be consistent it is possible that selecting one relation over another, where both have an occurrence of 0, could result in the final solution still being inconsistent. All relations that are considered here are marked as occurring in the search path. Lines 19-32 of the following code process this situation.

When there are no more triples left, the marked relations in the Removed list are then deleted from the list. The Removed list now only contains those relations that have no chance of being selected at an earlier stage. The Removed list is then passed to the ProcessRemoved algorithm which finds the final cost and solution. Lines 3-8 of the following code handle this situation.

```
Input:      Network M
            List of inconsistencies
            An occurrence matrix O
            NewNet a place to store the best solution
            Cost
            BestCost
            Removed a list of relations
RCost
1.  Begin
2.    If Cost >= BestCost then backtrack
3.    If there are no more triples left in List then
4.    begin
5.      remove all the relations from Removed that have been marked
6.      ProcessRemoved(M, NewNet, Removed, Cost, BestCost)
7.      backtrack
8.    end
9.    get and remove the next triple (A,B,C) from List
10.   If O_AB or O_AC or O_BC <= 0 then
11.   begin
12.     decrement all three relations in the occurrence matrix O by 1
13.     add the relations that have an occurrence > 0 to Removed
14.     RCost(M, List, O, NewNet, Cost, BestCost, Removed)
15.     remove the relations added to Removed
16.     increment all three relations in the occurrence matrix O by 1
17.     backtrack
18.   end
19.   For every relation R in {AB, AC, BC} do
20.   begin
21.     TRel = M_R
22.     TVal = O_R
23.     decrement O_AB, O_AC, O_BC by 1
24.     mark all three relations (AB, AC, BC)
```

```
        set O_R to 0
        set M_R to the relation I
        RCost(M, List, O, NewNet, Cost + 1, BestCost, Removed)
        M_R = TRel
        increment O_AB, O_AC, O_BC by 1
        O_R = TVal
        unmark all three relations
    end
End
```

Relations are marked incrementally not simply with a boolean value. Marking a relation indicates that it has no possibility of being excluded from a search.

When there are no more triples in List, the function ProcessRemoved is called to handle a rare occasion which could otherwise result in the best cost not being found. The problem occurs when a triple is removed where one of the relations has an occurrence of 0 or less. This makes it possible for a relation that should be weakened to gain the best cost to be excluded from a search. The ProcessRemoved algorithm initially checks to see if the current solution is consistent, if it is then the relations in the Removed list are not processed. If the solution is not consistent then one or more of the relations in the Removed list need to be weakened to allow a solution. Line 6 checks consistency by calling PathConsistent which checks that the supplied network is path-consistent.

```
Input:      Network M
            NewNet a place to store the best solution
            Removed a list of removed triples
            Cost
            BestCost
ProcessRemoved
1.  Begin
2.    If Cost >= BestCost then backtrack
3.    If Removed is empty then
4.    begin
5.      TemporyNetwork = M
6.      If PathConsistent(TemporyNetwork) does not fail then
7.      begin
8.        BestCost = Cost
9.        NewNet = TemporyNetwork
10.     end
11.     backtrack
12.   end
13.   get and remove the next relation R from Removed
14.   ProcessRemoved(M, NewNet, Removed, Cost, BestCost)
15.   If Cost < BestCost - 1 then
16.   begin
17.     set M_R to the relation I
18.     ProcessRemoved(M, NewNet, Removed, Cost + 1, BestCost)
19.     restore M_R to previous relation
20.   end
21.   Add relation R back to Removed
22. End
```

RealCost is similar to ApproximateCost in that it is really an interface to the functions that perform the main work.

```
Input:      Network M
            CurrentBestCost
Output:     BestCost
            NewNet a consistent network
RealCost
  Begin
    (List, O) = DetermineInconsistencies(M)
    BestCost = CurrentBestCost
    set list Removed to empty
    RCost(M, List, O, NewNet, 0, BestCost, Removed)
    return (Cost, NewNet)
  End
```

5 Experimental Results

In this section we present the preliminary results we have obtained by implementing the algorithms discussed and testing them with generated problems. The test problems where generated using Nebel's temporal reasoning problem generator [4]. The experiments were conducted on a Pentium 3 733 MHz processor with 256 megabytes of RAM running the Linux operating system. A label size (average number of atomic relations per relation) of 3 and 100 test cases were used for all experiments. Each graph uses a different degree, the degree of a problem being a percentage value indicating how many relations are unknown. For example a degree value of 1 indicates that all relations in the problem are known whereas a degree of .25 indicates that only 25% of relations are known. For each graph two types of problems were generated: a consistent problem which has a consistent solution and a random problem which may or may not contain a consistent solution. The Y axis for each graph represents the average run-time for a set of problems and uses a logarithmic scale. The X axis (k) shows the number of events used in a problem.

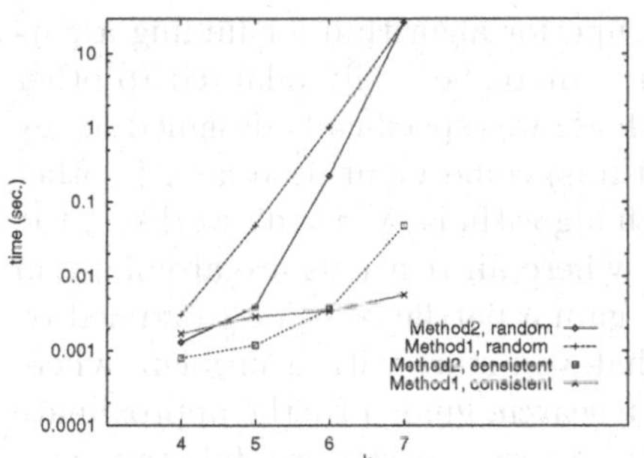

Fig. 2. Graph A: Degree = 1

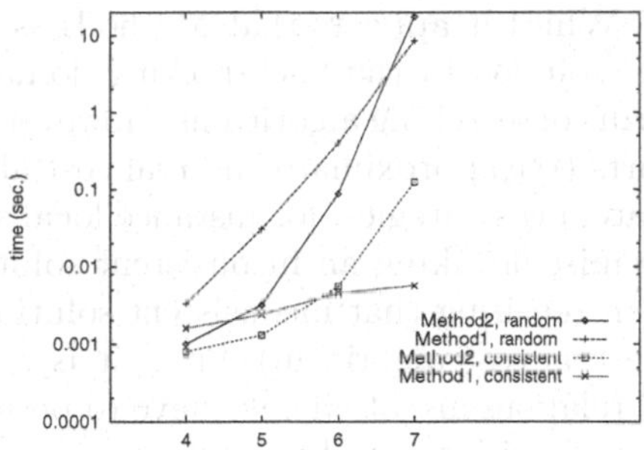

Fig. 3. Graph B: Degree = .75

The results of the four graphs show a trend where Method1 generally performs better at lower degrees and Method2 performs better at higher degrees. This is to be expected as lower degree problems contain a greater proportion of unknown relations and Method1 does not need to explicitly explore unknown relations (unlike Method2). Also at lower degrees there is a higher probability that the generated problem will be consistent (both algorithms appear to perform better on consistent problems). More significantly however, Method1 increasingly dominates Method2 as k increases, regardless of the problem degree.

Overall, the preliminary results indicate that Method1 is the better algorithm due to its predictable nature and better scaling. Whilst Method2 often outperforms Method1 on particular problems it is evident that as k gets larger Method1 will begin to dominate Method2. Analysing the raw data shows that

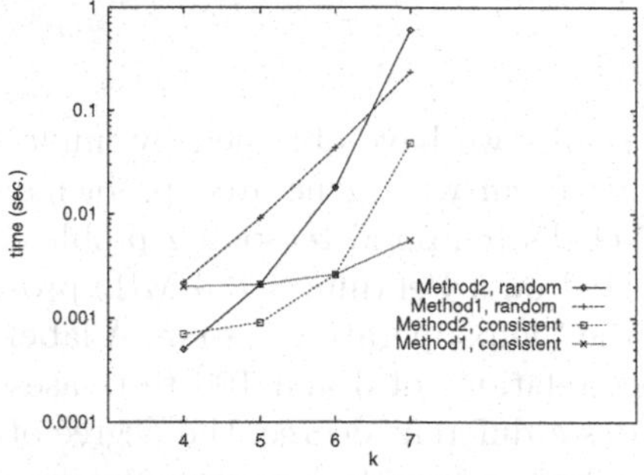

Fig. 4. Graph C: Degree = .5

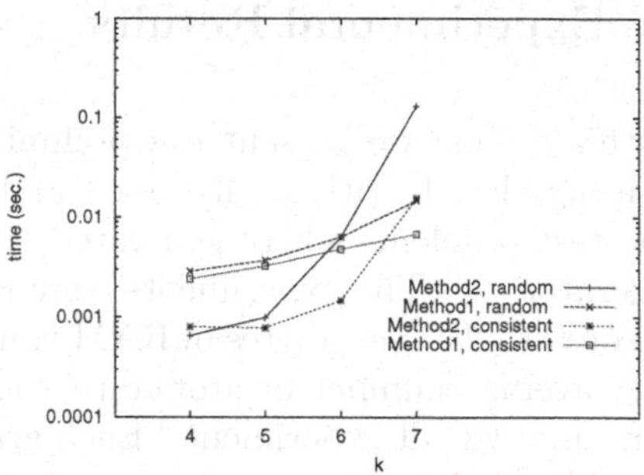

Fig. 5. Graph D: Degree = .25

in some cases Method2 takes an unusually long time to find a solution, significantly altering the average result. This may be occurring because Method2 is performing a detailed search in an unpromising part of the search tree. Such behaviour could be modified by using a random restart strategy, an option we are currently investigating.

Whilst it appears that Method1 is the superior algorithm for finding a partial solution in the backtracking domain, it cannot be easily adapted to other forms of searching algorithms. However Method2 was specifically designed so key parts (the approximate and real cost algorithms) could be utilized later in other searching strategies, for instance local search algorithms. Method2 works on the premise of taking an inconsistent solution (where all relations are atomic) and then repairing that inconsistent solution to gain a partial solution (obtained by the real cost algorithm). Since it is rare that you start with a problem where all relations are atomic we have to perform a search, guided by the approximate cost algorithm, to obtain this situation. If in a rare occasion we did start with such a problem Method2 would by far outperform Method1.

For the backtracking domain, as k gets larger Method2 has to search an increasingly larger search space without the aid of propagation techniques to reduce the search space. This is most likely the reason why Method1 starts to perform better for higher k values and makes it the better choice when a backtracking search must be used to gain an optimal partial solution.

6 Conclusion and Future Work

Finding a partial solution to a Temporal Reasoning problem has not been well investigated to date. In this paper we have outlined two algorithms that can be used in finding a solution to a TPCS problem. Both algorithms are guaranteed to find the optimal partial solution (optimal being the minimum number of relations violated).

The preliminary experimental results show using a traditional branch and bound type algorithm is only practical on small sized problems and so is not expected to be useful in more realistic situations. The results also show that Method1, while sometimes being slower than Method2, is more consistent in finding solutions and is probably the superior algorithm due its better scaling performance.

For future work we will be extending the experimental results and investigating ways to improve the performance of both algorithms. One idea is to employ ordering heuristics. These should improve the performance of both algorithms and particularly address the lack of consistency in Method2. We will also be investigating local search techniques to gain partial solutions. Whilst local search does not guarantee an optimal solution, experience in other CSP domains indicates it may be more effective on larger problems.

References

1. J. Allen. Maintaining knowledge about temporal intervals. *Communication of the ACM*, 26(11):832–843, 1983.
2. J. Allen and J. Kooomen. Planning using a temporal world model. In *Proceedings of the 8th International Joint Conference on Artificial Intelligence (IJCAI)*, pages 741–747, Karlsruhe, W.Germany, 1983.
3. Eugene Freuder and Richard Wallace. Partial constraint satisfaction. *Artificial Intelligence*, 58(1):21–70, 1992.
4. B. Nebel. Solving hard qualitative temporal reasoning problems: Evaluating the efficiency of using the ord-horn class. *Constraints Journal*, 1:175–190, 1997.
5. M. Poesio and R. Brachman. Metric constraints for maintaining appointments: Dates and repeated activities. In *Proceedings of the 9th National Conference of the American Association for Artificial Intelligence (AAAI-91)*, pages 253–259, 1991.
6. Fei. Song and Robin. Cohen. The interpretation of temporal relations in narrative. In *Proceedings of the 7th National Conference of the American Association for Artificial Intelligence (AAAI-88)*, pages 745–750, Saint Paul, MI, 1988.
7. P. van Beek and R. Cohen. Exact and approximate reasoning about temporal relations. *Computational Intelligence*, 6:132–144, 1990.
8. M. Vilain and H. Kautz. Constraint propagation algorithms for temporal reasoning. In *Proceedings of the 5th National Conference in Artificial Intelligence (AAAI-86)*, pages 377–382, Philadelphia, PA, 1986.

How the Level of Interchangeability Embedded in a Finite Constraint Satisfaction Problem Affects the Performance of Search

Amy M. Beckwith, Berthe Y. Choueiry, and Hui Zou

Department of Computer Science and Engineering, 115 Ferguson Hall,
University of Nebraska-Lincoln, Lincoln NE 68588-0115
{abeckwit | choueiry | hzou}@cse.unl.edu

Abstract. We investigate how the performance of search for solving finite constraint satisfaction problems (CSPs) is affected by the level of interchangeability embedded in the problem. First, we describe a generator of random CSPs that allows us to control the level of interchangeability in an instance. Then we study how the varying level of interchangeability affects the performance of search for finding one solution and all solutions to the CSP. We conduct experiments using forward-checking search, extended with static and dynamic ordering heuristics in combination with non-bundling, static, and dynamic bundling strategies. We demonstrate that: (1) While the performance of bundling decreases in general with decreasing interchangeability, this effect is muted when finding a first solution. (2) Dynamic ordering strategies are significantly more resistant to this degradation than static ordering. (3) Dynamic bundling strategies perform overall significantly better than static bundling strategies. Even when finding one solution, the size of the bundles yielded by dynamic bundling is large and less sensitive to the level of interchangeability. (4) The combination of dynamic ordering heuristics with dynamic bundling is advantageous. We conclude that this combination, in addition to yielding the best results, is the least sensitive to the level of interchangeability, and thus, indeed is superior to other searches.

1 Introduction

A Constraint Satisfaction Problem (CSP) [12] is the problem of assigning values to a set of variables while satisfying a set of constraints that restrict the allowed combinations of values for variables. In its general form, a CSP is NP-complete, and backtrack search remains the ultimate technique for solving it. Because of the flexibility and expressiveness of the model, Constraint Satisfaction has emerged as a central paradigm for modeling and solving various real-world decision problems in computer science, engineering, and management.

It is widely acknowledged that real-world problems exhibit an intrinsic non-random structure that makes most instances 'easy' to solve. When the structure of a particular problem is known in advance, it can readily be embedded in the model and exploited during search [3], as it is commonly done for the pigeon-hole

M. Brooks, D. Corbett, and M. Stumptner (Eds.): AI 2001, LNAI 2256, pp. 50–61, 2001.

problem. A challenging task is to *discover* the structure in a particular problem instance. In our most recent research [5, 2, 4], we have investigated mechanisms for discovering and exploiting one particular type of symmetry structure, called *interchangeability*, that allows us to bundle solutions, and have integrated these *bundling* mechanisms with backtrack search. We have investigated and evaluated the effectiveness of this integration and demonstrated its utility under particularly adverse conditions (i.e., random problems generated without any particular structure embedded *a priori* and puzzles known to be extraordinarily resistant to our symmetry detection techniques). In this paper, we investigate how the performance of these new search strategies is affected by the level of interchangeability embedded in the problem. We first show how to generate random problems with a controlled level of inherent structure, then demonstrate the effects of this structure on the performance of the various search mechanisms with and without interchangeability detection.

Section 2 gives a brief background to the subject and summarizes our previous work. Section 3 describes our random generator, designed to create random CSP instances with a pre-determined level of interchangeability. Section 4 introduces the problem sets used for testing, and demonstrates the performance of our search strategies across varying levels of interchangeability. Section 5 concludes the paper with directions for future research.

2 Background and Contributions

A finite Constraint Satisfaction Problem (CSP) is defined as $\mathcal{P}$=($\mathcal{V}$, $\mathcal{D}$, $\mathcal{C}$); where $\mathcal{V}$={V_1, V_2, ..., V_n} is a set of variables, $\mathcal{D}$={D_{V_1}, D_{V_2}, ..., D_{V_n}} is the set of their corresponding domains (the domain of a variable is a set of possible values), and $\mathcal{C}$ is a set of constraints that specifies the acceptable combinations of values for variables. A solution to the CSP is the assignment of a value to each variable such that all constraints are satisfied. The question is to find one or all solutions. A CSP is often represented as a constraint (hyper-)graph in which the variables are represented by nodes, the domains by node labels, and the constraints between variables by (hyper-)edges linking the nodes in the scope of the corresponding constraint. We study CSPs with finite domains and binary constraints (i.e., constraints apply to two variables).

Since a general CSP is NP-complete, it is usually solved by backtrack search, which is an exponential procedure. We enhance this basic backtrack search through the identification and exploitation of structure in the problem instance. This structure is in the form of symmetries. In particular, we make use of a type of symmetry called interchangeability, which was introduced and categorized by Freuder in [7]. We limit our investigations to interchangeability among the values in the domain of one given variable. Interchangeability between two values for the variable exists if the values can be substituted for one another without affecting the assignments of the remaining variables. Two such values are said to belong to the same *equivalence class.* Each equivalence class is a bundle of values that can be replaced by one representative of the bundle, thus reducing the size of the initial problem. We call the number of distinct equivalence classes in the domain of a variable the degree of *induced domain fragmentation*, IDF.

Freuder [7] proposed an efficient algorithm, based on building a discrimination tree, for computing one type of interchangeability, neighborhood interchangeability (NI). NI partitions the domain of a variable into equivalence classes given all the constraints incident to that variable. Haselböck [11] simplified NI to a weaker form that we call *neighborhood interchangeability according to one constraint* (NI_C). He showed how to exploit NI_C advantageously in backtrack search (BT), with and without forward-checking (FC) for finding all the solutions of a CSP. He also showed how NI_C groups multiple solutions of a CSP into *solution bundles*. In a solution bundle, each variable is assigned a specific subset of its domain instead of the unique value usually assigned by backtrack search. Any combination of one value per variable in the solution bundle is a solution to the CSP. Such a bundle not only yields a compact representation of this solution set, but is also useful in the event that one component of a solution fails, and an alternate, equivalent solution must be found quickly. In the bundling strategy proposed by Haselböck, symmetry relations are discovered *before* search is started. These are *static* interchangeability relations. We refer to this strategy as *static bundling*. Below we summarize our previous results [5, 2, 4], which motivate the investigations we report here.

In [5], we proposed to compute interchangeability *dynamically during* search using a generalized form of Freuder's discrimination tree, the joint discrimination tree of Choueiry and Noubir [6]. We called this type of interchangeability *dynamic neighborhood partial interchangeability* (DNPI). Since DNPI is computed during search, we say that it performs *dynamic bundling*. DNPI induces less domain fragmentation (larger partitions) than NI_C and is thus likely to find larger solution bundles. We designed a new search strategy that combines dynamic bundling (DNPI) with forward-checking, and compared it to searches without bundling and with static bundling (NI_C) for forward-checking search, see Fig. 1. We proved that the relations shown in Fig. 2 (left) hold when searching for all so-

Search		Comparison criteria
Non Bundling [10]	FC	Number of constraint checks CC, nodes visited NV, solution bundles SB, and CPU time.
Static bundling [11]	NI_C	
Dynamic bundling [5]	DNPI	

Fig. 1. *Search and bundling strategies.*

lutions (provided the variable and value orderings are the same for all searches), thus establishing that dynamic bundling is *always* worthwhile when solving for all solutions. In addition to the theoretical guarantees of Fig. 2 (left), we showed empirically that neither non-bundling (FC) nor static bundling (NI_C) search outperforms dynamic bundling search in terms of the quality of bundling (i.e., number of solution bundles generated) and in terms of the standard comparison criteria for search (i.e., number of constraint checks and number of nodes visited). CPU time measurements were reasonably in-line with the other criteria.

In [2], we modified the forward-checking backtrack-search procedures of Fig. 1 to allow the integration of *dynamic* variable-value orderings with bundling strategies, while looking for all solutions. We examined the following ordering heuris-

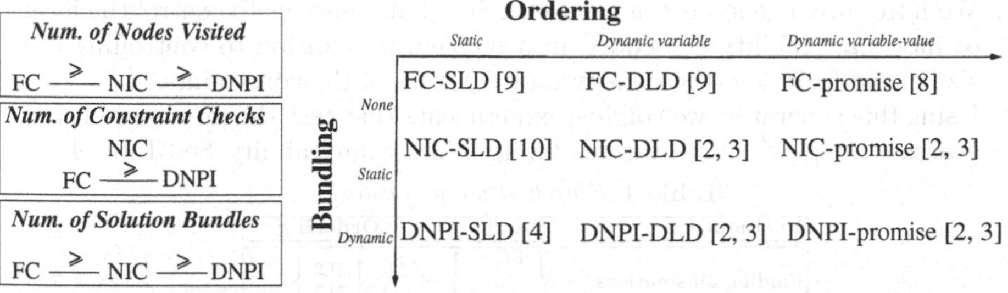

Fig. 2. *Left:* Comparison of search strategies assuming the same variable orderings for all strategies and while looking for all solutions. *Right:* Interleaving dynamic bundling with dynamic ordering.

tics: (1) static least-domain (`SLD`), (2) dynamic least-domain (`DLD`) and (3) dynamic variable-value ordering (`promise` of Geelen [9]). The search algorithms generated fell into the nine categories shown in Fig. 2 (right). Since the variable and value orderings can no longer be maintained across strategies, strong, theoretical results similar to the ones of Fig. 2 (left) cannot be made. We instead make empirical evaluations. Our experiments on these nine search strategies showed that dynamic least-domain ordering combined with dynamic bundling (DNPI-DLD) almost always yields the most effective search and the most compact solution space. Further, we noted that although `promise` reduces significantly the number of nodes visited in the search tree, it is harmful in the context of searching for all solutions because the number of constraint checks it requires is prohibitively large[1].

Finally, in [4], we addressed the task of finding a *first* solution. In addition to the ordering heuristics listed above (i.e., `SLD`, `DLD`, and `promise`), we proposed and tested two other ordering heuristics, specific to bundling: (1) Least-Domain-Max-Bundle (`LD-MB`) chooses the variable of smallest domain and, for this variable, the largest bundle in its domain; and (2) Max-Bundle (`Max-Bundle`) chooses the largest available bundle among all bundles of all variables. We found that the `promise` heuristic of Geelen [9] performs particularly well for finding one solution, consistently finding the largest first bundle with loosest bottlenecks[2], and nearly always yielding a backtrack-free search. This must be contrasted to its bad performance for finding all solutions in [2]. Further, dynamic bundling again proved to outperform static bundling, especially when used in combination with `promise`. Finally, we noted that `LD-MD`, our proposed new heuristic, is competitive with relatively few constraint checks, low CPU time, and good bundling.

The above summarized research established the utility of discovering and exploiting interchangeability relationships in general. In all of our past work, algorithms were tested on CSPs created with the random generator of Bacchus and van Run [1], which did not intentionally embed any structure in the problems. This paper furthers our investigation of interchangeability and adds the following contributions:

---

[1] The `promise` heuristic is by design best suited for finding one solution [9].

[2] The bottleneck of a solution bundle is the size of the smallest domain in the bundle.

1. We introduce a generator of random CSPs that allows us to control the level of interchangeability embedded in a problem in addition to controlling the size of the CSP, and the density and tightness of the constraints.
2. Using this generator, we conduct experiments that test the previously listed search strategies[3] across various levels of interchangeability. See Table 1:

Table 1. *Search strategies tested.*

Problem		Bundling		Ordering
Finding all solutions	×	{FC, NI_C, DNPI}	×	{SLD, DLD}
Finding first solution	×	{FC, NI_C, DNPI}	×	{SLD, DLD, LD-MB [4], promise [9]}

3. We show that: (a) Both static and dynamic bundling search strategies do indeed detect and benefit from interchangeability embedded in a problem instance. (b) the performance of dynamic bundling is significantly superior to that of static bundling when looking for a first solution bundle. (c) Problems with embedded interchangeability are not easier, or more difficult, to solve for the naive FC algorithm. And (d) Most algorithms are affected by the variance of interchangeability. However, DLD-ordered search is less sensitive and performs surprisingly well in all situations.

3 A Generator That Controls Interchangeability

Typically, a generator of random binary CSPs takes as input the following parameters $\langle n, a, p, t \rangle$. The first two parameters, n and a relate to the variables—n gives the number of variables, and a the domain size of each variable. The second two parameters, p and t control the constraints—p gives the probability that a constraint exists between any two variables (which also determines the number of constraints in the problem $C = p\frac{n(n-1)}{2}$), and t gives the constraint tightness (defined as the ratio of the number of tuples disallowed by the constraint over all possible tuples between the two variables).

In order to investigate the effects of interchangeability on the performance of search for solving CSPs, we must guarantee from the outset that each CSP instance contains a specific, controlled amount of interchangeability. Interchangeability within the problem instance is determined by the constraints. Indeed each constraint fragments the domain of the variable to which it applies into equivalence classes (as discussed below, Fig. 3) that can be exploited for bundling. Therefore, the main difficulty in generating a CSP for testing bundling algorithms resides in the generation of the constraints. We introduce an additional parameter to our random generator [14] that controls the number of equivalence

[3] LD-MB for finding all solutions collapses to DLD. Because of their poor behavior [2, 4], we exclude from our current experiments: (1) Max-Bundle for finding a first solution and (2) all dynamic strategies for variable-value orderings (e.g., promise and Max-Bundle) for finding all solutions.

classes induced by a constraint. This parameter, IDF, provides a measure of the interchangeability in a problem: a higher IDF means less interchangeability. In compliance with common practices, our generator adopts the following standard design decisions: (1) All variables have the same domain size and, without loss of generality, the same values. (2) Any particular pair of variables has only one constraint. (3) All constraints have the same degree of induced domain fragmentation. (4) All constraints have the same tightness. And, (5) any two variables are equally likely to be connected by a constraint.

3.1 Constraint Representation and Implementation

A constraint that applies to two variables is represented by a *binary matrix* whose rows and columns denote the domains of the variables to which it applies. The '1' entries in the matrix specify the tuples that are allowed and the '0' entries the tuples that are disallowed. Fig. 3 shows a constraint c, with $a = 5$ and $t = 0.32$. This constraint applies to V_1 and V_2 with domains $\{1, 2, 3, 4, 5\}$. The matrix is implemented as a list of row-vectors. Each row corresponds to a value in the domain of V_1. Each constraint partitions the domains of the variables

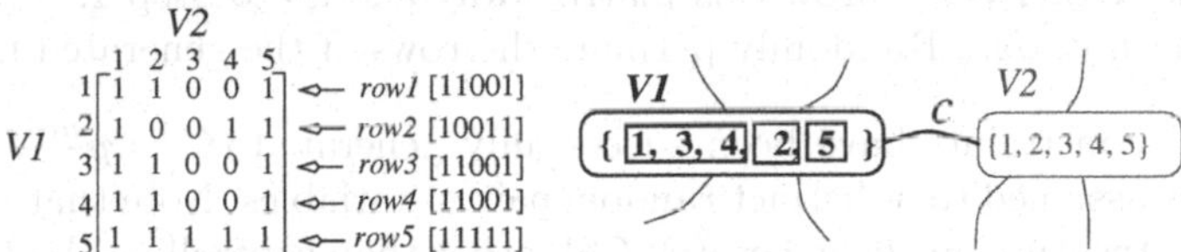

Fig. 3. *Constraint representation as a binary matrix.* Left: Encoding as row vectors. Right: Domain of V_1 partitioned by interchangeability.

to which it applies into equivalence classes. The values in a given equivalence class of a variables are consistent with the same set of values in the domain of the other variable. Indeed, c fragments the domain of V_1 into three equivalence classes corresponding to rows $\{1, 3, 4\}$, $\{2\}$ and $\{5\}$ as shown in Fig. 3.

We define the *degree of induced domain fragmentation* (IDF) of a constraint as the number of equivalence classes it induces on the domain of the variable *whose values index the rows of the matrix.* Thus the degree of induced domain fragmentation of c for V_1 is IDF = 3. Since we control the IDF for only one of the variables (the one represented in the rows), our constraints are not *a priori* symmetrical. The domain fragmentation induced on the remaining variable is not controlled. Our generator constitutes an improvement of the random generator with interchangeability of Freuder and Sabin [8], which inspired us. The latter creates each constraint from the conjunction of two components: one component controlling interchangeability and the other controlling tightness. The component controlling interchangeability is both symmetrical and non-reflexive (i.e., all diagonal entries in the matrix are 0). Therefore, both variables in a binary constraint have the same degree of induced domain fragmentation. This symmetry may affect the generality of the resulting constraint. Indeed, Freuder and Sabin introduce the second component of their constraint in order to achieve more generality and to control constraint tightness. This second component is a random constraint with a specified tightness t. The resulting constraint obtained by making the conjunction of the two components is likely to be tighter than specified and also contain less interchangeability than specified. To avoid this problem, our generator first generates a constraint with a specified tightness, imposes the degree of IDF requested, then checks the resulting tightness. Thus, in the CSPs generated, we guarantee that *both* t and IDF meet the specifications without sacrificing generality.

3.2 Constraint Generation

Constraint generation is done according to the following five-step process:

Step 1: *Matrix initialization.* Create an $a \times a$ matrix with every entry set to 1.
Step 2: *Tightness.* Set random elements of the matrix to 0 until specified tightness is achieved.
Step 3: *Interchangeability.* Modify the matrix to comply with the specified degree of induced domain fragmentation, see below.
Step 4: *Tightness check.* Test the matrix. If tightness meets the specification, continue. Otherwise, throw this matrix away and go to Step 1.
Step 5: *Permutation:* Randomly permute the rows of the generated matrix.

When C constraints have been successfully generated ($C = p\frac{n(n-1)}{2}$), each constraint is assigned to a distinct random pair of variables. Note that we do not impose any structure on the generated CSP other than controlling the IDF in the definition of the constraints. We also do not guarantee that the CSP returned is connected. However, when $C > n - 1$ extensive and random checks detected no unconnected CSPs among the ones generated. Obviously, when $C > \frac{(n-1)(n-2)}{2}$, connectedness is guaranteed. Below, we describe in further detail Steps 3 and 5 of the above process. Steps 1, 2, and 4 are straightforward.

Step 3: Achieving the degree of induced domain fragmentation (IDF). After generating a matrix with a specific tightness, we compute its IDF by counting the number of distinct row vectors. Each vector is assigned to belong to a particular induced equivalence class. In the matrix of Fig. 3, $row1$, $row3$ and $row4$ would be assigned to the equivalence class 1, $row2$ assigned to equivalence class 2, and $row5$ assigned to equivalence class 3. When the value of IDF requested different from that of the current matrix, we modify the matrix to increase or decrease its IDF by one as discussed below until meeting the specification. To increase IDF, we select any row from any equivalence class that has more than one element and make it the only element of a new equivalence class. This is done by randomly swapping distinct bits in the vector selected until obtaining a vector distinct from all other rows. Note this operation does not modify the tightness of the constraint. To decrease IDF, we select a row that is the only element of an equivalence class and set it equal to any another row. For example in Fig 3, setting $row2 \leftarrow row5$ decreases IDF from 3 to 2. This operation may affect tightness. When this is complete, Step 4 verifies that the tightness of the constraint has not changed. If it has, we start over again, generating a new constraint. If the tightness is correct, we proceed to the following step, *row permutation.*

Step 5: Row permutation. In order to increase our chances of generating random constraints and avoid that the fragmentation determined by one constraint on the domain of a variable coincidences with that induced by another constraint, the rows of each successfully generated constraint are permuted. The permutation process chooses and swaps random rows a random number of times. The input and output matrices of this process obviously have the same tightness and interchangeability as this process does not change these characteristics.

3.3 Constraint Generation in Action

An example of this 5-step process is shown in Figure 4, where we generate a constraint for $a = 5$, IDF $= 3$ and $t = 0.32$. Note that Step 3 and Step 4, which

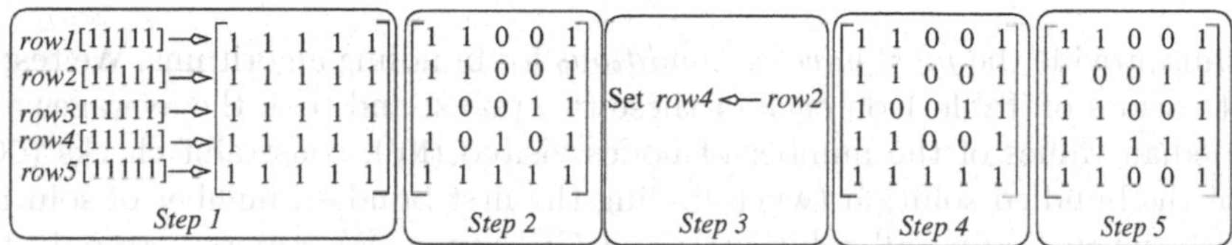

Fig. 4. *Constraint generation process.*

control the interchangeability and tightness of a matrix may fail to terminate successfully. This happens when: (1) No solution exists for the combination of the input parameters. It is easy to check that when $a = 5, t = 0.04$, there exists only solutions with IDF $= 2$, due to the presence of only one 0 in the matrix. And (2) although a solution may exist, the process of modifying interchangeability in the matrix continuously changes tightness. To avoid entering an infinite loop in either of these situations, we use a counter at the beginning of the process of constraint generation. After 50 attempts to generate a constraint, it times out, and the generation of the current CSP is interrupted. Our current implementation of the generator exhibits a failure rate below 5%, and guarantees constraints with both the specified tightness and degree of induced domain fragmentation.

4 Tests and Results

We generated two pools of test problems using our random generator, each with a full range of values for IDF, t, and p and 20 instances per measurement point. The first pool has the following input parameters: $n = 10$, $a = 5$, $p = [.1, 1.0]$ with a step of 0.1, IDF $= 2, 3, 4, 5$, and $t = [.04, .92]$, with a step of 0.08. The second pool has the input parameters: $n = 10$, $a = 7$, $p = [.1, 0.9]$ with a step of 0.2, IDF $=$ $2, 3, \ldots, 7$, and $t = [0.04, 0.92]$, with a step of 0.16. Recall that when p is small, the CSP is not likely to be connected, and when $p = 1$, the CSP is a complete graph. Note that instances with IDF $= a$ have *no* embedded interchangeability

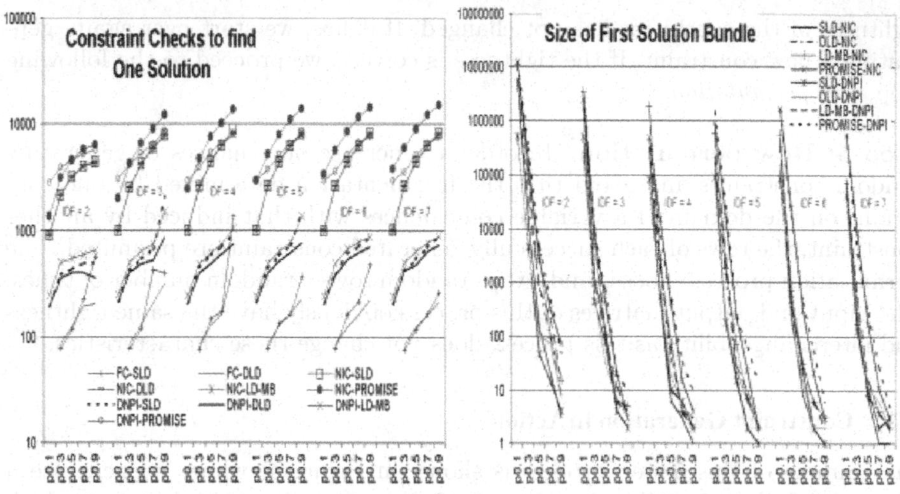

Fig. 5. *Comparing performance of search for finding one solution,* $t = 0.28$.

and thus provide the *most adverse conditions* for bundling algorithms. We tested the strategies of Table 1 on each of these two pools, and took the averages and the median values of the number of nodes visited (`NV`), constraint checks (`CC`), size of the bundled solution (when finding the first bundle), number of solution bundles (when finding all solutions), and CPU time. We report here only the average values since the median are qualitatively equivalent.

Constraint tightness has a large effect on the solvability of a random problem. Problems with loose constraints are likely to have many solutions. As tightness grows, the values of all measured parameters (`CC`, `NV`, CPU time, and bundle size) quickly die to zero because almost all problems become unsolvable (especially for $t \geq 0.5$). The behavior of the various algorithms is best visible at relatively low values for tightness. In Fig. 5 and Fig. 6 we display charts for tightness values of $t = 0.28$ with the second problem pool, where each variable has a domain size of 7 ($a = 7$). The patterns observed on this data set shown are consistent across all values for tightnesses for both problem pools and are not reported here for lack of space. Both figures show that the algorithms are affected by the increasing `IDF`. This effect is more visible in Fig. 6. This demonstrates that our generator indeed allows us to control of the level of interchangeability.

4.1 Finding the First Bundle

In our experiments for finding the first solution bundle, we report in Fig. 5 the charts for `CC` (left) and bundle size (right). Note the logarithmic scale of both charts. The the chart for CPU time is similar to that of `CC` and is not shown.

Three of the four DNPI-based searches (DNPI`promise` is the exception) reside toward the bottom of Fig. 5 proving DNPI performs better than NI_C in terms of the search effort measured as `CC` (left), CPU time (not shown), and size of the first bundle (right). DNPI seems also more resistant than NI_C to an increasing IDF. Even in the absence of embedded interchangeability (large IDF) and when density is high (large p), DNPI-based strategies still perform some bundling performed (bundle size > 1).

At the left Fig. 5, FC is shown slightly below DNPI at the bottom of the chart. One is tempted to think that FC outperforms all the bundling algorithms. However, recall that FC finds only one solution, while DNPI finds from 5 up to one million solutions per bundle for a cost of at most 5 times that of FC. Furthermore, DNPI is finding not only a multitude of solutions, but the similarity of these solutions makes particularly desirable in practical applications for updating solutions.

4.2 Finding All Solutions

The effects of increasing IDF are more striking when finding all solutions and are shown in Fig. 6. It is easy to see in all four charts of Fig. 6 that both static (NI_C) and dynamic (DNPI) bundling searches naturally perform better where there is interchangeability (low values of IDF) than when there is not (IDF approaches a). However, this behavior is much less drastic for DLD-based searches, which are less sensitive to the increase of IDF than SLD-based searches. Indeed the curves for DLD (both NI_C and DNPI) rise significantly slower than its SLD counterparts as the value of IDF increases. Additionally, we see here more clearly than reported in [2], that search with DLD outperforms search with SLD for all evaluation criteria and for all values of p and IDF.

From this data, one is tempted to think that the problems with high interchangeability (e.g., IDF $= 2$) are easier to solve in general than those with higher values of IDF. This is by no means the case. Our experiments have shown that non-bundling FC is not only insensitive to interchangeability, but also performs consistently several orders of magnitude worse than DNPI and NI_C. This data is not shown because it is 3 to 7 orders of magnitude larger than the other values.

Even when interchangeability was specifically not included in a problem (IDF $= a$), all bundling strategies, more significantly dynamic bundling, were able to bundle the solution space. This is due to the fact that as search progresses, some values are eliminated from domains, and thus more interchangeability may become present. This establishes again the superiority of dynamic bundling even in the absence of explicit interchangeability: its runtime is far faster than FC, and its bundling capabilities are clear.

5 Conclusions and Directions for Future Research

In this paper we describe a generator of random binary CSPs that allows us to embed and control the structure, in terms of interchangeability, of a CSP instance. We then investigate the effects of the level of interchangeability on the performance of forward-checking search strategies that are perform no bundling (FC) and that exploit static (NI_C) and dynamic (DNPI) bundling. These strategies are combined with the most common or best performing ordering heuristics.

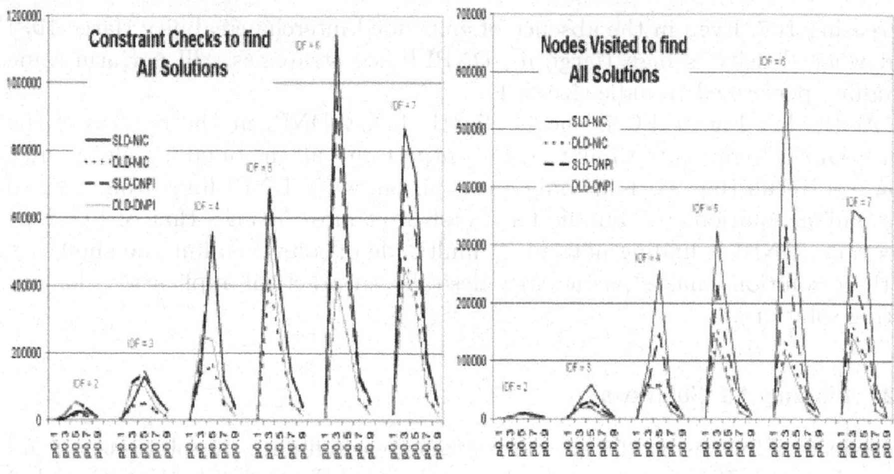

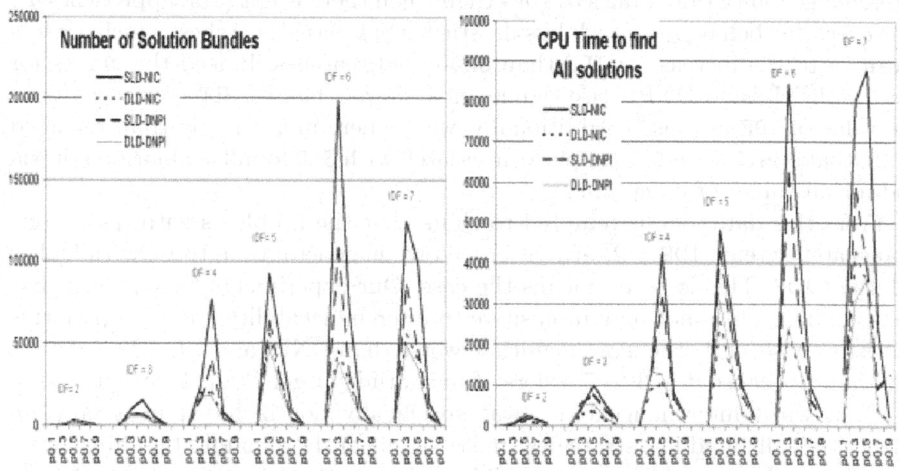

Fig. 6. *Comparing performance of search for finding all solutions, t = 0.28.*

We demonstrate that dynamic bundling strategies remain effective across all levels of interchangeability, even under particularly adverse conditions (i.e., IDF = domain size). While search with either static or dynamic ordering is able to detect and exploit the structure embedded in a problem, DLD-ordered search is less sensitive to the absence of interchangeability, performing quite well in all situations. In particular, we see that DNPI-DLD reacts slowly to the presence or absence of interchangeability while performing consistently well for finding either one or all solutions.

We intend to extend these investigations to non-binary CSPs and also to demonstrate that dynamic bundling may benefit from maintaining arc-consistency (MAC) of Sabin and Freuder [13]. Additionally, the flatness of the curves for

DNPI in Fig. 5 (left) makes us wonder how search strategies based on bundling may be affected by the famous phase-transition phenomenon.

References

1. Fahiem Bacchus and P. van Run. Dynamic Variable Ordering in CSPs. In *Principles and Practice of Constraint Programming, CP'95. Lecture Notes in Artificial Intelligence 976*, pages 258–275. Springer Verlag, 1995.
2. Amy M. Beckwith and Berthe Y. Choueiry. Effects of Dynamic Ordering and Bundling on the Solution Space of Finite Constraint Satisfaction Problems. Technical Report CSL-01-03`http://consystlab.unl.edu/CSL-01-03.ps`, University of Nebraska-Lincoln, 2001.
3. Cynthia A. Brown, Larry Finkelstein, and Paul W. Purdom, Jr. Backtrack Searching in the Presence of Symmetry. In T. Mora, editor, *Applied Algebra, Algebraic Algorithms and Error-Correcting Codes*, pages 99–110. Springer-Verlag, 1988.
4. Berthe Y. Choueiry and Amy M. Beckwith. On Finding the First Solution Bundle in Finite Constraint Satisfaction Problems. Technical Report CSL-01-03. `http://consystlab.unl.edu/CSL-01-04.ps`, University of Nebraska-Lincoln, 2001.
5. Berthe Y. Choueiry and Amy M. Beckwith. Techniques for Bundling the Solution Space of Finite Constraint Satisfaction Problems. Technical Report CSL-01-02. `http://consystlab.unl.edu/CSL-01-02.ps`, University of Nebraska-Lincoln, 2001.
6. Berthe Y. Choueiry and Guevara Noubir. On the Computation of Local Interchangeability in Discrete Constraint Satisfaction Problems. In *Proc. of AAAI-98*, pages 326–333, Madison, Wisconsin, 1998. Revised version KSL-98-24, `http://ksl-web.stanford.edu/KSL_Abstracts/KSL-98-24.html`.
7. Eugene C. Freuder. Eliminating Interchangeable Values in Constraint Satisfaction Problems. In *Proc. of AAAI-91*, pages 227–233, Anaheim, CA, 1991.
8. Eugene C. Freuder and Daniel Sabin. Interchangeability Supports Abstraction and Reformulation for Multi-Dimensional Constraint Satisfaction. In *Proc. of AAAI-97*, pages 191–196, Providence, Rhode Island, 1997.
9. Pieter Andreas Geelen. Dual Viewpoint Heuristics for Binary Constraint Satisfaction Problems. In *Proc. of the 10 th ECAI*, pages 31–35, Vienna, Austria, 1992.
10. Robert M. Haralick and Gordon L. Elliott. Increasing Tree Search Efficiency for Constraint Satisfaction Problems. *Artificial Intelligence*, 14:263–313, 1980.
11. Alois Haselböck. Exploiting Interchangeabilities in Constraint Satisfaction Problems. In *Proc. of the 13 th IJCAI*, pages 282–287, Chambéry, France, 1993.
12. Alan K. Mackworth. Consistency in Networks of Relations. *Artificial Intelligence*, 8:99–118, 1977.
13. Daniel Sabin and Eugene C. Freuder. Contradicting Conventional Wisdom in Constraint Satisfaction. In *Proc. of the 11 th ECAI*, pages 125–129, Amsterdam, The Netherlands, 1994.
14. Hui Zou, Amy M. Beckwith, and Berthe Y. Choueiry. A Generator of Random Instances of Binary Finite Constraint Satisfaction Problems with Controllable Levels of Interchangeability. Technical Report CSL-01-01. `http://consystlab.unl.edu/CSL-01-01.doc`, University of Nebraska-Lincoln, 2001.

Towards Learning Naive Physics by Visual Observation: Qualitative Spatial Representations

Paul A. Boxer

Department of Computer Science
Royal Melbourne Institute of Technology University
LaTrobe St Melbourne

pboxer@cs.rmit.edu.au

Abstract

Autonomous robots are unsuccessful at operating in complex, unconstrained environments. They lack the ability to learn about the physical behaviour of different objects. We examine the viability of using qualitative spatial representations to learn general physical behaviour by visual observation. We combine Bayesian networks with the spatial representations to test them. We input training scenarios that allow the system to observe and learn normal physical behaviour. The position and velocity of the visible objects are represented as discrete states. Transitions between these states over time are entered as evidence into a Bayesian network. The network provides probabilities of future transitions to produce predictions of future physical behaviour. We use test scenarios to determine how well the approach discriminates between normal and abnormal physical behaviour and actively predicts future behaviour. We examine the ability of the system to learn three naive physical concepts, 'no action at a distance', 'solidity' and 'movement on continuous paths'. We conclude that the combination of qualitative spatial representations and Bayesian network techniques is capable of learning these three rules of naive physics.

1 Introduction

The AI community has been unable to create successful, autonomous robots able to operate in complex, unconstrained environments. The main reason for this has been the inability of an agent to reason with Commonsense knowledge [McCarthy, 1968; Dreyfus, 1992]. A subset of Commonsense knowledge is the body of knowledge known as Naive Physics [Hayes, 1978; 1984; 1985]. This is the ability to learn and reason about the physical behaviour of objects. Humans generate rules about the physical behaviour of objects in the real world when they are infants [Bryant, 1974; Piaget and Inhelder, 1969; Vurpillot, 1976]. These rules are not as accurate as the laws of physics that one learns in school and in fact are often quite inaccurate. For this reason, the body of physical rules generated by humans is called Naive Physics and often represents a simplistic version of formal physics. Formal physics can only be learned through empirical experiments or education using high level concepts, such as forces and energy. It cannot be learned by visual observation alone, whereas most aspects of naive physics are learned by every normal human child by the age of 2.

Our research examines the task of learning naive physics by visual observation by combining both qualitative spatial representation and Bayesian networks.

In particular, our specific research questions are:

1. 'How viable is the use of qualitative spatial representations for reasoning in a dynamic, spatial domain?'
2. 'What is the critical sampling frequency for successful learning and prediction for this approach?'
3. 'Which physical concepts can be learned using this approach?'

Our contribution is significant for the following reasons:

- It covers a dynamic, spatial domain
- It confirms the viability of qualitative spatial representations in this domain
- It confirms the viability of probabilistic reasoning in this domain
- It is the first approach to learning general physical behaviour in a *dynamic*, spatial domain
- The knowledge base is learned entirely from observation. No *a priori* knowledge is used

2 Related work

2.1 Naive Physics

Human developmental psychology research [Bryant, 1974; Vurpillot, 1976] shows that infants develop naive physical concepts to understand the physical world. The goal of setting up a committee to build a naive physics knowledge base for AI use was first proposed twenty-two years ago in the *Naive Physics Manifesto* [Hayes, 1978]. This committee was never formed and twenty years later Davis [Davis, 1998] contends that it would be difficult to find more than 12 researchers who have pursued this type of research. One problem he lists is that physics relies heavily on spatial knowledge, which is difficult to express and represent. Furthermore, we do not have good, tractable algorithms

FROM:
B&T Pub Services
30 Amberwood Pkwy
Ashland, OH 44805

TO:
DATAMATION IMAGING SE
BOOKS RECEIVING
7700 GRIFFIN WAY STE B
WILLOWBROOK, IL 60527

(420) 60527

BTC
STANDARD

B/L #:

PRO #:

Purchase Order : MOM4011884

Department #:

Carton Qty:

Sales Order #: M1464562

Carton #:

Shipping Lane:

SSCC – 18
(00) 1 0082952 003353479 1

to handle dynamic, spatial reasoning. So far, no general knowledge base of naive physics exists.

2.2 Qualitative Spatial Reasoning

Qualitative Spatial Reasoning (QSR) [Cohn, 1995; Hernandez, 1994; Cohn, 1997] is a reasonably recent development within AI. It avoids quantitative measurement in its attempts to define the physical world in discrete regions labelled with qualitative terms[1]. This grouping of space into discrete regions greatly reduces the complexity of spatial reasoning. There are an infinite number of ways to carve up space into discrete regions. See Mukerjee [Mukerjee, 1997] for a summary of the different approaches for defining space. There are also a large number of other physical attributes that may be included in a qualitative spatial representation, including orientation [Zimmermann, 1993], shape [Schlieder, 1994], motion [Muller, 1998; Musto *et al.*, 1998; Rajagopalan and Kuipers, 1994] and even the behaviour of flexible bodies [Gardin and Meltzer, 1989].

Qualitative temporal representations have transitive properties due to natural ordering in one dimension [Allen, 1983]. Unfortunately, these are not carried over into three-dimensional space. Forbus, Nielsen and Falting's *Poverty Conjecture* [Weld and DeKleer, 1990] contends there is no powerful, general, purely qualitative spatial representation for more than one dimension. This would appear to limit the potential use of qualitative spatial representations in 2 or more dimensional spaces.

Randell, Cui and Cohn [Randell *et al.*, 1992] established the benchmark RCC8[2] calculus for static, topological worlds. RCC8 does not cater for dynamic factors, such as velocity, which are fundamental to physical behaviour. Furthermore, Renz and Nebel [Renz and Nebel, 1999] have shown reasoning in RCC8 to be NP-hard[3].

Given that RCC8-based spatial reasoning is intractable for static, 2-dimensional worlds, we believe that another approach is required for reasoning in dynamic, 3D worlds. When mapping RCC8 to a 3D world where objects cannot share the same space, the 8 states can be reduced to 2 relevant states, DC (DisConnected) and EC (Externally Connected or touching). These 2 states are the basis of the QSR types used in our work.

Almost all reasoning in the field of Qualitative Spatial Reasoning is based on logical inferencing. This is because QSR uses a discrete, expressive representation, ideal for logical inferencing. However, the real world is inaccessible. We believe any agent operating in it must be able to reason with missing or ambiguous evidence and uncertainty. Logical reasoning does not perform as well as certian types of probabilistic reasoning under these conditions. Probabilistic reasoning with qualitative spatial representations is an unexplored field. We examine the probabilistic reasoning approach. At this point our work diverges from the existing literature.

With the exception of a few researchers [Muller, 1998; Musto *et al.*, 1998], the majority of problem domains using QSR are static. The complexity of logical reasoning in static, spatial domains means that dynamic, spatial domains are still out of reach. Probabilistic tools may allow us to avoid some complexity issues in handling dynamic, spatial domains. This reduced complexity may allow us to extend beyond static domains to more realistic dynamic domains.

QSR representation also has the alleged advantage that it parallels the world representation models used by children under 6[4], *making it a suitable candidate for naive physics reasoning.*

2.3 The Tabula Rasa approach

Work on naive physics and commonsense has been centred around large, hand-generated knowledge bases, such as CYC [Lenat *et al.*, 1990; Lenat and Guha, 1990; Lenat, 1995]. These have proved difficult and expensive to create and have not yet achieved the desired results. Both Rene DeCartes and Bertrand Russell contended that human concepts are built up from a foundation of simpler concepts. We believe that a successful approach must be able to learn from observation, starting with a blank slate.

2.4 Bayesian Networks

Bayesian networks are a powerful probabilistic reasoning tool [Cheeseman, 1988; D'Ambrosio, 1999; Russell and Norvig, 1995] and have the characteristic of being able to handle uncertain, conflicting and missing evidence [Jensen, 1996]. Their performance in reasoning in these domains is better than logical reasoning. This makes them a suitable probabilistic reasoning tool for our work. We use Bayesian Networks for this work.

2.5 Event detection

Detection of events is the key to learning the rules of naive physics. [Tsotsos *et al.*, 1980] was a very early example of the use of qualitative methods in a spatial domain. Fernyhough, Cohn and Hogg [Fernyhough *et al.*, 1998] developed a qualitative vision system to identify traffic behaviour. This is one of the few recent attempts to use qualitative techniques for event detection observed through computer vision. The system focused on a very narrow domain but highlighted the potential of using discrete or qualitative spatial representations.

Siskind [Mann *et al.*, 1996; Siskind and Morris, 1996] developed a system using probabilistic reasoning tools for dynamic, spatial reasoning. Their system identifies 6 predefined, human interaction events. The 6 events are *push,*

[1] Instead of stating that a keyboard is 0.37 metres North of me, 0.12 metres West, which is a quantitative description of its location, QSR defines location in qualitative terms such as, the keyboard is 'in-front-of' me, 'on-the-desk'.

[2] Named after the authors, Randell, Cohn and Cui but often referred to as the Region-Connected Calculus

[3] Reasoning in both RCC8 and RCC5 is NP-hard in modal logic. They did identify a maximal, tractable set of relations through a transformation to propositional logic

[4] Up to 4 years of age, the human child appears to internally represent the world in a qualitative topological form where shape and distance are poorly represented. Later, a projective model is used, which can represent shape and relative position but is weak on measurement and scale. At the age of 10 to 12 the child attains an Euclidean model with full scale, measurement and vector abilities [Bryant, 1974; Piaget and Inhelder, 1969; Vurpillot, 1976]

pull, drop, throw, put down and *pick up*. Hidden Markov models (HMM) are used to provide a highest likelihood result to detect and classify an event. This use of probabilistic reasoning methods is the major similarity to our work. In contrast, Siskind's 6 events are at an ontologically higher level than ours and use *a priori* knowledge to define the events. Because of our Tabula Rasa approach, we believe our lower, foundational level is a more appropriate basis for a scalable general physical reasoning system. Furthermore, we suspect that Siskind's work is not expandable without adding code for each individual event to be detected. Our work uses no *a priori* knowledge of physical behaviour and learns from a blank slate. This gives our approach the potential to learn equally well in a world with vastly different physical behaviour, such as under water or in space.

3 Combining QSR and Probabilistic Reasoning

3.1 The Scenarios

The system uses simulated, animated scenarios of billiard ball motion for training and testing. Simulated scenarios are used to avoid the implementation problems of a computer vision system. The animated scenarios are generated from planar camera views of objects moving in a 3D virtual world. In this case, a billiard table is simulated. Because of the planar view point, all the scenarios used for this work are accessible and appear similar to 2D animations. Later work will investigate fully 3D scenarios. The scenarios capture a large range of examples of typical physical behaviour. There are 800 scenarios, each typically having 400 frames. Three typical (non-sequential) frames of one scenario, showing a collision, are shown in figure 1.

The position and velocity of all objects in the scenario are represented as discrete states, the amount of information being determined by the *QSR type*.

3.2 The Qualitative Spatial Representation

Definitions A *QSR type* is defined in this document as the way that a spatial relation is represented, usually as a vector containing 2 to 6 elements called *attributes*. We use the term 'qualitative spatial representation' even though all qualitative content is stripped from the representation and the state of each attribute is represented purely as a number. Each attribute has a discrete number of possible states, usually between 2 and 8, with 3 being very common [Cohn, 1995]. The total number of possible relations that a particular QSR type can represent is equal to the product of the number of states for each attribute.

$$N_{QSRtype} = N_0 \times N_1 \times N_2 \times N_3 \times .. \times N_n$$

For example, a QSR type with 6 attributes, each with 3 possible states, could represent 729 different spatial/motion relations (3^6).

Hernandez [Hernandez, 1994] lists the different dimensions used to classify different QSR types[5]. The following list

[5]citing Freska and Roehig

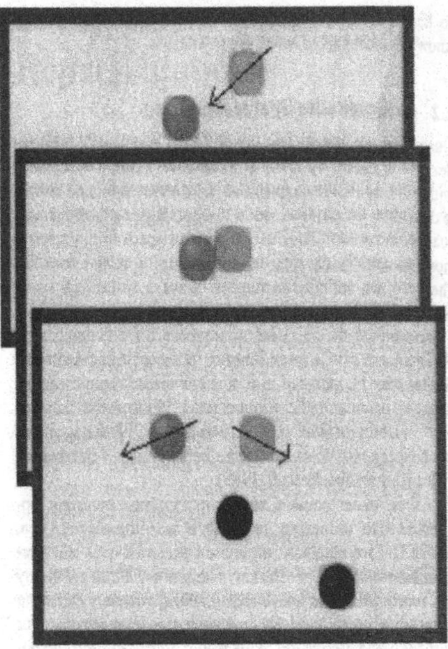

Figure 1: 3 frames from a typical scenario (arrows added to indicate velocity)

locates our QSR types within this framework:

- Frame Of Reference - We use locally-aligned Cartesian and polar coordinates.
- Representational Primitives - Our work is based on regions.
- Spatial Aspects Represented - We examine a topological QSR with the addition of velocity.
- Granularity - We use low resolution QSR types.
- Vagueness - Our QSR types have no ambiguity. All states are mutually exclusive.

4 different QSR types are examined, 2 using a cartesian representation and 2 using a polar representation. Because the scenarios are planar, the QSR types are only 2-dimensional. QSRO1 and QSRO2 use an orthogonal (cartesian) format and have 81 and 225 possible states, respectively. For both QSRO1 and QSRO2, the x and y dimensions are independent. These QSR types have 4 attributes. 2 attributes represent position in 2 dimensions, x and y and 2 attributes represent the respective velocities, V_x and V_y. The attributes have either 3 or 5 possible states. QSRO2 is shown in figure 2.

QSRP1 and QSRP2 are based on polar coordinates and have 384 and 960 possible states, respectively. Because of the nature of polar coordinates, both x and y dimensions are coupled.

The maximum number of transitions, shown in table 1 is the square of the number of possible states. That is, in a random world, each state could transition to any other state, including

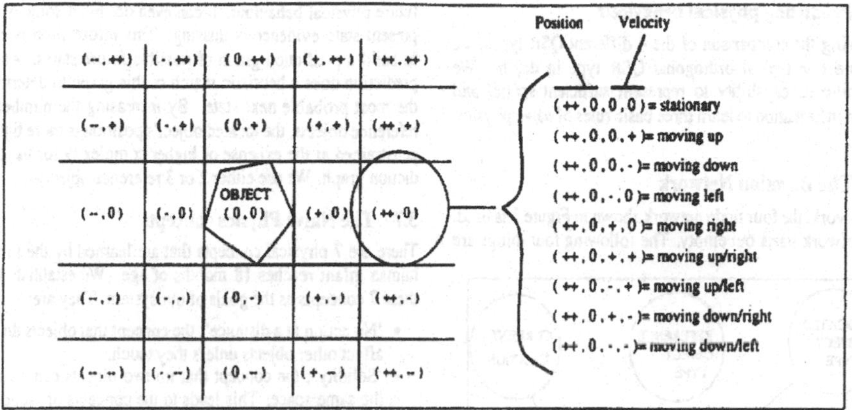

Figure 2: QSR type QSRO2, representing position and velocity in 225 states

itself. Given the ordered characteristic of the physical world, the number of transitions that one would expect to observe is considerably less, approximately 3-8% of the maximum number possible. This is discussed in the next section.

QSR Type	Number of States	Maximum number of transitions	Expected number of transitions
QSRO1	81	6,561	576
QSRO2	225	50,625	2,304
QSRP1	384	147,456	10,752
QSRP2	960	921,600	53,760

Table 1: Different QSR types tested

3.3 Complexity of QSR Composition Tables In Dynamic Domains

The natural ordering of QSR states [Cohn, 1995; Hernandez, 1994] greatly reduces the number of transitions from one state to another that should be observed. For QSRO2 that has 225 possible states, the actual number of observed transitions is only 2,300 instead of the 50,000 theoretical maximum. This characteristic of almost all QSR types is due to the fact that objects move along continuous curves in our physical world. Any change in position, when measured on a discretized scale, tends to be either an increment or a decrement of the previous position. This characteristic of QSR is very important for work in dynamic domains. There does not appear to be a consensus on the naming of this characteristic so we adopt the term 'transitive characteristic' based on the transitivity of ordering mentioned by Cohn [Cohn, 1995].

3.4 Transitivity Criterion

Because of the importance of this transitive characteristic, it is essential to use an image sampling rate that is fast enough compared to both the resolution of the QSR and the speed of the objects. There is a linear relationship between the sample rate, the object speed and resolution of a QSR type if the transitive characteristic is to be satisfied.

$$sample\ frequency(s^{-1}) = \frac{object\ speed(ms^{-1})}{minimum\ QSR\ resolution(m)}$$

If the sample frequency is too low or the resolution or object speed are too high, the observed object may pass through several states between observation samples. If it becomes possible for the object to move from any one state to any other state between sample times then the number of observable transitions climbs quickly. The problem deteriorates to an intractable level of complexity and probabilistic reasoning is degraded. For this reason, maintaining the transitive characteristic is very important for QSR work that involves motion. Because of the importance of this characteristic, we define it as the *transitivity criterion*. Unfortunately, velocity (and acceleration) attributes do not satisfy the transitivity criterion at normal sampling frequencies. Whilst position appears to change transitively, velocity appears to be discontinuous at normal sampling frequencies[6], typically 5-25 Hertz. For example, a ball may appear to change direction instantly as a result of a 'bounce' observed at normal sampling frequencies. Each position attribute usually has 3 expected next states, either an increment, a decrement or no change, whereas a velocity attribute could change to any value. This means we must monitor the potential combinatorial growth that may result from using QSR types that have high resolution velocity attributes. Therefore, there is a strong motivation for reducing the number of position attributes and increasing the resolution of those attributes while reducing both the number and resolution of velocity attributes.

[6] In fact, both velocity and acceleration are continuous and transitive for all objects with mass. However, satisfying the transitivity criterion for velocity or acceleration attributes requires resolution and sampling frequencies an order of magnitude higher than that for position attributes.

3.5 Predicting physical behaviour

Following the comparison of the 4 different QSR types, we examine one typical orthogonal QSR type in depth. We determine its capability to represent sufficient spatial and motion information to learn three basic rules of naive physics.

3.6 The Bayesian Network

In our work, the four node network shown in Figure 3 is used. The network starts out empty. The following four things are

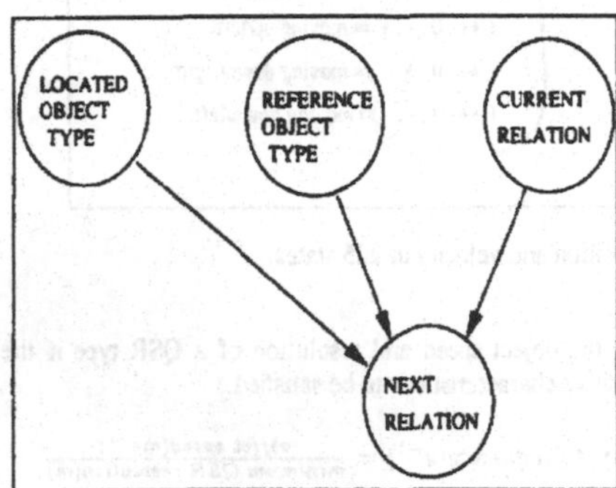

Figure 3: 4 Node Bayesian Network

represented in the network:

- 'Reference object (RO) type', the type of object acting as a reference point. For example, type 17 represents a billiard ball.
- 'Located object (LO) type', the type of the object to which the spatial relation refers.
- 'Current relation', the current state of the relation between the focal and reference object, represented in the relevant QSR type format.
- 'Next relation', the next state of the relation between the focal and reference object, represented in the relevant QSR type format. In a Bayesian network that includes all observed evidence, the number of states stored in this node would equal the number of transitions observed within all scenarios.

This network allows the system to use the object types, both reference and located, and their current relation in terms of a QSR type for prediction. The position and velocity of the objects shown in the scenarios are represented as qualitative states. Transitions between these states from frame to frame are used as updating evidence. The node probabilities are generated by fractional updating [Jensen, 1996]. Each node may grow to have many different node states.

Prediction of future relations is based on the Markov assumption that the future state is independent of the past state given the present state. By querying the Bayesian network based on the present state, the network can provide the probability of the next state in terms of the QSR type being used. The network thereby provides the probabilities of the future relative positions and motions of the located object, and hence, its future physical behaviour. It can even do this if some of the present state evidence is missing. This information is used to build a prediction graph of possible future states. Active prediction does a heuristic search of this graph to determine the most probable next state. By increasing the number of reference objects, the located object's position is more tightly constrained at the expense of higher complexity for the prediction graph. We use either 2 or 3 reference objects.

3.7 The Naive Physics concepts

There are 7 physical concepts that are learned by the time a human infant reaches 18 months of age. We establish 3 of these 7 concepts as the goals of our system. They are:

- 'No action at a distance', the concept that objects do not affect other objects unless they touch.
- 'Solidity', the concept that no two objects can occupy the same space. This leads to the concepts of 'support' and 'collision'.
- 'Movement on continuous paths', the concept that objects move along continuous curves.

The other four main, foundational concepts are 'object permanence', 'consistency', 'inertia' and 'gravity'.

4 Experimental Results

Two series of tests were conducted. The first series compared 4 QSR types, examining the growth in the number of observed states and observed transitions for the 4 types. The purpose of these tests was to confirm that the growth in observed transitions approached an asymptotic maximum far lower than the maximum number of possible transitions. Further, we wanted to demonstrate that this phenomenon applied to all the tested QSR types.

The second series examined the training, testing and prediction abilities of one of the QSR types when combined with a Bayesian network. This series of tests involved learning though observation, classifying abnormal behaviours and predicting future physical behaviour. The purpose of these tests was to demonstrate the viability of combining probabilistic reasoning and qualitative spatial representations to learn naive physical behaviour.

4.1 Comparing 4 different QSR types

A training set of 800 scenarios was generated for these tests. The tests were repeated 4 times, once with each QSR type. The system observed all 800 scenarios, using one of the selected QSR types to represent the spatial relations observed. As more scenarios were observed, both the number of observed states (spatial relations) and the number of observed transitions between these states increased. After viewing the 800 scenarios, the system will have observed almost all possible states and up to 900,000 transitions. The growth graphs for the 4 QSR types were compared.

The actual number of observed transitions after 800 scenarios is shown in table 2. It can be seen that the higher resolution QSR types have a far higher number of expected transitions.

From figure 4 it can be seen that, for all tested QSR types, the number of observed states grew quickly and approached a horizontal asymptote equal to the maximum number of

QSR Type	Expected number of transitions	Number of transitions after 800 scenarios
QSRO1	576	2,542
QSRO2	2,304	5,636
QSRP1	10,752	6,427
QSRP2	53,760	18,715

Table 2: Different QSR types tested

states. The simpler, lower resolution QSR types achieved the maximum number of observed states within a very low number of scenarios. For example, QSRO1 observes all 81 possible states within the first 3 scenarios alone.

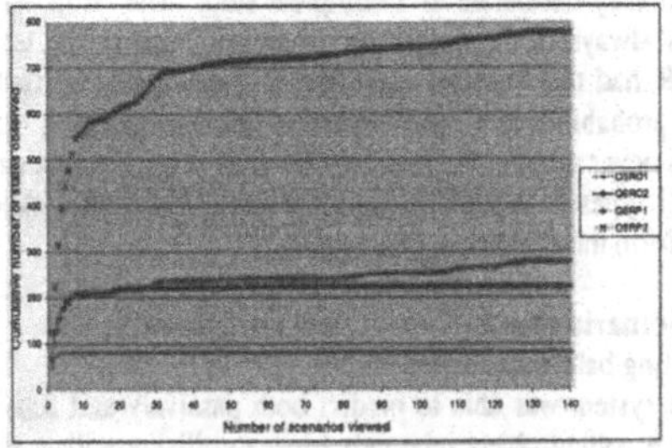

Figure 4: Growth in the number of observed states

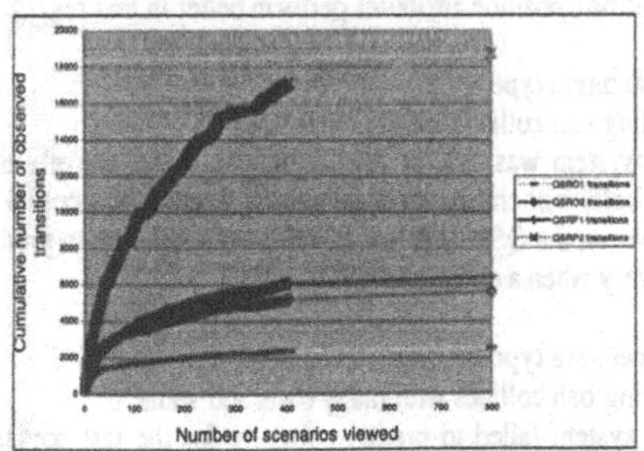

Figure 5: Growth in the number of observed transitions

The most significant result is that all transitions growth rates shown in figure 5 show a strong trend to approach a horizontal asymptote. Furthermore, this asymptote is far below the maximum number of possible transitions. This supports the contention that QSR types that meet the *transitivity criterion* will have a relatively low number of observed transitions compared to the maximum number of possible transitions. This keeps the computational requirements for probabilistic reasoning low.

Both the cartesian QSR types had more than twice as many observed transitions as expected. This is because many of the transitions that occured had changes in more than one attribute, usually x and y positions. The estimate of the expected number of observed transitions is based on only one attribute changing state at each transition. If two or more attributes can change state together, the number of observed transitions can be far greater than the expected number.

Both the polar QSR types had less observed transitions than the expected number. There are 2 factors that contribute to this. One is because the polar position can only change by an increment or a decrement (assuming the transitivity criterion is met). The other, in the case of QSRP2, is that the growth had not yet fully plateaued and was still increasing after 800 scenarios. Higher resolution QSR types need a larger number of training scenarios to oberve all the expected transitions.

For all QSR types, approximately 40% of the observed transitions were observed 5 or fewer times and 17% were only observed once. This fact could be used to prune rare transitions and further reduce the size of the Bayesian network, and hence the computational resources required for reasoning. Even with the large number of transitions observed, the system is able to make predictions at almost real-time speeds on a 233MHz Pentium II PC.

4.2 Training for prediction

Prior to running the tests, the system was prepared by purging the Bayesian network of all data, in effect clearing all knowledge of previously learned behaviour. The system was then subjected to a training process that involved observing 75 different training scenarios 14 times each. This exposes the system to 1,025 scenario runs. Each of these 75 scenarios showed a complex interaction of 4 rolling balls bouncing off cushions and hitting each other. The scenarios are not intended to be exhaustive. Our set of 75 training scenarios covers 83% of the expected transitions, calculated by comparing the number of expected versus actual observed transitions. At the completion of training, 400,000 pieces of evidence have been processed by the Bayesian Network.

4.3 Passive and active prediction

Our results revealed that there appear to be two levels of prediction of which the system is capable. The first one is the ability to detect and flag abnormal behaviour. We define this as *passive prediction*. The second level of prediction, called *active prediction*, is the ability to observe the first section of a scenario and predict the future motion of the objects involved [7].

4.4 Test Results

A series of 58 test scenarios was run. There were 34 'normal' scenarios, wherein the behaviour of the objects would be subjectively described as normal. There were also 24 'abnormal' scenarios, wherein the behaviour of the objects would be described as abnormal. That is, they were in conflict with the rules of naive physics.

[7] It is interesting to note that the standard psychological tests for human infants test only for passive prediction abilities [Bryant, 1974; Vurpillot, 1976].

Two passive prediction results were recorded for each test scenario. The first was the number of normal scenarios determined to be normal (true positives). The second was the number of abnormal scenarios that were detected as abnormal (true negatives). The results are shown in table 3.
The prediction graphs created during 23 'normal' scenarios were examined for each state to determine the accuracy of active prediction. These results are shown in table 4. In most cases the system correctly predicted the next state but there were few scenarios where the correct state was actively predicted for all transitions that occurred in the scenario. For this reason, the results show the total number of correct and incorrect predictions.

Scenario Type	Normal Scenarios accepted as normal	Abnormal Scenarios detected as anomalous
All Objects Stationary	4/4 100%	4/5 80%
Ball rolling to a stop	8/8 100%	8/8 100%
Ball bouncing off wall	10/10 100%	5/7 71%
Ball collides with ball	3/8 37%	4/4 100%
Multiple collisions	0/4 0%	

Table 3: Results for passive prediction

Overview of results
Overall the system is able to perform passive prediction very well using only probabilistic data. Exceptions specific to each scenario type are noted below.
Active prediction performance is dependent on the QSR attribute resolution. The low resolution attributes used for this work create low probabilities when predicting some valid state changes. This reduces the accuracy of active prediction. The most common active prediction (in 52% of the cases) was that the state will remain in the same state[8]. The 'same state' prediction is not a default prediction. It must also be learned. Also shown in table 4 are the number of correct and incorrect active predictions excluding 'same state' predictions.
In most cases, the limiting aspect is the resolution of the QSR type. Future work will investigate which aspects of QSR types most affect learning physical behaviour.

	Correct within QSR type resolution	Incorrect
All active predictions	142/184 77%	42/184 23%
All active predictions (excluding same state)	47/89 53%	42/89 47%

Table 4: Results for active prediction

[8]To avoid the high number of these 'same state' predictions overwhelming the results, a prediction that a state would remain constant for many frames of a scenario was counted as only one correct prediction

Scenario type 0
Stationary objects remain Stationary:
The system was able to predict both passively and actively that stationary objects will remain stationary.
It is interesting to note that the system failed to detect one abnormality in one of the test scenarios. The abnormality was the spontaneous relocation of a reference object. However the object remained in the same QSR region. This is an example of where a low resolution QSR type is unable to detect anomalous behaviour.

Scenario type 1
Rolling object decelerates and stops:
The system was able to predict both passively and actively that rolling objects will continue to roll in the same direction until they decelerate to a complete stop. The 'stop' event was always in the prediction graph but because the tested QSR had the coarsest resolution in the velocity attributes, the probability of a 'stop' was low. For this reason, a 'stop' was never actively predicted as the most probable next state. QSR types with higher resolution velocity attributes should perform much better in this regard.

Scenario type 2
Rolling ball rebounds off wall:
The system was able to predict both passively and actively that a rolling object rebounds from a collision with a wall. However, due to the coarse resolution of the position attributes, the probability of the collision was always low. As with the 'stop' event for scenario type 2, a 'collision' event was often not actively predicted. QSR types with higher resolution position attributes perform better in this regard.

Scenario type 3
Rolling ball collides with another ball:
The system was able to predict passively and actively that two balls will change their velocity as a result of a collision. However, the QSR type had insufficient resolution to predict actively when a collision would occur.

Scenario type 4
Rolling ball collides with many balls and walls:
The system failed to predict correctly for the last scenario type due to the movement of the reference objects. In the current implementation, other balls can be reference objects. When references move, the system is unable to establish a frame of reference and prediction deteriorates.

4.5 Testing the Transitivity Criterion

The training and testing were repeated with a configuration that ensured the transitivity criterion was not always satisfied. This was achieved by reducing the sampling speed by a factor of five. This slower sampling would allow a moving object to transition from one state to a non-neighbouring state between frames. The results, shown in table 5, show the expected deterioration of the prediction ability with the violation of the transitivity criterion.

The system is able to reliably detect anomalous behaviour

Scenario Type	Normal Scenarios accepted as normal
All Objects Stationary	4/4 100%
Ball rolling to a stop	4/4 100%
Ball bouncing off wall	4/7 57%
Ball collides with ball	1/4 25%

Table 5: Results with unsatisfied transitivity criterion

and actively predict future behaviour under the following conditions:

- Enough scenarios have been run to generate a comprehensive representation of physical behaviour within the Bayesian network.
- The transitivity criterion is satisfied for position attributes.
- The resolution of the QSR is high enough.

5 Conclusion

Our research questions were:

1. 'How viable is the use of qualitative spatial representations for reasoning in a dynamic, spatial domain?'
   If the system meets the transitivity criterion, the system does not suffer a combinatorial growth in the number of observed transitions. We conclude the approach is suitable for reasoning in this dynamic, spatial domain based on its ability to identify abnormal behaviour and predict future behaviour.
2. 'What is the critical sampling frequency for successful learning and prediction for this approach?'
   The sampling frequency is determined by the transitivity criterion. The transitivity criterion is a critical factor for qualitative, dynamic, spatial representations and the accuracy of probabilistic reasoning is degraded if the transitivity criterion is not satisfied.
3. 'Which physical concepts can be learned using this approach?'
   The approach was able to learn 3 of the foundational rules of naive physics, 'no action at a distance', 'solidity' and 'movement on continuous paths'. This knowledge was used to accurately identify abnormal behaviour and, in many cases, to actively predict future behaviour.

The prediction work was done with one QSR type. We intend to look at other QSR types to establish which QSR characteristics are important in learning physical behaviour.

References

[Allen, 1983] J. F. Allen. Maintaining knowledge about temporal intervals. *Communications of the ACM*, 26(11):832–843, November 1983.

[Bryant, 1974] Peter Bryant. *Perception and understanding in young children*. Methuen and Co Ltd, London, 1974.

[Cheeseman, 1988] Peter Cheeseman. An inquiry into computer understanding. *Computational Intelligence*, 4(1):58–66, 1988.

[Cohn, 1995] A. G. Cohn. The challenge of qualitative spatial reasoning. *ACM Computing Surveys*, 27(3):323–325, September 1995.

[Cohn, 1997] Anthony G. Cohn. Qualitative spatial representation and reasoning techniques. In Gerhard Brewka, Christopher Habel, and Bernhard Nebel, editors, *KI-97, Advances in Artificial Intelligence*, pages 1–30. Springer-Verlag, Berlin, 1997.

[D'Ambrosio, 1999] Bruce D'Ambrosio. Inference in bayesian networks. *AI Magazine*, 1999.

[Davis, 1998] E. Davis. The naive physics perplex. *AI Magazine*, 19(1):51–79, 1998.

[Dreyfus, 1992] H. L. Dreyfus. *What Computers Still Can't Do: A Critique of Artificial Reason*. MIT Press, 1992.

[Fernyhough *et al.*, 1998] J Fernyhough, AG Cohn, and DC Hogg. Building qualitative event models automatically from visual input. In *Sixth International Conference on Computer Vision*, pages 350–5. Narosa Publishing House, New Delhi, India, Jan 1998.

[Gardin and Meltzer, 1989] Francesco Gardin and Bernard Meltzer. Analogical representations of naive physics. *Artificial Intelligence*, 38:139–159, 1989.

[Hayes, 1978] Patrick J. Hayes. The naive physics manifesto. In D. Michie, editor, *Expert Systems in the Microelectronic Age*. Edinburgh University Press, Edinburgh, Scotland, 1978.

[Hayes, 1984] Patrick J. Hayes. The second naive physics manifesto. In *Formal Theories of the Commonsense World*. Ablex Publishing Corp., Norwood, New Jersey, 1984.

[Hayes, 1985] Patrick J. Hayes. Naive physics I: ontology for liquids. In Jerry R. Hobbs and Robert C. Moore, editors, *Formal Theories of the Commonsense World*, chapter 3, pages 71–107. Ablex, Norwood, New Jersey, 1985.

[Hernandez, 1994] Daniel Hernandez. *Qualitative Representation of Spatial Knowledge*. Number 804 in Lecture Notes in Artificial Intelligence. Springer-Verlag, 1994.

[Jensen, 1996] F. V. Jensen. *An introduction to Bayesian Networks*. UCL Press (Taylor & Francis Ltd), London, 1996.

[Lenat and Guha, 1990] Douglas B. Lenat and R. V. Guha. *Building Large Knowledge-Based Systems: Representation and Inference in the CYC Project*. Addison-Wesley, Reading, Massachusetts, 1990.

[Lenat *et al.*, 1990] D. B. Lenat, R. V. Guha, K. Pittman, D. Pratt, and M. Shepherd. CYC: towards programs with common sense. *CACM, August 1990*, 33(8):30–49, 1990.

[Lenat, 1995] Douglas B. Lenat. CYC: A large-scale investment in knowledge infrastructure. *Communications of the ACM*, 38(11):33–38, November 1995.

[Mann *et al.*, 1996] Richard Mann, Allan Jepson, and Jeffrey Mark Siskind. Computational perception of scene dynamics. In Roberto Cipolla Bernard Buxton, editor, *Computer Vision - ECCV '96 vol 2*, number 1065 in Lecture Notes in Computer Science, pages 528–39. Springer-Verlag, 1996.

[McCarthy, 1968] J. McCarthy. Programs with common sense. In M. Minsky, editor, *Semantic Information Processing*, pages 403–418. MIT Press, Cambridge, MA, 1968. Part of this article is a reprint from an an article by the same title, in *Proc. Conf. on the Mechanization of Thought Processes*, National Physical Laboratory, Teddington, England, Vol. 1, pp. 77–84, 1958.

[Mukerjee, 1997] Amitabha Mukerjee. Neat vs scruffy: A review of computational models for spatial expressions. 1997.

[Muller, 1998] Philippe Muller. A qualitative theory of motion based on spatio-temporal primitives. In Anthony G. Cohn, Lenhart Schubert, and Stuart C. Shapiro, editors, *KR'98: Principles of Knowledge Representation and Reasoning*, pages 131–141. Morgan Kaufmann, San Francisco, California, 1998.

[Musto *et al.*, 1998] A. Musto, K. Stein, A. Eisenkolb, K. Schill, and W. Brauer. Generalization, segmentation and classification of qualitative motion data. In Henri Prade, editor, *Proceedings of the 13th European Conference on Artificial Intelligence (ECAI-98)*, pages 180–184, Chichester, August 23–28 1998. John Wiley & Sons.

[Piaget and Inhelder, 1969] Jean Piaget and Baerbel Inhelder. *The Psychology of the Child*. Routledge and Kegan Paul, London, 1969.

[Rajagopalan and Kuipers, 1994] R. Rajagopalan and B. Kuipers. Qualitative spatial reasoning about objects in motion: Application to physics problem solving. In Dan O'Leary and Peter Selfridge, editors, *Proceedings of the 10th Conference on Artificial Intelligence for Applications*, pages 238–245, San Antonio, TX, March 1994. IEEE Computer Society Press.

[Randell *et al.*, 1992] David A. Randell, Zhan Cui, and Anthony G. Cohn. A spatial logic based on regions and connection. In William Nebel, Bernhard; Rich, Charles; Swartout, editor, *Proceedings of the 3rd International Conference on Principles of Knowledge Representation and Reasoning*, pages 165–176, Cambridge, MA, October 1992. Morgan Kaufmann.

[Renz and Nebel, 1999] Jochen Renz and Bernhard Nebel. On the complexity of qualitative spatial reasoning: A maximal tractable fragment of the region connection calculus. *Artificial Intelligence*, 108(1–2):69–123, 1999.

[Russell and Norvig, 1995] Stuart Russell and Peter Norvig. *Artifical Intelligence: A Modern Approach,*. Prentice-Hall, Englewood Cliffs, NJ, ISBN 0-13-103805-2, 912 pp., 1995, 1995.

[Schlieder, 1994] C. Schlieder. Qualitative shape representation. 1994.

[Siskind and Morris, 1996] J. M. Siskind and Q. Morris. A maximum likelihood approach to visual event classification. In Roberto Cipolla Bernard Buxton, editor, *Computer Vision - ECCV '96*, number 1065 in Lecture Notes in Computer Science, pages 347–62. Springer-Verlag, 1996.

[Tsotsos *et al.*, 1980] J. K. Tsotsos, J. Myopoulos, H. D. Covvey, and S. W. Zucker. A framework for visual motion understanding. *IEEE-T PAMI*, 2(6):563–573, 1980.

[Vurpillot, 1976] Elaine Vurpillot. *The Visual World of the Child*. George Allen and Unwin Ltd, London, 1976.

[Weld and DeKleer, 1990] Daniel Weld and J. DeKleer. *Qualitative Reasoning about Physical Systems, ed.* Morgan Kaufmann, 1990, 1990.

[Zimmermann, 1993] Kai Zimmermann. Enhancing qualitative spatial reasoning—combining orientation and distance. In Andrew U. Frank and Irene Campari, editors, *Spatial Information Theory. A Theoretical Basis for GIS. European Conference, COSIT'93*, volume 716 of *Lecture Notes in Computer Science*, pages 69–76, Berlin, September 1993. Springer.

Phased Array Sub-beam Optimisation

N. J. Bracken[1] and R. I. (Bob) McKay[2]

[1]CEA Technologies, 65 Gladstone St, Fyshwick, ACT Australia
njb@cea.com.au
[1,2]University of New South Wales at ADFA, Campbell ACT Australia
rim@cs.adfa.edu.au

Abstract. The subset of Elements used to form an independent sub beam of a Phased Array Radar Antenna can be found using a two stage Genetic Algorithm. The use of Pareto optimisation allows the determination of the minimum set of Elements to be used for the desired beam pattern. The outer GA optimises the selection of elements to be used in the sub beam, while the inner GA optimises the tuning parameters of the selected set of elements.

1 Introduction

This paper presents a method for the selection of a subset of elements to construct a reference beam for a phased array radar. A reference beam can be defined as a secondary beam that has a lower consistent power level over a wider field.

The continuing decreasing cost of phased array systems has led to increased investigation into the possible uses of this technology. One of the main advantages of a phased array system is the ability to shape the radiation pattern depending on the characteristics desired for the beam at any time. The application of beam shaping for radar systems has presented the radar engineer with many new possibilities and new requirements to improve systems. One of these requirements is the application of a secondary beam for use as a reference when tracking known targets without diverting the main search beam. This secondary beam or Reference Beam has different characteristics to those usually sought for a main beam, it is wider and does not focus its power into a small âpencil beam.

2 Aim

This paper aims to describe a method used to generate a reference beam that is independent of the main beam. The approach is based on the assumption that a small proportion of the nodes in an array tile can be diverted away from the main beam and used to create a secondary beam with little impact on the main beam. The actual impact on the main beam of the secondary beam is not within the scope of this paper.

The research uses an array configuration developed by CEA Technologies as its array topography. For an array of 512 transmitting elements arranged in a triangular

M. Brooks, D. Corbett, and M. Stumptner (Eds.): AI 2001, LNAI 2256, pp. 71–82, 2001.

grid, the optimum nodes to form a reference beam of a specified width and power are sought. This paper describes a method used to find this optimum set of nodes for any specified beam or tile pattern.

2.1 Phased Array Radars

A phased array radar is a collection of stationary antenna elements, which are fed coherently, and use variable phase or time-delay control at each element to scan a beam to given angles in space. The multiplicity of elements allows a more precise control of the radiation pattern.[1][2]. The power of the radiation at any point in space is the sum of the individual power from each element. This sum is a vector addition to take into account the effects of constructive and destructive interference induced by the different phases of elements. An example beam pattern is displayed in Figure 1.

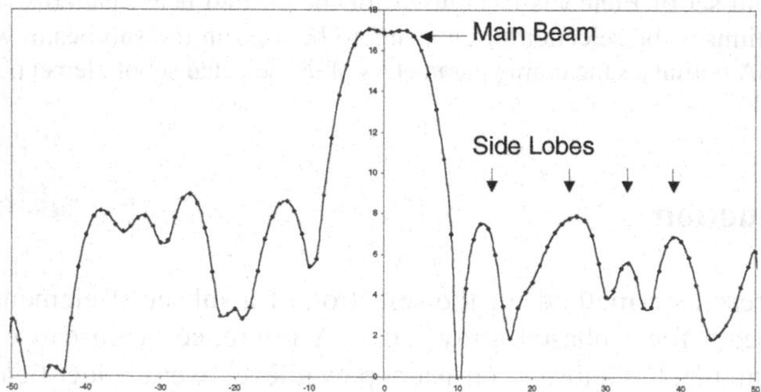

Fig. 1. Possible beam pattern at 0 elevation between 50 & 50 degrees of azimuth.

2.2 Genetic Algorithms

A genetic algorithm is a stochastic global search method using principles of natural selection. It has three main distinguishing features from other optimization methods.

Groups of answers are generated in parallel; the GA usually acts upon the encoding of parameters and not the parameters themselves, and it uses simple stochastic operators, Selection, Crossover, and Mutation, to explore the solution domain for an optimal solution [3][4][5].

An initial population is created at random. Each member of the population is an answer to the problem to be optimised. Parents are selected from the population for breeding. The child is produced via crossover and mutation to form a new answer. This answer is evaluated against a fitness function and the child replaces older members of the population. At some time after many generations the program is terminated and the best member of the population is the solution found.

The implementation of a GA can be broken into seven stages: the Encoding of Parameters, the determination of a Fitness Function, selection of the GA operators to be used: Selection, Crossover, Mutation and Replacement, and the determination of the Halting Criterion.

Parameter encoding

GAs use encoding of parameters, not the value of the parameters themselves. Where possible the coding should have some underlying relevance to the problem and as small an alphabet as practical. In most applications this means a binary representation which fits easily into a computer representation of the parameters.[6]

The represented parameters are often referred to as genes. The collection of genes which make up a single answer are correspondingly referred to as a chromosome.

Example: Phased array radar parameters

Tile of 4 * 4 elements. Each element has associated phase, amplitude and position:

```
Element {   Phase
            Amplitude
            Position}
Array {     Array of Elements}
```

The position of an element can be stored elsewhere as its value doesn t change and may be inferred from the position of the element within the array.

Phase and amplitude are often controlled by digital phase shifters and modulators and can be given values that reflect the number of states possible instead of a floating point value. This will reduce the search space for each parameter from the range of the floating representation to the actual number of states available. That is from approximately +/- 2^302 to 256.

The resulting representation is:

```
Element {   Phase = 8 bits
            Amplitude = 4 bits}
Array {     16 * 12 bits}
```

The position of each element in the array is inferred from its array index.

Fitness function

In a GA, the fitness function calculates a value or values to be used as a comparison between different solutions. The simplest form returns a value which represents how close the current solution is to the theoretical optimum. More complex functions return many values for comparison against multiple objectives. Using our simple radar example, a simple fitness function would return the amount of energy projected by the array at a set position. More advanced fitness functions might return the calculated beam pattern of the array or the maximum side lobe level.

Population selection

The selection of solutions for further optimisation is a stochastic process based on the relative fitness values of each member of the population. The fitter the solution, the more likely that member is going to reproduce and pass its genetic information onto the next generation.

Cross-over

The process of combining two parents to form a child is based on the recombination of genes in nature to form a new chromosome. This recombination basically consists of taking some of the genetic information from both parents and combing it together to form a new child.

Example :		
Parent 1:	ABC	DEFG
Parent 2:	123	4567
Crossover point		^
Child:	ABC	4567

Mutation
Mutation is useful in nature for adding new genetic material into a population. Positive mutations help an individual to survive and mutation is bred into the population as a whole. A bad mutation will usually result in the child being unfit for further reproduction. Mutation is achieved at the representation level with a binary bit of a gene being inverted.

Replacement
Once a child has been created the method in which it is placed in the population needs to be considered. In generational Gas, a number of children equal to the initial population are generated and then the old population is replaced completely. An elitist strategy may replace all but the best member of the population with children, thereby preserving a good solution for further optimisation. A steady state approach temporarily allows the population to increase and then performs some filtering on the population to remove members until a new level (usually the original population level) is reached.

Stopping criterion
Evolution will continue until some external event gets in the way. The timing of this event can be as simple as 'stop at generation 200'. More complicated stopping criteria may use measures of the genetic information present in the population (if members share 99% of the genes in a population then there will not be much pressure to evolve through reproduction). A common stopping condition is measuring if the best solution has changed in the last X generations, and stopping if it hasn t increased by a given amount or at all.

2.3 Implemented Algorithm Specifics

The implemented algorithm uses two nested GAs to accomplish its task. The inner GA is used to find an optimum phase and amplitude setting for a tile consisting of a set of nodes. This method of optimising a tile has been demonstrated previously for full array tiles [7][8][9]. It can be assumed that the optimisation of a limited number of nodes on a tile can be achieved in the same way [10][11]. The outer GA uses the inner GA as the fitness function for each of its chromosomes. The objective of the outer GA is to find a subset of nodes on the array that can be used to generate a sub beam of a desired shape. The fitness of any solution can be found by how well the beam pattern matches the objective pattern and the number of nodes in the array pattern. The fewer nodes the better.

2.4 Pareto Definition

A Pareto front distribution can be visualized as the boundary curve along which multiple different solutions lie. Each point on the curve neither dominates nor is dominated by any other point with regard to both objective functions. One or more points on or closer to the curve may dominate points not on the curve. Pareto curves allow the evolution of multiple alternative solutions to be presented to a human for further evaluation [12][13]. A Pareto curve has been used in this implementation, as there is no mathematically clear trade off between the number of nodes used and the shape of the beam. The selection of the best configuration can then be left to an expert, who is presented with the different results found by the GA.

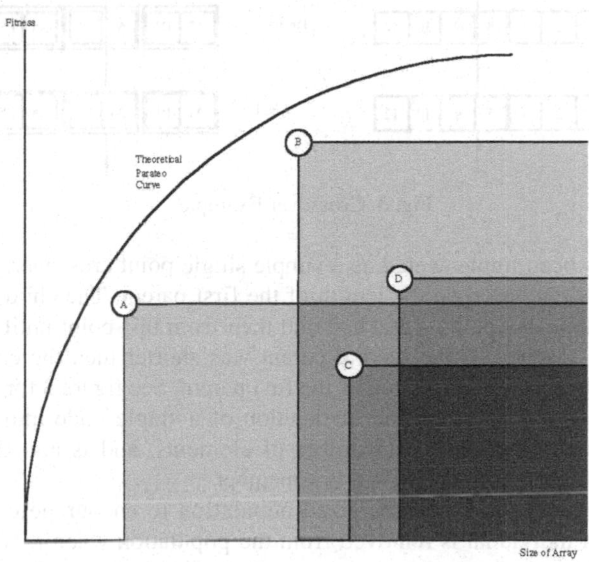

Fig. 2. Pareto Curve showing Dominance

The outer curve in Figure 2 represents a theoretical Pareto Front. Four points are depicted to illustrate the concept of dominance. Point A is better than point C in both size and fitness, therefore A dominates C. A is better than B and D in only one criterion, and therefore A does not dominate B or D. B dominates C and D, as it is smaller and fitter than they both are. C and D do not dominate any point. D may be considered better than C as it is only dominated by B where as C is dominated by both A and B.

2.5 The Outer GA

The outer GA is encoded as a variable sized list containing the elements that are present in the sub array. The size has been limited 30 80 elements as other sub array sizes are impractical for this specific problem.

Parents are selected from the population using the tournament selection criterion. Under this selection methodology, 4 possible parents are selected from the population,

A, B , C and D. AB and CD compete against each other for the selection of parent. The winner is determined to be the individual that is dominated by the least number of other members in the population. The winners of AB and CD then compete. If competitors are equal in their domination a winner is selected randomly.

The fitness function returns two attributes. The first is the size of the array pattern, the smaller the array pattern the better. The second is how closely the beam pattern formed by the array pattern matches an ideal pattern. This value is returned by the inner GA. Both attributes are used to position the result on the Pareto curve.

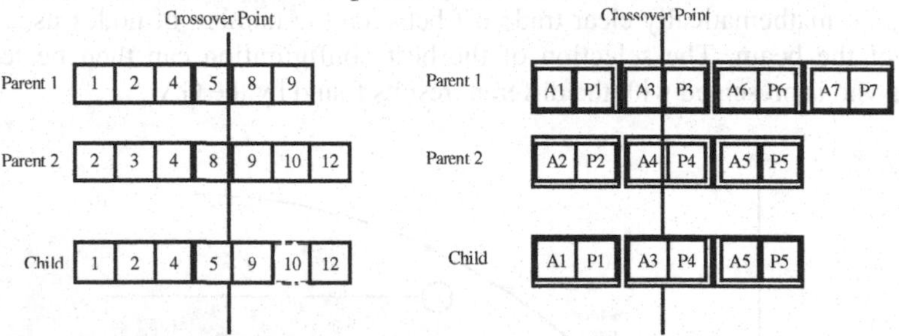

Fig. 3. Crossover Example

Crossover has been implemented as a simple single point crossover. The crossover is selected at random based on the length of the first parent. The child is made up of the first parent until this point is reached and then from this point until the end of the second parent is reached. If the second parent was shorter then the crossover point, the child is simply a truncated version of the first parent. See figure 3 for an example.

Mutation consists of the addition or deletion of a single node into the array. An element is selected from the total number of elements, and is added if it is not a member of the sub array, or deleted if it is a member.

The Outer GA utilizes a variable sized population to encourage coverage of the Pareto curve. An individual is removed from the population when it is dominated by X number of other individuals. X decreases slowly as the total population size increases. This mechanism allows a population to grow as it spreads out along the Pareto front, and to contract if a solution is found that dominates all others.

The stopping criterion is based simply on the number of generations processed. This could be modified to be based on a level of convergence, or allowed to keep evolving until an optimum child has been produced.

2.6 Inner GA

The inner GA is an adaptation of methods previously used for planar array optimisation for desired beam shapes. This work thus differs from other implementations in that rather than optimising an entire array, only a selected subset of the array is to be optimised. The objective function is also different although it is based on the same type of pattern specification.

There are two parameters to be encoded for each element, Phase and Amplitude. Amplitude is a 4 bit value and Phase is an 8 bit value. Each sub array to be optimised is therefore represented as a list of 12 bit binary numbers.

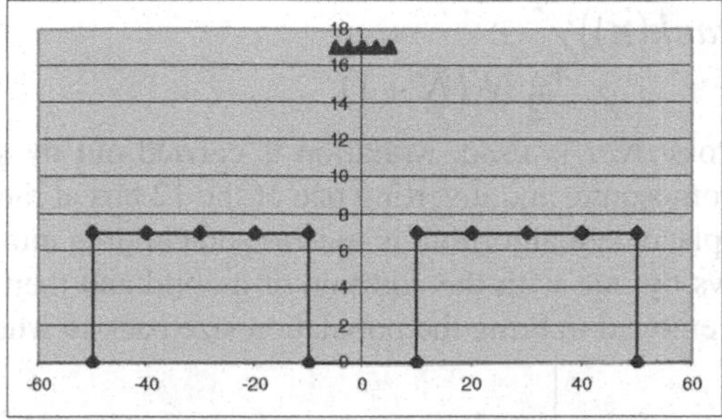

Fig. 4. Beam Pattern Objective

The fitness function is a penalty function where the calculated radiation pattern for a tile is compared to a desired pattern. Figure 4 shows the desired radiation levels for a 0 elevation cross section of the array pattern between -60 and 60 degrees of azimuth. The central region is a relatively wide, low power beam for the radar tile in question. The desired pattern will be as close to this level as possible any value not on this line will receive a penalty. The two outer regions specify an area we would like all side lobes to fall into. Any point above this area will incur a penalty.

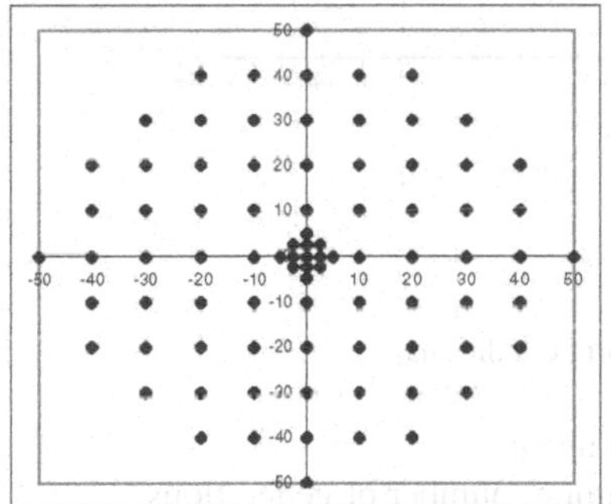

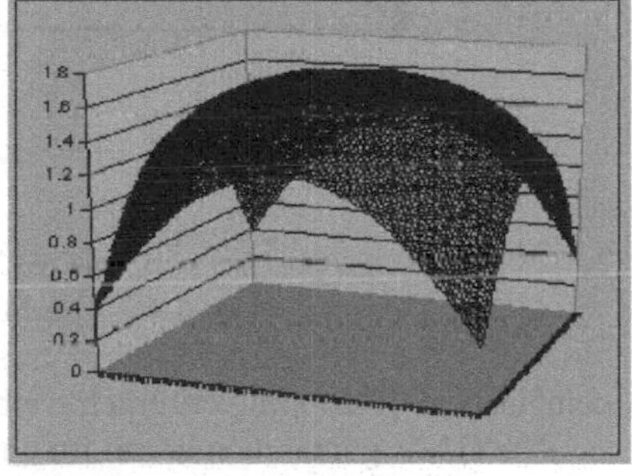

Fig. 5. Fitness function points in azimuth and elevation; Individual Element Gain Function

As it is not practical to test every point for its power level, a finite set of points needed to be selected. Figure 5 illustrates the points specified as an azimuth and elevation pair. The inner cluster is the reference beam, and as previously shown, a level of 17db is sought at each of these points. The outer donut area is the sidelobe area, where all sidelobes are desired to be less then 7db. The power levels used take into account the gains that can be achieved from the elements used in the array. The gain of a single element is a function of the angle from broadside (that is straight out from the array phase). This function is shown graphically in Figure 5.

Proportional selection is used to select parents from the population. Proportional selection involves ranking all the members of the population based on fitness function, and then selecting a member with probability of its rank over the sum of all ranks. That is, the probability of selecting the nth of N population members is:

$$P(n) = \frac{(N + 1 - rank(n))}{\frac{1}{2}N.(N+1)}$$

A single point cross over is used. Mutation is carried out by selecting a gene at random from the chromosome, and inverting one of the 12 bits at random.

A Steady state replacement algorithm is used to add children into the population. The population grows by one with the addition of a child and then the worst member of the population is removed to bring the population size back to where it started.

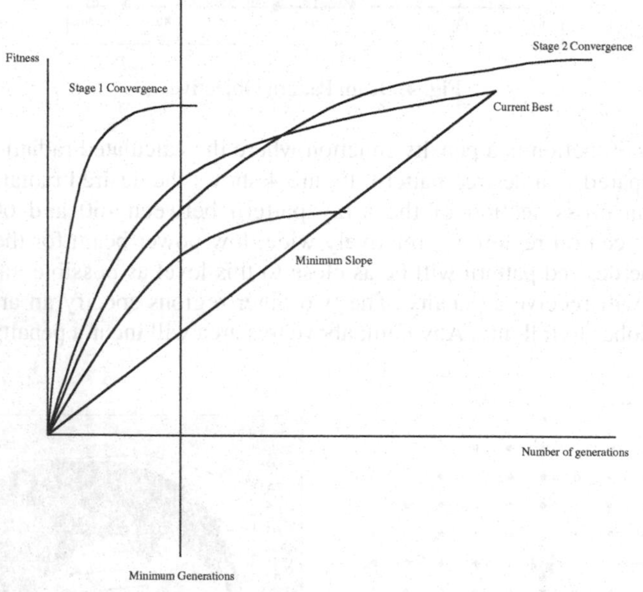

Fig. 6. Possible Stopping conditions

A combination of stopping criteria have been used:

1. The GA is guaranteed to run for a minimum number of generations.
2. The GA is not allowed to run more then a maximum number of generations.
3. The GA must improve per generation at a rate as good as the average rate from the previous best result obtained. This information is passed to the GA.
4. The GA may be terminated if there is no improvement in X number of generations even if it is performing above the slope in part 3.
5. If the GA passes the best position previously found the GA will terminate if there is no improvement in Y generations where Y is smaller the X.

Slope was used to halt solutions that did not appear likely to beat the best result so far. These sub optimal results were often taking twice as long to converge as better results. The slope is most effective when comparing element layouts for a sub array. Different sub arrays have different potential fitness and the slope usually filters out sub optimal layouts quickly. The two different generational convergence times (steps 4 and 5) were implemented so results that were looking better than previous results would not stop prematurely due to minor stagnations.

3 Results

3.1 Inner GA

Table 1. Varying Populations, with and without slope stopping criterion

Without Slope

Pop	20	40	60	80	100
Ave. Gens	6360	4705	4090	3700	3720
Ave. Fit	-380	-413	-429	-439	-443
Best	-353	-371	-395	-399	-403
Worst Gens	10800	7100	7100	5300	5200

With Slope

Pop	20	40	60	80	100
Ave. Gens	5895	4250	2865	3250	3185
Ave. Fit	-383	-416	-445	-445	-452
Best	-353	-371	-405	-399	-403
Worst Gens	7700	5800	3600	4700	4800

Differences

Population	Reduction in Generations	Decrease in Best Fitness
20	7.31%	0%
40	9.67%	0%
60	29.95%	2.62%
80	12.16%	0.09%
100	14.38%	0%

Initial results obtained from the inner GA showed that a small population produced similar results to a larger population but with much shorter convergence times. All population sizes obtained an increase in fitness when the convergence criteria were relaxed. Convergence time of the inner GA was improved by the introduction of the slope halting criterion. This addition resulted in an occasional small decrease in the best fitness reached and provided a 10 - 30% reduction in processing time. The actual reduction in processing was much higher when different sub array patterns were compared. Table 1 shows the results obtained from 20 runs of the inner GA with differing populations and with and without our slope stopping criterion.

The unusual results for population 60 can be explained by an exceptionally fast convergence to a good result in one of the early runs (run 4). All subsequent runs could not match the rate of improvement per generation and stopped where they met the slope line. There are many ways that this problem could have been avoided. The simplest would be to relax the halting condition, of no improvement in 100 generations. This would have caused a longer flatter period to be added to the end of run 4 decreasing its average slope. The graph also illustrates that run 4 was the only run that could have effected the best result obtained. Of course had the best result occurred before run 4 there would have been no problem. The results for population of 20 as used in the two stage GA are also presented in Figure 7.

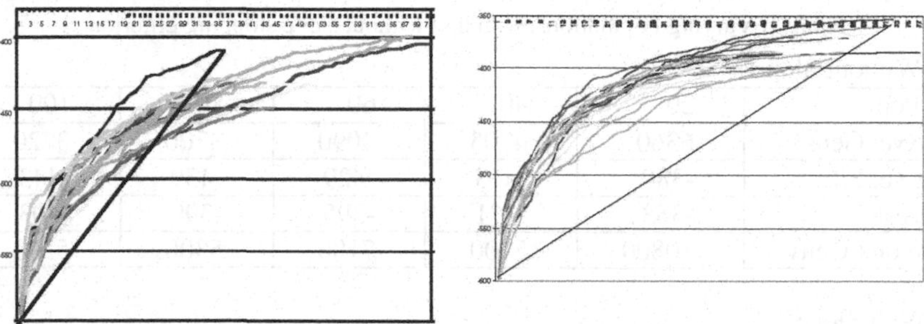

Fig. 7. Possible Stopping conditions; Population 20 Test Results

3.2 Outer GA

The outer GA produced a series of Pareto fronts that provide clear indications of an improving result. A sample curve mapped over 1000 generations of the outer GA is presented in Figure 8. It shows clearly the large outward movement of the curve during early generations. Improvements after this can be seen mainly around 40 to 50 nodes due to biases in the retention of favouring smaller array patterns and the natural drift to a single point on the Pareto front due to the lack of significant niche criteria. Figure 8 also shows a combined best and average Pareto Front for 16 runs of the combined GA. The array pattern for the highest rank individual is shown in Figure 9.

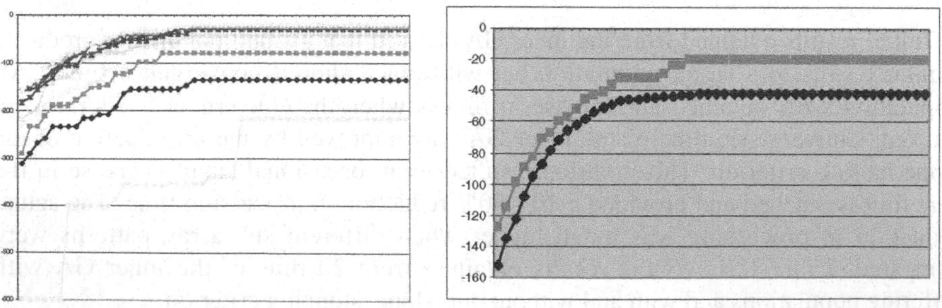

Fig. 8. Sample Pareto Front at 100 generation intervals; . Best and average Pareto Front found

The sidelobes produced by the beam are clearly above those that were desired. (There should be no peaks other then the central one). It is also easy to see that these sidelobes are between the points specified in the fitness function of the inner loop. This can be more clearly seen in the two dimensional representation taken across the plane of 0 elevation. The sidelobe positions specified to be below 7 db are 50, 40, 20 20, and 10 degrees on either side of 0. All these points are below 7 db and therefore fit the function given to be optimised.

To produce a more useful result for a radar engineer, the evaluation function will need to incorporate a finer mesh of points for evaluation within the inner GA s fitness function. The results produced clearly show that this method of optimisation can produce radar beam patterns specified by a penalty/fitness function.

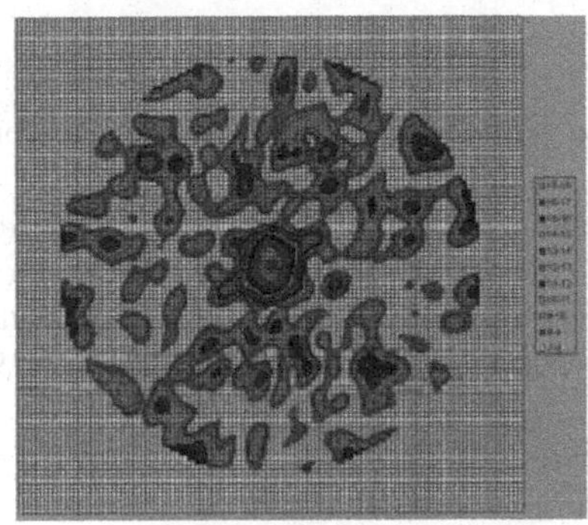

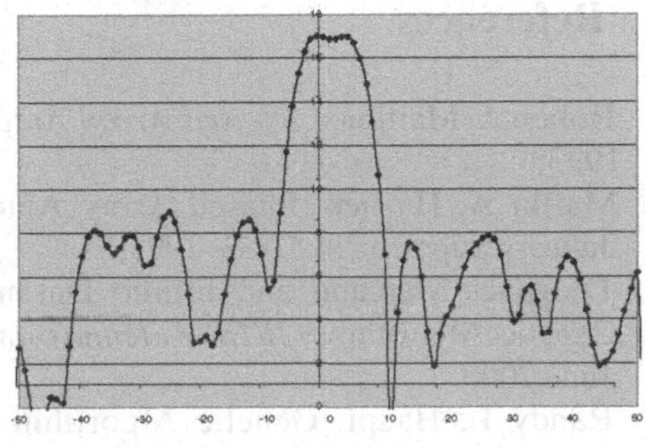

Fig. 9. Array Pattern for fittest individual found

3.3 Discussion and Further Work

The most limiting factor in this approach is the speed in which the inner GA converges to a minimum. A number of methods may be employed to increase this speed. The addition of a local search method into the inner GA should produce a simpler solution space and allow faster convergence to global optima [14][15].

The outer GA also has a large bias towards a smaller number of nodes in a sub array. The replacement policy used results in the removal of larger sub array sizes from the population when fitter small arrays have been found but there is no removal of small arrays with bad fitness, except by a small array with a better fitness.

The recombination function will on average produce a child with size the average of its two parents. Hence successive populations will have replacement pressure biasing the small members of the population. A niche mechanism could be implemented to prevent or balance this replacement pressure. It should be noted that selection pressure will usually favour the larger sized sub arrays as it is possible to shape these beams to at least the same extent as the smaller beams (as an amplitude can be zero). Natural drift along the Pareto Front would also be minimised or eliminated by the introduction of a niche mechanism.

4 Conclusion

A two staged GA approach to beam forming and element selection is a viable method of producing a good range of solutions against a multi objective criterion.

The limitation of an efficient fitness function is a problem that may be overcome by a hybrid algorithm in the inner GA.

5 References

[1] Robert J. Mailloux. *Phased Array Antenna Handbook.* Artech House, Boston, 1993.

[2] Martin A. Huisjen. Phased Array Antennas. *Journal of Electronic Defense*, January Supplement:51-53, 1995.

[3] Diogenes Marcano and Filinto Duran. Synthesis of Antenna Arrays Using Genetic Algorithms. *IEEE Antennas and Propagation Magazine*, 42(3):12-19, June 2000.

[4] Randy L. Haupt. Genetic Algorithm Design of Antenna Arrays. In *IEEE Aerospace Applications Conference Proceedings*, 1:103-109, 1996.

[5] Randy L. Haupt. An Introduction to Genetic Algorithms for Electromagnetics. *IEEE Antennas and Propagation Magazine*, 37(2):7-15, April 1995.

[6] J. Michael Johnson and Yahya Rahmat-Samii. Genetic Algorithms in Engineering Electromagnetics. *IEEE Antennas and Propagation Magazine*, 39(4):7-21, August 1997.

[7] R.L. Haupt. Optimum Quantised Low Sidelobe Phase Tapers for Arrays. Electronics Letters, 31(14):1117-1118, July 1995.

[8] Keen-Keong Yan and Yilong Lu. Sidelobe Reduction in Array-Pattern Synthesis Using Genetic Algorithm. *IEEE Transactions On Antennas and Propagation*, 45(7):1117-1122, July 1997.

[9] Masashi Shimizu. Determining the Excitation Coefficients of an Array using Genetic Algorithms. In *IEEE Antennas and Propagation Society International Symposium, APS Digest*, 1:530-533, 1994.

[10] T.K.Wu. A Thinned Multibeam Phased Array. *Microwave Journal*, :114-120, November 1999.

[11] Randy L. Haupt. Thinned Arrays Using Genetic Algorithms. *IEEE Transactions On Antennas and Propagation*, 42(7):993-999, July 1994.

[12] D.S.Weile and E.Michielssen. Integer Coded Pareto Genetic Algorithm Design of Constrained Antenna Arrays. *Electronics Letters*, 32(19):1744-1745, September 1996.

[13] Carlos Artemio Coello Coello, An Empirical Study of Evolutionary Techniques for Multiobjective Optimisation in Engineering Design. Department of Computer Science of the Graduate School of Tulane University Ph.D. Dissertation, 4 April 1996

[14] K-H. Liang, X.Yao, and C. Newton, Evolutionary Search of Approximated N-Dimensional Landscapes. International Journal of Knowledge-Based Intelligent Engineering Systems, Vol 4 No. 3:172-183 July 2000

[15] Yasuko Kimura and Kazuhiro Hirasawa. A CMA Adaptive Array with Digital Phase Shifters by a Genetic Algorithm and a Steepest Descent Method. In *IEEE Antennas and Propagation Society International Symposium*, 2:914-917, 2000.

Generation of Facial Expressions from Emotion Using a Fuzzy Rule Based System

The Duy Bui, Dirk Heylen, Mannes Poel, and Anton Nijholt

University of Twente
Department of Computer Science
The Netherlands
{theduy,heylen,mpoel,anijholt}@cs.utwente.nl

Abstract. We propose a fuzzy rule-based system to map representations of the emotional state of an animated agent onto muscle contraction values for the appropriate facial expressions. Our implementation pays special attention to the way in which continuous changes in the intensity of emotions can be displayed smoothly on the graphical face. The rule system we have defined implements the patterns described by psychologists and researchers dealing with facial expressions of humans, including rules for displaying blends of expressions.

1 Introduction

In this paper we introduce a fuzzy rule-based system that generates lifelike facial expressions on a 3D face of an agent based on a representation of its emotional state.

Within the Parlevink research group at the University of Twente, previous work has dealt with natural language interactions between humans and embodied conversational agents in virtual environments ([12], [13]). Our aim is to build believable agents for several application areas: information, transaction, education, tutoring and e-commerce. For an embodied agent to be believable it is necessary to pay attention not only to its capacities for natural language interaction but also to non-verbal aspects of expression. Furthermore, the mind of believable agents should not be restricted to model reasoning, intelligence and knowledge but also emotions and personality. We have therefore started exploring computational models of emotional behaviour, [10]. The representations used in this work form the basis for the results reported here on the facial expressions of emotions.

Based on the descriptive work by Ekman and Friesen in [2] we define rules to map emotion representations onto the contraction level of facial muscles. In the research reported on in this paper, we focus on two aspects of facial expression modeling. First, we want to take into account the continuous changes in expressions of an emotion depending on the intensity by which it is felt. Our fuzzy-rule based approach is chosen to assure smooth results. Secondly, we want to find a way to specify combinations of expressions, i.e. blends, in accordance with the literature mentioned.

Earlier work on computational models of emotion and facial expression includes the directed improvisation system of Hayes-Roth and van Gent [5], which makes an emotion-based selection among animation and audio sequences. Perlin and Goldberg's

M. Brooks, D. Corbett, and M. Stumptner (Eds.): AI 2001, LNAI 2256, pp. 83–94, 2001.

Improv animation system [16], [17] layers small animations under the control of scripts and state variables including mood and personality. Stern, Frank and Resner [22] develop an animated pets system named Petz, with facial expression, posture, and vocalizations corresponding to each personality profile and internal emotion state of the character. In most of this work, our concerns with modelling intensity as well as blends figure less prominently. Blends of emotions are often defined in terms of graphics algorithms combining single emotion expressions (using interpolation for instance, [6], [14], [18]) instead of relying on the empirical rules described in the literature. Hendrix et al. [6] use interpolation to display the intensity of emotions. For expressions of blends emotions the basic emotions are arranged on an Emotion Disc with the neutral face in the centre and maximal expressions of emotions on the perimeter. Each position in the Emotion Disc corresponds to an expression obtained by interpolation between the predefined expressions positioned on the disc. This method also does not rely on the empirical literature as the emotion intensity may be represented differently in different facial regions. Beside using interpolation, Pighin et al. [18] also use regional blending to create blends of expressions. However, this method creates uncorrelated facial regions which do not appear in the human face. Moreover, they need to use a very complex 3D face mesh and to collect photographs of expressions of each basic emotion using camera at different positions in order to generate blends of expressions. Therefore, this approach is not suitable for our project which aims at realtime animation of the agent.

The ideas from emotion theory and facial expression on which our work is based are summarised in section 2. In section 3 we give an overview of the complete system that we have implemented. We then discuss the fuzzy rule based system in section 4 in more detail. Some results and the evaluation of the system are presented in section 5.

2 Emotions and Facial Expressions

The rule-based system presented below is based on a collection of theories of emotion and facial expression proposed by [2], [7], [9] and others that has been labeled as "The Facial Expression Program" by Russell [21]. In this program, it is assumed that emotions can be distinguished discretely from one another. A limited number of these are called basic. Opinions differ on what it means for an emotion to be called basic. Russell (o.c.) summarises this discussion as follows: "Each basic emotion is genetically determined universal and discrete. Each is a highly coherent pattern consisting of characteristic facial behavior, distinctive conscious experience (a feeling), physiological underpinnings, and other characteristic expressive and instrumental actions."

In this paper we consider the following six emotions: Sadness, Happiness, Anger, Fear, Disgust and Surprise. These are said to be universal in the sense that they are associated consistently with the same facial expressions across different cultures ([2]). In this book, Ekman and Friesen also describe in details what the expressions for these emotions and certain blends look like.

Emotion feelings may differ in intensity. In [2] it is pointed out how for each of the basic emotions the expression can differ depending on the intensity of the emotion. It is therefore important for us to build our system on a representation that takes intensities into account.

The human face is also able to show a combination of emotions at the same time. These are called blends. Ekman and Friesen describe which blends of the basic emotions occur and what these blends look like universally. We have used their descriptions as the basis for our fuzzy rules.

3 Overview of the System

Our system maps a representation of the emotional state to a vector of facial muscle contraction intensities which is used to control the facial expressions of the 3D face. The system, as shown in figure 1, consists of six components:

1. The input is an Emotion State Vector (ESV). This is a vector of basic emotion intensities represented by a real number:
   $ESV = (e_1, e_2, ..., e_6)$ where $0 \leq e_i \leq 1$
2. The output is a Facial Muscle Contraction Vector (FMCV):
   $FMCV = (m_1, m_2, ..., m_{18})$ where $0 \leq m_i \leq 1$
   This is a vector of facial muscle contraction intensities.
3. The Expression Mode Selection determines whether a single emotion or blend of two emotions will be expressed in the 3D face model.
4. In the Single Expression Mode muscle contraction intensities from a single emotion intensity are produced.
5. In the Blend Expression Mode FRBS muscle contraction intensities from two emotion intensity values are produced.
6. The muscle based 3D face model expresses the emotions.

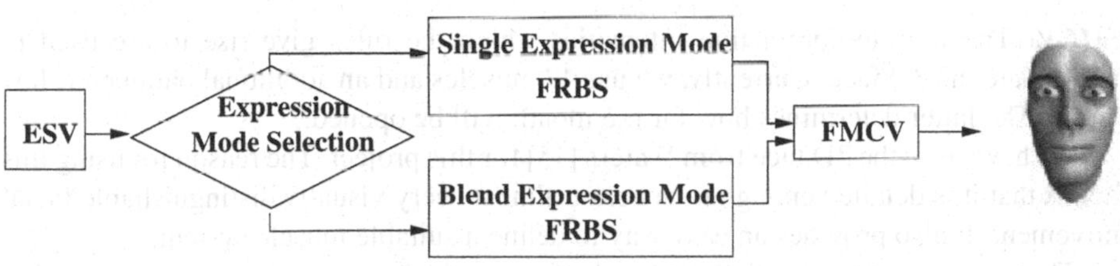

Fig. 1. The proposed system

FRBS. The core is formed by the fuzzy rule-based system (FRBS). Two collections of fuzzy if-then rules are used to capture the relationship between the ESV and the FMCV. During fuzzy inference, all the rules that are in one of the collections are fired and combined to obtain the output conclusion for each output variable. The fuzzy conclusion is then defuzzified with the Center of Area(COA) [11] method, resulting in a final crisp output.

The fuzzy if-then rules for both single and blend expressions are based on Ekman and Friesen's summary of the facial movements to express basic emotions [2]. We used several other information sources to map the descriptions of faces from Ekman and Friesen onto the values for the muscle contraction intensities that generate the expressions. These sources were the Facial Action Coding System (FACS)[3], and the book and tutorial by, respectively, Waters and Parke [15], and Prevost and Pelachaud [20]. Also our own observations on emotion expression in human faces have played a role. We will discuss these rules in more detail in section 4.

As can be seen from the system, the FRBS is actually broken up into three components: the Expression Mode Selection, the Single Expression Mode FRBS and the Blend Expression Mode FRBS. The expression of an emotion in a blend may differ in important ways from the expression of the emotion occurring on its own. Typically, for a single emotion expression several regions of the face are involved whereas in blends one of these regions may be used for the other emotion. We therefore do not want the single expression rules to fire when blends occur. It might be possible to build a system with just a single collection of fuzzy rules. However this will complicate the statement of the rules.

The emotional state vector, ESV, represents the emotional state of the agent. The human face cannot display all the combinations of emotion intensities that can be felt at the same time universally and unambiguously. It seems that only two emotions can be displayed at the same time, because the face has only a limited number of regions to display emotions. The mapping between emotional state and facial display is not direct also for other reasons. Several factors may be involved in real persons to decide for an emotion that is felt whether or not it will be displayed. There may be cultural rules for instance that inhibit showing certain emotions. An Expression Mode Selection module can mediate between the emotion state as it is felt and the rules for representing the emotions to be displayed. In our current implementation we select either the single or blend expression mode based on the intensities of the emotions felt[1].

FMCV. The muscle contraction intensities which the rules give rise to are used to manipulate the 3D face. Currently, we use 17 muscles and an additional parameter, Jaw Angle. The latter determines how far the mouth will be opened.

We have used the 3D face from Waters [15] for this project. The reason for using this face is that it is detailed enough to generate almost every visually distinguishable facial movement. It also provides an easy way to define a suitable muscle system.

The muscle system was defined for the face on the basis of anatomical information ([15] and [20]). We first created the muscles in the 3D face model at the positions similar to those of real muscles. Next we adjusted our muscle system until it produced reasonably lifelike effects on the 3D face model. For the adjustments we also relied on the photographs in [2].

[1] The Single Expression Mode is selected when a single emotion has to be expressed. This the case when only one emotion has an intensity bigger than 0.1 while other emotions have intensities close to zero (smaller than 0.1). In this case, the Single Expression Mode Fuzzy Rule Based System (FRBS) will be used, and the input of the FRBS is the single emotion with highest intensity. When the Blend Expression Mode FRBS is used, the input of the FRBS is the pair of emotions with highest intensity (in the case that more than two emotions have the same highest intensity, two emotions will be randomly selected to express). We certainly do not claim psychological realism here.

Some muscle types, such as the sphincter muscles, have not been implemented in Waters' 3D model. We therefore replaced the sphincter Orbicularis Oculi and Orbicularis Oris, by a collection of other muscle types combined into a circle to produce similar effects as the real sphincter muscles. The muscles that are implemented in our system can be seen in figure 2 and table 1.

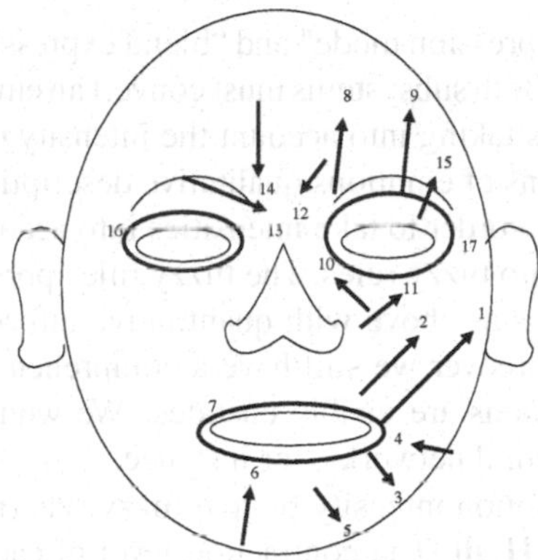

Fig. 2. Schematic of all implemented muscles

Table 1. Implemented muscles in the system

No.	Muscle name	No.	Muscle name
1	Zygomatic Major	10	Levator Labii Nasi
2	Zygomatic Minor	11	Levator Labii Superioris
3	Triangularis	12	Depressor Supercilli
4	Risorius	13	Corrugator Supercilli
5	Depressor Labii	14	Depressor Glabelle
6	Mentalis	15	Levator Palebrae Superios
7	Orbicularis Oris	16	Orbicularis Oculi Palebralis
8	Frontalis Medialis	17	Orbicularis Oculi Orbitalis
9	Frontalis Lateralis		

The system is designed to take into account future expansions. First, the introduction of the FMCV enables the combination of an agent's lip movements during speaking with facial emotion expression. Secondly, the use of the ESV and the Expression Mode Selection allows the integration of the agent's intention and personality into the model without changing the fuzzy rules for expressing emotions. This can be done by distinguishing the real ESV as felt from something like a "to-display" ESV. The "to-display" ESV which does not represent the agent's real emotion state but the emotion state the agent want to express. For example, with a strong personality, the agent may display a fake smile to mask sadness by increasing the intensity of happiness in the "to-display" ESV.

4 The Fuzzy Rule Based System

The subsystems "single expression mode" and "blend expression mode" are both implemented using fuzzy logic. Both subsystems must convert an emotion state to a contraction level for the facial muscles taking into account the intensity of the emotions. In the literature on facial expressions of emotions qualitative descriptions like "surprise then lift eyebrows" can be found. In order to take intensities into account as well these (logical) rules where transformed into fuzzy rules. The fuzzy rule approach allows us to incorporate qualitative descriptions as above with quantitative information (emotion intensity and contraction level). Moreover we still have a comprehensible rule-based system in which the logical descriptions are visibly encoded. We would miss out on that when using other models like neural networks, for instance.

First we model the emotion intensity by five fuzzy sets (figure 3): **VeryLow**, **Low**, **Medium**, **High**, and **VeryHigh**. The contraction level of each muscle is described by again five fuzzy sets (cf. figure 4): **VerySmall**, **Small**, **Medium**, **Big**, and **VeryBig**. The exact form of the membership functions and the support of each membership function are experimentally determined by hand.

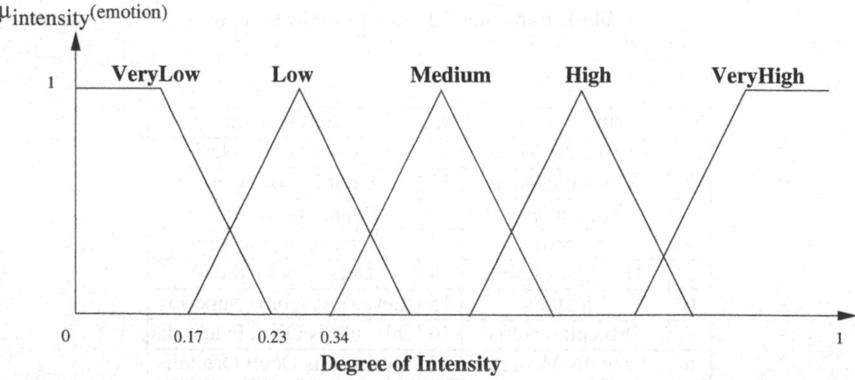

Fig. 3. Membership functions for emotion intensity

As we explained in the previous section, the Expression Mode Selector decides whether a single emotion has to be displayed or a blend. The rules in the single-expression mode FRBS take on the following form.

If Sadness is **VeryLow** then muscle 8's contraction level is **VerySmall**, muscle 12's contraction level is **VerySmall** ...

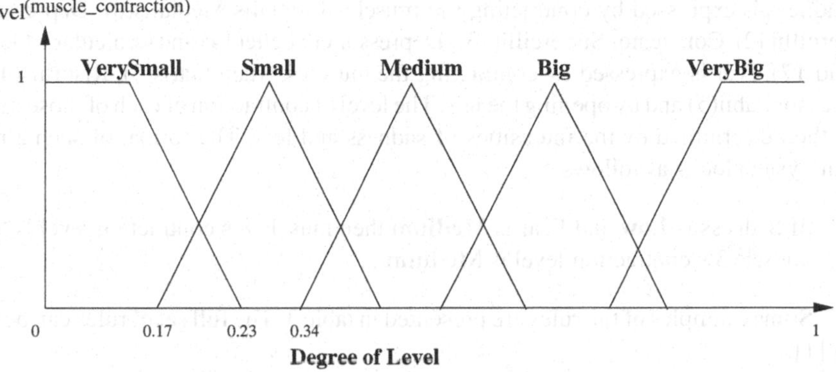

Fig. 4. Membership functions for muscle contraction level

The sample rule above encodes the information presented in the first row of table 2. Note that the relation between the emotion intensities and the muscle contraction level is not so straightforward that we can use a simple mapping system. The name and position of the muscles can be seen in table 1 and figure 2. All the rules for other single emotions are represented in the table form and can be found in [1].

Table 2. Fuzzy rules for emotion **Sadness**, vh:**VeryHigh** h:**High** m:**Medium** l:**Low** vl:**VeryLow** vs:**VerySmall** h:**Small** m:**Medium** l:**Big** vl:**VeryBig** -:no contraction

E. Intensity	m8	m12	m13	m14	m17	m16	m3
vl	vs	vs	vs	vs	vs	-	-
l	s	s	s	s	s	vs	-
m	m	m	m	m	m	s	-
h	b	b	b	b	b	m	m
vh	vb	vb	vb	vb	vb	m	b

If the Single Expression Mode is not used, then the Blend Expression Mode is selected. In this mode two emotions are displayed on the face. Normally each of the two emotions is displayed in a separate region of the face. The fuzzy rules for the blend of expressions reflect this fact. The contraction level of a muscle is determined by the intensity of the emotion that will be displayed in the facial region to which this muscle belongs. As the contraction level of each muscle is determined by the intensity of only one of the emotions, there will not be conflict values placing on any muscle's intensity. We will illustrate this with a description of the blend of sadness and fear.

Ekman and Friesen [2] describe how in a such a blend sadness is expressed in the brows and eyelids while fear is expressed in the mouth. Combining this with the specification of muscle movements in the FACS, we can define the emotions in muscle terms.

Sadness is expressed by contracting the muscles Frontalis Medialis(8), Depressor Supercilli(12), Corrugator Supercilli(13), Depressor Glabelle(14) and Orbicularis Oculi(16 and 17). Fear is expressed by contracting the muscles Triangularis(3), Risorius(4), Depressor Labii(5) and by opening the jaw. The level of contraction of each of those muscles is then determined by the intensities of sadness and fear. The format of such a rule in our system looks as follows.

> If Sadness is **Low** and Fear is **Medium** then muscle 8's contraction level is **Small**, muscle 3's contraction level is **Medium** ...

Some examples of the rules are presented in table 3. The full set of rules can be found in [1].

5 Result and Evaluation

The expressions of six basic emotions and a neutral face are displayed in figure 5. In figure 6, surprise is shown with increasing intensity. The increasing intensity of surprise can be seen in the increase in the raising of the eyebrows and the increase in the opening of the mouth. Figure 7 (left) shows the blend of anger and disgust. It can be seen that anger is represented in the eyebrows and eyelids while disgust is represented in the mouth. Blend of happiness and surprise are shown in figure 7 (right). This is a combination of surprised eyebrows and a happy smiling mouth.

Table 3. Fuzzy rules for blend of **Sadness** and **Fear**

Sadness	Fear	m8	m12	m13	m14	m17	m16	m3	m4	m5
vl	vl	vs	vs	vs	vs	vs	-	vs	vs	vs
vl	l	vs	vs	vs	vs	vs	-	s	s	s
m	l	m	m	m	m	s	vs	s	s	s
...	...	...	...	...	...	...	...	...	...	...

The results also show that the emotions are not only displayed in the main parts of the face like mouth and eyebrows but also in very detailed parts like eyelids and lips. The blends of expression are displayed according to the rules as described by psychologists instead of being computed by some graphics algorithm that combines values for single emotion expressions (morphing, interpolation). And finally, the quality of the facial expressions is improved by the smooth relationship function between emotion intensities and muscles contractions level. This smooth relationship function is obtained with fairly simple fuzzy if-then rules rather than with complicated formulas or intensively trained Neural Networks.

For a first evaluation, questionaires were set up to assess the recognizability of the expressions generated by the system. The expression of six basic emotions and a neutral

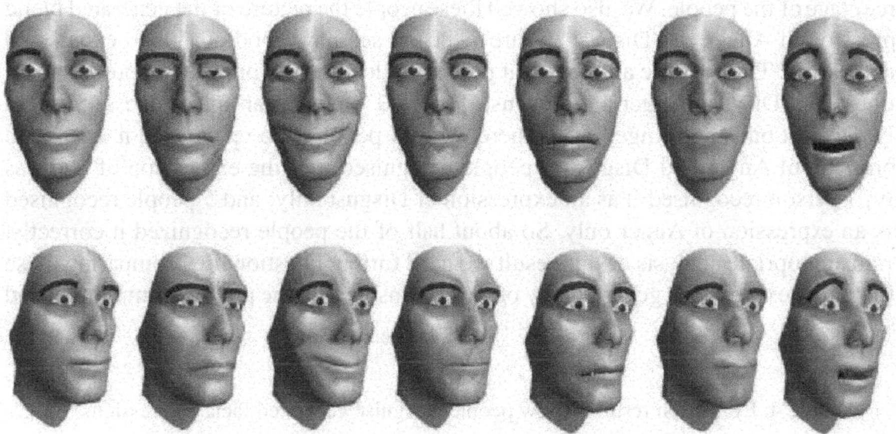

Fig. 5. Basic emotions: Neutral, Sadness, Happiness, Anger, Fear, Disgust, Surprise (from left to right)

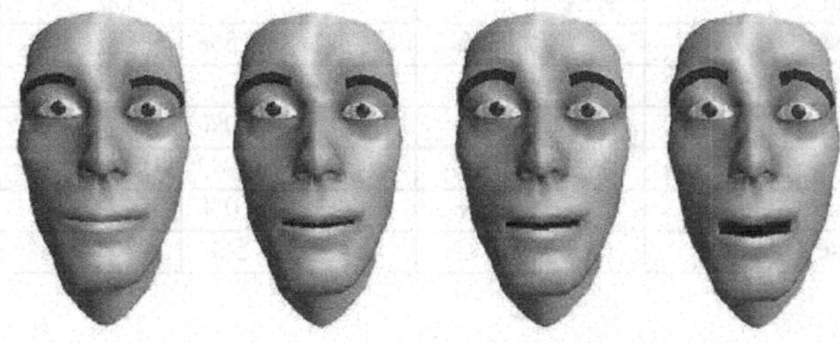

Fig. 6. Increasing surprise

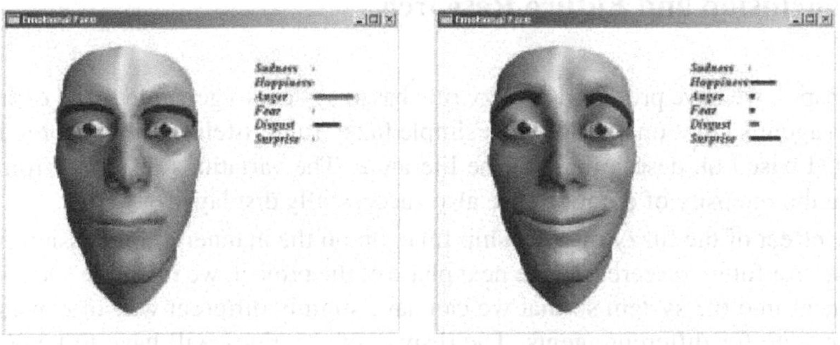

Fig. 7. Blend of anger and disgust(left), happiness and surprise(right)

face generated by the system were shown to 20 people. The result of how they recognised these emotional expressions is summarized in table 4. As can be seen from the table, the generated emotion expressions are recognised as what they are intended to be by a large percentage of the people. We also showed these people the picture of the generated blend expression of Anger and Disgust (figure 7 left) to see how good our blend expression generation is. The possible answers that people could choose from were expressions of: Sadness and Disgust, Anger and Disgust, Fear and Anger, Fear and Sadness, Sadness only, Disgust only, and Anger only. There were 11 people who recognised it as a blend expression of Anger and Disgust; 3 people recognised it as the expression of Sadness only; 1 person recognised it as an expression of Disgust only; and 5 people recognised it as an expression of Anger only. So about half of the people recognized it correctly. For an appropriate analysis of this result we need further questionaires comparing these with similar expressions generated by other systems or with the photos from Ekman and Friesen.

Table 4. Evaluation result on how people recognise generated facial expressions

	Intended	Neutral	Sadness	Happiness	Anger	Fear	Disgust	Surprise
Recognised as								
Neutral		95%	-	-	-	-	-	5%
Sadness		-	75%	-	15%	5%	5%	-
Happiness		-	-	100%	-	-	-	-
Anger		5%	5%		70%	10%	10%	-
Fear		-	15%	-	-	80%	-	5%
Disgust		-	5%	-	10%	5%	75%	5%
Surprise		-	-	-	5%	-	10%	85%

6 Conclusion and Future Research

In this paper, we have proposed a fuzzy rule based system to generate facial expressions from an agent's emotional state. With simple fuzzy rules, lifelike facial expressions are generated based on descriptions in the literature. The variations resulting from differences in the intensity of emotions are also successfully displayed.

The effect of the fuzzy membership function on the manner of expression is one of the issues for future research. In the next phase of the project, we intend to add a learning component into the system so that we can have slightly different way of expressing an emotion state for different agents. The display of emotions will have to be combined with other systems that influence what is shown on the face (like communicative signals and lip-movements). The expression mode selector will have to become more complex to take into account other factors besides intensity. Finally, other emotions besides the "universal" ones will have to be dealt with.

References

1. Bui, T.D (2001), Generation of facial expression from emotion using a Fuzzy Rule Based Sytem, Technical Report, Parlevink, Faculty of Computer Science, University of Twente.
2. Ekman, P. and W. Friesen(1975). *Unmasking the Face*. Prentice Hall.
3. Ekman, P., and W. Friesen, Facial Action Coding System. Consulting Psychologists Press, Inc., 1978.
4. Galernter, D.H. (1994), *The muse in the machine*. New York: Free Press.
5. Hayes-Roth, B. and R. van Gent(1997), Story-making with improvisational puppets, in *Proceedings of 9th Conference Uncertainty in Artificial Intelligence*, pp 122-127, San Francisco, Morgan Kaufmann.
6. J. Hendrix, Zs. Ruttkay, P. ten Hagen, H. Noot, A. Lelievre, B. de Ruiter (2000), A facial repertoire for avatars, Proceedings of the Workshop "Interacting Agents", Enschede, The Netherlands.
7. Izard, C.E. (1971), *The face of emotion*, New York: Appleton-Century-Crofts.
8. Izard, C.E. (1991), *The psychology of emotions*, New York: Plenum.
9. Izard, C.E. (1997), Emotions and facial expressions: A perspective from Differential Emotions Theory, in J.A. Russell and J.M. Fernandez-Dols (Eds.), *The Psychology of Facial Expression*, Maison des Sciences de l'Homme and Cambridge University Press.
10. Kesteren, A.J., R. Op den Akker, M. Poel and A. Nijholt (2000), Simulation of emotions of agents in virtual environments using neural networks. In: *Learning to Behave: Internalising Knowledge*. Proceeding Twente Workshops on Language technology 18 (TWLT18).
11. Lee, C.C. (1990), Fuzzy Logic in control systems: Fuzzy logic controller - parts i and ii. *Fuzzy Sets and Systems* 15:111-128,224-240
12. Nijholt, A., M. van den Berk and A. van Hessen (1998), A natural language web-based dialogue system with a talking face, *Proceedings Text, Speech and Dialogue*. Sojka et al (eds.), Brno, Czech republic, pp 415-420.
13. Nijholt, A., D. Heylen and R. Vertegaal (2000), Inhabited interfaces: Attentive conversational agents that help. In: Proceedings 3rd international Conference on Disability, Virtual Reality and Associated Technologies - CDVRAT2000, Alghero, Sardinia.
14. Paradiso, A. and M. L'Abbate (2001), A Model for the Generation and Combination of Emotional Expressions, In: *Proceedings of the Workshop on Multimodal Communication and Context in Embodied Agents*. C. Pelachaud and I. Poggi (eds.) - Autonomous Agents, Montreal, Canada.
15. Parke, F.I. and Waters, K. (1994) *Computer Facial Animation*, AK Peters. ISBN 1-56881-014-8.
16. Perlin, K., and A. Goldberg (1996), Improv: A system for scripting interactive actors in virtual worlds, in SIGGRAPH'96, *Proceedings of the 23rd Annual Conference on Computer Graphics*, pp 205-216, New York, ACM Press.
17. Perlin, K. (1997), Layered compositing of facial expression, SIGGRAPH'97 Technical Sketch, New York University Media Research Lab. Available: $< http://mrl.nyu.edu/improv/sig97 - sketch/ >$.
18. F.Pighin, J.Hecker, D.Lischinski, R. Szeliski, and D.Salesin (1998), Synthesizing realistic facial expressions from photographs, in *SIGGRAPH 98 Conference Proceedings, pages 75-84*, ACM SIGGRAPH, July 1998.
19. Plutchik, R. (1962), *The emotions: Facts, theories, and a new model*, New York: Random House.
20. Prevost, S. and C. Pelachaud. (1995). Talking Heads: Physical, Linguistic and Cognitive Issues in Facial Animation. Course Notes for Computer Graphics International 1995, Leeds, UK

21. Russell, J.A. and J.M. Fernández-Dols (1997), The meaning of Faces, in J.A. Russell and J.M. Fernandez-Dols (Eds.), *The Psychology of Facial Expression*, Maison des Sciences de l'Homme and Cambridge University Press.
22. Stern, A., A. Frank, and B. Resner(1998), Virtual Petz: A hybrid approach to creating autonomous, lifelike Dogz and Catz, in *Proceedings of the Second International Conference on Autonomous Agents*, AGENTS98, pp 334-335, New York, ACM Press.

An Efficient Form Classification Method Using Partial Matching

Yungcheol Byun[1], Sungsoo Yoon[2], Yeongwoo Choi[3], Gyeonghwan Kim[4], and Yillbyung Lee[2]

[1] Dept. of Computer Software Research Laboratory, ETRI, Korea
bcart@csai.yonsei.ac.kr
[2] Dept. of Computer Science, Yonsei University, Korea
[3] Dept. of Computer Science, Sookmyung Women's University, Korea
[4] Dept. of Electronic Engineering, Sogang University, Korea

Abstract. In this paper, we are proposing an efficient method of classifying form that is applicable in real life. Our method will identify a small number of local regions by their distinctive images with respect to their layout structure and then by using the DP (Dynamic Programming) matching to match only these local regions. The disparity score in each local region is defined and measured to select the matching regions. Genetic Algorithm will also be applied to select the best regions of matching from the viewpoint of a performance. Our approach of searching and matching only a small number of structurally distinctive local regions would reduce the processing time and yield a high rate of classification.

1 Introduction

There are some issues related to classifying form documents, such as the one involving a feature vector and a classifier. The process of feature extraction lightens the load of a classifier by decreasing the dimension of a feature vector and as a result enhances the performance of the classifier. In other words, the recognition rate becomes high while the computation time is reduced.

In [1] ten line corner junctions are used as features for document identification. Forms identification was implemented with a neural network, and 98% accuracy was acquired on the United States Internal Revenue Service forms. The time to calculate corner features was 4.1 CPU seconds on SPARCstation II. Horizontal and vertical line elements are easily distinguishable as textual images on a form. In [2], business forms were used as a test data, and the nine corner types by lines are extracted as features, which were converted as a representation by a string. A simple edit distance algorithm was used as a classifier. In this research, 1.75 CPU seconds or approximately 25 seconds in real time was needed to process a form. Also, matching of the model based on association graph was proposed for understanding of form image[3]. In this work, the information related to lines was extracted as a feature vector and represented by using a graph. The algorithm of graph matching was used as a recognizer and 14 categories of forms were used as a test data. In this research, the average rate

M. Brooks, D. Corbett, and M. Stumptner (Eds.): AI 2001, LNAI 2256, pp. 95–106, 2001.

of recognition was 98%, and the computation time was 5.76 CPU seconds. [4] proposed a method to recognize all the field items that are enclosed by lines and to construct a binary tree that represent neighboring relation among the field items by using the upper left coordinations of the field items. Furthermore, the binary trees can be used to recognize input forms.

Another method of form classification was proposed by [5]. In this paper, k-NN, MLP and a new structural classifier based on tree comparison are used as classifier. The three classifiers showed good rates of recognition ranging from 87.31% to 100% according to the related thresholds. However, the pixel by pixel operation to extract features is overall a time consuming operation.

Many methods and approaches in general treated all areas of a form document equally. Some methods are proficient at recognizing the form layout structure, and the resulting logical layout of a form is useful for interpretation. However, for form documents with complex structures, a new applicable system is needed to overcome the lengthy time of processing. Hence, we propose a system of form classification that centers on the method of partial matching. By performing structural recognition and form classification on only some areas of the input form, valuable time could be saved.

2 Overview of the Proposed Approach

Proposed here is a system for which the model is based on structural knowledge on forms to classify an input form. The model-based system operates in two stages as shown in Fig. 1: form registration and form classification. In the first stage, several local areas in the form image that are distinctive in their structure are found. Only these local areas are matched by using the DP matching so they may be further analyzed in the next phase, the form classification.

The process can be summarized as follows: First, structures of the layout of all the forms to be processed are identified. Each image is partitioned into rectangular-shaped local areas according to specific locations of horizontal and vertical lines. Next, the disparity in each partitioned local area of the forms is defined(cf., Sect. 4.1 and Eq. 3). This definition is used to look for all subsequent disparity measurements. Then, the preliminary candidates of the matching areas are selected according to the scores of disparity(cf., Eq. 5). The DP matching is used to calculate the disparity. The final candidates of the matching areas are selected by considering several approaches as follows: the Largest Score First(LSF) method is considered where the average of the disparity values in a matching area is used. And, a Maximal Disparity First(MDF) method is applied in which a matching area is used in order to classify the form documents which could be misinterpreted by the existing matching areas. Finally, the information that relates to the matching areas is registered as form models. In the step of classification, an input form is classified by using this registered form model.

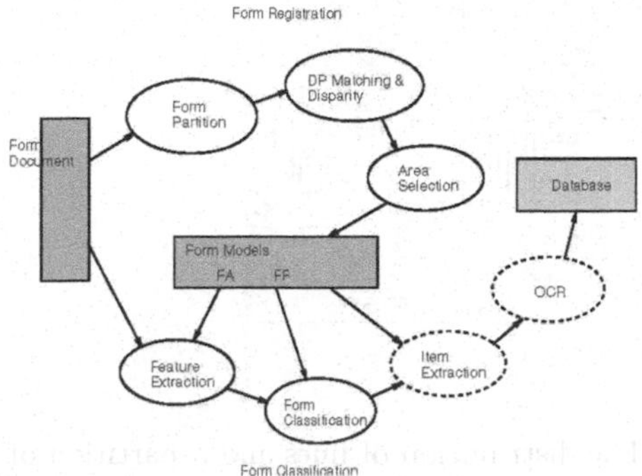

Fig. 1. A model-based system of form processing

3 Feature Extraction

3.1 Partition of Forms

Partition of forms is performed by the identified structures of the forms, which are composed of line segments. The following particulars should be done. First, the form document must be partitioned so that the feature of the form can be extracted robustly. The partitioned areas should contain at least one line that allows the matching process. Partitioning must also meet the requirement of conferring stability to forms and matching areas that are in transition.

In this case, necessary for the partitioning process are the location and the starting/ending point of the lines in a form. First, the adjacent line segments farthest away from each are bisected. Next, you repeat the process with the resulting halves. This process of partitioning is performed recursively until the distance between any two adjacent lines is smaller than a certain threshold(partition threshold). In detail, the vertical separators are defined to partition the center between the neighboring vertical lines and the starting/ending point of horizontal lines. The horizontal separators are defined to partition the center between the neighboring horizontal lines and the starting/ending point of vertical lines, as well. Fig. 2 shows an example of the partition. Fig. 2(a) indicates the form structure that is overlapped by two kinds of form documents to be processed. The dotted lines shown by Fig. 2(b) indicate the horizontal and vertical separators which are defined by a certain threshold for partition. Fig. 2(c) shows the partitioned result.

3.2 Feature Extraction

A feature vector consists of the location and starting/ending position of horizontal and vertical lines. For example, a vertical line is represented as (v_l, v_s, v_e). In this case, v_l stands for the location of a vertical line(x coordinates), v_s and v_e indicate the starting/ending position of a vertical line(y coordinates) respectively. Therefore, if m vertical lines exist in a partitioned area, a feature vector

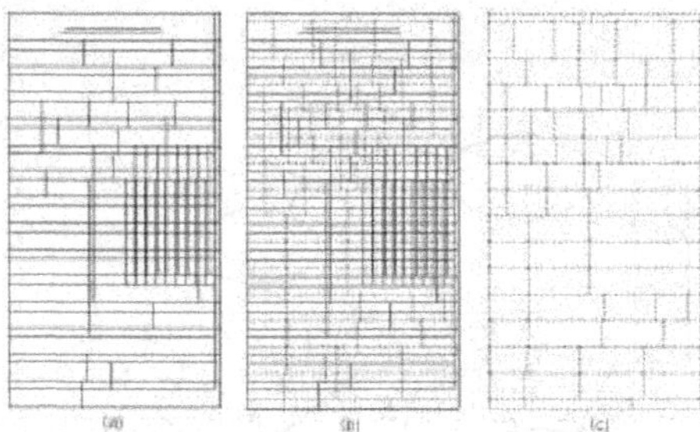

Fig. 2. The distribution of lines and a partition of forms

is constituted as follows.

$$((v_{l1}, v_{s1}, v_{e1}), (v_{l2}, v_{s2}, v_{e2}), \ldots, (v_{lm}, v_{sm}, v_{em}))$$

The extracted feature vector are normalized as follows: First, we search the maximal width and height of all the partitioned local areas. The x coordinates of vertical lines and the x coordinates of starting/ending position of horizontal lines are then divided by the maximal width. Also, y coordinates of horizontal lines and the y coordinates of starting/ending position of vertical lines are divided by the maximal height. As a result, all the elements in a feature vector are normalized between 0 and 1.

4 Form Classification

4.1 Calculation of Disparity Using DP Matching

The next step is a procedure to select the matching areas from the partitioned local areas. In this case, the selected matching areas should satisfy the following conditions: The matching areas should be selected so as to effectively classify an input form. More specifically, the input form must be classified individually in a reasonable span of time by the matching areas. It is desirable to keep the number of matching areas with large geometric differences small.

When performing the form classification using line information as a feature, the following problems must be considered: (1)Noises similar to a line could be added. (2)Lines could disappear for unknown reasons. (3)A line can be broken into two or more line segments. (4)A line can partially disappear. The computation of the disparity by the DP matching method offers a good solution to these kinds of problems.

The disparity represents the distance of a layout structure between two form documents in one partitioned area(see Fig. 3). Only two form documents exist and each form document is partitioned by n areas, then n disparity values are computed. If three form documents (for example A, B, and C) exist, the possible pairs are AB, BC, and CA, which means a total of $3n$ disparity values can be computed. A disparity plane is generated by comparing two form documents in which n disparity values exist. A disparity vector is constructed by all the values of disparity in the corresponding area of all disparity planes(see Fig. 3).

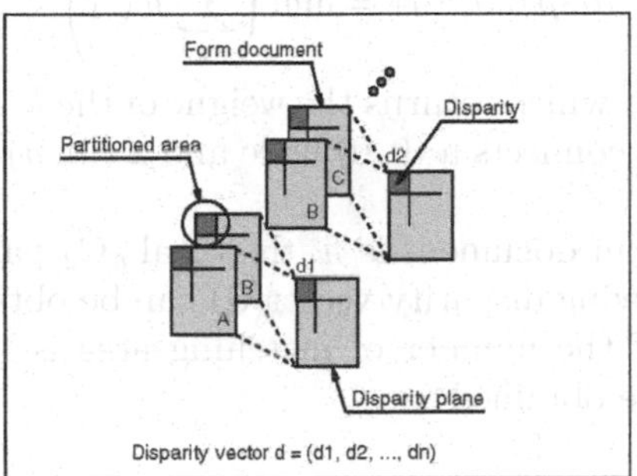

Fig. 3. Partitioned areas and disparity vectors for the local areas

The process of computation is summarized as follows: At first, the position and the starting/ending point of lines in each partitioned local area are extracted. And the values are next normalized. A feature vector is composed of the normalized relative positions of the lines in the particular partitioned area. At this point, the disparity could be computed using the DP matching algorithm, which is defined as follows:

$$g(i,j) = \min \left\{ \begin{array}{c} g(i-1,j)+C \\ g(i-1,j-1)+d(i,j) \\ g(i,j-1)+C \end{array} \right\} \tag{1}$$

where i and j represent two indices of the respective vectors, and C is a constant of DP matching. By $g(i,j)$, the weight in a weighted graph is computed. In the cases that the numbers of elements in the two feature vectors are m and n, $1 \leq i \leq m$, $1 \leq j \leq n$ are satisfied. For example, if the number of the form document to be processed is 2 and the two feature vectors for each area are $((a_{l1}, a_{s1}, a_{e1}), (a_{l2}, a_{s2}, a_{e2}), \ldots, (a_{lm}, a_{sm}, a_{em}))$ and $((b_{l1}, b_{s1}, b_{e1}), (b_{l2}, b_{s2}, b_{e2}), \ldots, (b_{ln}, b_{sn}, b_{en}))$ respectively, then $d(i,j)$ is defined as follows:

$$d(i,j) = |a_{li} - b_{lj}| + \alpha(|a_{s1} - b_{s2}| + |a_{e1} - b_{e2}|) \tag{2}$$

In the DP matching algorithm of line segments, the distance between two matching lines is added to the measure. In detail, the position and the length of a line would be determined from the the location and starting/ending points of the two lines and added to the measure. In this case, α represents the constant that indicates the extent to which the distance of starting/ending point is reflected in the equation. As a result of the DP matching, a weighted graph is generated. In the weighted graph, the shortest path, $k_1, k_2, \ldots, k_Q$ satisfying the following condition is found.

$$disparity(d) = \min\left(\sum_{i=1}^{Q} w(i)\right) \tag{3}$$

where $w(i)$ is a function which returns the weight of the k_i node. The path has a minimal penalty which connects a $(0,0)$ node and a (m,n) node in the weighted graph.

If the number of form document is n, the total ${}_n\mathrm{C}_2$ pairs of form document can exist, and the following disparity vector($\mathbf{d}$) can be obtained for each matching area(see Fig. 3). If the number of matching area is m, then a total of m disparity vectors can be obtained.

$$\mathbf{d} = (d_1, d_2, \ldots, d_{{}_n\mathrm{C}_2}) \tag{4}$$

4.2 Selection of Matching Area

Next, matching areas are selected by using the disparity vector. To select matching areas all the vector elements, that is, the values of the disparity in each disparity vector could be considered to compare the two local areas in each member of a pair. An important criterion is the recognition rate. Since the DP matching algorithm is used as a recognizer, the disparity affects the recognition rate. Therefore, an area that has a disparity vector with large values of disparity can be selected as a matching area. Some strategies to select the matching areas can be considered. We suggest the following three methods as strategies to select the matching areas.

Largest Score First(LSF) Method. The simplest method is to use the summation and average of all the vector elements(disparity) for each disparity vector as a score to select the appropriate matching areas, by which the input forms will be classified. That is, the local area with the largest score is selected as a matching area. Now we compute the score by using the equation as follows:

$$s_i = \frac{1}{{}_nC_2} \sum d_{Nij} \tag{5}$$
$$1 \leq i \leq n, 1 \leq j \leq_n \mathrm{C}_2$$

In this case the score satisfies $0 \leq s_i \leq 1$. s_i indicates the score for the ith area. For example, if there are four disparity vectors and the resulting scores are as illustrated in Table. 1, the first selection is a_2. When the number of the matching area is 2, a_2 and a_1 can be selected by the score. In this method, the order of selection is a_2, a_1, a_3, a_4(see Table 1), and only the selected areas are used in the form classification phase. This method is called the Largest Score First method.

Table 1. An example of the disparity values and scores.

area	AB	BC	CA	Score
a_1	0.50	1.00	0	0.50
a_2	1.00	0.80	0.13	0.64
a_3	0.50	0	0.88	0.46
a_4	0	0.20	1.00	0.40

Maximal Disparity First(MDF) Method. As illustrated in Table. 1, the area a_2 has three disparity values, 1.00, 0.80, 0.13 for AB, BC and CA form documents respectively. This means that the forms A and C can be distinguished well, but not the forms C and A in this local area. Therefore, if we select a_2 as the first matching area, the next matching area can be selected so as to enhance the recognition of the CA form documents. In this case, a_4 area can be the selection because in the areas C and A can be more clearly classified. Hence, the order of selection is a_2, a_4, a_1, a_3 by this method . The method is called the Maximal Disparity First method.

Genetic Algorithm Method. To determine the optimal matching areas with respect to the recognition rate and the computation time we use a Genetic Algorithm. The candidates for the matching areas are selected by using the score mentioned previously, and next the optimal matching areas are selected by a Genetic Algorithm. In the Genetic Algorithm, the optimal result can be produced by considering the recognition rate and the computation time. To compute the fitness of a gene during the generation, the following fitness function f is used.

$$f = \sigma \frac{r}{100} + (1 - \sigma)\left(1 - \frac{t}{T}\right) \tag{6}$$

where σ is a constant indicating the ratio of recognition rate to the computation time in the learning process, which satisfies $0 \leq \sigma \leq 1$. The recognition rate obtained by a gene is indicated by the r, and t stands for the average time of computation to classify an input form. The maximal computation time to classify an input form by genes is represented by a T.

5 Experiments and Results

5.1 Experimental Environment and Contents

We created a system in order to test the proposed method. Our system was implemented on Pentium PC(PII 366) using a C++ language. In this experiment, a total of six types of credit card slips were used because they had a similar size and/or structure and have the same function. More specifically, the slips of Hankook, Union, E-Mart, Easy, Kiss, and Yukong were used. A total of 246 form images that contain six training forms and 240 test forms were scanned in a 200 dpi mode. The average size of the image of the experimental form documents was 826 × 1139 pixels.

5.2 Partition of Forms and Computation of Disparity Scores

In the phase of form partition, the vertical and horizontal separators are obtained. At first, the threshold for partition, d_h and d_v, are defined based on an experimental result. The d_h stands for the distance between the two neighboring vertical lines and starting/ending points of the horizontal lines, and the d_v stands for the distance between the two neighboring horizontal lines and starting/ending points of the vertical lines.

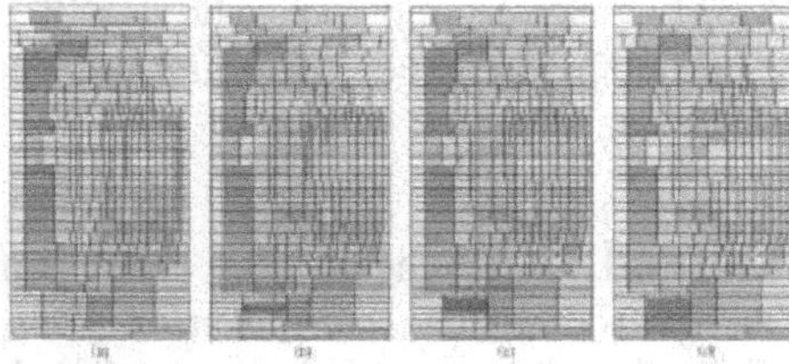

Fig. 4. Partition of forms and disparity score in each region

Fig. 4 shows the result of a partition when the d_h/d_w is 7/7, 8/8, 10/10, 12/12 and 13/13 respectively, which are decided by experiments. Fig. 4 also shows the values of disparity score. The white area means that the disparity score in the area is close to 0, and a black area means that the disparity score is close to 1. A total of 2583 areas could be obtained if all of the vertical and horizontal lines which are away from each are separated. When the d_v/d_h is 13/13, 432 areas could be generated.

Meanwhile, the computation time to partition a form is long when the threshold is small because the number of areas is large. Conversely, the computation time is short when the size of matching area is large as the number of matching area decreases. However, the length of the time increases again when the size of matching area is larger than a certain value by the DP matching due to the increased number of lines in a partitioned local area.

5.3 Form Classification by a LSF Method

Before computing the value of disparity for the corresponding parts in each member of a pair, form documents were partitioned with the threshold, d_h/d_v, which were as follows: 7/7, 8/8, 10/10, 12/12, 13/13 which were decided by experiments. All the values of disparity in the corresponding planes were used as elements of the disparity vector. The score was computed by summation and average of all the elements in the disparity vector. Finally, the 15 areas with the highest scores were selected as matching areas, and the form classification was performed according to the number of the matching areas. Fig. 5 shows the results of recognition for the first five partition thresholds.

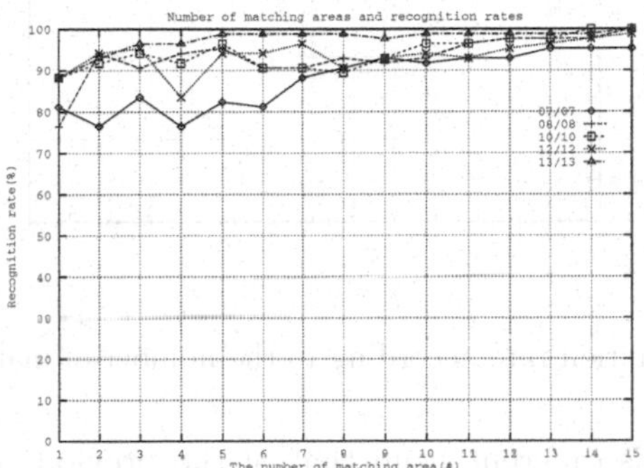

Fig. 5. The recognition rate according to the number of matching areas

Generally, the recognition rate is high if the size of a matching area is large and low if the size of matching area is small. Fig. 5 shows that the recognition rate is 95.29% in the case that the threshold is 7/7 with 15 matching areas.

Fig. 5 shows that the second, fourth, and sixth matching areas increase the error rate although the scores in those areas are high because those area are filled with data or pre-printed texts. Fig. 5 also shows that the recognition rate does not easily reach 100% even if more matching areas are used because the previous matching areas that caused the errors are still in use. The reason for the decreased recognition rate in this case of using the second matching area is that the size of matching area is too small and the filled data are incorrectly recognized as lines. The filled-in data in the 5th and 6th areas, which were spots for signatures, were recognized as line.

It was deduced from these experimental results that some matching areas could cause a poor result despite a high score in the areas. This is especially true when the size of matching area is relatively small, and when the filled data likes signatures are entered. On the contrary, the system can overcome the noise-induced error if the size of the matching area is relatively large, except that the computation time can be long.

5.4 Form Classification by an MDF Method

Another method of selecting matching areas, called the MDF, was examined in the study. In this approach, the matching areas are selected so as to classify the form document that could be confused with already existing matching areas. Fig. 6 shows the recognition result.

The first area is selected by the score, and the other matching areas are selected by the Maximal Disparity First method. As shown in Fig. 6, the result

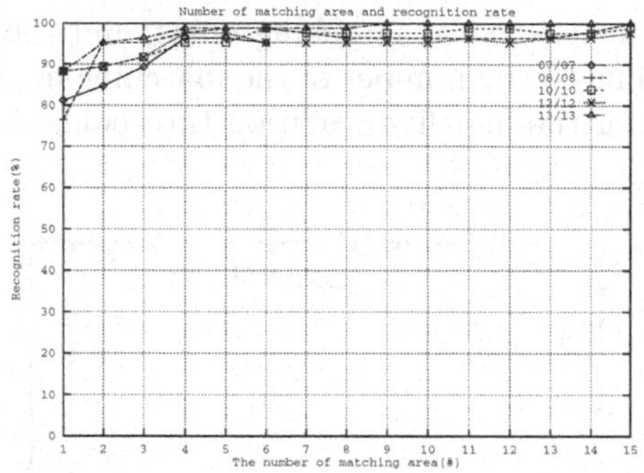

Fig. 6. Recognition rate according to the number of matching areas

of an MDF method is different from that of the previous method. When the score was used, the recognition rate vacillated significantly according to the increased number of matching areas. This is because the kinds of matching areas with superior classifying abilities for the mis-recognized forms were not selected beforehand. In fact, the Maximal Disparity First method shows a small change in the recognition rate and generally a better recognition rate than that by a score (compare Fig. 5 and Fig. 6). In both methods the recognition rate increases with the increase in the number of matching areas. When the threshold for partition is 13/13, a 100% rate of recognition is achieved by using only 9 matching areas which is 4% of the total size of a form image.

There are several explanations for the incorrect rate of recognition. (1)Erroneous lines can be extracted due to images of a poor quality. (2)Preprinted characters or user-entered data could be extracted as lines if the size of a matching area is too small. (3)Two or more form documents can be mis-recognized in a specific matching area due to similar form structures. To solve these problems we suggest the selection method with GA.

5.5 Selection of the Optimal Matching Areas with GA

In this method, the candidates of the matching areas are selected with the score and then the optimal matching areas are selected with GA automatically. The first step is to remove the redundant matching areas, and a total of 40 candidates are selected by a score. We could ascertain from the previous experiments that the maximal number of the matching areas is less than 20 to classify the input form document uniquely. A gene, therefore, consists of 20 bits, representing a range from the maximum of 20 matching areas to the minimal 1 area.

In the GA operation, we used a 50% rate of selection, a 0.1% rate of crossover, and a 0.005% rate of mutation. The fitness is computed by the recognition rates and computation time, so the value of fitness is large when the recognition rate is high and the computation time is short. The fitness converges into a certain value when the generation is performed. As a result of form recognition, the rate converges into 100% during the evolution process for all of the thresholds for partition. The speed of convergence can be either slow or fast. It becomes slow when gratuitous lines from noises or filled-in data are extracted and results in the incorrect recognition of the input with a high rate of error. On the other hand, when the error rate is small with respect to incorrect recognition, the speed of convergence becomes fast.

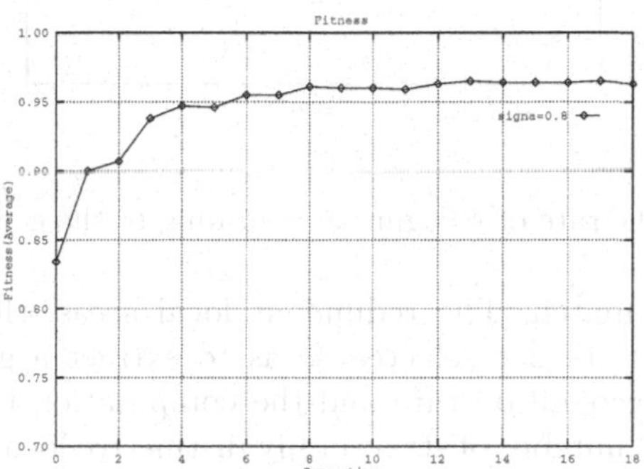

Fig. 7. The fitness of genes during the learning process

To select the optimal matching areas the following details were performed. First, a total of 30 filled images(5 images for each type of forms) were selected and used to the learning process. As a result of the process the genes with a high fitness remain alive at a certain generation. Next, form classification was performed by using the matching area represented by all of the genes alive. Figure 7 shows the fitness which is computed when the σ is 0.8. During the evolution process, the fitness value converges into 0.962 after the eighth generation.

The rate of recognition was measured by the summation and average of all of the recognition rates by genes at a generation. Figure 8 shows that the recognition rate converges into a certain value during the learning process. In this case, 100% recognition rate was acquired after eighth generation only. Interesting here is that the fitness at the second generation is not low in Figure 7 although the recognition at the same generation in Figure 8 is low. This is because the computation time needed to extract feature and to classify the input form is short. Consequently, we achieved a 100% rate of recognition after the 18th generation, when the average number of matching areas represented by genes was 5.2. The average time required to recognize a form was 0.76 seconds when the matching areas were used to match.

6 Conclusion

In this paper, we proposed a new method for processing form document efficiently using partial matching. Our method has feasible approaches for defining the

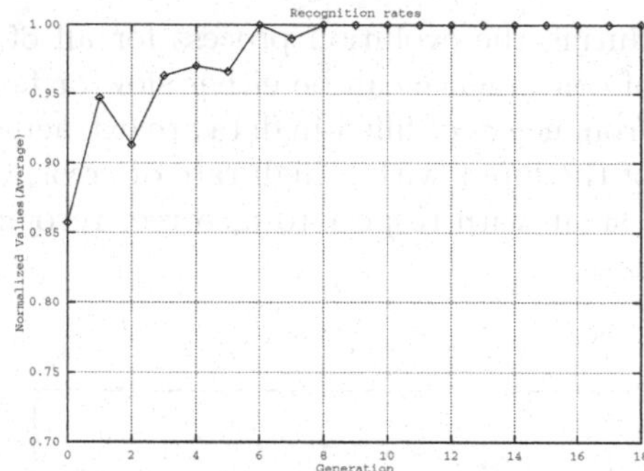

Fig. 8. The rate of recognition according to the generation

matching areas that match. The redundant local areas, the areas containing filled data and noises are not selected so as to extract a good feature vector with respect to the recognition rate and the computation time. Searching and matching only a small number of structurally distinctive local areas yields a high rate of classification with a reduced processing time.

From the experiments discussed in the previous chapter, the following matters were known in detail: By using areas with large differences in structural information among the form documents to be processed, a good feature can be extracted and used as an input of classifier, which would enable the system to process an input form document with a high rate of recognition within a reasonable span of time. Moreover, the optimal matching areas can be selected by using a Genetic Algorithm, which enables the form processing system to process an input form in a reasonable time span. As a result, the redundant matching areas are not processed, a feature vector of good quality can be extracted fast, and an efficient form processing system that is applicable in real environment can be constructed.

References

1. S. L. Taylor, R. Fritzson, J. A. Pastor, Extraction of data from preprinted forms, Proceedings of IAPR Workshop on Machine Vision and Applications, Vol. 5, pp.211-222
2. A. Ting, M. K. Leung, S. C. H, K. Y. Chan, A Syntactic Business Form Classifier, Proceedings of the International Conference on Document Analysis and Recognition, pp.301-304
3. Y. Ishitani, Model Matching Based on Association Graph for Form Image Understanding, Proceedings of the International Conference on Document Analysis and Recognition, pp.287-292
4. T. Watanabe, Document Analysis and Recogntion, IEICE Transaction on Information and Systems, Vol. E82-D, No. 3, pp.601-610
5. P. Heroux, S. Diana. A. Ribert, E. Trupin, Classification Method Study for Automatic Form Class Identification, Proceedings of the International Workshop on Frontiers in Handwrighing Recognition, pp.926-928

Gradient Descent Style Leveraging of Decision Trees and Stumps for Misclassification Cost Performance

Mike Cameron-Jones

School of Computing,
University of Tasmania,
Launceston,
Tasmania,
Australia
Michael.CameronJones@utas.edu.au

Abstract. This paper investigates the use, for the task of classifier learning in the presence of misclassification costs, of some gradient descent style leveraging approaches to classifier learning: Schapire and Singer's AdaBoost.MH and AdaBoost.MR [16], and Collins et al's multiclass logistic regression method [4], and some modifications that retain the gradient descent style approach. Decision trees and stumps are used as the underlying base classifiers, learned from modified versions of Quinlan's C4.5 [15]. Experiments are reported comparing the performance, in terms of average cost, of the modified methods to that of the originals, and to the previously suggested "Cost Boosting" methods of Ting and Zheng [21] and Ting [18], which also use decision trees based upon modified C4.5 code, but do not have an interpretation in the gradient descent framework. While some of the modifications improve upon the originals in terms of cost performance for both trees and stumps, the comparison with tree-based Cost Boosting suggests that out of the methods first experimented with here, it is one based on stumps that has the most promise.

1 Introduction

Much work within the field of machine learning focusses on methods for learning classifiers for attribute value data. The methods learn classifiers from examples of known class with attribute value descriptions, attempting to predict well the class of new examples from their attribute value descriptions. Although the most common goal is to learn classifiers with high accuracy, in which case all mistakes are considered equally bad, mistakes can have different degrees of significance, e.g. for the owner of a new car, paying a year's theft insurance for a year in which the car is not stolen will (usually!) be a less expensive mistake, than not paying for the insurance in a year in which the car is stolen and not recovered. Thus some recent work has considered the issue of there being different misclassification costs associated with the different ways of misclassifying, e.g. [6] and [13]. In

M. Brooks, D. Corbett, and M. Stumptner (Eds.): AI 2001, LNAI 2256, pp. 107–118, 2001.

some circumstances other forms of cost may be worth taking into account, see e.g. [22], but that is not pursued here, and henceforth costs will be assumed to be misclassification costs.

Recently, in the cost context there has been interest in the approach of learning classifiers that use the predictions of many component classifiers, e.g. Breiman's bagging [1] has been used for such problems in work involving the author [3], as have modifications of Freund and Schapire's boosting [9] by Fan et al [8], previously by Ting and Zheng [21], and subsequently by Ting individually [17,18], and Ting and Witten's form of Wolpert's stacking [19,20,23] in work also involving the author [2]. This paper continues the theme of combined classifiers and costs, taking a further look at the boosting-style approaches, considering methods which are applicable to problems with two or more classes, not just two classes as considered in e.g. [8,17]. In common with much of the previous work, the paper assumes a misclassification cost matrix representation of costs: for each class, there is a positive cost for each other class, representing the cost of misclassifying an item of the first class as being of the second class. The cost of correct classification is zero. The matrix is assumed to be available at the time the classifier is learned, but many of the methods here could be used in circumstances with differing costs per item, and only some need the cost information at learning time.

The original Adaboost method [9] and many of the subsequent variations aimed at accuracy maximisation have been interpreted as a form of gradient descent minimisation of a potential function, as in e.g. [7]; however, the previously successful boosting-style methods applicable to problems with misclassification costs and possibly more than two classes [21,18], do not appear to be able to be interpreted in such a manner. This paper investigates experimentally the misclassification cost performance of some boosting-style methods previously proposed outside the cost context, and suggests some variations on them for the cost context while retaining the notion of the gradient of a potential function. The previous work on boosting-style approaches in the presence of costs has combined the predictions of many decision trees learned using (modified versions of) C4.5 [15], and this paper follows this, basing the underlying learner on C4.5, either as in the previous work, growing (and pruning with C4.5's standard criterion) a full tree, or restricting the tree grown to be a "stump", a tree with only one decision node and the leaves immediately below it. While the use of stumps has been investigated in the accuracy context [16], it has not previously been considered for problems with costs.

As Duffy and Helmbold remark [7], not all potential functions that have been used in variations on Adaboost lead to the formal PAC boosting property, and they use the term "leveraging" for the broader category of methods that in some sense leverage an underlying classifier learning method, hence our use of the term. However, where other authors have described their own method as a "boosting" method, even where it lacks the formal property, we may also use the term boosting.

The paper continues with a description of the methods considered, then the experiments and results, including a comparison with the previous methods, and finishes with some conclusions and suggestions for further work.

2 The Methods

This section describes the leveraging methods and variations that will be compared experimentally for misclassification cost performance. First the general framework will be outlined, then the specific methods within it.

2.1 General Framework

The general framework to be outlined here is based on the multiple class methods of Schapire and Singer [16], but restricted to the case where each item can have only one class. It leverages a learning method that will take a set of m instances, each of which has an attribute value description, a class label y in the set of possible labels L, and a set of weights, one for each possible class label, and return a classifier, a hypothesis h, which when given the description of an instance i and a class label l returns a prediction $h(i,l)$, in some cases this may be a +1/-1 prediction, in others a real valued prediction. Each such hypothesis is given a weight α, in some cases $\alpha = 1$.

If a series of classifiers, $h_1, h_2, \ldots h_t$ have been formed, the sum of the weighted classifier predictions for item i, label l, is $s(i,l) = \sum_{j=1}^{j=t} \alpha_j h_j(i,l)$. For a label l, the "margin" is $[y = l]s(i,l)$, where $[\ldots]$ is used to stand for +1/-1 for the enclosed expression being true / false respectively. Thus a positive margin for a label corresponds to a correctly signed $s(i,l)$, thresholding about zero.

The "gradient descent" view is based upon consideration of a potential function expressing the current extent of training error as a function of the margins of the training examples. The leveraging process attempts to minimise the function in a series of steps, in each of which it attempts to learn an underlying classifier that approximates the direction of the (negative) gradient with respect to the margins, then takes an appropriately sized step in that direction by adding the classifier's predictions (perhaps appropriately weighted) to the current combined classifier. (Note that some might consider the gradient descent perspective more specifically to apply to the two class case.)

Given a potential function defined in terms of the $s(i,l)$ in such a way that the gradient of the potential function with respect to the margins can be found, the general leveraging process here consists of repeating for a number of rounds, the following steps for the jth round:

1. Set weight for each item label pair (i,l) to be the negative of the gradient of the potential with respect to the margin of (i,l)
2. Normalise the weights so that the sum of the weights is the number of items
3. Learn h_j using modified C4.5
4. Calculate α_j

When the learning process is completed the resulting combined classifier can be used to predict the class of a new item from the s's for the new item's different labels.

The differences between the methods that are now to be described further is in the potential functions, the modification to the C4.5 learning and predicting process, the calculation of α_j, and the way that the s's are used to predict the label of a new item. These are now described for each of the methods that we consider.

2.2 Schapire and Singer's Multi-class AdaBoosts and Variations

The AdaBoost.MH and AdaBoost.MR methods of Schapire and Singer [16] have not previously been tested in the cost context, and they and some modifications aimed at the cost context are the main methods examined here. Both methods follow the previous boosting approaches in using exponential style potential functions, leading to exponential gradients and instance-label pair weights that can be updated simply (e.g. multiplicatively) in the implementation rather than calculating the gradient from scratch as the general framework might suggest. The original paper gives a fuller description than that here, though it is not approached from the gradient descent perspective.

The original work evaluated the methods using decision stumps, of a slightly different form to the C4.5 stumps we consider here, e.g. when testing a multiple-valued discrete attribute, the stumps here form one leaf per value, and use the C4.5 approach to handling missing values, (splitting items amongst branches), whereas the original work formed a stump with three leaves, one for a value chosen to test against, another for all other known values, and the last for missing values. This work also considers full trees, not just stumps, as used by Schapire and Singer in the original work.

AdaBoost.MH. AdaBoost.MH, (Multi-class Hamming) is based upon the potential function $\sum_{i=1}^{i=m} \sum_{l \in L} \exp(-[y = l] s(i, l))$, reflecting a notion of Hamming style loss across instances and labels. Schapire and Singer suggest that for trees, each leaf can to some extent be considered as a separate classifier (making zero predictions on items that do not reach it) for the purposes of determining the appropriate prediction to make (i.e. step size to take) to minimise the potential function. The appropriate real valued leaf prediction for label l is $\frac{1}{2}\ln(\frac{W_+^l}{W_-^l})$ where W_+^l is the weight of items with class label l at the leaf and W_-^l is the weight of items with other class labels at the leaf. (In practice to avoid potentially infinite predictions a small constant weight is added to both Ws). Leaf predictions of this form lead to an appropriate splitting criterion based upon the Ws, which has been incorporated into our modified C4.5 along with the leaf predictions. The leaf predictions in effect render the αs redundant and they are set to 1. Predictions are made by the combined classifier by predicting the label with the greatest $s(i, l)$, (with simplistic tie-break here as in subsequent methods).

AdaBoost.MR. In the single label case AdaBoost.MR (Multi-class Ranking) simplifies to AdaBoost.M2 [9], but this paper sticks with the term MR. The method is based upon the potential function $\sum_{i=1}^{i=m} \sum_{l \in L: l \neq y} \exp(s(i,l) - s(i,y))$, reflecting a notion of ranking loss with respect to the incorrect labels versus the correct label for each instance.

Schapire and Singer do not suggest an appropriate real valued leaf prediction, just the use of +1/-1 predictions of $[W_+^l > W_-^l]$ for label l. Leaf predictions of this form lead to an appropriate splitting criterion based upon locally maximising r, the weighted sum over instance label pairs of the correctness of the predictions (+1 for a correct prediction for the instance label pair, -1 for incorrect), and the splitting criterion and prediction method have been incorporated into our C4.5 code. Here Schapire and Singer address the issue of the appropriate step size at the level of the entire classifier, with α being $\frac{1}{2}\ln(\frac{1+r}{1-r})$. Predictions are made by the combined classifier by predicting the label with the greatest $s(i,l)$.

Non-uniform Initialisation. The AdaBoost.M methods are designed to attach equal importance to each training example, and thus take no account of the relative importance in cost terms of getting different items right. Previous cost work, e.g. [12,18] has used non-uniform weight initialisation to get the non-uniform misclassification costs taken into account by the classifier learning method. In this previous work, the classifier learning has used only one weight per item, and hence in problems with more than two classes, the different costs of making different forms of errors for an individual item have not been able to be expressed in the weighting – each item has been weighted proportionately to the sum of the costs of the way in which it can be misclassified. As this method in effect collapses a cost matrix to a cost vector, it will be referred to as the "vector" approach of initialisation.

A vector approach can be applied to the AdaBoost.M methods, by weighting each of the terms in their potential functions by the relevant costs. Letting c_i stand for the sum of the costs of the ways of misclassifying instance i, the potential functions become $\sum_{i=1}^{i=m} c_i \sum_{l \in L} \exp(-[y = l]s(i,l))$ (MH) and $\sum_{i=1}^{i=m} c_i \sum_{l \in L: l \neq y} \exp(s(i,l) - s(i,y))$ (MR). However, unlike the previous approaches, the Adaboost.M methods offer the possibility of the different costs of the different ways of misclassifying the one item being reflected in the potential function and hence learning process. Letting $c_{(i,l)}$ stand for the cost of misclassifying instance i as label l, the potential function for MR becomes $\sum_{i=1}^{i=m} \sum_{l \in L: l \neq y} c_{(i,l)} \exp(s(i,l) - s(i,y))$. While an appropriate cost weighting of the instance-label pairs with incorrect labels in MH seems straightforward, that for the correctly labelled pairs is less clear. Here we define $c_{(i,l)}$ to be c_i for the correct labels in the potential function $\sum_{i=1}^{i=m} \sum_{l \in L} c_{(i,l)} \exp(-[y = l]s(i,l))$. (Alternatives for the correct label case could be investigated).

Logistic-like Reinterpretation of the Outputs. Although there do not appear to have been any experiments on the idea, Freund and Schapire [9] suggested that the outputs of the two class Adaboost procedure could be used in a logistic form as probabilistic predictions, and Friedman et al [10] have also drawn the connection between logistic regression and Adaboost. Thus the possibility of using the $s(i,l)$ in a multi-class logistic style approach is considered here, predicting the probability of an item i being of label l as $\frac{exp(s(i,l))}{\sum_{j\in L} exp(s(i,j))}$. These probabilistic predictions can then be used with a misclassification cost matrix to estimate for each class the expected cost of predicting that class, and then the class with least estimated expected cost can be predicted.

Real Leaf Prediction for MR. The real predictions from a single round for the MH method can potentially be different for each leaf and label, whereas the predictions for the MR method are just plus or minus the classifier weight α. The principle by which the weight α was chosen at the top level can be applied instead at the leaf level, yielding a (potentially) different (plus or minus) prediction for each leaf, though this does not go so far as the MH case where there is also the variation by label.

2.3 Logistic Regression Methods Based on Bregman Distances

Schapire and Singer have, along with Collins, placed their previous work in a mathematical framework based around minimisation of Bregman distances [4], and extended the work to include some related methods based explicitly upon potential functions using logistic regressions. The multi-class form is based on the (negative) log-prob potential function $-\sum_{i=1}^{i=m} \ln(\frac{exp(s(i,y))}{\sum_{j\in L} exp(s(i,j))})$. Like AdaBoost.MR, the function is based on the relative values of the s's and similarly to the situation with MR, +1/-1 predictions at leaves can be used, with the same form of splitting criterion and the same form of r-based weight α; however, the calculation of the instance-label pair weights at each round is no longer quite as simple. The use of the probability estimates is straightforward, and all the relevant code has been incorporated into our C4.5 based implementation.

The real leaf prediction mentioned for AdaBoost.MR can also be used with the logistic regression method.

An MH-like Variation. Given the close connection between the differing methods, it seems natural to consider the possibility of a more MH-like form of the logistic regression method. A possibility examined here, based upon the method proposed by Collins et al for the two class case is to use the potential function $-\sum_{i=1}^{i=m}\sum_{j\in L} \ln(\frac{1}{1+exp(-[y=j]s(i,j))})$, which is MH-like in considering separately the potential for the problems of predicting each of the different labels. This has been implemented in the C4.5 based code, using the corresponding real valued predictions from MH, and an appropriate multi-class style logistic prediction.

3 Experiments

This section presents the results of the experiments on the methods previously described, examining in summary the relevant comparative performance of the different variations, and comparing in full some of the methods against the previously successful "Cost Boosting" methods [21,18].

The commercial significance of true misclassification costs is such that, unfortunately for work in the area, very few data sets are made publically available with such costs. Hence in some of our previous work [2], and that of others, e.g. [21,11], publically available data sets without given cost matrices have been used with a range of cost matrices generated for each data set, and the performance in terms of average misclassification cost being determined. For two class data sets the alternative approaches of examining ROC curves [14] or some other forms of cost curves such as those proposed by Drummond and Holte [5] would give a better representation of the results, but the methods do not scale simply to problems with more than two classes.

The 16 data sets chosen in our previous work [2] for their variety of characteristics and use in others' previous relevant work are used again here. A description, omitted in our previous work due to lack of space, is given in table 1. These are used as obtained from public sources except for the mushroom data set of which only a sample (10% rounded up) is used, as the full data set is uninterestingly straightforward for most methods.

Table 1. Data Sets

Name	Instances	Classes	Attributes Discrete / Continuous	Missing Values (%)
Abalone	4177	3	0 / 8	0.0
Colic	368	2	15 / 7	23.8
Credit-Australian	690	2	9 / 6	0.6
Credit-German	1000	2	13 / 7	0.0
Diabetes-Pima	768	2	0 / 8	0.0
Heart-Cleveland	303	5	7 / 6	0.2
Hypothyroid	3772	4	22 / 7	5.5
LED-24	200	10	24 / 0	0.0
Mushroom	813	2	22 / 0	1.4
Sick-Euthyroid	3772	2	22 / 7	5.5
Sonar	208	2	0 / 60	0.0
Soybean	683	19	35 / 0	9.8
Splice	3190	3	60 / 0	0.0
Tumor	339	22	17 / 0	3.9
Vowel	990	11	3 / 10	0.0
Waveform-40	300	3	0 / 40	0.0

As in the previous work, the random cost matrices are generated, like those of [21], to have zero diagonal elements as the cost of correct classifications is zero, one off-diagonal element is chosen at random to be 1, and the rest are then chosen uniformly from the integers 1 to 10.

Each average cost reported is an average over ten experiments. Each experiment consists of randomly generating a cost matrix and determining the performance of each learning method using a ten-fold cross validation. The same cost matrices and splits of the data for the cross validation were used for all learning methods, hence the results for any two learning methods on a data set can be thought of as paired results, in that only the learning methods differed.

When using leveraging methods, the issue of how many classifiers should be combined arises, as often performance will improve to a point then deteriorate with over-fitting. Most of the previous work with trees suggests that the significant performance benefits arise in about the first 10 rounds. Here we run the methods for 30 rounds with trees, choosing on which round to make a prediction on the basis of an internal hold-out procedure. One third of the training data is kept aside and the method run on the remaining two thirds for 30 rounds, evaluating the performance at each round, on the hold-out one third, then the method is run on all the training data for 30 rounds with the prediction being made at the round that appeared best on the basis of the internal hold out procedure. The round that is used for different forms of prediction may vary between them, e.g. although we do not report the results here, we measured the accuracy performance of the original methods, and the best round for accuracy performance determined by the internal hold out procedure may well be different from that for cost performance of the original method, which again may differ from that for cost performance with a multi-class logistic style probabilistic prediction, etc. For the stumps a similar approach was used but the methods were run for 60 rounds as the greater simplicity of stumps can cause more to be appropriate.

To reduce the number of results to be presented to more manageable proportions, the results of many of the comparisons between pairs of similar methods will be considered here simply in summary form as win-lose-tie performances, i.e. on how many data sets one was better, on how many the other was better, and on how many they tied, (to the accuracy to which we later report fuller figures).

The first issue that we examine is the use of the cost based weighting with the AdaBoost.M methods. We compare the vector style weighting with the raw unweighted methods, and the matrix style weighting with the vector style. The aggregate results over the MH and MR methods and over trees and stumps for each of these, i.e. 4 results for each dataset, show vector strongly improving upon raw by 56-4-4. The corresponding figures for the comparison between matrix and vector, ignoring the two class data sets, on which the methods are the same, are 28-6-2, fairly strongly supporting the view that the multiple weights per instance of the methods can be advantageous for the cost based weighting approach. (The artificial LED and waveform data sets cause most of the wins for the vector method, but it is not clear whether there is something interesting in this.)

The second issue that we examine is the use of the logistic style probabilistic predictions to make least expected cost predictions with the AdaBoost.M methods, instead of the simple original approach to predicting. Aggregating again over MR and MH and trees and stumps, shows the probabilistic predictions ahead by 58-3-3, a strong indication of improvement.

Given the two previous results, the question of which improvement upon the base approaches is the better, the matrix based weighting or the logistic style probabilistic predictions, arises. Aggregating over MR and MH and trees and stumps suggests some overall advantage to the logistic style predictions 36-23-5.

Using this logistic style prediction, there appears to be no genuine advantage to the real leaf prediction instead of the +1/-1 for the tree and stump MR approaches, ahead only 17-15-0.

A similar comparison of the explicit logistic regression method with AdaBoost.MR suggests a possible small advantage 21-10-1, though as this is composed of 14-1-1 for trees and 7-9-0 for stumps, there is a possibility that there is a dependency on the underlying classifier in there.

The use of the real leaf prediction with the logistic regression method is perhaps slightly ahead, 20-10-2, of the +1/-1, and the use of the more MH style potential function yields very similar overall performance to the original, 16-15-1 by comparison.

Thus overall the clear advantages by comparison against similar methods are to the matrix weighting method over the vector, and the use of logistic-style predictions for the AdaBoost.M methods instead of the simpler original method. The other approaches may be worth evaluating in individual applications, but do not appear to be major improvements overall.

The final question is how the methods compare against the previously proposed successful "Cost Boosting" methods of Ting and Zheng [21] and Ting [18]. Here we give the full results for some of the previously compared methods, focussing in terms of Adaboost on the MH method, which was originally suggested to be slightly better overall by Schapire and Singer [16]: MHMatT (AdaBoost.MH with matrix style weighting, using trees), MHMatS (as previous but stumps), MHPrT (AdaBoost.MH with logistic style probabilistic predictions, using trees), MHPrS (as before using stumps), LgPrT (Logistic regression with probabilistic predictions, using trees), LgPrS (as before using stumps), CBTZ (Ting and Zheng's method), CBT (Ting's method). Note that the "Cost Boosting" methods only use trees as they have not been designed to work with stumps. Table 2 shows the average misclassification costs per instance of these methods.

A comparison of the methods using the full trees shows that while the cost matrix style weighting and logistic style probabilistic predictions have been shown to improve upon the basic AdaBoost.MH method, they are inferior overall to the previous cost boosting methods. However, the use of Adaboost.MH with stumps and logistic style probabilistic predictions, while frequently producing very different results to the previous methods has comparable performance overall to each of the previous methods, being ahead of each in 12 domains, and marginally in front in terms of the geometric mean of the ratios of average costs.

Table 2. Full cost results for some methods

Data set	MHMatT	MHMatS	MHPrT	MHPrS	LgPrT	LgPrS	CBTZ	CBT
abalone	2.393	1.880	2.060	1.691	1.846	1.705	1.798	1.785
colic	0.555	0.531	0.598	0.531	0.573	0.570	0.616	0.626
credit-a	0.389	0.317	0.379	0.317	0.444	0.317	0.337	0.423
credit-g	0.708	0.606	0.729	0.610	0.740	0.598	0.608	0.618
diabetes	0.668	0.537	0.747	0.542	0.684	0.497	0.554	0.572
heart	2.501	2.088	2.281	1.947	2.295	1.845	2.171	2.198
hypothyroid	0.024	0.024	0.025	0.024	0.024	0.046	0.021	0.024
led	2.030	1.590	1.874	1.520	1.800	1.431	1.654	1.879
mushroom	0.013	0.018	0.015	0.020	0.041	0.022	0.021	0.016
sick	0.030	0.055	0.030	0.052	0.030	0.046	0.031	0.026
sonar	0.366	0.383	0.346	0.386	0.377	0.322	0.529	0.491
soybean	0.400	0.273	0.397	0.225	0.361	0.414	0.350	0.300
splice	0.163	0.148	0.161	0.138	0.161	0.162	0.198	0.228
tumor	3.201	2.929	2.681	2.468	2.647	2.438	2.698	2.987
vowel	0.427	0.966	0.423	0.975	0.186	2.111	0.766	0.484
waveform	1.168	1.029	1.160	0.972	1.041	0.799	1.068	1.072

Thus the appropriate gradient descent based method with stumps is competitive with the previous tree based approaches that do not fit the gradient descent framework. A check on accuracy performance suggests that this is not simply a matter of stumps being better than trees in all ways for the data sets used, as AdaBoost.MH's overall accuracy performance is better with trees than stumps, so the advantage of stumps lies in their suitability for the method of making probabilistic predictions, while not being superior in simple accuracy terms. (A check on the number of classifiers chosen by the internal validations suggests that the stump based approaches might benefit from more rounds in some cases, especially on the vowel data set where the average number of classifiers chosen is close to the maximum possible – some further experiments will be conducted on this.)

4 Conclusions and Further Work

This paper has examined the use in the misclassification cost context of some gradient descent leveraging methods using decision trees and stumps as the underlying base classifiers, experimentally comparing on 16 data sets the cost performance of the original methods and some modifications of them, and previous cost boosting approaches. The results show that the use of multiple weight per item methods enables the use of a more matrix style weighting method that performs better than previous weighting methods that collapsed the matrix to a vector. The results show that the use of a multi-class logistic probabilistic prediction from the leveraging methods performs better than the simple original prediction methods intended for the accuracy context. When compared against previously proposed cost boosting methods using trees, the performance of one of the new stump based methods is competitive overall in cost terms. Accuracy performance results of the same method with trees suggest that the use of stumps may be particularly suited to the probabilistic prediction approach, as the trees perform better in accuracy terms.

Given the gap in performance between the tree based gradient descent approaches and the previous cost boosting approaches, an interesting possible direction to pursue seems to be in the creation of potential functions that better reflect the cost task in some way, and we are looking at some possibilities of this form at present. Given our previous results on stacking different forms of classifier [2], another fairly straightforward issue to investigate is whether the successful boosted stumps method constitutes a useful base classifier for the stacking approach.

Although this paper has put forward some successful cost based modifications to previous gradient descent leveraging methods, and experimentally demonstrated their potential, there are still some interesting possibilities to pursue in this area.

Acknowledgements. The work described in this paper was started while the author was on study leave at AT&T Labs Research, whom the author wishes to thank, particularly Rob Schapire and Michael Collins. Thanks are also due to the UCI repository maintainers, and the contributors, e.g. R. Detrano for the Cleveland data, and M. Zwitter and M. Soklic for the primary tumour data which was obtained from the University Medical Centre, Institute of Oncology, Ljubljana, Yugoslavia. Finally thanks are due to Robyn Gibson for comments on the paper.

References

[1] L. Breiman. Bagging predictors. *Machine Learning*, 24:123–140, 1996.

[2] M. Cameron-Jones and A. Charman-Williams. Stacking for misclassification cost performance. In *Advances in Artificial Intelligence: 14th Biennial Conference Canadian Society for Computational Studies of Intelligence, AI2001*, pages 215–224. Springer Verlag, 2001.

[3] M. Cameron-Jones and L. Richards. Repechage bootstrap aggregating for misclassification cost reduction. In *PRICAI'98: Topics in Artificial Intelligence – Fifth Pacific Rim International Conference on Artificial Intelligence*, pages 1–11. Springer Verlag, 1998.

[4] M. Collins, R.E. Schapire, and Y. Singer. Logistic regression, adaboost and bregman distances. In *Proceedings of the Thirteenth Annual Conference on Computational Learning Theory*, pages 158–169. Morgan Kaufmann, 2000.

[5] C. Drummond and R.C. Holte. Explicitly representing expected cost: An alternative to roc representation. Technical report, University of Ottawa, 2000.

[6] C. Drummond and R.C. Holte. Exploiting the cost (in)sensitivity of decision tree splitting criteria. In *Proceedings of the Seventeenth International Conference on Machine Learning (ICML-2000)*, pages 239–246. Morgan Kaufmann, 2000.

[7] Nigel Duffy and David Helmbold. Potential boosters? In *Advances in Neural Information Processing Systems 12*, pages 258–264. MIT Press, 2000.
[8] W. Fan, S.J. Stolfo, J. Zhang, and P.K. Chan. Adacost: Misclassification cost-sensitive boosting. In *Machine Learning: Proceedings of the Sixteenth International Conference (ICML '99)*, pages 97–105, 1999.
[9] Y. Freund and R.E. Schapire. A decision-theoretic generalization of on-line learning and an application to boosting. *Journal of Computer and System Sciences*, 55:119–139, 1997.
[10] J. Friedman, T. Hastie, and R. Tibshirani. Additive logistic regression. Technical report, Stanford University, 1998.
[11] D. Margineantu. Building ensembles of classifiers for loss minimisation. In *Proceedings of the 31st Symposium of the Interface: Models, Prediction and Computing*, pages 190–194, 1999.
[12] M. Pazzani, C. Merz, P. Murphy, K. Ali, T. Hume, and C. Brunk. Reducing misclassification costs. In *Proceedings of the Eleventh International Conference on Machine Learning (ML94)*, pages 217–225. Morgan Kaufmann, 1994.
[13] F. Provost and T. Fawcett. Robust classification for imprecise environments. *Machine Learning*, 42:203–231, 2001.
[14] F. Provost, T. Fawcett, and R. Kohavi. The case against accuracy estimation for comparing induction algorithms. In *Machine Learning: Proceedings of the Fifteenth International Conference (ICML'98)*. Morgan Kaufmann, 1998.
[15] J.R. Quinlan. *C4.5: Programs for Machine Learning*. Morgan Kaufmann, 1993. The Morgan Kaufmann Series in Machine Learning.
[16] R.E. Schapire and Y. Singer. Improved boosting algorithms using confidence-rated predictions. *Machine Learning*, 37:297–336, 1999.
[17] K.M. Ting. A comparative study of cost-sensitive boosting algorithms. In *Proceedings of the Seventeenth International Conference on Machine Learning (ICML-2000)*, pages 983–990. Morgan Kaufmann, 2000.
[18] K.M. Ting. An empirical study of metacost using boosting algorithms. In *Proceedings of the Eleventh European Conference on Machine Learning (ECML-2000)*, pages 413–425. Springer Verlag, 2000.
[19] K.M. Ting and I.H. Witten. Stacked generalization: when does it work? In *Proceedings of the Fifteenth International Joint Conference on Artificial Intelligence*, pages 866–871. Morgan Kaufmann, 1997.
[20] K.M. Ting and I.H. Witten. Issues in stacked generalization. *Journal of Artificial Intelligence Research*, 10:271–289, 1999.
[21] K.M. Ting and Z. Zheng. Boosting trees for cost-sensitive classifications. In *Machine Learning: ECML-98: Proceedings of the Tenth European Conference on Machine Learning*, pages 190–195. Springer-Verlag, 1998.
[22] P.D. Turney. Cost-sensitive classification: Empirical evaluation of a hybrid genetic decision tree induction algorithm. *Journal of Artificial Intelligence Research*, 2:369–409, 1995.
[23] D.H. Wolpert. Stacked generalization. *Neural Networks*, 5:241–259, 1992.

Postdiction Problems in Dynamic Logic

Samir Chopra and Dongmo Zhang

Knowledge Systems Group
School of Computer Science and Engineering
University of New South Wales
Sydney, NSW 2052, Australia
{schopra,dongmo}@cse.unsw.edu.au

Abstract. We present a framework for backward and forward temporal projection that combines dynamic and temporal logic. A propositional dynamic logic for reasoning about actions is extended with temporal modalities; the syntax of this extension differs from the syntax of the converse of programs, previously understood as backwards modalities. An application is carried out to benchmark postdiction examples such as the Stanford Murder Mystery [1] and the Two-Buses Problem [8]. A method for automatically generating frame axioms is used; the axioms so generated are treated as supplementary axioms in the associated proof theory. In future work, we hope to embed this system into a more comprehensive logic for reasoning about actions that enables a unified treatment of the frame, qualification and ramification problems and to work with more 'scaled-up' examples.

Keywords: temporal reasoning, commonsense reasoning

1 Introduction

In devising logical frameworks for temporal projection, our intuition is that when we inspect the current state of the world, we can reason about what states of affairs would obtain on the performance of a particular action and about what actions could have realized the current state (the latter is the classical form of the *explanation problem*). A logical framework, then, for temporal reasoning should be truly general. It should take the entire time line into consideration (not just a single step in the time line) and facilitate inferences about various target points in the time line, from partial information about other source points. When the target points are ahead of the source points in the time line, the inference problem is that of *prediction*; when it's the other way around, the problem is that of *postdiction*. These are vital components of commonsense reasoning: the latter requires reasoning from effects to causes and poses a special challenge for logical formalisms. Shanahan [17] provides a good discussion of the problems created by benchmark examples such as the Stanford Murder Mystery [1] and the Two-Buses problem [8].

Dynamic logic as a formalism for reasoning about action was proposed twenty years ago [7,16,9]. However, classical dynamic logic as originally proposed [14]

M. Brooks, D. Corbett, and M. Stumptner (Eds.): AI 2001, LNAI 2256, pp. 119–129, 2001.

can only directly express reasoning *forward* in time. For instance, $[\alpha]A$ means A is true *after* performing action α. If we view $[\alpha]$ as a temporal modality, some properties of $[\alpha]$ are identical to those of the future modality $[F]$. More precisely, $[\alpha]$ acts like a "nearest future": a combination of the 'Future' $[F]$ and 'Next' $\bigcirc$ modalities of temporal concurrent logic [13]. To reason backwards in dynamic logic, one can extend classical dynamic logic with inverse operations as in [11] (subsequently, *Converse PDL*): α^{-1} converts an action into its inverse. So to retrodict the state *before* an action is performed, we would perform the inverse action. Alternatively, we suggest, an *accompanying modality* to $[\alpha]$ can be introduced, which paralleling the role of $[P]$ in temporal logic, specifies the previous state *before* the performance of α. Syntactically these two approaches are different because *Converse PDL* extends the language by expanding the set of programs while our suggested alternative adds a new modality. They are also different in both methodology and ontology. The second approach allows us to reason about the past *directly* rather than *indirectly* via reversing changes to recover previous world states. More significantly, not all actions are coherently understood as being reversible whereas previous worlds always exist and so we need, and should be able to, reason about them.

In this study, we supplement the classical dynamic logic *PDL* with a temporal modality: a construct that allows us to speak coherently of fluents being true in *previous* or temporally prior, situations or states. In normal temporal logics, the modal operator $[F]$ is used to express the necessary truth of propositions in the future. So, $[F]A$ means that the proposition A must be true at *all* future times. The dual operator $\langle F\rangle$ expresses the possible truth of propositions in the future, that is, $\langle F\rangle A$ means A is true at *some* time in the future. Similarly, $[P]$ and $\langle P\rangle$ express the necessary and possible truth of propositions in the past. The relationship between these modalities is succinctly expressed by the following axiom schemes (these are precisely the axiom schemes used in *PDL* with program converses [11] with F, P replaced respectively by α, α^{-1}):

- $\mathbf{C_P}$: $A \to [P]\langle F\rangle A$
- $\mathbf{C_F}$: $A \to [F]\langle P\rangle A$

It is easy to see that the modal operators $[F]$ and $[P]$ are each the converse of the other. So, we could write $[P]$ as $[F]^{-1}$ in order to make the relationship between $[F]$ and $[P]$ more visible. These temporal modalities specify the state of a system in the *entire* future or *entire* past. A more refined temporal operator is $\bigcirc$ (Next) (considering time to be made up of discrete points). $\bigcirc A$ would then mean "A is true in the next step"; $\bigcirc^{-1}A$ would mean "A is true in the previous step". However, *these modalities are purely temporal.* They do not say *why* a proposition is true. So, to express the effect of an action, we can use the language of dynamic logic as follows:

- $[\alpha]A$: A must be true after performing action α.

Note that $[\alpha]A$ not only expresses the fact that A becomes true as the effect of action α but it also expresses the temporal relation between the current instant in time and the time *after* performing α. A similar temporal concept could be introduced as follows:

- $[\alpha]^{-1}A$: A must have been true before performing action α.

The dual modalities can then be defined:

- $\langle\alpha\rangle A$: α is executable and A *could be true after performing* α.
- $\langle\alpha\rangle^{-1}A$: α is executable and A *could have been true before performing* α.

For example, $[turn\_off]\neg light$ means that the action $turn\_off$ causes the light to be turned off. It also says that the light will be off *after* performing the turning off action. Similarly, $[turn\_off]^{-1}light$ means "the light was on in all worlds *before* the the $turn\_off$ action was taken" and $\langle turn\_off\rangle^{-1}light$ means "the light was on in some worlds before the the $turn\_off$ action was taken". The connection here between forward and backwards modalities and the postconditions and preconditions of actions should be apparent and intuitive.

We now present an intuitive semantics, supply an accompanying axiomatic deductive system and apply the framework to standard examples.

2 The Logic *TPDL*

In dynamic logic a modal connective is associated with each command α of a programming language, with the formula $[\alpha]A$ being read "after α terminates, A must be true." The dual operator $\langle\alpha\rangle$ of $[\alpha]$ is an abbreviation of $\neg[\alpha]\neg$. $\langle\alpha\rangle A$ means "there is an execution of α that terminates with A true". With the compound operators $;, \cup, ^*$, complex programs can be generated from atomic programs. If α, β are programs, $\alpha;\beta$ means "execute α followed by β", $\alpha \cup \beta$ means "execute either α or β nondeterministically", α^* means "repeat α finite times nondeterministically". $A?$ is a special program, meaning "test A proceed if A is true, else fail" [7] [5] .

2.1 The Language

The alphabet of the language $\mathcal{L}_{TPDL}$ consists of countable sets $\mathbf{Flu}$, $\mathbf{Act_P}$ of fluent and primitive action symbols respectively. Formulas ($A \in \mathbf{Fma}$) and actions ($\alpha \in \mathbf{Act}$) are defined by the following BNF rules:

- $A ::= f \mid \neg A \mid A_1 \to A_2 \mid [\alpha]A \mid [\alpha]^{-1}A$
- $\alpha ::= a \mid \alpha_1;\alpha_2 \mid \alpha_1 \cup \alpha_2 \mid \alpha^* \mid A^?$ where $f \in \mathbf{Flu}$ and $a \in \mathbf{Act_P}$

$\langle\alpha\rangle\top$ means "α is executable". The definitions of $\top, \bot, \vee, \wedge, \leftrightarrow$ are as usual. A literal is a fluent or its negation. The set of all literals in $\mathcal{L}_{TPDL}$ is denoted $\mathbf{Flu}_L$. A formula without modalities, termed a *proposition*, is denoted by $\varphi, \varphi_1, \varphi_2$ and ψ . The dual modal operators of $[\alpha]A$ and $[\alpha]^{-1}A$ are defined as usual: $\langle\alpha\rangle A =_{def} \neg[\alpha]\neg A$ and $\langle\alpha\rangle^{-1}A =_{def} \neg[\alpha]^{-1}\neg A$.

There are subtle differences between $TPDL$ and $Converse\ PDL$. $[\alpha^{-1}]$ is *not equivalent* to $[\alpha]^{-1}$. $Converse\ PDL$ uses inverse actions of the form α^{-1}. $TPDL$ uses only forward actions, and has the backward temporal operator $[\alpha]^{-1}A$. $TPDL$ is less expressive than $Converse\ PDL$. For instance, $[(\alpha^*)^{-1}]A = [(\alpha^{-1})^*]A$ is expressible in $Converse\ PDL$ but not in $TPDL$. We introduce the following notation:

- $\langle[\alpha]\rangle A =_{def} \langle\alpha\rangle\top \wedge [\alpha]A$, read as "$\alpha$ is executable and A will be true after peforming α".

2.2 Semantics

The semantics of $TPDL$ is a standard Kripkean semantics for PDL (see [5] for standard introductions) plus an added accessibility relation. A *model* is a triple $M = (W, \{R^F_\alpha : \alpha \in \mathbf{Act}\} \cup \{R^P_\alpha : \alpha \in \mathbf{Act}\}, V)$, where R^F_α and R^P_α are binary relations on W, and V is a function from $\mathbf{Flu}$ to 2^W (or equivalently, a two-place relation on $\mathbf{Flu} \times W$). Intuitively, performing an action takes the agent from one world to another (a state transformation). For instance, $(w_1, w_2) \in R^F_\alpha$ means that if the current world is w_1, then after performing action α the world will evolve to state w_2. $(w_1, w_2) \in R^P_\alpha$ means that if the current state is w_1, then before performing the action α the world was w_2. The satisfaction relation $M \models_w A$ is defined as follows: $M \models_w f$ iff $f \in V(f)$ for any $f \in \mathbf{Flu}$. We then have the following:

- $M \models_w [\alpha]A$ iff $\forall w' \in W, (wR^F_\alpha w' \Rightarrow M \models_{w'} A)$.
- $M \models_w [\alpha]^{-1}A$ iff $\forall w' \in W, (wR^P_\alpha w' \Rightarrow M \models_{w'} A)$.

As usual, $A \in \mathbf{Fma}$ is valid in a model M written $M \models A$ if $M \models_w A, \forall w \in W$. $\models A$ means A is valid in all models. Standard models are those in which the binary relation R_α has the intended meanings of programs or actions α with the added condition that $R^F_\alpha = (R^P_\alpha)^{-1}$ (as in [11]). The following hold in any standard model:

- $R_{\alpha;\beta} = R_\alpha \circ R_\beta$ (Composition)
- $R_{\alpha\cup\beta} = R_\alpha \cup R_\beta$ (Alternation)
- $R_{\alpha^*} = R^*_\alpha$ (Iteration)
- $R_{A?} = \{(w, w) : M \models_w A\}$ (Test)

2.3 A Deductive System for $TPDL$

The deductive system for $TPDL$ consists of the following axiom schemes and inference rules (where $A, B \in \mathbf{Fma}, \alpha \in \mathbf{Act}$):

1. Axiom Schemes
   - All tautologies of propositional dynamic logic.
   - Axiom schemata analogous to those for normal temporal logics:
     - $\mathbf{C_P}$: $A \rightarrow [\alpha]^{-1}\langle\alpha\rangle A$

- $\mathbf{C_F}$: $A \to [\alpha]\langle\alpha\rangle^{-1}A$
  - **FK**: $[\alpha](A \to B) \to ([\alpha]A \to [\alpha]B)$
  - **PK**: $[\alpha]^{-1}(A \to B) \to ([\alpha]^{-1}A \to [\alpha]^{-1}B)$

2. Inference Rules
   - **FN**: $\frac{A}{[\alpha]A}$
   - **PN**: $\frac{A}{[\alpha]^{-1}A}$
   - **MP**: $\frac{A, A \to B}{B}$

Provability in $TPDL$ is denoted $\vdash$. We note the presence of the new rules **FK, PK, FN, PN** which are extensions of the K, N rules of standard PDL. The following lemma is an obvious consequence of our definitions:

Lemma 1.

1. $\vdash \langle\alpha\rangle^{-1}[\alpha]A \to A$
2. $\vdash \langle\alpha\rangle[\alpha]^{-1}A \to A$
3. $\vdash \langle\alpha\rangle^{-1}\top \wedge [\alpha]^{-1}A \to \langle\alpha\rangle^{-1}A$
4. $\vdash [\alpha]^{-1}(A \to B) \to (\langle\alpha\rangle^{-1}A \to \langle\alpha\rangle^{-1}B)$

Theorem 1. *The following are theorems of* $TPDL$*:*

- $[\alpha;\beta]^{-1}A \leftrightarrow [\beta]^{-1}[\alpha]^{-1}A,$
- $[\alpha \cup \beta]^{-1}A \leftrightarrow [\alpha]^{-1}A \wedge [\beta]^{-1}A,$
- $[\alpha^*]^{-1}A \to A \wedge [\alpha^*]^{-1}[\alpha]^{-1}A,$

Soundness and completeness of the deductive system above is easily shown:

Theorem 2. *(Soundness and completeness of* $TPDL$*)* A *is valid in all standard models of* $\mathcal{L}_{TPDL}$ *if and only if* $\vdash A$.

Decidability in $TPDL$ has a time complexity similar to that of PDL:

Proposition 1. *Validity in* $TPDL$ *is decidable in exponential time.*

3 Reasoning with Action Descriptions in *TPDL*

Logics of action typically aim to provide *action descriptions* for describing the effects of actions and the causal relationships in a system, and *inference schemes* that enable the prediction of the effects of actions or explanations of observed phenomena. We describe these components in turn within the context of our framework. An action description for a dynamic system is a finite set of formulas, which specifies actions in the system and includes information about the direct and indirect effects of actions in the system. A formula in an action description is significantly different from an ordinary formula. The sentence $loaded \to [Shoot]\neg alive$ means that whenever $loaded$ is true (i.e., the fluent $loaded$ holds), performing the action $Shoot$ will result in a situation or state in which the value of the fluent *Alive* is $\neg Alive$. In the situation calculus a similar statement would read $\forall s(loaded(s) \rightarrow \neg alive(do(Shoot, s)))$. To recreate the same situation in dynamic logic, an extra modality **any** is used ([15,2]) to denote "any action". This lets us write expressions such as $[\,\mathbf{any}](loaded \rightarrow [Shoot]\neg alive$; such a modality is an S_5 modality. Introducing the **any** modality formally would involve adding all S_5 axioms and an extra axiom $([\mathbf{any}]A \rightarrow [\alpha]A)$. However, rather than introducing extra modalities which would make the system cumbersome, we use the techniques of [19], in which an action description is treated as a *set of axioms.* These function like domain axioms in the situation calculus and lets us define the notion of Σ -provability.

Definition 1. *Let Σ be a finite set of formulas. A formula A is a Σ -theorem, denoted $\vdash^{\Sigma} A$ if it belongs to the smallest set of formulas which contains, all theorems of $TPDL$, all elements of Σ and is closed under MP, FN and PN.*

For any $\Gamma \subseteq \mathbf{Fma}$, a sentence A is Σ-provable from Γ written $\Gamma \vdash^{\Sigma} A$ if $\exists A_1, \ldots A_n \in \Gamma$ such that $\vdash^{\Sigma} A_1 \rightarrow (\ldots(A_n \rightarrow A)\ldots)$. Γ is Σ-consistent if $\Gamma \nvdash^{\Sigma} \bot$.

Definition 2. *Let Σ be an action description. A standard model M is a Σ -model if $M \models A$ for any $A \in \Sigma$. A is Σ-valid i.e., $\models^{\Sigma} A$ if it is valid in every Σ-model.*

Soundness and completeness is then easily shown:

Theorem 3. *Σ-provability is sound and complete: $\vdash^{\Sigma} A$ iff $\models^{\Sigma} A$*

3.1 Frame Axioms

A reasonable requirement of any framework for reasoning about action is that it provide a solution to the frame problem. The following simple solution is proposed in [3] (L is a literal below) .

Definition 3. *A formula of the form $\varphi \wedge L \rightarrow [a]L$ is a frame axiom.*

Definition 4. *Let Σ be uniformly consistent (i.e., $\nvdash^{\Sigma} \bot$) and Γ be Σ-consistent (i.e., $\Gamma \nvdash^{\Sigma} \bot$). For an arbitrary formula A, and set Δ of frame axioms, such that Γ is $\Sigma \cup \Delta$-consistent and $\Gamma \vdash^{\Sigma \cup \Delta} A$ then A is Σ-provable from Γ with Δ, denoted by $\Gamma \vdash^{\Sigma}_{\Delta} A$. The elements of Δ are termed supplementary axioms.*

In [4], it is shown that $\Gamma \vdash^{\Sigma}_{\Delta} A$ if and only if there is a set Δ' of frame axioms which only contain the symbols occurring in Γ, Σ and A such that $\Gamma \vdash^{\Sigma}_{\Delta'} A$ (i.e., $\Gamma \vdash^{\Sigma}_{\Delta} A$ is reduced to $\Gamma \vdash^{\Sigma}_{\Delta'} A$) (some extra conditions are required to make this true, see [4]). Moreover, it is shown that if Σ is in normal form[1], Δ' can only contain the symbols in Γ and A. This means that for prediction and postdiction, there is no frame problem (representationally) if we postpone listing frame axioms till a query is made.

[1] The following kinds of formulas are said to be in *normal form*:

– $[\varphi]L$ (causal law)

3.2 Prediction and Postdiction

With Σ-provability, simple and desirable inferences involving prediction and postdiction become possible.

Example 1. Consider the Yale Shooting Problem [6]. Let $Flu = \{alive, loaded\}$ and $Act_P = \{Load, Shoot, Wait\}$. This problem is described by the following action description:

$$\Sigma = \left\{ \begin{array}{l} \neg loaded \rightarrow [Load]loaded \\ loaded \rightarrow [Shoot]\neg alive \\ loaded \rightarrow [Shoot]\neg loaded \\ \langle Load\rangle \top \\ \langle Wait\rangle \top \\ loaded \leftrightarrow \langle Shoot\rangle \top \end{array} \right\}$$

The first three sentences state the effects of the actions *Load* and *Shoot*. The last three state the feasibility of *Load*, *Wait* and *Shoot*. Among them, $\neg loaded \rightarrow \langle Load\rangle \top$ says that *Load* is performable if the gun is not already loaded. The action *Shoot* can cause $\neg Alive$ only if the gun is loaded.

We can prove that $\{\neg loaded\} \vdash^{\Sigma}_{\Delta} [Load; Wait; Shoot]\neg alive$ (i.e., that the sequence of actions *Load*, *Wait*, *Shoot* results in $\neg alive$ as desired), where $\Delta = \{loaded \rightarrow [Wait]loaded\}$ in the following:

1*.	$\vdash^{\Sigma}_{\Delta} \neg loaded \rightarrow [Load]loaded$	(AD)
2*.	$\vdash^{\Sigma}_{\Delta} loaded \rightarrow [Wait]loaded$	(FA)
3*.	$\vdash^{\Sigma}_{\Delta} loaded \rightarrow [Shoot]\neg alive$	(AD)
4*.	$\vdash^{\Sigma}_{\Delta} [Load]loaded \rightarrow [Load; Wait]loaded$	(2,FN)
5*.	$\vdash^{\Sigma}_{\Delta} [Load; Wait]loaded \rightarrow [Load; Wait; Shoot]\neg alive$	(3,FN)
6.	$\vdash^{\Sigma}_{\Delta} [Load; Wait; Shoot]\neg alive$	(Γ,1,4,5)

where *AD* indicates "Action Description in Σ"; *FN* is an inference rule of *TPDL*; Γ represent the premises. "*" means the formula is a Σ -theorem, so we can use the inference rules *FN* and *PN*. FA stands for "frame axiom". We can also prove that $\vdash^{\Sigma} [Shoot]^{-1} loaded$ (i.e., that *preconditions for actions can be inferred using past modalities*).

1*.	$\vdash^{\Sigma} [Shoot]^{-1}\langle Shoot\rangle \top \rightarrow [Shoot]^{-1} loaded$	(PN)
2*.	$\vdash^{\Sigma} [Shoot]^{-1}\langle Shoot\rangle \top$	(C_p)
3*.	$\vdash^{\Sigma} [Shoot]^{-1} loaded$	$(1,2)$

- $\varphi \rightarrow [a]L$ (deterministic action law)
- $\varphi \rightarrow \prec a \succ L$ (non-deterministic action law)
- $\varphi \rightarrow \langle a\rangle \top$ (qualification law).

where φ and ψ are propositional formulas, L is a literal and a is a primitive action. An action description Σ is *normal* if each formula in Σ is in normal form.

4 Application to Benchmark Examples

4.1 Stanford Murder Mystery

As demonstrated, the Yale Shooting Problem (as a prediction problem) is trivially handled. A far more interesting case is the Stanford Murder Mystery, which, as pointed out in [1] created problems for classical non-monotonic approaches (specifically, circumscription [10] and chronological minimization models [18]) and demonstrated the role of backward temporal projection. The status of the gun is unknown in the initial situation while it is known that the victim is initally alive and then is shot dead after a *Shoot* action followed by a *Wait* action.

Example 2. (Stanford Murder Mystery) Let $\mathbf{Flu} = \{Alive,\ Loaded,\ Walking\}$ and $\mathbf{Act}_P = \{Load,\ Shoot,\ Wait\}$. The action description is the one in Example 1. We want to be able to derive $\{[wait]^{-1}[shoot]^{-1}alive, \neg alive\} \vdash^{\Sigma} [wait]^{-1}[shoot]^{-1}loaded$. That is, we would like to draw the inference that the gun was loaded in the initial situation followed by the indicated sequence of actions above leading to the unfortunate victim's death.

As pointed out in [1], standard circumscription policy is unable to draw this conclusion–it cannot sanction the inference that the gun was initially loaded[2]. The chronological minimization model fails as well–in delaying abnormalities to fluents and postponing the victim's death to the waiting part of the scenario, it ends up concluding that the gun must have been unloaded. In contrast, in our system, we are able to formally prove the desired conclusion.

Proof for $\{[wait]^{-1}[shoot]^{-1}alive, \neg alive\} \vdash^{\Sigma}_{\Delta} [wait]^{-1}[shoot]^{-1}loaded$; in the following, the letter **L** stands for Lemma)

1*.	$\vdash^{\Sigma}_{\Delta} alive \to [wait]alive$	(FA)
2*.	$\vdash^{\Sigma}_{\Delta} [wait]^{-1}(alive \to [wait]alive)$	(1,PN)
3*.	$\vdash^{\Sigma}_{\Delta} \langle wait\rangle^{-1}alive \to \langle wait\rangle^{-1}[wait]Alive$	(2,**L** 1:4)
4*.	$\vdash^{\Sigma}_{\Delta} \langle wait\rangle^{-1}alive \to alive$	(3,**L** 1:1)
5.	$\vdash^{\Sigma}_{\Delta} \neg\langle wait\rangle^{-1}alive$	(Γ,4)
6*.	$\vdash^{\Sigma}_{\Delta} alive \wedge \neg loaded \to [shoot]alive$	(FA)
7*.	$\vdash^{\Sigma}_{\Delta} [shoot]^{-1}(alive \wedge \neg loaded \to [shoot]alive)$	(6,PN)
8*.	$\vdash^{\Sigma}_{\Delta} \langle shoot\rangle^{-1}(alive \wedge \neg loaded) \to \langle shoot\rangle^{-1}[shoot]alive$	(7,**L** 1:4)
9*.	$\vdash^{\Sigma}_{\Delta} \langle shoot\rangle^{-1}(alive \wedge \neg loaded) \to alive$	(8,**L** 1:1)
10*.	$\vdash^{\Sigma}_{\Delta} [wait]^{-1}(\langle shoot\rangle^{-1}(alive \wedge \neg loaded) \to alive)$	(PN)
11*.	$\vdash^{\Sigma}_{\Delta} \langle wait\rangle^{-1}\langle shoot\rangle^{-1}(alive \wedge \neg loaded) \to \langle wait\rangle^{-1}alive$	(10,**L** 1:4)
12.	$\vdash^{\Sigma}_{\Delta} \neg\langle wait\rangle^{-1}\langle shoot\rangle^{-1}(alive \wedge \neg loaded)$	(5, 11)
13.	$\vdash^{\Sigma}_{\Delta} [wait]^{-1}[shoot]^{-1}\neg(alive \wedge \neg loaded)$	(12)
14.	$\vdash^{\Sigma}_{\Delta} [wait]^{-1}[shoot]^{-1}loaded$	(Γ,13,PK)

where $\Delta = \{alive \to [wait]alive,\ alive \wedge \neg loaded \to [shoot]alive\}$ □

Our framework possesses an interesting feature vis-a-vis the existence of frame axioms. In addition to the standard frame axioms of the form "taking

[2] [1] then goes on to provide a circumscriptive formalization of the Stanford Murder Mystery.

action α has no effect on fluent A" we can generate axioms of the form "taking action α had no effect on fluent A in the past".

Proposition 2.

- $\vdash^{\Sigma} (\varphi \wedge A \to [\alpha]A) \to (\varphi \wedge \neg A \to [\alpha]^{-1}\neg A)$
- $\vdash^{\Sigma} (\varphi \wedge \neg A \to [\alpha]\neg A) \to (\varphi \wedge A \to [\alpha]^{-1}A)$

Proof: Immediate from definitions and axiom schemes. □

The proposition above says that whenever we have a frame axiom of the form $\varphi \wedge A \to [\alpha]A$, there exists one of the form $\varphi \wedge \neg A \to [\alpha]^{-1}\neg A$; for every frame axiom of the form $\varphi \wedge \neg A \to [\alpha]\neg A$, there exists one of the form $\varphi \wedge A \to [\alpha]^{-1}A$. These axioms can be used for shorter proofs of postdictive inferences.

4.2 The Two Bus Problem

We now demonstrate the efficacy of our approach by considering an example [8] that proves problematic for state-minimization [1] and narrative based approaches [12]). In the example below, the minimal models obtained by the circumscription policy of the state minimization models are adversely affected by the observation axioms (since non-deterministic actions are involved).

Example 3. There are two buses that take the agent to its workplace. The buses are of different colors: one red, the other yellow. To get to work, the commuter takes the first bus that comes by. It can board either bus only if it has a ticket. We use the fluents $HasTicket, OnRedBus$ and $OnYellowBus$ to express the state of the commuter. We consider two actions: $BuyTicket$ and $GetOnBoard$. This scenario is specified by the following action description:

$$\Sigma = \left\{ \begin{array}{l} \neg(OnRedBus \wedge OnYellowBus) \\ OnRedBus \to HasTicket \\ OnYellowBus \to HasTicket \\ \neg HasTicket \to [BuyTicket]HasTicket \\ [GetOnBoard](OnRedBus \vee OnYellowBus) \\ HasTicket \wedge \neg OnRedBus \wedge \neg OnYellowBus \leftrightarrow \langle GetOnBoard\rangle\top \\ \langle BuyTicket\rangle\top \end{array} \right\}$$

In the state minimization model, the erroneous deduction that the agent is on the red bus *immediately after buying the ticket* (without taking the action $GetOnBoard$) is not blocked. In contrast, our system allows the desired inferences and blocks the undesirable ones.

We can prove:

$\{\neg HasTicket, \neg OnRedBus, \neg OnYellow\} \vdash^{\Sigma}_{\Delta} \langle[BuyTicket; GetOnBus]\rangle(OnRedBus \vee OnYellowBus)$

where $\Delta = \{\neg OnRedBus \to [BuyTicket]\neg OnRedBus,\ \neg OnYellowBus \to [BuyTicket]\neg OnYellowBus\}$.

However, we can never prove that

$\{\neg HasTicket, \neg OnRedBus, \neg OnYellow\} \vdash^{\Sigma}_{\Delta} \langle [BuyTicket] \rangle OnRedBus$

or

$\{\neg HasTicket, \neg OnRedBus, \neg OnYellow\} \vdash^{\Sigma}_{\Delta} \langle [BuyTicket; GetOnBus] \rangle OnRedBus$

no matter what frame axioms are used in Δ.

Note too, that we can prove:

$\{OnRedBus\} \vdash^{\Sigma}_{\Delta} [GetOnBus]^{-1}(\neg OnRedBus)$

but

$\{OnRedBus\} \not\vdash^{\Sigma}_{\Delta} [BuyTicket]^{-1}(\neg OnRedBus)$,

which means if the passenger is on the red bus currently, before it got on the bus, it must not have been on the red bus, while buying a ticket can never cause the commuter to be off the bus. Furthermore, given that the passenger is on a bus (either one) we can draw the true inference that the commuter performed the action of boarding the bus, preceded by buying a ticket, before which the commuter was not on either of the buses:

$\{OnRedBus \vee OnYellowBus\}$

$\vdash^{\Sigma}_{\Delta} [GetOnBoard]^{-1}[BuyTicket]^{-1}(\neg OnRedBus \wedge \neg OnYellowBus)$.

We cannot strengthen the conclusion with the added conjunct $\neg HasTicket$ since buying a ticket is always possible even if the commuter already has a ticket. We can also infer that in order to board the bus, the commuter must have a ticket and must not be on either of the two buses: $\vdash^{\Sigma}_{\Delta} [GetOnBoard]^{-1}(\neg OnRedBus \wedge HasTicket \wedge \neg OnYellowBus)$.

5 Conclusion

In this paper, we have presented a framework for backward temporal projection that combines two existent frameworks for reasoning about action: dynamic logic and temporal logic. We have demonstrated the intuitive plausibility of the system by its application to standard examples in the literature and demonstrated its formal elegance and soundness. More work remains to be done however: embedding this system into a more comprehensive logic for reasoning about actions will enable a unified treatment of the frame, qualification and ramification problems. We would also like to apply the system to more 'scaled-up' examples. At a purely formal level, investigating the interaction of the iteration construct of standard PDL with the backward modalities of $TPDL$ is an interesting avenue of research.

Acknowledgements. The authors would like to thank Marcelo Finger, Norman Foo, Tomasz Kowalski, Rohit Parikh and R. Ramanujam for helpful discussions and comments. In addition, the authors would would like to thank Dexter Kozen, Vaughan Pratt and Moshe Vardi for the references they provided.

References

1. A.B Baker. Nonmonotonic reasoning in the framework of the situation calculus. *Artificial Intelligence*, 49:5–23, 1991.
2. M.A. Castilho, O. Gasquet, and A. Herzig. Formalizing action and change in modal logic I:the frame problem. *Journal of Logic and Computations*, 9:701–735, 1999.
3. N. Foo and D. Zhang. Dealing with the ramification problem in the extended propositional dynamic logic. In *Proceedings of Advances in Modal Logic,* pages 89–102,2000.
4. N. Foo and D. Zhang. Reasoning with extra frame axioms and qualification axioms manuscript. available at `ftp.cse.unsw.edu.au/pub/users/ksg/Working/action3.zip`, 2000.
5. R. Goldblatt. *Logics of Time and Computation.* Stanford University Press, 1987.
6. S. Hanks and D. McDermott. Nonmonotonic logic and temporal projection. *Artificial Intelligence*, 33(3):379–412, 1987.
7. D. Harel. *First-order dynamic logic.* Springer-Verlag, 1979.
8. G.N. Kartha. Two counterexamples related to baker 's approach to the frame problem. *Artificial Intelligence*, 69:379–391, 1994.
9. H.Kautz. A first order dynamic logic for planning. In *Proceedings of the CSCSI/SCEIO*, pages 19–26, 1982.
10. J. McCarthy. Circumscription - a form of nonmonotonic reasoning. *Artificial Intelligence*, 13, 1980.
11. Rohit Parikh. The completeness of propositional dynamic logic. In *Mathematical Foundations of Computer Science*, Lecture Notes in Computer Science, Number 64, pages 403–415. Springer-Verlag, 1978.
12. J. Pinto and R. Reiter. Reasoning about time in the situation calculus. *Annals of Mathematics and Artificial Intelligence*, 14(2-4:251–268, Sept 1995.
13. A. Pnueli. The temporal semantics of concurrent programs. *Theoretical Computer Science*, 13:45–60, 1981.
14. V.R. Pratt. Semantical considerations on floyd-hoare logic. In *Proceedings of the 17th IEEE Symposium on Foundations of Computer Science*, pages 109–121,1976.
15. H. Prendinger and G. Schurz. Reasoning about action and change: A dynamic logic approach. *Journal of Logic, Language, and Information*, 5:209–245, 1996.
16. S. Rosenschein. Plan synthesis:a logical approach. In *IJCAI-81*, pages 359–380, 1981.
17. Murray Shanahan. *Solving the Frame Problem: a mathematical investigation of the common sense law of inertia.* MIT Press,1997.
18. Y. Shoham. Chronological ignorance: experiments in nonmonotonic temporal reasoning. *Artificial Intelligence*, 36:279–331, 1988.
19. D. Zhang and N. Foo. EPDL: A logic for causal reasoning. In Proceedings of the *Seventeenth International Joint Conference on Artificial Intelligence-IJCAI-2001*, 2001.

A Method for Reasoning with Ontologies Represented as Conceptual Graphs

Dan Corbett

Advanced Computing Research Centre
School of Computer and Information Science
University of South Australia
Adelaide, South Australia 5095

Abstract. This paper discusses automated reasoning over ontologies. represented as Conceptual Graphs. We have designed and implemented reasoning tools using Conceptual Graphs as the underlying knowledge structure. This work demonstrates that the power of logic as implemented in Conceptual Graphs, and the tools available in Conceptual Graph Theory can be used as powerful ontology reasoning tools in a real-world domain. We show that ontologies can be constrained and unified using efficient methods, and that these methods provide the basis for an automated reasoning system. The Conceptual Graph techniques of concept join, partial order and subsumption are all exploited to create these reasoning tools.

We dicuss the implementation of our ideas, and demonstrate the reasoning tool that we created in two domains: building architecture and defence. The significance of our work is that the previously static knowledge representation of ontology is now a dynamic, functional reasoning system.

1. A Brief Overview of Conceptual Graphs

Conceptual Structures (or Conceptual Graphs, or "CGs") are a knowledge representation scheme, inspired by the existential graphs of Charles Sanders Peirce and further extended and defined by John Sowa [19-21]. Informally, CGs can be thought of as a formalization and extension of Semantic Networks, although the origins are different. They are labeled graphs with two types of nodes: concepts (which represent objects, entities or ideas) and relation nodes, which represent relations between the concepts. As an example, Figure 1 shows a Conceptual Graph which represents the knowledge that "The cat Felix is sitting on the mat which is known as mat 47."

Every concept or relation has an associated type. A concept may also have a specific referent or individual. A concept in a CG may represent a specific instance of that type (e.g., *Felix* is a specific instance, or individual, of type *cat*) or we may choose only to specify the type of the concept. That is to say that a concept may

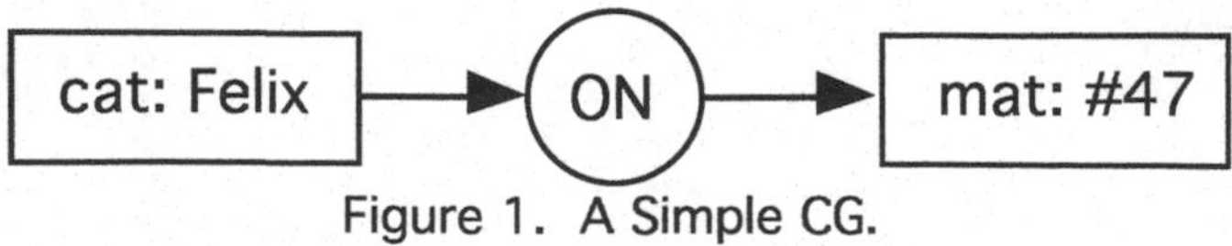

Figure 1. A Simple CG.

M. Brooks, D. Corbett, and M. Stumptner (Eds.): AI 2001, LNAI 2256, pp. 130–141, 2001.

simply represent a generic concept for a type, such as *mammal* or *room*, or a concept may represent a specific object or idea, such as *my cat* or *the kitchen at the Smith's house*. In the former case, the concepts in Figure 1 would be shown as "cat: * " and "mat: * " indicating non-specified entities of types *cat* and *mat*. In the standard canonical formation rules for Conceptual Graphs, unbound concepts are existentially quantified.

A relation may have zero or one incoming arcs, and one or more outgoing arcs. The type of the relation determines the number of arcs allowed on the relation. The arcs always connect a concept to a relation. Arcs cannot exist between concepts, or between relations.

A canon in the sense discussed here is the set of all CGs which are well-formed, and meaningful in their domain. Canonical formation rules specify how CGs can be legally built and guarantee that the resulting CGs satisfy "sensibility constraints." The sensibility constraints are rules in the domain which specify how a CG can be built, for example that the concept *eats* must have a theme which is *food*. Note that canonicity does not guarantee validity. A CG may be well-formed in the canononical formation rules for the domain, but still be false.

A type hierarchy is established for both the concepts and the relations within a canon. A type hierarchy is based on the intuition that some types subsume other types, for example, every instance of *cat* would also have all the properties of *mammal*. This hierarchy is expressed by a subsumption or generalization order on types.

For the reader interested in a formal treatment of these ideas (which we don't have room for here), Sowa discusses his original definitions in [20] but our work follows the further formalized and refined versions of Sowa's original ideas presented by Willems [24], by Chein and Mugnier [6, 17] and by Corbett [8, 10] .

2. Types and Inheritance

The set of types discussed in the previous section is arranged into a type hierarchy, ordered according to the specificity of each type. A type t is said to be more specific than a type s if t inherits information from s. We write $s \geq t$, and say that *s subsumes t* or is more general than t (or inversely, that t is *subsumed* by s, or is more specifc than s). We may also call s a *supertype* of t, or t a *subtype* of s. Equivalently to the above, one can write $t \leq s$.

In early pioneering work on the unification of first-order terms, Reynolds [18] used the natural lattice structure of first-order terms, which was a partial ordering based on subsumption of terms [11]. Many terms (or types in our case) are not in any subsumption relation, for example *cat* and *dog*, or *wood* and *mammal*. Unification corresponds to finding the greatest lower bound of two terms in the lattice [13]. The bottom of any lattice, which is represented with the symbol $\perp$, is the type to which all types can unify, and represents inconsistency. The top of the lattice, represented by $\top$, is the type to which all pairs of types can generalize, and is called the *universal* type. Every type is a subtype of $\top$. Inheritance hierarchies can be seen as lattices that admit unification and generalization [13]. The common specialization of two

Conceptual Graphs, s and t, is known as a join, and is represented as $s \vee t$. The common generalization of the two graphs is known as a meet, and is represented using the symbols $s \wedge t$.

The process of unifying Conceptual Graphs includes the process of finding the most general subtypes for pairs of types of concepts, which depends on the two types in question being consistent. We also allow constraints on the concepts in the graphs, which are processed during the unification and resolution process. Unification (by projection) is the mechanism we use to find the solution of the constraints. In our work, unification is a tool which performs the work of identifying two structures using subsumption, where the elements of the structure can be constrained.

3. Unification as Reasoning

Until very recently, CGs have had no formalism for constraining real values in the referent of a concept. The standard method for representing and validating constraints has been to use type subsumption to specify which concept types (or subsumed subtypes) are valid in a system. One could constrain values in a knowledge representation system by forcing the concepts to conform to a specified type, or else to be subsumed by that type. A similar method applies to relations. To extend a previous example, the concept *eats* is specified to occur only between an agent which is an *animal* and a theme which is a *food*. Any individual used in the animal concept must conform to the *animal* type, which means that it must either be *animal*, or be subsumed by *animal*, such as *cat* or *reptile*.

One generalization of unification constraints is the use of ordering constraints, i.e., constraints of the form $s \leq t$ where s and t are terms. Depending on the application, the ordering $\leq$ may have different interpretations. A concept may unify by subsumption with another concept if one of the concepts is a more general expression of the other, as defined in the partial order. There are also constraint approaches in logic programming where constraints are not interpreted over a single structure. An example for such an approach is H. Aït-Kaci's Login [2], where first-order terms are replaced by feature terms.

The formal definition of unification for Conceptual Graphs is set out in [7, 8, 10], however, it is essential to clarify the difference between the "join" operator and the general concept of unification. The difference between these two operators can be illustrated in the following way. In the standard canonical formation rules for Conceptual Graphs, unbound concepts are existentially quantified. We take for our example the two graphs in Figure 2, which can be interpreted as "Felix is on some object," and "There is some animal sitting on that particular mat." Joining these two graphs is not possible under the standard canonical formation rule for external join because there's no projection from one graph to the other. However, there are individual concepts which can be joined, such as the concept that "Felix is a cat" and "animal." However, as discussed in previous sections of this chapter, true unification is the knowledge conjunction of the two graphs. The unification of these two Conceptual Graphs would be similar to the unification of ψ-terms presented by Aït-Kaci [1]. The unification is therefore "Felix sat on mat number 47," as shown in

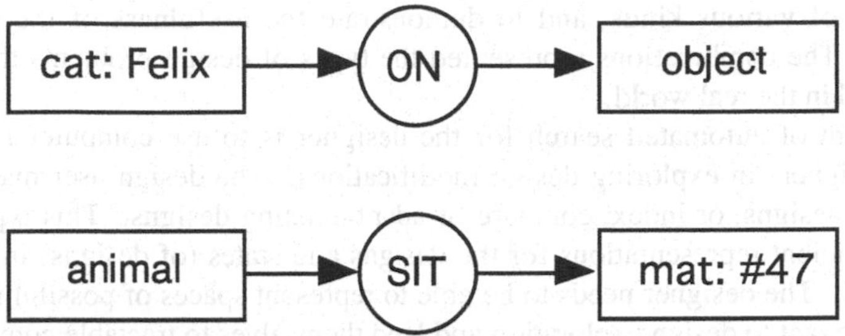

Figure 2. Is Felix on the mat?

Figure 3. Here, the more general concepts of "animal," "on," and "object" have been replaced by their more specific instances. This illustrates that unification is more than an external join, and is composed of several operations, including join.

Unification, however, is somewhat more complicated, and also more interesting and useful than merely an extension of the join operation. The unification of two graphs contains neither more nor less information than the two graphs being unified. Figure 3 shows that the unification of the two graphs in Figure 2 still retains all the information of the original two graphs. This is the idea behind knowledge conjunction [10].

4. The Architectural Design Tool

There have recently been many research forays by the design community into computational design tools which will give the designer useful structures which can be combined and constrained in useful ways [3, 5, 12]. There have also been attempts in the CG community to assist in defining methods and techniques which will be useful in computational design [8, 9, 14, 25].

The results discussed in this section are those recorded from the application of the Conceptual Graphs reasoning tool operating over the domain of architectural design. The domain knowledge is represented as Conceptual Graphs with constraints. Here, we demonstrate the idea behind the reasoning mechanism by employing order sorted unification and constraints within the domain of architectural design.

The concepts discussed previously were implemented in Allegro Common Lisp on a Sun Workstation. All of the relations were implemented as lisp functions, and all data structures were lisp lists. Many different types of designs were detailed, in order to cover a wide range of generic design problems, all type hierarchies and subsumption problems, and various relations. These designs were unified in various combinations, in order to test the functionality of unification with and without

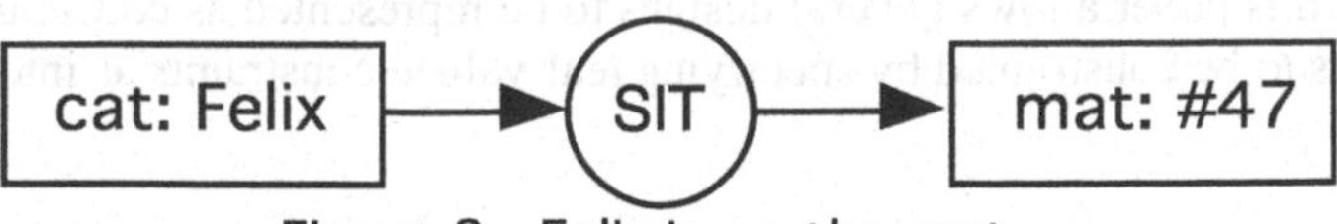

Figure 3. Felix is on the mat.

constraints of various kinds, and to demonstrate the usefulness of the reasoning technique. The combinations represented the types of design problems that can be encountered in the real world.

The point of automated search for the designer is to use computer media that engage designers in exploring design modifications. The design user may want to create new designs, or index, compare or adapt existing designs. This type of user requires efficient representations for the designs and states (of designs) in a symbol system [25]. The designer needs to be able to represent spaces of possibilities which are both relevant to design exploration and lend themselves to tractable computations. It is necessary for the design process that the information in the system can be ordered by specificity, since design exploration usually means starting from an under-specified design and proceeding to a more specialized state.

Consider a design for the kitchen of a custom-made house. In this design, the architect has specified some of the lighting design and that the floor area must be greater than 20 square meters. The architect has also retreived an old design, which specifies the remainder of the lighting design. The graphs specifying these two designs are shown in Figure 4. We assume that the portion of the graphs not shown in the diagram are compatible. The unification software discussed above combines these two graphs, with the result shown in Figure 5. In this graph, all the original knowledge of the first two graphs has been preserved, and the values in the concepts have been joined as specified.

Another example would have a design similar to the second in Figure 4, specifying most of the lighting design. Another graph would represent a kitchen design where only the plumbing design is specified. These two would unify since the two heads are compatible, and the remainder of the graphs would be included in the unified graph. All of the knowledge is represented in the unified graph, which would specify the design for the lighting and the plumbing.

These examples also illustrate how the interval type would allow real numbers to be represented in CGs. Any real number could be bounded inside an interval, similar to the concept of using floating point numbers to represent real numbers in software. Further, any concept containing a real value can be constrained in an interval. This allows the representation in CGs of constraint satisfaction problems. This use of interval constraints to represent real constraints has been used for some time in the Constraint Satisfaction Problem community. The work by van Hentenryck [22, 23] is a good example of intervals in CSP.

5. Results and Discussion: Architectural Design Tool

These graphs can be used to efficiently represent a building design ontology. The use of Conceptual Graphs is an efficient method for representing not only the designs, but also constraints on the designs and knowledge conjunction of designs. The system described in this paper allows general designs to be represented as concepts, and also allows values to be constrained by specifying real-valued constraints as intervals.

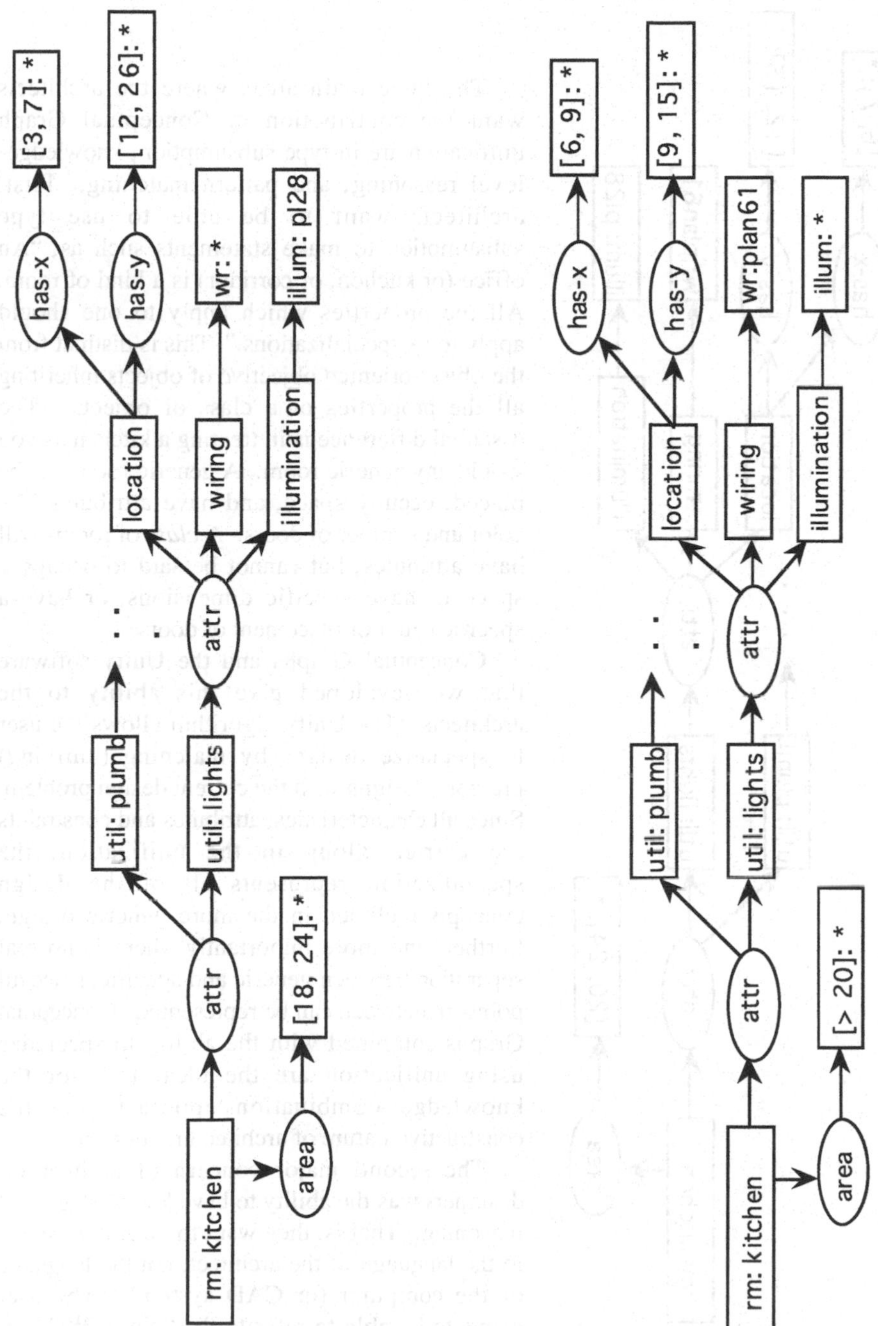

Figure 4. Two constrained partial designs to be unified.

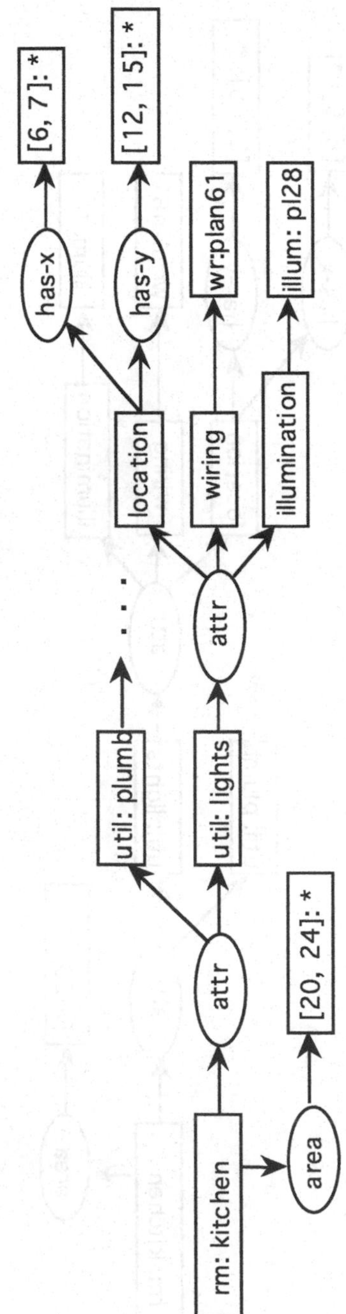

Figure 5. The unified design.

The three main areas where the architects want the contribution of Conceptual Graph unification are in type subsumption, knowledge-level reasoning, and pattern matching. First, architects want to be able to use type subsumption to make statements such as, "An office (or kitchen, or corridor) is a kind of room. All the properties which apply to one should apply to its specializations." This is distinct from the object-oriented objective of objects inheriting all the properties of a class of objects. The essential difference is in treating a kitchen as you would any generic room. A generic room can be placed, occupy space, and have attributes like color and number of doors. A *class* of rooms will have attributes, but cannot be said to occupy a space or have specific dimensions, or have a specific count or placement of doors.

Conceptual Graphs and the Unify software that we developed give this ability to the architects. The Unify algorithm allows the user to specialize designs by matching (unifying) previous designs with the current design problem. Since all characteristics, attributes and constraints are carried along in the unification, the specialization represents all of the design concepts included in the more generic design. Further, and more importantly, there is no real separation between generic and specific, since all points in between can be represented. Conceptual Graphs combined with the ability to specialize using unification are the ideal tool for the knowledge combination approach and the constructive nature of architectural design.

The second major concern of arcitectural designers was the ability to have knowledge-level reasoning. That is, they want to be able to speak in the language of the architect, not the language of the computer (or CAD system). The user wants to be able to refer to the "North Wall" or "door" without resorting to discussing geometric coordinates in space. The user wants to depart from previous CAD-based data-level processing, and work at the knowledge level in the architecture domain.

This is certainly another area where Conceptual Graphs and unification combine to bring a solution to this domain. While spatial coordinates (and their constraints) can be stored in a graphical representation of a room, there is no need for the user to bother with using them. The graph can be manipulated as a whole, and treated as a room, rather than a square in a diagram. The completed system will not deal with lines and boxes, but rather with specializing entire designs for rooms (or houses, or office buildings). This approach frees the architect from dealing with data-level concerns of numbers and coordinates, and allows the architect instead to deal with the architectural design.

Finally, the users want to be able to start with a high-level, generic description of a building, and then make queries such as, "Can this bay structure be used in the support structure?" or, "Do the constraints match up adequately for a particular technology to be used? If yes, tell me the constraints under which it is usable."

Once again, the work presented in this paper meets the requirements of the architects. A query is represented as a Conceptual Graph. The user can specify a type of structure for support, and make the query by attempting to unify the structure with the more generic design. If the unification fails, then the user knows that the proposed structure does not meet the constraints of the design problem. If the graphs unify, then the resulting graph will contain the constraints which must be met in order to make the design work.

Overall, the system of unification over constraints on Conceptual Graphs presented in this paper gives a set of tools to the designer. The ability to use knowledge combination with constraints to handle objects at the knowledge level greatly leverages the ability of the designer to work efficiently.

6. The Air Operations Officer

As our second knowledge domain, we discuss the use of unification and constraints for applying rules in a defense domain. An Air Operations Officer (usually known as an OPSO) is the defense officer responsible for deciding the appropriate defensive response to an air threat. A study of the Operations Officer decision-making methods was recently conducted, using a cognitive modeling technique [15, 16]. The study was used to show the usefulness of cognitive modeling in deriving rules from expert knowledge. In this section, we only make use of the rules which resulted from the study; the cognitive modeling technique is not discussed here.

In the domain of the Operations Officer, the magnitude of the response to an air threat is in proportion to the threat itself. So, if the opposing aircraft are very close, or if the aircraft is of a type which can cause a great deal of damage (known as a *strike* aircraft), then the response is large. If the threat is smaller, then the response is smaller. For example, Figure 6 shows a rule in this domain. (We have borrowed the style of Cao [4] to express the rule, although we do not employ Cao's fuzzy reasoning here.) This graph expresses the rule that if a fighter aircraft (small threat) is between 400 and 500 nautical miles distant, then assert a threat level of "alert 60" (the lowest level of alert, in which response fighters must be ready to take off within sixty minutes), and a single fighter is assigned to deal with this threat.

The assertion shown in Figure 6 unifies with the "if" portion of this rule. The "then" portion represents the response to the situation, and it is asserted into the current world knowledge. In this manner, we can represent the decision-making capabilities of the Operations Officer.

The rule shown in Figure 7 is used for a bigger and more impending threat. Any threat aircraft which is closer than 400 nautical miles is considered an immediate threat, and a response squadron must be ready very quickly. Further, a strike aircraft is one which can inflict a great deal of damage, and is therefore dealt with more severely than a fighter aircraft.

The assertion shown in Figure 7 states that a bomber is known to be between 380 and 390 nautical miles distant. Our type hierarchy indicates that a bomber is a type of strike aircraft. Because of the proximity of the threat, the response aircraft are put on "alert 10" status. Because of the enormity of the threat, two fighters are assigned to deal with the target aircraft. Again, the assertion unifies with the "if" portion of the rule, causing the "then" portion of the rule to be asserted.

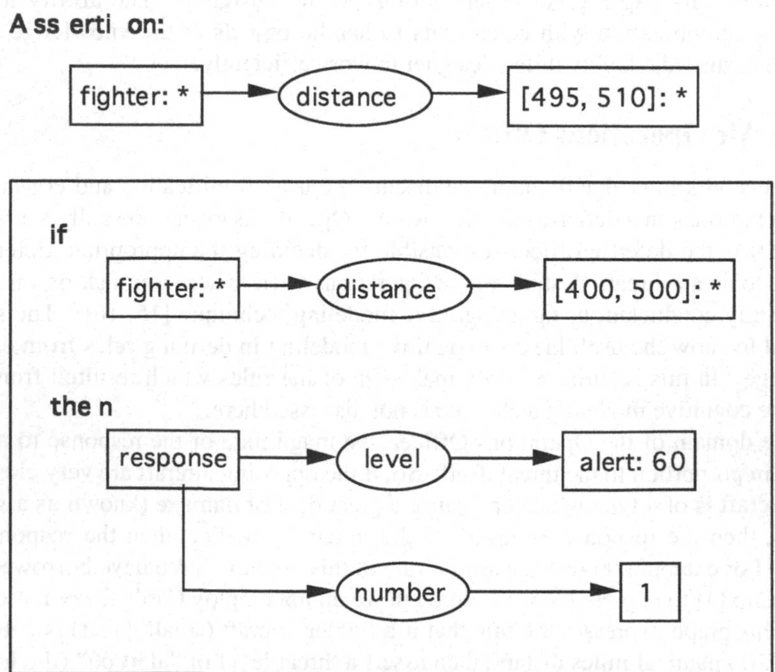

Figure 6. A rule in the defense domain, which uses constraints.

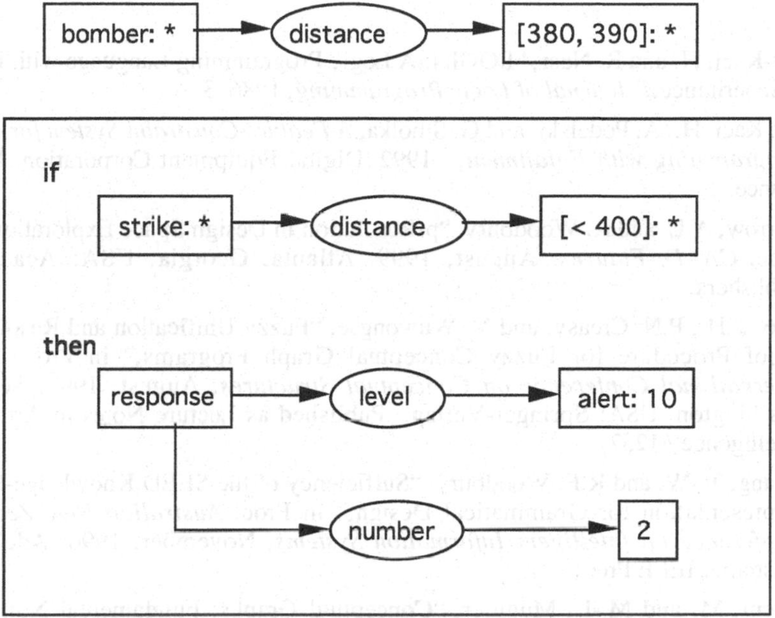

Figure 7. Another rule from the same domain.

7. Results and Discussion: The Air Operations Officer

Conceptual Graphs and the unification algorithm can be used to efficiently represent a set of rules in the domain of the Air Operations Officer. The use of Conceptual Graphs is an efficient method for representing the complete ontology of the OPSO, not only in the rules, but also in the exploration and use of the knowledge of types of aircraft and responses. General rules can be represented as Conceptual Graphs, and then specialized dynamically to match the current situation and describe an appropriate response.

8. Conclusions

We have demonstrated a method for automated reasoning on ontologies, using Conceptual Graphs to represent the underlying ontology. Type hierarchies and the canonical formation rules efficiently specialize graphs into concrete instances. A simple unification operation, using join and type subsumption, is used to validate real constraints over an entire unified graph. The significance of our work is that the previously static knowledge representation of ontology is now a dynamic, functional reasoning system.

References

1. Aït-Kaci, H. and R. Nasr, "LOGIN: A Logic Programming Language with Built-in Inheritance.," *Journal of Logic Programming*, 1986. **3**.
2. Aït-Kaci, H., A. Podelski, and G. Smolka, *A Feature Constraint System for Logic Programming with Entailment*, . 1992, Digital Equipment Corporation: Paris, France.
3. Burrow, A.L. and R. Woodbury. "p-Resolution in Design Space Exploration," in Proc. *CAAD Futures*, August, 1999. Atlanta, Georgia, USA: Academic Publishers.
4. Cao, T.H., P.N. Creasy, and V. Wuwongse. "Fuzzy Unification and Resolution Proof Procedure for Fuzzy Conceptual Graph Programs," in Proc. *Fifth International Conference on Conceptual Structures*, August, 1997. Seattle, Washington, USA: Springer-Verlag. Published as Lecture Notes in Artificial Intelligence #1257.
5. Chang, T.-W. and R.F. Woodbury. "Sufficiency of the SEED Knowledge-Level Representation for Grammatical Design," in Proc. *Australian New Zealand Conference on Intelligent Information Systems*, November, 1996. Adelaide, Australia: IEEE Press.
6. Chein, M. and M.-L. Mugnier, "Conceptual Graphs: Fundamental Notions," *Revue d'Intelligence Artificielle*, 1992. **6**(4): p. 365-406.
7. Corbett, D.R. "A Framework for Conceptual Graph Unification," in Proc. *Eighth International Conference on Conceptual Structures*, August, 2000. Darmstadt, Germany: Shaker Verlag.
8. Corbett, D.R., "Conceptual Graphs with Constrained Reasoning," *Revue d'Intelligence Artificielle*, 2001(to appear).
9. Corbett, D.R. and A.L. Burrow. "Knowledge Reuse in SEED Exploiting Conceptual Graphs," in Proc. *Fourth International Conference on Conceptual Structures*, August, 1996. Sydney, NSW, Australia: UNSW Press.
10. Corbett, D.R. and R.F. Woodbury. "Unification over Constraints in Conceptual Graphs," in Proc. *Seventh International Conference on Conceptual Structures*, July, 1999. Blacksburg, Virginia, USA: Springer-Verlag.
11. Davey, B.A. and H.A. Priestley, *Introduction to Lattices and Order*. 1990, Cambridge: Cambridge University Press.
12. Heisserman, J.A., "Generative Geometric Design," *IEEE Computer Graphics and Applications*, 1995. **14**(2): p. 37-45.
13. Knight, K., "Unification: A Multidisciplinary Survey," *ACM Computing Surveys*, 1989. **21**(1): p. 93-124.
14. Mineau, G.W. and C. Miranda, *Computer-Aided Design and Artificial Intelligence: Exploration in Architectural Plan Reuse*, . 1998.
15. Mitchard, H., *Cognitive Model of an Operations Officer*, 1998, Honours Thesis, Computer and Information Science, University of South Australia, Adelaide, South Australia.

16. Mitchard, H., J. Winkles, and D.R. Corbett. "Development and Evaluation of a Cognitive Model of an Air Defence Operations Officer," in Proc. *Fifth Biennial Conference of the Australasian Cognitive Science Society*, May, 2000. Adelaide, South Australia.

17. Mugnier, M.-L. and M. Chein, "Représenter des Connaissances et Raisonner avec des Graphes," *Revue d'Intelligence Artificielle*, 1996. **10**(6): p. 7-56.

18. Reynolds, J.C., "Transformational Systems and the Algebraic Structure of Atomic Formulas," *Machine Intelligence*, 1970. **5**.

19. Sowa, J. "Conceptual Graphs: Draft Proposed American National Standard," in Proc. *Seventh International Conference on Conceptual Structures*, July, 1999. Blacksburg, Virginia, USA: Springer-Verlag. Published as volume #1640 of Lecture Notes in Artificial Intelligence.

20. Sowa, J.F., *Conceptual Structures: Information Processing in Mind and Machine*. 1984, Reading, Mass: Addison-Wesley.

21. Sowa, J.F., *Conceptual Graphs Summary*, in *Conceptual Structures: Current Research and Practice*. 1992, Ellis Horwood: Chichester, UK.

22. Van Hentenryck, P., *Constraint Satisfaction in Logic Programming*. Logic Programming, ed. E. Shapiro. 1989, Cambridge, Massachusetts, USA: MIT Press.

23. Van Hentenryck, P., L. Michel, and Y. Deville, *Numerica*. 1997, Cambridge, Massachusetts, USA: MIT Press.

24. Willems, M. "Projection and Unification for Conceptual Graphs," in Proc. *Third International Conference on Conceptual Structures*, August, 1995. Santa Cruz, California, USA: Springer-Verlag. Published as Lecture Notes in Artificial Intelligence #954.

25. Woodbury, R., S. Datta, and A.L. Burrow. "Erasure in Design Space Exploration," in Proc. *Artificial Intelligence in Design*, June, 2000. Worcester, Massachusetts, USA.

Selection of Tasks and Delegation of Responsibility in a Multiagent System for Emergent Process Management

John Debenham
University of Technology, Sydney
debenham@it.uts.edu.au

Abstract. Emergent processes are high-level business processes; they are opportunistic in nature whereas production workflows are routine. Emergent processes may not be managed; they may contain goal-driven sub-processes that can be managed. A multiagent system supports emergent processes. Each player is assisted by an agent. The system manages goal-driven sub-processes and manages the commitments that players make to each other during emergent sub-processes. These commitments will be to perform some task and to assume some level of responsibility. The way in which the selection of tasks and the delegation of responsibility is done attempts to reflect high-level corporate principles and to 'sit comfortably' with the humans involved. Commitments are derived through a process of inter-agent negotiation that considers each individual's constraints and performance statistics. The system has been trialed on business process management in a university administrative context.

1. Introduction

Emergent processes are business processes that are not predefined and are ad hoc. These processes typically take place at the higher levels of organisations [1], and are distinct from production workflows [2]. Emergent processes are opportunistic in nature whereas production workflows are routine. How an emergent process will terminate may not be known until the process is well advanced. Further, the tasks involved in an emergent process are typically not predefined and emerge as the process develops. Those tasks may be carried out by collaborative groups as well as by individuals [3]. The support or management of emergent processes should be done in a way that reflects corporate priorities and that 'sits comfortably' with the humans involved.

From a process management perspective, emergent processes may contain "knowledge-driven" sub-processes as well as conventional "goal-driven" sub-processes. A *knowledge-driven process* is guided by its 'process knowledge' and 'performance knowledge'. The goal of a knowledge-driven process may not be fixed and may mutate. On the other hand, the management of a *goal-driven process* is guided by its goal which is fixed. A multiagent system to manage the "goal-driven" processes is described in [4]. In that system each human user is assisted by an agent which is based on a generic three-layer, BDI hybrid agent architecture. The term *individual* refers to a user/agent pair. That system is extended here to support knowledge-driven processes and so to support emergent process management. The general business of managing knowledge-driven processes is illustrated in Fig. 1, and will be discussed in Sec. 2. The following

M. Brooks, D. Corbett, and M. Stumptner (Eds.): AI 2001, LNAI 2256, pp. 142–152, 2001.

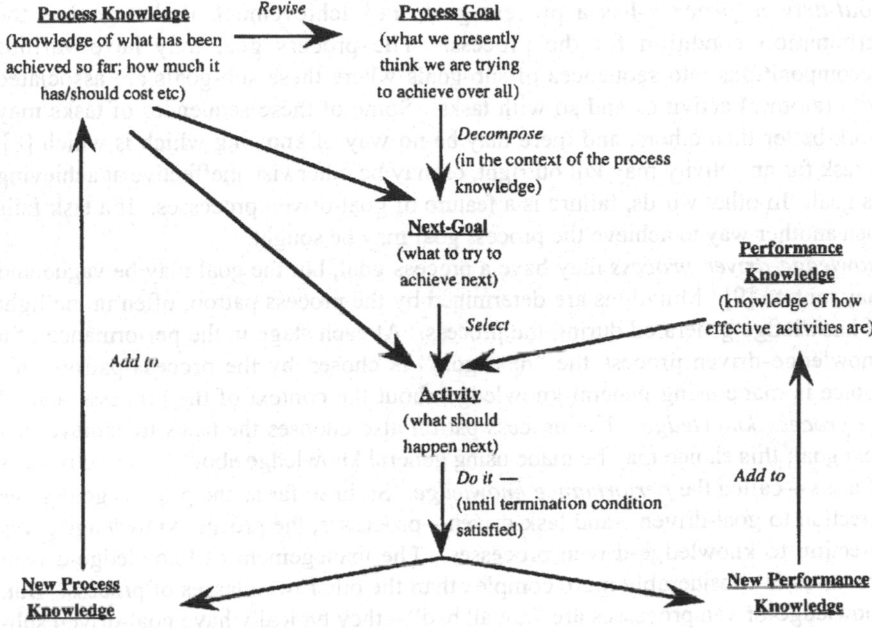

Fig. 1. Knowledge-driven process management (a simplified view)

sections are principally a description of how the system in [4] has been extended to support the management of knowledge-driven processes. Sec. 3 discusses the management of the process knowledge. Sec. 4 describes the performance knowledge which is communicated between agents in contract net bids for work. Sec. 5 compares various strategies for evaluating these bids.

Process management is an established application area for multi-agent systems [5]. One valuable feature of process management as an application area is that 'real' experiments may be performed with the cooperation of local administrators. The system described here has been trialed on emergent process management applications within university administration.

2. Process management

Following [2] a *business process* is "a set of one or more linked procedures or activities which collectively realise a business objective or policy goal, normally within the context of an organisational structure defining functional roles (also [6]) and relationships". Three classes of business process are defined in terms of their management properties [7] (ie in terms of how they may be managed).

- A *task-driven process* has a unique decomposition into a—possibly conditional—sequence of activities. Each of these activities has a goal and is associated with a task that "always" achieves this goal. Production workflows are typically task-driven processes.

- A *goal-driven process* has a process goal, and achievement of that goal is the termination condition for the process. The process goal may have various decompositions into sequences of sub-goals where these sub-goals are associated with (atomic) activities and so with tasks. Some of these sequences of tasks may work better than others, and there may be no way of knowing which is which [8]. A task for an activity may fail outright, or may be otherwise ineffective at achieving its goal. In other words, failure is a feature of goal-driven processes. If a task fails then another way to achieve the process goal may be sought.
- A *knowledge-driven process* may have a process goal, but the goal may be vague and may mutate [9]. Mutations are determined by the process patron, often in the light of knowledge generated during the process. At each stage in the performance of a knowledge-driven process the "next goal" is chosen by the process patron; this choice is made using general knowledge about the context of the process—called the *process knowledge*. The process patron also chooses the tasks to achieve that next goal; this choice may be made using general knowledge about the effectiveness of tasks—called the *performance knowledge*. So in so far as the process goal gives direction to goal-driven—and task-driven—processes, the process knowledge gives direction to knowledge-driven processes. The management of knowledge-driven processes is considerably more complex than the other two classes of process. But, knowledge-driven processes are "not all bad"—they typically have goal-driven sub-processes which may be handled in conventional way. A simplified view of knowledge-driven process management is shown in Fig. 1.

Properties of the three classes of process are shown in Fig. 2.

	Task-driven	Goal-driven	Knowledge-driven
Process goal	Determined by process patron, remains fixed	Determined by process patron, remains fixed	Determined by process patron, may mutate
Process termination condition	All tasks performed	Process goal achieved	Determined by process patron
Next goal	Determined by instance history	Determined by instance history	Determined by process patron
Next task	Determined by instance history—should achieve next goal	Chosen (somehow) on the basis of instance history and next goal—may not achieve next goal	Chosen by process patron to generate process knowledge.
Next activity termination condition	Next task performed	Next goal achieved, if it fails then try another way	Determined by process patron

Fig 2. Properties of the three types of process

Task-driven processes may be managed by a simple reactive agent architecture based on event-condition-action rules. Goal-driven processes may be modelled as state and activity charts [10] and managed by plans that can accommodates failure [11]. Such a planning system may provide the deliberative reasoning mechanism in a BDI agent architecture and is used in a goal-driven process management system [4] where tasks are represented as plans for goal-driven processes. But the success of execution of a plan for a goal-driven process is not necessarily related to the achievement of its goal. One reason for this is that an instance may make progress outside the process management system—two players could go for lunch for example. So each plan for a goal-driven process should terminate with a check of whether its goal has been achieved. Managing knowledge-driven processes is rather more difficult, see Fig. 1. The complete representation, never mind the maintenance, of the process knowledge would be an enormous job.

3. Process knowledge and the goals

This section refers to the left-hand side of Fig. 1, and to the relationship between the process knowledge, the process goal and the next-goal. This is the intractable part of knowledge-driven process management.

The process knowledge in any real application includes a significant amount of general and common sense knowledge. The system does assist in the maintenance of the process knowledge by ensuring that any virtual documents generated during an activity in a knowledge-driven sub-process arc passed to the process patron when the activity is complete. Virtual documents are either interactive web documents or workspaces in the LiveNet workspace system [6] which is used to handle virtual meetings and discussions.

The system records, but does not attempt to understand the process goal. Any possible revisions the process goal are carried out by the patron without assistance from the system. Likewise the decomposition of the process goal to decide "what to do next"—the next-goal. It may appear that the system does not do very much at all! If the next-goal is the goal of a goal-driven process—which it may well be—then the system may be left to manage it as long as it has plans in its plan library to achieve that next-goal. If the system does not have plans to achieve such a goal then the user may be able to quickly assemble such a plan from existing components in the plan library. The organisation of the plan library is a free-form, hierarchic filing system designed completely by each user. Such a plan only specifies what has to be done at the host agent. If a plan sends something to another agent with a sub-goal attached it is up to that other agent to design a plan to deal with that sub-goal. If the next-goal is the goal of a knowledge-driven process then the procedure illustrated in Fig. 1 commences at the level of that goal.

So for this part of the procedure, the agent provides assistance with updating the process knowledge, and if a next-goal is the goal of a goal-driven sub-process then the system will manage that sub-process, perhaps after being given a plan to do so.

4. Performance knowledge

This section refers to the right-hand side of Fig. 1. That is the representation and maintenance of the performance knowledge. The performance knowledge is used to support task selection—ie who does what—through inter-agent negotiation. Its role is comparative—to decide which choice is better than another. It is not intended to have absolute currency. With this use in mind, the *performance knowledge* comprises performance statistics on the operation of the system. These performance statistics are proffered by an agent in bids for work.

The system achieves its goal through the way in which the agents interact. Five groups of inter-agent communication types may be received by a particular agent A.

- Sub-goal distribution group. A *command* and an *invitation* for agent A to submit bids to assume responsibility for a sub-goal for a particular process instance. An *bid* and a *declination* to take responsibility for a sub-goal. A *commitment* that responsibility has been taken for a sub-goal.
- Activity completion group. A *declaration* that an activity initially intended to achieve a next-goal has been, or has yet to be, completed, and that certain associated process knowledge was derived during that activity. The *assent* that a declaration has been accepted by another agent. The *refusal* to accept a declaration by another agent for some reason.
- Declarative group. A *request* to another agent for a fact. An *assertion* by another agent of a fact. The *acknowledgment* that a communicated fact is satisfactory or is unsatisfactory for some reason.
- Authority group. The *delegation* and *retraction* of authority to bid for certain types of sub-goal.
- Priority group. An *instruction* (ie a command) and an *appeal* (ie a request) to modify the agent's priorities between sub-goals. The *agreement* and the *refusal* for some reason to comply.

The basis of the agent interaction is negotiation. Negotiation is achieved through the bidding mechanism of contract nets with focussed addressing [12]. A bid consists of the five pairs of real numbers (Constraint, Allocate, Success, Cost, Time). The pair Constraint is an estimate of the earliest time that the individual (ie. agent/human pair) could address the task—ie ignoring other non-urgent things to be done, and an estimate of the time that the individual would normally address the task if it "took its place in the in-tray". The agent receiving a bid attaches a subjective estimate of 'value' to that bid. The pair Allocate is an estimate of the mean density of work flowing into the agent (ie. delegated *to* the agent) and an estimate of the mean density of work flowing out of the agent (ie. delegated *by* the agent). A *success* parameter is the likelihood that an agent will complete work within the constraints prescribed. A *time* parameter is the total elapse time that the agent takes to complete work. A *cost* parameter is the cost—usually measured in time expended on the job—that the agent takes to complete the work. The three parameters *success*, *time* and *cost* are assumed to be normally distributed (*success* is binomially distributed but is approximately normal under the standard conditions). The pairs Success, Time and Cost are estimates of the means and standard deviations of these three parameters.

The estimates of the means and standard deviations of the three parameters *success*, *time* and *cost* are made on the basis of historical information and are useful as long as performance is statistically stable. If performance is unstable then an agent may have some idea of the *reason why*; such reasons may result from communication with other agents. These reasons may be used to revise the "historically based" estimates to give an *informed* estimate of performance that takes into account the *reasons why* things behaved the way they did [7]. The performance estimates are used for two distinct purposes. First, they are used by each agent's deliberative reasoning mechanism to decide which plan to use for what. Second, they are used by the bidding mechanism by which agents interact and so take responsibility for sub-processes.

Unfortunately, the important *value* parameter (ie. the value added to a process) is often very difficult to measure [12]. Some progressive organisations employ experienced staff specifically to assess the value of the work of others. The existing system does not attempt to measure *value*; each individual simply represents the perceived subjective *value* of each other individual's work as a constant for that individual. These constant subjective estimates are attached to each incoming bid.

The deliberative reasoning mechanism of the three-layer BDI agents is based on the non-deterministic procedure: "on the basis of current *beliefs*—identify the current *options*, on the basis of current options and existing commitments—select the current commitments (or *goals*), for each newly-committed goal choose a *plan* for that goal, from the selected plans choose a consistent set of things to do next (called the agent's *intentions*)". To apply this procedure requires a mechanism for *identifying* options, for *selecting* goals, for *choosing* plans and for *scheduling* intentions [9]. The problem of selecting a plan from a set of plans is equivalent to choosing a path through a 'large' composite plan that contains disjunctive nodes; this problem is expressed in terms of choosing such a path here. A plan or path may perform well or badly. A path's *performance* is defined in terms of: the likelihood that the path will succeed, the expected cost or time to execute the path, the expected value added by the path, or some combination of these measures. If each agent knows how well the choices that it has made have performed in the past then it can be expected to make decisions reasonably well as long as path performance remains reasonably stable. One mechanism for achieving this form of adaptivity is reinforcement learning [13]. An alternative approach based on performance estimates is described in [4].

Inferred explanations of *why* an observation is outside expected limits may sometimes be extracted from observing the interactions with the users and other agents involved. Inferred knowledge such as this gives *one possible cause* for the observed behaviour; so such knowledge enables us to *refine*, but *not* to *replace*, the historical estimates of parameters.

5. Task Selection

This section concerns the selection of a task for a given now-goal as shown in the middle of Fig. 1. The selection of a plan to achieve a next goal typically involves deciding *what* to do and selecting *who* to ask to assist in doing it. The selection of what to do and who to do it can not be subdivided because one person may be good and one form of task and bad at others. So the "what" and the "who" are considered together. The system provides assistance in making this decision. Sec. 5 describes how performance knowledge is attached to each plan and sub-plan. For plans that involve one individual only this is done for instantiated plans. That is there are estimates for each individual and plan pair. In this way the system offers advice on choosing between individual A doing X and individual B doing Y. For plans that involve more than one individual this is done for abstract, uninstantiated plans only.

This is something of a compromise but avoids the system attempting to do the impossible—for example, maintaining estimates on performance of every possible composition of committee. This does not weaken the system if a plan to form a committee is embedded in a plan that gives an individual the responsibility for forming that committee, because estimates are gathered for the performance of the second of these.

There are two basic modes in which the selection of "who" to ask is done. First the *authoritarian* mode in which an individual is told to do something. Second the *negotiation* mode in which individuals are asked to express an interest in doing something. This second mode is implemented using contract nets with focussed addressing [14] with inter-agent communication being performed in KQML [15]. When contact net bids are received the successful bidder has to be identified. So no matter which mode is used, a decision has to be made as to who to select. The use of a multi-agent system to manage processes expands the range of feasible strategies for delegation from the authoritarian strategies described above to strategies based on negotiation between individuals. Negotiation-based strategies that involves negotiation for each process instance are not feasible in manual systems for every day tasks due to the cost of negotiation. If the agents in an agent-based system are responsible for this negotiation then the cost of negotiation is may be negligible. A mechanism is described here to automate this negotiation.

If the agent making a bid to perform a task has a plan for achieving that task then the user may permit the agent to construct the bid automatically. As the bids consist of six meaningful quantities, the user may opt to construct the bid manually. A bid consists of the five pairs of real numbers (Constraint, Allocate, Success, Cost, Time). The pair *constraint* is an estimate of the earliest time that the individual could address the task—ie ignoring other non-urgent things to be done, and an estimate of the time that the individual would normally address the task if it "took its place in the in-tray". The pairs Allocate, Success, Cost and Time are estimates of the mean and standard deviation of the corresponding parameters as described above. The receiving agent then:

- attaches a subjective view of the *value* of the bidding individual;
- assesses the extent to which a bid should be downgraded—or not considered at all—because it violates process constraints, and
- selects an acceptable bid, if any, possibly by applying its 'delegation strategy'.

If there are no acceptable bids then the receiving agent "thinks again".

6. The delegation strategy

A *delegation strategy* is a strategy for deciding who to give responsibility to for doing what. A user specifies the delegation strategy that is used by the user's agent to evaluate bids. In doing this the user has considerable flexibility first in defining payoff and second in specifying the strategy itself. Practical strategies in manual systems can be quite elementary; delegation is a job which some humans are not very good at. A delegation strategy may attempt to balance some of the three conflicting principles: maximising payoff, maximising opportunities for poor performers to improve and balancing workload. Payoff is defined by the user and could be some combination of the expected value added to the process, the expected time and/or cost to deal with the process, and the expected likelihood of the process leading to a satisfactory conclusion [16].

The system provides assistance to the user by suggesting how delegation could be performed using a method that the user has specified in terms of the tools described below. The user can opt to let the system delegate automatically, or can opt to delegate manually.

Given a sub-process, suppose that we have some expectation of the payoff D_i as a result of choosing the i'th individual (ie agent and user pair) from the set of candidates $\{X_1,...,X_i,...,X_n\}$ to take responsibility for it. A *delegation strategy* at time τ is specified as $S = \{P_1,...,P_i,...,P_n\}$ where P_i is the probability of delegating responsibility at time τ for a given task to individual X_i chosen from

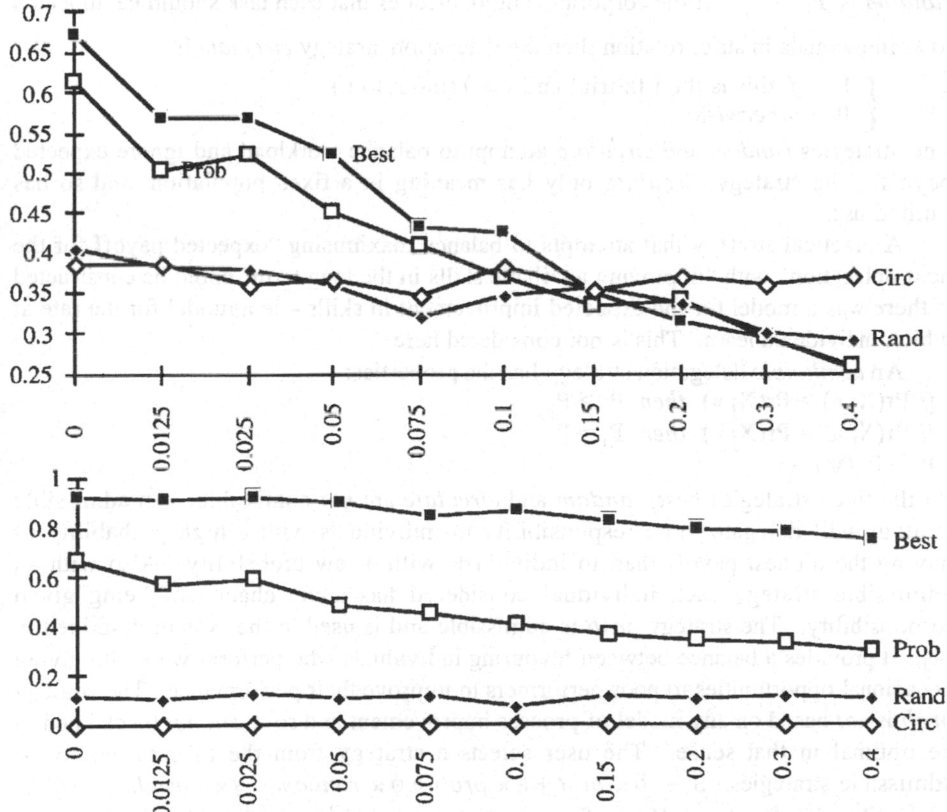

Fig 3. Payoff (top figure) and triple duplications (bottom figure) against the rebel factor for a learning rate = 0.1, death factor = 0.05, and α = 0.6.

$\{X_1,...,X_i,...,X_n\}$. The system suggests an individual/task pair stochastically using the delegation strategy.

Corporate culture may determine the delegation strategy. Four delegation strategies are described. If corporate culture is to choose the individual whose expected payoff is maximal then the delegation strategy *best* is:

$$P_i = \begin{cases} \frac{1}{m} & \textit{if } X_i \text{ is such that } \Pr(X_i \text{»}) \text{ is maximal} \\ 0 & \textit{otherwise} \end{cases}$$

where $\Pr(X_i \text{»})$ means "the probability that X_i will have the highest payoff" and m is such that there are m individuals for whom $\Pr(X_i \text{»})$ is maximal. In the absence of any other complications, the strategy *best* attempts to maximise expected payoff. Using this strategy, an individual who performs poorly may never get work. Another strategy *prob* also favours high payoff but gives all individuals a chance, sooner or later, and is defined by $P_i = \Pr(X_i \text{»})$. The strategies *best* and *prob* have the feature of 'rewarding' quality work (ie. high payoff) with more work. If corporate culture dictates that individuals should be treated equally but at random then the delegation strategy *random* is $P_i = \frac{1}{n}$. If the corporate culture dictates that each task should be allocated to m individuals in strict rotation then the delegation strategy *circulate* is:

$$P_i = \begin{cases} 1 & \textit{if} \text{ this is the i'th trial and } i \equiv 0 \text{ (modulo n)} \\ 0 & \textit{otherwise} \end{cases}$$

The strategies *random* and *circulate* attempt to balance workload and ignore expected payoff. The strategy *circulate* only has meaning in a fixed population, and so has limited use.

A practical strategy that attempts to balance maximising "expected payoff for the next delegation" with "improving available skills in the long term" could be constructed if there was a model for the expected improvement in skills—ie a model for the rate at which individuals learn. This is not considered here.

An *admissible* delegation strategy has the properties:

- *if* $\Pr(X_i \text{»}) > \Pr(X_j \text{»})$ *then* $P_i > P_j$
- *if* $\Pr(X_i \text{»}) = \Pr(X_j \text{»})$ *then* $P_i = P_j$
- $P_i > 0 \ (\forall i)$

So the three strategies *best, random* and *circulate* are *not* admissible. An admissible strategy will delegate more responsibility to individuals with a high probability of having the highest payoff than to individuals with a low probability. Also with an admissible strategy each individual considered has some chance of being given responsibility. The strategy *prob* is admissible and is used in the system described in [4]. It provides a balance between favouring individuals who perform well with giving occasional opportunities to poor performers to improve their performance. The strategy *prob* is *not* based on any model of process improvement and so it can *not* be claimed to be optimal in that sense. The user selects a strategy from the infinite variety of admissible strategies: $S = \delta \times \textit{best} + \varepsilon \times \textit{prob} + \phi \times \textit{random} + \gamma \times \textit{circulate}$ will be admissible if $\delta, \varepsilon, \phi, \gamma \in [0,1]$, $\delta + \varepsilon + \phi + \gamma = 1$ and if $\varepsilon > 0$. This leads to the question of how to select a strategy. As *circulate* is only meaningful in stable populations it is not considered here.

A world is designed in which the relative performance of the four strategies *best, prob, random* and *circulate* are simulated There are always three individuals in this world. If individuals die (ie they become unavailable) then they are replaced with new individuals. At each *cycle*—ie a discrete time unit—one delegation is made. There is a natural death rate of 5% for each individual for each cycle. The payoff of each individual commences at 0 and improves by 10% of "what there is still to learn" on each occasion that an individual is delegated responsibility. So an individual's recorded payoff is progressively: 0, 0.1, 0.19, 0.271, 0.3439, and so on, tending to 1.0 in the long term. The mean and standard deviation estimates of expected payoff are calculated as described above in Sec. 4 using a value of $\alpha = 0.6$. In addition the individuals have a strength of belief of the extent to which they are being given more work than the other two individuals in the experiment. This strength of belief is multiplied by a "rebel" factor and is added to the base death rate of 5%. So if work is repeatedly delegated to one individual then the probability of that individual dying increases up to a limit of the rebel factor plus 5%. A *triple duplication* occurs when work is delegated to the same individual three cycles running. The proportion of triple duplications is used as a measure of the lack of perceived recent equity in the allocation of responsibility. The payoff and proportion of triple duplications for the four strategies are shown against the rebel factor on the top and bottom graphs respectively in Fig. 3. The simulation run for each value is 2 000 cycles. The lack of smoothness of the graphs is partially due to the pseudo-random number generator used. When the rebel factor is 0.15—ie three times the natural death rate—all four strategies deliver approximately the same payoff. The two graphs indicate that the *prob* strategy does a reasonable job at maximising payoff while keeping triple duplications reasonably low for a rebel factor of < 0.15. However, *prob* may only be used when the chosen definition of payoff is normally distributed. The strategy *best* also assumes normality; its definition may be changed to "such that the expected payoff is greatest" when payoff is not normal.

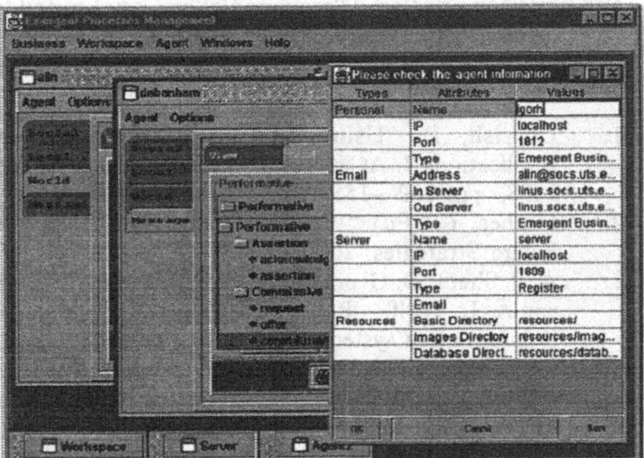

Fig 4. Setting up a task in the system

7. Conclusion

High-level business processes are analysed as being of three distinct types [17]. The management of knowledge-driven processes has been described. An existing multi-agent system for goal-driven process management [4] has been extended to support the management of knowledge-driven processes. The conceptual agent architecture is a three-layer BDI, hybrid architecture [18]. During a process instance the responsibility for sub-processes may be delegated. The system forms a view on who should be asked to do what at each step in a process. Each user defines payoff in some acceptable way. Payoff may be defined in terms of estimates of various parameters. These estimates are based on historic information; they are revised if they are not statistically stable. Using three basic built-in strategies, the user then specifies a delegation strategy for the chosen definition of payoff. In this way the system may be permitted to handle sub-process delegation automatically. The system has been trialed on an application in a university administrative context. Three delegation strategies [$\delta = 0.5$, $\varepsilon = 0.5$, $\phi = 0$], *prob* and [$\delta = 0$, $\varepsilon = 0.5$, $\phi = 0.5$] represent varying degrees of the "aggressive pursuit of payoff" and have been declared "reasonable" in very limited trials.

References

1. Dourish, P. "Using Metalevel Techniques in a Flexible Toolkit for CSCW Applications." ACM Transactions on Computer-Human Interaction, Vol. 5, No. 2, June, 1998, pp. 109—155.
2. Fischer, L. (Ed) "Workflow Handbook 2001." Workflow Management Coalition & Future Strategies, 2000.
3. A. P. Sheth, D. Georgakopoulos, S. Joosten, M. Rusinkiewicz, W. Scacchi, J. C. Wileden, and A. L. Wolf. "Report from the NSF workshop on workflow and process automation in information systems." SIGMOD Record, 25(4):55—67, December 1996.
4. Debenham, J.K. "Delegation of responsibility in an agent-based process management system", in proceedings 3rd Pacific Rim International Workshop on Multi-Agents PRIMA2000, Melbourne, 28-29 August 2000, pp170-181.
5. Jain, A.K., Aparicio, M. and Singh, M.P. "Agents for Process Coherence in Virtual Enterprises" in Communications of the ACM, Volume 42, No 3, March 1999, pp62—69.
6. Hawryszkiewycz, I.T. "Supporting Teams in Virtual Organisations." In Proceedings Tenth International Conference, DEXA'99, Florence, September 1999.
7. Debenham, J.K. "Supporting Strategic Process", in proceedings Fifth International Conference on The Practical Application of Intelligent Agents and Multi-Agents PAAM2000, Manchester UK, April 2000.
8. C. Bussler, S. Jablonski, and H. Schuster. "A new generation of workflow management systems: Beyond taylorism with MOBILE." SIGOIS Bulletin, 17(1):17—20, April 1996.
9. Debenham, J.K. "Knowledge Engineering: Unifying Knowledge Base and Database Design", Springer-Verlag, 1998
10. Muth, P., Wodtke, D., Weissenfels, J., Kotz D.A. and Weikum, G. "From Centralized Workflow Specification to Distributed Workflow Execution." In Journal of Intelligent Information Systems (JIIS), Kluwer Academic Publishers, Vol. 10, No. 2, 1998.
11. Rao, A.S. and Georgeff, M.P. "BDI Agents: From Theory to Practice", in proceedings First International Conference on Multi-Agent Systems (ICMAS-95), San Francisco, USA, pp 312—319.
12. Jennings, N.R., Faratin, P., Norman, T.J., O'Brien, P. and Odgers, B. Autonomous Agents for Business Process Management. Int. Journal of Applied Artificial Intelligence 14 (2) 145-189.
13. Sutton, R.S. and Barto, A.G. Reinforcement Learning. MIT Press, 1998.
14. Durfee, E.H.. "Distributed Problem Solving and Planning" in Weiss, G. (ed). Multi-Agent Systems. The MIT Press: Cambridge, MA.
15. Finin, F. Labrou, Y., and Mayfield, J. "KQML as an agent communication language." In Jeff Bradshaw (Ed.) Software Agents. MIT Press, 1997.
16. Koriche, F. "Approximate Reasoning about Combined Knowledge" in Intelligent Agents IV, Singh M.P, Rao, A. and Wooldridge, M.J. (Eds), Springer Verlag, 1998
17. Debenham, J.K. "Three Generations of Agent-Based Process Management" to appear in the International Journal of Applied Intelligence.
18. Müller, J.P. "The Design of Intelligent Agents" Springer-Verlag, 1996.

State Minimization Re-visited

Norman Foo[1], Abhaya Nayak[2], Maurice Pagnucco[1], and Dongmo Zhang[1]

[1] Artificial Intelligence Laboratory, School of Computer Science and Engineering, University of New South Wales, Sydney NSW 2052,
[2] Division of Information and Communication Sciences, Macquarie University, Sydney NSW 2109

Abstract. A well-known circumscription policy in situation calculus theories of actions is to minimize the Abnormality predicate by varying the Holds predicate. Unfortunately this admitted counter-intuitive models. A different policy of varying the Result function eliminated these models. Explanations of how it did this are not entirely satisfactory, but seem to appeal to informal notions of state minimization. We re-examine this policy and show that there are simple justifications for it that are based on classical automata theory. It incidentally turns out that the description "state minimization" for the varying Result policy is more accurate than the original nomenclature had intended.

1 Introduction

Logical approaches to reasoning about action in a discrete time setting have mostly adopted the situation calculus (SC) as the representation language. It was invented by McCarthy and Hayes [McCarthy and Hayes 69] as a formal language to capture discrete dynamics. The advantage of the SC is that it is based on a multi-sorted first-order language, a syntax with an established and unambiguous pedigree. Correspondingly, its semantics is conventional and its inference mechanism is a suitably augmented first-order logic. The aim of this paper is to explain, using routine ideas from classical automata theory, why a variant nonmonotonic minimization policy in reasoning about actions is successful. As a bonus, not only useful connections with automata theory are exposed, but the prospect of "compiling" this minimization policy into standard automata synthesis algorithms is enhanced. We assume some familiarity with the SC and circumscription, a contemporary and detailed account of which is the monograph by Shanahan [Shanahan 1997]. However, casual reviews of the relevant concepts will be made as we proceed. The automata theory assumed here is treated in standard texts such as [Arbib 1969a] and [Booth 68]. Again, we will informally review the required concepts as needed.

2 Situation Calculus and Models

The SC is a multi-sorted first-order theory in which the sorts are: *Sit* (*situations*), *Act* (*actions*), *Flu* (*fluents*). There is a binary function $Result : Act \times Sit \rightarrow Sit$,

M. Brooks, D. Corbett, and M. Stumptner (Eds.): AI 2001, LNAI 2256, pp. 153–164, 2001.

and a binary predicate *Holds* : $Flu \times Sit$. *Sit* has a distinguished member $s0$, called the *initial situation*. (In some formulations, *Result* is written as *Do*.) The intuition is that *Sit* is constructed from $s0$ as results of actions from *Act*, denoting the result of action a on situation s by $Result(a, s)$. Thus the ground terms of *Sit* is the Herbrand universe of this theory in which the constants are $s0$ and the action names, and the constructing function is *Result*. The fluents are intuitively the *potentially* observable properties of the situations, as it may be the case that a particular theory is not stringent enough to determine completely the status of all fluents in all situations. Fluent observation is via the *Holds* predicate, e.g., $\neg Holds(f, Result(a2, (Result(a1, s0))))$ says that the fluent f does not hold after the actions a1 and a2 are applied (in that order) to the initial situation. A *model* of a situation calculus theory is a Herbrand model. The unique names assumption (different constants denote different objects) for action and fluent sorts follows from the structure of the Herband universe, and likewise the observation that distinct situation terms denote distinct objects.

Consider the set Δ of formulas:

$$Holds(f, s0) \wedge Holds(g, s0) \tag{1}$$

$$\neg Holds(f, Result(a, s)) \leftarrow Holds(f, s) \wedge Holds(g, s) \tag{2}$$

$$Holds(g, Result(b, s)) \leftarrow Holds(f, s) \wedge Holds(g, s) \tag{3}$$

This is a simple example of an action specification using the SC. Here $Flu = \{f, g\}$ and $Act = \{a, b\}$. It is convenient for diagrammatic representation to adopt the notational convention that $Holds(\neg f, s)$ means $\neg Holds(f, s)$. Formula 1 is an *observation sentence*, while formulas 2 and 3 are *effect axioms*.

Figure 1 is a diagram that displays a fragment of $Th(\Delta)$, the deductive closure of Δ. This diagram sets down the minimal consequences of Δ, so that a fluent (output) F (respectively $\neg F$) appears in a situation (state) S if and only if $\Delta \models Holds(F, S)$ (respectively $\Delta \models \neg Holds(F, S)$).

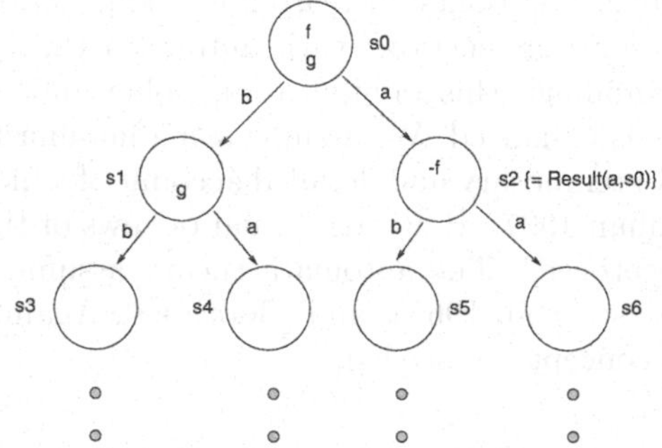

Fig. 1. Minimal information situation tree of $Th(\Delta)$

This tree is *incomplete* (even ignoring the fact that it represents only an initial fragment of action terms) in the sense that the status of fluents in some situations is unknown. These situations can be completed in any way that is consistent with Δ, and Figures 2 and 3 are two possibilities. The former is an *inertial* completion; no fluent changes from one situation to the next unless it is forced to do so by an effect axiom or other logical axiom (e.g. domain constraints or causal rules that are not discussed here). The latter completion is more arbitrary, and is not only non-inertial (fluent f in $s0$ changes after action b when it is not required to do so) but also *non-Markovian* in that two situations $s1$ and $s2$ that are identical in terms of fluent status nevertheless react differently to the same action b. In general, for any given SC action specification Δ, the class $Mod(\Delta)$ of its models (trees) comprises all the possible completions of the incomplete fragments as indicated by the examples.

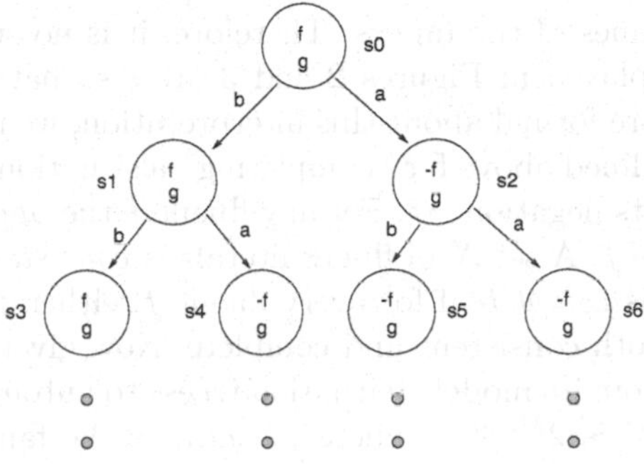

Fig. 2. One completion of the minimal information tree.

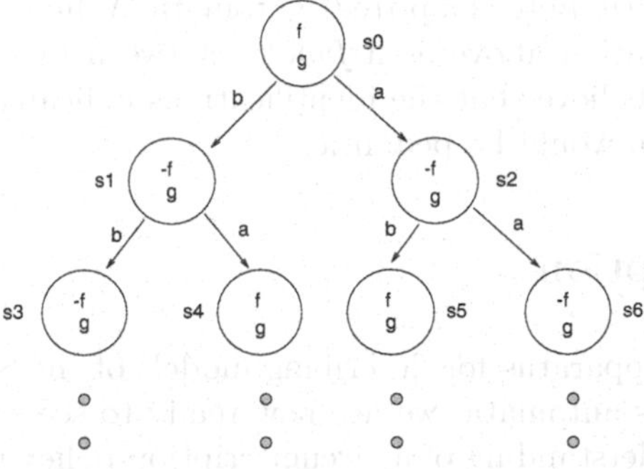

Fig. 3. Another completion of the minimal information tree.

In order to keep the exposition simple, we will impose a restriction on the theory Δ, that the actions are essentially *deterministic*. In terms of the situation trees this means that for each action, say a, there is at most one edge leading from a situation s to a successor situation $Result(a, s)$ labelled by a. We say "at most" because it may be the case that the action a cannot be performed in situation s, or in the parlance of action theories, s does not satisfy the preconditions of a. The restriction is inessential, but will help focus the discussion

3 Automata

A (Moore) automaton $\mathcal{M}$ is a quintuple $\langle I, Q, Y, \delta, \lambda \rangle$ where I is the set of inputs, Y is the set of outputs, Q is the state set, $\delta : Q \times I \rightarrow Q$ is the state transition function, and $\lambda : Q \rightarrow Y$ is the output function. The state set can be infinite. See [Booth 68] or [Arbib 1969a] for details. Diagrammatically, automata are traditionally represented by using labelled circles for states and labelled arcs for transitions. The labels in circles are the outputs for the states, and the arcs are labelled with names of the inputs. Therefore, it is no suprise that situation calculus models displayed in Figures 2 and 3 are also naturally interpreted as automata. To be more formal about this interpretation, we need the counterpart of the procedure outlined above for "completing" a situation. A fluent literal L is either a fluent f or its negation $\neg f$. For any fluent f the *opposite* of f is $\neg f$, and the opposite of $\neg f$ is f. A set X of fluent literals is *consistent* if it does not have opposite literals; it is *complete* if for every fluent f, either $f \in X$ or $\neg f \in X$. X is maximal if it is both consistent and complete. Now given a SC action theory Δ, the translation from its models (situation trees) to automata is a natural one: Q is Sit, I is Act, Y is 2^{MaxLit}, where $MaxLit$ is the family of maximal sets fluent literals. The transition function δ is just as naturally defined as follows: if q is the situation s, then $\delta(q, a) = q'$ where q' is the situation $Result(a, s)$. Likewise, the output function λ will say which fluent literals hold in the situation, viz., $L \in \lambda(s)$ iff $Holds(L, s)$. Informally, all this is saying is that one may choose to read the diagrams for completed situation trees either as models of an action theory or as (infinite, loop-free) automata. While it is possible to fully formalize the translation above as a *functor* between two categories (SC trees and automata), we believe that the identifications indicated are so natural that further formalization would be pedantic.

4 Circumscription

Having set up the apparatus for describing models of the SC and their alternative identification as automata, we are now ready to see how the latter can be used to simplify understanding of a circumscription policy used to reason about actions. We begin with a review of a circumstance which justified this policy. We assume acquaintance with *circumscription* for minimizing extensions of predicate and refer the reader to [Lifschitz 1994] and [Shanahan 1997] for contemporary summaries and details. McCarthy's paper [McCarthy 86] that introduced the fundamentals of circumscription has invaluable insights.

Historically, the idea behind a nonmonotonic rule for reasoning about actions was to capture *inertia* as we defined it above, viz., if there is no reason for a fluent literal to change after an action, then it should not. One way to do this is to introduce a formula

$$Ab(a, f, s) \leftarrow \neg[Holds(f, Result(a, s)) \leftrightarrow Holds(f, s)] \tag{4}$$

in which the predicate $Ab(a, f, s)$ essentially says that fluent f is abnormal in situation s under the action a because it changes. The idea is that most actions have only local effects, e.g., painting a shelf should not affect things other than the color of the shelf; so most fluents will be normal. Now, if among all models of Δ we were to choose those which minimized the extension $[\![Ab]\!]$ of Ab relative to set-containment, while letting the $Holds$ predicate vary, then in such a model M it will be the case that $M \models Ab(a, f, s) \leftrightarrow \neg[Holds(f, Result(a, s)) \leftrightarrow Holds(f, s)]$. It is plausible that this M would be inertial because of the following reasoning. Suppose that M is not inertial for a triple $\langle a, f, s\rangle$, say $M \models Holds(f, s)$, $\Delta \not\models \neg Holds(f, Result(a, s))$ but $M \models \neg Holds(f, Result(a, s))$. Observe that in this case we have $M \models Ab(a, f, s)$, so ostensibly there may be an alternative model M' which agrees with M everywhere except that $M' \not\models Ab(a, f, s)$. However, the Yale Shooting Problem (YSP) [Hanks and McDermott 1987] showed that this reasoning can be misleading. The SC theory of the YSP is:

$$Holds(L, Result(Load, s)) \tag{5}$$

$$\neg Holds(A, Result(Shoot, s)) \leftarrow Holds(Loaded, s) \tag{6}$$

$$Holds(A, S0) \tag{7}$$

$$\neg Holds(L, S0) \tag{8}$$

The YSP proved to be a fatal counter-example to the hope that by merely minimizing $[\![Ab]\!]$ it is possible to enforce global inertia. This was demonstrated by exhibiting two models I and II — see Figure 4 — for the YSP which were incomparable for their respective extensions $[\![Ab]\!]_I$ and $[\![Ab]\!]_{II}$, and yet both were minimal for these extensions. The situation tree fragments in the figure are laid out horizontally rather than vertically, and only some of the relevant actions are shown from each situation.

The problem is that in minimizing Ab across a *trajectory* (a sequence of actions) rather than a single action, it may be possible to trade off a later abnormality for an earlier one, or vice-versa.

Now, to recall one well-known way to overcome this, we review the vocabulary of *circumscription*. Instead of saying that we mimimize the predicate Ab, we can conform to the practice in nonmonotonic logic by saying that we *circumscribe* it. The notation $Circ(\Delta(P); P; Q)$ denotes a second-order formula which means the circumscription of the predicate P in action theory $\Delta(P)$ in which P appears as a predicate constant, letting the predicate (or function) Q vary — for details see [Lifschitz 1994] and [Shanahan 1997]. So, by adding $Circ(\Delta(Ab); Ab; Holds)$ to the YSP theory augmented with the abnormality formula 4, we find that there are two models I and II as shown. By "letting $Holds$ vary" is meant the

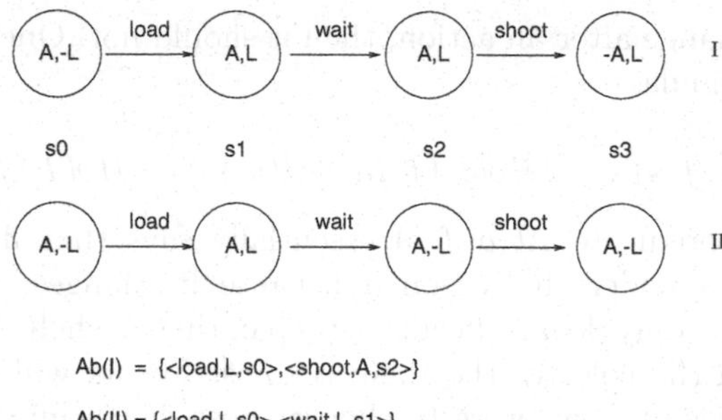

Fig. 4. Partial situation trees for the Yale Shooting Problem

policy of choosing (as far as possible consistent with the rest of the theory) which fluent literals should hold in any situation. This is equivalent to completing the circles in situation trees by filling in literals, or what amounts to the same thing, choosing certain completed trees. The choice is made to minimize or circumscribe the extension of *Ab*.

The flurry of research that followed the discovery of the YSP led to many alternative policies for circumscription. One line of attack which was remarkably successful was due to Baker [Baker 1991], to which we now turn.

5 Varying Result

Baker's idea was to change the circumscription policy to allow the *Result* function to vary rather than the *Holds* predicate. We illustrate the difference diagrammatically in Figure 5. In this figure, the situation s is a typical one in a situation tree, or equivalently a state in its corresponding automaton. Varying *Holds* is tantamount to filling in consistent fluent literals in the situation (state) $Result(a, s)$. Varying *Result* is to "re-target" the situation to which the function value $Result(a, s)$ should point. The corresponding automaton may then no longer be loop-free.

In either case, the objective is to circumscribe *Ab*. The formula that expresses varying *Result* is denoted by $Circ(\Delta(Ab); Ab; Result)$. If this is the policy that is used for the YSP, it is not hard to see that only one model survives, for the reason suggested by Figure 6. This policy is informally described by its advocates as *State Minimization*, presumably because it provided more compact situation configurations due to the permitted re-targettings. However, as we shall argue, this nomenclature is in fact more accurately descriptive than was initially imagined. In this figure, the second (unintended) model II of the YSP (we have added for a more complete picture the *shoot* action in situation $s1$) is modified to that of II' in which the abnormality $Ab(Wait, L, s1)$ is eliminated by retargetting $Result(Wait, s1)$ back to $s1$. This strictly reduces the extension of *Ab* in model II (nothing else has changed), so model II is not a circumscriptive model of

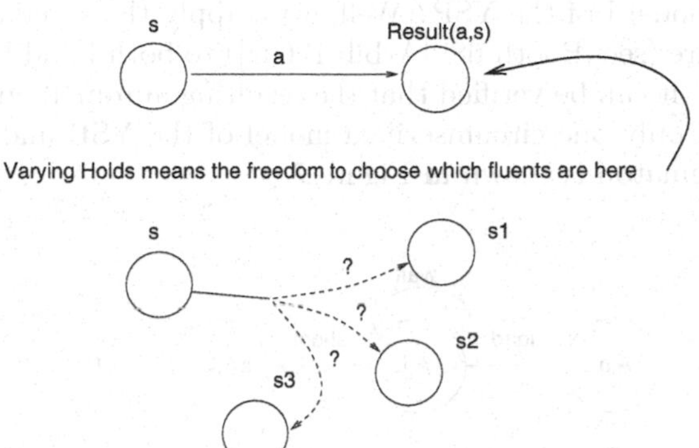

Fig. 5. Varying Holds vs. Varying Result

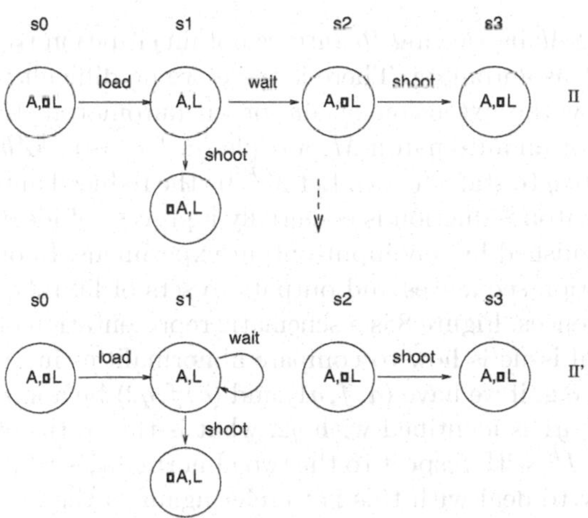

Fig. 6. Varying Result in model II of the YSP

the YSP (augmented by the abnormality axiom 4) if *Result* is allowed to vary. Observe that the corresponding automaton now has a "self-loop" at $s1$, and moreover, if $s0$ is regarded as an initial state, then $s2$ is no longer reachable.

What about model I of the YSP? Well, if we apply the standard *automaton reduction* procedure (see [Booth 68] [Arbib 1969a]) to both I and II' of Figures 4 and 6 respectively, it can be verified that the resulting automata are *isomorphic*, so in fact there is only one circumscribed model of the YSP under this policy. This reduced automaton is shown in Figure 7.

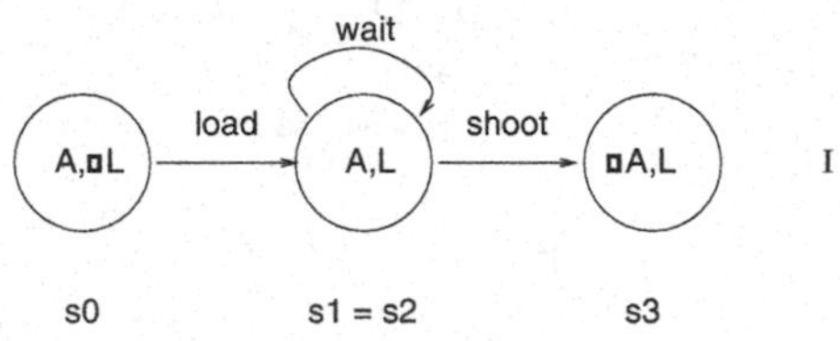

Fig. 7. Reduced Automaton of Models I and II'

It is natural to ask if there any general characterization of such models from the automaton-theoretic perspective? The next section addresses this.

6 Abnormality for Automata

In circumscribing *Ab* by varying *Result* we obtain situation tree models that are also interpretable as automata. There is therefore no difficulty in understanding what is meant by the extension of *Ab* for an automaton M. But to say the almost obvious, for an automaton M, a triple $\langle a, f, q\rangle$ is in $[\![Ab]\!]_M$ if the fluent f changes from state q to state $\delta(q, a)$. Let M^R be the reduced automaton of M. We recall that automaton reduction is essentially a process of identifying states that cannot be distinguished by any input-output experiment. In our context, inputs correspond to action sequences and outputs to sets of literals which hold at the ends of such sequences. Figure 8 is a schematic representation of this observation. A minor technical issue is how to compare abnormalities in an automaton with its reduced form, e.g, if we have $\langle a, f, q1\rangle$ and $\langle a, f, q2\rangle$ be abnormal in M, and in its reduction M^R $q1$ is identified with $q2$, what is the status of the abnormality $\langle a, f, [q1, q2]\rangle$ in M^R with respect to the two abnormalities which it inherits? The most elegant way to deal with this is to refer again to the idea in Figure 8. We can stipulate that $\langle a, f, [q1, q2]\rangle \in \{\langle a, f, q1\rangle, \langle a, f, q2\rangle\}$ since the input-output perspective permits one to interpret the former as any member of the latter set.

If $[\![Ab_M]\!]$ is the extension of abnormality in automaton M, and $[\![Ab_{M^R}]\!]$ is that in its reduced automaton M^R, the following is not hard to see.

Proposition 1 $[\![Ab_{M^R}]\!] \subseteq [\![Ab_M]\!]$.

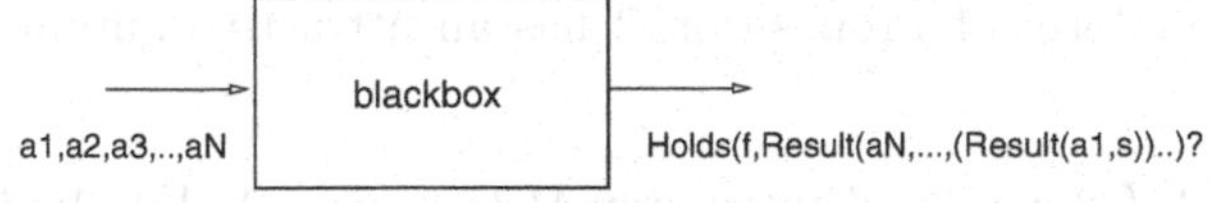

Identical answers from two blackboxes means they are Abnormality equivalent

Fig. 8. The Input-Output View of SC Models

The upshot of Proposition 1 is that nothing is lost in considering reduced automata as models of the SC under the circumscription policy of letting *Result* vary. Moreover, it suffices to search for such models of the SC within the class of reduced automata since these cannot be distinguished from those models by input-output queries.

Definition 1 *Let an automaton M be such that it has an a-labelled transition from state q to $\delta(q, a)$ and the fluent f has not changed between the two states. Then we say that the triple $\langle a, f, q\rangle$ is inertial.*

Observe that if such an M is also a model of a SC theory, then $\langle a, f, q\rangle$ is inertial if and only if this triple is not in $[\![Ab_M]\!]$.

Definition 2 *If $\langle a, f, q\rangle$ is inertial for every fluent f in an automaton M, then we say that the a-labelled transition is inertial.*

For a reduced automaton, an inertial transition is often (but not always) a "self-loop". It can be shown that this will be the case if the theory Δ admits Markovian models [Foo and Peppas 2001].

Proposition 2 *Let a reduced automaton M be a $Circ(\Delta(Ab); Ab; Result)$ model of action theory Δ. Consider any automaton M' which is obtained from M by transforming a non-inertial triple in M to an inertial one. Then M' cannot be a model of $Circ(\Delta(Ab); Ab; Result)$ unless it undergoes a further transformation in the reverse, i.e., at least one of its inertial triples is made non-inertial.*

Corollary 1 *No reduced automaton M can be a model of $Circ(\Delta(Ab);$ $Ab; Result)$ if it can be transformed to an automaton M' by changing a non-inertial triple to an inertial one, with M' also being a model of Δ.*

Corollary 1 guarantees that *Result*-varying circumscribed models cannot ignore all opportunities for local inertia. It entails the consequence below.

Corollary 2 *Suppose for some situation s and action a it is the case that for some fluent f, Δ is consistent with $\neg Ab(a, f, s)$. Then there is a reduced automaton M which is a model of $Circ(\Delta(Ab); Ab; Result)$ that is inertial for $\langle a, f, q\rangle$ where q is the state identified with s.*

The stronger form of Proposition 2 has an attractive automaton-theoretic flavor.

Proposition 3 *Let a reduced automaton M be a $Circ(\Delta(Ab); Ab; Result)$ model of action theory Δ. Consider any automaton M' which is obtained from M by transforming a non-inertial transition in M to an inertial one. Then M' cannot be a model of $Circ(\Delta(Ab); Ab; Result)$ unless it undergoes a further transformation in which at least one inertial triple is made non-inertial.*

Diagrammatically this simply means that one cannot change a non-self-loop in M to a self-loop and expect it to remain a circumscribed model, unless it also gives up at least one inertial triple elsewhere. The corollaries above also have corresponding strong forms below.

Corollary 3 *No reduced automaton M can be a model of $Circ(\Delta(Ab); Ab; Result)$ if it can be transformed to an automaton M' by changing a non-inertial transition to an inertial one, with M' remaining a model of Δ.*

Corollary 4 *Suppose for some situation s and action a it is the case that for all fluents f, Δ is consistent with $\neg Ab(a, f, s)$. Then there is a reduced automaton M which is a model of $Circ(\Delta(Ab); Ab; Result)$ with an a-labelled inertial transition at state q, the state identified with s.*

These corollaries provide simple explanations of why the policy of varying *Result* is successful in eliminating the undesired model II of the YSP. Corollary 4 says that there must be a model with local inertia at $Result(Load, s0)$ for the $Wait$ action, since this inertia is consistent with the YSP axioms. So there is a reduced automaton which is its model, viz., that in Figure 7. Moreover, it is not hard to verify that it is the *only* one with local inertia. The reason is that model II has a non-inertial triple $\langle Wait, Loaded, Result(Load, s)\rangle$ which can be made inertial and still satisfy the YSP axioms, so by Corollary 1, II cannot be a model of $Circ(\Delta(Ab); Ab; Result)$.

Another standard scenario is the Stolen Car Problem [Baker 1991]. In it, there is only one fluent, say f, representing the presence of a car in the initial situation $s0$. The only action is $Wait$ which has no formula constraining it, nor any effects, and is supposed to capture the passing of a day. However, in the theory one is told that $\neg Holds(f, Result(Wait, Result(Wait, s)))$, i.e., the car is gone at the end of the second day. So when was it stolen? Intuitively, there should be two models, one in which the fluent f changed at the end of the first day, and another in which it changed at the end of the second day, as shown in Figure 9. Incidentally, they are not Markovian. A circumscription policy should not eliminate either model, nor should it prefer one of them. [Baker 1991] shows that the policy of letting *Result* vary achieves this.

For the Stolen Car Problem Corollary 4 guarantees the existence of a model for each of the two possible days when the car could be stolen. Then Proposition 3 shows that they can only tranform to each other.

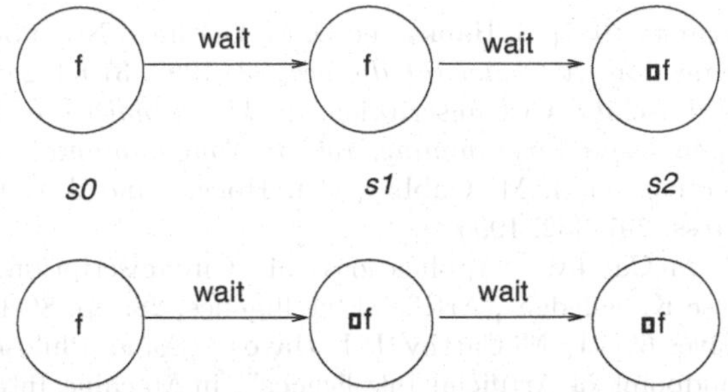

Fig. 9. The Two Models of the Stolen Car Problem

7 Conclusion

We have shown that classical automata theory can be used to explain a successful albeit variant policy for circumscription in SC-based theories of action. This has several advantages. The first is that it exposes this policy as really a method for constructing succinct automaton models of SC theories. It has therefore the potential to simplify the logic of circumscription by reducing it to automaton realization and reduction, for which efficient and transparent algorithms exist. The second is that some ostensibly rather puzzling features of this circumscription policy are de-mystified as simple properties of reduced automata with locally inertial state transitions.

This paper is an example of how the re-examination of circumscriptive models from a systems-theoretic perspective can clarify and highlight connections with standard computer science and engineering models. For instance, we alluded briefly to the Markov property, and its relationship with non-inertial actions. In fact, it can be shown that fully inertial systems are necessarily Markovian. In on-going work, we will delineate further similar considerations, among them simple explanations for certain delicate axioms that seem to be necessary for this circumscription. We also intend to show that it is closely connected with algebraic theories, thereby linking their models to algebras that have an ancient and familiar progeny.

References

[Arbib 1969a] M. Arbib. *Theories of Abstract Automata*, Prentice-Hall, 1969.

[Baker 1991] A. Baker. Nonmonotonic Reasoning in the Framework of the Situation Calculus. *Artificial Intelligence*, 49, 1991, 5-23.

[Booth 68] T. Booth, *Sequential Machines and Automata Theory*, John Wiley, 1968.

[Foo and Peppas 2001] N. Foo and P. Peppas. System Properties of Action Theories. *Proceedings NRAC'01 Workshop, IJCAI'01, Seattle, August 2001.*

[Hanks and McDermott 1987] S. Hanks and D. McDermott. Nonmonotonic Logic and Temporal Projection. *Artificial Intelligence*, 33, 1987, 379-412.

[Lifschitz 1994] V. Lifschitz. Circumscription. In *The Handbook of Logic in Artificial Intelligence and Logic Programming, vol. 3: Nonmonotonic Reasoning and Uncertain Reasoning*, ed. D.M. Gabbay, C.J. Hogger and J.A. Robinson, Oxford University Press, 297-352, 1994.

[McCarthy 86] J. McCarthy, "Applications of Circumscription to Formalizing Common-Sense Knowledge", Artificial Intelligence, 28, pp. 86-116, 1986.

[McCarthy and Hayes 69] J. McCarthy P.J. Hayes, "Some Philosophical Problems from the Standpoint of Artificial Intelligence", in Machine Intelligence 4, ed. B. Meltzer and D. Michie, pp. 463-502, Edinburgh University Press, Edinburgh, 1969.

[Shanahan 1997] M. Shanahan, *Solving the Frame Problem: a mathematical investigation of the commonsense law of inertia*, MIT Press, 1997.

Decidability of Quantifed Propositional Branching Time Logics

Tim French

Murdoch University, Murdoch, Perth, W.A. 6150,
Australia.
t.french@murdoch.edu.au

Abstract. We extend the branching temporal logics CTL and CTL* with quantified propositions and consider various semantic interpretations for the quantification. The use of quantificiation greatly increases the expressive power of the logics allowing us to represent, for example, tree-automata. We also show that some interpretations of quantification allow us to represent non-propositional properties of Kripke frames, such as the branching degree of trees. However this expressive power may also make the satisfiability problem for the logic undecidable. We give a proof of one such case, and also examine decidability in the less expressive semantics.

1 Introduction

Temporal logic has been particularly useful in reasoning about properties of systems. In particular, the branching temporal logics CTL* [4] and CTL [2] (a syntactic restriction of CTL*) have been used to verify the properties of non-deterministic and concurrent programs.

It is our goal to extend these results to a logic that allows propositional quantification. In the linear case PLTL [16] has been augmented with quantified propositions to get the significantly more expressive QPTL [18]. In [9] QPTL was shown to be able to reason about ω-automata, and prove the existence of refinement mappings [1]. A refinement mapping shows one system specification S_1 implements some other system specification S_2 by encoding the specifications in temporal logic where variables not common to S_1 and S_2 are quantified out. Propositional quantification has been shown to be related to logics of knowledge [8]. Finding decidable semantics for quantified propositional branching time logics is an important step to finding suitable semantics for the more expressive epistemic logics.

Previously branching temporal logics with quantified propositions have been examined in [11], [4], and [13], though only existential quantification was considered, and the structures were limited to trees. More powerful semantics for propositional quantification have been studied in intuitionistic propositional logic [19],

M. Brooks, D. Corbett, and M. Stumptner (Eds.): AI 2001, LNAI 2256, pp. 165–176, 2001.

[15]. In this paper we give three separate semantic interpretations for full propositional quantification. We show that one of these, the *Kripke semantics*, is highly undecidable. While the other two are decidable, the *tree semantics* can be used to reason about purely structural properties of the model (like the branching degree of trees). This can complicate the notion of refinement, so we introduce the *amorphous semantics* to overcome this, and sketch a decision process.

2 The Base Semantics, CTL*

We first describe the syntax and semantics of CTL*. The language CTL* consists of an infinite set of atomic variables $\mathcal{V} = \{x_0, x_1, ...\}$, the boolean operations $\neg, \vee$, the temporal operators $\bigcirc, \Box, \mathrm{U}$ (**next**, **generally** and **until** respectively) and the path quantifier E. The formulae of CTL* are defined by the following abstract syntax, where x varies over $\mathcal{V}$:

$$\alpha ::= x \mid \neg\alpha \mid \alpha_1 \vee \alpha_2 \mid \bigcirc\alpha \mid \Box\alpha \mid \alpha_1 \mathrm{U} \alpha_2 \mid \mathrm{E}\alpha \quad (1)$$

Definition 1. *A state formula of CTL* is a formula where every temporal operator ($\bigcirc$, $\Box$ or U) is in the scope of a path quantifier (E).*

The abbreviations $\wedge, \rightarrow, \leftrightarrow$ are defined as usual, and we define $\Diamond\alpha$ (future) to be $\neg\Box\neg\alpha$, and $\mathrm{A}\alpha$ to be $\neg\mathrm{E}\neg\alpha$. We also consider the formulas $\top, \bot$ (respectively "true" and "false") to be abbreviations for, respectively $x_0 \vee \neg x_0$ and $\neg(x_0 \vee \neg x_0)$. To give the semantics for CTL* we define *$\mathcal{V}$-labeled Kripke frames*:

Definition 2. *A Kripke frame is a tuple (S, R) where*

1. *S is a nonempty set of states, or moments.*
2. *$R \subseteq S^2$ is a total binary relation.*

A $\mathcal{V}$-labeled Kripke frame is a Kripke frame with a valuation $\pi : S \longrightarrow \wp(\mathcal{V})$.

Let $M = (S, R, \pi)$ be a $\mathcal{V}$-labelled Kripke frame. A *path* b in M is an ω-sequence of states $b = (b_0, b_1, ...)$ such that for all i, $(b_i, b_{i+1}) \in R$ and we let $b_{\geq i} = (b_i, b_{i+1}, ...)$. We interpret a formula α of CTL* with respect to a $\mathcal{V}$-labelled Kripke frame M and a path b in M. We write $M, b \models \alpha$ where:

$$M, b \models x \iff x \in \pi(b_0) \quad (2)$$
$$M, b \models \neg\alpha \iff M, b \not\models \alpha \quad (3)$$
$$M, b \models \alpha \vee \beta \iff M, b \models \alpha \text{ or } M, b \models \beta \quad (4)$$
$$M, b \models \bigcirc\alpha \iff M, b_{\geq 1} \models \alpha \quad (5)$$
$$M, b \models \Box\alpha \iff \forall i \geq 0,\ M, b_{\geq i} \models \alpha \quad (6)$$
$$M, b \models \alpha \mathrm{U} \beta \iff \exists i \geq 0,\ M, b_{\geq i} \models \beta \text{ and } M, b_{\geq j} \models \alpha \text{ for all } j < i \quad (7)$$
$$M, b \models \mathrm{E}\alpha \iff \text{ there is some path } b' \text{ s.t. } b'_0 = b_0 \text{ and } M, b' \models \alpha. \quad (8)$$

From the semantics given above we can see that the evaluation of a state formula only depends on the initial state of the path b, rather than the whole path. We restrict our attention to state formulas and define a *model* to be the tuple (S, R, π, s) (or (M, s)) where $s \in S$. A state formula α is *satisfied* by (M, s) (denoted $(M, s) \models \alpha$) if there is some path b in M with $b_0 = s$ and $M, b \models \alpha$. If for all models (M, s) we have $(M, s) \models \alpha$, then we say α is a *validity.*

The language CTL is a syntactic restriction of CTL*. Particularly, CTL requires that every temporal operator is paired with a path quantifier. To define CTL we only need to modify the abstract syntax (1) as follows:

$$\alpha ::= x \mid \neg\alpha \mid \alpha_1 \vee \alpha_2 \mid \mathrm{E}\bigcirc\alpha \mid \mathrm{E}\,\Box\alpha \mid \mathrm{A}\,\Box\alpha \mid \mathrm{E}(\alpha_1 \mathrm{U} \alpha_2) \mid \mathrm{A}(\alpha_1 \mathrm{U} \alpha_2)$$

The logic CTL is less expressive than CTL*, though it is frequently preferred as the model checking complexity is less than that for CTL*. We will show that this difference disappears when propositional quantification is considered.

3 Syntax and Semantics for Propositional Quantification

We add the operator $\exists$ to the languages defined above and define QCTL* to be the language consisting of the formulae defined by the abstract syntax above, where the following inductive step is included:

If α is a formula and $x \in \mathcal{V}$ then $\exists x\alpha$ is a formula.

The set of formulae of QCTL* is closed under complementation, and we let $\forall x\alpha$ be an abbreviation for $\neg\exists x\neg\alpha$. The logic QCTL is similarly defined to extend CTL.

The semantic interpretation of propositional quantification will rely on the following definition.

Definition 3. *Given some model $(M, s_0) = (S, R, \pi, s_0)$ and some $x \in \mathcal{L}$, an x-variant of (M, s_0) is some model $(M', s_0) = (S, R, \pi', s_0)$ where $\pi'(s)\backslash\{x\} = \pi(s)\backslash\{x\}$ for all $s \in S$.*

To complete the interpretation for formulae of QCTL* we augment the interpretation above (2-8) with

$$M, b \models \exists x\alpha \iff \text{There is some } x\text{-variant } M' \text{ of } M \text{ such that } M', b \models \alpha. \quad (9)$$

Since we will consider other possible interpretations below we refer to the set of semantics defined above as the *Kripke semantics.* We will show that QCTL* becomes highly undecidable over such a general semantic interpretation. There are two possible ways to overcome this.

3.1 Tree Semantics

The undecidability of the Kripke semantics results from the logic being able to specify structural properties of the model. By restricting the structures to trees, QCTL* becomes decidable. We give the following definitions and note the semantics for CTL* (2-8) can be restricted to $\mathcal{V}$-labelled trees without change.

Given some relation $R \subseteq S^2$ the *transitive closure* of R is $<_R \subseteq S^2$ where $(s,t) \in <_R$ if and only if for some $n > 0$ there exists $s_0, ... s_n \in S$ with $s_0 = s$, $s_n = t$ and for $i < n$, $(s_i, s_{i+1}) \in R$.

Definition 4. *A $\mathcal{V}$-labelled tree, (S, R, π, s) is a model that satisfies the following conditions:*

1. *S is a (countably) infinite set of nodes.*
2. *$<_R$ is irreflexive.*
3. *The past of $t \in S$, $\{s \in S | s <_R t\}$ is linerarly ordered by $<_R$.*
4. *Each maximally ordered subset of S is order-isomorphic to $\mathbb{N}$.*

We refer to this restriction as the *tree semantics.* Given any model, $(M, s) = (S, R, \pi, s_0)$ we can generate a $\mathcal{V}$-labelled tree $(M^T, s) = (S', R', \pi', s_0)$ (the *unwinding* of (M, s)) where:

- $S' \subseteq S^*$, $s_0 \in S'$, and for any word $w \in S^*$ and any $s \in S$ with $ws \in S'$ then $(s,t) \in R$ if and only if $wst \in S'$.
- $R' = \{(w, ws) \mid w \in S', ws \in S', s \in S\}$.
- $\pi'(s_0) = \pi(s_0)$ and $\pi'(ws) = \pi(s)$ for $s \in S$.

Lemma 1. *CTL* is insensitive to unwinding. That is $(M, s) \models \alpha$ if and only if $(M^T, s) \models \alpha$.*

This was proven in [3]. However QCTL* is not insensitive to unwinding, as was shown in [11]. For example consider a model consisting of a single state. For all possible valuations a proposition would be always true or always false, which is clearly not the case in tree semantics. While QCTL* becomes decidable in the tree semantics, it can still define purely structural properties of the model. Particularly, QCTL (and hence QCTL*) can define the number of successors a state has. For every $i \in \mathbb{N}$ we can define the state formula B_i such that $M, s \models B_i$ if and only if s has exactly i successors. For example $B_2 = \exists y B_2(y)$ where

$$B_2(y) = ((\mathrm{E}\bigcirc y \wedge \mathrm{E}\bigcirc \neg y) \wedge \forall x(\mathrm{E}\bigcirc(y \wedge x) \wedge \mathrm{E}\bigcirc(\neg y \wedge x) \rightarrow \mathrm{A}\bigcirc x)), \quad (10)$$

If there were only one successor of s, then $\mathrm{E}\bigcirc y$ and $\mathrm{E}\bigcirc \neg y$ could not both be true. If there were more than two successors, we could have x true at exactly two of the successors, and y true at exactly one of these. Then the left side of the implication would be satisfied, but $\mathrm{A}\bigcirc x$ would not.

3.2 Amorphous Semantics

The second way to avoid the undecidability of QCTL* is to give a different interpretation of propositional quantificiation. This will remove the ability of QCTL* to define any of the structural properties of the underlying model. The new interpretation requires the following definition:

Definition 5. *Given $X \subseteq \mathcal{V}$, the models $(M, s_0) = (S, R, \pi, s_0)$ and $(M', s') = (S', R', \pi', s'_0)$ are X-bisimilar if there exists some relation $B \subseteq S \times S'$ with $(s_0, s'_0) \in B$ and for all $(s, s') \in B$:*

1. $\pi(s)\backslash X = \pi'(s')\backslash X$.
2. *For all $t \in S$ such that $(s,t) \in R$, there exists $t' \in S'$ with $(s',t') \in R'$ such that $(t,t') \in B$.*
3. *For all $t' \in S'$ such that $(s',t') \in R'$, there exists $t \in S$ with $(s,t) \in R$ such that $(t,t') \in B$.*

The pairs (M, b) and (M', b') are X-bisimilar if there exists such a relation B for (M, b_0) and (M', b'_0) with $(b_i, b'_i) \in B$ for all $i \geq 0$. We write $\{x\}$-bisimilar as x-bisimilar, and $\emptyset$-bisimilar as bisimilar.

This definition is based on the notion of the bisimilarity of synchronization trees [14] and a similar notion of quantification has been considered in the case of intuitionistic propositional logic [19]. The amorphous semantics replace the interpretation of quantification (9) with

$$M, b \models \exists x\alpha \Leftrightarrow \text{ there is } (M', b'),\ x\text{-bisimilar to } (M, b),\ \text{with } M', b' \models \alpha. \quad (11)$$

The amorphous semantics allow us to disregard the purely structural properties of the model (for example, the formula B_2 (10) becomes unsatisfiable). This is particularly useful for proving the refinement of concurrent specifications, since the specifications do not have to be considered over identical structures. We give the following lemma without proof, though it is not hard to show.

Lemma 2. *1. X-bisimilarity is an equivalence relation.*
2. (M, s) and (M^T, s) are bisimilar.
3. QCTL is insensitive to unwinding in the amorphous semantics.*

4 Definability

Before addressing the decidability of QCTL* we simplify the syntax we must use. Particularly we show that in the case of the tree and the amorphous semantics, QCTL* is definable in a restriction of QCTL that does not include the U operators. We first claim that the U operator is definable by the other operators of QCTL*. The construction is taken from [9], and its soundness can easily be shown.

Given some pair (M, b) where $b = (b_0, b_1, ...)$ is a path in the model (M, b_0), and formulas α and β of QCTL* which do not contain the variable x_1, let $Until(\alpha, \beta) = \exists x_1(\Diamond \beta \wedge (x_1 \wedge \Box(x_1 \rightarrow (\beta \vee (\alpha \wedge \bigcirc x_1)))))$.

Lemma 3. *In the tree and amorphous semantics* $(M, b) \models \alpha U \beta \Leftrightarrow (M, b) \models \exists x_1 Until(\alpha, \beta)$.

We now show how every temporal operator can be paired with a path quantifier. By the above lemma we do not have to address the U operator.

Let Eα be any formula of QCTL* such that any subformula of α containing a branch quantifier is a formula of QCTL. For some $y \in \mathcal{V}$ that is not a variable of α we let $\alpha'(y)$ be the formula that results when all subformulas $\Box \beta$ of α, which are not directly preceded by a path quantifier are replaced with $\mathrm{A}\Box(y \rightarrow \beta)$, and likewise for the $\bigcirc$ operator. Let

$$\alpha^* = \exists z(z \wedge \mathrm{A}\Box(z \leftrightarrow \mathrm{E}\bigcirc z) \wedge \forall y(y \wedge \mathrm{A}\Box(y \leftrightarrow (\mathrm{E}\bigcirc y \wedge z)) \rightarrow \alpha'(y))). \quad (12)$$

Lemma 4. $(M, s) \models E\alpha \Leftrightarrow (M, s) \models \alpha^*$, *in the amorphous and tree semantics.*

Proof. (Tree Semantics) The formula (12) restricts the evaluation of $\alpha'(y)$ to models where y is true on a set of branches, and the formula $\mathrm{A}\Box(y \rightarrow \beta)$ restricts the interpretation only to paths where y is true. If we can restrict y to a single path the interpretation becomes equivalent to $\Box\beta$. Suppose $(M, s) \models \mathrm{E}\alpha$. We can choose z to be true only on a single path for which α is true. Then y can only be true along this path and the result follows. Conversely if $(M, s) \models \alpha^*$ then since we are considering all possible interpretations of y, then we must consider some interpretation which has y true on a single path, and Eα must be true. The $\bigcirc$ operator can be treated in the same way and the result follows. The proof for the amorphous semantics is similar, though the structure must be unwound first.

Corollary 1. *Given the amorphous semantics or the tree semantics, QCTL* is definable in QCTL.*

Proof. Given some formula α we first remove all occurences of U by using Lemma 3. The result can then be shown by induction over the complexity of formulas working from the inside out, and using the Lemma 4 to convert each branch quantified subformula to a formula of QCTL.

5 Decidability

We have defined three possible sets of semantics for QCTL*. The satisfiability problem for QCTL* will be shown to be highly undecidable for the Kripke semantics, while it is decidable for the tree and the amorphous semantics.

5.1 Undecidability

The consequence of the expressive power of the Kripke semantics QCTL is that the satisfiablity problem becomes undecidable. In fact Kremer [15] has shown that intuitionistic propositional logic with quantified propositions over Kripke structures is recursively isomorphic to full second-order logic. It is belived that QCTL can be shown to be just as powerful, though here we simply show that QCTL (and hence QCTL*) is not recursively enumerable. This is done by encoding the following tiling for $(\mathbb{N},<) \times (\mathbb{N},<)$ in QCTL.

We are given a finite set $\Gamma = \{\gamma_i | i = 1, ..., m\}$ of tiles. Each tile γ_i has four coloured sides: left, right, top and bottom, written γ_i^l, γ_i^r, γ_i^t, and γ_i^b. Each side can be one of n colours c_j for $j = 1, ..., n$. Given any set of these tiles, we would like to know if we can cover the plane $\mathbb{N} \times \mathbb{N}$ with these tiles such that adjacent sides share the same colour. Formally, given some finite set of tiles Γ we would like to decide if there exists a function $\lambda : \mathbb{N} \times \mathbb{N} \longrightarrow \Gamma$ such that for all $(x, y) \in \mathbb{N} \times \mathbb{N}$

1. $\lambda(x, y)^r = \lambda(x + 1, y)^l$
2. $\lambda(x, y)^t = \lambda(x, y + 1)^b$

where $\lambda(x, y)^t$ is the colour of the top side of the tile on (x, y), and likewise for the other sides. Finally we require that there is some specific tile γ_j that occurs infinitely often in the bottom row (i.e. $\lambda(x, 0) = \gamma_j$ for infinitely many x. In [7] this problem was shown to be highly undecidable, or Σ_1^1.

Theorem 1. *Given the Kripke semantics, the satisfiability problem for QCTL is highly undecidable.*

Given the set of tiles Γ we give a formula, $Tile^\Gamma$, of QCTL that is satisfiable if and only if the above tiling problem is satisfiable. To specify that some tile γ_j occurs infinitely often in the bottom row, we let γ_0 be a copy of γ_j, and suppose that γ_0 occurs only in the bottom row. This is clearly equivalent to the above problem.

We start by giving a formula that specifies the underlying Kripke structure to be a grid (i.e. a structure similar to a binary tree, but with the branches rejoining). To make a grid we have to specify that the two successors of any state have a common successor. This is done with the following formula:

$$G(y,z) = (y \wedge \mathrm{E}\bigcirc(y \wedge \mathrm{A}\bigcirc z)) \rightarrow \mathrm{E}\bigcirc(\neg y \wedge \mathrm{E}\bigcirc(z \wedge \neg y)) \quad (13)$$

$$S(y) = \mathrm{A}\,\Box(B_2(y) \wedge \forall z(G(y,z) \wedge G(\neg y, z)) \quad (14)$$

The formula $B_2(y)$ (10) specifies the branching degree to be two, and that y is true for exactly one successor of any state. This formula uses the universally quantified variable z to ensure that the two successors of any state share a successor, since any interpretation that makes z true for all the successors of the first successor of some point, makes z true for at least one successor of the second successor of that point.

To encode the tiling we let each tile γ_i be represented by the variable t_i and define the formula $T_i = t_i \wedge \neg \bigvee_{j \neq i} t_j$. Rather than explicitly encoding the colours we just place restrictions on which tiles can succeed other tiles:

$$C^\Gamma(y) = \bigvee_{i=0}^{m} \left(T_i \wedge y \wedge \mathrm{E}\bigcirc \left(y \wedge \bigvee_{\gamma_j^l = \gamma_i^r}^{j<m} T_j \right) \wedge \mathrm{E}\bigcirc \left(\neg y \wedge \bigvee_{\gamma_j^b = \gamma_i^t}^{j<m} T_j \right) \right) \quad (15)$$

$$B^\Gamma(y) = \mathrm{A}\,\Box(\neg y \rightarrow \mathrm{A}\,\Box\neg T_0) \wedge \mathrm{E}\,\Box\mathrm{E}\Diamond T_0 \quad (16)$$

$$\Lambda^\Gamma(y) = B^\Gamma(y) \wedge \mathrm{A}\,\Box(C^\Gamma(y) \vee C^\Gamma(\neg y)). \quad (17)$$

The first formula specifies the way tiles can fit together. The variable y is used to define rows and columns since the value of y is fixed along a row, and alternates along a column. The second formula specifies that the variable t_0 occurs only, and infinitely often, on the bottom row, since the only path where $\neg y$ is always true is the bottom row. We define the formula

$$Tile^\Gamma = y \wedge S(y) \wedge \Lambda^\Gamma(y). \quad (18)$$

Lemma 5. *The formula* $Tile^\Gamma$ *is satisfiable if and only if* Γ *can tile* $(\mathbb{N},<) \times (\mathbb{N},<)$, *with* γ_0 *occuring infinitely often on the bottom row.*

Proof. ($\longrightarrow$) Suppose that $Tile^\Gamma$ is satisfied by some model $M = (S, R, \pi, s_0)$. We define the function $\mu : \mathbb{N} \times \mathbb{N} \longrightarrow S$ recursively such that $\mu((0,0)) = s_0$, and $\mu((a,b)) = t$ where

$$\mu(a-1,b) = s,\ (s,t) \in R \text{ and } y \in \pi(s) \leftrightarrow y \in \pi(t) \quad (19)$$

$$\text{or} \quad \mu(a,b-1) = s,\ (s,t) \in R \text{ and } y \in \pi(s) \leftrightarrow y \notin \pi(t) \quad (20)$$

The function μ will be surjective and well defined since every $s \in S$ has exactly two successors, by $B_2(y)$ and y will always be true on exactly one of these successors. Therefore there is always exactly one successor of s satisfying (19), and exactly one successor satisfying (20). We can then define the tiling function as $\lambda((a,b)) = \gamma_i \iff t_i \in \mu((a,b))$. The use of T_i in $\Lambda^\Gamma(y)$ ensures that every point (a, b) is assigned exactly one tile, and the function $B^{\Gamma}(y)$, along with the definition of μ ensures that the tile γ_0 occurs infinitely often on the bottom row. All that is left to show is that the sides of the tiles match up. To do this suppose at some state $\mu(a, b)$, y and t_i are true. Then by the definition of μ, at $\mu(a{+}1, b)$ y is true and by $C^{\Gamma}(y)$ there is some j such that t_j is true where $\gamma_i^l = \gamma_j^r$. Similarly at $\mu(a, b+1)$ y is not true and there is some k with t_k true where $\gamma_i^t = \gamma_k^b$. By the formula $S(y)$, $\mu(a+1, b)$ and $\mu(a, b{+}1)$ have a common successor where y is not true. By the definition of μ this state must be $\mu(a+1, b+1)$, and suppose t_ℓ is true at this state. The formula $C^{\Gamma}(y)$ ensures $\gamma_k^t = \gamma_\ell^b$ and similarly $C^{\Gamma}(\neg y)$ ensures $\gamma_j^l = \gamma_\ell^r$. Likewise we can show the case for $\neg y$, so the sides of any four adjacent tiles match up, and by applying a similar argument recursively we can see that the generated tiling is sound.

($\longleftarrow$) Given that λ is a tiling for Γ of $(\mathbb{N}, <) \times (\mathbb{N}, <)$ we can construct the model $M = (S, R, \pi, s_0)$ where $S = \mathbb{N} \times \mathbb{N}$, $R = \{((a, b), (c, d)) | c = a + 1 \text{ or } d = b + 1\}$, and $s_0 = (0, 0)$. We define $y \in \pi((a, b))$ iff b is even, and $t_i \in \pi(a, b)$ iff $\lambda(a, b) = \gamma_i$. It is straightforward to show that $(M, s_0) \models \mathit{Tile}^{\Gamma}$.

This proof demonstrates the extensive expressive power of QCTL*. In fact the only formulae that were used were from QCTL, and there was only one propositional quantifier used. It is possible to give a similar proof where no path quantifiers are used, and hence QPTL [18] is undecidable when repeated states are allowed.

5.2 Decidability

The tree semantics are decidable. We do not go into details as the proofs are complicated [5]. The decidability can be shown by expressive equivalence with the language tree of automata [17], though this approach requires careful treatment as the branching degree of the model may not be fixed. In [4] the equivalence between the Rabin tree automata over binary trees and existentially quantified CTL* is shown. This does not relect the full the expressive ability of QCTL* over tree semantics since it does not allow for a varying branching degree.

In [6] the decidability of a similar logic over trees was proven. In this proof it was shown that the formulas of the language could be transformed so the satisfaction of any formula could be decided over binary trees. This approach is also applicable in the case of QCTL*.

To show QCTL* is decidable in the amorphous semantics we extend a method introduced in [9]. We define a new kind of tree automaton refered to as an *amorphous automaton*[1] such that for any formula α of QCTL* an amorphous

---

[1] Amorphous tree automaton were defined in [12] to act on trees of varying branching degree. As they are a generalization of the construction presented here we will retain the name.

automaton A_α can be constructed that will accept exactly the models of α. The decidability of QCTL* then reduces to the emptiness problem for the automaton, which in turn reduces to the satisfiability problem for CTL*. An amorphous automaton A is given by the tuple $(\Sigma, Q, q_0, \delta, C)$ where

1. $\Sigma = \wp(var(\alpha))$ is an alphabet, where $var(\alpha)$ is the set of the variables occuring in α.
2. $Q = \{q_0, ...q_n\}$ is a set of automaton states, (we refer to states of a model as moments from now on, to avoid confusion).
3. $q_0 \in Q$ is the initial state.
4. $\delta : Q \times \Sigma \longrightarrow \wp(\wp(Q))$ is the transition fuction.
5. $C = \{(L_i, U_i) \mid L_i, U_i \subseteq Q\}_{i=1}^k$ is the Rabin acceptence condition.

We define a run of the automaton A over some model (M, s_0) to be a Q-labelled tree (T, R^T, λ, t_0) along with some function $\mu : T \rightarrow M$ such that:

1. $\lambda : T \longrightarrow Q$, (i.e. each node is marked with a single automaton state).
2. $\mu(t_0) = s_0$ and $\lambda(t_0) = q_0$.
3. If $\mu(t) = s$ and $(s, s') \in R$ then there is some $t' \in T$ such that $(t, t') \in R^t$ and $\mu(t') = s'$.
4. If $\mu(t) = s$ and $(t, t') \in R^T$ then there is some $s' \in S$ such that $(s, s') \in S^t$ and $\mu(t') = s'$.
5. There is some set $a \in \delta(\lambda(t), \pi(\mu(t)))$ such that $a = \{\lambda(t') | (t, t') \in R^T\}$, where π' is the projection of π onto the variables of α (i.e. $\pi' : S \rightarrow \Sigma$).

Let $r = (T, R^t, \lambda, t_o, \mu)$ be some run of the automaton A over a model (M, s). We say r is an accepting run if for every path b of r there is some $i \leq k$ such that some state $\ell \in L_i$ occurs infinitely often along b and every state $u \in U_i$ occurs only finitely often along b.

For each automaton A we can define a characteristic formula χ_A in QCTL*, such that $M, s \models \chi_A$ if and only if A accepts (M, s). To do this we use a set of variables $P = \{p_0, ...p_n\}$ to represent the automaton states, and define the formula $at\_q_i = p_i \wedge \neg \bigvee_{j \neq i} p_j$ for each state $q_i \in Q$ and $in\_Q' = \bigvee_{q \in Q'} at\_q_i$ and for each subset $Q' \subseteq Q$. For each element $\sigma \in \Sigma$ we define the formula $\overline{\sigma} = \bigwedge\{x | x \in \sigma\} \wedge \bigwedge\{\neg x | x \in var(\alpha) \backslash \sigma\}$. The formula χ_A is given by

$$run = \bigvee_{\sigma \in \Sigma} \bigvee_{q \in Q} \left(at\_q \wedge \overline{\sigma} \wedge \bigvee_{a \in \delta(q, \sigma)} \left(\mathrm{A} \bigcirc in\_a \wedge \bigwedge_{q' \in a} \mathrm{E} \bigcirc at\_a' \right) \right) \tag{21}$$

$$acc = \mathrm{A} \bigvee_{i=1}^{k} (\Box \Diamond in\_L_i \wedge \Diamond \Box \neg in\_U_i) \tag{22}$$

$$\chi_A = \exists p_0 ... \exists p_n \, (at\_q_0 \wedge \mathrm{A} \Box run \wedge acc) \,. \tag{23}$$

Lemma 6. *An amorphous automaton A accepts some model (M, s) if and only if $M, s \models \chi_A$.*

This can be seen by comparision of the semantic defintions (2-8), (9) with the definition of the amorphous automata. Conversely for every formula α of QCTL* there is an automaton A_α that accepts exactly the models that satisfy α. To construct the automaton A_α we first convert α into a formula α' of QCTL, using Lemmas 3 and 4. A_α can then be constructed by induction over complexity of α'. We will give all the constructions for all operators except $\neg$. The complementation construction is double exponential, though it could possibly be optimized, and it has similarities with Klarlund's construction [10]. We let $A_\beta = (\Sigma, Q, q_0, \delta, C)$ and $A_\gamma = (\Sigma, Q^*, q_0^*, \delta^*, C^*)$.

1. Propositions. For $x \in \mathcal{V}$ we define $A = (\Sigma, \{q_0, q_1, q_2\}, q_0, \delta, \{(\{q_1\}, \emptyset)\})$, where for all $\sigma \in \Sigma$ $\delta(q, \sigma) = \{\{q_1\}\}$ if $q = q_0$ and $x \in \sigma$, or $q = q_1$, and $\delta(q, \sigma) = \{\{q_2\}\}$ otherwise.
2. $\beta \vee \gamma$. We define $A = (\Sigma, Q \cup Q^*, q', \delta', C \cup C^*)$, where for all $\sigma \in \Sigma$ $\delta'(q', \sigma) = \delta(q_0, \sigma) \cup \delta(q_0^*, \sigma)$, for all $q \in Q$ $\delta'(q, \sigma) = \delta(q, \sigma)$ and for all $q \in Q^*$ $\delta('q, \sigma) = \delta^*(q, \sigma)$.
3. $\mathrm{E}\bigcirc\beta$. We define $A = (\Sigma, Q \cup \{q_0', q_1'\}, q_0', \delta', C \cup \{(\{q_1\}, \emptyset)\})$, where for all $\sigma \in \Sigma$ $\delta'(q_0', \sigma) = \{\{q_0, q_1'\}\}$, $\delta'(q_1', \sigma) = \{\{q_1'\}\}$ and $\delta'(q, \sigma) = \delta(q, \sigma)$ for $q \in Q$. The construction for $\mathrm{E}\Diamond$ is similar.
4. $\mathrm{A}\Diamond\beta$. We define $A = (\Sigma, Q \cup \{q_0'\}, q_0', \delta', C)$, where for all $\sigma \in \Sigma$ $\delta'(q_0', \sigma) = \{\{q_0, q_0'\}, \{q_0\}, \{q_0'\}\}$ and $\delta'(q, \sigma) = \delta(q, \sigma)$ for $q \in Q$.
5. $\exists x \beta$. We define $A = (\Sigma, Q, q_0, \delta', C)$, where for all $\sigma \in \Sigma$ and all $q \in Q$ $\delta'(q, \sigma) = \delta(q, \sigma \backslash \{x\}) \cup \delta(q, \sigma \cup \{x\})$.

The complementation procedure and proofs of soundness for the above constructions will be given in [5]. To prove the decidability of the satisfiability problem for QCTL* in the amorphous semantics we have to show that we can decide whether or not an amorphous automaton A_α accepts the empty language (i.e. α is unsatisfiable). Rather than constructing such a decision process it is enough to note that α is equivalent to χ_{A_α}. Since χ_{A_α} is an existentially quantified formula of QCTL* we can reason that χ_{A_α} (and hence α) is satisfiable if and only if the unquantified part (i.e. $(at\_q_0 \wedge \mathrm{A}\,\Box run \wedge acc)$ from (21)) is satisfiable in CTL*. Since the CTL* is decidable the decidability of QCTL* follows and we are done.

6 Conclusion

We have defined three sets of semantics for QCTL*: Kripke semantics, tree semantics and amorphous semantics. While the Kripke semantics have been shown to be highly undecidable, there is good reason for further investigation. We have shown that QCTL* can reason about the structure of a model, but we do not yet know to what extent. For example, there is a formula of QCTL that is satisfied in the Kripke semantics by exactly the models that are trees. The variety of structures that are expressible may have applications in the theory of modal logic, or natural language processing.

In the case of the decidable semantics the complexity of the decision processes require further investigation. While there are some well known results in the case of the tree semantics, the amorphous semantics are relatively new and such issues are yet to be examined. The definition of amorphous automata is also of interest in its own right. The expressive power, complexity and applications are all yet to be fully explored.

References

1. M. Abadi and L. Lamport. The existence of refinement mappings. *Theorectical Computer Science*, 82(2):253–284, May 1991.
2. E. Clarke and E. Emerson. Synthesis of synchronization skeletons for branching time temporal logic. In *Proc. IBM Workshop on Logic of Programs, Yorktown Heights, NY*, pages 52–71. Springer, Berlin, 1981.
3. E. Emerson. Alternative semantics for temporal logics. *TCS*, 26, 1983.
4. E. Emerson and A. Sistla. Deciding full branching time logic. *Information and Control*, 61:175 - 201, 1984.
5. T. French. *The theory of branching time logics with quantified propositions.* PhD thesis, Murdoch University, In preparation.
6. Y. Gurevich and S. Shelah. The decision problem for branching time logic. *J. of Symbolic Logic*, 50:668–681, 1985.
7. D. Harel. Effective transformations on infinite trees, with applications to high undecidability, dominoes, and fairness. *J. A.C.M.*, 33(1):224–248, 1986.
8. R. van der Meyden K. Engelhardt and Y. Moses. Knowledge and the logic of local propositions. In *Conf. on Theoretical Aspects of Rationality and Knowledge*, 1998.
9. Yonit Kesten and Amir Pnueli. A complete proof systems for qptl. In *Proceedings, Tenth Annual IEEE Symposium on Logic in Computer Science*, pages 2–12, 1995.
10. N. Klarlund. Progress measures, immediate determinacy, and a subset construction for tree automata. *Annals of Pure and Applied Logic*, 69:243–268, 1994.
11. O. Kupferman. Augmenting branching temporal logics with existential quantification over atomic propositions. In *Computer Aided Verification, Proc. 7th Int. Conference*, pages 325–338, Liege, 1995. Springer-Verlag.
12. O. Kupferman and O. Grumberg. Branching time temporal logic and amorphous tree automata. In *Proceedings of the Fourth Conference on Concurrency Theory*, pages 262–277, Hildesheim, 1993. Springer-Verlag.
13. O. Kupferman and A. Pnueli. Once and for all. In *Proceedings of the Tenth IEEE Symposium on Logic in Computer Science*, San Diego, 1995.
14. R. Milner. A calculus of communicating systems. *Lecture Notes in Computer Science*, 92, 1980.
15. P.Kremer. On the complexity of propositional quantification in intuitionistic logic. *J. of Symbolic Logic*, 62(2):529–544, 1997.
16. A. Pnueli. The temporal logic of programs. In *Proceedings of the Eighteenth Symposium on Foundations of Computer Science*, pages 46–57, 1977.
17. M. Rabin. Decidability of second-order theories and automata on infinite trees. *Trans. AMS*, 141:1–35, 1969.
18. A. P. Sistla. *Theoretical Issues in the Design and Verification of Distributed Systems.* PhD thesis, Harvard University, 1983.
19. Albert Visser. Bisimulations, model descriptions and propositional quantifiers. Manuscript, see http://www.citeseer.nj.nec.com/visser96bisimulation.html.

Improved Techniques for an Iris Recognition System with High Performance

Gyundo Kee[1], Yungcheol Byun[2], Kwanyong Lee[3], and Yillbyung Lee[1]

[1] Dept. of Computer Science, Yonsei University, Seoul, Korea
[2] Dept. of Computer Software Research Laboratory, ETRI, Daejeon, Korea
[3] Dept. of Information and Telecommunication, Korea Cyber University, Seoul, Korea
{kigd,bcart,kylee,yblee}@csai.yonsei.ac.kr

Abstract. We describe in this paper efficient techniques for iris recognition system with high performance from the practical point of view. These techniques range every step for an iris recognition system from the image acquisition step to the final step, the pattern matching, and contain as follows: a method of evaluating the quality of an image in the image acquisition step and excluding it from the subsequent processing if it is not appropriate, a bisection-based Hough transform method on the edge components for detecting the center of the pupil and localizing the iris area from an eye image, an elastic body model for transforming the localized iris area into a simple coordination system, and a compact and efficient feature extraction method which is based on 2D multiresolution wavelet transform. By exploiting these techniques, we can improve the system performance in terms of computationally efficient, and more accurate and robust against noises.

1 Introduction

Controlling the access to secure areas or transacting electronically through the internet, a reliable personal identification infrastructure is required. Conventional methods of recognizing the identity of a person by using a password or cards are not altogether reliable. Biometrics measurements such as fingerprints, face, or retinal patterns are common and reliable ways to achieve verification of an individual's identity with a high level of accuracy. It provides a better way for the increased security requirements of our information society than traditional identification methods such as passwords or ID cards.

Since each individual has a unique and robust iris pattern, it has been considered as a good information for the identification of individuals among the various biometrics features. The highly randomized appearance of the iris makes its use as a biometric well recognized. Its suitability as an exceptionally accurate biometric derives from its extremely data-rich physical structure, stability over time, and genetic independence - no two eyes are same [1].

Most of works on personal identification and verification by iris patterns have been done in 1990s, and recent noticeable studies among them include those of [1], [2] and [3].

M. Brooks, D. Corbett, and M. Stumptner (Eds.): AI 2001, LNAI 2256, pp. 177–188, 2001.

In this paper we present some of effective and efficient techniques for improving the performance of human identification system based on the iris patterns in a practical point of views. To achieve the performance improvement of the systems, we give the following techniques; an evaluation method for the quality of images in the image acquisition stage to determine whether the given images are appropriate for the subsequent processing or not and then to select the proper ones, a bisection-based Hough transform method in the iris localization stage for detecting the center of the pupil and localizing the iris area from an eye image, an efficient and robust transformation method called the elastic body model for converting the localized iris area into a simple image so as to facilitate the feature extraction process, and a compact and effective feature extraction method which is based on 2D multiresolution wavelet transform. Through various experiments, we will show that the proposed methods can be used for iris-based personal identification systems in an efficient way.

The contents of this paper are as follows. In the following section, some related works are briefly mentioned. Section 3 gives the details of the various methods we proposed in the paper. Experimental results and analysis will be stated in section 4, and finally the conclusions are given in section 5.

2 Review of Past Work

Some works on human iris recognition have been found in the literatures [1] ~ [4]. We will take a brief look at the overall process from some of the representative systems.

Daugman used the circular edge detector to find out the boundaries and developed the feature extraction process based on information from a set of 2-D Gabor filter. He generated a 256-byte code by quantizing the local phase angle according to the outputs of the real and imaginary part of the filtered image, and compared by computing the percentage of mismatched bits between a pair of iris representation via XOR operator and by selecting a separation point in the space of Hamming distance.

On the contrary, the Wildes system exploited the gradient-based Hough transform for localizing the iris area, and made use of Laplacian pyramid constructed with four different resolution levels to generate iris code. It also exploited a normalized correlation based goodness-of-match values and Fisher's linear discriminant for pattern matching. Both of the iris recognition systems made use of bandpass image decompositions to avail multiscale information.

Boles used the knowledge-based edge detector for iris localization, and implemented the system operating the set of 1-D signals composed of normalized iris signatures at a few intermediate resolution levels and obtaining the iris representation of these signals via the zerocrossing of the dyadic wavelet transform. It made use of two dissimilarity functions to compare a new pattern and the reference patterns.

Boles' approaches have the advantage of processing 1-D iris signals rather than 2-D image used in both [1] and [2]. However, [1] and [2] proposed and implemented a whole system for personal identification or verifications including the configuration of image acquisition device, but [3] only focused on the iris representation and matching algorithm without an image acquisition module.

3 Analysis and Recognition of Iris Image

3.1 Image Acquisition

An image surrounding human eye region is obtained at a distance from a CCD camera without any physical contact to the device. To acquire more clear images through a CCD camera and minimize the effect of the reflected lights caused by the surrounding illumination, we suppose two situations as the surrounding lights; one exploits two halogen lamps locating on the right and left side of the camera at a distance, and the other uses two infrared lamps simply locating around the camera. The size of the image acquired under these circumstances is 320×240.

3.2 Evaluation of Image Quality

For fully automated systems for recognizing iris patterns to identify a person, it is required to minimize person's intervention in the image acquisition process. One simple way is to acquire a series of images within the specific interval and select the best one among them, but its approach is strongly required to have reasonable computational time for real applications.

In this paper, we propose a method for checking the quality of images to determine whether the given images are appropriate for the subsequent processing or not and then to select the proper ones among them in real time. Some images asserted to inappropriate ones are excluded from the next processing.

The images excluded from the subsequent processing include as follows; the images with the blink(Fig. 1(a)), the images whose the pupil part is not located in the middle thus some parts of the iris area disappear(Fig. 1(b)), the images obscured by eyelids or the shadow of the eyelids(Fig. 1(c)), and the images with severe noises like Fig. 1(d). Fig. 1 shows the examples of images with bad quality, and they can be caused to decrease the recognition rate and the overall system performance if they are excluded by the proposed method.

We define some basic cases of the inappropriate images for the recognition and then develop straightforward and efficient sub-modules to deal with each case by considering the pixel distribution and the directional properties of edge only on regions of interest. Each sub-module is combined in parallel and sequential depending on the characteristics of information used in the sub-modules. Our approach has the great potential of extending the functional modules simply by adding the corresponding mechanisms.

The eye image, at first, is divided into $M \times N$ blocks to get the pixel distribution of the specific areas. The process of the quality evaluation consists of three stages by combining three sub-modules sequentially. The first stage is to detect

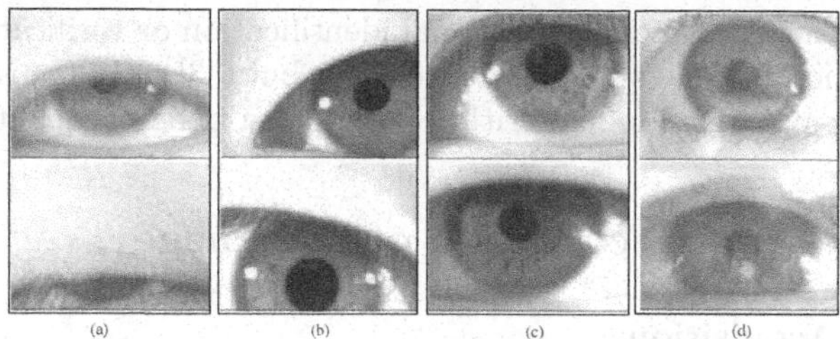

Fig. 1. Examples of images with bad quality

the blink using the information that the intensity of the eyelids is lighter than those of the pupil and the iris. The second stage is related to detect the location of the pupil approximately. The brightness of the pupil area is darker than those of the other areas in the normal cases, accordingly the darkest block around the center of the given image would be the best candidate of the pupil area. After finding out the darkest block, we give the score to other blocks depending on the distance from the center of the image. The third stage is to get the vertical and horizontal edge components using Sobel edge detector to compute the ratio of directional components as the form of score. Just applying the threshold to the sum of the scores obtained from each stage, we can decide the appropriateness of the given image eventually.

3.3 Iris Localization

The iris localization is to detect the iris area between pupil and sclera from an eye image. To find out that area exactly, it is important to precisely detect the inner boundary (between pupil and iris) and the outer boundary(between iris and sclera). At first, we need to get the exact reference point, the center of the pupil, and then compute the distance from that point to the boundaries as the radius.

We propose a three-step technique for detecting the reference point and localizing the iris area from an eye image. In the first step, the Canny edge detector is applied to the image to extract edge components and then the connected components are labeled. The next step is to use a 2D bisection-based Hough transform, not a 2D gradient-based Hough transform [5], to get the center of the pupil. The basic idea of the bisection method is that any line connecting to two points on the circle is bisected the perpendicular line to that line which passes through the center of the circle.

The frequency of each intersecting point among the perpendicular lines formed by two points at a specific distance on the edge components is computed. The most frequently intersected point above a threshold indicates the existence of a circle from the edge components, and the corresponding point can be considered as the center of the circle, the reference point. After detecting the candidate of the center, the radius histogram technique is applied to validate the existence of a circle and calculate its radius.

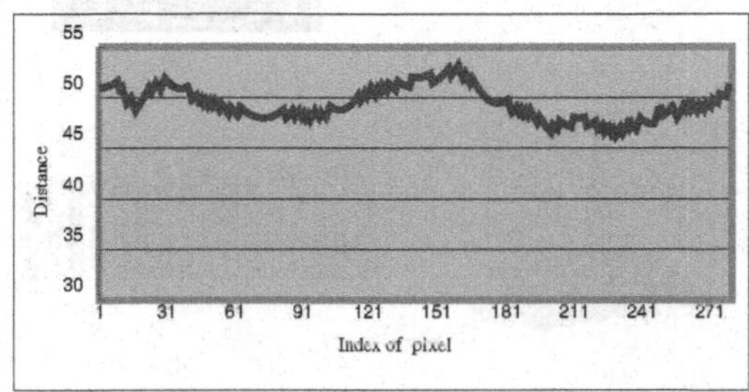

Fig. 2. Distance from the center to the tentative inner boundary

In order to compute the radius of the tentative circle, the inner boundary, one simple method is to average all of the distance from the center to the points on the connected edge components, but its method is sensitive to noise. Therefore, we propose a new method what we called the maximal frequency determination. The method is to divide the possible range of radius into lots of sub-ranges, and to select a sub-range with the maximal frequency and then determine the median of the corresponding sub-range as the radius. By using this method, we can get the radius less sensitive to noise. After determining the radius, we can easily find the inner boundary using the center of the pupil and the radius. For the outer boundary, the similar process of getting the inner boundary is applied. Finally, the iris area can be localized by separating the part of an image between the inner boundary and the outer boundary.

Fig. 3 shows each stage of the bisection-based Hough transform method.

3.4 Normalization

A normalization process is implemented to compensate for size variations due to the possible changes in the camera-to-face distance, and to facilitate the feature extraction process by converting the iris area represented by polar coordinate system into Cartesian coordinate system.

As you know in Fig 2, the deviation of the radius is about 14%, which means there is the possibility of losing information in the localized iris area due to the inclusion of the pupil area and the exclusion of the iris area. It is worthwhile, in addition to scale compensation, to point out transformation compensation.

To solve such problems caused by the use of virtual circle for the boundaries, we propose a new normalization method, the elastic body model for scale, rotation, and transformation compensation.

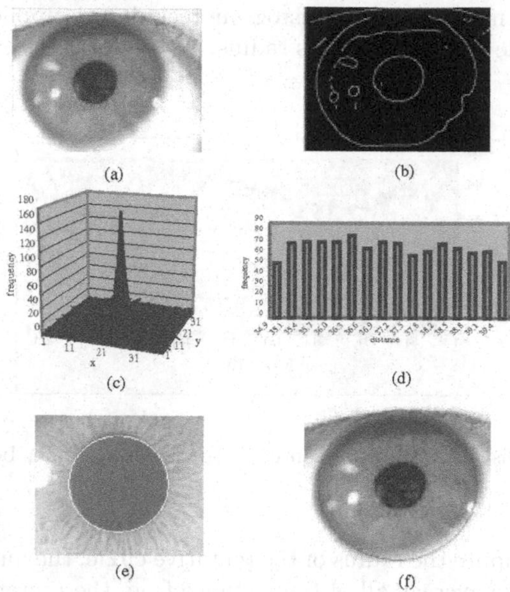

Fig. 3. Each stage of the bisection-based Hough transform: (a)Original image (b)Edge detected image (c)Plot of the frequency of the intersecting points (d)Radius histogram (e)Detected inner boundary (f)Detected outer boundary

Elastic Body Model. In the model, it is considered that there is one-to-one mapping between the inner boundary and the normalized mapping area despite of the actual distortions of the shape of the circle. Fig. 4 shows the conceptual diagram of the proposed method. We only consider the vertical direction of the inner boundary as the axis direction of an elastic body. The outer boundary corresponds to the outer frame of the elastic body, and the inner boundary corresponds to the edge of free movement of independent spring. Each point of the inner boundary connects to the corresponding point of the outer boundary by each spring.

We put two assumptions on the movement of iris muscles to the model. One is that the iris muscles consists of the elastic body connected by the pin joint of the outer frame, and the other is that the elastic bodies (iris patterns) can be transformed only in the direction of each spring, not the perpendicular direction, which means it is not permitted the bend of each spring.

The algorithm to apply the model to iris images is briefly described in Fig. 5 and Fig. 6.

In the Fig. 6, T_o is given by

$$T_o = arcsin(\frac{(Y_i - Y_{oc}) \times N_i - (X_i - X_{oc}) \times sinN_i}{R_o}) + N_i \quad (1)$$

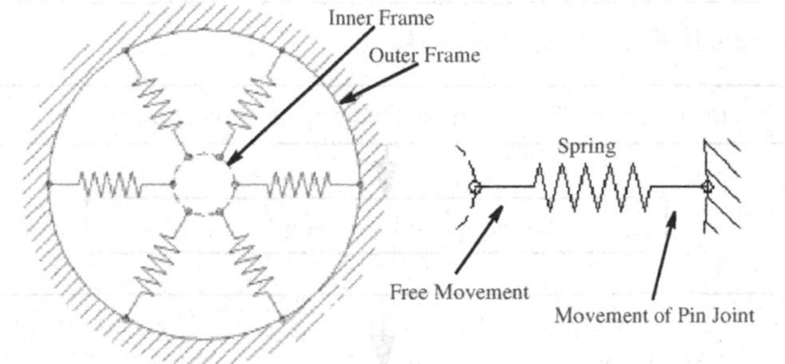

Fig. 4. Proposed normalization method: Elastic Body Model

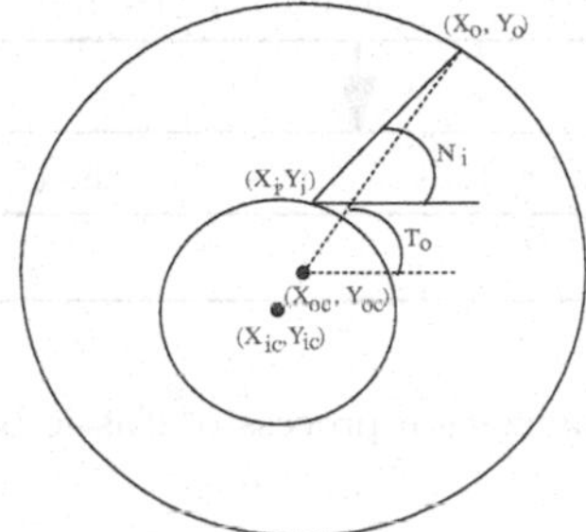

Fig. 5. Relationship between inner boundary and outer boundary from the elastic body's viewpoint

3.5 Feature Extraction

Various wavelets described in the literature have been reported to posses different properties of orthogonality, symmetry and compact support. The wavelet paradigm is now well established and has found many applications in signal and image processing [7]. We selected Daubechies's wavelet(tap-4), because this has shown high texture classification. This wavelet is based on orthogonalization and factorization conditions, and not symmetric but provide compact support [8].

Multiresolution techniques intend to transform images into a representation in which both spatial and frequency information is present [6]. In our scheme, all the iris images are first decomposed into subbands using wavelet transform. With the pyramid-structured wavelet transform, the original image is passed through the low-pass and high-pass filters to generate the low-low, low-high, high-low and high-high subimages. The decomposition is recursively applied on the low frequency channel to obtain the lower resolution subimages. Thus, we can analyze an iris image at both local and global scales simultaneously using the multiresolution approach.

Mallat's experiment [6] suggests that by using wavelet representation, statistics based on first order distribution of grey-levels might be sufficient for preat-

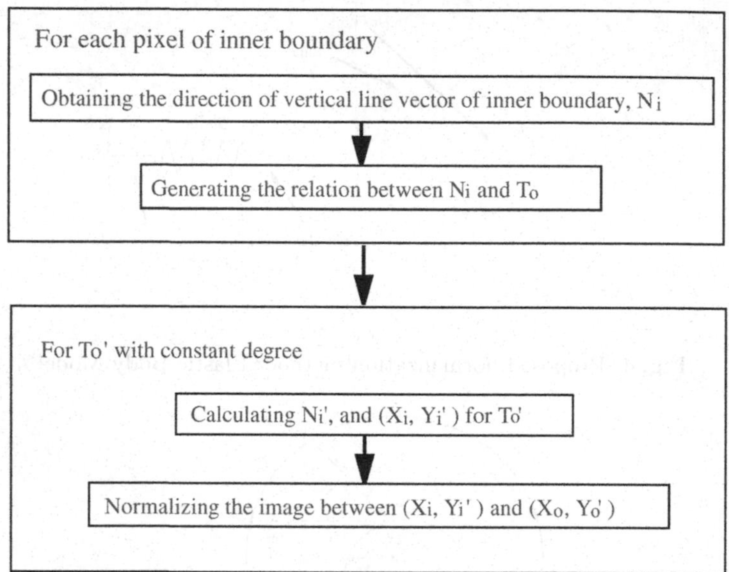

Fig. 6. The normalization process of elastic body model

tentive perception of textual difference. Hence we use four features i.e. mean, variance, standard deviation, and energy from the gray-level histogram of the subband images.

In this paper, each iris image was decomposed into three levels using Daubechies tap-4 filter which resulted in 12 subimages so as to extract iris features. We used the statistical features to represent feature vectors, thus four statistical features were computed from each subband image. In addition to that, we divide the subimages into local windows in order to get robust feature sets against shift, translation and noisy environment (Fig. 7). We extracted statistical features from local windows on the corresponding subimages, the subimages of the intermediate levels, to represent feature vectors.

3.6 Pattern Matching

The process of pattern matching consists of two phases: training and classification. In the training phase, we construct the registered patterns corresponding to the enrollment process of an iris recognition system based on a set of features obtained from the wavelet transformation on images. In the classification phase, the feature representation of an unknown iris is constructed in order to compare with the registered ones for identifying a person.

Denote the registered pattern by $\mathbf{y}_i = (y_{i,1}, \cdots, y_{i,J}), i = 1, \cdots, M$, and an unknown image pattern by $\mathbf{x} = (x_1, \cdots, x_J)$. Then we calculate the distance

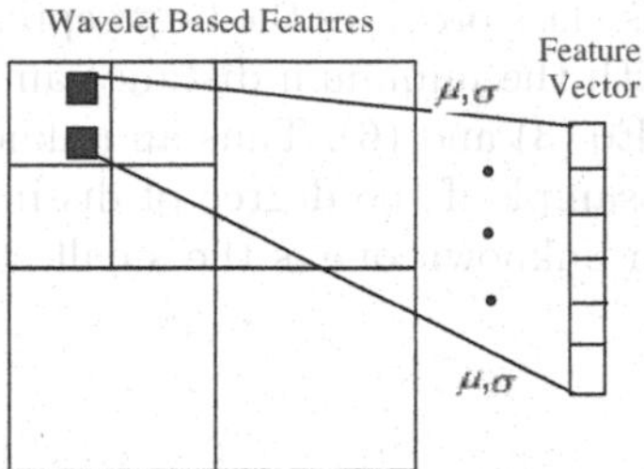

Fig. 7. Arrangement of feature vector by local windows

between the two patterns defined by the discrimination function in the feature space. The discrimination function for iris texture is listed by

$$D_i = distance(\mathbf{x}, \mathbf{y}_i) . \tag{2}$$

Several distance functions can be used in Eq.(2). We consider, first of all, the Euclidean distance function defined as

$$D_{1,i} = [(\mathbf{x} - \mathbf{y}_i)^T(\mathbf{x} - \mathbf{y}_i)]^{1/2} = \sqrt{\sum_{j=1}^{J}(x_j - y_{i,j})^2} . \tag{3}$$

The Euclidean distance between two features, however, can be greatly influenced by variables that have largest values [9]. Thus we consider that a more robust alternative in the presence of outliers is to divide the values by the standard deviation to reduce the effect of extreme values on the feature typical cases. Registered patterns are normalized by centering each component around its mean m_j and then scaling it by the inverse of its standard deviation σ_j,

$$\hat{y}_{i,j} = \frac{y_{i,j} - m_j}{\sigma_j} . \tag{4}$$

An unknown pattern is centered and scaled by

$$\hat{x}_j = \frac{x_j - m_j}{\sigma_j} . \tag{5}$$

The mean m_j for each component is computed by $m_j = \sum_{i=1}^{M} x_{ij}/M$ and the variance is obtained via the unbiased estimator $\sigma_j^2 = \sum_{i=1}^{M}(x_{ij} - m_j)/(M-1)$.

Therefore, the distance $D_{2,i}$ on the normalized features can be expressed as

$$D_{2,i} = \sqrt{\sum_{j=1}^{J}(\hat{x}_j - \hat{y}_{i,j})^2} . \tag{6}$$

To determine which iris class provides the best representation of an input image, we select the class with the minimum distance among all of the results for the registered vectors by Eq.(3) and (6). Thus an unknown iris will be matched with a specific registered sample if the degree of dissimilarity between the corresponding sample and an unknown one is the smallest distance in comparison with other samples.

4 Experimental Results

We use two kinds of iris data sets acquired from different environment for real applications. The first data set is obtained with two hallogen lamps as the surrounding illumination under irregular indoor lights, and is composed of 4500 iris data acquired from 150 persons(Data set 1). The second one is acquired from a constant illumination with two infrared lamps, and consists of 600 iris data from 20 persons(Data set 2). We used four samples from each other for training data, and the remaining ones are used for test data.

For the experiment of evaluating the image quality, the processing time on a Pentium-III 450 MHz PC with the windows 2000 is about 0.2 second. Table 1 shows the processing time according to each stage, and our method consists of three stages such as the blinking detection(F1), the detection of pupil location(F2), and the computation of the edge component ratio(F3).

Table 1. Processing time for evaluating the image quality

Step	F1	F1+F2	F1+F2+F3
Processing Time(sec)	0.04	0.8	0.16

For the iris localization stage, first of all, the images passed successfully from the quality evaluation were applied. When we applied the preprocessing techniques such as the bisection-based Hough transform and the elastic body model to these images, the success rate of the preprocessing stage was 97.3% from the subjective viewpoint. Some of the major causes of failing to iris localization include the distortion of the inner boundary by the intrusion of eyelashes, and inconsistency between the original image and the extracted outer boundary by the noises. On the contrary, all of the eye images which were asserted the inappropriate ones by the quality evaluation stage give the imperfect results even though they seemed to finished the localization process successfully. From these results, we noticed that the reliability and performance of the system was improved due to the evaluation module of image quality.

Fig. 8 illustrates the direction of all the vertical lines after compensating by the elastic body model. We noticed that the distorted edge components caused by reflected light made a convex shape by compensation.

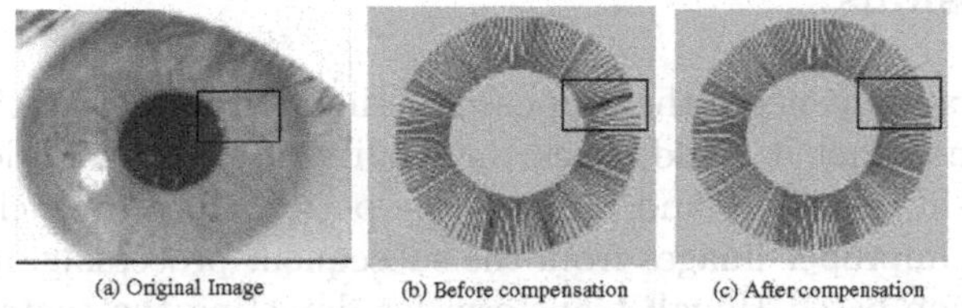

Fig. 8. Direction of vertical lines after compensating by elastic body model

From the practical viewpoints, it is strongly required for the systems to have the compact dimension of features as well as the best accuracy and reliability. To achieve these requirements, we conducted the four experiments to select the best strategy of selecting features. The first one is to arrange the statistical information of the entire subimages into a feature vector. The second experiment is to make a feature vector by mutually combining the decomposition coefficients of the low-level subimages. The third approach is to get a feature vector by combining the statistical information for some of the low-level subimages and the decomposition coefficients of the low-level subimages. The final thing is to combine the statistical information obtained from the low-level subimages by applying local windows.

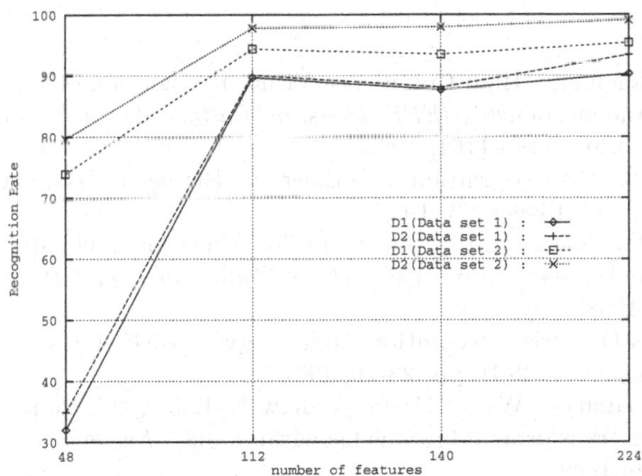

Fig. 9. Comparison of results using different feature vectors and distance function

Fig. 9 shows the recognition rate on the four above-mentioned experiments. As you can see the figure, we got the best recognition rate when exploiting a feature vector combined by mean and standard deviation value of local windows for the intermediate subbands.

5 Conclusions

Through the experiments of the proposed method for evaluating the image quality, we confirmed that it could check the quality of images and determine their appropriation in real-time, and improve the performance by excluding the unnecessary and improper images from the subsequent processing, accordingly.

The bisection-based Hough transform for detecting the centre of the circle and extracting the radius of the detected circular shape form iris images is more robust to noise than the existing methods while being more accurate. Furthermore, the proposed model of elastic body allows compensation for the transformation variations of iris shape resulting from asymmetric constriction and dilation, and for the rotation which is deviation in angular position about the optical axis.

By selecting some intermediate resolution levels based on multiresolution wavelet approach to get iris features, we can get a more compact features with robustness in a noisy environment, and reduce the computation time as the lower frequency bands are subsampled successively without loss of information. In addition, by normalizing the statistics values acquired from local windows of subimages, we achieve robustness against mismatches due to the shift and noise.

We showed that the proposed methods can be easily applied to the real problems of iris-based identification system in an efficient manner.

References

1. John G. Daugman, "High Confidence Visual Recognition of Persons by a Test of Statistical Independence", *IEEE Trans. on Pattern Analysis and Machine Intelligence*, 15(11), pp. 1148-1161, 1993.
2. Wildes, R.P., "Iris Recognition : An Emerging Biometric Technology", *Proc. of the IEEE*, 85(9), pp. 1348-1363, 1997.
3. Boles, W.W., Boashash, B., "A Human Identification Technique Using Images of the Iris and Wavelet Transform", *IEEE Trans. on Signal Processing*, 46(4), pp. 1185-1188, 1998.
4. Williams, G.O., "Iris Recognition Technology", *IEEE Aerospace and Electronics Systems Magazine*, 12(4), pp. 23-29, 1997.
5. Dimitrios Ioammou, Walter Huda, Andrew F. Laine, "Circle recognition through a 2D Hough Transform and radius histogramming", *Image and Vision Computing*, 17, pp.15-26, 1999.
6. Stephane. G. Mallet., "A Theory for Multiresolution Signal Decomposition: The Wavelet Representation", *IEEE Trans. Pattern Recognition and Machine Intelligence*, 11(4), pp.674-693, 1989.
7. Stephane. G. Mallet., "Wavelet for a Vision", *Proceedings of the IEEE*, 84(4), pp.604-614, 1996.
8. I. Daubechies., "Orthonormal bases of compactly supported wavelets", *Comm. Pure Appl. Math.*,41, pp. 909-996, 1988.
9. D. Randall Wilson, Tony R. Martinez, "Improved Heterogeneous Distance Functions", *Journal of Artificial Intelligence Research*, 6, pp.1-34, 1997

An Investigation of an Adaptive Poker Player

Graham Kendall and Mark Willdig

The University of Nottingham, School of Computer Science & IT, Jubilee Campus, Wollaton Road, Nottingham NG8 1BB, UK
gxk@cs.nott.ac.uk, Mark.Willdig@siemenscomms.co.uk

Abstract. Other work has shown that adaptive learning can be highly successful in developing programs which are able to play games at a level similar to human players and, in some cases, exceed the ability of a vast majority of human players. This study uses poker to investigate how adaptation can be used in games of imperfect information. An internal learning value is manipulated which allows a poker playing agent to develop its playing strategy over time. The results suggest that the agent is able to learn how to play poker, initially losing, before winning as the players strategy becomes more developed. The evolved player performs well against opponents with different playing styles. Some limitations of previous work are overcome, such as deal rotation to remove the bias introduced by one player always being the last to act. This work provides encouragement that this is an area worth exploring more fully in our future work.

1. Introduction

Game playing has a long research history. Chess has received particular interest culminating in Deep Blue beating Kasparov in 1997, albeit with specialized hardware (Hamilton, 1997) and brute force search. However, although arguably, being a 'solved game' chess still receives interest as researchers turn to adaptive learning techniques which allow computers to 'learn' to play chess, rather than being 'told' how it should play (Kendall, 2001). Adaptive learning was being used for checkers as far back as the 1950's with Samuel's seminal work (1959, re-produced in Samuel, 2000). Checkers research would lead to Jonathan Schaeffer developing Chinook, which claimed the world title in 1994 (Schaeffer, 1996). Like Deep Blue, it is arguable if Chinook used AI techniques. Chinook had an opening and ending database. In certain games it was able to play the entire game from these two databases. If this could not be achieved, a form of mini-max search, with alpha-beta pruning was used. Despite Chinook becoming the world champion, the search has continued for an adaptive checkers player. Chellapilla and Fogel's (Chellapilla, 2000) Anaconda was named due to the strangle hold it placed on its opponent. It is also named Blondie24, this being the name it used when competing in internet games (Fogel, 2001). Anaconda uses an artificial neural network (ANN), with 5000 weights, which are evolved by an evolutionary strategy. The inputs to the ANN are the current board position and it outputs a value which is used in a mini-max search. During the training period, using co-evolution, the program is given no information other than whether it won or lost.

M. Brooks, D. Corbett, and M. Stumptner (Eds.): AI 2001, LNAI 2256, pp. 189–200, 2001.

Once Anaconda is able to play at a suitable level, it often searches to a depth of 10, but depths of 6 and 8 are also common in play. Anaconda has been available to the delegates at the Congress on Evolutionary Computing (CEC) conference for the past two years (CEC'00, San Diego and CEC'01, Seoul) with Fogel offering a prize of $100 (CEC'00) and $200 (CEC'01) to anybody who could defeat it. The prize remains unclaimed and at the next conference (CEC'02, Hawaii), the prize rises to $300.

Poker also has an equally long research history with von Neumann and Morgensten (von Neumann, 1944) experimenting with a simplified, two-player, version of poker.

Findler (Findler, 1977) studied poker, over a 20 year period. He also worked on a simplified game, based on 5-card draw poker with no ante and no consideration of betting position due to the computer always playing last. He concluded that dynamic and adaptive algorithms are required for successful play and static mathematical models were unsuccessful and easily beaten.

In more recent times three research groups have been researching poker. Jonathan Schaeffer (of Chinook fame) and a number of his students have developed ideas which have led to Loki, which is, arguably, the strongest poker playing program to date. It is still a long way from being able to compete in the World Series of Poker (WSOP), an annual event held in Las Vegas, but initial results are promising. Schaeffer's work concentrates on two main areas (Billings, 1998a and Schaeffer, 1999). The first research theme makes betting decisions using probabilistic knowledge (Billings, 1999) to determine which action to take (fold, call or raise) given the current game state. Billings et. al. also uses real time simulation of the remainder of the game that allows the program to determine a statistically significant result in the program's decision making process. Schaeffer's group also uses opponent modeling (Billings, 1998b). This allows Loki to maintain a model of an opponent and use this information to decide what betting decisions to make.

Koller and Pfeffer (Koller, 1997), using their Gala system, allow games of imperfect information to be specified and solved, using a tree based approach. However, due to the size of the trees they state "...we are nowhere close to being able to solve huge games such as full-scale poker, and it is unlikely that we will ever be able to do so."

Luigi Barone and Lyndon While recognise four main types of poker player; Loose, Tight, Passive, and Aggressive. These characteristics are combined to create the four common types of poker players: Loose Passive, Loose Aggressive, Tight Passive and Tight Aggressive players (Barone & While, 1999; 2000). A **Loose Aggressive** player will overestimate their hand, raising frequently, and their aggressive nature will drive the pot higher, increasing their potential winnings. A **Loose Passive** player will overestimate their hand, but due to their passive nature will rarely raise, preferring to call and allow other players to increase the pot. A **Tight Aggressive** player will play to close constraints, participating in only a few hands which they have a high probability of winning. The hands they do play, they will raise frequently to increase the size of the pot. A **Tight Passive** player will participate in few hands, only considering playing those that they have a high probability of winning. The passive nature implies that they allow other players to drive the pot, raising infrequently themselves.

In their first paper Barone and While (Barone, 1998) suggest evolutionary strategies as a way of modelling an adaptive poker player. They use a simple poker variant where each player has two private cards, there are five community cards and one round of betting. This initial work incorporates three main areas of analysis; hand strength, position and risk management. Two types of tables are used, a loose table and a tight table. The work demonstrates how a player that has evolved using evolutionary strategies can adapt its style to the two types of table.

In (Barone, 1999) they develop their work by introducing a *hypercube* which is an *n* dimensional vector, used to store candidate solutions. The hypercube has one dimension for the betting position (early, middle and late) and another dimension for the risk management (selected from the interval 0..3). At each stage of the game the relevant candidate solutions are selected from the hypercube (e.g. middle betting position and risk management 2) and the decision is made whether to fold, call or raise. To make the decision the hypercube entry holds seven real valued numbers which are used as constants to three functions (fold, call and raise). In effect, the functions lead to a probability of carrying out the relevant action. It is the seven real values that are evolved depending on whether the player won the hand or not. Barone reports that this poker player improves on the 1998 version. Their 2000 paper (Barone, 2000) extends the dimensions of the hypercube to include four betting rounds (pre-flop, post-flop, post-turn and post-river) and an opponent dimension so that the evolved player can choose which type of player it is up against. The authors report this player out performs a competent static player.

Poker, being a game of imperfect information, is interesting as a game for the basis of research. Unlike chess and checkers, poker has some information that is unseen. Poker also contains other unknowns such as the playing styles of the other players who may use bluffing (and double bluffing) during the course of the game. These elements add to the research interest. Unlike complete information games where the techniques to solve the games (computational power allowing) have been known and understood for a long time (such as mini-max search and alpha-beta pruning), games of imperfect information have not received the same sort of analysis and, doing so, could prove relevant to many other areas such as economics, on-line auctions and negotiating.

2. The Rules of Poker

The exact rules for poker can be found in many poker books (see, for example, Sklansky, 1994; 1996) and we simply give here the basic rules of one variant (Texas Hold 'Em) so that the reader is able to follow the remainder of this paper. Each player is dealt two cards. These are private cards, only being visible to the player receiving those cards. These cards are normally referred to as hole cards. A round of betting follows this initial deal. Next, three community cards (called the flop) are dealt, face up, in the middle of the table. These cards are used by every player to make the best five card poker hand, using their hole cards. A round of betting follows the flop. Next, another community card (called the turn) is dealt face up in the middle of the table. Another round of betting follows. Finally, another community card (called the river) is dealt and a final round of betting follows. Once this final round of betting has taken place, assuming there are two or more players who still have an interest in the pot, the cards are shown and the highest poker hand wins. In forming a poker hand, the players can use any combination of their two hole cards and the five community cards to make the best five card poker hand. The various poker hands are as follows, in descending order.

Royal Flush: Ten, Jack, Queen, King and Ace, all in the same suit.

Straight Flush: any sequence of five cards, all of the same suit.

Four of a Kind: four cards having the same value, one from each suit.

Full House: three cards of the same value combined with two cards of the same value. For example, Three 2's and a pair of Queens.

Flush: all five cards have the same suit.

Straight: all five card values are in sequence, made up from at least two suits.

Three of a Kind: three cards all having the same value.

Two Pairs: two cards of the same value, combined with another two card of the same value. For example, two 9's and two 3's.

A Pair: two cards having the same value.

Single Card: the highest value card is used to value the hand.

When betting, the players have three choices to make. They can either fold (throw in their cards and relinquish all claims to the money in the pot), they can call (match the amount of money bet so far) or they can raise (increase the current bet, thus forcing all the other players to match this amount or fold). To start the betting it is usual to put in some form of ante. This is a mechanism to start the betting by giving the players an interest in the pot.

In this paper we have not implemented a full version of Texas Hold 'Em, preferring a version of poker, where the players are dealt five cards and, after a round of betting, are allowed to trade two cards before a final round of betting. This version is known as draw poker and was considered as a suitable test bed for this initial investigation.

3. Experiments

We have implemented the four playing styles (loose passive, loose aggressive, tight passive and tight aggressive) described above so that we can sit each of them at our tables and find out if our approach can adapt to each of these styles. Each playing style will play to a specific set of rules using the value of their current hand and the current value of the pot to decide whether to fold, call, or raise.

Table 1: The Loose Aggressive Players Strategy

1st Round Strategy		
Hand From	**Hand To**	**Action**
0	Pair 8's	Fold
Pair 9's	Pair K's	Call
Pair A's	2 Pairs Ace High	Raise 5 if Pot <= 100 otherwise Call
Three 2's	Three 4's	Raise 10 if Pot <= 150 otherwise Call
Three 5's	Three J's	Raise 15 if Pot <= 200 otherwise Call
Three Q's	Three A's	Raise 20 if Pot <= 250 otherwise Call
Straight	Royal Flush	Raise 25 if Pot <= 300 otherwise Call
2nd Round Strategy		
Hand From	**Hand To**	**Action**
0	Pair 8's	Fold
Pair 9's	Three 6's	Call
Three 7's	Three A's	Raise 5 if Pot <= 150 otherwise Call
Straight 6 High	Straight A High	Raise 10 if Pot <= 200 otherwise Call
Flush 6 High	Full House A High	Raise 15 if Pot <= 250 otherwise Call
Four 2's	Four A's	Raise 20 if Pot <= 300 otherwise Call
Straight Flush 6 High	Royal Flush	Raise 25 if Pot <= 400 otherwise Call

Table 2: The Loose Passive Players Strategy

1st Round Strategy		
Hand From	**Hand To**	**Action**
0	Pair 8's	Fold
Pair 9's	Three J's	Call
Three Q's	Flush A High	Raise 5 if Pot <= 100 otherwise Call
Full House 2 High	Royal Flush	Raise 10 if Pot <= 150 otherwise Call
2nd Round Strategy		
Hand From	**Hand To**	**Action**
0	Pair 8's	Fold
Pair 9's	Three A's	Call
Straight 6 High	Straight A High	Raise 5 if Pot <= 100 otherwise Call

Flush 6 High	Four 5's	Raise 10 if Pot <= 150 otherwise Call
Four 6's	Royal Flush	Raise 15 if Pot <= 200 otherwise Call

Table 3: The Tight Aggressive Players Strategy

1st Round Strategy		
Hand From	**Hand To**	**Action**
0	Pair A's	Fold
2 Pairs 3 High	Three 4's	Call
Three 5's	Three J's	Raise 5 if Pot <= 150 otherwise Call
Three Q's	Three A's	Raise 15 if Pot <= 200 otherwise Call
Straight 6 High	Royal Flush	Raise 25 if Pot <= 300 otherwise Call
2nd Round Strategy		
Hand From	**Hand To**	**Action**
0	Pair A's	Fold
2 Pairs 3 High	Three 10's	Call
Three J's	Three A's	Raise 5 if Pot <= 150 otherwise Call
Straight 6 High	Straight A High	Raise 10 if Pot <= 200 otherwise Call
Flush 6 High	Full House A High	Raise 15 if Pot <= 250 otherwise Call
Four 2's	Four A's	Raise 20 if Pot <= 300 otherwise Call
Straight Flush 6 High	Royal Flush	Raise 25 if Pot <= 400 otherwise Call

Table 4: The Tight Passive Players Strategy

1st Round Strategy		
Hand From	**Hand To**	**Action**
0	Pair A's	Fold
2 Pairs 3 High	Straight A High	Call
Flush 6 High	Four 5's	Raise 5 if Pot <= 100 otherwise Call
Four 6's	Straight Flush A High	Raise 10 if Pot <= 150 otherwise Call
Royal Flush	Royal Flush	Raise 15 if Pot <= 200 otherwise Call
2nd Round Strategy		
Hand From	**Hand To**	**Action**
0	2 Pairs A High	Fold
Three 2's	Three A's	Call
Straight 6 High	Flush A High	Raise 5 if Pot <= 100 otherwise Call

Full House 2 High	Four A's	Raise 10 if Pot <= 150 otherwise Call
Straight Flush 6 High	Royal Flush	Raise 15 if Pot <= 250 otherwise Call

In order to test our adaptive poker player, we adopt the following rules. At the start of each hand each player places an ante of one unit into the pot. There will be two rounds of betting. Each round will pass around the table a maximum of three times, unless every player except one decides to fold, or all players call.

Non-evolving players will play to the strategies described above (tables 1 thru 4). The evolving player considers three factors when deciding whether to fold, call or raise, these being hand strength, the number of players left at the table and the money in the pot. As well as these factors, a learning value will be evolved and will also dictate the actions of the evolving player. The learning value is manipulated throughout the training period of the evolving player, assisting in its decision whether to fold, call or raise. There is a learning value (ranging over the interval 1..10) associated with each possible hand. The algorithm, in deciding whether to fold, call or raise is as follows.

```
If lv < 6 then FOLD
   elseif lv >= 6 AND lv < 8 then CALL
   elseif lv >= 8 then
      ac = (lv/LOG(pv)/(np/lv)
      if ac < 10 then CALL
      else RAISE by SQRT(ac) * w
```

where

lv = learning value for the hand being played
pv = the current value of the pot
np = number of players left in the current game
ac = players action, returning a value greater than 0
w = a weighting factor dependant on *lv*

```
if lv < 8 then w = 1
if 8 < lv > 8.99 then w = 3
if 9 < lv > 9.99 then w = 4
if lv > 9.99 then w = 5
```

Example of the use of this algorithm is shown in figures 1 thru 3.

lv = 8, *np* = 5, *pv* = 50 *ac* = 7.53, player will call	*lv* = 8, *np* = 3, *pv* = 50 *ac* = 12.57, player will raise 11 units

Fig. 1: Player Calls

Fig. 2: Player Raises 11 units

lv = 9, *np* = 3, *pv* = 50 *ac* = 15.89, player will raise 16 units

Fig. 3: Player Raises 16 units

Figure 1 has more players participating in the current game resulting in the evolving player calculating it is less likely to win the pot so it decides to call. A reduced number of players contesting the pot increases the evolving players chances of winning, influencing its action to raise, as shown in figure 2.

Figures 3 highlights the difference in the raise value when the learning value is adjusted between the values of 8 (figure 2) and 9 (figure 3). The learning value of 9 is associated with better hand rankings, thus there is a better chance of winning. As the possibility of winning is increased with the higher learning value, more emphasis is placed on driving the pot harder, raising it, in the hope of increased winnings.

The learning values, *lv*, are associated with hand strength. Each hand is given a value, *lv*, which is used in the formulae outlined above. Initially, all values are set to 10, so that the evolving player will raise every time. Using this method every hand is assumed to be good until we find out otherwise. This is seen as preferable to assuming every hand is bad until we know otherwise as this was one of the criticisms that Barone made of his own work. He experienced a royal flush so infrequently that he folded it when one did appear, on the basis that the program had not learnt that this was good hand.

Our adaptation technique is simple. If the evolving player wins a game, with other players either calling or raising, then the learning value is incremented by 0.1, but will never exceed 10. If the player folds after raising or calling the learning value will be decreased by 0.1 unless it is already zero.

All our tests have five players seated at the table. Player 1, except for initial testing to confirm the system is operating fairly, will always be the evolving player. Players 2 thru 5 will be the non-evolving players as defined in tables 1 thru 4. Each player will have 10,000 units allocated to them making a total of 50,000 units at the table. The evolving player will have its learning values initialised to ten at the start of each training session. The deal and betting will move clockwise around the table. The player to the dealers left will always play first. Initial testing, using tables of similar players with no evolving player, showed that the game was fair, in that no single player or position dominated.

The evolving player must initially be trained by allowing manipulation of the learning values. It is interesting to monitor the evolving player during this learning period.

Initially, the evolving player plays every hand. This can be seen in epochs (hands played) 1 to 100 in table 5. After this, learning values are being reduced and the number of hands played gradually decreases.

Table 5 : Number of Games Played and Won During the Training Period

	25	**50**	**75**	**100**	**200**	**300**	**400**	**500**	**1000**	**1500**	**2000**	**2500**	**3000**
Hands Played	25	50	75	100	195	257	324	393	647	925	1187	1421	1664
Hands Won	5	12	19	28	60	81	102	123	216	312	409	484	560
% Played	100	100	100	100	97.5	85.6	81.0	78.6	64.7	61.6	59.3	56.8	55.5
% Won	20.0	24.0	25.3	28.0	30.7	31.5	31.5	31.3	33.3	33.7	34.5	34.0	33.6

Table 5 also shows another interesting result. The percentage of hands played gradually falls, yet the number of hands won increases, demonstrating that the player is learning. At the end of the training period less than half of the hands are being played with over 33% of them winning.

Next we consider how the training process affects the number of units the evolving player wins or loses over a specific time period. As highlighted above, the player will soon realise that playing in every pot (and raising it, due to the high learning values) is not the best method of playing poker. As the player begins to adapt, the losing streak eventually levels off and changes into a winning streak, creating a better player, maximising its winnings against a variety of players. Figures 4 and 5 show how the program learns to play poker against two different tables, where a table consists of players of the same playing style.

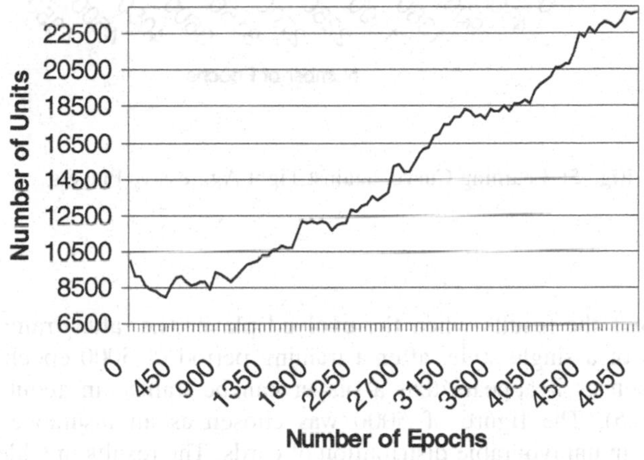

Fig. 4: Learning Curve, against Loose Aggressive Players

From figure 4 and 5 an obvious losing trend can be seen, particularly in figure 5. The evolving player initially loses, before the graph levels off and then rises. Figure 4 has an initial losing period until epoch 350, when the losing streak begins to level off as the learning starts to have an impact. By epoch 1300 the learning process is almost complete, and the program begins to win and eventually wins more units than it initially started with. Figure 5 takes slightly longer to learn, the initial losing streak continues until epoch 650. This losing streak levels off until epoch 2650, when the learning process allows the player to regain its earlier losses and by epoch 3600 the evolving player is back in the black. Figure 4 and 5 emphasises that learning against a table of Loose Aggressive players is quicker than that of a table of Tight Aggressive players due to the fact that tight players play less hands themselves. In addition, the evolving player wins more money against a loose player than a tight player.

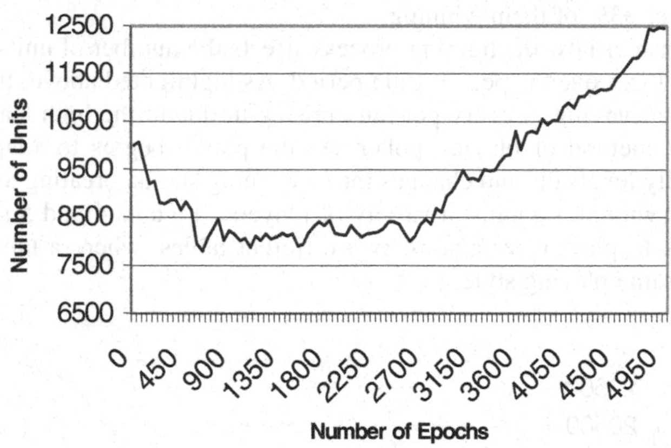

Fig. 5: Learning Curve, against Tight Aggressive Players

Table 6 shows the results when the evolved player (i.e. after training) is played against players of a single style, after a training period of 5000 epochs. A value of 5000 was chosen as it appears that a player can be trained in about 4000 epochs (figures 4 and 5). The figure of 5000 was chosen as an insurance against slow learning due to an unfavourable distribution of cards. The results in table 6 are played over 1000 hands, averaged over five runs

Table 6: Units Won by each player (Player 1 is the evolving player)

Player	Loose Aggressive ($^{played}/won$)	Tight Passive ($^{played}/won$)	Loose Passive ($^{played}/won$)	Tight Aggressive ($^{played}/won$)
1	13342 $^{507}/_{153}$	11123 $^{355}/_{196}$	15632 $^{500}/_{157}$	10816 $^{446}/_{167}$
2	9696 $^{362}/_{196}$	9536 $^{122}/_{83}$	8520 $^{376}/_{200}$	9527 $^{212}/_{147}$
3	8602 $^{386}/_{198}$	9459 $^{119}/_{80}$	8724 $^{373}/_{194}$	9730 $^{216}/_{115}$
4	8879 $^{343}/_{160}$	9420 $^{98}/_{64}$	8189 $^{342}/_{161}$	9837 $^{184}/_{122}$
5	9496 $^{341}/_{169}$	9706 $^{108}/_{68}$	8935 $^{345}/_{135}$	10079 $^{197}/_{129}$

The evolved player beats all the other players, whilst the non-evolving players perform evenly across all of the tables. It is also interesting to note that the evolving player participates in more games, due to a more aggressive nature. However, this does not mean that the player is guaranteed to win. In fact, the opposite is true; the more games played the more likely it is the player will be open to defeat, playing with lower rank cards. Therefore, it suggests that when the evolving player holds a strong hand it takes a very positive approach, by raising frequently.

It is an interesting observation that the non-evolving loose players play more hands than tight players due to an overestimation of their hand value. In general, the loose players lose more than tight players and the evolving player does better against the loose players. It is well known that tight poker players will do better than loose players but there is a balance to be struck otherwise a tight player would only ever bet with the best hand. It would appear that the evolving player has found such a balance.

So far, the players at a given table have all been of the same type. Figure 6 shows how the evolving player competes when there are four different types of player at the same table (we also tested a variety of different players at the same table and the results are similar).

The results confirm our intuition that the loose players do worse than the tight players. It is also pleasing to see that the evolved player beats all the other players.

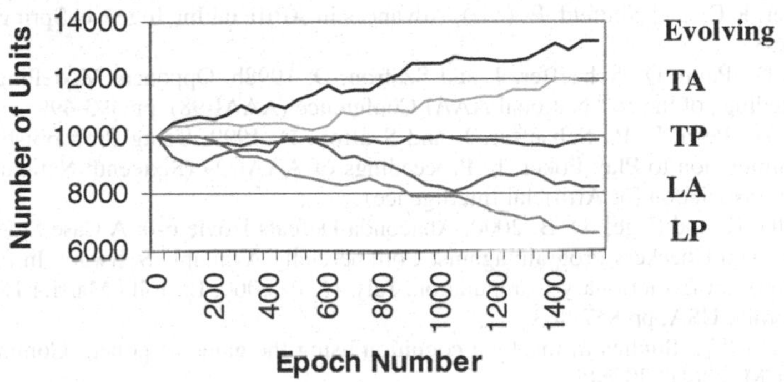

Fig. 6: A Table Consisting of each Type of Player

4. Conclusions and Discussion

This paper has carried out an initial investigation as to how a computer program can learn how to play poker. We realize that this is only an initial investigation but we feel that we have shown the method we propose, although simple in its implementation, does show that an adaptive poker player is a promising research direction. Not only would several competing research groups be able to promote the research domain but, a sustained research strategy could derive benefits in other areas such as bluffing, negotiation and dealing with imperfect information. These insights would be valuable in domains such as on-line auctions, game playing theory, negotiating and real world economics.

Our current research plans will consider using Texas Hold 'Em as a more suitable poker variant. We are also experimenting with evolutionary strategies in place of the simple learning technique we currently employ. We also plan to experiment with co-evolution so that different strategies have to fight to survive to a future generation. Finally, we will also incorporate bluffing and negotiation so as we feel these elements are needed in order to compete with the best human players.

References

Barone L. and While L. 1998. Evolving Computer Opponents to Play a Game of Simplified Poker. In proceedings of the 1998 International Conference on Evolutionary Computation (ICEC'98), pp 108-113

Barone L. and While L. 1999. An Adaptive Learning Model for Simplified Poker Using Evolutionary Algorithms. In proceedings of Congress of Evolutionary Computation 1999 (CEC'99), July 6-9, Washington DC, pp 153-160.

Barone L. and While L. 2000. Adaptive Learning for Poker. In proceedings of the Genetic and Evolutionary Computation Conference 2000 (GECCO'2000), July 10-12, Las Vegas, Nevada, pp 560-573

Billings, D., Papp, D., Schaeffer, J. and Szafron, D. 1998a. Poker as a Testbed for AI Research. In Proceedings of AI'98, The Twelfth Canadian Conference on Artificial Intelligence, Mercer, R.E., and Neufeld, E. (eds), Advances in Artificial Intelligence, Springer-Verlag, pp 228-238

Billings, D., Papp, D., Schaeffer, J. and Szafron, D. 1998b. Opponent Modelling in Poker. In Proceedings of the 15th National AAAI Conference (AAAI-98), pp 493-499

Billings, D., Pe•a, L, P., Schaeffer, J. and Szafron, D. 1999. Using Probabilistic Knowledge and Simulation to Play Poker. In Proceedings of AAAI-99 (Sixteenth National Conference of the Association for Artificial Intelligence).

Chellapilla, K. and Fogel, D. B. 2000. Anaconda Defeats Hoyle 6-0: A Case Study Competing an Evolved Checkers Program against Commercially Available Software. In Proceedings of Congress on Evolutionary Computation, July 16-19 2000, La Jolla Marriot Hotel, La Jolla, California, USA, pp 857-863

Findler N. 1977. Studies in machine cognition using the game of poker. Communications of the ACM, 20(4):230-245.

Fogel D. 2001. Blondie24: Playing at the Edge of AI, Morgan Kaufmann, ISBN 1-55860-783-8

Hamilton, S., Garber, L. 1997. Deep Blue's Hardware-Software Synergy. IEEE, pp 29-35

Kendall, G and Whitwell, G. 2001. An Evolutionary Approach for the Tuning of a Chess Evaluation Function using Population Dynamics. In proceedings of Congress of Evolutionary Computation 2001 (CEC 2001), May 27-30 2001, COEX, Seoul, Korea, pp 995-1002.

Koller, D. and Pfeffer, A. 1997. Representations and Solutions for Game-Theoritic Problems. Artificial Intelligence 94(1-2), pp 167-215

Neumann, J von and Morgenstern, O. 1944. Theory of Gamesand Economic Behavior. Princeton, N.J.: Princeton University Press

Samuel A. L. 1959. Some Studies in Machine Learning using the Game of Checkers. IBM Journal of Research and Development, 3(3), pp 210-229

Samuel A. L. 2000. Some Studies in Machine Learning using the Game of Checkers. IBM Journal of Research and Development, Vol. 44 No. 1/2 January/March, pp 207-226

Schaeffer, J. 1996. One Jump Ahead: Challenging Human Supremacy in Checkers, Springer, Berlin

Schaeffer, J., Billings, D., Pe•a, L, P. and Szafron, D. 1999. Learning to Play Strong Poker. In Proceedings of the Sixteenth International Conference on Machine Learning (ICML-99) (invited paper)

Sklansky, D. 1994. Theory of Poker. Two Plus Two Publishing, ISBN 1-880685-00-0

Sklansky, D. 1996. Hold'em Poker. Two Plus Two Publishing, ISBN 1-880685-08-6

Acquiring Adaptation Knowledge for CBR with MIKAS

Abdus Salam Khan and Achim Hoffmann

School of Computer Science and Engineering
The University of New South Wales, Sydney 2052, AUSTRALIA
{askhan,achim}@cse.unsw.edu.au

Abstract. This paper presents our approach and a fully implemented system for incrementally building complex adaptation functions for case-based reasoning (CBR) systems.
Building a CBR system still remains a difficult task due to the difficulties of developing suitable retrieval and adaptation mechanisms for a given application. To address these difficulties, we extended the basic Ripple Down Rules framework to allow the incremental development of an adaptation function during the use of the system for solving actual problems. In our approach the expert is only required to provide explanations of why, for a given problem, a certain adaptation step should be taken. Incrementally a complex adaptation function as a systematic composition of many simple adaptation functions is developed. Our approach is effective with respect to both, the development of highly tailored and complex adaptation functions for CBR as well as the provision of an intuitive and feasible approach for the expert.
The approach has been implemented in our CBR system MIKAS, for the design of menus according to dietary requirements.
In this paper we present experimental evidence for the suitability of our approach to address the adaptation problem in the development of CBR systems.

1 Introduction

Case-Based Reasoning (CBR) is an AI approach to build intelligent systems which increasingly finds entry into the industrial practice. The basic idea is to solve new problems by remembering solutions to problems which are similar to the current problem. Usually, one or multiple cases are remembered, which are similar to the current problem case and allow the derivation of a solution for the current problem case from the solutions of the remembered cases. If necessary, a remembered case is modified in a way that at least parts of the case is reused. This process is known as the case adaptation [4]. A major practical advantage in CBR is the fact that experts are often eager to tell their "war stories" - the cases they encountered. This is opposed to the situation where experts are asked to provide abstract general rules of what they do, which is a much harder task for them.

M. Brooks, D. Corbett, and M. Stumptner (Eds.): AI 2001, LNAI 2256, pp. 201–212, 2001.

However, the effectiveness of a CBR system depends not only on having and retrieving relevant cases but also on selecting which retrieved cases to apply and determining how to adapt them to fit new situation [5]. Both, suitable retrieval as well as adaptation of a case will usually require domain-dependent knowledge. Case-based reasoning systems generally do not refine the methods they use to retrieve or adapt prior cases, instead relying on static pre-defined rules or procedures [7]. It is generally impossible to anticipate all the difficulties and problems one may encounter in a domain. As a consequence, the knowledge represented in cases is often insufficient for an effective CBR system. In practice the problem of defining proper adaptation rules represents a major bottleneck for successfully developing CBR systems. The problems are so acute that many CBR applications simply omit case adaptation [11]. This demands the need of acquiring case specific and general domain knowledge as an ongoing process for effective CBR performance.

Experiences from knowledge acquisition for expert systems have also shown that it is very difficult to obtain the relevant knowledge from an expert, as experts are usually unable to provide precise rules which would describe their decisions.

Ripple-Down Rules have been developed as an extremely effective approach for the acquisition of classification knowledge, as they require the expert only to provide explanations of the decision taken in a given situation.

In this paper, we introduce a radically new approach for developing a suitable adaptation function. We encode adaptation knowledge in rules, which somewhat resemble the rules used in the INRECA approach [2]. The experiences in the INRECA project also showed the difficulty of actually encoding the suitable adaptation knowledge [2]. We address this experienced difficulty with our new approach: a new way, how an expert interacts with the system in order to provide suitable adaptation rules. Our approach for the *acquisition of adaptation knowledge* is based on ideas of Ripple-Down Rules [3].

The paper is organised as follows: In section 2, we present the motivation and technical details of our approach. Section 3 illustrates, how the approach is implemented in our menu design system MIKAS. Section 4 presents the results of our ongoing evaluation studies so far. The conclusions are found in section 5.

2 Incremental Knowledge Acquisition for Building CBR Adaptation Functions

2.1 Motivation

Building Case-Based Reasoning systems successfully often requires the development of a specialised retrieval function, which is complemented by a highly specialised adaptation function tailored to the domain. It must be ensured that the retrieved case can be successfully adapted if required.

For example, in our system MIKAS for designing menus according to dietary requirements, cases are menus along with patient descriptions. A suitable menu has not only to match the nutritional requirements but also a large number of special requirements for various health conditions need to be accommodated. Such special requirements may range from avoiding spicy food, over minimising the salt content, to ensuring that all foods come in sufficiently small parts which may even exclude thick drinks, such as milk shakes, due to the patient's difficulties when swallowing.

We lend ideas from Ripple-Down Rules [3], that ensures an incremental coverage of the expert's judgements and decision making. That is, for all problem cases for which the expert provided advice to the system on how to adapt a retrieved case, the system will have to reproduce the expert's performance.

We assume a domain expert will have a sufficient understanding of how to adapt a retrieved case in order to find a solution to the current problem.

2.2 Ripple-Down Rules

The basic idea of Ripple-Down Rules (RDR) [3,8] is to develop a knowledge base by allowing the expert to directly interact with the system and to incrementally add rules to a knowledge base. RDR has been applied successfully in building what appears to be the largest expert system in routine use [6]. It has also been applied to some construction tasks, such as the Sisyphus I problem in [12].

In RDR, the object space to be classified is incrementally subdivided into smaller and smaller partitions, until all objects in each single partition belong to the same class. The rules for subdividing the object space are specified by the expert, whenever an object is encountered, which the system classifies in disagreement with the expert. That is, the current object x falls into a partition p of the object space, which classifies the object incorrectly. Hence, this partition needs to be further subdivided into two partitions p_1, p_2, such that the partition to which x belongs, classifies x correctly. Such a subdivision can be provided by the expert competently and with minimal effort, as the expert is merely required to provide an explanation of why x is different from the previously presented object x_p, which led to the creation of the partition p in the first place. That is, the expert needs only to provide a criterion by which x differs from x_p and which justifies the different classification. To provide such an explanation is usually easy for an expert as it is not much different to explaining their decision to colleagues.

See Figure 1 for an RDR tree. An object is classified by this tree as follows: Initially the 'default rule' in node 1 is evaluated, i.e. class '-' is obtained. Before this becomes the final 'verdict', it is checked whether any 'except' link from the current node exists. If there is such a link, the connected node's condition is checked.

Here, we check the condition of node 2: if "C" is true, then the corresponding class '+' overwrites the previous 'verdict', unless this in turn is overwritten by another except link. If an except link exists, but the connected rule condition is not satisfied, say in node 3, then the nodes along a possibly existing chain of 'if not' links are checked. For instance, if the condition of 2 is satisfied, node 3 is checked. If the condition of node 3 is not satisfied, then node 5 is checked and, if node 5 is not satisfied, node 6 is checked. If any of these nodes 3, 5, or 6 is

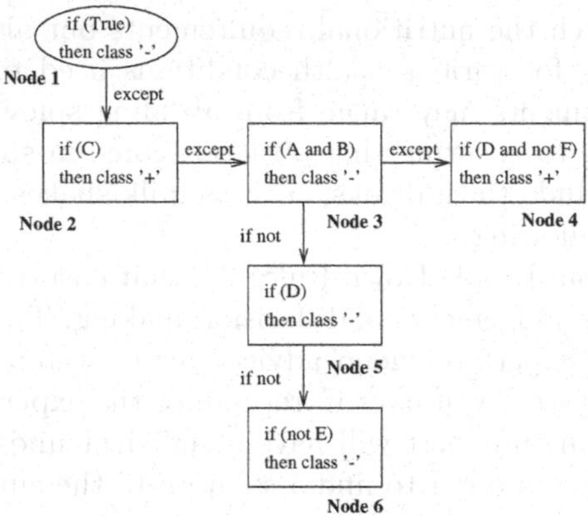

Fig. 1. An example of a Ripple Down Rules tree.

satisfied, the classification of the first satisfied node is the final verdict, unless this node has again an overwriting except link.

If the expert is not satisfied, say with the classification due to node 5, the system asks for a justification in terms of the current object's attributes. This explanation is then used as the condition to a new exception rule to node 5.

2.3 Formal Preliminaries

In general we consider attributes to be either numerical or discrete valued.[1]

We describe a case $C = \{\mathcal{P}, \mathcal{S}\}$ by two attribute vectors with the domains $P_1 \times P_2 \times ... \times P_n$ and $S_1 \times S_2 \times ... \times S_m$ respectively.

- The attribute vector $P = \langle p_1, ..., p_n \rangle$ represents the problem specification.
- The attribute vector $S = \langle s_1, ..., s_m \rangle$ is an ordered list of components and represents a solution to the problem P.

We call *Comps* the *available component list.* This is the general list of all possible types of components which can be included in the design. Hence, the components in the solution are also taken from the general list of available components, i.e. $s, ..., s_m \in Comps$.

Each component $c \in Comps$ is described by a number of attributes, called the *component attributes*, i.e. $c = \langle c_{a,1}, c_{a,2}, ..., c_{a,k} \rangle$. The domain of each component attribute $c_{a,i}$ is denoted by $C_{a,i}$. That is, each component is an element of $C_{a,1} \times ... \times C_{a,k}$.

In our case of diet construction, this is a database of possible foods, describing the nutrient content and food type of each food.

The case base contains cases, which are composed of a problem specification and a solution. The solution is a design, composed of a number of components

[1] Numerical valued attributes may be integer or continuously valued - the critical point is that the possible values have a meaningful order, while the discrete valued attributes have a finite value range without any meaningful order.

which are implicitly related to each other by their respective position in the ordered list of components S.

Generally speaking, the problem statement is composed of two parts:

- an attribute-value vector, stating certain properties of the problem, in order to choose the solution from an appropriate category.
- a collection of constraints, which either require certain values for certain slots in a solution and/or which forbid certain values for certain slots.

  Constraints may also specify that certain combinations of values of multiple attributes should or should not occur in a solution.

In the particular case of diet construction, our components are the various foods we have available and they are related to each other by composing the various meals of the day.

In diet construction, there are general constraints such as the required energy and nutrient level of the diet as well as specific constraints such as to choose an appropriate diet for vegetarians or diabetes patients, etc.

Some constraints are explicitly stated in the problem description, e.g., the amounts of the required daily intakes of nutrients for the task of diet construction. Other constraints are not explicitly stated but must be provided by a domain expert. For diet construction, this includes constraints on which types of foods to use for a specific meal to ensure that it represents a sensible composition of foods, such as meat combined with potatoes or rice combined with vegetables or salad.

2.4 Incremental Acquisition of Adaptation Knowledge

After cases have been retrieved, the system tries to adapt the few highest ranked cases in order to fit the current problem.

If the system cannot produce a satisfactory solution, additional adaptation knowledge must be provided to the system. Generally speaking, this can either be a refined retrieval function, or a refinement of the adaptation function. The expert has to decide whether the retrieved cases are feasible to be adapted or whether other cases need to be retrieved.

If the expert decides to adapt the solution of a retrieved case, he/she tries to manually adapt the solution so that a solution for the current problem is found. This adaptation is done by removing and adding components. Subsequently, the system requests explanations for each adaptation action the expert chose. To do so, the expert has to provide a condition under which the chosen adaptation action (the removal or addition of a component) should be executed. This condition is expressed, generally speaking, in terms of the current problem description as well as the retrieved solution to be adapted.

Furthermore, the action needs to be specified beyond being either a deletion or an addition of a component: The particular component which is added or deleted from the particular slot of the solution needs to be specified. This is done again by providing conditions which a component has to meet to be eligible for deletion or addition from or to a particular slot or class of slots. The new rule r' is integrated into the existing Ripple Down Rules structure as an exception to the rule r, which produced the undesired adaptation action, which the expert intends to supersede by the new rule. The system ensures that the expert entered conditions, which do not apply to all those cases, to which the previous rule r applied successfully, i.e. for which rule r led to an adaptation action, which was accepted by the expert.

Abstract actions. The purpose of *abstract actions* is to allow a way of generalisation. An adaptation rule is provided by an expert, who encounters an individual case which needs to be adapted, while observing the system's performance. The expert will be able to decide which component should be replaced by which new component.

However, just to provide the identity of those components will render the CBR system incapable to adapt a case which contains not exactly the same but perhaps a very similar component. Similarly, the new component may need some variation in a new case which need to be adapted. As a consequence, our system lets the expert specify the action, he/she suggests for adaptation of the given case, and then asks the expert to abstract from the individual action and to give a more abstract description of that action (usually a replacement of a component, an increase or decrease in the amount or size of a component).

An abstract action can be considered as a set of rules in itself. That is, depending on the features of the solution to be adapted, the abstract action may result in different changes to a different case. One important aspect is, that numerical feature values can be used to determine numerical aspects of the change. Most notably, the numerical attributes of components which are to be removed or added to the design can be determined by largely simple arithmetic calculations.

Formally, we allow to define abstract actions by a set of rules. Each rule has a condition part as described in the previous subsection and an action part. The action to be specified is either to delete, to add a certain component or to increase or decrease the amount/size of a component, which can be identified using certain attributes of the component and whose numerical attributes can be described using the attribute values of any part of the current case. A *replacement-action* is then composed of a *delete-action* and an *add-action*.

A *delete-action* just needs to identify the component to be deleted. This is done by specifying attribute value ranges for the attributes of components, which have to be matched by the component which is deleted from the current case.

The formal description is essentially the same as for the conditions of adaptation rules as mentioned earlier, although the involved attributes do not describe the case but rather the component. The first component $c = \langle c_{a,1}, \ldots, c_{a,n} \rangle \in Comps$ will be deleted, which is found in the component list of the case and for which the following condition holds:

$$(c_{a,i_{1,min}} \leq c_{a,i_1} \leq c_{a,i_{1,max}} \wedge \ldots \wedge c_{a,i_{k,min}} \leq c_{a,i_k} \leq c_{a,i_{k,max}}),$$

where $c_{a,i_1}, \ldots, c_{a,i_k} \in \{c_{a,1}, \ldots, c_{a,n}\}$.

Similarly, *add-actions* can be defined as follows: add the component $c = \langle c_{a,1}, \ldots, c_{a,n} \rangle$ from the *available component list*, for which the following condition holds:

$$(c_{a,j_{1,min}} \leq c_{a,j_1} \leq c_{a,j_{1,max}} \wedge \ldots \wedge c_{a,j_{k,min}} \leq c_{a,j_k} \leq c_{a,j_{k,max}}),$$

where $c_{a,j_1}, \ldots, c_{a,j_k} \in \{c_{a,1}, \ldots, c_{a,n}\}$.

3 MIKAS: Integrated KA and CBR Workbench

MIKAS implements the above sketched strategy for developing a CBR system. We used our RDR based approach for both phases, case retrieval [10] and adaptation [9]. In this paper, we will focus on the adaptation process and present first experimental results with the fully implemented system.

3.1 The Problem Domain of Diet Construction

A menu is recommended by a dietitian for a patient with specific health conditions. These health conditions represent stringent requirements on the menus to be designed. This does not only include certain amounts of various nutrients which should be contained in the diet. It may also refer to certain ways of preparing foods, e.g., use of spices, certain types of foods (vegetarian, kosher meat, etc.), or certain other aspects of the involved foods, such as their texture or flavour. The significance of this is that for 'normal' menus it seems appropriate to retrieve cases according to how well they match the required nutrients. However, adaptation may be necessary in order to scale the amount of foods to match nutrient requirements or to remove or replace certain types of foods which are unsuitable for the given patient.

Our system MIKAS accepts a description of the patient along with nutritional requirements. Applicable restrictions are not necessarily explicitly given, but acquired, largely in the form of adaptation rules, provided by the expert.

Once a problem description has been entered, the expert considers the retrieved menus. If he/she is not satisfied with the retrieval result, the retrieval function will be enhanced. Otherwise, he/she tries to adapt one of the retrieved menus, using various adaptation steps including the the addition, deletion of food or the increase/decrease of portions.

3.2 A Sketch of a Knowledge Acquisition Session with MIKAS

The patient description of a 60-years old duodenal ulcer patient, who usually has non-vegetarian, English meals was entered into MIKAS. The system retrieved menu 1. The expert did not agree with the retrieved menu for various reasons, including the coffee in the dinner, which is harmful for ulcer patients, etc.

So the expert modified the retrieved menu by taking out the breakfast grapefruit juice which is considered as harmful for the patient. The expert further

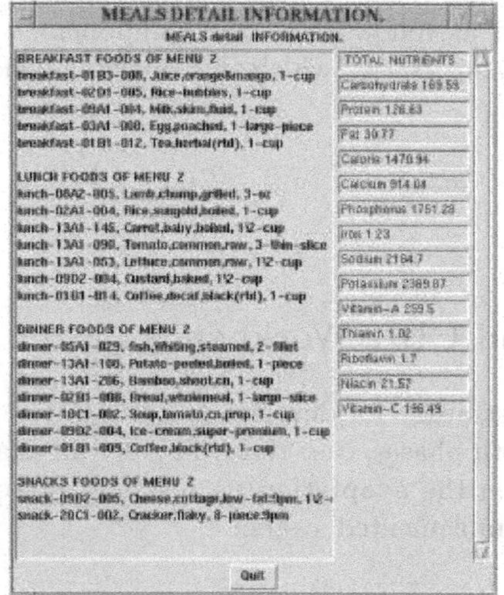

(a) Menu 2

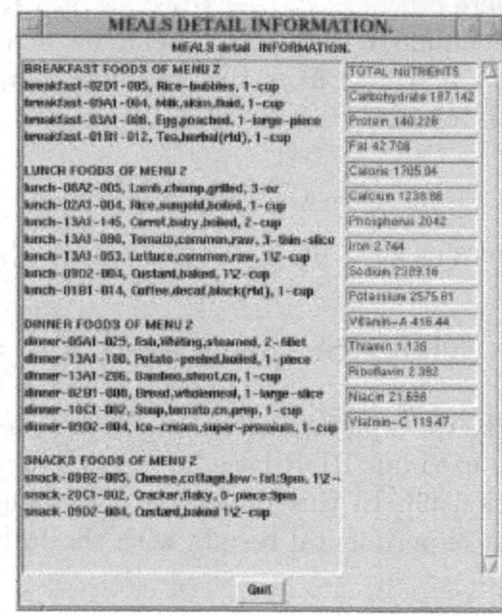

(b) Adapted menu 2

Fig. 2. (a) A new menu before and (b) after automatic adaptation using expert rules entered while adapting a previous case.

increased the portion size of the asparagus in the lunch in order to better match the nutrient requirements. He further deleted the dinner coffee for its caffeine content, and added baked custard to the snack slot for 11am, as an ulcer patient needs frequent meals in regular intervals. At the end of the adaptation steps, the expert found the resulting menu suitable for the patient.

After that, MIKAS asked the expert for justifications for each of the actions taken. That is, the expert was asked to provide conditions, which have to match the current case, under which the corresponding action should be taken. Furthermore, MIKAS asks the expert, to describe to taken action in more abstract terms. That is, if the expert deleted the grapefruit juice from the breakfast slot, the expert was asked whether only grapefruit juice or any fruit juice or even any fruit meeting specifiable characteristics, should be deleted. Furthermore, whether the action should only be applied to the breakfast or to other menu sections as well.

In another session a description of a patient, who is much younger in age but has similar health conditions was entered into MIKAS, together with nutrient requirements. The nutrient requirements for this patient were higher, because he is younger and, hence, needs more energy supply and more protein as he is more active. For this patient, MIKAS retrieved menu 2 in Figure 2 (a) and adapted it to Figure 2 (b). The rules entered before resulted in the following actions when applied to menu 2:

1. there was no grapefruit juice in the breakfast slot, but MIKAS deleted orange&mango juice instead. Reason being that it belonged to the same group of fruit juices, as specified in the abstract action by the expert.

2. MIKAS did not find asparagus in the lunch slot of menu 2, so baby carrots were taken instead and the portion size was increased.
3. MIKAS deleted coffee from the dinner slot.
4. MIKAS added baked custard to the snack slot.

If the expert finds the deletion of orange&mango juice inappropriate in the case of menu 2, he can say so and suggest an alternative action. MIKAS will then ask again for conditions under which the alternative action should be taken. These conditions must differentiate between menu 1 and menu 2 and/or between the first and second patient, so that the first rule would still apply in the first case and the new rule would only apply to menu 2. This is accommodated in the structure of the Ripple-Down Rules and ensures that the task to provide suitable conditions can be easily accomplished by a domain expert.

4 Experimental Studies

We developed a CBR system using the presented incremental knowledge acquisition approach. In our experiments we focussed on the development of the adaption process of our CBR system. The retrieval function was also developed incrementally, but for most cases the retrieval function was not changed, even if the retrieved case appeared rather inappropriate. This was done to better evaluate the potential of building adaptation knowledge bases with our approach.

One of the authors, Abdus Salam Khan, being a trained dietician served as the expert. We focussed on the following specific type of patients: The patients had an English food habit, were aged 35-45, had liver malfunction, and hence the fat and protein content of their diet need to be strictly complied with the given nutrient requirements. Due to varying body weight, physical activities and age of patients in this group different nutrient requirements were given which needed to be matched by a suitable menu.

Due to the varying nutrient requirements, the CBR system retrieved different menus which in turn needed to be adapted. It was usually not possible to simply scale all portion sizes because the nutrient requirements of one patient were not linearly related to other patient's nutrient requirements.

Figure 3 (a) shows how our adaptation knowledge base grew with the number of presented menus. The menus counted were either directly retrieved from the case base or they were already partially adapted by the system and needed further adaptation. Both is shown, the number of rules which were added to the knowledge base and the number of acceptable adaptation actions proposed by the system. Figure 3 (a) shows how the discrepancy between the two curves grows with increasing 'experience'. The increasing 'experience' here means a growing number of presented menus, for which the expert judged whether the system's knowledge base proposed an appropriate adaptation action or not.

After the knowledge base grew to some 180 rules, it was already capable of suggesting adaptation steps which were acceptable in the majority of the presented cases. Given the large variety of patient requirements and retrieved menus, this result is satisfactory. Currently, we are building a larger knowledge

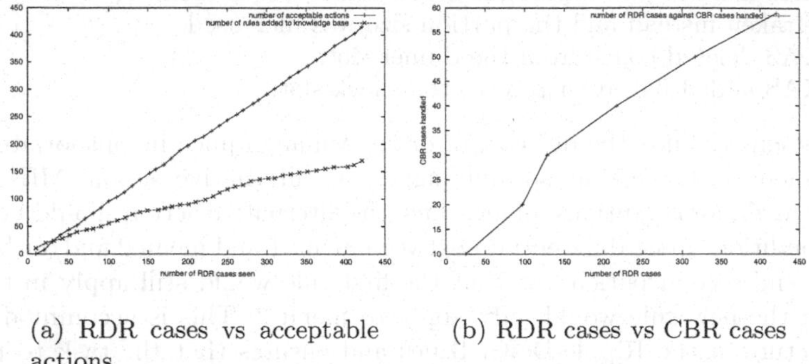

(a) RDR cases vs acceptable actions

(b) RDR cases vs CBR cases

Fig. 3. (a) The growth of the knowledge base and its competence to handle adaptation with the number of menus presented. An RDR case here is a menu that requires adaptation and is presented to the system and the expert. A retrieved menu (a CBR case) may require multiple adaptation steps, and thus would result in multiple presentations of modified menus to the expert. Accordingly, the various menu versions will be counted as multiple RDR cases. (b) How the competence of the adaptation knowledge base in handling cases increases with experience. A single CBR case usually involves a sequence of multiple adaptation actions to be determined by the knowledge base.

base which will also be able to handle a larger diversity of patient types. We will be able to report on the results with a larger knowledge base in the next few months. While the current knowledge base cannot handle the complete adaptation of every retrieved case, it can at least make some useful adaptation steps automatically. A system that assists an expert in semi-automatically constructing a suitable diet for a new patient is already a substantial help.

In Figure 3 (b) it is shown for how many different patients the adaptation was handled by the adaptation knowledge base. For most retrieved cases it took 3–8 adaptation steps to turn a retrieved menu into a satisfactory menu for the patient at hand. There was a relatively large number of retrieved cases where the expert decided at some stage that no further adaptation steps should be taken as the chances of successful adaptation of the retrieved menu appeared too slim. Instead the expert worked on the retrieval function of our CBR system to allow a more suitable case to be retrieved which then in turn can be adapted. We also found that for many problem instances our case base did initially not contain suitable cases at all.

We conducted our experiments with a constant case base to find how well our approach allows to build really flexible adaptation functions. However, in a practical situation, we would rather add a substantial number of the satisfactorily adapted menus to the case base to allow retrieval of a more suitable case for a similar problem instance. The results reported here are intermediate results of ongoing evaluation studies. By the time the camera ready copy is due, we will be able to report on more detailed results.

5 Conclusion

We presented our incremental approach for developing CBR systems where the expert directly interacts with the system and adds to its knowledge base during use of the system. Our implemented knowledge acquisition workbench MIKAS also allows the rapid development of expert support systems, which are not required to produce a complete design (or case adaptation more generally), but may produce an almost satisfactory design which is then manually completed by the domain expert. While completing the design, the system will interact with the expert in order to extend its knowledge base such that it is able to handle the current design automatically. Our experiments indicated the feasibility of our approach for complex design problems such as diet construction.

Our experiments showed that the acquisition of effective adaptation knowledge for a limited range of problem cases is effective. The required knowledge can be provided by an expert and can be organised into a Ripple Down Rules like structure with relative ease. While our experimental results need to be complemented by a more complete study which is currently underway, the preliminary results are very encouraging. Our approach offers an alternative to the traditional labour and time-intensive approaches for building CBR systems. We believe that the presented approach can also be adapted for allowing the development of CBR systems for many other design tasks, helpdesk systems and other applications, where CBR systems have been successfully employed recently, see e.g. [1,13]. The strengths of our approach include the following:

- it allows a domain expert to directly interact with the system without the need for a knowledge engineer or a system engineer. Adaptation rules are entered by the expert. The expert is guided by the system in providing suitable conditions for the rule's application.
- the expert is only required to explain, why certain solutions should be adapted in the demonstrated way for a given problem. This is much easier than to provide general rules for adaptation. In our approach, the expert needs only to justify the particular adaptation steps he chose.
- If an explanation results in overly general adaptation rules, this will be repaired as soon as the expert encounters a situation, in which the system would perform unsuitable adaptations.
- The integration of the incremental KA approach into a CBR system will hopefully result in substantially less effort on the side of the expert to build a satisfactory knowledge base compared to incremental KA that targets complete construction tasks from scratch such as [12].

Open problems which will be addressed in future research include the smooth integration of the case retrieval and case adaptation process. At this stage, we asked the expert to adapt a retrieved case if possible at all. Modifying the retrieval function in a CBR system may alleviate the difficulty of developing a suitable adaptation function substantially, as less adaptation is needed if a more suitable case can already be found in the case base.

In order to allow a balanced development of both, we envisage to provide support tools for the expert, such that the expert can quickly see what the system would do with a possible candidate case that has not been retrieved by the current retrieval function, but might be retrieved if the expert decides to modify the retrieval function. For the quick retrieval of a suitable case from the case base, a suitable query language is needed that allows the expert to try various queries in order to identify a case that should be retrieved.

References

1. Stefania Bandini and Sara Manzoni. A support system based on CBR for the design of rubber compounds in motor racing. In *Proceeding European Workshop on Case-Based Reasoning*, pages 348–357. Springer-Verlag, Germany, 2000.
2. R. Bergmann, S. Breen, E. Fayol, M. Goker, M. Manago, S. Schmitt, J. Schumacher, A. Stahl, S. Wess, and W. Wilke. Collecting experience on the systematic development of CBR applications using the INRECA methodology. In *Proceedings of the European Workshop on Case-Based Reasoning, EWCBR98*, 1998.
3. Paul Compton, Glen Edwards, Byeong Kang, Leslie Lazarus, Ron Malor, Phil Preston, and Ashwin Srinivasan. Ripple down rules: Turning knowledge acquisition into knowledge maintenance. *Artificial Intelligence in Medicine*, 4:463–475, 1992.
4. Marling C.R. *Integrating case-based and rule-based reasoning in knowledge-based systems development.* PhD thesis, Case Western Reserve University, Department of Computer Engineering and Science, August 1996.
5. Leake D.B., Kinley A., and Wilson D. Multistrategy learning to apply cases for case-based reasoning. In *Proceedings of the Third International Workshop on Multistrategy Learning*, Menlo Park, California, 1996. AAAI Press.
6. G. Edwards et. al. Peirs: a pathologist maintained expert system for the interpretation of chemical pathology reports. *Pathology*, (25):27–34, 1993.
7. Munoz-Avilla H. and Hendler J.A. Conversational case-based planning. *Review of applied Expert System*, 5:163–174, 1999.
8. Byeong Kang and Paul Compton. A maintenance approach to case-based reasoning. In J.P. Haton, K. Keane, and M. Manago, editors, *Advances in Case-Based Reasoning*, pages 226–239. Springer-Verlag, 1995.
9. Abdus Khan and Achim Hoffmann. A new approach for the incremental development of adaptation functions for CBR. In *Proceedings of the European Workshop on Case-Based Reasoning*, pages 260–272, Italy, 2000. Springer-Verlag.
10. A.S. Khan and A. Hoffmann. Incremental acquisition of retrieval knowledge for case-based reasoning. In *Proceedings of the Fourth Australian Knowledge Acquisition Workshop*, pages 72–86, Sydney, Australia, December 5-6 1999. University of New South Wales.
11. D.B. Leake. Combining rules and cases to learn case adaptation. In *Proceedings of the Seventeenth Annual Conference of the Cognitive Science*, pages 84–89, 1995.
12. Debbie Richards and Paul Compton. Revisiting sisyphus I - an incremental approach to resoruce allocation using ripple down rules. In *Proceedings of the* 12th *Workshop on Knowledge Acquisition, Modeling and Management*, pages 7.1–7.21, Banff, Canada, 1999.
13. Rainer Schmidt and Lothar Gierl. Evaluation strategies for generalised cases within a case-based reasoning antibiotics therapy advice system. In *Proceeding European Workshop on Case-Based Reasoning*, pages 491–503. Springer-Verlag, Germany, 2000.

A Real-Time Region-Based Motion Segmentation Using Adaptive Thresholding and K-Means Clustering

Jong Bae Kim [1], Hye Sun Park [1], Min Ho Park [2], and Hang Joon Kim [1]

[1] Kyungpook National University, Computer Engineering, 702-701, 1370, Sangyuk-dong, Puk-gu, Taegu, South Korea
{kjblove, hspark, kimhj}@ailab.knu.ac.kr
[2] Kyungpook National University, Computer Center
{mhpark}@knu.ac.kr

Abstract. This paper presents an approach for a real-time region-based motion segmentation and tracking using an adaptive thresholding and *k*-means clustering in a scene, with focus on a video monitoring system. In order to reduce the computational load to the motion segmentation, the presented approach is based on the variation regions application of a weighted *k*-means clustering algorithm, followed by a motion-based region merging procedure. To indicate motion mask regions in a scene, instead of determining the threshold value manually, we use an adaptive thresholding method to automatically choose the threshold value. To image segment, the weighted *k*-means clustering algorithm is applied only on the motion mask regions of the current frame. In this way we do not to process the whole image so that the computation time is reduced. The presented method is able to deal with occlusion problems. Results show the validity of the presented method.

1 Introduction

Segmentation and tracking of moving objects from an image sequences are a basic task for several applications of computer vision, e.g., video monitoring system, intelligent-highway system, intrusion surveillance, airport safety, etc [1-4]. Traditionally, the most important task of monitoring safety is based on human visual observation. However, an autonomous system that is able to detect anomalous or dangerous situations can help a human operator, even if it cannot completely replace the human's presence. To facilitate a monitoring system, efficient image detection and segmentation algorithms need to be used. Segmentation of an image usually divides the image contents into semantic regions that can be dealt with as separate objects. A region created by a segmentation algorithm is defined as a set of elements (pixel of images) which are homogeneous in the feature space and connected in the decision space. A region may not have any semantical meaning. One of the crucial elements of a monitoring system is the motion analysis component, which segments moving objects from an image sequence and estimates their motion on the image plane. Moreover, an accurate segmentation of the object is needed in order to estimate the motion accurately. On the other hand, a moving object is characterized by coherent motion characteristics

M. Brooks, D. Corbett, and M. Stumptner (Eds.): AI 2001, LNAI 2256, pp. 213–224, 2001.

over its entire region of support. Therefore, an accurate estimate of the motion is required in order to obtain an accurate segmentation of the object. These tasks are difficult for several reasons: there are multiple moving objects; the objects of interest are usually small (in the image plane) and poorly textured; illumination conditions may be poor and change rapidly; and multiple occlusions are likely and the environment may be cluttered. However, probably the most challenging obstacle is the requirement of real-time performance using relatively cheap hardware. Besides, many automatic surveillance applications operate in real-time, so good automatic segmentation algorithms are required. These specific difficulties and constraints mandate that a standard off-the-shelf algorithm cannot usually be applied. Instead, special motion segmentation algorithms must be designed. Most typical approaches to object segmentation are based mainly on motion information, segmentation by dominant motion analysis [5], MRF modeling [6-8], and Bayesian methods [9,8]. A major problem with all of the above methods is that their performances are limited by the accuracy of the motion estimation, which is itself an ill-posed problem. The pixel-based motion segmentation method, including [11], suffers from the drawback that the resulting segmentation map may contain isolated labels. Motion segmentation algorithms, including the temporal image difference-based method [12], motion-based method [13] and model-based method [14], were developed. These methods, however, suffers from poor detection in the real-world environment. What is worse, since the viewer moves in a dynamic scene, it is difficult to extract only the regions corresponding to moving objects using familiar methods of motion segmentation. These problems have made the visual perception of the real-world environment a difficult and challenging topic of computer vision. At present, the segmentation of moving objects from images is not satisfactory. Although the *k*-means clustering algorithm is simple in principle, it requires a lot of computation and the threshold is usual selection by trial and error.

In this paper, a procedure for region-based motion segmentation and tracking of image sequences is presented. As a basis for region-based motion segmentation, motion detection with an adaptive threshold method [15,16], region segmentation with the weighted *k*-means clustering algorithm and motion segmentation with motion information method are used. Region-based approaches define groups of connected pixels that are detected as belonging to a signal object that is moving with a different motion from its neighboring regions. Region tracking is less sensitive to occlusion due to the extensive information that regions supply. The rest of this paper is organized as follows. In Section 2, we present the method of region-based motion segmentation and tracking from an image sequence. The section includes four parts: *motion detection*, *region segmentation*, *motion estimation* and *motion segmentation*. Experimental results of this method are shown in Section 3 and finally, conclusions are given in Section 4.

2 Outline of the Process

Fig. 1 shows the process of the presented method. First, in the motion detection, the rough position of moving regions in an image is determined. From the motion detection a motion mask is created, to indicate the moving region position on the current frame. To indicate binary motion mask, instead of manually determining the threshold value, which is the case in most vision-based systems, we use an adaptive threshold to automatically choose the threshold value for motion detection. Then, we apply the weighted *k*-means clustering to the motion mask on gray level image of the current frame. By this way we do not need to process the whole image, which saves computation time. Only in the segmented regions, do estimate the motion by the heuristic measures (matching criteria). Thus, the regions that have similar motion vectors are merged. When the presented method tested on real image sequence, the performance is robust not only in the variation of luminance conditions and the change of environment condition, but also in the occlusion among the moving objects.

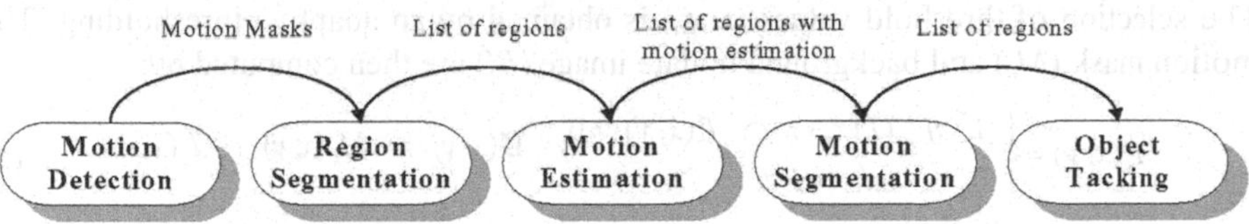

Fig. 1. The process sequence of the presented method

2.1 Motion Detection

The first phase of the presented algorithm indicates the moving objects' position in the current frame. In general, the motion of the moving object entails intensity changes in magnitude so that intensity changes are important cues for locating moving objects in time and space. These intensity changes can be represented not only by the differences between two successive images, but also by the differences between the current image and background image. To indicate the variation region from the background, instead of determining the threshold value manually, our present method used an adaptive thresholding to automatically choose the threshold value for the variation region detection method. In Fig. 2, we show the motion detection phase.

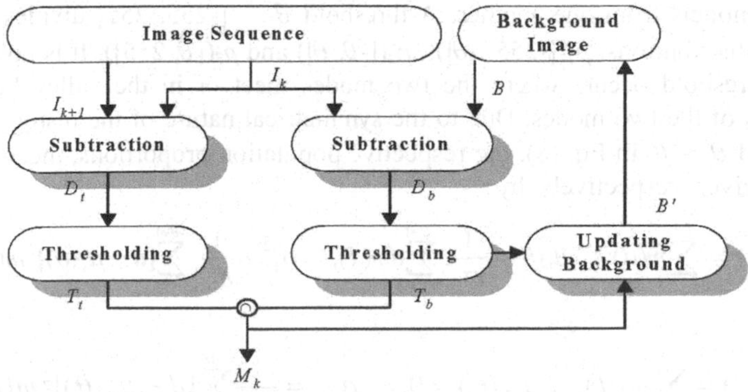

Fig. 2. Flow of the motion detection process

2.1.1 Variation Region Detection

The motion detection phase receives the input of a pair of gray-level images, I_k, I_{k+1}, and a predefined background image, B, in which no object exists. The output are the variance regions of the image area where significant changes have been detected. The two subtraction images ($D_t(x,y) = |I_k(x,y) - I_{k+1}(x,y)|$, $D_b(x,y) = |I_k(x,y) - B(x,y)|$) between the kth frame, k+1th frame and background image are computed. The two difference images (T_t, T_b) are then computed by:

$$T_t(x,y) = \begin{cases} 1, & if\ D_t(x,y) > t_t \\ 0, & otherwise \end{cases}, \quad T_b(x,y) = \begin{cases} 1, & if\ D_b(x,y) > t_b \\ 0, & otherwise \end{cases}. \tag{1}$$

The selection of threshold values (t_t, t_b) is obtained by an adaptive thresholding. The motion mask (M_k) and background update image (B') are then computed by:

$$M_k(x,y) = \begin{cases} 1, & if\ (T_t(x,y) \cap T_b(x,y)) \neq 0 \\ 0, & otherwise \end{cases}, \quad B'(x,y) = M_k(x,y) - T_b(x,y). \tag{2}$$

2.1.2 Adaptive Thresholding

This method is a histogram-based approach to thresholding for motion detection and can be used to discard temporal variations due to illumination. The method for threshold selection was derived under the assumption that the histogram generated from the difference between two gray-level images contains three values combined with additive Gaussian noise. The mixture probability density function of the difference value is

$$P(d) = \frac{\omega_1}{\sqrt{2\pi}\sigma_1}\exp\left[-\frac{(d-\mu_1)^2}{2\sigma_1^2}\right] + \frac{\omega_2}{\sqrt{2\pi}\sigma_2}\exp\left[-\frac{(d-\mu_2)^2}{2\sigma_2^2}\right] + \frac{\omega_3}{\sqrt{2\pi}\sigma_3}\exp\left[-\frac{(d-\mu_3)^2}{2\sigma_3^2}\right] \tag{3}$$

where ${}_i$ is the population proportion, ${}_i$ is mean value of the three difference levels and σ_i is the standard deviation about the means. As a result, the threshold problem is formulated as determination of the best thresholds, θ_1 and θ_2, separating the three Gaussian models from one another. A threshold θ [-255, 255] divides the image into three distributions: $p_1([-255, -\theta])$, $p_2([-\theta, \theta])$ and $p_3([\theta, 255])$. It is noted that the optimal threshold occurs where the two modes meet or in the valley between the maximums of the two modes. Due to the symmetrical nature of the histogram model, $\theta_1 = -\theta$ and $\theta_2 = \theta$. In Eq. (8), the respective population proportions, means and variances are given, respectively, by

$$\varpi_1(\theta) = \sum_{d=-255}^{-\theta-1} m(d), \quad \mu_1(\theta) = \frac{1}{\varpi_1}\sum_{d=-255}^{-\theta-1} dm(d), \quad \sigma_1^{\ 2} = \frac{1}{\varpi_1}\sum_{d=-255}^{-\theta-1}[d-\mu_1(\theta)]^2 m(d) \tag{4}$$

$$\varpi_2(\theta) = \sum_{d=\theta}^{-\theta} m(d), \quad \mu_2(\theta) = 0, \quad \sigma_2^{\ 2} = \frac{1}{\varpi_2}\sum_{d=\theta}^{-\theta}[d-\mu_2(\theta)]^2 m(d) \tag{5}$$

$$\varpi_3(\theta)=\sum_{d=\theta+1}^{255} m(d),\quad \mu_3(\theta)=\frac{1}{\varpi_3}\sum_{d=\theta+1}^{255} dm(d),\quad \sigma_3^{\ 2}=\frac{1}{\varpi_3}\sum_{d=\theta+1}^{255}[d-\mu_3(\theta)]^2 m(d)\cdot \tag{6}$$

Let *m(d)* be the probability of a difference values and *n* is the spatial domain of the difference image, which is defined as

$$m(d)=\frac{1}{n}num(d)\,. \tag{7}$$

In Eq. (12), *num(•)* is the function counting of the pixels. The threshold value (θ) is determined by fitting criterion defined as follows

$$e=\frac{1}{n}\sum_{d=-255}^{255}[P(d)-m(d)]^2\cdot \tag{8}$$

A best fit between the data and Gaussian model is found by minimizing the mean squared error between the mixture density (*P(d)*) and the probability of a difference value (*m(d)*). Fig. 3 shows the histogram probability distribution and the Gaussian model. θ in Fig. 3 that minimizes the fitting criterion is considered the threshold value separating Gaussian models from one another.

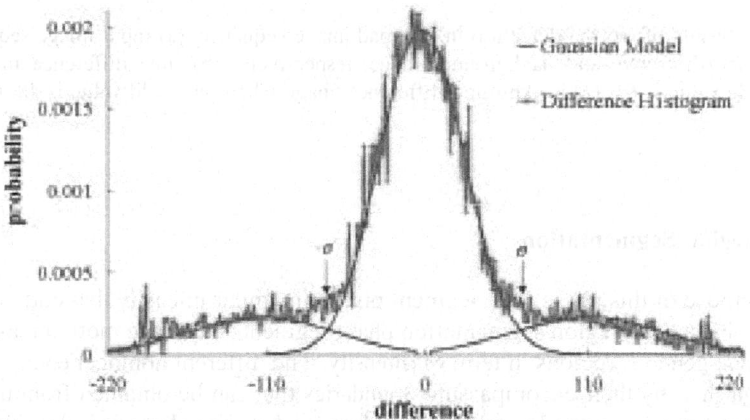

Fig. 3. Probability of difference values and Gaussian model for the image sequence of Fig. 4

At the end of this phase, a binary motion mask (M_k) is obtained where changing pixels are set to one and background pixels set to zero. This operator is spontaneously immune to noise due to the non-repeatability of noise in two subsequent different frames and filters isolated spots arising from small movements of sensors. Moreover, in the experiments on image sequences, the points of $M_k(x,y)$ occupied by moving objects, therefore, precisely locate moving objects. Next, a chain-code-based approach is able to separate loosely connected moving points with simple morphological operations. Then, we apply the morphological operation on the difference image to remove the noise and get the mask for the region segmentation. This technique locates the rough positions of the moving objects. The only area where both frame differences are meaningful is at the location of the *k*th frame. Fig. 4 shows the results of the motion detection phase using the threshold value (θ) in Fig. 3.

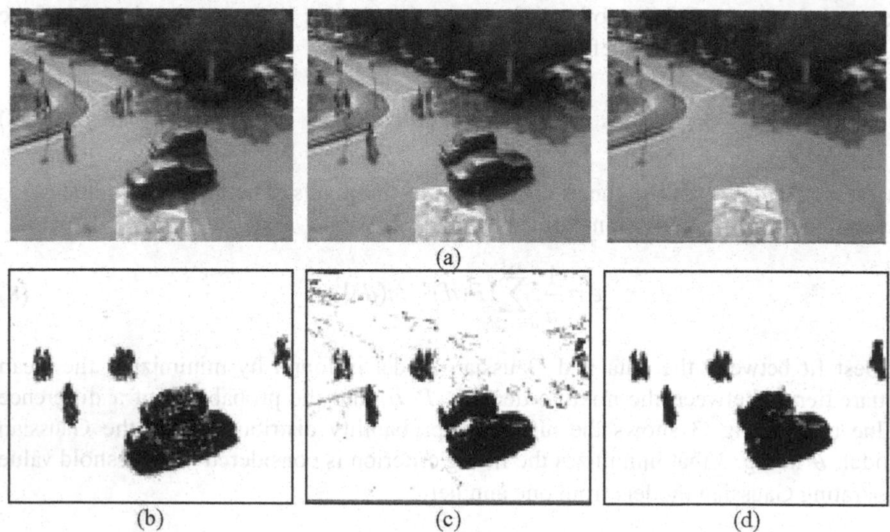

Fig. 4. Results of motion detection in the road image sequence. (a) input image sequence, *k*th frame, *k+1*th frame, and background image, respectively; (b) time difference image when threshold value is 61; (c) background difference image when threshold value is 48; (d) motion mask

2.2 Region Segmentation

The purpose of this phase is to segment pixels of similar intensity that correspond to a single object. The region segmentation phase segments the entire motion mask regions into homogeneous regions in term of intensity. The different homogeneous regions are distinguished by their encompassing boundaries that can be obtained from this phase. Our segmentation method is based on a classical *k*-means clustering algorithm. Pixel intensity allows the algorithm to separate the pixels of different regions as well as consider to the image coordinates concentration of the pixels in the motion mask region.

2.2.1 *K*-Means Clustering

The region segmentation algorithm can be thought of a variation of the *k*-means clustering algorithm [16,17] and incorporates three feature vectors for each pixel. The feature vectors are the coordinates and intensity. It is used to look for the region that minimizes a weighted squared Euclidean distance measure. The iteration stops when the maximum shift of the clusters drops blows a specified value. The initial cluster means choose arbitrarily. Pixel p^i is assigned to cluster c^j, j = 1, 2,..., number of clusters. In practice, each motion mask region to the number of j is determined by M_k, which is the number of detected motion mask regions, $j = M_k + 2$. At each iteration, a pixel (i) of the original cluster is assigned to that new cluster (j) which minimizes the following criterion:

$$e^{ij} = \left(p^i - f^j\right)W^j\left(p^i - f^j\right) \tag{9}$$

where p^i is a vector composed of the coordinates and the intensity of the pixel i, f^j is the vector composed of the mean coordinates and mean intensity of the cluster j, $f^j = \left(m_x^j, m_y^j, m_i^j\right)$ and W^j is a 3x3 diagonal matrix that contains a weight for each feature of clusters $\left(\omega_x^j, \omega_y^j, \omega_i^j\right)$. W^j is determined by minimizing the distance between the pixels in cluster c^j. These weights are given by [18].

$$\omega_x^j = \frac{c^j}{\sigma_x^j}, \quad \omega_y^j = \frac{c^j}{\sigma_y^j}, \quad \omega_i^j = \frac{c^j}{\sigma_i^j} \tag{10}$$

$$c^j = \left(\sigma_x^j \sigma_y^j \sigma_i^j\right)^{1/3} \tag{11}$$

$$\left(\sigma_x^j\right)^2 = \frac{1}{(N_j - 1)} \sum_{x \in c^j}^{N_j} (x - m_x^j)^2 \tag{12}$$

where N_j is the number of pixels in cluster j and σ_x^j, σ_y^j are the coordinates (x, y) variance and σ_i^j is intensity (i) variance of the cluster j. Every cluster has a matrix W. This matrix is recalculated every five iterations. Fig. 5 shows the segmenting results of a simplified image. The simplified image exhibits that the detailed texture of the moving object body and gray information of the original image are smoothed out, but the object shape is preserved. Moreover, the number of segmented regions are decreases in the detected moving region.

2.3 Motion Estimation

This phase is finding the motion information of segmented regions that minimizes the sum of displaced region differences. The summation is done over all pixels of the segmented region by the region segmentation phase. The regions are associated with a three-dimensional (3-D) feature vector describing the coordinates and the gray level. Our motion estimation method is based on the matching of the feature vector of regions by considering the displaced region difference as well. One fundamental approach is to math on portion of an image at time t, I_t, with each portion of the success sive image at $t+1$, I_{t+1}, using image features such as a coordinate and intensity. In estimating motion information, the algorithm used the matching window to compute t-

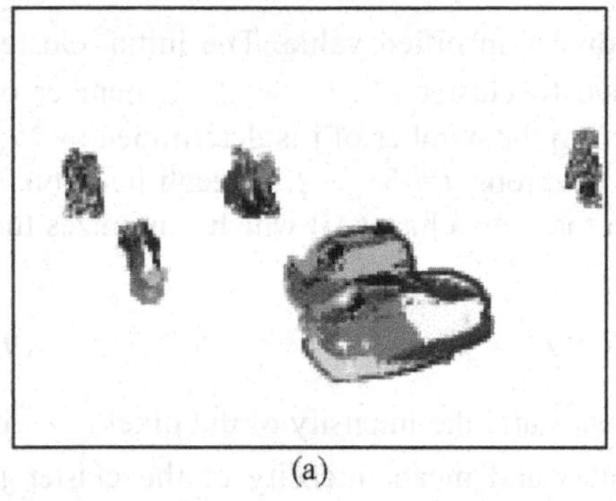

(a)

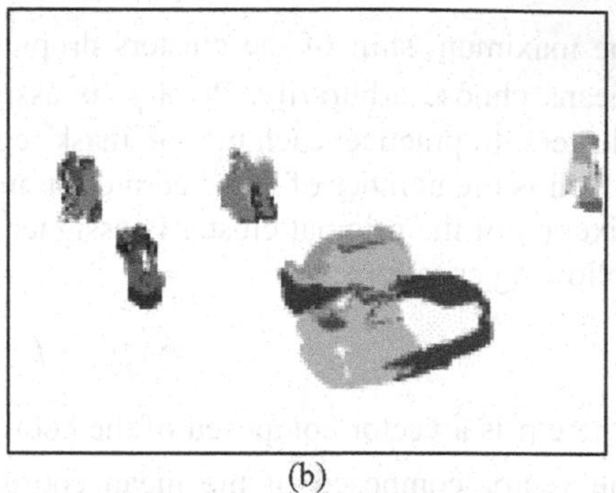

(b)

Fig. 5. Segmenting results of the original and simplified images when the number of clusters is five. (a) segmented image of original image in Fig 4; (b) segmented image of simplified image on motion mask regions

he similarity between the two portions in I_t and I_{t+1}. The motion mask region was used to limit the search for the possible location of a particular pixel in the frame I_{t+1}. Within the motion mask region, the new location of (*x*, *y*) is found by the displaced region difference. We minimize error measure, *ME*, defined as follows:

$$ME\,(u_x, v_y) = \frac{1}{N_j} \sum_{(x,y)\in c^j} \left(I_t(x,y) - I_{t+1}(x+u_x, y+v_y)\right) \qquad \textbf{(13)}$$

where c^j is the cluster *j*, u_x and v_y are motion vectors and $I_t(x,y)$ and $I_{t+1}(x,y)$ are pixel intensity values at location (*x*,*y*) in the segmented region. Fig. 6 (a) and (b) shows the motion information of the segmented region by the region segmentation phase. The motion information is able to separate occlusions with difference direction.

2.4 Motion Segmentation

As mentioned in the region segmentation phase, the *k*-means clustering algorithm was applied to partition the images into small regions that are homogenous in terms of intensity. Therefore, the image partition into many homogeneous regions results in oversegmentation. Since the *k*-means clustering algorithm leads image partition to oversegmentation, a region-merging step is required to solve the oversegmentation problem. The oversegmented partition can also be relaxed using a motion information similarity measure. In this phase, the motion information results from the motion estimation phase are merged into their neighboring regions where the small regions are most similar based on the motion information Fig. 6 (c) and (d) shows the result of motion segmentation.

3 Experimental Results

In order to verify the effectiveness of our present method, an experiment was perform-

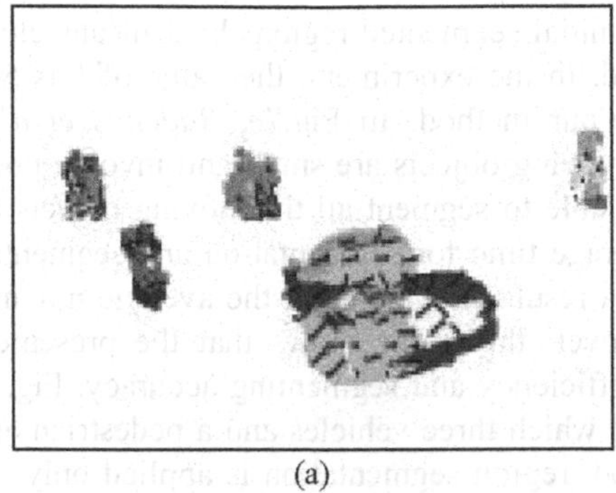
(a)

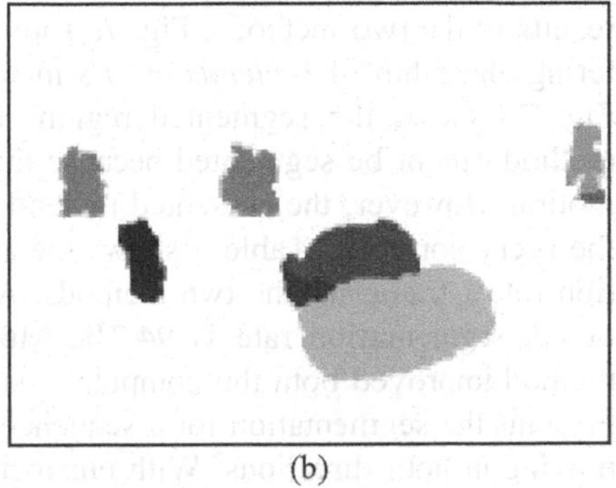
(b)

Fig. 6. Motion estimation and segmentation results. (a) segmented regions with motion vectors; (b) motion segmented image

ed on complex road scenes acquired from a fixed viewpoint. Image sequences are characterized by multiple moving objects, variable illumination conditions, noises, artificial lighting and presence of shadows. We achieve a frame rate of approximately eight frames per second. The acquired images were digitized into 320×240 pixels. The experiments were performed on a Pentium 333-MHz PC with Windows 98 and the algorithm was implemented using MS Visual C++ development tool. The processing each image frame takes 0.19 sec on average. The time depended on the number and size of moving objects present in the image. The average amount of processing time per algorithm phase is summarized in Table 1.

Table 1. Average processing time

Step	Time	Average time
Motion Detection	15-92 ms	48 ms
Region Segmentation	32-103 ms	71ms
Motion Estimation	24-81 ms	36 ms
Motion Segmentation	26-47 ms	32 ms

To show the robustness of the presented method, we performed a noise sensitivity test. The test scenes are a real road image containing multiple vehicles and a human corrupted by adding Gaussian noise with different SNR values. Table 2 gives the percentage of correct moving object region detection versus the increased Gaussian noise with different SNR values. As the rate of noise increased, the rate of correct location decreases. However, the presented method shows an average of 92.5% correct location on the SNR –3dB noise added road images. This shows the robustness of the present method with regard to noise. From the experiment results, we show that the rough position of the moving object is determined. With an adaptive threshold, this method provides better results under an environment with a change in illumination. The present method was effective in reducing the computation time and segmentation error when segmenting moving object in a scene. To prove its effectiveness, it was compared with *Badenas et al.'s* method [19] in average time for moving object segmentation and segmentation rate. Fig. 7 shows the moving object segmentation results of the two methods. Fig. 7*c* shows initial segmented regions by *k*-means clustering algorithm of *Badenas et al's* method. In the experiment, the value of *k* is 50. Fig. 7*d* shows the segmented regions by our method. In Fig.7*e*, *Badenas et al's* method cannot be segmented because the moving objects are small and involve poor motion. However, the presented method is able to segment all the moving objects in the scene correctly. Table 3 shows the average time for segmentation and segmentation rate a frame for the two methods. As a result of evaluation, the average moving object segmentation rate is 94.7%. Moreover, the result shows that the presented method improved both the computational efficiency and segmenting accuracy. Fig. 8 presents the segmentation for a sequence in which three vehicles and a pedestrian are moving in both directions. With our method, region segmentation is applied only on the motion detection regions. This way, It reduce not only the computation time but also the segmentation error of the moving object. The moving object segmentation rate was evaluated by our method. The following procedure was used.

$$\text{Moving object segmentation rate (\%)} = \frac{A}{B}\times 100 \,. \tag{14}$$

A: The number of pixels in the moving region segmented by this method
B: The number of pixels in the moving region extracted manually (Fig. 7(a) white boundary regions)

Table 2. The results of sensitivity analysis

SNR [db]	3	0	-3	-5	-10
Location rate (%)	96.7	96.2	92.5	73	54.7

Table 3. Evaluation of segmentation results

Method	*Badenas et al's* method	The presented method
Average time	0.78 ms	0.16 ms
Segmentation rate	91 %	94.8 %

4 Conclusions

In this work, we have presented an approach for a real-time region-based motion segmenting and tracking of moving objects using an adaptive thresholding and *k*-means clustering on images sequences, with focus on a video monitoring system. The method is based on gray level and motion information of the image sequence. The gray level information is used not only to detect variation regions, but also to segment moving regions. The motion information of our method is used to merge the adjacent regions that have a coherent motion vector. The present method has been tested on an outdoor environment at the intersection of two roads. Experimental results demonstrate the robustness in the noise and deal with occlusions.

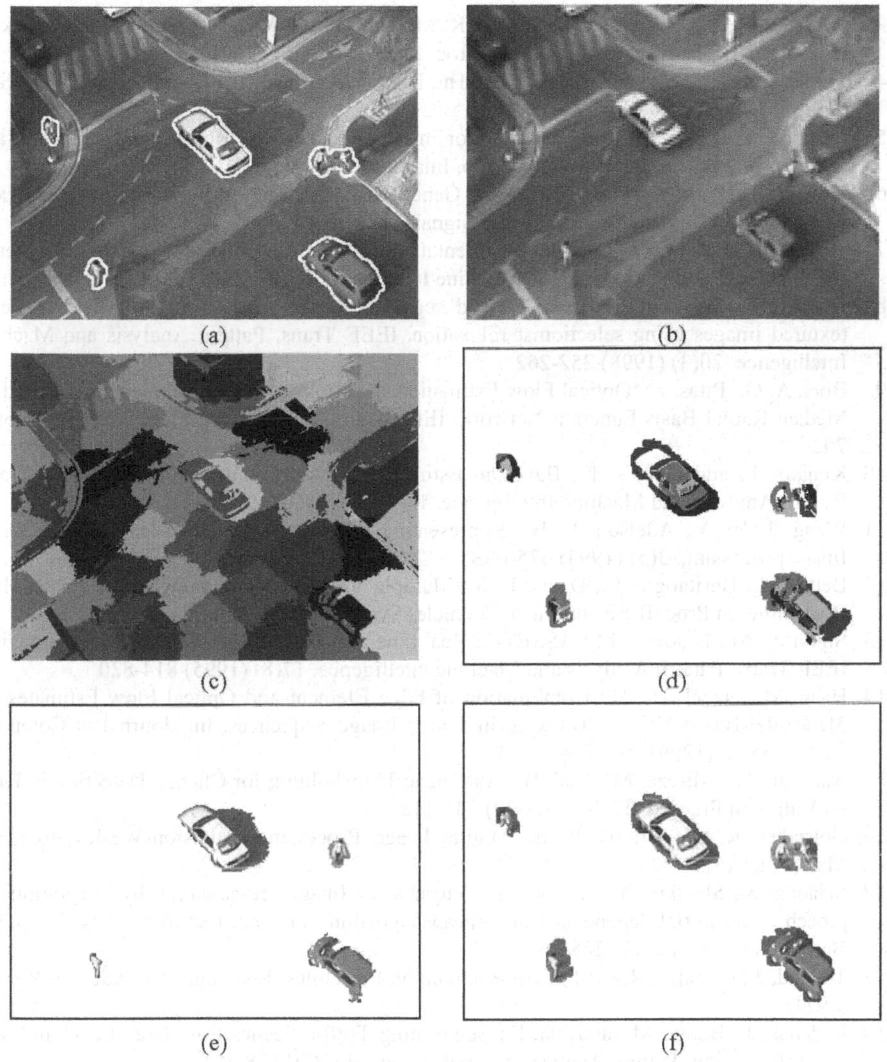

Fig. 7. Result of moving object segmentation. (a), (b) road image sequence; (c), (d) regions segmented by *Badenas et al's* method and the presented method; (e), (f) moving objects segmented by *Badenas et al's* method and the presented method

References

1. Haritaoglu, I., Harwood, D., Davis, L. S.: Real-Time Surveillance of People and Their Activities. IEEE Trans. Pattern Analysis and Machine Intelligence. 22(8) (2000) 809-830
2. Kim, J. B., Lee, C. W., Hwang, S. W., Kim, H. J.: A Real-Time Moving Object Detection for Video Monitoring System. in Proc. ITC-CSCC. 1 (2001) 454-457

3. Kim J. B., Lee, C. W., Yun. T. S., Lee, K. M., Kim, H. J.: Wavelet-based Vehicle Tracking for Automatic Traffic Surveillance. in Proc. IEEE Tencon. 1 (2001) 313-316
4. Sukthankar, R., Stockton, R.: Argues: The Digital Doorman. IEEE Trans. Intelligent System. 16(2) (2001) 14-19
5. Irani, M., Peleg, S.: Motion analysis for image enhancement: Resolution, occlusion, and transparency. Int. Journal of Vis. Comm. Image Rep. 4(4) (1993) 324-335
6. Kim, E. Y., Park, S. H., Kim, H. J.: A Genetic Algorithm based Segmentation of Markov Random Field Modeled Images. IEEE Signal Processing Letters. 7(11) (2000) 301-303
7. Gelgon M., Bouthemy. P.: Video Segmentation by MAP Labeling of Watershed Segments. IEEE Trans. Pattern Analysis and Machine Intelligence 23(3) (2001) 326-332
8. Andrey, P., Tarroux, P.: Unsupervised segmentation of markov random field modeled textured images using selectionist relaxation. IEEE Trans. Pattern Analysis and Machine Intelligence. 20(3) (1998) 252-262
9. Bors, A. G., Pitas, I.: 'Optical Flow Estimation and Moving Object Segmentation Based on Median Radial Basis Function Network. IEEE Trans. Image Processing. 7(5) (1998) 693-702
10. Konard, J., and Dubois, E.: Bayesian Estimation of Motion Vector Fields. IEEE Trans. Pattern Analysis and Machine Intelligence. 14(9) (1992) 910-927
11. Wang, J. Y. A., Adelson, E. H.: Representing moving images with layer. IEEE Trans. Image processing. 3(5) (1994) 625-638
12. Betke, M., Haritaoglu, E., Davis, L. S.: Multiple Vehicle Detection and Tracking in Hard Real-Time. in Proc. IEEE Intelligent Vehicles Symposium. (1996) 351-356
13. Smith, S. M., Brady, J. M.: ASSET-2: Real time motion segmentation and shape tracking. IEEE Trans. Pattern Analysis and Machine Intelligence. 17(8) (1995) 814-820
14. Haag, M., Nagel, H. -H.: Combination of Edge Element and Optical Flow Estimates for 3D-Model-Based Vehicle Tracking in Traffic Image Sequences. Int. Journal of Computer Vision. 35(3) (1999) 295-319
15. Nariman, H., Alireza, M., Neil, B.: Automatic Thresholding for Change Detection in Digital Video. in Proc. SPIE. 4067 (2000) 133-142
16. Gonzalez, R. C., Woods, R. E.: Digital Image Processing. Addision-Wesley, Reading, Massachusetts.
17. Salaoda, S., Shisikui, Y., Tanaka, Y., Yuyama, I.: Image segmentation by integration approach using initial dependence of k-means algorithm. in Proc. Picture Coding Symp.'97. Berlin. Germany. (1997) 265-269
18. Tounad, J., Gonalez, R. C.: Pattern Recognition Principles. Reading. MA: Addison-Wesley (1974)
19. Badenas, J., Bober, M., and Pla, F.: Segmenting Traffic Scenes from Grey Level and Motion Information. Pattern Analysis & Applications. 4 (2001) 28-38

Automatic Cell Classification in Human's Peripheral Blood Images Based on Morphological Image Processing

Kyungsu Kim[1], Jeonghee Jeon[1], WanKyoo Choi[2], Pankoo Kim[3], Yo-Sung Ho[1]

[1] Kwangju Institute of Science and Technology (K-JIST), 1 Oryong-dong Puk-gu, Kwangju, 500-712, Korea,
{arieskim, jhjeon, hoyo}@kjist.ac.kr,

[2] Division of Computer, Electronics & Communiation Engineering, Kwangju University, 591-1 Jinwol-dong Nam-gu, Kwangju, 503-703, Korea,
wkchoi@kwangju.ac.kr

[3] College of Electronics and Information Engineering, Chosun University, Kwangju, 501-759, Korea,
pkkim@chosun.ac.kr

Abstract. A new scheme for automatic analysis and classification of cells in peripheral blood images is presented in this paper. The proposed method can analyze and classify mature red-blood and white-blood cells efficiently. After we identify red-blood and white-blood cells in a blood image captured by a CCD camera attached to a microscope, we extract their features and classify them by a neural network model based on back-propagation learning. While we have fifteen different clusters including the normal one for red-blood cells, there are five different categories for white-blood cells. We also propose a new segmentation algorithm to extract the nucleus and cytoplasm for white-blood cell classification. In addition, we apply the principal component analysis to reduce the dimension of feature vectors efficiently without affecting classification performance. Experimental results demonstrate that the proposed method outperforms the learning vector quantization-3 and the k-nearest neighbor algorithms for blood cell classification.

1 Introduction

Various algorithms for automated analysis and recognition of medical images have been proposed in conjunction with advanced artificial intelligence, image processing, and computer graphics techniques [1], [4], [9], [13]. As consequences, several automatic medical diagnosis systems have been developed to help doctors to diagnose diseases. Especially, red-blood and white-blood cells of human beings provide valuable information to pathologists. Such information is used to diagnose patients' diseases and allows pathologists to identify morphological variations of blood cells. However, the inspection is time-consuming and requires technical knowledge. With computer-aided inspection systems, pathologists can have objective analysis results of blood cell images and the false inspection ratio can be reduced significantly. If some part of the inspection job is automated, a technician can save his or her time and effort substantially. Recently, there was an attempt to differentiate the normal white-blood cell from three kinds of leukemia cells. However, it is a very difficult task even for a specialist [1].

Generally, we can observe red-blood cells, white-blood cells, platelets, and plasmas in the image of the human peripheral blood sample by the microscope. Based on the shape and color of the nucleus and cytoplasm, we can classify white-blood cells into five different types: neutrophil, eosinophil, basophil, lymphocyte, and monocyte, as shown in Figure 1.

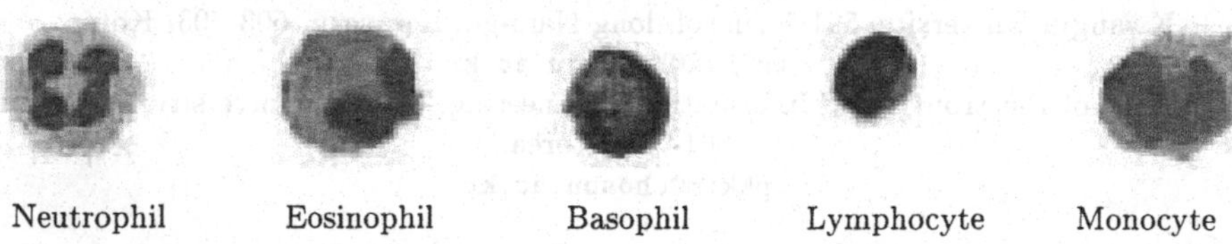

Fig. 1. Mature white-blood cells.

In this paper, we focus on building a practical system that can be used in the hospital. We classify fifteen different types of red-blood cells including the normal one, as shown in Figure 2, referencing hematology literatures and using pathologist's aids [5].

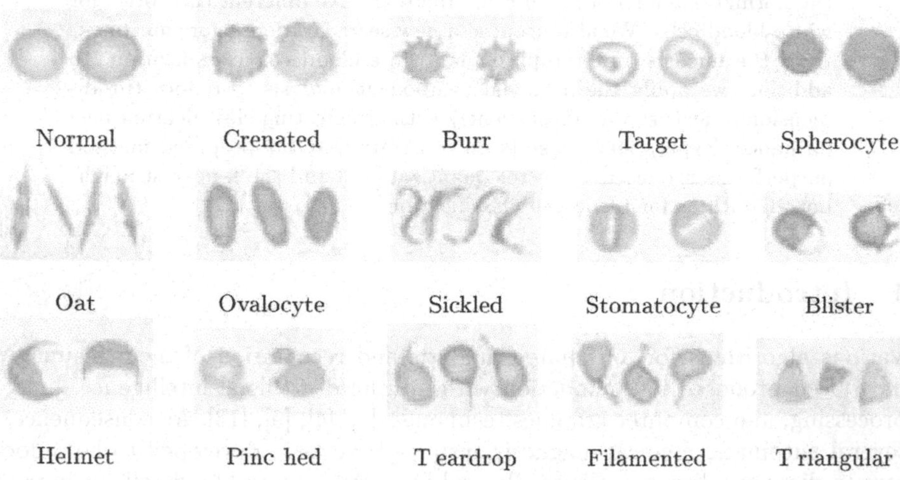

Fig. 2. Morphological shapes of red-blood cells

In the proposed system, we classify and count red-blood and white-blood cells automatically. In our experiment, we design a cell classifier using a neural network model and compare its performance with two other classifiers: learning vector quantization-3 (LVQ-3) and k-nearest neighbor (K-NN) algorithms. We also reduce the number of multi-variate features using the principal component analysis (PCA) to construct a more efficient classifier.

This paper is organized as followings. Section 2 describes preprocessing, feature extraction and classification algorithms for blood cell analysis. After we present experimental results in Section 3, we draw conclusions in Section 4.

2 Classification of Blood Cells

2.1 Preprocessing

Input images are captured from the color CCD camera attached to a microscope, magnified four hundred times with the resolution of 640x480 pixels. Figure 3(a) shows an input image. Since the clinical pathologist generally examines the ideal zone that has quite a few folded cells, we select the image that is noise free and well focused.

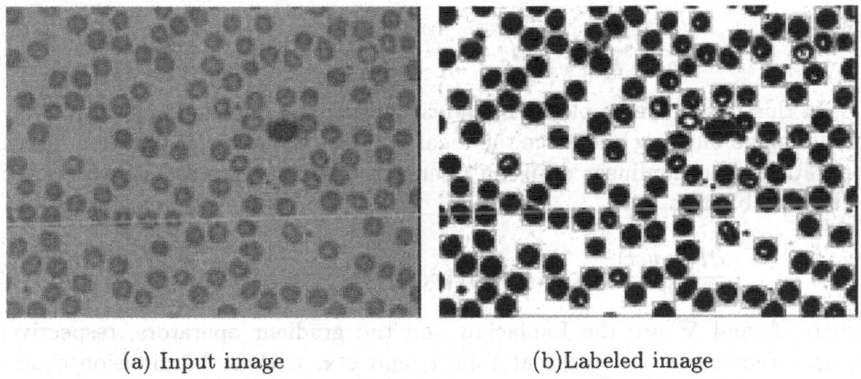

(a) Input image (b)Labeled image

Fig. 3. Preprocessing of the input image.

For the input image, we apply a luminance thresholding method using a fuzzy measure [3] to separate red-blood and white-blood cells from the background of the image. In the labeling step, we exclude boundary cells of the target image. Each labeled cell is classified into one of red-blood cells, white-blood cells, platelets and plasmas based on its size and color. While the white-blood cell has the biggest size and has a nucleus in it, the plasma and the platelet are considerably smaller compared to red-blood and white-blood cells, as demonstrated in Figure 3(a). Figure 3(b) displays labeled cells enclosed by the minimum bounding rectangular boxes.

2.2 Segmentation

In order to separate the white-blood cell into the nucleus and cytoplasm, we propose a hybrid segmentation scheme based on regions and edges. After we enhance image edges and remove noises by the nonlinear anisotropic diffusion algorithm [10], we apply a watershed transform to the image [6], [8]. We then merge the nearest regions by the k-means algorithm based on color information.

Once we apply PCA and the nonlinear anisotropic diffusion algorithm to the input image, we can obtain important edge information by fusing the first component and other two components with appropriate weighting factors. Comparing to other noise filtering methods, the nonlinear diffusion algorithm has good characteristics of removing noises while preserving the edge information. Since the proposed segmentation method employs the watershed transform, PCA and the nonlinear diffusion algorithms are very effective. PCA, also known as the Karhunen-Loeve decomposition, can be used to find eigenvectors of the covariance matrix. In this paper, we employ the linear PCA and use the covariance matrix of each RGB color component to obtain eigenvectors and eigenvalues.

After the PCA operation, a fused image A_n is generated. Regardless of the color model adopted, we can assume that e_1, e_2, and e_3 are the eigenvalues of three principal components of the color. Weighting factors for those color components are calculated by

$$\alpha_1 = \frac{e_1}{e_1 + e_2 + e_3}, \ \alpha_2 = \frac{e_2}{e_1 + e_2 + e_3}, \ \alpha_3 = \frac{e_3}{e_1 + e_2 + e_3}. \tag{1}$$

In this paper, we employ a nonlinear anisotropic diffusion algorithm [10] to avoid image blurring and solve the local problem of the linear diffusion filtering operation. The nonlinear diffusion operation can be expressed in terms of the time variable t as

$$\frac{\partial I(x,y,t)}{\partial t} = c(x,y,t)\Delta I(x,y,t) + \nabla c(x,y,t)\nabla I(x,y,t) \tag{2}$$

where Δ and ∇ are the Laplacian and the gradient operators, respectively, I(x,y,t) represents the image at time t, and c(x, y, t) is the diffusion conductance coefficient and is globally changed by the local edge analysis. Perona and Malik proposed a function for the intensity gradient [10] as

$$g(\nabla I) = \frac{1}{1 + (\|\nabla I\|/K)^2} \ or \ g(\nabla I) = exp\left(-\left(\frac{|\nabla f|}{K}\right)^2\right) \tag{3}$$

where K is a conductance variable that controls the gradient of the image. Ideally, K should be selected to reflect the gradient over the whole image or neighboring gradient values of each pixel. The time variable t controls the quantity of diffusion and it plays as the scale variable of the Gaussian blurring operation. If we set a larger value for t, the image will get more diffused. The nonlinear anisotropic diffusion algorithm has advantages in two aspects. It can reduce noises effectively while preserving the edge information, compared to other noise filtering algorithms: median filtering and Gaussian filtering. The popular watershed algorithm may result in oversegmention, if noises in the input image are not properly removed. However, we do not have the oversegmentation problem with the nonlinear anisotropic diffusion algorithm.

In general, an edge-based segmentation algorithm needs a robust edge linking operation due to edge discontinuity. However, the watershed transform does not need any edge linking opeation, since regions are defined by closed curves. The watershed transform can be implemented by rain falling or hill climbing operation. In this paper, we employ the rain-falling method that consists of the following two steps. Firstly, we define a threshold value. If one pixel has a smaller value than its neighboring pixels, it is considered to belong to the same region. In the next step, remaining pixels are merged to neighboring pixels that have the biggest slope. It is analogous that water in the surface of topology flows to the direction of lower slope.

In order to prevent oversegmenation by the watershed transform, we need to apply a postprocessing algorithm over segmented regions. In this paper, we employ the k-means algorithm, and the average intensity value of each segmented region is used as the measure for merging.

We compare the proposed method with the nonparametric clustering algorithm that was originally proposed for leukemia diagnosis [1]. As shown in Figure 4(a), the nonparametirc algorithm does not segment the input image properly into the nucleus and cytoplasm. Although the region merging algorithm affects the result, the proposed method segments regions intuitively. Figure 4(a) and Figure 4(b) demonstrate the segmentation results of white-blood cells by the nonparametric clustering method and the proposed method, respectively. Figure 5 shows another segemntation result by the proposed method.

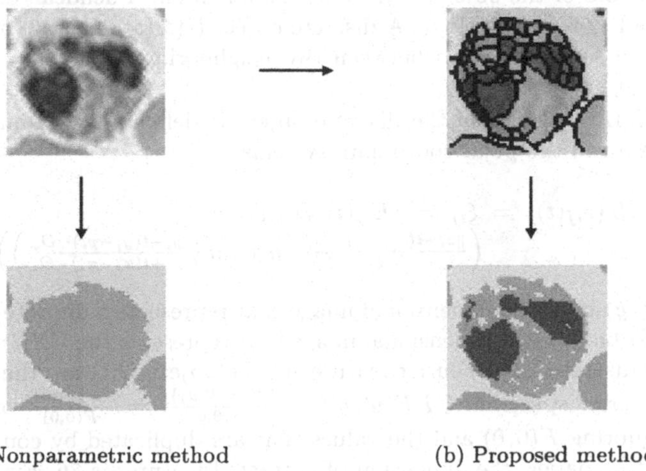

(a) Nonparametric method (b) Proposed method

Fig. 4. Comparison of segmentation results

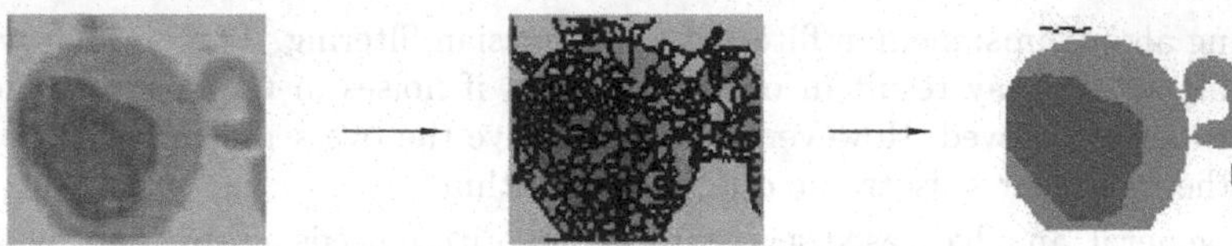

Fig. 5. Segmentation of white-blood cells

2.3 Feature Extraction

Once we label red-blood cells in the input image, we extract image features from each red-blood cell. The red-blood cells are then classified in two steps. Features extracted in the first step are different from those extracted in the second step. We assume that they belong to the same class.

In the first step, since normal, spherocyte, target and stomatocyte cells have the circular shape, the contour information of each cell is used for classification. In the second step, we use all edge information including interior edges as well as their contour information. In order to extract image features, we employ the Universidade Nova de Lisboa (UNL) Fourier transform [11] that is an improved extension of the Fourier descriptor to handle open curves and lines.

We obtain image features as follows. The input image consisting of binary curve patterns is transformed from the Cartesian coordinate system to the polar coordinate system by the UNL transform. After an analytic curve equation is estimated, the transformed curve is instantiated in the polar coordinate system.

Let $\Omega(t)$ be a discrete object composed of n pixels $z_i = (x_i, y_i)$, $O = (O_x, O_y)$ be the centroid of the object, and M be the maximum Euclidean distance from the centroid Ω to all pixels z_i. A discrete object $U(\Omega(t))$ consists of $(U(z_{ij}(t))$, a set of line segments $z_{ij}(t)$ between two neighboring pixels $z_i = (x_i, y_i)$ and $z_j = (x_j, y_j)$.

The UNL transform of the discrete object is defined by the mapping from the Cartesian to the polar coordinate systems.

$$(U(z_{ij}(t)) = \xi_{ij} = (E_{ij}(t), \Theta_{ij}(t)) = \left(\frac{\|z_i+t(z_j-z_i)-O\|}{M}, \ arctan\left(\frac{y_i+t(y_j-y_i)-O_y}{x_i+t(x_j-x_i)-O_x}\right)\right) \tag{4}$$

Let $i(x, y)$ be a two-dimensional image that represents a discrete object $\Omega(t)$ and $f(R, \theta)$ be the two dimensional image that represents the UNL transform of $\Omega(t)$. The discrete UNL Fourier features of the object $\Omega(t)$ are the normalized discrete Fourier spectrum $UFF(u', v') = \frac{\|F\{f(R,\theta)\}\|}{F(0,0)} = \frac{\|F(U,v)\|}{F(0,0)}$ of the image $f(R, \theta)$, ignoring $F(0, 0)$ and the values that are duplicated by conjugate symmetry. In this paper, the dimension of extracted features is 76. Figure 6 shows the process to extract edge information of red-blood cells as a preprocessing step for feature extraction.

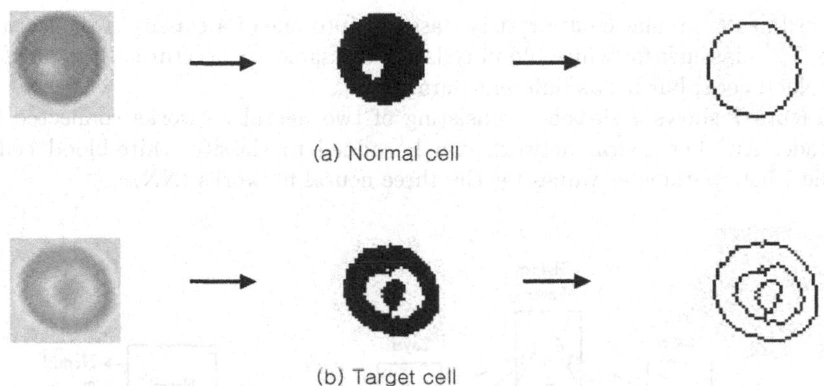

(a) Normal cell

(b) Target cell

Fig. 6. Feature extraction process of red-blood cells

We have also tested various features of white-blood cells. We categorize the set of features into three groups. Basic features, such as color, size, intensity, ratio of the nucleus and cytoplasm, are included in first category. Second group features are circularity, eccentricity, elongatedness, convexity, and invariant moment features for the shape of the nucleus. Texture features of the nucleus and cytoplasm are included in the third category, where we choose the best 60 features among them.

In order to construct the classifier efficiently, we can extract image features by filtering and wrapping[11]. In this paper, we use the principal component analysis (PCA), one of the popular filtering methods, to extract lower dimensional features by analyzing multi-dimensional features statistically [12]. For red-blood cells, we reduce the extracted 76 dimensional features to 38 dimensional features in the first recognition step by applying PCA. In the second step, we can reduce the initial 76 dimensional features to 67 dimensional features. For white-blood cells, we reduce the 60 dimensional features to 52 dimensional features. Finally, each feature value is normalized to a number between 0 and 1.

2.4 Classification

In this chapter, we introduce a neural network classifier based on the back-propagation learning algorithm and compare the performance of the classification model with the k-nearest neighbor (K-NN) and the learning vector quantization-3 (LVQ-3) algorithms. While K-NN is one of the statistical pattern classification methods, LVQ-3 is one of the clustering algorithms.

Our classifier is a hierarchical neural network model to classify red-blood and white-blood cells using the back-propagation learning algorithm [2]. Classification of red-blood cells consists of two steps. We assume that normal, target, spherocyte and stomatocyte cells of circular contour are included in the same class in the first step. Therefore, each input cell is classified into one of 12 classes.

If a cell has a circular contour, it is classified into one of 4 classes in the second step. The classifier for white-blood cells has the same architecture as the one for red-blood cells, but it has different parameters.

Figure 7 shows a classifier consisting of two neural networks connected in cascade. Another neural network can be added to classify white-blood cells. Table 1 lists parameter values for the three neural networks (NN).

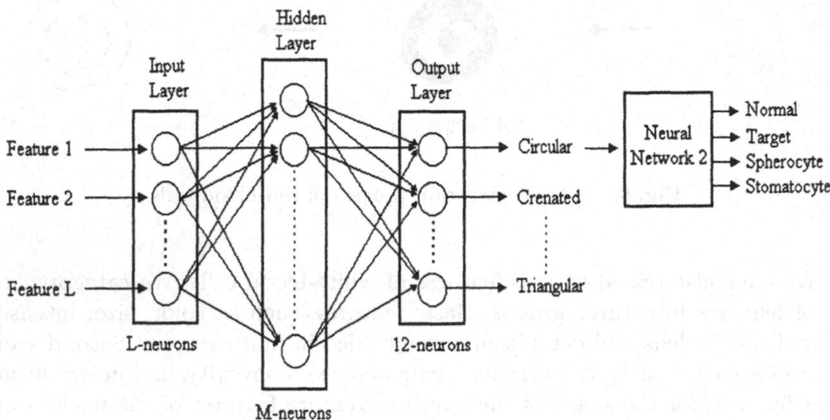

Fig. 7. Neural network architecture to classify red-blood cells

The back-propagation learning algorithm is a general delta rule that controls the weighting factor by the following equation.

$$W(new)_{ij} = W(old)_{ij} + \alpha\delta_j a_i \tag{5}$$

where i,j : a neuron in the hidden and output layer, respectively,
$W(new)_{ij}$: modified weight between neuron i and neuron j,
$W(old)_{ij}$: previous weight between neuron i and neuron j,
$e_j = t_j - a_j$: neuron error in output layer,
$e_j = \sum_k W_{jk}\delta_k$: neuron error in hidden layer,
$\delta_j = a_i(1 - a_j)e_j$: delta of neuron j,
α : learning rate,
a_i: activation value of neuron i,
a_j: activation value of neuron j,
e_j: error of neuron j,
t_j: value of target pattern if neuron j is in output layer,
W_{jk}: weight of neuron k in previous layer if neuron j is in the hidden layer,
δ_k: delta of neuron k in previous layer if neuron j is in the hidden layer.

We use an adaptive learning algorithm to reduce the learning time of the neural network and to find the local minima. Let $W_{ij}(old)$ be the current weight and $W_{ij}(older)$ be the previous weight. The current momentum is the difference between the current weight and the previous weight. Therefore, the general delta rule can be modified as

$$W(new)_{ij} = W(old)_{ij} + \alpha\delta_j a_i + \beta \Delta W_{ij}(old) \quad (6)$$

where β is a constant that controls the momentum.

Table 1. Parameter values for neural networks

Classifier	Parameter						
	Slope of activation function	Learning constant	Nodes for input layer	Hidden layer	Nodes for hidden layer	Nodes for output layer	Momentum constant
NN 1	0.1	0.5	38	2	125	12	0.9
NN 2	0.1	0.5	38	1	120	4	0.9
NN 3	0.1	0.5	52	1	80	5	0.9

3 Experimental Results

In our experiment, we have used Wright dyed blood images collected from two hundred patients in the hospital. In order to train the classifier, we use 680 test cells for fifteen classes of red-blood cells, and 70 of monocyte, 50 of basophil, 120 of neutrophil, 50 of esinophil, and 120 of lymphocyte for five classes of white-blood cells. The data set is verified by human expert. We select the leave-one-out method for the test and apply PCA to reduce the feature dimension. The original feature dimension of 76 has been reduced to 38 in the first recognition step, 67 in the second one for the red-blood cells. The initial 60 dimensional features for white-blood cells are reduced to 52 dimension.

We have compared our classifier to other two classifiers, K-NN and LVQ-3 for classifying red-blood cells. Figure 8 shows recognition rates for red-blood cells in the first and the second steps, respectively. Figure 9 shows the improved recognition rates acquired with the reduced features after applying PCA. MLP in Figure 8 and Figure 9 indicates our classifier based on the multiplayer perceptron.

After classification, the result is compared with that of human expert. Our experimental results show that we can obtain improved recognition rates using features of reduced dimension. However, the recognition rate is low in the first step, since it is difficult to distinguish burr cells from crenated cells with nearly the same contour shape. This problem can be improved by more precise contour extraction. Table 2 and Table 3 list the average recognition rates with the original features and the reduced features, respectively.

Table 4 presents the final recognition result of white-blood cells by a confusion matrix with the reduced features. As we can observe in Table 4, most recognition errors are between monocyte and lymphocyte and between neutrophil and esinophil, since they have the same characteristics in the shape, the size and the color of the nucleus and cytoplasm. Moreover, it is very difficult even for a human expert to distinguish the monocyte from the abnormal lymphocyte, because they have the same characteristics in terms of the size, color and ratio of neucleus and cyteoplasm.

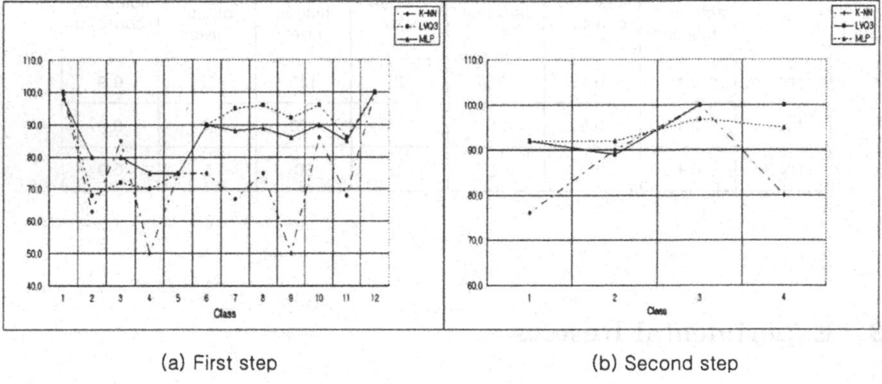

(a) First step (b) Second step

Fig. 8. Recognition rate (%) of red-blood cells

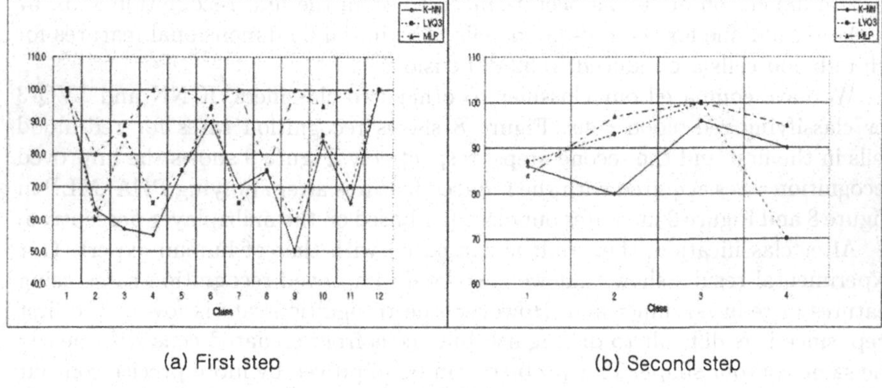

(a) First step (b) Second step

Fig. 9. Recognition rate (%) after PCA

Table 2. Average recognition rate (%) before PCA

Recognition Step	Classifier		
	K-NN	LVQ-3	MLP
Second Step (12 Classes)	75	87	87
Second Step (4 Classes)	90	91	94

Table 3. Average recognition rate (%) after PCA

Recognition Step	Classifier		
	K-NN	LVQ-3	MLP
Second Step (12 Classes)	73	78	87
Second Step (4 Classes)	88	87	94

Table 4. Confusion matrix for white-blood cells

Input \ Output	Monocyte	Basophil	Neutrophil	Esinophil	Lymphocyte
Monocyte	55	0	2	0	13
Basophil	0	38	2	10	0
Neutrophil	11	0	97	8	4
Esinophil	0	2	6	42	0
Lymphocyte	8	0	4	0	98

4 Conclusions

In this paper, we have proposed a new scheme to recognize and classify red-blood and white-blood cells in the human peripheral blood image. We have also described a classification model based on the neural network. We classify red-blood cells in two steps using inner edges and contour information, and white-blood cells using various features of the nucleus and cytoplasm. We have proposed a new algorithm to segment the nucleus and cytoplasm of white-blood cells. In addition, we show that complexity of the neural network can be reduced and a more efficient system can be constructed by applying PCA to features extracted from cells. The recognition rate for red-blood and white-blood cells is 91% and 81% on average, respectively.

Acknowledgment

This work was supported in part by the Korea Science and Engineering Foundation (KOSEF) through the Ultra-Fast Fiber-Optic Networks (UFON) Research Center at Kwangju Institute of Science and Technology (K-JIST), and in part by the Ministry of Education (MOE) through the Brain Korea 21 (BK21) project.

References

1. Comaniciu, D., Meer, P., Foran, D.: Image Guided Decision Support System for Pathology, Machine Vision and Applications, Vol. 11, No. 4 (2000) 213-224
2. Freeman, J.A., Skapura, D.M., Neural Networks: Algorithms, Applications and Programming, Techniques. Addision-Wesley Publishing (1991)
3. Huang, L.K, Wang, M. J.: Image Thresholding by Minimizing the Measures of Fuzziness, Pattern Recognition, Vol.28 (1995) 1:41-51
4. Jang, Y.H.: Optimal Neural Network Classifier for Chromosome Karyotype Classification, KIEE Journal, Vol.46, No.7, Jul. (1997) 1129-1134
5. Korea Medical Publisher: Illustrated Hematology Book. Korea Publishing (1995)
6. Majman, L., Schmitt, M.: Geodesic Saliency of Watershed Contours and Hierarchical Segmentation, IEEE Trans. on Pattern Analysis and Machine Intelligence, Vol.18, No.12 (1996) 1163-1173
7. Mehtre, B.M., Kankanhalli, M.S., Lee, W. F.: Shape Measures For Content Based Image Retrieval: A Comparison, Technical Report 95-195-0, Institute of Systems Science, National University of Singapore (1995)
8. Moga, N.A., Gabbouj, M. : Parallel Image Component Labeling with Watershed Transformation, IEEE Trans. on Pattern Analysis and Machine Intelligence, Vol.19, No.5 (1997) 441-450
9. Nagata, H., Mizushima, H.: World Wide Microscope: New Concept of Internet Telepathology Microscope and Implementation of the Prototype, MEDIINFO 98 (1998) 286-289
10. Perona, P., Malik, M.: Scale-Space and Edge Detection using Anisotropic Diffusion, IEEE Trans. on Pattern analysis and machine intelligence, Vol.12, No.7 (1990) 629-639
11. Rauber, T.W.: Two-Dimensional Shape Description, Technical Report Gruninova-RT-10-94, Universidade Nova de Lisboa, Lisboa, Portugal (1994)
12. Seker, S., Bagriyanik, M., Gabgriyanik, F.G.: An Application of Shannon's Entropy for Neural Architecture, Proc. of the 15th IASTED, Innsbruck (1997) 33-36
13. Stewart, B.K., Langer, S.G.: Medical Image Databases and Informatics, IEEE International Conf. on image processing, Oct. 4-7, Chicago, Illinois (1998) 29-33

Formal Concept Analysis for Domain-Specific Document Retrieval Systems

Mihye Kim and Paul Compton

School of Computer Science and Engineering
University of New South Wales
Sydney NSW 2052 Australia
+61 2 9385 6531
{mihyek, compton}@cse.unsw.edu.au

Abstract. Domain-specific information retrieval normally depends on general search engines, or systems which support browsing using handcrafted organisation of documents, but such systems are costly to build and maintain. An alternative approach for specialised domains is to build a retrieval system incrementally and dynamically by allowing users to evolve their own organisation of documents and to assist them in ensuring improvement of the system's performance as it evolves. This paper describes a browsing mechanism for such a system based on the concept lattice of Formal Concept Analysis (FCA) in cooperation with incremental knowledge acquisition mechanisms. Our experience with a prototype suggests that a browsing scheme for a specific domain can be able to be collaboratively created and maintained by multiple users over time. It also appears that the concept lattice of FCA is a useful way of supporting the flexible open management of documents required by individuals, small communities or in specialised domains.

1 Introduction

Broadly speaking there are two ways in which a user interacts with document retrieval systems. In one the user formulates a specific query and some documents are retrieved in response. This process is normally iterative in that the user refines (or changes) the query on the basis of the documents retrieved by each query. In the second approach the documents are grouped and the document groups organised into some sort of structure that can be browsed. That is, from any point in the structure at least some other related parts of the structure can be identified and moved to.

The ideal would be that specific queries would always produce the most relevant documents. Despite improvements in this area (e.g. Google), specific queries remain very frustrating: the only search terms the user can think of occur in myriad other contexts and perhaps even do not occur in some relevant documents. As a result a browsing approach is supported in many information retrieval systems. With browsing users quickly explore the search domains and can easily acquire domain knowledge [18]. Typically, a hierarchy is used for browsing and documents are grouped using some sort of clustering algorithms. Hierarchical Agglomerative Clustering algorithms are probably the most commonly used. The problem with a hierarchical clustering is category mismatch [7, 12]. If one goes down the wrong path

M. Brooks, D. Corbett, and M. Stumptner (Eds.): AI 2001, LNAI 2256, pp. 237-248, 2001.

one must go back up the hierarchy and start again. There is no mechanism for navigating to other clusters, as there is only a simple taxonomy structure. A further critical issue in a browsing scheme is the origin of the terms by which the documents are grouped. One can attempt to arrive at some global taxonomy to satisfy all possible users as used by sites like Yahoo and the Open Directory Project (http://dmoz.org/). In these global systems the category mismatch problems can be very severe.

As an alternative, documents can be organised using ontologies for browsing for a specific domain. That is, one can build a specialised ontology to be used by a specific community, with the assumption that within the community there will be consensus on the terms. A good example is the $(KA)^2$ initiative [2]. $(KA)^2$ starts out with an ontology appropriate to the domain with the expectation that people in the community will annotate documents according to the ontology. These same users should also be able to use the ontology to retrieve documents entered by others and an end-user can retrieve relevant documents by navigating an ontological browser formulated in a hierarchy. There are likely to be considerable practical advantages to even very large communities committing to specific ontologies, and part of education would be to learn these ontologies. Despite the practical advantages of a community committing to ontology, we have long held the view that at base any knowledge structure is a construct which should be allowed to evolve over time [6].

Hence rather than committing to an *a priori* ontology and expecting that all documents will be annotated according to the ontology, our aim is to explore the possibilities of a system where the user can annotate a document however they like and that the ontology will evolve accordingly. Rather than this being totally *ad hoc*, we would like the system to assist the user to make extensions to the ontology that are in some way improvements. We are not concerned with automated or semi-automated ways of discovering an ontology appropriate to a document or corpus [1, 17]. Despite the potential of such approaches, from our more deconstructionist perspective, we are more interested in the role of the reader or user interpreting documents and deciding on their annotation and development of an ontology. However, this does not preclude the inclusion of ontologies either constructed by an expert or an ontology imported from elsewhere, as part of the ontological structure preferred by the user.

An alternative to a hierarchy for browsing is a lattice-based navigation scheme using Formal Concept Analysis (FCA). In this approach, a document is annotated by an expert with a set of controlled terms. From this a concept lattice is constructed using the given mathematical formulae of FCA. The significant advantage of this approach is that the mathematical formulae produce a conceptual structure which automatically provides generalisation and specialisation relationships among the concept nodes. This lattice structure allows one to reach a group of documents via one path, but then rather than going back up the same hierarchy and guessing another starting point, one can go to one of the other parents of the present node reducing the problem of category mismatch. In this paper we describe a system based on the lattice browsing supported by FCA but supporting incremental development of the system over time. The system assists users in ensuring improvement of the system's performance as it evolves.

We have previously demonstrated incremental development of document management systems based on selecting keywords that discriminate between documents [14, 15] using the Ripple-Down Rule (RDR) knowledge acquisition and maintenance methodology. The RDR approach was initially developed for knowledge acquisition for knowledge based systems [6]. Although, as demonstrated in other RDR work, RDR greatly assists context-specific knowledge acquisition it does not organise the knowledge in a way that is suitable for browsing. One of the aims here is to integrate the RDR incremental approach with the browsing advantage of FCA. FCA has previously been used with RDR expert systems as an explanation tool [20].

A prototype has been implemented (http://pokey.cse.unsw.edu.au/servlets/Search) and demonstrated with a test domain of around 200 papers from the Banff Knowledge Acquisition Workshops (http://ksi.cpsc.ucalgay.ca:80/KAW). Another test domain (http://pokey.cse.unsw.edu.au/servlets/RI) is for research topics in the School of Computer Science and Engineering, UNSW. There are around 150 research staff and students in the School who generally have homepages indicating their research projects. The aim here was to allow staff and students to freely annotate their pages so that they would be found appropriately within the evolving lattice of research topics. The goal is a system to assist prospective students and potential collaborators in finding research relevant to their interests.

2 System Overview

Figure 1 shows an overview of the system. A user can annotate his/her own document with a set of keywords by selecting keywords already used in the system which have been added by others or by entering further textwords which in turn will be available to future users. The user is provided with a list of keywords already available. After an initial selection, the system indicates keywords that have been used together with the keywords already selected for other documents. Through these and further knowledge acquisition steps, the initial keywords can be refined. Then the case (a document with a set of keywords) is added into the system. After that, the system rebuilds the concept lattice to cope with the new case. Figure 2 (a) shows an example of a lattice. The concept lattice is a data structure either for indexing documents or for browsing. The keywords set is used for the indexing as shown in Figure 2 (b).

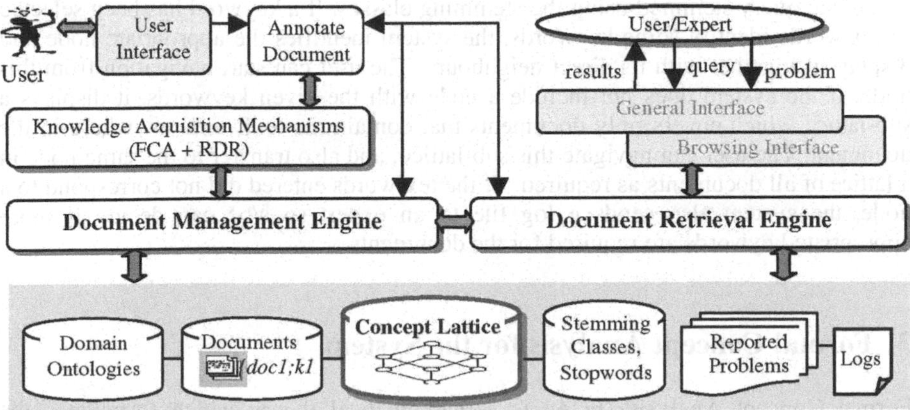

Fig. 1. An overview of the system

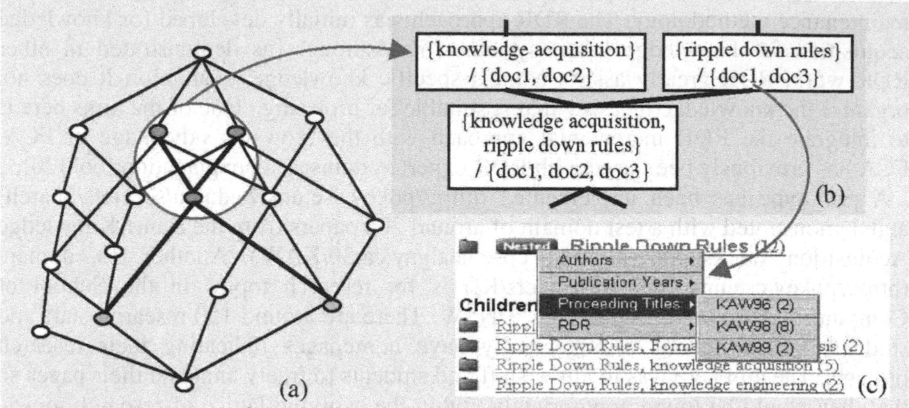

Fig. 2. Examples of the browsing structure (a) Lattice structure (b) Indexing of the lattice (c) Nested structure

The concept lattice is incrementally and automatically reformulated whenever a new case is added or the existing cases are changed. The user can also to give values for properties (attributes) defined for the domain ontology by an expert or the system can automatically extract the values of attributes from the content of documents. This requires a prior domain ontology in the same way as $(KA)^2$ and is included in our system only for completeness. We suggest that it will be used only the most obvious attributes rather than for implementing a fully developed ontology. The attributes are accessed via nested browsing as shown in Figure 2 (c). The nested structure is constructed dynamically corresponding to the search results. That is, we build a concept lattice using the resulting documents with their keywords as an outer structure and from this produce a nested structure.

The user specifies a query by entering any textwords in a conventional information retrieval fashion or by selecting a keyword from those that had used for annotating the documents. For a textword search a set of words is entered separated by ',' and assuming the AND Boolean operator. Stopwords are first eliminated and the remaining query stemmed using the stemming classes. If a keyword has been selected or textwords identify some keywords, the system identifies the appropriate node and displays it together with its direct neighbours. The user can start navigation from this node. If the system does not include a node with the given keywords, it displays a sub-lattice which covers only documents that contain the textwords anywhere in the document. The user can navigate this sub-lattice, and also transfer to the same node in a lattice of all documents as required. If the textwords entered did not correspond to a node, the system also sends a log file to an expert so s/he can decide if more appropriate keywords are required for the documents.

3 Formal Concept Analysis for the System

Formal Concept Analysis (FCA) is a mathematical theory which formulates the understanding of 'concept' as a unit of thought comprising its extension and intension as a way of modelling a domain [11, 22]. The extension of a concept is formed by all objects to which the concept applies and the intension consists of all attributes existing in those objects. FCA generates a conceptual hierarchy of the domain by finding all possible formal concepts which reflect the relationships between attributes and objects. The resulting subconcept-superconcept relationships between formal concepts are expressed in a concept lattice which can be seen as a semantic net providing "hierarchical conceptual clustering of the objects… and a representation of all implications between the attributes" [23]. More detailed definitions and examples can be found in [11].

3.1 Formal Contexts and Formal Concepts

The most basic data structure of FCA is a formal context. The set of objects and their attributes constitute a formal context (K) = (G, M, I). G is a set of objects, M is a set of attributes and I is a binary relation between G and M which indicates where an object *g* has an attribute *m* by the relationship *gIm* (also by $(g, m) \in I$). In the original formulation of FCA, objects were implicitly assumed to have some sort of unity or identity so that the attributes applied to the whole object; e.g. a dog has four legs. Clearly documents do not have the sort of unity where attributes will necessarily apply to the whole document. However at this stage of this work we suppose that documents correspond to objects and the keywords or terms attached to documents by a user constitute attribute sets. We define a formal context (C) for our document retrieval system as follows.

Definition 1: A formal context is a tripe C = (D, K, I) where D is a set of documents, K is a set of keywords and I is a binary relation which indicates where a document *d* has a keyword *k* by the relationship ${}_dI_k$ (also by $(d, k) \in I$).

For example, Table 1 shows the formal context of C where D is {1, 2, 3, 4}, K is {artificial intelligence, information retrieval, machine learning, decision tree, natural language processing, speech recognition, signal representation} and the relation I is {(1, artificial intelligence), (1, information retrieval),..., (4, artificial intelligence), (4, natural language process), (4,speech recognition), (4, signal representation)}.

Then, formal concepts are derived from the formal context using the basic definition $X \subseteq D$: $X \mapsto X' := \{k \in K \mid \forall d \in X: (d, k) \in I\}$, $Y \subseteq K$: $Y \mapsto Y' := \{d \in D \mid \forall k \in Y: (d, k) \in I\}$. A formal concept is defined as a pair (X, Y) such that $X \subseteq D$, $Y \subseteq K$, $X' = Y$ and $Y' = X$ where X and Y are called the extent and the intent of the concept (X, Y). More detail mathematical formulae and procedures can be found in [11, 22]. A node in Figure 3 represents a formal concept.

Table1. Part of formal context in our application

	Artificial intelligence	Information retrieval	Machine learning	Decision tree	Natural language processing	Speech recognition	Signal representation
1	X	X					
2	X		X	X			
3	X	X			X		
4	X				X	X	X

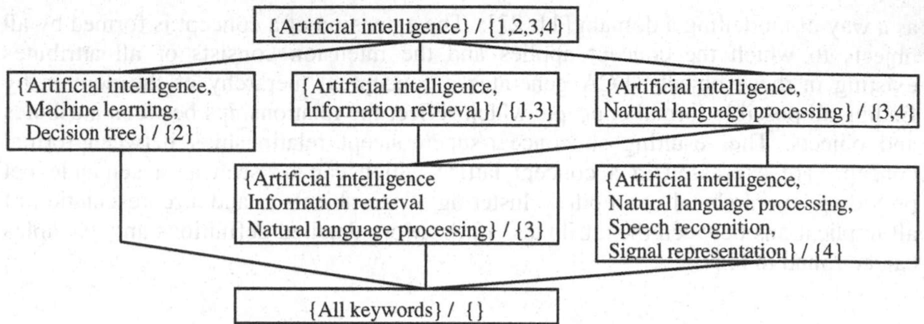

Fig. 3. Concept lattice of the formal context in Table 1

3.2 Concept Lattice

The formal concepts of C are expressed in a concept lattice £ (D, K, I) which is the conceptual structure of FCA and ordered by the smallest set of attributes. The structure is reformulated incrementally and automatically by adding a new case and refining the existing cases. To build a concept lattice we need to find the subconcept-superconcept relationship between the formal concepts. This is formalised by $(X_1, Y_1) \leq (X_2, Y_2) \Leftrightarrow X_1 \subseteq X_2$ $(\Leftrightarrow Y_2 \subseteq Y_1)$ where (X_1, Y_1) is called a subconcept of (X_2, Y_2) and (X_2, Y_2) is called a superconcept of (X_1, Y_1). Figure 3 shows the concept lattice of the formal context C in Table 1.

3.3 Conceptual Scaling

Conceptual scaling has been introduced in order to deal with many-valued attributes [10]. A many-valued context is defined as a formal context (K) = (G, M, W, I) where G is a set of objects, M is a set of attributes, W is a set of attribute values. I is a ternary relation between G, M and W which indicates where an object *g* has the attributes value *w* for the attribute *m*. Then, if a user is interested in analysing the interrelationship between attributes, he/she can choose the required attribute(s) from the multi-valued context and build a formal context for the attribute(s). This process is called conceptual scaling. The concept lattices are structured for each of the separate formal contexts. A concept lattice is derived by combing several concept lattices into 'nested line diagrams' (e.g. TOSCANA) or a new form of a lattice structure. Table 2 is an example of many-valued contexts in our domain. We build a concept lattice with a set of documents with their keywords as an outer structure. Then, we scale up using other attributes into a nested structure. The nested structure is constructed dynamically in response to the outer structure. Conceptual scaling is also applied to one-valued contexts in order to reduce the complexity of the visualisation [21]. In our present system, an expert can group relevant attribute values from the formal context C = (D, K, I) in the definition 1. The process is incorporated with building a thesaurus which is not addressed here as it is beyond the scope of this paper. Then, when a query is associated with the thesaurus, conceptual scales are derived on the fly to group the relevant terms as the nested attributes.

Table 2. An example table for many-valued contexts

	Keywords	Authors	Proceeding title	Publication year
Document1	k1, k2, k3	a1, a2	KAW	1998
Document2	k1, k3, k4	a3, a2	EKAW	1999
Document3	k1, k2, k5, k6	a4, a5, a6	PKAW	2000
...	...	...	...	...

3.4 Incremental Construction of the Concept Lattice

Many different algorithms exist for generating a concept lattice from a given formal context [3, 9, 13]. However, we have developed a further incremental algorithm to construct the concept lattice. In our approach, the concept lattice is incrementally changed by adding a new case and refining the existing cases. The following is a brief explanation of the algorithm.

Assume the existing formal context C = (D, K, I) where D is a set of documents, K is a set of keywords and I is a binary relation between D and K. Then, let ß(C) be the set of all formal concepts of the formal context C. A formal concept of the context C consists of a pair (X, Y) where X and Y are called the extent and the intent respectively. Now let X^a be all extents and Y^a be all intents of ß(C). In adding a new document, let *d* be a new document and Γ be the set of keywords of *d*. Then, an extended formal context of C is defined as $C^+ = (D^+, K^+, I^+)$ where $D^+ = D \cup \{d\}$, $K^+ = K \cup \Gamma$ and $I^+ = I \cup \{(d, k) \mid k \in \Gamma\}$. In the case of refining an existing case, $D^+ = D$ and $K^+ = (K - \Gamma^o) \cup \Gamma^n$ where Γ^o is the set of keywords associated with the document from among existing keywords and Γ^n is the new set of keyword for this document.

Then the following procedure is applied for each element *k* of Γ. The system formulates a formal concept (X, Y) where X is the set of documents which is associated with the element *k* and Y is {*k*}, and determines the intersection of X with the X^a of ß(C). If the intersection does not exist in X^a, the system reformulates the formal concept (X, Y) where X is the intersection and Y is {*k*} and adds the concept into £(C). After this process, the extended set of all formal concepts $ß^+(C)$ is composed. But $ß^+(C)$ can include a common attribute component contrary to FCA. We eliminate the formal concepts in the common attribute component except for the maximal concept of $ß^+(C)$ defined with the largest object component. For reference, the object components of the common attribute component are in a total subsumption relationship. Then, subconcept and superconcept relationships are reformulated for all formal concepts which include the keywords Γ of *d*. This results in a new lattice $£(D^+, K^+, I^+)$ of the context C^+.

4 Incremental Knowledge Acquisition Mechanisms

Knowledge acquisition is carried out when a new document is added with a set of keywords or the keywords of existing documents are refined. When an expert/user assigns the set of keywords for a document, some keywords may be missed. The system guides the user to discover possible missed concepts through a number of steps. The knowledge acquisition mechanisms are based on FCA and RDR techniques. The following definitions are used.

Definition 2: Let C = (D, K, I) be a formal context, and d be a new document ($d \notin$ D) and Γ be the set of keywords of d. The set of keywords is not necessarily a subset of K. Then, the extended formal context of C is defined as $C^+ = (D^+, K^+, I^+)$ where $D^+ = D \cup \{d\}$, $K^+ = K \cup \Gamma$ and $I^+ = I \cup \{(d, k) \mid k \in \Gamma\}$.

Definition 3: Let C = (D, K, I) be a formal context and Γ be a set of keywords (Γ ⊆ K). Then the set of documents associated with Γ is defined to be $\Delta_\Gamma = \{d \in D \mid \exists k \in \Gamma \text{ such that } (d, k) \in I\}$.

We introduced Δ_Γ to get a set of documents, which has at least one keyword of Γ. If Γ is a singleton (i.e. Γ= {γ}), then we will abbreviate $\Delta\gamma = \Delta_\Gamma = \{d \in D \mid (d, \gamma) \in I\}$.

Definition 4: Let C = (D, K, I) be a formal context. We define a function f from D to 2^K as f: D→ 2^K such that $f(d) = \{k \in K \mid (d, k) \in I\}$.

That is, $f(d)$ returns the set of keywords of d. Let the new document be d ($\notin$ D) with the set of keywords Γ. We formulate the sub-formal context C′ = (D′, K′, I′) with $D' = \Delta_\Gamma + \{d\}$ where Δ_Γ is in definition 3 and $K' = \bigcup_{d \in D'} f(d)$ where f is the function in definition 4. In order to get a set of relevant keywords of d, we obtain a set of keywords which are associated with Δ_Γ as $f(\Delta_\Gamma) = \bigcup_{d \in \Delta_\Gamma} f(d)$ from the context C′. Now the set of relevant keywords is defined as $\Re = f(\Delta_\Gamma) - \Gamma$. Then, the function *Freq* introduced below is used for each keyword of $\Re$ (k) to compute the number of common keywords of Γ with the keywords of all the documents that have the keyword k from the context C′.

Definition 5: We define a function *Freq* from $2^K \times K$ to the set of natural numbers N as follows: *Freq*: $2^K \times K \rightarrow N$ such that $Freq(\Gamma, k) = \sum_{d \in \Delta_k} |f(d) \cap \Gamma|$ where |X| is the cardinality of X.

The user can annotate his/her document with a set of keywords by entering any terms or selecting known terms. The system displays all the keywords used by other annotators to be able to share and reuse them. After this initial assignment, the user can view the other terms that co-occur with the terms s/he has provided and can annotate the document with these further terms if desired. The terms are presented to the user ordered by their frequency in the lattice, normalised for the number of terms at the node, and their 'closeness' to the node to which the document is assigned by the user's initial choice of terms in the conceptual hierarchy.

In a more detailed explanation, an ordered set of documents and a set of keywords which are relevant to the new document are obtained. A sub-lattice £′ (D′, K′, I′) of the formal context C′ described in above is then constructed. This step is divided into two stages. In the first stage, the ordered documents are shown to the user along with the features that are different between the new document and each of the set of documents. Given a new document d, we are interested in finding the set of documents D_d that share some commonalties. We formulate a formal concept ζ ({d},f (d)) with the newly added document d and its set of keywords Γ. Starting from the concept ζ we recursively go up to the direct superconcepts of its subconcept in the lattice to find the next level of the relevant documents. This procedure is done until the superconcept reaches the top node of the lattice.

At the second stage, we elicit the relevant keywords which are associated with the newly added document *d*. Then, a weight for each relevant keyword is calculated by definition 5. Then, the ordered relevant keywords are presented to the user with their relevant weight. After that, the system asks the user the relevancy for each extracted keyword. The user can also view the sub-lattice and the relevant documents for each of the relevant keywords during this process. The similarity relation between keywords and documents can be easily observed through the lattice.

When the above stage is complete the document is located at a node. If there is another document(s) already at the node, the user adding the new document is presented with the previous document and asked to include keywords that distinguish the documents. The user can chose to leave the two documents together with the same keywords. Ultimately however, every document is unique and offers different resources to other documents and probably should be annotated to indicate the differences. The approach used here is derived from Ripple-Down Rules, but the location of the document is determined by the lattice structure rather than the history of the development.

Another knowledge acquisition we have addressed is when a new term is entered for a new document; this term may also appropriately apply to other documents already in the system. This problem can be left until the system fails to provide an appropriate document for a later search as the RDR approach. However, in our approach, the system passes a log of the addition of a new document to a meta-expert. The expert then considers whether any document at the parent nodes for the new nodes should also have the term added. The following definitions are used in formulating the relevant documents and their associated new terms for the new added case.

Definition 6: Let $\pounds = < V, \leq >$ be a lattice. Given a node $\theta \in V$, the set of direct parents of θ denoted $DP_{\pounds}(\theta)$ is defined as follows: $DP_{\pounds}(\theta) = \{\alpha \in V \mid \theta < \alpha$ and there does not exist any $\beta \in V$ such that $\theta < \beta$ & $\beta < \alpha\}$.

Definition 7: Let $\pounds(C)$ be a concept lattice of the formal context $C = (D, K, I)$ and *d* be the new document. For each document $\delta \in D$, we can define the set of relevant keywords for δ with respect to *d* denoted $Rel_d(\delta)$ as follows:

$$Rel_d(\delta) = \{ f(d) \setminus \bigcup_{(X,Y) \in DP_{\pounds(C)}(<\{d\}, f(d)>) \,\&\, \delta \in X} Y \}$$

As the system evolves, new terms are being added. As a consequence, there is a necessity to handle synonyms or to group the relevant terms together for extending the users' query. For this reason, we support a tool for experts of the system to build a thesaurus for the involved domain whenever it is required. We have developed a mechanism to discover new concepts when a new case is added by connecting to this process that is to hold the compatibility condition (is-a relationship) in the thesaurus hierarchy. Another mechanism is motivated from when the system can not find a node in the lattice with a query. In this case, the system sends a log file to an expert so s/he can decide if more appropriate keywords are required for documents. The expert then sends e-mail to the author (annotator of the document) by attaching a hyperlink which can facilitate to refine the keywords of the document if it desires. All interactions between the system and users are also logged. We are analysing the log file to find effective factors or users' behaviours to influence the performance of the system. The user can immediately view the changed concept lattice and further decide whether the set of keywords they have assigned for the document is appropriate.

5 Related Work

Formal concept analysis has developed to have a wide range of application in medicine, psychology, libraries, software reengineering and ecology, and has applied to a variety of methods for data analysis, information retrieval and knowledge discovery in databases. A number of researchers have proposed this lattice structure for information retrieval. Here we consider only where FCA has been applied to documents [4, 5, 12, 19].

Godin et al. [12] studied the advantage of the lattice method against hierarchical classification and also evaluated retrieval performance. Hierarchical classification retrieval showed significantly lower recall compared to the lattice-based retrieval and Boolean querying. Between the lattice-based retrieval and Boolean retrieval no significant performance difference was found, but they strongly argued the advantages of a lattice structure for browsing. Carpineto and Romano [4] determined that the performance of lattice retrieval was comparable to or better than Boolean retrieval on two medium-sized databases. Carpineto and Romano [5] also used a thesaurus as background knowledge in formulating a browsing structure and presented experimental evidence of a substantial improvement after the introduction of the thesaurus. Godin et al. [12], and Carpineto and Romano [4] systems were both implemented on a stand-alone microcomputer. More recently FCA has been used for document retrieval culminating in faceted information retrieval system (FaIR) [19]. This classifies the documents using a faceted knowledge representation based on a thesaurus or knowledge base, but a browsing scheme is not yet deployed.

The focus in previous work was to examine the advantages and capabilities of the lattice-based retrieval. The main difference in the work here is an emphasis on incremental development and evolution, and knowledge acquisition tools to support this for specialised domains. Our aim is a browsing scheme which can be collaboratively created and maintained and where users evolve their own organisation of documents but are assisted in this to facilitate improvement of the system's performance as it evolves.

Another difference is that our focus is on a web-based system using a hypertext representation of the links to a node, but without a graphical display of the overall lattice. Lin [16] discussed how visualisation through a graphical interface could enhance information retrieval and generally the browsing mechanism in the application of FCA is based on exploring the lattice graph itself. However, we anticipate that most web users are unfamiliar or uncomfortable with concept lattice diagrams and viewing of the whole lattice diagrams will also remain a problem. Even though we agree the lattice diagram (graphical relationships of the concepts) can be a useful tool to review and explore the whole map of a domain, we believe that the hyperlink technique is a fairly natural simplification for a lattice display and is also very natural for Web users.

A further difference is that we also support a textword search which is invoked automatically to identify the relevant documents from the context of the documents when the system fails to get a result from the lattice nodes. Conceptual scaling is also supported to handle multi-valued attributes which are obvious in the domain and to allow related values of single-valued contexts to be grouped together as the system evolves.

6 Conclusion

The system described above has been implemented and demonstrated with two test domains. There is little doubt that it seems to facilitate browsing and that users adding documents enjoy seeing how their document fits into the lattice and are motivated to make sure it is appropriately positioned. FCA is widely used for knowledge acquisition to discover concepts and rules related to objects and their attributes. Its advantage comes from the way it shows how the presence or absence of attributes distinguishes objects in the various super-concept sub-concept relations. In the system here a key feature is the incremental development of the knowledge base via a web-based interface. The key extension to FCA that we have implemented is similar to the philosophy of both RDR and Repertory grids [8] where an expert is asked to gradually build up axes of differentiation (constructs) between objects. Our system suggests keywords that the document may have in common with other documents and also indicates documents that have the same annotation and which the author may wish to differentiate. These techniques are very simple but their utility is well established in these other areas of incremental knowledge acquisition.

A more substantial evaluation is being undertaken. In this evaluation, the FCA browsing scheme is being used as the search mechanism for research interests in a research institution. The researchers themselves add the keywords related to their home page, the target document. We anticipate that more complex ontologies may be useful in applications such as this. We are investigating techniques whereby the ontology can be constructed as the system develops, as suggested in this paper, but also techniques where ontology can be imported and used for making suggestions to the user, but where the user retains complete control in using existing or adding new terms.

From our experience so far with this development it is clear to us that Formal Concept Analysis is a useful way of supporting the flexible open management of documents required by individuals, small communities or in specialised domains. It also appears that our approach can apply to conceptual modelling of domain taxonomies to be collaboratively created and maintained over time by multiple users (or authors) without the mediation of knowledge engineers. However, these apparent strengths and further possibilities still require a more thorough evaluation.

Acknowledgments. The authors would like to thank Bao Vo and Dr. Rex B.H. Kwok for helping in formalising of mathematical formulas used in definitions. This research is supported by an Australian Research Council (ARC) grant.

References

1. Aussenac-Gilles, N., Biebow B. and Szulman S. Revisiting Ontology Design: A Methodology Based on Corpus Analysis, *12th European Conference on Knowledge Acquisition and Knowledge Management* (*EKAW 2000*), Springer, 172-188, 2000.

2. Benjamins, V. R., Fensel, D., Decker, S. and Perez, A. G. (KA)²: building ontologies for the Internet: a mid-term report. *International journal of human computer studies*, Vol. 51, No. 3, 687-712, 1999.
3. Carpineto, C. and Romano, G. GALOIS: An Order-Theoretic Approach to Conceptual Clustering, *In Proceedings of the Machine Learning Conference*, 33-40, 1993.
4. Carpineto, C. and Romano, G. Information retrieval through hybrid navigation of lattice representations. International Journal of Human-Computer Studies, 45, 553-578, 1996.
5. Carpineto, C. and Romano, G. A Lattice Conceptual Clustering System and Its Application to Browsing Retrieval. *Machine Learning*, 24(2), 95-122, 1996.
6. Compton, P. and Jansen, R. A Philosophical Basis for Knowledge Acquisition. Knowledge Acquisition 2:242-257, 1990.
7. Furnas, G. W., Landauer, T. K., Gomez, L. M. and Dumais, S. T. Statistical semantics: analysis of the potential performance of key-word information systems, *Bell System Technical Journal*, 62, 1753-1806, 1983.
8. Gaines, B. and Shaw, M. Cognitive and Logical Foundation of Knowledge Acquisition. *The 5th Knowledge Acquisition for Knowledge Based Systems Workshop*, 9.1-9.25, 1990.
9. Ganter, B. Computing with Conceptual Structures, *Proceedings of the 8th International Conference on Conceptual Structure (ICCS 2000)*, Darmstadt, Springer, 453-467, 2000.
10. Ganter, B. and Wille, R. Conceptual Scaling, In: F. Roberts (ed.): *Application of Combinatorics and Graph Theory to the Biological and Social Sciences*, Springer, 139-167, 1989.
11. Ganter, B. and Wille, R. Formal Concept Analysis: mathematical foundations. Springer, Heidelberg, 1999.
12. Godin, R., Missaoui, R. and Alaoui, H. Learning algorithms using a Galois lattice structure, *Proceedings of the Third International Conference on Tools for Artificial Intelligence*, San Jose, CA: IEEE Computer Society Press, 22-29, 1991.
13. Godin, R., Missaoui, R. and Alaoui, H. Incremental concept formulation algorithms based on Galois (concept) lattices. Computational Intelligence, 11(2), 246-267, 1995.
14. Kang, B. H., Yoshida, K., Motoda, H. and Compton, P. Help Desk System with Intelligent Interface, *Applied Artificial Intelligence*, 11: 611-631, 1997.
15. Kim, M., Compton, P. and Kang, B. H. Incremental Development of a Web Based Help Desk System, *Proceedings of the 4th Australian Knowledge Acquisition Workshop (AKAW99)*, University of NSW, Sydney, 13-29, 1999.
16. Lin, X. Map Displays for Information Retrieval, *Journal of the American Society of Information Science*, 48:40-54, 1997.
17. Maedche, A. and Staab, S. Mining Ontologies from Text, *12th European Conference on Knowledge Acquisition and Knowledge Management (EKAW)*, Springer, 189-202, 2000.
18. Marchionini, G. and Shneiderman, B. Finding facts vs. browsing knowledge in hypertext systems, *IEEE Computer*, 21, 70-80, 1988.
19. Priss, U. Faceted Information Representation, In: Stumme, Gerd (ed.), working with Conceptual Structures. *Proceedings of the 8th International Conference on Conceptual Structures*, Shaker Verlag, Achene, 84-94, 2000.
20. Richards, D. and Compton, P. Knowledge acquisition first, modelling later, *Knowledge Acquisition, Modeling and Management*, E. Plaza and R. Benjamins, Berlin, Springer: 237-252, 1997.
21. Stumme, G. Hierarchies of Conceptual Scales. *12th Banff Knowledge Acquisition, Modelling and Management,* Eds. B Gaines; R Kremer; M Musen, Banff Canada, 16-21 Oct., SRDG Publication, University of Calgary, 1999.
22. Wille, R. Restructuring lattice theory: an approach based on hierarchies of concepts. In: Ivan Rival (ed.), Ordered sets, Reidel, *Dordrecht-Boston*, 445-470, 1982.
23. Wille, R. Concept lattices and conceptual knowledge systems. *Computers and Mathematics with Applications*, 23, 493-515, 1992.

Learner's Self-assessment: A Case Study of SVM for Information Retrieval

Adam Kowalczyk and Bhavani Raskutti
{Adam.Kowalczyk, Bhavani.Raskutti}@team.telstra.com

Telstra Corporation, 770 Blackburn Road, Clayton, Victoria 3168, Australia

Abstract. The paper demonstrates that the predictive capabilities of a typical kernel machine on the training set can be a reliable indicator of its performance on the independent test set in the region where scores are larger than 1 in magnitude. We present initial results of a number of experiments on the popular Reuters newswire benchmark and the NIST handwritten digit recognition data set. In particular, we demonstrate that the values of recall and precision estimated from the training and independent test sets are within a few percent of each other for the evaluated benchmarks. Interestingly, this holds for both separable and non-separable data cases, and for training sample sizes an order of magnitude smaller than the dimensionality of the feature space used (e.g. using $\approx$ 2000 samples versus $\approx$ 20000 features for Reuters data).
A theoretical explanation of the observed phenomena is also presented.

1 Introduction

Many of us can recall school days, when studying for a biology or chemistry test, we were quite conscious of which parts of the task at hand we have learned well and which we have not. And the satisfactory (or not) solutions of previously unseen problems in the school test the next day confirmed that our self-assessment was quite correct. Whether a learning machine is capable of similar introspection and can assess what it has learnt without referring to an external (independent) test is a fundamental question bordering on the issue of self awareness. What we have in mind here is not a test based on a hold-out validation set, or a cross-validation assessment, like it is done in the case of decision tree generation, but an assessment based on uniform treatment of all of the training set and some simple information on the state of the machine. The message from this paper is that in some situations of practical interest such self-assessment can be done efficiently for support vector machines, even for small training samples.

This is somewhat contrary to the accepted machine learning idea that estimates based on training sets are notoriously optimistic when compared with true values. For instance, in supervised learning of a classification the experimental training errors are much smaller than the test (true) errors. Similarly, in the theory of learning systems, a typical upper bound on generalisation error consists of a training error plus a significant penalty term. This penalty becomes non-trivial (i.e. < 1) only in the "thermodynamic limit" of unrealistically large training samples. In particular, the penalty term in the well known uniform bounds produced by VC-theory becomes ≤ 1 only for a training sample many times the size of VC-dimension of the learning machine, which is normally much larger than the number of available training samples for practical machines.

Against this background kernel machines seem to be a notable exception. It has been noticed recently [10] that in the case of support vector machines [13] or regularisation networks [4,8], training *margin error* rate can be proven to be an almost unbiased estimator of the true margin error rate. Interestingly, proofs hold for small training samples, explicitly smaller than the VC-dimension of the function class. This can be extended to estimators of various other risks which can be used to define measures of interest for information retrieval, e.g. recall and precision.

Can such estimators be of practical relevance? The answer is not straightforward. Firstly, practical machines are only suboptimal approximations of ideal solutions, and the imperfections may adversely impact on the properties of interest. Secondly, the proof of the above result relies essentially on assumptions, such as the *iid* sampling from continuous probability density, which are not satisfied in practice [7]. Thirdly, the estimators although unbiased may have variance too large to be of practical relevance. The prime aim of this paper is to test them experimentally in some domains of practical interest such as text categorisation (Section 3) and recognition of handwritten digits (Section 4), and offer some theoretical corroboration of the observed phenomena (Section 5).

2 Support Vector Machines and Estimators

Consider an m-sample

$$\overrightarrow{xy}^m := \big((x_1, y_1), ..., (x_m, y_m)\big) \in (X \times \{\pm 1\})^m \tag{1}$$

of patterns $x_i \in X \subset \mathbb{R}^n$ and target values $y_i = \pm 1$. The learning algorithms used by *support vector machines* (SVM) [1,2,14] minimise the regularised risk functional:

$$f_{\overrightarrow{xy}^m} = \arg\min_{f \in \mathcal{H}} R_{\overrightarrow{xy}^m}[f] := ||f||^2_{\mathcal{H}} + C \sum_{i=1}^{m} L([1 - y_i f(x_i)]_+). \tag{2}$$

Here $\mathcal{H}$ denotes a reproducing kernel Hilbert space (RKHS) [14] of real valued functions $f : X \to \mathbb{R}$, $||.||_{\mathcal{H}}$ the corresponding norm, $C > 0$ is a regularisation constant, $L : \mathbb{R} \to \mathbb{R}^+$ is a *non-negative*, convex *cost function* penalising for the deviation $1 - y_i f(x_i)$ of the estimator $f(x_i)$ from target y_i and $[\xi]_+ := \max(0, \xi)$. For $L(\xi) := \xi^p$ with $p = 1$ (*linear cost*) or $p = 2$ (*quadratic cost*), the minimisation (2) can be solved by quadratic programming [1] with the formal use of the following expansions holding for the minimiser (2):

$$f_{\overrightarrow{xy}^m}(x) = \sum_{i=1}^{m} \alpha_i y_i k(x_i, x), \tag{3}$$

$$||f_{\overrightarrow{xy}^m}||_{\mathcal{H}} = \sum_{i,j=1}^{m} \alpha_i \alpha_j y_i y_j k(x_i, x_j), \tag{4}$$

where $k : X \times X \to \mathbb{R}$ is kernel corresponding to the RKHS $\mathcal{H}$ [8]. Likewise, the quadratic programming gives a solution to the *hard margin* case [1, 2, 14] which, in terms of (2) corresponds to the cost $L(\xi) := 1$ for $\xi > 0$ and $L(\xi) := 0$, otherwise, and the constant $C > 1/\rho$, where $\rho := \max_{(\alpha_i)} y_i f_{\overrightarrow{xy}^m}(x_i)/||f_{\overrightarrow{xy}^m}||_{\mathcal{H}}$ is the margin with which data can be separated by the kernel machines.

3 Experiments with Reuters News-wires

For our experiments, we have used the widely used text categorisation benchmark, the modApte split of the *Reuters*-21578 news-wires collection available from http://www.research.att.com/lewis [3, 12, 16]. This split has 9603 training documents (*ApteTrain*) and 3,299 test documents (*ApteTest*) spread over 135 diverse categories with varying frequency of occurrence. The modApte split assigns documents from April 7, 1987 and before to the training set, and the remainder to the ApteTest set. This introduces a systematic bias in a sense used in statistics. (For instance, contrary to the common sense expectation, for some categories the training set is harder to classify than the test set, cf. Figures 1 and 2.) Hence, in experiments we have used systematically two independent test sets, one was on the remainder of the ApteTrain after the training subset was randomly selected from it, and another on the ApteTest collection.

The feature vector in these experiments consists of the 20197 unique words extracted from the ApteTrain documents, where the extraction involved case conversion, stemming and removal of words in a standard stop list [12]. We have used exclusively SVMs with linear kernel, $k(x, x') = 1 + x \cdot x'$, since this is the simplest kernel machine and previous experiments have shown that more complicated kernels do not necessarily give better performance [3]. Hence our optimal machine has an expansion $f_{\overrightarrow{xy}^m}(x) = \sum_{i=1}^{l} \alpha_i y_i (1 + x \cdot x_i)$, where the Lagrangian coefficients (α_i) are given as a solution of the following optimisation:

$$\min \Big(\sum_{i,j=1}^{m} y_i y_j \alpha_i \alpha_j (1 + x_i \cdot x_j) + C \sum_{i=1}^{m} [1 - y_i \sum_{j=1}^{m} \alpha_j y_j (1 - x_i \cdot x_j)]_+^p \Big), \tag{5}$$

where $p = 1$ or 2.

For a predictor $f : X \to \mathbb{R}$ and a data sequence $\overrightarrow{xy}^m \in \big(X \times \{\pm 1\}\big)^m$ we shall be evaluating estimators of *recall*

$$Rec_{\overrightarrow{xy}^m}[f, \theta] := \frac{\big|\{i\ ;\ f(x_i) > \theta\ \&\ y_i = 1\}\big|}{\big|\{i\ ;\ y_i = 1\}\big|}, \tag{6}$$

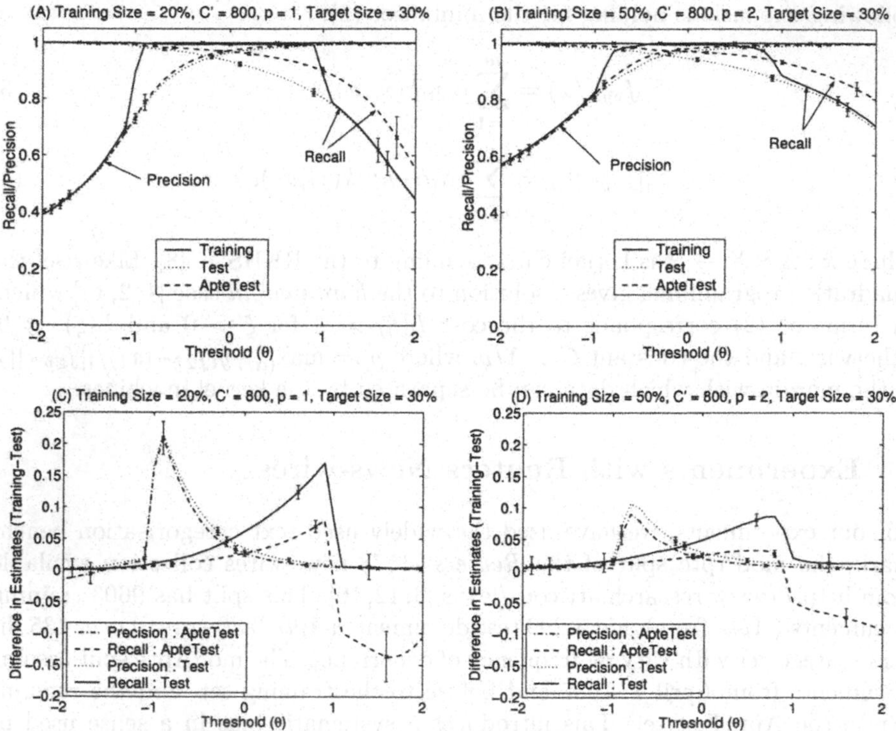

Fig. 1. Precision and Recall estimates and the corresponding differences for Reuters benchmark, category = 'earn' (30%), the largest category. Experimental settings were $C' = 800$, $p = 1$, $m = 1920$ for Figures A and C and $p = 2$, $m = 4801$ for Figures B and D. The systematic bias in ApteTest is clearly evident, e.g. contrary to the common sense expectations, we observe the better recall for ApteTest than for the training set.

and *precision*:

$$Prec_{\bar{x}\bar{y}^m}[f, \theta] := \frac{\left|\{i \,;\, f(x_i) > \theta \;\&\; y_i = 1\}\right|}{\left|\{i \,;\, f(x_i) > \theta\}\right|}. \tag{7}$$

First, we have generated 100 random splits of ApteTrain collection into the training (20% or 50% of the data) and test sets (the remaining 80% or 50%, respectively). Estimators were calculated for the the training, the test and, additionally, for ApteTest sets for thresholds in the range $-2 \leq \theta \leq +2$. This has been repeated for each experimental setting: $p = 1, 2$, learning constants $C = C'/m$, where $C' = 10,800$ and m is the number of training examples, $m = 1920, 4801$ for the 20% and 50% split respectively. In our Figures we show the averages and standard deviations over those 100 splits.

Figure 1 shows precision and recall estimates (Figures 1(A) and 1(B)) and their differences (Figures 1(C) and 1(D)) for Reuters benchmark, category =

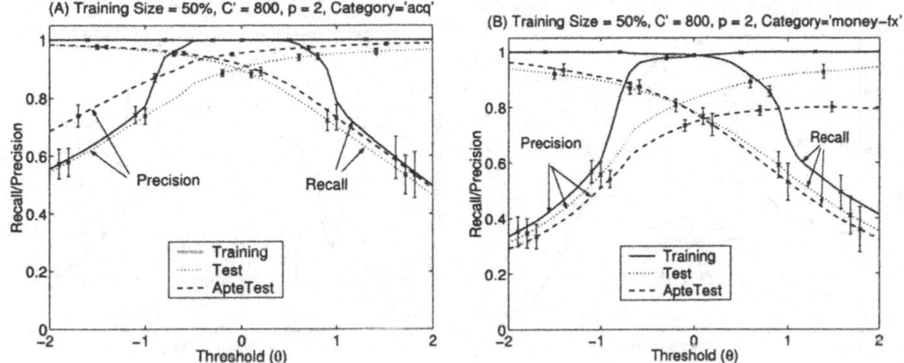

Fig. 2. Precision and Recall estimates for acq' and 'money-fx' the second and third largest categories in Reuters benchmark. Experimental settings were $C' = 800$, $m = 4801$ and $p = 2$. The systematic bias in ApteTest is clearly visible for category = 'acq', e.g. we observe the better precision for ApteTest than for the training set.

'earn' (30%), which is the largest category. The systematic bias in ApteTest for this category is clearly visible, e.g. contrary to expectations, we observe the better recall for ApteTest than for the training set. In order to examine if such bias exists for other categories, Figure 2 plots the precision and recall estimates for the second and third largest categories, category = 'acq' and 'money-fx'. Experimental settings were $C' = 800$, $m = 4801$ and $p = 2$. Note that the systematic bias in ApteTest is clearly visible for category = 'acq', e.g. we observe the better precision for ApteTest than for the training set. No such bias is evident for category = 'money-fx', although the empirical estimates for this category are very optimistic indicating that this is one of the hardest of the top 10 Reuters categories [3].

For learning constant $C' = 800$ we observe a well defined phase transition at $\theta = 1$ for recall and at $\theta = -1$ for precision. For the learning constant $C = 10$ those phase transitions are smoother, however the gap between estimates for the training and test sets is much smaller (compare Figure 1(D) with Figure 3(C)).

Figure 3 plots the precision and recall estimates for two different SVM settings, and the corresponding differences between the training and test estimates when different amounts of training data is used. From the differences graph for training size = 20% and 50% in the two Figures 3(C) and 3(D), it is evident that the greater the amount of training examples, the closer the training estimate is to the test estimate. Figure 3(A) and 3(C) are for the settings $C' = 10$, $p = 2$ and category = 'earn', while Figure 3(B) and 3(D) are for the settings $C' = 800$, $p = 1$ and category = 'crude'. Note that the differences in estimates when the minority class size is 4% is much larger (Figure 3(B) and 3(D)), again highlighting the need for estimates to be based on a large number of positive training examples.

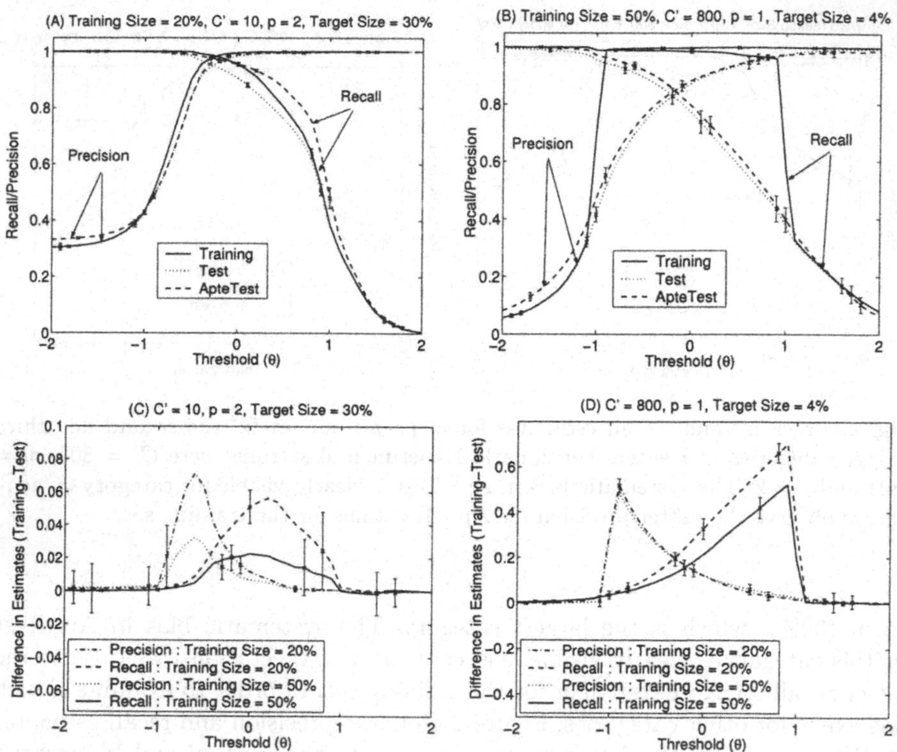

Fig. 3. Precision and Recall estimates and the corresponding differences for the largest category 'earn' (30%) and the fifth largest category 'crude' (4%) in Reuters benchmark for two different SVMs.

4 Recognition of NIST digits

In this section we present results of a test of a support vector machine with a non-linear kernel on a popular benchmark data set of handwritten digits[1]. Each data entry is a 784 pixel grey scale image, with a pixel represented by an integer between 0 and 255. We have decided to use the fourth order polynomial kernel $k(x_i, x_j) := (1+x_i \cdot x_j)^4$, which was the best performing for this data in [1].In this case data is separable hence we have decided to use hard threshold SVM. Such a machine can be obtained by optimisation of (2) with loss $L(\xi) := 1$ if $\xi > 0$ and $L = 0$, otherwise, and sufficiently large C, but there is also a possibility of using dedicated algorithms instead. In our research an algorithm described in [9] has been used.

In Figure 4 we give a sample of results obtained. Two target tasks have been set: one to retrieve images of digit 0 and another to retrieve images of digit 4. The training was on 30K samples randomly selected from 60K in the training

[1] Available from http://www.research.att.com/~yann/exdb/mnist/

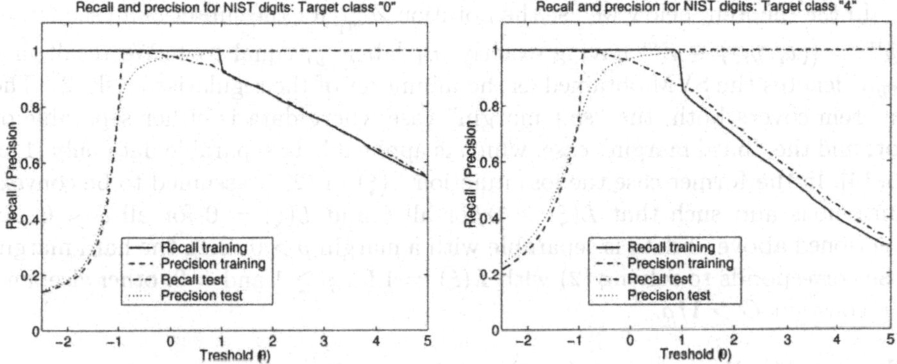

Fig. 4. Plots of averages precision and recall estimators for NIST digit data test. Results of a single run are shown for the task of discrimination of digit 0 from the remaining nine digits. The SVM was trained on 30,000 randomly selected samples from the standard training set of 60,000 and then tested on the standard test set of 10,000 patterns.Note that for the digit 4, recall for threshold $\theta > 1$ is systematically lower for the training set, then for the independent test set.

corpus, and the test was on the standard set 10K samples from *different* writers. In the case of 0 the trained network used 1038 support vectors, made 41 errors on the test set and achieved > 80% of the optimal margin. Similarly, in the case of 4 the trained network used 1396 support vectors, made 71 errors on the test set and achieved > 80% of the optimal margin.

5 Theoretical Explanation

It is convenient to introduce the notation $Z := X \times \{\pm 1\}$ and $\overrightarrow{z}^m := \overrightarrow{xy}^m := ((x_1, y_1), ..., (x_m, y_m))$ for the training m-sequence from $Z^m = (X \times \{\pm 1\})^m$. We shall always assume that our *target* or *minority* samples have label $y_i = +1$ and reserve the label -1 for the majority (background) samples.

We assume that there is given a probability distribution P on the input space $Z = X \times \{\pm 1\}$. The *true or expected recall* of a predictor $f : X \rightarrow \mathbb{R}$ is defined by the conditional probability:

$$Rec[f, \theta] := \mathbb{P}[f(x) > \theta | y = 1]$$

for every $\theta \in \mathbb{R}$. We shall also study a modification the *empirical* estimator (6):

$$Rec^*_{\overrightarrow{xy}^m}[f, \theta] := \frac{|\{i \; ; \; f(x_i) > \theta \; \& \; y_i = 1\}|}{m_1}, \tag{8}$$

where m_1 is an integer $0 < m_1 < m$. The most interesting is the case when $m_1 \approx m\,\pi_1$, where $\pi_1 := \mathbb{P}[y = 1]$ denotes *the prior* of the target class. For large m, this modification of recall makes little difference.

In the theorem below we use the notation $Z^m_{|m_1}$ for the subset of all sequences $\overrightarrow{xy}^m = ((x_i, y_i)) \in Z^m$ having exactly m_1 labels y_i equal to 1. We recall that $f_{\overrightarrow{xy}^m}$ denotes the SVM obtained as the minimiser of the regularised risk (2). The theorem covers both, the "soft margin" case where data is either separable or not, and the "hard margin" case, which is applicable to separable data only [1, 2, 13, 14]. In the former case the loss function $L(\xi)$ in (2) is assumed to be convex, continuous and such that $L(\xi) \geq 0$ for all ξ and $L(\xi) = 0$ for all $\xi \leq 0$. As mentioned above, if data is separable with a margin $\rho > 0$, then the hard margin case corresponds to solving (2) with $L(\xi) := 1$ for $p \geq 1$ and $= 0$, otherwise, and the constant $C > 1/\rho$.

Theorem 1. *For every $\theta > 1$ and every integer $0 < m_1 < m$:*

$$\mathbb{E}\big[Rec^*_{\overrightarrow{xy}^m}[f_{\overrightarrow{xy}^m}, \theta] \mid \overrightarrow{xy}^m \in Z^m_{|m_1}\big] = \frac{m_1 - 1}{m\pi_1}\mathbb{E}\big[Rec[f_{\overrightarrow{xy}^{m-1}}, \theta] \mid \overrightarrow{xy}^{m-1} \in Z^{m-1}_{|m_1-1}\big] \quad (9)$$

We shall outline the proof in the subsequent subsection. Now we concentrate on the discussion of the above result.

If $m_1 \approx \lfloor m\pi_1 \rfloor \gg 1$, then $\frac{m_1-1}{m\,\pi_1} \approx 1$ and

$$\mathbb{E}\big[Rec[f_{\overrightarrow{xy}^{m-1}}, \theta] \mid \overrightarrow{xy}^{m-1} \in Z^{m-1}_{|m_1-1}\big] \approx \mathbb{E}\big[Rec[f_{\overrightarrow{xy}^m}, \theta] \mid \overrightarrow{xy}^m \in Z^m_{|m_1}\big].$$

Hence with "high" accuracy (9) implies

$$\mathbb{E}\big[Rec^*_{\overrightarrow{xy}^m}[f_{\overrightarrow{xy}^m}, \theta] \mid \overrightarrow{xy}^m \in Z^m_{|m_1}\big] \approx \mathbb{E}\big[Rec[f_{\overrightarrow{xy}^m}, \theta] \mid \overrightarrow{xy}^m \in Z^m_{|m_1}\big]$$

and subsequently

$$\mathbb{E}\big[Rec^*_{\overrightarrow{xy}^m}[f_{\overrightarrow{xy}^m}, \theta]\big] \approx \mathbb{E}\big[Rec[f_{\overrightarrow{xy}^m}, \theta]\big]$$

since $\mathbb{P}\big(\bigcup_{|m_1 - m\pi_1| < m\epsilon} Z^m_{|m_1}\big) \approx 1$ for an $\epsilon > 0$ and sufficiently large m. This can be interpreted as a theoretical corroboration of experimental observation that there is no systematic bias in the empirical estimator of the recall for $\theta > 1$. In other words, empirical recall is sometimes pessimistic, sometimes optimistic estimator of the true recall, but on average neutral. Needless to say, that our experimental results in Figures 1, 2, and 3 are consistent with this statement.

5.1 Outline of the proof of Theorem 1

The proof is based on leave-one-out estimator and involves a number of steps.

A. The SVM $f_{\overrightarrow{xy}^m}$ obtained as the minimiser of the functional (2) is unique. This can be derived from the strict convexity of functional $f \mapsto R_{\overrightarrow{xy}^m}[f]$ [14].

B. Let $\overrightarrow{xy}^{m\setminus i} Z^{m-1}$ denote the training sequence (1) with the ith training instance removed. Then

$$y_i f_{\overrightarrow{xy}^{m\setminus i}}(x_i) \leq y_i f_{\overrightarrow{xy}^m}(x_i) \qquad (\forall \overrightarrow{xy}^m \in Z^m).$$

The crux is to show that if this inequality does not hold, then $R_{\overrightarrow{xy}^m}[f_{\overrightarrow{xy}^m\setminus i}] \leq R_{\overrightarrow{xy}^m}[f_{\overrightarrow{xy}^m}]$, which contradict the uniqueness of the minimiser $f_{\overrightarrow{xy}^m}$ (since $f_{\overrightarrow{xy}^m\setminus i} \neq f_{\overrightarrow{xy}^m}$ in such a case).

C. If $y_i f(x_i) > 1$, then

$$y_i f_{\overrightarrow{xy}^m\setminus i}(x_i) = y_i f_{\overrightarrow{xy}^m}(x_i).$$

This can be derived from the convexity of the functional $\xi \mapsto L(\xi)$ in the region $\xi > 0$ and the uniqueness of SVM solution and the Khun-Tucker conditions [1, 2, 14].

D. Let us consider the leave-one-out estimator of the number of recalled patterns:

$$L_\theta(\overrightarrow{xy}^m) = \sum_{i=1}^{m} \mathbb{I}[f_{\overrightarrow{xy}^m\setminus i}(x_i) > \theta \ \&\ y_i = 1],$$

for every $\theta \in \mathbb{R}$, where $\mathbb{I}[\,\cdot\,]$ denotes the indicator function equal to 1 if its argument is *true* and 0, otherwise. Then from the last two Steps we get

$$\frac{L_\theta(\overrightarrow{xy}^m)}{m_1} = Rec^*_{\overrightarrow{xy}^m}[f_{\overrightarrow{xy}^m}, \theta] \qquad (10)$$

for every $\overrightarrow{xy}^m \in Z^m_{|m_1}$ and $\theta > 1$.

E. We show a variant of Luntz-Brailovski theorem [14]:

$$\mathbb{E}[\frac{L_\theta(\overrightarrow{xy}^m)}{m_1} \mid \overrightarrow{xy}^m \in Z^m_{|m_1}] = \frac{m_1 - 1}{m\,\pi_1}\mathbb{E}[Rec[f_{\overrightarrow{xy}^{m-1}}, \theta] \mid \overrightarrow{xy}^{m-1} \in Z^{m-1}_{|m_1-1}] \qquad (11)$$

for every $\theta > 1$, where $\pi_1 = \mathbb{P}[y = 1]$ is the prior of class 1.

The proof involves a chain of transformations:

$$\mathbb{E}\,[\frac{L_\theta(\overrightarrow{xy}^m)}{m_1} \mid \overrightarrow{xy}^m \in Z^m_{|m_1}]$$

$$= \frac{1}{m_1 \mathbb{P}(Z^m_{|m_1})}\int \cdots \int_{\overrightarrow{z}^m = \overrightarrow{xy}^m \in Z^m_{|m_1}} \sum_{i=1}^{m} \mathbb{I}[f_{\overrightarrow{xy}^m\setminus i}(x_i) > \theta \ \&\ y_i = 1] dP(z_1)...dP(z_m)$$

$$= \frac{1}{m_1 \mathbb{P}(Z^m_{|m_1})}\int \cdots \int_{Z^{m-1}_{|m_1-1}} (\int_Z \sum_{i=1}^{m} \mathbb{I}[f_{\overrightarrow{xy}^m\setminus i}(x_i) > \theta \ \&\ y_i = 1] dP(z_i))$$
$$dP(z_1)...dP(z_{i-1})dP(z_{i+1})...dP(z_m)$$

$$= \frac{m_1 - 1}{m_1 \mathbb{P}(Z^m_{|m_1})}\int \cdots \int_{Z^{m-1}_{|m_1-1}} Rec[f_{\overrightarrow{xy}^{m-1}}, \theta] dP(z_1)...dP(z_{i-1})dP(z_{i+1})...dP(z_m)$$

$$= \frac{(m_1 - 1)\,\mathbb{P}(Z^{m-1}_{|m_1-1})}{m_1 \mathbb{P}(Z^m_{|m_1})}\mathbb{E}\left[Rec[f_{\overrightarrow{xy}^{m-1}}, \theta] \mid \overrightarrow{xy}^{m-1} \in Z^{m-1}_{|m_1-1}\right]$$

$$= \frac{(m_1 - 1)}{m\pi_1}\mathbb{E}[Rec[f_{\overrightarrow{xy}^{m-1}}, \theta] \mid \overrightarrow{xy}^{m-1} \in Z^{m-1}_{|m_1-1}]$$

For the last equality we use the relation $\mathbb{P}(Z^m_{|m_1}) = \binom{m}{m_1}\pi_1^{m_1}(1 - \pi_1)^{m-m_1}$.

The equation (9) of Theorem 1 follows from (10) and (11).

6 General Discussion

Below we analyse the various issues highlighted by our experimental findings. **Early stopping.** The (preliminary) experiments reported in this paper involved generation of thousands of different SVMs, which forced us to use early stopping heuristics. This could affect our results though we do not believe that it is significant. Our view is that with more exact solutions, the observed phenomena, such as the phase transition, should become sharper.

Link to support vectors. We recall the a data point (x_i, y_i) is called a support vector if the coefficient α_i in the data expansion (3) of the SVM is non-zero. From the Khun-Tucker conditions it follows that for the (ideal) minimiser of (2) this is equivalent to $y_i f(x_i) \leq 1$. Thus we can summarise our empirical results in the following "rule of thumb": the empirical estimates of recall are "accurate" as long as they are based on non-support vectors, however, once the support vectors are involved, the estimates are optimistically biased.

Phase transition. The "sudden jump" (a "first order phase transition" in physics parlance) in the training estimates of the recall for threshold $\theta \approx 1$ is directly linked to the concentration of support vectors with positive label around value $f(x_i) = 1$. Note the for the small values of training constant C those jumps become smoother, as support vectors are less concentrated (cf. Figures 3).

Correction for support vectors. The training estimates of the recall for $\theta < 1$ can be potentially improved using various theoretical corrections and lower bounds for leave-one-out estimator [5, 6, 11, 15]. Joachims in [6] has investigated recall for Reuters benchmark at threshold $\theta = 0$, hence he overlooked the phenomena studied in this paper.

Theoretical corroboration for precision. The extension of our theory to the case of precision is harder, since it's definition involves a denominator dependent on threshold θ (cf. Eqn.7). However, rough approximations can be derived for this case from our result for recall.

Linear vs. quadratic penalty. In our experiments, we have used two soft margin SVMs ($p = 1, 2$) and additionally, a hard margin SVM for the NIST digit recognition task, and our observations regarding estimators are valid across all of these SVMs. Due to space limitations, we have not addressed the issue of performance differences due to different SVMs.

Break-even point. Interestingly, break-even point, i.e. the point at which recall is equal to precision, is roughly the same for the test set for all settings (cf. category = 'earn', in Figures 1(A), 1(B) and 3(A)). This raises the utility of the extensively used break-even point as a text categorisation performance evaluation measure.

Bias in the standard test sets. Result in Figure 4 for digit 4 and in Figures 1 and 2 for Reuters show that standard test sets for both data collections used are biased in a way that empirical estimates of both retrieval and recall for $\theta > 1$ are pessimistic. In the context of Theorem 1 the explanation is that the standard training and test sets for these benchmarks are not iid sampled from the same distribution, which is consistent with the way they have been created.

NIST digits. More systematic study of NIST digits benchmark in the context of estimators considered in the paper will be reported soon, including both soft and hard margin SVMs. The result reported in [1] that very accurate soft margins SVMs trained on the whole training set of 60K patterns use 1 to 2 thousand of support vectors. Hence, the bulk of the training data (more than 95%) are non-support vectors, for which training estimates should be very accurate. However one should remember, that this may be obscured by the bias which exists in the standard NIST digit test set (cf. Figure 4).

Practical implications. Due to the prevalent belief that estimates based on training sets are notoriously optimistic, a common practise in machine learning is to use tests on a validation set rather than on the training set in order to assess quality of the classifier. In practice this is fine as long as the training data is abundant, however this is not always the case. Moreover, if we try to subtly fine-tune our classifier involving multiple tests on our validation set, then we tacitly introduce additional bias and our validation set will not be truly independent any more. The point we want to make here is that in practise, the training set is a valuable and scarce resource, which should be utilised for assessment of classifier performance whenever possible.

7 Conclusion

The paper has introduced a novel topic of reliable performance estimation from training set. The preliminary experimental results presented here confirm a theoretical prediction that the support vector machine performance on training data is a reliable indicator of its performance on independent test data, in the region where allocated score is larger than 1 in magnitude. This has been demonstrated for practical benchmarks of Reuters news-wires and NIST hand-written digits.

We have shown that empirical estimates of recall and precision from the training set can be of high accuracy, with errors below a few percent. For Reuters benchmark these results have been demonstrated for relatively small training sample sizes, an order of magnitude smaller than the dimensionality of the feature space.

We have demonstrated that the standard test sets for popular Reuters news-wires and NIST hand-written digit benchmark have systematic bias, making for instance, the performance on the test set better than on the training set. Such an anomaly can obscure some subtle properties of learning machines, and researchers should exercise care while dealing with these data sets.

A number of new questions have been raised by this research and should be investigated further. In particular, future research should investigate other data sets including other real data sets and carefully designed artificial data. Also kernels other than the linear kernel studied in this paper should be tested. In addition, the well pronounced phenomenon of phase transition in accuracy of estimation that has been observed consistently should be investigated further.

Acknowledgements

The permission of the Chief Technology Officer, Telstra Corporation, to publish this paper is gratefully acknowledged.

References

1. C. Cortes and V. Vapnik. Support vector networks. *Machine Learning*, 20:273 – 297, 1995.
2. N. Cristianini and J. Shawe-Taylor. *An Introduction to Support Vector Machines and other kernel-based learning methods.* Cambridge Uni. Press, Cambridge, 2000.
3. S. Dumais, J. Platt, Heckerman D., and M. Sahami. Inductive learning algorithms and representations for text categorization. In *Seventh International Conference on Information and Knowledge Management*, 1998.
4. F. Girosi, M. Jones, and T. Poggio. Regularization theory and neural networks architectures. *Neural Computation*, 7(2):219–269, 1995.
5. T. Jaakkola and D. Haussler. Estimating the Generalization Performance of an SVM Efficiently. In *Proc. of the Seventh International Conference on Machine Learning*, San Francisco, 1999. Morgan Kaufman.
6. T. Joachims. Estimating the Generalization Performance of an SVM Efficiently. In P. Langley, editor, *Seventh Int. Conf. on Machine Learning*, pages 431–438, Morgan Kaufman, 2000.
7. M. Kerns. A bound on error of cross validation using the approximation and estimation rates, with consequences for the training-test split. *Neural Computation*, 9:1143–1162, 1997.
8. G. Kimeldorf and G. Wahba. A correspondence between Bayesian estimation of stochastic processes and smoothing by splines. *Ann. Math. Statist.*, 41:495–502, 1970.
9. A. Kowalczyk. Maximal margin perceptron. In P.Bartlett, B. Schölkopf, D. Schuurmans, and A. Smola, editors, *Advances in Large Margin Classifiers*, pages 61–100, Cambridge, MA, 2000. MIT Press.
10. A. Kowalczyk. Sparsity of data representation of optimal kernel machine and leave-one-out estimator. In T.G.Dietterich T.K. Leen and V. Tresp, editors, *Advances in Neural Information Processing Systems 13*, Cambridge, MA, 2001. MIT Press.
11. M. Opper and O. Winther. Gaussian process classification and svm: Mean field results and leave-one out estimator. In A. Smola, P.Bartlett, B. Schölkopf, and D. Schuurmans, editors, *Advances in Large Margin Classifiers*, pages 301–316, Cambridge, MA, 2000. MIT Press.
12. B. Raskutti, H. Ferrá, and A. Kowalczyk. Second Order Features for Maximising Text Classification Performance . In *Proceedings of the Twelfth European Conference on Machine Learning ECML01*, 2001.
13. V. Vapnik. *The Nature of Statistical Learning Theory.* Springer Verlag, New York, 1995.
14. V. Vapnik. *Statistical Learning Theory.* Wiley, New York, 1998.
15. V. Vapnik and O. Chapelle. Bounds on error expectation for svm. In A. Smola, P.Bartlett, B. Schölkopf, and D. Schuurmans, editors, *Advances in Large Margin Classifiers*, pages 261–280, Cambridge, MA, 2000. MIT Press.
16. S. M. Weiss, C. Apte, F. Damerau, D.E. Johnson, F. J. Oles, T. Goetz, and T. Hampp. Maximizing text-mining performance. *IEEE Intelligent Systems*, 14, 1999.

A Semiotic Model of Communication and Its Implications for the Digital City Development

Victor V. Kryssanov[1], Masayuki Okabe[1], Koh Kakusho[2], and Michihiko Minoh[2]

[1] Japan Science and Technology Corporation, Japan
[2] Center for Information and Multimedia Studies, Kyoto University, Japan
{kryssanov, okabe, kakusho, minoh}@mm.media.kyoto-u.ac.jp

Abstract. This study attempts to find a theoretical basis for the development of digital cities. The ultimate function of a digital city is to support navigation in an environment. Navigation builds on meanings of the environment resulted from semiosis processes. These processes may affect each other when combined so that become able to communicate. Communication is performed with signs and depends on the behavioral co-ordination of communicating parties. The classical theories do not satisfactory explain communication. The paper introduces a new model of communication appropriate for computer treatment.

1 Introduction

In the last few years, a great deal has been written in the academic and popular literature about the extension of the urban space-economies and social institutions into the new "virtual areas" called "digital cities" [11]. A digital city is usually understood as a collection of digital products and information resources deployed for a collaborative use. The principal mission of a digital city is to provide services aimed at facilitating social and/or spatial navigation in a virtual (e.g. "information") or physical (e.g. geographical) space. Typically, a digital city comprises a large distributed database of heterogeneous documents of various digital genres – texts, maps, animated images, and the like. It uses a computer network and a client-server protocol and allows for browsing across digital documents through appropriately ordered hyperlinks to search, retrieve, and manipulate information as needed. Networking and information retrieval are often pointed to as key issues for the development of digital cities.

As part of the information delivery, a digital city usually assists in interpretation of the results of a user's query. To facilitate understanding the results (or even the query itself, as in exploratory search), a digital city may provide the user with the related context or employ an illustrative metaphor or suitable analogy. Besides, it may utilize the user's feedback (or some data about the user) for adjusting retrieving or displaying the obtained information to make it more accessible and meaningful to the user. Another important issue that is thus often discussed by digital city developers is human-computer interaction.

Reflecting the present understanding of the concept of digital city (which is, however, far from being unified), reference [10] reports a number of implemented or pro-

M. Brooks, D. Corbett, and M. Stumptner (Eds.): AI 2001, LNAI 2256, pp. 261-272, 2001.

jected digital cities. Different authors approach the task of the development in a similar manner, defining a digital city through its functions or else through its contents with vague terms, such as "useful information," "cyberspace," "community," and the like, and with *ad hoc* design decisions. These decisions may be of arbitrary relevance to the users' needs, and they may have unpredictable (especially, on a long-term scale) social, technical, and economical consequences. Owing to the speculative definitions of basic concepts, with which they are defined, reported digital cities readily loose their identities and become almost indistinguishable from other digital products, such as map repositories and digital libraries. The study of digital cities obviously lacks conceptual clarity, and hence, the developed digital cities are not necessarily useful and usable. Another drawback common to the current implementations is that although it is usually admitted by default that a digital city is set up for a group of users rather than for a single user, the reported projects were focused on and addressed specific aspects related to the individual needs (e.g. planning a sightseeing tour) and personal adaptation (e.g. of the interface). The issue of the appropriateness of a digital city to a particular society has not been explored. Even more obscure remains the question of possible mutual influences of a digital city and the society of its users. All this could be a serious reason to question the very expediency of the digital cities.

Our work first seeks to develop a theoretical basis for the creation of digital cities. Through the study, we examine a digital city as an organization of interacting social agents and propose a semiotic model explicating communication of the agents. It is argued that the semiotic approach not only allows for building a powerful theory of communication, but suggests important implications for the digital city development.

The rest of the paper is structured as follows. Section 2 investigates the concept and identifies communication as a definitive function of a digital city. Section 3 discusses different models of communication. The core of the paper then follows, introducing a semiotic model of communication in Section 4. The model helps us better understand the dynamics of communication. Some ideas on how to apply the theoretical findings are reported in Section 5. Finally, Section 6 outlines related work and summarizes the study.

2 Navigation with a Digital City

The general task of navigation in an environment[1] can be described as a four-stage iterative process that includes [20]: 1) perception of the environment, 2) interpretation of the perception, 3) deciding whether the current goal has been reached, and 4) appropriately adjusting the behavior. Among the four stages, the last two have obviously a subjective character, whereas the other two depend on "objectively" available – sensed – information about the environment. Perception first receives and represents raw sensory data and provides for the further interpretation by combining (i.e. putting

[1] For the purpose of this study, we will not distinguish the environment of a digital city as surroundings from the environment as navigation space. In both cases the environment is "that, which is not the digital city," and the latter is often part of the former.

into a context) the obtained representations. When information available through the senses is not enough for establishing or re-establishing meanings (i.e. "knowledge") of the environment necessary for the decision-making, the navigator may ask for help a guide – someone, who (presumably) knows more about the environment. A digital city may be seen as such a guide: it works to enhance the navigator's sensing capabilities.

Perceptual Control Theory [17] proposes an explanation of the control mechanism for the navigation process. The theory tells us that a perceiving entity seeks to bring the perceived situation to its goal (or preferred state) by utilizing negative feedback from the environment: if the situation deviates from the goal, the entity acts and adapts, possibly changing its own state and the state of the environment, and the new situation is again sensed and estimated in respect to the goal. The loop repeats and keeps the system in a stable goal-directed (or motivated) state. A digital city can, in principle, sense its environment directly (e.g. through cameras and transducers – in the case of spatial navigation). There is, however, no other way for it to determine the context and, hence, semantics necessary for making the sensed information meaningful, but (ultimately) by drawing on the expertise of its users and utilizing feedback from them. In this aspect, the users (together with their knowledge) are constitutive parts of the digital city that should then be considered a social system.

Each user's knowledge is a subjective reconstruction of the locally and selectively perceived environment. No user possesses the perfect knowledge, but being connected by means of the digital city, the users can interact with each other, thus accessing to the collective "knowledge" – once sensed or created information about the environment – that is usually far more complete and encompassing than the knowledge of a solitary user. There can be different social interactions between users of a digital city, but most typical interactions are the following [7]: communication of the goal (or motivation), communication of the relevant knowledge, and the location of a source (e.g. another user) of relevant knowledge. Given the diversity and apparent subjectivism of each user's knowledge, to understand how a digital city should operate, one must clarify (at least) three principal issues: 1) what is communication (and how it goes on), 2) what is(are) the rôle(s) of a digital city in communication, and 3) how communication reconciles the diversity of the subjective views of reality.

3 Modeling Communication

There are two major approaches to understanding and modeling communication processes [6]: statistical "signal-oriented" and interpretive "meaning-based." The Shannon-Weaver theory with its conveyor tube model [19] represents the former class of the approaches. The theory (and the model) assumes the following (see also Figure 1):

- There are the (information) source and the target parties involved in communication that is seen as the "exchange of information" between them through a channel. It is generally possible for a third party – an observer – to judge about the correctness of information, whether sent or received.
- The source is active and initiates communication.

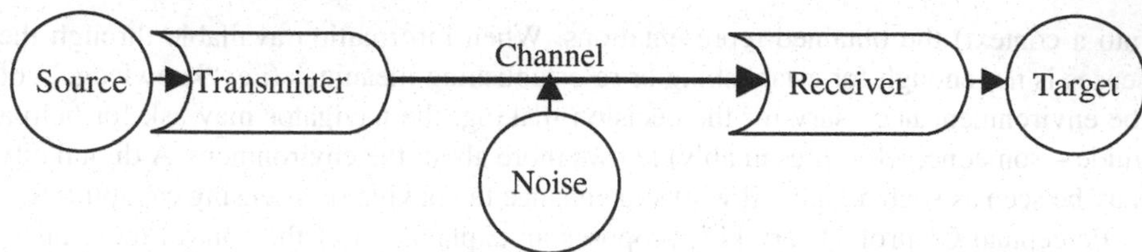

Fig. 1. The conveyor tube model

- The channel is passive and unstructured: "useful information" can be extracted from the transmitted signal, provided it statistically differs from (physical or semantic) noise.
- At the target side, received information is utilized by embedding it into predefined information structures.

Although criticized by many (see [24]), the Shannon-Weaver theory currently dominates over any other theory of communication in terms of its conceptual development and significance for practice. Among the most noticeable shortcomings of the conveyor tube model, we would mention its inability to explain the phenomena of (mis)understanding, lying, and psychological effects of verbalizing thoughts and emotions. More significant (though evident) for us is, however, the fact that the Shannon-Weaver theory can contribute little, if anything, to clarifying and coping with the complexity of communication in a social context [5]. Often, neither the target nor the source can uniquely be identified in the case of digital city (rather, there can be many sources and targets, which may or may not coincide), and it is unclear what is the rôle (apart from the straightforward "information channel" rôle) a digital city can play in communication. This makes the statistical approaches ineffective for the study of a digital city as a social system.

Striving to compensate for the limitations of the conveyor tube model, a number of interpretive models of communication have recently been developed (e.g. [1, 14]). Rooted in the human sciences, an interpretive model postulates that:

- There are no physical target and source but interpretants – that, which follow semantically from interpretation processes.
- The observer cannot judge about the correctness and incorrectness of information: these two are subject to individual interpretation. Besides, there is no direct access to reality, and the decisive notions, like "truth" and "false," are only socially determinable.
- The target, rather than source, is active.
- Not mere information, but meaning is produced, sent, and interchanged in the course of interaction between a carrier (e.g. text or sound) and culture.

Operating with meaning, interpretive models are often defined in terms of semiotics – a science about signs, which (in the Peircian interpretation [16]) departs from the naïve treatment of signs as utter signifiers of their objects by introducing a third aspect of the representation process – the interpretant – that corresponds to the meaning connecting a sign with its object. While a more detailed introduction into semiotics will be given in the next section, declaring that a sign can have many different meanings depending on the socio-cultural context should suffice to understand Figure 2, which presents an interpretive model of communication proposed in [1].

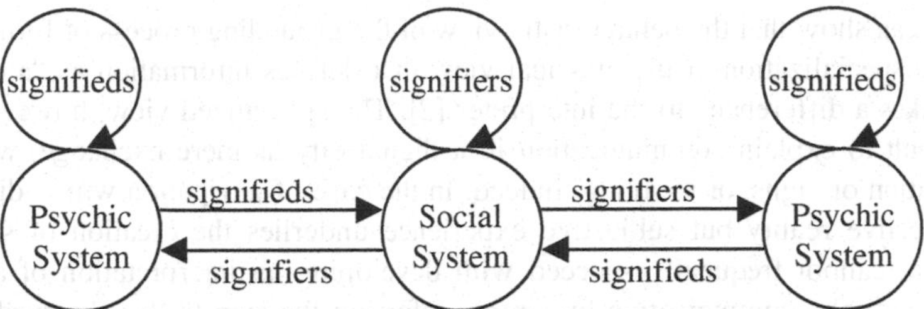

Fig. 2. The interpretive model

The model sees communication as the interaction of two or more psychic systems with a shared communicative – social (cultural) – system, in course of which signifieds (products of the psychic systems) become signs (products of the social system), which have socially (culturally) determinable meaning. In this view, a digital city is to play the rôle of the social system, and the interpretive approach can (and does) explicate many of the communication phenomena overlooked in the conveyor tube framework (see [1] for details). At the same time, however, the model appears too speculative to be useful in practice: it says little about mutual influences of the social and psychic systems (and, hence, about the dynamics of these systems), yet leaving one confused by specifying the functioning of a psychic system in terms of "signifieds" understood as either "objects" with which meaning is expressed (e.g. sound-waves) or "objects" of interpretation (i.e. that which is expressed). This, as well as the poorly matched formalization of interpretive models suggests us that to meet the modeling needs of the digital city development, a new approach, which would assimilate the advantages but remove the shortcomings of the different communication theories, needs to be devised.

4 Towards a Semiotic Theory of Communication

4.1 Insight from Systems Theory

From a behavioristic viewpoint, an individual engaged in navigation develops an internal representation using those distinctions – "signs" – of the environment, which turn up solutions to the problem that are successful behaviors [3]. Signs of such a representation arrive as "tools for indication purposes" [18]. When met in an environment, these signs (i.e. the distinctions they stand for) serve to orient the navigator, regardless of their other possible (or "actual") meanings and rôles. The navigator is not really interested in "getting to the truth," but in knowing what happens or what are possible consequences – expectations, when a sign is encountered. In this aspect, signs come up as signifiers of once successful interaction between an individual and an environment: a sign is an orientational "pointer" to not merely an object standing in a referential relation with it, but to the outcome desired for the user (e.g. "turn left after the sign-post" but not "follow the sign-post"). Signs can be considered "anticipations of successful interactions of referral" [18], emphasizing their origin and expected influence on behavior.

One can show that the behavioristic view of the grounding process of forming signs is just a specialization of the classical view that defines information as "a difference that makes a difference" to the interpreter [2]. The specialized view, however, makes it difficult to explain communication in a digital city as mere exchange, whether of information or signs, or meaning. Indeed, in the case of navigation with a digital city, not objective reality but subjective experience underlies the creation of signs. The navigator cannot frequently succeed with developing an interpretation of a sign received through communication by simply referring the sign to the observed environment – the navigator's personal experience has first to be coordinated (up to a point) with the experience of the "creator" of the sign. The latter requires something else than just sending and receiving information (signs, meaning, etc).

An advanced explanation of communication that includes aspects of information (sign) exchange as well as behavioral coordination between *autopoietic systems* can help us shed more light on the phenomenon. An autopoietic system is a dynamic system maintaining its organization on account of its own operation: each state of such a system depends on its current structure and a previous state only [13]. The structure of an autopoietic system determines the system possible (i.e. self non-destructive) behaviors that are triggered by its interactions with the environment. If the system changes its state, causing changes of the structure, without breaking autopoiesis, the system is structurally coupled with the environment. If the environment is structurally dynamical (e.g. is itself an autopoietic or self-organizing system), then both the system and the environment may mutually trigger their structural changes, sustaining the system's self-adaptation. When there are more than one autopoietic system in the environment, the adaptation processes of some of the presented systems may become coupled, acting recursively through their own states. All the possible changes of states of such systems, which do not destroy their coupling, create a consensual domain for the systems. Behaviors in a consensual domain are mutually oriented. Communication, in this view, is the behavioral coordination resulting from the interactions that occur in a consensual domain (see [5] for details). This definition can be used to refine and improve the interpretive model described in the previous section by introducing the dynamic aspects. To do so, let us first make clear the terminology.

4.2 Terminology and Basic Assumptions

In Peirce's formulation [16], semiotics studies the process of interaction of three subjects: the sign itself – the signifier, its object – that which is signified by the sign, and the interpretant – the meaning made of the sign. No sign is directly connected to an object: signs acquire meanings only when they are re-represented in (referred to) a system of interpretance that is a sign system, which creates a context (e.g. by establishing relations on signs). Naturally, the same sign may have different meanings while signifying different objects, or the same sign may have different meanings while signifying the same object, or different signs may have the same meaning while signifying the same object, and so on. Designated semiosis processes determine the meaning(s) of a sign in all the specific situations.

A semiosis process is the process of establishing the meaning of some distinctions in an environment that entails representation and re-representation of these distinctions over levels of interpretation (that form different systems of interpretance), where every level is governed by and adopts certain developmental rules and axioms called norms. The norms reflect different aspects of human behavior and can be classified into five major groups [21]: perceptual (to respond to peculiarities of sensing), cognitive (to deal with cultural knowledge and beliefs), evaluative (to explain personal preferences, values, and goals), behavioral (to delineate behavioral patterns), and denotative (to specify the choice of signs for signifying). Semiosis comes as a natural organizational process: it organizes signs in a partial level-hierarchy by ordering them so that signs of objects (which can also be signs) of level N-1 for processes and structures of level N+1 are placed on level N. The lowest-level signs, e.g. (manifestations of) physical objects, behaviors, emotions, and the like, are perceived or realized through their distinctions and may get a representation at an "intermediary" level of norms, reflecting interpretive laws of a higher, experiential and environmentally (physiologically, socially, technically, economically, etc.) induced level, which determines "meanings" for the lower-level signs. This simplified three-level structure corresponds to a single semiosis process, whereas navigation in an environment engenders multiple semiosis processes and results in the creation of a multi-level sign system with a potentially infinite hierarchy of dynamic interpretive levels [12].

A user of a digital city deals with a fragment of the global, i.e. loosely shared through the environment by all the users, system of signs. The fragment is, however, distinctively ordered in an interpretive hierarchy peculiar to the user's experience and norms adopted. Hierarchies created by different users may be different in terms of the order and the coverage, and they may run on different time-scales. Unlike the case of individual navigation, where perceived and conceived signs may need not be articulated – "externalized" – explicitly, the operation of a digital city neatly builds on communicative use of the global sign system representing the environment and the digital city itself. This sign system is a projection of a consensual domain of the communicating parties onto the domain of physical objects and phenomena that comes as a language defined in a very general "behavioristic" way. The digital city "describes" its environment with such a language, which has a syntax reflecting the organization of the environment, semantics establishing meanings of the environment, and pragmatics characterizing the effect of the language use. The language is to reconcile the subjectivism and diversity of individual perceptions through communication.

4.3 Semiotic Model

Let $y(t)$ be the state of an autopoietic system at time t, and $\mathbf{x}(t)$ be the vector of states of the system parts, which constitute its structure. Following the definition of an autopoietic system [13], we can write:

$$\begin{cases} \mathbf{x}(t+1) = \mathrm{f}(\mathbf{x}(t), y(t)), \\ y(t+1) = \mathrm{g}(y(t), \mathbf{x}(t+1)), \end{cases} \tag{1}$$

where f and g are some functions, specifying the behavior of the system parts and the system as a whole, respectively. If f and g are properly specified, these equations allow one to characterize the dynamics of the system.

By the system-theoretic explanation (see Section 4.1), communication is an interaction between autopoietic systems taken place in a dynamic environment. The psychic system of a human is an instance of an autopoietic system [13], a social system is an autopoietic system [23], and a digital city, seen as a "digital realization" of a social system, may be considered an autopoietic system, too. The interpretive model of communication described in Section 3 can then be re-formulated.

Let t be a discrete time-mark corresponding to a single semiosis process S_t={*Object*(t),*Sign*(t),*Meaning*(t)} in a partial time-sequence of communication $\{S_1,S_2,S_3,\ldots, S_k\}$. Let us also assume that the abstract notion of psychic state is equivalent to the totality of subjectively valid interactions (behaviors), and the notion of social state is equivalent to the totality of socially valid (i.e. appropriate for communication) signs. In line with (1), the dynamics of a psychic system involved into communication can semiotically be characterized as follows:

$$\begin{cases} \mathbf{Objects}(t+1) = \text{Externalizing}(\mathbf{Objects}(t), \mathit{PsychicState}(t)), \\ \mathit{PsychicState}(t+1) = \text{Interpreting}(\mathit{PsychicState}(t), \mathbf{Signs}(t+1)), \end{cases} \quad (2a)$$

where "Externalizing" and "Interpreting" are some parametric relational mappings that specify the uttering process and the (personal) understanding process, respectively. "**Objects**" is a state vector representing the behaviors, which are (expected to be) individually effective (by feedback), and "**Signs**" is a state vector representing the behaviors socially effective.

Analogously, for the social system:

$$\begin{cases} \mathbf{Signs}(t+1) = \text{Externalizing}(\mathbf{Signs}(t), \mathit{SocialState}(t)), \\ \mathit{SocialState}(t+1) = \text{Interpreting}(\mathit{SocialState}(t), \mathbf{Objects}(t+1)), \end{cases} \quad (2b)$$

where "Externalizing" and "Interpreting" are some parametric relational mappings that specify the processes of social "filtering" and "adaptation," respectively.

Equations (2*a*) and (2*b*) permit us to fully characterize the communication process, provided the corresponding relational mappings have thoroughly been defined. It is important to note that neither "social" nor "personal" time is represented explicitly in the model, but by the effect they have on the semiosis process. The model states that (also see Figure 3 for a graphical illustration):

- The correctness and incorrectness of information are subject to both, individual and social interpretations.
- There are no "meanings" in the social system, and there are no objects in the psychic system. Semantics of the communication language is a result of a social convergence of understanding the environment, while its syntax is a social convergence of the interactions (behaviors). The semantics and syntax may overlap.
- There is no target or source: communication is seen as a partial time-sequence of interdependent (recurrent) semiosis processes.
- The social system plays the rôle of an active communication channel: it filters communications out of interactions (behaviors) and buffers perception against "noise" – processes and phenomena not immediately related to the communication.

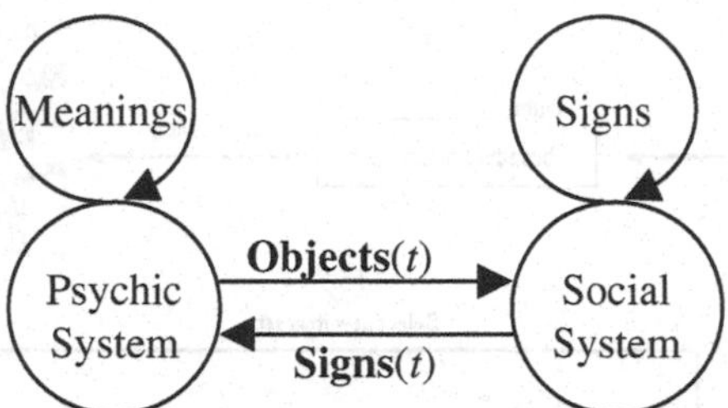

Fig. 3. The semiotic model

- "Meanings" change owing to perturbing a psychic system with signs; signs change owing to perturbing the social system with objects (behaviors).

A digital city creates a social system and can now precisely be defined as an autopoietic organization of social agents communicating via the digital medium, such that every social agent is a realization of a semiosis process caused by navigation taken place in a common (for all agents) environment.

5 Example

The main problem of the semiotic model introduced in the previous section is that it is difficult to implement. Indeed, the relational parametric mappings "Externalizing" and "Interpreting" of (2*a*) and (2*b*) are not fixed but depend on the internal "hidden" dynamics of the social and psychic systems that, although can in principle be estimated for a period of time by observation, are generally unpredictable, as unpredictable is the dynamics of any autopoietic or self-organizing system [4]. While the latter problem can, to an extent, be addressed within approaches of systems theory, such as synergetics, chaos modeling, and cellular automata (see [8] for a survey), in this section we will discuss an interface design that is a partial realization of the semiotic model made under certain simplified conditions.

Let us first confine our consideration to a single individual interaction (and, thus, to one psychic system) in the sequence of semiosis processes representing a communication. Substituting the second equation of (2*a*) into the first results in the following:

$$\text{Object}(t+1) \leftarrow \text{Externalizing}\left(\begin{array}{l}\mathbf{Objects}(t),\\ \text{Interpreting}(\mathit{PsychicState}(t-1), \mathbf{Signs}(t))\end{array}\right) \quad (3)$$

Let us assume that during communication, both the psychic and the social systems do not change their states, and that the socially valid interactions (i.e. "**Signs**") do not change. Let us then set the beginning (for the psychic system) of the communication at time t (note that generally, $\mathbf{Objects}(t) \neq \varnothing$). As $\mathit{PsychicState}(t\text{-}1)$ appears, in this interpretation, nothing but relations and constraints imposed on (a subset of) the signs (which are supposed not to change under the postulated "zero dynamics"), (3) can be reduced to the following form:

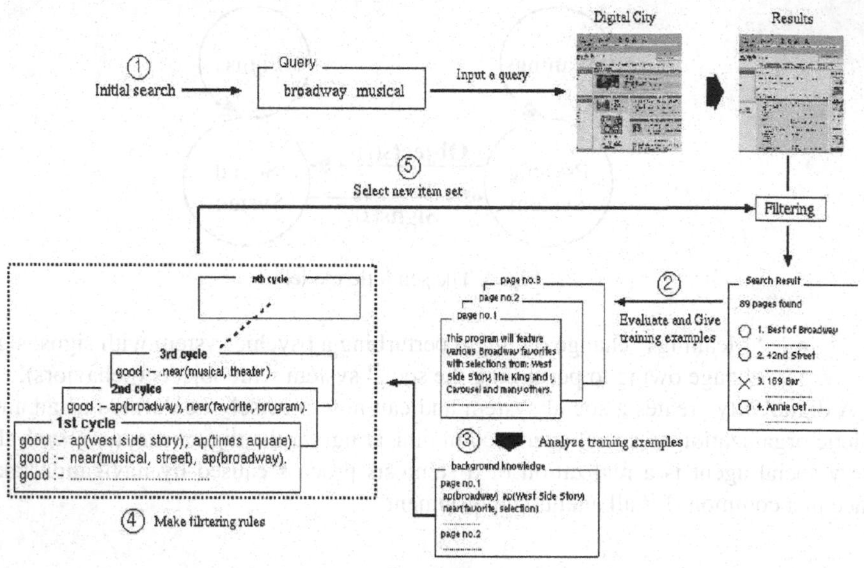

Fig. 4. Modeling communication with an intelligent interface

$$\text{Object}(t+1) \xleftarrow{\mu(\textbf{Objects}(t))} \textbf{Signs}(t), \tag{4}$$

where μ is some set of rules controlling the selection.

Figure 4 shows an interactive Web-page filtering process with an "intelligent" interface, which realizes the model specified by (4). The user starts the interaction by inputting a query to a search engine that then produces a (usually vast) set of digital documents (e.g. texts or hyperlinks). The system then suggests the user to evaluate the relevancy of arbitrary chosen elements of the set in order that some μ' is build based on the relevance feedback. μ' is applied to filter the retrieved documents, and the procedure may be repeated until a satisfactory μ is found.

The interface was originally developed by one of this paper authors for the general purposes of information retrieval. It demonstrated the ability to facilitate the process of man-machine communication by reducing the number of interactions necessary to obtain information of interest. A more detailed account on the implementation can be found in [15].

Although the simplified treatment of the semiotic model appears reasonable and natural in many cases (the probability of changing the social state is far less than the probability of changing the psychic state [12], and the latter probability is quite small when the goal – see Section 2 – does not change), a weak point of the implementation is that the user is required to know (at least, to a degree) the communication language, i.e. to know some of the relevant elements of the "**Signs**" to initiate communication. This problem could be subdued with a realization of the second part of the semiotic model – the equations (2*b*) – that we plan to accomplish in the near future: an advanced version of the interface is to be deployed in a digital city. (It is easy to see that (2*b*) can be reduced to a form similar to (4), e.g. $\text{Sign}(t+1) \xleftarrow{\pi(\textbf{Signs}(t))} \textbf{Objects}(t)$, under certain conditions.)

6 Related Work and Conclusions

Our semiotic model of communication resembles the one of "dynamic semiotics" proposed in [1], although our ultimate goal is more pragmatic: to develop an effective digital city rather than to explain communication phenomena. Besides, the approach that we advocated in this paper is, in our opinion, theoretically better sound as it relies on the results independently obtained in several disciplines, such as cognitive and social sciences [17, 7], semiotics [12], and complex system theory [9]. The work [23] on Niklas Luhmann's theory of social systems is also closely related; however, we have a different vision of communication and apply a different apparatus to explicate it. We do not concentrate on the generic social phenomena but study their "projection" and effect on the digital media. One may find this work as an effort to somewhat widen but specialize the idea of modeling the society as the "global superorganism" [9] – we believe that our research has fewer only intuitively understood points and, therefore, better suits for the developmental needs. Among information systems related to our study, we should mention the so-called recommender systems (see a survey in [22]), which usually utilize some specific method (e.g. data mining) or "common sense" knowledge rather than a communication theory or model. All these works have influenced our research, and [1] actually inspired us to apply the apparatus of semiotics. Unfortunately, we have not found reports which have theoretically approached the development of digital cities.

Among the results of the study, we would first like to point to the clarification of communication as a socio-cognitive phenomenon, and to the determination of the rôle of a digital city as a socio-culturally controlled communication channel that is, on the other hand, a "realization" of the social system in the form of a language. Some implications of these results for the design of digital cities are as follows. A digital city should be able to utilize relevance feedback from its users to co-ordinate communication at both the personal (by adjusting to the social system) and the social (by adjusting to the user) levels. This will reduce the cost of communication by decreasing the number of necessary interactions. The semantics of the communication language (and, therefore, the structure of the user-system interactions) is determined by the users of the digital city rather than by some "objective" laws or "universal" ontologies. The digital city should be able to adjust the semantics as it evolves. Finally, more studies on the semiosis of communication are necessary, as well as the design of new techniques to implement the semiotic model.

The presented work is part of the Universal Design of Digital City project in the Core Research for Evolutional Science and Technology programme funded by the Japan Science and Technology Corporation.

References

1. Andersen, P.B.: Dynamic semiotics. Semiotica (2001, to appear)
2. Bateson, G.: Steps to an Ecology of Mind. Ballantine Books New York (1972)
3. Bickhard, M.H.: The emergence of representation in autonomous agents. In: Prem, E. (ed.): Epistemological Issues of Embodied AI. Cybernetics and Systems. 28(6) (1997)
4. Dendrinos, D.S. and Sonis, M.: Chaos and Socio-Spatial Dynamics. Springer-Verlag, New York (1990)
5. Di Paolo, E.A.: An investigation into the evolution of communication. Adaptive Behavior. 6(2) (1998) 285-324
6. Fiske, J.: Introduction to communication studies. Routledge, London (1990)
7. Hemingway, C.J: Toward a Socio-cognitive Theory of Information Systems: An Analysis of Key Philosophical and Conceptual Issues. In: Proc. of the IFIP Conference on Information Systems: Current Issues and Future Changes. IFIP, Helsinki (1999) 275-286
8. Heylighen, F.: Evolutionary Transitions: how do levels of complexity emerge? Complexity. 6(1) (2000)
9. Heylighen, F.: The Global Superorganism: an evolutionary-cybernetic model of the emerging network society. Posted at URL http://pespmc1.vub.ac.be/Papers/Superorganism.pdf (2000)
10. Ishida, T. and Isbister, K. (eds): Digital Cities: Experiences, Technologies and Future Perspectives. Lecture Notes in Computer Science, Vol. 1765. Springer-Verlag (2000)
11. Ishida, T.: Understanding Digital Cities. In: Ishida, T. and Isbister, K. (eds): Digital Cities: Experiences, Technologies and Future Perspectives. Lecture Notes in Computer Science, Vol. 1765. Springer-Verlag (2000) 7-17
12. Lemke, J.L.: Opening Up Closure: Semiotics Across Scales. In: Chandler, J.L.R., van de Vijver, G. (eds): Closure: Emergent Organizations and Their Dynamics. Annals of the New York Academy of Sciences, Vol. 901. The New York Academy of Sciences, New York (2000) 100-111
13. Maturana, H. and Varela, F.J.: Autopoiesis and Cognition: The Realization of the Living. D. Reidel Publishing Company, Dordrecht (1980)
14. Nehaniv, C.L.: Meaning for observers and agents. In: Proc. IEEE International Symposium on Intelligent Control/Intelligent Systems and Semiotics. (1999) 435-440
15. Okabe, M. and Yamada, S.: Interactive Web Page Filtering with Relational Learning. In: Proc. The First Asia-Pacific Conference on Web Intelligence. (2001, to appear)
16. Peirce, C.S.: The essential Peirce: Selected philosophical writings, Vol. 2. Indiana University Press, Bloomington (1998)
17. Powers, W.T.: Behavior: the Control of Perception. Aldine, Chicago (1973)
18. Prem, E.: Semiosis in embodied autonomous systems. In: Proc. of the IEEE International Symposium on Intelligent Control. IEEE, Piscataway NJ (1998) 724-729
19. Shannon, C.E. and Weaver, W.: The Mathematical Theory of Communication. University of Illinois Press, ILL (1963)
20. Spence, R.: A framework for navigation. Int. J. H.-Comp. Studies. 51(5) (1999) 919-45
21. Stamper, R.: Signs, Information, Norms and Systems. In: Holmqvist, B., Andersen, P.B., Klein, H., Posner, R. (eds): Signs of Work. de Gruyter, Berlin (1996) 349-399
22. Terveen, L. and Hill, W.: Human-Computer Collaboration in Recommended Systems. In: Carroll, J. (ed.): Human-Computer Interaction in the New Millenium. Addison-Wesley (2001)
23. Viskovatoff, A.: Foundations of Niklas Luhmann's Theory of Social Systems. Philosophy of the Social Sciences. 29(4) (1999) 481-516
24. Woodward, K. (Ed.): The Myths of Information: Technology and Post-industrial Culture. Routledge, London (1980)

Simulations for Comparing Knowledge Acquisition and Machine Learning

Achim Hoffmann, Rex Kwok, and Paul Compton

School of Computer Science and Engineering
University of New South Wales, 2052 NSW, Australia
E-mail: {achim,rkwok,compton}@cse.unsw.edu.au

Abstract. This paper introduces a new class of systematic experimental studies targeted towards a better understanding of the strengths and weaknesses of knowledge acquisition (KA) methods. We model a domain along with the behaviour of a domain expert. Using these models we can simulate the KA process and observe which factors of the domain, the expert or the KA technique, affect the overall result of the KA process. On the basis of our models, we can also compare the performance of our KA techniques against the performance of automatic KA techniques, i.e. against machine learning techniques.
We present a number of results from our modelling approach. These results include the surprising fact that in some domains, building a decision tree by consulting an expert for providing a correct discriminating attribute along with a correct threshold value for a presented case, may still be inferior to an automatic method, such as C4.5, using the same set of cases. Furthermore, we obtained new insights into characteristics of the knowledge representation scheme being used (Ripple Down Rules) as well as guidelines for experts when providing knowledge. Finally, we advocate our methodological approach for studying KA techniques to also being much more widely used in machine learning research. We consider our approach as an important methodological complement to the extensive performance comparisons in machine learning research using 'natural datasets'.

1 Introduction

The careful evaluation of the effectiveness of a new approach in AI is important but often difficult to conduct in practice. Empirical studies have been conducted in a large number of subfields of AI, including theorem proving, constraint satisfaction, vision, machine learning and neural networks. Often UCI datasets are used to allow comparison of approaches and evaluation studies. The UCI machine learning (ML) repository, contains a number of datasets obtained from real applications. Evaluations in knowledge acquisition (KA) have been very limited in regards to the actual knowledge acquisition process and those few studies that have been done, were using real data, partly from the UCI ML repository.

This paper demonstrates the use of simulated domains in investigating the strengths and weaknesses of knowledge acquisition techniques. A model of a domain is developed that provides a source of cases, a target function which is the goal of the induction or knowledge acquisition process and also a simulated expert, which can be consulted

M. Brooks, D. Corbett, and M. Stumptner (Eds.): AI 2001, LNAI 2256, pp. 273–284, 2001.

in the knowledge acquisition process. The major insight that has arisen from the work reported in this paper is that the simulated domain approach enables one to investigate how the domain structure affects knowledge acquisition much more readily than using 'real-world' data where the target function is unknown. Webb [18] is one of the few evaluation studies that have been done with human subjects as experts. Simulated experts may suffer somewhat from inaccurate expert models but allow more comprehensive and detailed studies.

In this paper, the knowledge acquisition technique of Ripple Down Rules (RDRs) will be studied in regards to how quickly an accurate knowledge base can be developed, depending on the structure of the domain. We also compare RDR's performance against the performance of an automatic technique, i.e. the decision tree learner C4.5 [13]. Section 2 provides a survey of previous evaluation studies in KA. It is assumed that the reader is familiar with C4.5 but may not be familiar with RDR. Hence, a brief overview will be presented in Section 3. The target concepts used in the studies presented in section 4 will be hyper-rectangles in an n-dimensional space and decision trees. Section 5 contains the conclusions.

2 Previous Evaluation Studies

There has been a strong emphasis on evaluation in the KA community [15]. However, the used approaches do not really evaluate the actual process of knowledge acquisition from an expert [12]. The major focus of the KA community at the time was on problem solving methods so that the major focus of evaluation was on evaluating the appropriateness of the problem solver for the problem rather than evaluating the process of building the actual problem solver.

The origins of this work are investigations into a class of KA techniques known as Ripple-Down Rules (RDR) [3]. Since RDR is critically concerned with populating a knowledge base, a different approach to evaluation was developed early on [4]. In this approach knowledge bases were first developed by machine learning using some UC Irvine data sets. These knowledge bases were then used as 'experts' to build further knowledge bases using one or more RDR techniques. Similar recent work is found in [17]. Comparisons of the knowledge bases built by knowledge acquisition (RDR) were made with machine learning techniques using training sets of various sizes. These approaches demonstrated that RDR produced surprisingly compact knowledge bases and, because of the use of an expert, the early performance of the RDR system was always better than that of machine learning alone. As with machine learning studies using these data sets, the techniques perform differently on different data sets and one is faced with trying to understand what features of the domains cause the variations in performance. The hypothesis of the present study is that by building various domain models or target functions, and using these both to produce data and to act as the 'expert' one will be able to better understand why various learning and knowledge acquisition techniques perform as they do. Indeed, this paper presents results that contradict some of the conclusions drawn from those studies using the 'real data sets'.

Recently a more general simulation study has been conducted where the key measures have been the tendency of the expert to over-generalise or over-specialise in the rules they provide [2]. In the present work, however, a much 'finer-grained' simulation approach is presented which allows much deeper insights into the domain structure and its impact on the KA process.

There have been many studies using simulated data in machine learning evaluation. However, in most cases these have not been used to explore the way in which the domain structure affects the induction and in general the machine learning community has preferred real world data. There are few exceptions to this work, such as the early in depth studies by Rendell and Cho [14] or the studies of boosting by statisticians [7], but also some other ML studies, such as [5]. Perhaps most notably in this regard is the field of reinforcement learning in which artificial domains are rather the norm than an exception. Langley [11] wrote a brief but very good motivation for experimental studies using artificial data.

3 Ripple Down Rules

3.1 Background

The key features of the various Ripple Down Rules (RDR) techniques are:

1. the expert monitors the system while in use. Whenever the system does not perform to the satisfaction of the expert, e.g. when it misclassifies a case, the expert adds another rule to the so-called RDR tree.
2. the use of exception structures so that errors in the system are corrected by adding refinement rules. Rules are not edited to correct errors. All corrections to the system are made by adding new rules.
3. the incremental development while the knowledge base is in actual use. RDR systems can be built off-line, but the technique is aimed at building systems by correcting errors while in use.

RDR systems have been implemented for a range of application areas and tasks. The first industrial demonstration of this approach was the PEIRS system, which provided clinical interpretations for reports of pathology testing [6]. By now there is a quite substantial history of success with this approach to knowledge acquisition, despite the considerable initial skepticism in the knowledge acquisition community about an incremental development where the only form of correction was the addition of new rules. The approach has also been adapted to tasks including multiple classification [8], control [16], heuristic search [1], spoken-language dialogue systems [10], and document management [9]. The essential idea of RDR is exhibited in the Single Classification Ripple Down Rules. Hence, we used those for the studies presented in this paper.

3.2 Single Classification Ripple Down Rules

A Single classification ripple down rule (SCRDR) tree is a finite binary tree with two distinct types of edges. These edges are typically called *exception* (or *true*) and *false* edges. They are used for evaluating cases and will be discussed later. Associated with each node in a tree is a *rule*. A rule has the form: *if* α *then* β where α is called the *condition* and β the *conclusion*. In this study, binary classification is often used. In such cases, β can be considered as having a value of *positive* or *negative*. The condition will typically be either a single attribute-value test or a conjunction of such tests. See Figure 1.

An *example* (or synonymously *case*) is a point in an n-dimensional space and a SCRDR tree is used to assign a conclusion to such points. A case in SCRDR is evaluated by passing it to the root of the tree. At any node in the tree, if the example entails the condition of the node, the node is said to *fire*. If a node fires, the example is passed to the next node following the except (or true) branch. Otherwise, the case is passed down the false branch. This determines a path through a SCRDR tree for an example. The conclusion given by this process is the conclusion from the last node which fired on this path. To ensure that a conclusion is always given, the root node typically contains a trivial condition which is always satisfied. This node is called the *default* node.

A SCRDR tree is revised when the evaluation process returns the wrong conclusion. When this happens a new node is placed at the end of the evaluation path which gave this wrong answer. The example causing this change (call this example *e*) is associated with the new node and is called the *cornerstone case* for the node. To determine the rule for the new node, the expert formulates a rule which is satisfied by *e* but not by the cornerstone case for the last node which fired in the evaluation path[1].

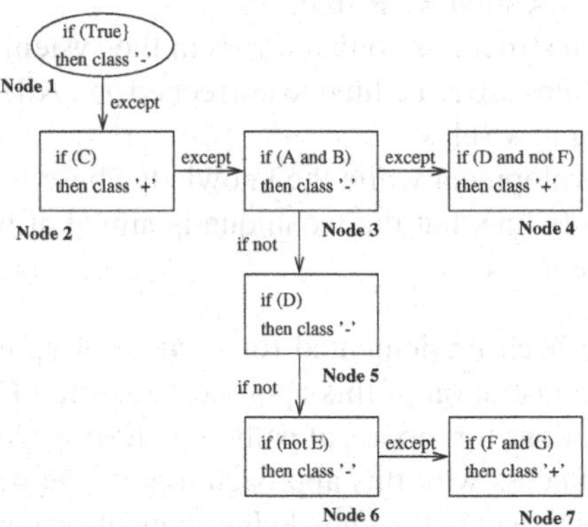

Fig. 1. An example SCRDR tree. Node 1 is the default node.

The strength of the RDR approach lies in the fact that it is usually rather easy for an expert to provide discriminating conditions between two presented cases, while it is difficult for an expert to provide valid and complete classification rules for the general case.

[1] Note that if the last node to fire in the evaluation path is a leaf node, the new node is attached to the true branch of that node. Otherwise, the new node is attached to the false branch of the last node in the evaluation path.

4 Simulation Studies

The following studies consider an n-dimensional feature space ranging from 0.0 to 100.0 in each dimension. Examples were randomly drawn according to a uniform distribution in the feature space. Different types of models were again randomly created and used to classify the randomly generated examples. The results plotted in the following graphs are the averaged results over 20 randomly generated target concepts of the same type as explained below. Experiments indicated that further averaging over trials with different seeds for the generation of examples has only a negligible effect on the results. The simulated expert is assumed to derive answers to the KA requests from the generated models as explained in the following.

In the following we study three types of target concepts: a) Sets of hyper-rectangles, which correspond to disjunctive concepts in numerical domains; a rather natural class of concepts - at least for human conceptualisation. b) Sets of nested rectangles, a class of concepts where one would expect the Ripple Down Rules to perform better that decision tree learning. c) Decision trees, i.e. concepts which use the same representational scheme as our decision tree learner C4.5.

4.1 Sets of Hyper-Rectangles

We considered the following class of domains: In the n-dimensional Euclidean space we assume a number of rectangular areas (hyper-rectangles) to cover all positive examples while the negative examples lie in the remaining area. See Figure 2.

Each hyper-rectangle is randomly generated as follows: For some dimensions, the hyper-rectangle will extend over the entire value range, while for other dimensions, a constraining interval will be imposed. Which dimensions are chosen for the constraining intervals is decided randomly using a uniform distribution. To define a constraining interval two numbers are randomly generated between 0.0 and 100.0.

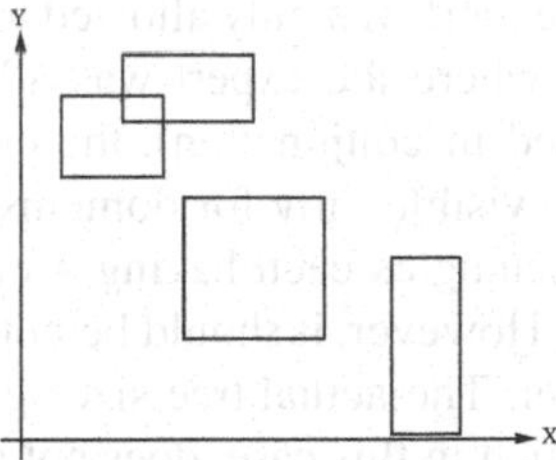

Fig. 2. A set of four hyper-rectangles in the 2-dimensional space. The area inside any of the rectangles belongs to class 1, while the remaining area belongs to class 0.

Expert model: The expert is always asked to provide one or multiple *significant* differences between two cases belonging to two different classes. That is, the expert is presented one case which is inside one of the hyper-rectangles and a second case which lies outside. It appears plausible that in such a case, the expert is able to provide at least one of the edges of the cube containing the positive example. I.e. the expert provides both, the relevant attribute and the correct threshold value. This seems plausible, as the expert will usually be able to articulate discriminatory conditions, but only in the context of two concrete cases. For example, in a medical domain, given two cases the expert may realize that body temperature is critical in assessing the case and the expert will usually be able to provide sensible threshold values of the critical fever level. Practical experiences with the RDR approach confirm the plausibility of our hypothesis.

In the following experiments we varied a constraint on the number of conditions (to be used in conjunction), which the expert may provide for a single pair of cases that need to be discriminated.

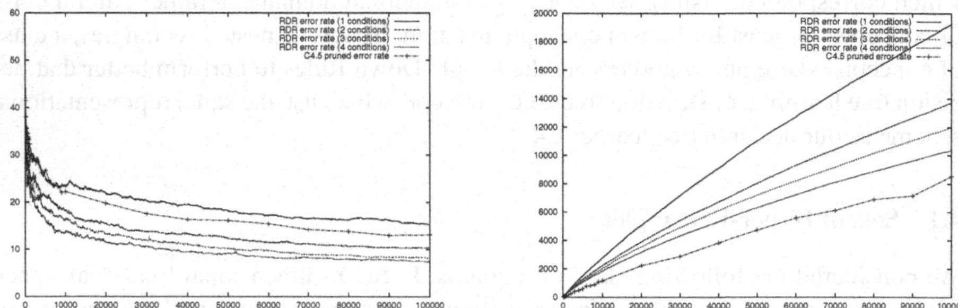

Fig. 3. A 20 hyper-rectangles problem with 4 constraining attributes each. (Left) Number of examples (x-axis) against error rate of RDR (y-axis). (Right) Number of examples (x-axis) against RDR tree size (y-axis).

One of the more surprising result we obtained is shown in Figure 3, where C4.5 outperformed RDR when the expert was only allowed to provide a single attribute plus threshold as condition. Only where the expert was allowed to provide two or more discriminating conditions (used in conjunction), the error of RDR was less than the error of C4.5. This effect was visible only for domains of relatively high complexity, i.e. with 20 or more hyper-rectangles each having 4 constraining intervals randomly chosen from the 20 attributes. However, it should be noted that the 20 hyper-rectangles have only 160 edges altogether. The actual tree sizes generated are much larger. This is due to the tree structure, which in this case, does not allow a compact representation of the domain. With fewer hyper-rectangles, all versions of RDR outperformed C4.5, which we expected, as RDR appears to have superior resources, by being able to consult the expert. With more hyper-rectangles, the discrepancies between the three methods increased further.

In Figure 3 the tree sizes are shown. C4.5 comes out the smallest, while RDR with single attribute conditions grows more than double the nodes from 100 000 examples. Both results contradict conclusions from earlier studies in [4] which used ‘real world’ data sets.

4.2 Nested Hyper-Rectangles

The next class of domains we studied are described by a set of nested hyper-rectangles which classify cases in alternating order. That is, the outer most hyper-rectangle C_1 classifies positively, while hyper-rectangle C_2 inside C_1 classifies negatively, while hyper-rectangle C_3 inside C_2 represents an exception to C_2 and classifies again positively, etc. We expected that RDR performs well on this type of domain, as the nested structure of hyper-rectangles corresponds to the exception structure, for which RDR seems so well-suited. At least if multiple attributes were allowed to be provided as conjunction by the expert, RDR should outperform C4.5.

Surprisingly, the simulation studies showed that in such domains RDR does not perform any better than C4.5. See Figure 4. What is even more surprising is the fact that the number of attributes to be provided per rule does not make any substantial difference.

One would think that RDR can tap into much richer resources (asking the expert for a discriminating attribute plus the exact threshold value) and the provision of multiple attributes in a condition appears ideally suited to the domain. In contrast, C4.5 has to do that job merely on the basis of the available, and often somewhat insufficient, training data. It is also surprising that for this class of domains the tree sizes are essentially the same, regardless whether developed by C4.5 or grown by RDR.

From the studies of the non-nested hyper-rectangles we can derive the guideline for the expert to provide as many discriminating conditions as possible when presented with two cases of different classes.

4.3 Decision Trees

Another way of defining a target concept is as a decision tree. In the study presented here, random decision trees are generated given parameters for the number of attributes present, the depth of the decision tree, and the number of attributes which may occur in a test at internal nodes in the decision tree. A random binary conclusion is then assigned to each leaf node.

Expert model: In the RDR framework, the only task of the expert is to differentiate pairs of examples. Given two examples, an expert creates a rule which one example satisfies and which the other contradicts. One way of generating such a rule from a decision tree is to traverse the tree from the root and return the first attribute test which sends the two examples down different branches.

This simulated expert who picks the first test in the model tree as described, called *expert 1*, has the property that the rules generated for two examples (depending on which case is misclassified) are negations of each other. This renders the order of presentation of the two cases irrelevant for the chosen discriminating condition in contrast to the following approach.

Another way of generating a rule is to place emphasis on the misclassified example. Such an expert would make rules which are more specific to the misclassified example. More formally, consider the evaluation path of a misclassified example. The attribute test which is closest to the leaf of this path and which distinguishes the cornerstone case could be used. We call the expert who follows this approach *expert 2*.

We are interested in the performance of the two experts in regards to the error rate and RDR tree size depending on the complexity of the domain and the number of presented examples. Figure 5 shows the result of running trials of increasing target concept complexity. The number of training examples and the number of attributes in the state

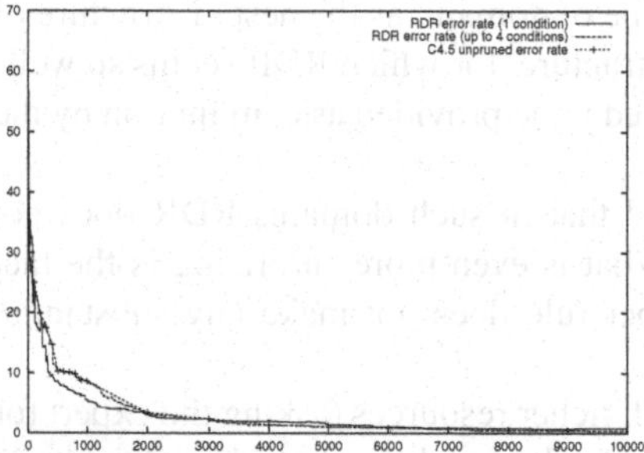

Fig. 4. Number of examples (x-axis) against RDR error rate (y-axis) on a 10 nested hyper-rectangles problem with 4 constraining attributes for each hyper-rectangle. Similar results were obtained for varied numbers of nested hyper-rectangles and varied numbers of constraining attributes.

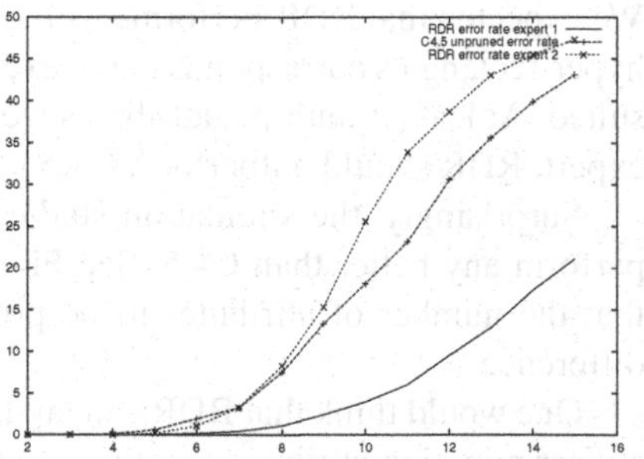

Fig. 5. Increasing error rate (y-axis) with increasing target concept complexity (depth of the balanced decision tree on x-axis) based on a fixed number of 10 000 training examples.

space were kept constant for each trial. In this case, there were 20 attributes and 10 000 training examples. The results of varying the number of training examples can be seen in Figure 6. For this graph, the complexity of the target concept was kept constant at a depth of 10 with 20 attributes available. In both tests, the pruned error rate has not been plotted because the difference is tiny. Similar shapes were found for the graphs for trees of less complexity, although, as one would expect, the convergence speed was greater.

The immediate and striking feature of these results is that expert 1 for RDR produces the lowest error rate. C4.5 sits in the middle with expert 2 performing the worst. This conclusion has to be weighed and balanced. One advantage gained by RDR is that it has greater resources. The simulated expert has direct access to the target concept and generates rules which are attribute tests in the target concept. This is tempered by the fact that RDR is an incremental learner. Depending on the order of examples, different rules will be returned by the simulated expert. Of particular importance are the rules returned by the first few training examples. These rules will occur close to the root of the RDR tree and have a greater impact on classification and on the structure (and size) of the emerging RDR tree. With expert 1, these rules will more than likely come from near the top of the target decision tree. Starting from the root of the decision tree, each attribute test has (on average) a 50% chance of distinguishing two examples[2]. In contrast, expert 2 will generate rules which come from close to the bottom of the

[2] For any two examples, the chances that some attribute test above depth i will distinguish them is $1 - \frac{1}{2^i}$.

decision tree. These results suggest that, when the target concept is a decision tree, the expert should give equal weight to the cornerstone case and the misclassified case and not pay special attention to the misclassified case.

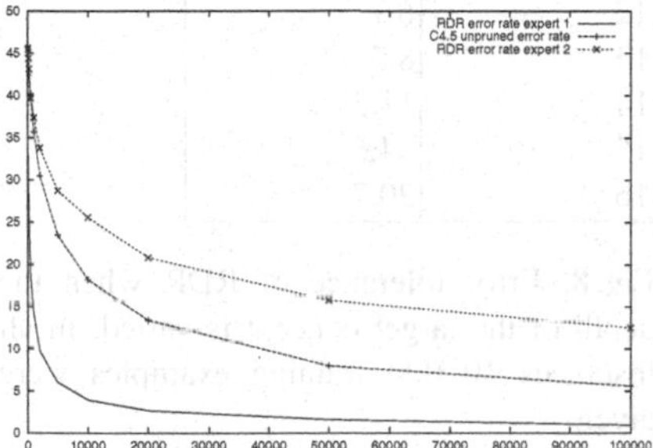

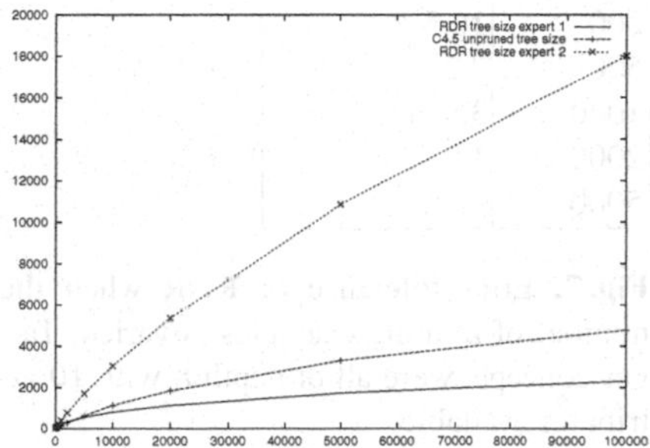

Fig. 6. A model decision tree of depth 10. (Left) Decreasing error rate (y-axis) with the increasing number of training examples (x-axis). (Right) Increasing tree size(y-axis) with the number of training examples (x-axis).

Another interesting finding concerns the tree size. An example of our results is shown in Figure 6. The data comes from the same trials used to generate the error rates in Figure 6. The results are quite typical and show that, besides giving lower error rates, expert 1 generates rather compact theories, while the size of the RDR tree for expert 2 is some 4 times greater than C4.5 trees. Once again this result corroborates the conclusion that the expert should view the cornerstone case and the misclassified case symmetrically.

Simulation results also show that the comparative performance of RDR is better when there are fewer examples and when the target concept is more complex. Figure 5 shows that expert 1 always outperforms C4.5. To determine how much RDR outperforms C4.5, errors can be introduced into the simulated expert to degrade the performance of RDR. The degree to which RDR outperforms C4.5 can then be measured by the amount of error needed to make RDR give the same error rate as C4.5. The error model used here is to vary the threshold value in rules created by the simulated expert. If the correct threshold is x, an error of 5 will mean that the threshold returned has a random value between $x-5$ and $x+5$. The results obtained show that the error tolerance of RDR is far greater when there are fewer examples or when the target concept is more complex. Figures 7 and 8 show typical results of varying the number of examples and the depth of the target concept respectively. The error tolerance figures are approximations because linear extrapolation was used between consecutive integer error values.

Increasing the number of conclusions (increasing the range of values a leaf node in the target concept can take) produces an improved result for C4.5 and a slightly deteriorating result for RDR. Typical results can be seen in Figure 9. This result for C4.5 is surprising for three reasons. Firstly, the number of cuts and divisions to the

Examples	Error tolerance
50	> 50
100	29.0
200	16.3
500	7.2
1000	3.9
2000	1.7
5000	< 1

Fig. 7. Error tolerance of RDR when the number of training examples is varied. Target concepts were all of depth 8 with 10 attributes available.

Concept Depth	Error tolerance
7	< 1
8	1.6
9	2.1
10	4.2
11	4.9
12	6.7
13	8.5
14	11.3
15	14.6
16	20.7

Fig. 8. Error tolerance of RDR when the depth of the target concept is varied. In all instances 10 000 training examples were given.

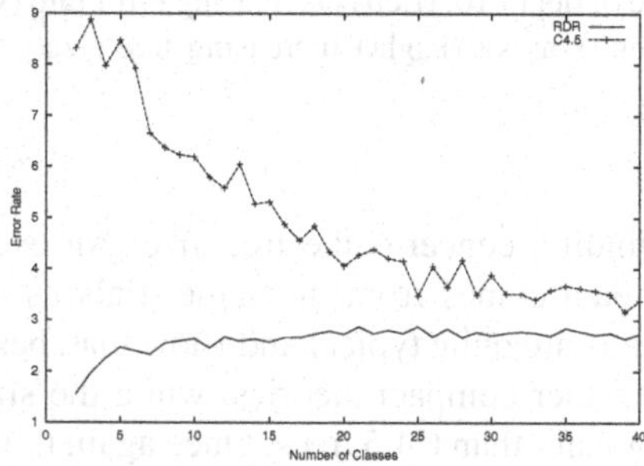

Fig. 9. Varying the number classes. Target concepts of depth 7 with 12 available attributes and 5 000 training examples.

state space is determined by the depth of the target concept. Increasing the conclusion number only increases the number of labels with which the divisions can be named. Secondly, guessing becomes harder. With fewer conclusions, a guess is more likely to produce the correct answer than when there are more conclusions. At this stage, we suspect that the slight tendency of RDR to deteriorate is due to this factor. Finally, when there are fewer conclusions, the target concept often receives some pruning. For instance, consider a target concept with two conclusions. When two adjacent leaf nodes are attributed the same class (there is a 50% chance of this happening), the last attribute test is rendered redundant.

With fewer conclusions, the regions in the state space ascribed any one particular conclusion will tend to be more numerous and more scattered. Any single attribute test is unlikely to demarcate the regions for one conclusion. In contrast, when C4.5 deals with many conclusions, it is more likely that C4.5 will find a split on an attribute which does not split apart the examples belonging to the same conclusion.

5 Conclusions

We presented a new approach to systematic studies in knowledge acquisition research and we believe that more studies using models of experts will allow substantial progress towards a better understanding of the strengths and weaknesses of a KA technique. While using artificial data sets is not new in machine learning research, it has not been widely used as a tool to obtain a better understanding of the domain characteristics that determine the relative success or lack of success of a given technique. We expect that important insights into characteristics of ML techniques can be obtained using our presented methodology.

We demonstrated the usefulness of our simulations by presenting a number of counter-intuitive results, which were partly in contradiction to conclusions drawn from previous studies based on poorly understood 'real world' data.

i) Despite the fact that RDR seems to have significantly more resources to draw information from, in some domains, C4.5 achieves a lower error rate and more compact trees than RDR, based on the same training examples. This can be interpreted as showing the inadequacy of the used knowledge representation scheme and suggests further research towards enhancing the SCRDR knowledge representation.

ii) In the hyper-rectangles study, it was demonstrated that an expert who provides as many discriminating conditions as possible, would build a more compact and more accurate knowledge base faster.

iii) In the decision tree studies, we demonstrated that it will be beneficial if the expert would not so much focus on the misclassified case as an exception to the existing knowledge base, but considers both cases on a rather equal footing when formulating a discriminating condition. Furthermore, results show that RDR performs better, when compared to C4.5, on domains with fewer examples, greater complexity or fewer classes.

These guidelines for the experts when interacting with the system depend on the structure of the domain, which is in practice not exactly known. However, we believe that often some insight into a domain is available which may suffice to assess roughly what type of domain one is dealing with. For example the hyper-rectangles represent disjunctions of multiple interval constraints. If one is to classify objects broadly, such as cars into fast and slow cars, hyper-rectangles seem to be a reasonable model, where one can formulate, e.g. intervals in engine power depending on other features such as type of car, etc.

Future research will develop in a number of directions. For knowledge acquisition in the style of RDR, it is desirable to represent a number of hyper-rectangles in a more compact form than a single RDR tree, to allow suitable treatment of the disjunctive nature of the domain. The effects of non-uniform distributions of examples using the presented models will also be of significant interest. Another interesting direction to push this work is to see how sensitive RDR is to errors which an expert can make in formulating rules. For instance, the threshold for an attribute test could be perturbed by some degree. This may result in larger RDR trees and higher error rates.

References

1. G. Beydoun and A. Hoffmann. Acquisition of search knowledge. In *Knowledge Acquisition, Modeling and Management, 10th European Workshop (EKAW'97)*, pages 1–16, Spain, 1997. Springer-Verlag. LNAI 1319.
2. P. Compton. Simulating expertise. In *Proceedings of the 6th Pacific Knowledge Acquisition Workshop*, pages 51–69, Sydney, Austrlia, 2000. ISBN: 0-7334-1734-5.
3. P. Compton and R. Jansen. A philosophical basis for knowledge acquisition. *Knowledge Acquisition*, 2:241–257, 1990.
4. P. Compton, P. Preston, and B. Kang. The use of simulated experts in evaluating knowledge acquisition. In *Proceedings of the 9th AAAI-Sponsored Banff Knowledge Acquisition for Knowledge–Based Systems Workshop*, pages 12.1–12.18, 1995.
5. T. Dietterich. Approximate statistical tests for comparing supervised classification learning algorithms. *Neural Computation*, 7(10):1895–1924, 1998.
6. G. Edwards and P. Compton *et al.* PEIRS: a pathologist maintained expert system for the interpretation of chemical pathology reports. *Pathology*, 25:27–34, 1993.
7. J. Friedman, T. Hastie, and R. Tibshirani. Additive logistic regression: a statistical view of boosting. Technical report, Stanford University, August 1998.
8. B. Kang, P. Compton, and P. Preston. Multiple classification ripple down rules: Evaluation and possibilities. In *Proceedings of the 9th Banff Knowledge Acquisition for Knowledge Based Systems Workshop*, pages 17.1–7.20, 1995.
9. B. Kang and K. Yoshida *et al.* A help desk system with an intelligent interface. *Applied Artificial Intelligence*, 11(7–8):611–631, 1997.
10. S. Kaspar and A. Hoffmann. Using knowledge acquisition to build spoken language systems. In *Knowledge Acquisition, Modeling and Management, 10th European Workshop (EKAW'97)*, pages 353–358, Spain, 1997. Springer-Verlag. LNAI 1319.
11. P. Langley. Relevance and insight in experimental studies. *IEEE Expert*, 11(5):11–12, October 1996.
12. T. Menzies and F. van Harmelen. Editorial: Evaluating knowledge engineering techniques. *International Journal of Human-Computer Studies*, 51(4):715–727, 1999.
13. J. R. Quinlan. *C4.5: Programs for Machine Learning*. Morgan Kaufmann Publishers, 1993.
14. L. Rendell and H. Cho. Empirical learning as a function of concept character. *Machine Learning*, 5:267–298, 1990.
15. N. Shadbolt and K. O'Hara *et. al.* The experimental evaluation of knowledge acquisition techniques and methods: history, problems and new developments. *International Journal of Human-Computer Studies*, 51(4):729–755, 1999.
16. G. Shiraz and C. Sammut. Combining knowledge acquisition and machine learning to control dynamic systems. In *Proceedings of the 15th IJCAI*, 1997.
17. T. Wada, T. Horiuchi, H. Motoda, and T. Washio. Integrating inductive learning and knowledge acquisition in the ripple down rule method. In *Proceedings of the 6th Pacific International Knowledge Acquisition Workshop*, pages 325–340, 2000.
18. G. Webb, J. Wells, and Z. Zheng. An experimental evaluation of integrating machine learning with knowledge acquisition. *Machine Learning*, pages 5–23, 1999.

Application of Genetic Algorithms to the Optimisation of Neural Network Configuration for Stock Market Forecasting

Daniel Hulme and Shuxiang Xu

Locked Bag 1-359, School of Computing, University of Tasmania, Newnham Drive, Newnham, Tasmania, 7248.
Daniel.Hulme@utas.edu.au

Abstract. Neural networks are recognised as an effective tool for predicting stock prices (Shin & Han, 2000), but little is known about which configurations are best and for which indices. The present study uses genetic algorithms to find a near optimal learning rate, momentum, tolerance and network architecture for 47 indices listed on the Australian Stock Exchange (ASX). Some relationships were determined between stock index and neural network attributes, and important observations were made for the further development of a methodology for determining optimal neural network configurations.

Keywords. genetic algorithms, neural networks, stock forecasting.

1. Introduction

Many attempts have been undertaken at adopting artificial intelligence methods for forecasting share prices on the stock market, which are starting to supersede traditional computational methods. For the neural network (NN) method it is not known how to produce a near optimal configuration. The present study uses genetic algorithms (GAs) to near-optimally configure NNs for particular forecasts. A qualitative analysis of the configurations corresponding to particular indices seeks to explain the factors in the GAs' selection of that configuration.

1.1. Genetic Algorithms

GAs are an abstraction of the principles of genetic evolution (Kuo et al., 2001). A genetic algorithm is a string of binary digits (bits) that encode an algorithm. The fitness of that algorithm is determined by its performance on a given task, and a population of GAs can be evolved to improve the fitness of individual algorithms.

The process undertaken for each generation is as follows:

1. Determine the "fitness" of each algorithm according to a fitness function.

M. Brooks, D. Corbett, and M. Stumptner (Eds.): AI 2001, LNAI 2256, pp. 285–296, 2001.

2. Take random pairs of the fittest algorithms out of the population and cross over random portions to produce progeny.
3. Mutate a small number of bits by making random changes.

All three steps ensure the fitness improves. By only breeding the fittest algorithms, the aspects that make them the fittest remain. By crossing over algorithms, portions that contribute to fitness can be combined. By mutating bits, aspects that contribute to fitness can emerge.

1.2. Neural Networks

Neural networks in a computing sense are an abstraction of the biology of the brain (Rogers, 1997). The network is made up of a number of layers. Each layer contains several neurons, each of which has connections to every neuron in the adjacent layer. Each connection has a certain weight associated with it, which is multiplied by the output value of the neuron at one end and forms the input for the neuron at the other end. The sum of the inputs, x, of a particular neuron determine the output of that neuron according to a transfer function, $f(x)$. It is the changes in the connection weights that allow the network to learn.

A back propagation neural network (BPNN) contains at least one input layer of neurons, one output layer, and any number of hidden layers (Figure 1). The network is trained by comparing observed and expected output values, and adjusting the weights of the links according to the error. The change in weight, •, is equal to the product of the initial weight, the learning rate and the error. These changes in weights propagate back through the network after comparing the observed and expected output, hence the name.

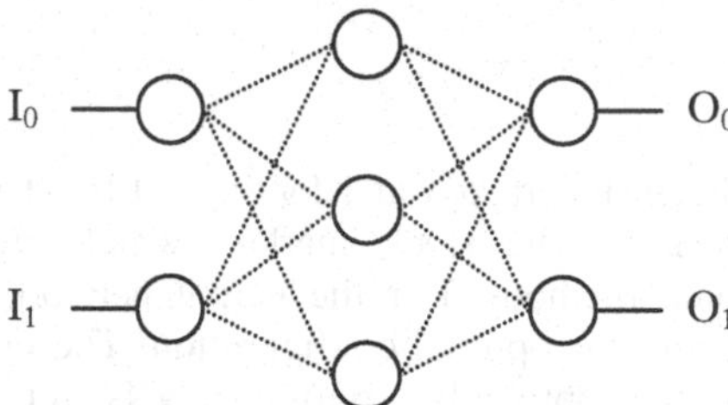

Fig. 1. Back propagation neural network

1.3. Financial Forecasting

There seems to be consensus among many researchers that NNs are superior to other methods of stock market forecasting or, at the very least, a reliable method. Aiken & Bsat (1999) explain the advantage NNs have over traditional statistical models for financial forecasting: they are "fault tolerant," do not "require assumptions about the data," and can "deal with missing data." Wittkemper & Steiner (1996) demonstrated this advantage, applying GAs to NNs and producing better predictive results than traditional statistical methods.

There are several other statements that back the superiority of NNs for financial forecasting and their popularity amongst researchers. "The application of NNs for decision support is well documented" (Kumar et al., 1997). "NNs are gaining popularity for solving several business and technical problems that involve prediction" (Sexton & Gupta, 2000). "NNs are an ideal choice for flexible non-linear modelling and are gaining attention in the area of stock prediction" Qi (1999).

Despite their performance, NNs are not the perfect solution to forecasting. Wong & Selvi (1998) point out two limitations to neural networks: they require large data sets (strategic decision-making is non-routine); and they are unable to explain their decisions. An extensive literary analysis shows that neural networks generally outperform statistical models (Wong & Selvi, 1998).

The availability of material relating to what data should be analysed by NNs to produce good results is limited. According to Shin & Han (2000), multi-resolution learning significantly improves the generalisation ability of NNs. Kuo, et al. (2001) were the first to suggest that the consideration of qualitative factors improve the forecasting ability of NNs. The present study uses historical share price data.

Researchers have given little attention to the reasoning behind their choice of NN configuration. However, according to Qi (1999), "It has been widely accepted that a three-layer feedforward network with an identity transfer function in the output units can approximate any continuous function arbitrarily well given sufficiently many middle-layer units" – an hypothesis that will be tested by this study.

Methodology

Stocks from the top 50 leaders in the ASX June 2001 were used, excluding AXA Asia Pacific, News Corporation Preferred and NRMA Insurance Group, as data was not available for these indices for the period from which data was obtained. The indices and their corresponding ASX codes are listed in Table 1.

For each index, 50 generations of 20 genetic algorithms were run. Each genetic algorithm contained 80 binary digits (bits). The first 32 bits represented the hidden layers of a neural network (NN), and the last 48 bits represented the learning rate (*L*), momentum term (*M*) and tolerance (*T*) for the NN.

The first 32 bits were divided into groups of four. The digital representation of the first three bits of each group gave the number of neurons in each hidden layer from 0 to 7. A value of 0 represented the non-existence of the corresponding layer. The fourth bit in each group indicated whether the number of neurons in that layer should be added to the number of neurons in the next layer (Figure 2).

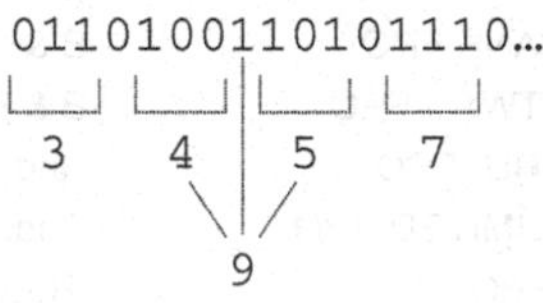

Fig. 2. Conversion of GA to NN configuration

Table 1. ASX codes and names of stock indices used.

ASX Code	ASX Name	Group	Dur.	β	ES (%)
AGL	AUSTRALIAN GAS LIGHT FPO	Ind.	10.00	0.76	75
ALL	ARISTOCRAT LEISURE FPO	Ind.	10.00	1.19	62
AMC	AMCOR LIMITED FPO	Ind.	15.00	1.72	75
AMP	AMP LIMITED FPO	B & F	3.05	0.90	89
ANZ	AUSTRALIA AND NZ FPO	B & F	18.00	0.99	80
BHP	BHP BILLITON LIMITED FPO	Res.	14.00	1.46	67
BIL	BRAMBLES INDUSTRIES FPO	Ind.	10.00	0.68	77
CBA	COMMONWEALTH BANK. FPO	B & F	9.81	0.99	80
CCL	COCA-COLA AMATIL FPO	Ind.	10.00	0.47	71
CML	COLES MYER LTD. FPO	Ind.	10.00	0.45	74
CPU	COMPUTERSHARE LTD FPO	B & F	7.10	1.11	61
CSL	CSL LIMITED FPO	Ind.	7.07	0.86	74
CSR	CSR LIMITED FPO	Ind.	20.00	1.17	54
CWO	CABLE & WIRELESS OPTUS FPO	Ind.	2.63	1.08	60
ERG	ERG LIMITED FPO	Ind.	10.00	1.08	60
FBG	FOSTER'S BREWING FPO	Ind.	10.00	0.52	86
FXJ	FAIRFAX (JOHN) FPO	Ind.	10.00	1.00	71
GMF	GOODMAN FIELDER FPO	Ind.	10.00	0.47	71
GPT	GENERAL PROP. TRUST UNIT	B & F	10.00	0.58	NA
HVN	HARVEY NORMAN FPO	Ind.	10.00	0.45	74
LLC	LEND LEASE CORP. FPO	B & F	14.00	1.12	65
MBL	MACQUARIE BANK LTD FPO	B & F	4.93	0.99	80
MGR	MIRVAC GROUP STAPLED	B & F	2.04	0.58	NA
MIM	M.I.M. HOLDINGS LTD FPO	Res.	10.00	1.42	56
NAB	NATIONAL AUST. BANK FPO	B & F	10.00	0.99	80
NCP	NEWS CORPORATION FPO	Ind.	14.00	1.00	71
NDY	NORMANDY MINING FPO	Res.	10.00	1.10	51
ORI	ORICA LIMITED FPO	Ind.	3.41	0.94	78
PBL	PUBLISHING & BROAD FPO	Ind.	10.00	1.00	71
PDP	PACIFIC DUNLOP FPO	Ind.	12.00	0.70	78
QAN	QANTAS AIRWAYS FPO	Ind.	5.93	0.68	77
QBE	QBE INSURANCE GROUP FPO	B & F	10.00	0.90	89
RIO	RIO TINTO LIMITED FPO	Res.	4.08	1.46	67
SGB	ST GEORGE BANK FPO	B & F	9.01	0.99	80
SME	SUNCORP-METWAY FPO	B & F	4.15	0.99	80
SMI	SMITH (HOWARD) FPO	Ind.	10.00	0.70	78
SRP	SOUTHCORP LIMITED FPO	Ind.	7.59	0.70	78
STO	SANTOS LTD FPO	Res.	20.00	0.97	58
TAH	TABCORP HOLDINGS LTD FPO	Ind.	10.00	1.19	62
TLS	TELSTRA CORPORATION. FPO	Ind.	2.68	1.08	60

WBC	WESTPAC BANKING CORP FPO	B & F	20.00	0.99	80
WES	WESFARMERS LIMITED FPO	Ind.	10.00	0.70	78
WFT	WESTFIELD TRUST UNIT	B & F	10.00	0.58	NA
WMC	WMC LIMITED FPO	Res.	14.00	1.46	67
WOW	WOOLWORTHS LIMITED FPO	Ind.	10.00	0.45	74
WPL	WOODSIDE PETROLEUM FPO	Res.	10.00	0.97	58
WSF	WESTFIELD HOLDINGS FPO	B & F	10.00	1.12	65
Median			10.000	0.990	74.0
Mean			9.883	0.930	71.75
SD			4.310	0.301	9.61

The last 48 bits were divided into three groups of 16. The reciprocal of the digital representation of each group represented *L, M* and *T* respectively.

Each NN contained 14 input layers and 7 output layers. The stock index data was organised into 19 groups for the months of June 1999 to January 2001. Each group contained the closing price for the stocks on the 21 trading days beginning on the first trading day of each month. If data was not available for a particular index for a particular trading day, that data was filled in from the most recent previous trading day.

Because the NN software only accepts input and output values between 0 and 1, the stock prices were converted thus:

$$T_n = \frac{S_n - \min(S)}{\max(S) - \min(S)} \tag{1}$$

A sigmoid transfer function was used for the firing of neurons:

$$f(x) = \frac{1}{1 + e^{-x}} \tag{2}$$

Each NN was trained using backpropogation (BP) over a maximum of 100,000 epochs using the 12 data sets from the 1999-2000 financial year. The fitness of the algorithm was determined as the error of the NN when applied to the 6 data sets for the first 6 months in the 2000-2001 financial year. The error for each data set was specified by the NN software as:

$$E_s = \sum f'(n_{l-1,j})(o_{s,j} - n_{l-1,j}) \tag{3}$$

For the error over the six data sets, the negative Root Mean Squared Error (RMSE) was taken. The negative RMSE was used because a low error should indicate a high fitness, and vice-versa:

$$RMSE = -\sqrt{\sum E_s^{\ 2}} \tag{4}$$

The aim of the to determine a relationship between the attributes of the optimal NN configurations and the attributes of the stock indices. The attributes considered were the learning rate (*L*), momentum (*M*) and tolerance (*T*) chosen by the algorithm, the number of layers, *l* (depth) of the network, the mean number of neurons in each layer (5) the accentuation (6) of the network configuration and the left (7) and right (8) triangular orientations.

$$n = \frac{n_1 + n_2 + \ldots + n_l}{l} \tag{5}$$

$$\text{If } l = 1 \text{ then } A = 0 \tag{6}$$

$$\text{If } l > 1 \text{ then } A = \frac{|(n_2 - n_1)| + |(n_3 - n_2)| + \ldots + |(n_l - n_{l-1})|}{n(l-1)}$$

$$\text{If } l = 1 \text{ then } TL = 0 \tag{7}$$

$$\text{If } l > 1 \text{ then } TL = \frac{(n_1 - \frac{n_l}{l}) + (n_2 - \frac{2n_l}{l}) + \ldots + (n_{l-1} - \frac{(l-1)n_l}{l})}{n_l(l-1)}$$

$$\text{If } l = 1 \text{ then } TR = 0 \tag{8}$$

$$\text{If } l > 1 \text{ then } TR = \frac{(n_l - \frac{n_1}{l}) + \ldots + (n_3 - \frac{(l-2)n_1}{l}) + (n_2 - \frac{(l-1)n_1}{l})}{n_1(l-1)}$$

The nearest-optimal NN, determined by the fitness function, was selected for each index. Its performance on forecasting the July 2001 data set was compared with the performance of a NN generated by another arbitrary algorithm-generated NN.

For each attribute, the optimal NN configurations were classified as being "high" or "low" for that attribute according to whether they had a value for that attribute above (or equal to) or below the median respectively. The low and high values were reversed for *TL* and *TR*, as a low value implies a high triangular orientation and vice versa.

This categorisation was compared against attributes of the stock indices, shown in Table 1. The attributes used for the stock indices were market sector grouping (Industrials, Resources or Building & Finance), approximate duration in years (high or low) up to July 2001, sector •-volitility in July 2001 (high or low), and sector earnings stability (high or low). As with the NN attributes, categorisation into high and low values for index attributes was determined by the median.

The indices covered 22 market sectors, however, no sector covered enough indices to make any reasonable analysis, as the most indices covered by any sector was Banks & Finance, which covered seven. The Building & Finance grouping included Banks & Finance, Developers & Contractors, Insurance, Investment & Financial Services and Property Trusts. The Industrials grouping included Alcohol & Tobacco, Building Materials, Chemicals, Diversified Industrials, Food & Household, Healthcare & Biotech, Infrastructure & Utilities, Media, Paper & Packaging, Retail, Transport, Telecommunications and Tourism & Leisure. The Resources grouping included Diversified Resources, Energy, Gold and Other Metals.

Results

The difference in fitness of random networks and the near-optimal networks tested on the July 2001 data set for each share index (Table 2) was statistically significant ($p < 10^{-8}$). A paired t-test with one tail was used to take into consideration the one to one correspondence of data elements based on the index to which they are applied. This result suggests some significance in the GA's choice of NN configuration as opposed to the chosen NN having a similar fitness to a randomly generated NN. In other words, the GA had to some extent optimised the configuration of the NN.

The optimised NNs and corresponding stock indices were categorised as HIGH or LOW for each attribute. This was done according to the median. The exception was the sector group attribute of the stock indices, which was divided into Building & Finance, Industrials and Resources. The values for the NN attributes are listed in Table 1, whereas the values for the index attributes are listed in Table 3.

Table 4 shows the frequency of stock indices falling into particular categories for both NN and stock index attributes. For the purposes of this analysis, it is expected that particular attributes of stock indices lead to particular attributes of optimised NNs. Therefore a •^{2} test on all category frequencies for each NN attribute for each stock index attribute category should show if the latter affects the former. The expected frequencies for the •^{2} test are taken as the total frequency of the NN attribute category times the total frequency of the index attribute category divided by the total number of indices. The total number of indices was 47 except in the case of Earnings Stability, where there was no data for three indices in the Property Trusts Sector.

The most significant •^{2} results ($p < 0.3$) are listed in Table 5. Only two comparisons were statistically significant with $p < 0.1$ and another two with $0.1 < p < 0.2$.

Table 2. Performance of random and near-optimal NN configurations on each stock index.

ASX code	Random	optimized
AGL	-1.244	-0.479
ALL	-1.158	-2.013
AMC	-0.439	-1.067
AMP	-0.834	-0.675
ANZ	-1.077	-0.600
BHP	-1.266	-1.077
BIL	-1.560	-1.447
CBA	-0.925	-0.752
CCL	-1.262	-0.097
CML	-1.497	-0.110
CPU	-1.240	-0.868

CSL	-1.103	-0.794
CSR	-1.249	-0.520
CWO	-1.021	-0.155
ERG	-1.292	-1.056
FBG	-1.253	-0.998
FXJ	-0.663	-0.660
GMF	-1.239	-1.130
GPT	-1.762	-1.648
HVN	-0.912	-0.121
LLC	-1.555	-0.269
MBL	-1.202	-0.967
MGR	-1.323	-0.973
MIM	-0.297	-0.091
NAB	-1.594	-0.749
NCP	-1.144	-0.621
NDY	-0.274	-0.107
ORI	-0.433	0.000
PBL	-1.930	-0.939
PDP	-0.367	-0.057
QAN	-1.069	-0.102
QBE	-1.175	-0.578
RIO	-1.177	-0.285
SGB	-0.863	-0.700
SME	-0.511	-0.260
SMI	-0.675	-0.338
SRP	-1.165	-0.822
STO	-0.610	-0.201
TAH	-0.965	-0.323
TLS	-1.552	-0.402
WBC	-0.823	-0.731
WES	-0.943	-0.113
WFT	-2.181	-1.061
WMC	-1.077	-0.849
WOW	-0.658	-0.160
WPL	-0.913	-0.786
WSF	-0.749	-0.659
Mean	-1.068	-0.626
SD	0.415	0.449

Table 3. Attributes of optimised NN configurations for each stock index.

ASX code	*L*	*M*	*T*	*l*	*n*	*A*	*TL*	*TR*
AGL	0.75	0.56	0.45	2	16.00	0.50	0.10	1.17
ALL	0.11	0.37	0.04	4	3.75	0.98	0.67	0.75
AMC	0.68	0.93	0.01	1	24.00	0.00	0.00	0.00
AMP	0.77	0.99	0.40	3	13.33	0.41	0.42	1.86
ANZ	0.77	0.99	0.39	4	6.50	0.77	0.65	-0.05
BHP	0.16	0.91	0.09	3	11.33	1.94	2.00	7.50
BIL	0.13	0.19	0.10	4	7.25	1.47	2.64	8.75
CBA	0.00	0.43	0.31	4	9.50	0.46	0.08	1.19
CCL	0.98	0.75	0.39	5	8.80	0.80	-0.04	1.30
CML	0.92	0.78	0.06	6	6.00	0.83	-0.02	0.30
CPU	0.09	0.98	0.47	4	7.00	1.10	0.13	-0.14
CSL	0.52	0.96	0.59	6	5.00	1.04	0.38	0.60
CSR	0.81	0.98	0.60	2	11.00	1.45	-0.34	5.83
CWO	0.96	0.95	0.25	1	42.00	0.00	0.00	0.00
ERG	0.21	0.15	0.73	3	10.33	2.71	14.67	14.50
FBG	0.56	0.66	0.54	5	4.20	0.77	0.60	-0.38
FXJ	0.98	0.71	0.09	3	13.67	1.57	4.29	1.28
GMF	0.71	0.59	0.21	3	6.33	1.26	-0.27	8.50
GPT	0.52	0.27	0.09	4	3.25	0.82	0.50	-0.19
HVN	0.30	0.48	0.11	6	8.00	0.53	2.03	-0.39
LLC	0.14	0.09	0.02	2	18.00	1.78	-0.44	16.50
MBL	0.21	0.35	0.41	4	6.00	0.56	0.31	0.68
MGR	0.00	0.82	0.29	4	4.25	0.55	5.08	-0.21
MIM	0.99	0.97	0.25	6	5.67	0.99	-0.03	2.50
NAB	0.36	0.97	0.51	6	7.00	0.77	0.10	0.78
NCP	0.42	0.98	0.20	5	4.00	0.38	0.26	4.10
NDY	0.98	0.75	0.39	4	4.50	0.59	0.17	0.58
ORI	0.99	0.82	0.09	1	44.00	0.00	0.00	0.00
PBL	0.22	0.36	0.75	4	8.00	0.63	0.24	1.75
PDP	0.49	0.72	0.06	5	8.20	0.58	1.26	-0.30
QAN	0.95	0.85	0.22	5	9.00	0.81	0.09	0.98
QBE	0.21	0.69	0.43	6	6.00	0.57	0.15	1.50
RIO	0.90	0.99	0.03	6	6.67	0.63	0.17	1.10
SGB	0.06	0.30	0.27	3	8.33	1.14	-0.24	5.25
SME	0.79	0.94	0.56	1	36.00	0.00	0.00	0.00
SMI	1.00	0.88	0.17	1	51.00	0.00	0.00	0.00
SRP	0.99	0.35	0.25	3	13.67	1.35	-0.29	19.50
STO	0.95	0.94	0.70	1	23.00	0.00	0.00	0.00
TAH	0.91	0.89	0.85	1	44.00	0.00	0.00	0.00
TLS	0.92	0.97	0.39	5	7.00	0.71	-0.01	1.29

WBC	0.00	0.12	0.30	4	3.50	1.14	-0.06	3.75
WES	0.97	0.99	0.99	1	41.00	0.00	0.00	0.00
WFT	0.10	0.70	0.35	2	13.00	1.08	-0.20	2.83
WMC	0.87	0.87	0.09	5	7.00	0.79	0.01	0.85
WOW	0.65	0.11	0.04	4	6.00	0.11	1.02	0.23
WPL	0.51	0.99	0.39	5	5.80	0.65	0.36	0.31
WSF	0.77	0.99	0.38	5	4.40	0.91	0.24	1.85
Median	0.685	0.821	0.296	4.000	8.000	0.769	0.100	0.850

Table 4. Frequency of NN attributes for each category in stock index attributes.

		Group			Duration		β-volatility		Earn. Stab.	
		B & F	Ind.	Res.	HIGH	LOW	HIGH	LOW	HIGH	LOW
L	HIGH	4	14	5	15	8	12	11	10	13
	LOW	11	11	2	18	6	13	11	13	8
M	HIGH	6	11	6	14	9	15	8	10	13
	LOW	9	14	1	19	5	10	14	13	8
T	HIGH	10	10	3	16	7	13	10	11	11
	LOW	5	15	4	17	7	12	12	12	10
I	HIGH	3	9	4	12	4	7	9	8	8
	LOW	12	16	3	21	10	18	13	15	13
n	HIGH	6	14	2	14	8	11	11	12	9
	LOW	9	11	5	19	6	14	11	11	12
A	HIGH	8	12	3	18	5	13	10	9	12
	LOW	7	13	4	15	9	12	12	14	9
TL	HIGH	8	11	4	17	6	12	11	10	11
	LOW	7	14	3	16	8	13	11	13	10
TR	HIGH	8	12	3	16	7	14	9	9	13
	LOW	7	13	4	17	7	11	13	14	8

Table 5. Comparisons of index attribute categories and NN attributes by $\bullet^2$ test with $p < 0.3$.

Index Attribute	Index Attribute Category	NN Attribute	NN Attribute Value	*p*
Group	Resources	Momentum	HIGH	0.0515
Group	Building & Finance	Learning Rate	LOW	0.0844
Group	Building & Finance	Tolerance	HIGH	0.1695
Group	Resources	Depth	HIGH	0.1971
Group	Resources	Learning Rate	HIGH	0.2339
Earnings Stability	LOW	Learning Rate	HIGH	0.2343
Earnings Stability	LOW	Momentum	HIGH	0.2343
Earnings Stability	LOW	Right Triangular	HIGH	0.2343
β-volatitiliy	LOW	Momentum	LOW	0.2381
Duration	LOW	Momentum	HIGH	0.2506
Group	Building & Finance	Depth	LOW	0.2511
β-volatitiliy	HIGH	Momentum	HIGH	0.2685

Discussion

It has been demonstrated that configuration is an important consideration when forecasting stock prices with NNs. The present study has not, however, completely produced all the useful rules for configuring a NN for stock market forecasting based on the attributes of the stock index. Despite the results, the present study has managed to "test the water" so to speak in developing a methodology to determine the causes of NN optimisation

The apparent lack of strength in the relationship between the NN attributes and some stock index attributes possibly suggests that the given NN attributes are not strongly determined by those index attributes. To find stronger relationships, more attributes should be considered in any future study.

It is interesting to note that the five most significant relationships listed in Table 5 were determined by market sector groupings, suggesting that this attribute is a stronger determinant than the others. Therefore another possible contribution to the lack of strength in these relationships is that the other three attributes are dynamic, and were taken from a particular point in time. Unfortunately, no archived data were available for previous measures of •-volatility or earnings stability.

Also, the present study does not take into consideration whether there is some kind of interrelationship between the attributes of the indices or between the attributes of the NNs. Given the possibility of this consideration, there would be potential value in conducting a more detailed analysis. A proposed method of analysis that takes this consideration into account would be some form of machine learning.

The categorisations of some attributes into HIGH and LOW do not allow an examination of the variations within these groupings. There would be more qualitative integrity to the analysis if a less simplified approach were taken. For three of the stock index attributes, relationships between these and NN attributes could be determined in terms of correlation. This unfortunately does not apply to market sectors, as there is no apparent translation from these categories to quantitative values.

Training values such as momentum, learning rate and tolerance featured more prominently in significant relationships, suggesting that these attributes should be examined separately to those that determine attributes of the network itself.

A casual observation of the GAs at work would show that in many cases the fittest generation was towards the earlier or middle generations. This suggests a high prevalence of local minima, which could be caused by the convolution of network architecture fitness by training data fitness, and possibly furthers the case for interrelationships between such attributes. Nonetheless, there is little to be gained from studying such convoluted data until the training values and network architectures are examined as separate considerations.

In conclusion, there are several limiting factors to determining strong relationships between index and NN attributes: the lack of importance of the index attributes studied in determining NN configurations, dynamic attributes being considered as static attributes, the lack of consideration of interrelationships between index attributes or NN attributes, the integration of training values with NN architecture.

It is suggested that any future studies into the optimisation of neural network configuration for stock market forecasting:

a) separate the optimisation of NN training values and architectures;
b) use different stock index attributes to find network configuration determinants;
c) conduct a more detailed analysis of the relationship between stock index and NN attributes, possibly taking into account attribute interrelationships, and examining relationships by correlation, not frequency.

Further study will take these matters into consideration and refine the methodology.

Acknowledgments

Thank you to:

- Des Fitzgerald and Barrie Robinson for their help with statistical analysis
- Tony Gray and Christian McGee for their help with hardware

Software obtained from Object Oriented Neural Networks in C++ by Joey Rogers.

References

Aiken, M. & Bsat, M. (1999). *Forecasting market trends with neural networks*. Information Systems Management. 16(4): 42-48.

Kumar, N., Krovi, R. & Rajagopalan, B. (1997). *Financial decision support with hybrid genetic and neural based modeling tools*. European Journal of Operational Research. 103(2): 339-349, Dec 1.

Kuo, R. J. Chen, C. H. & Hwang, Y. C. (2001). *An intelligent stock trading decision support system through integration of genetic algorithm based fuzzy neural network and artificial neural network*. Fuzzy Sets & Systems. 118(1): 21-45, Feb 16.

Rogers, J. (1997). *Object Oriented Neural Networks in C++*. Academic Press, Sydney.

Qi, M. (1999). *Nonlinear predictability of stock returns using financial and economic variables*. Journal of Business & Economic Statistics. 17(4): 419-429, Oct.

Sexton, R. S. & Gupta, J. N. D. (2000). *Comparative evaluation of genetic algorithm and backpropagation for training neural networks. Information Sciences*. 129(1-4): 45-59, Nov.

Shin, T. & Han I. (2000). *Optimal signal multi-resolution by genetic algorithms to support artificial neural networks for exchange-rate forecasting*. Expert Systems with Applications. 18(4): 257-269, May.

Wittkemper, H. G. & Steiner, M. (1996). *Using neural networks to forecast the systematic risk of stocks*. European Journal of Operational Research. 90(3): 577-588, May 10.

Wong, B. K. & Selvi, Y. (1998). *Neural network applications in finance: a review and analysis of literature (1990-1996)*. Information & Management. 34(3):129-140, Oct.

Updating epistemic states

Jérôme Lang[1], Pierre Marquis[2], and Mary-Anne Williams[3]

[1] IRIT - Université Paul Sabatier -Toulouse, France
[2] CRIL - Université d'Artois - Lens, France
[3] University of Newcastle - Newcastle, Australia

Abstract. Belief update is usually defined by means of operators acting on belief sets. We propose here belief update operators acting on epistemic states which convey much more information than belief sets since they express the relative plausibilities of the pieces of information believed by the agent. In the following, epistemic states are encoded as rankings on worlds. We extend a class of update operators (dependency-based updates) to epistemic states, by defining an operation playing the same role as knowledge transmutations [21] do for belief revision.

1 Introduction

While belief revision is meant to integrate new knowledge about a static world, belief update is usually thought of as taking account of a piece of information representing the effect of an evolution of the world (which may be caused by an event or an action) [13]. It has been shown in many places (e.g., [2] [5]) that iterated applications of belief revision operations need a representation of initial beliefs more informative than flat belief sets, namely, *epistemic states*. A (flat) belief set is a closed logical theory, which, when the language is propositional and generated by a finite number of propositional symbols (which is assumed here), is equivalently expressed by a propositional formula. An epistemic state is a full encoding of what the agent believes and how she is likely to revise her beliefs accordingly, which calls for a gradation of beliefs. This gradation is usually expressed by a preorder on formulas, i.e., a reflexive and transitive relation, or more specifically by a ranking function on formulas.

Oddly enough, while the distinctions between revision and update have been extensively studied, as well as postulates and strategies for iterated belief revision, the KR community has devoted much less attention on iterated belief update (exceptions being [9], [17] and [19]) and even less on update on epistemic states. This raises the following questions, in order.

1. *Is iterated belief update as worth investigating as iterated belief revision?*

2. *Can usual update operators, mapping a pair (belief set, input formula) to a belief set, be applied iteratively without trivialization?*

3. *If so, does iteration sometimes need belief update operators acting on epistemic states rather than on belief sets?*

M. Brooks, D. Corbett, and M. Stumptner (Eds.): AI 2001, LNAI 2256, pp. 297–308, 2001.

The answer to Question 1. is obvious when one thinks of a belief update operator as a tool for computing the effects of an action given the initial beliefs of the agent. Actions are meant to be performed in sequence, especially when it comes to planning, and in this context, iterate dupdates naturally arise.

Question 2. is more complex. W e propose the following answer. The process of belief revision *acting on belief sets* is not Markovian, because revising a belief set by an input formula will not lead to the same result whether it comes from a certain sequence of revision or from another one. This can be overcome either by storing the whole history of the revision process or by representing knowledge by epistemic states, which actually amounts to the same kind of information (see [14] for a general discussion), namely, not only the pure beliefs are stored but also the way they should be revised; now, belief revision *acting on epistemic states or on sequences of belief sets* can be seen as Markovian. That belief revision on belief sets should not be a Markovian process is not surprising, since belief revision is concerned with a static world and "old" beliefs still play an important role since they bear on the very same world as new ones. The latter intuition does not carry on to belief update, or at least not with the same strength. Indeed, since iterated belief updates amount to performing successive actions, the obtained belief states represent the beliefs after each action is performed, and considering this process as Markovian is generally harmless.

Now, the paper could well stop at this point, since updating epistemic states could be seen as a formal exercise with no other interest than making students work with worlds, formulas, rankings and so on. As the reader expects, this is not the case, and here is our answer to Question 3: *there are some contexts where belief update on flat belief sets is insufficient.* We give here two such contexts:

Context 1: *Successive applications of belief revisions and updates*: Planning with nondeterministic actions in *partially observable environments* calls for plans that interleave "traditional" (or *ontic*) actions acting on the world only and *knowledge-gathering* (or *epistemic*) actions that do not change the state of the world, but the beliefs of the agent, only – their role is to render the agent informed enough so as to help her choose what to do next. Therefore, it may well be the case that a belief update will be followed by a revision, or even a sequence of revisions, which obviously calls for the need of working on rich structures such as epistemic states rather than on flat belief sets.

Example 1 (*Saturday night shooting*).
Bill is a good shooter but he is sometimes drunk. When he is not drunk, sho oting at a turkey results in the turkey being dead. When he is drunk, however, shooting at a turkey results in the turkey hiding. Today, Bill does not look drunk – so that in the initial belief it is more plausible, yet not totally certain, that he's not drunk; the turkey is initially alive and not hidden (and these latter beliefs are certain). Bill shoots, which may be expressed by updating the initial belief by the formula $(\mathtt{drunk} \wedge \mathtt{hidden}) \vee (\neg\mathtt{drunk} \wedge \neg\mathtt{alive})$, *with the further constraint that* **drunk** *(as well as* $\neg$**drunk***) cannot be changed by the action of shooting. After a*

few seconds, one hears the turkey goobling, which leads to a revision by **alive**. *Is the turkey hidden in the final state?*
With belief change operators on flat belief sets, the initial belief is **alive** $\wedge\neg$**hidden** $\wedge\neg$**drunk**, which after update according e.g. to Forbus' operator leads to the belief set $\neg$**drunk** $\wedge\neg$**hidden** $\wedge\neg$**alive**; after revision by **alive**, the new belief set is $\neg$**drunk** $\wedge\neg$**hidden** $\wedge$**alive** while the intended result is **drunk** $\wedge$**hidden** $\wedge$**alive**.

Context 2: *Evaluation of the satisfaction of a goal after a sequence of updates.* After a sequence of updates, we may want to evaluate to what point a given goal is satisfied (this is typically looked for in decision-theoretic planning). What we want at the end is an epistemic state where the worlds violating the goals are the least entrenched ones, which needs of course to work on epistemic states. Consider the same example as above, with the goal of having the turkey dead at the end, and suppose that we have also the action **bomb** always resulting in the turkey being dead – thus performing **bomb** amounts to updating by $\neg$**alive**. We should be able to conclude that the plan **shoot** normally succeeds but sometimes fails, while the plan **bomb** always succeed.

We choose to model epistemic states by ranking functions on the set of propositional worlds, or *Ordinal Conditional Functions* (OCF) – sometimes called *kappa* functions. This model is among the simplest ones, and it is frequently chosen for modelling epistemic states. For computational efficiency reasons, OCFs will not be represented explicitly but by a more compact way, namely by means of *stratified belief bases* that induce a full OCF (see for instance [22]).

In Section 2, we give the necessary background about OCFs and stratified belief bases; next, we give the necessary background about dependency-based update. In Section 3, we show how epistemic states are updated, not only by single propositional formulas but more generally by pairs consisting of a propositional formula and a rank, and we thus propose a counterpart to belief update of what is known under the name of *transmutation* for belief revision. We proceed first by extending the notion of variable forgetting to epistemic states, and then we are in a position to define transmutations for belief update. We briefly show that our update operators on epistemic states are relevant for reasoning about action, and we conclude by discussing related work.

2 Background and notations

Let VAR be a finite set of propositional variables and $\mathcal{L}_{VAR}$ the propositional language built upon these variables and the usual connectives. For every $X \subseteq VAR$, $\mathcal{L}_X$ denotes the sublanguage of $\mathcal{L}_{VAR}$ generated from the variables of X only. For every formula φ of $\mathcal{L}_{VAR}$, $Var(\varphi)$ is the set of variables occurring in φ. $\varphi_{x\leftarrow 1}$ (resp. $\varphi_{x\leftarrow 0}$) denotes the formula from $\mathcal{L}_{VAR}$ obtained by substituting in a uniform way the variable $x \in VAR$ by the boolean constant $\top$ (resp. $\bot$) in φ. Full instantiations of variables of VAR are called worlds, and are denoted by ω, ω' etc. Full instantiations of variables of $X \subseteq VAR$ are called X-worlds, and are denoted by ω_X, ω'_X etc. 2^X denotes the set of all possible truth assignments of variables of X. $Mod(\varphi)$ is the set of models of φ, i.e., the worlds satisfying φ.

Let X and Y be two disjoint subsets of VAR, and let $\omega_X \in 2^X$, $\omega_Y \in 2^Y$. We define the concatenation of ω_X and ω_Y as the world $\omega_X \,.\, \omega_Y \in 2^{X \cup Y}$ assigning to each variable of X (resp. Y) the same value as ω_X (resp. ω_Y). If ω is a world from 2^{VAR} and $x \in VAR$ then we define $switch(\omega, x)$ as the world obtained from ω by switching the truth value of the variable x. If $X \subseteq VAR$, we say that ω and ω' agree on X, denoted by $\omega \approx_X \omega'$, if and only if ω and ω' assign the same truth value to every variable of X.

2.1 Ordinal conditional functions and stratified belief bases

Definition 1

- *An* ordinal conditional function (OCF) r *is a mapping from* 2^{VAR} *to* $I\!N \cup \infty$. r *is said to be* normalized *if and only if* $\exists \omega \in 2^{VAR}$ *such that* $r(\omega) = 0$;
- *A normalized OCF* r *induces an* entrenchment ranking E_r *on* $\mathcal{L}_{VAR}$ *defined by* $E_r(\varphi) = \min_{\omega \models \varphi} r(\omega)$;
- *If* r *and* r' *are two normalized OCFs,* r *is said to be* at least as specific *as* r', *noted* $r \geq r'$, *if and only if for every world* $\omega \in 2^{VAR}$ *we have* $r(\varphi) \geq r'(\varphi)$.

Unless the contrary is explicitly stated, all OCFs considered in this paper will be normalized.

The higher $r(\omega)$, the less plausible ω represents the actual state of the world. In particular, if $r(\omega) = \infty$ then ω is totally impossible. The usual interpretation of OCFs is in terms of order of magnitude of infinitesimal probabilities [20]: $r(\omega) = i < \infty$ means that the order of magnitude of the probability of ω being the actual world is in $\mathcal{O}(\varepsilon^i)$ where ε is an infinitesimal, and $r(\omega) = \infty$ if ω is an impossible world. This interpretation implies that r should be necessarily normalized.

From a practical point of view, it is not possible to ask the agent to express her beliefs under the form of a full OCF explicitly, since it is exponentially large in the number of propositional variables. Instead, it is more efficient and natural to represent them implicitly by means of stratified belief bases.

Definition 2 (stratified belief bases)

- *A* stratified belief base *(SBB)* B *is a finite sequence* $\langle B_1, ..., B_n, B_\infty \rangle$ *of propositional formulae* B_i. *Each* i *in* $\{1, \ldots, n, \infty\}$ *is called a* rank. B_∞ *represents fully certain beliefs,* B_n *the* most *entrenched among the uncertain beliefs and* B_1 *the* least *entrenched ones;*
- *The* cut *of level* i *of a SBB* B *is defined by* $Cut(B, i) = \bigwedge_{j \geq i} B_j$; B *is said to be* consistent *if and only if* $Cut(B, 1)$ *is consistent;*
- *The OCF* r_B *induced by the SBB* B *is defined by* $\forall \omega \in 2^{VAR}, r_B(\omega) = \max\{i \mid \omega \models \neg B_i\}$ *if such an index exists, and* 0 *otherwise;* r_B *is normalized if and only if* B *is consistent.*
- *if* B *is a SBB,* φ *a formula and* i *a rank in* $\{1, \ldots, n, \infty\}$ *then we let*

$$Add(B, \varphi, i) = \langle B_1, ..., B_{i-1}, B_i \wedge \varphi, B_{i+1}, ..., B_n, B_\infty \rangle.$$

2.2 Formula-variable independence and variable forgetting

Definition 3 (FV-independence) *[16] Let φ be a formula from $\mathcal{L}_{VAR}$ and $X \subseteq VAR$. φ is said to be* independent from X *if and only if there exists a formula ψ from $\mathcal{L}_{VAR}$ logically equivalent to φ which does not mention any variable from X.*

It is shown in [16] that φ is independent from X if and only if φ is independent from $\{x\}$ for each $x \in X$; we denote by $DepVar(\varphi)$ the set of variables φ is dependent on. It is also shown in [16] that φ is independent from x if and only if $\varphi_{x \leftarrow 0}$ and $\varphi_{x \leftarrow 1}$ are logically equivalent, from which it can be derived that checking whether $x \in DepVar(\varphi)$ is coNP-complete.

The notion of variable elimination (also referred to as forgetting, projection or marginalization) is central in the following:

Definition 4 (variable forgetting) *[18] Let φ be a formula from $\mathcal{L}_{VAR}$ and $X \subseteq VAR$. $Forget(\varphi, X)$ is the formula inductively defined as follows:*
(i) $Forget(\varphi, \emptyset) = \varphi$;
(ii) $Forget(\varphi, \{x\}) = \varphi_{x \leftarrow 1} \vee \varphi_{x \leftarrow 0}$;
(iii) $Forget(\varphi, \{x\} \cup X) = Forget(Forget(\varphi, X), \{x\})$.

The following characterization of variable forgetting [15] helps to understand how it works in practice: if φ is under DNF, i.e., $\varphi = \gamma_1 \vee \ldots \vee \gamma_n$ where each γ_i is a conjunction of literals, then $Forget(\varphi, X)$ can be obtained by deleting from the γ_i's all occurrences of literals $x, \neg x$ for all $x \in X$. For instance, let $\varphi = (\neg a \vee b) \wedge (a \vee c) \wedge (b \vee c \vee d)$ and $X = \{a, d\}$. Since φ is logically equivalent to $(\neg a \wedge c) \vee (a \wedge b) \vee (b \wedge c)$, we have $Forget(\varphi, X) \equiv (b \vee c)$. $Forget(\varphi, X)$ is the strongest consequence of φ being independent from X [16].

2.3 Belief update

A *belief update operator* $\diamond$ maps the propositional belief base (a formula) K representing the initial beliefs of a given agent and an input formula α reflecting some explicit evolution of the world [13], to a new set of beliefs $K \diamond \alpha$ held by the agent after this evolution has taken place.

Katsuno and Mendelzon [13] proposed a general semantics for update. The most prominent feature of KM-updates (distinguishing updates from revision) is that update must be performed modelwise, i.e., $Mod(K \diamond \alpha) = \bigcup_{\omega \models K} \omega \diamond \alpha$. Given that updates are performed modelwise, what remains to be defined is the way models are updated, i.e., how $\omega \diamond \alpha$ is defined.

Update operators proposed in the literature can be (roughly) classified in two main families. *Minimisation-based updates* $\diamond_{Min}$ (such as Winslett's PMA [23]), stemming from the direct instantiation of the Katsuno-Mendelzon semantics, compute $\omega \diamond_{Min} \alpha$ by selecting the models of α "closest" to ω (this notion of closeness being modelled by a collection of preorders $\geq_\omega$ on 2^{VAR}). *Dependency-based updates* $\diamond_{Dep}$ ([10], [11], [6], [24], [12]) compute $\omega \diamond \alpha$ by first forgetting (from ω) the truth value of all variables that are "relevant" to α (leaving unchanged the truth value of variables not relevant to the update), and then expanding the result with α; the notion of "being relevant to" is modelled by a mapping Dep from $\mathcal{L}_{VAR}$ to 2^{VAR}. Many choices for Dep are possible (see [11] for details). The most frequent choice for Dep is *semantical dependence*: $Dep(\alpha) = DepVar(\alpha)$, and by default we let $Dep = DepVar$. Whatever the choice of Dep, the *dependence-based update* $\omega \diamond_{Dep} \alpha$ of a world ω by a formula α w.r.t. Dep is the set of all worlds ω' such that $\omega' \models \alpha$, and for every propositional variable x from VAR such that $x \notin Dep(\alpha)$, ω and ω' assign the same truth value to x.

Interestingly, $\diamond_{Dep}$ operators can be characterized through the notion of variable forgetting defined above. Indeed, the following holds [6]:

$$K \diamond_{Dep} \alpha \equiv (Forget(K, Dep(\alpha))) \wedge \alpha$$

This result gives an intuitive understanding of how dependency-based update works: first, one forgets the variables concerned by the update, and then one expands by the input.

3 Updating OCFs

We are now going to apply the principle "forget, then expand", at work in dependency-based update, to epistemic states consisting of OCFs. Therefore what we have to do first is to generalize variable forgetting to OCFs.

3.1 Independence of an OCF from a set of v ariables

Recall that variable forgetting can be characterized by the following result: $Forget(\varphi, X)$ is the strongest consequence of φ that is independent from X. We may thus define variable forgetting from an OCF by a similar construction, which requires first to define independence of an OCF from a set of variables.

Definition 5 *Let $X \subseteq VAR$.*

- *An OCF r is* independent *from X if and only if there is a SBB B inducing r not mentioning any variable from X.*
- *A SBB B is* independent from *X if and only if its generated OCF r_B is independent from X.*

Example 2: $B = \langle B_1, B_2, B_\infty \rangle$ *with* $B_\infty = a \rightarrow b$, $B_2 = (a \rightarrow \neg b) \wedge (a \rightarrow b \vee c) \wedge (b \rightarrow d)$, $B_1 = b$. *The OCF induced by B is the following:*

$r(\omega) = \infty$ *for each* $\omega \models a \wedge \neg b$	$r(\omega) = 2$ *for each* $\omega \models b \wedge \neg d$
$r(\omega) = 1$ *for each* $\omega \models \neg a \wedge \neg b$	$r(\omega) = 0$ *for each* $\omega \models \neg a \wedge b \wedge d$

The following simple result states that it is sufficien t to focus on independence from a single variable.

Proposition 1 *r (resp. B) is independent from X if and only if r (resp. B) is independent from $\{x\}$ for all $x \in X$.*

Therefore, all the information about sets of variables an OCF r is dependent on which can be summarized by the set of variables $DepVar(r) = \{x \in VAR \mid r \text{ depends on } \{x\}\}$ (and we define $DepVar(B)$ similarly).

It is not difficult to verify that the SBB $B' = \langle B'_1, B'_2, B'_\infty \rangle$ with $B'_1 = B_1$, $B'_2 = (a \rightarrow \neg b) \wedge (b \rightarrow d)$ and $B'_\infty = B_\infty$, induces the same OCF, i.e., $r_B = r_{B'}$. Therefore, B and B' are equivalent, and since c is not mentioned in B', B is independent from $\{c\}$ (and so is the OCF r_B). On the other hand, it is dependent on $\{a\}$, $\{b\}$ and $\{d\}$, i.e., $DepVar(B) = \{a, b, d\}$.

The following result gives semantical characterizations of independence of an OCF from a variable.

Proposition 2 *Let r be an OCF and $X \subseteq VAR$. The following four statements are equivalent.*

1. *r is independent from X.*
2. *For any X-worlds $\omega_X, \omega'_X \in 2^X$, we have $r(\omega_{VAR\setminus X} \cdot \omega_X) = r(\omega_{VAR\setminus X} \cdot \omega'_X)$.*
3. *For any variable $x \in X$ and any $\omega \in 2^{VAR}$, we have $r(\omega) = r(switch(\omega, x))$.*
4. *For any nontautological φ such that $Var(\varphi) \subseteq X$, we have $E_r(\varphi) = 0$.*

In the case where the OCF is defined implicitly by a SBB, the next result gives a practical way of computing whether it is independent from $\{x\}$ without having to write r explicitly.

Proposition 3
The SBB B is independent from X if and only if for all $i \in \{1, ..., n, \infty\}$, $Cut(B, i)$ is independent from X.

Therefore, the problem of checking independence of a SBB from a variable can be reduced to a linear number of "classical" independence problems. This result enables us to draw generalizations of several results about formula-variable independence stated in [16]. In particular, determining whether B is independent from X is coNP-complete.

3.2 Forgetting in OCFs

Definition 6 *Let $X \subseteq VAR$ and r be an OCF. $Forget(r, X)$ is the minimal OCF r' (w.r.t. $\leq$) such that $r' \geq r$ and r' is independent from X.*

The following result gives a semantical characterization of forgetting.

Proposition 4 *Let r be an OCF and $X \subseteq VAR$. Then*

$$Forget(r, X)(\omega) = \min\{r(\omega') \mid \omega' \in 2^{VAR} \text{ and } \omega' \approx_{VAR\setminus X} \omega\}$$

Note that when X is a singleton $\{x\}$, the latter identity becomes $Forget(r, \{x\})(\omega) = \min(r(\omega), r(switch(\omega, x)))$. The previous definition and characterization are not operational when the OCF is represented implicitly under the form of a SBB. The next result tells us how to implement variable forgetting from a SBB in practice, namely by forgetting from the n classical propositional formulas $Cut(B, i)$.

Proposition 5 *Let B be a SBB and $X \subseteq VAR$. Let $BForget(B, X) = \langle Forget(Cut(B, i), X)\rangle_{i=1,2,\dots,n,\infty}$. Then we have*

$$Forget(r_B, X) = r_{BForget(B,X)}$$

Example 3: Let $B = \langle B_1, B_2, B_\infty\rangle$ with $B_\infty = \top$, $B_2 = a \wedge c$, $B_1 = a \rightarrow b$. We have $BForget(B, \{a\}) = \langle b \wedge c, c, \top\rangle$; $BForget(B, \{b\}) = \langle a \wedge c, a \wedge c, \top\rangle$; $BForget(B, \{a, c\}) = \langle c, \top, \top\rangle$.

Note that it is important to take the conjunction of the strata before forgetting: since $Forget(B_2, \{a\}) = c$ and $Forget(B_1, \{a\}) = \top$, $BForget(B, \{a\})$ is not equivalent to $\langle Forget(B_1, \{a\}), Forget(B_2, \{a\}), Forget(B_\infty, \{a\})\rangle$.

3.3 Updating an epistemic state by a formula and a rank

Let's remind that a *transmutation* operator maps an OCF r, a consistent formula φ and a rank i to a new OCF $r^*(\varphi, i)$ such that $E_{r^*(\varphi,i)}(\varphi) = i$ (see [21]). On this ground, we define the update of r by α with rank i as the transmutation of $Forget(r, Dep(\alpha))$ by the new belief α together with its OCF degree i. This supposes that a transmutation operator has been previously fixed.

Definition 7 (U-transmutation)
Let $*$ be a transmutation operator, Dep a dependency function, r an OCF, α a consistent, nontautological formula and i a rank. The U-transmutation *of r by (α, i) with respect to Dep and $*$ is defined by*

$$r^\diamond(\alpha, i)(\omega) = Forget(r, Dep(\alpha))^*(\alpha, i)$$

After the forgetting process has pushed $E_{Forget(r,Dep(\alpha))}(\alpha)$ down to 0 (see last point of Proposition 2), the transmutation process pushes it up to the specified level i, i.e., enforces $E_{r^\diamond(\alpha,i)}(\alpha) = i$. Importantly, note that the higher i, the less entrenched α and the more entrenched $\neg\alpha$. Hence, when learning a new fact φ with some entrenchment degree i reflecting the evolution of the world, the initial knowledge base has to be U-transmuted by $(\neg\varphi, i)$. The higher i, the more entrenched the new information φ and the more unlikely the more plausible $\neg\varphi$-worlds. The limit case of updating by a certain input φ consists in U-transmuting by $(\neg\varphi, \infty)$ which enforces $r^\diamond(\neg\varphi, \infty)(\omega) = \infty$ for all models of $\neg\varphi$, i.e., $E_{r^\diamond(\neg\varphi,\infty)}(\neg\varphi) = \infty$.

We consider now two of the most common transmutation schemes, namely conditionalization [20] and *adjustment* [21]. The following expressions can be derived from the above definition, the general formulations of conditionalization and adjustment (omitted for the sake of brevity), and the fact that for any consistent, nontautological formula α, $E_{Forget(r,Dep(\alpha))}(\alpha) = E_{Forget(r,Dep(\alpha))}(\neg\alpha) = 0$ (last point of Proposition 2):

$*$ = conditionalization [20]

$$r^\diamond(\alpha, i)(\omega) = \begin{cases} Forget(r, Dep(\alpha))(\omega) & \text{if } \omega \models \neg\alpha \\ Forget(r, Dep(\alpha))(\omega) + i & \text{if } \omega \models \alpha \end{cases}$$

$*$ = adjustment [21]

$$r^\diamond(\alpha, i)(\omega) = \begin{cases} Forget(r, Dep(\alpha))(\omega) & \text{if } \omega \models \neg\alpha \\ \max(i, Forget(r, Dep(\alpha))(\omega)) & \text{if } \omega \models \alpha \end{cases}$$

Two limit cases are worth considering:
1. When $i = \infty$ – meaning, as said above, that the information $\neg\alpha$ is certain in the new state of affairs – then $r^\diamond(\alpha, i)(\omega)$ is independent from the choice for $*$:

$$r^\diamond(\alpha, \infty)(\omega) = \begin{cases} Forget(r, Dep(\alpha))(\omega) & \text{if } \omega \models \neg\alpha \\ \infty & \text{if } \omega \models \alpha \end{cases}$$

2. When $i = 0$, the transmutation step (whatever the choice of $*$) has no effect on $Forget(r, Dep(\alpha))$ since $E_{Forget(r,Dep(\alpha))} = 0$. This merely means that everything about the variables concerned with α has been forgotten. Note that, as a consequence, $r^\diamond(\alpha, 0)$ and $r^\diamond(\neg\alpha, 0)$ coincide and are equal to $Forget(r, Dep(\alpha))$.

Now, when the initial OCF r is given implicitly under the form of a SBB, its U-transmutation by (α, i) can be computed without generating r explicitly, in both particular cases where $*$ is a conditionalization and an adjustment.

Proposition 6 *Let B be a consistent SBB. Let r be an OCF, α a consistent, nontautological formula and i a rank.*
1. if $*$ = conditionalization then $r^\diamond_B(\alpha, i) = r_{Add(BForget(B,Dep(\alpha)),\neg\alpha,i)}$;
2. if $*$ = adjustment and $i \neq \infty$ then $r^\diamond_B(\alpha, i) = r_{ShiftAdd(BForget(B,Dep(\alpha)),\neg\alpha,i)}$ where $ShiftAdd(K, \alpha, i) = \langle K_1 \vee \neg\alpha, \ldots, K_{i-1} \vee \neg\alpha, K_i \wedge \alpha, (K_{i+1} \vee \neg\alpha) \wedge (K_1 \vee \alpha), \ldots, (K_n \vee \neg\alpha) \wedge (K_{n-i} \vee \alpha), K_{n-i+1} \vee \alpha, \ldots, K_n \vee \alpha, K_\infty\rangle$.

Example 4 (Door and window)
Suppose that initially, the agent knows for sure that the door is open or the window is open, and that normally *the door is open. Thus, the initial epistemic state r_B is induced by the SBB*

$B = \langle B_1 =$ `door-open`, $B_\infty =$ `door-open`$\vee$`window-open`$\rangle$

Closing the door amounts to update the epistemic state by the certain piece of information $\neg$`door-open`*. We get: (i) $DepVar(\neg$`door-open`$)$ =\{*`door-open`*\}; (ii) $BForget(B,$ \{*`door-open`*\}$) = \langle\top,\top\rangle$; (iii) $r^\diamond_B($*`door-open`*$,\infty)$ is the OCF induced by the SBB $\langle\top,$*$\neg$`door-open`*$\rangle$. Now, closing the window amounts to update the epistemic state by the certain piece of information* $\neg$`window-open`*, i.e., to U-transmute it by* (`window-open`, ∞)*: (i) $DepVar(\neg$`window-open`$)$ =* \{`window-open`\}*; (ii) $BForget(B,$*\{`window-open`\}*$) = \langle$*`door-open`*$,\top\rangle$;*
(iii) $r^\diamond_B($`window-open`*$,\infty)$ is associated to the OCF induced by the SBB* $\langle\neg$`window-open`,`door-open`$\rangle$*. Note that whereas we do not know anything more*

about the window after we closed the door, we still know that the door is normally open after we closed the window – which is intended.
Let us now consider the action "do something with the window" which results nondeterministically in the window being closed or open, none of these results being exceptional. We U-transmute the initial belief base by (`window-open`,0) *(note that, obviously, it would work as well with* ($\neg$`window-open`,0)*):* $r^{\diamond}_{B}$(`window-open`, 0) *is the OCF induced by the SBB* ⟨`door-open`, $\top$⟩.

3.4 Application to reasoning about action

When reasoning about action, the formula representing the knowledge about the initial state of the world is updated by the explicit changes caused by the actions. Now, it is often the case that the possible results of a nondeterministic action do not all have the same plausibility. Rather, typical nondeterministic actions have, for a given initial state, one or several normal effects, plus one or several exceptional effects, with possibly different levels of exceptionality. In this case, one has to update the initial belief base by a SBB rather than with a single formula. For the purpose of applying U-transmutations to reasoning about action, we extend U-transmutations to the case where some of the variables are not allowed to be forgotten, because they are static. We first need to partition the set of literals between *static* and *dynamic* variables, i.e., $VAR = SVAR \cup DVAR$. Static variables are persistent, i.e., their truth value does not evolve. Such a distinction is meant to forget only dynamic variables relevant to the update (static variables should not be forgotten). These static and dynamic variables may depend on the action performed and be specified together with the action description (see [12]). Note that the standard case is recovered when $SVAR = \emptyset$.

Definition 8 *The* U-transmutation *of B by (α, i), w.r.t. the static variables $SVAR$, a dependency relation Dep and a given transmutation $*$, is defined by* $r^{\diamond}(\alpha, i)(\omega) = Forget(r, Dep(\alpha) \setminus SVAR)^{*}(\alpha, i)$.

Example 5 *(Saturday night shooting).*
Let us consider the problem mentioned in the introduction. Let the initial epistemic state r_B be represented by the SBB

$$B = \langle B_1 = \texttt{alive} \wedge \neg\texttt{hidden},\ B_\infty = \neg\texttt{drunk}\rangle$$

Furthermore, `drunk` *is a static variable:* $SVAR = \{\texttt{drunk}\}$*, which means that none of the actions considered in the action model can influence the truth value of* `drunk`*. Updating by the result of the action* `shoot`*, namely*

$$\varphi = (\texttt{drunk} \rightarrow \texttt{hidden}) \wedge (\neg\texttt{drunk} \rightarrow \neg\texttt{alive})$$

gives the following result: $r^{\diamond}_{SVAR}(\neg\varphi, \infty)$ *is the OCF induced by the SBB*

$$\langle \neg\texttt{drunk}),\ (\texttt{drunk} \rightarrow \texttt{hidden}) \wedge (\neg\texttt{drunk} \rightarrow \neg\texttt{alive})\rangle$$

which is equivalent to (i.e., induced the same OCF) this other SBB:

$$\langle \neg\texttt{drunk} \wedge \neg\texttt{alive},\ (\texttt{drunk} \rightarrow \texttt{hidden}) \wedge (\neg\texttt{drunk} \rightarrow \neg\texttt{alive}\rangle.$$

Thus, in the final belief state, it is believed (yet with no certainty) that the turkey is dead, which is intended.

4 Related work

Changing epistemic states has been considered many times for *belief revision*, especially when it comes to iteration. In particular, the recent work of Benferhat, Konieczny, Papini and Pino-Perez [1] investigates the revision of an epistemic state by an epistemic state.

As to belief update, the closest approach to ours is Boutilier's generalized update [3]. Generalized update is more general than both belief revision and belief update. It models epistemic states by OCFs. A generalized update operation considers (i) the (explicit) description of the initial epistemic state; (ii) the dynamics of a given set of events (each of which having its own plausibility rank) expressed by a collection of transition functions mapping an initial and a final world to a rank; (iii) a formula representing an observation made after the evolution of the dynamic system; now, the output consists of the identification of the events that most likely occurred, a revised initial belief state and an updated new belief state. In the absence of observations (i.e., when updating by $\top$), generalized update merely computes the most likely evolution of the system from its dynamic and the initial belief state, which is not far from the goals of our approach. The crucial difference is in the way this most likely evolution is computed: in [3] epistemic states are represented explicitly (by fully specified ordinal conditional functions), while in our approach the dynamics of the system is represented in a very compact way: requiring that fluents dependent (resp. independent) of the input formula be forgotten (resp. remain unchanged) is a compact way to encode the dynamics of the system – it is a kind of a solution to the frame problem. In further work we plan to integrate observations (as in generalized update) in our model, and thus develop an efficient way, based on dependence relations, of performing generalized update.

Another related line of work is [7] who show that Lewis' imaging operations can be viewed as belief updates on belief states consisting of probability distributions. They propose a counterpart of imaging to possibility theory. Both classes of operations map a belief state and a flat formula to a belief state, and they are based on minimization.

Acknowledgements

The second author has been partly supported by the Région Nord/Pas-de-Calais, the IUT de Lens and the European Communities.

References

1. Salem Benferhat, Sébastien Konieczny, Odile Papini and Ramon Pino-Perez. Iterated revision by epistemic states: axioms, semantics and syntax. *Proceedings of ECAI'2000*, 13-17.
2. Craig Boutilier. Revision sequences and nested conditionals. *Proceedings of IJCAI'93*, 519-525.

3. Craig Boutilier. Generalized update: belief change in dynamic settings. *Proceedings of IJCAI'95*, 1550-1556.
4. Gerhard Brewka and Joachim Hertzberg. How to do things with worlds: on formalizing actions and plans. *Journal of Logic and Computation*, 3 (5), 517-532, 1993.
5. Adnan Darwiche and Judea Pearl. On the logic of iterated belief revision. *Proceedings of TARK'94*, 5-23.
6. Patrick Doherty and Witold Lukaszewicz and Ewa Madalinska-Bugaj. The PMA and relativizing change for action update. *Proceedings of KR'98*, 258-269.
7. Didier Dubois and Henri Prade. Belief revision and updates in numerical formalisms. *Proceedings of IJCAI'93*, 620-625.
8. Hélène Fargier, Jérôme Lang and Pierre Marquis. Propositional logic and one-stage decision making. *Proceedings of KR'2000*, 445-456.
9. Nir Friedman and Joseph Halpern. Modeling beliefs in dynamic systems. Part 2: revision and update, *Journal of Artificial Intelligence Research*, 10, 117-167, 1999.
10. Andreas Herzig. The PMA revisited. *Proceedings of KR'96*, 40-50.
11. Andreas Herzig and Omar Rifi. Propositional belief base update and minimal change. *Artificial Intelligence*, 115(1), 107-138, 1999.
12. Andreas Herzig, Jérôme Lang, Pierre Marquis and Thomas Polacsek. Actions, updates and planning. *Proceedings of IJCAI'2001*, 119-124.
13. Hirofumi Katsuno and Alberto Mendelzon. On the difference between updating a knowledge base and resvising it. *Artificial Intelligence* 52:263-294, 1991.
14. Sébastien Konieczny. *Sur la logique du changement : révision et fusion de bases de connaissances*. Thèse de l'Université des Sciences et Technologies de Lille, 1999. In French.
15. Jérôme Lang, Paolo Liberatore and Pierre Marquis. Complexity results for propositional independence. In preparation.
16. Jérôme Lang and Pierre Marquis. Complexity results for independence and definability in propositional logic. *Proceedings of KR'98*, 356-367.
17. Shai Berger, Daniel Lehmann and Karl Schlechta. Preferred history semantics for iterated updates. *Journal of Logic and Computation*, 9(6), 817-833.
18. Fangzhen Lin and Ray Reiter. Forget it! *Proceedings of the AAAI Fall Symposium on Relevance*, New Orleans, 1994, 154-159.
19. Steven Shapiro, Maurice Pagnucco, Yves Lespérance and Hector Levesque. Iterated change in the situation calculus. *Proceedings of KR'2000*, 527-538.
20. W. Spohn. Ordinal conditional functions: a dynamic theory of epistemic states. In *Causation in Decision, Belief Change, and Statistics*, vol. 2, 105-134, Kluwer Academic Publishers, 1987.
21. Mary-Anne Williams. Transmutations of knowledge systems. *Proceedings of KR'94*, 619-629.
22. Mary-Anne Williams. Iterated theory base change: a computational model. *Proceedings of IJCAI'95*, 1541-1547.
23. Marianne Winslett. Reasoning about action using a possible model approach. *Proceedings of AAAI'88*, 89-93.
24. Yan Zhang and Normal Foo. Reasoning about persistence: a theory of actions. *Proceedings of IJCAI'93*, 718-723.

Fast Text Classification Using Sequential Sampling Processes

Michael D. Lee*

Department of Psychology, University of Adelaide

Abstract. A central problem in information retrieval is the automated classification of text documents. While many existing methods achieve good levels of performance, they generally require levels of computation that prevent them from making sufficiently fast decisions in some applied setting. Using insights gained from examining the way humans make fast decisions when classifying text documents, two new text classification algorithms are developed based on sequential sampling processes. These algorithms make extremely fast decisions, because they need to examine only a small number of words in each text document. Evaluation against the Reuters-21578 collection shows both techniques have levels of performance that approach benchmark methods, and the ability of one of the classifiers to produce realistic measures of confidence in its decisions is shown to be useful for prioritizing relevant documents.

1 Introduction

A central problem in information retrieval is the automated classification of text documents. Given a set of documents, and a set of topics, the classification problem is to determine whether or not each document is about each topic. This paper presents two fast text document classifiers inspired by the human ability to make quick and accurate decisions by skimming text documents.

2 Existing Methods

A range of artificial intelligence and machine learning techniques have been applied to the text classification problem. A recent and thorough evaluation of five of the best performed methods is provided in [1]. The classifiers examined are:

* This research was supported by the Australian Defence Science and Technology Organisation. The author wishes to thank Peter Bruza, Simon Dennis, Brandon Pincombe, Douglas Vickers, and Chris Woodruff. Correspondence should be addressed to: Michael D. Lee, Department of Psychology, University of Adelaide, SA 5005, AUSTRALIA. Telephone: +61 8 8303 6096, Facsimile: +61 8 8303 3770, E-mail: michael.lee@psychology.adelaide.edu.au, URL: http://www.psychology.adelaide.edu.au/members/staff/michaellee

M. Brooks, D. Corbett, and M. Stumptner (Eds.): AI 2001, LNAI 2256, pp. 309–320, 2001.

- Support Vector Machines (SVM), which use a training set to find optimal hyperplanes that separates documents into those about a topic, and those not about a topic. These hyperplanes are then applied to classify new documents.
- k-Nearest Neighbor classifiers (kNN), which classify new documents according to the known classifications of its nearest training set neighbors.
- Linear Least Squares Fit classifiers (LLSF), which generate a multivariate regression model from a training set that can be applied to new documents.
- Neural Network classifiers (NNet), which learn the connection weights within a 3-layer neural network using a training set, and then applies this network to classify new documents.
- Naive Bayes classifiers (NB), which use a training set estimate the probabilities of words indicating documents being about topics, and uses a simple version of Bayes theorem with these probabilities to the classify new documents.

Different performance measures show different levels of relative performance for the five classifiers, although the SVM and kNN are generally the most effective, followed by the LLSF, with the NNet and NB classifiers being the least effective [1]. What is important, from an applied perspective, is the considerable degree of computation undertaken by each classifier, either during the training process, the process of classifying new documents, or both. SVMs, for example, require the solution to a quadratic programming problem during training, LLSF classifiers must solve a large least-squares problem, and NNets are notoriously time consuming to train.

In classifying new documents, most existing techniques consider every word in the document, and often have to calculate involved functions. This means that they take time to process large corpora. In many applied situations, analysts require fast 'on-line' text document classification, and would be willing to sacrifice some accuracy for the sake of timeliness. The aim of this paper is to develop text classifiers that emphasize speed rather than accuracy, and so the results in [1] are used as guides on acceptable performance, rather than benchmarks to be exceeded.

3 Some Insights from Psychology

As with many artificial intelligence and machine learning problems, there is much to be learned from examining the way in which humans perform the task of text classification. In particular, it is worth making the effort to understand how people manage to make quick and accurate decisions regarding which of the many text documents they encounter every day (e.g., newspaper articles) are about topics of interest.

3.1 Bayesian Decision Making

A first psychological insight involves the relationship between the decisions "this document is about this topic" and "this document is not this topic". When people are asked to make this decision, they actively seek information that would help them make either choice. They do not look only for confirming information in the hope of establishing that the document is about the topic, and conclude otherwise if they fail to find enough information.

For example, if people are asked whether a newspaper article is about the US Presidential Elections, consider the following three scenarios:

- The first word is "The". In this case, most people would not be able to make any decision with any degree of confidence.
- The first word is "Cricket". In this case, most people would confidently respond 'No'.
- The first word is "Gore". In this case, most people would confidently respond 'Yes'.

The fact that people are able to decide to answer 'No' in the second scenario suggests that they are actively evaluating the word as evidence in favor of the document not being about the topic (in the same way they actively evaluate the word "Gore" in the third scenario). This behavior suggests that people treat the choices "this document is about this topic" and "this document is not this topic" as two competing models, and are able to use the content of the document, in a Bayesian way, as evidence in favor of either model. Many established text classifiers, including the kNN, LLSF and NNet classifiers, do not operate this way. In general terms, these classifiers construct a measure of the similarity between the document in question, and some abstract representation of the topic in question. When the measure of similarity exceeds some criterion value, the decision is made that the document is about the topic, otherwise the default decision is made that the document is not about the topic. The text classifiers developed here, however, actively assesses whether the available information allows the decision "this document is not about this topic" to be made. Adopting this approach dramatically speeds text classification, because it is often possible to determine that a document is not about a topic directly, rather than having to infer this indirectly from failing to establish that it is about the topic.

At the heart of the Bayesian approach are measures of the evidence individual words provide for documents either being about a topic, or not being about a topic. The evidence that the i-th word in a dictionary provides about topic $\mathbf{T}$, denoted by $V_{\mathbf{T}}(w_i)$, may be calculated on a log-odds scale as follows:

$$V_{\mathbf{T}}(w_i) = \ln \frac{p(w_i \mid \mathbf{T})}{p(w_i \mid \bar{\mathbf{T}})} \approx \ln \frac{|w_i \in \mathbf{T}| / |\mathbf{T}|}{|w_i \in \bar{\mathbf{T}}| / |\bar{\mathbf{T}}|},$$

where $\mathbf{T}$ is "about a topic", $\bar{\mathbf{T}}$ is "not about a topic", $|w_i \in \mathbf{T}|$ is the number of times word w_i occurs in documents about topic $\mathbf{T}$, and $|\mathbf{T}|$ is the total number of words in documents about topic $\mathbf{T}$. Note that these evidence values are symmetric about zero: Words with positive values (e.g., "Gore") suggest that the document is about the topic, words with negative values (e.g., "cricket") suggest that the document is not about the topic, and words with values near zero (e.g., "the") provide little evidence for either alternative.

3.2 Non-compensatory Decision Making

A second psychological insight is that, when people decide whether or not a text document is about a topic, they often make non-compensatory decisions. This means that people are able to make a decision without considering all of the content of a document. For example, if asked whether a newspaper article is about the US Presidential Elections, and the first 11 words read are "Alan Border yesterday questioned the composition of the Australian cricket team ...", most people would choose to answer 'No', even if they were permitted to examine the remainder of the article. In making non-compensatory decisions,

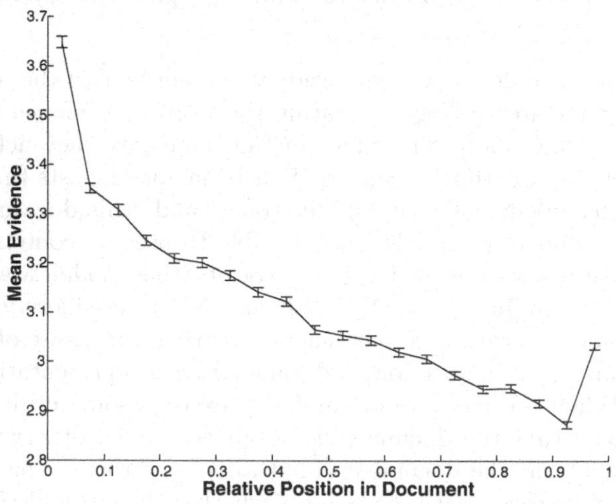

Fig. 1. The mean absolute evidence provided by words in the Reuters-21578 Corpus, as a function of their relative position in the document.

people rely on regularities in their environment [2]. In the case of text documents, they assume that words near the beginning will provide some clear indication of the semantic topic. This assumption is borne out by the analysis of the entire Reuters-21578 collection presented in Figure 1, which shows the mean absolute evidence provided by words according to their relative position in the documents. Words at the beginning of documents provide relatively more evidence than those in the middle or near the end, although there is a small increase for words at the very end, presumably associated with the 'summing up' of documents. The important point, for the purposes of fast text classification, is that it is possible to know *a priori* those words in a document that will be the most useful for making a decision. Figure 1 suggests that, at least for news-style documents, they will be words at or near the beginning of the document.

3.3 Complete Decision Making

A final psychological insight is that when people decide whether or not a text document is about a topic, they undertake a decision process that generates more information than just a binary choice. People give answers with a certain level of accuracy, having taken a certain period of time, and are able to express a certain level of confidence in their decision. An automatic text classification system capable of providing the same sort of response outputs seems likely to have advantages in many applied situations.

4 Sequential Sampling Process Models

Within cognitive psychology, the most comprehensive accounts of human decision making are provided by sequential sampling models. In particular, a number of 'random-walk' and 'accumulator' models have been developed, and demonstrated to be successful in a variety of experimental situations [3,4]. These models are based on the notion of accruing information through the repeated sampling of a stimulus, until a threshold level information in favor of one alternative has been collected to prompt a decision.

Both random walk and accumulator models naturally capture the three psychological insights into the text classification problem. Both models use a Bayesian approach to model selection, in the sense that they establish explicit thresholds for both of the possible decisions. The use of thresholds also means that non-compensatory decisions are made, since the stimulus is only examined until the point where the threshold is exceeded. Furthermore, by examining the words in a text document in the order that they appear in the document, those words that are more likely to enable a decision to be made will tend to be processed first. Finally, both models are able to generate measures of confidence in their decisions.

This integration of the psychological insights suggests text classifiers that operate by examining each word in a text document sequentially, evaluating the extent to which that word favors the alternative decisions "this document is about the topic" and "this document is not about the topic", and using the evidence value to update the state of a random-walk or accumulator model.

4.1 Random Walk Text Classifier

In random walk models, the total evidence is calculated as the difference between the evidence for the two competing alternatives, and a decision is made once it reaches an upper or lower threshold. This process can be interpreted in Bayesian terms [5], where the state of the random walk is the log posterior odds of the document being about the topic. Using Bayes' theorem, the log posterior odds are given by

$$\ln \frac{p\left(\mathbf{T} \mid \mathbf{D}\right)}{p\left(\bar{\mathbf{T}} \mid \mathbf{D}\right)} = \ln \frac{p\left(\mathbf{T}\right)}{p\left(\bar{\mathbf{T}}\right)} \frac{p\left(\mathbf{D} \mid \mathbf{T}\right)}{p\left(\mathbf{D} \mid \bar{\mathbf{T}}\right)},$$

where **D** is the document being classified in terms of topic **T**. Assuming the document is appropriately represented in terms of its n words $w_1, w_2, \ldots, w_n$, which is probably the most justifiable assumption, although it is certainly not the only possibility, this becomes

$$\ln \frac{p(\mathbf{T} \mid \mathbf{D})}{p(\bar{\mathbf{T}} \mid \mathbf{D})} \approx \ln \frac{p(\mathbf{T})\, p(w_1, w_2, \ldots, w_n \mid \mathbf{T})}{p(\bar{\mathbf{T}})\, p(w_1, w_2, \ldots, w_n \mid \bar{\mathbf{T}})}.$$

If it is further assumed that each word provides independent evidence, which is more problematic, but is likely to be a reasonable first-order approximation, the log posterior odds becomes

$$\begin{aligned} \ln \frac{p(\mathbf{T} \mid \mathbf{D})}{p(\bar{\mathbf{T}} \mid \mathbf{D})} &= \ln \frac{p(\mathbf{T})}{p(\bar{\mathbf{T}})} + \ln \frac{p(w_1 \mid \mathbf{T})}{p(w_1 \mid \bar{\mathbf{T}})} + \ln \frac{p(w_2 \mid \mathbf{T})}{p(w_2 \mid \bar{\mathbf{T}})} + \ldots + \ln \frac{p(w_n \mid \mathbf{T})}{p(w_n \mid \bar{\mathbf{T}})} \\ &= \ln \frac{p(\mathbf{T})}{p(\bar{\mathbf{T}})} + V_{\mathbf{T}}(w_1) + V_{\mathbf{T}}(w_2) + \ldots + V_{\mathbf{T}}(w_n). \end{aligned}$$

This final formulation consists of a first 'bias' term, given by the log prior odds, that determines the starting point of the random walk, followed by the summation of the evidence provided by each successive word in the document.

Once a random walk has terminated, and a decision made according to whether it reached an upper or lower threshold, a measure of confidence in the decision can be obtained as an inverse function of the number of words examined. For documents that require many words to classify, confidence will be low, while for documents classified quickly using few words, confidence will be high.

Figure 2 summarizes the operation of the random walk classifier on a document from the Reuters-21578 collection that is about the topic being examined. The state of the random-walk is shown as the evidence provided by successive words in the document are assessed. A threshold value of 50 is shown by the dotted lines above and below. This example highlights the potential of noncompensatory decision making, because the first 100 words of the documents allow the correct decision to be made, but the final state of the random-walk, when the entire document has been considered, does not lead to the correct decision being made.

4.2 Accumulator Text Classifier

The accumulator text classifier is very similar to the random walk version, except that separate evidence totals are maintained, and a decision is made when either one of them reaches a threshold. This means that evidence provided by each successive word $V_{\mathbf{T}}(w_i)$ is added to the "is about topic" accumulator $A_{\mathbf{T}}$ if it is positive, and to the "is not about accumulator" $A_{\bar{\mathbf{T}}}$ if it is negative. Once either $A_{\mathbf{T}}$ reaches a positive threshold, or $A_{\bar{\mathbf{T}}}$ reaches a negative threshold, the corresponding decision is made. The confidence in this decision is then measured according to the difference between the evidence totals accumulated for each decision, as a proportion of the total evidence accumulated, as follows: $(A_{\mathbf{T}} - |A_{\bar{\mathbf{T}}}|) / (A_{\mathbf{T}} + |A_{\bar{\mathbf{T}}}|)$.

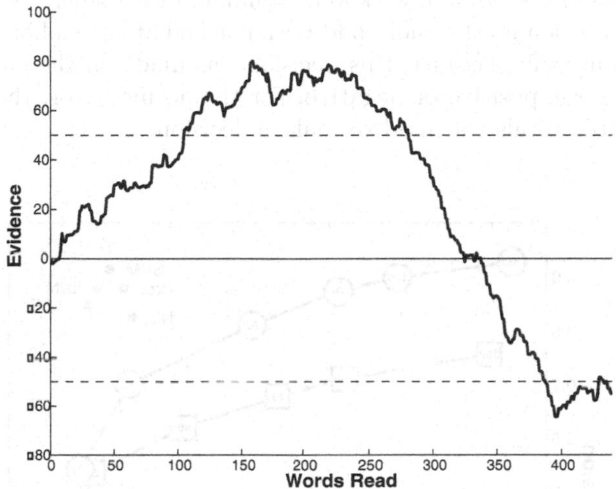

Fig. 2. Operation of the random walk text classifier in a case where the document is about the topic in question

5 Evaluation against Reuters-21578

5.1 Standard Information Retrieval Measures

The random walk and accumulator classifiers were evaluated using the ModApte training/test split detailed in [6] to enable comparison with the benchmark results presented in [1]. In the interests of ensuring speed, the corpus was not pre-processed to the same extent as [1]. In particular, no word-stemming was undertaken. The only pre-processing was to filter the documents into lower case characters {a...z} together with the space character. The performance of the text classifiers was measured in five standard ways [7]: recall, precision, macro F1, micro F1, and error rate.

Precision, p, measures the proportion of documents the classifier decided were about a topic that actually were about the topic. Recall, r, measures the proportion of documents actually about a topic that were identified as such by the classifier. The two versions of the F1 measure, $\mathrm{F1} = 2rp/\left(r+p\right)$ were obtained by different forms of averaging. The first was obtained by 'micro-averaging', where every decision made by the classifier was aggregated before calculating recall and precision values. The second was obtained by 'macro-averaging', where recall and precision values were calculated for each topic separately, and their associated F1 values were then averaged. As argued in [1], it is important to consider both approaches when using corpora, such as Reuters-21578, where the distribution of topics to documents is highly skewed. The error was simply measured as the percentage of incorrect decisions made by the classifier over all document-topic combinations. These measures were based on modified 'forced-choice' versions of the random walk and accumulator classifiers, where a decision was made even when no threshold had been reached at the end of the document. For the random walk classifier, this decision was made on the basis of whether the final state was positive or negative. For the accumulator, the larger of the two accumulated totals was used to make a decision.

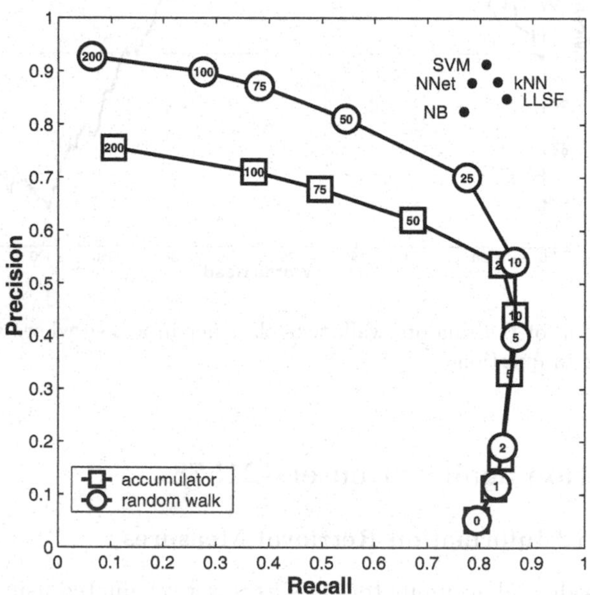

Fig. 3. Precision-recall performance of the random walk and accumulator text classifiers, together with existing benchmarks.

Figure 3 shows the precision and recall performance of the random walk and accumulator text classifiers for a range of different threshold values, together with the benchmark performances reported in [1]. While different applied settings can place different degrees of emphasis on recall and precision, the best balance probably lies at about the threshold value of 25. In terms of the existing benchmarks, both classifiers have competitive recall performance, but fall short in terms of precision. In practical terms, this means that the random walk and accumulator classifiers find as many relevant documents, but return 3 or 4 irrelevant documents in every batch of 10, whereas benchmark performance only return 1 irrelevant document in every batch of 10.

Figure 4 shows the micro F1 and macro F1 performance of the random walk and accumulator text classifiesr for the threshold values up to 25, together with the benchmarks. On these measures, both classifiers are very competitive and, in fact, outperform some existing methods on the macro F1 measure.

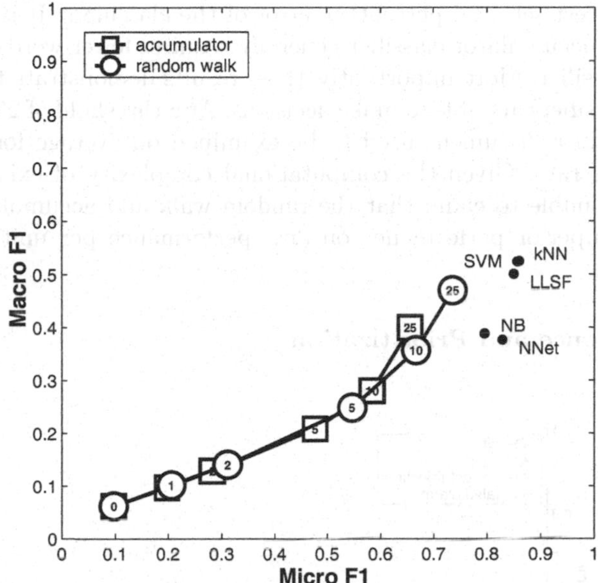

Fig. 4. Micro and Macro F1 performance of the random walk and accumulator text classifiers, together with existing benchmarks.

Table 1. Mean number of words examined, mean percentage of words examined, and mean percentage error of the forced choice random walk and accumulator text classifiers.

	Random Walk			Accumulator		
Threshold	Words	Percentage	Error	Words	Percentage	Error
0	1.06	0.8%	18.5%	1.06	0.8%	18.5%
1	1.59	1.3%	8.1%	1.54	1.3%	8.5%
2	1.99	1.7%	4.7%	1.88	1.6%	5.4%
5	3.45	2.9%	1.8%	2.96	2.5%	2.4%
10	6.72	5.6%	1.1%	5.48	4.6%	1.6%
25	15.7	13.1%	1.0%	12.8	10.7%	1.2%
50	29.0	24.2%	1.0%	24.9	20.8%	1.1%
75	40.4	33.6%	1.0%	35.9	29.9%	1.1%
100	49.9	41.6%	1.0%	45.3	37.8%	1.1%
200	75.1	62.6%	1.0%	71.2	59.4%	1.1%

Table 1 presents the mean number of words examined by each of the classifiers at each threshold, this mean count as a percentage of the average document length of the test set, and percentage error of the classifiers. It is interesting to note that the accumulator classifier generally requires fewer words than the random walk classifier. More importantly, these results demonstrate the speed with which the classifiers are able to make decisions. At a threshold of 25, only 10–13% of the words in a document need to be examined on average for classification at a 1% error rate. Given the computational complexity of existing methods, it seems reasonable to claim that the random walk and accumulator classifiers would have superior performance on any 'performance per unit computation' measure.

5.2 Confidence and Prioritization

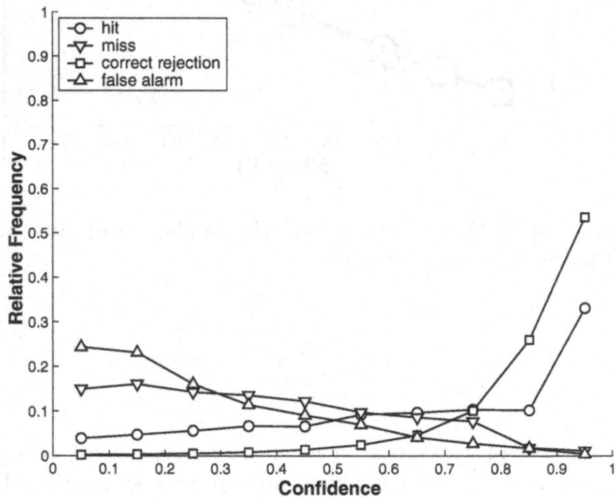

Fig. 5. Confidence distributions for the forced-choice version of the accumulator classifier.

For the forced choice versions of the classifiers, it is informative to examine the distribution of confidence measures in terms of the standard signal detection theory classes of 'hit', 'miss', 'correct rejection' and 'false alarm'. These distributions are shown at a threshold of 25 for the accumulator classifier in Figure 5, and for the random walk classifier in Figure 6. The measures of confidence generated by the accumulator are meaningful, in the sense that hits and correct rejections generally have high confidence values, while misses and false alarms generally have low confidence values. The random walk confidence measures, in contrast, do not differ greatly for any of the four decision classes and, in fact, the classifier is generally more confident when it misses than when it hits.

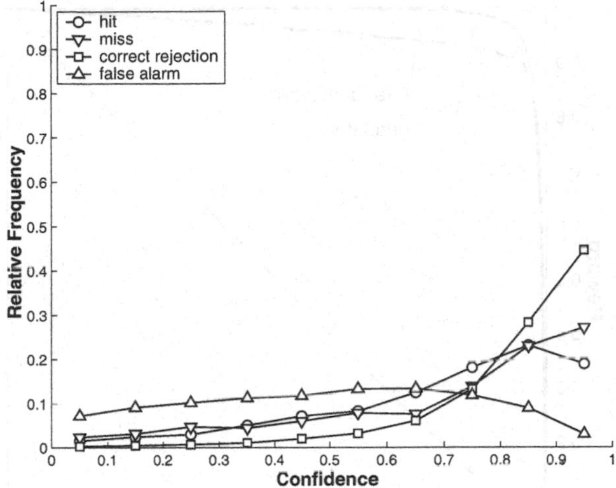

Fig. 6. Confidence distributions for the forced-choice version of the random walk classifier.

The ability of accumulator models to provide more realistic confidence measures than random walk models has been observed within psychology [4], and has practical implications for text classification. In particular, the confidence measures can be used as 'relevancy' scores to order or prioritize the decisions made by the classifiers. The obvious way of doing this is to return all of the documents that were classified as being about topics first, ranked from highest confidence to lowest confidence, followed by the documents not classified as being about topics, ranked from lowest confidence to highest.

This prioritization exercise was undertaken for both of the classifiers on all of the possible document-topic combinations, and the results are summarized by the 'effort-reward' graph shown in Figure 7. The curves indicate the proportion of relevant documents (i.e., the reward) found by working through a given proportion of the prioritized list (i.e., the effort). It can be seen that both classifiers return almost 90% of the relevant documents in the first 5% of the list, but that the accumulator then performs significantly better, allowing all of the relevant documents to be found by examining only the top 20% of the list.

6 Conclusion

This paper has presented two text classifiers based on sequential sampling models of human decision making. Both techniques achieve reasonable levels of performance in comparison to established benchmarks, while requiring minimal computational effort. In particular, both classifiers are capable of making extremely fast decisions, because they generally need to examine only a small proportion

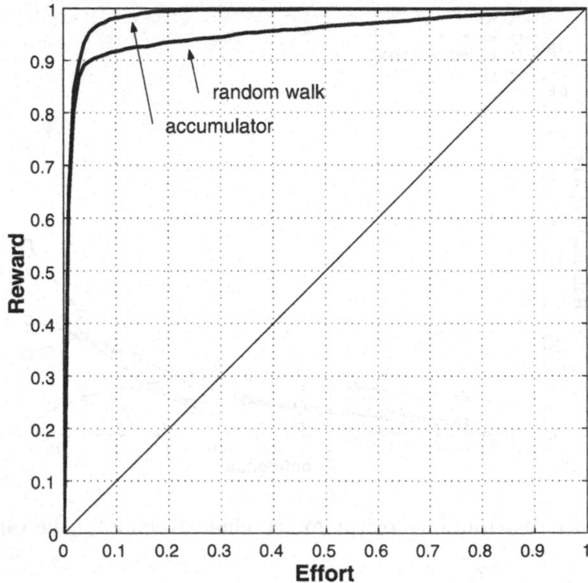

Fig. 7. Effort-reward performance for priorization using the forced-choice accumulator and random walk classifiers.

of the words in a document. The ability of the accumulator classifier to generate meaningful confidence measures has also been demonstrated to be useful in presenting prioritized lists of relevant text documents.

References

[1] Y Yang and X Liu, "A re-examination of text categorization methods," in *SIGIR '99: Proceedings of the 22nd Annual International ACM SIGIR Conference on Research and Development in Information Retrieval*, Berkley, CA, 1999, pp. 42–49, ACM.

[2] G Gigerenzer and P M Todd, *Simple Heuristics That Make Us Smart*, Oxford University Press, New York, 1999.

[3] P L Smith, "Stochastic dynamic models of response time and accuracy: A foundational primer," *Journal of Mathematical Psychology*, vol. 44, pp. 408–463, 2000.

[4] D Vickers and M D Lee, "Dynamic models of simple judgments: I. Properties of a self-regulating accumulator module," *Non-linear Dynamics, Psychology, and Life Sciences*, vol. 2, no. 3, pp. 169–194, 1998.

[5] R E Kass and A E Raftery, "Bayes factors," *Journal of the American Statistical Association*, vol. 90, no. 430, pp. 773–795, 1995.

[6] D D Lewis, "Reuters-21578 text categorization test collection," 1997, Available at http://www.research.att.com/~lewis/reuters21578/readme.txt.

[7] C J Van Risjbergen, *Information Retrieval*, Butterworths, London, 1979.

Agents in a Multi-cultural World: Towards Ontological Reconciliation

Kendall Lister and Leon Sterling

Department of Computer Science and Software Engineering,
The University of Melbourne, Victoria, 3010, Australia,
krl,leon@cs.mu.oz.au,
Intelligent Agent Laboratory: http://www.cs.mu.oz.au/agentlab

Abstract. In order to function effectively, agents, whether human or software, must be able to communicate and interact through common understandings and compatible conceptualisations. In a multi-cultural world, ontological differences are a fundamental obstacle that must be overcome before inter-cultural communication can occur. The purpose of this paper is to discuss the issues faced by agents operating in large-scale multi-cultural environments and to argue for systems that are tolerant of heterogeneity, illustrating the discussion with a running example of researching and comparing university web sites as a realistic scenario representative of many current knowledge management tasks that would benefit from agent assistance. We then discuss the efforts of the Intelligent Agent Laboratory toward designing such tolerant systems, giving a detailed presentation of the results of several implementations.

"In an ill-structured domain you cannot, by definition, have a pre-compiled schema in your mind for every circumstance and context you may find ... you must be able to flexibly select and arrange knowledge sources to most efficaciously pursue the needs of a given situation." [8]

1 The Reality of Distributed Knowledge Systems

That useful knowledge systems inevitably incorporate vast amounts of information is becoming a generally acknowledged phenomenon. The evolution of the computer as a data processing device, and computer networks as communication media, has provided the technical means to aggregate enormous quantities of information. Similarly acknowledged is that our capacity for accumulation, storage and reproduction of data and information has out-paced our ability to perceive and manipulate knowledge. This is not a new realisation; Vannevar Bush identified just such a glut of knowledge and information over fifty years ago and proposed a technological solution in the form of the memex, an enlarged intimate supplement to memory that anticipated the hypertext systems of today [3]. The need for contextualising data remains thoroughly applicable to the World Wide Web and other large-scale information networks.

M. Brooks, D. Corbett, and M. Stumptner (Eds.): AI 2001, LNAI 2256, pp. 321–332, 2001.

By implementing a (pseudo-)global communication infrastructure that provides means for the publication, comparison and aggregation of apparently limitless amounts of data, we have discovered the potential to ask questions as individuals conducting our daily lives that previously would have been dismissed as infeasible for anyone less than a dedicated organisation. For example, with the entry cost of publishing a web site effectively negligible, the university that does not do so is the exception rather than the rule. This means that dozens, if not hundreds, of descriptions of courses, programs and facilities are available for us to peruse. As we learn this, we immediately see a possibility for comparison, and want to ask reasonable and seemingly simple questions such as "Which faculties offer courses in applied machine vision?" or "Which campuses provide accommodation facilities for post-graduate students?".

To answer questions like these, we could fairly easily compile a list of university web sites; the list might even be complete. We could then visit each site in turn, browsing or searching and recording what information we think will answer our question. Finally, we could compare the results of our research from each site to formulate an answer. Many people perform this very task every day. The question that interests this paper is why our computers can't do this for us yet, and how we can approach the issue of enabling them to do so. The example of university service descriptions is an appropriate one for the purposes of this paper, as the issues described can be readily seen to be present in the real world. Additionally, universities as institutions tend naturally to develop and often then actively promote their individuality; this local culture flavours their presentation of information that must then be reconciled with information from other institutions that apply their own cultural characteristics to their publications. If we are to manage knowledge from a variety of sources effectively, we will need the assistance of software that is culturally aware and is capable of negotiating the conflicts that arise when such heterogeneous knowledge is juxtaposed.

2 How Organisational Culture Affects Communication

The reality of distributed information systems is an environment in which knowledge from large numbers of heterogeneous sources must be integrated in such a way that we can efficiently reconcile any differences in representation and context in order to incorporate foreign knowledge into our own world-view. To be able to work with knowledge from incongruous sources is becoming increasingly necessary [15] as the focus of information processing moves beyond intra-organisational interaction and begins to transgress borders, whether departmental, corporate, academic or ethnic.

Organisational cultures arise as individual organisations develop mechanisms, procedures and representations for dealing with the issues that they face. Inevitably, because these cultures are generally developed in isolation, each organisation will invariably arrive at different solutions to what are often very similar problems. In order to stream-line organisational activities and focus group efforts on a common goal, it is necessary for individuals to internalise their own personal intuited approach to a situation in lieu of an agreed common understanding shared by the other members of the group. We do this naturally when we work together on a problem; some are more able than others, and we recognise teamwork and the ability to understand another's point of view as desirable qualities. Such qualities are also becoming desirable in software as agents play an increasing role in our communication and collaboration.

When we suppress our own intuitive understanding of a situation and attempt to adopt a standardised, agreed upon approach, we increase our ability to interact with others who have similarly adapted their individual understanding to that of the group or community. But we also lose something in the process: context and generality. An efficient understanding of a situation is like a model, in that the more closely it describes a particular situation, the less effectively it describes a general class of situations. Additionally, as we move from a general conceptualisation of a situation rich with semantic flexibility to a specific understanding, we tend to eschew context. We do this because the very generality that gives us the ability to deal with many varied and new situations is a barrier to communication; at the same time that ambiguity allows adaptation, it prohibits individuals from establishing the certainty of agreement that is necessary for confidence that each understands the other.

However, as organisations discover, standardisation of practices and understandings does not create a panacea for the difficulties of communication and collaboration. On a small scale, adoption of standardised approaches helps individuals to cooperate and achieve goals too large for a single person. On a larger scale, the effort required to establish and prescribe global standards and common approaches grows rapidly beyond feasibility as the number of participants and the amount of data being manipulated increases. As our ability to communicate and interact across cultural borders increases, so does our desire to do so. And as we come to terms with the necessities of increased interoperation and develop coping strategies, if our software tools are to scale similarly we must provide them with equivalent reconciliation capabilities.

3 Our Software Colleagues

In many respects, computers are an extreme example of co-workers with poor teamwork and communication skills. When specifying a task for a software application or agent we must specify every step in precise detail, detail that will generally remain constant throughout the life of the software. Whilst humans are able to adjust the level of abstraction at which they conceptualise a particular situation, computers traditionally have the capacity only for comparatively very low levels of abstraction. As machines that follow explicit instructions to the letter, their operation is analogous to the most procedural organisational standards, and unsurprisingly they too have great difficulty adapting to new situations.

Traditional computational paradigms require that computer-mediated representations of information and knowledge be exact and literal; for a computer to process information requires simplistic structuring of data and homogeneous representations of concepts. In order to maintain consistency during processing, traditional approaches require that each participant in a system, whether human or software, subscribe to a common understanding of the concepts within the system. In other words, traditional information systems require the adoption of an absolute ontological world-view; deviation from a priori agreed terms and understandings results in a breakdown in communication and loss of consistency through the system.

This ontological homogeneity has worked well for systems with little direct human interaction, when the computers can be left to sort out technical details and humans can work at a level removed from the coal face. In fact, isolating technically detail areas of a system from those areas with which humans interact permits engineering of the technical aspects to create an optimised environment. The World Wide Web is an example of a large-scale system in which the level at which humans interact with the system is greatly separated from the level at which machines interact. We write web pages and read them, navigating along hypertextual paths, while machines manage domain name resolution, protocol selection, transmission of data and rendering of text and images. The gap between the activities of humans and machines is highlighted by the problems that occur when we try to make machines work closer to our level as we attempt to automate various functions that we currently perform manually. The example of this most recognisable to the ordinary web user is the task of searching for information, an obviously difficult problem that has yet to be solved to our satisfaction. But a more far-reaching problem is that of integrating the vast quantities of information available in such a way that we can seamlessly assimilate whatever sources of data are most appropriate to the task at hand, whatever that task may be.

4 Automating Conceptualisation

Automation of data processing is desirable because it frees humans from the morass of detail and permits them to utilise their capacity for abstraction. The ability to manipulate concepts at varying levels of detail and to match the level of detail to the needs of the situation at hand is one of our most effective tools for processing knowledge and communicating. Being able to subsume detail within conceptual units of knowledge allows us to overcome the natural limits of our processing capacity; although there appear to be clear cognitive limits on the number of concepts we can articulate at any given time, we have the critical ability to 'chunk' collections of knowledge into single units [11,5], effectively providing a capacity to search through information webs both widely and deeply as necessary. Similarly, when the scope of an information or data problem becomes too great for us to process in a reasonable amount of time, we bring computers to bear on the problem to assist us with storage, recall and simple processing. Automation of data processing provides increased speed and accuracy, and also permits the not insignificant relief of boredom resulting from repetitive tasks.

By handing low-level information processing tasks to machines, humans are freed to consider issues at higher levels of abstraction. If we are to continue to advance the level of assistance that our computers can provide to us as we work, we must elevate our tools to higher levels of abstraction to accommodate the ever-increasing complexity of the situations we face.

As knowledge travels through progressively lower levels of abstraction, its context degrades as generality is replaced by specificity and logical operability. Humans require some specification in order to communicate successfully, but the desired degree of consistency of conceptualisations determines the extent of specification that is necessary. Indeed, it is suggested that even consensus between participants is not always necessary for successful collaboration [1,12]. As discussed earlier, one of our greatest strengths as humans is our ability to adapt to new situations and reconcile new ontological concepts with our own history of previous experiences. We are also capable of identifying mismatches of understanding in our communications and negotiating shared perspectives as we interact with others [2]. We use the term *ontological reconciliation* for the process of resolving conceptual differences. Human natural language is neither precise nor predictable, and this seems to reflect the way that we understand the world though our internal representations and conceptualisations. When we express ourselves in natural language, we often encounter confusion and difficulty as others attempt to understand us. This requires us to explore alternative expressions, searching for representations that others understand. We do this naturally, and our attention is drawn to the process only when it fails. But we are generally capable of finding enough common ground for communication of knowledge to proceed; we are often even able to convey basic information without a common language, as any tourist who has managed to gain directions to a restaurant or train station with much waving of hands can attest.

Fitting knowledge to logical representations is a subjective process. Decisions must be made about how to express complex concepts in relatively constrained languages; these decisions are made by people whose choices of representation and expression are influenced by their own cultural background. Consequently, as context is lost problems then arise as other organisations with different cultures, or even just individuals with different conceptualisations, attempt to understand the logical representation and rebuild the original knowledge.

To return to the case of university web sites, it seems reasonable to assume that all universities partake in the teaching of students and in research. Most universities offer undergraduate degrees in the areas of engineering, arts, science and commerce. But when it comes to describing their activities, where one university may use the word *course* to refer to a particular degree program, another will use *course* to mean an individual subject within a degree; a third institution may use *course* to describe a particular stream or program within a degree. Some institutions will say *unit* where others say *subject* and others say *class*. Simply due to their own individual organisational cultures, different institutions use different vocabularies to describe their activities. The researcher wishing to compare the services provided by different universities will generally quickly identify the differences and through an understanding of the knowledge domain concerning university activities and services will be able to translate between terms, usually assimilating them into the researcher's own personal ontological understanding, which itself will be shaped by their personal experiences (if they are from a university that uses *course* to mean a unit of teaching and *program* to describe an undergraduate degree, they will probably translate the descriptions from other institutions into this ontology - if they are not from a particular university, they will probably draw on whatever experience they have of academic institutions, and if they have none, they may build their own ontology from the collection of university representations).

To create software agents that can handle this level of ontological complexity would seem to be very difficult. Why then is it preferable to simply agreeing upon a global ontology to which all agents subscribe, a centralised language of understanding and representation, or even a global directory of multiple re-usable ontologies from which agents select as necessary? Ontology creation itself is very difficult. It requires the ability to define many concepts precisely and consistently. It requires the ability to predict appropriate assumptions and generalisations that will be acceptable to most, if not all, people. It also requires universal access and distribution infrastructure, and a well-established and accepted knowledge representation format. It requires some way to address the desire for agents and humans to interact at variable levels of abstraction as particular situations demand. It requires constant maintenance to ensure freshness and currency, yet also must provide backward compatibility for old agents. It requires that agent developers familiarise themselves with the prescribed knowledge representation formats, ontologies and protocols and adapt their own development efforts to suit them. These issues make a global ontology infrastructure unsuitable as the sole approach, and it is our belief that effort spent adding tolerance of heterogeneity to systems will provide greater benefit as we begin to introduce agents to our multi-cultural world.

In addition to the practical benefits, one of our strongest desires for tolerance of heterogeneity for software systems is rooted unashamedly in idealism: humans manage to resolve ontological differences successfully, in real time and 'on the fly'. This ability gives us much flexibility and adaptability and allows us to specialise and optimise where possible and yet generalise and compromise when necessary. Therefore, it seems both feasible and desirable to have as a goal a similar capability for software agents.

If we are to make effective use of multi-cultural data from heterogeneous sources, we need ways and means to reconcile the differences in representation. If we are to work efficiently to solve large information problems, we need the assistance of automated mechanisms. To achieve both, we need systems that are tolerant of heterogeneity.

Reconciling ontological differences requires understanding the difference between concepts and their representations; in semiotic terms, appreciating the difference between the signified and the signifier. Reconciling ontological differences means reading multiple texts that represent identical, similar or related concepts and being able to work with them at the concept level rather than at the level of representation.

For an XML documents or databases, it might be as simple as realising that two fields in different data sources actually contain the same class of data. On the other hand, it might be as complex as deciding that articles from an economics magazine and an automotive magazine are discussing different topics even though they both have 'Ford' and 'analysis' in their titles, something that current search technologies would be unlikely to realise.

As the number of data sources available to us and our ability to access them on demand and in real time is increasing, the overhead of pre-constructing a complete ontology for a given interaction becomes less and less viable. Large scale interconnectedness and increased frequency of data transactions across organisational and cultural borders leads to a reduction in the useful life of any context constructed for a particular transaction. Just as we are able to establish contexts and construct suitable local ontologies as needed for particular interactions, if we want to be able to include software agents in our higher level communication and knowledge management, they will need to be capable of similar conceptualisation.

5 Results and Thoughts from the Intelligent Agent Laboratory

The Intelligent Agent Laboratory at the University of Melbourne has been working for a number of years on knowledge representation and manipulation for information agents [13,14]. When considering how best to structure knowledge for information agents, two questions arise: what types of knowledge should be pre-defined and what should be left to be learned dynamically? The work of the Intelligent Agent Laboratory addresses these questions in both theory and practice; the remainder of this paper describes two recent projects.

5.1 CASA

Classified Advertisement Search Agent (CASA) is an information agent that searches on-line advertisements to assist users in finding a range of information including rental properties and used cars [4]. It was built as a prototype to evaluate the principle of increasing the effectiveness and flexibility of information agents while reducing their development cost by separating their knowledge from their architecture, and discriminating between different classes of knowledge in order to maximise the reusability of constructed knowledge bases. CASA is able to learn how to interpret new HTML documents, by recognising and understanding both the content of the documents and their structure. It also represents a framework for building knowledge-based information agents that are able to assimilate new knowledge easily, without requiring re-implementation or redundant development of the core agent infrastructure. In a manner that draws on similar principles to object-oriented analysis and design methodologies and component-based development models, an agent shell developed from CASA [9] allows simple construction of agents that are able to quickly incorporate new knowledge bases, both learnt by the agent itself and incorporated from external sources.

CASA classifies knowledge into three categories: general knowledge, domain specific knowledge and site or source specific knowledge. Each category is independent from the others, and multiple instances of each category can exist. General knowledge gives a software agent enough information to understand and operate in its environment. General knowledge is knowledge that is true for all information sources, and is independent of specific domains and sites. The set of general knowledge developed for CASA describes on-line web documents, and includes knowledge of the components that make up an HTML document such as what are tables, paragraphs and lines, as well as knowledge of what a web page is and how one can be accessed.

Domain specific knowledge provides an information agent with a basic understanding of the area in which is required to work. This knowledge is true for a particular field and is independent of site or source specifics. For the case of university services, domain knowledge would generally include the concepts of students, lectures, theatres, semesters, professors and subjects, as well as ontological relationships such as the idea that students take classes, classes cover particular topics and occur at certain times during the week at certain locations, and that particular subjects make up a course. Because domain knowledge is independent of site specific knowledge, it can be re-used across numerous sites and should remain useful into the future.

Site specific knowledge is true for a particular information source only. Site knowledge is specific and unique, but necessary for negotiating the contents of a particular information source; it provides a means of understanding the basic data that comprise an information source, for a particular representation. Continuing the university web site example, site specific knowledge might encode the particular pattern or format in which a certain institution presents a description of a unit of teaching, or of a degree, including information such as table structures, knowledge unit sequences and marker text that locates certain classes of information.

The three categories of knowledge that CASA manages provide different levels of operational assistance for the information agent. General knowledge enables an agent to act and interact in a particular environment, providing the basis for navigation and perception and giving the agent a means by which to internalise its input. Site specific knowledge permits an agent to assimilate and process information from a particular source, which is a necessary ability if the agent is to perform useful tasks. Domain specific knowledge sits between general and site specific knowledge, giving a conceptual framework through which an agent can reconcile information from different sources. Domain specific knowledge can also assist an agent to negotiate unfamiliar information sources for which it has no site specific knowledge. Domain knowledge can be used in conjunction with general knowledge to analyse a site's conventions and representations and to attempt to synthesise the site knowledge necessary to utilise the new information source. Because domain knowledge is not tied to a particular representation, it can be adapted and applied to a variety of different sites or data sources, significantly reducing development time for information agents.

5.2 AReXS

Automatic Reconciliation of XML Structures (AReXS) is a software engine that attempts to reconcile differences between XML structures that encode equivalent concepts. It is able to identify differences of expression and representation across XML documents from heterogeneous sources without any predefined knowledge or human intervention [6]. It requires no knowledge or experience of the domain in which it works, and indeed is completely domain independent. It uses Example-Based Frame Matching (EBFM) [7] and is able to achieve very high recall with modest precision on real world data collected from commercial web sites.

By requiring no domain knowledge, AReXS is suitable for application to any field; its success relies on its ability to identify and resolve the differences in representation that result from sourcing data from a multi-cultural environment. For example, a pair of XML documents from different sources, both describing services offered by universities, might contain attributes named `SUBJECT` and `UNIT` respectively. If the two attributes happen to both signify self-contained units of course work, an agent with no prior domain experience or knowledge will have little hope of realising this. AReXS resolves this discontinuity by considering the values of instances of the attributes as well as the attribute names, deriving confidence in a match from similarities in either comparison. If one document contains the statement `<SUBJECT>Introductory Programming</SUBJECT>` and another contains a similar statement `<UNIT>Introduction to Programming </UNIT>`, AReXS is able to consider the possibility that the two attributes `SUBJECT` and `UNIT` are in this context signifying the same concept. If further correspondences could be found between other instances of these same attributes, the confidence of a conceptual match would increase.

AReXS works by analysing two XML structures and identifying matching attributes, generating a map of equivalence between concepts represented in the two documents. Identification of conceptual equivalence is based on a consideration of lexicographical similarity between both the names and the values of attribute XML tags in each document. Matches are then assessed to deduce structural similarities between documents from different sources. By repeating this search for semiotic correspondence across other pairs of attributes generated from the contents of the XML documents under consideration, AReXS is able to build a local context for data and then use this context to reconcile the ontological differences between XML documents.

To establish the extent of the context shared by pairs of documents, the AReXS engine uses the Character-Based Best Match algorithm [10] to evaluate textual similarity between the names and values of attributes. Such a string based comparison works well to filter out simple manifestations of local cultures; for example, one university web site may choose to include the identification number of a subject in the name of the subject while another may not, opting instead to have a second attribute containing a numeric identification code for each unit. While AReXS will not be able to realise that the number in the name of a subject from one university corresponds to the numeric unit code from another, it will generally conclude from the similarity of the names that *units* and *subjects* are conceptually compatible in this context.

Applying a textual similarity analysis on real data is likely to generate a large number of candidate concepts that may or may not contribute to the local context of the data. AReXS increases its confidence in a candidate for equivalence depending on the uniqueness of the matches between attribute pairs. The uniqueness function described by [7] is used to establish the likelihood of a textual match between attributes actually revealing a shared, unique concept, based on the principle that the more common a concept is across significantly different attributes, the less rich the concept is and thus the less there is to be gained from considering it as part of the data context.

The results of tests based on sample real world data from web sites including amazon.com, barnesandnoble.com, angusandrobertson.com.au and borders.com show that AReXS is capable of accurately identifying conceptually equivalent attributes based on both the attribute names and sample instances of the attributes. These web sites were chosen as useful examples for two reasons. Firstly, they are live, international representatives of the types of data source with which people desire to interact (and in fact already do interact) on a regular but casual basis, and secondly they provide data that by its nature is open to subjective decisions during the process of choosing a logical representation. The casual nature of the interaction that people generally have with sites such as these is important, as discussed earlier in this paper.

The AReXS algorithms allow identification of concept matches regardless of the ordering of concepts or attributes, and its consideration of both names and values of attributes allows it to identify equivalences even if one of the name or the value is absent; in other words, AReXS is tolerant of inconsistent data. The AReXS engine has also demonstrated partial success in identifying many-to-one conceptual equivalences, which can occur in situations like that described earlier in which multiple concepts are represented by multiple attributes in one data source but only one attribute in the other data source.

6 Further Thoughts

AReXS is in reality only a prototype that serves as a demonstration of the potential for automated reconciliation of the ontological differences that manifest in data sources from a culturally heterogeneous environment. Because the effectiveness of the concept matching algorithm is improved by examining more instances of the data, and each data attribute must be examined to increase the confidence of the conceptual matches, AReXS currently suffers from poor scalability as the complexity of data objects increases. The CBBM algorithm used for comparing attribute names and values is heavily biased toward text strings and struggles with variations of numerical data. Due to the modular design of AReXS, this component of the engine could be significantly improved with a combination of simple heuristics, alternative matching algorithms and possibly even the capacity to pre-populate the data context with concepts previously observed or learned. AReXS currently can only work with flat or un-nested XML structures, although it is quite reasonable to imagine extending the principles it demonstrates to more complex data structures, or even incorporating the AReXS concept matching engine as a component in a more sophisticated data analysis system.

Although AReXS only supports reconciling pairs of data sources, the EBFM algorithm on which it is based does allow for comparison of multiple sources and so extending AReXS to support this feature is feasible. While AReXS is partially able to recognise many-to-one equivalences, it will require further work to actually capitalise on this recognition. Finally, the principles implemented in AReXS could quite readily be adapted to allow the extension of data structures based on identification of concept matches within attribute names or values. Drawing on the example described earlier of university service descriptions, if one institution chose to present teaching units with an attribute of the form `<UNIT>Machine Vision (Semester 1)</UNIT>` and a second institution opts for two attributes `<SUBJECT>Machine Vision</SUBJECT>` and `<SEMESTER>1</SEMESTER>`, it is possible to see that a software agent could use analysis techniques similar to those implemented in AReXS to realise that both attributes from the second source are encoded within a single attribute of the first source.

A significant benefit of classifying knowledge into categories is that knowledge can be more readily reused and incorporated into other agents. Compartmentalising knowledge also allows agents to teach each other about new information sources or even new knowledge domains. Domain knowledge is reusable by design, and general knowledge is similarly useful. Given the modular approach to information agent construction presented in CASA, once an agent has been taught about a certain domain of knowledge, that knowledge can be applied to a variety of environments just as easily as it can a variety of sites. By plugging in a different general knowledge base, a web-based information agent could easily become an SQL- or XML-based information agent, with the cost of redevelopment greatly reduced by the re-applicability of the domain knowledge base. It also seems quite feasible for an information agent to be armed with a variety of general knowledge bases permitting it to work in multiple environments as appropriate, or even at the same time, utilising its knowledge as applicable both to process recognised information and to interpret and negotiate unfamiliar conceptual representations.

Acknowledgements. This paper was supported by a University of Melbourne Research Development Grant. Thanks to the members of the Intelligent Agent Laboratory at the University of Melbourne for many useful discussions.

References

1. Beck, Eevi E.: *Changing documents/documenting changes: using computers for collaborative writing over distance*, in Susan Star Leigh (ed.), The Cultures of Computing, Blackwell Publishers, Oxford UK, 1995, 53-68
2. Boisot, Max H.: *The Sharing of Information*, in Information space: A Framework for Learning in Organizations, Institutions and Culture, Routledge, London, 1995, 93-164
3. Bush, Vannevar: *As We May Think*, The Atlantic Monthly, Vol. 176 No. 1, 1945
4. Gao, X., and Sterling, L.: *Classified Advertisement Search Agent (CASA): A Knowledge-Based Information Agent for Searching Semi-Structured Text*, Department of Computer Science, The University of Melbourne, Technical Report 98/1, 1998
5. Hofstadter, Douglas R.: Godel, Escher, Bach: an eternal golden braid, Basic Books, New York, 1979
6. Hou, Dominic: *Automatic Reconciliation of XML Structures*, Honours thesis, Department of Computer Science and Software Engineering, The University of Melbourne, 2001
7. Ikeda, Yuji, Itoh, Fumiyaki, and Ueda, Takaya: *Example-based frame mapping for heterogeneous information agents*, Proceedings of the International Conference on Multi-Agent Systems, IEEE Press, 1998
8. Jones, Robert Alun, and Spiro, Rand J.: *Contextualization, cognitive flexibility, and hypertext: The convergence of interpretive theory, cognitive psychology, and advanced information technologies*, in Susan Leigh Star (ed.), The Cultures of Computing, Blackwell Publishers, Oxford UK, 1995, 146-157
9. Loke, Seng Wai, Sterling, Leon, Sonenberg, Liz, and Kim, Hoon: *ARIS: a shell for information agents that exploits web site structure*, Proceedings of the Third International Conference on Practical Applications of Intelligent Agents and Agent Methodology, London, 1998, 201-219
10. Sato, S.: *CTM: An example-based translation aid system*, Proceedings of the Fifteenth International Conference on Computational Linguistics, 1992
11. Simon, Herbert A.: *The Psychology of Thinking*, The Sciences of the Artificial, MIT Press, Cambridge Mass., 1996, 69
12. Star, Susan Leigh: *Cooperation without consensus in scientific problem solving: Dynamics of closure in open systems*, in Easterbrook, S. (ed.), CSCW: Cooperation or Conflict?, Springer-Verlag, London, 1993, 93-105
13. Sterling, Leon: *On Finding Needles in WWW Haystacks*, Advanced Topics in AI, Proceedings of the 10th Australian Joint Conference on Artificial Intelligence, Abdul Sattar (ed.), Springer-Verlag LNAI, Vol 1342, 1997, 25-36
14. Sterling, Leon: *A Knowledge-Biased Approach to Information Agents*, 1999
15. Weinstein, Peter C., and Birmingham, William P.: *Agent Communication with Differentiated Ontologies*, submitted for journal review December 1998

Logical Foundations for Reasoning about Trust in Secure Digital Communication

Chuchang Liu

Information Technology Division
Defence Science and Technology Organisation
PO Box 1500, Salisbury, SA 5108, Australia
Chuchang.Liu@dsto.defence.gov.au

Abstract. This paper investigates foundations for the description of, and reasoning about, trust in secure digital communication. We propose a logic, called the Typed Modal Logic (TML), which extends first-order logic with typed variables and modal operators to express agent beliefs. Based on the logic, the theory of trust for a specific security system can be established. Such trust theories provide a foundation for reasoning about trust in digital communication.

1 Introduction

Trust is essential to a communication channel. Modern secure digital communication is usually based on cryptography. Investigating foundations for trust in secure digital communication, we need to answer the following questions: (1) What kind of trust is involved in a secure digital communication? (2) How should we specify trust and trust relations among agents involved in such communications? (3) Can trust be transferred as required? (4) How should we manage trust? (5) How should we reason about trust in such communications?

This paper intends to address these questions by providing a formal theory and methodology for specifying and reasoning about trust in a system. In order to develop a formal theory of trust, we first start with a logic upon which the theory can be based. What kind of a logic is suitable for modelling trust in digital communication? One of the most desirable properties for a formal theory is an ability to capture what agents intend to say and what they are thinking about. This indicates that reasoning about trust involves reasoning about the notion of belief, and the theory of trust should therefore be based on a kind of belief logic.

There are several logics, such as the BAN logic [1] and Rangan's Logic [9], which can be use for reasoning about belief in secure communications. However, there is a lack of "standard" logical foundations and techniques which can generally be used for specifying and reasoning about trust in modern secure digital communication. In this paper, we propose a new belief logic, called the Typed Modal Logic (TML), on which a trust theory for any particular security system, (such as a public key infrastructure), can be established. These trust theories provide a foundation for analysing and reasoning about trust in particular environments and systems.

M. Brooks, D. Corbett, and M. Stumptner (Eds.): AI 2001, LNAI 2256, pp. 333–344, 2001.

The rest of this paper is organized as follows. Section 2 discusses the notion of trust in general, and talks about why we need a logic of belief. Section 3 presents the logic TML, including its syntax, semantics, and proof system. Section 4 discusses trust theories with an example. Section 5 discusses the process and techniques for reasoning about trust. The last section concludes with a short discussion about future work.

2 Trust and Belief

The notion of trust is fundamental for understanding the interactions between agents such as human beings, machines, organizations, and other entities [7]. Linguistically, "trust" is closely related to "true" and "faithful", with a usual dictionary meaning of "assured reliance on the character, the integrity, justice, etc., of a person, or something in which one places confidence." So, in common English usage "trust" is what one places his confidence in, or expects to be truthful [3,11].

Digital communication involves computer systems. A computer system can be regarded as an interconnection of people, hardware, and software, together with their external connections. We view a secure digital communication environment (e.g., the Internet) as a large complex system consisting of a number of agents, i.e., entities who are involved in the system. Agents need to trust others in certain aspects if they are to have confidence that such interactions will lead to a desirable outcome. When we say that agent A trusts another agent B, this means that (in some sense) the two agents are situated in a state in which, from A's perspective, certain actions by B will be chosen under certain circumstances. In other words, A may believe that B will truthfully do certain actions which concern A. For instance, if a data service system (DS) trusts an authentication server (AS) to verify the ID claim of any user who wants to access DS, then DS may believe that the information provided by AS can be used. As an example, DS may believe "*Alice* is a legal user" because it knows AS says this.

Discussing formal descriptions of trust in digital communication, we need to note the following features within the notion of trust:

- No global trust exists in a secure digital communication environment. In other words, there is no agent who can be trusted by all others. This is obvious in distributed systems. In fact, even in a hierarchical system, such as a hierarchical PKI, although it is more likely that we may assume that all agents would trust the top Certification Authority, in practice there may still be some agents who do not trust it and may try to check its behavior in a variety of ways.
- Trust is not static. The trust of an agent can be changed dynamically. For example, for two weeks agent A trusts agent B, but this morning A found that B lied to him, so A no longer trusts B.
- There is no full trust. A's full trust in B means that A believes everything B says. However, in most cases, this is impossible – an agent cannot trust

all statements provided by another agent. We choose a limited trust model, where "agent A trusts agent B" means that A will only trust B on some topics.
- Trust relations lack the properties of transitivity and symmetry. That is, we cannot derive the conclusion "A_1 trusts A_3" from "A_1 trusts A_2" and "A_2 trusts A_3", and cannot assert that we should have "B trusts A" from "A trusts B".

Let us consider the case in a Public Key Infrastructure (PKI) which manages public keys, where agent *Alice* wants to communicate securely with agent *Bob*, then *Alice* has to obtain *Bob*'s public key first. The PKI provides a mechanism for users to retrieve required certificates, so *Alice* can retrieve any certificates required. Once *Alice* has *Bob*'s certificate, in which *Bob*'s public key is bound, if *Alice* believes that the certificate is valid, then she may use the public key contained in *Bob*'s certificate to send secure messages to *Bob*.

Consider an agent's assertion about the truth of the proposition $\texttt{Valid}(C)$, where C is a certificate and the semantic interpretation of $\texttt{Valid}(C)$ gives $true$ if and only if C is indeed valid. Such an assertion made by an agent is obviously related to the agent's belief. In fact, *Alice* would use *Bob*'s certificate only in the case she cannot prove $\texttt{Valid}(Bob's\ certificate)$ to be false from her beliefs. More strongly, *Alice* is not prepared to use *Bob*'s certificate unless she can prove $\texttt{Valid}(Bob's\ certificate)$ from her own beliefs. To infer $\texttt{Valid}(Bob's\ certificate)$ from her belief, *Alice* has to use some assumptions. In our approach, such assumptions will be encapsulated in a notion of trust for the system.

From the above analysis, we may see that reasoning about trust actually involves reasoning about beliefs. Therefore, a theory of trust may be based on a logic that possesses the ability to represent beliefs. What kind of a logic can play the role? As Rangan [9] has pointed out, belief represents a disposition of an agent to a proposition, so a logic of expressing propositional dispositions should be able to expressing the required relations between believers and attitudes. Classical first-order logic cannot handle such relations well. The modal logic approach is able to enhance propositional and first-order logics with modal operators to represent agent beliefs. Considering this fact, we will attempt to develop an appropriate modal logic as a basis for establishing trust theories of secure digital communications.

3 The Logic TML

The logic we present in this paper is the Typed Modal Logic (TML), which is an extension of first-order logic with typed variables and modal operators expressing beliefs of rational agents. In this section, we discuss the syntax and semantics of TML, and present its proof system.

3.1 Types

In TML, all variables as well as functions are typed. A type can simply be viewed as a certain set of elements. Examples of simple types are numerical numbers and boolean values. We first introduce several *primitive* types, which are used throughout this paper, as follows: Ω (a set of agents), $\mathcal{K}$ (a set of keys), $\mathcal{S}$ (string set), and $\mathcal{N}$ (the set of natural numbers). In particular, we assume that the agent set $\Omega = \{A_1, \ldots, A_k\}$. Other primitive types can be introduced at any time as the need arises. We can also construct new types (so called *constructive* types) from existing types by using the recursive rule: if $\mathcal{T}_1$ and $\mathcal{T}_2$ are types, so are $\mathcal{T}_1 \times \mathcal{T}_2$ and $\mathcal{T}_1 \rightarrow \mathcal{T}_2$ (cartesian products, and functions).

The type of each variable is assigned in advance; the type of each constant is the type it belongs to. The type of a function is determined based on its definition, i.e., the types of all variables involved in it and the type corresponding to its range. For example, given a function $f(X_1, \ldots, X_n)$, if the types of variables $X_1, \ldots, X_n$ are $\mathcal{T}_1, \ldots, \mathcal{T}_n$, respectively, and the type of corresponding to the range of the function is $\mathcal{T}$, then the type of $f(X_1, \ldots, X_n)$ is $\mathcal{T}_1 \times \ldots \times \mathcal{T}_2 \rightarrow \mathcal{T}$.

The type of any predicate is defined in the same way, but the type corresponding to the range is $\mathcal{B}$, the Boolean type. Boolean type $\mathcal{B}$ consists of two elements, *true* and *false*. Thus, for any n-ary predicate $p(X_1, \ldots, X_n)$, if $\mathcal{T}_1, \ldots, \mathcal{T}_n$ are the types of $X_1, \ldots, X_n$, respecively, then the type of the predicate is $\mathcal{T}_1 \times \ldots \times \mathcal{T}_n \rightarrow \mathcal{B}$.

3.2 Syntax

In our logic, we distinguish two different concepts, *messages* (in the first-order logic, called terms) and *formulae*. Messages can be names of agents, certificates, public keys, private keys, dates, strings having particular meanings, or other things. They can also be a combination (or sequence) of other messages. Messages are not formulae although formulas are built from messages. Only formulae can be true or false or have agent's beliefs attributed to them. Formally, messages can inductively be defined as follows:

- If X is a variable or a constant of type $\mathcal{T}$, then X is a message of type $\mathcal{T}$.
- If $X_1, \ldots, X_n$ are messages of type $\mathcal{T}_1, \ldots, \mathcal{T}_n$ respectively, and the type of an n-ary function f is $\mathcal{T}_1 \times \ldots \times \mathcal{T}_2 \rightarrow \mathcal{T}$, then $f(X_1, \ldots, X_n)$ is a message of type $\mathcal{T}$.
- X is a message (of a certain type) iff it is generated by the above formation rules.

In the vocabulary of our logic, apart from typed variables, function and predicate symbols, we have the primitive propositional connectives, $\neg$ and $\rightarrow$, universal quantifier "$\forall$" and modal operators: $\mathbf{B}_{A_i}$, for all $A_i \in \Omega$. The formulae of the logic are therefore inductively defined as follows:

- $p(X_1, \ldots, X_n)$ is a formula if p is a n-ary predicate symbol and $X_1, \ldots, X_n$ are the terms (messages) with corresponding types to p. In particular, we have: (1) $X \in S$ is a formula if X is a message of type $\mathcal{T}$ and S is a set that consists of some elements of $\mathcal{T}$; and (2) $X = Y$ is a formula if X and Y are messages.

- $\neg\varphi$ and $\varphi \rightarrow \psi$ are formulae if φ and ψ are formulae.
- $\forall X \varphi(X)$ is a formula if X is a free variable in the formula $\varphi(X)$.
- $\mathbf{B}_{A_i}\varphi$ is a formula if φ is a formula, $i = 1, \ldots, k$.

Here, most of the expressions are standard notation, so we only need to give a brief description for '$\mathbf{B}_{A_i}\varphi$'. $\mathbf{B}_{A_i}$ is read as "agent A_i believes", so $\mathbf{B}_{A_i}\varphi$ means that the agent A_i believes φ. In the language, other connectives, $\wedge, \vee$ and $\leftrightarrow$, and $\exists$ can be defined in the usual manner.

3.3 Semantics

An agent's beliefs arise primarily from the agent's assumptions about the global state of the system. Thus an agent's state of belief corresponds to the extent to which, based on its local state, the agent can determine what global state the system is in. In this view, we can associate with each agent a set of possible global states that according to the agent's beliefs, it could possibly be the real global state. Based on a local state, an agent cannot determine the real global state it is in; the agent can only conclude that some global states are possible. Therefore, an agent believes φ if and only if φ is true in all the global states that the agent consider possible. The agent does not believe φ if and only if there is at least one global state it consider possible where φ does not hold.

From this analysis, a formal definition of the semantics for the Logic TML would be referred to as the possible-world semantics [6], using the notion of possible global states for the semantics interpretation of belief.

Let S be a set of states, $\mathcal{T}_1, \mathcal{T}_2, \ldots$ be the types over which variables range, and $[\mathcal{Q} \rightarrow \mathcal{T}]$ denote the set of functions from the type $\mathcal{Q}$ to the type $\mathcal{T}$. We now define interpretations on the state set S as follows: An *interpretation* π on S comprises

- assigning an element for each variable from its corresponding type;
- assigning an element of $[\mathcal{T}_{i_1} \times \ldots \times \mathcal{T}_{i_n} \rightarrow \mathcal{T}]$ for each n-ary function with type $\mathcal{T}_{i_1} \times \ldots \times \mathcal{T}_{i_n} \rightarrow \mathcal{T}$, and
- for each state $s \in S$, assigning an element of type $[\mathcal{T}_{i_1} \times \ldots \times \mathcal{T}_{i_n} \rightarrow \mathcal{B}]$ for each n-ary predicate symbol, if the n variables are involved in the predicate have the types $\mathcal{T}_{i_1}, \ldots, \mathcal{T}_{i_n}$ respectively.

The reader should note that giving an interpretation of our logic needs to carefully deal with types of variables, functions and predicates. In particular, we should note that assignments to predicates must be made for all states in S. Therefore, assignments can be different at different states.

A *Kripke structure* with k agents $A_1, \ldots, A_k$ is a tuple $\langle S, \pi, R_{A_1}, \ldots, R_{A_k} \rangle$, where S is the set of all global states, π is an interpretation on S, and R_{A_i}, $i = 1, \ldots, k$, are relations on the global states in S. R_{A_i}, called the *possibility relation* according to agent A_i, is defined as follows: $(s, t) \in R_{A_i}$ if and only if, in the global state s, A_i considers the global state t as possible (note that the global state s includes the local state information of A_i).

Let $\langle S, \pi, R_{A_1}, \ldots, R_{A_k} \rangle$ be a Kripke structure. If $f(e_1, \ldots, e_n)$ is a term, then $\pi(f(e_1, \ldots, e_n)) = \pi(f)(\pi(e_1), \ldots, \pi(e_n))$, where f is an n-ary function symbol. In the following, $\models_w \varphi$ stands for "φ is true at w" or "φ holds at w", and iff for "if and only if". The semantics of formulae in TML can inductively be given as follows: For any $s \in S$, we have

(1) For any n-ary predicate symbol p and terms $e_1, \ldots, e_n$, $\models_s p(e_1, \ldots, e_n)$ iff, at s, $p(e_1, \ldots, e_n)$ has the truth value "*true*" under the interpretation π. We write it as $\pi(s)(p(e_1, \ldots, e_n)) = true$.
(2) $\models_s \neg\varphi$ iff it is not the case that $\models_s \varphi$.
(3) $\models_s \varphi \rightarrow \psi$ iff $\models_s \neg\varphi$ or both $\models_s \varphi$ and $\models_s \psi$.
(4) $\models_s \forall X \varphi(X)$, where X is a free variable appearing in φ, iff, for all $d \in \mathcal{T}$ (we assume that X has the type $\mathcal{T}$), $\models_s \varphi(d)$, where $\varphi(d)$ is obtained replacing all X by d in $\varphi(X)$.
(5) $\models_s \mathbf{B}_{A_i}\varphi$ iff, for all t such that $(s,t) \in R_{A_i}$, $\models_t \varphi$

Furthermore, for the given structure $(S, \pi, R_{A_1}, \ldots, R_{A_k})$, we say that φ is valid under the structure, and write $\models \varphi$ if $\models_s \varphi$ for every state $s \in S$; we say that φ is satisfiable under the structure if $\models_s \varphi$ for some state $s \in S$.

The proof system for a logic of belief depends on the properties of the possibility relations. We say that a binary relation R on a set S is *reflexive* if $(s,s) \in R$ for all $s \in S$; R is is *symmetric* if, for all $s, u \in S$, if $(s,u) \in R$, then $(u,s) \in R$; R is is *transitive* if, for all $s, u, v \in S$, if $(s,u) \in R$ and $(u,v) \in R$, then $(s,v) \in R$; and R is is *Euclidean* if, for all $s, u, v \in S$, if $(s,u) \in R$ and $(s,v) \in R$, then $(u,v) \in R$. Based on the semantics definition given above, we can show that the possibility relation for our notion of belief is *symmetric*, *transitive*, and *Euclidean*. We leave the proofs for the reader. Here we only point that an actual state may not be one of the possible states, therefore, the possibility relation is *not reflexive*. In fact, from the semantics definition, we can see that the fact "an agent believes that a formula is true" does not mean the formula is really true. The reason is that the agent's cognition is "local" and only based on those "possible states" it has considered.

3.4 Axioms and Rules of Inference

The proof system of TML consists of a set of axioms and a set of rules of inference. The axiom set consists of the following axiom schemata:

A1. $\varphi \rightarrow (\psi \rightarrow \varphi)$
A2. $(\varphi \rightarrow (\psi \rightarrow \chi)) \rightarrow ((\varphi \rightarrow \psi) \rightarrow (\varphi \rightarrow \chi))$
A3. $(\neg\varphi \rightarrow \neg\psi) \rightarrow (\psi \rightarrow \varphi)$
A4. $\forall X \varphi \rightarrow \varphi$, where φ does not contain any free occurrence of X.
A5. $\forall X \varphi(X) \rightarrow \varphi(Y)$, where Y is free against $\varphi(X)$.
A6. $\forall X(\varphi \rightarrow \psi) \rightarrow (\varphi \rightarrow \forall X \psi)$, where φ does not contain any free occurrence of X.
A7. $\mathbf{B}_{A_i}(\varphi \rightarrow \psi) \wedge \mathbf{B}_{A_i}\varphi \rightarrow \mathbf{B}_{A_i}\psi$, $i = 1, \ldots, k$.
A8. $\mathbf{B}_{A_i}(\neg\varphi) \leftrightarrow \neg(\mathbf{B}_{A_i}\varphi)$, $i = 1, \ldots, k$.

The first six axioms are axiom schemata from the classical first-order logic; Axiom A7 involves transition of agent belief and is so called the belief transitive axiom; Axiom A8 deals with negation of belief, and it says that an agent believes $\neg\varphi$ iff it is not the case that the agent believes φ, i.e., the agent does not believe φ.

Each axiom schema generates infinite instances, so there are infinite axioms contained within the proof system.

The rules of inference in this logic include:

R1. From $\vdash \varphi$ and $\vdash \varphi \rightarrow \psi$ infer $\vdash \psi$ (Modus Ponens)
R2. From $\vdash \forall X\varphi(X)$ infer $\vdash \varphi(Y)$ (Instantiation)
R3. From $\vdash \varphi(X)$ infer $\vdash \forall X\varphi(X)$ (Generalisation)
R4. From $\vdash \varphi$ infer $\vdash \mathbf{B}_{A_i}\varphi$, $i = 1, \ldots, k$ (Necessitation)

where X is a free variable. $\vdash$ is a metalinguistic symbol. '$\Gamma \vdash \varphi$' means that φ is derivable from the set of formulae Γ (and the axioms). '$\vdash \varphi$' means that φ is a theorem, i.e., derivable from axioms alone.

For a logic, soundness and completeness are important issues. Our logic is sound and complete. The correction (soundness) of all axioms and rules of inference can be expressed through the following results: For any formulae φ, ψ and any agent $A_i (i = 1, \ldots, k)$,

1. if φ is an instance of one of the axioms A1–A6, then $\models \varphi$.
2. $\models \varphi$ and $\models \varphi \rightarrow \psi$, then $\models \psi$.
3. if $\models \forall X\varphi(X)$ where the type of variable x is $\mathcal{T}$, then $\models \varphi(d)$, d is an arbitrary constant in the type $\mathcal{T}$.
4. if $\models \varphi(X)$ for any $X \in \mathcal{T}$, then $\models \forall X\varphi(X)$, where $\mathcal{T}$ is the type of X.
5. $\models (\mathbf{B}_{A_i}\varphi \wedge \mathbf{B}_{A_i}(\varphi \rightarrow \psi)) \rightarrow \mathbf{B}_{A_i}\psi$.
6. if $\models \varphi$ then $\models \mathbf{B}_{A_i}\varphi$.

The proofs of these assertions are not difficult, and we omit them. Also, we do not attempt to discuss completeness of our logic, which would be covered in an extended version of this paper.

4 Trust Theory

As we stated before, in a given system supporting secure digital communication, if an agent wants to derive a conclusion from its belief, the agent has to use some assumptions regarding what the system should satisfy (and/or it should truthfully do). All agents have to trust these assumptions unless they do not need the system. When an agent uses such assumptions, the agent actually places its trust in the system: it believes that the behavior of the system can be trusted. For example, in a public key infrastructure, agents may use such an assumption: "if a certificate is a valid, so is the public key contained in the certificate." This actually comes from a implicit assumption that all agents trust that all CAs (Certification Authorities) to faithfully execute their operations and that it is not viable to tamper with certificates as the cryptography protecting the certificate is sound.

In our approach, such assumptions are encapsulated in the notion of trust and represented by a set of trust axioms of the system. Thus, a trust theory for the system consists of the logic TML, together with the set of axioms of the particular system. As an example, in the following, we present a theory for a PKI system, called the PKI Theory.

A PKI refers to an infrastructure for distributing public keys where the authenticity of public key is certified by Certification Authorities (CAs). Without loss of generality, we define a PKI certificate to have the following form:

$$\mathtt{Cert}\ \{\mathtt{I}, \mathtt{DS}, \mathtt{DE}, \mathtt{S}, \mathtt{PK}, \mathtt{E}, \mathtt{Sig}\}$$

where I is the issuer, DS and DE are the start date and expiry date respectively, S is the subject of the certificate, PK is the value of the public key for S, E is the value of the extension field, and Sig holds the signature of the issuer I. We introduce a constructive type $\mathcal{C}$ as $\Omega \times \mathcal{N} \times \mathcal{N} \times \Omega \times \mathcal{K} \times \mathcal{S} \times \mathcal{S}$, which is intended to represent the set of certificates.

The types of variables are assigned as follows: let $A, B, A_1, A_2, \ldots$ be agent variables ranging over the type Ω; $C, C_1, C_2, \ldots$ certificate variables ranging over the type $\mathcal{C}$; $PK, PK_1, PK_2, \ldots$ public key variables ranging over the type $\mathcal{K}$; $SK, SK_1, SK_2, \ldots$ private key variables ranging over the type $\mathcal{K}$; and $T, T_1, T_2, \ldots$ time variables ranging over the type $\mathcal{N}$. The constants we use in this paper include agent constants, such as *alice*, *bob*; certificate constants $c, c_1, c_2, \ldots$, and time constants $t, t_1, t_2, \ldots$, etc. A special time constant *today* is employed to represent the current time.

With certificates we have eight projection functions defined as follows: for any certificate $C = \mathtt{Cert}\ \{\mathtt{I}, \mathtt{DS}, \mathtt{DE}, \mathtt{S}, \mathtt{PK}, \mathtt{E}, \mathtt{Sig}\}$,

$$\begin{array}{lll} \overline{\mathtt{I}}(C) = \mathtt{I} & \overline{\mathtt{DS}}(C) = \mathtt{DS} & \overline{\mathtt{DE}}(C) = \mathtt{DE} \\ \overline{\mathtt{S}}(C) = \mathtt{S} & \overline{\mathtt{PK}}(C) = \mathtt{PK} & \overline{\mathtt{E}}(C) = \mathtt{E} \\ \overline{\mathtt{Sig}}(C) = \mathtt{Sig} & \overline{\mathtt{tbs}}(C) = (\mathtt{I}, \mathtt{DS}, \mathtt{DE}, \mathtt{S}, \mathtt{PK}, \mathtt{E}) & \end{array}$$

The meanings of these functions are obvious. We only point that $\overline{\mathtt{tbs}}$ represents "to be signed".

We may wirte $K = (PK, SK)$ to mean that the public key of key pair K is PK and the private key corresponding to PK is SK (sometimes write SK as $SK(PK)$ to indicate the correspondence). Note that no one can calculate the private key from the public key although the correspondence has been represented. $\{M\}_X$ and $\langle M \rangle_X$ represent M encrypted under the key X and M decrypted under the key X respectively, where X is a public key or a private key. CRL_{A_i} denotes the certificate revoked list of an agent A_i, i.e., at the current state, all certificates listed in CRL_{A_i} have been revoked by agent A_i.

To verify a required certificate, agents should agree with the following assumptions concerning trust within the PKI, which form the set of trust axioms of the system:

T1. $\forall C(\mathtt{Valid}(C) \to \mathtt{Valid}(\overline{\mathtt{PK}}(C)))$
T2. $\forall K(K = (\overline{\mathtt{PK}}(C), SK(\overline{\mathtt{PK}}(C))) \wedge \mathtt{Valid}(\overline{\mathtt{PK}}(C)) \to \mathtt{Valid}(K))$
T3. $\forall K \forall M(K = (PK, SK) \wedge \mathtt{Valid}(K) \to (\langle\{M\}_{SK}\rangle_{PK} = M))$
T4. $\forall K \forall M(K = (PK, SK) \wedge \mathtt{Valid}(K) \to (\langle\{M\}_{PK}\rangle_{SK} = M))$
T5. $\forall C(\exists C'(\mathtt{Valid}(C') \wedge (\overline{\mathtt{I}}(C) = \overline{\mathtt{S}}(C')) \wedge (\overline{\mathtt{tbs}}(C) = \langle\overline{\mathtt{Sig}}(C)\rangle_{\overline{\mathtt{PK}}(C')}))$ $\to \mathtt{Valid}(\overline{\mathtt{Sig}}(C)))$
T6. $\forall C(\mathtt{Valid}(\overline{\mathtt{Sig}}(C)) \wedge today \geq \overline{\mathtt{DS}}(C) \wedge today < \overline{\mathtt{DE}}(C) \wedge \neg(C \in CRL_{\overline{\mathtt{I}}(C)})$ $\to \mathtt{Valid}(C))$

The meanings of these axioms are as follows. Axiom T1 says that, if a certificate is valid, then the public key contained in the certificate is valid. Axiom T2 says that, if the public key bound to the subject of a certificate is valid, then the key pair consisting of the public key and the private key corresponding to it is valid. Axiom T3 says that, for any message M, we have $\langle\{M\}_{SK}\rangle_{PK} = M$ if the key pair (PK, SK) is valid. The meaning of T4 is symmetric to T3. Axioms T5 and T6 allow agents to verify the signature of a certificate as well as the certificate itself based on another certificate whose validity has been established.

Digital signature algorithms usually involve use of a hash function, however, in order to simplify our discussion, we do not consider this. So, in axiom T5, to verify the signature of the certificate C, one is required only to check whether $\overline{\mathtt{tbs}}(C) = \langle\overline{\mathtt{Sig}}(C)\rangle_{\overline{\mathtt{PK}}(C')}$ holds.

Let TA $= \{T1 \ldots, T6\}$, then TML and TA together construct the PKI theory, a trust theory for the PKI. In the next section, we discuss reasoning about trust through demonstrating a practical example based on this theory.

5 Reasoning about Trust: An Example

Suppose that *maris* holds a certificate, c_1, and *chuchang* holds a certificate, c_2, which is signed by *maris* with his private key corresponding to the public key bound to c_1. Consider the case: *john* requires *chuchang*'s certificate, he trusts *maris* and he in particular trusts *maris*' certificate, i.e., he believes that c_1 is valid, but at the moment, he does not trust *chuchang*'s certificate c_2. Therefore, in order to use c_2, *john* must verify it.

Based on the PKI theory, the verification process can be outlined as follows:

(1) $\mathbb{B}_{john}\mathtt{Valid}(c_1)$. (assumption)
(2) $\overline{\mathtt{I}}(c_2) = \overline{\mathtt{S}}(c_1)(= maris)$. (assumption)
(3) $\mathbb{B}_{john}(\overline{\mathtt{I}}(c_2) = \overline{\mathtt{S}}(c_1))$. (by Rule R4)
(4) $\overline{\mathtt{tbs}}(c_2) = \langle\overline{\mathtt{Sig}}(c_2)\rangle_{\overline{\mathtt{PK}}(c_1)}$. (be checked and assumed to be true)
(5) $\mathbb{B}_{john}(\overline{\mathtt{tbs}}(c_2) = \langle\overline{\mathtt{Sig}}(c_2)\rangle_{\overline{\mathtt{PK}}(c_1)})$. (by Rule R4)
(6) $\mathbb{B}_{john}(\mathtt{Valid}(c_1) \wedge (\overline{\mathtt{I}}(c_2) = \overline{\mathtt{S}}(c_1)) \wedge (\overline{\mathtt{tbs}}(c_2) = \langle\overline{\mathtt{Sig}}(C_2)\rangle_{\overline{\mathtt{PK}}(c_1)}))$. (from (1), (3) & (5))
(7) $\mathtt{Valid}(c_1) \wedge (\overline{\mathtt{I}}(c_2) = \overline{\mathtt{S}}(c_1)) \wedge (\overline{\mathtt{tbs}}(c_2) = \langle\overline{\mathtt{Sig}}(c_2)\rangle_{\overline{\mathtt{PK}}(c_1)}))$ $\to \mathtt{Valid}(\overline{\mathtt{Sig}}(c_2))$. (by axiom T5 & rule R2)

(8) $\mathbb{B}_{john}(\texttt{Valid}(c_1) \wedge (\overline{\texttt{I}}(c_2) = \overline{\texttt{S}}(c_1)) \wedge (\overline{\texttt{tbs}}(c_2) = \langle\overline{\texttt{Sig}}(c_2)\rangle_{\overline{\texttt{PK}}(c_1)}))$
$\rightarrow \texttt{Valid}(\overline{\texttt{Sig}}(c_2)))$. (by rule R4)
(9) $\mathbb{B}_{john}\texttt{Valid}(\overline{\texttt{Sig}}(c_2))$. (from (6) & (8), and by axiom A7 and rule R1)

Furthermore, if the formulae $today \geq \overline{\texttt{DS}}(c_2)$, $today < \overline{\texttt{DE}}(c_2)$ and $\neg(c_2 \in CRL_{maris})$ are all checked and hold, then we have

(10) $(today \geq \overline{\texttt{DS}}(c_2) \wedge today < \overline{\texttt{DE}}(c_2) \wedge \neg(c_2 \in CRL_{maris}))$.

Thus, we can have

(11) $\mathbb{B}_{john}(today \geq \overline{\texttt{DS}}(c_2) \wedge today < \overline{\texttt{DE}}(c_2) \wedge \neg(c_2 \in CRL_{maris}))$. (by R4)
(12) $\mathbb{B}_{john}(\texttt{Valid}(\overline{\texttt{Sig}}(c_2)) \wedge today \geq \overline{\texttt{DS}}(c_2) \wedge today < \overline{\texttt{DE}}(c_2) \wedge$
$\neg(c_2 \in CRL_{maris}))$. (from (9) & (11))
(13) $\texttt{Valid}(\overline{\texttt{Sig}}(c_2)) \wedge today \geq \overline{\texttt{DS}}(c_2) \wedge today < \overline{\texttt{DE}}(c_2) \wedge \neg(c_2 \in CRL_{maris})$
$\rightarrow \texttt{Valid}(c_2)$. (by axiom T6 and rule R2)
(14) $\mathbb{B}_{john}(\texttt{Valid}(\overline{\texttt{Sig}}(c_2)) \wedge today \geq \overline{\texttt{DS}}(c_2) \wedge today < \overline{\texttt{DE}}(c_2) \wedge$
$\neg(c_2 \in CRL_{maris}) \rightarrow \texttt{Valid}(c_2))$. (by rule R4)
(15) $\mathbb{B}_{john}\texttt{Valid}(c_2)$. (from (12) & (14), by axiom A7 and rule R1)

Having completed the proof, we can therefore have

(*) $\mathbb{B}_{john}\texttt{Valid}(c_1) \vdash \mathbb{B}_{john}\texttt{Valid}(c_2)$.

The expression (*) can formally be read as follows: the fact "*john* believes that c_2, *chuchang*'s certificate, is valid" is derived from the fact "*john* believes that c_1, *maris*'s certificate, is valid". Intutively, such a expression represents a trust transfer: an agent's trust in a certificate may be transferred from its trust in another certificate. In general, an expression '$\mathbb{B}_{A_i}\varphi \vdash \mathbb{B}_{A_i}\psi$' represents that an agent's trust in ψ is transferred from its trust in φ (or its belief in ψ is transferred from its belief in φ).

Trust axioms T2–T4 are not directly used in the proof process. However, we have to point out that checking if $\overline{\texttt{tbs}}(C_2) = \langle\overline{\texttt{Sig}}(C_2)\rangle_{\overline{\texttt{PK}}(C_1)}$ holds lies in the validity of the key $K = (\overline{\texttt{PK}}(C_1), SK(\overline{\texttt{PK}}(C_1)))$, and the fact that the agent believes that if K is valid, then $\langle\{M\}_{SK(\overline{\texttt{PK}}(C_1))}\rangle_{\overline{\texttt{PK}}(C_1)} = M$ for any message M. Therefore, these axioms are also needed.

In general, verifying the validity of a required certificate involves obtaining and verifying the certificates from a trusted certificate to the target certificate. Obtaining the certificates is referred to as *certificate path development* and checking the validity of the certification path is referred to as *certification path validation.* A *certification path* is usually defined to be a non-empty sequence of certificates $\langle C_0, \ldots, C_n\rangle$, where C_0 is a *trusted* certificate, C_n is the *target* certificate, and for all i $(0 \leq l < n)$ the subject of C_l is the issuer of C_{l+1}. Once a certification path $\langle C_0, \ldots, C_n\rangle$ bas been developed for agent A_i to verify cerificate C_n, then from the fact that C_0 is a certificate trusted by A_i we can assert that

$\mathbf{B}_{A_i}\texttt{Valid}(C_0)$.

That is, A_i believes that C_0 is valid. The path validation involves checking whether A_i's trust in C_0 can be transferred to its trust in C_n, i.e., it needs to prove the following trust transferring:

$$\mathbf{B}_{A_i}\texttt{Valid}(C_0) \vdash \mathbf{B}_{A_i}\texttt{Valid}(C_1),$$
$$\mathbf{B}_{A_i}\texttt{Valid}(C_1) \vdash \mathbf{B}_{A_i}\texttt{Valid}(C_2),$$
$$\ldots\ldots$$
$$\mathbf{B}_{A_i}\texttt{Valid}(C_{n-1}) \vdash \mathbf{B}_{A_i}\texttt{Valid}(C_n).$$

Unless all proofs of these trust transferring are successfully completed, the agent A_i cannot accept C_n as valid by this path.

PKIs provide a mechanism for agents to transfer their trust from where it exists to where it is needed, while our logic allows agents to check the correctness of such trust transfer based on the trust theory. However, we have to note that PKIs do not create trust [5]. Any PKI is only able to propagate it: agents must initially trust something. Usually, initial trust is established off-line. In our approach, initial trust can also be formalized as proper axioms in the trust theory of the PKI. Once the set of trust axioms for a given PKI is given, agents can obtain their trust bases as well as the initial trusted certificate set. For detailed discussion about this, we refer the reader to Liu *et al.* [7].

6 Conclusion

We have presented a typed modal logic that can be used for describing and reasoning about trust in secure digital communication. The modal logic is sound and complete and, based on this logic, a trust theory for a given system can be established. Thus, from agents' initial beliefs, trust can be transferred from where the trust exists initially to somewhere else where it may be needed, and the correctness of the transfer process can formally be proved. Our approach is flexible, as it not only applies to a range of applications, such as analysing and designing authentication protocols, but also can be easily modified by deleting or add trust axioms for any specific purpose. The examples given in the paper also show that the proof process based on a trust theory can automatically be implemented once we have mechanized our logic and trust axioms in a certain prover, such as Isabelle [8].

As we pointed before, there are a number of logics which have been developed for specifying and reasoning about agents' beliefs, especially BAN Logic family [1,2,4,10] have widely been discussed and applied for the analysis of identification/authentication protocols, particularly authenticated key distribution protocols. BAN logic is a many-sorted modal logic. It includes several sorts of objects: principals, encryption keys, and statements (formulae). Our typed logic is close to such logic, but we have separated the trust axioms from the logic which is regarded as the basis for building the theory of trust. The advantage of our approach is to make the logic more flexible. Rangan [9] treated a theory of trust as consisting of a logic and a set of trust axioms, but did not consider types.

Future work may include completing the theoretical study of the logic TML, and investigating techniques for reasoning about trust in a well-constructed theory. We may consider different distributions of trust points within a specific system and continue to investigate trust models. Mechanizing trust theories is also planned.

Acknowledgements. The author would like to thank Dr. Maris Ozols and Peter Drewer, the Head of Trusted Computer Systems Group, for their support and valuable comments. Thanks are also due to an anonymous referee for the useful comments and suggestions to improve the final version of this paper.

References

1. M. Burrows, M. Abadi, and R. M. Needham. A logic of authentication. *ACM Transactions on Computer Systems*, 8(1):18–36, 1990.
2. A. Dekker. C3PO: A tool for automatic sound cryptographic protocol analysis. In *Proceedings of the 13th IEEE Computer Security Foundations Workshop*, pages 77–87, Cambridge, UK, 3-5 July 2000. IEEE Computer Society.
3. E. Gerck. Overview of Certificate Systems: X.509, CA, PGP and SKIP. Available from `http://mcg.org.br/`.
4. L. Gong, R. Needham, and R. Yahalom. Reasoning about belief in cryptographic protocols. In *Proceedings of the IEEE Society Symposium on Research in Security and Privacy*, pages 234–248, Los Alamitos, California, 1990. IEEE Computer Society Press.
5. A. Jøsang, I. G. Pedersen, and D. Povey. PKI seeks a trusting relationship. In *Proceedings of the 5th Australasian Conference on Information Security and Privacy (ACISP 2000)*, volume 1841 of *Lecture Notes in Computer Science*, pages 191–205. Springer, 2000.
6. S. Kripke. Semantical considerations of modal logic. *Acta Philosophica Fennica*, 16:83–94, 1963.
7. C. Liu, M. A. Ozols, and T. Cant. An axiomatic basis for reasoning about trust in PKIs. In *Proceedings of the 6th Australasian Conference on Information Security and Privacy (ACISP 2001)*, volume 2119 of *Lecture Notes in Computer Science*, pages 274–291. Springer, 2001.
8. L. C. Paulson. *ML for Working Programmer*. Cambridge University Press, 1991.
9. P. V. Rangan. An axiomatic basis of trust in distributed systems. In *Proceedings of the 1988 IEEE Computer Society Symposium on Research in Security and Privacy*, pages 204–211, 1988.
10. P. F. Syverson and P. C. van Oorschot. On unifying some cryptographic protocol logics. In *Proceedings of the IEEE Society Symposium on Research in Security and Privacy*, pages 234–248, Oakland, CA USA, 1994. IEEE Computer Society Press.
11. R. Yahalom, B. Klein, and Th. Beth. Trust relationships in security systems - A distributed authentication prespective. In *Proceedings of the 1993 IEEE Computer Society Symposium on research in Security and Privacy*, pages 151–164, 1993.

Phe-Q : A Pheromone Based Q-Learning

Ndedi Monekosso and Paolo Remagnino

Digital Imaging Research Centre
School of Computing and Information Systems
Kingston University, United Kingdom
{n.monekosso, p.remagnino}@king.ac.uk

Abstract. Biological systems have often provided inspiration for the design of artificial systems. On such example of a natural system that has inspired researchers is the ant colony. In this paper an algorithm for multi-agent reinforcement learning, a modified Q-learning, is proposed. The algorithm is inspired by the natural behaviour of ants, which deposit pheromones in the environment to communicate. The benefit besides simulating ant behaviour in a colony is to design complex multi-agent systems. Complex behaviour can emerge from relatively simple interacting agents. The proposed Q-learning update equation includes a belief factor. The belief factor reflects the confidence the agent has in the pheromone detected in its environment. Agents communicate implicitly to co-operate in learning to solve a path-planning problem. The results indicate that combining synthetic pheromone with standard Q-learning speeds up the learning process. It will be shown that the agents can be biased towards a preferred solution by adjusting the pheromone deposit and evaporation rates.

Keywords: Machine Learning, Reinforcement Learning, Multi-agent system

1 Introduction

An ant colony displays collective problem solving ability [4, 9]. Complex behavioural patterns emerge from the interaction of relatively simple behaviour of individuals. A characteristic that artificial multi-agent systems seek to reproduce. The ant colony exhibits among other features, co-operation and co-ordination, and communicate implicitly by depositing pheromones. An ant foraging will deposit a trail of pheromones. The problem is that of learning the shortest path between nest and food whilst minimising effort. The aim of the work described in this paper is to develop an algorithm for multi-agent learning inspired by the search strategies of foraging ants, using synthetic pheromones. In particular we use Q-Learning augmented with a belief factor. The belief factor is a function of the pheromone concentration on the trail and reflects the extent to which an agent will take into consideration the information lay down by all agents within the environment. Reinforcement learning and synthetic pheromone have been combined for action selection strategies [15, 20]. The usefulness of the

M. Brooks, D. Corbett, and M. Stumptner (Eds.): AI 2001, LNAI 2256, pp. 345–355, 2001.

belief factor is that it allows an agent to selectively make use of communication from other agents where the information may not be reliable due to changes in the environment. An important issue when designing intelligent agents for the real world.

Section 2 presents related work in ant behaviour modelling and ant systems that have applied ant foraging mechanisms to optimisation problems. Section 3 describes the natural behaviour of ants in a colony. Section 4 discusses reinforcement learning, specifically Q-learning, followed in Section 5 by the pheromone-Q learning update equation. Experiments and results obtained with this algorithm are described in Sections 6 and 7 respectively. Section 9 gives some indication of future work and finally the paper concludes in Section 10.

2 Related Work

The work described in this paper is inspired by ant foraging mechanisms. The aim is to produce useful problem-solving behaviours from relatively simple behaviours in software agents. In common with all works described in this action, it uses synthetic pheromones for communication in a multi-agent environment. The agents can detect pheromone deposited on the agent trails. Ant behaviour has been researched both for the understanding of the ant colony behaviour and also to develop intelligent systems.

Ollason, in [16, 17], reports a deterministic mathematical model for feeding ants. The model predicts the behaviour of ants moving from one regenerating food source to the next. Anderson [1] extends Ollason's work to simulate a colony of ants feeding from a number of regenerating food sources.

Though not intended for ant behaviour modelling or simulation, a methodology inspired by the ant behaviour was developed in [7, 11, 13]. While foraging for food, certain ant species find the shortest path between a food source and the nest [2]. Some of the mechanisms adopted by foraging ants have been applied to classical NP-hard combinatorial optimisation problems with success. In [10] Ant Colony Optimisation is used to solve the travelling salesman problem, a quadratic assignment problem in [13], the job-shop scheduling problem in [6], and the Missionaries and Cannibals problem in [18].

In [12] Gambardella suggests a connection between the ant optimisation algorithm and reinforcement learning (RL) and proposes a family of algorithms (Ant-Q) related to the RL Q-learning. The ant optimisation algorithm is a special case of the Ant-Q family. In these works, synthetic pheromone is used in the action selection strategy whereas in the work presented in this paper, the pheromone detected is integrated into the update equation.

The merging of Ant foraging mechanisms and reinforcement learning is also described in [15]. Three mechanisms found in ant trail formation were used as exploration strategy in a robot navigation task. In this work as with the Ant-Q algorithm, the information provided by the pheromone is used for the action selection mechanism.

Another work inspired by ant behaviour is reported in [20]. It is applied to a multi-robotic environment where robots transport objects between locations. Rather than physically laying a trail of synthetic pheromones, the robots communicate path information via a shared memory.

3 Ant Behaviour

Ants are able to find the shortest path between a nest and a food source by an autocatalytic process [3, 14]. This process comes about because ants deposit pheromones on the trail as they move along in the search for food or resources to construct a nest. The pheromone evaporates with time nevertheless ants follow a pheromone trail and at a branching point prefer to follow the path with the highest concentration of pheromone. On finding the food source, the ants return laden to the nest depositing more pheromone along the way thus reinforcing the pheromone trail. Ants that have followed the shortest path return quicker to the nest, reinforcing the pheromone trail at a faster rate than those ants that followed an alternative longer route. Further ants arriving at the branching point choose to follow the path with the highest concentration of pheromone thus reinforcing even further the pheromone and eventually most ants follow the shortest path. The amount of pheromone secreted is a function of an angle between the path and a line joining the food and nest locations [5]. Deneubourg [8] found that some ants make U-turns after a branch, and a greater number will make a U-turn to return to the nest or to follow the shorter path after initially selecting the longer path. This U-turn process reinforces the aggregation of pheromone on the shortest path.

So far two properties of pheromone secretion were mentioned: aggregation and evaporation [19]. The concentration adds when ants deposit pheromone at the same location, and over time evaporation causes a gradual reduction in pheromone concentration. A third property is diffusion [19]. The pheromone at a location diffuses into neighbouring locations.

4 Reinforcement Learning

Reinforcement Learning (RL) is a machine learning technique whereby an agent learns by trial and error which action to perform by interacting with the environment. Models of the agent or environment are not required. At each discrete time step, the agent selects an action given the current state and execute the action, causing the environment to move to the next state. The agent receives a reward that reflects the value of the action taken. The objective of the agent is to maximise the sum of rewards received when starting from an initial state and ending in a goal state. One form of RL is Q-Learning [21]. The objective in Q-learning is to generate Q-values (quality values) for each state-action pair. At each time step, the agent observes the state s_t, and takes action a. It then receives a reward r dependent on the new state s_{t+1}. The reward may be discounted into the future, meaning that rewards received n time steps into the future are worth less by a factor γ^n than rewards received in the present. Thus the cumulative discounted reward is given by (1)

$$R = r_t + \gamma r_{t+1} + \gamma^2 r_{t+2} + \cdots + \gamma^n r_{t+n} \tag{1}$$

where $0 \leq \gamma < 1$. The Q-value is updated at each step using the update equation (2) for a non-deterministic Markov Decision Process (MDP)

$$\begin{aligned} \hat{Q}_n(s_t, a) \longleftarrow &\ (1 - \alpha_n)\hat{Q}_{n-1}(s_t, a) + \\ &\ \alpha_n(r_t + \gamma \cdot max_{a'} \hat{Q}_{n-1}(s_{t+1}, a')) \end{aligned} \tag{2}$$

where $\alpha_n = \frac{1}{1+visits_n(s_t,a)}$. Q-learning can be implemented using a look-up table to store the values of Q for a relatively small state space. Neural networks are also used for the Q-function approximation.

5 The Pheromone-Q (Phe-Q) Learning

The main difference between the Q-learning update equation and the pheromone-Q update equation is the introduction of a belief factor that must also be maximised. The belief factor is a function of synthetic pheromone. The synthetic pheromone ($\Phi(s)$) is a scalar value, where s is a state(a cell in the grid world) that comprises three components: aggregation, evaporation and diffusion. The pheromone $\Phi(s)$ has two possible discrete values, a value for the pheromone deposited when searching for food and when returning to the nest with the food.

The belief factor (B) dictates the extent to which an agent believes in the pheromone that it detects. An agent, during early training episodes, will believe to a lesser degree in the pheromone map because all agents are biased towards exploration. The belief factor is given by (3)

$$B(s_{t+1}, a) = \frac{\Phi(s_{t+1})}{\sum_{\sigma \in N_a} \Phi(\sigma)} \tag{3}$$

where $\Phi(s)$ is the pheromone concentration in a cell/state, s, on the grid and N_a is the set of neighbouring cells.

The Q-Learning update equation modified to take into account the synthetic pheromone is given by (4)

$$\begin{aligned} \hat{Q}_n(s_t, a) \longleftarrow &\ (1 - \alpha_n)\hat{Q}_{n-1}(s_t, a) + \\ &\ \alpha_n(r_t + \gamma\prime \cdot max_{a'}(\hat{Q}_{n-1}(s_{t+1}, a') + \xi B(s_{t+1}, a')) \end{aligned} \tag{4}$$

where the parameter, ξ, is a sigmoid function of time (*epochs* ≥ 0). The value of ξ increases as the number of agents successfully accomplish the task.

6 Methodology

It will be shown that the modified update equation converges. Speed of convergence determines how fast an agent learns. The objective of the experiments is to evaluate the modified updating equation for Phe-Q and confirm empirically convergence. Phe-Q will be compared to standard Q-learning for speed of convergence.

For the experiments reported the agent environment is a $N \times N$, grid where $N = 10, 20, 40$. Each cell has an associated pheromone strength (a scalar value). The agents are placed at a starting cell (the nest) on the grid. The aim is for the agents to locate 'food' occupying one or more cells throughout the grid space and return to the starting cell. The agents move from cell to cell depositing discrete quantities of pheromone in each cell. There are two pheromone values, one associated with the search for a food location (outbound pheromone) and the other associated with the return to the nest (return pheromone). The values for the outbound and return pheromone concentrations were 'manually' adjusted to optimise the Phe-Q agent's search performance. This will be further discussed in the section 8. The pheromone adds linearly (aggregates) in a cell up to an upper bound, and evaporates at a rate (evaporation rate (φ_a) until there is none remaining if the cell pheromone is not replenished. Each agent has a set of tasks to accomplish, each task has an associated Q-table. The first task is to reach the 'food' location, and the second task is to return to the nest laden with food.

More than one agent can occupy a cell within the $N \times N$ grid. The pheromone strength is $\Phi \in [0, 100]$ at a location. Pheromone is de-coupled from the state at the implementation level so that the size of the state space is $N \times N$, a single cell corresponds to a state. For a small grid, e.g. $N \leq 40$, a lookup table is used for maintaining the Q values.

The agent receives a reward on completing the tasks i.e. when it locates the food and when it returns to the nest. Each experiment consists of a number of agents released into the environment and running in parallel for 500 to 1000 epochs. Each epoch is the time from the agent's release from the nest to the agent's return to the nest.

In the experiments, the search is achieved with pheromone aggregation and evaporation. Diffusion has not yet been implemented. The outbound pheromone strength was varied between 0.5 and 1.5 units, and the return pheromone strength was varied between 5.0 and 40.0 units. While returning to the nest the agents do not make 'use' of pheromone for guidance. The experiment was run with and without obstacles in the grid space. An agent cannot occupy the same cell as an obstacle. It must navigate around the obstacle.

Table 1. Pheromone variables : fast convergence

Pheromone	Phe(food)	Phe(nest)	Phe(evaporation)
Phe-Q agent	1.0	10.0	1.0

Table 2. Pheromone variables : location search bias

Pheromone	Phe-food	Phe-nest	Phe-evaporation
Phe-Q agent	1.5	30.0	0.3

7 Results

To demonstrate empirically convergence of the update equation Phe-Q, the RMS of the error between successive Q-values is plotted against epoch (an epoch is a complete cycle of locating food and returning to the nest). The RMS curve for Phe-Q (averaged over 10 agents) seen in Figure 1 shows convergence. For comparison, the Q-learning RMS curve is also shown in the same graph. Phe-Q learning converges faster than Q learning. This particular experiment was run with a number of obstacles scattered throughout the grid. With fewer obstacles, Phe-Q converges at a faster rate and the difference between Phe-Q learning and Q-learning is greater. For a given grid size, there is a limit to the number of agents for which Phe-Q performs better than Q-Learning with or without obstacles. In a 20×20 grid space, the performance of the Phe-Q agent degrades to that of Q-learning with approximately 30 agents. The graph in Figure 2 shows the RMS curves for an increasing number of Phe-Q agents maintaining a constant grid size (for clarity only the RMS curves for 5, 40, and 60 agents are shown on the graph). Between 5 and 20 agents, the speeds of convergence of Phe-Q are comparable. Above that number, the trend is slower convergence, a phenomenon that does not occur with Q-learning. The reason for this is explained in the next section.

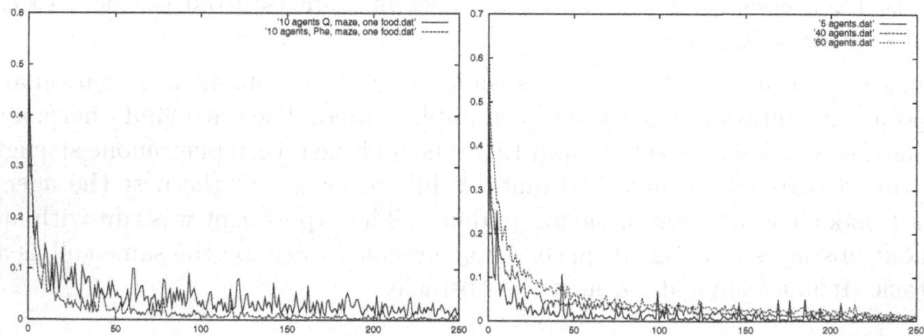

Fig. 1. RMS curve for Phe-Q learning

Fig. 2. Performance scaling

The graph in Figure 3 shows the search performance of the Q-learning and the Phe-Q learning agents with two food sources in a 20×20 grid. The first food source was located at the opposite corner (cell 399) diagonally to the nest (cell 0), and the second food source was located midway, at the centre of the grid. Phe-Q learning converges faster than Q learning. The objective of the experiment was to determine which food location the two types of agents would prefer.

In Figure 4, the number of visits per episode (locate food and return) is plotted. Results indicate that for a relatively simple 'world' e.g. as described above one food source located centrally, both types of agents learn to visit mainly the closest food location as expected but the Q-agent visited the closer food location more frequently than the Phe-Q agent. However when the closest centrally located food source was surrounded by obstacles on three sides (the unobstructed side was facing away from the nest) and the more distant food source was unobstructed, the Q-agent visited the hidden food sources with similar frequency as in the previous experiment with no obstacles however the Phe-Q agent visited the hidden food source less frequently as shown in Figure 4. It was also found that the Phe-Q agents converged faster with two or more food sources. These results were obtained with the outbound and return pheromone values shown in Table 1. From the table it can be seen that the outbound pheromone is low (1 unit) and the return pheromone is 10 times higher (10 units). The evaporation rate was set to 1 unit at each discrete time step, which meant that the outbound pheromone plays a minor role. Experimental results showed that by increasing the pheromone concentration deposited on their return, Phe-Q agent performed less well in terms of speed of convergence, degrading to that of the Q-agent. However in both cases, as with real ants, the agents have preferred the shortest path by a ratio from 20:1 to 25:1 even when the path to the closest food was partially obstructed. An important point to note is that the Phe-Q agent learnt to avoid the obstacles more frequently and opted for a more distant but easily located food source.

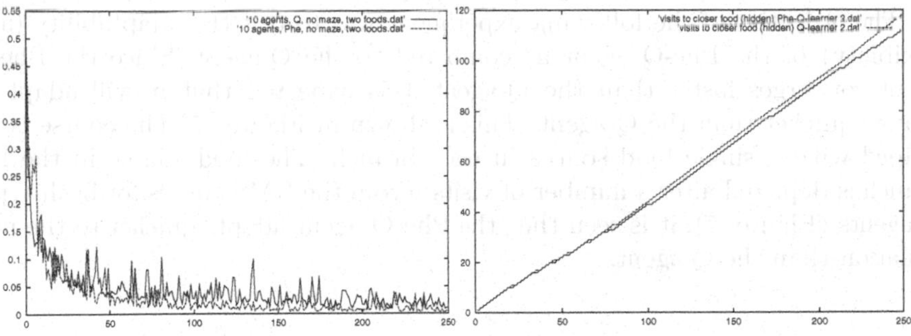

Fig. 3. Two competing food sources

Fig. 4. Visits to closest but hidden food source

In the above experiments, speed of convergence i.e. faster learning was the main goal and the pheromone variables were selected by experimentation for that purpose. It was found that by selecting a range of pheromone variables, the behaviour of the Phe-Q agents could be biased towards a preference for one or another food source. For example using the pheromone variables set in Table 2, the Phe-Q agent preferred the closest food source even if it was partially obstructed as shown in Figure 5. Note that with the pheromone variables in Table 1, the Phe-Q agent preferred the distant unobstructed food. In particular with three food sources, two of which were hidden, the Phe-Q agents with variables in Table 2 were biased towards the closest, most obscured food location as shown in Figure 6.

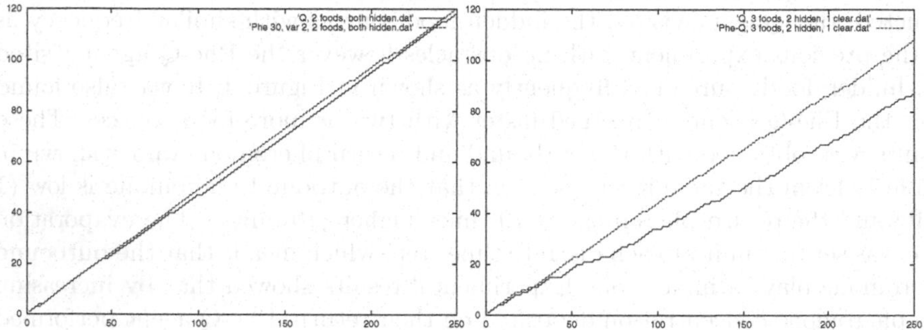

Fig. 5. Two competing food sources

Fig. 6. Three competing food source, one hidden

The effective use of pheromone aggregation and evaporation rates influence the search patterns i.e. which item an agent searches for. The pheromone variables can be chosen to meet a particular application.

The objective of the following experiment was to test the adaptability (and flexibility) of the Phe-Q agent as compared to the Q-agent. Since the Phe-Q agent converges faster than the Q-agent it is expected that it will adapt to change quicker than the Q-agent. This is shown in Figure 7. The course is Y-shaped with a single food source in each branch. The food source in the left branch is depleted after a number of visits. From the RMS curves for both types of agents (Figure 7), it is seen that the Phe-Q agent adapts quicker to the new situation than the Q-agent.

8 Discussion

The synthetic pheromone guides the agents. It is implicit communication. At the implementation level, a pheromone map is produced. This map is de-coupled from the grid 'world' thus reducing the state space. The information exchange via pheromone enables the agents to learn faster as demonstrated by faster convergence. Phe-Q was compared with Q-learning, in both cases using the greedy and Boltzmann action selection mechanisms. Phe-Q using Boltzmann was seen to perform better than all three other combinations. There is however a price to be

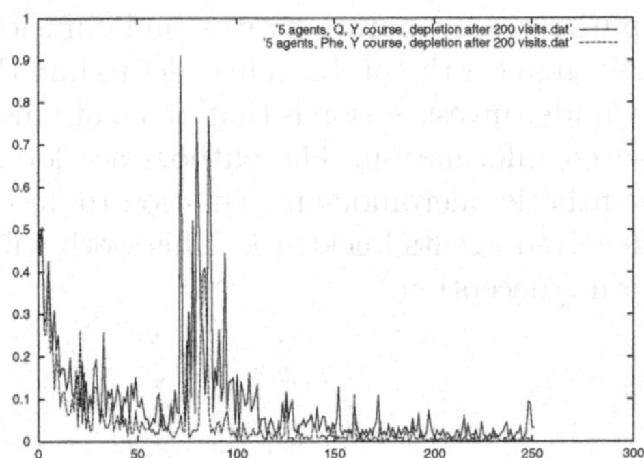

Fig. 7. Food source depletion after 200 visits

paid for this information sharing. Too much information i.e. too high pheromone deposits rate or low pheromone evaporation rates causes not unexpectedly poorer results especially in the earlier learning stages. Agents are 'mislead' by exploring agents. However it was seen that the agents were not highly sensitive to the degree of pheromone information belief. In addition, it was expected that the agent may be 'deceived' by its own pheromone, influenced by pheromone just previously deposited. It was anticipated that this could lead to cycling. However the higher exploration rates in the early learning phases prevents cycling from becoming a problem.

Whereas with non-interacting Q-learning agents, the convergence speed does not change with number of agents, with Phe-Q learning, it was seen that there is an upper limit to the number of agents searching a space while maintaining faster convergence (with respect to Q-learning). Too high a number of agents slows down learning (convergence). The pheromone deposited by large numbers of exploring agents 'mislead' agents. In addition, with a high number of agents the solution also becomes computationally intensive.

The results show that the Phe-Q agent adapts quicker to changes than the Q-agent. This is to be expected as it learns faster. This is a useful characteristic in a dynamic, changing environment.

9 Future Work

Phe-Q will be compared to other reinforcement learning techniques specifically eligibility traces. An advantage of a multi-agent system compared to a single monolithic agent is the emergence of a more 'complex' behaviour. In this particular case the agents are required to communicate and co-ordinate to solve a problem. The more complex the problem, the greater the benefits of the multi-agent solution. It remains to be seen if the performance of Phe-Q can be applied to different types of problems.

There are several variables to be tweaked in order to optimise the problem solving capability of the Phe-Q agent. Particularly with respect to pheromone concentrations, dropping rates, evaporation rates, and diffusion rates across cells. It is intended to reverse engineer the problem in order to find the optimum values.

An issue currently under investigation is that of agent trust. So far the agents have believed the shared information. The authors are looking into deception whereby agents use synthetic pheromone information to deceive agents inhabiting the 'world' and deceived agents backtrack. This work will lead to modelling deception and countering deception.

10 Conclusions

The work described in this paper set out to investigate the use of synthetic pheromone for implicit communication to speed up multi-agent learning. Rather than using pheromone information directly for the action selection strategies, each agent calculates a belief value for the information based on pheromone concentration in the four surrounding cells. The belief is maximised together with the Q-value. This technique, Phe-Q learning, was shown to converge faster than Q-learning when searching for food at different locations in virtual spaces with varying degrees of complexity (obstacles). With two food sources, Q-agents had a preference for the closest source almost to the exclusion of the furthest food source, irrespective of whether the closer food source was hidden or not, in the process taking more time to learn the solution. Phe-Q agents can be biased towards a particular food source.

The Phe-Q agent also showed greater adaptability to changes in the environment. This is an important characteristic for agents inhabiting a noisy real world.

References

1. C. Anderson, P.G. Blacwell, and C. Cannings. Simulating ants that forage by expectation. In *Fourth Conf. on Artificial Life*, pages 531–538, 1997.
2. R. Beckers, J. L. Deneubourg, S. Goss, and J. M. Pasteels. Collective decision making through food recruitment. *Ins. Soc.*, 37:258–267, 1990.
3. R. Beckers, J.L. Deneubourg, and S. Goss. Trails and u-turns in the selection of the shortest path by the ant lasius niger. *Journal of Theoretical Biology*, 159:397–4151, 1992.
4. E. Bonabeau, M. Dorigo, and G. Theraulaz. *Swarm intelligence, From Natural to Artificial Systems.* Oxford University Press, 1999.
5. M. C. Cammaerts-Tricot. Piste et pheromone attraction chez la fourmi myrmica ruba. *Journal of Computational Physiology*, 88:373–382, 1974.
6. A. Colorni, M. Dorigo, and V. Maniezzo. Ant system for job-shop scheduling. *Belgian Journal of OR, statistics and computer science*, 34:39–53, 1993.
7. A. Colorni, M. Dorigo, and G. Theraulaz. Distributed optimzation by ant colonies. In *Proceedings First European Conf. on Artificial Life*, pages 134–142, 1991.
8. J.L. Deneubourg, R. Beckers, and S. Goss. Trails and u-turns in the selection of a path by the ant lasius niger. *Journal of Theoretical Biology*, 159:397–415, 1992.
9. J.L. Deneubourg and S. Goss. Collective patterns and decision making. *Ethol. Ecol. and Evol.*, 1:295–311, 1993.

10. M. Dorigo and L. M. Gambardella. Ant colony system: A cooperative learning approach to the travelling salesman problem. *IEEE Trans. on Evol. Comp.*, 1:53–66, 1997.
11. M. Dorigo, V. Maniezzo, and A. Colorni. The ant system: Optimization by a colony of cooperatin agents. *IEEE Trans. on Systems, Man, and Cybernetics*, 26:1–13, 1996.
12. L. M. Gambardella and M. Dorigo. Ant-q: A reinforcement learning approach to the traveling salesman problem. In *Proceedings 12Th ICML*, pages 252–260, 1995.
13. L. M. Gambardella, E. D. Taillard, and M. Dorigo. Ant colonies for the qap. *Journal of Operational Research society*, 1998.
14. S. Goss, S. Aron, J.L. Deneubourg, and J. M. Pasteels. Self-organized shorcuts in the argentine ants. *Naturwissenschaften*, pages 579–581, 1989.
15. L. R. Leerink, S. R. Schultz, and M. A. Jabri. A reinforcement learning exploration strategy based on ant foraging mechanisms. In *Proceedings 6Th Australian Conf. on Neural Nets*, 1995.
16. J.G. Ollason. Learning to forage - optimally? *Theoretical Population Biology*, 18:44–56, 1980.
17. J.G. Ollason. Learning to forage in a regenerating patchy environment: can it fail to be optimal? *Theoretical Population Biology*, 31:13–32, 1987.
18. H. Van Dyke Parunak and S. Brueckner. Ant-like missionnaries and cannibals: Synthetic pheromones for distributed motion control. In *Proceedings of ICMAS'00*, 2000.
19. H. Van Dyke Parunak, S. Brueckner, J. Sauter, and J. Posdamer. Mechanisms and military applications for synthetic pheromones. In *Fifth International Conference Autonomous Agents, Montreal, Canada, 29 May 2001*, 2001.
20. R. T. Vaughan, K. Stoy, G. S. Sukhatme, and M. J. Mataric. Whistling in the dark: Cooperative trail following in uncertain localization space. In *Proceedings 4Th International Conf. on Autonomous Agents*, 2000.
21. C. J. C. H. Watkins. *Learning with delayed rewards*. PhD thesis, University of Cambridge, 1989.

Specification of Kansei Patterns in an Adaptive Perceptual Space

Tomoko Murakami, Ryohei Orihara, and Naomichi Sueda

Information-Base Functions Toshiba Laboratory,
Real World Computing Partnership,
1, Komukai Toshiba-cho, Saiwai-ku Kawasaki 212-8582, Japan
{tomoko, orihara, sueda}@eel.rdc.toshiba.co.jp

Abstract. In this paper, we apply the algorithms to facilitate learning to kansei modeling and experimentally investigate constructed kansei model itself. We introduce using a vector space as a scheme of the mental representation and place still images in the perceptual space by generating perceptual features. Furthermore we propose a method to manipulate the perceptual data by optimizing modeling parameters based on the kansei scale. After this adaptation we compare the similarity between the kansei clusters using their distance in the space to evaluate if the adapting perceptual space is appropriate for one's kansei. We have conducted preliminary experiments utilizing image data of TV commercials and briefly evaluated the mental space constructed by our method through the kansei questionnaire.

1 Introduction

Human perceives objects or images through not only sensory perception but also judgment based on their memory, experience and preferences[1]. For example, one person may consider a picture to be attractive and another may not. This occurs due to differences in people's viewpoints even though they have similar sensors.

In a research project, we have identified various viewpoints of users and apply them to multimedia data[2, 4, 3]. We have also constructed a decision support system for creators of TV commercial films using data including still images and consumers' reports to evaluate our method. Since TV commercial creators are expected to produce attractive TV commercials for the target consumers of the product, that is important for them to grasp the target consumers' kansei[1] and to make TV commercials that appeal to those kansei. TV commercial creators are required to propose the factor that arouses those kansei first of all.

To specify the factor, kansei modeling representing subjective perceptions is studied in human media project[5, 6]. They consider subjective interpretation as

[1] Kansei is a Japanese word and implies human reaction under various stimuli ranging from sensory to mental state, that is sensitivity, sense, sensibility, feeling, esthetics, emotion, affection and intuition.

M. Brooks, D. Corbett, and M. Stumptner (Eds.): AI 2001, LNAI 2256, pp. 356–367, 2001.

a ratio of regarding as important for each physical features of the image, such as color, direction and position in related to stimuli. This is realized by using statistical method[7] or neural network[8] in the previous studies, but there are still difficulties in performance to predict subjective interpretation according to the experiments in the way of evaluating learning algorithms. Furthermore they have not conducted the experiments to analyze constructed kansei model itself yet.

Regarding the construction of good human perceptual models, artificial intelligence researchers have seldom studied how to construct a suitable model for a learning system despite of the excellent results achieved through the improvement of learning algorithms. Various well-constructed machine learning algorithms(e.g. ID3[9], C4.5[10], Progol[11]) have been proposed and used widely. Although these algorithms show sufficient learning ability if the world is modeled accurately, it is still quite difficult to represent the real world due to noisy data and irrelevant features. Even if those problems were solved, the personal preferences would be a bigger obstacle. If a machine constructs the model adaptively, that is, if the machine interprets one's mental model and creates a suitable model of it, the machine can capture one's preference, judgment or behavior. One approach to achieve this is constructive induction[12], i.e., the automatic computation of suitable feature representations for machine learning tasks. On the other, we introduced representation of instance data in a perceptual vector space by generating perceptual features and proposed a method to manipulate the perceptual data by adapting modeling parameters to the task[2]. The algorithms to construct a model to facilitate learning and the experiments to confirm their high performance were reported[13].

In this paper, we apply the algorithms to facilitate learning to kansei modeling and experimentally investigate constructed kansei model itself. We represent the TV commercial images in the perceptual space by generating perceptual features and adapt the perceptual data by optimizing the modeling parameters based on the kansei scale[14]. After this adaptation, we compare the similarity between kansei clusters using their distance in the space to evaluate if the adapting perceptual space is appropriate for one's kansei. We describe the representation of TV commercial image data in a perceptual instance space and how to implement it in section2. We show an algorithm to manipulate the perceptual data by adapting modeling parameters for the task in section3. Preliminary experiments utilizing real-world data and a brief evaluation are presented in section4. Section5 identifies future directions for this work and presents conclusions.

2 Perceptual Modeling of TV Commercial Data

2.1 Perceptual Instance Space

We propose to use a vector space as a scheme of the mental representation. A CM image data perceived by a person corresponds to a point in the vector space. This approach has the following advantages.

- Similarity between situations in the software's mental space can be easily measured by means of Euclidean distance between corresponding points in the vector space.
- It is easy to manipulate the points by something other than the input stimuli, if it is related to the axes composing the vector space.
- A set of points in the vector space can be seen as a private concept of the software. This view allows us to give it a simple means to form a new concept, i.e., by standard clustering techniques.

In this approach, the nature of a perception is characterized by the axes of a vector space and how input stimuli are transformed into points in the space. Ideally the software should be able to construct the axes on demand. In this paper we simplify the problem by giving the software a reasonably large space and letting the software use its subspaces freely.

Regarding the transformation, behavior of the transformers should be systematically controllable because we implicitly want to adjust the behavior to optimize efficiency of the software at a task, so that the software can gradually improve its perception through the task executions. This can be done by parameterizing the procedures. We are thinking that adaptation of the transformers is more important and investigating the possibility of achieving that.

2.2 Design of Features of Space

A human obtains millions of items of information from vision[15] and simulating all of them exceeds this study's scope. Besides verbal information contained in a TV commercial, we consider that the factors that affect human perception are mainly involved with color and TV personalities in the image. From this point of view we introduce features respecting index colors and TV personalities in the TV commercial as perceptual axes in the space. For numerical data related to the personalities such as the age or popularity, we applied sigmoid function denoted as follows to map the value in the range of $(0, 1)$. Intuitively, the value of the function stands for the representation of the data in the mental space.

$$y = \frac{1}{1 + \exp(-k(x - x_0))} \tag{1}$$

Here x_0 represents the mean of x and k indicates the slope of the curve in $x = x_0$. For the index colors, we extract them by means of a modeling program involving parameters. We built a model of human perceptions of the index color in the image. The algorithm consists of two steps, which are described in the following subsections. The steps involve parameters. The parameters are adjusted to make a space of index colors useful for a task. We also propose to use a vector space as a scheme of the internal representation — the mental space — of the system. This makes it easy to judge the similarity of kansei patterns, because the similarity can be easily measured by means of Euclidean distance between corresponding points in the vector space.

2.3 Reducing the Number of Colors

A TV commercial image usually includes a number of colors. However, people do not distinguish most of them and index colors are determined by perceiving some similar colors as one color and by reducing their number[15]. In order to work with reasonable efficiency, the system should set an appropriate color resolution.

Although there are various methods to extract index colors, such as the Popularity algorithm or the MC algorithm[16], we adopt the following algorithm[17] to avoid losing minor colors that are perceptually important.

1. Representation of color space
   All colors for every pixel in an image are input to RGB color space. Those colors are converted to L*a*b* color space, where distance between two colors is a reflection of human intuition.
2. Making color list
   A color list for an image consist of the value of color space coordinates and its frequency, that is the number of pixels the color occupies. The color list is constructed by the mixing of two colors whose distance is under threshold p, regarding the frequencies of the colors. The number of colors registered in the list is reduced to 1% of the number of input colors after the procedure.
3. Noise removal and color reduction
   Since less frequent colors in the list are considered to be noise, if the frequency of a color is under 0.5% of all pixels in an image, the colors are mixed with the nearest neighbor color in the list in the way described above. Furthermore, two nearest neighbor colors in the list are mixed in the same way until the number of registration colors in the list becomes m.
4. Color reduction by histogram
   A histogram for each axis $L^*a^*b^*$ is created by partitioning the axis into $2m$ regions and counting the number of colors in them. The nearest neighbor two colors in the list are mixed in the same way until the number of registered colors in the list becomes the maximum value among the number of convexity in each histogram because the number of convexity is considered to be the number of distinctive colors in an image intended by a designer[17]. Then the histograms are recreated and the maximum number of convexity is recalculated. The procedure is iterated until the maximum number of convexity remains constant through the recalculation.

2.4 Conspicuousness of Colors

The index colors must be conspicuous. Conspicuousness of a color L is defined as follows.

$$L = \sqrt{(e \cdot C_1)^2 + (f \cdot C_2)^2 + (g \cdot C_3)^2}$$

where C_1 denotes frequency of the color, C_2 denotes temptation of the color and C_3 denotes contrast of the color, and e, f and g are parameters. C_1, C_2 and C_3 are defined as follows.

– Frequency

$$C_1 = \frac{\text{Frequency of the color}}{\text{The number of pixels in the image}}$$

– Temptation

First the color is converted into HSV(Hue, Color Saturation, Value) color space. Then

$$C_2 = \frac{s \cdot H' + t \cdot S + u \cdot V}{s + t + u}$$

where the H' denotes the affection value of H (predefined for all colors) and s, t and u are parameters.

– Contrast

Let V' denote the V value of the color created by mixing all the colors in the list but the color under consideration. Then

$$C_3 = |V - V'|$$

2.5 Specifying Index Colors

L is calculated for all the colors in the list. Index colors are n colors with larger L values in the list. Let us emphasize that we have introduced controllable parameters p, e, f, g, s, t, u and m for flexible modeling of images.

3 Adaptive Mental Space

3.1 Previous Works

In machine learning approaches, it is widely considered that only a domain expert who has great knowledge regarding how to solve the problems can design appropriate input information for a learning system. In other words, good modeling leads to sufficient learning performance.

In previous studies, various modeling approaches were applied in order to obtain sufficient learner's performance. One is feature selection, which reduces the number of features by selecting a subset of existing features[18]. Algorithms to select a subset have been developed include heuristics[19], exhaustive search[20] and Relief algorithm[21]. Among them, the Relief algorithm shows the best since, unlike exhaustive search, it does not involve expensive computation and, unlike heuristics, it does not suffer from poverty of concept description. But feature selection approaches assume that an initial feature set is given, and it will only be successful if this initial set is a suitable starting point for selection. Insufficient training instances fool Relief and it is important for Relief to pick real near-hit instances.

The other modeling approach is feature construction to add the relationships between features by generating features as combination of features[18]. By generating good new features, the number of peaks of the target concept is reduced.

The concept having few peaks is learned more easily than the concept that is spread out all over the instance space. It is reported that concept concentration can affect learning drastically[22]. But how to decrease the number of peaks of the target concept has not been studied.

From the kansei modeling point of view, representing subjective perceptions is said to be necessary because each person has his or her own viewpoints. One approach is to construct a model that realizes a human-adaptive system dealing with subjective interpretation based on visual perception[8]. In that approach, a visual perception model is composed of a physical level and a mental feeling level and the subjective interpretations are represented by a ratio for each features in the physical level, such as color, direction and position in relation to stimuli. These ratio is calculated by statistics[7] or neural network [8]. In the sense that it specifies the relation between physical features and kansei patterns, it is related to our method. But there are still difficulties in performance to predict subjective interpretation according to their experiments in the way of evaluating learning algorithms. Furthermore they have not conducted the experiments to analyze constructed kansei model itself yet.

3.2 Smoothness-Driven Adaptive Model(SAM)

We consider the case that perceptual evaluation for data, such as subjective evaluation of a TV commercial, is given as a label with scale. Our TV commercial data include images in advertisements and consumers' reports. We define kansei as discriminated subjective interpretation, which can be categorized as groups of adjectives, for our environments. The semantic differential(SD) method[23] provides us with the discriminated interpretations for our environments, such as preference or openness, and they can be represented as groups of paired adjectives such as like-dislike or simple-complicated.

In the following $\boldsymbol{r}_i (i = 1 \cdots n)$ denotes raw data and $F_j(\boldsymbol{r}_i)$ denotes the perceptual representation for each raw data based on the j-th feature.

With the perceptual evaluation, the program reconstructs the space according to the scale of the evaluation. Let $E_1 \geq E_2 \geq \ldots \geq E_n$ be evaluation values for each $F_j(\boldsymbol{r}_i)$ first. Then F_j is adjusted to make a curved surface of E in the space it generates as smooth as possible. Here we introduce the following formula to consider the smoothness.

$$\hat{d}_{j,i} = \frac{F_j(\boldsymbol{r}_{i+1}) - F_j(\boldsymbol{r}_i)}{E_{i+1} - E_i}$$

When $F_j(\boldsymbol{r}_i)$ increase or decrease smoothly in terms of E, the formula returns $\hat{d}_{j,i}$ close to a constant. The constant can be anything but 0, because with d being 0 any inputs are indistinguishable. Let the constant be 1. We define the following function $G(\hat{d}_{j,i})$ to evaluate the smoothness of the curved surface. If $\hat{d}$ is near to 0,

$$G(\hat{d}) = (\hat{d} + 1 - p)^2 + \frac{-A(\hat{d} + 1 - p)}{1 + e^{\hat{d} + B + 1 - p}}$$

Otherwise,

$$G(\hat{d}) = (\hat{d} - p)^2 + \frac{-A(\hat{d} - p)}{1 + e^{\hat{d}+B-p}}$$

A and B defines the shape of G. In the following experiments, we use $A = 20$ and $B = 2$. p is a constant to be set so that G takes the smallest value at $\hat{d} = 1$ in equation. The closer to 1 $\hat{d}$ becomes, the better an evaluation value is. $G(x)$ also increases gently for $x \geq 1$ and exponentially according to the absolute value of x for $x < 1$.

With G, the evaluation function for F_j is defined as the following. Here, the lower the value of H_j, the smoother the space is.

$$H_j = \sum_{i=1}^{n-1} G(\hat{d}_{j,i})$$

4 Empirical Results

4.1 Experimental Preparation

We introduce kansei scale[14] as a label with scale E. Kansei scale represents a human's intuitive description of the images, which are denoted by paired adjectives. In this experiment a questionnaire was prepared for 100 representative samples using the 14 well-used kansei scales listed in table.1. 60 men's testees in their twenties answered these questions, that means the experimental result is based on men's kansei in their twenties.

Table 1. Paired adjectives.

Bright - Dark	Man - Woman
Warm - Cold	Artificial - Natural
New - Old	Loud - Quiet
Vivid - Dull	Simple - Complicated
Hard - Soft	International - Japanese
Rustic - Urban	Artistic - Scientific
Beautiful - Ugly	Open - Closed

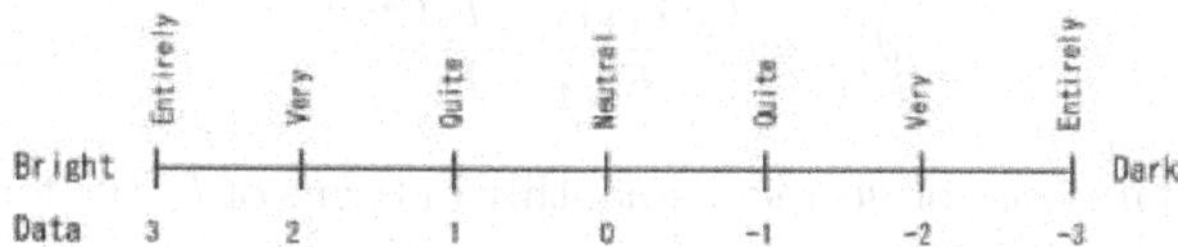

Fig. 1. Scaling for paired adjective.

Values from -3 to 3 were allocated respectively to each point on the questionnaire's horizontal scale. Figure.1 shows *bright* $\leftrightarrow$ *dark* kansei scale. *bright* $\leftrightarrow$ *dark* evaluation $(3, -3)$ which is one of the kansei scales and a larger positive number shows stronger relationship toward *bright*, whereas a larger negative number shows stronger relationship toward *dark*. We define a set of TV commercial images corresponding to the value over 1.5 on a kansei scale by the testees as a positive cluster for that kansei, whereas a set of images corresponding to the value under -1.5 on it is defined as a negative cluster for that kansei. For example, TV commercial images corresponding to the value over 1.5 are labeled *bright* and those corresponding to the value under -1.5 are labeled *dark* for *bright* $\leftrightarrow$ *dark* kansei scale.

When we apply kansei scale to a label with scale E and reconstruct the space according to E to evaluate SAM, we adopt Genetic Algorithm(GA), that is, simplex crossover for real-coded GA, to optimize modeling parameters based on [24]. According to [24] a parameter set is represented as a chromosome in real-coded GA and the alternation of generation preserves the distribution of the population. It also shows that the performance is more advantageous than that by bit-string coding.

The specification of GA in the experiment is as follows.

- A parameter set is represented as a chromosome.
- An initial population is uniformly generated in a certain range.
- Mutation is not implemented.
- The alternation of generation is performed by
  1. selecting randomly n individuals as a parent set from the population set,
  2. generating child individual by crossover of the parent set,
  3. selecting randomly 2 parents from the parent set,
  4. replacing 2 parents with an individual returning the most adapting value($G(x)$) and an individual selected among 2 parents and a child.

4.2 Similar Kansei Patterns

In this experiment, we firstly place 110 TV commercial image data in the perceptual space by generating perceptual features and adapt the perceptual space by SAM based on men's kansei scale in their twenties.

The number of index colors of the images n is fixed to 2. Value and saturation of the two index colors are used to define the vector space. Furthermore, four attributes of a TV personality — age, body proportion, physical attractiveness and popularity — are also used. As a result, the adaptation takes place in an 8-dimensional vector space.

Figure.2 shows how the parameter set is optimized to smooth a curved surface of *bright* $\leftrightarrow$ *dark* in the space by GA. The initial population and the limit of the number of generations are set to 100 and 12000, respectively. The horizontal axis shows the number of generations in GA and the vertical axis represents smoothness evaluation G for each generation. As a result the smoothness became minimum $G = 137.8483$ where parameter $k0 = 0.2$, $x0 = 30.0021$, $k1 = 15.0036$, $x1 = 0.7$, $k2 = 100.021$, $x2 = 0.055$, $k3 = 0.06$, $x3 = 50.0021$. Table.2 shows the results of optimization based on 14 different scales.

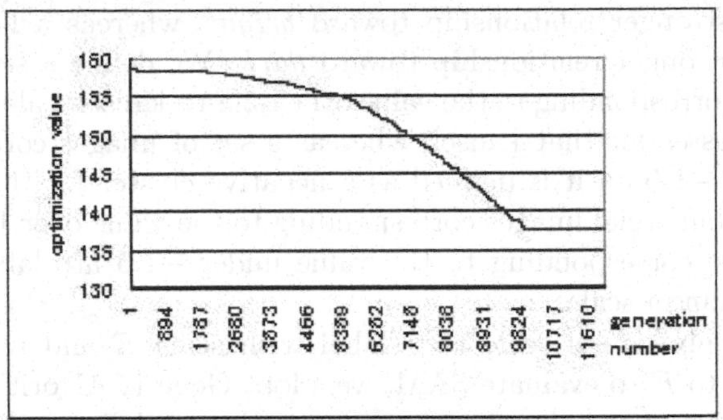

Fig. 2. Optimization based on bright-dark scale by GA.

Table 2. Optimized value in adaptation.

	personality	color
Bright - Dark	137.8483	615.3609
Man - Woman	142.0269	1126.0935
Warm - Cold	144.8203	786.4428
Artificial - Natural	108.8662	905.5394
New - Old	126.2598	430.0494
Loud - Quiet	148.2697	563.5461
Vivid - Dull	162.5275	844.4679
Simple - Complicated	99.6125	552.5917
Hard - Soft	120.1523	659.8007
International - Japanese	106.9665	813.6292
Rustic - Urban	137.2776	652.1892
Artistic - Scientific	72.3130	470.1387
Beautiful - Ugly	106.7876	777.5336
Open - Closed	163.6887	889.2479

We secondly specify similar kansei patterns in the perceptual space by comparing kansei clusters and experimentally evaluate if the adapting perceptual space is appropriate for men's kansei in their twenties. We also specify the factors related to the similarity.

We compare the kansei clusters in the space related to color and personality, respectively, by calculating the center of each kansei cluster and Euclidean distance between the centers of the clusters as the dissimilarity of those clusters. Table.3 indicates the 7 most similar kansei clusters in the perceptual space of color and personality. The experimental result in table.3 shows that there are differences among similar kansei clusters in the space of color and personality. To determine which factor, color or personality, mainly affects kansei patterns we obtained information by means of questionnaires for 22 men's testees in their twenties. The questionnaire is composed of 14 questions that ask if 2 images are

Table 3. Similar kansei clusters in each space.

rank	personality		color	
1	woman — open	0.14477	artistic — international	0.06458
2	bright — warm	0.20881	artificial — bright	0.07406
3	natural — quiet	0.28458	artistic — bright	0.09225
4	quiet — simple	0.31252	woman — simple	0.09273
5	bright — open	0.32875	scientific — soft	0.09397
6	natural — simple	0.33772	loud — bright	0.10438
7	beautiful — woman	0.36461	artificial — loud	0.10653

similar, dissimilar or illegible. Those 2 images in each question are representative images in the similar kansei clusters in the space of color or personality in table.3. The result of the questionnaire is shown in table.4. The result shows that people mainly judged similar kansei clusters in the space of personality to be similar. Personality in the TV commercial, rather than color, strongly affects to kansei patterns for men in their twenties.

Table 4. Evaluation of similar kansei clusters in each space.

personality				color			
kansei pattern	sim.	dissim.	illeg.	kansei pattern	sim.	dissim.	illeg.
woman — open	17	0	5	artistic — international	6	12	4
bright — warm	12	4	6	artificial — bright	0	19	3
natural — quiet	15	1	6	artistic — bright	3	16	3
quiet — simple	7	10	5	woman — simple	3	16	3
bright — open	5	10	7	scientific — soft	2	20	0
natural — simple	9	5	8	loud — bright	1	20	1
beautiful — woman	18	1	3	artificial — loud	3	18	1

(the number of people)

Figure.3 shows 7 similar kansei clusters in the perceptual space of personality. Although most kansei clusters are characterized by *age* or *proportion*, *warm* and *bright* kansei clusters are mainly characterized by popularity. 4 similar kansei patterns, such as *woman* $\leftrightarrow$ *open*, *bright* $\leftrightarrow$ *warm*, *natural* $\leftrightarrow$ *quiet* and *beautiful* $\leftrightarrow$ *woman*, are affected the similarity of popularity and *woman* $\leftrightarrow$ *open* is also affected the similarity of age.

5 Conclusion

In this paper we proposed the use of a vector space as a scheme for the internal representation of the system, where the features of index colors and TV personalities in TV commercial images are introduced as perceptual axes of the space. We also represented the TV commercial images in the perceptual space based on the kansei scale and analyzed the similarity of kansei clusters using their distance in the perceptual space.

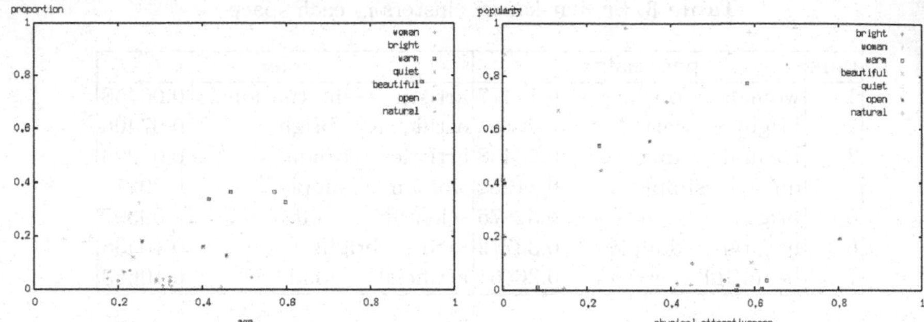

Fig. 3. Perceptual space of personality.

We constructed an experimental system for still image perception to identify the similarity of kansei patterns in the space and to investigate its impact on real-world applications. The data adaptation was performed based on the kansei scale in the perceptual vector space, so that a kansei cluster is compactly represented in the space, rather than spread out all over the space. This is done by creating perceptual axes based on the kansei scale. The axes help to create a space with fewer peaks where characteristics of the kansei can be identified easily. We specified not only similar kansei but also their factors related to the similarity by comparing the kansei cluster in the perceptual space. The result shows that personality strongly affects the similarity rather than color in TV commercial images.

However, we have to say that our study is still in its preliminary stage. We intend to carry out the experimental studies with SAM based on other kansei scales. We should also extend the range of data we can handle, i.e., extend the method so that it can handle multimedia data such as movies and sounds. Our final goal is to construct a decision support system, which can analyze multimedia data from various viewpoints that are implemented as parameters of modeling functions.

References

1. B. Indurkha: Metaphor and Cognition. Volume 13 Studies in Cognitive Systems, Kluwer Academic Publishers (1992)
2. R. Orihara et al.: Improvement of Perception through Task Executions. Proceedings of the 17th Workshop on Machine Intelligence, pp.70-73, (2000)
3. T.Murakami et al.: Friendly information retrieval through adaptive restructuring of information space. In *Proc. of AIEIEA 2000*, (2000)
4. T. Murakami and R. Orihara.: Friendly information retrieval through adaptive restructuring of information space. *New Generation Computing*, Vol.18, No.2, pp.137-146, (2000)
5. T. Kato, S. Hirai: Human Media Technology – Human centred Approach to Information Infrastructure –. Proceedings of 1st International Symposium on Digital Libraries, (1995)

6. T. Kato: Multimedia Database with Visual Interaction Facilities. Proceedings of International Symposium on Cooperative Database Systems for Advanced Applications, (1996)
7. T. Shibata, T. Kato: General Model of Subjective Interpretation for Street Landscape Image. DEXA, pp.501-510, (1998)
8. T. Kato: Cognitive user interface to cyber space database: human media technology for global information infrastructure . in *Proceedings of the International Symposium on Cooperative Database Systems for Advanced Applications*, pp.184-190, (1996)
9. Quinlan,J.R.: Learning Efficient Classification Procedures and Their Application to Chess End Games. Machine Learning:An Artificial Intelligence Approach, pp.463-482, (1983)
10. Quinlan,J.R.: C4.5: Programs for Machine Learning. Morgan Kaufmann, San Mateo, CA (1993)
11. S. Muggleton: Inverse entailment and Progol. New Generation Computing, Vol.13, pp.245-286, (1995)
12. R.Michalski: A theory and methodology of inductive learning. In R.S.Michalski,J.G.Carbonell,and T.M. Mitchell, editors, *Machine Learning: An Artificial Intelligence Approach, Vol.I*, Morgan Kaufmann, Palo Alto, (1983)
13. T.Murakami et al.: Model Construction Suitable for Learning through Adapting Parameters. Proceedings of the 15th Annual Conference of Japanese Society for Artificial Intelligence, in Japanese, pp.70-73, (2000)
14. H. Yamazaki and K. Kondo. A method of changing a color scheme with kansei scales. In *Proceedings of eighth International Conference on Engineering Computer Graphics and Descriptive Geometry*, pp.210-214, (1998)
15. M. Ikeada: Foundation of Color Engineering. Asakura Shoten, in Japanese, (1980)
16. P. Heckbert.: Color Image Quantization for Frame Buffer Display, *Computer Graphics*, Vol.16, No.3, (1982)
17. Y. Morohara et al: Automatic picking of index colors in textile pictures. Proceedings of the 6th International Conference on Engineering Computer Graphics and Descriptive Geometry, pp.643-647, (1994)
18. H.Liu and H.Motoda: Feature Extraction, Construction, and Selection. Kluwer Academic Publishers, (1998)
19. Devijver, P.A. and Kittler, J.: Pattern Recognition:A Statistical Approach. Prentice Hall, (1982)
20. Almuallim, H. and Dietterich, T.G.: Learning With Many Irrelevant Features. Proceedings of the Ninth National Conference on Artificial Intelligence, pp.547-552, (1991)
21. K.Kira and L.A.Rendell. The Feature Selection Problem:Traditional Methods and New Algorithm. Proceedings of the National Conference on Artificial Intelligence, American Association for Artificial Intelligence, pp.129-134, (1992).
22. L.A.Rendell and H.Cho. The Effect of Data Character on Empirical Concept Learning. Proceedings of the National Conference on Artificial Intelligence, American Association for Artificial Intelligence, pp.199-205, (1989)
23. C.E.Osgood, G.J.Suci, and P.H.Tannenbaum: The Measurement of Meaning. University Illinois, Urbana, (1957)
24. S. Tsutsui et al.: Multi-parent Recombination with Simplex Crossover in Real Coded Genetic Algorithms. Proceedings of Genetic and Evolutionary Computation Conference, pp.657-664, (1999)

Embodying the JACK Agent Architecture

Emma Norling[1] and Frank E. Ritter[2]

[1] Computer Science and Software Engineering
The University of Melbourne
E.Norling@csse.unimelb.edu.au

[2] School of Information Sciences and Technology
The Pennsylvania State University
ritter@ist.psu.edu

Abstract. Agent-based models of human operators rarely include explicit representations of the timing and accuracy of perception and action, although their accuracy is sometimes implicitly modelled by including random noise for observations and actions. In many situations though, the timing and accuracy of the person's perception and action significantly influence their overall performance on a task. Recently many cognitive architectures have been extended to include perceptual/motor capabilities, making them embodied, and they have since been successfully used to test and compare interface designs. This paper describes the implementation of a similar perceptual/motor system that uses and extends the JACK agent language. The resulting embodied architecture has been used to compare GUIs representing telephones, but has been designed to interact with any mouse-driven Java interface. The results clearly indicate the impact of poor design on performance, with the agent taking longer to perform the task on the more poorly designed telephone. Initial comparisons with human data show a close match, and more detailed comparisons are underway.

1 Introduction

Although it is difficult to find a definition of a software agent that all researchers will agree upon, one aspect that seems to be universally accepted is that an agent is *situated* — it operates within an environment that it senses in some way, and in which its actions are performed. Despite this agreement on the importance of being situated, when it comes to using software agents to model human operators the details of perception and action are too often ignored.

In many cases, software agents are simply given perfect vision, able to see all objects within their field of vision equally clearly, and precise action, with every action being completely accurate and instantaneous. For some types of simulation, these simplifications may have little impact on the results, but in many applications the effects can be significant. In human-computer interaction, for example, the time taken to find an object on the display and move the mouse to this object can be significant in the overall timing of the task, even for experts. In a driving simulation, the accuracy and speed of steering might make

M. Brooks, D. Corbett, and M. Stumptner (Eds.): AI 2001, LNAI 2256, pp. 368–377, 2001.

the difference between safe driving and an accident. As Gray discusses [9], small differences in interface design can have a significant impact on the time taken to perform common tasks.

Perceptual/motor extensions to cognitive architectures, most notably ACT-R/PM [4], have allowed researchers to build models that interact with simulations of the interfaces an operator would use (such as Salvucci's work on telephone use while driving [15]), and in some cases with the interface itself (e.g. the work of Byrne [6,5] and Amant and Riedl [2] on user interface evaluation). The growing interest in this approach is illustrated in a recent special edition of the *International Journal of Human-Computer Studies* [14]. Although a significant amount of work has focused on GUI testing and evaluation, there are also models which manipulate (simulations of) physical objects, e.g. [11,15]. These studies all illustrate the importance of including perception and action in the model in order to get a better match between the model and the operator being modelled.

This paper describes an implementation of an initial set of functional perceptual/motor capabilities with the JACK agent language [1]. An agent with these capabilities was used to compare graphical representations of telephone interfaces, such as those shown in Fig. 1. Although we limited the motor capabilities to simple mouse movement and clicking (this is all that was needed for the interface), the addition of further motor abilities will now be straightforward. These capabilities will be particularly useful in the JACK agent language because it is designed for modelling human operators. These capabilities allow a more complete model of the operator.

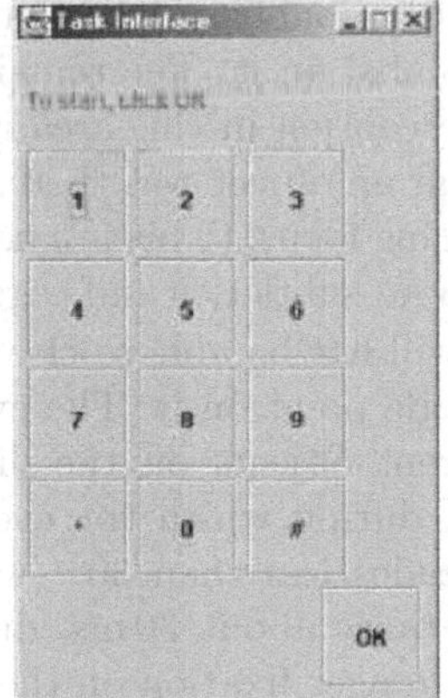

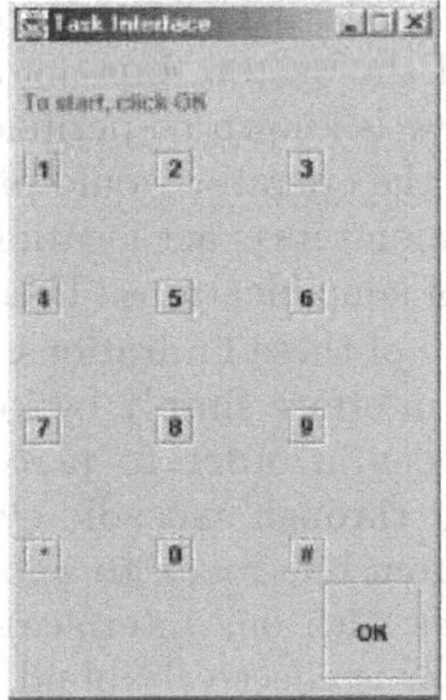

Fig. 1. Two sample interfaces with which the agent and human can interact

In the remainder of this paper, we first discuss perception and action from the perspective of interaction with these GUIs, and then discuss our implementation of perception and action using JACK. We present the results showing the impact of simple good and bad GUI designs on agent performance, and some preliminary work showing that the embodied JACK agent's performance predicts the human performance on the same interfaces. From these results, we note how including perceptual/motor components helps to model human operators, and that similar effects will influence models of human operators in other types of environments.

2 Interaction with Example Interfaces

The interfaces in Fig. 1 require only simple interaction: reading the instruction at the top of the window, performing the appropriate sequence of mouse clicks (which always ends with clicking "OK"), then getting the next instruction, and repeating this loop until "Finished" appears in the instruction area. The interface does not require any keyboard input, nor does it include any complex mouse navigation, such as pull-down menus. For a description of how keyboard interaction could be included in the model, see the work of Baxter, Ritter and their colleagues [3,13] or John [10].

2.1 Visual Perception

The model of visual perception added to the agent corresponds to the three regions people have in their field of view. The first of these is the fovea, a narrow region approximately two degrees in diameter, which is the region of greatest visual acuity. The next is the parafovea, which extends approximately five degrees beyond the fovea, and provides somewhat less acuity. For example, if a button lay in the parafovea, the operator would probably see the shape, size and location of the button, but not recognise the label on it. The remainder of the field of view is known as peripheral vision. Perception in this area is extremely limited — the operator would probably see that an object was there, but not be able to pinpoint its exact location without shifting focus. (This is a necessary but gross set of simplifications. There are many more subtleties and regularities.)

Because of these limitations, an operator will not be able to clearly perceive the entire interface simply by looking at a single point on it. The eye will have to shift focus in order to perceive the different objects on the display. This is achieved through saccadic eye movements, during which the eye effectively "jumps" from one focus to another. For saccades less than 30° (which covers all saccades with our interface), the "jump" takes about 30 ms, during which the operator is effectively blind, followed by a longer fixation on the new focus, typically of about 230 ms duration [7].

These capabilities and limitations allow models in JACK to find information on interfaces, but they require effort. The model must know where to look, or it must search: it must move its eye, and it must then process what it sees. These efforts take time and knowledge, corresponding to similar time and knowledge that the operator has.

2.2 Manual Input

The only manual input required for this interface is mouse movement and clicking. Mouse movements by operators are not accurate, relying heavily on visual feedback. Rather than moving in a single linear motion to the object, the human operator will move the mouse in a series of shorter segments, with a correction at the end of each one, until the mouse pointer appears on the target. Studies have shown that each of these segments has length approximately $1 - \epsilon d$, where d is the remaining distance to the centre of the target, and ϵ is a constant 0.07 [7], p. 53. Each of these movements takes roughly the same amount of time, approximately 70 ms, plus a delay for visual feedback, before the next movement begins. This means that although the final position of the mouse will be within the target, it will not necessarily be at the centre of the target, as shown in Fig. 2.

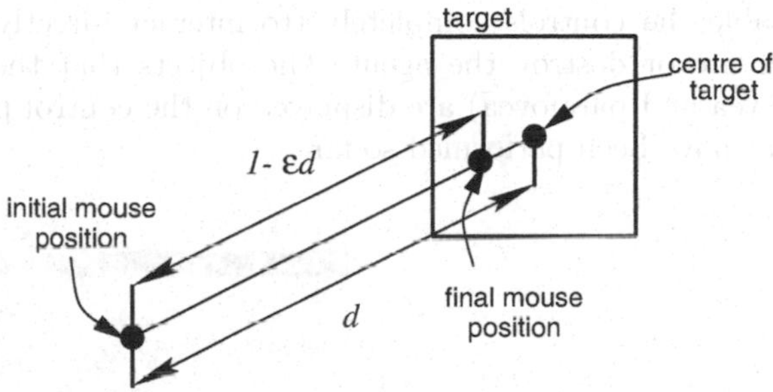

Fig. 2. Moving the mouse to a target

Of course, because of error in the movement, the distance will not be exactly $1 - \epsilon d$, nor will the point lie directly on the line between the origin and the centre of the target. Unfortunately, as discussed by MacKenzie et al [12], while there have been many studies which report error *rates* when using a mouse or other pointing device, very few report the types or magnitudes of errors. We have extrapolated from the results of MacKenzie et al to get a mean variability in final position that is equal to 5% of the distance travelled — further studies are required to confirm this figure.

3 Implementation

The implementation of the system consists of two parts: a simple GUI that was used for testing purposes, and the embodied JACK agent that interacts with this GUI.

3.1 Interface

The telephone GUI was written in Java 1.3 using Swing components. The user can specify the size of the telephone buttons and the spacing between the buttons as command line arguments. A transparent pane overlays this GUI, and it is via this pane that the agent interacts with the GUI. When the agent "looks" at the GUI, the pane returns the details of objects in the fovea and parafovea. When the agent moves or clicks the mouse, the pane passes this information to the GUI. The eye position of the agent is displayed on the pane, as well as the current position of the agent's mouse pointer. Although the agent was tested only using the telephone GUIs, it is designed to interact with any mouse-driven GUI written in Java, by overlaying this same pane.

A control panel is also provided to control the agent and test the interface. (See Fig. 3.) This allows the user to adjust the fovea and parafovea size, switch between a crosshair display for eye position or a full indication of fovea and parafovea boundaries, manually control the eye and mouse positions (for testing purposes), disable the controls completely (to interact directly with the telephone), and create or destroy the agent. The objects that the agent can see (both in the fovea and parafovea) are displayed on the control panel, as well as the actions that have been performed so far.

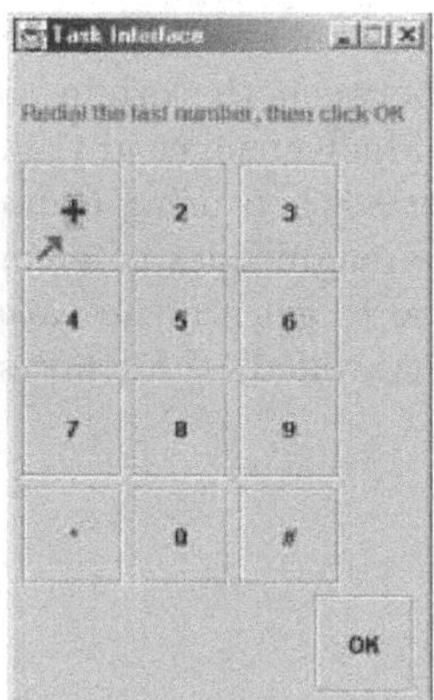

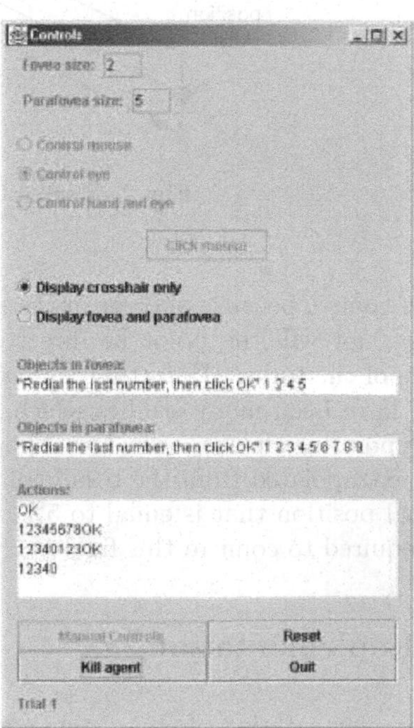

Fig. 3. An agent interacting with the interface, and the associated control panel

3.2 Agent

The agent was written in the JACK agent language, a language implementing a BDI (beliefs-desires-intentions) architecture as an extension to the Java programming language. Other than the perception and action capabilities, the agent is extremely simple, with just two plans: one that interprets the instructions and another that dials a number (retrieving it from memory).

Interaction with the GUI is provided through two capabilities: a vision capability which controls eye position and fixations, and an action capability which controls mouse position and clicks.

The vision capability can achieve three goals: to look at a particular object on the screen, to look at a particular position on the screen, and to simply observe at the current eye position, storing information to memory. The times for eye movements and fixations are included using JACK `@waitfor(`*time*`)` statements, so that the agent takes the appropriate time to achieve these goals.

Similarly, the actions capability can achieve a limited number of goals: to move the mouse to a particular point or object, to click on a particular object, and to click at the current mouse position. Timing to perform these tasks is incorporated for these actions as for the eye movements.

4 Comparison of Model Predictions and Human Data

For preliminary testing, we created a short sequence of tasks for both the agent and human operator to perform using our telephone interface. These tasks were displayed in the instruction section at the top of the interface. The instructions (in order) were:

- To start, click OK
- Dial home, then click OK
- Dial work, then click OK
- Redial the last number, then click OK
- Dial directory enquiries, then click OK
- Call your mother, then click OK

After this sequence, "Finished" appeared in the instruction section. The user was told in advance which numbers they would be asked to dial, and in one case "your girlfriend" was substituted for "your mother" because the user did not know that number — the aim was to use numbers that were known "by heart," so that the time to recall them was short and uniform.

Each of the three users was asked to perform this sequence of tasks 20 times — 10 for the interface with the "standard" size buttons, and 10 for the one with small, widely-spaced buttons. (The two interfaces in Fig. 1 show the scale of differences but are smaller than the real size of 5.5 cm by 9.5 cm.) Every user encountered the standard interface first. The users were instructed not to pause between starting a sequence of tasks and seeing "Finished" appear, but to take as long as they wished between sequences. The time was recorded each time the user clicked "OK." The results for each user were then averaged over each group of 10 sequences.

The JACK agent performed the same sequences of tasks, but in this case there were 30 repetitions for each version of the interface, and these were averaged. Because the number dialled can have a significant impact on the performance of this task (e.g. "555" is dialled more quickly than "816"), the agent was compared against individual users, dialling the same numbers, rather than aggregating all users [8]. Figures 4 and 5 show results from two subjects — the first is the worst fit of all subjects, and the second is the best.

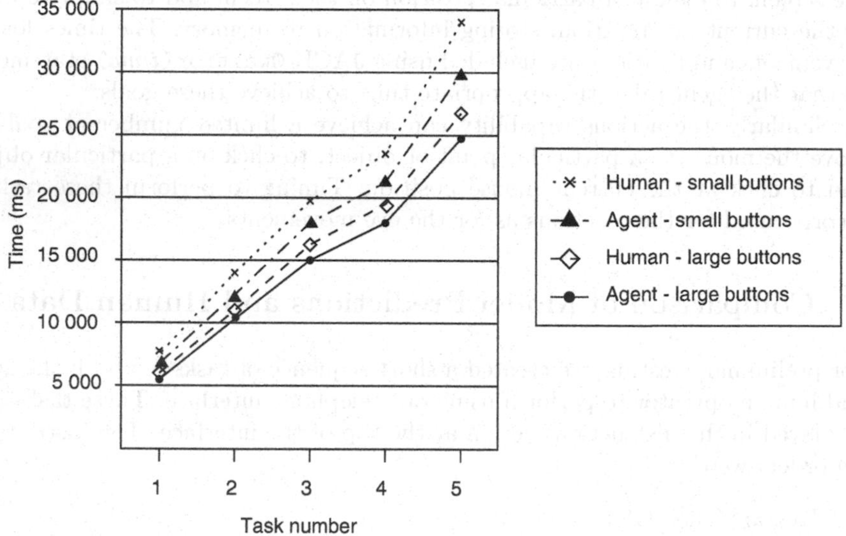

Fig. 4. Time taken to perform the sequence of tasks (the worst fit, subject 1)

In all cases, the time taken to perform the tasks was significantly lower for both the human and agent using the GUI with large buttons. The agent has a tendency to out-perform the human user on both interfaces, and we suspect that this is because the error that we introduce during mouse movement is too small. As mentioned previously, further studies are needed to get an accurate figure for the magnitude of the error. The raw data (not presented here) also shows more variation in the human timing than that of the agent, further reinforcing the suspicion that our error magnitude is too small.

These results are only preliminary results, and we have only used a very small sample of three users, but these results are extremely promising. We are now gathering more detailed human data, logging all mouse actions, and using an eye tracker to record eye movements, so that more detailed comparisons between the users and the model can be made. We will also collect more data

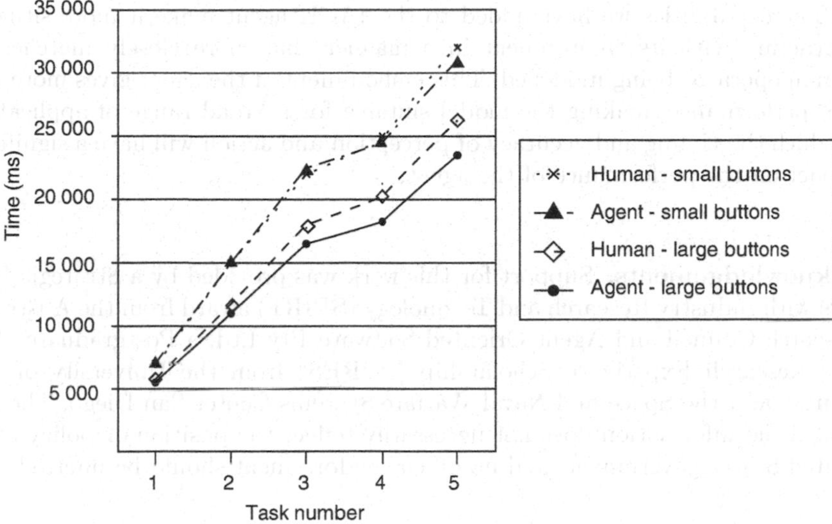

Fig. 5. Time taken to perform the sequence of tasks (the best fit, subject 3)

on the magnitude of errors in mouse movement. The detailed comparison will allow us to further validate the model.

5 Conclusion

The work presented here represents a first step in embodying a JACK agent, giving it the ability to interact with a GUI by "looking" at the interface, seeing it as a human would, and moving and clicking a mouse on the interface. As discussed, the early results are promising, and we expect the more detailed comparison with human users to further refine the model. Although we have focused on visual perception and mouse input, other modes of perception and action could be added in a similar fashion, using the vast wealth of human engineering data that has been collected over the years.

The initial results here clearly indicate the impact of a "bad" user interface design, with the agent taking significantly longer to perform the task on the bad interface (as did the human users). Our results suggest that an embodied agent of this type can be used to test user interfaces, in time eliminating much (though probably not all) of the costly user testing stage of GUI design.

Another application of an agent that is embodied in this way is in a simulation environment where the agent replaces a human operator, for example, in a training simulator. If the agent does not have accurate delays for its actions, or perceives the environment in an unrealistic manner, the value of the training may be questioned. The trainee may develop unrealistic expectations of their team members' abilities, or they may use tactics that would be unnecessary or inappropriate to beat a real world opponent.

The capabilities we have added to the JACK agent make it more situated, interacting with its environment in a manner that more closely matches the human operator being modelled. This embodiment of the agent gives more realistic performance, making the model suitable for a broad range of applications in which the timing and accuracy of perception and action will have a significant impact on the performance of the agent.

Acknowledgements. Support for this work was provided by a Strategic Partners with Industry Research and Technology (SPIRT) award from the Australian Research Council and Agent Oriented Software Pty Ltd, a Postgraduate Overseas Research Experience Scholarship (PORES) from the University of Melbourne, and the Space and Naval Warfare Systems Center San Diego. The content of the information does not necessarily reflect the position or policy of the United States government, and no official endorsement should be inferred.

References

1. Agent Oriented Software Pty. Ltd. JACK Intelligent Agents. http://agent-software.com.au/jack.html.
2. Robert St. Amant and Mark O. Riedl. A perception/action substrate for cognitive modeling in HCI. *International Journal of Human-Computer Studies*, 55:15–39, 2001.
3. Gordon D. Baxter and Frank E. Ritter. Designing abstract visual perceptual and motor action capabilities for use by cognitive models. Technical Report 36, ERSC Center for Research in Development, Instruction and Training, Department of Psychology, University of Nottingham, 1996.
4. Michael D. Byrne. The ACT-R/PM project. In Michael Freed, editor, *Simulating Human Agents: Papers from the 2000 Fall Symposium*, pages 1–3, North Falmouth, Massachusetts, November 2000.
5. Michael D. Byrne. ACT-R/PM and menu selection: Applying a cognitive architecture to HCI. *International Journal of Human-Computer Studies*, 55:41–84, 2001.
6. Michael D. Byrne, Scott D. Wood, Piyawadee Sukaviriya, James D. Foley, and David Kieras. Automating interface evaluation. In *Proceedings of the CHI'94 Conference on Human Factors in Computer Systems*, pages 232–237, New York, NY, 1994.
7. Stuart K. Card, Thomas P. Moran, and Allen Newell. *The Psychology of Human-Computer Interaction.* Lawrence Erlbaum Associates, 1983.
8. Fernand Gobet and Frank E. Ritter. Individual data analysis and unified theories of cognition: A methodological proposal. In N. Taatgen and J. Aasman, editors, *Proceedings of the Third International Conference on Cognitive Modelling*, pages 150–157, Groningen, Netherlands, March 2000.
9. Wayne D. Gray and Deborah A. Boehm-Davis. Milliseconds matter: An introduction to microstrategies and to their use in describing and predicting interactive behavior. *Journal of Experimental Psychology: Applied*, 6(4):322–335, 2000.

10. Bonnie E. John. TYPIST: A theory of performance in skilled typing. *Human-Computer Interaction*, 11:321–355, 1996.
11. Gary Jones and Frank E. Ritter. Over-estimating cognition time: The benefits of modelling interaction. In Michael Freed, editor, *Simulating Human Agents: Papers from the 2000 Fall Symposium*, pages 67–74, North Falmouth, Massachusetts, November 2000.
12. I. Scott MacKenzie, Tatu Kauppinen, and Miika Silfverberg. Accuracy measures for evaluating computer pointing devices. In *Proceedings of CHI 2001*, pages 9–16, Seattle, Washington, April 2001.
13. Frank E. Ritter, Gordon D. Baxter, Gary Jones, and Richard M. Young. Supporting cognitive models as users. *ACM Transactions on Computer-Human Interaction*, 7(2):141–173, 2000.
14. Frank E. Ritter and Richard M. Young. Embodied models at simulated users: Introduction to this special issue on using cognitive models to improve interface design. *International Journal of Human-Computer Studies*, 55:1–14, 2001.
15. Dario D. Salvucci. Predicting the effects of in-car interface use of driver performance: An integrated model approach. *International Journal of Human-Computer Studies*, 55:85–107, 2001.

Towards an Ontology of Part-of

Chris Nowak[1] and Richard Raban[2]

[1] Defence Science & Technology Organisation,
Information Technology Division,
PO Box 1500, Salisbury SA 5108, Australia
nowak@itd.dsto.defence.gov.au
http://www.int.gu.edu.au/~nowak/
[2] University of Technology, Sydney,
School of Computing Sciences,
PO Box 123, Sydney NSW 2007, Australia
richard@socs.uts.edu.au

Abstract. It is accepted that ontologies are vitally important for interoperability and information integration. The major part of every ontology is its taxonomy, a hierarchy of the *kind-of* relation. A conceptual relation seldom omitted from ontological considerations of a domain is the *part-of* relation. Guarino and Welty provide an *ontology of properties* which facilitates dealing with *kind-of*—we summarise their proposal from an order-theoretic perspective, and employ it to address *part-of*. We propose criteria and analyse the resulting classifications of the *part-of* relation. The result is a step towards an ontology of *part-of*.

1 Introduction

It is commonly accepted that *ontologies* are crucial for successful interoperability and information integration [10,5,6]. There is however no consensus yet on what ontology is—we believe [5] provides a proper way of defining an ontology, and improves upon [3]. Whichever definition of ontology one accepts, building an ontology includes building a *taxonomy* (of terms). We refer to the relationship between terms that results in a taxonomy hierarchy as a *kind-of* relation and denote it with a symbol $\sqsubseteq$. Guarino's definition of ontology [5] involves a *domain* of objects and a set of *conceptual relations* on the domain. Selecting an appropriate set of relations is application dependent. There is however a relation that is seldom omitted from ontological considerations on the domain, the relation of *part-of*, sometimes referred to as *part-whole* relation. We denote *part-of* with a symbol $\preceq$.

The paper is structured as follows. In Section 2 we mainly review the results of Guarino and Welty [7], but present them from an *order-theoretic* perspective. In Section 3 we make use of the results reviewed in Section 2, and decide to focus on $\preceq$ restricted to *types*. We propose criteria for classifying $\preceq$ relations, and derive the resulting classifications. We then compare our results with those proposed by others [13,11,8]. We conclude the paper with directions for future research.

M. Brooks, D. Corbett, and M. Stumptner (Eds.): AI 2001, LNAI 2256, pp. 378–389, 2001.

2 Kind-of Relation $\sqsubseteq$

This section considers the *kind-of* relation, denoted $\sqsubseteq$. The discussion is based on research described in [7]. The research offers an ontology of properties, and therefore is crucial for understanding taxonomies and ontologies.

We provide an order-theoretic view of the ontology. Adding explicit orderings (on criteria for classifying properties, and on properties themselves) can enhance and facilitate our understanding of the ontology, and becomes a real advantage when the proposed ontology of properties needs to be modified or extended.

The classification of properties offered in [7] is essential for understanding taxonomies; it is also helpful in our analysis of the *part-of* relation in Section 3.

2.1 Criteria on Properties for $\sqsubseteq$

The criteria considered in [7] are those of *identity (I), rigidity (R)* and *dependence (D)*, see Table 1.

Table 1. Criteria on and classification of properties for $\sqsubseteq$

criteria											
I				R			D			property	
$+O$	$+I$	(lower)	$-I$	$+R$	$-R$	$\otimes R$	$-D$	(top)	$+D$		
•				•				•		type	t
		•		•				•		mere essential sortal	u
		•			•		•			attribution-type mixin	x
•						•	•			phase sortal	h
	•					•			•	material role	m
			•	•				•		category	c
			•		•		•			attribution	a
			•			•			•	formal role	l

It seems beneficial to see criteria as ordered sets of meta-properties (properties of properties), e.g. *non-rigidity* is a property of (the property) *student*; apart from *rigidity* (denoted $+R$) and *non-rigidity* ($-R$), there are *anti-rigidity* ($\otimes R$) and *strict non-rigidity* ($\oslash R$), and there is an ordering on these. The three orderings are depicted in the upper part of Table 1. The definitions [7] follow.

Identity is a binary relation that holds between two objects if they are the same, or equivalently, that does not hold between two objects if they are different. A *named* identity relation is called an *identity condition.* We say that ι is an *identity condition* for p, if for all objects x, y of p we have that $\iota(x, y) \leftrightarrow x = y$.

A given property p can have not only the meta-property $+I$ of identity, but also a meta-property $+O$ of *own identity*—this happens when a property (class) introduces its own identity. Therefore, the criterion of *identity* can be seen as an ordered set of meta-properties, namely $(I, \leq) = (\{\cdot I, +I, -O, +O, +I{-}O, -O\}, \leq)$, i.e., I has 6 elements, and for instance $\cdot I \leq +I \leq +O$. The relation $\leq$ is an *information ordering*, $+O$ is more specific (carries more information) than $+I$, which is in turn more specific than $\cdot I$ (we assign a meta-property $\cdot I$ to a property p, if we don't know whether p has identity).

A *rigidity* criterion R includes the meta-properties of *rigidity* (denoted $+R$), *non-rigidity* ($-R$), *anti-rigidity* ($\otimes R$), and *strict non-rigidity* ($\oslash R$), where a property is strictly non-rigid if it is non-rigid but not anti-rigid. Therefore, $(R, \leq) = (\{\cdot R, +R, -R, \otimes R, \oslash R\}, \leq)$, for the ordering see the upper part of Table 1.

A property is *rigid* if instances of the corresponding class must necessarily be instances of the class [7]. Let $p(x)$ denote the fact that an object x has the property p. Then p is *rigid* (has $+R$) if $\forall_x\, p(x) \rightarrow \Box p(x)$, where $\Box$ is a modal *necessity* operator, in this context usually seen as a temporal necessity operator *always*. Then p is *non-rigid* (has $-R$) if $\exists_x\, p(x) \wedge \neg\Box p(x)$ (there are objects that can move out of the class p, without ceasing to exist). A property p is *anti-rigid* ($\otimes R$) if $\forall_x\, p(x) \rightarrow \neg\Box p(x)$, for every object in p there is a world (time moment) in which it is not in p (note that $\neg\Box p(x) \equiv \Diamond\neg p(x)$, where $\Diamond$ denotes the *possibility* operator).

Dependence is defined as follows. A property is *dependent* if every object in the corresponding class require an object of another class to exist. We say that p_1 depends on p_2 if $\forall_x\, p_1(x) \rightarrow \exists_y\, p_2(y)$, where $p_1 \neq p_2$ and x and y are not parts of each other.

The above definitions can be summarised as follows.

- ι is an *identity condition* for p if
  $\forall_{x,y}\, p(x) \wedge p(y) \rightarrow (\iota(x,y) \leftrightarrow x = y)$;
- ι is p's *own identity condition* if it is an identity condition for p not inherited from $p_2 \sqsupseteq p$;
- p has $+I$ if it has an identity condition;
- p has $+O$ if it has its own identity condition;
- p has $+R$ if $\forall_x\, p(x) \rightarrow \Box p(x)$;
- p has $\otimes R$ if $\forall_x\, p(x) \rightarrow \neg\Box p(x)$;
- p has $\oslash R$ if it has $-R$ but does not have $\otimes R$;
- p depends on p_2 if $\forall_x\, p(x) \rightarrow \exists_y\, p_2(y)$,
  where $p_1 \neq p_2$ and x, y not parts;
- p has $+D$ if there is p_2 such that p depends on p_2;
- p has $-I/O/R/D$ if it does not have $+I/O/R/D$;

Given our interest in $\sqsubseteq$ we need to know whether *identity, rigidity* and *dependence* get inherited, because this would help us to decide whether a given property subsumes (is more general than) another property. We return to this issue in Section 2.3.

2.2 Classification of Properties for $\sqsubseteq$

Given the criteria described in Section 2.1, properties can be classified as shown in Table 1.

The resulting taxonomy of properties for $\sqsubseteq$ is presented in Table 2, taken from [7]. Notice that the taxonomy has a form of a tree. Notice also that Table 1 shows only leaves of the tree of Table 2. In both tables we indicate whether a given property carries an identity condition, is rigid, is dependent.

Table 2. Taxonomy of properties for $\sqsubseteq$

property	(p)
sortal $(+I)$	(s)
essential $(+R)$	(e)
type $(+O)$	(t)
merely essential sortal $(-O)$	(u)
non-essential $(-R)$	(n)
type-attribute mixin $(-D, -O)$	(x)
anti-essential $(\oslash R)$	(i)
phase sortal $(+O, -D)$	(h)
material role $(+D)$	(m)
formal property $(-I)$	(f)
category $(+R)$	(c)
attribute $(-D, -R)$	(a)
formal role $(\oslash R, +D)$	(l)

Given that the criteria I, R and D determine the ordered sets $(I, \leq), (R, \leq)$ and $(D, \leq)$ it is natural to consider the product $I \times R \times D$ of the three ordered sets. An ordering on properties derived from the $I \times R \times D$ ordering is presented in Figure 1—it gives more information about the classification than Table 2 does. For instance, it not only shows that t and u are essential sortals (below e), but also that t and h join at a node stricly below s (the node that could be called s_{+O}, a sortal that has $+O$), and that u and x join at a node stricly below s (the node that could be called s_{-O}, a sortal that has $-O$). Also, *formal role* and *material role* are subsumed by *role*—the corresponding node can be found in the bottom part of Figure 1 as the join of m and l. The ordering can enhance our understanding of the classification of properties for $\sqsubseteq$.

An interesting, order-theoretic method for data anaylysis is offered by *Formal Concept Analysis (FCA)* [2,1]. We employ FCA to analyse properties (employed as *FCA-objects*) and meta-properties (*FCA-attributes*)—see Figure 2.

Figure 2 shows a resulting *concept lattice*. For instance, a node marked h represents an FCA-concept "phasal sortal." This FCA-concept consists of an *FCA-extent* and an *FCA-intent*—its extent is $\{h\}$ (collect FCA-objects below or at the node), its intent is $\{+O, +I, -D, \otimes R\}$ (collect FCA-attributes above

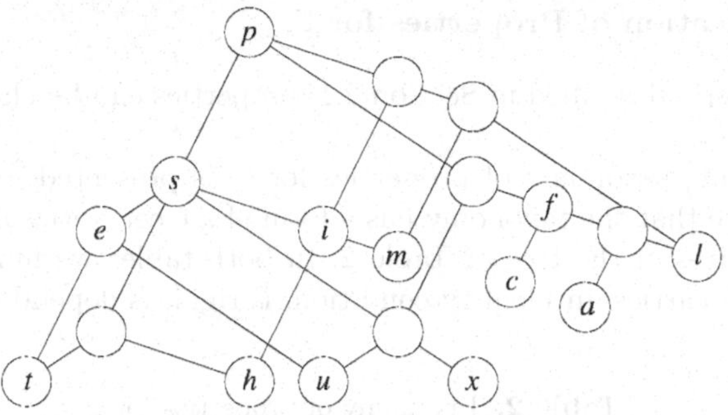

Fig. 1. Ordering on properties for $\sqsubseteq$

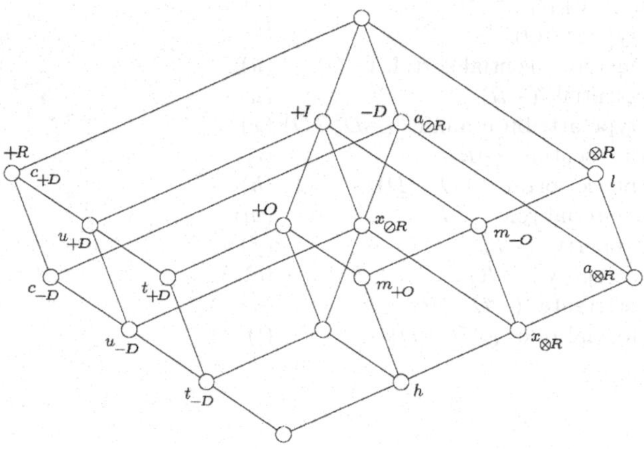

Fig. 2. FCA ordering on properties for $\sqsubseteq$

or at the node). One can also read from the lattice that, for instance, t_{+D} and t_{-D} both have $+O$, $+I$ and also $+R$, but only t_{-D} has $-D$.

2.3 Classification of Kind-of Relations

We need to classify not only properties, but also sub-relations of $\sqsubseteq$. Figure 3 shows the containment between various subsets of P obtained by classifying properties for $\sqsubseteq$—the containments correspond exactly to the taxonomy on properties presented in Table 2, but the only subsets of P that now interest us are those corresponding to the leaves of the taxonomy, namely the subsets T, U, X, H, M, C, A and L; we need answers to questions like the following: if p_1 and p_2 are elements of those subsets, is it the case that p_1 subsumes, or is subsumed by, p_2?

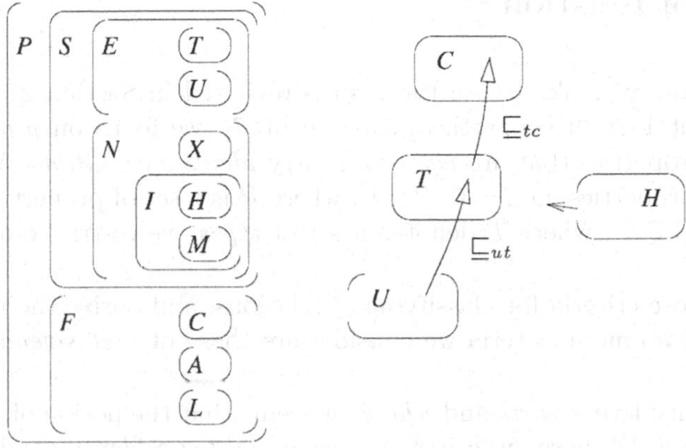

Fig. 3. Containment & taxonomy hierarchy

As mentioned in Section 2.1, we need to know whether *identity, rigidity* and *dependence* get inherited. It is easy to see that identity and dependence is inherited. Rigidity is not inherited. However, anti-rigidity is inherited; to see this, let p be anti-rigid, $p \sqsupseteq q$, and x be an element of the domain. We have that $q(x)$ implies $p(x)$ (because $p \sqsupseteq q$), implies $\Diamond\neg p(x)$ (by anti-rigidity of p), implies $\Diamond\neg q(x)$ (because $p \sqsupseteq q$)—hence anti-rigidity of q. Therefore, we have the following:

- sortals never subsume formal properties;
- anti-rigid properties never subsume rigid properties;
- dependent properties never subsume independent ones.

The above restricts subsumption relation between elements of P. In particular, *categories* are never subsumed by *types*. The practice of ontological modeling tells us that *categories* always subsume *types* (simply put *entity* at the top of the taxonomy). Hence, we can consider $\sqsubseteq_{tc} = \sqsubseteq_{|T\times C}$; similarly, one can introduce $\sqsubseteq_{ut}$. Such results add *structure* to taxonomies, i.e., they allow to partition $\sqsubseteq$ by restricting it to properties for which it holds.

Taxonomy hierarchy is an ordered set of properties P, with $\sqsubseteq$ being the order relation, i.e., it is $(P, \sqsubseteq)$. When $p_1 \sqsubseteq p_2$, this is sometimes represented graphically by drawing a (pointing upwards) arrow line —▷ from the node representing p_1 to the node representing p_2, i.e., p_1 —▷ p_2. Sections 2.2 and 2.3 discussed classifying properties (for $\sqsubseteq$), and classifying sub-relations of $\sqsubseteq$. We have identified, for instance, two more specialised *kind-of* relations $\sqsubseteq_{tc}$ and $\sqsubseteq_{ut}$, with *kind-of* links from *types* to *categories*, and from *merely essential sortals* to *types*. Selecting such specific subsets of $\sqsubseteq$ adds structure to the process of taxonomy building.

Figure 3, the right hand part, shows a fragment of the taxonomy building process. As suggested in [7], one should first construct inheritance ($\sqsubseteq$, *kind-of*) links from *types* to *categories*, and from *merely essential sortals* to *types*. After having this done *phase sortals* should be added, resulting in a *backbone ontology.*

3 Part-of Relation $\preceq$

In this section we make use of the results reviewed in Section 2. In particular, given the ontology of properties proposed in [7], we focus on *properties* called *types*, i.e., properties that are *rigid* and carry *identity conditions*. We see $\preceq$ as a relation on properties, i.e., $\preceq \subseteq P \times P$, where P is a set of properties. Therefore, given that $T \subseteq P$, where T denotes a set of *types*, we restrict our attention to $\preceq|_{T\times T}$.

We propose criteria for classifying $\preceq$ relations, and derive the resulting classifications. Two main criteria we consider are those of *exclusiveness* and *essentiality*.

When considering *parts* and *wholes* it seems that the notion of *dependence* is highly relevant. We base our criterion of *essentiality* on *identity* and *functionality* and it is therefore the essentiality criterion that strongly connects to *dependence*. One can certainly ask "dependence-oriented" questions. Does the part "identity-depend" on the whole, i.e., does it cease to exist when the whole does? Does the part "functionality-depend" (stops functioning) on the whole? Does the part "location-depend" on the whole, i.e., can we locate the part (separability issue) given that we know the location of the whole?

Given two sets, the set of *parts* and the set of *wholes*, the term "exclusiveness" relates to certain properties of mappings between the sets of parts and wholes. For instance, there can be a *1–1 onto* mapping between parts and wholes, or the mapping from wholes to parts is *1–1*—in the latter case we have that "wholes do not share parts," or that given a part and its whole, the part belongs "exclusively" to that whole. Although *dependence* can mainly be captured by *essentiality* and *separability*, one can make use of *exclusiveness*, as well, because it tells us whether parts (wholes) can be shared. If a part is shared by two wholes, does one whole *depend* on the other one? If two parts share a whole, does one part *depend* on the other one?

Our criteria of *exclusiveness* and *essentiality* not only provide a way of classifying $\preceq$, but also *order* various kinds of $\preceq$-relation. When one needs to consider a specific *part-of* relation, one can find its place in the *exclusiveness* and *essentiality* orderings. The advantage of being able to do the classification is that different inferences can be performed in different *part-of* relations. This is similar to the driving force behind the problem of transitivity of *part-of* [13, 8]—computing transitive closure of *part-of* can give us useful inferences, but it only makes sense if the relation *is* transitive, for otherwise *invalid* inferences are derived. But transitive closure on *part-of* (finding parts of the given whole, and parts of the parts, recursively) is not the only way to obtain useful inferences. One might also be interested in updating the database of assets when some of them cease to exist (*identity*), stop to function (together with *identity* it gives our *essentiality*), or their parts get *separated* (where separation either affects identity / functioning or not).

We then compare our results with those proposed by others [13,11,8]. We also indicate directions for future research.

3.1 Exclusiveness

In this section we discuss a criterion called "exclusiveness" and obtain a resulting ordering, as presented in Figure 4.

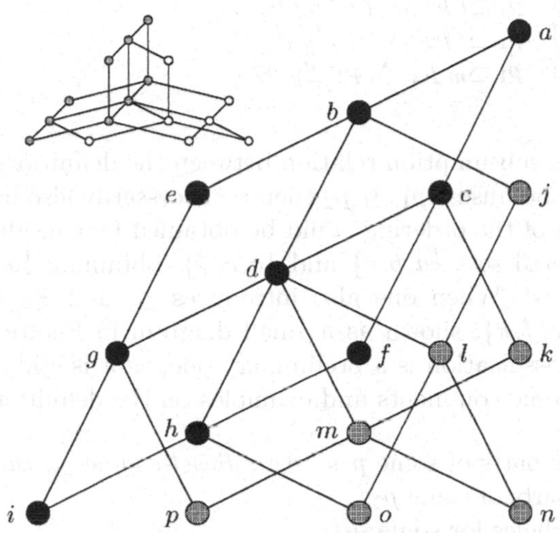

Fig. 4. Exclusiveness ordering for $\preceq$

Suppose that given two objects x_1 and x_2, we can decide[1] whether x_1 is a part of x_2, denote this by $x_1 \leq x_2$. Let $\preceq$ denote a given *part-of* relation we are interested in. We understand $\preceq$ as a relation on *properties*, i.e., $\preceq \subseteq P \times P$, or more specifically $\preceq \subseteq T \times T$. Then, when we say that $p_1 \preceq p_2$, what we mean is that an object x_1 that has p_1 (that is, $p_1(x_1)$), is a part of x_2 that has p_2. Let X_1 collects all parts—objects having p_1 which are parts of objects having p_2—and let X_2 collects all wholes. The criterion of *exclusiveness* is obtained by considering what mapping between X_1 and X_2 the relation $\preceq$ offers, i.e., is it *1–1, onto, total*? This leads to the following definitions.

(a) $p_1 \preceq_a p_2$ iff $\exists_{x_1} \exists_{x_2}\ x_1 \leq x_2$
(b) $p_1 \preceq_b p_2$ iff $\forall_{x_1} \exists_{x_2}\ x_1 \leq x_2$
(c) $p_1 \preceq_c p_2$ iff $\forall_{x_2} \exists_{x_1}\ x_1 \leq x_2$
(d) $p_1 \preceq_d p_2$ iff $p_1 \preceq_b p_2 \ \wedge\ p_1 \preceq_c p_2$
(e) $p_1 \preceq_e p_2$ iff $\forall_{x_1} \exists!_{x_2}\ x_1 \leq x_2$
(f) $p_1 \preceq_f p_2$ iff $\forall_{x_2} \exists!_{x_1}\ x_1 \leq x_2$
(g) $p_1 \preceq_g p_2$ iff $p_1 \preceq_e p_2 \ \wedge\ p_1 \preceq_d p_2$
(h) $p_1 \preceq_h p_2$ iff $p_1 \preceq_f p_2 \ \wedge\ p_1 \preceq_d p_2$

[1] We can decide whether x_1 is a part of x_2 for instance on the base of whether they are identity/functionality/separability dependent on each other, see Section 3.2.

(i) $p_1 \preceq_i p_2$ iff $p_1 \preceq_g p_2 \wedge p_1 \preceq_h p_2$
(j) $p_1 \preceq_j p_2$ iff $p_1 \preceq_b p_2 \wedge p_1 \not\preceq_e p_2$
(k) $p_1 \preceq_k p_2$ iff $p_1 \preceq_c p_2 \wedge p_1 \not\preceq_f p_2$
(l) $p_1 \preceq_l p_2$ iff $p_1 \preceq_j p_2 \wedge p_1 \preceq_d p_2$
(m) $p_1 \preceq_m p_2$ iff $p_1 \preceq_k p_2 \wedge p_1 \preceq_d p_2$
(n) $p_1 \preceq_n p_2$ iff $p_1 \preceq_l p_2 \wedge p_1 \preceq_m p_2$
(o) $p_1 \preceq_o p_2$ iff $p_1 \preceq_l p_2 \wedge p_1 \preceq_h p_2$
(p) $p_1 \preceq_p p_2$ iff $p_1 \preceq_m p_2 \wedge p_1 \preceq_g p_2$

Figure 4 presents subsumption relation between the definitions, e.g., $\preceq_a$ is more general than $\preceq_b$, because if $p_1 \preceq_b p_2$ then we necessarily also have that $p_1 \preceq_a p_2$. A simple version of the ordering could be obtained by considering a product of the linearly ordered sets $\{a, b, e\}$ and $\{a, c, f\}$, obtaining $\{a, b, e, c, f, d, g, h, i\}$ (black-filled nodes). When one also introduces $\preceq_j$ and $\preceq_k$ then the result is $\{a, b, e, j\} \times \{a, c, f, k\}$, shown as a small diagram in Figure 4, and its bigger variation; this classification is a preliminary one, as it is still incomplete.

We provide some comments and examples on the definitions:

(a) some p_1s are parts of some p_2s, e.g.: *diesel-engine* $\preceq_a$ *car*;
(b) all p_1s are parts of some p_2s;
(c) all p_2s are wholes for some p_1s;
(e) all p_1s are *not-shared* parts of some p_2s, e.g.: *carburator* $\preceq_e$ *engine*;
(f) all p_2s are *not-shared* wholes for some p_1s, e.g.: *engine* $\preceq_f$ *car*;
(i) all p_1s are *not-shared* parts of some p_2s, all p_2s are *not-shared* wholes for some p_1s, mapping between p_1s and p_2s is *1–1 onto*, e.g.: *mind* $\preceq_i$ *person*;
(j) all p_1s are parts of some p_2s, some parts p_1s shared by wholes p_2s, e.g.: *computer-printer* $\preceq_j$ *computer-network*;
(k) all p_2s are wholes for some p_1s, some wholes p_2s shared by parts p_1s, e.g.: *engine* $\preceq_k$ *speed-boat*;
(n) all p_1s are parts of some p_2s, all p_2s are wholes for some p_1s, some parts p_1s shared by wholes p_2s, some wholes p_2s shared by parts p_1s e.g.: *processor* $\preceq_n$ *computer*;
(o) all p_1s are parts of some p_2s, some parts p_1s shared by wholes p_2s, all p_2s are *not-shared* wholes for some p_1s, e.g.: *heart* $\preceq_o$ *person*;
(p) all p_2s are wholes for some p_1s, some wholes p_2s shared by parts p_1s, all p_1s are *not-shared* parts of some p_2s, e.g.: *spark-plug* $\preceq_o$ *petrol-engine*.

3.2 Essentiality and Separability

In this section we discuss a criterion called "essentiality" (see Figure 5) and derive a resulting ordering (see Figure 6).

Consider the top part of Figure 5. We intend to capture how identity / functionality changes of the part (whole) affect the whole (part). Let $+f$ denote the fact that the part *functions* properly, $-f$ that it does not (i.e., it has lost some

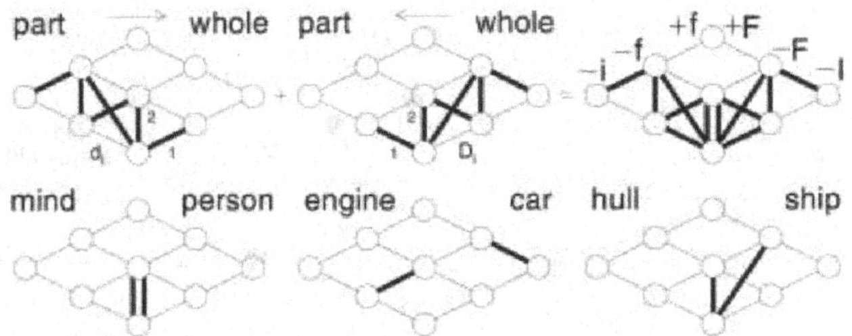

Fig. 5. Essentiality criterion

functionality), and $-i$ that it has lost its *identity* (and therefore, it ceased to exist); similarly, we employ $+F, -F, -I$ for the whole. To capture the *identity* and *functionality dependence*, consider the functions $d\colon \{-f, -i\} \longrightarrow \{+F, -F, -I\}$ and $D\colon \{-F, -I\} \longrightarrow \{+f, -f, -i\}$. We use d to describe how the whole depends on its part, and D to describe how the part depends on its whole. For instance, if $d(-f) = -F$ then we say that when the part stops functioning properly, then so does the whole. Given that we can order $\{+f, -f, -i\}$ and $\{+F, -F, -I\}$ to indicate how drastic the change to the part and whole is, $+f < -f < -i$ and $+F < -F < -I$, it is appropriate to require that both mappings are *order-preserving*, so we restrict d and D to functions that satisfy $d(-f) \leq d(-i)$ and $D(-F) \leq D(-I)$, respectively. For instance, one would not like to allow both $d(-f) = -I$ and $d(-i) = -F$, because if the part ceases to exist $(d(-i))$, then it also ceases to function $(d(-f))$, and therefore we should have $d(-i) = -I$, (because $d(-f) = -I$) rather than only $d(-i) = -F$. Therefore, we get the following functions $d_1, \ldots, d_6$.

$$d_1 = \{(-i, -I), (-f, -I)\},$$
$$d_2 = \{(-i, -I), (-f, -F)\},$$
$$d_3 = \{(-i, -I), (-f, +F)\},$$
$$d_4 = \{(-i, -F), (-f, -F)\},$$
$$d_5 = \{(-i, -F), (-f, +F)\},$$
$$d_6 = \{(-i, +F), (-f, +F)\}.$$

and we can order them: $d_i > d_j$ iff $d_i(-i) > d_j(-i)$ or $d_i(-i) = d_j(-i) \wedge d_i(-f) > d_j(-f)$. In an analogous way we obtain $D_1, \ldots, D_6$ and an ordering on them. Figure 5 illustrates the functions, and provides examples.

Given the ordered sets of functions $\{d_i\}_i$ and $\{D_i\}_i$ the essentiality ordering is given by $\{d_i\}_i \times \{D_i\}_i$, a product of the ordered sets of functions. This is shown in Figure 6, with examples of Figure 5. In the figure three nodes are marked *mp*, *ec* and *hs*, and represent the examples of Figure 5, namely, *mind* $\preceq$ *person*, *engine* $\preceq$ *car* and *hull* $\preceq$ *ship*, respectively.

In this way we can capture whether parts and wholes depend on each other—w.r.t. identity and functionality. The final result is that we can, given a particular *part-of* relation, see how strong the dependence is. It is important to make use

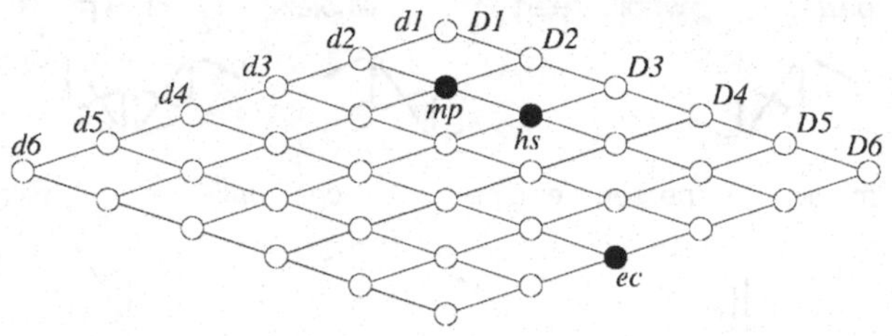

Fig. 6. Essentiality ordering for $\preceq$

of this information: depending on where our specific $\preceq$ is, different computations might be performed for $\preceq$.

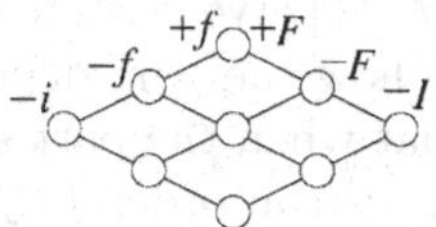

Fig. 7. Separability ordering for $\preceq$

Figure 7 presents a simple way of ordering $\preceq$-relations w.r.t. *separability*—when a part and its whole are separated, do they still function properly, or do they loose their functionality or identity? The same notation as in the discussion of essentiality is employed. For instance, marking a node labelled $(+f, +F)$ would mean that the part and the whole are fully separable, as they can continue to function properly after separation; a node labelled $(-i, -I)$ corresponds to the case of non-separability, as both the part and the whole would cease to exist when separated.

3.3 Classification of Part-of Relations

The criterion of *exclusiveness* results in an ordered set $\{\preceq_a, \dots, \preceq_p\}$ of *part-of* relations, while essentiality gives us $\{\preceq_{i,j} | \; i, j \in \{1, \dots, 6\}\}$, c.f. Figures 4 and 6. Comparing our results with e.g.: [11,9,13,8] it should be noted that [11] and [9] include topological concepts that would be crucial for more detailed treatment of *separability.* Both [13] and [8] focus on *transitivity* of the *part-whole* relation, which is only one of the possible ways of employing $\preceq$ in automated inferencing. The issue of transitivity, from our *exclusiveness* and *essentiality* perspective, converts to the issue of composition of $\preceq$-relations, i.e., given $\preceq_1, \preceq_2$ as elements of the set $\{\preceq_a, \dots, \preceq_p\} \cup \{\preceq_{i,j} | \; i, j = 1, \dots, 6\}$, what is $\preceq_1 \circ \preceq_2$, or which element of the set it is? We certainly have that, e.g., $\preceq_i' \circ \preceq_i''$ is a $\preceq_i$ (see Figure 4) and $\preceq_{22}' \circ \preceq_{22}''$ is a $\preceq_{22}$ (see Figure 6) but we do not provide the whole composition table here.

4 Conclusion

In this paper we have discussed some aspects of *ontology of properties* [7] and its use in constructing a *taxonomy*, providing some simple order-theoretic view of the criteria. We have then employed the ontology to restrict our treatment of *part-of* to *types*. We then proposed some criteria for classifying *part-of* $\preceq$, and derived the classification.

There is a large number of relevant issues that have been given no treatment in this paper. For instance, an axiomatic perspective on *mereologies* and *mereotopologies* presented in [11] provides an ordering on them. The approach would be crucial for a proper treatment of *separability*, where topological notions such as *overlap, connection* and *boundary* are needed. Other relevant references include [9] and [4]; for a recent paper on *separability*, addressing *identity* (does the *tail* of a *cat* exist?) see [12]. Summarising, vindicating ordered structures and exploring *kind-of* and *part-of* are important for ontological modeling and information integration.

References

1. B.A. Davey and H.A. Priestley. *Introduction to Lattices and Order*. Cambridge University Press, 1990.
2. Bernhard Ganter and Rudolf Wille. *Formale Begriffsanalyse. Mathematische Grundlagen*. Springer, 1996.
3. M. R. Genesereth and N. J. Nilsson. *Logical Foundations of Artificial Intelligence*. Morgan Kaufmann, 1987.
4. N. Guarino, S. Pribbenov, and L. Vieu. Modeling parts and wholes. *Data and Knowledge Engineering*, 20(3), 1996. Special issue.
5. Nicola Guarino. Formal ontology and information systems. In Nicola Guarino, editor, *Formal Ontology in Information Systems*, pages 3–15. IOS Press, 1998.
6. Nicola Guarino, editor. *Formal Ontology in Information Systems. Proceedings of the First International Conference (FOIS'98), Trento, Italy*. IOS Press, 1998.
7. Nicola Guarino and Christopher Welty. A formal ontology of properties. In R. Dieng and O. Corby, editors, *Proceedings of EKAW-2000: The 12th International Conference on Knowledge Engineering and Knowledge Management*, LNCS, pages 97–112. Springer Verlag, 2000.
8. Renate Motschnig-Pitrik and Jens Kaasboll. Part-whole relationship categories and their application in object-oriented analysis. *IEEE Transactions on Knowledge and Data Engineering*, 11(5), 1999.
9. Barry Smith. Mereotopology: A theory of parts and boundaries. *Data and Knowledge Engineering*, 20(3), 1996.
10. Mike Uschold and Michael Gruninger. Ontologies: Principles, methods and applications. *Knowledge Engineering Review*, 11(2), 1996.
11. Achille C. Varzi. Parts, wholes, and part-whole relations: The prospects of mereotopology. *Data and Knowledge Engineering*, 20(3):259–86, 1996.
12. Achille C. Varzi. Undetached parts and disconnected wholes. *Almen Semiotik*, 2000. To appear.
13. M. E. Winston, R. Chaffin, and D. Herrmann. A taxonomy of part-whole relations. *Cognitive Science*, 11:417–444, 1987.

Actions Made Explicit in BDI

Vineet Padmanabhan[1], Guido Governatori[2], and Abdul Sattar[1]

[1] Knowledge Representation & Reasoning Unit (KRRU)
School of Information Technology
Griffith University, Gold Coast Campus, Queensland, Australia.
{vineet,sattar}@cit.gu.edu.au

[2] Cooperative Information System Research Centre
Queensland University of Technology, Queensland, Australia
g.governatori@qut.edu.au

Abstract. The Belief, Desire, Intention (*BDI*) architecture is increasingly being used in a wide range of complex applications for agents. Many theories and models exist which support this architecture and the recent version is that of *Capability* being added as an additional construct. In all these models the concept of action is seen in an endogenous manner. We argue that the *Result* of an action performed by an agent is extremely important when dealing with composite actions and hence the need for an explicit representation of them. The Capability factor is supported using a RES construct and it is shown how the components of a composite action is supported using these two. Further, we introduce an OPP (opportunity) operator which in alliance with *Result* and *Capability* provides better semantics for practical reasoning in BDI.

1 Introduction

A paradigm shift is happening in both Artificial Intelligence and mainstream computer science with the advent of agents and agent-oriented approaches to developing systems, both on a theoretical and practical level. One such approach called *BDI* takes mental attitudes like *Belief*, *Desire* and *Intention* as the primitives and has given rise to a set of systems called *Intentional Agent Systems* [2, 5, 7, 9]. Of these the one by Rao and Georgeff [13] has been widely investigated due to its strong links with theoretical work. Many modifications have been made since the initial work, the most recent being the addition of a *Capability* [11] construct along with the three primitive modalities. In all these systems the concept of action is seen in an endogenous manner. Though it is possible to come up with accounts of action without representing them explicitly, many problems that plague endogenous formalisations can be avoided in exogenous ones. The later work by Rao [12] makes this shift but then it is restricted to the planning domain.

This paper can be viewed as a further extension of the existing BDI theory whereby we reason about the mental state of an agent during the execution of an action in an exogenous way. We investigate the close connection between the *result* of an action performed by a BDI agent and its capability of achieving that result. We argue that though the agent might have a capability to perform an action it need not be the case that the *opportunity* should always accompany it. This view gets importance when we

M. Brooks, D. Corbett, and M. Stumptner (Eds.): AI 2001, LNAI 2256, pp. 390–401, 2001.

take into consideration composite actions where one action follows the other ($\phi_1;\phi_2$), which means an agent performs ϕ_1 followed by ϕ_2. In such cases the *result* of the component parts of the action is needed for the overall success of the action. It also seems reasonable to declare that the agent has the relevant *opportunity* to perform the component actions in such a way that the execution leads to an appropriate state of affairs. By making actions explicit in BDI we try to avoid some of the problems that plague the endogenous systems when dealing with composite actions. We describe a formal relationship between the *Result, Opportunity, Belief, Desire* and *Intention* modalities. It is important to note the close connection between *Intention* and *Result*. For instance, if an agent intends to perform a plan, we can infer under certain conditions he intends the result of the plan. Similar is the case with Goals and Results.

This work is partially motivated by the KARO architecture of Van Linder [10] whereby we indicate how *Result* and *Opportunity* can be integrated to the existing BDI framework. Such an addition definitely paves way for a better understanding of the dynamics of BDI Systems. The rest of the paper is organised as follows. In section 2 we make a distinction between *intentional action* (actions with a pre-defined intention) and *intending an action* (actions with future Intention) and claim that composite actions fit well under *actions with future intention*. Section 3 gives a brief summary about the original BDI logic as developed by Rao [13] and the recent version of it with the *Capability* construct [11]. Sections 4 and 5 integrate two new operators RES and OPP with the existing BDI architecture. Section 6 gives the full picture of the new semantics. We have purposefully avoided the use of any temporal operators as it remains part of the future work. In section 7 we formalise the commitment axioms according to the new semantics and the conclusion and future work is depicted in section 8.

2 Intentional Action & Intending an Action

When one takes into account the compositional nature of actions $\phi_1;\phi_2$ (ϕ_1 followed by ϕ_2), it seems contradictory to believe that endogenous logics alone can account for the mental state of an agent during the execution of such actions. The problem with the current formalisms is in their failure to differentiate *Intentional Action* (Predefined Intention) from *Intending to do an Action* (Future Intention). Most of the work in BDI represent actions in the former manner. In the work of Rao [13] formulas like BEL(Φ), GOAL(Φ) etc. are used to denote the belief and goal of an agent performing an action ϕ. The formalism remains true for single actions, but when it comes to composite actions like ($\phi_1;\phi_2$) it fails to do justice as it is taken for granted that the execution of the first action necessarily leads to the second without mentioning anything about the *result* of the first action on the second. Based on the existing BDI architecture the concept of composite actions could be formalised as

$$\mathrm{INT}(does(\phi_1;\phi_2)) \Rightarrow does(\phi_1;\phi_2).$$

This need not be the case as the performance of ϕ_1 could result in a counterfactual state of affairs. It seems crucial to consider the *result* of the first action for the overall success of the composite action. In the same manner the formulas like

$$\mathrm{GOAL}(\phi_1;\phi_2) \Rightarrow \mathrm{CAP}(\mathrm{GOAL}(\phi_1;\phi_2))$$

seem to be problematic as the formulation doesn't tell anything about the ability of the agent if the first action results in a counterfactual state of affairs. It doesn't mention anything regarding the *Opportunity* the agent has in performing the second action.

It is important to make a division between the two action constructs of *Intentional* and *Intending* for our framework. The former relates to a predefined intention, where the *Result* of an action is taken for granted, whereas the latter concerns a future intention, where further deliberation is done as to what the result would be before an action is performed. Davidson [6] oversees such a division and extends the concept of *intentionally doing* to that of *intending to*. Though Bratman [1] points out this disparity the current formalisms does not allow for sound representation using the existing modal operators. Hence the need for additional constructs like RES and OPP. In intentional action, there is no temporal interval between what Davidson terms as *all-out evaluation and action*. So there is no room for further practical reasoning in which that all-out evaluation can play a significant role as input. The BDI framework gives primary importance to practical reasoning and hence to means-end reasoning which is important to avoid further deliberation at the time of action. Therefore it seems appropriate to categorise composite actions under future intentions as they play a crucial role in our practical thinking. More importantly, we form future intentions as part of larger plans whose role is to aid co-ordination of our activities over time. As elements in these plans, future intentions force the formation of yet further intentions and constrain the formation of other intentions and plans.

3 The BDI Logic

The logic developed by Rao and Georgeff [13] is based on Computational Tree Logic (CTL^*) [4] extended with a first order variant for the basic logic and a possible-worlds framework for the Belief, Goal and Intention operators. The world is modelled using a temporal structure with a branching time future and a single past called a *time-tree*. A situation refers to a particular time point in a particular world. Situations are mapped to one another by occurrence of events. The branches in a time tree can be viewed as representing the choices available to the agent at each moment in time. There are two kinds of formulae in the logic called the *state formulae* and *path formulae*. The former are evaluated at a specified time point in a time tree and the latter over a specified path in a time tree. Two modal operators *optional* and *inevitable* are used for path formulas. *optional* is said to be true of a path formula Φ at a particular point in a time-tree if Φ is true of at least one path emanating from that point. *inevitable* is said to be true of a path formula Φ at a particular point in a time-tree if Φ is true of all paths emanating from that point. The standard temporal operators $\diamond$ (eventually), $\Box$ (always), $\bigcirc$ (next) and $\bigcup$ (until), operate over state and path formulae. These modalities can be combined to describe the options of an agent.

Beliefs, Goals and Intentions are modelled as a set of belief-, goal- and intention accessible worlds associated to an agent in each situation. An agent x has a belief Φ, at a time point t (BEL(Φ)), if Φ is true in all belief-accessible worlds. It is the same case for *goals* (GOAL(Φ)) and *intentions* (INT(Φ)). The logic is based on the concept of strong realism which requires the goals to be compatible with beliefs, and intentions with goals. This is done by requiring that for every belief-accessible world w at time-point t, there is a desire-accessible world w' at that time point which is a sub-world for w. The converse does not hold as there can be desire-accessible worlds that do not have corresponding belief-accessible worlds. There are similar relationships between goal-accessible and intention-accessible worlds. The axiomatization of beliefs is the standard weak-S5 (or KD45) modal system [8]. The D and K axioms are adopted for goals and intentions, which means that goals and intentions have to be closed under implication and have to be consistent. We are concerned with the semantics of the mental attitudes and the details concerning the possible worlds semantics for various state and path formulae, is given in Appendix A. The set of belief-accessible worlds of an agent x from world w at time t, is denoted by $B_t^w(x)$. Similarly we use $G_t^w(x)$ and $I_t^w(x)$ to denote set of Goal and Intention-accessible worlds of agent x in world w at time t, respectively. When we state the rules and axioms the world w is taken for granted and the formalism is based on the agent, action and time. The semantics for beliefs, goals and intentions can be defined formally as follows

Definition 1 *For an interpretation M, with a variable assignment v, a possible world w and a temporal variable t, the semantics for the mental attitudes can be given as:*

- $M, v, w_t \models \mathrm{BEL}(\Phi)$ *iff* $\forall w' \in B_t^w(x), \langle M, v, w'_t \rangle \models \Phi$;
- $M, v, w_t \models \mathrm{GOAL}(\Phi)$ *iff* $\forall w' \in G_t^w(x), \langle M, v, w'_t \rangle \models \Phi$;
- $M, v, w_t \models \mathrm{INT}(\Phi)$ *iff* $\forall w' \in I_t^w(x), \langle M, v, w'_t \rangle \models \Phi$.

The rules and axioms depicting the semantic conditions is given as in [13]. The temporal variable t stands for a constant. We do not make any explicit representation of time as it remains part of future work.

Definition 2 *Let Φ be a formula,* BEL, INT *and* GOAL *be the modal operators for the mental constructs, done, do es be the operators for event types, and* inevitable *be the modal operator for a path formulae; then we have the following axioms:*

A1 $\mathrm{GOAL}(\Phi) \Rightarrow \mathrm{BEL}(\Phi)$
A2 $\mathrm{INT}(\Phi) \Rightarrow \mathrm{GOAL}(\Phi)$
A3 $\mathrm{INT}(does(e)) \Rightarrow do\,es(e)$
A4 $\mathrm{INT}(\Phi) \Rightarrow \mathrm{BEL}(\mathrm{INT}(\Phi))$
A5 $\mathrm{GOAL}(\Phi) \Rightarrow \mathrm{BEL}(\mathrm{GOAL}(\Phi))$
A6 $\mathrm{INT}(\Phi) \Rightarrow \mathrm{GOAL}(\mathrm{INT}(\Phi))$
A7 $done(e) \Rightarrow \mathrm{BEL}(done(e))$
A8 $\mathrm{INT}(\Phi) \Rightarrow inevitable \Diamond(\neg \mathrm{INT}(\Phi))$

Axiom A3 seems to be problematic because of the fact that the event e need not be necessarily restricted to a single action. If the agent has a choice of actions at the current time point, he/she would be incapable of acting *intentionally* until she deliberates and chooses one of them. It is the same case when the particular event is a composite action. The agent needs to deliberate on the result of the first action for the successful execution of the second one. It might also be the case that the agent lacks the relevant opportunity at that particular time point of doing the specific action. It becomes more relevant with the addition of the capability construct as given below.

The basic axioms with the capability construct are the same as those given in [11]. The temporal variable has been added in the semantics.

C1 CAP(Φ) $\Rightarrow$ BEL(Φ)
C2 GOAL(Φ) $\Rightarrow$ CAP(Φ)
C3 CAP(Φ) $\Rightarrow$ BEL(CAP(Φ))
C4 GOAL(Φ) $\Rightarrow$ CAP(GOAL(Φ))
C5 INT(Φ) $\Rightarrow$ CAP(INT(Φ))

The semantic condition of C2 and C3 can be given as follows

Definition 3 *Let $C_t^w(x)$ be the set of capability-accessible worlds of agent x in world w at time t.*

- $\forall w' \in C_t^w(x), \exists w'' \in G_t^w(x)$ *such that* $w'' \sqsubseteq w'$;
- $\forall w' \in B_t^w, \forall w'' \in C_t^{w'}(x)$ *we have* $w'' \in C_t^w(x)$

The first constraint means that for every capability-accessible world w' at time-point t, there is a goal-accessible world w'' at that time-point which is sub-world of w'. The converse doesn't hold as there can be goal-accessible worlds that do not have corresponding capability-accessible worlds. The second constraint is more complicated and deviates from the original interpretation as in [13]. It means that for every belief-accessible world w' at time-point t, all the capability-accessible worlds w'' which is a member of the belief (capability)-accessible worlds w' at time-point t is a member of the capability-accessible worlds w at time-point t, i.e., if the agent has a capability to achieve Φ, then the agent believes that she has such a capability.

4 Integrating Results

The BDI logic and the semantic conditions stated in the previous section shows that the compositional behaviour of actions has not been dealt within the BDI architecture. With the recent addition of the *Capability* construct we believe that it is worthwhile exploring this concept. Whereas the BDI framework is concerned with finding out what it means exactly to have the ability to perform some action, we try to focus on the compositional behaviour of actions. In other terms we are concerned with finding a relation between the capability to perform a composite action and relate it with the capability for the components of that action. Not all actions are treated equally in our approach but instead the result of each action is determined individually and then the conclusion is made whether the agent succeeds in performing that action. Three types of actions are dealt with ($\phi_1; \phi_2$) (ϕ_1 followed by ϕ_2), (*while* Φ *do* ψ) (ψ as long as Φ holds) and (*if* Φ *then* ϕ_1 *else* ϕ_2) (ϕ_1 if Φ holds and ϕ_2 otherwise). The composite action ($\phi_1; \phi_2$) is discussed in detail. An additional operator RES (*result*) is introduced to show the success/failure of the component actions. The RES operator functions as a *practition* operator which indicates the sequence of actions being performed, i.e., which action is performed next. The existing BDI architecture doesn't mention anything about the actual execution of actions. Since the transition caused by the execution of the action ($\phi_1; \phi_2$) equals the *sum* of the transition caused by ϕ_1 and the one caused by ϕ_2 in the state brought about by execution of ϕ_1, the RES operator helps in acting as a filter which checks whether the first action results in a counterfactual state or not. Such a filtering helps in avoiding further deliberation at the time of action as would otherwise be in situations arising from counterfactual states. For example, the success of the printer command (*lpr*), in a unix environment, depends on the result of the execution of the command in the spooler phase followed by the recognition of the command by the printer in the communication phase. Here the action needs to be broken down into compartments and the success of each action should be validated for the overall success. In such circumstances the RES operator helps in providing the necessary specification. This goes in alliance with our view of categorising composite actions under future intentions, where the scope of practical reasoning is more.

Definition 4 *Let ϕ_1, ϕ_2 be actions, then the axioms for the operator* RES *are:*

R1 $\mathrm{CAP}(does(\phi_1;\phi_2)) \Rightarrow \bigwedge_{i=1,2} \mathrm{BEL}(does(\phi_i)) \wedge \mathrm{BEL}(\mathrm{RES}(does(\phi_1))) \neq \perp$

R2 $\mathrm{GOAL}(does(\phi_1;\phi_2)) \Rightarrow \bigwedge_{i=1,2} \mathrm{CAP}(does(\phi_i)) \wedge \mathrm{RES}(does(\phi_1)) \neq \perp$

R3 $\mathrm{CAP}(does\phi_1;\phi_2)) \Rightarrow \bigwedge_{i=1,2} \mathrm{BEL}(\mathrm{CAP}(does(\phi_i))) \wedge \mathrm{RES}(does(\phi_1)) \neq \perp$

R4 $\mathrm{GOAL}(does(\phi_1;\phi_2)) \Rightarrow \bigwedge_{i=1,2} \mathrm{CAP}(\mathrm{GOAL}(does(\phi_i))) \wedge \mathrm{RES}(does(\phi_1)) \neq \perp$

R5 $\mathrm{INT}(does(\phi_1;\phi_2)) \Rightarrow \bigwedge_{i=1,2} \mathrm{CAP}(\mathrm{INT}(does(\phi_i))) \wedge \mathrm{RES}(does(\phi_1)) \neq \perp$

The first axiom states that an agent has the capability of performing a composite action $\phi_1;\phi_2$ then at some point of time the agent believes in doing ϕ_1 and ϕ_2 and believes that the performance of ϕ_1 does not end in counterfactual state of affairs (i.e, it does not end in falsity). Similarly the third axiom states that an agent has the capability of performing a composite action $\phi_1;\phi_2$, then at some point of time, the agent believes that it has the capability of doing ϕ_1 and believes in the capability of doing ϕ_2 and the result of ϕ_1 does not end up in a counterfactual state of affairs.

The semantic conditions for RES are similar to those given in Definition 3. For instance it can be shown that the semantic condition for R2 is

$$\forall w' \in C_t^w(x), \exists w'' \in G_t^w(x), \exists w''' \in R_t^w(x) \text{ such that } w'' \sqsubseteq w' \text{ and } w''' \sqsubseteq w'$$

where $R_t^w(x)$ is the set of result-accessible worlds of agent x in world w at time t.

This constraint means that for every capability-accessible world w' at time-point t, there is a goal-accessible world w'' at that time-point which is a sub-world of w' and a result-accessible world w''' which is a sub-world of w'. The converse doesn't hold as there can be Goal-accessible worlds that do not have corresponding capability as well as result-accessible worlds that do not have corresponding capability but only has the opportunity. We shall deal with the opportunity construct in the next section.

The action constructors dealing with *while Φ do ψ* (which means that ψ as long as Φ holds) and *if Φ then ϕ_1 else ϕ_2* (ϕ_1 if Φ holds and ϕ_2 otherwise) is crucial from computational point of view. For an agent to be able to perform an action *while Φ* do ψ it has to have the ability to perform some finite actions constituting the body of the while-loop as well as the opportunity to perform all the steps. Agents should not be able to perform an action that goes indefinitely. These specifications are formally represented by the following two axioms.

R6 $\mathrm{CAP}(\mathit{while}\ \Phi\ \mathit{do}\ \psi) \Rightarrow [\neg\Phi \vee (\Phi \wedge \mathrm{BEL}(\mathrm{CAP}(\mathit{does}(\psi)))) \wedge \mathrm{RES}(\mathit{done}(\phi)) \neq \bot]$
R7 $\mathrm{CAP}(\mathit{if}\ \Phi\ \mathit{then}\ \phi_1\ \mathit{else}\ \phi_2) \Rightarrow$
$[\Phi \wedge \mathrm{BEL}(\mathrm{CAP}(\mathit{does}(\phi_1))) \wedge \mathrm{RES}(\mathit{done}(\phi_1)) \neq \bot] \vee$
$[\neg\Phi \wedge \mathrm{BEL}(\mathrm{CAP}(\mathit{does}(\phi_2))) \wedge \mathrm{RES}(\mathit{done}(\phi_2)) \neq \bot]$.

The first proposition states that an agent is capable of performing an action *while* Φ *do* ψ, as long as Φ holds and the agent believes that it has the capability of ψ and result of ψ does not end in falsity. Similarly R7 can be read as, an agent has the capability of performing an action *if* Φ *then* ϕ_1 *else* ϕ_2, if Φ holds and the agent believes that it has the capability of ϕ_1 and the result of ϕ_1 is true, or it is the case that, Φ does not hold and the agent believes that it has the capability of ϕ_2 and result of ϕ_2 does not end in a counterfactual state of affairs.

5 Integrating Opportunity

Though in many cases it seems reasonable to assume that Capability implies Opportunity, when it comes to practical reasoning Opportunity seem to play a significant role. Van Linder [10] explains opportunity in terms of the correctness of action. An action is correct for some agent to bring about some proposition iff(*if and only if*) the agent has the opportunity to perform the action in such a way that its performance results in the proposition being true. Integrating opportunity lays further constraint on the part of the agent to think about an action before getting committed. Consider the example of a lion in a cage, which is perfectly well capable of eating a zebra, but ideally never has the opportunity to do so.[1] Using the BDI formalism we would have to conclude that the lion is capable of performing the sequential composition *eat zebra* ; *fly to the moon* which hardly seems to be intuitive. In such situations it is very important to know the combination of Capability and Opportunity so that no unwarranted conclusions can be drawn. We introduce an operator OPP whose intuitive meaning is agent x has the opportunity. The axioms for the OPP operator together with the Capability construct can be given as follows

Definition 5 *Let* ϕ_1, ϕ_2 *be actions, then we have*

O1 $\mathrm{CAP}(\mathit{does}(\phi_1;\phi_2)) \Rightarrow \bigwedge_{i=1,2} \mathrm{BEL}(\mathrm{OPP}(\mathit{does}(\phi_i)))$

O2 $\mathrm{GOAL}(\mathit{does}(\phi_1;\phi_2)) \Rightarrow \bigwedge_{i=1,2} \mathrm{CAP}(\mathit{does}(\phi_i)) \wedge \mathrm{OPP}(\mathit{does}(\phi_i))$

O3 $\mathrm{CAP}(\mathit{does}(\phi_1;\phi_2)) \Rightarrow \bigwedge_{i=1,2} \mathrm{BEL}(\mathrm{CAP}(\mathit{does}(\phi_i))) \wedge \mathrm{OPP}(\mathit{does}(\phi_i))$

[1] The example is taken from [10].

O4 $\text{GOAL}(does(\phi_1;\phi_2)) \Rightarrow \bigwedge_{i=1,2} \text{CAP}(\text{GOAL}(does(\phi_i))) \wedge \text{OPP}(does(\phi_i))$

O5 $\text{INT}(does(\phi_1;\phi_2) \Rightarrow \bigwedge_{i=1,2} \text{CAP}(\text{INT}(does(\phi_i))) \wedge \text{OPP}(does(\phi_i))$

O6 $\text{CAP}(\textit{while } \Phi \textit{ do } \psi) \Rightarrow [\neg\Phi \vee (\Phi \wedge \text{BEL}(\text{CAP}(does(\psi)))) \wedge \text{OPP}(does(\psi))]$

O7 $\text{CAP}(\textit{if } \Phi \textit{ then } \phi_1 \textit{ else } \phi_2) \Rightarrow [\Phi \wedge \text{BEL}(\text{CAP}(does(\phi_1))) \wedge \text{OPP}(does(\phi_1))] \vee [\neg\Phi \wedge \text{BEL}(\text{CAP}(does(\phi_2))) \wedge \text{OPP}(does(\phi_2))]$

The third axiom states that an agent has the capability of performing $\phi_1;\phi_2$ then the agent believes that he has the capability of ϕ_1, if he has the opportunity of ϕ_1, and, he has the capability of ϕ_2, if he has the opportunity of ϕ_2. Similarly O7 can be interpreted as an agent has the capability of doing the action (if Φ then ϕ_1 else ψ_2) then either Φ holds and the agent believes that he/she has the capability of ϕ_1 provided the opportunity exists or $\neg\Phi$ holds and the agent has the capability of ϕ_2 provided the opportunity exists. The other axioms can be interpreted in a similar manner.

6 Opportunity + Results

In [10] a division is made between *optimistic* and *pessimistic agents* and the interpretation of the OPP formulae is done accordingly. They make use of two dynamic operators $\langle do_i(\alpha)\rangle\varphi$ and $[do_i(\alpha)]\varphi$. The first one denotes that an agent i has to have the opportunity to perform the action α in such a way that φ will result from the performance (*Pessimistic Approach*): A pessimistic agent needs certainty. The second one is the dual of the first and states that if the opportunity to do α is present then φ would be among the results of $do_i(\alpha)$ (*Optimistic Approach*). The formula $[do_i(\alpha)]\varphi$ is noncommittal about the opportunity of the agent i to perform the action α. We do not go for such a division and interpret the OPP formulae in a realistic manner linked with the RES operator. Such a formalism helps in avoiding unwarranted results as were seen in the earlier examples. In what follows we present the axioms capturing this intuition.

OR1 $\text{CAP}(does(\phi_1;\phi_2)) \Rightarrow$

$$\begin{bmatrix} \text{BEL}(does(\phi_1)) \wedge \text{OPP}(does(\phi_1)) \wedge \text{RES}(done(\phi_1)) \neq \bot \\ \wedge\, \text{BEL}(does(\phi_2)) \wedge \text{OPP}(does(\phi_2)) \end{bmatrix}$$

OR2 $\text{GOAL}(does(\phi_1;\phi_2)) \Rightarrow$

$$\begin{bmatrix} \text{CAP}(does(\phi_1)) \wedge \text{OPP}(does(\phi_1)) \wedge \text{RES}(done(\phi_1)) \neq \bot \\ \wedge\, \text{CAP}(does(\phi_2)) \wedge \text{OPP}(does\phi_2) \end{bmatrix}$$

OR3 $\text{CAP}(does(\phi_1;\phi_2)) \Rightarrow$

$$\begin{bmatrix} \text{BEL}(\text{CAP}(does(\phi_1))) \wedge \text{OPP}(does(\phi_1)) \wedge \text{RES}(done(\phi_1)) \neq \bot) \\ \wedge\, \text{BEL}(\text{CAP}(does(\phi_2))) \wedge \text{OPP}(does(\phi_2)) \end{bmatrix}$$

OR4 $\text{GOAL}(does(\phi_1;\phi_2)) \Rightarrow$

$$\begin{bmatrix} \text{CAP}(\text{GOAL}(does(\phi_1)) \wedge \text{OPP}(does(\phi_1)) \wedge \text{RES}(done(\phi_1)) \neq \bot) \\ \wedge\, (\text{CAP}(\text{GOAL}(does(\phi_2)) \wedge \text{OPP}(does(\phi_2)) \end{bmatrix}$$

OR5 $\mathrm{INT}(does(\phi_1;\phi_2)) \Rightarrow$

$$\begin{bmatrix} \mathrm{CAP}(\mathrm{INT}(does(\phi_1)) \wedge \mathrm{OPP}(does(\phi_1)) \wedge \mathrm{RES}(done(\phi_1)) \neq \bot) \\ \wedge (\mathrm{CAP}(\mathrm{INT}(does(\phi_2)) \wedge \mathrm{OPP}(does(\phi_2)) \end{bmatrix}$$

OR6 $\mathrm{CAP}(while\ \Phi\ do\ \psi) \Rightarrow$

$$\begin{bmatrix} (\Phi \wedge \mathrm{BEL}(\mathrm{CAP}(does(\psi)) \wedge \mathrm{OPP}(does(\psi)) \\ \wedge \mathrm{RES}(done(\psi)) \neq \bot) \vee (\neg\Phi) \end{bmatrix}$$

OR7 $\mathrm{CAP}(if\ \Phi\ then\ \phi_1 else\ \phi_2) \Rightarrow$

$$\begin{bmatrix} \Phi \wedge \mathrm{BEL}(\mathrm{CAP}(does(\phi_1)) \wedge \mathrm{OPP}(does(\phi_1)) \wedge \\ \mathrm{RES}(done(\phi_1)) \neq \bot) \vee \\ (\neg\Phi \wedge \mathrm{BEL}(\mathrm{CAP}(does(\phi_2)) \wedge \mathrm{OPP}(does(\phi_2)) \wedge \\ \mathrm{RES}(done(\phi_1)) \neq \bot) \end{bmatrix}$$

Axioms OR1–OR7 are a formalisation of the results and opportunities together with the capability operator for composite actions. OR3 states that agents have the capability of doing a composite action $(\phi_1;\phi_2)$ to achieve Φ then the agent believes that it has the capability, provided the right opportunity, in each of the atomic states and the resulting condition is in alliance with its beliefs, i.e., it does not result in counterfactual situations. The actual execution of actions is made explicit through such a formalisation. Similarly OR6 states that if an agent has the Capability and Opportunity to perform a while-loop then it keeps this opportunity under execution of the body of the loop as long as the condition holds, i.e., as long as the result is true.

7 Commitment Axioms Revisited

In [13] a division is made in the commitment strategies of an agent, categorising an agent as *blindly committed agent*, *single minded agent*, and *open-minded agent*. A *blindly* committed agent maintains her intentions until she *actually* believes that she has achieved them; the *single minded* agent maintains her intentions as long as she believes that they are still options; finally an *open-minded agent* maintains her intentions as long as the intentions are still her goals. Based on the semantics given in the previous section the formalisation can be given as follows

CA1 $\mathrm{INT}(inevitable\Diamond\Phi) \Rightarrow$
$inevitable(\mathrm{INT}(inevitable\Diamond\Phi) \bigcup \mathrm{BEL}(\mathrm{RES}(\Phi)))$
CA2 $\mathrm{INT}(ineveitable\Diamond\Phi) \Rightarrow$
$inevitable(\mathrm{INT}(inevitable\Diamond\Phi) \bigcup \mathrm{BEL}(\mathrm{CAP}(\Phi)) \vee \neg\mathrm{BEL}(\mathrm{OPP}(optional\Diamond\Phi)))$
CA3 $\mathrm{INT}(ineveitable\Diamond\Phi) \Rightarrow$
$inevitable(\mathrm{INT}(inevitable\Diamond\Phi) \bigcup \mathrm{BEL}(\mathrm{GOAL}(\Phi)) \vee \neg\mathrm{CAP}(optional\Diamond\Phi))$

The *self-aware agent* mentioned in [11] can be added to the above set of commitment strategies directly. It seems that the formalisation depicted above is much more intuitive than the one given by Rao and Georgeff [13]. For instance the axiom of blind commitment states that, if an agent intends that inevitably Φ be eventually true, then the agent will inevitably maintain its intentions until she believes in the *result* of Φ. The addition of *result* is important in the sense that the blindly committed agent maintains the intentions until the agent *actually* believes that she has achieved them, i.e., until the agent has a justified true belief. This condition is needed for an agent blindly-committed to her means to inevitably eventually *believe* that she has achieved her means or ends. It also seems to be in alliance with the philosophical theories concerning the nature of belief. Similarly a single-minded agent maintains her intentions as long as she believes that she has got the capability for it. Since we do not say anything about an agent *optionally* achieving particular means or ends, even if the opportunity is present, the agent does not believe that optionally Φ be eventually true which is captured by the $\neg$BEL(OPP(*optional*$\Diamond\Phi$)). Finally, an open-minded agent maintains her intentions as long these intentions are still her goals or as long as she lacks the ability of optionally achieving them.

8 Conclusion and Future Work

The representation and reasoning about composite actions in a BDI environment forms the primary contribution of this work. Our work is motivated by the fact that many BDI systems provide no clue as to the actual execution of actions, and are only able to perform actions in an endogenous manner. When dealing with composite actions the actual execution of actions need to be represented and reasoned about for the overall success of the action. The addition of the two operators RES and OPP strengthens the semantics and functions as a filter in avoiding counterfactual situations. Though some mention has been done in [3] about the composite action construct $(\phi_1; \phi_2)$, it has been restricted to the Intention domain and nothing has been mentioned regarding the result of the actions. The only other comparable work is given by [10].

An explicit representation of temporal constructs can be seen as a further extension to this work. We have used the temporal operator as a static variable. When it comes to composite actions it is important to mention explicitly the time of each action and the temporal duration of the commitment an agent has towards each action. The interpretation of the $\bigcirc$ (next) operator in the original logic needs to be verified. For example when it comes to composite actions like $(\phi; \psi)$ the temporal operator $\bigcirc$ can be interpreted either as $\Diamond(\phi \Rightarrow \bigcirc\psi)$ or $(\phi \Rightarrow \bigcirc\psi)$. The temporal notion as to whether the action is performed now or eventually needs to be clarified. It would also be worthwhile to investigate *does*$(\phi; \psi)$ in terms of (*done*ϕ; *does*ψ), i.e., to find whether *does*$(\phi; \psi)$ is concurrent or sequential.

9 Acknowledgments

This work was partially supported by the Australian Research Council (ARC) **grant A49601783**. We would like to thank the members of the Knowledge Representation and Reasoning Unit (KRRU) for valuable suggestions.

A Possible World Semantics

A structure M is a tuple $M = \langle W, \{S_w\}, \{R_w\}, \mathbf{B}, \mathbf{D}, \mathbf{I}, \mathbf{L}\rangle$ where W is a set of possible worlds, S_w is a set of time points in world w; $R_w \subseteq S_w \times S_w$ is a total binary *temporal accessibility* relation; **L** is a truth assignment function that assigns to each atomic formula the set of world-time pairs at which it holds. **B** is a *belief-accessibility* relation that maps a time-point in a world to a set of worlds that are belief accessible to it; and **D** and **I** are *desire* and *intention* accessibility relations, respectively, that are defined in the same way as **B**.

There are two types of formulas: *state formulas* (which are evaluated at a state in a time-tree) and *path formulas* (which are evaluated against a path in a time-tree). They are defined as follows.

- any propositional formula is a state formula; if $\Phi \wedge \Phi'$ are state formulas then so too are $\Phi \vee \Phi'$ and $\neg\Phi$
- if Φ is a state formula then so too are BEL(Φ) and INT(Φ)
- if Ψ is a path formula then *optional*(Ψ) and *inevitable*(Ψ) are state formulas.
- Any state formula is also a path formula
- if Ψ and Ψ' are path formulas then so too are $\Psi \vee \Psi'$, $\neg\Psi$, $\bigcirc\Psi$, $\Diamond\Psi$ and $\Box\psi$

A *full path* in w is an infinite sequence of time points such that $(w_i, w_{i+1}) \in R_w$ for all i. Satisfaction of a state formula Φ is defined with respect to a structure M, a world w and a time point t, denoted by $M, w_t \models \Phi$.

Satisfaction of a path formula Ψ is defined with respect to a structure M, a world w, and a full path $(w_{t_0}, w_{t_1}, \ldots)$ in world w.

- $M, w_t \models \Phi$ iff $(w,t) \in \mathbf{L}(\Phi)$, where Φ is an atomic formula.
- $M, w_t \models \neg\Phi$ iff $M, w_t \not\models \Phi$
- $M, w_t \models \Phi_1 \vee \Phi_2$ iff $M, w_t \models \Phi_1$ or $M, w_t \models \Phi_2$
- $M, (w_{t_0}, w_{t_1}, \ldots) \models \Phi$ iff $M, w_{t_0} \models \Phi$, where Φ is a state formula.
- $M, (w_{t_0}, w_{t_1}, \ldots) \models \bigcirc\Phi$ iff $M, (w_{t_1}, \ldots) \models \Phi$
- $M, (w_{t_0}, w_{t_1}, \ldots) \models \Diamond\Psi$ iff $\exists w_{t_k} \in (w_{t_0}, w_{t_1}, \ldots)$ s.t. $M, (w_{t_k}, w_{t_{k+1}}, \ldots) \models \Psi$
- $M, w_{t_0} \models \Box\Psi$ iff $M, (w_{t_0}, w_{t_1}, \ldots) \models \Psi$, for all full paths $(w_{t_0}, w_{t_1}, \ldots)$
- $M, (w_{t_0}, w_{t_1}, \ldots) \models \Phi_1 \bigcup \Phi_2$ iff for some $i \geq 0$, $M, w_t \models \Phi_2$ and for all $0 \leq j < i$, $M, w_{t_j} \models \Phi_1$
- $M, w_{t_0} \models$ *optional*(Ψ) iff there exists a full path $(w_{t_0}, w_{t_1}, \ldots)$ such that $M, (w_{t_0}, w_{t_1}, \ldots) \models \Psi$.

References

1. M. E. Bratman. *Intentions, Plans and Practical Reason.* Harvard University Press, Cambridge, MA, 1987.
2. M.E. Bratman, D.J. Israel, and M.E Pollack. Plans and resource-bounded practical reasoning. *Computational Intelligence*, 4:349–355, 1988.
3. Lawrence Cavedon, Lin Padgham, Anand Rao, and Elizabeth Sonnenberg. Revisiting rationality for agents with intentions. In *Eight Australian joint conference on Artificial Intelligence*, 1995.

4. E. A. Emerson. *Temporal and Modal Logic*. Elsevier, Cambridge, 1990.
5. M. Georgeff and F. Ingrand. Decision making in an embedded reasoning system. In *In proc. of the International Joint Conference on Artificial Intelligence- IJCAI*, pages 972–978, 1989.
6. Bruce Vermazen & Merril Hintikka. *Essays on Davidson: Actions and Events*. Clarendon Pres, Oxford, 1985.
7. M. Huber. Jam: A bdi-theoretic mobile agent architecture. In *In Proceedings of the Third International Confernce on Autonomous Agents - Agents 99*, pages 236–243, Seattle, WA, 1999.
8. G.E. Hughes and M.J. Cresswell. *An Introduction to Modal Logic*. Routledge, London, 1968.
9. Fischer K. and Muller J. P. & Pischel M. A pragmatic bdi architecture. In Michael J. Woodridge, Muller J. P., and Milind Tambe, editors, *Intelligent Agents II, Agent theories, Architectures, and Languages, IJCAI'95 Workshop (ATAL),Montreal, Canada*, volume 1037 of *Lecture notes in Computer Science*, pages 203–218. Springer-Verlag, 1996. subseries of Lecture notes in Artificial Intelligence (LNAI).
10. Bernardus Van Linder. *Modal Logic for Rational Agents*. PhD thesis, Department of Computer Science, Utrecht University, 19th June 1996.
11. Lin Padgham and Patrick Lambrix. Agent capabilities: Extending bdi theory. In *Proceedings of Seventeenth National Conference on Artificial Intelligence(AAAI-2000)*, pages 68–73, Austin, Texas USA, July 30-August 3 2000. AAAI Press/The MIT Press.
12. Anand S. Rao. Means-end plam recognition- towards a theory of reactive recognition. Technical note - 49, Australian Artificial Intelligence Institute, 1994.
13. A.S. Rao and M.P. Georgeff. Modelling rational agents within a bdi-architecture. In Allen J. Fikes R. Sandewall E., editor, *Proceedings of the Second International Conference on Principles of Knowledge Representation and Reasoning (KR'91)*, pages 473–484. Morgan Kaufmann, 1991.

Wrapping Boosters against Noise

Bernhard Pfahringer, Geoffrey Holmes, and Gabi Schmidberger

University of Waikato, Hamilton, New Zealand,
{bernhard, geoff, gabi}@cs.waikato.ac.nz,
http://www.cs.waikato.ac.nz/~ml

Abstract. Wrappers have recently been used to obtain parameter optimizations for learning algorithms. In this paper we investigate the use of a wrapper for estimating the correct number of boosting ensembles in the presence of class noise. Contrary to the naive approach that would be quadratic in the number of boosting iterations, the incremental algorithm described is linear.
Additionally, directly using the k-sized ensembles generated during k-fold cross-validation search for prediction usually results in further improvements in classification performance. This improvement can be attributed to the reduction of variance due to averaging k ensembles instead of using only one ensemble. Consequently, cross-validation in the way we use it here, termed wrapping, can be viewed as yet another ensemble learner similar in spirit to bagging but also somewhat related to stacking.

Keywords: machine learning.

1 Introduction

Boosting can be viewed as an induction method that sequentially generates a set of classifiers by reweighting the training set in accordance with the performance of each intermediate set of classifiers. Theoretical attempts at explaining boosting's superior performance, based on so-called *margins* [17], would imply the following relationship between predictive performance of an ensemble and its size: given sufficiently expressive base classifiers, in the limit (i.e. the ensemble consists of infinitely many classifiers) each training example will have a margin of 1. This infinite ensemble will also be optimal in terms of predictive error on new test examples.

Obviously, one would expect this relationship to hold only in noise-free cases, and quite a few recent studies (e.g. [3]) have shown boosting's potential for over-fitting noisy data. Consequently, quite a few authors have proposed and investigated various modifications of the original AdaBoostM1 algorithm [5].

Some of these attempts focus on the reweighting policy, which in the original algorithm utilises an exponential function. Modified reweighting policies try to be less aggressive [4,6]. Usually the modified algorithm includes an additional parameter for regularization, which could, for example, be an estimate of the optimal ensemble size, or the maximal percentage of training examples, that the ensemble is allowed to misclassify. Also, Friedman's additive regression in-

M. Brooks, D. Corbett, and M. Stumptner (Eds.): AI 2001, LNAI 2256, pp. 402–413, 2001.

terpretation of boosting [8] adding a *shrinkage* parameter, can be seen as a counter-measure to exponential fast fitting of the training data. Alternatively, others have attempted to counter noise problems by using some kind of bagging *around* boosting. Whereas [12] directly bags boosted ensembles, MultiBoost [19] utilizes a bagging variant called *wagging* which simulates bagging's sample-with-replacement by poisson-distributed weights.

What all these methods have in common is their *indirect* approach of solving the anticipated problem: all force the user to specify additional parameters. Most of these parameters have an obvious interpretation, so we can expect the user to supply reasonable values. Take the case of BrownBoost as an example: the user is supposed to supply the true noise-level c as a parameter, thus allowing the algorithm to classify c% of the training examples incorrectly. Thus, we have only shifted the burden of selecting a reasonable ensemble size upfront to estimating another parameter. Still, there is no guarantee that the supplied estimates are effective for a given dataset.

Alternatively, in this paper we investigate a more direct approach: we try to estimate the appropriate size of the boosted ensemble directly by standard cross-validation. We will show how cross-validation can be computed efficiently for boosters, and we will also show that it naturally leads to ensembles of boosters at no extra induction time cost. The next section defines the algorithm. In section 3 we report on experiments involving various boosters and various levels of noise in datasets. Section 4 discusses our findings and in section 5 we draw our final conclusions.

2 Wrapping

Usually, boosting seems to be pretty stable even in the presence of noise: if enough boosting iterations are performed, a boosted ensemble outperforms an unboosted base-level learner most of the time, sometimes by an impressive amount. Even in the presence of noise the behaviour does not seem to deteriorate too much. But judging by the results cited above, boosting could have performed better in cases with noise. Recently, it has been shown that if the optimal Bayes error for some dataset is different from zero, the boosted ensemble will *not* be optimal in the limit, but some initial prefix of the same ensemble will [9].

We try to directly estimate this optimal size of the boosting ensemble by simple cross-validation. This is reminiscent of so-called early stopping in neural network induction (see e.g. [16]), where some portion of the training set is set aside and used as an independent evaluation set for judging whether performance is still improving or not. Standard k-fold cross-validation seems to be a more principled estimator, but of course involves a k-fold higher runtime cost. Trying to optimize parameters by cross-validation is not new, either. Most importantly, it has been formalized and called the *wrapper* approach for feature subset selection [10]. Also, in [7] cross-validation is used to determine the optimal size of an ADTree for a given dataset.

Table 1. Pseudo-code for two ways of estimating the optimal ensemble size: standard cross-validation, which is $O(k * N^2)$, and wrapping - incremental cross-validation - which is $O(k * N)$.

Standard CV	Wrapping (incremental CV)
	`func Wrap(k,data,booster,N)`
	`let bestSize = 0`
	`let minError = 1.0`
	`let boosters = new booster[k]`
`func estimateSize(k,data,booster,N)`	
	`for i from 1 upto k`
`let bestSize = 0`	`  boosters[i].initCV(data,i,k)`
`let minError = 1.0`	`endfor`
`for T from 1 upto N`	`for T from 1 upto N`
`  error =`	`  let error = 0.0`
`    cvEstimate(k,data,booster,T)`	`  for i from 1 upto k`
`  if (error =< minError)`	`    boosters[k].iterate()`
`    minError = error`	`    error += boosters[k].estimate()`
`    bestSize = T`	`  endfor`
`  endif`	`  error = error/k`
`endfor`	`  if (error < minError)`
	`    minError = error`
`return bestSize`	`    bestSize = T`
	`  endif`
	`endfor`
	`return bestSize`

Simple-minded application of cross-validation is hampered by excessive runtime needs. The issue here is not the multiplication due to k folds being used, but the fact that using simple-minded cross-validation for determining the right ensemble size shows quadratic behaviour in the number of calls to the underlying base-level learner: one call for an ensemble of size one, two calls for an ensemble of size two, and so on, yielding a total of $k * (n-1) * n/2$ calls for estimating all ensemble sizes from 1 up to n using k-fold cross-validation. This will clearly be a prohibitive cost for most datasets.

Luckily, there is a simple remedy available, due to the additive nature of boosting ensembles: for a given set of examples, the ensemble of size m is the union of the ensemble of size $m-1$ plus one more base-level classifier. Both ensembles use exactly the same $m-1$ classifiers. So the smart way to implement cross-validation is to do it incrementally, simply adding one base-level classifier after the other, interleaving these steps with performance estimation on the respective test-fold. Thus we can reduce the complexity of our estimation down

Table 2. Pseudo-code for the ensemble-returning variant of wrapping.

$W_{ensemble}$

```
func WrapEnsemble(k,data,booster,N)

let minError = 1.0
let boosters = new booster[k]

for i from 1 upto k
   boosters[i].initCV(data,i,k)
endfor

let bestBoosters = boosters.clone()     // <== CHANGED

for T from 1 upto N
   let error = 0.0
   for i from 1 upto k
      boosters[k].iterate()
      error += boosters[k].estimate()
   endfor
   error = error/k
   if (error < minError)
      minError = error
      bestBoosters = boosters.clone()  // <== CHANGED
   endif
endfor

return bestBoosters                     // <== CHANGED
```

to $k*n$ calls of the base-level learner, i.e. a linear number of calls. Therefore this cost is identical to the cost of just *one* k-fold cross-validation for the maximal ensemble size n, meaning that we get all the other estimates for sizes 1,2, up to $n-1$ at *no additional cost*. Also, bagging k times a boosted ensemble of size n would involve exactly the same cost.

We will call this improved implementation of cross-validation *wrapping*. Basically, we are estimating a single integer parameter in the range from 1 to N, where N is user-specified. This improved version is applicable whenever the algorithm in question is incremental in that parameter, which is obviously true for boosted ensembles due to their additive nature.

Pseudo-code comparing standard cross-validation to its incremental variant termed wrapping is given in Table 1. We assume that incremental boosters implement an interface that supports at least the following operations[1]:

[1] Of course, in practise the interface may also include additional functions for book-keeping, cleanup, general outputting, and so on.

- `initCV(data,i,k)`: which initializes the data-structures of the respective boosting algorithm, as well as separates the training data into the ith-fold for later testing and the remaining data as the ith-fold training set (it is sufficient to just keep the index and a local boosting weight for each training example, full copies are not required here).
- `iterate()`: which performs one boosting iteration, e.g. adding the next best test to an ADTree, or adding another C4.5 generated tree to an AdaBoosted C4.5 ensemble. Each iteration will only use its ith-fold training data subset for induction.
- `estimate()`: which returns an estimate of the predictive error rate of the ensemble at the current size, using the previously set-aside ith-fold test set.

Additionally, we can further improve the utility of wrapping in the following way: with the above scheme we first estimate a good size, and then induce one ensemble of exactly that size using *all* of the training data. Alternatively, quite similar to bagging [2], we can also just directly use these k ensembles of optimal size m as computed during cross-validation, yielding a $k * m$ size ensemble reminiscent of a bagged boosting ensemble. In that case we don't even have to perform the final induction step over all the training data. This variant is depicted in Table 2. As an alternative implementation, this variant might extract the best-sized ensemble for each fold separately, i.e. estimate the best size for each fold independently from all other folds. Thus the ensembles of each fold might vary in size. We have experimented with this alternative variant as well, but found that the estimates computed in such a manner were a lot more unstable, consequently causing inferior predictive behaviour.

So, in summary, wrapping (using k-fold cross-validation) allows us to both estimate the best size m for a boosted ensemble as well as compute a k-sized ensemble of such m-sized boosted ensembles, all in one go. Best of all, the total runtime cost of wrapping is about the same as that of k-times bagging the booster to the respective maximal size n.

In the next section we will investigate the utility of wrapping in terms of predictive error rates.

3 Experiments

This section compares the performance, in terms of predictive error rates[2], of three different boosting algorithms and their bagged and wrapped versions respectively.

The datasets used and their properties are listed in Table 3. All these sixteen datasets are taken from the UCI repository [1]. The datasets were evaluated using five times ten-fold cross validation. All datasets are two-class problems only, as some of the boosters we use are limited to such problems (currently). The noisy variants of these datasets were generated as follows: as we only deal

[2] Runtime increased by an order of magnitude: averaged factors are e.g. 8.43 for Bagging, 8.01 for Wrapping, and 9.04 for $W_{ensemble}$ normalized against AdaBoostM1.

with class-noise here, X% of the examples were chosen at random and their class-value was *flipped*. This noisification was done in a preprocessing step prior to experimentation, i.e. both training and testing was done on noisy data. This specific noise model (which has been used previously, e.g. in [14]) was chosen because of both its simplicity and its guaranteed noise levels: if X% is specified, exactly X% of all examples will be given a new, different class label.

Table 3. Datasets used for the experiments

Dataset	Instances	Missing values (%)	Numeric attributes	Nominal attributes
breast-cancer	286	0.3	0	9
breast-wisc	699	0.2	9	0
cleveland	303	0.2	6	7
credit	690	0.6	6	9
diabetes	768	0.0	8	0
hepatitis	155	5.4	6	13
hypothyroid	3772	5.4	7	22
ionosphere	351	0.0	34	0
kr-vs-kp	3196	0.0	0	36
labor	57	33.6	8	8
promoters	106	0.0	0	57
sick-euthyroid	3163	6.5	7	18
sonar	208	0.0	60	0
splice	3190	0.0	0	61
vote	435	5.3	0	16
vote1	435	5.5	0	15

To investigate the sensitivity of bagging and wrapping with respect to the underlying booster, we have conducted experiments with three different boosters:

- ADTree (our WEKA version of it [13]) using randomized search and a maximal ensemble size of 100.
- AdaBoostM1 over C4.5 (in their respective WEKA incarnations) with a maximal ensemble size of 10.
- An ADTree variant that triples the size of the tree at each iteration, with a maximal ensemble size of 8.

Unfortunately, it is somewhat tricky to depict all the variations along all axes available for comparison: noise-levels, algorithms, datasets. Therefore we will only give exemplary full tables of results for one base algorithm, namely for ADTree induction, for noise-free data and data with 30% class noise (the extreme cases), and only summary tables for everything else. So, Tables 4 and 5 depict predictive error rates (all tabulated results are considered significant if the difference between two pairs is statistically significant at the 1% level according to a paired two-sided *t*-test) for the following four versions of ADTree induction:

Table 4. Predictive error, no noise. The best entry in each line is set in boldface, a prefix star marks values that are significantly different from the value in the first column.

Dataset	ADTree	Bagging	Wrapping	$W_{ensemble}$
BREAST-CANCER	31.59	* 28.57	* 26.02	* **25.32**
BREAST-W	3.83	* **3.49**	* 4.32	3.63
CLEVE	21.78	* 17.15	* 17.28	* **16.03**
CREDIT-A	15.10	* **13.22**	15.68	15.07
CREDIT-G	25.50	* **23.58**	26.62	24.60
DIABETES	26.22	* **24.55**	26.45	* 24.58
HEART-STATLOG	20.30	* 18.00	* **17.11**	* 17.33
HEPATITIS	18.45	* **17.27**	17.53	18.09
IONOSPHERE	8.25	* 7.46	8.43	* **7.40**
KR-VS-KP	0.86	0.79	0.84	* **0.73**
LABOR	12.33	**10.47**	13.27	12.33
PROMOTERS	**6.76**	7.71	* 9.22	5.84
SICK	1.13	* 1.44	* 1.37	**1.11**
SONAR	13.66	14.50	* 16.64	**12.86**
VOTE	4.05	**3.96**	4.32	4.28
VOTE1	9.33	* 8.60	9.43	* **8.43**

- ADTree: using randomized search boosted 100 times. In ADTrees one boosting iteration adds exactly one test to the current tree.
- Bagged ADTrees: generate an ensemble of 10 ADTrees, each of size 100, by means of bagging.
- Wrapped ADTree: use wrapping to determine the optimal ADTree size of up to 100 tests, then induce a single ADTree of that size using the full training set.
- Wrapped ADTree ensemble: use wrapping to determine the optimal ADTree size of up to 100 tests, but instead of consequently inducing another tree, simply use the ensemble of the 10 trees of optimal size generated during cross-validation as the final ensemble.

Table 6 depicts the number of significant wins, draws, and losses over all noise levels and base-learners in a pair-wise manner for the two pairs we think are the most reasonable pairwise competitors: the sole booster versus its simple wrapped form, as well as the bagged booster versus the wrapped ensemble. Finally, Table 7 depicts the number of significant wins, draws, and losses for all pairwise combinations.

We can summarize all the figures of these tables into the following qualitative findings:

- Wrapping seems to be able to choose a reasonable size for the underlying boosting algorithm, as it rarely performs significantly worse than the booster itself.

Table 5. Predictive error, 30% noise. See Table 4 for more explanation.

Dataset	ADTree	Bagging	Wrapping	$W_{ensemble}$
BREAST-CANCER	48.82	* 45.83	* **44.34**	* 44.69
BREAST-W	36.71	* 35.34	* 34.43	* **33.71**
CLEVE	43.87	42.08	44.04	* **41.37**
CREDIT-A	40.03	* 37.91	* 37.42	* **36.20**
CREDIT-G	44.78	43.72	* **43.40**	* **43.40**
DIABETES	45.65	**44.61**	45.42	45.03
HEART-STATLOG	47.85	* 45.04	* 41.56	* **40.96**
HEPATITIS	36.80	* 34.12	35.13	* **33.24**
IONOSPHERE	44.45	* 40.97	* 41.31	* **39.84**
KR-VS-KP	33.63	* 32.44	* 31.97	* **31.91**
LABOR	50.73	**49.60**	52.20	51.53
PROMOTERS	52.44	**51.36**	51.45	52.60
SICK	33.92	* 32.51	* 31.36	* **31.14**
SONAR	37.89	38.66	* 40.26	**37.56**
VOTE	38.20	* 35.77	* 36.28	* **34.75**
VOTE1	36.68	* 35.13	* 30.61	* **30.43**

- Bagging also improves performance over just boosting most of the time, and it seems to perform better than simple wrapping.
- Wrapped ensemble performs as well as Bagging at low noise levels, and even better at higher noise levels.

Interestingly, there is also the odd dataset where boosting simply outperforms every method, even in the presence of noise. We suspect that this behaviour will occur mostly in situations were the available training set is actually too small. As it has been shown in [18], usual learning curves are pretty steep initially up to a point where they finally level out asymptotically to the best value a specific algorithm can achieve for a particular dataset. Now if the size of the given training set lies within this first steep region of the learning curve, a few additional examples can make a big difference. So bagging, which on average only includes about two-thirds of the training set in each bag, may be disadvantaged. Similarly, ten-fold cross-validation only uses 90% of the training set for inducing a classifier for each fold, so it too may be disadvantaged, but to a lesser degree. Still, cross-validation seems to exhibit an over-fitting tendency for smaller training sets.

We have repeated the same experimental setup (original algorithm, bagged version, wrapped version, wrapped ensemble) for two other boosting algorithms as well: AdaBoostM1 over C4.5, as well as a variant of ADTree induction, where instead of choosing the globally best test at each boosting iteration all locally (at each prediction node) best tests are added, thus tripling the size of the tree at each iteration. Consequently, we have limited the total number of boosting iterations to 8 for this variant, and set it to 10 for AdaBoostM1, which seems to be a reasonable value reported for AdaBoostM1 over C4.5 induction [15].

Table 6. Significant wins, draws, and significant losses for various pair-wise comparisons at various noise-levels. An entry “i-j-k” means that the first algorithm wins significantly i times, draws j times, and significantly looses k times against the second algorithm.

Noise	ADTree vs. Wrapping	Bagging vs. $W_{ensemble}$
00%	4-9-3	3-8-5
10%	0-10-6	2-12-2
20%	0-4-12	2-7-7
30%	1-6-9	0-10-6
	AdaBoost vs. Wrapping	Bagging vs. $W_{ensemble}$
00%	3-9-4	3-11-2
10%	2-6-8	0-5-11
20%	1-8-7	0-14-2
30%	1-9-6	0-13-3
	tADTree vs. Wrapping	Bagging vs. $W_{ensemble}$
00%	3-9-4	5-5-6
10%	1-7-8	4-7-5
20%	0-8-8	1-6-9
30%	0-6-10	0-8-8

4 Discussion

In this section we discuss two further opportunities offered by wrapping. First, wrapping allows for a more interactive approach to ensemble induction. As error estimates are computed sequentially for increasing ensemble sizes, these estimates can be displayed or graphed online, providing immediate feedback. This allows a user to immediately withdraw from investigating larger ensembles once the error estimates are either good enough or seem to have reached a plateau. Such interaction is valuable in exploratory data analysis.

Second, the additive nature of both wrapping and bagging also allows for further compression of ensembles, provided the underlying base-level learner itself is also additive. This is not the case for Adaboost in general, but it is certainly the case for ADTrees. Ensembles of ADTrees can be merged into a single ADTree, which usually reduces the total size by 20 to 30% (we compare the total number of prediction nodes in a wrapped ensemble of ADTrees to the total number of prediction nodes in the equivalent single merged ADTree). We are currently looking into more sophisticated ways of merging, thus hopefully compressing ensembles even further.

Regarding the apparent success of wrapped ensembles over bagging in high noise cases, an explanation of this fact would be most welcome, as both methods seem to be quite similar. Wrapping seems to enjoy a better variance reduction than bagging under these circumstances. At least, some experimental bias plus variance decompositions that we have computed in the same way as described in [11] seem to indicate that. On the other hand, we are reluctant to put too much trust in these results, as their overall error sums seem to be of high variance, varying considerably with the specific split chosen for estimation.

5 Conclusions

Our empirical investigation of wrapping seems to indicate that wrapping is a viable (and efficient) alternative to bagging boosters, especially when we suspect considerable levels of class-noise in our data. Simple wrapping allows us to choose an appropriate size, and the wrapped ensemble variant looks even more promising: at zero noise they are equivalent to bagged ensembles, and at higher noise levels they significantly outperform bagged ensembles, and their induction times are about equal. So consequently, wrapped ensembles provide an effective and efficient safeguard for boosters against noise.

In future work we hope to compare wrapping with some of the more sophisticated regularization approaches we have mentioned in the introduction, especially a comparison with BrownBoost and MultiBoost should be most interesting. Furthermore, we want to concentrate more on larger KDD-class datasets. Such experiments might be able to further strengthen our hypothesis that cross-validation is prone to overfitting small datasets. Additionally, we want to investigate the potential of merging, especially as a means of reducing total ensemble sizes, thus hopefully improving the comprehensibility of these merged ensembles. Furthermore, we are researching the applicability of wrapping to general complexity class estimation, a problem that is obviously not limited to boosting algorithms alone. Perhaps the most valuable achievement would be to find a way of replacing the currently user-specified maximal ensemble-size by some principled estimation. Unfortunately, our attempts in that direction have not been successful so far. We believe that something better than just presetting the maximal ensemble size to some ridiculously high value must exist.

A WRAPPER1D class as well as an appropriate interface for iterative classifiers, and a few exemplar iterative classifiers will all be included in the next version of the WEKA machine learning workbench [20], which is available[3] under the Gnu Public License.

References

1. Blake, C. L., Keogh, E., Merz, C.J.: UCI Repository of Machine Learning DataBases. Irvine, CA: University of California, Department of Information and Computer Science. [http://www.ics.uci.edu/ mlearn/MLRepository.html] (1998).
2. Breiman L.: Bagging Predictors, Machine Learning, 24(2), 1996.
3. Dietterich T.G.: An Experimental Comparison of Three Methods for Constructing Ensembles of Decision Trees: Bagging, Boosting, and Randomization, Machine Learning, 40(2), 139-158, 2000.

[3] WEKA can be downloaded from `http://www.cs.waikato.ac.nz/~ml`

4. Domingo C., Watanabe O.: MadaBoost: A Modification of AdaBoost, in Proceedings of the Thirteenth Annual Conference on Computational Learning Theory", Morgan Kaufmann, San Francisco, 2000.
5. Freund Y., Schapire R.E.: Experiments with a New Boosting Algorithm, in Saitta L.(ed.), Proceedings of the 13th International Conference on Machine Learning (ICML'96), Morgan Kaufmann, Los Altos/Palo Alto/San Francisco, pp.148-156, 1996.
6. Freund, Y.: An adaptive version of the boost by majority algorithm. In Proceedings of the Twelfth Annual Conference on Computational Learning Theory, Morgan Kaufmann, San Francisco, 1999.
7. Freund, Y., Mason, L.: The alternating decision tree learning algorithm. Proceedings of the Sixteenth International Conference on Machine Learning, Bled, Slovenia, (1999) 124-133.
8. Friedman J., Hastie T., Tibshirani R.: Additive logistic regression: a statistical view of boosting. Technical Report, 1998.
9. Jiang W.: Some theoretical aspects of boosting in the presence of noisy data, in Proceedings: The Eighteenth International Conference on Machine Learning (ICML-2001), Morgan Kaufmann, 2001.
10. Kohavi R., John G.H.: Wrappers for feature subset selection, in Subramanian D., et al.(eds.), Special Issue on Relevance, Artificial Intelligence, 97(1-2), 273-324, 1997.
11. Kohavi R., Wolpert D.: Bias plus variance decomposition for zero-one loss functions, in Proc. of the Thirteenth International Machine Learning Conference, Morgan Kaufmann, 1996.
12. Pfahringer B.: Winning the KDD99 Classification Cup: Bagged Boosting, SIGKDD explorations, 1(2), 65-66, 2000.
13. Pfahringer B., Holmes G., Kirkby R.: Optimizing ADTrees, Proceedings of the Fifth Pacific-Asia Conference on Knowledge Discovery and Data Mining, Springer, 2001.
14. Quinlan J.R.: The Minimum Description Length Principle and Categorical Theories, in Cohen W.W. and Hirsh H.(eds.), Proceedings of the 11th International Machine Learning Conference (ICML'94), Rutgers University, Newark, NJ, pp.233-241, 1994.
15. Quinlan J.R.: Bagging, Boosting, and C4.5, in Proceedings of the 13th National Conference on Artificial Intelligence, AAAI Press/MIT Press, Cambridge/Menlo Park, 1996.
16. Raudys S., Cibas T.: Regularization by Early Stopping in Single Layer Perceptron Training, in Malsburg C.van der, et al.(eds.), Artificial Neural Networks - ICANN 96, Springer, pp.77-82, 1996.
17. R.E. Schapire, Y. Freund, P. Bartlett, and W. S. Lee.: Boosting the margin: A new explanation for the effectiveness of voting methods. The Annals of Statistics, 26(5):1651-1686, October 1998.
18. Ting K.M., Low B.T.: Model Combination in the Multiple-Data-Batches Scenario, in Someren M.van and Widmer G.(eds.), Machine Learning: ECML-97, Springer, Berlin/Heidelberg/New York/Tokyo, pp.250-265, 1997.
19. Webb G.I.: MultiBoosting: A Technique for Combining Boosting and Wagging, Machine Learning, 40(2), 159-196, 2000.
20. Witten, I.H., Frank, E.: Data Mining: Practical Machine Learning Tools and Techniques with Java Implementations. Morgan Kaufmann Publishers, San Francisco, California (2000).

Table 7. Significant wins, draws, and significant losses for all four noise-levels and the following four algorithms: ADTree, bagged ADTree, wrapped ADTree, and a wrapped ensemble over ADTree. An entry "i-j-k" means that the row algorithm wins significantly i times, draws j times, and significantly looses k times against the column algorithm.

ADTree

no noise	Bagging	Wrapping	$W_{ensemble}$	10% noise	Bagging	Wrapping	$W_{ensemble}$
ADTree	1-5-10	4-9-3	0-9-7	ADTree	0-3-13	0-10-6	0-3-13
Bagging		8-7-1	3-8-5	Bagging		8-6-2	2-12-2
Wrapping			0-6-10	Wrapping			0-5-11
20% noise	**Bagging**	**Wrapping**	$W_{ensemble}$	**30% noise**	**Bagging**	**Wrapping**	$W_{ensemble}$
ADTree	0-2-14	0-4-12	0-1-15	ADTree	0-6-10	1-6-9	0-4-12
Bagging		3-9-4	2-7-7	Bagging		0-11-5	0-10-6
Wrapping			0-7-9	Wrapping			0-10-6

AdaBoost

no noise	Bagging	Wrapping	$W_{ensemble}$	10% noise	Bagging	Wrapping	$W_{ensemble}$
AdaBoost	2-2-12	3-9-4	1-4-11	AdaBoost	0-2-14	2-6-8	0-5-11
Bagging		8-6-2	3-11-2	Bagging		6-9-1	1-14-1
Wrapping			1-8-7	Wrapping			0-12-4
20% noise	**Bagging**	**Wrapping**	$W_{ensemble}$	**30% noise**	**Bagging**	**Wrapping**	$W_{ensemble}$
AdaBoost	0-6-10	1-8-7	0-6-10	AdaBoost	0-15-1	1-9-6	0-8-8
Bagging		5-9-2	0-14-2	Bagging		2-10-4	0-13-3
Wrapping			0-13-3	Wrapping			0-15-1

tADTree

no noise	Bagging	Wrapping	$W_{ensemble}$	10% noise	Bagging	Wrapping	$W_{ensemble}$
tADTree	2-4-10	3-9-4	0-7-9	tADTree	0-3-13	1-7-8	0-5-11
Bagging		7-8-1	5-5-6	Bagging		6-7-3	4-7-5
Wrapping			0-8-8	Wrapping			0-8-8
20% noise	**Bagging**	**Wrapping**	$W_{ensemble}$	**30% noise**	**Bagging**	**Wrapping**	$W_{ensemble}$
tADTree	0-6-10	0-8-8	0-4-12	tADTree	0-12-4	0-6-10	0-5-11
Bagging		1-11-4	1-6-9	Bagging		1-7-8	0-8-8
Wrapping			0-10-6	Wrapping			0-14-2

Continuous Temporal Models

Mark Reynolds

Murdoch University, Murdoch, Perth, W.A. 6150,
Australia.
m.reynolds@murdoch.edu.au

Abstract. We develop notation for describing a temporal structure over the real numbers flow of time. This forms a basis for various reasoning tasks including synthesizing a model from a given temporal or first-order specification. We announce an efficient procedure for finding a manageable description of such a model. There are applications in reasoning about multi-agent systems, understanding natural language, analogue devices, robotics and artificial reasoning.

1 Introduction

Linear temporal logic with a real-numbers flow of time is one of the most important and applicable of the many and varied temporal logics. A continuous model of time respects everyday human intuitions, allows dense activity by any number of parallel components (agents or threads as well as hardware) or by the environment, and can support arbitrary overlapping intervals of states and so, as argued in [16] or [8], may be suited for many applications, ranging from philosophical, natural language and AI modelling of human reasoning to computing and engineering applications of concurrency, refinement, open systems, analogue devices and metric information. In contrast to the situation with discrete time steps [25], or discrete branching of discrete steps, the continuous model and its temporal logics have not been well understood.

Any dense model of time may be appropriate for many of these applications but the real-numbers are probably the most specifically correct in terms of intuitions and classical physics. There are interesting differences between the temporal logics of the reals and of other dense flows ([8], [11] or [12]) but here our primary concern is the logic over the real numbers and the technical results will be about that logic.

For some applications it is sufficient to impose a "finite variability" requirement on the truth values of atoms and hence reduce (albeit messily) the problems to standard discrete time tasks. See [28] and [16] for examples. The idea is that each atom is only allowed to change its truth value a finite number of times during each bounded interval of time. This assumption is acceptible when we are considering a closed system of discretely ticking components taking on binary valued states. However, the finite variability assumption is not appropriate when we want to reason about the unlimited environment of a typical robot, the unbounded openness of an agent exposed to the Internet, an information system

M. Brooks, D. Corbett, and M. Stumptner (Eds.): AI 2001, LNAI 2256, pp. 414–425, 2001.

which includes one or many human users, a system with some states defined in terms of ranges of continuous valued measurements, a careful argument about new laws of physics in unfamiliar domains or the full richness of behaviour expressible in human language. So we make no such finite variability assumption: valuations are unrestricted and the logic general. In fact, in our logic it is possible to easily specify which components do satisfy finite variability while leaving other components (including the environment) unrestricted.

The most natural and useful such temporal logic is propositional temporal logic over real-numbers time using the Until and Since connectives introduced in [15]. We will call this logic RTL in this paper. We know from [15] that this logic is as expressive as the first-order monadic logic of the real numbers and so at least as expressive as any other usual temporal logic that could be defined over real-numbers time (see [35] for a brief account of a less expressive logic). RTL is decidable [8] and complete axioms systems are given in [11] and [29].

The decision procedure in [8] uses Rabin's non-elementarily complex decision procedure for the second-order monadic logic of two successors. In fact, deciding validity in the first-order monadic logic of the reals is a non-elementary problem [37]. The surprising recent result in [32] is that deciding (validity or satisfiability in) the equally expressive RTL is PSPACE-complete.

In this paper we move the development on another step and consider how to usefully describe possible models of a satisfiable formula in the language. This is not straightforward as we are dealing with the vissisitudes of propositional atoms over a richly complicated and uncountable flow of time. One of the main contributions of this paper is a straightforward recursive notation which allows the description of some real-flowed structures in terms of simple combinations of simpler structures. We also announce that any temporal formula (and hence also any first-order monadic formula) satisfiable over the reals is satisfiable in one of these constructible real-flowed structures.

The main result is a synthesis procedure or way of building a model of a satisfiable RTL formula. We sketch an EXPTIME procedure for finding the description of a model from any given satisfiable RTL formula. EXPTIME is shown to be a best possible bound.

The proofs of these results use the new mosaic techniques for temporal logic developed in [30], [17] and [32]. These mosaics are small pieces of a real-flowed structure. We try to find a finite set of mosaics which is sufficient to be used to build a real-numbers model of a given formula. Then we build the model. Unfortunately, the proofs of these results are too long and complicated to give in full in this paper and will be presented in a longer version [31].

In the next section we define RTL. We then describe some of the many important application areas for the logic and carefully contrast the use of RTL in these areas with some of the established techniques (such as interval logics). The new notation for describing an RTL model is given in section 6 where we also give a brief sketch of the important new synthesis result. Finally we describe some potential applications of the notation and the synthesis construction.

2 The Logic

Fix a countable set $\mathcal{L}$ of atoms. Here, frames $(T, <)$, or flows of time, will be irreflexive linear orders. Structures $\mathcal{T} = (T, <, h)$ will have a frame $(T, <)$ and a valuation h for the atoms i.e. for each atom $p \in \mathcal{L}$, $h(p) \subseteq T$. Of particular importance will be *real* structures $\mathcal{T} = (\mathbb{R}, <, h)$ which have the real numbers flow (with their usual irreflexive linear ordering).

The language $L(U, S)$ is generated by the 2-place connectives U and S along with classical $\neg$ and $\wedge$. That is, we define the set of formulas recursively to contain the atoms and for formulas α and β we include $\neg\alpha$, $\alpha \wedge \beta$, $\beta U \alpha$ and $\beta S \alpha$. As we will see $\beta U \alpha$ means that β holds at all times until a time when α holds. Hence the "β until α" reading. Similarly for "since".

Formulas are evaluated at points in structures $\mathcal{T} = (T, <, h)$. We write $\mathcal{T}, x \models \alpha$ when α is true at the point $x \in T$. This is defined recursively as follows. Suppose that we have defined the truth of formulas α and β at all points of $\mathcal{T}$. Then for all points x:

$\mathcal{T}, x \models p$ iff $x \in h(p)$, for p atomic;
$\mathcal{T}, x \models \neg\alpha$ iff $\mathcal{T}, x \not\models \alpha$;
$\mathcal{T}, x \models \alpha \wedge \beta$ iff both $\mathcal{T}, x \models \alpha$ and $\mathcal{T}, x \models \beta$;
$\mathcal{T}, x \models \beta U \alpha$ iff there is $y > x$ in T such that $\mathcal{T}, y \models \alpha$
and for all $z \in T$ such that $x < z < y$ we have $\mathcal{T}, z \models \beta$; and
$\mathcal{T}, x \models \beta S \alpha$ iff there is $y < x$ in T such that $\mathcal{T}, y \models \alpha$
and for all $z \in T$ such that $y < z < x$ we have $\mathcal{T}, z \models \beta$.

Definitions, results or proofs will often have a *mirror image* in which U and S are exchanged and $<$ and $>$ swapped. There are also plenty of abbreviations including "truth" $\top = p \wedge \neg p$; "falsity" $\bot = \neg\top$; "will" $F\alpha = \neg(\bot U \alpha)$; "will always" $G\alpha = \neg F \neg\alpha$; "for a while" $\Gamma^+\alpha = \alpha U \top$; and "arbitrarily soon" $K^+\alpha = \neg\Gamma^+(\neg\alpha)$.

In [15] it is shown that RTL is as expressive as the first-order monadic logic of the reals order. See [10] for details. This means that in terms of expressiveness it is the right temporal logic for such structures. It is important to note that there is a very similar looking but less expressive [32] temporal logic built from so called non-strict until and non-strict since which we do not consider in this paper.

A formula ϕ of $L(U, S)$ is $\mathbb{R}$-*satisfiable* if it has a real model: i.e. there is a real structure $\mathcal{S} = (\mathbb{R}, <, h)$ and $x \in \mathbb{R}$ such that $\mathcal{S}, x \models \phi$. A formula is $\mathbb{R}$-*valid* iff it is true at all points of all real structures. Of course, a formula is $\mathbb{R}$-valid iff its negation is not $\mathbb{R}$-satisfiable. The set of RTL formulas which are $\mathbb{R}$-valid has been axiomatized with the help of a special irreflexivity rule in [11] and also in [29] where only traditional inference rules are used. Let RTL-SAT be the problem of deciding whether a given formula of $L(U, S)$ is $\mathbb{R}$-satisfiable or not. The main result in [32] is:

Theorem 1. *RTL-SAT is PSPACE-complete.*

3 RTL Instead of Intervals

It is common to see interval based temporal logics and related formalisms used in AI applications which may have dense time semantic underpinning. These include artificial planning tasks [1], semantics for tense and aspect in natural language [19] and reasoning about the evolution of spatial relationships[36]. The density of time allows the arbitrary overlap of different actions or states.

There has been much discussion about the relative merits of point-based versus interval-based temporal logics in such applications [38]. It is probably generally accepted that in many applications an interval-based representation can be interpreted in terms of states holding at the points which make up the interval. (See [13], chapter 8, for a rare exception).

For constraint problems in planning it is often sufficient to just reason in terms of networks of intervals and the order relations between each pair. In fact, there are some very efficient procedures [23] for answering specific planning questions [22]. However, for more sophisticated or more general reasoning about intervals an interval temporal logic is necessary [14]. There is a modal diamond in Halpern and Shoham's logic HS for each of the thirteen of Allen's relations between intervals [2]. For example, $\langle D \rangle p$ is true of an interval x iff there is another interval y making p true such that x is a subinterval of y, ie x is related to y by Allen's "during" relation.

Unfortunately HS is highly undecidable: it is not even recursively axiomatizable. Because of this, researchers have often imposed restrictions on the temporal structures which are reasoned about and thus been able to define more manageable interval logics. For example, there is often a "homogeneity" assumption (see, for example, [18]) which does not allow properly overlapping intervals to satisfy the same atomic propositions unless they are both properly included in a larger interval which also satisfies that proposition. It thus becomes possible to recast such structures in a point-based way instead: a proposition holds at a point iff there is some interval containing that point which satisfies the proposition.

Another approach to making interval logics more manageable (in this case axiomatizable) is Venema's "flat" interval logic [39] in which a proposition holds at an interval iff it holds at the start point. Again this can easily be recast in point-based form.

Yet another approach to interval logics (usually in the discrete case) seen in [21] and [7] is based directly on evaluating truth of atomic propositions at points.

If it is the case as we have seen that the kind of reasoning about structures done using intervals can often be done with atomic propositions being evaluated at points then the expression and specification of properties can equally be done using the first-order monadic logic. For example, suppose that under our assumption we represent proposition p holding of the interval (u, v) by the monadic condition $\forall z((u < z < v) \rightarrow P(z))$ using a 1-ary predicate. The HS formula $\langle D \rangle p$ holding at (u, v) then becomes $\exists x \exists y((x < u < v < y) \wedge \forall z((x < z < y) \rightarrow P(z)))$.

Thanks to Kamp's theorem [15], we see then that we can equally well use point-based temporal logics such as RTL to express these properties. To say that now is the beginning of an interval satisfying $\langle D \rangle p$ becomes simply $pSp \wedge p \wedge pUp$.

4 RTL and Timing

In many applications of complex systems, timing or metric considerations are important. Reasoning about the behaviour of safety critical systems [24] and multimedia specifications [6] are just two examples. A good account of this so-called real-time logic area appears in [3]. Most of the timing work is built on discrete time temporal logics and indeed any move to a dense order of times usually results in highly undecidable logics [3].

Despite these sorts of results it is not hard to add a limited form of metric expressiveness to RTL: in fact it can be added within RTL with no loss of decidability. The basic idea is that we add a proposition whose truth represents the ticking of a clock and then we express timing requirements between events in terms of the number of ticks inbetween. The constraints can be made more strict by introducing grades of granularity of ticking.

We introduce a new proposition `tick`, say. Let us suppose that we start ticking at a certain time: it is not hard to change this construction if ticking forever into the past is required instead. By including the following conjuncts we impose a simple metric on our real structure:

$$\mathtt{tick} \wedge G((\neg\mathtt{tick})U\mathtt{tick}) \wedge G((\neg\mathtt{tick})S\mathtt{tick}).$$

The last conjunct is just a so-called non-Zeno condition which ensures "finite variability" of the ticking.

With a ticking clock we can now introduce some simple metric information into RTL formulas. For example, to approximate the condition that p must be followed within 1 tick by a q we can use $G(p \to \Diamond_{<2} q)$ with $\Diamond_{<2} q$ an abbreviation for $\neg((\neg q \wedge \neg\mathtt{tick}))U(\mathtt{tick} \wedge (\neg q) \wedge (\neg q \wedge \neg\mathtt{tick})U\mathtt{tick}))$.

If finer granularity of metrics are required then obviously we can introduce a finite few finer layers by requiring a certain number of sub-ticks between ticks and sub-sub-ticks between them and so on. The kind of logics needed for such granular reasoning can be found in [20]. They are usually computationally complex.

Of course, using abbreviations in terms of ticks as above does not allow us to quantify over metric values. However, as pointed out in [3] it is just this facility which makes metric temporal logics undecidable. It is also arguably the case that most practical applications of the metric logics can be specified without recourse to quantification.

5 RTL and Open or Compositional Systems

The suggestion that dense time temporal logics might be useful for compositional reasoning (as in distributed or multi-agent systems) was first made in [5]. If discrete time is used instead, then all sorts of difficulties arise when the steps(or ticks) of one component do not match up with the steps of another component or what is taken to be the steps of the combined system. The notation can become quite messy when proof rules have to allow for this mismatch as in [9] for example. The alternative with discrete time is the draconian supposition that there is a universal clock for all modules as in [24]. In contrast, if we use dense time then we do not need any such assumption. The proof rule is perfectly simple: from α holding of one component and β of another we can simply deduce that $\alpha \wedge \beta$ holds of the combined system.

Open systems, those in the presence of an unpredictable environment, present even more difficulties for discrete time formalisms as there is not necessarily any appropriate notion of its steps. As discussed in the introduction there are many circumstances when any sort of finite variability assumption becomes untenable. Once again, when we move to a dense model of time, a formal account is straightforward. For example, to say that no matter how soon we measure after the water boils, the steam pressure will have become detectable, simply use

$$\text{boil} \rightarrow \neg((\neg\text{detectable}) U \text{measure}).$$

In the near future, verification of properties of neural networks [33] may become an important application area for formal metric compositional reasoning in dense time.

6 Building Structures

We now introduce a notation which allows the description of a temporal structure in terms of simple basic structures via a small number of ways of putting structures together to form larger ones. In all cases the underlying flow of time of each structure will be an interval of the real numbers. Crucially we also allow the possibly of a singleton interval in which the flow of time is one point.

The general idea is simple: using singleton structures we build up to more complex structures by the recursive application of four operations. They are:

- the sum of two structures, consisting of one followed by the other;
- ω repeats of some structure laid end to end towards the future or alternatively towards the past;
- and making a densely thorough *shuffle* (see below) of copies from a finite set of structures.

These sorts of operations are familiar in the study of linear orders (see, for example, [8]) and the details of the notation and operations could have been done in a variety of ways.

There are slight complications to do with the need to join structures up end to end in the right way without leaving a gap. We choose to solve this problem by classifying our structures according to whether the end points are included or not. Thus we have open-open, open-closed, closed-open and closed-closed interval structures depending on whether the left end or right end respectively is included. Singleton structures are closed-closed. We want to end up with an open-open structure whose flow of time will thus be isomorphic to the whole real numbers.

Yet another unimportant complication is the fact that in giving a description of a particular and well-defined structure we must give a particular and well-defined concrete form to the shuffle. In this paper we will ignore this complication because, as we show in the longer paper, it turns out that any sufficiently thorough mixture of the sub-structures would do equally well.

The only really important detail is that the shuffle must involve at least one singleton structure. Copies of this are distributed as a sort of background filler throughout the shuffle thus guaranteeing the two crucial properties of intervals of the reals: Dedekind completeness and separability. Recall that we say a linear order $(T, <)$ is Dedekind complete if any subset $S \subseteq T$ with an upper bound (ie there is $t \in T$ such that for all $s \in S$, $s \leq t$) has a least upper bound. Recall also that the reals are separable ie have a countable suborder (eg the rationals) which are distributed densely throughout the reals.

So now we are interested in structures $(T, <, h)$ with $(T, <)$ being order isomorphic to some interval of the real numbers.

A *singleton structure* is just a structure $X = (\{x\}, \emptyset, h)$.

Assume we have interval structures $\mathcal{T}_1 = (T_1, <_1, h_1)$ and $\mathcal{T}_2 = (T_2, <_2, h_2)$ with $\mathcal{T}_1$ closed on the right and $\mathcal{T}_2$ open on the left. The *sum* $\mathcal{T}_1 + \mathcal{T}_2$ of $\mathcal{T}_1$ and $\mathcal{T}_2$ is then defined to be $(T, <, h)$ where:
$T = \{(1, t) | t \in T_1\} \cup \{(2, t) | t \in T_2\}$;
$(i, t) < (j, s)$ iff $i < j$ or $i = j$ and $t < s$;
$h(p) = \{(1, t) | t \in h_1(p)\} \cup \{(2, t) | t \in h_2(p)\}$.
This is clearly an interval structure itself: with a classification dependent on the left end of $\mathcal{T}_1$ and the right end of $\mathcal{T}_2$. Similarly we can find the sum of an interval open on the right with one which is closed on the left.

Given an interval structure $\mathcal{T}_1 = (T_1, <_1, h_1)$ which is closed on the left and open on the right we define the structure *wax* $(\mathcal{T}_1)$ to be $\mathcal{T} = (T, <, h)$ given by:
$T = \{(-i, t) | t \in T_1\}$;
$(i, t) < (j, s)$ iff $i < j$ or $i = j$ and $t < s$;
$(i, t) \in h(p)$ iff $t \in h_1(p)$.
This is an open-open interval structure.

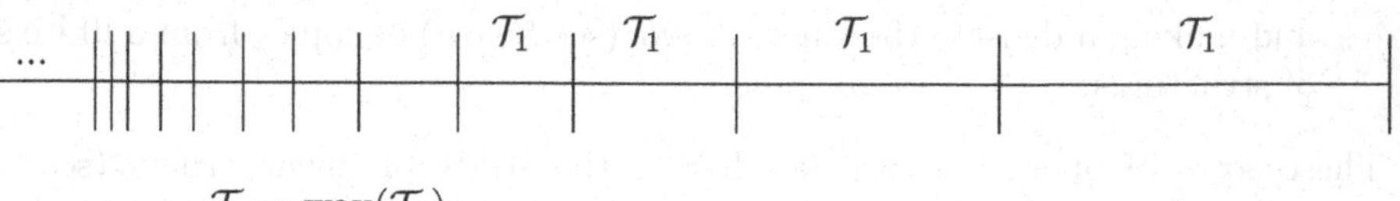

$\mathcal{T} = \text{wax}(\mathcal{T}_1)$

The mirror image is the open-open interval structure *wane* $(\mathcal{T}_1)$.

Now suppose that we have singleton structures $X_0, ..., X_r$ $(r \geq 0)$ and non-singleton closed-closed interval structures $\mathcal{T}_1, ..., \mathcal{T}_s$ $(s \geq 0)$. In the full version of the paper [31] we define the *shuffle* shuff$(X_0, ..., X_r, \mathcal{T}_1, ..., \mathcal{T}_s,)$ to be a particular open-open interval structure $\mathcal{T} = (T, <, h)$ which has a dense thorough mixture of copies of all the intervals (i.e. all X_i and all $\mathcal{T}_j$) in between. However, as mentioned above, any thoroughly dense mixture of the X_i and $\mathcal{T}_j$ will do: between any two copies of any X_i or any $\mathcal{T}_j$ must lie copies of each of the X_i and each of the $\mathcal{T}_j$. The singleton structure X_0, which must be present, is used as a sort of background filler to ensure that the combined order is Dedekind complete while still being separable. The case of $s = 0$ is allowed in which case the shuffle is built from just singletons.

We define the set of constructible interval structures to contain all the singletons and be closed under constructing sums, waxes, wanes and shuffles. Define the set of *Constructible real structures* to be the open-open constructible interval structures.

It is straightforward to make the notation completely formal in the case of a finite set of atoms, and this is the case when we are considering a particular temporal formula. For example, let $[p, \neg q]$ represent a singleton structure with the obvious valuation. We might then suggest

$$\text{shuff}([p,q]) + [p,q] + \text{shuff}([p,\neg q],[p,q]) + [p,q] + \text{shuff}([p,q])$$

as a model of $Gp \wedge (\neg((\neg q)Uq) \wedge \neg(qUq))Uq$.

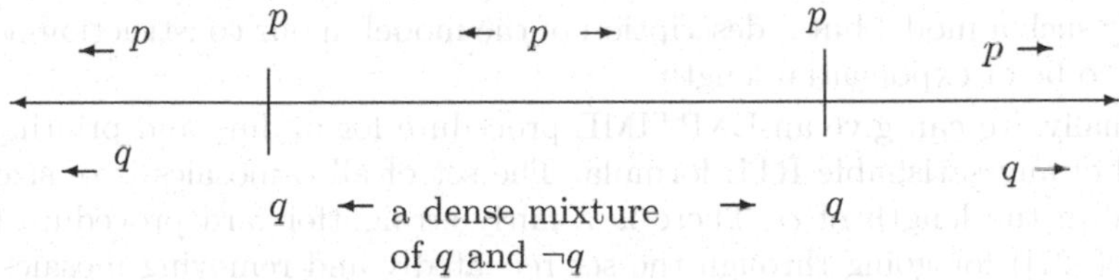

The main result announced in this paper is that an RTL formula has a real-flowed model iff it has a constructible real model. Thus we can describe a model in our new notation.

Theorem 2. *A formula ϕ from $L(U, S)$ is $\mathbb{R}$-satisfiable iff there is a constructible real model of ϕ. There is some c such that, in that case, a model can be described by an expression of shuffles, waxes, wanes and sums of length $< 2^{c|\phi|^2}$ (this bound is best possible).*

Furthermore, there is an EXPTIME procedure for finding such an expression.

The proof of the theorem is long, complex and technical in parts. It relies on the new temporal mosaic techniques developed in [30], [17] and [32] as well as some deep reasoning about properties of the real numbers. Much of the groundwork is laid in the proof of the complexity of the decision problem [32]. However, there is also important new work on the properties of shuffles, back and forth morphisms and a procedure for enumerating representations of models constructed from sets of mosaics. The full details will be presented in [31].

We only have space here to give a brief sketch of the proof. Suppose that we want a model of ϕ. Only a small finite closure set of subformulas of ϕ and their negations will be of interest to us. Mosaics are triples of sets of formulas from the closure set representing the formulas which are true at two points in a model and the formulas which hold at all points in between. That is the intuition behind the concept of a mosaic: the actual definition is just in terms of several conditions, called coherency conditions, on the relationship between the formulas which may appear in the three sets. For example, if $G\alpha$ is in the set representing the earlier time point then α must be in the set representing the later point.

We are able to show that the satisfiability of ϕ is equivalent to the existence of a finite set of such mosaics called a real mosaic system (RMS) which is closed under certain conditions (called saturation conditions). The saturation conditions impose a hierarchy of layers on the set of mosaics and require that mosaics in one layer can be decomposed in terms of shuffles, waxes, wanes and sums of mosaics in lower layers. The required model construction expression can be extracted recursively from these decompositions.

The bound on the length of the expression can be extracted from a linear bound on the number of levels needed in the set and a bound on the length of each decomposition from one level in terms of those below.

We can also show that length bound is best possible by considering a formula describing a binary counter. Given n, use n atoms to describe a counter which increases at discrete intervals. A formula of quadratic length (in n) can be used to specify such a model but a description of the model in our construction notation needs to be of exponential length.

Finally, we can give an EXPTIME procedure for finding and printing out a model of any satisfiable RTL formula. The set of all ϕ-mosaics is of size exponential in the length of ϕ. There is a fairly straightforward procedure (in the style of [27]) for going through the set repeatedly and removing mosaics which can not be fully decomposed in terms of other simpler ones in the set. If ϕ is satisfiable we will eventually end up with an RMS and another straightforward EXPTIME procedure reads out the description of a model of ϕ. By repeatedly decomposing mosaics as specified in the RMS we can produce the expression in a top-down manner.

Note that thanks to the expressive completeness result in [15], we know that any satisfiable sentence of the first-order monadic logic of the reals also has a constructible real model. To find a description of a model from the sentence must be a hard problem as deciding validity in this logic is non-elementarily complex [37]. One could use the separation technique of [10] to first find an equivalent temporal formula and then use the procedure above. The translation to the temporal formula must be the time-consuming part of the process.

Other results from [31] allow us to conclude that if we find all possible starting points (ie relativized mosaics in the RMS) and follow all possible ways of decomposing the mosaics then we will eventually output a list of possible models of the formula which is in a certain sense exhaustive. Any real model of ϕ will be back-and-forth equivalent to one of the constructible models which is listed.

It is worth noting that there is a similar sort of result to our theorem in [8] where it is shown that a RTL formula has a real-flowed model iff it has a model with the valuation of each atom being a Borel set, ie one obtained from open sets by iterated application of complementation and countable union. The important advantages of our new result are that we can give a finite representation in our notation and we give an efficient means for finding it.

We have space for a few more brief descriptions of the notation in action. The formula qUp has a model shuff($[p,q]$) (where, as above, $[p,q]$ is the singleton model with p and q holding at the point). The formula $K^+q \wedge \Gamma^+((\neg q)Uq) \wedge \Gamma^+(\neg\Gamma^+p \wedge \neg\Gamma^+(\neg p))$ has a model

$$\text{shuff}([p,q]) + [p,q] + wax([p,q] + \text{shuff}([p,\neg q],[\neg p,\neg q])).$$

The formula $\Gamma^+(p \vee ((\neg p)Up)) \wedge K^+((\neg p)Up) \wedge \Gamma^+(p \to K^+p) \wedge \neg((\neg p)Up)$ has a model

$$\text{shuff}([p],[\neg p] + \text{shuff}([\neg p]) + [p]).$$

7 Conclusion

We have seen that reasoning with continuous time has many and varied important applications across computing, AI and systems engineering.

Deciding satisfiability (or validity), as investigated in [32], is one of the most important reasoning tasks but others include synthesis, model-checking and deciding realizability. These three all involve notions of a formal representation of a model and so we consider how our new notation helps with these tasks.

Our main theorem above is a *synthesis* result: it shows how to make a model of a given formula (assuming the formula is satisfiable). In many application areas it is helpful to be able to check and develop formal specifications in terms of intuitions. One way to do this is to build a model (or several models) of the specification and see what other properties the model has. Identifying a preferred model of a statement is itself one of the main tasks of natural language processing. The RTL synthesis procedure can be used for this purpose. It is also useful for giving concrete counter-examples to incorrect consequences such as a desired property supposedly following from a detailed specification. Efficient systhesis techniques in limited sublanguages may also give rise to executable continuous temporal logics (c.f. [4]).

In fact, now that we we know RTL is no harder to reason with than well-known discrete time logics—discrete time formulas also can have models which take exponential size expressions to describe [34]—we can follow the suggestions in [16] and use continuous time for many of the compositional reasoning tasks associated with verification of specifications.

The construction notation itself might also be useful as a way of for describing real-flowed structures which can then be "model-checked" against a temporal or monadic specification. Techniques for model-checking in RTL need to be developed.

Other important future work includes development of the idea of "realizability" in continuous time. This is the question which arises when a temporal specification is given and we want to know whether a system in control of only some of the propositions in the specification can guarantee that the specification can be met whatever the behaviour of the environment which controls the rest of the propositions. Early work in a special case has been done in [26] but a fuller account will need development of continuous branching time logics.

References

1. J. Allen, H. Kautz, R. Pelavin, and J. Tenenberg. *Reasoning about Plans.* Morgan Kaufman, 1991.
2. J. F. Allen. Towards a general theory of action and time. *Artificial Intelligence*, 23(2):123–154, 1984.
3. R. Alur and T. A. Henzinger. Real-time logics: Complexity and expressiveness. *Information and Control*, 104:35–77, 1993.
4. H. Barringer, M. Fisher, D. Gabbay, R. Owens, and M. Reynolds, editors. *The Imperative Future.* Research Studies Press, Somerset, 1996.
5. H. Barringer, R. Kuiper, and A. Pnueli. A really abstract concurrent model and its temporal logic. In *Proceedings of 13th ACM symposium on the principles of Programming Languages, St. Petersberg Beach, Florida*, January 1986.
6. H. Bowman, H. Cameron, and S. Thompson. Specification and prototyping of structured multimedia documents using interval temporal logic. In H. Barringer, M. Fisher, D. Gabbay, and G. Gough, editors, *Advances in Temporal Logic*, pages 435–453. Kluwer, 2000.
7. H. Bowman and S. Thompson. A tableaux method for interval temporal logic with projection. In *TABLEAUX'98*, volume 1397 of *LNAI*, pages 108–123. Springer Verlag, 1998.
8. J. P. Burgess and Y. Gurevich. The decision problem for linear temporal logic. *Notre Dame J. Formal Logic*, 26(2):115–128, 1985.
9. J. Fiadeiro and T. Maibaum. Sometimes "tomorrow" is "sometime" – action refinement in a temporal logic of objects. In D. Gabbay and H. Ohlbach, editors, *Temporal Logic, Proceedings of ICTL '94*, number 827 in LNAI, pages 48–66. Springer-Verlag, 1994.
10. D. Gabbay, I. Hodkinson, and M. Reynolds. *Temporal Logic: Mathematical Foundations and Computational Aspects, Volume 1.* Oxford University Press, 1994.
11. D. M. Gabbay and I. M. Hodkinson. An axiomatisation of the temporal logic with until and since over the real numbers. *J. Logic and Computation*, 1(2):229 – 260, 1990.
12. D. M. Gabbay, I. M. Hodkinson, and M. A. Reynolds. Temporal expressive completeness in the presence of gaps. In J. Oikkonen and J. Väänänen, editors, *Logic Colloquium '90, Proceedings ASL European Meeting 1990, Helsinki*, number 2 in Lecture Notes in Logic, pages 89–121. Springer-Verlag, 1993.
13. D. Gabbay, M. Reynolds, and M. Finger. *Temporal Logic: Mathematical Foundations and Computational Aspects, Vol. 2.* Oxford University Press, 2000.
14. J. Halpern and Y. Shoham. A propositional modal logic of time intervals. In *Proceedings, Symposium on Logic in Computer Science.* IEEE, Boston, 1986.
15. H. Kamp. *Tense logic and the theory of linear order.* PhD thesis, University of California, Los Angeles, 1968.
16. Y. Kesten, Z. Manna, and A. Pnueli. Temporal verification of simulation and refinement. In J. de Bakker, W. de Roover, and G. Rozenberg, editors, *A decade of concurrency*, pages 273–346. Springer–Verlag, 1994.

17. M. Marx, S. Mikulas, and M. Reynolds. The mosaic method for temporal logics. In R. Dyckhoff, editor, *Proceedings of TABLEAUX 2000, Saint Andrews, Scotland, July 2000*, pages 324–340. Springer, 2000.
18. M.Leith and J. Cunningham. Modelling linguistic events. In H. Barringer, M. Fisher, D. Gabbay, and G. Gough, editors, *Advances in Temporal Logic*, pages 207–222. Kluwer, 2000.
19. M. Moens and M. Steedman. Temporal ontology and temporal reference. *Journal of Computational Linguistics*, 14, 1988.
20. A. Montanari, A. Peron, and A. Policriti. Extending Kamp theorem to linear orders with binary predicates to model time granularity. In *ICTL 2000, Proceedings of the Third International Conference on Temporal Logic*, 2000.
21. B. Moszkowski. *Executing Temporal Logic Programs*. Cambridge, 1986.
22. B. Nebel and C. Bäckström. On the computational complexity of temporal projection, planning, and plan validation. *Artificial Intelligence*, 66(1):125–160, 1994.
23. B. Nebel and H-J. Bürckert. Reasoning about temporal relations: A maximal tractable subclass of Allen's interval algebra. *J. of the ACM*, 42(1):43–66, January 1995.
24. J. Ostroff. Composition and refinement of discrete real-time systems. Technical report, DCS, York University, Ontario, Canada, 1998. CS-1998-10.
25. A. Pnueli. The temporal logic of programs. In *18th Symposium on Foundations of Computer Science*, pages 46–57, 1977. Providence, RI.
26. A. Pnueli and R. Rosner. On the synthesis of an asynchronous reactive module. In *ICALP89*, volume 372 of *LNCS*, pages 652–671. Springer-Verlag, 1989.
27. V. R. Pratt. Models of program logics. In *Proc. 20th IEEE. Symposium on Foundations of Computer Science, San Juan*, pages 115–122, 1979.
28. A. Rabinovich. On the decidability of continuous time specification formalisms. *Journal of Logic and Computation*, 8:669–678, 1998.
29. M. Reynolds. An axiomatization for Until and Since over the reals without the IRR rule. *Studia Logica*, 51:165–193, May 1992.
30. M. Reynolds. A decidable temporal logic of parallelism. *Notre Dame Journal of Formal Logic*, 38(3):419–436, 1997.
31. M. Reynolds. Synthesis of a continuous temporal model, in preparation.
32. M. Reynolds. The complexity of the temporal logic over the reals, submitted. Version available at http://www.it.murdoch.edu.au/~mark/research/online.
33. P. Rodrigues, J. Felix Costa and H. Sigelmann. Verifying Properties of Neural Networks. In J. Mira Mira, editor, *IWANN2001, 6th International Work-Conference on Artificial and Natural Neural Networks*, LNCS, Springer-Verlag, 2001.
34. A. Sistla and E. Clarke. Complexity of propositional linear temporal logics. *J. ACM*, 32:733–749, 1985.
35. A. Sistla and L. Zuck. Reasoning in a Restricted Temporal Logic. *Information and Computation*, 102:167–195, 1993.
36. O. Stock, editor. *Spatial and Temporal Resaoning*. Kluwer, 1997.
37. L. Stockmeyer. *The complexity of decision problems in automata and logic*. PhD thesis, M.I.T., 1974.
38. J. van Benthem. Temporal logic. In D.M. Gabbay, C.J. Hogger, and J.A. Robinson, editors, *The Handbook of Logic in Artificial Intelligence and Logic Programming, vol. 4*, Oxford University Press, 1995.
39. Y. Venema. Completeness through flatness in two-dimensional temporal logic. In D. Gabbay and H.-J. Ohlbach, editors, *Temporal Logic, First International Conference, ICTL '94*, volume 827 of *LNAI*, pages 149–164. Springer-Verlag, 1994.

Language and Commonsense Knowledge

Walid S. Saba

Knowledge and Language Engineering Group
School of Computer Science, University of Windsor, Windsor, ON N9B-3P4 Canada
saba@cs.uwindsor.ca

Abstract. It is by now widely accepted that a number of tasks in natural language understanding (NLU) require the storage of and reasoning with a vast amount of background (commonsense) knowledge. While several efforts have been made to build such ontologies, a consensus on a scientific methodology for ontological design is yet to emerge. In this paper we suggest an approach to building a commonsense ontology for language understanding using language itself as a design guide. The idea is rooted in Frege's conception of compositional semantics and is related to the idea of type inferences in strongly-typed, polymorphic programming languages. The method proposed seems to (*i*) resolve the problem of multiple inheritance; (*ii*) suggest an explanation for polysemy and metaphor; and (*iii*) provide a step towards establishing a systematic approach to ontological design.

1 Introduction

Recent work in natural language understanding (NLU) seems to be slowly embracing what we like to call the 'understanding as reasoning' paradigm, as it is quite clear by now that understanding natural language is, for the most part, a commonsense reasoning process at the pragmatic level, for example in such tasks as reference resolution, plan recognition, lexical disambiguation, prepositional phrase attachments, temporal coherence, and the resolution of quantifier scope ambiguities. For instance, consider the resolution of 'He' in the following:

John shot a policeman. He immediately
a) *fled away.* (1)
b) *fell down.*

It is quite difficult to imagine how children effortlessly resolve such references, if not by recourse to the commonsense facts that, typically, when *shot*(x,y) holds between some x and some y, x is the more likely subject to flee and y is the more likely subject to fall down. Other examples of commonsense reasoning in language understanding involve the resolution of quantifier scope ambiguities. Consider the following:

$$\left\{\begin{matrix} every \\ few \\ two \end{matrix}\right\} \textit{graduate student(s) at MIT submitted a paper to ACL'99} \qquad (2)$$

M. Brooks, D. Corbett, and M. Stumptner (Eds.): AI 2001, LNAI 2256, pp. 426–437, 2001.

We argue that the plausibility of wide scope *a* (implying a single paper) increases as the number of students involved in the relation decreases. Lacking a syntactic or a semantic explanation, this inference must be a function of our commonsense knowledge of how the 'submit' relation between students and 'papers' is typically manifested in the real world. Specifically, this inference is based on our commonsense belief that the *submit* relation between a *student* and a *paper* is typically [1..m]-to-1, where m is some small number. Moreover, different individuals seem to have a slightly different value for m, which is consistent with the findings of Kurtzman and MacDonald (1993) that different individuals seem to have different scope preferences in the same textual context.[1]

The 'understanding as reasoning' paradigm is certainly not entirely new in NLU research. Within the AI community, this paradigm was implicitly embraced by a number of authors (e.g., see Charniak, 1986; Hirst, 1986; Wilks, 1975; Schank, 1982). Unfortunately, however, these approaches were largely based on *ad hoc* algorithms built on top of *informal* knowledge representations. Due to the lack of formality, these procedures were hopelessly unscalable, and scalability was for the most part attempted by pushing the problem from the procedures to the data; which consequently led to the so-called *knowledge bottleneck*. The lack of progress in solving the *knowledge bottleneck* problem generally led AI researchers to either abandon inferential and knowledge-based approaches in favor of more quantitative approaches (e.g., Charniak, 1993), or to focus almost exclusively on the development of large commonsense knowledge bases (e.g., Lenet and Ghua, 1990). Within linguistics and formal semantics, one the other hand, little or no attention was paid to the issue of commonsense reasoning at the pragmatic level. Indeed, the prevailing wisdom (which might be partly due to lack of progress in AI-based NLU) was that a number of NLU tasks require the storage of and reasoning with a vast amount of background knowledge (van Deemter, 1996), an opinion that led some (e.g., Reinhart, 1997) to conclude that pragmatic approaches are 'highly undecidable'.

In our view both trends were partly misguided. In particular, we hold the view that while language understanding is for the most part a commonsense reasoning process at the pragmatic level, this reasoning process and the underlying knowledge structures that it utilizes must be formalized if we ever hope to build scalable systems. In this light we believe the work on integrating logical and commonsense reasoning in language understanding (e.g., Allen, 1987; Pereira & Pollack, 1991; Zadrozny & Jensen, 1991; Hobbs, 1985; Hobbs *et al.*, 1993; and more recently Asher & Lascarides, 1998; and Saba & Corriveua, 1997) is of paramount importance. Much of this work is directed towards formulating commonsense inferencing strategies to resolve a number of ambiguities at the pragmatic level. Although it has been shown (see Saba & Corriveau, 2001) that these inferences do not always require the storage of and reasoning with a vast amount of background knowledge, it is clear that a number of tasks do require such a knowledgebase. Indeed, substantial effort has been made towards building ontologies of commonsense knowledge (e.g., Lenat & Ghua, 1990; Mahesh & Nirenburg, 1995; Sowa, 1995), and a number of promising trends that advocate ontological design based on sound linguistic and logical foundations have started to emerge in recent years (e.g., Guarino & Welty, 2000; Pustejovsky, 2001). However, a systematic and objective approach to ontological design is still lacking. In particular, we believe that an ontology for commonsense knowledge must be *discovered* rather than *invented*, and thus

---

[1] An inferencing strategy that models individual preferences in the resolution of scope ambiguities at the pragmatic level has been suggested in (Saba and Corriveau, 2001).

it is not sufficient to establish some principles for ontological design, but that a strategy by which a commonsense ontology might be **systematically** and **objectively** designed must be developed.

2 Language Use as Guide to Ontological Design

Our basic strategy for designing an ontology of commonsense knowledge is rooted in Frege's conception of Compositionality. According to Frege (see Dummett, 1981, pp. 4-7), the sense of any given sentence is derived from our previous knowledge of the senses of the words that compose it, together with our observation of the way in which they are combined in that sentence. The cornerstone of this paradigm, however, is an observation that has not been fully appreciated regarding the manner in which words are supposed to acquire a sense. In particular, the principle of Compositionality is rooted in the thesis that "our understanding of [those] words consists in our grasp of the way in which they may figure in sentences in general, and how, in general, they combine to determine the truth-conditions of those sentences." (Dummett, 1981, pp. 5). This simple idea forms the basis of our strategy in designing an ontology for commonsense knowledge: what language allows one to say about a concept, tells us a lot about the concept under consideration. In other words, the meanings of words (i.e., the concepts), can be discovered from the manner in which the words are **used** in everyday language. As Bateman (1995) has suggested, *language* is the best-known theory on everyday knowledge. Assuming that language reflects thought, therefore, analyzing patterns of everyday language 'use' should provide useful clues to the structure of commonsense knowledge. As a motivating example, consider the nouns *table* and *elephant*, and the adjectives *smart* and *large*, out of which four syntactically well formed and semantically valid adjective-noun combinations can be made. One of these combinations, namely *smart table,* is typically rejected on pragmatic grounds, as it is at odds with our commonsense view of what tables are[2]. In particular, while it is sensible to say *large elephant* and *large table*, a *table* is not the kind of object for which *smart* applies. This analysis results in the fragment hierarchy shown in figure in 1 below.

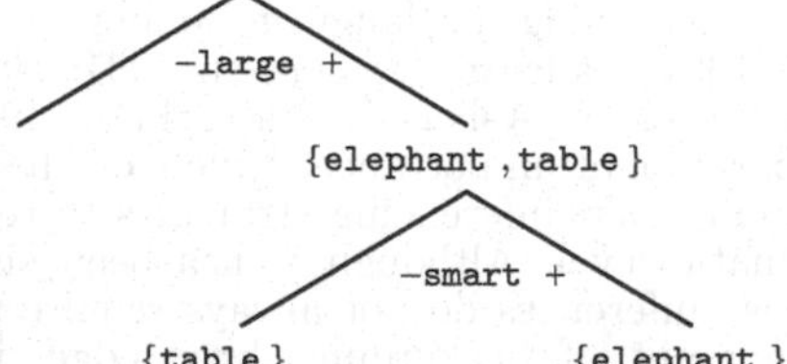

Figure 1. A simple analysis of four adjective-noun combinations.

Note that this kind of analysis is not much different from the type inferencing process that occurs in strongly typed, polymorphic programming languages. For example, consider the linguistic patterns and the corresponding type inferences shown in table 1. From $x + 3$, for example, one can infer that x is a `number` since numbers are the "kinds of things" that can be added to 3. In

[2] For the moment we are not concerned with metaphor.

general, the most generic type possible is inferred (i.e., these operations are assumed to be polymorphic).

Linguistic Pattern	Type Inference
$x + 3$	x is **number**
reverse(x)	x is a **sequence**
insert(x,y)	x is an **object**; y is **sequence** of x objects
head(x)	x is a **sequence**
even(x)	x is **number**

Table 1. Linguistic patterns and the corresponding type inferences.

For example, all that can be inferred from *reverse*(x) is that x is the generic type **sequence**, which could be a **list**, a **string** (a sequence of **characters**), a **vector**, etc. Note also that in addition to actions (methods), properties (truth-valued functions) can also be used to infer the type of an object. For example, from *even*(x) one can infer that x is a **number**, since lists, sequences, etc. are not the kinds of objects which can be described by the predicate *even*. Consider a set of concepts C and a set P of properties (or actions) that may or may not be sensibly applied to concepts in C:

$C = \{\texttt{list}, \texttt{string}, \texttt{set}\}$

$P = \{\texttt{empty}, \texttt{memberOf}, \texttt{size}, \texttt{tail}, \texttt{head}, \texttt{reverse}, \texttt{toUpperCase}\}$

Shown in figure 2 below is a number of sets $C_p = \{c \mid app(p,c)\}$ that are generated by the predicate $app(p,c)$ which is true if the property p is applicable to the concept c (figure 2a); and the concept hierarchy implied by the subset relationship among these sets (figure 2b). Note that each (unique) set corresponds to a class in the hierarchy. Equal sets (e.g. $C_{\texttt{tail}}$ and $C_{\texttt{head}}$) correspond to the same class. A class could be given any meaningful label that intuitively represents all the concepts in the class. For example, in figure 2b **sequence** is used to collectively refer to sets, strings and lists.

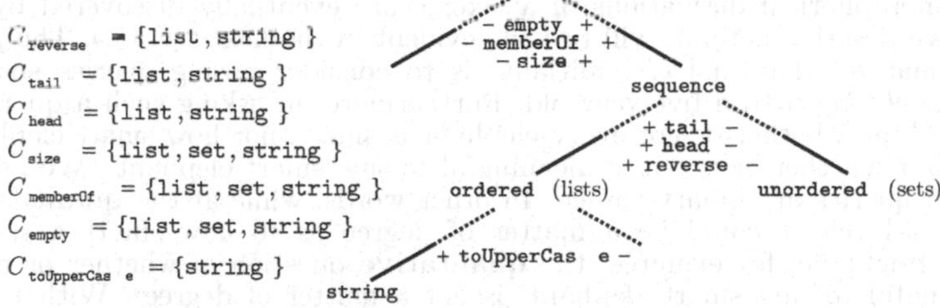

Figure 2. Sets generated by $app(p,c)$ and the hierarchical structure implied by them.

Clearly, there are a number of rules that can be established from the concept hierarchy shown in figure 2. For example, one can state the following:

$$(\forall c)(app(reverse,c) \supset app(size,c)) \tag{3}$$

$$(\exists c)(app(size,c) \wedge \neg app(reverse,c)) \tag{4}$$

$$(\forall c)(app(tail,c) \equiv app(head,c)) \tag{5}$$

Here (3) states that whenever *it makes sense* to *reverse* an object *c*, then it also makes sense to ask for the *size* of *c*. This essentially means that an object to which the *size* operation can be applied must be a parent of an object to which the *reverse* operation can be applied. (4), on the other hand, states that there are objects for which the *size* operation applies, but for which the *reverse* operation does not apply. Finally, (5) states that whenever it makes sense to ask for the *head* of an object then it also makes sense to ask for its *tail*, and vice versa. Thus while there must be at least one property that defines a concept, there could be many (we will have more to say about this below.) Finally, it must be noted that in performing this analysis we have assumed that the predicate *app(p,c)* is a Boolean-valued function, which has the consequence that the type hierarchy is a strict binary tree. In fact, this is one of the main characteristics of our method, and has led to two important results: (*i*) multiple inheritance is completely avoided; and (*ii*) by not allowing any ambiguity in the interpretation of *app(p,c)*, lexical ambiguity, polysemy and metaphor are explicitly represented in the hierarchy.

3 Language and Commonsense Knowledge

The work described here was motivated by the following two assumptions: (*i*) the process of language understanding is for the most part a commonsense reasoning process at the pragmatic level; and (*ii*) since children master spoken language at a very young age, children must be performing commonsense reasoning at the pragmatic level, and consequently, they must posses all the commonsense knowledge required to understand spoken language[3]. In other words, we are assuming that deciding on a particular *app(v,c)* should not be controversial, and that children can easily and consistently answer simple questions such as *do elephants fly*, *do mountains talk*, *do books run*, etc. Note that in answering these questions it is clear that one has to be coconscious of metaphor. For example, while tables, people, and feelings can be strong (i.e., it is quite meaningful to say *strong table, strong person, strong feeling*), it is clear that the senses of *strong* in these three cases are quite distinct. In fact, the various metaphorical derivations of a lexeme are eventually discovered by the process we describe here, as will become evident in the next sections. The point here is that all that matters, initially, is to consider posing queries such as *app*(*smart*,*elephant*) to a five-year old. Furthermore, in asking such a query we are not asking whether or not every elephant is smart, nor how smart elephants can be, but whether or not it is meaningful to say 'smart elephant'. We believe that such queries are binary-valued. In other words, while at the **quantitative** (or a data-level) it could be a matter of degree as to how smart a specific elephant might be, for example, the **qualitative** question of whether or not it is meaningful to say 'smart elephant' is not a matter of degree[4]. With this in

[3] It may very well be the case that "everything we know we learned in kindergarten"!

[4] We will not dwell on this issue too much here except to say that as Elkan (1993) has convincingly argued, to avoid certain contradictions logical reasoning must at some level collapse to a binary logic. While Elkan's argument seemed to be susceptible to some criticism (e.g., Dubois *et al.* (1994)), there are more convincing arguments supporting the same result. For example, consider the following:

(1) *John likes every famous actress*
(2) *Liz is a famous actress*
(3) *John likes Liz*

mind, our basic approach to discovering the ontology of commonsense knowledge can be summarized as follows:

- Select a set of adjectives and verbs, $V = \{v_1,\dots,v_m\}$.
- Select a set of nouns $C = \{c_1,\dots,c_n\}$.
- Generate sets $C_i = \{c \in C \mid app(v_i,c)\}, 1 \le i \le m$ for every $v_i \in V$
- Analyse the subset relationship between all sets $C_i \in \{C_1,\dots,C_m\}$

As an initial example, consider the set of verbs $V =$ {**move**, **walk**, **run**, **talk**, **reason**} and the set of nouns $C =$ {**Rational**, **Bird**, **Elephant**, **Shark**, **Animal**, **Ameba**}. Repeated application of *app*(v,c) results in the following sets:

$C_{\texttt{move}} = \{\texttt{Rational}, \texttt{Animal}, \texttt{Bird}, \texttt{Elephant}, \texttt{Shark}, \texttt{Ameba}\}$
$C_{\texttt{talk}} = \{\texttt{Rational}\}$
$C_{\texttt{reason}} = \{\texttt{Rational}\}$
$C_{\texttt{think}} = \{\texttt{Animal}\}$
$C_{\texttt{walk}} = \{\texttt{Rational}, \texttt{Bird}, \texttt{Elephant}\}$
$C_{\texttt{run}} = \{\texttt{Rational}, \texttt{Bird}, \texttt{Elephant}\}$

First we note that while some decisions could 'technically' be questioned (say by a biologist), our strategy was to simply consider the question from the point of view of commonsense. In deciding on a particular *app*(v,c) we considered the query poised to a five-year old: do elephants fly, do they run, do they talk, etc. Questionable situations were simply ignored. This initial process resulted in the hierarchy shown in figure 3 below. Some of the sets indicating positive left and right attributes are given in figure 4 below. Note that some powerful inferential patterns that can be used in language processing are implicit in the structure shown in figure 3. For example, what does not think does not hurt (L_7), what walks also runs (L_8), anything that lives evolves (L_3 and L_4), etc. Note that according to our strategy every concept at the knowledge- (or commonsense-) level must 'own' some unique property, and this must also be linguistically reflected by some verb or adjective. This might be similar to what Fodor (1998, p. 126) meant by "having a concept is being locked to a property." In fact, it seems that this is one way to test the demarcation line between commonsense and domain specific knowledge. In particular, it seems that domain-specific concepts are not uniquely locked to any word in the language.

4 Polysemy and Metaphor

In our approach the occurrence of a verb/adjective at any place and at any level in the hierarchy always refers to a *unique sense* of that verb/adjective. Therefore one expects similar senses of a lexeme to apply to concepts along the

Clearly, (1) and (2) should entail (3), regardless of how famous Liz actually is. Using any quantitative model (such as fuzzy logic), this intuitive entailment cannot be produced (we leave the details of formulating this in fuzzy logic as an exercise!) The problem here is that at the qualitative level the truth-value of *famous*(x) must collapse to either true or false, since at that level all that matters is whether or not Liz is famous, not how famous she actually is.

same path, albeit at different levels in the hierarchy. In particular, one would expect that highly ambiguous verbs to apply to concepts higher-up in the hierarchy, where various similar senses of a verb v should end-up applying at various levels below v.

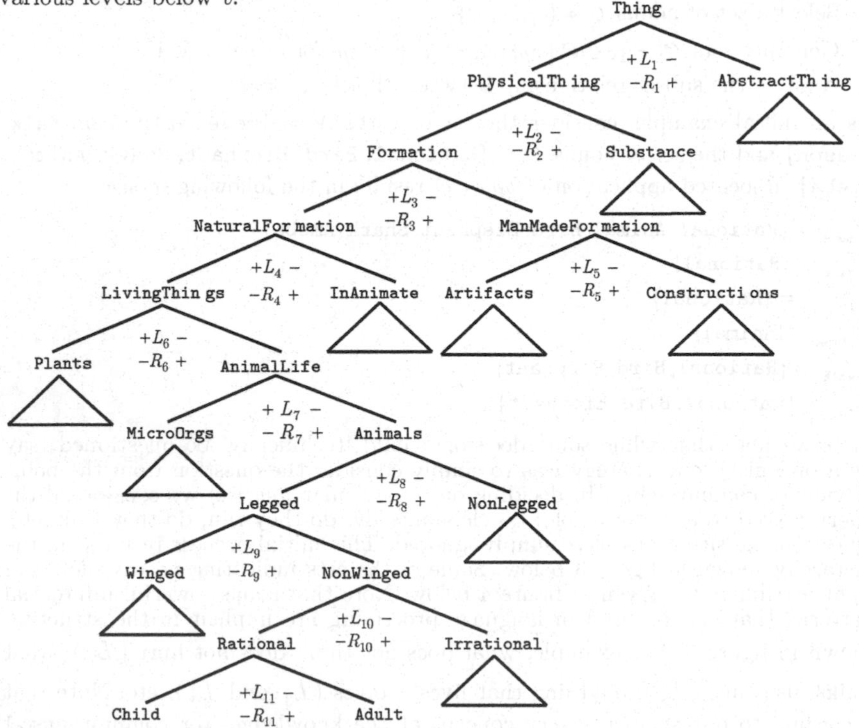

Figure 3. An adult is a physical, living thing that is formed. It evolves, it grows, it develops, moves, it can walk, run, hear, see, talk, think, reason, etc.

Consider for example `form` and `formulate`, in the sense of forming and formulating ideas. Since our method is based on the idea of using such verbs to discover the nature of concepts, `form` and `formulate` must both apply to `ideas`. Note that if everything that can be 'formed' can be 'formulated' and vice versa, then these two verbs would be synonymous. However, in this case this is not so, since there are things that can be formed but not formulated. For example, consider the small fragment shown in figure 5, where it is shown that 'developing', 'formulating', 'forming', etc. are all specific ways of 'making' (in other words, one sense of 'make' is 'develop'). Note the eventual split however. In particular, while we `make`, `form`, and `develop` both `ideas` and `feelings`, `ideas` are `formulated` while `feelings` are `fostered`.

While the occurrence of similar senses of verbs at various levels in the hierarchy indicates polysemy, the occurrence of the same verb (the same lexeme) at structurally isomorphic places in the hierarchy indicates metaphorical derivations. Consider the following:

app(**run**,**LeggedThing**) (6)
app(**run**,**Machine**) (7)
app(**run**,**Show**) (8)

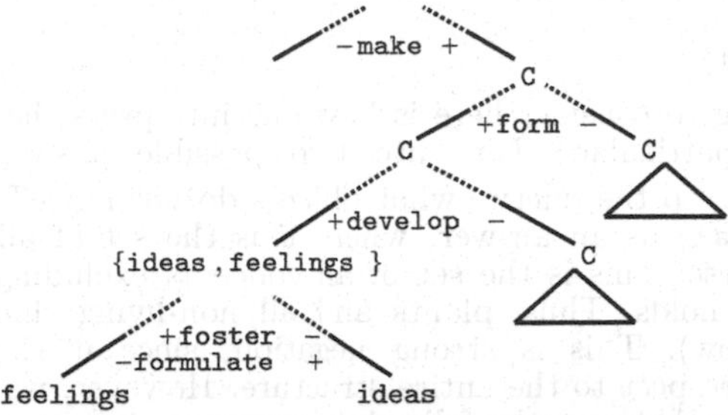

Figure 5. An explanation of polysemy.

(6) through (8) state that we can speak of a legged thing, a machine and a show running. Clearly, however, these examples involve three different senses of the verb **run**. It could be argued that the senses of **run** that are implied by (7) and (8) correspond to a metaphorical derivation of the actual running of natural kinds, the sense implied by (6). It is also interesting to note that these metaphorical derivations occur at various levels: first from natural kinds to artifacts; and then from physical to abstract. Moreover, the mass/count distinction on the physical side seems to have a mirror image of a mass/count on the abstract side. For example, note the following similarity between **water** (physical substance) and **information** (abstract substance):

- **water/information** flows, can be diverted, filtered, processed, etc.
- we can be flooded by, or drown in **water/information**
- a little bit of water/information is (still) water/information

One interesting aspect of these findings is to further investigate the exact nature of this metaphorical mapping and whether the map is consistent throughout; that is, whether same-level hierarchies are structurally isomorphic, as the case appears to be so far (see figure 6)[5].

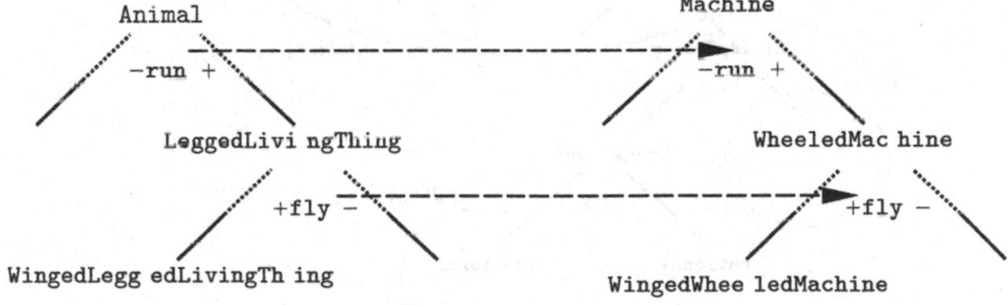

Figure 6. Isomorphic structures explaining metaphors.

6 Negation, Immutable Features and Surprise

The model proposed here allows us to have a very interesting model of the negation. To illustrate, consider the following propositions implied by the concept hierarchy given in figure 3, namely that generally animals move, and people talk:

app(Move,Animal) (9)

[5] Conservatively, the mapping might be a homomorphism and not an isomorphism.

app(`Talk`,`Rational`) (10)

What is interesting to consider here is how one interprets the negation of such propositions. In particular, there are two possible answers to the query $\neg$*app*(`Move`,?`X`), i.e., to the query "what objects do not move?" One can simply provide (`U - Animal`) as an answer, where `U` is the set of all concepts in the universe of discourse. This is the set of all concepts excluding those for which *app*(`Move`,`Animal`) holds. Thus, plants and all non-living things do not move (see figure 7 below). This is strong negation, since it simply returns the complement with respect to the entire structure. However, we argue that there is a subtle difference between the following queries:

Do mountains talk? (11)
Do elephants talk? (12)

Although a rational agent would answer "no" in both cases, one might imagine a child replying "nah, mountains do not talk" in response to (11). This must be function of the following: elephants fall directly under the negative polarity of **talk**; while this property is not even applicable to mountains (see figure 7 below). From a Gricean point of view, it seems that "elephants do not talk" is somewhat more meaningful than "mountains do not talk." This subtle difference in the two cases of negation is crucial in performing commonsense reasoning in language understanding. This is also related to the notion of the *immutability* of a feature (Sloman *et al.*, 1998), which is thought to reflect the degree to which a concept depends on a certain feature (or, conversely, how central is a certain feature to the definition of a concept).

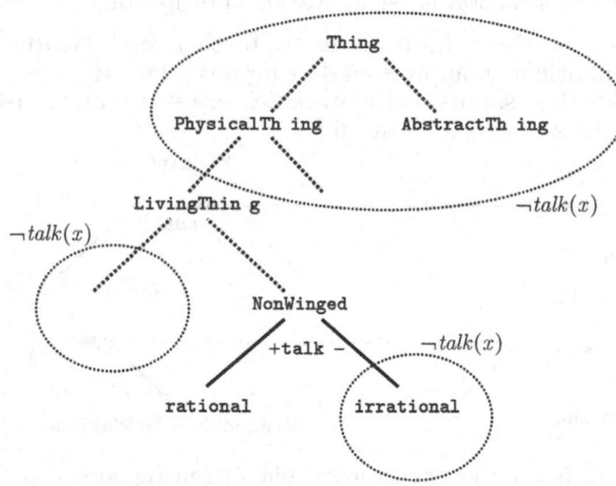

Figure 7. Mountains, elephants, and poems do not talk.

7 Reasoning with Commonsense Knowledge

What we are suggesting in this paper is a process that would hopefully lead to the *discovery* of the ontology of commonsense knowledge. This alone would clearly do little to building natural language understanding systems unless an inferencing strategy that utilizes this ontology is properly formulated. While the ontology provides the synthetic knowledge that an NLU system might need, an NLU system must clearly use quite a bit of analytic knowledge. A typical example would be the following:

$$(\forall p, c_1, c_2)(app(p, c_1) \wedge isa(c_1, c_2) \supset app(p, c_1)) \tag{13}$$

That is, any property that applies to a concept applies to all its subtypes. Clearly there are numerous other such rules that could be added. Another important observation here is that the system that will eventually emerge will yield a much richer type structure than the (flat) type systems typically assumed in formal semantics (e.g., Montague, 1973). For example, form the hierarchy in figure 3 one can clearly establish the following:

$$\texttt{Walk} : (e_{\texttt{LeggedThing}} \rightarrow t) \tag{14}$$

$$\texttt{Write} : (e_{\texttt{Human}} \rightarrow (e_{\texttt{Content}} \rightarrow t)) \tag{15}$$

That is, 'write' is not simply a relation between two entities, but a relation between two specific types of entities. Note the importance of this step (of combining formal semantics with a rich type hierarchy), however. For example, (15) states that *write(x,y)* is well-typed as long as $\texttt{isa}(x,\textbf{Human})$ and $\texttt{isa}(y,\texttt{Content})$. In general,

$$wellTyped(\mathrm{v}(e)) \equiv_{df} type(\mathrm{v}, (e_m \rightarrow t)) \wedge type(e, a) \wedge \texttt{isa}(a, m)$$

$$wellTyped(\mathrm{v}(e_1, e_2)) \equiv_{df} type(\mathrm{v}, (e_m \rightarrow (e_n \rightarrow t))) \wedge type(e_1, a) \wedge type(e_2, b) \wedge \texttt{isa}(a, m) \wedge \texttt{isa}(b, n)$$

More importantly, however, the combination of a rich type hierarchy and a rigorous semantics should shed some light on the semantics of compound nominals. For instance, type information might explain why removing the middle noun form (16) changes the subject considerably while the same is not true in (17).

Computer book sale (16)
Information management system (17)

Such rules are important in a variety of language processing tasks, and in particular in topic-based information retrieval. A compositional semantics that exploits a rich type hierarchy should therefore facilitate the development of a meaning algebra; for example to explain why *fake gun* is not (exactly) a gun, whereas *imported gun* is very much a gun. These are precisely the kinds of issues that have prompted this work, and much of this is currently under development.

8 Concluding Remarks

In this paper we argued for and presented a new approach to the systematic design of ontologies of commonsense knowledge. The method is based on the basic assumption that "language use" can guide the classification process. This idea is in turn rooted in Frege's principle of Compositionality and is similar to the idea of type inference in strongly-typed, polymorphic programming languages. The experiment we conducted shows this approach to be quite promising as it seems to have answered a number of questions simultaneously. In particular, the approach seems to (*i*) completely remove the need for multiple inheritance; (*ii*) provide a good model for lexical ambiguity and polysemy; and (*iii*) suggest a plausible explanation of metaphor in natural language. Much of what we presented here is work in progress, more so than a final result. Therefore, we are well aware that it might be quite ambitious to expect this process to yield a complete classification in a strict binary tree (no multiple inheritance, and no lexical ambiguity). We must also note that a number of other aspects of this work were not discussed here, such as the part-whole relationship. In particular, it seems that some, but not all, verbs that apply to a concept apply to their parts. For example, *grow* in *app*(*grow*,*leg*) and *app*(*grow*,*arm*) is very much related to *grow* in *app*(*grow*,*person*). That is, when we refer to a person growing, aging, etc. we are indirectly referring to the growing or aging of the parts. Another important part of this work is to also discover the nature of the relationship between (genuine) types (e.g., `Human`) and roles that concepts play (e.g., `Teacher`, `Father`, etc.) In this regard a number of temporal aspects must also be formalized.

A great deal of work is still needed to formalize the entire approach as well as work out the various inference rules that will eventually be needed in a natural language understanding system. We have already successfully used some of the ideas presented here in NLU tasks, such as developing an efficient and cognitively plausible inferencing strategy to resolve quantifier scope ambiguities at the pragmatic level (see Saba & Corriveau, 2001). While our immediate goal is to discover the ontology of commonsense knowledge, our ultimate goal is to build systems that can *understand* spoken language. This task has proven to be more challenging than has ever been imagined. Turing might have had it right all along: a machine that can converse in spoken language, must be an intelligent machine!

References

Allen, J. (1987), *Natural Language Understanding*, Benjamin/Cummings.

Asher, N. and Lascarides, A. (1998), The Semantics & Pragmatics of Presupposition, *Journal of Semantics*, 15:239-299.

Charniak, E. (1993), *Statistical Language Learning*, Cambridge, MA: MIT Press.

Charniak, E. (1986), A neat theory of marker passing. In *Proceedings of the 5th National Conference on Artificial Intelligence*, pp. 584--588, Los Altos, CA, Morgan Kaufmann.

Dubois et al. (1994), Fuzzy logic vs. possibilistic logic, *IEEE Expert*, 9(4), pp. 15-19

Dummett, M. (1981), *Frege: Philosophy of Language*, Harvard Univ. Press, Cambridge: MA.

Elkan, C. (1993), The Paradoxical Success of Fuzzy Logic, In *Proceedings of the 11th National Conf. on Artificial Intelligence*, AAAI-93, pp. 698-703. AAAI Press.

Fodor, J. A. (1998), *Concepts - where cognitive science went wrong*, Oxford University Press: NY.

Guarino, N. and Welty, C. (2000), A Formal Ontology of Properties, In *12th Int. Conf. on Knowledge Engineering and Knowledge Management, LNCS*, Verlag.

Hirst, G. (1986). *Semantic Interpretation and the Resolution of Ambiguity.* Cambridge University Press, Cambridge

Hobbs, J. (1985), Ontological Promiscuity, In *Proceedings of the 23rd Annual Meeting of the Association for Computational Linguistics*, pp. 61-69, Chicago, Illinois, 1985. ACL.

Hobbs, J. R., *et al.* (1993), Interpretation as Abduction, *Artificial Intelligence*, **63**:69-142.

Kurtzman, H. and MacDonald, M. (1993), Resolution of Quantifier Scope Ambiguities, *Cognition*, 48, 243-279.

Lenat, D. B. and Guha, R.V. (1990), *Building Large Knowledge-Based Systems: Representation and Inference in the CYC Project.* Addison-Wesley.

Mahesh, K. and Nirenburg, S. (1995), A Situated Ontology for Practical NLP, In *IJCAI-95 Workshop on Basic Ontological Issues in Knowledge Sharing*, IJCAI-95, August 1995, Montreal, Canada.

Montague, R. (1973). The Proper Treatment of Quantification in Ordinary English, In Thomason (1974).

Montague, R. (1970), English as a Formal Language, In Thomason (1974).

Pereira, F. C. N. and Pollack, M. E. (1991), Incremental Interpretation, *Artificial Intelligence*, **50**:37-82.

Pustejovsky, J. (2001), Type Construction and the Logic of Concepts, In P. Bouillon and F. Busa (eds.), *The Syntax of Word Meanings*, Cambridge University Press.

Reinhart, T. (1997), Quantifier Scope: How Labor is Divided between QR and Choice Functions, *Linguistics and Philosophy*, **20**(4): 335-397

Saba, W. S. and Corriveau, J.-P. (1997), A Pragmatic Treatment of Quantification in Natural Language, In *Proceedings of the 15th National Conference on Artificial Intelligence* (AAAI-97), pp. 610-615, Morgan Kaufmann.

Saba, W. S. and J-P. Corriveau (2001), Plausible Reasoning and the Resolution of Quantifier Scope Ambiguities, *Studia Logica*, **67**:271-289.

Schank, R. C. (1982), *Dynamic Memory: A Theory of Learning in Computers and People*, Cambridge University Press, New York.

Sloman, AS., Love, B. and Ahn, W-K. (1998), Feature Similarity and Conceptual Coherence, *Cognitive Science*, **22**(2):189-228.

Sowa, J. F. (1995). *Knowledge Representation: Logical, Philosophical, and Computational Foundations.* Boston, MA: PWS Publishing Company.

Thomason, R. (1974), Editor with an Introduction, *Formal Philosophy: Selected Papers of Richard Montague*, Yale University Press.

van Deemter, K. (1996), Towards a Logic of Ambiguous Expressions, In K. van Deemter and S. Peters (eds.), *Semantic Ambiguity and Underspecification*, pp. 55-76, CSLI, Stanford, CA.

Wilks, Y. (1975), A Preferential, Pattern-Seeking, Semantics for Natural Language Interface, *Artificial Intelligence*, **6**:53-74.

Zadronzy, W. and Jensen K. (1991), Semantics of Paragraphs, *Computational Linguistics*, **17**(2):171-209.

Simulation of Network Security with Collaboration among IDS Models

Hee Suk Seo and Tae Ho Cho

School of Electrical and Computer Engineering Modeling & Simulation Lab,
Sungkyunkwan University Suwon, 440-746, South Korea.
{histone , taecho}@ece.skku.ac.kr

Abstract. IDS (Intrusion Detection System) plays a vital role in network security in that it monitors system activities to identity unauthorized use, misuse or abuse of computer and network system. For the simulation of IDS a model has been constructed based on the DEVS (Discrete EVent system Specification) formalism. With this model we can simulate whether the intrusion detection, which is a core function of IDS, is effectively done under various different conditions. As intrusions become more sophisticated, it is beyond the scope of any one IDS to deal with them. Thus we placed multiple IDS agents in the network where the information helpful for detecting the intrusions is shared among these agents to cope effectively with attackers. Each agent cooperates through the BBA (Black Board Architecture) for detecting intrusions. If an agent detects intrusions, it transfers attacker's information to a Firewall. Using this mechanism attacker's packets detected by IDS can be prevented from damaging the network.

1 Introduction

As e-business being rapidly developed the importance of security is on the rise in network[1],[2]. IDS monitors system activities to identify unauthorized use, misuse or abuse of computer and network system[3],[4]. It accomplishes these by collecting information from a variety of systems and network resources then analyzing the information for symptoms of security problems[4],[5].

Usually, the input data in simulation is abstracted from the actual intrusion. In this paper, however, we compose a real intrusion environment by generating non-abstracted intrusion packets and accordingly non-abstracted version of IDS core. Another characteristic in the proposed simulation is the modeling of multiple IDSs which share attacker's information to effectively detect the intrusion.

2 DEVS Formalism

The DEVS formalism, developed by Zeigler is a theoretical, well grounded means of expressing hierarchical, modular discrete-event models[6],[7],[8],[9]. In DEVS, a

M. Brooks, D. Corbett, and M. Stumptner (Eds.): AI 2001, LNAI 2256, pp. 438-448, 2001.

system has a time base, inputs, states, outputs and functions. The system function determines next states and outputs based on the current states and input. In the formalism, a basic model is defined by the structure:

$$M = < X, S, Y, \delta_{int}, \delta_{ext}, \lambda, ta >$$

where X is an external input set, S is a sequential state set, Y is an external output set, δ_{int} is an internal transition function, δ_{ext} is an external transition function, λ is an output function and ta is a time advance function. A coupled model is defined by the structure:

$$DN = < D, \{M_i\}, \{I_i\}, \{Z_{i,j}\}, select >$$

where D is a set of component name, Mi is a component basic model, I_i is a set of influences of I, $Z_{i,j}$ is an output translation, select is a tie-breaking function. Such a coupled model can itself be employed in a larger coupled model. Several basic models can be coupled to build a more complex model, called a coupled model. A coupled model tells how to couple several models together to form a new model.

3 Classification of Intrusion

The intrusions used in the simulation are classified into three types according to the number of packets needed to detect the intrusion as shown in Table 1. The first type can be identified by analyzing one packet which contains one or more abnormal flags in packet's header information and the second type by analyzing many packets like DoS (Denial of Service). The third type can be identified by analyzing packet's data in which the attacker tries to acquire the privilege of system administrator using bugs of system[10].

Table 1. Classification of Intrusions

	One packet needed for detection	Multiple packets needed for detection		
	Packet header analyzed	Packets header analyzed		Packets data analyzed
Attack type	-probing	-scan	-DoS	·door knob rattling
	·port probing	·port scan	·ICMP flood	·buffer overrun
	·protocol probing	·address scan	·web-port DoS	·password cracking
		·ftpd scan	·mail-port DoS	·environment variable overflow attack
	-DoS	·CGI-Query	·DNS DoS	
	·winnuk	·mscan	·mailbomb	·use commands which can be used by administrator himself
	·X-mas tree	·sscan	·UDP bomb	
	·ping of death	·popd scan	·SYN Flood	

	·land attack ···	·imapd scan ·smurf ·trinoo ·spam mail ···	use commands which are frequently used by intruders ···

4 The Structure of Target Network and Simulation Model

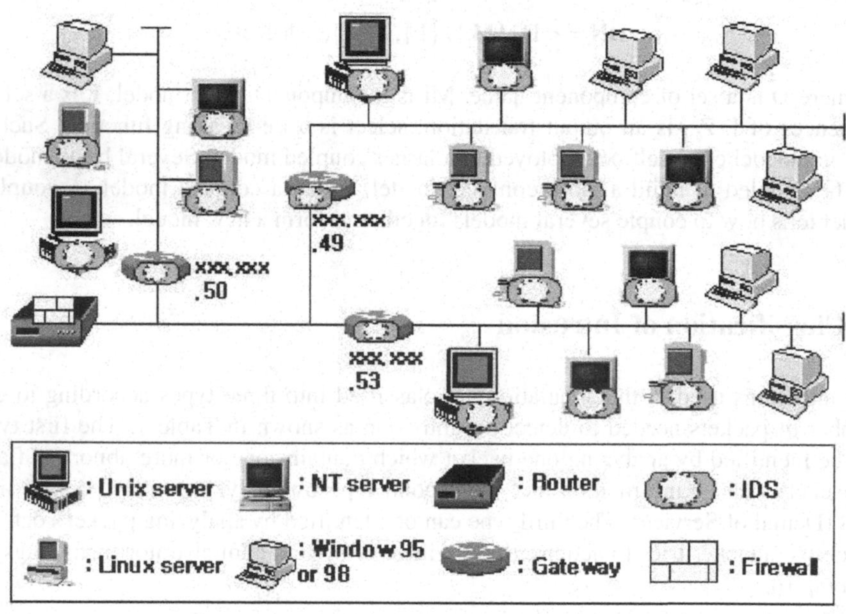

Fig. 1. The structure of target network

Fig. 1 is the structure of the target network which has three subnets. The types of component models in the network are IDS, Firewall, Router and Gateway model[11]. A IDS is loaded within each host and it cooperates with other IDSs in detecting the intrusion.

Fig. 2 shows the structure of the model that are based on the network described in Fig. 1. The model is constructed based on the DEVS formalism. Each subnet has several ID models. Fig. 3 shows the structure of ID model within each host, its subcomponents and their interconnections. The subcomponent models are explained in the following subsections

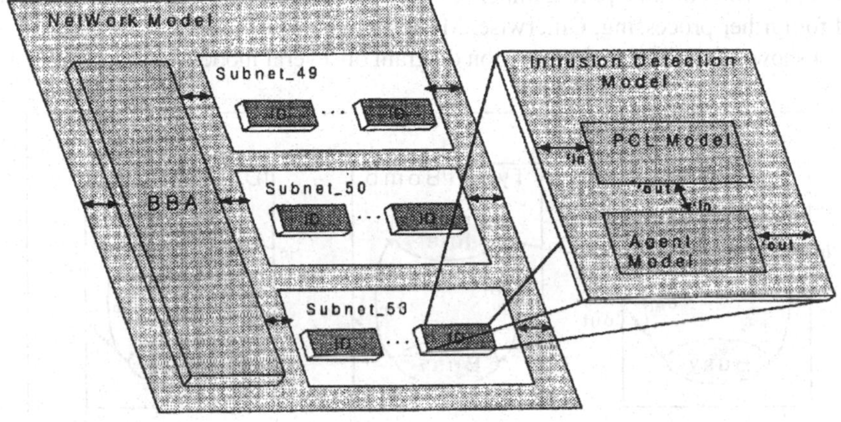

Fig. 2. The overall structure of network model

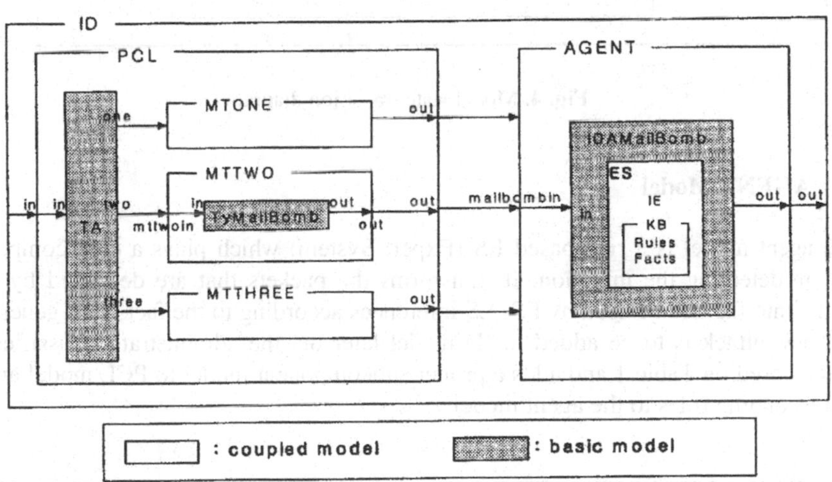

Fig. 3. The structure of intrusion detection model

4.1 PCL Model

PCL (Packet Classify Library) model receives network's packets that are generated by the intrusion generator model and classifies them according to Table 1. Then it filters sorted packets to reduce processing time as the following process. For example, for the mailbomb case, TA (Task Allocator) of PCL model receives packets from the generator model and then it transmits the packets to one of the three different types of models. These are MTONE, MTTWO, MTTHREE. If the packets, send to MTTWO, are of TCP protocol and port number 25 then it transfers the packets to an agent model for further processing. Otherwise, MTTWO ignores it.

Fig. 4 shows the model state transition diagram of several models.

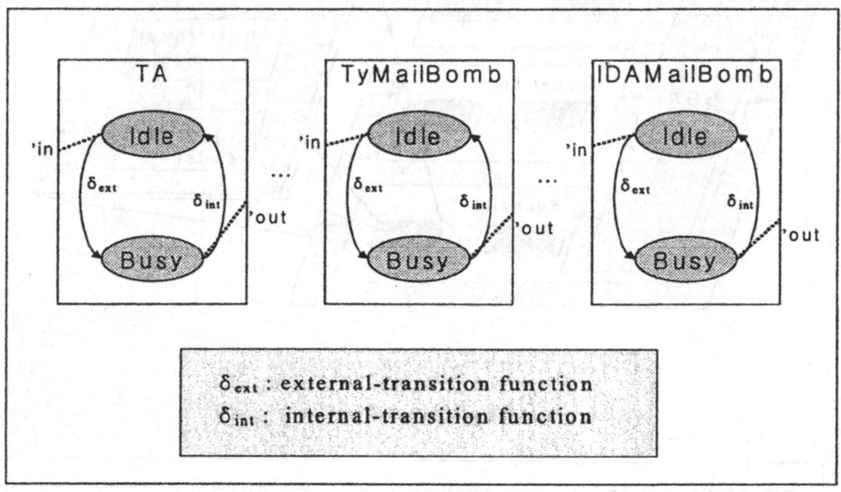

Fig. 4. Model state transition diagram

4.2 AGENT Model

The agent model is a rule-based ES (Expert System) which plays a core component role in detecting the intrusion. It transforms the packets that are delivered by PCL model into facts to be used by ES. ES inferences according to the facts thus generated. If a new attack is to be added to ID model later on, the administrator classifies the attack based on Table 1 and adds a proper subcomponent model to PCL model and its corresponding rules to the agent model.

```
void MBRule::Rule1(Slot_List& fact){
... if(protocol==6) PtlId = true; ...}

void MBRule::Rule2(Slot_List& fact){
... if( PtlId && port==25) PrtId = true; ...}

void MBRule::Rule3(Slot_List& fact){
... if(PrtId && Time==nowtime)
      if(timecount >= localThreshold){
        S_add.insert( Source_IP );
        InAttack = true; ...}
...}
```

```
void MBRule::Rule4(Slot_List& fact){
... //check the buffer clearing time. ...}

void MBRule::Rule5(Slot_List& fact){
... if(!BufCT && IsDanger()>= Minimal)
    InMin = true; ...}

. . . .

void MBRule::Rule9(Slot_List& fact){
... if(InSer && IsDanger()>=Catastrophic)
     InCat = true; ...}
```

Fig. 5. The rules of Expert System

Fig. 5 shows the part of the rules of mailbomb attack. The Rule3, for example, receives the facts and checks whether PtlId is true and the value of the fact "Time" represents the network is under attack currently. If the number of packets is more than "localThreshold", Rule3 stores "Source_IP" and sets the variable "InAttack" to be true. Rule4 is the rule which checks buffers periodic clearing time.

5 The Collaboration among the Security Models

5.1 Communication among Agents of BB (Black Board)

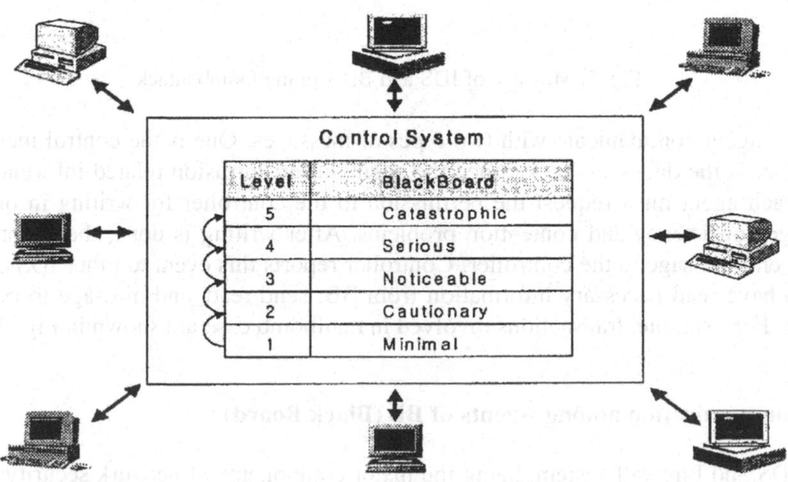

Fig. 6. Communication by Black Board

There have been large volume of research works done for detecting intrusions within distributed environment[12],[13],[14]. This section presents the mechanism in which IDSs communicate by BBA which is one of the architecture that allows collaboration among distributed agents[15],[16],[17].

BB (Black Board) in BBA, the field of the distributed AI (Artificial Intelligence), is hierarchically structured shared working memory through which the agents communicate by writing and reading the information relevant in detecting the intrusions.

The hierarchy in BB is set according to Joseph Barrus & Neil C. Rowe[18] as shown in Fig. 6. They proposed Danger values to be divided into five different levels. The level in the BB is based on these divisions. These five BB levels are Minimal, Cautionary, Noticeable, Serious, Catastrophic.

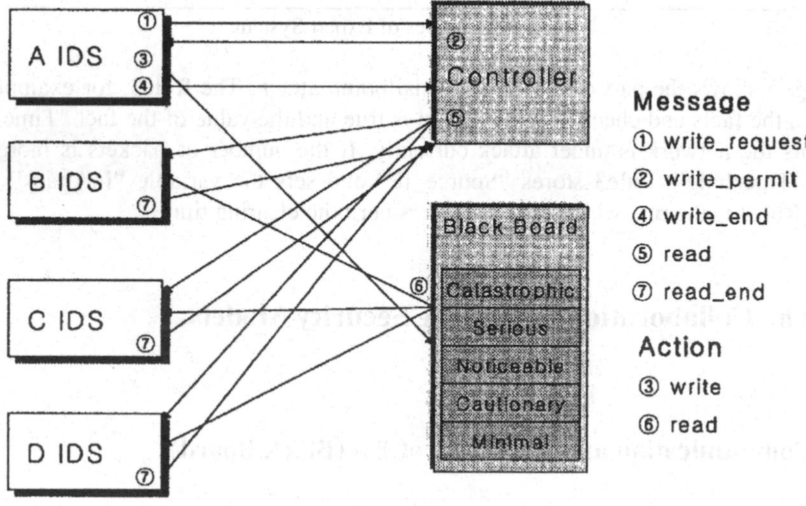

Fig. 7. Message of IDS and BBA in mailbomb attack

Each agent communicate with two types of messages. One is the control messages, the other is the data messages. Since the agents insert intrusion related information to BB, each agent must request the permission to the controller for writing in order to manage consistency and contention problems. After writing is done, the agent sends write_end message to the controller. Controller reports this event to other IDSs. IDSs, which have read necessary information from BB, send read_end message to the controller. For example, transactions involved in mailbomb case are shown in Fig. 7.

5.2 Communication among Agents of BB (Black Board)

The IDS and Firewall system, being the major components of network security, cooperate to enhance the security level. If IDS detects the intrusion through BBA, its agent modifies the security policy of the Firewall. So that the intrusion packets detected by IDS can be prevented.

In order to reduce the damage of the network to a minimum level, we have prevented attacker's packets from getting into the computer when BB is at beyond Serious level. When BB is at Serious level, the agent adds the source IP (Internet Protocol) address to the blacklist of the Firewall, then all packets coming from these source IP address are blocked. Fig. 8 shows that IDS detects an intrusion and responses according to this attack.

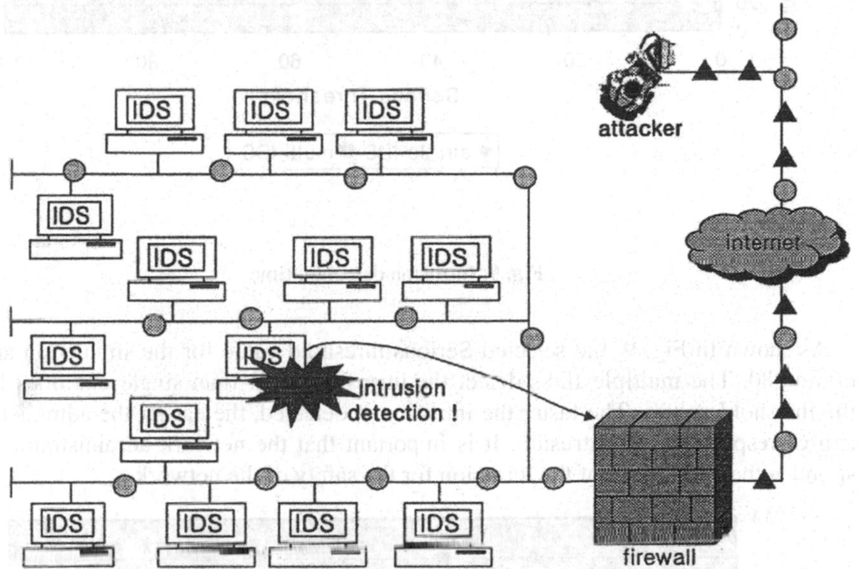

Fig. 8. Intrusion detection and response

6 Simulation Result

We have executed simulations for two cases. One is the case for a single IDS to detect the intrusion, the other is the case for multiple IDSs to detect the intrusion by cooperation. Mailbomb attack was used for the simulation in both cases. Mailbomb attack is a type of DoS attacks. It attacks by sending many mails to the mail server. For the generation of mailbomb packets, Kaboom version 3.0 is used. The intrusion detection time, false positive and false negative ratio are measured for the performance indexes in the simulation.

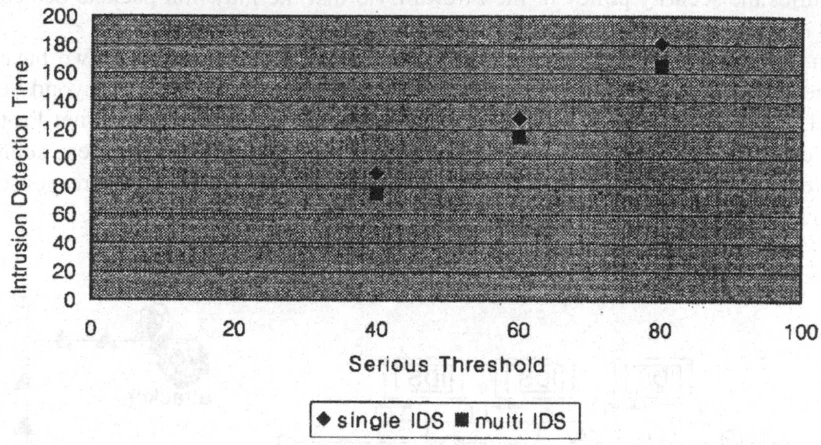

Fig. 9. Intrusion detection time

As shown in Fig. 9, the selected Serious threshold value for the simulation are 40, 60 and 80. The multiple IDSs detect the intrusion faster than single one does for all the threshold values. The faster the intrusion is detected, the earlier the administrators can correspond to the intrusion. It is important that the network administrator to respond at the early stage of the intrusion for the safety of the network.

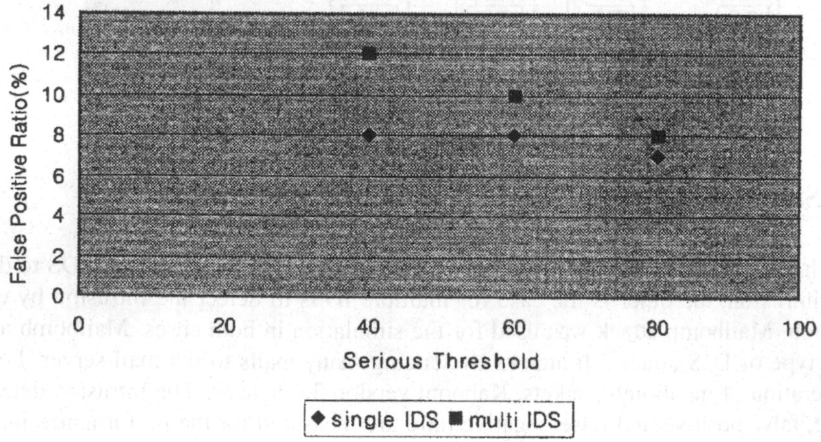

Fig. 10. False positive ratio

Fig. 10 shows that the false positive ratio has been increased by the strengthening of the security level (lessening the threshold in our system). Fig. 11 shows the decrease of the false negative ratio as the security level is strengthened. In the figure, the error ratio of multi IDS is lower than that of single IDS since the intrusions are detected based on the shared information.

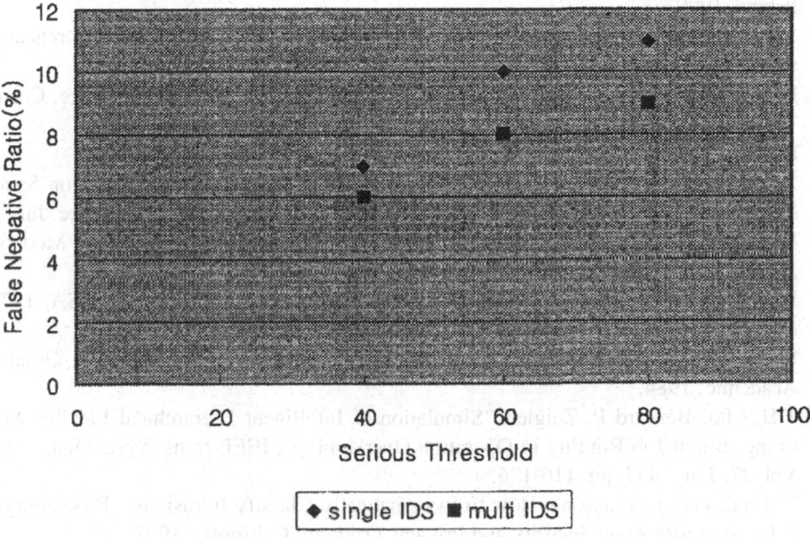

Fig. 11. False negative ratio

7 Conclusion and Future Work

As the usage of the network increases, intrusions occur more frequently and become more widespread and sophisticated. If multiple agents share the information with one another, the detection capability can be enhanced. The system which uses BBA for the information sharing can be easily expanded by adding new agents and increasing the number of BB levels. The cooperation between the Firewall component and IDS will provide added efficiency in the safe guarding the network. In the future, the generator model should generate the intrusion packets similar to real world packets, detailness and the simulation environment should also provide a proper set of threshold values according to the specific target system being modeled. Simulation results in this paper show that the false positive ratio of multi IDS is worse than that of single IDS and the performance of false negative is increased by lowering the Serious threshold level. The false positive ratio of multi IDS became worse with the lowering of the same threshold level. Therefore, the multi IDS performance of false positive case needs improvement in the further research of IDS core. The current simulation result, however, still shows the performance improvement in multi IDS case since if one of the performance index has to be enhanced it should be false negative ratio than false positive ratio in respect to the security.

References

1. S. Northcutt, "Network Intrusion Detection - An Analyst's Handbook", New Riders Publishing, 1999.
2. S Mclure, J. Scambray, G. Kurtz, "Hacking Exposed: Network Security Secrets and Solutions", McGraw-Hill, 1999.
3. E. Amoroso, "Intrusion Detection - An Introduction to Internet Surveillance, Correlation, Traps, Trace Back, and Response", Intrusion.Net Books, 1999.
4. R. Bace, "Intrusion Detection", Macmillan Technical Publishing, 2000.
5. Seo, Hee Suk, Yi, Mi Ra, Cho, Tae ho, "Simulation of Intrusion Detection System for Network Security", Proceedings of Summer Computer simulation Conference, July 2001.
6. B. P. Zeigler, "Object-Oriented Simulation with Hierarchical, Modular Models", San Diego, CA, USA:Academic Press, 1990.
7. B. P. Zeigler, "Theory of Modeling and Simulation", John Wiley, NY, USA, 1976, reissued by Krieger, Malabar, FL, USA, 1985.
8. B. P. Zeigler, "Multifacetted Modeling and Discrete Event Simulation". Orlando, FL: Academic, 1984.
9. T.H. Cho, Bernard P. Zeigler, "Simulation of Intelligent Hierarchical Flexible Manufacturing: Batch Job Routing in Operation Overlapping", IEEE trans. Syst. Man, Cybern. A, Vol. 27, Jan. 1997, pp. 116-126.
10. U. Lindqvist, E. Jonsson, "How to Systematically Classify Intrusions", Proceedings of the IEEE Symposium on Security and Privacy, Oakland, California, 1997.
11. B. A. Forouzan, "TCP/IP Protocol Suite", McGrawHill, 2000.
12. U. Lindqvist, P. A. Porras, "Detecting Computer and Network Misuse Through the Production-Based Expert System Toolset(P-BEST)", Proceedings of the IEEE Symposium on Security and Privacy, Oakland, California, May 9-12, 1999.
13. P. Porras and P. Neumann, "EMERALD: Event Monitoring Enabling Responses to anomalous live disturbances", Proceedings of the 20th National Information Systems Security Conference. National Institute of Standards an Technology, 1997.
14. M. Crosbie and G. Spafford, "Active Defence of a Computer System using Autonomous Agents", Technical Report No. 95-008, COAST Group, Dept. of Computer Science, Purdue University, Feb. 15, 1995.
15. G. Van Zeir, J. P. Kruth, J. Detand, "A Conceptual Framework for Interactive and Blackboard Based CAPP", International Journal of Production Research, Vol. 36(6), 1998, pp. 1453-1473.
16. K. Decker, A. Garvey, M. Humphrey, V. R. Lesser, "Control Heuristics for Scheduling in a Parallel Blackboard System", International Journal of pattern Recognition and Artificial Intelligence, Vol. 7, No. 2, pp. 243-264, 1993.
17. F. Klassner, V. R. Lesser, S. H. Nawab, "The IPUS Blackboard Architecture as a Framework for Computational Auditory Scene Analysis", IJCAI-95 Workshop on Computational Auditory Scene Analysis, Montreal, Canada, August 1995.
18. J. Barrus, N. C. Rowe, "A Distributed Autonomous-Agent Network-Intrusion Detection and Response System", Proceedings of Command and Control Research and Technology Symposium, Monterey CA, June 1998, pp. 577-586.
19. P. Neumann and D. Parker, "A Summary of computer misuse techniques", In Proceedings of the 12th National Computer Security Conference, October 1989, pp. 396-407.
20. N. Puketza, M. Chung, R. Olsson, B. Mukherjee, "A Software Platform for Testing Intrusion Detection Systems", IEEE Software, September/October, 1997, pp.43-51.
21. F. Cohen, "Simulating Cyber Attacks, Defences, and Consequences", Computer & Security, Vol.18, pp. 479-518 , 1999.

Programming Spoken Dialogs Using Grammatical Inference

Bradford Starkie

Telstra Research Laboratories, Box 249 Rosebank MDC 770 Blackburn Road Clayton Victoria, Australia
BradStarkie@team.telstra.com

Abstract. Over-the-telephone Large Vocabulary Spoken Dialog Systems have now become a commercial reality. A major obstacle to the uptake of the technology is the effort required to construct spoken dialog applications, in particular the grammars. To overcome this obstacle, a spoken dialogue toolkit has been developed that uses grammatical inference in combination with a templating technique to build transaction based services. As part of this development a new grammatical inference technique know as the "Lyrebird" algorithm has been developed. Experimental results contained show that the Lyrebird algorithm outperforms the only other known algorithm for inferring context free attribute grammars. We also present the results of a comparison between the performance of the Lyrebird algorithm and an experienced speech application developer, showing that the algorithm creates grammars of a similar quality in a significantly reduced time.

1 Introduction

Developers of large vocabulary spoken dialog systems have available to them several commercially available speech recognition products. These products are available as stand alone applications or are integrated into Integrated Voice Response platforms for over-the-telephone applications. To build an application, the developer is required to specify the expected language and the dialog.
The expected language is typically defined using a set of attribute grammars, with one grammar per question in the dialog. Attribute grammars [1] are used in large vocabulary speech recognition to

1) improve speech recognition accuracy by constraining the expected language;
2) attach meanings to phrases by attaching a set of key-value pairs to a parsed phrase.

For instance, the expression;

```
        i'd like to fly from melbourne to sydney
```

might be represented by the attributes :

```
  { op=bookflight from=melbourne to=sydney}
```

M. Brooks, D. Corbett, and M. Stumptner (Eds.): AI 2001, LNAI 2256, pp. 449-460, 2001.

Commercially available speech recognition development systems typically come with drag and drop GUI tools to enable the user to develop the dialogs. Developers use a graphical language based upon procedural flow to define the application. Although this style of programming has proven successful for tone based applications, it is unsuitable for natural language applications due to the large amount of branching in mixed mode initiative spoken dialogues. The drag and drop interface in its current form is starting to be replaced by finite state dialog managers due to the wide acceptance of the VoiceXML standard. The VoiceXML standard has been designed as a means of accessing Internet content using speech recognition.

In this paper, we describe a toolkit that uses a radically different concept for developing spoken dialog systems. This toolkit starts from a simple description of the goals of the application and then learns from examples to improve the interface. We will also describe the grammatical inference algorithm in more detail. The performance of the algorithm is then compared to the Bayesian Model Merging Algorithm [2],[3]. Finally the results of a comparison between the Lyrebird algorithm and an experienced human application developer are presented. The results suggest that the use of the grammatical inference can significantly reduce development effort time without sacrificing grammar quality.

1.1 Attribute Grammars

Each symbol in an attribute grammar (terminal or nonterminal) has a fixed number of attributes with corresponding values. Attribute grammars contain copy rules which are attached to context free production rules, and assign an attribute value or a constant to another attribute.

Figure 1 below shows a simple attribute grammar capable of being inferred using the Lyrebird algorithm. The notation used in this paper is as follows: symbols beginning in upper case are nonterminals while those beginning in lower case are terminals. Top level nonterminals begin with a period.

In our notation a nonterminal "Y1" can have a variable "x" attached to it denoted as "Y1:x".

```
.S -> i'd like to fly S2:s {from=$s.from,to=$s.to,
op=bookflight}
S2-> from Location:l { from=$l.location }
S2-> from Location:l1 to Location:l2
{from=$l1.location to=$l2.location }
Location -> melbourne { location=melbourne }
Location -> sydney { location=sydney }
```

Fig. 1. Example attribute grammar.

The attribute values returned by a rule are defined using copy rules that are contained within curly braces. These copy rules can assign a value to the attribute returned by the rule either as a constant (e.g. location=melbourne) or by referencing the values of attributes attached to nonterminals (e.g. from=$l.location). In addition, the value of an attribute can be set to the result of a function that takes one or more arguments that are

either constants or the value attached to a nonterminal (e.g. number=add($n1.number $2.number)).
Methods for attaching attribute values to a phrase given an attribute grammar are described in [4]. In our algorithm we used a bottom up chart parser to create a syntax tree, and a parse stack to attach attributes to the phrase.

Attribute copy rules can also be used to constrain the ways in which rules can be expanded. For instance when a noun phrase is attached to a verb phrase in a valid english sentence they should either be both singular or both plural. This interelationship can be implemented using attribute copy rules that are defined top down rather than bottom up. These top down attributes are known as inherited attributes, while those described in the notation used in this paper are known as synthesised attributes and are defined bottom up.

Inherited attributes are useful for language generation systems. Although they can be used to deambigufy complex phrase structures, they are not commonly used in speech recognition systems, and therefore are not considered in this research.

1.2 Inferring Attribute Grammars

The grammatical inference of attribute grammars involves supplying to an algorithm a set of tagged phrases (observations) from which an attribute grammar is inferred that can generate not only the training data but other phrases similar to it. Although there is a substantial body of work on attribute grammars as well as grammatical inference of regular and context free grammars, there is very little work on the grammatical inference of context free attribute grammars for natural language phrases [5]. Stolcke's [2] Bayesian model merging (BMM) algorithm is an exception. Both BMM and our algorithm can be described as minimum description length (MDL) algorithms. Other examples of MDL algorithms include the algorithms of Cook [6] and Grünwald [7], although these algorithms infer context free grammars rather than attribute grammars.
The minimum description length principle can be considered to be a rearrangement of Bayes' law. With grammatical inference the aim is to find a suitable model (M) to describe a set of observed phrases (X). If there are a number of candidate models to select from then Bayes' laws states that you would select the model that maximised the probability P(M|X). Using Bayes' law.

$$P(M|X) \propto P(M)P(X|M) \qquad (1)$$

Maximising this function is equivalent to minimising

$$-\log P(M) - \log P(X|M) \qquad (2)$$

Information theory tells us that –log P(E) is the optimal code length for communicating an instance of E. Therefore –log P(M) can be seen as the optimal code length for describing the model (complexity), and –log P(X|M) can be seen as the optimal code length for describing the data using the model (discrepancy or cross entropy). The optimal solution may therefore be found by choosing the model that has the shortest total description length of both the model and the data [2]. In the absence of negative data the MDL principle can be used to indicate when generalisation should stop. This is because the MDL is a hypothetical mid-point between the most restrictive model, in which only the training data can be generated by the grammar, and the most general model that can generate any phrase and therefore requires the training data to be described explicitly.

MDL grammatical inference algorithms typically use a greedy search whereby a starting grammar is improved one step at a time using a cost function that describes the total description length. Candidate grammars are then compared for their effect upon the cost function, and the model that creates the greatest reduction in the cost function is chosen. If none of the candidate grammars leads to a reduction in the cost function generalisation stops.

In both Stolcke's [2] algorithm and Cook's [6] algorithm a starting grammar that generates the training data explicitly is created (i.e. each rule represents a number of identical observations). Progression from one candidate grammar to another is via a set of operators. These operators can be described as either chunking or merging.

Chunking involves the identification of commonly repeated sequences (chunks). New rules are created that represent these chunks and a new rule is substituted into the existing rules. This adds hierarchical structure to the grammar without increasing discrepancy and commonly reducing the complexity of the grammar.

Merging involves the merging of two non-terminals based upon patterns. When two non-terminals are merged, the grammar is often generalised.

Some related research includes the work of Dulz et Al.[8] and Ross[9]. Dulz infers attribute grammars to model the performance characteristics of protocol implementations but his work differs in that he infers regular grammars and attribute copy rules are used only to define average arrival times of protocol units.

Ross uses attribute grammars in conjunction with genetic programming to infer stochastic regular grammars. He uses attribute grammars to ensure the validity of his inferred regular grammars, and in doing so he creates a more concise implementation of his code. He does not use attribute grammars to attach meaning to parsed phrases.

2 Building Applications Using the Lyrebird Tool

The Lyrebird tool has been designed to develop spoken dialog systems where the tasks to be performed are well defined, and a spoken natural language interface is required.

In order to construct the application, the developer defines the tasks to be performed as a series of operations, along with the parameters required to perform the task and their types. For instance, in a stock broking application the developer might define that there are three tasks to perform, such as buying, selling and listing stock prices. Each of these operations have a set of slots that need to be filled. The "buy" operation might require a stockname, the number of stocks and the price of each stock. The types of the parameters can include predefined types, such as integers, money amounts and dates, or they can be defined as part of the application description as a list of items, such as stocknames, locations or products. Parameters are defined as either mandatory or optional. Mandatory parameters need to be specified explictly by speakers, while

optional parameters can be set to default values, or left unfilled. Applications that can be defined this way include voice commerce applications, bill paying, ordering, messaging and scheduling.
From the application description presented to it, the Lyrebird tool builds an initial finite state machine dialog manager, along with a set of prompts and grammars. This initial application is a menu driven dialog in which speakers are prompted for each slot to be filled. Likewise the grammars are simple predictable responses to these questions and the prompts follow a simple pattern. From this simple description, a more sophisticated mixed mode initiative dialog can be learnt by supplying example phrases to the Lyrebird tool.
For instance the developer might supply the phrase:

```
"buy three hundred shares of acme dot com at the going
rate"
```

This might be represented by the attributes :

```
{operation=buy, stockname="acme.com", price="market
rate"}
```

From this phrase the Lyrebird tool would be able to generalise the phrase to include other phrases describing the purchasing of different quantities of other stocks. With additional phrases, the Lyrebird tool will learn the equivalence of phrases such as *"the going rate"* and *"market value"*. The Lyrebird algorithm also has the ability to learn prepositional phrases by identifying synonyms and complex phrase structures that describe structured types. It can also extend grammars that include integer types and concatenated strings.
In addition to being able to generalise expressions, the Lyrebird tool typically does not require the developer to modify the dialog manager to accommodate the mixed mode initiative input.

The approach taken by the Lyrebird tool, is to generate all of the regular parts of the application automatically using a templating approach, and to learn the irregular parts of the application through example. This technique requires the collection of phrases from a trial service to improve the application. This process of collecting example phrases from a trial however is commonly performed when an application is manually built so the grammatical inference technique results in a reduced development time.

2.1 The Grammatical Inference Algorithm

The Grammatical inference algorithm will now be briefly described. For a more detailed description of the algorithm the reader should refer to [10]&[11].
The Lyrebird Algorithm infers an attribute grammar from a set of tagged training data, plus an optional starting grammar. It does this in the following manner;

1) An intermediate grammar is created that generates the training data (Incorporation phase).

2) Hierarchical structure is then added to the intermediate grammar (Chunking phase).
3) Generalisation then occurs through the merging of rules (merging phase).
4) Redundant rules are then removed by reestimating rule probabilities and deleting zero probability rules (Reestimation Phase).

The process is then repeated until the grammar is as compact as possible, while still attaching the correct meanings to all of the training data. The algorithm does not use a minimum description length cost function explicitly to determine when to stop inference. Instead it uses several inductive biases for adding hierarchical structure which have their basis in the MDL principle. The algorithm also uses a MDL checksum to prevent endless looping.
The algorithm can use negative examples, but can equally operate without them. The algorithm can detect overgeneralisation, by detecting when training phrases are assigned two or more meanings, only one of which corresponds to the meaning attached to it in the training data.

During the incorporation phase the grammar is extended to include previously unpredicted phrases. When a starting grammar is supplied to the algorithm each training observation is parsed using a bottom up chart parser. In the case of a partial parse, this creates a small number of parse-trees, which return attributes. When such a parse-tree exists, and the attributes it produces exist in the observation, the phrase can be replaced by a reference to the non-terminal, and the copy rules updated.
For instance, if there was a starting grammar that included rules for describing numbers and stocknames, and the observation `"buy three hundred shares of acme dot com"` was observed in the dialog state `".TopLevelStock"` with the attributes `"{ op=buy, stock="acme.com" number=300 }"`
a rule of the form given below might be added.

```
TopLevelStock -> buy Number:x1 of StockName:x2 {op=buy,
stock=$x2.stock number=$x1.number}
```

When there is no starting grammar, a new rule is created that reproduces the observation explicitly.

During the chunking phase, three different techniques are used to attach hierarchical structure to the grammar, only two of which are described here for the sake of brevity.

The first method of generating hierarchical structure is to attach meanings to individual words in the grammar. This is found by determining correlations between the attributes of observed phrases and the words within those phrases. To enable this problem to be solved the Lyrebird algorithm builds a class of attribute grammars where;

1. Each attribute has a type and copy rules can only assign values of the appropriate type to an attribute.

2. Copy rules cannot refer to functions. (i.e. they are all of the form x=$y.z or x=Z)
3. The result of a copy rule is visible on all observations it generates.

When these conditions hold true each copy rule may contribute zero or more attributes or attribute values. For instance in Figure 1 the rule

```
.S -> i'd like to Fly S2:s {from=$s.from,to=$s.to,
op=bookflight}
```

contributes the attribute `op=bookflight` to the phrase

```
i'd like to fly from melbourne to sydney
```

The rule

```
Location -> melbourne { from= melbourne }
```

contributes the value "`melbourne`" to it.

The contribution a rule makes to an observation can be described using an ordered pair notation as described in Table 1.

Table 1. Attribute contribution notation

Notation	Name	Meaning
(f,v)	Static contribution	Contributes the attribute f with value v
(*,v)	Wildcard contribution	Contributes the value v

Consider the scenario of two observed phrases as follows:

```
from melbourne to sydney { from=mel, to=syd }
from perth to melbourne { from=pth, to=mel}
```

The first phrase could only be generated with rules with the following attribute contributions

```
A1 = { (from,mel), (to,syd), (*,mel) (*,syd) }
```

This is defined as the attribute contributions of the phrase, and includes one static contribution and one wildcard contribution for each attribute. Similarly the attribute contributions of the second phrase is

```
A2= { (from,pth), (*,pth), (to,mel), (*,mel) }
```

A list of possible attribute contributions of a rule being considered for chunking can be created from the intersection of all the attribute contributions of all the phrases that would be generated by it.

For instance if we considered a rule of the form

```
X -> melbourne
```

Then given the two phrases above its attribute contributions would be contained in the set

A3= A1 ∩ A2= { (*,mel) }

This reduces the search space by eliminating impossible scenarios. For instance the new rule could not contribute (*,syd), otherwise the second phrase would contain this attribute contribution also.
A copy rule can then be generated from this attribute, either from=mel or to=mel. After chunking this would give the grammar of figure 2 below.

```
.S-> from X:x to sydney { from=$x.from,to=syd }
.S->from perth to X:x { from=pth, to=$x.from}
X -> melbourne { from=mel }
```

Fig. 2. Grammar after chunking

It should be noted that, with sparse training data, correlations between phrases and attribute contributions can occur that would disappear with more data. For instance in the example above, the contribution (*,mel) is also attached to the words "from" and "to". In the grammar shown in figure 2 however, the contribution (*,melb) can only be attached to one rule.
The second way in which hierarchical structure is added to the grammar is by replacing repeated phrases by a reference to a new rule which contains the repeated phrase. This enables phrases of two or more symbols to be assigned consistent meaning throughout the grammar. The creation of these new rules is a form of compression, and the technique used in the Lyrebird algorithm, borrows some techniques from the Sequitur algorithm[12]. The Lyrebird algorithm uses a bigram table to count the number of occurrences of two consecutive symbols in the grammar to ensure the most commonly occurring sequence of symbols are chunked first. Chunking the most commonly occurring sequence of symbols first gives the greatest reduction in the description length of the grammar without affecting discrepancy.

During the merging phase, symbols are merged that can be considered to be equivalent. Merging reduces the complexity of a grammar and generalises it so that it can handle additional phrases. The merging phase uses a set of evidence patterns to determine which non-terminals should be merged. An example evidence pattern along with its required merger action is shown in Table 2 below.

Table 2. Example Merging Evidence Pattern

Evidence	Action
X -> A B & X -> A C	Merge B and C,X -> A Y Y -> B ,Y -> C

If there is evidence for the merge, the merge is executed. Prior to the completion of merge, tests are applied to determine the suitability of the merge. The most critical test is that the grammar can still generate all of the training examples, and attach the same meaning to them.

After merging the algorithm removes redundant and less desirable rules, by attaching probabilities to rules and deleting zero probability rules. Probabilities are estimated using emperical relative frequency estimates [13] and expectation maximisation using the Viterbi parse [14].

3 Experimental Results

Our algorithm was first tested on grammars used by Stolcke and included in the BOOGIE [15] software. The Lyrebird algorithm consistently outperforms the BMM, on these grammars and similar grammars. Figure 3 below shows the grammar coverage of the two algorithms on a natural language date grammar where the difference is most noticeable. The training set included expressions such as

```
march the twenty fifth of two thousand and five {
month="march" day=25 year=2005}
```

&

```
next sunday the twenty fifth {day=25
day_of_week="sunday" modifier="next"}
```

The grammar contained 84 rules and could generate 197,150 possible phrases.
The grammar was chosen because the correlation between some words and the attributes attached to them are inconsistent. For instance;

```
DayOrd -> second { day=2}
DayOrd -> twenty second { day=22}
```

A number of sample and test sets were generated from the grammars, such that the first hundred samples in the training sets included observations generated by each rule in the target grammar. Both tools were tested with training sets of various sizes. A phrase was considered to be in grammar if the grammar could generate it, and the attributes attached to the phrase in the training set were the same as those attached to it by the highest probability parse.

Figure 3 show the results of these tests. The lines labelled "grammar coverage" indicate the percentage of phrases generated by the target grammar that were parsed with the correct meaning by the inferred grammar. The lines labelled "reverse grammar coverage" show the percentage of phrases generated by inferred grammar that are parsed with the correct meaning by the target grammar. These two measurements are equivalent to the concepts of recall and precision in information retrieval respectively. Of these two measures grammar coverage (recall) is more important, and speech recognition accuracy will more closely track it as demonstrated in figure 4.
Each point on figure 3 is the average of four tests. It can be seen that the Lyrebird algorithm significantly outperforms the Bayesian Model Merging algorithm for this data. With 700 training samples, the Lyrebird algorithm could produce 99.9% of the

phrases in the test sets on average. On some training sets the algorithm could generate a grammar with 100% coverage with as little as 500 training samples.
The reverse grammar coverage plotted in figure 3 shows that the inferred grammar is slightly more general than the target grammar. All of the overgeneralised phrases inferred by Lyrebird were the result of the inference of the equivalence of "*two thousand*" and "*twenty*". This was due to the inclusion in the training data of phrases such as

```
april the ninth of twenty eleven { month="april" day=9
year=2011}
```

The grammars inferred by the Bayesian Model Merging differed significantly from the target grammar, and included large amounts of recursion.

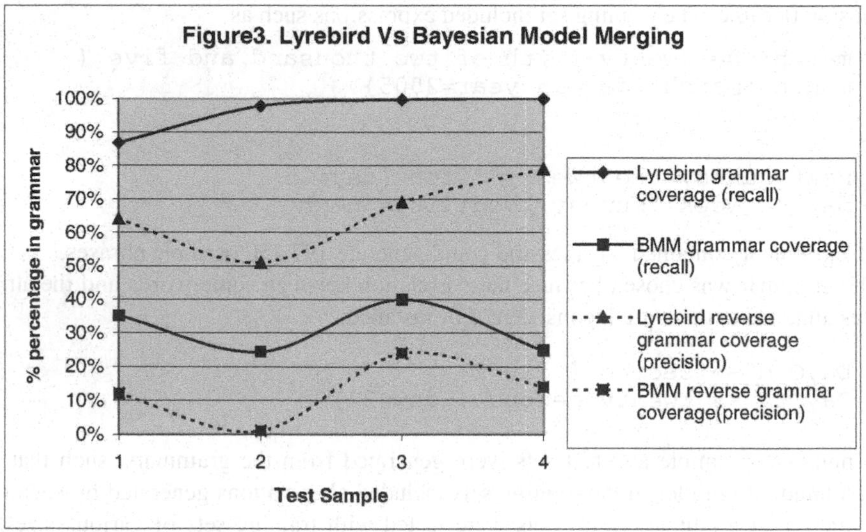

The performance of the Lyrebird algorithm was then compared against an experienced human developer. Two identical train timetable applications were built both manually and using the lyrebird tool. The two applications were then compared on,

1) The time taken to develop the application.
2) The quality of the application developed.

The time taken to develop the application for the start of the learning curve test is shown in table 3. Application quality was measured using percentage of utterances in grammar (recall) and natural language speech recognition accuracy. Precision cannot be measured with real world natural language phrases because the target grammar is unknown. Twelve different speakers were given twelve tasks each (144 tasks). They then interacted with one of the prototype systems, to get the information they wanted. After they completed these tasks they were then encouraged to "try to say it all in one sentence", and "say it the way you (they) would like the system to understand". This resulted in the collection of 1074 utterances, which were transcribed into text and divided into four sets. Both the manually crafted and automatically learnt grammars were then tested on one of the four test sets. The grammars were then modified using the previously seen utterances, and tested on another utterance set. This was repeated four times including the initial grammar. A learning curve was then plotted to show the predictive power of both the manually developed and automatically acquired grammars. This learning curve can be seen in figure 4.

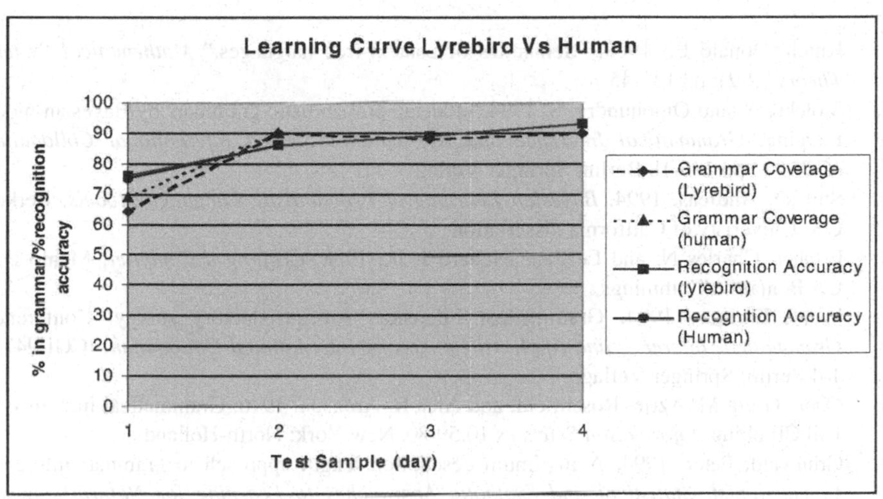

Table 3. Development time Lyrebird Vs Manual (starting application).

	Lyrebird (hrs)	Manual(hrs)
Specification & Data Collection	0.47	0.47
Dialog Manager and Prompts	2.00	21.5
Grammar construction	0.75	9
total (hrs)	3.22	30.97

Conclusion

This paper describes a grammatical inference algorithm created for use in a toolkit for the development of spoken dialogue systems, and compares its performance to both another algorithm for inferring attribute grammars, and an experienced human developer.

The comparison of the algorithm with Bayesian model merging illustrates both its improved performance, and the ability of the algorithm to infer grammars that tightly define the training data. The development of the attribute grammars for an application is the most critical and time consuming task. In addition the work is not easily distributed amongst more than one developer.

The comparison of the algorithm against a human operator illustrates the algorithms ability to learn natural spoken language, in a shorter time frame than a human with a similar quality.

References

1. Knuth, Donald E., 1968, "Semantics of context-free languages." *Mathematical Systems Theory* , 2(2): pp 127-45.
2. Stolcke, A. and Omohundro, S. 1994, Inducing probabilistic grammars by Bayesian model merging, *Grammatical Inference and Applications. Second International Colloquium, ICGI-94* , pp 106-18 Berlin: Springer Verlag.
3. Stolcke, Andreas, 1994, *Bayesian Learning of Probabilistic Language Models*. Berkely CA: Univeristy of California dissertation.
4. Fischer, Charles N. and LeBlanc,Richard J. Jr., 1988, *Crafting a Compiler,* Menlo Park CA Benjamin/Cummings,.
5. Vidal, Enrique, 1994, Grammatical Inference: An introductory survey, Conference: *Grammatical Inference and Applications. Second International Colloquium*, ICGI-94, pp 1-4 Berlin: Springer Verlag.
6. Cook, Graig M.,Azriel Rosenfield, and Alan R. Aronson. 1976. Grammatical inference by Hill Climbing. *Information Sciences* 10.59-80. New York: North-Holland
7. Grünwald, Peter, 1994, A minimum description length approach to grammar inference, *Connectionist, Statistical and Symbolic Approaches to Learning for NaturalLanguage Processing* , volume 1004 of Lecture Notes in AI, pp 203-16 Berlin: Springer Verlag.
8. Dulz, Winfried and Hoffmann, Stefan 1991, Grammar-based Workload Modelling of Communication Systems, Conference: *Computer Performance Evaluation. Modelling Techniques and Tools. Proceedings of the Fifth International Conference* , pp 17-31 Amsterdam: North-Holland
9. Ross, Brian J. 2001, Logic-based Genetic Programming with Definite Clause Translation grammars, *New Generation Computing* (in press),
10. Starkie, Bradford C., 1999. *A method of developing an interactive system*, International Patent WO 00/78022.
11. Starkie, Bradford C., 2001. Developing Spoken Dialog Systems using Grammatical Inference, *Proceedings of the 2001 Australasian Natural Language Processing Workshop (ANLP 2001)*,pp 25-32 Maquarie University Language Technology Group.
12. Nevill-Manning, Craig G., 1996 *Inferring Sequential Structure* , University of Waikato doctoral dissertation.
13. Abney, Steven 1997, Stochastic Attribute-Value Grammars, *Computational Linguistics* , vol.23, no.4 , pp 597-618 MIT Press for Assoc. Comput. Linguistics
14. Charniak, Eugene 1993, Statistical Language Learning, Cambridge, Mass. : MIT Press.
15. Stolcke, Andreas, June 1994, How to BOOGIE: A manual for Bayesian Object-oriented Grammar Induction and Estimation, Internal memo, International Computer Science Institute.

Towards Genetic Programming for Texture Classification

Andy Song, Thomas Loveard, and Vic Ciesielski

School of Computer Science
RMIT University
GPO Box 2476V, Melbourne Victoria 3001, Australia
{asong,toml,vc}@cs.rmit.edu.au

Abstract. The genetic programming (GP) method is proposed as a new approach to perform texture classification based directly on raw pixel data. Two alternative genetic programming representations are used to perform classification. These are dynamic range selection (DRS) and static range selection (SRS). This preliminary study uses four brodatz textures to investigate the applicability of the genetic programming method for binary texture classifications and multi-texture classifications.
Results indicate that the genetic programming method, based directly on raw pixel data, is able to accurately classify different textures. The results show that the DRS method is well suited to the task of texture classification. The classifiers generated in our experiments by DRS have good performance over a variety of texture data and offer GP as a promising alternative approach for the difficult problem of texture classification.

1 Introduction

Textural information is an important aspect of visual processing in both human and artificial applications. The capability of recognising and categorising textures is a key requirement to the use of textural data in a visual system, be it natural or artificial.

Genetic programming (GP) has emerged as a flexible method of problem solving for a diverse range of complex problems [6]. In this approach a population of computer programs are evolved over a number of generations to perform a specific task, in a process analogous to natural evolution.

One task that GPs have previously been applied to is that of classification. In classification tasks, each example to be classified consists of a feature vector pertaining to various attributes of the example, and a class label, indicating which, of a set of possible classes, the example belongs. A classifier is trained from a given set of examples where the class of the example is known, and the accuracy of the classifier can then be determined by the application of the resulting classifier on unseen data. In previous investigations GPs have shown to be capable of producing accurate classifiers in a variety of domains such as medical diagnosis [7,8], object detection and image analysis [11,13].

M. Brooks, D. Corbett, and M. Stumptner (Eds.): AI 2001, LNAI 2256, pp. 461–472, 2001.

Texture is observed as homogeneous visual patterns of scenes that we perceive, such as grass, cloud, wood and sand. The repetition of such patterns somehow produces the uniformity of sense which is very important for a observer to understand the scenes.

The textural property of an image is one of the most informative cues for machine vision tasks, such as visual inspection, medical image analysis and remote sensing. However, there is no universally accepted definition of texture and no universal model to describe texture. Analysing texture information of images still remains a complex problem.

Texture classification is one of the main areas of texture analysis problems, in which image textures are categorized into different classes and an observed image will be determined to belong to one of the given set of texture classes. The conventional method of texture classification involves obtaining an a priori knowledge of each class to be recognized. Normally this knowledge is some set of texture features of one or all of the classes. Once the knowledge is available and texture features of the observed image are extracted, then classical classification techniques , e.g. nearest neighbors and decision trees, can be used to make the decision [12]. The fields that texture classification has been applied to include the classification of satellite images [10], radar imagery [1], inspection [3] and content based image retrieval [5],

In this paper we propose a new method towards texture classification problems by the use of genetic programming in a one step process, directly based on raw pixel data. As a result the process of classifier production by this method does not require manual interruption or detailed domain knowledge.

The aim of this research investigation is to explore the application of GP towards the texture classification problem, and to determine a GP methodology that can be appropriately applied to this complex domain. Additionally this work aims to provide support for the suitability of the GP approach to the texture domain and for applicability of the method in general.

2 Methodologies

2.1 Genetic Programming: Static Range Selection

In the general case, genetic programs return numeric (real) values as program output, such as can be seen in the example program in figure 1. In previous works into GP for classification the real values returned by GPs have been used to interpret the class value by arbitrarily segmenting the range of reals. Each segment correspond to class labels. For this investigation we term this method of classification static range selection (SRS).

For a two class (binary) classification problem the division point for the classes in SRS is generally made to be the zero point, which forms a suitable decision boundary for the two classes. A training example that results in a negative output from the program will be classified class 1, while a non-negative result will be classified class 2. For problems with more than two classes, meaningful division points over the set of reals are not readily available, and the choosing of arbitrary division points has been shown to produce less accurate classifiers [7]. For this reason the SRS method is seen to be suitable for only binary classification problems.

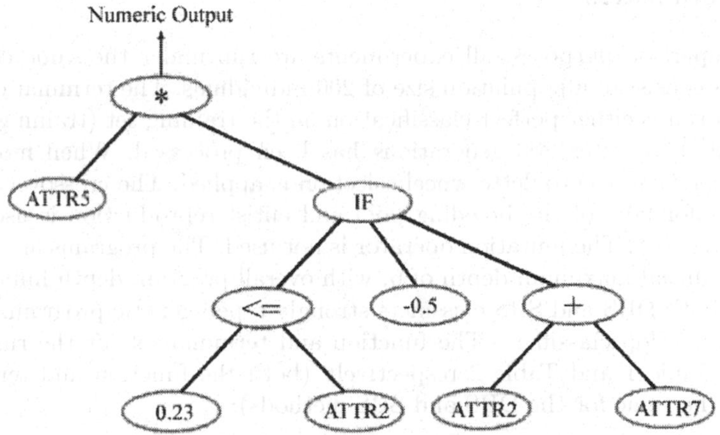

Fig. 1. An example genetic program for classification

2.2 Genetic Programming: Dynamic Range Selection

An alternative to SRS for performing classification using genetic programming is the method of dynamic range selection (DRS) [7]. Similar to the SRS approach to classification, real values are returned by a GP which must then be interpreted as one of a possible set of class labels. In this instance however the ranges for class labels over the set of reals are determined dynamically, and can be different for each program. The segmentation of the range of reals is performed using a subset of the training data termed the segmentation subset. For any individual within the GP population, each data example of the segmentation subset is presented to the GP classifier and the output value is recorded, along with the known class label. In the interests of limiting complexity, in this investigation the output values are rounded to the nearest integer value, and output values greater then +250 are considered to be +250. Likewise values less than -250 are considered to be the value -250.

Once all elements from the segmentation subset have been presented to the GP the output range [-250,250] is segmented into class labels. This segmentation is performed such that any given point over the range [-250,250] corresponds to the class label of the nearest output value obtained from the segmentation subset. The resulting range segmentation may thus contain multiple class labels, and multiple regions for any given class label.

The DRS method of classifier representation was shown to be capable of producing accurate results over a variety of datasets in the medical and image processing domains [7].

2.3 Parameters

For comparison purposes, all experiments are run under the same conditions. All runs consist of a population size of 200 individuals. The termination criteria for each run is either perfect classification on the training set (training accuracy was 100%), or after 200 generations has been processed. When moving to a new generation, the roulette wheel selection is applied. The crossover operation accounts for 90% of the breeding pool and elitist reproduction is used for the remaining 10%. The mutation operator is not used. The programs are generated with an initial maximum depth of 6, with overall program depth limited to 17.

For both DRS and SRS classifiers strongly typed genetic programming [9] is used to develop classifiers. The function and terminal set for the runs can be seen in Table 1 and Table 2 respectively (both the function and terminal set remain the same for the DRS and SRS methods).

Table 1. Function Set

Name	Return Type	Argument Types	Description
Plus	Double	Double, Double	Arithmetic addition
Minus	Double	Double, Double	Arithmetic subtraction
Mult	Double	Double, Double	Arithmetic multiplication
Div	Double	Double, Double	Protected arithmetic division (divide by zero returns zero)
IF	Double	Boolean, Double, Double	Conditional. If arg1 is true return arg2, otherwise return arg3
<=	Boolean	Double, Double	True if arg1 is <= arg2
>=	Boolean	Double, Double	True if arg1 is >= arg2
=	Boolean	Double, Double	True if arg1 is equal to arg2
Between	Boolean	Double, Double, Double	True if the value of arg1 is between arg2 and arg3

Table 2. Terminal Set

Name	Return Type	Description
Random(-1, 1)	Double	Randomly assigned constant between -1 and 1
Attribute[x]	Double	Value of attribute x

2.4 The Datasets

Fig. 2. The four textures (a)French Canvas(D21) (b)Soap Bubbles(D73) (c)Cotton Canvas(D77) (d)Plastic Bubbles(D112) (From Left to Right)

Four kinds of texture from Brodatz album [2] are used to test the classification performance of genetic programming method. They are French canvas(D21), Soap bubbles(D73), Cotton canvas(D77) and Plastic bubbles(D112). All these textures are grey level images, of the value from 0 to 255 (See Figure 2).

For each class of texture, 400 distinct sub-images are sampled from the original 640×640 picture. These sub images can be considered as the texture elements, called texels [4]. To determine the size or appropriate resolution of texels could be an extensive research topic itself. In our work, we simply use 16 pixels by 16 pixels as the sampling size.

2.5 Fitness Function

The fitness value measures the performance of the generated program in terms of the ability to solve the problem. The fitter individual programs have a probabilistically greater opportunity to pass genetic material to future generations.

The fitness measure for texture classification is straightforward. The performance can be determined by the success made by the program, which is, in this case, the classification accuracy (the percentage of the cases that have been correctly classified). As a result the fitness value can be expressed by the following formula:

$$f = \frac{TP + TN}{TOTAL} \times 100\% \tag{1}$$

Where TP is the true positive rate, TN is the true negative rate and TOTAL is the total number of the cases.

2.6 Classification Accuracy

To evaluate the classification accuracy of the methods trialed, ten fold cross validation is applied. In experiments using SRS nine folds of data are used in training and one is used as test (unseen) data. In experiments using DRS one fold is used as the segmentation subset, eight folds are used for training and one fold is used for test.

Due to the probabilistic nature of GP systems, results can vary from run to run. To reduce the variation of results due to random sampling, all experiments are run ten times and the final accuracy for training and test are given as an average of these ten runs (giving a total of 100 independent GP runs for each experiment).

3 Experiments and Results

3.1 Binary Classifications

The first stage of this investigation involved the use of a GP classifier to differentiate one texture from another. Each run selected two from the four textures used until all possible combinations were exhausted. The resulting dataset for each run consisted of 800 examples (400 examples from each texture class). The results of these experiments were shown in Table 3.

Table 3. Classifying Two Textures: Classifier Accuracy (Test Data), average of 10 runs

	D21 vs D73	D21 vs D77	D21 vs D112	D73 vs D77	D73 vs D112	D77 vs D112
SRS	87.74%	80.74%	87.72%	71.73%	87.86%	80.72%
DRS	91.73%	89.59%	98.24%	84.35%	99.75%	99.11%

3.2 Multiclass Classifications

Binary problems are rare in the domain of texture classification and to account for this we extended the GP approach to multiclass classification.

Five additional experiments, shown in Table 4, used all 1600 samples from the four textures. The first four experiments were the extension of binary classification, in which one texture was labelled as 0, while all other textures were labelled as class 1, resulting in a binary classification problem. In contrast, the texture samples used in the fifth experiment were labelled from 0 to 3, in which four classes were included.

Both methods, SRS and DRS, were applied in the first four experiments. In fifth experiment, only DRS was used as the SRS is considered to be unsuited to the method of multi-class classification.

For the experiment classifying the texture D112 against the other three textures we also present, in Figure 3, the progression of classification accuracy over generations for the DRS and SRS methods. The accuracy figures are given as

Table 4. Classifying Four Textures: Classifier Accuracy (Test Data), average of 10 runs

	D21 vs D73 D77 D112	D73 vs D21 D77 D112	D77 vs D21 D73 D112	D112 vs D21 D73 D77	All Four Classes
SRS	90.0%	77.4%	79.7%	85.9%	-
DRS	91.8%	85.1%	81.7%	99.36%	71.82%

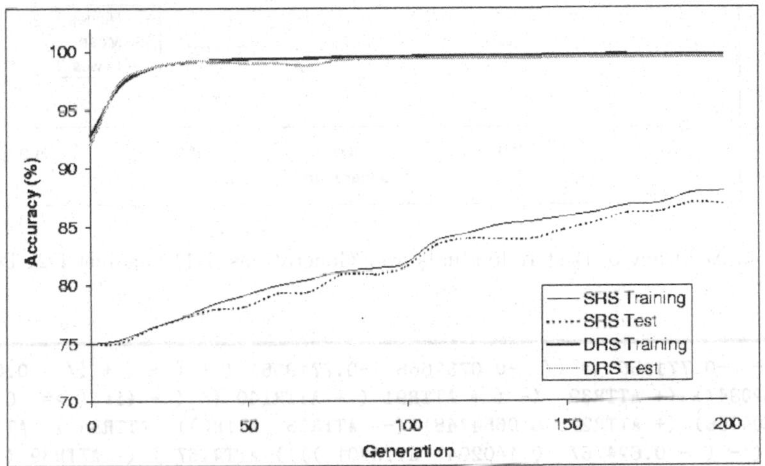

Fig. 3. Accuracy of Best Individuals over Generations: D112 against D21 D73 D77

the best individual (based on training fitness) of each generation for the run. Figures for both training and test accuracy for such individuals are presented, although it should be noted that these figures are given as the average over 10 runs.

Additionally, for this experiment (D112 vs D21, D73, D77) Figure 4 showed the trend of test accuracy over the ten runs. The top line represented the highest test accuracy in the ten, the bottom line showed the lowest, while the middle represented the mean.

4 Discussion and Analysis of Results

In the application of the two methods of genetic programming to the texture classification task it can be seen that classifiers of a high degree of accuracy were produced, particularly when the DRS method of training was employed. The results shown in Figure 3 indicate that the DRS method not only had a higher accuracy than SRS, but also converge at a faster rate than the SRS method. It can be seen that in this experiment the average classification accuracy of the DRS method reached 99% in 40 generations. Subsequently, from generation 40 to 200,

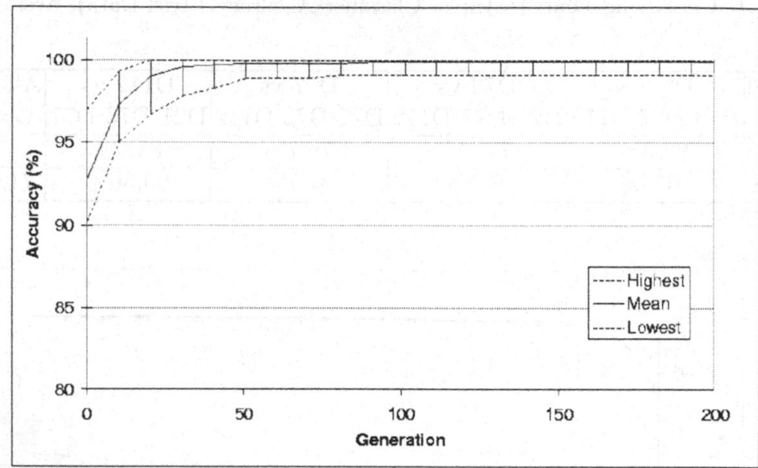

Fig. 4. Accuracy of Best Individuals over Generations: D112 against D21 D73 D77

```
(+ (+  -0.771955 (* (/  -0.0752668  -0.771955) ( + ( + ( + (/  -0.0752668
-0.820847) (+ ATTR39  (- ( + ATTR91 ( - ATTR140 (/ ( + (if ( >= -0.552571
-0.704058) (+ ATTR215 0.0654748) (-  ATTR35  ATTR0))  ATTR84 )  ATTR247 )
) ) ( - ( - 0.624757  0.140204) ATTR201 )))) ATTR167 ) (+ ATTR39 (+ ATTR8
ATTR30 ))))) ( * ( / -0.0752668 -0.820847) ( + ( - ( + (+ ATTR42 ATTR167)
ATTR59) (- (- 0.624757 0.140204) ATTR201)) ATTR85)))

          Ranges: Class 1: D112           : -213 ~ +250
                  Class 2: Other Textures : -250 ~ -214
```

Fig. 5. A program generated by the DRS method which can achieve 100% accuracy

the accuracy was only very slighted improved. In the ten runs of the experiment, there were four runs which were able to achieve 100% accuracy on training data and terminated within 40 generations. In comparison, classifiers trained with the SRS method converged at a slower rate, and were never capable of exceeding the accuracy achieved by the DRS method. This pattern is consistent with results in all other experiments run in this investigation.

Figure 3 shows the progression of training and test accuracy for both the SRS and DRS. It can be noted that for both DRS and SRS, the curves of training accuracy and test accuracy are very close, which indicates that the classifiers generated in the training process generalise well to unseen data. An additional point of interest is that, even after many generations of near perfect classification, the DRS method did not tend to begin the over-train on the training data. If

```
(* -0.208533 (if (n= (- ATTR39 ATTR69) (+ ATTR114 0.299995)) (- ATTR222
0.253174) ( + ( + (if (Between ( * ATTR189 ( + ATTR205 ATTR74)) ATTR164
ATTR12) ATTR108 ( if (Between ( - (* 0.253174 ATTR129) 0.9875) 0.128228
(/ ATTR189 0.940897)) ( + ATTR39 (if (Between -0.947054 ATTR164 ATTR12)
ATTR160 ATTR124)) (* 0.5979 0.230855))) ( + ( + (if (Between (+ ATTR205
ATTR74) ATTR164 ATTR12) ATTR108 ( if ( Between -0.947054 ( if ( Between
-0.947054  ATTR164  ATTR12) ATTR160  ATTR124)  ATTR12) ( + ATTR39 (if (
Between -0.947054 ATTR164 ( - (/ ATTR149 ( if (Between -0.947054 (if (
Between -0.947054  ATTR164  ATTR12) ATTR160  ATTR124)  ATTR12)  ATTR108
0.135714)) (* ATTR164 ATTR129))) ATTR160 ATTR124))(* 0.5979 0.230855)))
(if (Between (* ATTR189 (+ (if (Between (- (* 0.253174 ATTR129) 0.9875)
0.128228 ( / ATTR189 ( - 0.987674 0.747389))) ( + ATTR39 ( if ( Between
-0.947054  ATTR164  ATTR12)  ATTR160  ATTR124)) ( *  0.5979  0.230855))
ATTR74)) ATTR164 ATTR12) ATTR205 ( + ( + ( if (Between (* (* ATTR189 (+
ATTR205 ATTR74)) ( + ATTR205  ATTR74 )) ATTR164  ATTR12 ) ATTR108 (if (
Between (- (* 0.253174 ATTR129) 0.9875) 0.128228 (/ ATTR189 (- 0.987674
0.747389))) ( +  ATTR39 (if ( Between -0.947054 ATTR164 ATTR12) ATTR160
ATTR124)) ( * 0.5979 0.230855))) ( + ( + ATTR160 (if (Between -0.947054
ATTR164 ATTR12) ATTR160  ATTR114))  ( * 0.253174  ATTR129))) ATTR205)))
(* 0.253174 ATTR129))) ATTR205))

      Ranges: Class 1: D112            : -250 ~ +146
              Class 2: Other Textures : +147 ~ +250
```

Fig. 6. Another program generated with the DRS method

this had occurred the test error rate in Figure 3 would be seen to decline in later generations, which is not the case here.

In this same experiment using DRS methods for distinguishing D112 with other three textures, ten classification programs were created at the end of each run (one for each fold of test data). Fig 5 and 6 are two examples of such programs. These programs were selected from different runs and were the best individuals of their run. These two classifiers achieved 100% training accuracy and 100% test accuracy before 200 generations. Each program has a separate range of values corresponding to class labels, which are generated by the dynamic selection process. In the case of these programs it appears that a single threshold value is sufficient to accurately classify the textures. However it is possible that some textures could require more than one threshold e.g. -250 to -100 with 100 to 150 being the range of one class, and -99 to 99 with 150 and above being the range of another class. For such a multi-threshold problems it is certainly most difficult for the SRS method to achieve high classification accuracy and easy convergence.

Although these two programs in Fig 5 and 6 have good performance, they are in relatively simple forms. Program 1 only uses *IF* and one >= function (which are actually redundant as they compare two constant values) and a combination of arithmetic functions. The program only utilises 17 attributes, which corresponds to 17 pixels of the 256 pixels of texel input images. Program 2 looks much more complicated than the program1, but it requires only 20 pixels of the 16×16 raw image as the input for its 20 attributes. It can also be noted that the set of input attributes used by each program differ substantially. All programs from runs that were assessed made use of a different set of attributes and adhered to a variety of associated ranges. This variability in the approach to classification can be seen as an advantage for the further generalisation of the method. Having a flexible and varied approach from run to run should allow the method to be applied to a wide variety of texture classification problems.

The four textures used in this investigation have varied levels of difficulty for classification. The accuracy of classifying the two textures D73 and D77 is the lowest of the two texture classification problem, at 84.4%. With the addition of the two other textures, the accuracy didn't change by anything but a relatively small amount. The lower accuracy in this problem may be partially due to the size of sampling window (16×16), which is possibly not large enough to extract the information needed to distinguish between these two textures. In contrast it appears that the texture D112 is relatively simple for genetic programming to classify, particularly with the DRS method. This would indicate that the GP method is able to classify textures, although the accuracy of this classification is dependent upon some further factors.

In an attempt to verify that the GP systems were utilising meaningful textural information from the problem, and not simply memorising attributes of the training dataset, four additional experiments were conducted in which the each of the four textures was classified against itself. For all four textures, the training accuracy obtained from both DRS and SRS method was around 50%. The inability of the method to distinguish one texture from that same texture indicates that the accuracy of the classifier is based on the texture information present in the texels, rather than any specifically remembered elements of the data. Additional support for this is found in the fact that test and training error rates remain similar, even when large periods of training are given.

One interesting consideration of the four multi-class experiments where one texture was classified against all other textures is that the generated classifiers, with a high degree of classification accuracy can potentially be considered as the texture description function for a particular texture. According to our results, such classifiers are relatively small in size and do not require all pixel information of a texture image. Moreover, such classifiers are able to directly work on pixel data, indicating that the conventional texture feature extraction process is not necessary in the genetic approach.

5 Conclusions and Future Work

The aim of this study was to explore the genetic programming paradigm towards classification, and in particular, the difficult problem of texture classification.

In this work two approaches of representation, static range selection (SRS) and dynamic range selection(DRS), were investigated. The results from all the experiments indicate that DRS can generate a more accurate classifier compared to SRS. Moreover, DRS has quicker convergence, which means a classifier with higher performance can be generated more quickly by DRS than by SRS.

This work also proposed genetic programming as a new method towards texture classification. The results indicate this method was able to classify texture images directly based on raw pixel information. Within the limited training process, some texture could be classified to a near perfect degree of accuracy.

In the future work, the investigation will involves the inclusion of more textures, using larger population and more training generations, using different sampling window size and resolution, the inclusion of some simple features such as local statistical data or simple feature extraction functions into classifiers. The investigation will also address the understanding of the generated programs, which could answer why the genetic programming approach has good performance. Analyzing of these programs could also be helpful to understand textural properties of images. This study could further improve the applicability of the genetic programming method to the texture classification problem.

References

1. D Blacknell. Texture anomaly detection in radar imagery. In *Texture Classification: Theory and Applications, IEE Colloquium on , 1994*, pages 7/1 –7/4. 1994.
2. Phil Brodatz. *Textures: A Photographic Album for Artists and Designers.* Dover, NY, 1966.
3. L. Hepplewhite and T.J. Stonham. Magnetic disk inspection using texture recognition. In *Texture Classification: Theory and Applications, IEE Colloquium on , 1994*, pages 8/1 –8/4. 1994.
4. Anil K. Jain. *Fundamentals of Digital Image Processing.* Prentice-Hall, Englewood Cliffs, NJ, 1989.
5. J.You, H. Shen and H. A. Cohen. An efficient parallel texture classification for image retrieval. In *Advances in Parallel and Distributed Computing, 1997. Proceedings*, pages 18–25, 1997.
6. John R. Koza. *Genetic Programming: On the Programming of Computers by Means of Natural Selection.* MIT Press, 1992.
7. Thomas Loveard and Victor Ciesielski. Representing classification problems in genetic programming. In *Proceedings of the Congress on Evolutionary Computation*, Volume 2, pages 1070–1077, COEX, Seoul, Korea, 27-30 May 2001. IEEE Press.
8. Robert E. Marmelstein and Gary B. Lamont. Pattern classification using a hybrid genetic program decision tree approach. In John R. Koza, Wolfgang Banzhaf, Kumar Chellapilla, Kalyanmoy Deb, Marco Dorigo, David B. Fogel, Max H. Garzon, David E. Goldberg, Hitoshi Iba and Rick Riolo (editors), *Genetic Programming 1998: Proceedings of the Third Annual Conference*, pages 223–231, University of Wisconsin, Madison, Wisconsin, USA, 22-25 July 1998. Morgan Kaufmann.

9. David J. Montana. Strongly typed genetic programming. *Evolutionary Computation*, Volume 3, Number 2, pages 199–230, 1995.
10. M.A. Shaban and O. Dikshit. Textural classification of high resolution digital satellite imagery. In *Geoscience and Remote Sensing Symposium Proceedings, 1998*, Volume 5, pages 2590 –2592, 1998.
11. Walter Alden Tackett. Genetic programming for feature discovery and image discrimination. In Stephanie Forrest (editor), *Proceedings of the 5th International Conference on Genetic Algorithms, ICGA-93*, pages 303–309, University of Illinois at Urbana-Champaign, 17-21 July 1993. Morgan Kaufmann.
12. Mihran Tuceryan and Anil K. Jain. Texture analysis. In C. H. Chen, L. F. Pau and P. S. P. Wang (editors), *Handbook of Pattern Recognition and Computer Vision*, Chapter 2, pages 235–276. World Scientific, Singapore, 1993.
13. Mengjie Zhang and Victor Ciesielski. Genetic programming for multiple class object detection. In Norman Foo (editor), *Proceedings of the 12th Australian Joint Conference on Artificial Intelligence*, Volume 1747, Lecture Notes in Artificial Intelligence, pages 180–191. Springer, Heidelberg, Dec 1999.

Using Design Information to Identify Structural Software Faults*

Markus Stumptner
University of South Australia
Advanced Computing Research Centre
5095 Mawson Lakes SA
Email: mst@cs.unisa.edu.au

Abstract

The use of model-based diagnosis techniques for software debugging has been an active research area for several years. This paper describes the extension of model-based debugging by the utilization of object-oriented design information for the identification of structural faults. The typical structural software fault is the incorrect assignment, both a frequent and hard to identify problem if no extra information about the fault is present. We analyze the different types of faults, use heuristics about pre- and postconditions to infer missing or additional state variable assignments, and use statechart diagrams as additional constraints over the permissible method execution sequences.

1 Introduction

Detecting, locating, and repairing faults in software is a difficult and time consuming task. Detecting an incorrect behavior of a given program is done by using testing techniques or formal verification methods, e.g., model checking [CGL94]. Whereas much effort has been made on test theory, test methodology, and algorithms for automatic test-case generation, somewhat less work has been published on locating and repairing software faults. Because debugging is not only performed in the implementation and test phases of a project, but also in maintenance, saving debugging time naturally results in saving time and money over the whole product life cycle. Especially in maintenance, where the original developers may no longer be involved, debugging is very costly. An automated debugger for locating and fixing faults can help in such a situation.

Automatic debugging approaches introduced in the past include program slicing [Wei84], algorithmic debugging [Sha83], dependency-based techniques [KR97, Jac95], probability-based methods [BH95], and others. These traditional approaches

*This work was partially supported by Austrian Science Fund projects P12344-INF and N Z29-INF.

M. Brooks, D. Corbett, and M. Stumptner (Eds.): AI 2001, LNAI 2256, pp. 473–486, 2001.

are either specific to a programming language, use specialized algorithms, or require explicit user-interaction to locate a bug. In order to overcome these drawbacks and to improve the results of the abovementioned approaches, the use of model-based diagnosis (MBD) for debugging was suggested [CFD93]. Model-based diagnosis [Rei87, dKW87] provides a general theory for diagnosis that has sucessfully been applied to various engineering areas.

We have previously described the use of a model of Java programs that is based on recording dependencies between variables [MSW00a]. We convert the Java program into a logical description that afterwards is used together with a model-based diagnosis engine [Rei87, dKW87] for computing diagnoses, i.e., finding possible bug locations given an observed incorrect execution outcome. An alternate model that was based on the actual values being computed for a given test case was described in [MSW00b].

In Model-based Diagnosis [Rei87], the structural or bridge fault has been justly considered as a special problem that requires special methods to be effectively solved. The original bridge fault, as described by Davis [Dav84], occurs in circuits where a short circuit exists across multiple lines and thus forces them to an identical state, despite the fact that they are not functionally connected according to the original description of the artifact. Such a fault can therefore only be handled by the use of a separate, second model that allows to identify special situations (such as physical adjacency in the case of the brigde fault) which can then be examined more closely. This approach was generalized by Boettcher [Böt95], where the notion of physical layout was converted into an abstract context that activated additional model fragments suitable to capturing specific types of what was appropriately called "hidden interactions".

Applying model-based diagnosis to software emphasizes the necessity to come to terms with structural faults, due to the different nature of buggy software - by definition an unfinished artifact for which unlike in hardware diagnosis a complete description cannot even exist. As mentioned, above, our recent work has developed diagnosis models applicable for imperative programs written in the Java language at different levels of abstraction: dependency-oriented [MSW99], i.e., the model used for diagnosis only expresses dependencies between variables, and parts of the program that are assumed to be correct propagate correct values through the system until they contradict observations of bugs, at which point diagnoses can be computed in terms of components that are assumed to be incorrect; and value-oriented [MSW00a], where the semantics of the language are modeled in detail so that effectively the complete execution of a program is simulated and examined dynamically. Both approaches, as the authors note, are of limited applicability with regard to structural faults, although this issue was examined in [SW99], where structural faults were explicitly addressed by considering name misspellings, variable switchings, or searching for repair expressions (i.e., synthesizing missing parts) to provide correct functionality. This paper takes a different approach in that it uses available sources of information for focusing on structural faults. Nonetheless it should be noted that the focus is still on diagnosis, i.e. error *location*, compared to verification approachs, which deal with error *detection* and by means of checking whether the program formally satisfies external special purpose specifications.

The rest of the paper is structured as follows: We first examine the different types of structural errors that can occur in software and show how their influence on a dependency-based diagnosis model. We then examine the use of object-oriented design documentation in augmenting diagnosis models. First we consider contracts and give an example of how their incorporation in the diagnosis process can exclude diagnoses, thus improving the process. We then examine the use of high-level models such as UML statecharts. The paper closes with a discussion of related results.

2 Structural errors and software diagnosis

Structural faults are faults that do not occur because a component is functioning incorrectly, but because there is a missing or *additional* connection between two components, as in a bridge fault in electrical engineering. More than in traditional domains it is relevant when diagnosis is applied to designs, and in particular, software designs (which Davis mentioned as one particular area in his article). The use of an incorrect argument in an expression (e.g., by using a different variable name, switching the ordering of arguments), or the omission of part of a complex expression constitute typical examples of such faults.

In conventional model-based diagnosis, the system description is an exact specification not only of the overall behavior of the system, but of its individual parts. For example, when diagnosing the hardware implementation of a 16-bit adder, the adder's system description will describe the behavior of the logical gates from which the adder is composed. A fault is assumed to occur because one of the components does not act according to its specification.

In diagnosing a program, the assumption that the specification will be a complete representation of the structure of the artifact is invalid. The internal structure and the way in which the behavior is described will differ widely between a specification and its implementation in a programming language – the implementation will usually contain many auxiliary variables and data structures and signals which have no explicit counterpart at all in the functional specification. The only "part" of the specification that is directly usable are, generally, test cases which are produced manually (sometimes by software tools). One is therefore forced to base the model of the implementation on analysis of the code of the implementation itself. That implies, however, that it is the model that reflects the incorrectness of the design and whose output (the implementation trace) is confronted with observations that are correct (the specification trace), whereas in traditional diagnosis problems, the model is correct and it is the observations, made from the behavior of the actual system, that reflect on the incorrect behavior.

The usual way for dealing with structural faults is to assume the existence of a different, complementary model that allows to reason about the likelihood of such faults (i.e., modelling of spatial neighbourhood in the case of bridge faults). Before we consider this issue we first want to examine structural errors more closely.

2.1 Classifying Structural Errors

We consider the execution of a sequential program P to be represented by a sequence $\rho_1, \ldots, \rho_n$ of states of its variables. We write $\rho_i < \rho_j$ if $i < j$. Note that the set of variables in the program is not constant over time since local variables will be created by entering subroutines (methods in Java) and instance variables will be created when objects are created.

We first want to examine how structural errors make themselves felt in the code for detection purposes. In hardware diagnosis, methods that attempt to solve structural diagnosis problems are generally applied only to diagnosis candidates postulating multiple faults.

For the purpose of this discussion, we do not make a distinction between different types of variables (local, global, static, instance or class variables, or reference parameter to methods). We basically examine independent (local or static variables) and, later, as part of our example, variables that are associated with a particular object (instance variables). We call an incorrect assignment to a variable `x` *masked* at a point ρ in the execution of program P if the variable had its value overwritten by a different assignment without being accessed, or if the scope containing the variable was left/destroyed without the variable being accessed again. We write that `x` is *masked** in ρ if there is a sequence of variables $x_1 = \mathtt{x}, \ldots, x_n$ s.t. x_{i+1} depends on x_i, but x_n is masked in ρ. We write that a variable `x` is *observed* to be incorrect in a particular state ρ of P if the value of `x` in ρ is incorrect. We write that a variable `x` is *felt incorrect* in a state ρ of P if `x` is not masked* in ρ.

We examine the different types of structural errors that may result from assignments. Note that other types of assignment than assignment statements exist, e.g., use of reference parameters in a subroutine, just as it is possible to access a variable outside a statement (e.g., in a loop condition). However, these cases can in general be expressed in terms of an assignment statement simply in terms of postulating the introduction of an auxiliary variable. E.g., a call `findName(name,user2)` that is supposed to alter the value of `name` by reference can be replaced by the sequence `findName(aux,user2); name = aux,` or a condition **if** `i < j` can be written as `aux = j;` **if** `i < aux`. The only situation where this is not possible is a variable access in a loop condition: `z = 0; while (i < z) {`⟨body⟩`; z =` ⟨some expression⟩`}` would require *both* assigments to `z` replaced by assignments to `aux` and therefore lose the property of having only one position changed.

We do omit intricate situations that are possible in expression-oriented languages like C or Java, where assignments are expressions too and therefore can be used inside other expressions, since in usage is hard to understand for the programmers themselves and therefore frowned upon[1]. The exception are `for` loops, but we omit these for space reasons, since for theoretical purposes they can be simulated by `while` loops, although a specific treatment will be more effective in practice. Finally, we do assume that the variables and constants involved in the errors are type compatible, since that type of error can routinely be caught by current compilers.

2.2 Structural assignment faults

For illustration purposes, we examine the simple case of an incorrect assignment statement. The first case is the classical case of a statement that has been inadvertently added.

[1]One could argue that a debugger could then help here a lot, which is true, but then we do not claim that being better at semantic understanding of programs than programmers possible with current technology. Some situations are just too hard.

Assignment added: `x=z;` is contained in the program, but should not be.

In all other cases we consider a variation of an intended correct assignment statement s with textual representation `x = y;` in program state ρ. This is a stand in for the whole class of statements of type `x =` $\langle exp \rangle$ where $\langle exp \rangle$ is a complex expression containing an access of `y`. Given that $s \equiv$ `x = y;` is the statement that should actually be contained in the code, we have basically five possible erroneous statements s' that could be considered to be produced instead of s by "atomic" errors. The first four assume that `y` is a variable. The fifth assumes that `y` is a named constant or a literal (we refer to both cases simply as "constant" from here on).

Wrong target: $s' \equiv$ `z=y;` where `z` is a different variable.

Wrong source: $s' \equiv$ `x=z;` where `z` is a different variable.

Constant source: $s' \equiv$ `x=c;` where `c` is a constant.

Switch: $s' \equiv$ `y=x;` .

Variable source: (Remember that `y` is a constant in this case.) $s' \equiv$ `x=z;` where `z` is a variable.

Assignment omitted: s is not contained in the code.

We will refer to these cases by their abbreviations: WT, WS, CS, S, VW, AA, AO. Regardless of the type of error present there must be some test case such that the value assigned to `x` will be incorrect (or we are not dealing with an error but have merely uncovered a case of redundant data storage in the supposedly correct program).

The WT and WS case remove one dependency between variables in the program state and add another. The AO and VS case add one, while the CS and AO case drop one and the S case reverses the direction of one.

Note that if the WT, WS, and S case result in `z` being incorrect in program state $\tau > s'(\rho)$, then the value of `x` in $s'(\rho)$ is also incorrect and if `x` is not masked*, `x` will also be felt incorrect in τ.

The WS, CS, VS, and AO case result in only `x` being incorrect in program state $s'(\rho)$. An observation in $s'(\rho)$ will therefore identify `x` as a potential single fault candidate.

As can be seen, examining single test cases does not necessarily result in multiple fault candidates. The identification of structural faults with multiple fault candidates only applies in domains where the structural faults have the semantics of bridge faults in the original model, namely that both ends of the new connection are influenced. A positive effect of this is that a dependency- or value-based model will still propose s' as one of its set of single fault diagnosis candidates. A negative effect is that it means the standard recognition method from hardware diagnosis is not applicable. The counterpart of, say, a VS fault in hardware diagnosis would be that of being shorted to ground in a circuit domain, or a tank leaking into the outside world in the domain described in [Böt95]. But even a tank leaking to the outside world would still result in a multiple error if no explicit *leak* fault mode were present (because it would imply a fault in all valves and pumps downstream of the tank, or perhaps in the absence of physical impossibility constraints, the water being sucked out of the tank by the input pipe).

In software, on the other hand, we cannot make that assumption since auxiliary information is constantly created and destroyed (e.g., when a scope containing auxiliary local variables is lost). Not only do we need a separate model level to localize the

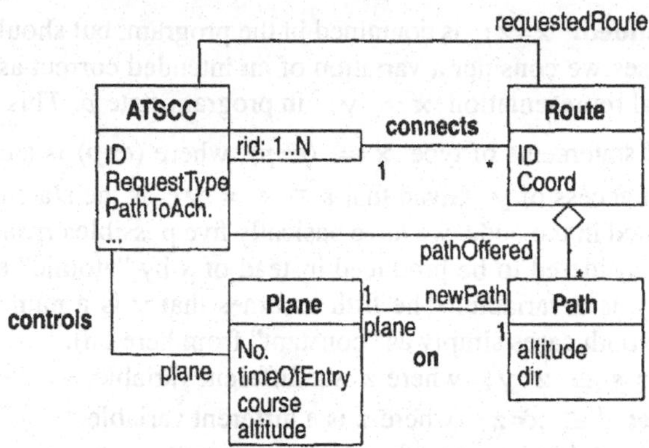

Figure 1: ATSCC Class Diagram

faults, we do need a separate model level to better hypothesize about their existence in the first place.

3 Utilizing Design Documentation

Thankfully, there is a potential source of additional information that we can use if only we can relate its semantics to the type of problem we are facing. The development of object-oriented software led to the development of methods for designing object-oriented software, and a central issue of these methods generally consists of the production of design descriptions for documentation purposes, both during development and for maintenance.

Example: Consider a strongly simplified version of a real-world Air Traffic Service Control Center (ATSCC) which controls the traffic flow across an intersection point among a group of air routes intersecting, controlling and tracking the aircraft until they leave the immediate vicinity of the ATSCC along one of the incident routes. For brevity we assume that only one aircraft travels through the airspace of the ATSCC at one point. The UML class diagram in Figure 1 shows the entities involved, with their attributes and their associations which represent links between entities, e.g., references stored in instance variables. A plane that enters the airspace of the ATSCC registers its flight ID, is asked by the ATSCC for its intended route, responds by which route it wants to exit, is assigned a flight path (route and altitude, not necessarily the one requested if multiple acceptable routes exist), and is tracked until it has attained that flight path and exited the ATSCC airspace along that route. We now consider different types of applicable design specifications.

3.1 Pre- and Postconditions

A widespread textual specification technique is the use of *Contracts* [Mey92], also known in terms of their constituents as pre- and postconditions (and invariants). Contracts describe for individual methods in an object-oriented program the conditions which must be satisfied to execute a particular method without causing an error, as well as the conditions which are satisfied by the state of the program after execution of the method. Invariants would describe conditions which hold throughout the lifecycle of an object, e.g., the requirement that a stack cannot hold a negative number of elements. The degree of detail in writing contracts is generally left to the user, since the conditions are, with exceptions (such as the programming language Eiffel) not considered as runtime checks but as documentation aids.

Below we have a list of specifications for methods of the ATSCC class, written in the UML Object Constraint Language (OCL), expressing pre- and post-conditions in terms of so-called state variables. Subsets of the method parameters are listed. The state variables are here, as is often the case, directly derived from the class diagram, and intuitively correspond to instance variables of the object in question. These instance variables can either contain values or references (i.e., state changes can express attribute or link changes in the terminology of the class diagram). It would also be conceivable that the "state variables" would express some aggregate property of the object; in that case they would roughly correspond to a user defined predicate.

```
Plane: Plane.
RequestedRoute: integer.
PathOffered: FltPath.
RequestType: {unknown,land,continue}.

Op register
  pre:   Plane = nil
  post:  Plane ≠ nil and RequestType ≠ unknown
Op processRouteRequest(R: 0..N)
  pre:   RouteSelected = nil
  post:  RouteSelected = R and PathOffered.plane = Plane
Op trackCourse
  pre:   PathOffered ≠ nil
  post:  PathOffered = nil and Plane.course = PathOffered.dir
Op scanArrival
  pre:   PathOffered = nil and Plane = nil
Op askRoute
  pre:   RouteSelected = nil
Op dropControl
  pre:   RequestType ≠ unknown
  post:  PathOffered = nil and RequestType=unknown
         and plane = nil.
```

A specification for the AssignPath operation of the plane could be as follows:

```
Op assignPath(P: FltPath)
  pre:   controller.RouteSelected ≠ nil and newPath = nil
  post:  newPath = P
```

Consider the following code example. It picks a path for a plane among those available for a route, that (if the plane has no approach warning transponder) guarantees sufficient separation to earlier planes sent along it.

```
void processRouteRequest(routeID rid);
{ fltPath path;
  plane p2;
  integer i;
1. route = self.findRoute(rid);
2. while (p.path = nil) && (i < noOfPaths){
3.   path = route.getPath(i);
4.   p2 = path.plane;
5.   if (p.noTP() && (time - p2.timeOfEntry >= 10) {
6.     path.plane = plane;
     } }
7.   pathOffered = path }
```

Structural errors that could happen in this method (focusing only on the planes) would include replacing statement 4 by `plane = path.plane;` (a WT error), `path.plane = p2;` (S), `p2 = plane;` (WS), or statement 6 by `path.plane = p2;` (WS), `plane = path.plane;` (S), `p2 = plane;` (WT), and of course omitting either statement (AO errors).

Let us consider the errors for statement 6. The first (WS) will lead to an incorrect time check when the next plane selects that route. The second (S) means that the ATSCC is tracking the wrong plane; this might lead to an error when it sends a course change command to that plane. The AO case hase the same effect as the first in this example. The WT case means also that statement 7 is executed on the wrong plane and has no effect.

Now assume that either the AO or WT case has happened, and the error is noticed in testing (e.g., because the next plane is assigned an incorrect height or the path's `last_plane` has the wrong flight number). In the WT case tracing the dependencies will not include the replaced statement 6 as a potential diagnosis candidate, and of course the same holds in the AO case (where statement 6 is not present).

It should be noted that CASE tools which automatically complete the code update the inverse pointer of a link such as the "on" link between plane and path do not prevent such an error from occurring, since the incorrect assignment can of course result in an incorrect completion. However the code would be organized differently (the path assignment would not be in a separate method).

3.1.1 Heuristic Modeling

How can we use the contract information to restrict the diagnosis candidates? It should be recognized beforehand that any such use is necessarily heuristic since there is no guarantee that the design information is more correct than the program, except that it usually predates the program and therefore can be assumed to be more mature, and that it will be more abstract and therefore easier to check for inconsistency (although not necessarily for completeness). There is an obvious heuristic which can be applied to a correct and nonredundant contract specification.

– If a state variable is mentioned in a postcondition but not precondition then it will be tested or changed in that method.

This is because otherwise the method could not guarantee its own postcondition; for that the variable would either have to be correct before execution, be changed during execution, or at least tested during execution to see that no change is necessary.

– If a state variable is mentioned in a precondition but not postcondition, then it will be accessed (because a particular value is expected and needs to be protected) during execution.

We accommodate these heuristics as follows. (Any reference to "variable" in the following description refers to a state variable visible outside the method.) If a variable v is in the postcondition of method m but not assigned, add a dependency $v \Leftarrow m_{body}$. If m calls other methods with the same condition on v then only the innermost method call is preferred. If v is mentioned in the precondition of v but not accessed, add v to all dependencies in the body of m and prefer those dependencies in diagnosis. In the other cases, do nothing.

Example: Consider the two method calls below. These would be part of the ATSCC code, first identifying a path for the plane to take based on its chosen route and then assigning the path to the plane (which include informing the plane about needed course changes).

```
processRouteRequest(rid);
p.assignPath(path);
```

The post condition for `processRouteRequest` included RouteSelected, which was indeed changed in the method. The precondition for `assignPath` includes newPath, which is indeed changed in the method (assigned a value which it did not previously have).

Assume we have a version of `processRouteRequest` where statement 6 has been replaced by the WT error `p2 = p;`. If we use a dependency-based system description as mentioned in Section 1 for diagnosing the ATSCC code, we receive the variable dependencies $p_1 \Leftarrow \{p_0, rid_0, path(i)_0\}$ and $pathOffered_1 \Leftarrow \{rid_0, path(i)_0\}$ for the call of `processRouteRequest` (using p for "plane" and s_1 to refer to the first line). The dependency $pathOffered_1.plane \Leftarrow \{rid_0, path(i)_0, p_0\}$ is missing and a dependency-based diagnosis will not return $s1$ as a source for the error. If we add a special dependency $pathOffered_1.plane \Leftarrow$ $\texttt{processRouteRequest}_{body}$ because pathOffered is listed in the post condition, then the method will be included in the search, and diagnoses containing such a special method reference can be preferred to other diagnoses.

3.1.2 Value-oriented Modeling

Harder constraints than these two heuristics can be obtained when looking at the conditions themselves. The precondition to assignPath mentions that newPath should be nil; this condition will obviously be violated if statement 6 is replaced by `p2 = p;`. In general it will not be possible to analyze such cases statically.

When using a value-based model, the nature of pre- and postcondition changes. They are in effect used as runtime constraints. Once diagnosis is started, they are tested whenever values are propagated forward out of a procedure call or backward before the procedure call, leading to contradictions when the constraint is not satisfied.

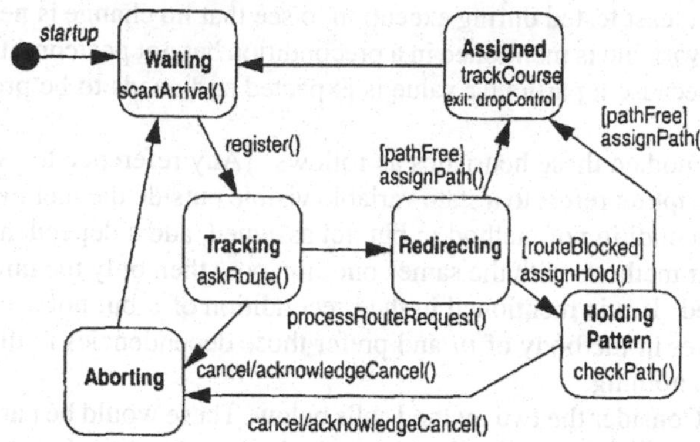

Figure 2: Statechart of class ATSCC

3.2 UML statecharts

The class diagram depicted above uses the notation of the currently the most widely used and examined of OO design notations, the Universal Modeling Language (UML) [RJB99] which resulted from the merger of several older methodologies. It provides a variety of diagram types. Here we are interested in three, of the most important diagram types: class diagrams, statecharts which describe the dynamic behavior of the individual object classes, and collaboration diagrams which show message interaction between a group of objects in a particular application situation.

The statechart diagram in Figure 2 shows the behavior of the ATSCC entity. Transitions in the statechart can be labeled in the form trigger event[guard]action(). Events cause transitions, guards have to be satisfied to permit an event to fire a transition, and actions or activities depict the operations executed on an object as a result of undergoing the transition or while in a state. By default, events are assumed to correspond to outside method calls and the actions or activities show the code that is being executed, and that is the assumption we make here. Unlabeled completion transitions depict a state change caused by completion of an internal activity (e.g., completion of trackCourse leading to state Waiting. The set of statecharts for all objects in a system represents a high level model of the causal structure of the system.

The designers arrive at statecharts by a process of compilation (manual and generalization from the set of collaboration diagrams in which a class is involved. The existence of the collaboration diagram guarantees that we know which class is the receiver of a particular method corresponding to an action in the statechart diagram. We do not show a graphical example of a collaboration diagram but instead simply define it formally. Given a set of classes C, a collaboration diagram is a sequence of message sends $m_1, \ldots, m_n$ where each m_i is a tuple $\langle s_i, r_i, \langle p_{ij} \rangle \rangle$, with s_i the sender, r_i the receiver, and $\langle p_{ij} \rangle$ the list of parameters of the message send.

The semantics of UML statecharts are not formally defined, although for our purposes we can approximate them by considering them as finite automata annotated with methods: transition, entry, exit, and completion actions.

The basic concept of using statecharts in addition to contracts is the realization that a statechart effectively constitutes a constraint on the sequence of method calls in a program. The states do generally correspond to particular attribute/link constellations but this information cannot be gleaned from the diagram without further annotations. In the simplest manner we can therefore use statecharts as additional constraints on the method call sequences in the program.

3.3 Using Statecharts alone

Importantly, both contracts and statechart diagrams are abstractions of code behavior. However, they abstract different issues. Statecharts are more likely to abstract state information but retain causality, Contracts are more likely to ignore causal information and focus on specifications of individual operations.

While the conditions expressed in contracts *at design level* may well be real abstractions of the actual object state (i.e., the variables referred to in pre-and postconditions may not be actually represented in the code), this is much more likely in the case of statechart diagrams. The gain in causal information is therefore offset by the need to construct a mapping between the abstract states and the conditions in terms of state variables they represent; in other words, contracts.

3.4 Static Tests

An obvious question is why, in those cases where we are using a dependency-based system description (which is statically computed), contracts and state diagrams are not just used statically. In principle a comparison of dependencies should give us a set of possible fault locations. That is correct and can in fact be done. However, neither contracts nor statechart diagrams are semantically complete and therefore actual observed testcases provide additional information. Static dependency analysis always implies overestimation. In the traditional debugging community this led to the development of methods like dynamic program slicing [KR97] to overcome the restrictions of static slicing [Wei84].

In other words, static dependency analysis lists all methods where the contract specifications do not fit our heuristics. A diagnosis run using a testcase with incorrect output will list those parts of the code which could possibly contribute to that testcase.

When examining contracts at the level of state variable values, then of course static analysis is not possible.

4 Discussion

In [Böt95], the diagnosis of structural faults was treated as the discovery of hidden interactions. The HiDe&Seek approach hypothesized about structural faults only when multiple faults occurred, a particular contextual constellation (e.g., physical layout) of components was given, and the behavioural modes of the components were matched. This layering was used for effective implementation that introduced hidden interactions as particular working hypotheses that activated a model of the particular fault.

In our case, the implementation side is somewhat simpler. The interactions are not really hidden since all assignments are visible. What is not clear is which of the assignments are correct, in fact the assumption that a structural fault must be indicated by multiple fault diagnoses does not hold, and the prior presence of separate models must be exploited to specifically mark those cases as relevant. Apart from the introduced priority ordering among diagnoses the implementation therefore simply takes place in terms of extending the existing dependency-based [MSW99] or value-based [MSW00a] diagnosis models. In both cases the overhead is limited. When working with the value-based model, the design information plays the role of additional constraints during the propagation of the model. When working with the dependency-based model, the number of rules added is linear in terms of the size of the contract conditions (i.e., the number of variables involved), whereas the number of rules in the model is not linear in terms of the size of the methods due to the way in which loops are handled.

In comparison to repair-based approaches [SW99] the flexibility of the approach presented here is drastically constrained. It is also more rarely applicable than the models of [MSW99, MSW00a], since it requires the existence of separate design information. On the other hand that is its advantage; it does not require additional effort in cases where these widespread techniques are in use and the search space is limited. Information from earlier design stages was also used in [FSW99] which used model-based techniques to debug VHDL circuit designs. However, the information there was only available and presented to the system in terms of execution traces (i.e,. test cases), not as a high level description. Also, most importantly, the abstraction levels in the VHDL case were different. The "high level" functional specification was fully executable and programmed in terms of conventional code using loops (i.e., providing a degree of detail comparable to what we are working with at the *implementation level*, most software design documentation is much less detailed, whereas the implementation level (RT level) replaces the loops by concurrently executing smaller components. Finally, the execution trace information was not used (and not suitable) to identifying structural faults.

Other work includes [PW90], where the classical bridge faults were considered in terms of a framework that simply included all possible interaction paths, and of course the classical work by Davis [Dav84] addressed the modeling issue in terms of "adjacency" in a second model that showed different interactions. His concept of adjacency would correspond to the fact that the design notations we utilize attempt to address the basic causal structure of the application, e.g., the requirements for methods to interface or the sequence of states in a diagram. Of course this means that interactions outside the realm of the diagrams (e.g., in auxiliary data structures) are not covered.

4.1 Future Work

At the moment the work presented here is purely conceptual and not implemented. Due to the richness of OO design processes the number of possible avenues for further research is huge. Issues include the effects ofthe fact that specifications can be formulated at differing levels of abstraction depending on application or process model. UML-based CASE tools automatically created code stubs from certain modeling constructs that may help or hinder the application. We have not considered the possibility of analyzing explicitly represented iteration in diagrams (cyclic state sequences).

5 Conclusion

This paper has described an approach that uses available design information produced by contemporary OO design processes to deal with the concept of the structural fault in software. We have examined different types of structural faults involving assignment statements as the basic type to which others can be traced. We have examined the use of pre- and postconditions for method calls as the basis for heuristics that allow focusing on structural faults that result in omission of variables mentioned in the pre- and postconditions, and have extended this concept to UML statecharts, using both dependency- and value-based diagnosis models.

References

[BH95] Lisa Burnell and Eric Horvitz. Structure and Chance: Melding Logic and Probability for Software Debugging. *Communications of the ACM*, pages 31 – 41, 1995.

[Böt95] Claudia Böttcher. No faults in structure? How to diagnose hidden interaction. In *Proc. IJCAI*, Montreal, August 1995.

[CFD93] Luca Console, Gerhard Friedrich, and Daniele Theseider Dupré. Model-based diagnosis meets error diagnosis in logic programs. In *Proceedings* 13th *International Joint Conf. on Artificial Intelligence*, Chambery, August 1993.

[CGL94] Edmund M. Clarke, Orna Grumberg, and David E. Long. Model Checking and Abstraction. *ACM Transactions on Programming Languages and Systems*, 16(5):1512–1542, September 1994.

[Dav84] Randall Davis. Diagnostic reasoning based on structure and behavior. *Artificial Intelligence*, 24:347–410, 1984.

[dKW87] Johan de Kleer and Brian C. Williams. Diagnosing multiple faults. *Artificial Intelligence*, 32(1):97–130, 1987.

[FSW99] Gerhard Friedrich, Markus Stumptner, and Franz Wotawa. Model-based diagnosis of hardware designs. *Artificial Intelligence*, 111(2):3–39, July 1999.

[Jac95] Daniel Jackson. Aspect: Detecting Bugs with Abstract Dependences. *ACM Transactions on Software Engineering and Methodology*, 4(2):109–145, April 1995.

[KR97] Bogdan Korel and Jurgen Rilling. Applications of Dynamic Slicing in Program Debugging. In *Proceedings of the Third International Workshop on Automatic Debugging (AADEBUG-97)*, Linköping, Sweden, 1997.

[Mey92] B. Meyer. Applying "Design by Contract". *IEEE Computer*, 25(10):40–51, October 1992.

[MSW99] Cristinel Mateis, Markus Stumptner, and Franz Wotawa. Debugging of Java programs using a model-based approach. In *Proceedings of the Tenth International Workshop on Principles of Diagnosis*, Loch Awe, Scotland, 1999.

[MSW00a] Cristinel Mateis, Markus Stumptner, and Franz Wotawa. Modeling Java Programs for Diagnosis. In *Proceedings of the European Conference on Artificial Intelligence (ECAI)*, Berlin, Germany, August 2000.

[MSW00b] Cristinel Mateis, Markus Stumptner, and Franz Wotawa. A Value-Based Diagnosis Model for Java Programs. In *Proceedings of the Eleventh International Workshop on Principles of Diagnosis*, Morelia, Mexico, June 2000.

[PW90] C. Preist and B. Welham. Modelling bridge faults for diagnosis in electronic circuits. In *Proc. DX'90 Workshop*, Stanford, 1990.

[Rei87] Raymond Reiter. A theory of diagnosis from first principles. *Artificial Intelligence*, 32(1):57–95, 1987.

[RJB99] J. Rumbaugh, I. Jacobson, and G. Booch. *The Unified Modeling Language Reference Manual*. Addison-Wesley Publishing Company, 1999.

[Sha83] Ehud Shapiro. *Algorithmic Program Debugging*. MIT Press, Cambridge, Massachusetts, 1983.

[SW99] Markus Stumptner and Franz Wotawa. Debugging Functional Programs. In *Proceedings* 16th *International Joint Conf. on Artificial Intelligence*, Stockholm, Sweden, August 1999.

[Wei84] Mark Weiser. Program slicing. *IEEE Transactions on Software Engineering*, 10(4):352–357, July 1984.

The Application of AI to Automatically Generated Animation

Adam Szarowicz[1], Juan Amiguet-Vercher[1], Peter Forte[2], Jonathan Briggs[2], Petros Gelepithis[2], and Paolo Remagnino[2]

[1]WhiteSpace Studio, Kingston University, Penrhyn Road, Kingston-Upon-Thames, KT1 2EE, UK
{a.szarowicz, jamiguet}@kingston.ac.uk, tel. +48 (0) 20 8547 7984
[2]School of Computing and Information Systems, Kingston University, Penrhyn Road, Kingston-Upon-Thames, KT1 2EE, UK
{pforte, j.h.briggs, p.gelepithis, p.remagnino}@kingston.ac.uk

Abstract. Modern animation packages provide partial automation of action between key frames. However the creation of scenes involving many interacting characters still requires most of the work to be hand-done by animators and any automatic behavior in the animation sequence tends to be hard-wired and lacking autonomy. This paper describes our "FreeWill" prototype which addresses these limitations by proposing and implementing an extendable cognitive architecture designed to accommodate goals, actions and knowledge, thus endowing animated characters with some degree of autonomous intelligent behavior.

Keywords: cognitive modeling, lifelike characters, multiagent systems, planning

1 Introduction

Modern animation packages for film and game production enable the automatic generation of sequences between key frames previously created by an animator. Applications for this exist in computer games, animated feature films, simulations, and digitized special effects, for example synthesized crowd scenes or background action. However, automated animation has, until very recently, been limited to the extent that characters move without autonomy, goals, or awareness of their environment. For example in moving from A to B a character might come into unintended contact with obstacles, but instead of taking avoiding action or suffering a realistic collision the animation package generates a scene in which the character simply passes through the obstacle (Figure 1a). Such incidents must be repaired manually by the human animator (Figure 1b). Although recent versions of commercially available animation packages have incorporated limited environment awareness and a degree of collision avoidance, there remains considerable scope for applying AI to animated characters to endow them with a full animation oriented

M. Brooks, D. Corbett, and M. Stumptner (Eds.): AI 2001, LNAI 2256, pp. 487-494, 2001.

cognitive model, as advocated by Funge *et al* (Funge, 1998; Funge *et al,* 1999). The role of the cognitive model is to provide perception, goals, decision making, and autonomous interaction with their surroundings and other characters. This paper describes our "FreeWill" prototype (Forte *at al,* 2000, Amiguet-Vercher *at al*, 2001) which has recently been initiated with the eventual aim of adding such capability to commercially available animation packages.

Fig. 1a. Avatar colliding with an obstacle

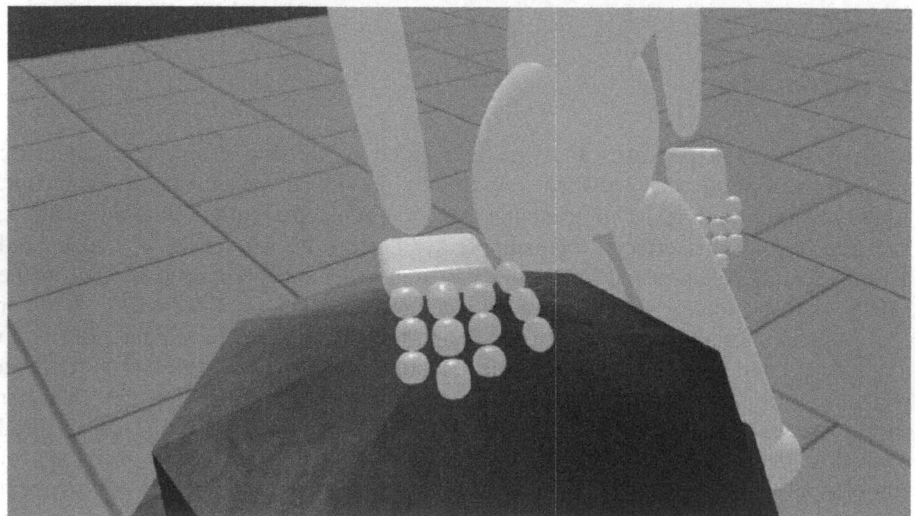

Fig. 1b. The scene corrected manually

2 Components of the System

An animated sequence consists of characters (avatars) interacting within a graphically defined setting. In our system, avatars are implemented as agents, *i.e.* something: "that can be viewed as perceiving its environment through sensors and acting upon that environment through effectors" (Russel and Norvig, 1995). In the example illustrating this paper, the setting is a city street populated by avatars walking in either direction. Their behavior consists of walking towards a set destination, avoiding collisions, and stopping to shake hands with designated "friends". Subject to fulfilling these goals, an avatar's behavior is otherwise autonomous. The action is simulated in our software, and the information then translated to a file format that is understandable by the animation package. Several standard formats are available in the industry. In our present prototype we use 3D Studio Max as an animation package and we interface with it through step files and scripts written in MaxScript (e.g. as in Figure 2). We could also interface with other packages available in the market such as Maya. The animation package then renders each frame and produces a video of the simulated interaction of the avatars. A scene from one such video is shown in Figure 3.

```
biped.AddNewKey LarmCont3 0
biped.AddNewKey RarmCont3 0
      sliderTime = 10
rotate RForearm3 30 [-1,0,0]
biped.AddNewKey LarmCont3 10
biped.AddNewKey RarmCont3 10
      sliderTime = 20
rotate RForearm3 80 [0,0,-1]
biped.AddNewKey LarmCont3 20
biped.AddNewKey RarmCont3 20
```

Fig. 2. Sample script for generating avatar behavior

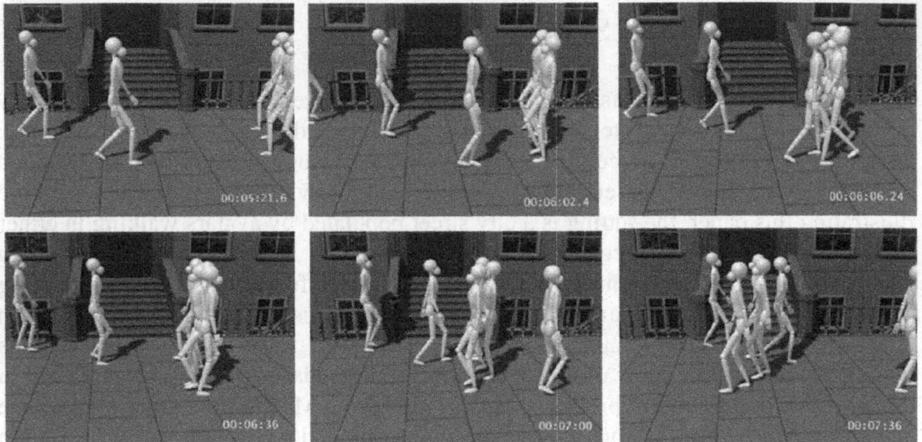

Fig. 3. Avatar interaction

The class structure underpinning our system is depicted in Figure 4, which presents a UML (Unified Modeling Language) model currently implemented in Java. As shown in Figure 4 the principal classes of the system are:

- *World* comprising all physical *objects*, including avatars, participating in the scene. Details stored for each object include a complete description of shape, dimensions, colour, texture, current position etc, sufficient to render the object.
- *Avatar*, which consists of a physical *body* together with an *AI engine*, instantiated as a separate AI object (on-board "brain") for each avatar. The body provides the AI engine with all necessary sensing and actuator services, while the AI engine itself is responsible for perception (interpretation of information) and the issue of appropriate motion commands based on goal planning. As a subsystem, the AI engine is built of an *action planner*, a *motion controller*, and a *knowledge base* storing *goals* and *facts*, and the avatar's *private world model* (which represents the fragment of the virtual world currently seen and remembered by the avatar).
- A *scheduler* based on discrete event simulation and a queue handler enabling the autonomous behavior to unfold within the virtual world by passing control to appropriate world objects (including avatars) according to the *event* which is currently being processed.
- There is also one external component used to generate the final animation – the animation package or more generally *visualization engine* – this part of the system is responsible for displaying the world model and the interacting avatars. At the moment this is performed by the package 3D Studio Max as described above. The system can also interface other products and other formats, *e.g.* those using motion capture files. The visualization engine must also allow for rendering the scenes and for saving the final animation.

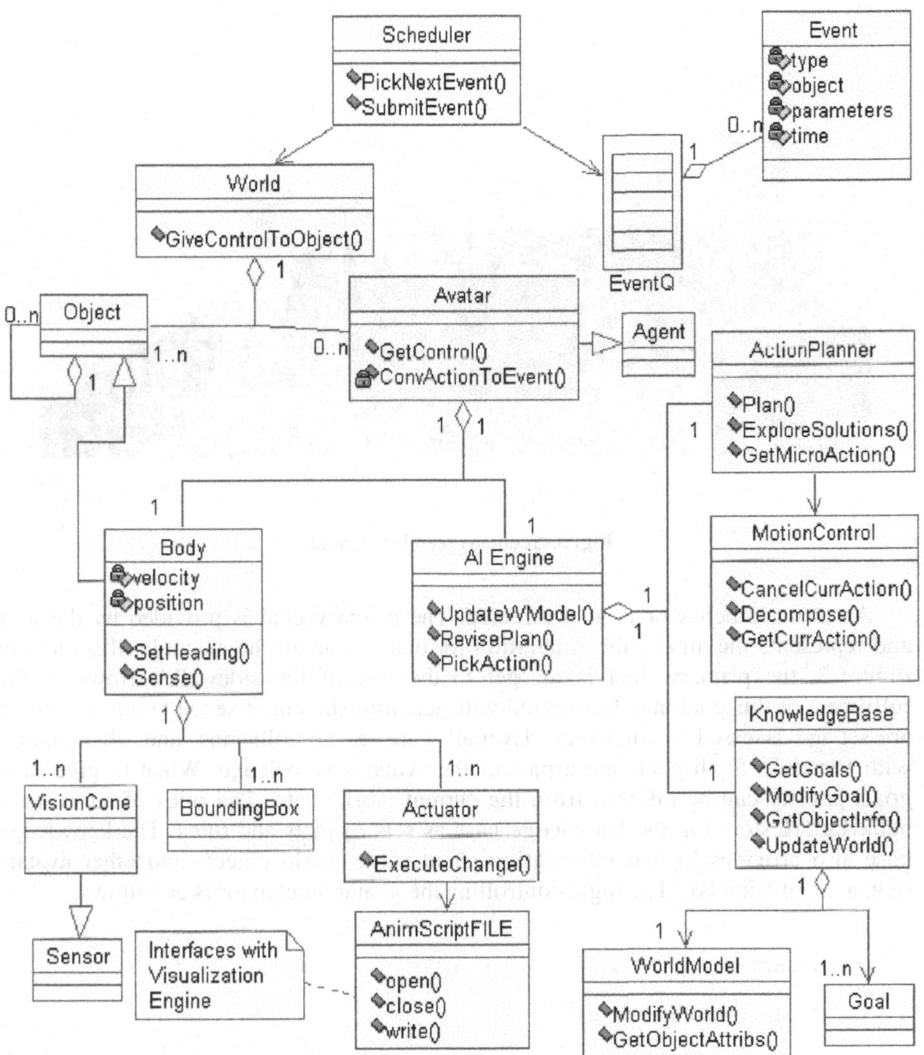

Fig. 4. UML model of the system

3 Logic Controlling an Avatar's Behavior

One of the key elements of the knowledge base is the internal world model. Every time an avatar performs an action, the process is initiated by first updating the avatar's world model. The avatar senses the world via a vision cone, through which it gains awareness of immediate objects in its path (see Figure 5). The information obtained from the vision cone is then used to modify the avatar's plan and perform the next action.

Fig. 5. Scene as seen by an avatar

An avatar's behavior is goal directed. The primary goal is provided by the user and represents the aim of the simulation for that avatar. In the example illustrated in Figure 3, the primary goal is to 'get to the end of the sidewalk'. However the fulfilment of this goal may be enacted with accomplishment of secondary goals which are set and assessed by the avatar. Examples are 'avoid collisions' and 'shake hands with friends'. Such goals are a part of the avatar's knowledge. When to give such goals priority can be inferred from the current world state. The rules of an avatar's behavior are stored in the knowledge base as sets of facts and rules. The knowledge base also provides logical information about static world objects and other avatars (e.g. a list of friends). The logic controlling the avatar's behavior is as follows:

```
DoSensing()
{
     image = Body.Sense()
     {
             return VisionCone.GetImage()
     }
     Mind.UpdateWorldModel(image)
     {
             KnowledgeBase.ModifyWorld(image)
             {
                     WorldModel.ModifyWorld(image)
             }
     }
     Mind.RevisePlan()
     {
             ActionPlanner.Plan()
             {
                     KnowledgeBase.GetGoals()
                     ExploreSolutions()
                     KnowledgeBase.GetObjectInfo()
                     {
```

```
                    WorldModel.GetObjectAttribs()
                }
                CreatePlan()
                lastAction = SelectLastPlannedAction()
                MotionControl.Decompose(lastAction)
            }
    }
    action = Mind.PickAction()
    {
                microA = ActionPlanner.GetMicroAction()
                {
                    return MotionControl.GetCurrentAction()
                }
            return microA
    }
    return ConvertActionToEvent(action)
}
```

Fig. 6. Logic controlling an avatar's behavior

The main simulation loop is located within the Scheduler class which consecutively picks events from an event queue. Control is then passed to the appropriate world object to which the event refers (which in most cases is an avatar) and necessary actions are taken. These can be

- an 'act' action – such as move a hand or make step. The action is rolled out (the avatar's state variables are updated) and a new line is added to the MaxScript file. This action returns a new sensing event to be inserted in the event queue
- a 'sense' action – which means that the avatar should compare the perceived fragment of the world with its own internal model. Then the avatar has a chance to rethink its plan and possibly update goals and the planned set of future actions. This action returns a new acting event.

The returned actions are inserted in the event queue and the time is advanced so that the next event can be selected. A PeriodicEventGenerator class has been introduced to generate cyclic sensing events for each avatar so that even a temporarily passive avatar has its internal world model updated.

The goal-planning algorithm constructs plans using the notion of an action as a generic planning unit. An action can be defined on various levels of specialization – from very general ones (e.g. 'get to the end of the sidewalk') to fairly detailed activities ('do the handshake'). The most detailed actions (microactions) are said to be at level 0. They correspond to action events in the event queue and also to MaxScript file entries. In general every action is specified by a pre and postcondition and is implemented by an avatar's member function, which will perform the action and update the state of objects affected by it. These objects can be world objects or parts of the avatar's body. The planning unit (ActionPlanner) operates on actions from level N to 1 – creating general plans and then refining them. The ActionPlanner maintains the chosen plan from which the last action is submitted to the MotionControl unit. It is then decomposed into a set of level 0 microactions (e.g. handshake consists of a set of arm and hand movements) which can be executed one by one. Any change in the plan may cause the list of microactions to be dropped and new ones to be generated.

If an action event is pulled from the queue then the scheduler updates the appropriate property of the world object that owns the event. At the same time the scheduler passes the information of that movement to the interface with the animation package so as to update the state of the world that will be displayed in the animation.

4 Conclusion and Future Direction

This paper has explained our framework for supporting autonomous behavior for animated characters, and the mechanisms that drive the characters in the simulation. The resulting actions are rendered in an animation package as illustrated. Our current prototype indicates that there is considerable scope for the application of AI to the automatic generation of animated sequences. In the current system the implementation of goal based planning is inspired by STRIPS (Fikes and Nilsson, 1971; Fikes, Hart and Nilsson, 1972). As a next step it would be interesting to extend our framework to experiment with planning activity that is distributed across several agents and takes place in a dynamic complex environment requiring the intertwining of planning and execution. Such requirements imply that goals may need to be changed over time, using ideas described for example by Long *et al* (Long, 2000). The prototype we have developed is a useful environment for developing and testing such cognitive architectures in the context of a practical application.

References

1. Amiguet-Vercher J., Szarowicz A., Forte P., Synchronized Multi-agent Simulations for Automated Crowd Scene Simulation, AGENT-1 Workshop Proceedings, IJCAI 2001, Aug 2001.
2. Fikes R., and Nilsson, N., STRIPS: A new approach to the application of theorem proving to problem solving, Artificial Intelligence, Vol. 2, pp 189-208, 1971.
3. Fikes R., Hart, P., Nilsson, N., Learning and executing generalised robot plans, Artificial Intelligence, Vol. 3, pp 251-288, 1972.
4. Forte P., Hall J., Remagnino P., Honey P., VScape: Autonomous Intelligent Behavior in Virtual Worlds, Sketches & Applications Proceedings, SIGGRAPH 2000, Aug 2000.
5. Funge J., Making Them Behave: Cognitive Models for Computer Animation, PhD thesis, Department of Computer Science, University of Toronto, 1998.
6. Funge J., Tu X., Terzopoulos D., Cognitive Modeling: Knowledge, reasoning and planning for intelligent characters, Computer Graphics Proceedings: SIGGRAPH 99, Aug 1999.
7. Long D., The AIPS-98 Planning Competition, AI magazine, Vol. 21, No. 2, pp 13-33, 2000.
8. Object Management Group, OMG Unified Modeling Language Specification, June 1999. Version 1.3. See also http://www.omg.org
9. Russell S., Norvig P., Artificial Intelligence, A Modern Approach, Prentice Hall, 1995.

Planning with Noisy Actions
(Preliminary Report)

Michael Thielscher

Dresden University of Technology
mit@inf.tu-dresden.de

Abstract. Ignoring the noise of physical sensors and effectors has always been a crucial barrier towards the application of high-level, cognitive robotics to real robots. We present a method of solving planning problems with noisy actions. The approach builds on the Fluent Calculus as a standard first-order solution to the Frame Problem. To model noise, a formal notion of uncertainty is incorporated into the axiomatization of state update and knowledge update. The formalism provides the theoretical underpinnings of an extension of the action programming language FLUX. Using constraints on real-valued intervals to encode noise, our system allows to solve planning problems for noisy sensors and effectors.

1 Introduction

Research into Cognitive Robotics aims at explaining and modeling intelligent acting in a dynamic world. Whenever intelligent behavior is understood as resulting from correct reasoning on correct representations, the classical Frame Problem [12] is a fundamental theoretical challenge: Given a representation of the effects of the available actions, how can one formally capture a crucial regularity of the real world, namely, that an action usually does not have arbitrary other effects? Explicitly specifying for each single potential effect that it is actually not an effect of a particular action, is obviously unsatisfactory both as a representation technique and as regards efficient inferencing [3]. The predicate calculus formalism of the Fluent Calculus [15], which roots in the logic programming approach of [7], provides a basic solution to both the representational and the inferential aspect of the Frame Problem. This solution also forms the theoretical underpinnings of the action programming language FLUX (the *Fluent Calculus Executor*) [16], which is based on constraint logic programming and allows to specify and reason about actions with incomplete states, and thus to solve planning problems under incomplete information.

In order to make it possible for a robot to reason about the correct use of its sensors, the Fluent Calculus has been extended by an axiomatization of how sensing affects the robot's knowledge of the environment [17]. A corresponding extension of FLUX has been developed in [18], which allows to solve planning problems with sensing actions. However, the method shares a common assumption of high-level approaches to sensing, namely, that sensors are ideal. This ignoring the noise of physical sensors and effectors has always been a crucial

M. Brooks, D. Corbett, and M. Stumptner (Eds.): AI 2001, LNAI 2256, pp. 495–506, 2001.

barrier towards the application of cognitive robotics to real robots, because noisy sensors and effectors may take influence on the correctness of plans.

In this paper, we extend the existing model for acting and sensing in the Fluent Calculus to the representation of noise in both sensors and effectors. Actions with noise result only in limited certainty about the values of the affected state variables. As part of the approach we define a notion of executable plans in which the robot may condition its further actions on previously obtained sensor readings. In the second part of the paper, we present an extension of the action programming language and system FLUX which allows to solve planning problems with noisy actions, using constraints on real-valued intervals to encode noise. Prior to presenting these results, we give a brief introduction to the basic Fluent Calculus and FLUX.

2 FLUX

The action programming language FLUX [16] is a recent implementation of the Fluent Calculus using constraint logic programming. The Fluent Calculus combines, in classical logic, elements of the Situation Calculus [9] with a STRIPS-like solution to the Frame Problem [15]. The standard sorts ACTION and SIT (i.e., situations) are inherited from the Situation Calculus along with the standard functions $S_0 : \text{SIT}$ and $Do : \text{ACTION} \times \text{SIT} \mapsto \text{SIT}$ denoting, resp., the initial situation and the successor situation after performing an action; furthermore, the standard predicate $Poss : \text{ACTION} \times \text{SIT}$ denotes whether an action is possible in a situation. To this the Fluent Calculus adds the sort STATE with sub-sort FLUENT. The Fluent Calculus also uses the pre-defined functions $\emptyset : \text{STATE}$; $\circ : \text{STATE} \times \text{STATE} \mapsto \text{STATE}$; and $State : \text{SIT} \mapsto \text{STATE}$; denoting, resp., the empty state, the union of two states, and the state of the world in a situation. As an example, let the function $Dist : \mathbb{R} \mapsto \text{FLUENT}$ denote the current distance of a robot to a wall. If z is a variable of sort STATE, then the following incomplete state specification says that initially the robot is somewhere between 4.8m and 5.1m away from the wall:[1]

$$(\exists x, z)\,(\,State(S_0) = Dist(x) \circ z \,\wedge\, \mathtt{4.8m} \leq x \leq \mathtt{5.1m}\,) \tag{1}$$

That is, the state in the initial situation is composed of the fluent $Dist(x)$ and sub-state z representing arbitrary other fluents that may also hold.

Based on the general signature, the Fluent Calculus provides a rigorously logical account of the concept of a state being characterized by the set of fluents that are true in the state. This is achieved by a suitable subset of the Zermelo-Fraenkel axioms, stipulating that function $\circ$ behaves like set union with $\emptyset$ as the empty set (for details see, e.g., [18]). Furthermore, the macro *Holds* is used to specify that a fluent is contained in a state:

$$Holds(f, z) \stackrel{\text{def}}{=} (\exists z')\, z = f \circ z' \tag{2}$$

[1] Free variables in formulas are assumed universally quantified. Variables of sorts ACTION, SIT, FLUENT, and STATE shall be denoted by the letters a, s, f, and z, resp. The function $\circ$ is written in infix notation.

A second macro, which reduces to (2), is used for fluents holding in situations:

$$Holds(f, s) \stackrel{\text{def}}{=} Holds(f, State(s))$$

As an example, consider the following so-called state constraint, which stipulates that the distance to the wall be unique in every situation:

$$(\forall s)\,(\exists! x)\, Holds(Dist(x), s)$$

The Frame Problem is solved in the Fluent Calculus using so-called state update axioms, which specify the difference between the states before and after an action. The axiomatic characterization of negative effects, i.e., facts that become false, is given by an inductive abbreviation which generalizes STRIPS-style update to incomplete states:

$$z' = z - f \stackrel{\text{def}}{=} [z' \circ f = z \vee z' = z] \wedge \neg Holds(f, z')$$

$$z' = z - (f_1 \circ \ldots \circ f_n \circ f_{n+1}) \stackrel{\text{def}}{=}$$
$$(\exists z'')\,(z'' = z - (f_1 \circ \ldots \circ f_n) \wedge z' = z'' - f_{n+1})$$

This is the general form of a state update axiom for a (possibly nondeterministic) action $A(\vec{x})$ with a bounded number of (possibly conditional) effects:

$$\begin{aligned}
&Poss(A(\vec{x}), s) \supset \\
&\quad (\exists \vec{y}_1)\,(\Delta_1(\vec{x}, \vec{y}_i, State(s)) \wedge State(Do(A(\vec{x}), s)) = (State(s) - \vartheta_1^-) \circ \vartheta_1^+) \\
&\quad \vee \ldots \vee \\
&\quad (\exists \vec{y}_n)\,(\Delta_n(\vec{x}, \vec{y}_n, State(s)) \wedge State(Do(A(\vec{x}), s)) = (State(s) - \vartheta_n^-) \circ \vartheta_n^+)
\end{aligned}$$

where the sub-formulas $\Delta_i(\vec{x}, \vec{y}_i, State(s))$ specify the conditions on $State(s)$ under which $A(\vec{x})$ has the positive and negative effects ϑ_i^+ and ϑ_i^-, resp. Both ϑ_i^+ and ϑ_i^- are STATE terms composed of fluents with variables among $\vec{x}, \vec{y}_i$. If $n = 1$ and $\Delta_1 \equiv True$, then action $A(\vec{x})$ does not have conditional effects. If $n > 1$ and the conditions Δ_i are not mutually exclusive, then the action is nondeterministic.

Consider, as an example, the function $MoveFwd : \mathbb{R}^+ \mapsto$ ACTION denoting the action of the robot moving a certain (positive) distance towards the wall. Under the assumption that the effectors are ideal, the effect of this axiom can be axiomatized by the following state update axiom:

$$\begin{aligned}
&Poss(MoveFwd(d), s) \supset \\
&\quad (\exists x, y)\,(Holds(Dist(x), s) \wedge y = x - d \wedge \\
&\qquad\qquad State(Do(MoveFwd(d), s)) = (State(s) - Dist(x)) \circ Dist(y))
\end{aligned} \tag{3}$$

Put in words, moving the distance d towards the wall has the effect that the robot is no longer x units away from the wall and will end up at $x - d$. Recall, for example, formula (1) and suppose for the sake of argument that $Poss(MoveFwd(\mathtt{2m}), S_0)$. After combining the inequations, our state update axiom and the foundational axioms imply

$$\begin{aligned}
(\exists y, z)\,(\, & State(Do(MoveFwd(\mathtt{2m}), S_0)) = z \circ Dist(y) \\
& \wedge\ \mathtt{2.8m} \leq y \leq \mathtt{3.1m}\,)
\end{aligned} \tag{4}$$

A crucial property of this new state equation is that sub-state z has been carried over from (1). Thus any additional constraint on z in (1) equally applies to the successor state $State(Do(MoveFwd(2\mathtt{m}), S_0))$. This is how the Frame Problem is solved in the Fluent Calculus.

Based on the theory of the Fluent Calculus, the distinguishing feature of the action programming language FLUX is to support incomplete states, which are modeled by *open* lists of the form

```
Z0 = [F1,...,Fm | Z]
```

(encoding the state description $\mathtt{Z0} = \mathtt{F1} \circ \ldots \circ \mathtt{Fm} \circ \mathtt{Z}$), along with constraints

```
not_holds(F, Z)
not_holds_all([X1,...,Xk], F, Z)
```

encoding, resp., the negative statements $(\exists \vec{y})\, \neg Holds(\mathtt{F}, \mathtt{Z})$ (where $\vec{y}$ are the variables occurring in F) and $(\exists \vec{y})(\forall \mathtt{X1}, \ldots, \mathtt{Xk})\, \neg Holds(\mathtt{F}, \mathtt{Z})$ (where $\vec{y}$ are the variables occurring in F except X1, ..., Xk). These two constraints are used to bypass the problem of 'negation-as-failure' for incomplete states. In order to process these constraints, so-called declarative Constraint Handling Rules [4] have been defined and proved correct under the foundational axioms of the Fluent Calculus. In addition, the core of FLUX contains definitions for `holds(F,Z)`, by which is encoded macro (2), and `update(Z1,ThetaP,ThetaN,Z2)`, which encodes the state equation $\mathtt{Z2} = (\mathtt{Z1} - \mathtt{ThetaN}) \circ \mathtt{ThetaP}$.

As an example, the following is the FLUX encoding of our state update axioms (3) (ignoring preconditions) and the initial specification (1):[2]

```
state_update(Z1, move_forward(D), Z2) :-
  holds(dist(X), Z1), Y = X - D,
  update(Z1, [dist(Y)], [dist(X)], Z2).

init(Z0) :- X :: 4.8..5.1, holds(dist(X), Z0),
            duplicate_free(Z0).
```

where the constraint `duplicate_free(Z)` means that list Z does not contain multiple occurrences. The following sample query computes the conclusion made in (4):

```
[eclipse 1]: init(Z0), state_update(Z0, move_forward(2), Z1).

Z0 = [dist(X{4.8..5.1}) | _Z]
Z1 = [dist(Y{2.8..3.1}) | _Z]
```

[2] Throughout the paper we use ECLIPSE-Prolog notation. The interval expression ;X::L..R; is taken from the library RIA, the constraint solver for interval arithmetic (see Section 4 below).

3 Update for Noisy Actions

The Fluent Calculus provides a simple and elegant means to axiomatize noisy effectors. Uncertainty regarding the values of affected fluents can be represented in a state update axiom as existentially quantified and constrained variables. For example, suppose that the effectors of our robot are noisy in that the actual position after moving towards the wall may differ from the ideal one by the factor 0.05. The following is a suitable state update axiom for this noisy action:

$$\begin{array}{l} Poss(MoveFwd(d), s) \supset \\ \quad (\exists x, y)\,(\,Holds(Dist(x), s) \wedge \\ \qquad State(Do(MoveFwd(d), s)) = (State(s) - Dist(x)) \circ Dist(y) \wedge \\ \qquad |y - (x - d)| \leq d \cdot 0.05\,) \end{array} \tag{5}$$

Moving a distance d thus has the effect that the robot will end up at some distance y which is at most $d \cdot 0.05$ units away from the goal position $x - d$.

To represent knowledge in the Fluent Calculus and to reason about sensing actions, the predicate $KState : \text{SIT} \times \text{STATE}$ has been introduced in [17]. An instance $KState(s, z)$ means that according to the knowledge of the planning robot, z is a possible state in situation s. On this basis, the fact that some property of a situation is known to the robot is specified using the macro $Knows$, which is defined as follows:

$$Knows(\varphi, s) \stackrel{\text{def}}{=} (\forall z)\,(KState(s, z) \supset HOLDS(\varphi, z)) \tag{6}$$

where

$$\begin{array}{rll} HOLDS(\alpha, z) & \stackrel{\text{def}}{=} \alpha & (\alpha \text{ arithmetic constraint}) \\ HOLDS(f, z) & \stackrel{\text{def}}{=} Holds(f, z) & \\ HOLDS(\neg\varphi, z) & \stackrel{\text{def}}{=} \neg HOLDS(\varphi, z) & \\ HOLDS(\varphi \wedge \psi, z) & \stackrel{\text{def}}{=} HOLDS(\varphi, z) \wedge HOLDS(\psi, z) & \\ HOLDS((\forall x)\,\varphi, z) & \stackrel{\text{def}}{=} (\forall x)\,HOLDS(\varphi, z) & \end{array}$$

This model of knowledge uses pure first-order logic. As an example, the precondition for the action $MoveFwd$ can be specified in such a way that the robot always keeps a safety distance to the wall. This of course requires to take into account the uncertainty of the effectors:

$$Poss(MoveFwd(d), s) \equiv Knows(\,(\forall x)(Dist(x) \supset x - 1.05 \cdot d \geq 0.1\mathtt{m}), s)$$

Hence, moving forward is possible only if the robot *knows* that it will end up at least 0.1m away from the wall. Suppose given that the robot knows that its initial position is somewhere between 4.8m and 5.1m away from the wall, that is,

$$KState(S_0, z) \supset (\forall x)\,(Holds(Dist(x), z) \supset 4.8\mathtt{m} \leq x \leq 5.1\mathtt{m}\,) \tag{7}$$

With the help of macro (6) it follows that $Poss(MoveFwd(2\mathtt{m}), S_0)$.

The Frame Problem for knowledge is solved by axioms that determine the relation between the possible states before and after an action. More formally, the effect of an action $A(\vec{x})$, be it sensing or not, on the knowledge is specified by a *knowledge update axiom* of the form

$$Poss(A(\vec{x}),s) \supset \\ [\,(\forall z)\,(KState(Do(A(\vec{x}),s),z) \equiv (\exists z')(KState(s,z') \wedge \Psi(z,z',s)))\,] \tag{8}$$

In case of non-sensing actions, formula Ψ defines what the robot knows of the effects of the action. E.g., state update axiom (5) for moving with unreliable effectors corresponds to the following knowledge update axioms:

$$\begin{array}{l} Poss(MoveFwd(d),s) \supset \\ \quad [\,(\forall z)\,(KState(Do(MoveFwd(d),s),z) \equiv \\ \qquad (\exists x,y,z')\,(\,KState(s,z') \wedge Holds(Dist(x),z') \wedge \\ \qquad\qquad z = (z' - Dist(x)) \circ Dist(y) \wedge \\ \qquad\qquad |y-(x-d)| \le d \cdot 0.05\,))\,] \end{array} \tag{9}$$

The generic ACTION term $Sense(f)$ has been introduced in [17] to denote the action of sensing whether a fluent f holds. The corresponding knowledge update axiom,

$$\begin{array}{l} Poss(Sense(f),s) \supset \\ \quad [\,KState(Do(Sense(f),s),z) \equiv \\ \qquad KState(s,z) \wedge [Holds(f,z) \equiv Holds(f,s)]\,] \end{array} \tag{10}$$

says that among the states possible in s only those are still possible after sensing which agree with the actual state of the world as far as the sensed fluent is concerned. An important implication is that after sensing f either the fluent or its negation is known to hold [17]. Thus axiom (10) can be viewed as modeling an ideal sensor.

In order to model sensing with noise, axiom schema (8) needs to be used in a different manner, where formula Ψ restricts the possible states to those where the value of the sensed property may deviate from the actual value within a certain range. To this end, we introduce the generic ACTION function $Sense_F$ where F can be any domain function of type $\mathbb{R} \mapsto$ FLUENT.[3] For later purpose, we assume that for any fluent which can thus be sensed there is an additional fluent $SensorReading_F(x)$ denoting the last sensor reading. Let ϱ_F denote the maximal deviation of the noisy sensor reading from the actual value. The effect of noisy $Sense_F$ is then specified by this knowledge update axiom:

$$\begin{array}{l} Poss(Sense_F,s) \supset \\ \quad [\,(\exists r)\,(\forall z)\,(KState(Do(Sense_F,s),z) \equiv \\ \qquad (\exists r',x,y,z')\,(\,KState(s,z') \wedge \\ \qquad\qquad Holds(F(x),s) \wedge \\ \qquad\qquad Holds(F(y),z') \wedge Holds(SensorReading_F(r'),z') \wedge \\ \qquad\qquad z = (z' - SensorReading_F(r')) \circ SensorReading_F(r) \wedge \\ \qquad\qquad |x-r| \le \varrho_F \wedge |y-r| \le \varrho_F\,))\,] \end{array} \tag{11}$$

[3] For the sake of simplicity, we assume that each sensor delivers just a unary value. The generalization to perceivable fluents with multiple arguments, such as the position in a two-dimensional space, is straightforward.

Put in words, after sensing, a sensor reading r is obtained which differs from the actual value x by at most ϱ_F, and only those states are still considered possible where the value y of the sensed fluent deviates from r by at most ϱ_F and where the old sensor reading r' has been updated to r. The accompanying state update axiom says that a new sensor reading is obtained within the allowed range:

$$\begin{aligned}
&Poss(Sense_F, s) \supset \\
&\quad (\exists r, r', x)\,(Holds(F(x), s) \wedge Holds(SensorReading_F(r'), s) \wedge \\
&\qquad\qquad State(Do(Sense_F, s)) = (State(s) - SensorReading_F(r')) \\
&\qquad\qquad\qquad\qquad\qquad\qquad\qquad \circ SensorReading_F(r) \\
&\qquad \wedge |x - r| \leq \varrho_F\,)
\end{aligned} \tag{12}$$

While precise knowledge of the sensed property is thus no longer guaranteed, an important consequence of the generic knowledge update axiom (11) is that sensing never cause loss of possibly more precise initial knowledge wrt. the sensed fluent.

Proposition 1. *Let* α *be an arithmetic constraint with free variable* x*, then (11) and the foundational axioms entail*

$$Knows((\exists x)\,(F(x) \wedge \alpha), s) \supset Knows((\exists x)\,(F(x) \wedge \alpha), Do(Sense_F, s))$$

A second crucial consequence is that the sensor reading itself will be known by the robot.

Proposition 2. *(11) and the foundational axioms entail*

$$(\exists x)\,Knows(SensorReading_F(x), Do(Sense_F, s))$$

Suppose, for example, that the noise of the robot's sensor for measuring the distance to the wall is given by $\varrho_{Dist} = \mathtt{0.1m}$, and recall the specification of initial knowledge given in (7). Then after moving 2m towards the wall and sensing the distance, the robot will know the distance to the wall within a range of 0.1m. Moreover, this distance must be between 2.7m and 3.2m (as above) while the possible sensor readings are between 2.6m and 3.3m due to the noise of the sensor. Formally, let $S_2 = Do(Sense_{Dist}, Do(MoveFwd(\mathtt{2m}), S_0))$, then the state and knowledge update axioms for $MoveFwd$ and $Sense_{Dist}$ entail

$$\begin{aligned}
&(\exists x)\,(\,\mathtt{2.7m} \leq x \leq \mathtt{3.2m} \;\wedge\; Knows((\exists y)\,(Dist(y) \wedge |y - x| \leq \mathtt{0.1m}), S_2)\,) \\
&\wedge (\exists r)\,(\mathtt{2.6m} \leq r \leq \mathtt{3.3m} \;\wedge\; Knows(SensorReading_{Dist}(r), S_2)\,)
\end{aligned}$$

Solutions to planning problems with noisy sensing actions may require to condition an action on the outcome of sensing. Suppose, for example, the goal of our robot is to be at a point where it is between 2.8m and 3.2m away from the wall. Given the initial knowledge state (7), this problem is solvable only by a plan which includes reference to previous sensing readings. A possible solution along this line would be for the robot to advance 2m, measure the distance, and if necessary adjust its position according to the obtained reading r. A suitable choice of the argument for the second *MoveFwd* action is $r - 3\text{m}$: As we have seen above, the robot knows that it will be between 2.7m and 3.2m away from the wall after the initial move. Moreover, the sensor reading r will measure the actual position x within the range $x \pm 0.1\text{m}$. Thus, even with the added uncertainty caused by the new movement, the robot can be sure without further sensing that it will end up at a distance which is between 2.885m and 3.12m.

In order to allow for the use of sensor readings as parameters for actions, we need to make precise when formal actions such as $MoveFwd(r - 3\text{m})$ can be considered executable by the robot. To this end, we introduce the macro $Kref(\tau, s)$ (inspired by [14]) with the intended meaning that the arithmetic expression τ can be evaluated by the robot on the basis of its knowledge in situation s. The macro is inductively defined as follows:

$$\begin{aligned} Kref(c, s) &\stackrel{\text{def}}{=} True && (c \text{ constant}) \\ Kref(F, s) &\stackrel{\text{def}}{=} (\exists x)\, Knows(F(x), s) && (F \text{ value fluent}) \\ Kref(op(\tau_1, \tau_2), s) &\stackrel{\text{def}}{=} Kref(\tau_1, s) \wedge Kref(\tau_2, s) && (op \in \{+, -, \cdot, \ldots\}) \end{aligned} \tag{13}$$

The executability of a plan $Do(a_n, \ldots, Do(a_1, S_0) \ldots)$ is then defined as the macro *EXEC* as follows:

$$\begin{aligned} EXEC(S_0) &\stackrel{\text{def}}{=} True \\ EXEC(Do(A(\tau_1, \ldots, \tau_k), s) &\stackrel{\text{def}}{=} EXEC(s) \wedge Poss(A(\tau_1, \ldots, \tau_k), s) \\ &\qquad \wedge Kref(\tau_1, s) \wedge \ldots \wedge Kref(\tau_k, s) \end{aligned}$$

4 Planning with Noise in Flux

Encoding state update axioms for noisy actions requires to state arithmetic constraints. A constraint solver is then needed to deal with these constraints. A suitable choice for FLUX is the standard ECLIPSE constraint system RIA (for real number interval arithmetic). Incorporating this constraint module, the following is a suitable encoding of state update axiom (5), specifying an action with unreliable effectors:

```
:- lib(ria).

state_update(Z1, move_forward(D), Z2) :-
   holds(dist(X), Z1),
   abs(Y-(X-D)) *=< 0.05*D,
   update(Z1, [dist(Y)], [dist(X)], Z2).
```

In comparison with the computed answer shown at the end of Section 2, the new state update axiom causes a higher degree of uncertainty wrt. the resulting position:

```
init(Z0) :- X :: 4.8..5.1, holds(dist(X), Z0),
            duplicate_free(Z0).
```

```
[eclipse 1]: init(Z0), state_update(Z0, move_forward(2), Z1).

Z0 = [dist(X{4.8..5.1}) | _Z]
Z1 = [dist(Y{2.7..3.2}) | _Z]
```

While the explicit notion of possible states leads to an extensive framework for reasoning about knowledge and noisy sensing, automated deduction becomes considerably more intricate by the introduction of the modality-like *KState* predicate. As a consequence, in [18] we have developed an inference method which avoids separate update of knowledge and states. In what follows, we extend this result to noisy sensors and effectors and show how knowledge updates are implicitly obtained by progressing an incomplete state through state update axioms.

Our approach rests on two assumptions. First, the planning robot needs to know the given initial specification $\Phi(State(S_0))$, and this is all it knows of S_0, that is, $KState(S_0, z) \equiv \Phi(z)$. Second, the robot must have accurate knowledge of its own actions. That is, formally, the possible states after a non-sensing action are those which would be the result of actually performing the action in one of the previously possible states:

Definition 1. [17] *A set of axioms* Σ represents accurate effect knowledge *if for each non-sensing* ACTION *function* A, Σ *contains a unique state update axiom*

$$Poss(A(\vec{x}), s) \supset \Gamma_A\{z/State(Do(A(\vec{x}), s)), z'/State(s)\} \tag{14}$$

(where $\Gamma_A(\vec{x}, z, z')$ *is a first-order formula with free variables among* $\vec{x}, z, z'$ *and without a sub-term of sort* SIT*) and a unique knowledge update axiom which is equivalent to*

$$\begin{aligned} Poss(A(\vec{x}), s) \supset \; [\,(\forall z)\,(KState(Do(A(\vec{x}), s), z) \equiv \\ (\exists z')(KState(s, z') \wedge \Gamma_A(\vec{x}, z, z'))\,)\,] \end{aligned} \tag{15}$$

Accurate knowledge of effects suffices to ensure that the possible states after a non-sensing action can be obtained by progressing a given state specification through the state update axiom for that action. The effect of sensing, on the other hand, cannot be obtained in the same fashion. To see why, let S be a situation and consider the knowledge specification

$$\begin{aligned} & KState(S, z) \equiv \\ & \quad (\exists x, y)\,(z = Dist(x) \circ SensorReading_{Dist}(y) \wedge \mathtt{4.8m} \leq x \leq \mathtt{5.1m}\,) \end{aligned} \tag{16}$$

Suppose that $Poss(Sense_{Dist}, S)$, then knowledge update axiom (11) yields different models reflecting the possible sensing result r, which run from 4.7m to 5.2m. However, in each model the distance is known up to an error of just $\varrho_{Dist} =$ 0.1m! Hence, while we cannot predict the sensing outcome, it is clear that the sensed value will be known within the precision of the sensor. This knowledge is not expressible by a specification of the form $KState(Do(Sense_{Dist}, S), z) \equiv \Phi(z)$ entailed by (16) and (11). Hence, the effect of a sensing action cannot be obtained by straightforward progression.

In order to account for different models for *KState* caused by sensing, we introduce the notion of a *sensing history* ς as a finite, possibly empty list of real numbers. A history is meant to describe the outcome of each sensing action in a sequence of actions. For the sake of simplicity, we assume that the only sensing action is the generic $Sense_F$ with knowledge update axiom (11) and state update axiom (12).

For the formal definition of progression we also need the notion of an *action sequence* σ as a finite, possibly empty list of ground ACTION terms. An action sequence corresponds naturally to a situation, which we denote by S_σ:

$$S_{[]} \stackrel{\text{def}}{=} S_0 \quad \text{and} \quad S_{[A(\vec{t})\,|\,\sigma]} \stackrel{\text{def}}{=} Do(A(\vec{t}), S_\sigma)$$

We are now in a position to define, inductively, a *progression operator* $\mathcal{P}(\sigma, \varsigma, z)$ along the line of [18], by which an initial state specification $\Phi(State(S_0))$ is progressed through an action sequence σ wrt. a sensing history ς, resulting in a formula specifying z:

$$\mathcal{P}([\,], \varsigma, z) \stackrel{\text{def}}{=} \Phi(z) \quad \text{if } \varsigma = [\,] \tag{17}$$

$$\mathcal{P}([A(\vec{t})\,|\,\sigma], \varsigma, z) \stackrel{\text{def}}{=} (\exists z')\,(\mathcal{P}(\sigma, \varsigma, z') \wedge \Gamma_A(\vec{t}, z, z')) \quad \text{if } A \text{ non-sensing with state update (14)} \tag{18}$$

$$\begin{aligned} &\mathcal{P}([Sense_F\,|\,\sigma], \varsigma, z) \stackrel{\text{def}}{=} \\ &\quad (\exists r', x, y, z')\,(\mathcal{P}(\sigma, \varsigma', z') \wedge \\ &\qquad Holds(F(x), s) \wedge \\ &\qquad Holds(F(y), z') \wedge Holds(SensorReading_F(r'), z') \wedge \\ &\qquad z = (z' - SensorReading_F(r')) \circ SensorReading_F(r) \wedge \\ &\qquad |x - r| \leq \varrho_F \wedge |y - r| \leq \varrho_F\,) \\ &\qquad\qquad \text{where } \varsigma = [r\,|\,\varsigma'] \end{aligned} \tag{19}$$

In case the length of the history ς does not equal the number of sensing actions in σ, we define $\mathcal{P}(\sigma, \varsigma, z)$ as *False*. Progression provides a provably correct inference method for knowledge update.

Theorem 1. *Consider the initial state and knowledge* $\Sigma_0 = \{\Phi(State(S_0)), KState(S_0, z) \equiv \Phi(z)\}$ *and let* Σ *be the foundational axioms plus a set of domain axioms representing accurate effect knowledge. Let* σ *be an action sequence such that* $\Sigma \cup \Sigma_0 \models EXEC(S_\sigma)$. *Then for any model* $\mathcal{M}$ *of* $\Sigma_0 \cup \Sigma$ *and any valuation* ν,

$$\mathcal{M}, \nu \models KState(S_\sigma, z) \quad \textit{iff} \quad \mathcal{M}, \nu \models \mathcal{P}(\sigma, \varsigma, z) \textit{ for some } \varsigma$$

The proof is by simple induction on σ.

This theorem serves as the formal justification for the FLUX encoding of knowledge and sensing. The sensing action $Sense_{Dist}$, for example, is encoded by a state update axiom which carries as additional argument the result of sensing, that is, the sensor reading:

```
state_update(Z1, sense_dist, Z2, SV) :-
   holds(dist(X), Z1), holds(reading(Y), Z1),
   abs(X-SV) *=< 0.1,
   update(Z1, [reading(SV)], [reading(Y)], Z2).
```

The definition of progression is a direct encoding of (17)–(19):

```
p([], [], Z) :- init(Z).
p([A|S], H2, Z2) :- p(S, H1, Z1),
                    ( state_update(Z1, A, Z2), H2=H1 ;
                      state_update(Z1, A, Z2, SV), H2=[SV|H1] ).
```

In principle, the FLUX clauses we arrived at can readily be used by a simple forward-chaining search algorithm. Enumerating the set of plans, including all possible sensing actions, a solution will eventually be found if only the problem is solvable. However, planning with incomplete states usually involves a considerable search space, and the possibility to generate conditional plans only enlarges it. The concept of nondeterministic robot programs has been introduced in GOLOG as a powerful heuristics for planning, where only those plans are searched which match a given skeleton [10]. This avoids considering obviously useless actions such as ineffectual sensing. In [18] we have shown how this concept can be adopted in FLUX on the basis of a progression operator, in order to make planning with sensing more efficient. These heuristics can be directly applied to planning with noisy actions in FLUX.

5 Summary and Discussion

We have presented an approach to planning with noisy actions by appealing to the Fluent Calculus as a basic solution to the Frame Problem. The axiomatization has be shown to exhibit reasonable properties. Moreover, we have extended the action programming language FLUX to obtain a system for solving planning problems that involve noisy actions.

Both the axiomatic approach as well as the realization in FLUX are an extension of the solution to the Frame Problem for knowledge [17,18]. A distinguishing feature of this approach is its expressiveness in comparison to most existing approaches to planning with knowledge and sensing. Unlike other systems, FLUX is not tailored to restricted classes of planning problems (as opposed to, e.g., [6, 5,2,11,8]) and allows to search for suitable sensing actions during planning (as opposed to [13]).

Closest to our work is [1], where an extension of the Situation Calculus is presented that allows to axiomatize noisy actions. The crucial difference to our approach is the indirect way of modeling a noisy action as a non-deterministic selection among actions with determined effects. To this end, the approach uses the non-deterministic programming constructs of GOLOG for modeling noise. Consequently, these programs can no longer be used as planning heuristics, and therefore the theory cannot be straightforwardly integrated into GOLOG to provide a planning system that deals with noise. On the other hand, the approach of [1] includes a notion of probability distribution for noisy effects. The extension of our approach along this line is an important goal for future work.

References

1. F. Bacchus, J. Halpern, and H. Levesque. Reasoning about noisy sensors and effectors in the situation calculus. *Artif. Intell.*, 111(1–2):171–208, 1999.
2. C. Baral and T. C. Son. Approximate reasoning about actions in presence of sensing and incomplete information. In *Proc. of ILPS*, pp. 387–401, 1997. MIT Press.
3. W. Bibel. Let's plan it deductively! *Artif. Intell.*, 103(1–2):183–208, 1998.
4. T. Frühwirth. Theory and practice of constraint handling rules. *J. of Logic Programming*, 37(1–3):95–138, 1998.
5. G. De Giacomo, L. Iocchi, D. Nardi, and R. Rosati. Planning with sensing for a mobile robot. In *Proc. of ECP*, vol. 1348 of *LNAI*, pages 158–170. Springer, 1997.
6. K. Golden and D. Weld. Representing sensing actions: The middle ground revisited. In *Proc. of KR*, pp. 174–185, 1996. Morgan Kaufmann.
7. S. Hölldobler and J. Schneeberger. A new deductive approach to planning. *New Generation Computing*, 8:225–244, 1990.
8. G. Lakemeyer. On sensing and off-line interpreting GOLOG. In *Logical Foundations for Cognitive Agents*, pages 173–189. Springer, 1999.
9. H. Levesque, F. Pirri, and R. Reiter. Foundations for a calculus of situations. *Electronic Transactions on Artif. Intell.*, 3(1–2):159–178, 1998. URL: `http://www.ep.liu.se/ea/cis/1998/018/`.
10. H. Levesque, R. Reiter, Y. Lespérance, F. Lin, and R. Scherl. GOLOG: A logic programming language for dynamic domains. *J. of Logic Programming*, 31(1–3):59–83, 1997.
11. J. Lobo. COPLAS: A conditional planner with sensing actions. In *Cognitive Robotics*, vol. FS–98–02 of *AAAI Fall Symposia*, pp. 109–116. AAAI Press 1998.
12. J. McCarthy and P. Hayes. Some philosophical problems from the standpoint of artificial intelligence. *Machine Intell.*, 4:463–502, 1969.
13. R. Reiter. On knowledge-based programming with sensing in the situation calculus. In *Cognitive Robotics Workshop at ECAI*, pp. 55–61, Berlin, Germany, August 2000.
14. R. Scherl and H. Levesque. The frame problem and knowledge-producing actions. In *Proc. of AAAI*, pp. 689–695, 1993.
15. M. Thielscher. From Situation Calculus to Fluent Calculus: State update axioms as a solution to the inferential frame problem. *Artif. Intell.*, 111(1–2):277–299, 1999.
16. M. Thielscher. The Fluent Calculus: A Specification Language for Robots with Sensors in Nondeterministic, Concurrent, and Ramifying Environments. Technical Report CL-2000-01, Dept. of Computer Science, Dresden Univ. of Tech., 2000. URL: `http://www.cl.inf.tu-dresden.de/~mit/publications/reports/CL-2000-01.pdf`.
17. M. Thielscher. Representing the knowledge of a robot. In *Proc. of KR*, pp. 109–120, 2000. Morgan Kaufmann.
18. M. Thielscher. Inferring implicit state knowledge and plans with sensing actions. In *Proc. of KI*, vol. 2174 of *LNAI*, pp. 366–380, 2001. Springer.

Getting the Job Done in a Hostile Environment

Steven Versteeg and Alan Blair

Department of Computer Science
University of Melbourne
Parkville 3010 Australia
scv@cs.mu.oz.au
blair@cs.mu.oz.au

Abstract. In nature animals going about their daily routine need to avoid predators in order to survive. Many animals have evolved some kind of startle response, which enables them to escape from dangerous situations. As robots are required to operate in more hostile environments, mechanisms analogous to startle responses may be critical to building robust systems. This paper presents some preliminary work exploring (1) how some reactive evasive behaviours can be added to an agent operating in a hostile environment, and (2) how evasive measures can be integrated with the agent's other activities.

1 Introduction

Almost every animal is required to escape from predators from time to time in order to survive and reproduce. Animats may also need to escape from sources of danger, such as malevolent passers by and curious children [18]. The key is not only to have effective escape mechanisms but also to integrate escape with the animat's other activities. An animal that spends all its time running away without stopping to eat and find food will not survive very long.

A startle response for escaping quickly in critical situations is an adaptation which has arisen in many different animals from disparate parts of the evolutionary tree [7]. The startle responses vary greatly. In common they usually have simple reliable triggers, very fast activation and often produce a stereotyped response [3]. The fact that almost all animals have some kind of startle response suggest that there is an advantage to having a dedicated subsystem for detecting and responding to hazardous situations. Hoy [13] argues that startle responses will have a significant role in designing robust robot architectures.

A relatively 'simple' invertebrate animal that is particularly well studied by neuroscientists is the crayfish. (This is because they have relatively few neurons, some of the neurons are very large and crayfish make a delicious meal at the end of the experiment.) The crayfish is equipped with a variety of evasion techniques including (but not limited to): spending large amounts of time in hiding; retreating to safety if it notices a far away predator; and an escape response [19]. The escape response is a last resort mechanism that is used in extreme conditions. It is activated by a sharp tap to the abdomen or sudden visual stimuli. The

M. Brooks, D. Corbett, and M. Stumptner (Eds.): AI 2001, LNAI 2256, pp. 507–518, 2001.

response is a stereotyped tailflip that rapidly propels the crayfish away from the source of danger. The trigger for the escape reflex is controlled by giant command neurons in the abdomen. These neurons are responsible for integrating a large group of stimuli and making a snap decision. For a detailed reference to the neural organisation of the crayfish escape mechanism refer to [25,24,17,15, 16].

Some previous studies that have drawn inspiration from invertebrate neural circuits have yielded promising results. Beer [1] successfully modelled the neurons controlling insect walking with an R-C network. The circuit was fully distributed, efficient and robust; later it was used to control a real hexapod robot. There has also been work on modelling the escape response of the cockroach. [2]

There have been many previous studies of evasion in isolation. A couple of examples of evolving optimal strategies in scenarios with fixed predator behaviour include [14] and [12]. Miller and Cliff [18] co-evolved pursuer and evader tactics using noisy neural network controllers. The pursuer-evader problem has been reformulated as a one-dimensional, time-series prediction game. [10] There has been exploration of the evolution of evasion strategies when the game is made slightly asymmetric between the pursuer and evader. [23]

This paper presents some preliminary work in exploring how some simple reactive evasive behaviours can be added to an agent operating in a hostile environment. The mechanisms used are loosely inspired by the evasive tactics and reactions of the crayfish.

2 The Scenario

The scenario is a simple predator-prey simulation. There is one predator and one prey. The prey has the task of collecting enough food to survive while being hunted by a predator. The predator has a greater maximum velocity and a further seeing distance than the prey. The prey has superior acceleration over the predator and may choose to hide in a shelter where it is safe from the predator.

The environment is a continuous two-dimensional plane of $n \times m$ units. It has wraparound edges (this is to avoid the artifact of the prey being trapped in a corner.) The world contains pieces of food located at random locations. New pieces of food are added and old ones are removed at random time intervals. Also situated in the environment is a shelter. When the prey is in the shelter the predator is unable to see it and unable to kill it.

The predator and prey are able to move within the world and are able to make some limited interactions with the other entities in the world. The prey is able to eat a piece of food if it is close enough. The predator is able to kill the prey if it is close enough. The simulation is updated in discrete time steps. At each time step the predator and prey are queried by the simulation engine about their intended movements and other actions they want to take. All updates to positions and interactions are executed simultaneously. If the predator or prey elect to change their velocity, they are not able to do it instantly but instead accelerate to new velocities. It may take several time steps for the predator or prey to reach their new velocity. The predator and prey each have maximum rates of acceleration.

The predator follows a very simple behaviour pattern. This behaviour pattern is fixed for all the experiments. The predator roams around at half-speed travelling in a straight line. At random time intervals it changes to a new random direction. The predator is continuously looking for the prey. If at any point the predator spots the prey it will immediately change its direction to head directly toward it and accelerate to its maximum velocity. When the predator gets within a distance of k_{kill} units of the prey, the predator kills the prey and then eats its. The predator is present somewhere in the world for the entire duration of the simulation.

The prey has an internal energy level. To avoid starving it must maintain its energy level above zero. At each time interval the prey consumes an amount of energy determined by equation 1.

$$\Delta E = -(B + Av^2) \tag{1}$$

The base energy consumption (determined by B) forces the prey to occasionally go and collect food. The other term is dependent on the square of the prey's velocity to penalise travelling at high speeds. The prey replenishes its energy level by eating food. The prey needs to move close to a piece of food before it can eat it. When a piece of food is eaten the food is removed and the prey gains k units of energy. If E drops below zero the prey starves to death.

The simulation was written in Java. There are two interfaces: a graphical applet interface and a command line interface. The applet interface can be accessed on the web at `http://www.cs.mu.oz.au/~scv/botsim/`

3 Architecture of the Prey

The prey uses a layered architecture which we build up incrementally [20], [4]. The prey operates in distinct behavioural modes. It monitors the level of some simple stimuli, such as 'hunger', to determine which behavioural mode to operate in. At the most basic stage the prey ignores the predator completely and is solely focused on collecting enough food to avoid starving. At each stage, another behavioural mode or stimulus is added to the prey's repertoire to assist it in avoiding the predator. New behaviours are able to subsume or suppress behaviours introduced at previous levels.

3.1 The Hiding Bot

First we consider a very simple bot. The hiding bot looks for food when it is hungry and hides in the shelter when it is not. It does not detect an approaching predator. The hiding bot's survival strategy is basically to spend as much time in the shelter as possible, while avoiding starvation.

The hiding bot uses one stimulus with which to make its decisions: the internal energy level (E). It uses this information to choose between one of two behavioural modes in which it can operate:

Forage. The prey searches for food and eats it. The prey follows the odour gradient emitted by the food until it reaches an item of food which it then eats. The prey travels at half speed to conserve energy.

Hide. The prey moves to the shelter and hides there when it arrives. The prey travels at half speed to conserve energy.

Figure 1a shows the hiding bot's control architecture.

3.2 The Running Away Bot

The running away bot actively keeps an eye out for the predator while it is outside of the shelter. The bot operates in the same way as the hiding bot in that it ventures out of the shelter for food when it is hungry, but if while the bot is out of the shelter it detects the predator it will scurry back to the shelter for safety.

The running away bot may use the behavioural modes of the hiding bot: hide and forage, and in addition may use: *run away* mode.

Run Away. The prey runs to the shelter at maximum velocity.

To determine when to run away, the bot uses the stimulus *predator fear*. It is dependent on the distance (d_{pred}) between the prey and the predator as shown in equation 2.

$$P = A_P e^{-\frac{d_{pred}}{L}} \tag{2}$$

The algorithm uses to control the running away bot is shown in figure 1b.

3.3 The Memory Bot

The hiding bot and the running away bot are stateless. The memory bot explores what advantage a simple piece of state information can give an agent. [6] demonstrated that adding even a few memory bits can give a significant improvement to the performance of a reactive object tracking system.

The memory bot remembers when it last saw the predator. This affects the stimulus *memory fear*. When the predator is seen memory fear instantly rises to the maximum. It decays exponentially with time (t_{pred}) from when the predator was last seen as shown in equation 3

$$M = A_M e^{-\frac{t_{pred}}{\tau}} \tag{3}$$

The memory bot operates in the same way as the running away bot but if its memory fear is still above a threshold T_M then it will continue to hide. Figure 1c shows the control algorithm.

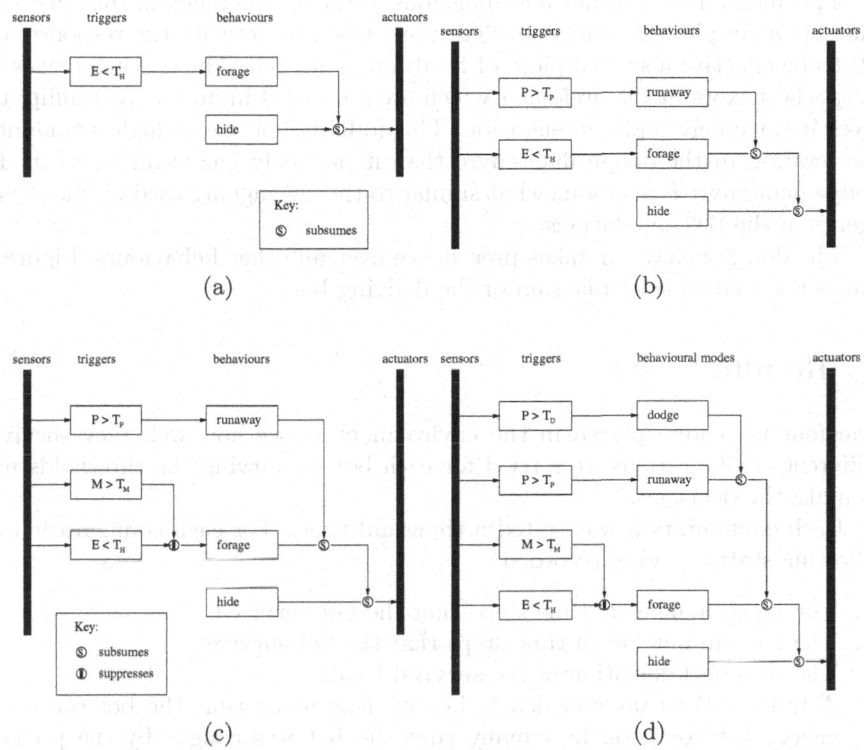

Fig. 1. The architecture of the prey. (a) Hiding bot. By default the bot hides; if the bot is hungry, the forage behaviour takes control of the actuators. (b) The running away bot. *Run away* takes control of the actuators if the predator is seen. (c) The memory bot. If the predator was seen recently the forage behaviour is suppressed. (d) The dodging bot. Dodge takes precedence over all other behaviours.

3.4 The Dodging Bot

The dodging bot has a reflex action with which it attempts to evade the predator if it gets too close.

If the predator fear stimulus crosses a threshold T_D then the prey will go into *dodge* mode:

Dodge. The prey immediately changes to a new direction which is orthogonal to the direction of the approaching predator. The prey very rapidly accelerates to maximum velocity. (It is in effect a jump to the side.)

This manœuvre is somewhat analogous to the escape reflex in the crayfish in that (1) a simple test is used to determine when to activate the response, and (2) to be effective a special piece of hardware is needed. The crayfish makes use of special flexors in the abdomen which are only used in an escape tailflip; this gives it extremely rapid acceleration. The dodging bot uses a higher amount of acceleration in the dodge manœuvre than it normally has available to it. The dodge manœuvre is also somewhat similar to the zig-zagging used by the evasive agents in the [18] simulations.

The dodge behaviour takes precedence over all other behaviours. Figure 1d shows the control layer diagram of the dodging bot.

4 Results

The four bots were placed in the environment to see how well they survived. Different configurations were tried for each bot by varying the thresholds used to make the decisions.

Each configuration was tested a thousand times. For each configuration the following statistics were recorded:

1. The mean number of time steps that the bot survived.
2. The median number of time steps that the bot survived.
3. The standard deviation of the survival time.
4. A tally of the causes of death, i.e., on how many runs the bot ran out of energy (*starved*), on how many runs the bot was caught by the predator (*killed*) and on how many runs the bot reached the end of the simulation still alive (*survived*).

Refer to Appendix A for the values of constants used in the simulation.

4.1 The Hiding Bot

Since the hiding bot is unable to detect the predator its behaviour is governed only by the hunger threshold, which determines when it will hide in the shelter and when it will venture out to look for food. Figure 2a shows how the survival time and cause of death vary as the hunger threshold (T_H) changes. If the hunger threshold is very low, then the bot will wait until it is almost completely out of energy before venturing out to look for food. There is a very high chance that the bot will starve to death before finding the food. If the hunger threshold is very high, then the bot will spend most of its time out of the shelter looking for food and there is a greater chance of it being eaten by the predator. The bots that do the best are the ones that stay in the shelter as long as possible while still having a good chance of finding food in time before starving.

Figure 2a shows how the survival rate of the hiding bot varies by adjusting the hunger threshold. A curious feature of the graph in figure 2a is that as the hunger threshold goes from 0 to about 2, the median declines slightly but the mean rises. The explanation of this phenomenon is at very low hunger thresholds

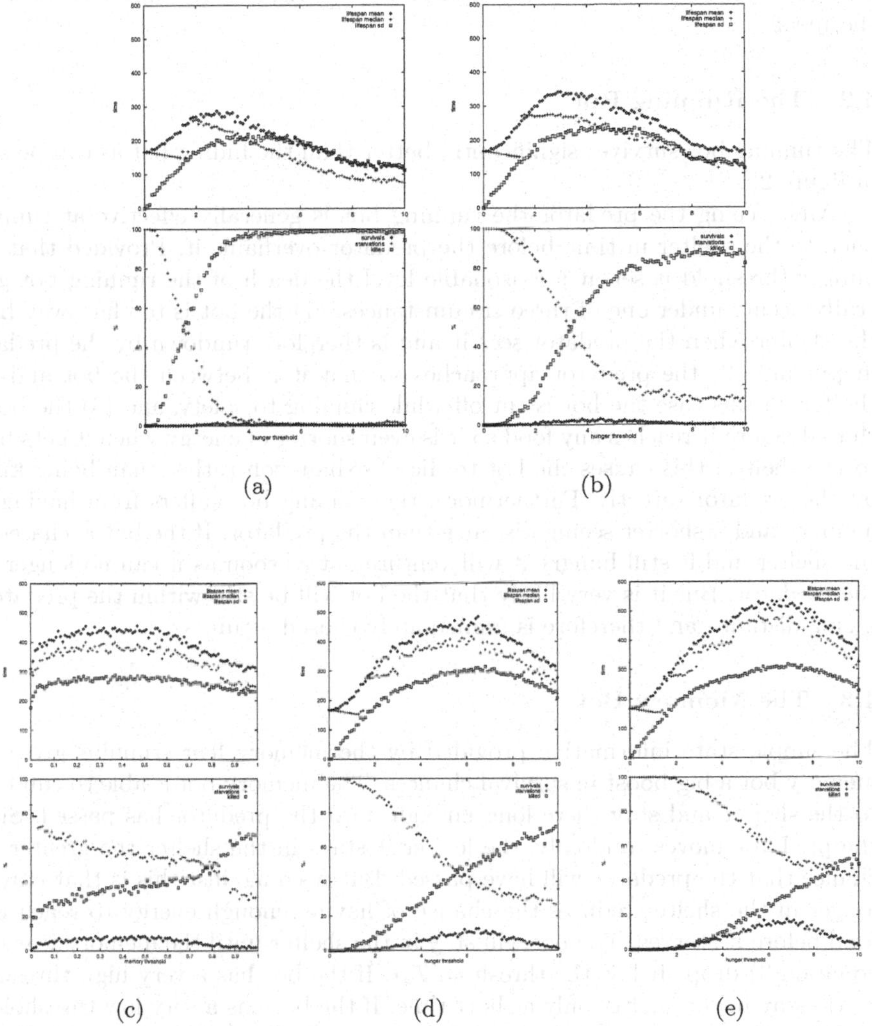

Fig. 2. Plots of the survival times and the causes of death versus the hunger threshold for each bot: (a) the hiding bot, (b) the running bot, (d) the memory bot and (e) the dodging bot. (c) The survival times and cause of death versus memory threshold for the memory bot ($T_H = 6$).

when the bot ventures out it is more likely that the bot will starve than that it will find food. While most of the bots die of this cause the median will stay low. However the lucky few who find food live significantly longer so push up the mean.

4.2 The Running Bot

The running bot survives significantly better than the hiding bot as can be seen in figure 2b.

After seeing the predator the running bot is generally effective at running back to the shelter in time before the predator overhauls it. Provided that the hunger threshold is set at a reasonable level the death of the running bot generally occurs under one of three circumstances: (1) the bot is too far away from the shelter when the predator sees it and is therefore rundown by the predator in pursuit, (2) the predator approaches so that it is between the bot and the shelter; in this case the bot is cut off while running to safety, and (3) the bot is chased before it reaches any food so it is even shorter of energy when it gets back to the shelter; this causes the bot to die of exhaustion rather than being killed by the predator directly. Furthermore, the running bot suffers from having no memory and a shorter seeing distance than the predator. If the bot is chased to the shelter and is still hungry it will venture out as soon as it can no longer see the predator. But it is very likely that the bot will be still within the predator's seeing distance and therefore is immediately chased again.

4.3 The Memory Bot

The simple state information provided by the memory fear stimulus gives the memory bot a big boost in survival chances. The memory bot is able to run back to the shelter and stay there long enough until the predator has passed. Since the predator moves randomly, the longer it stays in the shelter the greater the chance that the predator will have passed. Balanced against this is that staying longer in the shelter reduces the chance of having enough energy to reach new food before it starves. The bot will stay in the shelter until the memory fear (see equation 3) drops below the threshold T_M. If the bot has a very high threshold it will stay in the shelter only a short time. If the bot has a very low threshold it will stay in the shelter a very long time. Figure 2c shows how the survival rate is affected by the value chosen for the memory threshold. Note that the survival rate is fairly even for thresholds between 0.2 and 0.6, reflecting that the tradeoff between waiting out the predator and risk of starvation is fairly evenly balanced.

Figure 2d shows how the survival rate is affected by the hunger threshold for the memory bot. The optimal hunger threshold is greater for the memory bot than for the running bot. This can be explained by two factors: (1) the memory bot has got a better chance of surviving an encounter with the predator so it can risk spending more time out of the shelter and (2) if the memory bot collects more energy then it can spend more time in the shelter after it has been chased by a predator, giving it higher chance of the predator having left.

The memory bot is still killed if it is too far away from the shelter when pursuit begins or if the predator is in between it and the shelter. It is fairly successful in waiting in the shelter until the predator has passed. It sometimes starves while waiting for the predator to pass and sometimes is unlucky and finds the predator still waiting outside after it has waited.

4.4 The Dodging Bot

The dodge manœuvre of the dodging bot allows it to survive in one of the situations where the memory bot is frequently killed. If the predator attacks the prey coming from the direction of the shelter, the dodging bot is able to evasively side-step the predator. The predator coming at full speed is unable to adjust its direction in time to catch the prey. The dodge manœuvre is less successful in evading the predator chasing from behind. However as with the running bot and the memory bot, in most cases when the prey is being chased from behind it will be able to reach the shelter in time. It is usually only when the prey is very far from the shelter that it is caught in pursuit.

Figure 2e shows how the survival rate of the dodging bot varies with the hunger threshold. The dodging bot has a higher optimal hunger threshold again compared to the memory bot.

5 Discussion and Conclusions

A trend that emerges is the prey spends more time outside of the shelter foraging for food as it gets better at avoiding the predator. This phenomenon may be caused by two factors: (1) for the evasion tactics to be advantageous the prey needs enough energy to do the evasive manœuvres and still collect food, and (2) because the prey is more likely to survive an encounter with the predator it can afford to spend more time outside the shelter foraging for food, thereby reducing its risk of starvation.

To optimise its survival time the prey needs to balance its primary task, collecting food, with taking evasive action. If the predator were nonexistent the optimal survival strategy for the prey would be to spend all its time collecting food to nullify any risk of starvation. In the presence of a predator, collecting food becomes a risky task. This causes the bots with poor predator avoidance to wait until they are really hungry before they will venture out to look for food. As the prey is equipped with more evasive capabilities the risk in collecting food diminishes. This increased confidence allows the prey to act more like it would if there were no predator. As more evasive capabilities are added, the prey's behaviour pattern (when it is not taking evasive action) approaches what it would be if the predator did not exist.

A more general implication of this result is that having separate subsystems to deal with dangerous situations allows an agent to be less obstructed in undertaking its primary activities. Robots presumably have a set of primary tasks which they have to perform. However some robots while undertaking their work robots may periodically have to face obstructions or even dangers. A hypothetical example is a rescue robot sent into a burning building that may have to dodge falling debris. Having separate subsystems to deal with obstructions may allow robots to be minimally affected in the way they achieve their primary tasks. Animals have dedicated neural circuits to deal with unexpected hazardous situations. [3,13]

One of the biggest improvements given to the prey in this simulation is the addition of some simple memory information. In this memory model the time that the predator was last seen is used implicitly as a predictor of the predator's present proximity.

The fixed hierarchical model used for the agents seems suboptimal for this scenario. One kind of behaviour should not always have precedence over another. For example because hiding in a shelter after seeing a predator has a higher precedence than foraging, in some cases the bot would starve to death in the shelter. A better model would be more flexible: wait longer in the shelter if energy reserves are relatively high, and shorter if energy reserves are low. Different actions need different precedence at different times.

There is biological evidence that in animals the precedence of actions is much more flexible. [21] review biological findings about parts of the vertebrate brain and argue that the basal ganglia acts as a central decision making point for arbitrating between conflicting actions. They argue that a similar specialised switching mechanisms might be employed in layered robot architectures (such as [4]) to provide more flexible action selection.

In the crayfish the giant command neurons responsible for triggering the escape response are modulated by other parts of the nervous system [22,11,9]. The trigger threshold adjusts according to various circumstances, such as during feeding and restraint [24] and also adjusts according to longer term conditions such as the mating cycle and social dominance [26].

Edwards [8] proposes a model for behavioural choice in crayfish that uses mutual inhibition amongst the neural command centres. In Edwards' model there is one command neuron for seven different behavioural modes. Each neuron receives excitatory stimuli from sensors. Each neuron is able to inhibit other command neurons and also receives inhibitory signals from the excited command neurons. After summing the excitations and the inhibitions, the command neuron with the greatest excitation wins. Edwards' model is able to give actions different precedence at different times. An attempt was made to write a bot based on Edwards' architecture for the scenario described in this paper. Preliminary results indicate that in this scenario it performs slightly better, but the results are inconclusive.

The scenario examined in this paper is very specific. Previous pursuit-evasion experiments [5] have shown that effective evasion strategies are often very sensitive to the parameters of the environment. Future work may consider what kind of escape measures work best when faced with different kinds and variable sources of danger. The prey currently uses 'magic' perception to get the position of the predator. This is unrealistic. In future simulations the prey will have to infer the presence of a predator from noisy sensors.

The work presented in this paper is a preliminary step in exploring the role of integrating evasive actions in the context of doing other activities. As robots move out of the laboratory into more hostile environments, handling evasive actions may prove an important component of the robot architecture.

A Constants Used in Simulation

Constant	Value	Equations used
A	0.001	(1)
B	0.03	(1)
A_P	1	(2)
L	40	(2)
A_M	1	(3)
τ	15	(3)

References

1. Randall D. Beer. Intelligence as adaptive behaviour: An experiment in computational neuroethology. In *Perspectives in Artificial Intelligence*, volume 6. Academic Press, 1990.
2. Randall D. Beer and Hillel J. Chiel. Simulations of cockroach locomotion and escape. In *Biological Neural Networks in Invertebrate Neuroethology and Robotics*, pages 267–285. Academic Press, San Diago, 1993.
3. Michael V. L. Bennett. Escapism: Some startling revelations. In *Neural Mechanisms of Startle Behavior*, pages 353–363. New York: Plenum Press, 1984. edited by R. C. Eaton.
4. Rodney A. Brooks. A robust layered control system for a mobile robot. *IEEE Journal of Robotics and Automation*, RA-2(1):14–23, Marth 1986.
5. Dave Cliff and Geoffrey F. Miller. Co-evolution of pursuit and evasion ii: Simulation methods and results. In *Animals to Animats IV: Proceedings of Fourth International Conference on Simulation of Adaptive Behaviour*, pages 506–515. MIT Press, 1996.
6. M Dorigo and M Colombetti. Robot shaping: developing autonomous agents through learning. *Artifical Intelligence*, 71:321–370, 1994.
7. R. C. Eaton, editor. *Neural mechanisms of startle behaviour*. Plenum Press, New York, 1984.
8. Donald H. Edwards. Mutual inhibition among neural command systems as a possible mechanism for behavioral choice in crayfish. *Journal of Neuroscience*, 11(5):1210–1223, May 1991.
9. Donald H. Edwards, William J. Heitler, Esther M. Leise, and Russell A. Fricke. Postsynaptic modulation of rectifying synaptic inputs to the lg escape command neuron in crayfish. *Journal of Neuroscience*, 11(7):2117–2129, July 1991.
10. Sevan G. Ficici and Jordan B. Pollack. Coevolving communinative behavior in a linear pursuer-evasion game. In *Animals to Animats V: Proceedings of Fifth International Conference on Simulation of Adaptive Behaviour*, pages 557–561. MIT Press, 1998.

11. David L. Glanzman and Franklin B. Krasne. Serotonin and octopamine have opposite modulatory effects on the crayfish's lateral giant escape reaction. *Journal of Neuroscience*, 3(11):2263–2269, November 1983.
12. J. J. Grefenstette, C. L. Ramsey, and A. C. Schultz. Learning sequential decision rules using simulation models and competition. *Machine Learning*, 5(4):355–391, 1990.
13. Ronald R. Hoy. Acoustic startle: an adaptive behaviour act in flying insects. In *Biological neural networks in invertebrate neuroethology and robotics*, pages 139–158. Academic Press, San Diago, 1993.
14. J. Koza. Evolution and co-evolution of computer programs to control independently-acting agents. In *Animals to Animats: Proceedings of First International Conference on Simulation of Adaptive Behaviour (SAB92)*, pages 366–375. MIT Press, 1991.
15. Franklin B. Krasne and Sunhee Cho Lee. Response-dedicated trigger neurons as control points for behavioural actions: selective inhibition of lateral giant command neurons during feeding in crayfish. *Journal of Neuroscience*, 8(10):3703–3712, October 1988.
16. Franklin B. Krasne and Terri M. Teshiba. Habituation of an invertebrate escape reflex due to modulation by higher centers rather than local events. In *Proceedings of the National Academy of Science, USA*, volume 92, pages 3362–3366, 1995.
17. Franklin B. Krasne and Jeffrey J. Wine. The production of crayfish tailflip escape response. In *Neural Mechanisms of Startle Behaviour*, pages 179–211. New York: Plenum Press, 1984. edited by R. C. Eaton.
18. Geoffrey F. Miller and Dave Cliff. Protean behaviour in dynamic games: coevolution of pursuit-evasion tactics. *From Animals to Animats 3*, pages 411–420, 1994.
19. P. Olszewski. *A Salute to the humble yabby.* London Angus & Robertson, 1980.
20. Rolf Pfeifer and Christian Scheier. *Understanding Intelligence.* MIT Press, 1999.
21. Tony J. Prescott, Peter Redgrave, and Kevin Gurney. Layered control architectures in robots and vertebrates. *Adaptive Behaviour*, 7(1):99–127, 1999.
22. Eric T. Vu and Franklin B. Krasne. Crayfish tonic inhibition: Prolonged modulation of behavioural excitability by classical gabaergic inhibition. *Journal of Neuroscience*, 13(10):4394–4402, October 1993.
23. Mattias Wahde and Mats G. Nordahl. Evolution of protean behavior in pursuit-evasion contests. In *Animals to Animats V: Proceedings of Fifth International Conference on Simulation of Adaptive Behaviour*, pages 557–561. MIT Press, 1998.
24. Jeffrey J. Wine. The structural basis of an innate behavioural pattern. *Journal of Experimental Biology*, 112:283–319, 1984.
25. Jeffrey J Wine and Franlin B Krasne. The cellular organisation of crayfish escape behaviour. In *The Biology of Crustacea*, volume 4, pages 241–292. Academic Press, 1982.
26. S-R Yeh, B. E. Musolf, and D. H. Edwards. Neuronal adaptations to changes in the social dominance status of crayfish. *Journal of Neuroscience*, 17(2):697–708, January 1997.

Solving the Qualification Problem
(In the Presence of the Frame Problem)

Quoc Bao Vo and Norman Y. Foo

Knowledge Systems Group
School of Computer Science and Engineering
University of New South Wales - Sydney NSW2052 Australia
{vqbao | norman}@cse.unsw.edu.au

Abstract. We present a uniform nonmonotonic solution for the problem of reasoning about action on the basis of argumentation-theoretic approach in a series of paper. This paper is the first one in which we solve the frame and the qualification problems in a simplifying setting without domain constraints or ramifications. Our theory is provably correct relative to a sensible minimisation policy introduced on top of a temporal propositional logic.

1 Motivation and Introduction

The need for a good reasoning about action formalism is apparent for research in artificial intelligence (AI). Alongside the logicist point of view to artificial intelligence, more recently, there emerges the cognitivist and situated action-based approaches (see [10] and the references therein). The latters provide some immediate and practical answers to certain issues of AI. The current problem domains for (Soccer) Robot Cup seem to be an area where these approaches promise to gain fruitful results. On the other hand, the logicist approach aims at long term solutions for the general problems of AI. From a logicist approach, formalising dynamic domains for reasoning about action can be realised within a logical knowledge representation. The general idea is that intelligent agents should be able to represent all kinds of knowledge in a uniform way such that some general problem solver can fully employ and find a solution based on their knowledge. As it turns out, there are difficulties with such a general approach to AI. Consider the task of formalising dynamic domains in some logical language. To formalise the dynamics of an action (or event) in a language with n fluents[1], one will need to axiomatise not only about the fluents that are effected by the action but also about those that are not. Essentially, it requires that n axioms be asserted. Such a formalisation can hardly be considered a good representation. Hence, there is the need to solve this problem in logic-based reasoning about action formalisms. This is the well known frame problem as introduced by McCarthy and Hayes ([15]). Moreover, there is still a problem in axiomatising the effects of an action, called the effect axiom. A logical axiomatisation requires that

[1] fluent is a technical term referring to functions or predicates whose values can be varied relative to time.

M. Brooks, D. Corbett, and M. Stumptner (Eds.): AI 2001, LNAI 2256, pp. 519–531, 2001.

the conditions under which the effects will take place after executing the action be precisely speciified. However, there are potentially infinitely many such conditions, some of which the reasoner may have never thought about. No realistic formalisation would ever be able to exhaustively enumerate all of those conditions. Nonetheless, to start a car, most people only worry about whether they have the key to that car. They never bother checking whether there is something blocking the tailpipe or checking all electric circuits to make sure that they are all well connected. Such a story has long been well-known within the community of common-sense reasoning, in particular reasoning about action. This is known as ther qualification problem and was introduced by McCarthy (cf. [13]).
While there have been a number of solutions to the frame problem (see e.g. [19],[16] and [3]), the qualification problem has largely been ignored. Some people argue that the frame problem is already very challenging and it would be a good approach to thoroughly solve the frame problem before complicating a formalism with the qualification problem. We argue that there is a danger of approaching these problems from that point of view for (at least) two reasons: (1) it may be very hard to come up with a uniform solution for all problems: while many existing solutions for the frame problem are monotonic (e.g. [3] and [16]), the qualification problem inherently requires a non-monotonic solution; and (2) these solutions of the frame problem can only succeed under some precise assumptions:
- Actions always succeed. This is the *action omniscience* assumption. More precisely, this assumption dictates that the qualification problem is skipped.
- Fluents change if and only if the reasoner knows that there exists an action that possibly changes its value. This can be termed as *domain omniscience* assumption. It assumes that the reasoner has complete (ontological) knowledge about the domain on which he is reasoning about.

The above two reasons are of course closely related as (1) arises due to the underlying assumptions in (2) which can no longer hold once the qualification problem is taken into consideration.

In this paper, a uniform nonmonotonic solution for the two most basic problems of reasoning about action is proposed. Basically, when performing common sense reasoning, the reasoner is based on a number of plausible assumptions. E.g., assuming that an instance of birds flies, or assuming that shooting a turkey with a loaded gun causes it to die, etc. The proposed representation formalism aims at making these assumptions explicit so that an automated reasoner is conscious (at least) about what assumptions it relies on when performing reasoning. It is also the basic idea of assumption-based frameworks which are at heart of Bondarenko *et al.*'s (1997) argumentation-theoretic approach. As a first step towards a comprehensive framework, we show how the frame and the qualification problems are solved in the absence of domain constraints and ramifications.

2 Domain Descriptions

We introduce a propositional action description language based on a more comprehensive representation formalism proposed by Sandewall (1994). In particular, we extend Drakengren and Bjäreland's (1999) language so that it is possible to describe narratives in our framework.

2.1 Syntax

Following Sandewall's, the underlying representation of time is a (*discrete*) *time structure* $\mathbf{T} = \langle \mathcal{T}, <, +, - \rangle$ consisting of

- a *time domain* $\mathcal{T}$ whose members are called *timepoints* which are integers in this paper;
- $<, +, -$ are as usual for integers.

Given a time structure $\mathbf{T} = \langle \mathcal{T}, <, +, - \rangle$, a *signature* with respect to $\mathbf{T}$ is a tuple $\sigma = \langle T, \mathcal{F}, \mathcal{A} \rangle$, where T is a set of *timepoint variables*, $\mathcal{F}$ is a set of *propositional fluent names*, and $\mathcal{A}$ is a set of *action names*. We assume that all sets in σ are countable. We denote $\overline{\mathcal{F}} = \{\neg f \mid f \in \mathcal{F}\}$. A member of $\mathcal{F}^* = \mathcal{F} \cup \overline{\mathcal{F}}$ is a *fluent literal*. Moreover, $\mathcal{A} = \mathcal{A}_0 \cup \mathcal{DA}$, where is the set of domain dependent action names, called *basic actions*, e.g. *load*, *shoot*, etc. and $\mathcal{DA} = \{da_\varphi \mid \varphi \in \mathcal{F}^*\}$ is the set of *dummy actions*.

For each fluent literal $\varphi \in \mathcal{F}^*$, we introduce the following two propositions: AQ_φ, and FA_φ. AQ_φ is associated with the assumed qualifications upon the preconditions of an action regarding the fluent φ. FA_φ is associated with the frame assumptions regarding φ. Given a set of fluent literals $\Gamma \subseteq \mathcal{F}^*$, we denote $FA_\Gamma \stackrel{def}{=} \{FA_\varphi \mid \varphi \in \Gamma\}$ and $AQ_\Gamma \stackrel{def}{=} \{AQ_\varphi \mid \varphi \in \Gamma\}$.

A *timepoint expression* is one of the following:

- a member of $\mathcal{T}$,
- a timepoint variable in T,
- an expression formed from timepoint expressions using $+$ and $-$. For convenience, we will also write τ^+ and τ^- instead of $\tau + 1$ and $\tau - 1$, respectively.

We denote the set of timepoint expressions by $\mathcal{TE}$.

Definition 1 Let $\sigma = \langle T, \mathcal{F}, \mathcal{A} \rangle$ be a signature and $\tau, \upsilon \in \mathcal{TE}$, $f \in \mathcal{F}$, $A \in \mathcal{A}$, $R \in \{=, <\}$, $\otimes \in \{\wedge, \vee, \rightarrow, \leftrightarrow\}$. Define the *basic (domain description) language* Λ over σ by:

$\Lambda ::= \mathtt{T} \mid \mathtt{F} \mid f \mid [\tau, \upsilon]A \mid \tau R \upsilon \mid \neg\Lambda \mid \Lambda_1 \otimes \Lambda_2 \mid [\tau]\Lambda$,

and the *assumption base* $\mathcal{AB}$ by:

$\mathcal{AB} = \mathcal{AB}_{AQ} \cup \mathcal{AB}_{FA}$, where $\mathcal{AB}_{AQ} = \{[\tau, \upsilon]AQ_\varphi \mid \tau, \upsilon \in \mathcal{TE} \text{ and } \varphi \in \mathcal{F}^*\}$ and $\mathcal{AB}_{FA} = \{[\tau]FA_\varphi \mid \tau \in \mathcal{TE} \text{ and } \varphi \in \mathcal{F}^*\}$.

The *domain description language* $\mathcal{L}$ (over σ) is defined: $\mathcal{L} = \Lambda \cup \mathcal{AB}$.

$[\tau, \upsilon]A$ means the action A is performed during the time interval $[\tau, \upsilon]$. $[\tau, \upsilon]AQ_\varphi$ means the fluent literal φ is assumed to be qualified to hold by the end of the interval $[\tau, \upsilon]$. $[\tau]FA_\varphi$ means the fluent literal φ is assumed by default to persist from the time point τ to the next, i.e. the *principle of inertia*.

A formula that does not contain any connectives (i.e. $\wedge, \vee, \rightarrow, \leftrightarrow, \neg$, and $[.]$) is *atomic*. If γ is atomic and $\tau \in \mathcal{TE}$, then the formula γ, $[\tau]\gamma$, $[\tau]\gamma$, $\neg\gamma$, $\neg[\tau]\gamma$, and $[\tau]\neg\gamma$ are *literals*.

Let γ be a formula. A fluent $f \in \mathcal{F}$ occurs *free* in γ iff it does not occur within the scope of a $[\tau]$ expression in γ. $\tau \in \mathcal{TE}$ *binds* f in γ if a formula $[\tau]\psi$ occurs as a subformula of γ, and f is free in ψ. If no fluent occurs free in γ, γ is *closed.* If γ does not contain any occurrence of $[\tau]$ for any $\tau \in \mathcal{TE}$, then γ is *propositional.*

2.2 Semantics

Definition 2 Let $\sigma = \langle T, \mathcal{F}, \mathcal{A}\rangle$ be a signature. A *state* over σ is a function from $\mathcal{F}$ to the set $\{\mathtt{T},\mathtt{F}\}$ of truth values. A *history* over σ is a function h from $\mathcal{T}$ to the set of states. A *valuation* is a function ϕ from $\mathcal{TE}$ to $\mathcal{T}$. A *narrative assignment* is a function η from $\mathcal{T}\times\mathcal{A}\times\mathcal{T}$ to the set $\{\mathtt{T},\mathtt{F}\}$. In addition, we define $\varepsilon_q : \mathcal{T}\times AQ_{\mathcal{F}^*}\times\mathcal{T} \to \{\mathtt{T},\mathtt{F}\}$ and $\varepsilon_f : \mathcal{T}\times FA_{\mathcal{F}^*} \to \{\mathtt{T},\mathtt{F}\}$. An interpretation over σ is a tuple $\langle h, \phi, \eta, \varepsilon_q, \varepsilon_f\rangle$ where h is a history, ϕ is a valuation, η is a narrative assignment and $\varepsilon_q, \varepsilon_f$ are defined as above.

Definition 3 Let $\gamma, \delta \in \Lambda$ and $I = \langle h, \phi, \eta, \varepsilon_q, \varepsilon_f\rangle$ an interpretation. Assume $\tau, \upsilon \in \mathcal{TE}$, $f \in \mathcal{F}$, $A \in \mathcal{A}$, $R \in \{=,<\}$, $\varphi \in \mathcal{F}^*$, $\otimes \in \{\wedge,\vee,\rightarrow,\leftrightarrow\}$, and $\chi \in \{\mathtt{T},\mathtt{F}\}$. Define the truth value of γ in I for a timepoint $t \in \mathcal{T}$, denoted $I(\gamma, t)$ as follows:

$$I(\chi,t) = \chi$$
$$I(f,t) = h(t)(f)$$
$$I([\tau,\upsilon]A,t) = \eta(\tau, A, \upsilon)$$
$$I([\tau,\upsilon]AQ_\varphi,t) = \varepsilon_q(\tau, AQ_\varphi, \upsilon)$$
$$I([\tau]FA_\varphi,t) = \varepsilon_f(\tau, FA_\varphi)$$
$$I(\tau R \upsilon,t) = \phi(\tau) R \phi(\upsilon)$$
$$I(\neg\gamma,t) = \neg I(\gamma,t)$$
$$I(\gamma\otimes\delta,t) = I(\gamma,t)\otimes I(\delta,t)$$
$$I([\tau]\gamma,t) = I(\gamma,\phi(\alpha))$$

Two formulas γ and δ are equivalent iff $I(\gamma,t) = I(\delta,t)$ for all I and t. An interpretation I is a *model* of a set $\Gamma \subseteq \Lambda$ of formulas, denoted $I \models \Gamma$, iff $I(\gamma,t) = \mathtt{T}$ for every $t \in \mathcal{T}$ and $\gamma \in \Gamma$. A formula $\gamma \in \Lambda$ is *entailed* by a set $\Gamma \subseteq \Lambda$ of formulas, denoted $\Gamma \models \gamma$, iff γ is true in all models of Γ.

Definition 4 Let $I = \langle h, \phi, \eta, \varepsilon_q, \varepsilon_f\rangle$ be an interpretation. The set $Occ^I = \{(t, A, u) \in \mathcal{T}\times\mathcal{A}\times\mathcal{T} \mid \eta(t, A, u) = \mathtt{T}\}$ is called *action occurrence denotation* of I. The set $FA^I = \{(t, FA_\varphi) \in \mathcal{T}\times FA_{\mathcal{F}^*} \mid \varepsilon_f(t, FA_\varphi) = \mathtt{T}\}$ is called *FA-denotation* of I. The set $AQ^I = \{(t, AQ_\varphi, u) \in \mathcal{T}\times AQ_{\mathcal{F}^*}\times\mathcal{T} \mid \varepsilon_q(t, AQ_\varphi, u) = \mathtt{T}\}$ is called *AQ-denotation* of I. ■

2.3 Background

Bondarenko *et al.* (1997) propose a unified framework for default reasoning called argumentation-theoretic approach which we will use as the underlying inference mechanism for our system. We reproduce the relevant definitions from Bondarenko *et al.*'s work for completeness.

A *deductive system* is a pair $\langle\mathcal{L},\mathcal{R}\rangle$, where
-$\mathcal{L}$ is a formal language consisting of countably many sentences, and
-$\mathcal{R}$ is a set of inference rules of the form

$$\frac{\alpha_1,\ldots,\alpha_n}{\alpha}$$

where $\alpha, \alpha_1, \ldots, \alpha_n \in \mathcal{L}$ and $n \geq 0$.

Any set of sentences $T \subseteq \mathcal{L}$ is called a *theory*. A *deduction* from a theory T is a sequence $\beta_1, \ldots, \beta_m$, where $m > 0$, such that, for all $i = 1, \ldots, m$,

- $\beta_i \in T$, or
- there exists $\frac{\alpha_1, \ldots, \alpha_n}{\beta_i}$ in $\mathcal{R}$ such that $\alpha_1, \ldots, \alpha_n \in \{\beta_1, \ldots, \beta_{i-1}\}$.
- $T \vdash_{\langle \mathcal{L}, \mathcal{R} \rangle} \alpha$ means that there is a deduction from T whose last element is α. $Th_{\langle \mathcal{L}, \mathcal{R} \rangle}(T)$ is the set $\{\alpha \in \mathcal{L} \mid T \vdash_{\langle \mathcal{L}, \mathcal{R} \rangle} \alpha\}$. Since the language $\mathcal{L}$ is generally kept fixed whereas the set of inference rules $\mathcal{R}$ is likely to vary depending on the description of the domain, when there is no possible confusion we will abbreviate $\vdash_{\langle \mathcal{L}, \mathcal{R} \rangle}$ and $Th_{\langle \mathcal{L}, \mathcal{R} \rangle}$ as $\vdash_{\mathcal{R}}$ and $Th_{\mathcal{R}}$, respectively. Thus the classical inference relation $\vdash$ can also be written as $\vdash_{\mathcal{R}_C}$ where $\mathcal{R}_C$ is the set of inference rules of classical propositional logic. Note also that every set of inference rules considered in this paper will be a super set of $\mathcal{R}_C$.

Given $r = \frac{\alpha_1, \ldots, \alpha_n}{\alpha} \in \mathcal{R}$, we will also denote $prem(r) = \{\alpha_1, \ldots, \alpha_n\}$, the premises of r, and $cons(r) = \alpha$, the consequence of r.

Definition 5 [2] Given a deduction system $\langle \mathcal{L}, \mathcal{R} \rangle$, an *assumption-based framework* with respect to $\langle \mathcal{L}, \mathcal{R} \rangle$ is a tuple $\langle T, Ab, ^- \rangle$ where

- $T, Ab \subseteq \mathcal{L}$ and $Ab \neq \emptyset$,
- $^-$ is a mapping from Ab into $\mathcal{L}$, where $\overline{\alpha}$ denotes the contrary of α.

Definition 6 [2] Given an assumption-based framework $\langle T, Ab, ^- \rangle$,

- a set of assumptions $\Delta \subseteq Ab$ *attacks* an assumption $\alpha \in Ab$ iff $T \cup \Delta \vdash_{\mathcal{R}} \overline{\alpha}$,
- a set of assumptions $\Delta \subseteq Ab$ attacks a set of assumptions $\Delta' \subseteq Ab$ iff $\Delta \subseteq Ab$ attacks some assumption $\alpha \in \Delta'$.

As assumptions are expressed in terms of usual propositions, we will replace the notion of contrariness $^-$ in Bondarenko *et al.*'s system with the classical negation $\neg$ and omit it from the specification of assumption-based framework.

3 Reasoning about Action with Argumentation-Theoretic Approach

In the rest of this paper, we introduce a uniform framework for solving the frame and qualification problems using the frame and qualification assumptions. General solutions for the frame and the qualification problems can be obtained by computing plausible sets of assumptions which guarantee that extensions computed from plausible sets of assumptions will be consistent when the given theory is consistent.

Definition 7 A deductive system $\langle \mathcal{L}, \mathcal{R} \rangle$ is *well-defined* iff for each subset $S \subseteq \mathcal{R}$, if the set $\bigcup_{r \in S} prem(r)$ is consistent then the set $CONS(S) = \{cons(r) \mid r \in S\}$ is also consistent.

We will assume that a deductive system is well-defined. Being formalised in terms of the argumentation-theoretic approach, the representation requires an extended notion of consistency.

Definition 8 Let $\langle \mathcal{L}, \mathcal{R} \rangle$ be a deductive system, (a) a set of sentences $\Gamma \subseteq \mathcal{L}$ is *$\mathcal{R}$-consistent* iff $\Gamma \not\vdash_{\mathcal{R}} \mathrm{F}$; (b) an assumption-based framework $\langle T, Ab, \neg \rangle$ with respect to $\langle \mathcal{L}, \mathcal{R} \rangle$ is *consistent* iff T is $\mathcal{R}$-consistent. ■

Definition 9 Given an assumption-based framework $\langle T, Ab, \neg \rangle$, a set of assumptions $\Delta \subseteq Ab$ *rejects* an assumption $\alpha \in Ab$ iff (a) Δ does not attack itself, and (b) $\Delta \cup \{\alpha\}$ attacks itself.

Observation 1 *Given an assumption-based framework $\langle T, Ab, \neg \rangle$ and a set of assumptions $\Delta \subseteq Ab$, if Δ attacks an assumption $\alpha \notin \Delta$ then Δ rejects α.*

We are interested in the assumptions which are rejected by a given set of assumptions without being attacked by that set.

Definition 10 Given an assumption-based framework $\langle T, Ab, \neg \rangle$, a set of assumptions $\Delta \subseteq Ab$ *leniently rejects* an assumption $\alpha \in Ab$ iff (a) Δ rejects α, and (b) Δ does not attacks α.

We denote $Lr(\Delta) \stackrel{def}{=} \{\alpha \in Ab \mid \alpha \text{ is leniently rejected by } \Delta\}$.

The frame assumptions are the essence of the inertia problem, and their role in the argumentation approach is illustrated below by the Yale Shooting Problem (YSP) [9]. In this formalisation we intentionally ignore the qualification problem (it is addressed in the next section) to highlight how the frame problem is solved. We consider a well-worn example to motivate our approach to the frame problem.

Example 1

$AD_{YSP} = \{[\tau, \upsilon]load \rightarrow ([\upsilon]loaded \wedge \neg[\tau]FA_{\neg loaded}),$
$([\tau, \upsilon]shoot \wedge [\tau]loaded) \rightarrow (\neg[\upsilon]alive \wedge \neg[\tau]FA_{alive}), \}$

The following rules representing the frame assumptions are added:

$FR_{YSP} = \{\frac{[\tau]loaded, [\tau]FA_{loaded}}{[\tau^+]loaded}, \frac{[\tau]alive, [\tau]FA_{alive}}{[\tau^+]alive},$
$\frac{\neg[\tau]loaded, [\tau]FA_{\neg loaded}}{\neg[\tau^+]loaded}, \frac{\neg[\tau]alive, [\tau]FA_{\neg alive}}{\neg[\tau^+]alive}\}$

Given a theory $T_{YSP} = \{[0]alive, [0,1]load, [1,2]wait, [2,3]shoot\}$, the argumentation-theoretic approach will yield the following preferred set of assumptions (cf. [2]): $\Delta_{YSP} = \{[\tau]FA_{loaded} \mid \tau \in Tme\} \cup \{[\tau]FA_{\neg loaded} \mid \tau \in Tme\} \cup \{[\tau]FA_{alive} \mid \tau \in Tme\} \cup \{[\tau]FA_{\neg alive} \mid \tau \in Tme\} \setminus \{[0]FA_{\neg loaded}, [2]FA_{alive}\}$. They give rise to the following preferred extension (cf. [2]): $Th(T_{YSP} \cup \{[\tau]loaded \mid \tau \geq 1\} \cup \{[1]alive, [2]alive\} \cup \{\neg[\tau]alive \mid \tau \geq 3\} \cup \Delta)$. This extension is also the stable extension and well-founded semantics (cf. [2]) of the given theory under the argumentation-theoretic approach. Note that in case one would like to be uncertain about whether the gun is still loaded after the shooting action, one just simply needs to add an axiom: $[\tau, \upsilon]shoot \rightarrow \neg[\tau]FA_{loaded}$ to dictate that the persistence of the fluent *loaded* after the action shooting is not guaranteed. In that case, we can still derive that $[\tau]loaded$ for $\tau = 1, 2$, but we can no longer give a definite assertion about $[\tau]loaded$ for $\tau \geq 3$. □

As the above formalisation of YSP resembles that using default logic, it may be surprising that the problem of unintended models pointed out by Hanks and McDermott for circumscription, default logic, autoepistemic logic does not happen here. The principal reason is the interaction of the inference rules and the notion of attack in the argumentation-theoretic framework, which invalidates undesired assumptions. Notice that even if $\neg[2]loaded$ can be (magically) derived, it cannot lead to $\neg[1]FA_{loaded}$. Therefore, the set of assumptions corresponding to this case does not satisfy the conditions of preferred set of assumptions, thus ruling out this unintended model.

We adopt the following guidelines in seeking for a sensible solution for the problems of reasoning about action:

- The derived pieces of information don't conflict with the given facts;
- Occurrences of events are minimised; and
- The inertia of fluents is maximised though the minimality of the event occurrences will be of higher priority.

However, while the preferred model semantics copes successfully with the YSP, it can not properly account for the explanation problem, e.g. the Stanford Murder Mystery, the Stolen Car Problem. The subtlety lies in the derivation of the contrary of the frame assumption FA_φ. The contrary of a frame assumption is derived only when both the occurrence of the event that brings about the change (absent in the Stolen Car Problem) and the preconditions required to be satisfied for the change to actually take place (absent in the Stanford Murder Mystery) are explicitly derivable. This is where the notion of (leniently) rejected assumptions is called into service.

Definition 11 Given an assumption-based framework $\langle T, Ab, \neg\rangle$, a set of assumptions $\Delta \subseteq Ab$ is *presumable* iff (a) $\Delta = \{\alpha \in Ab \mid T \cup \Delta \vdash_{\mathcal{R}} \alpha\}$ (in Bondarenko *et al.*'s terms, Δ is closed), (b) Δ does not attack itself, and (c) for each assumption $\alpha \notin \Delta$, α is rejected by Δ. ■

Definition 12 Given an assumption-based framework $\langle T, Ab, \neg\rangle$, a set of assumptions $\Delta \subseteq Ab$ is *plausible* iff (a) Δ is presumable, and (b) there exists no $\Delta' \subseteq Ab$ such that Δ' is presumable and $Lr(\Delta') \subset Lr(\Delta)$. ■

4 Technical Framework

Aside from the trivial case of occurrences of events causing the frame assumptions to be rejected, two aspects of events can be distinguished:

(a) An event happens but the change it is supposed to cause does not take place. We call this *expectation failure* and this is more or less the qualification problem; and

(b) No events that are known to cause a change happen but the change does take place. We call this *surprise* and this is usually known as the explanation problem.

The following assumption represents our underlying intuition behind reasoning about action formalisms.

Assumption 1 *Intuitive models contain minimal (with respect to set inclusion) sets of surprises.* □

Definition 13 Let $\sigma = \langle \mathcal{T}, \mathcal{F}, \mathcal{A}\rangle$ be a signature. Assume $\tau, \upsilon \in \mathcal{TE}$, $A \in \mathcal{A}$, $R \in \{=, <\}$, $\Phi \subseteq \Lambda$, and $\varphi \in \mathcal{F}^*$. A *domain description* D is defined to be a tuple $\langle \mathcal{L}, \mathcal{R}, \mathcal{AB}, \Gamma\rangle$, where:

1. $\mathcal{L}$ is the domain description language and $\mathcal{AB}$ an assumption base over σ;
2. $\mathcal{R} = \mathcal{R}_C \cup \mathcal{R}_F \cup \mathcal{R}_A \cup \mathcal{R}_Q$, where
   (a) $\mathcal{R}_C$ is the set of inference rules of (classical) propositional logic;
   (b) $\mathcal{R}_F$ is the set of *frame-based inference rules* of the form: $\frac{[\tau]\varphi, [\tau]FA_\varphi}{[\tau^+]\varphi}$, i.e. those that represent the frame axioms in terms of inference rules;
   (c) $\mathcal{R}_A$ is the set of *action descriptions* which are inference rules of the form: $\frac{\Phi, [\tau,\upsilon]A, [\tau,\upsilon]AQ_\varphi}{[\upsilon]\varphi \wedge \neg[\tau]FA_{\neg\varphi}}$, i.e. those that represent the conditions for an action to bring about some effect on a fluent; and
   (d) $\mathcal{R}_Q$ is the set of *qualification-based inference rules* of the form: $\frac{\Phi}{\neg[\tau,\upsilon]AQ_\varphi}$, i.e. those that represent the (dis-)qualifications regarding the fluent literal φ.
3. The theory $\Gamma \subseteq \Lambda$. ■

Given a set of assumptions Δ, we denote $\Delta_{FA} = \Delta \cap \mathcal{AB}_{FA}$ and $\Delta_{AQ} = \Delta \cap \mathcal{AB}_{AQ}$.

Definition 14 Let $\sigma = \langle \mathcal{T}, \mathcal{F}, \mathcal{A} \rangle$ be a signature and $D = \langle \mathcal{L}, \mathcal{R}, \mathcal{AB}, \Gamma \rangle$ a domain description over σ. An interpretation $I = \langle h, \phi, \eta, \varepsilon_q, \varepsilon_f \rangle$ is a *model* of D iff

1. I is a model of Γ;
2. for each $r \in \mathcal{R}$, if $I \models prem(r)$ then $I \models cons(r)$. ■

The following definition captures one of several aspects of the (model-theoretic) solution of the frame problem. This aspect is known as the action-oriented frame problem in Lin and Shoham's (1995) terms. The proposed minimisation policy formalises the intuition that change does not happen by itself but is caused by some kind of event. Thus, for each fluent, if its value is changed between two timepoints τ and υ, (at least) an occurrence of some event must end at υ that brings about that change.

Definition 15 Let $D = \langle \mathcal{L}, \mathcal{R}, \mathcal{AB}, \Gamma \rangle$ be a domain description and I a model of D. I is a *coherent model* of D iff

1. for each basic action $\alpha \in \mathcal{A}_0$ and $\tau, \upsilon \in \mathcal{TE}$, if $\Gamma \not\models [\tau,\upsilon]\alpha$ then $I \not\models [\tau,\upsilon]\alpha$; and
2. for each $\varphi \in \mathcal{F}^*$ and $\tau \in \mathcal{TE}$, if $I \models [\tau]\varphi \wedge \neg[\tau^+]\varphi$ then either (i) there is $A \in \mathcal{A}_0$ and $\upsilon_1, \upsilon_2 \in \mathcal{TE}$ such that $\upsilon_2 = \tau^+$, and $r = \frac{\Phi, [\upsilon_1,\upsilon_2]A, [\upsilon_1,\upsilon_2]AQ_{\neg\varphi}}{\neg[\upsilon_2]\varphi \wedge \neg[\upsilon_1]FA_\varphi} \in \mathcal{R}$, and $I \models prem(r)$, or (ii) $I \models [\tau,\tau^+]da_{\neg\varphi}$. ■

Thus, in a coherent model (1) all satisfiable basic actions must follow from the given theory, and (2) all changes are attributable to events.

Given an interpretation I, we want to extract the sets of assumptions satisfiable in I.

Definition 16 Let $\sigma = \langle \mathcal{T}, \mathcal{F}, \mathcal{A} \rangle$ be a signature and $I = \langle h, \phi, \eta, \varepsilon_q, \varepsilon_f \rangle$ an interpretation over σ. The set of frame assumptions satisfiable in I, denoted Δ^I_{FA}, is defined as follows: $\Delta^I_{FA} = \{[\tau]FA_\varphi \mid (\tau, FA_\varphi) \in FA^I\}$ and the set of qualification assumptions satisfiable in I, denoted Δ^I_{AQ}, is : $\Delta^I_{AQ} = \{[\tau,\upsilon]AQ_\varphi \mid (\tau, AQ_\varphi, \upsilon) \in AQ^I\}$. We also write $\Delta^I_{QF} = \Delta^I_{AQ} \cup \Delta^I_{FA}$. ■

Conversely, given a theory Γ and a set of assumptions Δ, a reasoner can also construct his models about the domain of interest.

Definition 17 Let $D = \langle \mathcal{L}, \mathcal{R}, \mathcal{AB}, \Gamma \rangle$ be a domain description and $\Delta \subseteq \mathcal{AB}$. A model I of D is *Δ-relativised* iff

1. for each $\alpha \in \mathcal{AB}$, $I \models \alpha$ iff $\alpha \in \Delta$; and
2. $Occ^I = OA_D \cup DAS(\Delta)$, where: (i) $OA_D = \{(t, A, u) \in \mathcal{T} \times \mathcal{A}_0 \times \mathcal{T} \mid \Gamma \models [t, u]A\}$, and (ii) $DAS(\Delta) = \{(t, da_\varphi, t^+) \in \mathcal{T} \times \mathcal{DA} \times \mathcal{T} \mid [t]FA_\varphi \notin \Delta$ and there exists no action $A \in \mathcal{A}_0$ such that the following hold: $\frac{\Phi, [\tau,v]A, [\tau,v]AQ_{\neg\varphi}}{\neg[v]\varphi \wedge \neg[\tau]FA_\varphi} \in \mathcal{R}$, and $v = t^+$, and $\Gamma \cup \Delta \models \{\Phi, [\tau, v]A, [\tau, v]AQ_{\neg\varphi}\}\}$.■

4.1 The Frame Problem

Initially we address the frame problem in a simple setting viz. without qualifications, but will lift the restrictions later.

Definition 18 Let $D = \langle \mathcal{L}, \mathcal{R}, \mathcal{AB}, \Gamma \rangle$ be a domain description. D is a *simple domain description*, or *S-domain*, iff $\mathcal{R}_Q = \emptyset$ and AQ does not occur any where in $\mathcal{R}$ or Γ. ■

Definition 19 Let $D = \langle \mathcal{L}, \mathcal{R}, \mathcal{AB}, \Gamma \rangle$ a domain description. An interpretation $I = \langle h, \phi, \eta, \varepsilon_q, \varepsilon_f \rangle$ is a *simple model*, or *S-model*, of D iff
1. I is a model of D; and
2. $\varepsilon_q(t, AQ_\varphi, u) = \mathrm{T}$ for every $(t, AQ_\varphi, u) \in \mathcal{T} \times AQ_{\mathcal{F}^*} \times \mathcal{T}$. ■

This effectively isolates the frame problem from the qualification problem. Note also that if I is an S-model then $\Delta^I_{AQ} = \mathcal{AB}_{AQ}$. A *coherent S-model* is an S-model which is coherent.

Example 1 (*continued.*) Let $D_{YSP} = \langle \mathcal{L}, FR_{YSP}, \mathcal{AB}, \Gamma \rangle$ be an S-domain formalising the YSP scenario, where $\Gamma = AD_{YSP} \cup T_{YSP}$. The following is part of one of the coherent models of D_{YSP}:
$\{[0, 1]load, \neg[0]loaded, [1]loaded, [0]alive, [1]alive,$
$[1, 2]wait, [1, 2]da_{\neg loaded}, \neg[2]loaded, [2]alive,$
$[2, 3]shoot, \neg[3]loaded, [3]alive\}$,
which corresponds to one of the anomalous models of this scenario (the one pointed out by Hanks and McDermott). □

But it is not desirable to admit the occurrence of an event when there is no evidence for it. Thus we need to minimise the set of action occurrences in a given action theory.

Definition 20 Let D be an S-domain. A coherent S-model I of D is a *prioritised minimal model* (or simply *PMM*) of D iff there does not exist any coherent S-model I' of D such that $Occ^{I'} \subset Occ^I$. ■

Note that the above model-theoretic minimisation policy isn't based on the frame assumptions. This solution to the frame problem is thus amenable to well-known techniques such as circumscription[2], but we believe an argumentation-theoretic approach is not only more direct but has wider applicabilty. In order to

[2] in combination with the introduction of occurences of dummy actions.

provide the connection between the above (model-theoretic) minimisation policy and the (argumation-theoretic) notion of plausible sets of assumptions we need to maximise the set of assumptions satisfiable in a PMM.

Definition 21 Let D be an S-domain. A PMM I of D is a *canonical prioritised minimal model* (or simply *CPMM*) of D iff there does not exist any PMM I' of D such that $FA^I \subset FA^{I'}$. ■

We now want to see how the account of plausible sets of assumptions connects to this account of minimality.

Theorem 1 *Let D be an S-domain. If I is a CPMM of D then Δ^I_{QF} is plausible.*

We now prove that not only can we derive a plausible set of assumptions from a given CPMM but we can also construct CPMMs from a plausible set of assumptions of a given S-domain.

The set of Δ-relativised models of an S-domain D is denoted as $Mod^S_\Delta(D)$.

Observation 2 *Let D be an S-domain and Δ a set of assumptions of D. For each $I \in Mod^S_\Delta(D)$, $\Delta = \Delta^I_{QF}$.* □

Theorem 2 *Let $D = \langle \mathcal{L}, \mathcal{R}, \mathcal{AB}, \Gamma \rangle$ be an S-domain and $\Delta \subseteq \mathcal{AB}$. Δ is plausible iff $Mod^S_\Delta(D) \neq \emptyset$ and for each $I \in Mod^S_\Delta(D)$, I is a CPMM of D.* □

Theorem 3 *Let D be an S-domain. Furthermore, suppose that $CPMM(D)$ is the set of CPMMs of D and $Plaus(D)$ is the set of plausible sets of assumptions of D, then $CPMM(D) = \bigcup_{\Delta \in Plaus(D)} Mod^S_\Delta(D)$.* □

4.2 Solving the Qualification Problem (in the Presence of the Frame Problem)

The results reported in the previous section are established in a simple setting. If we add the following observation to the theory in example 1: $[3]alive$, i.e. after the *shoot* action, the victim is still alive, then like most existing formalisms, the above account of plausibility would come up with a contradiction. In fact, it would be more reasonable that such a failure is explained as an occurrence of some (dis-)qualification. In this section, we remove certain restrictions on the qualifications of actions in order to achieve a more general framework.

There are some subtleties in the way action theories are represented in our proposed assumption-based framework. Note first that there is a potential difficulty if frame assumptions and qualification assumptions are not distinguished, which can be illustrated by a version of the YSP. Consider the following action description:
$\{\frac{[\tau]alive, [\tau]FA_{alive}}{[\tau^+]alive}, \frac{[\tau]loaded, [\tau,v]shoot, [\tau,v]AQ_{\neg alive}}{\neg[v]alive \wedge \neg[\tau]FA_{alive}}\} \subseteq \mathcal{R}$
$\{[0]loaded, [0]alive, [0,1]shoot\} \subseteq \Gamma$.

From this, we have (at least) two stable set of assumptions: one contains the frame assumption $[0]FA_{alive}$ which rejects the qualification assumption

$[0,1]AQ_{\neg alive}$ and another contains $[0,1]AQ_{\neg alive}$ which attacks $[0]FA_{alive}$. Only the latter is intuitive in this case but we do not have any explicit criterion to prefer one over another.

Given the presence of several kinds of assumptions, i.e. frame and qualification, we will adopt the following convention: we will write $Lr_P(\Delta)$ instead of $(Lr(\Delta))_P$ for $P \in \{FA, AQ\}$. Since we no longer exclude qualification assumptions from our assumption-based domain descriptions, we will simply refer to assumption-based domain descriptions as *Q-domains.*

Definition 22 Let $D = \langle \mathcal{L}, \mathcal{R}, \mathcal{AB}, \Gamma \rangle$ be a Q-domain. A presumable set of assumptions $\Delta \subseteq Ab$ is *semi-Q-plausible* iff $Lr_{FA}(\Delta)$ is minimal (with respect to set inclusion). ∎

Definition 23 Let $D = \langle \mathcal{L}, \mathcal{R}, \mathcal{AB}, \Gamma \rangle$ be a Q-domain. A set of assumptions $\Delta \subseteq Ab$ is *Q-plausible* iff (a) Δ is semi-Q-plausible, (b) Δ_{AQ} is maximal, i.e. there does not exist any $\Delta' \subseteq Ab$ such that Δ' is semi-Q-plausible and $\Delta_{AQ} \subset \Delta'_{AQ}$, and (c) Δ_{FA} is maximal relative to the above two conditions, i.e. there does not exist any $\Delta' \subseteq Ab$ such that Δ' satisfies the above two conditions and $\Delta_{FA} \subset \Delta'_{FA}$. ∎

We will now refer to models of a Q-domain as *Q-models.* A *coherent Q-model* is a Q-model which is coherent. We minimise the set of action occurrences in coherent Q-models of a given action theory.

Definition 24 Let D be a Q-domain. A coherent Q-model I of D is a *prioritised minimal Q-model* (or simply *PMQM*) of D iff there does not exist any coherent Q-model I' of D such that $Occ^{I'} \subset Occ^{I}$. ∎

Definition 25 Let D be an S-domain. A PMQM I of D is a *canonical prioritised minimal Q-model* (or simply *CPMQM*) of D iff (a) there does not exist any PMQM I' of D such that $AQ^{I} \subset AQ^{I'}$, and (b) there does not exist any PMM I' of D such that $FA^{I} \subset FA^{I'}$. ∎

Now we can proceed to results for CPMQMs regarding Q-plausible sets of assumptions which are similar to those for CPMMs regarding plausible sets of assumptions.

Theorem 4 *Let D be a Q-domain. If I is a CPMQM of D then Δ^{I}_{QF} is Q-plausible.* □

Similar to the previous section, we now prove that not only can we derive a plausible set of assumptions from a given CPMQM but we can also construct CPMQMs from a plausible set of assumptions of a given domain description. The set of Δ-relativised models of a Q-domain D is denoted as $Mod^{Q}_{\Delta}(D)$.

Observation 3 *Let D be a Q-domain Δ a set of assumptions of D. For each $I \in Mod^{Q}_{\Delta}(D)$, $\Delta = \Delta^{I}_{QF}$.* □

Theorem 5 *Let $D = \langle \mathcal{L}, \mathcal{R}, \mathcal{AB}, \Gamma \rangle$ be a Q-domain and $\Delta \subseteq \mathcal{AB}$. Δ is Q-plausible iff $Mod^{Q}_{\Delta}(D) \neq \emptyset$ and for each $I \in Mod^{Q}_{\Delta}(D)$, I is a CPMQM of D.*

Theorem 6 *Let D be a Q-domain. Furthermore, suppose that $CPMQM(D)$ is the set of CPMQMs of D and $Plaus^Q(D)$ is the set of Q-plausible sets of assumptions of D, then $CPMQM(D) = \bigcup_{\Delta \in Plaus^Q(D)} Mod^Q_\Delta(D)$.* □

Q-plausible sets of assumptions allow one to overcome scenarios in which expectation failures (or, qualification surprises) arise, e.g. shooting a turkey with a loaded gun and it can be observed that the turkey is still alive. When such surprises arise, the reasoner knows who's to blame: qualification assumptions. He can then accordingly remove the "guilty" assumptions.

5 Related Work

The frame problem has been addressed in numerous research papers formalised under various frameworks for reasoning about actions, including the Situation Calculus (see [17]), the Event Calculus (see [19]), a temporal logic introduced by Sandewall (see [18]), the action language family (see [8]), the Fluent Calculus (see e.g. [20]). Attempts to solve the original version of the qualification problem (in contrast to the narrowed version of this problem as introduced by Ginsberg and Smith [7] and Lin and Reiter [11]) include Kvarnström and Doherty's work in tackling the qualification problem in a version of the temporal logic introduced by Sandewall. The solution proposed in this work, however, is still largely fragmented from the solution to other problems of reasoning about actions such as the frame and the ramification problems. A more uniform solution to the qualification problem in accordance to other accounts of reasoning about actions is introduced by Thielscher [21] for the Fluent Calculus. The solution proposed by Thielscher is based on a monotonic solution to the frame problem. The idea with Thielscher's solution to the frame problem is similar to the idea behind the STRIPS problem solver. The fluents that hold in a state will be manipulated by rules that add (resp. delete) certain fluent (literals) from the preceding state in order to obtain the resulting state. On the other hand, the solutions to the ramification problem and the qualification problem rely on the causal expressions. The idea is to exploit the directional characteristic of causal expression to eliminate the unintended models (aka. the anomalous models). The solution to the qualification problem is non-monotonic while the solution to the ramification problem remains monotonic. Thielscher's argument in favour of this approach is largely due to the fact that minimisation of abnormalities in the traditional way as originally performed by McCarthy under circumscription [14] leads to anomalous models. However, as pointed out by Baker [1], a clever minimisation policy will overcome the problem. For a more formal analysis of the related issues from a system-theoretic point of view, the reader is referred to Foo *et al.*'s paper [6].

Our solution is distinctive from the above approaches in the sense that it offers solution to the major problems of reasoning about actions in a uniform manner. With the introduction of explicit assumptions and the use of reasonable arguments, only intended models should emerge and allow the reasoner to arrive at correct conclusions about the dynamic world.

6 Conclusion

We developed a uniform framework for reasoning about action using an argument-ation-theoretic approach (more precisely, assumption-based approach) in a series of papers. The present paper is the first of this series in which we have presented how our framework copes with the frame and the qualification problems in a simple setting without indirect effects or domain constraints. We have shown how our framework can be naturally extended to become more and more expressive.

References

1. A. Baker. A Simple Solution to the Yale Shooting Problem. In KR'89: 11-20.
2. A. Bondarenko, P. Dung, R. Kowalski, and F. Toni. An Abstract, Argumentation-Theoretic Approach to Default Reasoning. *AIJ*, 93: 63-101, 1997.
3. M. Castilho, O. Gasquet and A. Herzig. Formalizing action and change in modal logic I: the frame problem. *Journal of Logic and Computation*, to appear.
4. T. Drakengren and M. Bjäreland. Reasoning about action in polynomial time. *AIJ*, 115: 1-24, 1999.
5. J. Kvarnström and P. Doherty. Tackling the Qualification Problem Using Fluent Dependency Constraints. *Computational Intelligence*, 16(2): 169-209 (2000).
6. Foo, N., Peppas, P., Vo, B.Q. and Zhang, D. Circumscriptive Models and Automata. *Proc. of NRAC, IJCAI-01*: 1-7, Seattle, Sept 2001.
7. M. Ginsberg, D. Smith. Reasoning About Action II: The Qualification Problem. *AIJ*, 35(3): 311-342 (1988).
8. M. Gelfond and V. Lifschitz. Action languages. *Electronic Trans. on AI*, 3(16), 1998.
9. S. Hanks, and D. McDermott. Nonmonotonic logic and temporal projection. *AIJ*, 33(3): 379-412, 1987.
10. N. Kushmerick. Cognitivism ans situated action: two views on intelligence agency. *Computers and Artificial Intelligence*, 15(5): 1-20, 1996.
11. F. Lin and R. Reiter. State Constraints Revisited. *Journal of Logic and Computation*, 4(5): 655-678 (1994).
12. F. Lin and Y. Shoham. Provably Correct Theories of Action. *JACM*, 42(2): 293-320, 1995.
13. J. McCarthy. Epistemological Problems of Artificial Intelligence. In *Proc. of the IJCAI*, 1977: 555-562.
14. J. McCarthy. Applications of Circumscription to Formalizing Common-Sense Knowledge. *AIJ*, 28(1): 89-116 (1986).
15. J. McCarthy and P. Hayes. Some philosophical problems from the standpoint of artificial intelligence. In *Machine Intelligence*, v.4, 1969: 463-502.
16. R. Reiter. The frame problem in the situation calculus: A simple solution. In V. Lifschitz, ed., *AI and Mathematical Theory of Computation: Papers in Honor of John McCarthy*, pp.418-420. Academic Press, 1991.
17. R. Reiter. *Knowledge in Action: Logical Foundations for Specifying and Implementing Dynamical Systems.* MIT Press, 2001.
18. E. Sandewall. *Features and Fluents.* Oxford University Press, 1994.
19. M. Shanahan. *Solving the Frame Problem: A Mathematical Investigation of the Common Sense Law of Inertia.* The MIT Press, Cambridge, Massachusetts, 1997.
20. M. Thielscher. Ramification and Causality. *AIJ*, 89(1-2): 317-364 (1997).
21. M. Thielscher. The Qualification Problem: A solution to the problem of anomalous models. *AIJ*, 131(1-2): 1-37 (2001).

Dialogue Modelling for a Conversational Agent

Peter Wallis[1], Helen Mitchard[2], Jyotsna Das[2], and Damian O'Dea[2]

[1] Agent Oriented Software, Pty. Ltd.
Carlton, Victoria
peter.wallis@agent-software.com.au
[2] Information Technology Division
Defence Science and Technology Organisation
Salisbury, South Australia
<firstName>.<lastName>@dsto.defence.gov.au

Abstract. There is growing agreement that dialogue management is critical to speech enabled applications. This paper describes a novel approach to knowledge acquisition in the natural language processing domain, and shows the use of techniques from *cognitive task analysis* to capture politeness protocols from a "dialogue expert." Acknowledging the importance of intentions in mixed initiative systems, our aim was to use an off-the-shelf Belief, Desire, and Intention (BDI) framework from Agent Oriented Software to provide the planning component, and introduce *plan library cards* as a means of capturing expertise in this context.

1 Introduction

Being able to hold a conversation with a computer has been a dream of AI research from the very beginning when Turing proposed what has become known as the Turing Test. It turned out to be harder than expected, and in this year when HAL was to be on his way to Jupiter, the GUI is still the primary means of interfacing to a computer, and call centres employ people to answer telephones.

Two things have changed in recent years that make dialogue more attractive as a research area. First, with the rise of the call centres, there is more research funding available, not only for speech recognition, but also for the software that decides what to say, and when to say it. Second, the research community now accepts there will be no silver bullet, and that a working AI system will require a concerted effort by a team of people doing sometimes dull things.

The work described here is part of an ongoing project to create a conversational agent using the beliefs, desires, and intentions (BDI) architecture introduced by Rao and Georgeff [1]. BDI systems fall within a long tradition in AI of modelling human decision making by selecting plans from a plan library to match current goals. Populating that library is a key issue, and this paper describes our approach to this task.

For the last ten years the natural language processing (NLP) community has been using *corpus analysis* as its primary data acquisition tool. This approach collects a large body of naturally occurring text, and then uses tools such as sta-

M. Brooks, D. Corbett, and M. Stumptner (Eds.): AI 2001, LNAI 2256, pp. 532–544, 2001.

tistical models [2,3] or sequential analysis [4] to infer things about text in general. In this paper we introduce a different approach to knowledge acquisition. We use a technique called Cognitive Task Analysis (CTA) in which a subject matter expert (SME) is *interviewed* to discover their thought processes while performing a task. Similar techniques have been used to populate the rule bases of expert systems [5,6] and Cognitive Work Analysis has been used to develop software agents for system simulation [7]. Mitchard [8] used Cognitive Task Analysis to create BDI models of human decision making in the air operations domain, and, following on from Mitchard, we use *Applied Cognitive Task Analysis* [9,10] to elicit knowledge from our dialogue expert.

Our SME's task — let us call her *KT* — was to take bookings for company cars by telephone. Booking cars is, naturally, of little direct use to the Australian Defence Forces and, like many other tasks, is more conveniently done with a GUI. This particular task should be seen as the pilot study for a more useful embodied conversational agent performing data access on behalf of decision makers.

As far as dialogue is concerned, we find that expressions like "OK," "Yea," "I see," and "Really" not only ground knowledge in the shared space, but can also fulfill the goal of encouraging the other party to say more. This technique is, we claim, key to *KT*'s strategy for being polite.

2 Background – The BDI Architecture

Beliefs, Desires, and Intentions, have long been used as an framework for embedded systems. Bratman's original aim [11] was to describe resource-bounded decision making. Architectures based on his writing provide a way to balance planning and reactive behaviour. It provides a model of making decisions with partial knowledge of the environment, and with insufficient time to make the best decision.

Since it was first introduced, the BDI approach has found a niche in the software agent community. Two common themes in the definition of "agent" are autonomy, which suggests goal driven behaviour, and a separation between the agent entity and its environment. The environment, being outside the control of the agent, provides inputs to which the agent may want to react. BDI is designed to pursue goals while at the same time exploiting opportunities as they arise.

A second reason BDI is closely linked with software agents is that, like SOAR [12], it is a candidate model of human cognition. For many years Air Operations Division at DSTO have been using BDI agents to implement the human element in simulations [13]. Such simulations involve classic software agents with a complex task, and programming them is non-trivial. Domain experts are often brought in to verify the behaviour of agents, and these SMEs tend to find the BDI scripts intuitively clear. Why? One explanation is that the BDI approach explicitly models how we humans think others think. It can be seen as an implementation of the folk psychological view that a rational agent will *do* what it *believes* is in its *interests*. This understanding is so ingrained in us humans that it is often difficult to see why it is interesting, hard, or even useful [14].

Using Dennett's example [15], seeing two children tugging at a toy, we know they both *want* it. We reason about other minds in terms of mental attitudes, and the BDI approach attempts to capture models of decision making at that level of abstraction. When pilots look at a BDI plan in Air Operations simulations, what they see makes intuitive sense because it describes what they would expect another pilot to do. Writing agents in terms of BDI utilises our inbuilt human ability to understand, in a common-sense way, other people's behaviour.

3 Background – Dialogue

Probably the most infamous dialogue system is Weizenbaum's Eliza [16]. This system was implemented using quite a simple procedure; the text is read and inspected for the presence of a keyword. If such a word is found, the sentence is transformed in accordance with a rule associated with the keyword, if it is not, a content-free remark or an earlier transform is retrieved. The text from this retrieval or transform is then printed out as the reply. Since 1966 when Eliza first appeared, there would appear to have been general agreement in the AI community that, although an interesting curiosity, the technique Wiezenbaum used did not bear on the nature of dialogue. Although pattern/action rules could implement a Rogerian psychologist, that role was seen as simply an interesting exception with little relevance to more general skills that would allow a machine to, for instance, book cars.

Much of the work on dialogue since then has concentrated on text generation. This kind of dialogue is often described as goal driven and is known as discourse planning. Consider writing this text. As authors, we have a goal to convince the reader of something and some plans and sub-plans on how to do it. The text planning process can be modelled as a hierarchical set of goals that bottoms out with the production of words on the page. Dialogue, by contrast, involves multiple agents who can interrupt and block each other's goals. It has the added complexity of continual plan failure and re-evaluation — something BDI was explicitly developed to handle. Research on the interactive nature of dialogue includes work on the way the "common ground" is developed between the participants [17], the nature and role of obligation, and what Allan calls "practical dialogue" systems [18]. Research on the latter emphasizes the way people use language to cooperatively solve problems. This is seen as not only practical, but also significantly simpler to achieve than general human conversational competence. The work described here falls squarely in this last camp.

As mentioned above, the primary tool of the NLP community is corpus analysis. In the case of dialogue, a popular approach is for researchers to use *sequential analysis* [4] and mark up transcripts with *dialogue moves* [19,20], or *rhetorical devices* [21]. This is the set of dialogue moves from a research project for a major Telco:

REQUEST-SERVICE, OFFER-SERVICE, EXPRESS-PROBLEM, ASK-DETAILS, CHECK, ACCEPT-REQUEST, REFUSE-REQUEST, GIVE-DETAILS, COR-

Child's plan #176

goal: eat
precondition: near mum
trigger: hungry
actions:

tell mum "I'm hungry"
get her to approve
ask her what I can have
if I like it, continue
else post goal "eat chocolate"
get it
eat it

Fig. 1. The outline of one of a child's plans for getting food.

RECT-INFO, ECHO, ACKNOWLEDGE, PARDON, HOLD, FULFILL, SOCIAL, UNCLASSIFIABLE

Although these types of speech act may seem straight forward, the reliability of the mark-up process still raises questions about the validity of many such tag sets. Better classifications and more effective training and instruction manuals are a hot research topic.

Probably the theory of dialogue structure that comes closest to a BDI approach, is that of dialogue as *dialogue games* [22,23,24].

Here is an example from Mann [23] introducing dialogue games:

1 *I'm hungry.*
2 Did you do a good job on your geography homework?
3 *Yeah. What's to eat?*
4 Let me read it. What is the capital of Brazil?
5 *Rio de Janeiro.*
6 Think about it.
7 *It's Brasilia. Can I eat now?*
8 I'll let you have something later. What is the capital of Venezuela?
9 *Caracas.*
10 Fine.
11 *So what can I eat?*
12 You want some cereal?
13 *Sure.*
14 O.K.

In this dialogue between a mother and child, the child's desire to eat is only satisfied after mum has checked the homework. At line 1 the child instantiates a plan, something along the lines of that in Figure 1, with the goal of eating. At line 2 Mum has a different goal: to check the child's homework. At line 3 the child tries to stonewall Mum's question, and continues on with her plan. Mum is having none of that, and continues the "check homework" game. At line 7 there is evidence that the child has a plan to wear Mum down — the strategy is that if the child asks often enough, Mum will get sick of saying no. At line 8 Mum explicitly tells her that the wear-Mum-down game is not going to work ("I'll let you have something later") and at line 9 the child has abandoned that plan. With line 10, Mum is indicating that her plan to check homework is finished and the child returns to her plan to get something to eat.

Dialogue *games*, in contrast to dialogue *moves*, are explicitly goal based, longer term, and succeed, fail or are abandoned. Dialogue games are consequently not as explicitly "in" the text, and coding schemes that mark up intentions of the speaker have been found to be unreliable. Rather than looking for games in transcripts, we introduce the idea of explicitly asking a "dialogue expert" about the dialogue games they use. Before looking at the study however, it is informative to consider exactly what it is the study intends to achieve.

3.1 Mixed Initiative and Politeness

Mixed initiative is often seen as the "Holy Grail" in the quest for better dialogue systems. Our primary premise is that a BDI architecture will provide the control structure to enable a mixed initiative dialogue. The concept of a dialogue game describes what the required BDI plans would look like, and ACTA provides the tools to populate the plan library. It is still not clear what *kind* of thing we are looking for however. In human to human conversations, why does initiative shift from one participant to another? When can a participant propose a new goal and when are they obliged to stick with the current one? The hypothesis is that *politeness* is a key motivation in initiative shift in human dialogue. Politeness is not just a matter of saying please and thank you. Brown and Levinson in their seminal work [25] list 30 or so universal strategies for maintaining the "face" of conversants. Interestingly many of these strategies are goal based and so, for instance, if a conversant expresses a desire for X, *positive face* can be expressed by the other person if they also consider X desirable.

The importance of getting politeness right is perhaps demonstrated by the Microsoft Paper Clip. It goes without saying that Mr. Clipit is (was) not popular, but on examination it appears to work quite well as a mechanism for accessing the Microsoft help system. So why the user reaction? One explanation is that it is not playing the social games we expect rational agents to play. On reflection, it appears that the Microsoft Paper Clip is annoying rather than ineffectual.

If user satisfaction is a product of both effectiveness and social skills, it is instructive to consider whether social skills can compensate for poor effectiveness. Evidence from our study suggests this is the case. The car booking scenario can be seen as a slot filling task (in the cases were the caller wanted to book a car — see below) in which the aim of the conversation is to fill in a form with five or so slots: name, destination, time, duration, and contact details. One measure of effectiveness in this context is the proportion of data provided by the caller that makes it into the appropriate slot. *KT*'s error rate can be measured as the number of times the caller provides a piece of data that *KT* does not pick up, divided by the number of pieces of slot fill data provided. Going through the transcripts, it turns out that she misses 20% of the data callers provide. Keep in mind that *KT* was approached for these experiments because she is recognised as being good at her job, and although user satisfaction was not explicitly measured, there seems little doubt people were happier dealing with *KT* than they would have been working with a machine with a 20% fail rate[1] This has significant consequences for organisations that want to improve user satisfaction with their speech enabled systems.

4 A BDI Model of *KT*

We wanted to look at *KT* booking cars over the phone as a pilot study for an intelligent assistant project in the Division. Given time limits, car bookings were not going to give enough samples from our Division alone, and so we approached Electronic Warfare Division for assistance. As a carrot we promised a carton of beer (funded from our own pockets) for the Division that made the most phone calls. The beer becomes important.

A separate recording telephone was installed in *KT*'s office and email sent to both Divisions asking people ring that number to book cars rather than doing it through the existing Outlook calendar. Over two weeks there were 25 calls, 2 of which were taken by a stand-in operator while *KT* was away.

KT was told that the aim of the exercise was to look at politeness and that she would be interviewed after the data was collected to see if we could identify her goals and procedures, and what cues she used to select them. The tapes were transcribed, and this shows a transcript (with names changed) of one of the more successful calls that gives a feeling for the car booking process. When looking at transcripts, bear in mind that a dialogue that seems perfectly natural and comprehensible when spoken, can appear quite awkward when transcribed..

1 *Morning ITD KT speaking*
2 Morning KT, it's PD again
3 *Hello, how are you? [laughter]*
4 Can I book the car for 10 o'clock again please?
5 *Yes, which one was it that you like?*
6 Okay, ZKJ292
7 *292. Um for 10.30?*
8 No, no. 10 till 12
9 *10 till 12. And is it to go to the same place?*
10 Yes, same place. Elex Adelaide
11 *Not a problem, I'll put it in.*
12 Thanks for that KT
13 *Okay, thank you, bye*
14 Bye

[1] The reason *KT* misses data is of course the limitations of human memory and attention when trying to use Outlook and hold a conversation at the same time. Computers of course do not have these limitations.

As usual in AI, the straightforward cases are not interesting; it is the exceptions that require common-sense and where AI systems let us down.

4.1 The Knowledge Elicitation Process

Of the various tools under the ACTA banner, it seemed inappropriate to use the Knowledge Audit probes. Dialogue management skills are primarily skills we humans do not need to think about when we use them, and so it seemed inappropriate to ask *KT* what basically she would think was "obvious." Using the transcripts and preliminary interview data, Das and Wallis used their "naïve" understanding of dialogue to produce a *Task Diagram* overview of the task and to identify the cognitively interesting components of the task. Figure 2 provides the sub-tasks that help frame the car booking dialogue process.

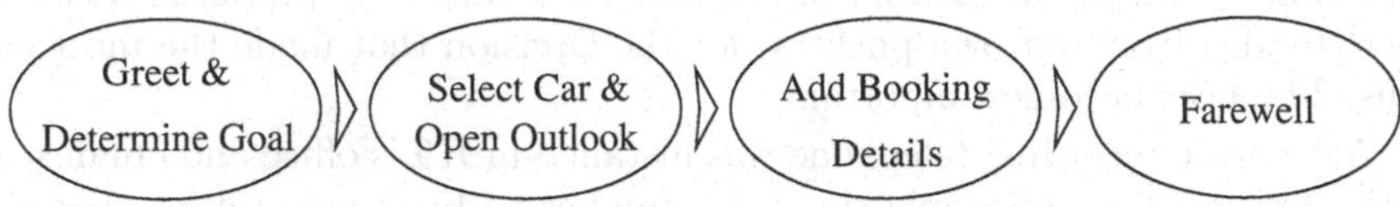

Fig. 2. The Task Diagram for booking-a-car dialogues.

Task diagrams bear a strong resemblance to state transition diagrams, which have been used by some to represent the structure of dialogue for a particular application. Although at this level of description there is a natural order to the sub-tasks, elaborating on the nature of the add-booking-details reveals no such restriction.

The next stage in the analysis was to use techniques from the *Critical Decision Method* (CDM) and ask *KT* why she did things when she did, and to identify her goals when performing some action, her procedures for achieving goals, and the cues she used to initiate procedures and goals. These issues are explored in the context of a "story" and the transcripts provided the context for the interview. In effect the approach was naturalistic observation with supplemental interviews. Phase one was to go through the transcripts and make a first pass at the BDI plans that would implement the necessary dialogue games for the car booking task. Given a set of plans, we could then interview *KT* using probes for CDM to check and develop the model.

4.2 An Interesting Transcript

Going through the transcripts, the very first call caused problems with identifying the goal. It was from a person who had already booked a car but rang anyway. We suspect the caller was after the beer, but *KT* (being nice) thinks he just wanted to help with the experiment.

Before looking at the transcript, keep in mind that *KT* is expecting callers who want to book a car. Figure 3 shows what happens.

1	*Good afternoon ITD, KT speaking*
2	Oh good afternoon, I have booked a car for tomorrow, a divisional car;
3	*[Right](1)*
4	[I](1) have to ring you here?
5	*Yes*
6	So I booked a COMMS division car, ZKJ292 for 9.30 till 12.00
7	*9.30 to 12.00*
8	We are going to Adelaide
9	*And it was the ZKJ?*
10	Yeah. 292
11	*292. And what was your name?*
12	Ah PD
13	*Right and your extension number?*
14	97313
15	*97313. Um did you want to just wait while I um check that it's available?*
16	I have booked it [not clear] I did this this afternoon before I got the message
17	*[laughter] Okay*
18	Okay
19	*Not a problem*
20	That'll be okay?
21	*Thank you*
22	Okay, thank you KT
23	*Yes, bye*
24	Bye

Fig. 3. Transcript No. 1 — the caller wants the beer.

What is happening in this conversation? Has *KT* not heard the past tense in the callers opening statement? According to our model, what was going on here is that *KT* has no plan that fits with the situation. The initial view was that she was simply going with the plan she had, and getting the details in order to make a booking – a booking she knew, at some level, she was not going to have to make.

There were other cases where the model did not fit neatly with the transcripts, but this paper concentrates on this particular case as it is the most general, and demonstrates how we used CTA in the context of dialogue.

4.3 The Interview

The interview threw a new light on the situation. We used probes similar to those in O'Hare et al. [26]. Looking at the transcripts, *KT* was asked things like "What were your specific goals when you said this?" and "What else might you have said at this point?"

When asked what was going on in the transcript in Figure 3, she said that she was thinking "Oh no! what am I going to do here!" She pointed out that she was aware the car was already booked and that indeed she had used the past tense on line 9. There was no intention to get all the details for a car booking, and even when pressed she would not state an actual goal that would fit with the Dialogue Games approach. So what motivated her responses? If she had decided to go with the plan she had, shouldn't she have been able to say as much? One might posit subconscious goals, but that would not be in keeping with using BDI as a model of cognition. It seemed that *KT* uses BDI for goal based behaviour, but when all else fails, she has a plan — enabled and disabled by the BDI mechanism — that simply fills in and encourages the caller to say more. In the same way as Eliza hands the initiative back to the user, it seems *KT*'s goal, for her first 2 or 3 responses at least, is simply to encourage.

At some point in this dialogue — about line 9 perhaps — she has developed a new plan to add to her plan library. Here is a call, the next day, from some one from ITD who is also after the beer:

1 *Good afternoon ITD KT speaking*
2 G'day, my name's AD, I'm also in ITD, over in
3 *Oh yes*
4 Um, we've just booked a car
5 *Right*
6 And ah we got that e-mail, so, uh can we do that ah [laughter] terrible thing?
7 *[laughter] Um yeah. Can I just go through it with you and just check that you've got it booked okay?*
8 Yep, sure
9 *Is that alright? Um which car were you, did you just book?*
...

Some time between line 9 of the first call, and this call, *KT* has created a plan to confirm someone's booking if they have already made a booking with Outlook, but ring up anyway.

We conclude that a key mechanism for human dialogue is the ability to hand initiative back to the other person and simply encourage the other person to say more. Eliza's success relied upon exploiting this social protocol to the hilt. In a BDI model of dialogue, one plan — in fact the default plan for when a goal is not identified — should be to encourage the user to say more.

Figure 4 is a caller ringing to cancel a booking with *KT*'s stand-in. At line 7 *PP* has no idea what to do with the caller and, we propose, is simply encouraging the caller to say more. Similarly at lines 13 and 15. Once again, at line 9, there is a tendency to go with whatever plan is even partly appropriate, but it is not clear how this would generalize. In this case *PP* is likely to have a plan with a strong link between the cue of a registration number being said, and bringing up the appropriate Outlook entry. There is also a very low cost to doing this, and there is also a tendency for people to want more information. All of these may contribute to *PP* apparently going with the book-a-car plan when the caller obviously doesn't intend to.

Here is a case where *KT* cannot recognize the destination, and uses the encourage technique:

1 *Good morning, customer service point, PP speaking*

2 Oh, um I'm ringing for KT actually

3 *Yes, KT is*

4 Car bookings, yeah

5 *Yep, I can take that for you*

6 Okay, fine, I've just had a car out

7 *Yep*

8 A CD car, ZKJ292

9 *One moment, I'll just bring that up. Sorry, the car number was?*

10 Ah ZKJ292

11 *Yep, and your name was?*

12 Ah PD. I'm back from Adelaide now, so the car can be reused, like.

13 *Okay?*

14 Okay

15 *Yep*

16 Okay I didn't need it as long as I thought

17 *Righty oh*

18 Okay, thanks

19 *Thank you for letting us know*

20 Bye-bye

Fig. 4. KT's stand-in using the encourage strategy.

1 *... and where were you going to be going?*

2 Ah the, it's called the UWB facility

3 *UWB*

4 Yeah

5 *Facility*

6 Which is on the RAAF Base.. and also be going to store 2

7 *Okay and do you know where the keys are for the car?*

Imagine a more direct approach — popular in computer interfaces — that "helpfully" suggests the known options:

1 *... and where were you going to be going?*

2 Ah the, it's called the UWB facility

3 *The available options are ...*

There can be no doubt *KT*'s approach is dramatically more polite.

4.4 Knowledge Representation

Having analysed the data, the conclusion from the analysis needs to be written down. This is what Klien refers to as "knowledge representation" and Militello and Hutton [9] recommend using a *cognitive demands table* to sort through and analyse the data. For each situation, the table lists the cues and strategies used by the expert, and the common errors a novice might make. In our case the target BDI architecture requires that cues and strategies be associated with procedures. To this end we introduce *Plan Library Cards* (PLCs) which map directly into BDI plan structures. The use of cards was inspired by experience with CRC[2] cards as used in the software engineering community. Figure 5 shows some of the more obvious PLCs for the car booking task. Each card represents a

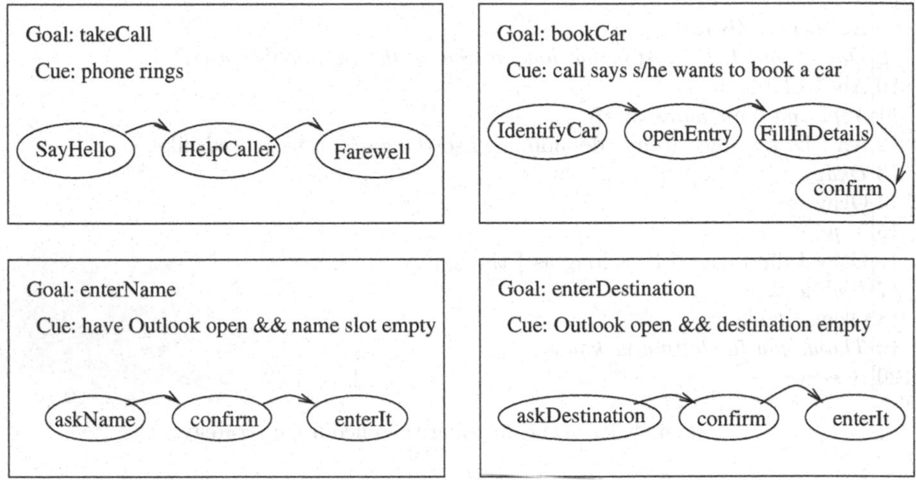

Fig. 5. Four example Plan Library Cards (PLCs) for the car booking task.

procedure; the goal it might achieve; and the cues which determine when it can be used. Note that using the BDI approach, multiple plans might be relevant at any instant but only one is used, and that a procedure can fail or be abandoned at any point — there is no guarantee of completion.

To walk through a transcript, the cards are grouped by goal. When the speaker adopts a goal, the appropriate pile of cards becomes active. Each active pile is then searched for a card with matching cues, and the procedure is executed. That is, in our case, things are said and subsidiary goals are posted. As new cues are discovered, either by looking at the transcript or by interview, they are added to the appropriate card. New cards can be introduced as required and the process repeated until a satisfactory description of the dialogue process is obtained.

Once the analysis is complete the next step is to apply it. Although it would have been nice to implement a phone based car booking system as a demonstrator, we did not have the appropriate resources to do this. We have however been working on the parts of the system that would be portable to other domains. One such component is a Java Speech API [28] based implementation of dialogue which allows "barge-in" statements like those seen in the car booking transcripts. Turning PLCs into an operational system is straight forward using

[2] Class-Responsibility-Collaboration cards. See *UML Distilled* [27, pp64-66] for details.

Agent Oriented Software's product JACK [29] and marrying JACK to the speech system is under way.

5 Conclusion

This paper introduces the use of techniques from Cognitive Task Analysis for knowledge elicitation in the context of BDI systems for dialogue. Intentions are explicitly modelled in a BDI approach, but intentions are hard to capture with more conventional corpus techniques.

We found that one strategy our SME uses is to encourage the other person to say more. It is used when our expert has no plan for furthering shared goals. Such a strategy is more polite than those currently in use in human computer interfaces, and as such would appear to be able to improve user satisfaction independently of system effectiveness.

References

1. Rao, A., Georgeff, M.: BDI agents:from theory to practice.Technical Report TR-56, Australian Artificial Intelligence Institute, Melbourne, Australia (1995)
2. Kupiec, J.: Robust part-of-speech tagging using a hidden markov model. Computer Speech and Language **6** (1992)225–242
3. Charniak, E.: Statistical Language Learning. MIT Press (1993)
4. Bakeman, R., Gottman, J.M.: Observing Interaction:An Introduction to Sequential Analysis. Cambridge University Press (1997)
5. O'Hara, K., Shadbolt, N.R.: Interpreting generic structures: Expert systems, expertise and context. In Feltovich, P., Ford, K., Hoffman, R., eds.: Expertise in Context. AAAI & MIT Press (1997)
6. Hoffman, R.R., Crandall, B., Shadbolt, N.R.: Use of the critical decision method to elicit expert knowledge: A case study in the methodology of cognitive task analysis authors.Human Factors **40** (1998)254 -276
7. Sanderson, P., Naikar, N., Lintern, G., Goss, S.: Use of cognitive ork analysis across the system life cycle: Requirements to decommissioning. In: Proceedings of the 43rd Annual Meeting of the Human Factors and Ergonomics Society, Houston, TX (1999)
8. Mitchard, H., Winkles, J., Corbett, D.: Development and evaluation of a cognitive model of an air defence operations officer. In Davis, C., van Gelder, T. ,Wales, R., eds.: Proceedings of the 5th Biennial Australasian Cognitive Science Conference, www.causal.on.net, Causal Productions (2000)
9. Militello, L.G., Hutton, R.J.: Applied cognitive task analysis (ACTA): a practitioner's toolkit for understanding cognitive task demands. Ergonomics **41** (1998) 1618–1641
10. Klein, G., Militello, L.: Cognitive task analysis orkshop. Course notes (2000)
11. Bratman, M.E., Israel, D.J., Pollack, M.E.: Plans and resource-bound practical reasoning. Computational Intelligence **4** (1988)349–355
12. Rosenbloom, P.S., Laird, J.E., Newell, A., eds.: The Soar Papers: Readings on Integrated Intelligence. The MIT Press, Cambridge, Massachussetts (1993)
13. Tidhar, G., Heinze, C., Selvestrel, M.: Flying together: Modelling air mission teams.Applied Intelligence **8** (1998)195–218

14. Fodor, J.: Psychosemantics. MIT Press, Cambridge,Mass (1987) A Bradford Book.
15. Dennett, D.C.: The Intentional Stance. The MIT Press, Cambridge, Massachussetts (1987)
16. Weizenbaum, J.: ELIZA - a computer program for the study of natural language communication bet een man and machine. Communications of the ACM 9 (1966)
17. Traum, D.R.: A Computational Theory of Grounding in Natural Language Conversation. PhD thesis, Computer Science, University of Rochester, New York (1994)
18. Allen, J.F., Schubert, L.K., Ferguson, G., Heeman, P., H ang, C.H., Kato, T., Light, M., Martin, N.G., Miller, B.W., Poesio, M., Traum, D.R.: The TRAINS project: A case study in defining a conversational planning agent. Journal of Experimental and Theoretical AI **7** (1995)7–48
19. Carletta, J., Isard, A., Isard, S., Kowtko, J.C., Doherty-Sneddon,G., Anderson, A.H.:The reliability of a dialogue structure coding scheme. Computational Linguistics **23** (1997)13–31
20. Core, M., Ishizaki, M., Moore, J., Nakatani, C., Reithinger, N., Traum, D., Tutiya, S.:Chiba corpus project technical report no. 3. Technical Report CC-TR-99-1, Department of Cognitive and Information Sciences, Faculty of Letters, Chiba University, Japan (1999)
21. Zukerman, I., McConachy, R.: WISHFUL: A discourse planning system that considers a user's inferences. Computational Intelligence 17 (2001)
22. Levin, J.A., Moore, J.A.: Dialogue games: Metacommunication structures for natural language interaction. Cognitive Science 1 (1977)395–420
23. Mann, W.C.: Dialogue games: Conventions of human interaction. Argumentation **2** (1988)511–532
24. Levin, L., Ries, K., Thym'e-Gobbel, A., Lavie,A.: Tagging of speech acts and dialogue games in spanish callHome. In: Towards Standards and Tools for Discourse Tagging (Proceedings of the Workshop at ACL '99), Association for Computational Linguistics (1999)42–47
25. Brown, P., Levinson, S.C.: Politeness: Some Universals in Language Usage. Cambridge University Press (1987)
26. O'Hare, D., Wiggins, M., Williams, A., Wong, W.: Cognitive task analyses for decision centred design and training. Ergonomics 41 (1998)1698–1718
27. Fowler, M., Scott, K.: UML Distilled: Applying The Standard Object Modeling Language. Addison Wesley Longman, Inc.(1997)
28. Sun-microsystems: The java speech application programmer interface (2001) `http://java.sun.com/products/java-media/speech/`.
29. Howden, N., Rönnquist, R., Hodgson, A., Lucas, A.: JACK intelligent agents - summary of an agent infrastructure.In:Proceedings of the 5th International Conference on Autonomous Agents, Montreal, Canada (2001)

Candidate Elimination Criteria for Lazy Bayesian Rules

Geoffrey I. Webb

School of Computing and Mathematics
Deakin University
Geelong Vic. 3217
webb@deakin.edu.au

Abstract. Lazy Bayesian Rules modifies naive Bayesian classification to undo elements of the harmful attribute independence assumption. It has been shown to provide classification error comparable to boosting decision trees. This paper explores alternatives to the candidate elimination criterion employed within Lazy Bayesian Rules. Improvements over naive Bayes are consistent so long as the candidate elimination criteria ensures there is sufficient data for accurate probability estimation. However, the original candidate elimination criterion is demonstrated to provide better overall error reduction than the use of a minimum data subset size criterion.

Keywords: machine learning

1 Introduction

Naive Bayes [4] is a simple and efficient approach to classification learning that has clear theoretical motivation and support. It has been demonstrated to provide competitive prediction error to more complex learning algorithms [8,11], especially when training set sizes are small [17].

Lazy Bayesian Rules (LBR) [17,18] modifies naive Bayes, seeking to retain its simplicity, efficiency, and clear theoretical foundations, while weakening the attribute independence assumption that can reduce naive Bayes' prediction accuracy. LBR has been demonstrated to provide prediction accuracy comparable to boosting decision trees [18].

This paper describes naive Bayes and LBR. It then examines one of the components of LBR, the candidate elimination criterion by which LBR determines whether an attribute should be a candidate for factoring out of the attribute independence assumption. Experiments demonstrate that improvements over naive Bayes are consistent so long as the candidate elimination criterion ensures there is sufficient data for accurate probability estimation. The original candidate elimination criterion is demonstrated to be better at determining when to stop than the use of a minimum data subset size criterion.

M. Brooks, D. Corbett, and M. Stumptner (Eds.): AI 2001, LNAI 2256, pp. 545–556, 2001.

2 Naive Bayes

Naive Bayes is motivated as follows. When classifying an instance $X = x_1, x_2, \ldots x_n$, whose class y is unknown, classification error will be minimized by selecting

$$argmax_y(P(y \mid X)) \tag{1}$$

the class that is most probable given X. A problem arises where $P(y \mid X)$ is to be estimated from the frequencies of X and y in a set of data $\mathcal{D} = \langle X_1, y_1\rangle, \langle X_2, y_2\rangle, \ldots \langle X_k, y_k\rangle$. In the limit, when the dataset contains the entire domain with respect to which probabilities are to be determined,

$$P(W) = F(W) \tag{2}$$

where $F(W)$ is the frequency with which W occurs in $\mathcal{D}$. As $P(W \mid Z) = P(W \wedge Z)/P(Z)$, $P(y \mid X)$ might be estimated by the approximation

$$P(y \mid X) \approx \frac{F(y \wedge X)}{F(X)} . \tag{3}$$

However, in many cases X and $y \wedge X$ will not occur frequently enough in the data for accurate estimation of the probabilities from the frequencies. In fact, unless the set of data is very comprehensive, X and $y \wedge X$ may not occur at all. In this context, Bayes rule

$$P(y \mid X) = \frac{P(y)P(X \mid y)}{P(X)} \tag{4}$$

may be used to derive alternative probabilities, by estimation of which the target probability can be estimated. As P(X) is invariant across different values of y,

$$P(y \mid X) \propto P(y)P(X \mid y) \tag{5}$$

and hence we need not estimate the denominator. However, this still leaves the problem of estimating $P(X \mid y)$ when $y \wedge X$ does not occur frequently in the data. By making the conditional independence assumption

$$P(x_1, x_2, \ldots x_n \mid y) = \prod_{i=1}^{n} P(x_i \mid y) \tag{6}$$

$P(X \mid y)$ can be estimated by estimation of each $P(x_i \mid y)$, latter estimates being more reliable as each conjunct is likely to occur with relatively high frequency.

Naive Bayes is classification using (1), estimating $P(y \mid X)$ by (4) and (6). As (1) minimizes prediction error, naive Bayes will minimize prediction error except in so far as the conditional independence assumption is violated and the estimation from data of probabilities $P(y)$ and $P(x_i \mid y)$ is inaccurate.

However, while the conditional independence assumption makes the estimation of $P(X \mid y)$ feasible, and naive Bayes delivers competitive classification performance for small data sets, the independence assumption is likely to be violated for many real world classification tasks. Notwithstanding Domingos & Pazzani's [3] observation the such violations are harmless so long as they do not affect the relative rank of each estimate of $P(y \mid X)$, research into semi-naive Bayesian learning has demonstrated that such violations are frequent and that explicit actions to alleviate their effect can reduce error [6,7,9,10,11,12,13,14,16].

3 Lazy Bayesian Rules

LBR utilizes an alternative to Bayes theorem (4),

$$P(y \mid Z_1 \wedge Z_2) = \frac{P(y \mid Z_2)P(Z_1 \mid y \wedge Z_2)}{P(Z_1 \mid Z_2)}. \tag{7}$$

The derivation of this equality is given in Zheng & Webb [17]. Given that $P(Z_1 \mid Z_2)$ is invariant across values of y,

$$P(y \mid Z_1 \wedge Z_2) \propto P(y \mid Z_2)P(Z_1 \mid y \wedge Z_2). \tag{8}$$

Where Z_1 is a conjunction of terms, $Z_1 = z_1 \wedge z_2 \wedge \ldots z_m$, a conditional attribute indpendence assumption

$$P(Z_1 \mid y \wedge Z_2) \approx \prod_{i=1}^{m} P(z_i \mid y \wedge Z - 2) \tag{9}$$

can be used to estimate $P(Z_1 \mid y \wedge Z_2)$.

Like naive Bayes, LBR estimates $P(y \mid X)$ for each y, selecting the y that maximizes the estimate. LBR differs from naive Bayes by segmenting the conjuncts of X into two groups, Z_1 and Z_2, and then using (7) in place of (4) and (9) in place of (6). Like naive Bayes, LBR will minimize classification error except in so far as its independece assumption is violated and the estimation of the required probabilities is incorrect.

A principal advantage of LBR over naive Bayes is that its independence assumption is weaker. Whereas naive Bayes assumes independence between all conjuncts given the class, LBR assumes independence only between the conjuncts in Z_1 given both the class and the conjuncts in Z_2.

The assumption of independence between fewer attributes is an advantage as fewer attribute interdependencies will be assumed incorrectly.

The assumption of independence under stronger conditions is also a major advantage. Consider the conditions $age > 70$, *senile*, and *nocturia*. Each of these three conditions will be highly interdependent with the others, as senility and nocturia are both correlated with age. However, given $age > 70$, *senile* and *nocturia* may be independent, as the interdependence of senility and nocturia may solely result from the respective interdependencies with age. That is, while $P(senile \wedge nocturia) \neq P(senile)P(nocturia)$, $P(senile \wedge nocturia \mid age > 70) = P(senile \mid age > 70)P(nocturia \mid age > 70)$. If this is the case (and conditioning on y does not produce independence between these attributes),

$$P(y \mid age > 70 \wedge senile \wedge nocturia) \neq \frac{P(y)P(age > 70 \mid y)P(senile \mid y)P(nocturia \mid y)}{P(age > 70 \wedge senile \wedge nocturia)} \quad (10)$$

so naive Bayes will be inaccurate. However, LBR may be accurate because

$$P(y \mid age > 70 \wedge senile \wedge nocturia) = \frac{P(y \mid age > 70)P(senile \mid age > 70 \wedge y)P(nocturia \mid age > 70 \wedge y)}{P(senile \wedge nocturia \mid age > 70)} . \quad (11)$$

If these two advantages were the only consideration, it would be advantageous to factor out all conditional interdependencies by placing all attributes in Z_2. However, placing an attribute in Z_2 carries one disadvantage in addition to its advantages. Each conditional probability $P(Z_1 \mid y \wedge Z_2)$ will be estimated by the approximation $P(z_i \mid y \wedge Z_2) \approx F(z_i \wedge y \wedge Z_2)/F(y \wedge Z_2)$. The more attributes in Z_2 the lower the frequency in $\mathcal{D}$ of both $z_i \wedge y \wedge Z_2$ and $y \wedge Z_2$ and hence the lower the expected accuracy of the approximation. Hence, LBR engages in a process of seeking to balance gains in expected accuracy due to factoring out harmful attribute interdependencies against losses in expected accuracy due to decreased expected accuracy of estimation of the required parameters.

LBR manages this trade-off by performing leave-one-out cross-validation once for each attribute-value using the conditional formula that results from including that value in Z_2. An attribute-value v is only considered as a candidate if the number of examples misclassified by including v in Z_2 but correctly classified by excluding it is significantly lower than the number correctly classified by including it but misclassified by excluding it. A matched-pair binomial sign test with significance level 0.05 is used to assess significance. The candidate with the lowest error is selected and the process repeated until no candidates remain.

LBR uses *lazy learning*. Calculation is performed when an object is to be classified. Only the attribute-values of that object are considered for inclusion in Z_2. The algorithm is presented in Table 1. Note that this algorithm does not explicitly maintain Z_2. Each A_{best} found is added to Z_2. Z_1 is the values of the attributes in *Att* for E_{test}. Z_2 is the remaining attribute values for E_{test}. The effect of factoring out Z_2 is achieved by selecting for $D_{training}$ the subset of instances that satisfy the conditions in Z_2. When the probability of an attribute value conditional on a class is estimated from a training set, the m-estimate [2] with m = 2 is used. When the probability of a class is estimated, the Laplace estimate [2] is used. When applying naive Bayesian classification, if two or more classes obtain equal highest probability estimates, one is selected at random.

4 Alternative Candidate Elimination Strategies

LBR eliminates from consideration as candidates for A_{best} attribute values that fail to reduce error by a statistically significant amount using leave-one-out cross-

Table 1. The Lazy Bayesian Rule learning algorithm

```
LBR(Att, D_training, E_test)
    INPUT: Att: a set of attributes,
           D_training: a set of training examples described using Att and classes,
           E_test: a test example described using Att.
    OUTPUT: a predicted class for E_test.
LocalNB = a naive Bayesian classifier trained using Att on D_training
Errors = errors of LocalNB estimated using N-CV on D_training
Cond = true
REPEAT
  TempErrors_best = the number of examples in D_training + 1
  FOR each attribute A in Att whose value v_A on E_test is not missing DO
      D_subset = examples in D_training with A = v_A
      TempNB = a naive Bayesian classifier trained using Att − {A} on D_subset
      TempErrors = errors of TempNB estimated using N-CV on D_subset +
                   errors from Errors for examples in D_training − D_subset
      IF ((TempErrors < TempErrors_best) AND
         (TempErrors is significantly lower than Errors))
      THEN
         TempNB_best = TempNB
         TempErrors_best = TempErrors
         A_best = A
  IF (an A_best is found)
  THEN
     Cond = Cond ∧ (A_best = v_{A_best})
     LocalNB = TempNB_best
     D_training = D_subset corresponding to A_best
     Att = Att − {A_best}
     Errors = errors of LocalNB estimated using N-CV on D_training
  ELSE
     EXIT from the REPEAT loop
classify E_test using LocalNB
RETURN the class
```

validation on the training data. The condition that enforces this strategy is set in bold type in Table 1.

This approach was motivated by the desire to eliminate from consideration attribute values for which factoring out appears to reduce error only by chance. Inevitably different formulae will result in variability in prediction performance, and by chance some will perform better than others. By eliminating candidates for which the difference in performance was not significantly greater than the baseline performance, we reduce the risk of selecting an attribute value that appears to improve performance only by chance. By using leave-one-out cross-validation classification performance as the selection criterion we aimed to measure the effect of both the improvement brought about by weakening the attribute independence assumptions and the decrease in accuracy of estimation brought about by decreased data.

Our previous experiments indicate that this strategy is very effective at managing this trade-off and results in very strong classification performance [17,18]. However, an alternative argument can be constructed that as the only harm in moving an attribute-value to Z_2 lies in the reduction in accuracy of estimation of the parameters, the candidate elimination strategy should be aimed directly at combating this problem. In other words, an attribute-value should remain a candidate for inclusion in Z_2 so long as there is sufficient data to reliably estimate the required parameters.

This paper tests this proposal by substituting for the LBR candidate elimination test (set in bold type in Table 1) an alternative test that is based solely on the number of examples in $D_{training}$ that have the relevant value. This is predicated on the assumption that if there are sufficient examples of a given value, estimation of the frequency of that value and the probability of each class given that value will be sufficiently accurate for accurate classification. Three values are considered, 30, 100, and 500. The first value, 30, was selected as 30 is commonly held to be the minimum sample from which one should draw statistical inferences. The last value, 500, was selected as a sufficiently large number that accurate estimation of parameters should be possible. 100 was selected as an intermediate value. This new strategy was implemented by substituting the condition $|D_{subset}| \geq MinSize$ for the candidate elimination condition set in bold type in Table 1, where $MinSize$ was set respectively to 30, 100, and 500. This approach will default to naive Bayes when the dataset size is less than $MinSize$ as all candidates will be eliminated.

5 Experiments

For the first experiment, naive Bayes and the four variants of LBR (the original candidate elimination criterion, called hereafter LBR, and candidate elimination using $MinSize$ set to each of 30, 100, and 500, called hereafter $MinSize = 30$, $MinSize = 100$, and $MinSize = 500$, respectively). The 29 datasets from the UCI repository [1] were used that have been used in previous LBR experiments [17,18] (a selection based on those used in prior semi-naive Bayesian learning research). These datasets are described in Table 2. The experimental method of [18] was replicated, ten repetitions of three-fold cross-validation, with different random selection of folds during each repetition. Numeric attributes were discretized using Fayyad & Irani's [5] MDL discretization algorithm on the training data for a given fold. Each algorithm was evaluated with the same sequence of thirty training and test set pairs formed in this manner.

The average error rates of each algorithm for each data set are presented in Table 3. Also presented for each algorithm is the mean error across all data sets, the geometric mean error ratio compared with naive Bayes, the win/loss record between the algorithm and naive Bayes, and the win/loss record between the algorithm and LBR. The mean error is a very gross measure of performance

Table 2. Description of data sets

Domain	Size	No. of Classes	No. of Attributes	
			Numeric	Nominal
Lung cancer	32	3	0	56
Labor negotiations	57	2	8	8
Postoperative patient	90	3	1	7
Zoology	101	7	0	16
Promoter gene sequences	106	2	0	57
Echocardiogram	131	2	6	1
Lymphography	148	4	0	18
Iris classification	150	3	4	0
Hepatitis prognosis	155	2	6	13
Wine recognition	178	3	13	0
Sonar classification	208	2	60	0
Glass identification	214	6	9	0
Audiology	226	24	0	69
Heart disease (Cleveland)	303	2	13	0
Soybean large	307	19	0	35
Primary tumor	339	22	0	17
Liver disorders	345	2	6	0
Horse colic	368	2	7	15
House votes 84	435	2	0	16
Credit screening (Australia)	690	2	6	9
Breast cancer (Wisconsin)	699	2	9	0
Pima Indians diabetes	768	2	8	0
Annealing processes	898	6	6	32
Tic-Tac-Toe end game	958	2	0	9
LED 24 (noise level = 10%)	1000	10	0	24
Solar flare	1389	2	0	10
Hypothyroid diagnosis	3163	2	7	18
Splice junction gene sequences	3177	3	0	60
Chess (King-rook-vs-king-pawn)	3196	2	0	36

as error rates on different domains are incommensurable, but provides an approximate indication of relative performance. The geometric mean error ratio is the geometric mean of the value for each data set of the error of the algorithm divided by the error of naive Bayes. The geometric mean is more appropriate than the mean as an aggregate measure of ratio values [15]. The win/loss records with respect to naive Bayes and LBR list the number of domains for which the error of the algorithm is lower than the error of, respectively, naive Bayes and LBR.

The first point of interest is that LBR has scored slightly fewer wins and slightly more losses with respect to naive Bayes than in previous experiments [17,18]. However, it is notable that all of LBR's losses to naive Bayes occur with smaller data sets. The largest is credit screening, containing 690 examples, and for which the training set size in three-fold cross-validation will be 430. It is also

Table 3. Error rates

	NB	LBR	MinSize 30	100	500
Lung cancer	0.534	0.544	0.534	0.534	0.534
Labor negotiations	0.098	0.098	0.105	0.098	0.098
Postoperative patient	0.378	0.386	0.383	0.378	0.378
Zoology	0.059	0.059	0.063	0.059	0.059
Promoter gene sequences	0.109	0.112	0.170	0.109	0.109
Echocardiogram	0.296	0.297	0.306	0.296	0.296
Lymphography	0.182	0.182	0.196	0.182	0.182
Iris classification	0.066	0.066	0.065	0.066	0.066
Hepatitis prognosis	0.144	0.144	0.175	0.144	0.144
Wine recognition	0.023	0.023	0.030	0.023	0.023
Sonar classification	0.245	0.245	0.240	0.248	0.245
Glass identification	0.238	0.237	0.240	0.246	0.238
Audiology	0.277	0.277	0.290	–	0.278
Heart disease (Cleveland)	0.171	0.171	0.200	0.177	0.171
Soybean large	0.143	0.101	0.149	0.115	0.143
Primary tumor	0.534	0.535	0.568	0.551	0.534
Liver disorders	0.361	0.363	0.359	0.355	0.361
Horse colic	0.208	0.199	0.197	0.192	0.208
House votes 84	0.100	0.067	0.086	0.057	0.100
Credit screening (Australia)	0.146	0.147	0.166	0.154	0.146
Breast cancer (Wisconsin)	0.026	0.026	0.041	0.034	0.026
Pima Indians diabetes	0.252	0.251	0.267	0.253	0.252
Annealing processes	0.030	0.028	0.030	0.026	0.030
Tic-Tac-Toe end game	0.295	0.185	0.145	0.220	0.295
LED 24 (noise level = 10%)	0.261	0.260	0.265	0.263	0.259
Solar flare	0.039	0.015	0.020	0.017	0.031
Hypothyroid diagnosis	0.018	0.015	0.020	0.017	0.018
Splice junction gene sequences	0.046	0.044	0.077	0.057	0.043
Chess (King-rook-vs-king-pawn)	0.124	0.028	0.021	0.021	0.032
Mean	0.185	0.174	0.186	0.178	0.183
Geo mean vs NB		0.930	1.081	0.960	0.975
W/L vs NB		12/7	8/19	10/9	4/1
W/L vs LBR			8/21	10/13	9/11

notable that of the seven losses to naive Bayes, only three are by more than 0.002, a very small margin. While the win loss record is not significant at the 0.05 level using a one-tailed binomial sign test (p=0.1796), the mean across all data sets is substantially lower, and, more significantly, the geometric mean error ratio strongly favours LBR. It is notable that for the largest data sets LBR is consistently winning, halving naive Bayes' error with respect to solar flare and quartering it with respect to chess.

These results suggest that the LBR's candidate elimination strategy might be suboptimal for small numbers of examples. In other words, it is credible that the candidate elimination strategy does not take adequate account of whether there is sufficient data for reliable estimation of the required parameters. It was this supposition, derived from previous experiments, that motivated the current study.

Of the three minimum example settings, it seems clear that $MinSize = 30$ provides the worst performance. On all metrics it performs worse than naive Bayes. The geometric mean error ratio strongly favours naive Bayes as does the win/loss record (significantly at the 0.05 level, one-tailed binomial sign test p=0.0261). The win/loss record against LBR strongly and significantly favours LBR (p=0.0120).

The situation with respect to $MinSize = 100$ is less clear cut. It wins as often as it loses against naive Bayes. The mean, and more significantly, the geometric mean error ratio, both favour $MinSize = 100$ over naive Bayes, indicating that the magnitude of its wins tends to be greater than the magnitude of its losses. The win/loss record with respect to LBR favours the latter, but not significantly so (p=0.3388).

The results with respect to $MinSize = 500$ appear much more straightforward, however. First, it is necessary to consider the outcome for audiology. It might initially appear anomalous that $MinSize = 500$ achieves a different outcome to naive Bayes for a dataset with fewer than 500 examples. The explanation, however, is straightforward. For this dataset there is one classification during the ten sets of three-fold cross-validation for which naive Bayes scores two classes as equi-probable and for which the random resolution of this draw selected different classes for naive Bayes and $MinSize = 500$. In this case the random outcome favoured naive Bayes. Of the larger datasets, for which $MinSize = 500$ had the opportunity to move attribute-values to Z_2, $MinSize = 500$ consistently wins over naive Bayes. Restricting the analysis to datasets for which $MinSize = 500$ modifies the behaviour of naive Bayes, the win/loss record is 4/0, which approaches significance at the 0.05 level (p=0.0625).

Table 4 presents the average size of Z_2 ($|Z_2|$) and the average number of examples from which the probabilities are estimated ($|\mathcal{D}|$) for each dataset for LBR and its three variants. It is striking that when there is sufficient data for the constraint on minimum numbers of examples to be satisfied, this alternative approach tends to add many more values to Z_2. Consider, for example, $MinSize = 500$ on the King-rook-vs-king-pawn data. More than three times the number of attribute values are added to Z_2 even though there is not a large difference in the average number of examples selected by each Z_2. This is because $MinSize = 500$ can keep selecting additional attribute values so long as they cover sufficient cases while LBR requires that the selection results in a significant reduction in error.

Of the six datasets for which $MinSize = 500$ is able to select attribute values for Z_2, LBR obtains lower error for four and higher for two. However, for the two for which LBR obtains higher error, the magnitude of the difference is very small whereas the magnitude is relatively high for those datasets for which LBR achieves lower error. These results suggest that the significance test in LBR's candidate elimination strategy does confer an advantage. Further support

Table 4. Mean $|Z_2|$ and examples available for estimation of parameters

	LBR		MinSize=30		MinSize=100		MinSize=500	
	$\|Z_2\|$	$\|\mathcal{D}\|$	$\|Z_2\|$	$\|\mathcal{D}\|$	$\|Z_2\|$	$\|\mathcal{D}\|$	$\|Z_2\|$	$\|\mathcal{D}\|$
Lung cancer	0.07	20.7	0.00	21.3	0.00	21.3	0.00	21.3
Labor negotiations	0.00	38.0	0.24	36.4	0.00	38.0	0.00	38.0
Postoperative patient	0.05	58.9	1.25	40.9	0.00	60.0	0.00	60.0
Zoology	0.00	67.3	4.13	35.0	0.00	67.3	0.00	67.3
Promoter gene sequences	0.01	70.2	0.47	53.5	0.00	70.7	0.00	70.7
Echocardiogram	0.02	87.1	1.85	49.7	0.00	88.0	0.00	88.0
Lymphography	0.05	97.8	4.31	43.0	0.00	98.7	0.00	98.7
Iris classification	0.00	100.0	0.84	48.9	0.00	100.0	0.00	100.0
Hepatitis prognosis	0.02	102.2	4.28	36.4	0.00	103.3	0.00	103.3
Wine recognition	0.00	118.7	0.74	86.2	0.00	118.7	0.00	118.7
Sonar classification	0.27	126.3	12.39	40.0	5.91	102.4	0.00	138.7
Glass identification	0.12	135.3	3.41	58.1	1.01	118.8	0.00	142.7
Audiology	0.18	145.6	43.33	48.5	26.24	103.0	0.00	150.7
Heart disease (Cleveland)	0.05	175.5	3.31	47.2	1.66	128.1	0.00	180.0
Soybean large	0.99	161.0	13.38	47.6	8.37	109.9	0.00	204.7
Primary tumor	0.10	221.3	3.30	136.8	2.51	161.9	0.00	226.0
Liver disorders	0.28	217.5	4.60	61.3	2.97	138.8	0.00	230.0
Horse colic	0.47	192.4	3.59	54.1	2.01	130.5	0.00	245.3
House votes 84	0.67	188.5	5.44	54.8	2.43	115.7	0.00	290.0
Credit screening (Australia)	0.20	425.2	4.51	84.9	3.06	160.6	0.00	460.0
Breast cancer (Wisconsin)	0.00	466.0	2.38	150.6	1.82	269.9	0.00	466.0
Pima Indians diabetes	0.23	455.3	2.83	100.0	1.76	187.2	0.00	512.0
Annealing processes	0.09	570.0	5.05	121.4	4.76	208.1	2.52	545.0
Tic-Tac-Toe end game	1.65	165.1	2.86	45.3	1.85	121.0	0.00	638.7
LED 24 (noise level = 10%)	0.50	571.1	5.11	129.8	3.54	197.8	0.50	603.9
Solar flare	0.80	534.6	4.71	235.1	4.35	267.4	3.01	695.0
Hypothyroid diagnosis	0.28	1923.7	14.92	532.5	14.61	616.7	14.04	832.6
Splice junction gene sequences	0.39	1686.8	1.98	413.3	1.75	448.4	1.14	878.1
Chess (King-rook-vs-king-pawn)	3.67	572.5	15.62	136.2	15.30	169.2	11.28	551.7

for this conclusion is provided by a second study that compared naive Bayes, LBR, and $MinSize = 500$ in five larger datasets: phoneme (5438 examples), mush (8124), pendigits (10992), adult (48842), and shuttle (58000). As ten runs of three-fold cross-validation was infeasible for such large data sets, leave-one-out cross-validation was performed for 1000 randomly selected examples from each data set. For each of these examples, each algorithm was presented all the remaining examples in the dataset as a training set and the withheld example was then classified. The resulting error rates are presented in Table 5. As can be seen, both LBR and $MinSize = 500$ consistently achieve lower error than naive Bayes for these larger datasets. The win loss records of 5/0 are in both cases statistically significant at the 0.05 level using a one-tailed sign test (p=0.0313). While $MinSize = 500$ obtains marginally lower error than LBR on one dataset, LBR obtains substantially lower error on one and slightly lower on two.

Table 5. Error for large datasets

Dataset	**NB**	**LBR**	**MinSize=500**
phoneme	0.265	0.215	0.244
mush	0.014	0.000	0.000
pendigits	0.123	0.028	0.025
adult	0.163	0.132	0.137
shuttle	0.002	0.000	0.001

6 Conclusions

This paper makes two contributions to the literature on lazy Bayesian rules. First, it presents empirical results on much larger datasets than previously explored, providing statistically significant support for the hypothesis previously advanced [17] that LBR provides consistent advantage over naive Bayes for large datasets.

The primary motivation for the paper, however, was to investigate alternatives to the candidate elimination criteria employed in LBR, exploring the hypothesis that it will never be harmful to select candidate attribute values for inclusion in Z_2 that retain sufficient examples for reliable estimation of the required parameters. While some support for this hypothesis was obtained by the consistent capacity of $MinSize = 500$ to reduce error relative to naive Bayes, the error reduction capacity of LBR remains higher. This suggests that the significance test serves a useful function in implicitly assessing the relative gains from factoring out a harmful attribute interdependence against the losses from reducing the amount of data from which parameters are estimated.

Nonetheless, the $MinSize = 500$ strategy may offer computational advantages in some applications. This is because the overheads of assessing how many training cases are selected by a candidate attribute value are very low in comparison to the computational overheads associated with performing a matched-pair binomial sign test. For the extremely large datasets employed in some online datamining applications these computational considerations may outweigh the error reduction capacity of the significance test strategy.

Acknowledgements. I am grateful to Zijian Zheng for developing the lazy Bayesian rules software that was used in these experiments.

References

1. C. Blake and C. J. Merz. UCI repository of machine learning databases. [Machine-readable data repository]. University of California, Department of Information and Computer Science, Irvine, CA., 2001.

2. B. Cestnik, I. Kononenko, and I. Bratko. ASSISTANT 86: A knowledge-elicitation tool for sophisticated users. In I. Bratko and N. Lavrač, editors, *Progress in Machine Learning*, pp. 31–45. Sigma Press, Wilmslow, 1987.
3. P. Domingos and M. Pazzani. Beyond independence: Conditions for the optimality of the simple Bayesian classifier. In *Proc. Thirteenth International Conference on Machine Learning*, pp. 105–112, Bari, Italy, 1996. Morgan Kaufmann.
4. R. Duda and P. Hart. *Pattern Classification and Scene Analysis.* John Wiley and Sons, New York, 1973.
5. U. M. Fayyad and K. B. Irani. Multi-interval discretization of continuous-valued attributes for classification learning. In *IJCAI-93: Proc. 13th International Joint Conference on Artificial Intelligence*, pp. 1022–1027, Chambery, France, 1993. Morgan Kaufmann.
6. N. Friedman and M. Goldszmidt. Building classifiers using Bayesian networks. In *AAAI-96*, pp. 1277–1284, 1996.
7. R. Kohavi. Scaling up the accuracy of naive-Bayes classifiers: A decision-tree hybrid. In *KDD-96*, Portland, Or, 1996.
8. I. Kononenko. Comparison of inductive and naive Bayesian learning approaches to AUtomatic knowledge acquisition. In B. Wielinga, J. Boose, B. Gaines, G. Schreiber, and M. van Someren, editors, *Current Trends in Knowledge Acquisition.* IOS Press, Amsterdam, 1990.
9. I. Kononenko. Semi-naive Bayesian classifier. In *ECAI-91*, pp. 206–219, 1991.
10. P. Langley. Induction of recursive Bayesian classifiers. In *Proc. 1993 European Conference on Machine Leanring*, pp. 153–164, Vienna, 1993. Springer-Verlag.
11. P. Langley and S. Sage. Induction of selective Bayesian classifiers. In *Proc. Tenth Conference on Uncertainty in Artificial Intelligence*, pp. 399–406, Seattle, WA, 1994. Morgan Kaufmann.
12. M. J. Pazzani. Constructive induction of Cartesian product attributes. In *ISIS: Information, Statistics and Induction in Science*, pp. 66–77, Melbourne, Aust., August 1996. World Scientific.
13. M. Sahami. Learning limited dependence Bayesian classifiers. In *Proc. 2nd International Conference on Knowledge Discovery and Data Mining*, pp. 334–338. AAAI Press, 1996.
14. M. Singh and G. M. Provan. Efficient learning of selective Bayesian network classifiers. In *Proc. 13th International Conference on Machine Learning*, pp. 453–461, Bari, 1996. Morgan Kaufmann.
15. G. I. Webb. Multiboosting: A technique for combining boosting and wagging. *Machine Learning*, 40(2):159–196, 2000.
16. G. I. Webb and M. J. Pazzani. Adjusted probability naive Bayesian induction. In *Proc. Eleventh Australian Joint Conference on Artificial Intelligence*, pp. 285–295, Brisbane, Australia, 1998. Springer.
17. Z. Zheng and G. I. Webb. Lazy learning of Bayesian Rules. *Machine Learning*, 41(1):53–84, 2000.
18. Z. Zheng, G. I. Webb, and K. M. Ting. Lazy Bayesian Rules: A lazy semi-naive Bayesian learning technique competitive to boosting decision trees. In *Proc. Sixteenth International Conference on Machine Learning (ICML-99)*, pp. 493–502, Bled, Slovenia, 1999. Morgan Kaufmann.

Simplifying the Development of Intelligent Agents

Michael Winikoff, Lin Padgham, and James Harland

RMIT University, Melbourne, AUSTRALIA
{winikoff,linpa,jah}@cs.rmit.edu.au,
http://www.cs.rmit.edu.au/~{winikoff,linpa,jah}

Abstract. Intelligent agents is a powerful Artificial Intelligence technology which shows considerable promise as a new paradigm for mainstream software development. However, despite their promise, intelligent agents are still scarce in the market place. A key reason for this is that developing intelligent agent software requires significant training and skill: a typical developer or undergraduate struggles to develop good agent systems using the Belief Desire Intention (BDI) model (or similar models). This paper identifies the concept set which we have found to be important in developing intelligent agent systems and the relationships between these concepts. This concept set was developed with the intention of being clearer, simpler, and easier to use than current approaches. We also describe briefly a (very simplified) example from one of the projects we have worked on (RoboRescue), illustrating the way in which these concepts are important in designing and developing intelligent software agents.

Keywords: AI Architectures, distributed AI, multiagent systems, reactive control, software agents.

1 Introduction

Intelligent agents is a powerful Artificial Intelligence technology which shows considerable promise as a new paradigm for mainstream software development. Agents offer new ways of abstraction, decomposition, and organisation that fit well with our natural view of the world and agent oriented programming is often considered a natural successor to object oriented programming [6]. It has the potential to change the way we design, visualise, and build software in that agents can naturally model "actors" – real world entities that can show autonomy and proactiveness. Additionally, social agents naturally model (human) organisations ranging from business structure & processes to military command structures. A number of significant applications utilising agent technology [5] have already been developed, many of which are decidedly non-trivial.

An intelligent agent is one which is able to make rational decisions, i.e., blending proactiveness and reactiveness, showing rational commitment to decisions made, and exhibiting flexibility in the face of an uncertain and changing environment.

Despite their promise, intelligent agents are still scarce in the market place[1]. There is a real technical reason for this: developing intelligent agent software currently requires significant training and skill. Our experience (and the experience of others) is that a

[1] Although abuse of buzzwords is, alas, all too common.

M. Brooks, D. Corbett, and M. Stumptner (Eds.): AI 2001, LNAI 2256, pp. 557–568, 2001.

typical developer or final-year undergraduate student struggles to develop good agent systems using the Belief Desire Intention (BDI) model (or similar models).

Decker [3] discusses problems that undergraduate students have in approaching agent oriented development. These include a lack of suitable background in AI (planning and goal oriented programs), poor software engineering skills, and a lack of experience at dealing with concurrent and distributed programming/debugging, and with communication protocols.

We have found the key problem to be that students cannot clearly identify the necessary pieces to break the program into and thus tend to build monolithic plans which try to handle all contingencies internally, rather than create an appropriate collection of plans which can be applied in different contexts. They also have significant difficulty with interfacing the agent to its environment. Other reasons why developing intelligent agent systems is difficult include:

- Immature tool support: There is a lack of good debugging tools and of tools which integrate an internal agent architecture with suitable middleware & infrastructure. Additionally, many tools are research prototypes and lack efficiency, portability, documentation, and/or support.
- The need for processes and methodologies: Programmers are familiar with designing object oriented systems. However, the design of agent oriented systems differs in a number of ways. For example, identifying roles, goals, and interaction patterns.
- Design guidelines and examples: Designing a collection of plans to achieve a goal is different to designing a single procedure to perform a function. This difference is fundamental – developing intelligent agents is a different programming paradigm and needs to be learnt and taught as such.
- Complex concepts such as intentions are difficult to explain; this isn't helped by a lack of agreement on concepts and inconsistent terminology.
- Lack of a suitable[2] text book: much of the work on intelligent agents is scattered across many research papers (sometimes collected into volumes).

In the process of working on a number of agent programs, teaching students and assisting them to build agent programs, and developing and running workshops for academia and industry[3], we have developed an initial process of agent design and development for BDI systems.[4] This process is explained more fully in the technical report [8] and is still being refined and developed.

This paper identifies the concept set which we have found to be important in developing intelligent agent systems and the relationships between these concepts. These of course rely heavily on the standard Belief Desire Intention (BDI) concepts [9,10] though we have found it necessary to clarify some of the differences between just what these concepts are in the initial philosophical work [1], the logical theories [9,13,2] and the implementations such as PRS, dMars and JACK. We have also found it important to place some emphasis on the concepts of percepts and actions which appear in many

[2] Suitable: Aimed at undergraduates or professional developer and contains enough detail to answer the question "How would I actually go about building an intelligent agent?".

[3] Workshops have been developed and delivered in association with Agent Oriented Software

[4] Using primarily dMars from the Australian Artificial Intelligence Institute, and more recently JACK from Agent Oriented Software.

generic models of agents (e.g. [12]) and which are very important in the interfacing of the agent deliberation to the external environment. We have found a need to separate more clearly between events and goals than is done in dMars or JACK and to provide greater support within the execution engine for reasoning about goals than is usually done in BDI agent systems [14].

Our work in general is focussed on multi-agent systems although this paper concentrates on the concepts required for the internals of each intelligent agent - a necessary pre-requisite for multi-agent systems with teams or societies containing such agents.

2 Background: The BDI Model

The BDI model [9,10] is a popular model for intelligent agents. It has its basis in philosophy [1] and offers a *logical theory* which defines the mental attitudes of Belief, Desire, and Intention using a modal logic; a *system architecture*; a *number of implementations of this architecture* (e.g. PRS, JAM, dMars, JACK); and *applications* demonstrating the viability of the model. The central concepts in the BDI model are:

Beliefs: Information about the environment; *informative*.

Desires: Objectives to be accomplished, possibly with each objective's associated priority/payoff; *motivational*.

Intentions: The currently chosen course of action; *deliberative*.

Plans: Means of achieving certain future world states. Intuitively, plans are an abstract specification of both the means for achieving certain desires and the options available to the agent. Each plan has (i) a body describing the primitive actions or sub-goals that have to be achieved for plan execution to be successful; (ii) an invocation condition which specifies the triggering event[5], and (iii) a context condition which specifies the situation in which the plan is applicable.

The BDI model has developed over about 15 years and there are certainly strong relationships between the theoretical work and implemented systems. The paper [10] describes an abstract architecture which is instantiated in systems such as dMars and JACK and shows how that is related to the BDI logic. However, the concepts we have found useful for development within these systems do not necessarily match the concepts most developed in the theoretical work. Neither are they necessarily exactly the concepts which have arisen within particular implemented systems such as JACK. An additional complication is small differences between similar concepts, such as Desires and Goals, which receive differing emphasis in different work at different times.

Desires are understood to be things the agent wants to achieve. They play an important role in the philosophical foundations, but the logical theory deals primarily with Goals, which are assumed to be a consistent set of desires. At the implementation level the motivational concept is reduced to events – goals are implicit and the creation of a new goal is treated as an event which can trigger plans. Events are ignored in the theoretical framework although they play a key role in implementations. In the theoretical model plans are simply beliefs or intentions. However in the implementations plans are a central

[5] Some events are considered as goal-events.

concept. Some key differences between the philosophy, theory, and implementation viewpoints of BDI are shown in the table below.

Philosophy:	Belief	Desire	Intention
Theory:	Belief	Goal	Intention
Implementation:	Relational DB (or arbitrary object)	Event	Running Plan

3 Concepts for Intelligent Agents

We describe the set of concepts which we have come to use in developing intelligent agent applications. We believe that these are necessary and sufficient for building the sort of applications appropriately approached using BDI agents, and we hope that they are simple, and clearly explained. The work to develop a formal semantic framework for these concepts, thus developing closer links between a theoretical framework and an implemented development platform, is work in progress.

We build up our description of an intelligent agent by beginning with a basic, and universally agreed upon (see for example [12]), property of agents: they are situated (see figure 1). Thus, we have **actions** and **percepts**. Internally, the agent is making a **decision**: from the set of possible actions As it is selecting an action (or actions) to perform ($a \in As$). Loosely speaking, where the description of the agent's internal workings contains a statement of the form "[select] $X \in Y$" then we have a decision being made. Thus the type of decisions being made depend on the *internal agent architecture*.

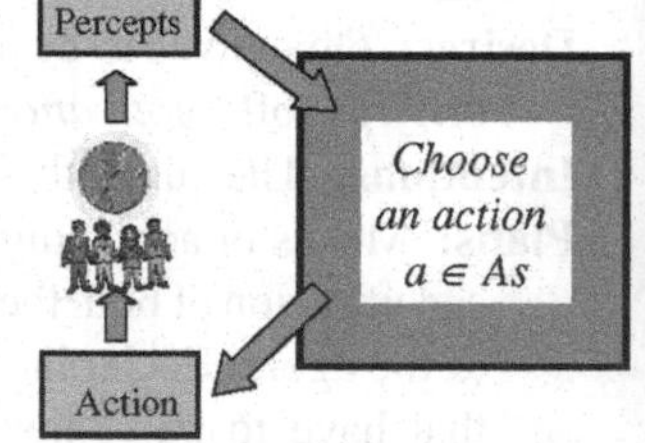

Fig. 1. Agents are Situated

An **action** is something which an agent does, such as *move_north* or *squirt*. Agents are situated, and an action is basically an agent's ability to effect its environment. In their simplest form actions are atomic and instantaneous and either fail or succeed. In the more general case actions can be durational (encompassing behaviours over time) and can produce partial effects; for example a failed *move_to* action may well have changed the agent's location. In addition to actions which directly affect the agent's environment, we also want to consider "internal actions". These correspond to an ability which the agent has which isn't structured in terms of plans and goals. Typically, the ability is a piece of code which either already exists or would not benefit from being written using agent concepts, for example image processing in a vision sub-system.

A **percept** is an input from the environment, such as the location of a fire and an indication of its intensity. The agent may also obtain information about the environment through sensing actions.

A **decision**: The essence of intelligent agents is rational decision making. There are a number of generic, non-application-specific questions which intelligent agents must answer, such as: *Which* action shall I perform now? *Which* goal do I work on now? *How* shall I attempt to realise this goal? *Where* shall I go now (for mobile agents)? And *who* shall I interact with (for social agents)?

Mechanisms to answer these kinds of questions are core intelligent agent processes. They result in decisions which must fulfil rationality conditions, in that we expect that decisions be persistent and only be revisited when there is a good reason for doing so. It is also important that the answer to the questions not be trivial: if an agent only has a single goal at a time and a single means of realising this goal then we have reduced the agent to the special case of a conventional program and there is no scope for decision making or for flexible, intelligent behaviour.

Note that although the concept of a decision is fundamental to intelligent agents, it is not always necessary to represent the decisions explicitly. For example, the decision regarding choice of goal could be represented using a "current goal" variable which is updated when a decision is made.

We now consider the internal workings of the agent (see figure 2). We want our intelligent agents to be both *proactive* and *reactive*. A proactive agent is one which pursues an agenda over time. The agent's proactiveness implies the use of **goals** and modifies the agent's internal execution cycle: rather than select an action one at a time, we select a goal which is persistent and constrains our selection of actions. A *reactive* agent is one which will change its behaviour in response to changes in the environment. An important aspect in decision making is balancing proactive and reactive aspects. On the one hand we want the agent to stick with its goals by default, on the other hand we want it to take changes in the environment into account. The key to reconciling these aspects, thus making agents suitably reactive, is to identify *significant* changes in the environment. These are **events**. We distinguish between percepts and events: an event is an interpreted percept which has significance to the agent. For example, seeing a fire is a percept. This percept could give rise to a *new fire* event or a *fire under control* event depending on history and possibly other factors.

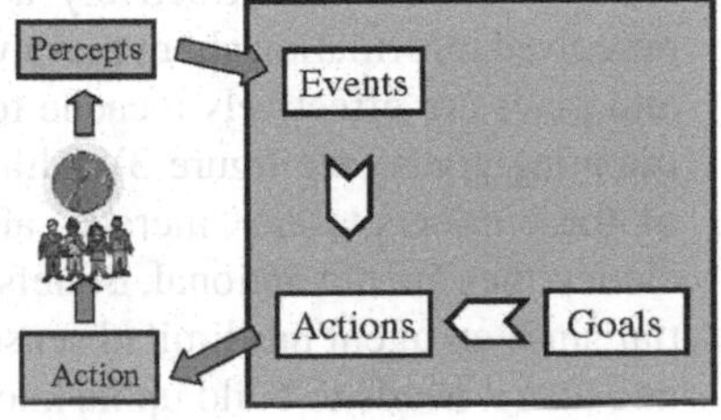

Fig. 2. Proactive Agents have Goals, Reactive Agents have Events

A **goal** (variously called "task", "objective", "aim", or "desire") is something the agent is working on or towards, for example *extinguish_fire*, or *rescue_civilian*. Often goals are defined as states of the world which the agent wants to bring about; however, this definition rules out maintenance goals (e.g. "maintain cruising altitude") and avoidance goals, or safety constraints (e.g. "never move the table while the robot is drilling"). Goals give the agent its autonomy and proactiveness. An important aspect of proactiveness is the persistence of goals: if a plan for achieving a goal fails then the agent will consider alternative plans for achieving the goal in question. We have found that goals require greater emphasis than is typically found in existing systems. It is important for the developer to identify the top level goals of the agent as well as subsidiary goals which are used in achieving main goals. Our modified execution engine does significantly more reasoning about goals than is usual in BDI implementations [14], including reasoning about interference between goals and how to select goals when it is not consistent to pursue them simultaneously. We differentiate between top level goals and subsidiary goals in that subsidiary goals are not important in their own right and may therefore be treated differently in the reasoning process than top-level goals.

An **event** is a significant occurrence. Events are often extracted from percepts, although they may be generated internally by the agent, for example on the basis of a clock. An event can trigger new goals, cause changes in information about the environment, and/or cause actions to be performed immediately. Actions generated directly by events correspond to "reflexive" actions, executed without deliberation. Events are important in creating reactive agents in that they identify important changes which the agent needs to react to.

Agents in realistic applications usually have limited computational resources and limited ability to sense their environment. Thus the auxiliary concepts of **plan** and **belief** are needed. Beliefs are effectively a cache for perceived information about the environment, and plans are effectively a cache for ways of pursuing goals (see figure 3). Although both of these concepts are "merely" aids in efficiency, they are not optional. Beliefs are essential since an agent has limited sensory ability and also it needs to build up its knowledge of the world over time. Plans are essential for two reasons. The first is pure computational efficiency: although planning technology and computational speed are improving, planning from action descriptions is still incompatible with real time decision making. The second reason is that by providing a library of plans we avoid the need to specify each action's preconditions and effects: all we need to provide for an action is the means to perform it. This is significant in that representing the effects of continuous actions operating over time and space in an uncertain world in sufficient detail for first principles planning is unrealistic for large applications.

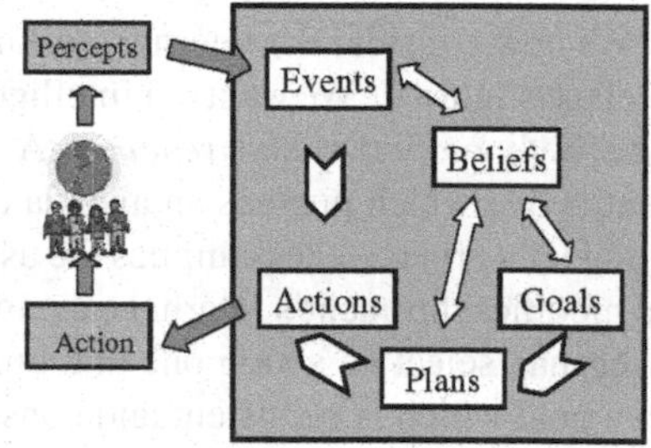

Fig. 3. Adding Plans and Beliefs

A **plan** is a way of realising a goal, for example a plan for achieving the goal *extinguish_fire* might specify the three steps: plan a route to the fire, follow the route to the fire, and squirt the fire until it has been put out. Although the concept of a plan is common there is no agreement on the details. From our point of view it is not necessary to adopt a specific notion of a plan, rather we can specify abstractly that a plan for achieving a goal provides a function which returns the next action to be performed. This function takes into account the current state of the world (beliefs), what actions have already been performed, and might involve sub-goals and further plans. For computational reasons it is desirable for this to at least include a "library of recipes" approach, rather than requiring construction of plans at runtime from action descriptions.

A **belief** is some aspect of the agent's knowledge or information about the environment, self or other agents. For example an agent might believe there is a fire at X because she saw it recently, even if she cannot see it now.

These concepts (actions, percepts, decisions, goals, events, plans, and beliefs) are related to each other via the **execution cycle** of the agent. An agent's execution cycle follows a sense-think-act cycle, since the agent is situated. The think part of the cycle involves rational decision making, consisting of the following steps: (depicted in figure 4)

1. Percepts are interpreted (using beliefs) to give events
2. Beliefs are updated with new information from percepts
3. Events yield reflexive actions and/or new goals
4. Goals are updated, including current, new and completed goals.
5. If there is no selected plan for the current goal, or if the plan has failed, or if reconsideration of the plan is required (due to an event) then a plan is chosen.
6. The chosen plan is expanded to yield an action
7. Action(s) are scheduled and performed

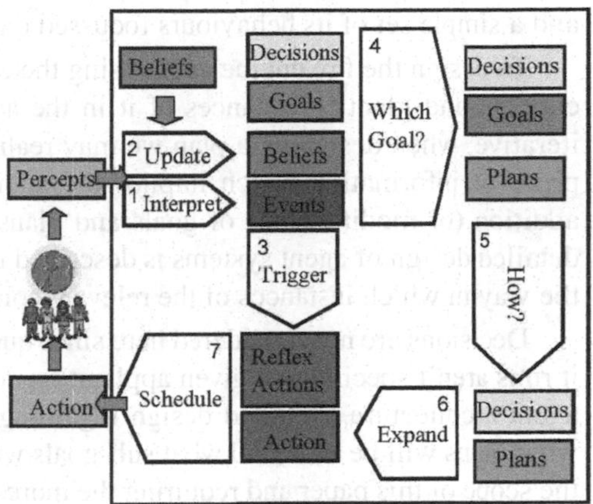

Fig. 4. Agent Execution Cycle

By comparison, the BDI abstract execution cycle [10] consists of the following steps: (1) use events to trigger matching plans (options), (2) select a subset of the options, (3) update the intentions and execute them, (4) get external events, and (5) drop successful and impossible attitudes. The execution cycle presented here differs from the BDI execution cycle in a number of ways including the use of reflexive actions, the derivation of events by interpreting percepts, the process of going from goals to plans to actions, and increased reasoning about goals. However, the two primary contributions are the role of top level goals (which are distinguished from events and from sub-goals, and are persistent) in achieving proactiveness, and the role of events (as *significant* occurrences) in creating suitably reactive agents.

4 A Case Study: RoboRescue

One of the applications we have worked on recently is RoboRescue. We describe a greatly simplified version of a part of this application in order to illustrate concretely the concepts we have identified.

RoboRescue [11] is a long-term (50 years!) project which has the goal of creating robotic squads which could be deployed in the aftermath of a disaster such as an earthquake. Tasks to be carried out include rescuing & evacuating people and controlling fires. Challenges faced include the lack of information and an environment which contains obstacles (including collapsed buildings, obstructed roads, fires, etc.) and potentially limited communication.

The RoboRescue simulator has a number of components which simulate different aspects of a disaster scenario. The intention is that these aspects combine synergistically to provide a realistically complex and challenging environment. There are a number of different types of agents in the system including fire engines, ambulances, civilians, and police agents. At each simulator cycle agents receive visual information and possibly heard information.

Due to space limitations in this paper we focus on a single agent type (fire engine) and a simple set of its behaviours focussed on fire extinguishing.

To design the fire engine agent using the concepts described earlier we look at each concept and identify instances of it in the agent system. This process is, in general, iterative: when designing a plan we may realise that the agent needs to know a certain piece of information which implies the addition of a belief which might imply the addition (or modification) of goals and plans. A comprehensive methodology for the detailed design of agent systems is described in [8]. Here we concentrate on illustrating the way in which instances of the relevant concepts are identified and defined.

Decisions are not considered here since questions which an agent needs to answer as it runs aren't specific to a given application domain; rather, they are specific to a given agent architecture. Detailed design regarding how agents will work together, exactly what plans will be used and what sub-goals will be needed is a design task well beyond the scope of this paper and requiring the more extensive methodology of [8]. Rather, we focus on the initial aspects of the process and the identification of some of the relevant concepts in each class. More concept instances will inevitably be identified as the design progresses.

Percepts: Percepts represent an interface to the environment, so are often, as in this case, at least partially predefined. There are two types of percepts in RoboRescue - visual and auditory. Auditory information may be broadcast information which in the case of a fire-engine agent may be a message from another fire-engine agent, the fire-engine center, or a civilian either crying for help or stating that they have heard a cry for help. It may also be a message directed specifically to that agent from another fire-engine agent. The content of messages from fire-engine agents and the fire-engine center is an aspect of perceptual information which is under the control of the designer and must be decided. Visual information contains a current view of the environment including such things as roads, buildings, fires and their intensity, etc.

Percepts must be processed to build up knowledge of the environment (beliefs) and to extract events. In the case of the visual information in RoboRescue it is first processed in order to add any information to the map of the world that is built incrementally. It is then processed to extract the position of each fire which is assessed to see whether there is a fire-related event which should be generated and to further update the knowledge of the environment.

Actions: The actions which an agent can perform are also part of its interface to the environment. As indicated earlier, there may be additional actions defined beyond those that affect the environment, but these are a starting point. In this case the agent can perform the external actions of *squirting* which reduces the fire at the current location, *moving* which moves the agent an unspecified number of steps along a given route, *telling* (broadcasting) and *saying* (sending) a message. The move and squirt actions may need to be applied repeatedly to achieve the desired goal, for example a fire may need to be squirted multiple times before it is extinguished and the agent may need to move several times before it reaches its destination.

We also identified early on the action of planning a route between two points as an internal action. A route is a necessary parameter for the move action, code existed for planning a route given the map, a current position and a destination, and there seemed to be no clear advantage in using goals and plans to achieve this task, particularly given the existing code. Thus we had an initial set of five actions, four that were part of the external interface to the simulator and one which was internal.

Goals: An obvious major goal of the fire engine agent is to put out any fire. We also identified a goal of discovering fires. Additional thought yielded for us the further goals of assisting a team-mate to put out a fire and coordinating a team effort to extinguish a fire. The goals of the agent obviously have to do with the motivation for the system, but are not externally defined in the way that at least some of the percepts and actions are. Choosing the appropriate set of top-level goals is one of the early design decisions that need to be made.

It is tempting to treat goals as being implied by the beliefs: any belief in the existence of a fire implies a goal extinguish the fire. However, this approach has a number of issues. Firstly, it is hard to indicate that certain fires should not be pursued (e.g. because another agent is dealing with them). Secondly, it is difficult to add goals which are not directly prompted by environmental cues. For example, the goal to find fires exists independent of cues in the environment, and should result in exploratory behaviour if no other goals are inhibiting this goal.

In addition to identifying the goals of an agent, we need to specify when to adopt and drop goals (including how to recognise when they are achieved), plans for achieving these goals, sub-goals that may be part of achieving each goal and relative priorities and interactions between the goals.

As indicated in section 3, events, i.e. significant things which happen in the environment, often result in the adoption of goals. Thus the event of receiving a message from a team-mate requesting help in extinguishing a fire is likely to result in a goal to assist that team mate to put out his fire. The event of noticing a fire is likely to result in a goal to extinguish that fire. Thus we move onto events.

Events: Here we are identifying significant occurrences that are likely to make the agent add or delete goals, change goal priorities, or change how the agent is pursuing a goal. We also look for significant occurrences which affect our beliefs. Many events will be the result of processing percepts - e.g. extracting information about fires and their locations, checking these against a list of fires we already know about, and obtaining any "new-fire" events. Some events will also be generated internally as a result of the agent's own behaviour. For example after sending a request for assistance with a fire, the agent may generate a "help-requested" event. As events are used to update beliefs, trigger plans and generate reflexive actions there are likely to be a large set of events which are developed iteratively in the process of developing the full design. The detailed design methodology in [8] allows for a layered identification of events in conjunction with incremental refinement of sets of plans.[6]

The initial events that we identify typically have to do with the significant occurrences that will alert the agent to the need to instantiate one of its top level goals, recognise one of its top level goals as achieved, or indicate a need for reconsideration.

[6] These sets of plans and related events are actually JACK capabilities.

In this example such events include

- "new-fire" which causes instantiation of an "extinguish" goal and also causes a reflexive action to broadcast the existence of the fire to other fire-engine agents;
- "fire-extinguished" event which causes the agent to recognise that a goal has been achieved;
- "fire-urgent" event which indicates fire is growing and is larger than a given threshold. This indicates a need for reconsideration and in our design may lead to a goal to co-ordinate a team effort to extinguish the fire;
- "help-requested" which leads to a reconsideration of current priorities and may lead to a goal to assist team-mates;

Identification of events determines what interpretation or processing we need to do with the percepts received in order to be able to recognise events. This in turn also often affects what information about the environment we need to represent - e.g. to be able to generate a new fire event from a visual percept we need to explicitly represent which fires we already know about.

Beliefs: Beliefs are really any knowledge the agent maintains. Some of this information may be kept in the form of a special purpose knowledge database, other information may be kept in arbitrary suitable data structures. For this application the primary information needed is an internal map of the environment including the location of fires, roads, buildings, etc. Updating of this data structure is part of the important processing of percepts.

Beliefs tend to be used primarily in two ways. The first is in extracting events from percepts: to recognise a new fire we have to have knowledge about existing fires. The second is in determining which plan should be used to achieve a goal in a particular situation. Information that allows us to choose between two alternative ways of achieving a goal - or even whether there is any way of achieving a goal, depends on some representation of beliefs.

Some of the beliefs we have identified as important here (in addition to the map) are: which fires are being attended to and by who; current priority of fires; and whether a route is available to a particular location (it may not be, either due to blockages, or insufficient information about the environment).

Plans: Plans describe various ways for us to achieve our goals. To get the full power of the BDI approach it is advantageous to define simple plans, with use of sub-goals wherever possible. Initially there may only be one straightforward way to achieve each goal, but new variations can be added in a modular fashion. This allows development of a simple agent that manages straightforward cases first, with addition of variations for more complex cases afterwards. Plan sets need to be checked for coverage and overlap regarding the situations which can arise.

A very simple pair of plans for achieving the goal to extinguish a fire at X would be one plan which simply squirts until the fire is extinguished (suitable if the agent is already at location X), and another plan which obtains a route to X, moves to X, then squirts until the fire is extinguished (suitable if the agent is not already at X). Alternatively we could have a plan for putting out a fire and a plan for extinguishing a fire as shown below:

Goal: put-out_fire(position)	**Goal:** extinguish_fire(position)
plan_route(position)	**Condition:** location = position
move(route)	squirt
extinguish_fire(position)	extinguish_fire(position) **unless** nofire(position)

In fact this plan is simple enough that it can be implemented reactively using a set of trigger response rules, all that needs to be stored for this approach is the target's coordinates. However this approach is unable to handle sequences of actions where the triggers aren't in the environment and is unable to manage commitment. For these reasons plans need internal state to track what has been done, and need to be able to specify a sequence of actions to be done.

5 Discussion

We have presented the concepts we have found important in building BDI agent systems and the relationships between these concepts. We have found these concepts to be clearer and easier to teach and use than the BDI model. The concepts presented:

- Distinguish between goals and sub-goals, between percepts and events, and between events and goals. BDI implementations, by comparison, do not distinguish these and merge them all into an "event" type. We feel that this distinction is important since goals and events play roles in achieving reactivity and proactiveness and have rather different properties: for example, goals persist until they are achieved.
- Explicitly represent goals. This is vital in order to enable selection between competing goals, dealing with conflicting goals, and correctly handling goals which cannot be pursued at the time they are created and must be delayed [14].
- Highlight goal selection as an important issue. By contrast, BDI systems simply assume the existence of a selection function.
- Emphasise the importance of percepts and actions.
- Highlight the role of events in creating reactive agents.

We also introduced reflex actions, generalised the concept of a plan, decomposed the concept of intentions (which we have found to be difficult to explain and teach) into the simpler notion of a decision, and provided a hierarchical, staged presentation of the concepts.

Our design process (which is still being refined and developed, and which is explained more fully in [8]) is focussed on the detailed design and we view it as complementary to methodologies such as GAIA [15] and Tropos [7] which focus more on the higher level design and analysis and on the requirements aspects of agent systems.

The choice of concepts was driven by three sources. Primarily, our experience working on a number of agent programs, teaching students and assisting them to build agent programs, and developing and running workshops for academia and industry. Secondly, a survey of a range of agent systems (see below); and finally, "bottom up" derivation of concepts from first principles.

Although there is some degree of consensus in the deliberative agent research community that the BDI model is a reasonable common foundation for intelligent agents there are also known shortcomings of the model [4]. Thus, in order to avoid being "BDI-biased" we surveyed a range of agent systems which address the internals of an intelligent software agent. For more details see *http://www.cs.rmit.edu.au/~winikoff/SAC*.

There is much further work to be done including continuing to apply the concepts and design process to various applications. We are also starting to survey students and professionals regarding the concepts they regard as natural for developing agent systems. Developing a formal semantics for the concepts we have identified, as well as developing support tools (design, development, and debugging) are also high priorities. Finally, the concepts identified need to be extended (and revised) to support the creation of social intelligent agents.

Acknowledgements. We would like to acknowledge the support of Agent Oriented Software Pty. Ltd. and of the ARC (under grant CO0106934).

References

1. M. E. Bratman. *Intentions, Plans, and Practical Reason*. Harvard University Press, Cambridge, MA, 1987.
2. P. R. Cohen and H. J. Levesque. Intention is choice with commitment. *Artificial Intelligence*, 42:213–261, 1990.
3. K. Decker. DECAF update: Agents for undergrads & planning for a smart scheduler. Presentation at the Workshop on Infrastructure for Agents, MAS, and scalable MAS at Autonomous Agents 2001.
4. M. Georgeff, B. Pell, M. Pollack, M. Tambe, and M. Wooldridge. The belief-desire-intention model of agency. In ATAL, 1999.
5. N. Jennings and M. Wooldridge. Applications of intelligent agents. Chapter 1 in *Agent Technology: Foundations, Applications, and Markets*. Springer, 1998.
6. N. R. Jennings. An agent-based approach for building complex software systems. *Communications of the ACM*, 44(4):35–41, 2001.
7. J. Mylopoulos, J. Castro, and M. Kolp. Tropos: Toward agent-oriented information systems engineering. In *Second International Bi-Conference Workshop on Agent-Oriented Information Systems (AOIS2000)*, June 2000.
8. L. Padgham and M. Winikoff. A methodology for agent oriented software design. Technical Report TR-01-2, School of Computer Science and Information Technology, RMIT University, 2001.
9. A. S. Rao and M. P. Georgeff. Modeling rational agents within a BDI-Architecture. In J. Allen, R. Fikes, and E. Sandewall, editors, *Principles of Knowledge Representation and Reasoning, Proceedings of the Second International Conference*, pages 473–484, Apr. 1991.
10. A. S. Rao and M. P. Georgeff. An abstract architecture for rational agents. In C. Rich, W. Swartout, and B. Nebel, editors, *Proceedings of the Third International Conference on Principles of Knowledge Representation and Reasoning*, pages 439–449, San Mateo, CA, 1992. Morgan Kaufmann Publishers.
11. RoboCup-Rescue home page. *http://robomec.cs.kobe-u.ac.jp/robocup-rescue/*, 2001.
12. S. Russell and P. Norvig. *Artificial Intelligence: A Modern Approach*. Prentice Hall, 1995.
13. Y. Shoham. Agent-oriented programming. *Artificial Intelligence*, 60:51–92, 1993.
14. J. Thangarajah. Representation of goals in the belief-desire-intention model, 2000. Honours thesis, supervised by Lin Padgham.
15. M. Wooldridge, N. Jennings, and D. Kinny. The Gaia methodology for agent-oriented analysis and design. *Autonomous Agents and Multi-Agent Systems*, 3(3), 2000.

An Operational Semantics for a PRS-Like Agent Architecture

Wayne Wobcke

Department of Information Systems, University of Melbourne
Parkville VIC 3052, Australia
e-mail: wobckew@unimelb.edu.au

Abstract. In recent years, there have been increased efforts towards defining rigorous operational semantics for a range of agent programming languages. At the same time, there have been increased efforts to develop logical frameworks for modelling belief, desire and intention (and related notions) that make closer connections to the workings of particular architectures, thus aiming to provide some computational interpretation of these abstract models. However, there remains a substantial gap between the more abstract logical approaches and the more computationally oriented operational approaches. In this paper, we develop an operational semantics for a simplified language based on PRS that is derived directly from a high-level abstract interpreter; thus taking one step towards bridging this gap in the case of a simplified agent programming language sufficiently expressive to incorporate a simple notion of intention.

1 Introduction

In recent years, there have been increased efforts towards defining rigorous operational semantics for a range of agent programming languages. In this paper, we focus on languages based on the BDI (Belief, Desire, Intention) agent architecture as embodied in PRS and its variants, Georgeff and Lansky [8], Georgeff and Ingrand [7]. Such languages include AgentSpeak(L), Rao [13], Vivid, Wagner [17], dMARS, d'Inverno *et al.* [5], 3APL, Hindriks *et al.* [9], and Ψ, a PRS-style programming language defined using process algebra, Kinny [10].[1] Operational semantics have also been given for Concurrent METATEM, Wooldridge [20], using approaches from distributed computing, and for *ConGolog*, de Giacomo *et al.* [4], using the situation calculus.

However, especially for languages based on BDI architectures, there remains a substantial gap between operational descriptions and semantic descriptions at the higher "intentional" level. This gap means that "cognitive" properties of agents, such as rationality and commitment, that are typically modelled at this higher level, are not systematically connected to the properties of implemented agents as described at the operational level, raising doubts as to the efficacy and accuracy of such higher-level modelling in relation to practice. In part because operational definitions are designed to be self-contained, they are not explicitly related to more high-level descriptions of agent behaviour.

[1] Most of these operational definitions are incomplete, thus leaving some choices of computation mechanism up to the particular implementation.

M. Brooks, D. Corbett, and M. Stumptner (Eds.): AI 2001, LNAI 2256, pp. 569–580, 2001.

In this paper, we provide an operational description for a simplified language based on PRS that is derived directly from a high-level description of its abstract interpreter. This goes part way towards bridging the gap between the operational and intentional levels of description – in future work, we intend to investigate closer connections between the two levels of description. The organization of the paper is as follows. In section 2, we motivate our simplified, reconstructed version of PRS by relating it to the descriptions of PRS given in the literature. In section 3, we define more precisely the operational semantics of our language using Plotkin-style transition systems to define plan execution. We conclude in section 4 with a discussion of Bratman's theory of intention in relation to our reconstructed architecture.

2 PRS: A Reconstruction

PRS (*Procedural Reasoning System*) was initially described in Georgeff and Lansky [8], with further elaboration given in Georgeff and Ingrand [7]. Here we give a reconstruction of PRS along lines of the implementation of UM-PRS [11], and will speak of a 'PRS-like' architecture and 'PRS-like' plans to acknowledge both their roots and the differences between our reformulation and the original language specification and implementation.[2]

Basically, we consider a PRS agent program to be a collection of plans, originally called Knowledge Areas (KAs). These plans are essentially the same as standard plans in the Artificial Intelligence literature (though also allowing conditional and iterative actions), in that they have a *precondition* (a condition under which the plan can be executed), an *postcondition* (a condition that indicates successful execution of the plan – note that this is quite different from the expected outcome of executing the plan), and a *body* (a collection of actions which when successfully executed will normally achieve the postcondition). The body of a plan is also very similar to a standard computer program, except that there can be special actions of the form *achieve* γ, meaning that the system should achieve the goal γ in whichever way is convenient: these are the analogues of procedure calls.

To enable decisions about plan execution to be made at runtime, PRS-like plans extend standard planning formalisms in having a *context* (a condition that must be true when each action in the plan is initiated),[3] a *trigger* (a condition that, in conjunction with the precondition, indicates when the interpreter should consider the plan for execution), a *termination condition* (a condition indicating when the plan should be dropped), and a *priority* (a natural number indicating how important the plan's goal is to achieve). The context is important in dynamic settings: when there are a number of ways of achieving a particular goal, the context helps the interpreter to find the "best" way of achieving the goal in the current environment, which, due to unforeseen changes in the world, cannot always be predicted in advance. The priority of each plan enables the

[2] Thanks to David Kinny for clarifying differences between the different versions of PRS and other PRS-like languages/systems.

[3] Contexts are similar to maintenance conditions in PRS, but differ in that maintenance conditions must be true throughout the execution of a plan.

system to determine which plan to pursue given a choice of potential plans (usually a plan with the highest priority is chosen for execution).

The original definition of PRS allowed for meta-KAs, or plans that are used to determine which plans to invoke and execute.[4] But in practice, meta-plans have not been widely used, and this is partly because they are not available in implementations of PRS such as UM-PRS, Lee *et al.* [11]. Instead, we assume that each plan has a state-dependent *utility* used in conjunction with its (state-independent) priority to further discriminate between potential plans at runtime, and a state-dependent *cost* used to indicate the loss involved in temporarily suspending a current plan in favour of a newly triggered plan. More precisely (and this should be clearer with the operational definition given below), we assume that in any given state, the interpreter considers as options all plan instances whose precondition and context hold in the current belief state and whose trigger condition is satisfied in virtue of the most recent observations of external events. Further, we assume that the agent chooses to act, in any given state, upon the plan with the highest priority that has the highest value, where, for a current plan, the value is simply the plan's utility in that state, and, for a newly triggered plan, the value is the plan's utility minus the cost of temporarily suspending the highest valued viable current plan, again relative to that state (if this does not yield a unique selection, one such plan is chosen at random). Thus priorities, utilities and costs together determine a simple "commitment strategy" for the agent.

The agent's computation cycle can be conveniently described with reference to the simplified interpreter for BDI agents shown in Figure 1, presented by Rao and Georgeff [15] (note that here there is also no mention of meta-plans). In this abstract interpreter, the system state consists of sets of beliefs B, goals G and intentions I. Each element of I corresponds to a partially executed concrete hierarchical plan, towards which the agent has made some prior commitment, that is either currently active or has been suspended due to an alternative goal being pursued: for consistency, we will call such items *(concrete) plans* rather then intentions, reserving this term for the mental analogues of individual actions in such plans. Each cycle of the interpreter runs as follows. The process begins with a collection of external events stored in a queue, any or all of which may trigger pre-existing abstract plans: along with the currently active and suspended concrete plans that are feasible in the current state and the refinements of such plans (defined below), these constitute the options available to the agent. Then, "deliberation" determines which such plan is chosen for execution, the set I is updated to reflect this choice, and the agent executes the next action in the chosen plan. After obtaining new external events, the set of current intentions is further updated, first by removing those that have successfully completed (whose postcondition holds), then by dropping those which are impossible to complete (whose termination condition holds).

The above description of the interpreter leaves many computational issues unresolved. Hence we make the following additional assumptions concerning PRS-like programs, many of which hold for practical implementations of PRS.

- the belief set B is updated as new events are added to the event queue (so B represents the agent's beliefs about the current world state);

[4] In the original descriptions of PRS, KAs do not have priorities, so meta-KAs were necessary for fulfilling this purpose.

```
Abstract BDI Interpreter:
    initialize-state();
    do
        options := option-generator(event-queue, B, G, I);
        selected-options := deliberate(options, B, G, I);
        update-intentions(selected-options, I);
        execute(I);
        get-new-external-events();
        drop-successful-attitudes(B, G, I);
        drop-impossible-attitudes(B, G, I)
    untilquit
```

Fig. 1. Abstract BDI Interpreter

- the belief set B is consistent (i.e. it is assumed that inconsistencies in the set of events observed in any one cycle are resolved when updating beliefs);
- the event queue is cleared after options are generated (this ensures the agent's internal processing does not lag behind its observations of the world);
- the generated options consist of all concrete instantiations of newly triggered plans, all plans in the set I whose next action is feasible (its precondition and the context of the subplan in which it occurs are consequences of B), and all refinements of the current plans with respect to the current belief set B (the definition of a refinement is given below);
- each element of the set I is a concrete hierarchical plan (defined below);
- the set of goals G consists of the postconditions of the concrete plans in the set I;
- for each plan in the set I, if P' is a maximal subplan of P with respect to the property of being believed successful (its postcondition is a consequence of B), or impossible (its termination condition is a consequence of B), the updated set of intentions, instead of containing P, contains P with P' and all its subplans removed;
- the updated set of intentions I includes all plans from the previous cycle that have not been modified (i.e. suspended plans persist unless believed to be successful or impossible).

To define the auxiliary concepts used in the above description, we first assume a finite predicate language $\mathcal{L}$ incorporating the usual connectives $\wedge$, $\vee$, $\neg$ and $\Rightarrow$ but no quantifiers, i.e. each atomic formula of $\mathcal{L}$ is of the form $r(t_1, \cdots, t_n)$, where r is a relation name and t_i is a term that may contain function symbols, constant symbols and variables. The agent's belief set B at any time is assumed to be a consistent set of ground literals of $\mathcal{L}$, and it is assumed that for any ground formula α of $\mathcal{L}$, the issue of whether α is a consequence of B (denoted $\mathsf{B} \vdash \alpha$) is decidable (and that such α can be generated from non-ground formulae of $\mathcal{L}$). Goals and actions are also represented by formulae of $\mathcal{L}$ (possibly non-ground in the case of abstract plans).

We next assume that the agent has a plan library containing a set of abstract plans. The conditions associated with each plan are formulae of $\mathcal{L}$, and each plan body is a program, defined below.

Definition 1. *The language of* programs *is defined as follows. First, the atomic action formulae of $\mathcal{L}$, including the special formulae* achieve γ *for formulae* γ *of* $\mathcal{L}$*, plus a symbol* Λ *denoting the "null" action, are (atomic) programs. Second, if* π *and* χ *are programs and* α *is a formula of* $\mathcal{L}$*, the following are all programs (and no other expressions are programs).*

$$\begin{array}{ll} \pi;\chi & \textit{(sequential)} \\ \textbf{if } \alpha \textbf{ then } \pi \textbf{ else } \chi & \textit{(conditional)} \\ \textbf{while } \alpha \textbf{ do } \pi & \textit{(iterative)} \end{array}$$

The precondition of the sequence $\pi;\chi$ is that of π; its postcondition that of χ. The precondition and postcondition of Λ and of any conditional or iterative program is assumed to be *true*. The precondition of *achieve* γ is *false* and its postcondition is γ.

Definition 2. *A* (hierarchical) plan *is a nonempty sequence of programs* $[\pi_1,\cdots,\pi_n]$*, each with an associated precondition, postcondition and context, whose initial element is* achieve γ *for some goal formula* γ *of* $\mathcal{L}$ *(with precondition true, postcondition* γ *and context true).*

Definition 3. *The* active program *of a plan* $[\pi_1,\cdots,\pi_n]$ *is its final element* π_n*.*

Definition 4. *A plan* P' *is a* subplan *of a plan* $P = [\pi_1,\cdots,\pi_n]$ *if* P' *is a nonempty suffix* $[\pi_i,\cdots,\pi_n]$ *of the sequence* P*.*

Definition 5. *A plan is* concrete *if all its contained programs and associated conditions are ground formulae; otherwise the plan is* abstract.

Definition 6. *A plan* $P' = [\pi_1,\cdots,\pi_n,\pi]$ *is a* refinement *of a concrete hierarchical plan* $P = [\pi_1,\cdots,\pi_n]$ *with respect to the belief set* B *under the following conditions.*

- *if* π_n *is* achieve $\gamma;\chi$, π *is a program corresponding to the body of an (instantiated) plan from the plan library whose (instantiated) postcondition implies* γ*, whose (instantiated) precondition and context are consequences of* B *and whose (instantiated) trigger is implied by the beliefs corresponding to the most recently observed events (the program* achieve γ *is assumed to be equivalent to* achieve $\gamma;\Lambda$*);*
- *if the context of* π_n *is not a consequence of* B*,* π *is a program corresponding to the body of an (instantiated) plan from the plan library whose (instantiated) postcondition implies the context of* π_n*, whose (instantiated) precondition and context are consequences of* B*, and whose (instantiated) trigger is implied by the beliefs corresponding to the most recently observed events (in this case, the plan acts as a recovery plan for* π_n *by restoring its context).*

Finally, the PRS-like agent's "commitment strategy" is embodied in the following assumptions.

- In any state, the utility of any refinement of a plan is at most that of the original plan;
- Deliberation chooses for execution a plan with the highest value amongst those highest priority options generated.

Here, the *state* refers to the mental state of the agent rather than the state of the world, i.e. all values, utilities and costs are subjective.

That is, the PRS-like agent is assumed to have some commitment to its intentions in the sense that once a plan is chosen for execution by deliberation, the agent continues to attempt to fulfil the corresponding intention, through performing the actions contained in the plan body and achieving its various subgoals and attempting to recover from failures, *unless* an alternative option of higher priority (or of equal priority and higher value) becomes available, in which case, the plan is (or may be) suspended, or the plan is believed impossible to complete, in which case it is abandoned.

3 Operational Semantics

The previous section provides a fairly complete intuitive operational definition of the execution of PRS-like agents, but a more formal definition is needed if such execution strategies are to be shown to correspond to a logical modelling. In this section, we give such a formal operational semantics, for plan execution using the structured operational semantics style of definition due to Plotkin [12], and following the approach of Wagner [17]. This requires the definition of the PRS-like agent's internal states, then the definition of the transitions between states corresponding to each step in the abstract BDI interpreter described above.

Definition 7. *A* state *is a pair* $\langle \mathsf{B}, \mathsf{I} \rangle$ *where* B *is a consistent set of literals of* $\mathcal{L}$ *and* I *is a set of concrete hierarchical plans.*

The agent's state, together with the event queue, contains all *and only* the information the agent uses in planning and acting. Thus the PRS-like agent does not have complex beliefs, for example, introspective beliefs about its beliefs or intentions, beliefs about the possible effects of its actions in various states, or beliefs about the past or the future. This has the consequence that all conditions associated with plans (such as preconditions and context conditions) can refer only to the current state of the environment, not to other aspects of the agent's state such as its current intentions. One motivation for this is speed of computation: option generation is meant to be a simple process based on the newly observed events occurring in the environment (as recorded in the event queue). It is the role of the deliberation step to make a "decision" concerning which option to pursue, or whether to continue pursuing an existing plan.

Let us now define a transition function from states to states that formalizes the operational semantics of one cycle of the PRS-like agent interpreter. We assume that the input belief set to this function is the belief set computed on the previous cycle, after new observations have been used to modify the old belief set, and after plans considered successful or impossible have been dropped. For the very first cycle, we can assume the agent has no plans and some arbitrary set of beliefs.

The general form of the transition function is the composition of a series of functions, each corresponding to one step in the abstract interpreter as described by Rao and Georgeff [15]. That is, the operation of the interpreter is characterized by a triggering function τ (that returns a set of plans and leaves the state unchanged), a deliberation function δ (that returns a plan π and leaves the state unchanged), an update function for intentions prior to action ι, a plan execution function ϵ, a belief update function β (which also accepts a consistent set of literals representing events), and a plan update function υ, all of which return a modified state.

We now define each of the component functions in turn. The most complicated function is the plan execution function, being defined recursively on the structure of programs. In the following, let E be the set of literals in the logical language $\mathcal{L}$ (i.e. the atomic formulae of $\mathcal{L}$ and the negations of such formulae), let Φ be the class of concrete hierarchical plans, let Σ be the class of states (i.e. the set of pairs $\langle \mathsf{B}, \mathsf{I} \rangle$ where B is a consistent set of literals of $\mathcal{L}$ and I is a set of concrete hierarchical plans), and for a given state σ, let $\mathsf{B}(\sigma)$ and $\mathsf{I}(\sigma)$ denote the belief set and intention set in σ, respectively.

3.1 Triggering, Deliberation, and Intention Update

The interpreter is assumed to have access to an event "queue" containing a set of ground literals of $\mathcal{L}$ corresponding to the events observed on the previous computation cycle, which collectively trigger various concrete plans. For each concrete plan instantiating a plan in the plan library (the plan library is assumed fixed), let $\mathit{trigger}(\pi)$, $\mathit{pre}(\pi)$ and $\mathit{context}(\pi)$ denote the trigger, precondition, and context of π, respectively.

Definition 8. *The* triggering function τ *is the function* $\tau : 2^E \times \Sigma \to 2^\Phi$ *defined as follows.*

$$\tau(e, \sigma) = \{\phi \in \Phi : e \vdash \mathit{trigger}(\phi) \text{ and } \mathsf{B}(\sigma) \vdash \mathit{pre}(\phi) \wedge \mathit{context}(\phi)\}$$

In the "deliberation" step, a plan is selected for execution from amongst the newly triggered plans, the current plans eligible for execution, and the possible refinements of the current plans. We define a deliberation function δ whose inputs are the newly triggered plans Ψ and the initial state σ. We use auxiliary functions τ' and τ'' that return, respectively, the current plans eligible for execution and the refinements of the current plans. Assume that $\rho(B, \phi)$ returns the set of refinements of a hierarchical plan ϕ with respect to a belief set B, as defined above.

$$\tau'(\sigma) = \{\phi \in \mathsf{I}(\sigma) : \mathsf{B}(\sigma) \vdash \mathit{pre}(\phi) \wedge \mathit{context}(\phi)\},\ \tau''(\sigma) = \bigcup_{\phi \in \mathsf{I}(\sigma)} \rho(\mathsf{B}(\sigma), \phi)$$

Here it is understood that the precondition of a plan ϕ is that of its active program, and the context that of the instantiated plan in the plan library from which the active program was derived.

For any given concrete hierarchical plan ϕ, let the priority of ϕ be denoted $p(\phi)$ (that of the plan from which its active program was derived) and let the value of ϕ in state σ be denoted $v(\phi, \sigma)$ (i.e. subtracting a penalty cost from the utility of each newly triggered plan). The deliberation function returns a randomly chosen plan that has maximal value amongst those with maximal priority amongst the input plans (or the empty plan $[\Lambda]$ if no such plan exists). Let the choice function be denoted 'ran'.

Definition 9. *The* deliberation function δ *is the function* $\delta : 2^\Phi \times \Sigma \to \Phi$ *defined as follows.*

$$\delta(\Psi, \sigma) = \begin{cases} \text{ran } \delta'(\Psi, \sigma) & \text{if } \delta'(\Psi, \sigma) \neq \emptyset \\ [\Lambda] & \text{otherwise} \end{cases}$$

where

$$\delta'(\Psi, \sigma) = \arg\max_{v(\psi,\, \sigma)} \arg\max_{p(\psi)} \{\psi \in \Psi \cup \tau'(\sigma) \cup \tau''(\sigma)\}$$

Finally, the intention update function either adds the selected newly triggered plan to the set of intentions or else replaces a plan by one of its refinements (depending on which plan is selected by deliberation), and returns the plan selected and the new state.

Definition 10. *The* intention update function ι *is the function* $\delta : \Phi \times \Sigma \to \Phi \times \Sigma$ *defined as follows.*

$$\iota(\phi, \sigma) = \langle \phi, \langle \mathsf{B}(\sigma), \iota'(\phi, \sigma)\rangle\rangle$$

where

$$\iota'(\phi, \sigma) = \begin{cases} \mathsf{I}(\sigma) - \{\phi'\} \cup \{\phi\} & \textit{when } \phi \in \rho(\phi') \\ \mathsf{I}(\sigma) \cup \{\phi\} & \textit{otherwise} \end{cases}$$

3.2 Plan Execution

The operational semantics of plan execution is defined by means of a transition function ϵ that specifies the effect of executing one atomic step of the agent's plan in a given state, returning the remainder of the plan to be executed and the resulting state (a *continuation*). The auxiliary function ϵ' defines the execution of a single step in a program.

Definition 11. *The* plan execution transition function ϵ *is the function* $\epsilon : \Phi \times \Sigma \to \Sigma$ *defined as follows.*

$$\epsilon(\phi, \sigma) = \langle \mathsf{B}(\sigma), \mathsf{I}(\sigma) - \{\phi\} \cup \{\phi'\}\rangle$$

where π *is the active program of* ϕ, ϕ' *is the same as* ϕ *except that* $\epsilon'(\pi)$ *replaces* π *as the active program, and* ϵ' *is an auxiliary function* $\epsilon' : \Pi \times \Sigma \to \Pi$ *defined as follows.*

$$\epsilon'(\pi, \sigma) = \pi \textit{ when } \pi \textit{ is an atomic action}$$

$$\epsilon'(\pi; \chi, \sigma) = \pi'; \chi \textit{ where } \epsilon'(\pi, \sigma) = \pi'$$

$$\epsilon'(\textbf{if } \alpha \textbf{ then } \pi \textbf{ else } \chi) = \begin{cases} \pi & \textit{if } \mathsf{B}(\sigma) \vdash \alpha \\ \chi & \textit{otherwise} \end{cases}$$

$$\epsilon'(\textbf{while } \alpha \textbf{ do } \pi) = \begin{cases} \pi; \textbf{while } \alpha \textbf{ do } \pi & \textit{if } \mathsf{B}(\sigma) \vdash \alpha \\ \Lambda & \textit{otherwise} \end{cases}$$

One of the peculiarities of PRS-like plan "execution", in contrast to the execution of standard computer programs, is that execution does not necessarily advance the state of the computation. This can be seen in the rule for atomic actions, which returns the continuation π, i.e. the same as the initial plan. This is because for an agent embedded in the world, execution counts as an *attempt* to perform the corresponding action, and it is only through *successful* execution of a plan that an agent achieves its goals (the computation will be advanced if and when an observation confirms successful execution). A second feature of the PRS-like interpreter that is a consequence of this rule concerns the agent's actions on the failed execution of an action: no matter how many times an action fails, it is simply retried on the following cycle (assuming no alternative of higher priority arises). Thus it is possible for the PRS-like agent to be stuck in an infinite loop of continually trying and retrying the same failed action.

The rules for conditional and iterative statements also embody an assumption about PRS-like agents that may lead to undesirable consequences. The rules effectively state that execution of a conditional or iterative statement amounts to determining whether the condition α in the statement is a consequence of the belief set B or not (so for the conditional statement, if α is believed, the **then** branch is selected, otherwise the **else** branch is selected). However, no action of the chosen branch is taken until a subsequent cycle. One reason for this is that the selected action might be a special action of the form *achieve* γ, in which case its execution requires a further triggering/deliberation cycle. The problem this raises is that between the time the branch is selected and the time the first action in the branch is executed, the belief set may have changed (and the agent might have selected the other branch had the test been done in the new state). Thus in this case, the agent's processing lags behind its observations of the environment.

3.3 Belief and Plan Update

Finally, the functions for belief and plan update are specified. Belief revision involves the serious complication that approaches to belief revision in the literature, e.g. Gärdenfors [6], lead to revision functions that are computationally expensive and, moreover, indeterminate (not specified uniquely in terms of just the agent's beliefs). To address both issues, PRS-like systems typically restrict the language of events and beliefs to make belief revision both determinate and simple. One such simplification, e.g. Wagner [17], is to insist that the observations on each cycle correspond to a consistent set of literals e. Then revision can be defined, c.f. Gärdenfors [6], as the function that removes the complement $\bar{l}$ of each literal l in e from B (if it is contained in B) and then adds each (now consistent) literal l of e to B.

Definition 12. *The* belief update function β *is the function* $\beta : 2^E \times \Sigma \rightarrow \Sigma$ *defined as follows.*

$$\beta(e, \sigma) = \langle \mathsf{B}(\sigma) - \bar{e} \cup e, \mathsf{I}(\sigma) \rangle$$

where

$$\bar{e} = \{\bar{l} : l \in e\}$$

The plan update function is more straightforward. This function is mainly concerned with "housekeeping" which consists of removing those actions whose programs have finished execution, or those plans that have achieved their goals or which are believed to be impossible to complete. Actions that have completed successfully are those whose postconditions are a consequence of the belief set (it is assumed, of course, that the beliefs are accurate); in addition, if the active program of a plan is Λ, the empty program, then that program requires no further execution. Subplans that are believed to be impossible are those whose termination conditions are a consequence of the belief set.

For a concrete hierarchical plan ϕ, let $\mathit{successful}(\phi)$ be the set of subplans ψ of ϕ for which $\mathsf{B}(\sigma) \vdash \mathit{post}(\psi)$, and let $\mathit{impossible}(\phi)$ be the set of subplans ψ of ϕ for which $\mathsf{B}(\sigma) \vdash \mathit{termination}(\psi)$ (as above, for any plan, the conditions are those of the instantiated plan in the plan library from which the active program of the plan was derived).

Definition 13. *The* plan update function υ *is the function* $\upsilon : \Sigma \rightarrow \Sigma$ *defined as follows.*

$$\upsilon(\sigma) = \langle \phi, \omega(\{\varrho(\phi - \upsilon'(\phi)) : \phi \in \mathsf{I}(\sigma)\})\rangle$$

where, for each plan ϕ, $\upsilon'(\phi)$ *is the largest subplan contained in* $successful(\phi) \cup impossible(\phi)$ *if this exists, or else is the empty plan,* $\phi - \phi'$ *is* ϕ *with the subplan* ϕ' *removed, and for any plan* ϕ, $\varrho(\phi)$ *returns* ϕ *with the active program* $\pi; \chi$ *replaced by* χ *if* $\mathsf{B}(\sigma) \vdash post(\pi)$ *for an atomic action* π, *and otherwise returns* ϕ *(again, the program* achieve γ *is assumed to be equivalent to* achieve $\gamma; \Lambda$*). Finally, the function* ω *removes, from a given set of plans, any plan that consists of a singleton sequence whose only element is the program* Λ*.*

Note that nowhere is it described when and how the PRS-like agent abandons its goals. This is because, whereas the termination condition is associated with a plan, there is no corresponding termination condition associated with a goal, so there is no belief the agent can use to determine that a goal is infeasible. The only way a goal can be abandoned is when it occurs as a subgoal of a plan that is abandoned.

4 Discussion

The exercise of developing an operational semantics for an agent programming language of the PRS variety raises fundamental questions about such languages and their architectures *qua* rational agent architectures. This is because intentional notions such as knowledge, belief, desire and intention are given specific meanings with reference to an underlying architecture in terms of transitions on internal states. The question of interest then is whether these so-called BDI agents really have these mental attributes, as seems to be commonly presumed. This question can only be answered with respect to a specific theory of beliefs, desires and intentions such as that provided by Bratman [1]. Recall that Bratman characterizes intention with reference to three functional roles, e.g. Bratman [1, p. 141]: (i) intentions pose problems for deliberation, i.e. how to fulfil them, (ii) existing intentions constrain the adoption of further intentions, and (iii) intentions control conduct: an agent endeavours to fulfil its intentions. To some degree, the plan structures used by PRS-like agents do possess these roles. For property (i), the plans adopted by PRS-like agents may include special actions of the form *achieve* γ, which can be construed as posing problems to be solved by the agent. For property (ii), the structure of a single plan constrains the adoption of further intentions corresponding to refinements of the plan. For property (iii), the computation cycle of the PRS-like interpreter ensures some persistence of intention, normally leading to attempts by the agent to fulfil its intentions.

However, Bratman also emphasizes that these are the roles of intention in *reasoning*, i.e. mental processing of a certain degree of complexity is involved in reasoning with intentions, and it is this which is absent from the PRS-like agent architecture. In particular, Bratman [1, p. 31] emphasizes that intentions play a role in coordinating the overall activities of the agent, such that the agent's overall plan should be strongly consistent (believed feasible). But to establish this property of a single course of actions, the agent must reconcile the competing requirements of all its adopted intentions in order to ensure that they can all be fulfilled in a coordinated manner – this aspect of determining the overall coherence of an agent's plans is entirely absent from the PRS-like system, whilst present (again, to some degree) in a system such as IRMA, Bratman, Israel and Pollack [2]. Let us take a closer look at the three functional roles of intention with this in mind. For property (i), the case of *achieve* γ subgoals, the PRS-like agent solves such subproblems only when it is time to execute the *achieve* action, which entails triggering relevant plans and selecting one that achieves γ. Thus such subgoals do not generate further intentions or constraints on future intentions adopted during the agent's intermediate "planning". On the other hand, PRS-like agents are assumed to be situated in an environment where, perhaps, decisions about how best to achieve a subgoal are best deferred until execution time; if so, this is not as the world is commonly assumed. For property (ii), while the structure of a *single* plan constrains the adoption of future intentions related to that plan, the multiple plans of PRS-like agents are never reconciled in one overarching plan, and the plans of the PRS-like agent are not necessarily ever mutually compatible. For property (iii), the computation cycle embodied in the PRS-like interpreter ensures some persistence of plans, but also that the agent may attempt to execute an action incompatible with one of its own plans, leading to the needless abandonment of a plan.

Thus the operational semantics accorded to PRS-like languages and architectures makes plain that systems based on PRS have intentions in Bratman's sense only to an extremely limited extent. Whether PRS-like systems embody BDI agents then turns on whether fulfilling the three roles posited by Bratman as functions of intentions *in humans* is a constitutive requirement of intentions, or merely additional to the role intentions play in human reasoning. In the latter case, an alternative, weaker, theory of intention would be needed to justify the claim that PRS-like agents have intentions.

5 Conclusion and Further Work

In this paper, we provided an operational description for a simplified language based on PRS that is derived directly from a high-level description of its abstract interpreter. This goes part way towards bridging the gap between the operational and intentional levels of description. In comparison to other operational descriptions of PRS-like systems, our language is more expressive in allowing conditional and iterative constructs, and is more explicit about action selection, through the use of utility functions to formalize this aspect of the computation cycle.

In future work, we intend to investigate closer connections between the operational and intentional levels of description. The main problem to be addressed is that there is no clear way of mapping abstract logical models onto the computational states of an implemented agent. The work of Rao and Georgeff [14] on modelling intention, of Singh [16] on modelling strategies, and of Cavedon and Rao [3] on modelling plans provides a starting point, and earlier work showed how to define such mappings in simplified cases, e.g. Wooldridge [19], Wobcke [18].

References

1. Bratman, M.E. (1987) *Intention, Plans and Practical Reason.* Harvard University Press, Cambridge, MA.
2. Bratman, M.E., Israel, D.J. & Pollack, M.E. (1988) 'Plans and Resource-Bounded Practical Reasoning.' *Computational Intelligence*, **4**, 349–355.
3. Cavedon, L. & Rao, A.S. (1996) 'Bringing About Rationality: Incorporating Plans Into a BDI Agent Architecture.' in Foo, N.Y. & Goebel, R.G. (Eds) *PRICAI'96: Topics in Artificial Intelligence.* Springer-Verlag, Berlin.
4. De Giacomo, G., Lespérance, Y. & Levesque, H.J. (2000) '*ConGolog*, a Concurrent Programming Language Based on the Situation Calculus.' *Artificial Intelligence*, **121**, 109–169.
5. d'Inverno, M., Kinny, D.N., Luck, M.M. & Wooldridge, M.J. (1997) 'A Formal Specification of dMARS.' in Singh, M.P., Rao, A.S. & Wooldridge, M.J. (Eds) *Intelligent Agents IV.* Springer-Verlag, Berlin.
6. Gärdenfors, P. (1988) *Knowledge in Flux.* MIT Press, Cambridge, MA.
7. Georgeff, M.P. & Ingrand, F.F. (1989) 'Decision-Making in an Embedded Reasoning System.' *Proceedings of the Eleventh International Joint Conference on Artificial Intelligence*, 972–978.
8. Georgeff, M.P. & Lansky, A.L. (1987) 'Reactive Reasoning and Planning.' *Proceedings of the Sixth National Conference on Artificial Intelligence (AAAI-87)*, 677–682.
9. Hindriks, K.V., de Boer, F.S., van der Hoek, W. & Meyer, J.-J.Ch. (1998) 'Formal Semantics for an Abstract Agent Programming Language.' in Singh, M.P., Rao, A.S. & Wooldridge, M.J. (Eds) *Intelligent Agents IV.* Springer-Verlag, Berlin.
10. Kinny, D.N. (2001) 'The Ψ Calculus: An Algebraic Agent Language.' *Proceedings of the Eighth International Workshop on Agent Theories, Architectures, and Languages*, 230–244.
11. Lee, J., Huber, M.J., Kenny, P.G. & Durfee, E.H. (1994) 'UM-PRS: An Implementation of the Procedural Reasoning System for Multirobot Applications.' *Conference on Intelligent Robotics in Field, Factory, Service, and Space*, 842–849.
12. Plotkin, G.D. (1981) 'A Structural Approach to Operational Semantics.' Technical Report DAIMI FN-19, Department of Computer Science, University of Aarhus.
13. Rao, A.S. (1996) 'AgentSpeak(L): BDI Agents Speak Out in a Logical Computable Language.' in Van de Velde, W. & Perram, J.W. (Eds) *Agents Breaking Away.* Springer-Verlag, Berlin.
14. Rao, A.S. & Georgeff, M.P. (1991) 'Modeling Rational Agents within a BDI-Architecture.' *Proceedings of the Second International Conference on Principles of Knowledge Representation and Reasoning (KR'91)*, 473–484.
15. Rao, A.S. & Georgeff, M.P. (1992) 'An Abstract Architecture for Rational Agents.' *Proceedings of the Third International Conference on Principles of Knowledge Representation and Reasoning (KR'92)*, 439–449.
16. Singh, M.P. (1994) *Multiagent Systems.* Springer-Verlag, Berlin.
17. Wagner, G. 'A Logical and Operational Model of Scalable Knowledge- and Perception-Based Agents.' in Van de Velde, W. & Perram, J.W. (Eds) *Agents Breaking Away.* Springer-Verlag, Berlin.
18. Wobcke, W.R. (1996) 'Plans and the Revision of Intentions.' in Zhang, C. & Lukose, D. (Eds) *Distributed Artificial Intelligence: Architecture and Modelling.* Springer-Verlag, Berlin.
19. Wooldridge, M.J. (1995) 'This is MyWorld: The Logic of an Agent-Oriented DAI Testbed.' in Wooldridge, M.J. & Jennings, N.R. (Eds) *Intelligent Agents.* Springer-Verlag, Berlin.
20. Wooldridge, M.J. (1997) 'A Knowledge-Theoretic Semantics for Concurrent MetateM.' in Müller, J.P., Wooldridge, M.J. & Jennings, N.R. (Eds) *Intelligent Agents III.* Springer-Verlag, Berlin.

A Model of Unconstrained Digit Recognition Based on Hypothesis Testing and Data Reconstruction

Sungsoo Yoon[1], Yungcheol Byun[1], Gyeonghwan Kim[2], Yeongwoo Choi[3], and Yillbyung Lee[1]

[1] Dept. of Computer Science, Yonsei University, 134 Shinchon-dong, Seodaemun-gu, 120–749, Seoul, Korea
gomdoli,bcart,yblee@csai.yonsei.ac.kr

[2] Dept. of Electronic Engineering, Sogang University, 1-1 Sinsu-dong, Mapo-gu, 121–110, Seoul, Korea
gkim@ccs.sogang.ac.kr

[3] Dept. of Computer Science, Sookmyung Women's University, 53-12 Cheongpa2-dong, Yongsan-gu, 140–132, Seoul, Korea
ywchoi@cc.sookmyung.ac.kr

Abstract. We propose a model for the recognition of unconstrained digits that may be touched with neighbor ones or damaged by noises such as lines. The recognition of such digits seems to be rather paradoxical because it requires the segmentation of them into understandable units, but proper segmentation needs a priori knowledge of the units and this implies recognition capability. To break up the loop of their interdependencies, we combine two schemes, hypothesis testing and data reconstruction, motivated by the human information system. Hypothesis is set up on the basis of the information obtained from the results of the basic segmentation, and reconstruction of the information is carried out with the knowledge of a guessed digit and then testing for its validity is performed. Since our model tries to construct a guessed digit from input image it can be successful in a variety of situations such as that a digit contains strokes that do not belong to to it, that neighbor digits are touched with each other, and that there are some occluding things like lines. The recognition results of this model for 100 handwritten numeral strings belonging to NIST database and for some artificial digits damaged by line demonstrate the potential its capacity.

1 Introduction

Compared to a isolated one, recognizing a digit among noises or other digits is very difficult problem. Moreover, if the digit is touched or overlapped by noises or other digits, it even seems to be some paradoxical because it requires to separate what is to recognize from other things, but proper separation requires a priori knowledge of the patterns that form meaningful units and this implies recognition capability. Lecolinet and Crettez [1] pointed out that segmenting words

M. Brooks, D. Corbett, and M. Stumptner (Eds.): AI 2001, LNAI 2256, pp. 581–592, 2001.

before recognizing them can be paradoxical, because without any recognizable symbols, one would have to resort to an arbitrary segmentation process, which in turn may result in numerous errors. Recognition-based segmentation also has the same drawbacks: Recognizing a word that contains illegal characters is even more difficult because proper segmentation is not known for the non-recognized parts of the word.

The root cause is that the segmentation and the recognition are interdependent and require the results of the others to complete their work as shown in Fig. 1(a)(inner loop).

The rest of this paper is organized in the following manner: Section 2 reviews the past work, Section 3 gives an overview of the proposed model, Section 4–6 describes its modules, experiments are reported in Section 7, and finally, the paper is concluded in Section 8.

2 Review of Past Work

So far, so many studies have been done to tackle this dilemma. According to Casey and Lecolinet [2], there are three main strategies for character segmentation, and numerous hybrids of the three.

The three main strategies are the holistic method, the dissection approach, and recognition-based segmentation. The pure holistic method does not require segmentation because the system tries to recognize words as a whole. However, the holistic method is only applicable to the restricted cases that predefined lexicon is available or the string length is known [3].

The two remaining ones are basically used for numeral recognition. Most recent researches have a tendency to combine them to complement and compensate for the abovementioned inadequacies that each method exhibits. Arica and Yarman Vural's method [4] considers several candidates for segmentation paths which are then confirmed by the Hidden Markov Model (HMM). The source of their errors may be traced to missed segmentation regions, i.e. the assumption that each digit can be segmented into at most two segments. Yu and Yan [5] detect a candidate touching point based on geometrical information. In cases where the left or right lateral numeral of a single-touching handwritten string can be recognized, recognition information may be used to correct the position of the candidate touching point. But this is limited to single touching cases. Ha, Zimmermann and Bunke [6] combine segmentation-based and segmentation-free methods in a cascading manner to obtain the efficiency of the former method and the accuracy of the latter, and to avoid the defects of the latter such as a higher computational complexity and the increasing segmentation error with the number of numerals. In the segmentation-free module singular points after thinning are employed as clues to extracting the partial strokes, and then weighted graph whose node present the partial strokes and whose arc is the linking cost of two nodes is used to recognition. Rocha et al. [7,8] and Filatov et al. [9] all use a graph to describe symbol prototypes, but in [7,8] the skeletonization of the initial image with help of singular points and in [9] the predefined symbols representing the local graph shape are used to recognize, respectively.

The main differences between existing methods and ours are as follows: Firstly, we use the dynamic tracking method to avoid defects of skeletonization, and adopt the principle of good continuation, which is an underlying property of perceptual grouping in line segregation, for the line segmentation instead of singular points such as an end point, a T-joint, and a crossing point. Secondly recognition is carried out by extracting what needs to build up the assumed digit from the input image instead of by attempting to determine the most consistent combination of the blindly over-segmented subimages. Finally existing works for the recognition of characters damaged by lines has the intrinsic limitation, namely not extendable to curves or other shapes such as that of stains of ink [10], but ours is carried out regardless of the shapes of noises relatively.

3 Overview of Proposed Model

As we mentioned, the segmentation and the recognition are interdependent and so these are paradoxical. The hint as to a solution to these dilemma can be taken from the human information system.

When the stimulus is given to our sensor we might get the basic features that are called *primitives* - simple, basic units of perception, and then hypothesize tentatively based on the *primitives* that there is the object that is most likely to be the cause of our sensory stimulation and then verify the hypothesis by making an attentive analysis of the *primitives*, their compounds, results of partial perception and the knowledge of the assumed object [11,12]. In human case, not only the bottom-up information like *primitives* but also the top-down information such as knowledge about a object play a important role in the recognition, and the bottom-up information is positively reconstructed for effective recognition. We make the virtual information in the absence of any real stimulus. This fact demonstrates that human system has the means to reconstruct the input information [13].

It is believed that all of these faculties make it possible to segment and recognize a certain object among other things efficiently. Our model is based on these facts above. As shown in Fig. 1(a)(outer loop), the rough information is gained by the basic segmentation. Since digits are mainly composed of lines we use for the basic principle of segmentation the property of good continuation which is a fundamental intuitive property of perceptual grouping in line segregation, as advocated by the Gestalt school of psychology [11]. Some numerals can be guessed on the basis of the rough information from the preceding segmentation, and the rough information is reconstructed by the knowledge of the assumed numerals and then testing for its validity is performed.

We define the seven basic elements(BE) according to the shapes of strokes that can be obtained by splitting the strokes of numerals by the criterion of good continuation, and build up a digit prototype(DP) with the BEs and the information of their interrelationship as a priori knowledge. To get the rough information is that the line primitives(LPs) are extracted from the given image after preprocessing. Partial perception is carried out through the similarities between BEs and LPs. The candidate digits are inferred from the similarities of LPs to BEs and their interrelationship information described in DP. The rough information from the image is reconstructed to accord with the knowledge of assumed digits and then testing for the validity of some candidates is performed and the final decision is made. The algorithm proposed in this article can be summarized in Fig. 1(b):

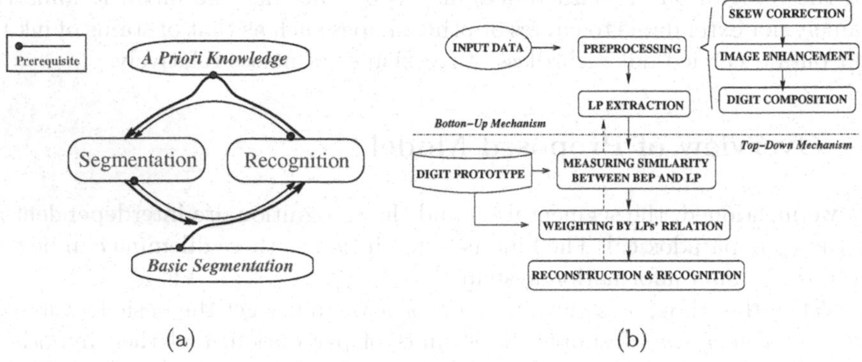

Fig. 1. (a)Segmentation and recognition model, (b)Organization of proposed model

4 Preprocessing

4.1 Stroke Width Estimation

In our application lines are main objects, and so stroke width is one of important parameters to handle images. But it can vary locally depending on writing devices and pressure within a line. It is reasonable, therefore, to use average stroke width. Through projection of horizontal and vertical the number of occurrences of each stroke width are obtained and then average stroke width is estimated base on the peak of histogram which is come from the frequency of stroke width. In case there are many small fragments this estimation may be wrong. So noise removal and defragment method must be followed by this estimation.

4.2 Skew Correction

Handwritten numeral strings often have a number of slants specific to each writing style. This makes it difficult to extract invariant features from the strings and analyze them. Our slant estimation is performed by extracting the contour pixels from the entire string as shown in Fig. 2(b) and by calculating their gradients using a gradient operator like Sobel. Applying the gradient operator to only the contour pixels, which gives the most information about its direction, helps to save time. Estimated global slant is the average of all pixels' angles between 15° and 165° or 195° and 345°(Fig. 2(c)), weighted by their length in the vertical direction. The longer the line, the more accurate the angle [14]. The skewed string is corrected based on the estimated slant angle θ by adjusting x-coordinates of all black pixels with Eq. (1).

$$x_n = x - (y - Height/2) \times tan(\theta) \quad (1)$$
$$y_n = y$$

where x_n and y_n are the coordinates after the correction of a component at (x,y).

There are two problems incurred during the skew correction. First, some digits may touch their neighbors after the slant correction because of the new 8-connected neighbor relationship between the boundary pixels of them. Second, an error in quantization may result in contour jaggedness.

We solve the first problem by applying a connected component technique to the original string images before the correction. Connected components with different indices may be treated as distinct entities even though they may actually be connected after the slant correction.

The second problem is overcome using the linear interpolation method [15]. The linear interpolation assumes that the contribution of a pixel in the neighborhood varies directly with its distance. As a result of the transformation a pixel is given a noninteger address. The intensity of the transformed black pixel is derived from the four nearest pixels according to their relative distances from the calculated address of the transformed pixel. Tow-dimensional interpolation is performed. If the intensity of the transformed pixel is less than a threshold, then it should be given 0(white) and otherwise 1(black). Fig. 2(a) and (d) show the original image and the slant-corrected image, respectively.

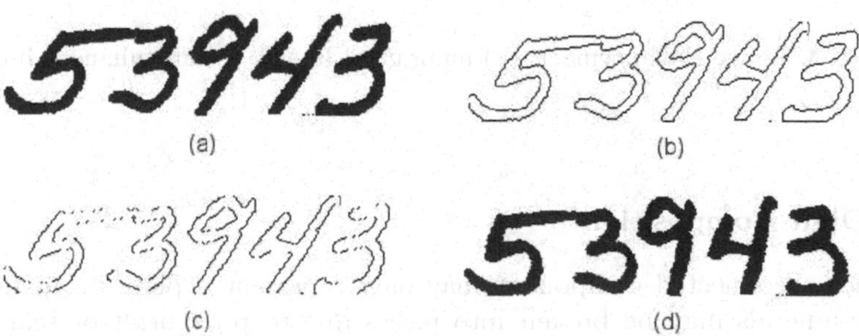

Fig. 2. Skew handling: (a) an original image, (b) a result of edge extraction, (c) Edge points with the vertical factor, (d) an image after skew correction

4.3 Image Enhancement

We need to link together small fragments separated from main strokes and remove noises. The small gaps and fragments of strokes caused by input devices or imperfect binarization may result in errors when analyzing the structure of digits, especially in the case of a connected component-based method like ours. We adopt the selective region growing method [16], which dynamically selects one of four differently shaped neighborhood operators, based on the properties of the neighborhood. As in the case of skew correction, when digits in the input string are very close to each other, region-growing methods usually make the mistake of linking two regions(digits). This problem can be overcome using the connected component information. Only if Eq. 2 is satisfied, two connected components under consideration can be joined together.

$$\begin{aligned} & C_1.i = C_2.i \\ & C_1.s + C_2.s \leq Average\_Blob\_Size \\ & (C_1.lx \leq C_2.lx \text{ and } C_2.rx \leq C_1.rx) \\ & or\ (C_2.lx_1 \leq C_1.lx \text{ and } C_1.rx \leq C_2.rx) \end{aligned} \tag{2}$$

where $C.i$ is the connected component index, $C.s$ is the size of the component, $C.lx$ and $C.rx$ are the left or right x-coordinate of the component, respectively, Average_Blob_Size refers to the average number of foreground pixels in the components whose height is greater than, or equal to, their width. The example of image enhancement is shown in Fig. 3.

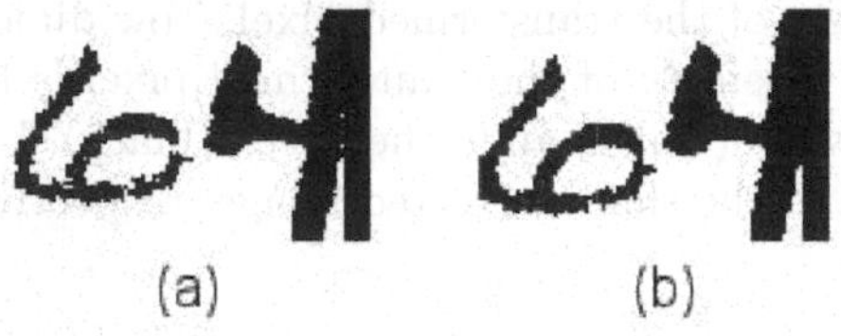

Fig. 3. Image Enhancement: (a) an original Image, (b) an enhanced image

4.4 Digit Composition

At times a connected component may only represent a piece of an individual digit. Numerals may be broken into pieces due to poor print or scan quality, or their strokes may be written in such a way that they appear detached. This frequently happens in the case of digits with long horizontal strokes such as '4' and '5'. So these components should be merged together in order to construct complete digits. The task of composing digits is carried out by the same criteria in Garris' work[17].

5 Segmentation for Rough Information

5.1 Stroke Representation

A scanned image of a drawing is initially an ordered array of pixels representing the an average intensity over a small region. The ability to build up a representation from these individual pixels which exploits relationships such as local proximity and highlights the structure of the underlying components is important for the extraction of features during interpretation and recognition. In our model we use a dynamic line tracking method which do not need a line fitting. As shown in Fig. 4, a circularly symmetric Gaussian bead(GB) with a variable radius is used as a processing unit instead of a pixel and a graph is built up with the GBs. The fitness of each foreground pixel in the image is determined independently from a distribution defined by circularly symmetric Gaussian beads. The bead that has the highest fitness in the searching area is chosen as new neighbor one. Each node of the graph represents GB and its arc between two nodes stands for their connection and direction. The local direction is the same as that of a line passing through center of two GBs. The bead whose diameter is over the *average stroke width* has virtual multi-center.

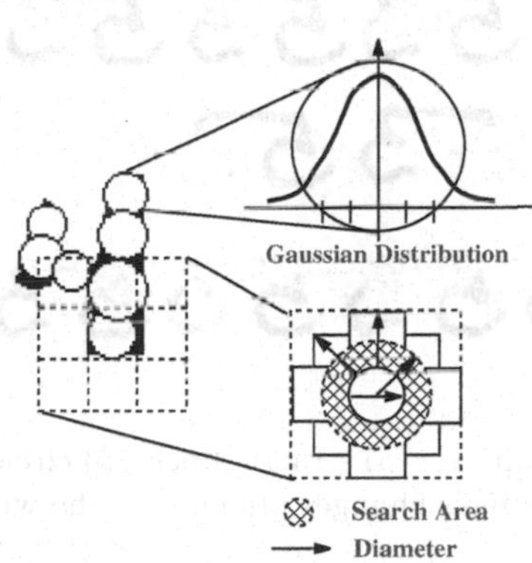

Fig. 4. Stroke representation and construction

5.2 Method

Chen and Hsu [18] have proven that good continuation is feasible and reasonable for smooth line segregation, and satisfied if a line has smooth property of orientation over it. But their hypothetical model is implemented using pixel-based operation. This makes it difficult to interpret the line being segregated as a meaningful unit. The ability to interpret is required for proper segmentation as described in the previous section. So we employ the GB for stroke representation as described above.

Two steps are taken to get smooth lines from the graph obtained in the previous stage. In the first step, straight lines are extracted by gathering the nodes whose direction differences are less than the threshold which is determined by the diameters of the current beads. In the next, smooth curves are obtained by means of merging straight lines into big ones if they have monotonous and smooth changes of direction. Fig. 5 (a) shows the instances of the straight lines and the smooth curves.

In addition to the smooth lines, circles and half circles whose smoothness properties are violated by a specific area need to be detected when the prototype of the assumed digit is composed of them(Fig. 5 (b)). Two kinds of LPs, namely smooth and not smooth, are all used as units in matching between input data and the digit prototypes, as described in the following section. But their scopes of application are different: The LPs with a smooth property are used for all digit prototypes, additional LPs are used exclusively for those prototypes which have circle(s) or half circle(s).

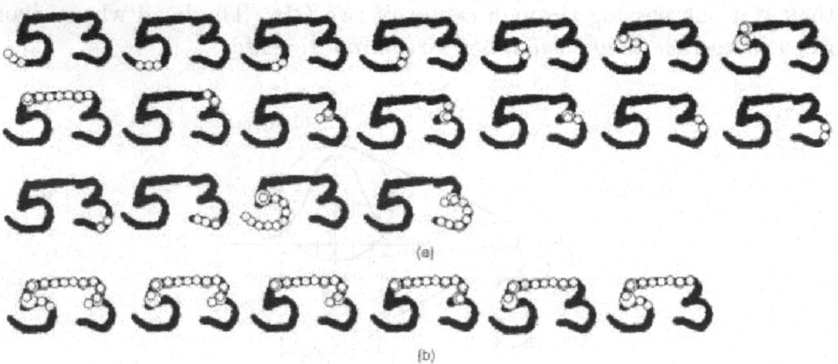

Fig. 5. Extracted line primitives: (a) straight lines, (b) circles and half circles that have no smoothness but monotonous changes of angle on the whole

6 Hypothesis Testing and Data Reconstruction

There are two main processes, top-down and bottom-up, for hypothesis testing as shown in Fig. 6. Among all LPs, including additional half circles and circles, we search the LPs homomorphic for the elements of previously defined prototype(BEPs) with the knowledge of the interconnecting relationships of the BEPs, such as their position, size and connection.

6.1 A Priori Knowledge

The abstract seven elements are defined as the basic element of prototype(BEP). They are composed of three smooth curves and four straight lines : circle,

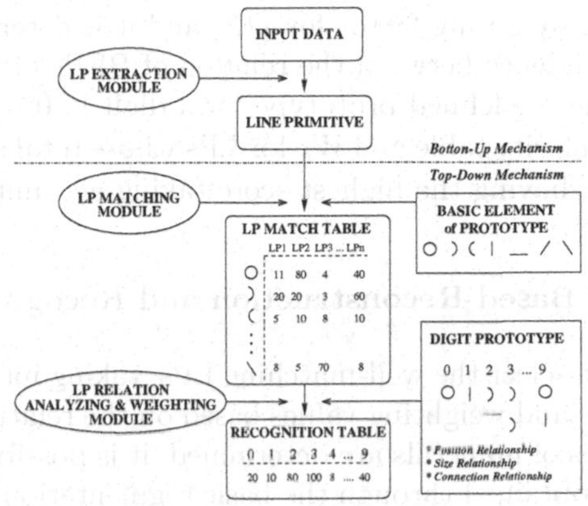

Fig. 6. Top-down and bottom-up mechanism

left(right) open half circle, vertical line, horizon and two diagonal. Their types are derived from the shapes of lines that can be obtained by splitting the strokes of undistorted digits by the criterion of smoothness.

The contents of prototype(DP) for each digit are composed of four fields, namely, basic elements, size relationship, connection relationship and position relationship. Knowledge about which BEPs are required to build up the digit is stored in the the basic elements field. The relative size and relative position information of the BEPs in the DP are stored in the corresponding fields, respectively. On the other hand, connection information is represented by a table in the connection field.

6.2 Digit Inference

To find out which DPs correspond to an input image, the similarity of each LP to BEP should first be calculated individually and then evaluated that of each combination of LPs to the DPs. We use not only LP matching scores but also the weights of their relationship in evaluating the total scores for each of DPs. The steps taken are summarized as follows:.

(i) Let S_{ij} be the similarity of LP_i to BEP_j and define as follows:

$$S_{ij} = \begin{cases} C_1 \times SizeRatio_{ij} & \text{if } BEP_j \text{ is curve} \\ \times AngleScope_i / AngleScope_j & \\ C_2 \times SizeRatio_{ij} \times & \text{otherwise} \\ Average(90 - |AngleScope_i - AngleScope_j|) & \end{cases}$$

where $C_{1,2}$ is constant, $AngleScope_j$ is the angle range of the predefined BEP_j, $AngleScope_i$ is the angle range of LP_i belonging to $AngleScope_j$ and $SizeRatio_{ij}$ is LP_i / BEP_j.

(ii) Make a similarity table by evaluating S_{ij} for all i and j, $0 < i \leq \#$ of extracted LPs, $0 < j < \#$ of predefined BEPs.

(iii) Let W_k be the weighting factor for DP_k and it is determined in proportion to the correspondence between the relation of BEPs of the DP_k and that of LPs. DP_k is the predefined prototype for a digit k, $0 \leq k \leq 9$.
(iv) Search the similarity table and W_k for LPs whose total scores are maximum.
(v) Select the DP_k having the highest score taking account of the W_k.

6.3 Knowledge Based Reconstruction and Recognition

For each of DPs, we select the well-matching LPs, taking into account their similarities to the BEPs and weighting values based on the relationship among them. Once the candidates of numerals are determined, it is possible to reconstruct the rough information obtained through the basic segmentation on the basis of their knowledge. The most reliable LP of a candidate is taken as starting point and LPs are reconstructed to coincide with the BEP of its DP as possible. In our model segmentation is done naturally during the reconstruction. Fig. 7 shows the examples of segmentation through reconstruction. Finally, we select the best one among candidates whose total scores are recalculated on the basis of the reconstructed LPs in the same way as before.

The total scores have four parts: total sum of match scores(TM), each score of LPs corrcsponding BEPs of DP(M), weighting scores between two LPs(W) and indices of LP used(P). To decide whether the input blob is touching and needs to segment or not, we first assume that each DP whose TMs is above a threshold and relatively large represents its own single digit and then investigate the extent of LPs' overlapping. In cases where there is little or no overlapping, each of them represents a single digit and segmentation is done naturally. If the shared parts of LPs that belong to different digits are too big for an individual digit then it is one digit having the the highest matching score. If some LPs share a bit which is significant enough to affect the shape of BEP heuristic knowledge is applied to segmentation and recognition. Because it is known that the shared parts are which part of the digits segmentation and recognition can be safely done. For example, as shown in Fig. 7(a), the shared parts is understood to be horizontal stroke and so it is little risk to split it in two.

7 Experimental Results

The proposed model is tested using the artificial digits damaged by line and the NIST SD3 database, provided by the American National Institute of Standards and Technology (NIST) in 1992. We use 10 artificial digits and 100 numeral strings with 2 ~10 lengths, where 21 strings have broken strokes, 29 contain small fragments, 34 exhibit two-digit touching and 1 data has three-digit touching. In our model one prototype per class is used to recognize numerals. The results show that 95.5% of all strings are correctly recognized at zero-reject level. The details are summarized in Table 1. The causes of errors are incorrect LP extraction and digit composition failure.

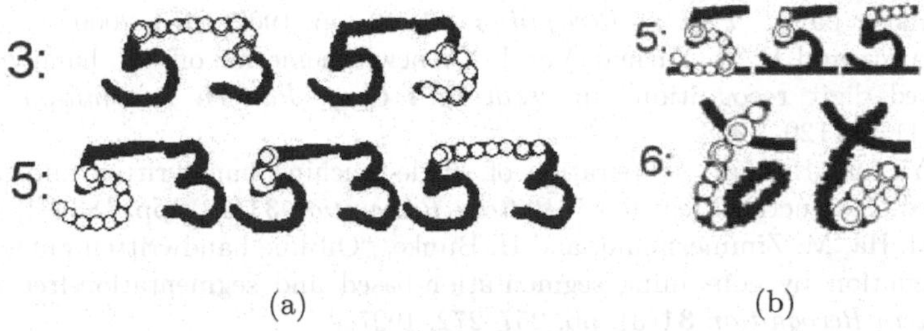

Fig. 7. Reconstruction and recognition: (a)Example of touching digits, (b)Example of digits damaged by line

Table 1. Recognition results

String length	Number of tested string	Recognition rate(in %)
Artifical digit	10	100
2	24	92
3	21	100
4	21	95
5	17	94
6	12	92
10	5	100
Total	110	95.5

8 Conclusions

Segmentation and recognition are mutually dependent. Proper segmentation would need the help of a recognizer, who in turn can give critical help only if segmentation is well done. So we combine two schemes, hypothesis testing and data reconstruction, motivated by the human information system. Since our model tries to construct the assumed digit from input image it can be successful in a variety of situations such as that a digit contains strokes that do not belong to to it, that neighbor digits are touched each other, and that there are some occluding things like lines. The experimental results demonstrate the performance and capacity of our model.

References

1. E. Lecolinet and J. Crettez, "A grapheme-based segmentation technique for cursive script recognition," in *1st Int'l Conf. Document Analysis and Recognition, Saint-Marlo, Frances*, pp. 740–748, Sept. 1991.
2. R. G. Casey and E. Lecolinet, "A survey of methods and strategies in character segmentation," *IEEE Trans. on Pattern Analysis and Machine Intelligence* **18**(7), pp. 690–706, 1996.

3. X. Wang, V. Govindaraju, and S. Srihari, "Holistic recognition of handwritten character pairs," *Pattern Recognition* **33**(12), pp. 1967–1973, 2000.
4. N. Arica and F. T. Yarman-Vural, "A new scheme for off-line handwritten connected digit recognition," in *14th Int'l Conf. Pattern Recognition, Australia*, pp. 1127–1129, 1998.
5. D. Yu and H. Yan, "Separation of single-touching handwritten numeral strings based on structural features," *Pattern Recognition* **31**(12), pp. 1835–1847, 1998.
6. T. M. Ha, M. Zimmermann, and H. Bunke, "Off-line handwritten numeral strings recognition by combining segmentation-based and segmentation-free methods," *Pattern Recognition* **31**(3), pp. 257–272, 1997.
7. J. Rocha and T. Pavlidis, "A solution to the problem of touching and broken characters," in *2nd Int'l Conf. Document Analysis and Recognition, Tsukuba, Japan*, pp. 602–605, Oct. 1993.
8. J. Rocha and T. Pavlidis, "Character recognition without segmentation," *IEEE Trans. on Pattern Analysis and Machine Intelligence* **17**(9), pp. 903–909, 1995.
9. A. Filatov, A. Gitis, and I. Kil, "Graph-based handwritten digit string recognition," in *3rd Int'l Conf. Document Analysis and Recognition, Montreal, Canada*, pp. 845–848, Aug. 1995.
10. K. Lee, H. Byun, and Y. Lee, "Robust reconstruction of damaged character images on the form documents," *Graphics Recognition: Algorithms and Systems, Selected Papers from 2nd Int'l Workshop on Grephics Recognition, 1997, LNCS* **1389**, pp. 149–162, 1998.
11. E. B. Goldstein, *Sensation and Perception*, ch. Perceiving Objects, pp. 175–213. Brooks/Cole, 5 ed., 1999.
12. R. L. Gregory, *Eye and brain*, McGraw-Hill, NewYork, 2 ed., 1973.
13. L. Spillmann and J. S. Werner, *Visual Perception: The Neurophysiological Foundations*, ch. Form Perception and Attention: Striate Cortex and Beyond, pp. 273–316. Academic Press, Inc, San Diego, 1990.
14. G. Kim and V. Govindaraju, "Efficient chain code based image manipulation for handwritten word recognition," in *Proc. SPIE Symp. on Electronic Image Science and Technology (Document Recognition III), San Jose, California*, pp. 2660, 262–272, Feb. 1996.
15. C. A. Lindley, *Practical Image Processing in C: Acquisition,Manipulation, Storage*, pp. 424–426. Wiley press, 1991.
16. Z. Shi and V. Govindaraju, "Character image enhancement by selective region-growing," *Pattern Recognition Letters* **17**, pp. 523–527, 1996.
17. M. D. Garris, "Component-based handprint segmentation using adaptive writing style model." NIST Internal Report 5843, June 1996.
18. Y. S. Chen and W. H. Hsu, "An interpretive model of line continuation in human visual perception," *Pattern Recognition* **22**(5), pp. 619–639, 1989.

Collecting Quality Data for Database Mining

Chengqi Zhang and Shichao Zhang

School of Computing and Mathematics
Deakin University, Geelong Victoria 3217, Australia
{chengqi, scz}@deakin.edu.au

Abstract. Data collecting is necessary to some organizations such as nuclear power plants and earthquake bureaus, which have very small databases. Traditional data collecting is to obtain necessary data from internal and external data-sources and join all data together to create a homogeneous huge database. Because collected data may be untrusty, it can disguise really useful patterns in data. In this paper, breaking away traditional data collecting mode that deals with internal and external data equally, we argue that the first step for utilizing external data is to identify quality data in data-sources for given mining tasks. Pre- and post-analysis techniques are thus advocated for generating quality data.
Keywords: Data preprocessing, data collecting, data mining, quality data, data sharing.

1 Introduction

In knowledge discovery in databases (KDD), data preprocessing includes data collecting, data cleaning, data selection, and data transformation [4]. So data collecting is very important in the process of knowledge discovery in databases. It is to obtain necessary data from various internal and external sources and join data together to create a homogeneous huge dataset. Data preprocessing [2] may be more time consuming and presents more challenges than data mining.

In existing techniques, while internal and external data are together joined into a single dataset for mining tasks, they play equally roles in the dataset. However, because collected data may be untrusty even fraudulent, it can disguise really useful patterns in data. In particular, if external data is not preprocessed before it is applied, it causes that identified patterns from data can conduct an application high-risk.

In this paper, breaking away traditional data collecting mode that deals with internal and external data equally, we argue that the first step for utilizing external data is to identify quality data in data-sources for given mining tasks, called as *quality data model*. Pre- and post-analysis techniques are thus advocated for generating quality data. Due to the fact that only relevant, uncontradictable and high-trusty data-sources are suggested to be mined in our approach, it can not only reduce the search cost, but also generate quality patterns. The approach is particularly useful to companies/organizations such as nuclear power plants and earthquake bureaus, which have some very small databases but require trusty knowledge for their applications.

M. Brooks, D. Corbett, and M. Stumptner (Eds.): AI 2001, LNAI 2256, pp. 593–604, 2001.

The rest of this paper is organized as follows. We begin with stating the problems statement in Section 2. In Section 3 we present effectiveness of collecting quality data. In Section 4, we illustrate how to identify believable data-sources by pre-analysis. Section 5 also advocates a post-analysis for identifying believable data-sources. Section 6 evaluates the effectiveness of the proposed framework. We summarize this paper in last section.

2 Problems Statement

In this section, we formulate the problems in data collecting and our approach.

2.1 Problems Faced by Data Collecting

Traditional data collecting among data-sources is directly to borrow data from external data-sources to form a big dataset for a given mining task. This means that internal and external data play equally important roles in the mining task.

Indeed, data collecting is necessary to some companies/organizations such as nuclear power plants and earthquake bureaus, which have very small databases. For example, because accidents in nuclear power plants cause many environmental disasters and create economical and ecological damage as well as endangering people's life, automatic surveillance and early nuclear accident detection have received much attention. To reduce nuclear accidents, we need trusty knowledge for controlling nuclear accidents. However, a nuclear accident database often contains data too little to form trustful patterns. So, mining the accident database in the nuclear power plant must depend on external data.

Also, a company that has a large database may want to collect external data for high-profit purpose when a decision is made. So, employing external data has become a challenging topic in data mining.

Joining all data together from internal and external data-sources directly to form a single dataset for mining task has three main limitations below.

1. Low-quality (including noisy, erroneous, ambiguity, untrusty, and fraudulent) data disguises really useful patterns in data.
2. Which of the collected data-sources are relevant to a given mining task is not made clear. In other words, data in irrelevant data-sources plays equally important role in the mining task.
3. Also, it doesn't confirm that which of collected data-sources are really useful to the mining task.

For the sake of noise and related issues, external data is certainly dirty. Dirty data can disguise really useful patterns in data and cause failing applications. For example, if a stock investor gathers fraudulent information and the information is directly applied to his/her investment decisions, he/she may, however, go bankruptcy. Hence, it is very important that selects quality external data.

Based on the above analysis, the problem for our research can be formulated as follows.

Given a mining task on dataset DS and n data-sources collected for the mining task, we are interested in identifying quality data in external data by pre-analysis and post-analysis.

There are diverse techniques useful to other steps of the process of KDD in such as [5][6]. This paper focuses on identifying believable data-sources collected.

2.2 Our Approach

This paper proposes an approach for identifying believable external data-sources as the first step of utilizing external data, which is toward databases mining.

1. *Pre-analysis,* which is an insight into such as the relevant and uncontradictable data-sources collected. It is useful when we have no any other information about the data-sources.
2. *Post-analysis,* which is to learn the data-sources upon historical data (training set).

Our experiments show that our quality data model is effective and promising.

3 Effectiveness of Identifying Quality Data

To show the effectiveness of identifying quality data, an example is used below. Without loss of generality, we often call a data-source as a database or a relation.

Consider an internal database (data-source) $ID = \{(A, B, C); (A, C)\}$ and six external (collected) databases (data-sources) D_1, D_2, $\cdots$, D_6 as follows.

$$D_1 = \{(A, B, C, D); (B, C); (A, B, C); (A, C)\}$$
$$D_2 = \{(A, B); (A, C); (A, B, C); (B, C); (A, B, D)\}$$
$$D_3 = \{(B, C, D); (A, B, C); (B, C); (A, D)\}$$
$$D_4 = \{(A, F, G, H, I, J); (E, F, H); (F, H)\}$$
$$D_5 = \{(B, E, F, H, J); (F, H); (F, H, J); (E, J)\}$$
$$D_6 = \{(C, F, H, I, J); (E, H, J); (E, F, H); (E, I)\}$$

where each database has several transactions, separated by semicolon; each transaction contains several items, separated by commas.

Let $minsupp = 0.5$. We can search local frequent itemsets in D_1 as follows: A, B, C, AB, AC, BC, and ABC, where "XY" means the conjunction of X and Y. Local frequent itemsets in D_2 are searched as follows: A, B, C, and AB. Local frequent itemsets in D_3 are searched as follows: A, B, C, and BC.

Local frequent itemsets in D_4 are searched as follows: F, H, and FH. Local frequent itemsets in D_5 are searched as follows: E, F, H, J, EJ, FH, FJ, and

FHJ. Local frequent itemsets in D_6 are searched as follows: E, F, H, I, J, EH, FH, and HJ.

Local frequent itemsets in internal database ID are searched as follows: A, B, C, AB, AC, BC, and ABC.

Let's examine the existing techniques check if some of them can serve the purpose of selection, pretending no knowledge about which database contains interesting information.

1. The first solution (traditional data collecting technique) is to put all data together from the given database and the six collected databases to create a single database $TD = ID \cup D_1 \cup D_2 \cup \cdots \cup D_6$, which has 26 transactions. We now search the above (local) frequent itemsets in TD listed in Table 1.

Table 1. The information of local frequent itemsets in the database TD

Itemsets	Frequency	$\geq minsupp$	Itemsets	Frequency	$\geq minsupp$
A	12	n	B	12	n
C	13	y	AB	7	n
AC	8	n	BC	9	n
ABC	5	n	E	6	n
F	8	n	H	9	n
I	3	n	J	6	n
EH	4	n	EJ	3	n
FH	8	n	HJ	5	n
FHJ	4	n			

There is only one frequent itemset C when $minsupp = 0.5$. To discover the database TD, we need another minimum support specified by users or experts. For example, $minsupp = 0.115$. Then all the above itemsets listed in Table 1 are frequent itemsets. And itemsets such as AD, BD, and EF are also frequent itemsets in TD.

Actually, in the above six external databases, only the former three databases are likely relevant to the internal database. The later three databases are unlikely relevant to the internal database. The technique developed in this paper can meet the requirement of the above application. It is regarded as the third solution as follows.

2. The second solution is the quality data model proposed in this paper. The approach works as follows. Firstly, it selects believable databases: $class_1 = \{D_1, D_2, D_3\}$. Secondly, the databases and internal database are put into a single database TD_1, which TD_1 has 13 transactions. Finally, it discovers TD_1. In this way, we can receive a better effectiveness from the quality data model. Table 2 illustrates the effectiveness of identifying quality data in TD_1.

Table 2. The information of local frequent itemsets in the database TD_1

Itemsets	Frequency	$\geq minsupp$	Itemsets	Frequency	$\geq minsupp$
A	11	y	B	11	y
C	12	y	AB	7	n
AC	8	y	BC	9	y
ABC	5	n			

By $minsupp = 0.5$, A, B, C, AC, and BC are frequent itemsets in TD_1.

From the above, commonly used technique can not only increase search cost, but also disguise the useful patterns due the fact that huge amounts of irrelevant data are included. quality data model presented a significant effectiveness. The following sections will explore basic techniques for identifying quality data.

4 Data-Source Pre-analysis

As have seen, quality data model is toward database mining. So, we propose to determine which of data-sources are trusty by pre- and post-analysis in this paper.

For a given data-source DS and the set $DSSet$ of collected data-sources DS_1, $DS_2, \cdots, DS_m$, we first pre-analyze the data-sources from $DSSet$ using their features and rules when we have no any other information about the data-sources. It is to select external data-sources that are relevant and uncontradictable to DS.

4.1 Relevant Data-Sources Selecting

Let $Feature(DS_i)$ be the set of all features [1] in DS_i $(i = 1, 2, \cdots, m)$. We need to select data-sources from $DSSet = \{DS_1, DS_2, \cdots, DS_m\}$ for DS such that each data-source is relevant to a data-source DS under a measurement. The features of data-sources can be used to measure the closeness of a pair of data-sources. We call the measure as sim that is defined as follows.

1. A function for the similarity between the feature sets of two data-sources DS_i and DS_j is defined as follows.

$$sim(DS_i, DS_j) = \frac{|Feature(DS_i) \cap Feature(DS_j)|}{|Feature(DS_i) \cup Feature(DS_j)|}$$

where "$\cap$" denotes set intersection, "$\cup$" denotes set union, "$|Feature(DS_i) \cap Feature(DS_j)|$" is the number of elements in set $Feature(DS_i) \cap Feature(DS_j)$.

[1] The features of a data-source is often selected from its data. If we can only share the rules (patterns) of the data-source, the features of the data-source can selected from the rules (patterns).

In the above definition of similarity $sim : DSSet \times DSSet \rightarrow [0, 1]$, we take the size of the intersection of a pair of the feature sets of data-sources to measure the closeness of the two data-sources. That is, a large intersection corresponds to a high degree of similarity, whereas two data-sources with a small intersection are considered to be rather dissimilar.

We now illustrate the use of the above similarity by an example as follows.

Example 1 *Let* $Feature(DS_1) = \{a_1, a_2, a_3\}$ *and* $Feature(DS_2) = \{a_2, a_3, b_1, b_2\}$ *be two sets of features of two data-sources* DS_1 *and* DS_2*, respectively. The similarity between* DS_1 *and* DS_2 *is as follows.*

$$sim(DS_1, DS_2) = \frac{|Feature(DS_1) \cap Feature(DS_2)|}{|Feature(DS_1) \cup Feature(DS_2)|} = \frac{2}{5} = 0.4.$$

Note that, if $sim(DS_i, DS_j) = 1$, it only means that $Feature(DS_i) = Feature(DS_j)$ or, DS_i and DS_j can be certainly relevant under measure sim. It doesn't mean that $DS_i = DS_j$ when $sim(DS_i, DS_j) = 1$.

We have proposed a simple and understandable function for measuring the similarity of pairs of data-sources. Certainly, we can construct more functions for similarity using such as the weights of features. It is not the goal of this paper. Our work in this paper is only to advocate how to construct measures for similarity. Using the above similarity on data-sources, we define data-sources α-relevant to DS below.

Definition 1 *A data-source* DS_i *is* α*-relevant to* DS *under the measure* sim *if* $sim(DS_i, DS) > \alpha$*, where* α (> 0) *is a threshold.*

For example, let $\alpha = 0.4$. Consider the data $Feature(DS_1) = \{i_1, i_2, i_3, i_4, i_5\}$ and $Feature(DS) = \{i_1, i_3, i_4, i_5, i_6, i_7\}$, because $sim(DS_1, DS) = 0.571 > \alpha = 0.4$, the data-source DS_1 is 0.4-relevant to DS.

Definition 2 *Let* $DSSet$ *be the set of* m *data-sources* $D_1, D_2, \cdots, D_m$*. The set of the selected data-sources in* $DSSet$ *that are* α*-relevant to a data-source* DS *under the similarity measure* sim*, denoted as* $RDS(DS, DSSet, sim, \alpha)$*, is defined as follows:*

$$RDS(DS, DSSet, sim, \alpha) = \{ds \in DSSet | ds \textit{ is } \alpha\textit{-relevant to } DS\}.$$

4.2 Uncontradictable Data-Sources Selecting

Selecting relevant data-sources considers their features. Also, we can check the contradiction between pairs of data-sources by comparing their knowledge if we have no any other information about the data-sources. For two data-sources DS_i and DS_j, they are contradictive if there is at least one proposition A such that A holds in DS_i and $\neg A$ holds in DS_j. A is called as a contradictive proposition in data-sources DS_i and DS_j. We use the ratio of contradictive propositions in data-sources DS_i and DS_j to measure the contradiction between the two data-sources. We now define a function for contradiction $contrad$ below.

Let $Rule(DS_i)$ be the set of all propositions in DS_i $(i = 1, 2, \cdots, m)$. We need to select data-sources from $DSSet = \{DS_1, DS_2, \cdots, DS_m\}$ for DS such that each data-source is uncontradictable to a data-source DS under a measurement.

2. We can construct contradiction *contrad* by the ratio of contradictive propositions in data-sources DS_i and DS_j as follows.

$$contrad(DS_i, DS_j) = \frac{\text{number of contradictive propositions in } DS_i \text{ and } DS_j}{|Rule(DS_i) \cup Rule(DS_j)|}$$

In the above definition of contradiction $contrad : DSSet \times DSSet \to [0, 1]$, we take the number of contradictive propositions in data-sources to measure the contradiction of the two data-sources. That is, a large number of contradictive propositions correspond to a high degree of contradiction, whereas two data-sources with a small intersection are considered to be rather uncontradiction.

We illustrate the use of the contradiction *contrad* by an example below.

Example 2 *Let* $Rule(DS_1) = \{A, B, \neg C, D\}$ *and* $Rule(DS_2) = \{A, \neg B, C, E, F\}$ *be two sets of propositions of two data-sources* DS_1 *and* DS_2 *respectively. The contradiction between* DS_1 *and* DS_2 *is measured as follows.*

$$contrad(DS_1,\ DS_2) = \frac{number\ of\ contradictive\ propositions\ in\ DS_1\ and\ DS_2}{|Rule(DS_1) \cup Rule(DS_2)|}$$
$$= \frac{2}{6} = 0.3333.$$

Using the above contradiction on data-sources, we define data-sources β-uncontradictable to DS below.

Definition 3 *A data-source* DS_i *is* β*-uncontradictable to a data-source* DS_j *under the measure contrad if* $1 - contrad(DS_i, DS_j) > \beta$, *where* β (> 0) *is a threshold.*

For example, let $\beta = 0.8$. Consider the data in Example 2, because $1 - contrad(DS_1, DS_2) = 1 - 0.3333 = 0.6667 < \beta = 0.8$, the data-source DS_1 is not 0.8-uncontradictable to DS_2.

Definition 4 *Let* $DSSet$ *be the set of* m *data-sources* $DS_1, DS_2, \cdots, DS_m$. *The set of the selected data-sources in* $DSSet$ *that are* β*-uncontradictable to a data-source* DS *under the contradiction measure contrad, denoted as* $UDS(DS, DSSet, contrad, \beta)$, *is defined as follows:*

$$UDS(DS, DSSet, contrad, \beta) = \{ds \in DSSet | ds\ is\ \alpha\text{-}uncontradictable\ to\ DS\}.$$

Table 3. Past data of using external knowledge

	$DS1$	$DS2$	$DS3$	$DS4$	result
a_1		1	1	1	yes
a_2	1	1	1	1	yes
a_3	1	1			no
a_4	1		1		no
a_5	1		1		no
a_6	1			1	yes
a_7		1	1	1	yes
a_8	1	1	1		yes
a_9	1	1			no
a_{10}	1	1	1	1	yes

5 Data-Source Post-analysis

When we have some information such as cases of applying external data-sources (it is often a training set), collected data can be post-analyzed. Suppose we have applied external data-sources $DS1$, $DS2$, $DS3$, and $DS4$ for ten real-world applications in Table 3.
where, DSi stands for the ith data-source; a_i indicates the ith application; "1" stands for that the knowledge in a data-source is applied to an application, we use $DSi = 1$ to indicate that ith data-source is applied to an application; "*result*" measures the success of the applications, "$result = yes$" means that an application is successful and, "$result = no$" means that an application is failure. For application a_1, three data-sources $DS2$, $DS3$, and $DS4$ have been applied.

Using historical data in tables such as Table 3, we can post-analyze the collected knowledge and determine which of data-sources are trusty and which of patterns collected are believable. The above instance only elucidates how to use possible information to judge the trustfulness of a data-source. If we can obtain more information, we can make a judgement on trustfulness by synthesizing.

We now advocate a method for solving trusty degrees of data-sources by the above historical data. The cases of applying the four data-sources $DS1$, $DS2$, $DS3$, and $DS4$ in Table 3 are listed in Table 4.

Table 4. The cases of applying the four data-sources $DS1$, $DS2$, $DS3$, and $DS4$

	frequency	*success*	*fail*	success-ratio
$DS1$	8	4	4	0.5
$DS2$	7	5	2	0.714
$DS3$	7	5	2	0.714
$DS4$	5	5	0	1

where, *frequency* is the number of applications that use a data-source; *success* is the success times of applications when a data-source was applied; *failure* is the fail times of applications when a data-source was applied; "success-ratio" is *success*/*frequency*.

From the above table, $DS1$ was applied 8 times with success-ratio 0.5, $DS2$ was applied 7 times with success-ratio 0.714, $DS3$ was applied 7 times with success-ratio 0.714, $DS4$ was applied 5 times with success-ratio 1.

Certainly, we can use the success-ratios to determine the trusty degrees of the data-sources. One way is to normalize the success-ratios as the trusty degrees of the data-sources below.

$$td_{DS1} = \frac{0.5}{0.5 + 0.714 + 0.714 + 1} = 0.167,$$
$$td_{DS2} = \frac{0.714}{0.5 + 0.714 + 0.714 + 1} = 0.238,$$
$$td_{DS3} = \frac{0.714}{0.5 + 0.714 + 0.714 + 1} = 0.238,$$
$$td_{DS4} = \frac{1}{0.5 + 0.714 + 0.714 + 1} = 0.357,$$

where td_{DSi} stands for the trusty degree of the ith data-source ($i = 1, 2, 3, 4$).

We have seen that, data-source $DS4$ has the highest success-ratio and it has the highest trusty degree; $DS1$ has the lowest success-ratio and it has the lowest trusty degree.

Furthermore, the the trusty degree of DS_i ($i = 1, 2, \cdots, n$) can be defined as follows.

$$td_{DS_i} = \frac{\text{success-ratio of } DS_i}{\sum_{j=1}^{n} \text{success-ratio of } DS_j}.$$

6 Algorithm Designing

In our approach, we focus on only three factors: relevance, uncontradictability, and trustfulness when data-sources are ranked. Other factors are as similar as the above. To synthesize the three factors for ranking, we can use weighting techniques in [3]. We now design the algorithm of ranking the external data-sources by pre- and post-analysis as follows.

Algorithm 1 *Data-sourcesRank*
begin
Input: *DS: data-source; DS_i: m data-sources;*
Output: *S: a set of data-sources;*
(1) **input** the collected data-sources DS_i relevant to DS;
(2) **transform** the data in each data-source into rules;
(3) **pre-analyze** the data-source DS_1, $\cdots$, DS_m;

(4) **rank** the data-sources by synthesizing the pre-analyzing results decreasingly;
(5) **post-analyze** the data-sources according to the ranking by pre-analysis;
(6) **rank** the data-sources by synthesizing the post-analyzing results decreasingly;
(7) **let** $S \leftarrow$ all high-rank data-sources;
(8) **output** S;
end

The algorithm *Data-sourcesRank* is to rank the collected m data-sources $DS_1, DS_2, \cdots, DS_m$ relevant to the data-source DS according to the proposed framework, where S is the set of all high-rank data-sources.

Step (1) inputs the collected data-sources $DS_1, DS_2, \cdots, DS_m$ relevant to the data-source DS. Step (2) transforms the data in data-sources into rules by mining for the purpose of uncontradiction analysis. Step (3) pre-analyzes the data-sources using their features and knowledge to select data-sources that are relevant and uncontradictable to DS. Step (4) first synthesizes the results of pre-analysis by weighting and then rank the external data-sources according to the synthesizing results decreasingly. Step (5) is to generate the trusty degrees of the selected data-sources in Step (4) by historical data. For convenience, Step (6) ranks the data-sources by synthesizing the pre-analysis (including relevance and uncontradictability) and post-analysis (trusty degrees) decreasingly. Step (7) selects all high-rank data-sources and saves them into S. And the final result S is output in Step (8), where the data-sources in S are suggested to user as believable data-sources.

7 Experiments

To evaluate the effectiveness of the proposed framework, we have done some experiments by Java in DELL. Our experiments are designed to test the effectiveness of the proposed approach in applications, which is with respect to the preprocessing by the algorithm *Data-sourcesRank* from three aspects: relevance, uncontradiction, and trustfulness of external data-sources by pre- and post-analysis.

We select 10 data-sources, in which each data-source has a set of rules. 8 data-sources of them are trusty. 2 data-sources of them contain rules contradictable to a given data-source, where the contradictable rules always cause failing applications, which is used to demonstrate the profit from the proposed framework. The parameters of experimental data-sources are summarized as follows.
where DSi is the ith data-source, "size" is the number of rules in a data-source, "trusty" is the trustfulness of a data-source. "yes" indicates trusty, and "no" stands for non-trusty.

Firstly, we can classify the data-sources into three classes $c_1 = \{DS1, DS2, DS4, DS5, DS6, DS8, DS9, DS10\}$, $c_2 = \{DS3\}$, and $c_3 = \{DS7\}$ according to the relevance and contradiction.

Table 5. The Experimental data-sources

data-source	size	trusty	data-source	size	trusty
$DS1$	41	yes	$DS2$	50	yes
$DS3$	25	no	$DS4$	34	yes
$DS5$	57	yes	$DS6$	23	yes
$DS7$	44	no	$DS8$	29	yes
$DS9$	40	yes	$DS10$	18	yes

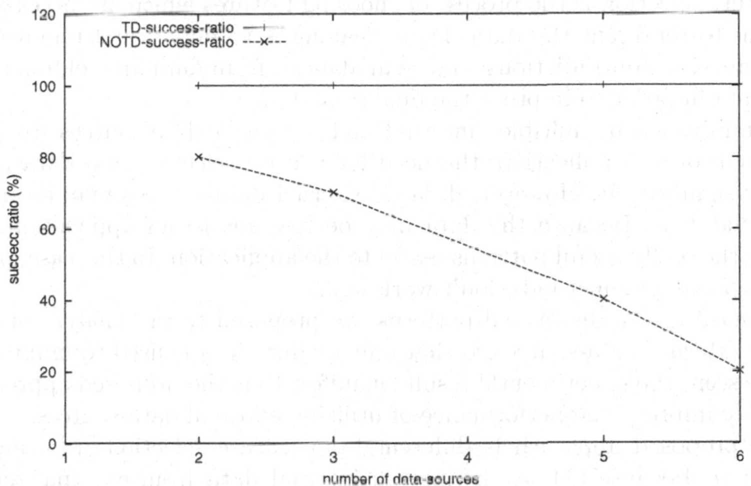

Fig. 1. The success ratios of TD and $NOTD$

Secondly, we use the rules of data-sources in a class as possible for applications. After several applications, we rank the data-sources in a table by trustfulness. The data-sources in the class c_1 have high-rank and the data-sources in the class c_2 and c_3 have low-rank.

Thirdly, the data-sources in the class c_1 are recommended to be trusty. And then the rules in the data-sources are used to applications.

We have done two sets of experiments for four classes of applications of a data-source DS, where the data-source has 14 rules. One is that DS uses only rules from trusty data-sources, called as TD. Another is called as $NOTD$, which DS randomly borrows external rules from other data-sources. Each class of applications consists of ten reasoning tasks. The first class of application needs rules from 2 data-sources. The second class of application needs 3 from two data-sources. The third class of application needs rules from 5 data-sources. The fourth class of application needs rules from 6 data-sources. The success ratios of TD and $NOTD$ are depicted in Figure 1.

In Figure 1, TD model received a 100% success-ratio because (1) the proposed technique is utilized and (2) the given reasoning tasks can be finished in class c_1. $NOTD$ model obtained a low success-ratio decreasingly because the fraudulent rules in $DS3$ and $DS7$ are also used to the tasks.

8 Conclusions

To our knowledge, little work on identifying believable external data-sources has been reported in current literature. However, the efforts on feature selection [1][6] and data cleaning [7] seem quite related to this work.

Feature selection is the process of choosing features which are necessary and sufficient to represent the data. Data cleaning is to detect and remove errors, inconsistencies, contradictions, and redundancies from data and, eliminate irrelevant data in order to improve the quality of data.

Certainly, when multiple (internal and external) data-sources need to be integrated for an application, the need for feature selection and data cleaning increase significantly. However, data in external data-sources may be untrusty even fraudulent. Because the data may be relevant to an application, it can disguise the really useful patterns useful to the application. In this case, previous data preprocessing methods don't work well.

To make use of discovered patterns, we proposed to pre-analyze and post-analyze external data-sources so that only quality data is used to mining tasks. As have seen, the experimental results manifest that the proposed approach can effectively improve the performance of utilizing external data-sources.

The proposed approach is different from feature selection [1][6] and data cleaning [7] because (1) we distinguish internal data from external data; (2) our operating objects may be datasets (data-sources); and (3) untrusty and fraudulent data are eliminated by pre-analysis and post-analysis.

References

1. A. Blum and P. Langley, Selection of relevant features and examples in machine learning. *Artificial Intelligence*, Vol. 97 (1997): 245-271.
2. U. M. Fayyad and E. Simoudis, Data mining and knowledge discovery. *Proc. of 1st International Conf. Prac. App. KDD& Data Mining*, 1997: 3-16.
3. I. Good, Probability and the weighting of evidence. Charles Griffin, London, 1950.
4. J. Han, " Data Mining ", in J. Urban and P. Dasgupta (eds.), *Encyclopedia of Distributed Computing*, Kluwer Academic Publishers, 1999.
5. J. Han, J. Pei, and Y. Yin, Mining frequent patterns without candidate generation. In: *Proceedings of ACM SIGMOD*, 2000: 1-12.
6. H. Liu and H. Motoda *Feature Selection for Knowledge Discovery and Data Mining*, Kluwer Academic Publishers, July 1998.
7. X. Wu and D. Urpani, Induction by Attribute Elimination, *IEEE TKDE*, Vol. 11, 5(1999): 805-812.

Further Pruning for Efficient Association Rule Discovery

Songmao Zhang and Geoffrey I. Webb

School of Computing and Mathematics, Deakin University
Geelong, Victoria 3217, Australia

Abstract. The Apriori algorithm's frequent itemset approach has become the standard approach to discovering association rules. However, the computation requirements of the frequent itemset approach are infeasible for dense data and the approach is unable to discover infrequent associations. OPUS_AR is an efficient algorithm for association rule discovery that does not utilize frequent itemsets and hence avoids these problems. It can reduce search time by using additional constraints on the search space as well as constraints on itemset frequency. However, the effectiveness of the pruning rules used during search will determine the efficiency of its search. This paper presents and analyses pruning rules for use with OPUS_AR. We demonstrate that application of OPUS_AR is feasible for a number of datasets for which application of the frequent itemset approach is infeasible and that the new pruning rules can reduce compute time by more than 40%.

Keywords: machine learning, search.

1 Introduction

Association rule discovery has been dominated by the frequent itemset strategy as exemplified by the Apriori algorithm [2]. OPUS_AR utilizes an alternative association rule discovery strategy to find associations without first finding frequent itemsets [16]. This avoids the need to retain the set of frequent itemsets in memory, a requirement that makes the frequent itemset strategy infeasible for dense data [4]. This paper presents and evaluates pruning rules and other strategies that improve the computational efficiency of OPUS_AR.

We characterize the association rule discovery task as follows.

- A *dataset* is a finite set of *records* where each record is an element to which we apply Boolean predicates called *conditions*.
- An *itemset* is a set of conditions. The name *itemset* derives from association rule discovery's origins in market basket analysis where each condition denotes the presence of an item in a market basket.
- *coverset*(I) denotes the set of records from a dataset that satisfy itemset I.
- An *association rule* consists of two conjunctions of conditions called the *antecedent* and *consequent* and associated statistics describing the frequency with which the two co-occur within the dataset. An association rule with antecedent A, consequent C, and statistics S is denoted as $A \to C[S]$.

The task involves finding all association rules that satisfy a set of user defined constraints with respect to a given dataset.

M. Brooks, D. Corbett, and M. Stumptner (Eds.): AI 2001, LNAI 2256, pp. 605–618, 2001.

The frequent itemset strategy has become the standard approach to association rule discovery. This strategy first discovers all *frequent itemsets*. A frequent itemset is an itemset whose support exceeds a user defined threshold. The association rules are then generated from the frequent itemsets. If there are relatively few frequent itemsets this approach can be very efficient. However, it is subject to a number of limitations.

1. The user is required to nominate a minimum frequency. Associations with support lower than this frequency will not be discovered. For some applications there may not be any natural lower bound on support and hence pruning the search space on minimum frequency in this manner may not be appropriate. Also, for some applications infrequent itemsets may actually be especially interesting. For example, especially high value transactions are likely to be both relatively infrequent and of high interest. This is known as the *vodka and caviar problem*.
2. Even when a minimum frequency is applicable, there may be too many frequent itemsets for computation to be feasible. The frequent itemset approach requires that all frequent itemsets be maintained in memory. This imposes unrealistic memory requirements for many applications [4].
3. It is difficult to utilize search constraints other than minimum frequency to improve the efficiency of the frequent itemset approach. Where other constraints can be specified, potential efficiencies are lost.

Most research in association rule discovery has sought to improve the efficiency of the frequent itemset discovery process [1,9, for example]. This has not addressed any of the above problems, except the closed itemset approaches [11,17], which reduce the number of itemsets required, addressing point 2, but not 1 or 3.

OPUS_AR provides an alternative approach to association rule discovery based on the efficient OPUS search algorithm [15]. This extends previous work in rule discovery search [5,8,10,12,13,14,15] by searching for rules that optimize an objective function over a space of rules that allows alternative variables in the consequent. Previous algorithms have all been restricted to a single target consequent variable per search.

OPUS_AR does not have significant memory requirements other than the requirement that all data be retained in memory. While it does not achieve the same degree of pruning as Apriori from a constraint on minimum frequency, it can utilize other constraints more effectively than Apriori. In particular, it can utilize constraints on the number of associations to be discovered, returning the n associations that optimize some criterion of interestingness. This provides a desirable contrast to the frequent itemset approach that is prone to generate extraordinarily large numbers of associations. In practice, only a small number associations are likely to be utilized by a user. A large number of associations is more likely to be a hindrance than an asset.

Search space pruning rules are critical to the efficiency of OPUS_AR. Webb [16] utilized four such pruning rules. This paper presents two new pruning rules and additional mechanisms for reducing the computational requirements of OPUS_AR.

This paper is organised as follows. Section 2 introduces the Apriori algorithm and analyzes its advantages and disadvantages. Section 3 introduces the OPUS search algorithm on which OPUS_AR is based. Section 4 presents the OPUS_AR algorithm for discovering association rules. Section 5 describes the new pruning rules and other efficiency measures and presents experiments that demonstrate the effectiveness of these measures when discovering association rules on several large datasets. Section 6 presents conclusions.

2 The Apriori Algorithm

The Apriori algorithm discovers associations in a two-step process. First, it finds the frequent itemsets $\{I \subseteq \mathcal{C} : \frac{|coverset(I)|}{|\mathcal{D}|} \geq min\_support\}$, where $\mathcal{C}$ is the set of all available conditions, $\mathcal{D}$ is the dataset, and *min_support* is a user defined minimum support constraint. In the second stage the frequent itemsets are used to generate

```
     ┌{a}
     ├{b}─{a, b}
     │     ┌{a, c}
─{}─┤{c}─┤
     │     └{b, c}─{a, b, c}
     │     ┌{a, d}
     └{d}─┤{b, d}─{a, b, d}
           │        ┌{a, c, d}
           └{c, d}─┤
                    └{b, c, d}─{a, b, c, d}
```

Fig. 1. A fixed-structure search space

the association rules. The minimum support constraint on the frequent itemsets guarantees that all associations generated will satisfy the minimum support constraint. Other constraints, such as minimum confidence are enforced during the second stage.

The frequent itemset strategy can limit the number of rules that are explored, and cache the support values of the frequent items so that there is no need to access the dataset in the second step. It is very successful at reducing the number of passes through the data. The frequent itemset approach has become the predominant approach to association rule discovery.

However, the frequent itemset approach is only feasible for sparse data. For dense datasets where there are numerous frequent itemsets, the overheads for maintaining and manipulating the itemsets are too large to make the system efficient and feasible [4]. This is also apparent in the experiments presented below. Dense datasets are common in applications other than basket data analysis or when basket data is augmented by other customer information. Another problem of Apriori is that it lists numerous association rules to the user and it may be very difficult for the user to identify the interesting rules manually. Take the covtype dataset for example. Covtype has 581,012 records containing 125 items. The number of the association rules generated by Apriori with the minimum support set to 0.01, minimum confidence 0.8, and maximum itemset size 5 is 88,327,710. Since the Apriori algorithm generates itemsets by considering features of itemsets in isolation, the inter-relationships between the itemsets are not taken into account. In consequence, many association rules generated may not be of interest to the user.

3 The OPUS Search Algorithm

OPUS [15] provides efficient search for subset selection, such as selecting a subset of available conditions that optimizes a specified measure. It was developed for classification rule discovery. Previous algorithms ordered the available conditions and then conducted a systematic search over the ordering in such a manner as to guarantee that each subset was investigated once only, as illustrated in Fig. 1.

Critical to the efficiency of such search is the ability to identify and prune sections of the search space that cannot contain solutions. This is usually achieved by identifying subsets that cannot appear in a solution. For example, it might be determined that $\{b\}$ cannot appear in a solution in the search space illustrated in Fig. 1. Under previous search algorithms [8,10,12,13,14], subsets that appear below such a subset were pruned, as illustrated in Fig. 2. In this example, pruning removes one subset from the search space.

This contrasts with the pruning that would occur if all subsets containing the pruned subset were removed from the search space, as illustrated in Fig. 3. This optimal pruning almost halves the search space below the parent node.

```
     ┌{a}
     ├{b}— ×
     │      ┌{a, c}
-{}-─┼{c}-─┤
     │      └{b, c}—{a, b, c}
     │      ┌{a, d}
     └{d}-─┼{b, d}—{a, b, d}
            │        ┌{a, c, d}
            └{c, d}-─┤
                     └{b, c, d}—{a, b, c, d}
```

Fig. 2. Pruning a branch from a fixed-structure search space

```
     ┌{a}
     ├{b}— ×
     │      ┌{a, c}
-{}-─┼{c}-─┤
     │      └ × — ×
     │      ┌{a, d}
     └{d}-─┼ × — ×
            │        ┌{a, c, d}
            └{c, d}-─┤
                     └ × — ×
```

Fig. 3. Pruning all nodes containing a single condition from a fixed-structure search space

OPUS achieves the pruning illustrated in Fig. 3 by maintaining a set of available items at each node in the search space. When adding an item i to the current subset s results in a subset $s \cup \{i\}$ that can be pruned from the search space, i is simply removed from the set of available items at s which is propagated below s. As supersets of $s \cup \{i\}$ below s can only be explored after $s \cup \{i\}$, this simple mechanism with negligible computational overheads guarantees that no superset of a pruned subset will be generated in the search space below the parent of the pruned node. This greatly expands the scope of a pruning operation from that achieved by previous algorithms which only extended to the space below the pruned node. Further pruning can be achieved by reordering the search space, but this proves to be infeasible in search for association rule discovery, as explained by Webb [16].

4 The OPUS_AR Algorithm

OPUS_AR extends the OPUS search algorithm to association rule discovery [16]. To simplify the search problem, the consequent of an association rule is restricted to a single condition. Association rules of this restricted form are of interest for many data mining applications.

Whereas OPUS supports search through spaces of subsets, the association rule search task requires search through the space of pairs $\langle I \subseteq \mathit{conditions}, c \in \mathit{conditions}\rangle$, where I is the antecedent and c the consequent of an association. OPUS_AR achieves this by performing OPUS search through the space of antecedents, maintaining at each node a set of potential consequents, each of which is explored at each node.

The algorithm relies upon there being a set of user defined constraints on the acceptable associations. These are used to prune the search space. Such constraints can take many forms, ranging from the traditional association rule discovery constraints on support and confidence to a constraint that only the n associations that maximize some statistic be returned. To provide a general mechanism for handling a wide variety of constraints, we denote associations that satisfy all constraints *target associations*. Note that it may not be apparent when an association is encountered whether or not it is a target. For example, if we are seeking the 100 associations with the highest lift, we may not know the cutoff value for lift until the search has been completed. Hence, while we may be able to determine in some circumstances that an association is not a target, we may not be able to determine that an association is a target until the search is completed. To accommodate this, pruning is only invoked when it is determined that areas of the search space cannot contain a target. All associations encountered are recorded unless the system can determine that they are not targets. However, these associations may be subsequently discarded as progress through the search space reveals that they cannot be targets. When seeking the n best associations with respect to some statistic, we can determine that a new association is not a target if its value on that statistic is lower than the value of the nth best recorded so far, as the value of the nth best for the search space cannot be lower than the value of the nth best for the subset of the search space examined so far.

Table 1 displays the algorithm that results from applying the OPUS search algorithm [15] to obtain efficient search for this search task. The algorithm is presented as a recursive procedure with three arguments:

CurrentLHS: the set of conditions in the antecedent of the rule currently being considered.

AvailableLHS: the set of conditions that may be added to the antecedent of rules to be explored below this point.

AvailableRHS: the set of conditions that may appear on the consequent of a rule in the search space at this point and below.

Table 1. The OPUS search algorithm adjusted for search for association rules

```
Algorithm: OPUS AR (CurrentLHS,AvailableLHS,AvailableRHS)
 1. SoFar := {}
 2. FOR EACH P in AvailableLHS
 2. 1 IF pruning rules cannot determine that ∀x ⊆ AvailableLHS: ∀y ∈
    AvaiableRHS: ¬target (x ∪ CurrentLHS ∪ {P} → y) THEN
 2. 1.1 NewLHS := CurrentLHS ∪ {P}
 2. 1.2 NewAvailableLHS := SoFar - P
 2. 1.3 IF pruning rules cannot determine that ∀x ⊆ NewAvailableLHS: ∀y ∈
    AvailableRHS: ¬target (x ∪ NewLHS → y) THEN
    (a) NewAvailableRHS := AvailableRHS - P
    (b) IF pruning rules cannot determine ∀y ∈ NewAvailableRHS: ¬target
        (NewLHS → y) THEN
    (b. 1) FOR EACH Q in NewAvailableRHS
       i. IF pruning rules determine that ∀x ⊆ NewAvailableLHS: ¬target (x
          ∪ NewLHS → Q) THEN
          A. NewAvailableRHS := NewAvailableRHS - Q
      ii. ELSE IF pruning rules cannot determine that ¬target (NewLHS → Q)
          THEN
          A. IF target (NewLHS → Q) THEN
             A.1 record NewLHS → Q
             A.2 tune the settings of the statistics
          B. IF pruning rules determine that ∀x ⊆ NewAvailableLHS: ¬target
             (x ∪ NewLHS → Q) THEN
             NewAvailableRHS := NewAvailableRHS - Q
    (c) IF NewAvailableLHS ≠ {} and NewAvailableRHS ≠ {} THEN
          OPUS AR (NewLHS,NewAvailableLHS,NewAvailableRHS)
    (d) SoFar := SoFar ∪ {P}
```

The initial call to the procedure sets CurrentLHS to {}, and AvailableLHS and AvailableRHS to the set of conditions that are to be considered on the antecedent and consequent of association rules, respectively.

The algorithm OPUS_AR is a search procedure that starts with the associations with one condition in the antecedent and searches through successive associations formed by adding conditions to the antecedent. It loops through each condition in AvailableLHS, adds it to CurrentLHS to form the NewLHS. For the NewLHS, it loops through each condition in AvailableRHS to check if it could be the consequent for NewLHS. After the AvailableRHS loop, the procedure is recursively called with the arguments NewLHS, NewAvailableLHS and NewAvailableRHS. The two latter arguments are formed by removing the pruned conditions from AvailabeLHS and AvailableRHS, respectively. Step 2.1.3(b.1)ii.A.1 records the potential target associations.

5 Pruning in Search for Association Rules

Webb [16] utilized four pruning rules to prune the search space explored by OPUS_AR. We present two new pruning rules and two data access saving rules for improving the efficiency of OPUS_AR. In order to evaluate their impact, experiments are performed on five large datasets from the UCI ML and KDD repositories [6,3]. These datasets are listed in Table 2.

The four pruning rules presented in Webb [16] are taken as the basic pruning rules in our experiments. Column "basic pruning" of Table 3 lists the times of running OPUS_AR with these basic pruning rules on the five datasets. We test on the same datasets the running times of OPUS_AR with the basic pruning plus each of the pruning mechanisms introduced below. We also compare the performance with the publicly available apriori system developed by Borgelt [7]. In all the experiments OPUS_AR seeks the top 1000 associations on lift within the constraints of minimum confidence set to 0.8, minimum support set to 0.01, and the maximum number of conditions in antecedent of an association set to 4. The same minimum support, minimum confidence, and maximum antecedent size are used for Apriori, thus the maximum itemset size is 5 for Apriori because itemsets are required that contain up to 4 antecedent conditions as well as the single consequent condition. The experiments were performed on a Linux server with 2 CPUs each 933MHz in speed, 1.5G RAM, and 4G virtual memory.

5.1 Formal Description of Association Rule Discovery Based on OPUS_AR

A formal description of association rule discovery based on OPUS_AR is given in the following.

Definition 1. *An association rule discovery task based on OPUS_AR (abbreviated as AR_by_OPUS) is a 4-tuple* $(\mathcal{C}, \mathcal{D}, \mathcal{A}, \mathcal{M})$, *where*
$\mathcal{C}$*: nonempty set of conditions;*
$\mathcal{D}$*:nonempty set of records, called the dataset, where for each record* $d \in \mathcal{D}$, $d \subseteq \mathcal{C}$. *For any* $S \subseteq \mathcal{C}$, *let* $coverset(S) = \{d | d \in \mathcal{D} \wedge S \subseteq d\}$, *and let* $cover(S) = \frac{|coverset(S)|}{|\mathcal{D}|}$;
$\mathcal{A}$*: set of association rules, where each association rule takes the form*

$$X \rightarrow Y[coverage, support, confidence, lift]$$

where $X \subset \mathcal{C}$, $X \neq \emptyset$, $Y \subset \mathcal{C}$, $|Y| = 1$, $X \cap Y = \emptyset$, *and* $coverage, support, confidence,$ *and* $lift$ *are statistics for the association rule,*

Table 2. Datasets for experiments

name	records	attributes	values
covtype	581012	55	125
ipums.la.99	88443	61	1883
ticdata2000	5822	86	709
connect-4	67557	43	129
letter-recognition	20000	17	74

satisfying $coverage(X \rightarrow Y) = cover(X)$, $support(X \rightarrow Y) = cover(X \cup Y)$, $confidence(X \rightarrow Y) = \frac{support(X \rightarrow Y)}{coverage(X \rightarrow Y)}$, *and* $lift(X \rightarrow Y) = \frac{confidence(X \rightarrow Y)}{cover(Y)}$;
$\mathcal{M}$*: constraints, composed of* $maxAssocs$ *denoting the maximum number of target association rules (which will consist of the association rules with the high-*

est values for lift of those that satisfy all other constraints), $maxLHSsize$ denoting maximum number of conditions allowed in the antecedent of association rule, $minCoverage$ denoting the minimum coverage, $minSupport$ denoting the minimum support, $minConfidence$ denoting the minimum confidence, and $minLift = \max(1.0, \beta(RS, maxAssocs))$, where RS is the set of associations $\{R : coverage(R) \geqslant minCoverage \wedge support(R) \geqslant minSupport \wedge confidence(R) \geqslant minConfidence\}$, and $\beta(Z, n)$ is the lift of the nth association in Z sorted from highest to lowest by lift. An association rule $X \to Y[coverage, support, confidence, lift]$ is a target iff it satisfies $|X| \leqslant maxLHSsize$, $coverage(X \to Y) \geqslant minCoverage$, $support(X \to Y) \geqslant minSuport$, $confidence(X \to Y) \geqslant minConfidence$, and $lift(X \to Y) \geqslant minLift$.

Theorem 1. *Suppose $AR\_by\_OPUS = (\mathcal{C}, \mathcal{D}, \mathcal{A}, \mathcal{M})$. For any $S_1 \subseteq \mathcal{C}$, $S_2 \subseteq \mathcal{C}$, and $S_1 \subseteq S_2$, $coverset(S_2) \subseteq coverset(S_1)$ holds. This is to say, $cover(S_2) \leqslant cover(S_1)$ holds.*

Proof. For any $d \in coverset(S_2)$, according to Definition 1, $S_2 \subseteq d$ holds. Since $S_1 \subseteq S_2$, $S_1 \subseteq d$ holds. Hence $d \in coverset(S_1)$. So $coverset(S_2) \subseteq coverset(S_1)$ holds. □

Theorem 2. *Suppose $AR\_by\_OPUS = (\mathcal{C}, \mathcal{D}, \mathcal{A}, \mathcal{M})$. For any nonempty $S_1, S_2, S_3 \subseteq \mathcal{C}$ satisfying $S_1 \cap S_2 = \emptyset$, $S_2 \cap S_3 = \emptyset$, and $S_1 \cap S_3 = \emptyset$, if*

$$cover(S_1) = cover(S_1 \cup S_2) \tag{1}$$

the following holds.

$$cover(S_1 \cup S_3) = cover(S_1 \cup S_2 \cup S_3) \tag{2}$$

Proof. From (1) and Definition 1, we have

$$|coverset(S_1)| = |coverset(S_1 \cup S_2)| \tag{3}$$

From Theorem 1,

$$coverset(S_1) \supseteq coverset(S_1 \cup S_2) \tag{4}$$

From (3) and (4), we get

$$coverset(S_1) = coverset(S_1 \cup S_2) \tag{5}$$

For any $d \in \mathcal{D} \wedge S_1 \cup S_3 \subseteq d$, $S_1 \subseteq d$ and $S_3 \subseteq d$ hold. From $S_1 \subseteq d$ and (5), we get $S_1 \cup S_2 \subseteq d$. From $S_3 \subseteq d$, $S_1 \cup S_2 \cup S_3 \subseteq d$ holds. Hence

$$coverset(S_1 \cup S_3) \subseteq coverset(S_1 \cup S_2 \cup S_3) \tag{6}$$

From Theorem 1, we have

$$coverset(S_1 \cup S_2 \cup S_3) \subseteq coverset(S_1 \cup S_3) \tag{7}$$

From (6) and (7), $coverset(S_1 \cup S_3) = coverset(S_1 \cup S_2 \cup S_3)$ holds. Hence (2) is proved. □

5.2 Pruning the Consequent Condition Before the Evaluation of Association Rule

One of the pruning rules at Step 2.1.3(b.1)i is used to prune the consequent condition according to the current lower bound on *minSupport* before the evaluation of the association rule. This pruning rule is based on the following theorem.

Theorem 3. *Suppose* $AR\_by\_OPUS = (\mathcal{C}, \mathcal{D}, \mathcal{A}, \mathcal{M})$. *For any association rule* $X \to Y$, *if* $cover(Y) < minSupport$, $X \to Y$ *is not a target.*

Proof. According to Definition 1 and Theorem 1, we get

$$support(X \to Y) = cover(X \cup Y) \leqslant cover(Y) < minSupport$$

Hence $X \to Y$ is not a target. □

From this theorem, we get the following pruning rule.

Pruning 1 *In OPUS_AR for* $AR\_by\_OPUS = (\mathcal{C}, \mathcal{D}, \mathcal{A}, \mathcal{M})$, *for any condition* $Q \in AvailableRHS$, *if* $cover(Q) < minSupport$, *then* Q *can be pruned from* $NewAvailableRHS$.

According to Theorem 3, any association rule with such Q as the consequent can not be a target, therefore Q can be pruned. The "pruning 1 added" column of Table 3 lists the times for OPUS_AR on the five datasets with the basic pruning and pruning 1.

5.3 Pruning the Consequent Condition after the Evaluation of Association Rule

This pruning rule at Step 2.1.3(b.1)ii.B is used to prune the consequent condition after the evaluation of the current association rule. It is based on the following theorem.

Theorem 4. *Suppose* $AR\_by\_OPUS = (\mathcal{C}, \mathcal{D}, \mathcal{A}, \mathcal{M})$. *For any association rule* $X \to Y$, *if* $confidence(X \to Y) = 1$, *for any* $X_1 \subset \mathcal{C}$ *satisfying* $X_1 \cap X = \emptyset \wedge X_1 \cap Y = \emptyset \wedge cover(X \cup X_1) \neq 0$, *the following holds.*

$$lift(X \cup X_1 \to Y) = lift(X \to Y)$$

Proof. From $confidence(X \to Y) = 1$, we get

$$support(X \to Y) = coverage(X \to Y)$$

that is to say,

$$cover(X) = cover(X \cup Y) \tag{8}$$

From (8) and Theorem 2, $cover(X \cup X_1) = cover(X \cup X_1 \cup Y)$ holds. Since $cover(X \cup X_1) \neq 0$, hence

$$support(X \cup X_1 \to Y) = coverage(X \cup X_1 \to Y) \neq 0$$

Therefore $confidence(X \cup X_1 \to Y) = 1$. From Definition 1, the following two equations hold.

$$lift(X \cup X_1 \to Y) = \frac{confidence(X \cup X_1 \to Y)}{cover(Y)} = \frac{1}{cover(Y)}$$

$$lift(X \to Y) = \frac{confidence(X \to Y)}{cover(Y)} = \frac{1}{cover(Y)}$$

Hence $lift(X \cup X_1 \to Y) = lift(X \to Y)$ holds. □

From this theorem, we get the following pruning rule.

Pruning 2 *In OPUS_AR for* $AR\_by\_OPUS = (\mathcal{C}, \mathcal{D}, \mathcal{A}, \mathcal{M})$, *after the evaluation of the current association rule* $NewLHS \to Q$, *if* $confidence(NewLHS \to Q) = 1$ *and* $lift(NewLHS \to Q) < minLift$, *$Q$ can be pruned from* $NewAvailableRHS$.

According to the above theorem, all of the association rules with Q as the consequent in the search space below the current node take the same lift value as $NewLHS \to Q$. Therefore if $lift(NewLHS \to Q) < minLift$, none of these rules can be target association, Q can be pruned from $NewAvailableRHS$. The "pruning 2 added" column of Table 3 lists the times for OPUS_AR on the five datasets with the basic pruning and pruning 2. For "covtype," the compute time is reduced by this pruning to less than 55% of that supported by the basic pruning rules, for "ipums.la.99," the compute time is reduced to less than 66% of the basic pruning.

5.4 Saving Data Access for the Current Association Rule by $minConfidence$

In order to evaluate the number of records covered by set of conditions, the dataset is normally accessed by OPUS_AR at least once for each association rule antecedent and once for the union of the antecedent and consequent. Techniques for saving such data access can improve the efficiency of the algorithm. Whereas the pruning rules save data access by discarding the region of the search space below a node, the saving rules save data access for a node without removing its branch.

Step 2.1.3(b.1)ii is for saving data access for the current association rule $NewLHS \to Q$. We are going to introduce two of the saving rules adopted at this step, one is by $minConfidence$, based on the following theorem, and the other is by the antecedent of the current association rule, described in the next section.

Theorem 5. *Suppose* $AR\_by\_OPUS = (\mathcal{C}, \mathcal{D}, \mathcal{A}, \mathcal{M})$. *For any association rule* $X \to Y$, *if* $\frac{cover(Y)}{cover(X)} < minConfidence$, $X \to Y$ *is not a target.*

Proof. According to Definition 1, we have

$$confidence(X \to Y) = \frac{support(X \to Y)}{coverage(X \to Y)} = \frac{cover(X \cup Y)}{cover(X)}$$

According to Theorem 1, $cover(X \cup Y) \leqslant cover(Y)$ holds. Since $\frac{cover(Y)}{cover(X)} <$ $minConfidence$,

$$confidence(X \to Y) \leqslant \frac{cover(Y)}{cover(X)} < minConfidence$$

Therefore $X \to Y$ is not a target. □

From this theorem, we get the following data access saving rule.

Saving 1 *In OPUS_AR for AR_by_OPUS* $= (\mathcal{C}, \mathcal{D}, \mathcal{A}, \mathcal{M})$*, for the current association* $NewLHS \to Q$*, if* $|NewLHS| = maxLHSsize$ *and* $\frac{cover(Q)}{cover(NewLHS)} < minConfidence$*, there is no need to access data to evaluate* $NewLHS \to Q$*, as it is not a target.*

The reason that the saving is adopted instead of pruning under this situation is in the branch below the current $NewLHS \to Q$, some of the supersets of $NewLHS$ with lower values of coverage might make the association have confidence larger than $minConfidence$. While saving data access, the pruning based on the results of the data access is not available anymore, thus the overall efficiency might be slowed down accordingly. Due to this, $|NewLHS| = maxLHSsize$ is added to the above saving rule to ensure that it is applied only at the maximum search depth where no pruning is necessary.

The "saving 1 added" column of Table 3 lists the times for OPUS_AR on the five datasets with the basic pruning and this saving rule.

5.5 Saving Data Access for the Current Association Rule by the Antecedent

Another saving rule at Step 2.1.3(b.1)ii for the current associations rule $NewLHS \to Q$, where $NewLHS = CurrentLHS \cup \{P\}$, $P \in AvailableLHS$, functions according to the relation between $CurrentLHS$ and P. It is based on the following theorem.

Theorem 6. *Suppose AR_by_OPUS* $= (\mathcal{C}, \mathcal{D}, \mathcal{A}, \mathcal{M})$*. For any association rule* $X \to Y$ *and* $X \cup \{P\} \to Y$ *where* $P \in \mathcal{C}$*,* $P \notin X$ *and* $P \notin Y$*, if* $cover(X) = cover(X \cup \{P\})$*, the following hold.*

$$coverage(X \to Y) = coverage(X \cup \{P\} \to Y) \tag{9}$$

$$support(X \to Y) = support(X \cup \{P\} \to Y) \tag{10}$$

$$confidence(X \to Y) = confidence(X \cup \{P\} \to Y) \tag{11}$$

$$lift(X \to Y) = lift(X \cup \{P\} \to Y) \tag{12}$$

Proof. According to $cover(X) = cover(X \cup \{P\})$, (9) holds. From $cover(X) = cover(X \cup \{P\})$ and Theorem 2, the following holds.

$$cover(X \cup Y) = cover(X \cup \{P\} \cup Y) \tag{13}$$

From (13), (10) holds. Hence (11) and (12) are proved. □

From this theorem, we get the following data access saving rule.

Saving 2 *In OPUS_AR for AR_by_OPUS* $= (\mathcal{C}, \mathcal{D}, \mathcal{A}, \mathcal{M})$*, for the current association* $NewLHS \rightarrow Q$ *where* $NewLHS = CurrentLHS \cup \{P\}$, $P \in AvailableLHS$*, if* $|NewLHS| = maxLHSsize$*, the number of current target associations is less than* $|coverset(NewLHS)|$*, and* $cover(CurrentLHS) = cover(NewLHS)$*, instead of accessing data to evaluate* $NewLHS \rightarrow Q$*, check if* $CurrentLHS \rightarrow Q$ *exists in the current target associations, and if yes, copy all the statistic values of* $CurrentLHS \rightarrow Q$ *to* $NewLHS \rightarrow Q$*, otherwise,* $NewLHS \rightarrow Q$ *is not a target.*

Since $CurrentLHS \rightarrow Q$ is investigated before $NewLHS \rightarrow Q$ in OPUS_AR, and they share the same statistic values, $NewLHS \rightarrow Q$ will be a target if and only if $CurrentLHS \rightarrow Q$ is a target. Due to the same reasons as in the above section, we add $|NewLHS| = maxLHSsize$ in the saving rule to make sure that application of the saving rule can not slow down the overall efficiency. If the number of current target associations is larger than $|coverset(NewLHS)|$, searching current target associations might become less efficient than accessing data of the amount of $|coverset(NewLHS)|$ for computing $cover(NewLHS \cup Q)$.

The "saving 2 added" column of Table 3 lists the times for OPUS_AR on the five datasets with the basic pruning and this saving rule. For both "covtype" and "connect-4," the compute times are reduced by this saving to less than 66% of that supported by the basic pruning rules.

Table 3. Efficiency improvements by pruning in OPUS_AR and efficiency of Apriori

datasets	OPUS_AR						Apriori
	basic pruning	pruning 1 added	pruning 2 added	saving 1 added	saving 2 added	all added	
covtype	7:33:50	5:28:21	4:6:58	6:25:16	4:59:19	3:4:19	77:56:3
ipums.la.99	11:38:31	9:2:37	7:40:12	11:27:9	9:25:16	6:28:38	19:45:5
ticdata2000	25:28:43	24:34:12	23:41:12	24:56:10	22:34:7	23:18:29	—
connect-4	1:48:51	1:24:59	1:10:9	1:30:35	1:11:37	0:48:33	3:15:26
letter-recognition	0:0:23	0:0:20	0:0:20	0:0:23	0:0:22	0:0:20	0:0:35

5.6 Efficiency Comparison between OPUS_AR and Apriori

The "all added" column of Table 3 lists the times on the datasets for OPUS_AR with the new pruning mechanisms composed of pruning 1 and 2 and saving rule 1 and 2 all added to the four original pruning rules. For all datasets other than "ticdata2000," combining all rules results in more efficient search than utilizing any of the rule alone. The interaction between rules than increases compute times for "ticdata2000" merits further investigation. For "covtype," "connect-4," and "ipums.la.99," the compute times are reduced to less than 41%, 45% and 56% of that supported by the original pruning rules, respectively.

The CPU times of running Borgelt's Apriori system on the five datasets are listed in the "Apriori" column of Table 3. The inefficiency of Apriori for dense datasets is demonstrated by the fact that on every dataset OPUS_AR is more efficient than Apriori, and that for "ticdata2000," Apriori runs out of memory when processing itemsets of size 4.

6 Conclusions

OPUS_AR provides an alternative to the frequent itemset approach to association rule discovery. Our experiments have demonstrated that OPUS_AR can provide more efficient association rule discovery than apriori for dense datasets, and can make association rule discovery feasible where the memory requirements of the frequent itemset approach can make its application infeasible. OPUS_AR has the further advantage that it can utilize constraints other than minimum frequency to prune the search space. This makes feasible association rule discovery where there is no natural lower limit on the support for an association.

This paper has presented new pruning rules and data access saving rules for OPUS_AR, which result in the reduction of compute times by as much as 41% compared with those resulting from the original mechanisms only. These results again demonstrate that OPUS_AR can support fast association rule discovery from large dense datasets.

References

1. R. Agarwal, C. C. Aggarwal, and V. V. V. Prasad. Depth first generation of long patterns. In *Proc. Sixth ACM SIGKDD Int. Conf. Knowledge Discovery and Data Mining (KDD2000)*, pages 108–118, Boston, MA, August 2000. ACM.
2. R. Agrawal, T. Imielinski, and A. Swami. Mining associations between sets of items in massive databases. In *Proc. 1993 ACM-SIGMOD Int. Conf. Management of Data*, pages 207–216, 1993.
3. S. D. Bay. The UCI KDD archive. [http://kdd.ics.uci.edu] Irvine, CA: University of California, Department of Information and Computer Science., 2001.
4. R. J. Bayardo. Efficiently mining long patterns from databases. In *Proc. 1998 ACM-SIGMOD Int. Conf. Management of Data*, pages 85–93, 1998.
5. R. J. Bayardo, R. Agrawal, and D. Gunopulos. Constraint-based rule mining in large, dense databases. *Data Mining and Knowledge Discovery*, 4(2/3):217–240, 2000.
6. C. Blake and C. J. Merz. UCI repository of machine learning databases. [Machine-readable data repository]. University of California, Department of Information and Computer Science, Irvine, CA., 2001.
7. C. Borgelt. apriori. (Computer Software) http://fuzzy.cs.Uni-Magdeburg.de/ borgelt/, February 2000.
8. S. H. Clearwater and F. J. Provost. RL4: A tool for knowledge-based induction. In *Proc. Second Intl. IEEE Conf. on Tools for AI*, pages 24–30, Los Alamitos, CA, 1990. IEEE Computer Society Press.
9. J. Han, J. Pei, and Y. Yin. Mining frequent patterns without candidate generation. In *Proc. 2000 ACM-SIGMOD Int. Conf. on Management of Data (SIGMOD'00)*, Dallas, TX, May 2000.
10. S. Morishita and A. Nakaya. Parallel branch-and-bound graph search for correlated association rules. In *Proc. ACM SIGKDD Workshop on Large-Scale Parallel KDD Systems*, volume LNAI 1759, pages 127–144. Springer, Berlin, 2000.
11. J. Pei, J. Han, and R. Mao. CLOSET: An efficient algorithm for mining frequent closed itemsets. In *Proc. 2000 ACM-SIGMOD Int. Workshop on Data Mining and Knowledge Discovery (DMKD'00)*, Dallas, TX, May 2000.
12. F. Provost, J. Aronis, and B. Buchanan. Rule-space search for knowledge-based discovery. CIIO Working Paper IS 99-012, Stern School of Business, New York University, New York, NY 10012, 1999.

13. R. Rymon. Search through systematic set enumeration. In *Proc. KR-92*, pages 268–275, Cambridge, MA, 1992.
14. R. Segal and O. Etzioni. Learning decision lists using homogeneous rules. In *AAAI-94*, Seattle, WA, 1994. AAAI press.
15. G. I. Webb. OPUS: An efficient admissible algorithm for unordered search. *Journal of Artificial Intelligence Research*, 3:431–465, 1995.
16. G. I. Webb. Efficient search for association rules. In *The Sixth ACM SIGKDD Int. Conf .Knowledge Discovery and Data Mining*, pages 99–107, Boston, MA, 2000. The Association for Computing Machinery.
17. M. J. Zaki. Generating non-redundant association rules. In *Proceedingsof the Sixth ACM SIGKDD Int. Conf. Knowledge Discovery and Data Mining (KDD2000)*, pages 34–43, Boston, MA, August 2000. ACM.

Pattern Discovery in Probabilistic Databases

Shichao Zhang and Chengqi Zhang

School of Computing and Mathematics
Deakin University, Geelong, Vic 3217, Australia
{scz, chengqi}@deakin.edu.au

Abstract. Modeling probabilistic data is one of important issues in databases due to the fact that data is often uncertainty in real-world applications. So, it is necessary to identify potentially useful patterns in probabilistic databases. Because probabilistic data in 1NF relations is redundant, previous mining techniques don't work well on probabilistic databases. For this reason, this paper proposes a new model for mining probabilistic databases. A partition is thus developed for preprocessing probabilistic data in a probabilistic databases. We evaluated the proposed technique, and the experimental results demonstrate that our approach is effective and efficient.

1 Introduction

Association analysis for large databases has received much attention recently [1]. Recently, there are also much work on mining special databases. For example, spatial data mining [5] and image data mining [2].

However, there is no work on mining probabilistic databases. Indeed, today's database systems must handle uncertainties in the data they store. Such uncertainties arise from different sources such as measurement errors, approximation errors, and the dynamic nature of real world. For example, in an image retrieval system, an image processing algorithm may fetch images that are similar to a given sample image, and feed the results into a relational database. The results are generally uncertain. Because probabilistic data in 1NF (First Normal Form) relations is redundant, traditional mining techniques don't work well on probabilistic databases. For this reason, a new mining model for probabilistic databases is established in this paper, which the probabilistic data model in [3] is adopted. A dependent rule is thus identified in a probabilistic database, represented in the form $X \rightarrow Y$ with conditional probability matrix $M_{Y|X}$. We now illustrate the above argument with the following example.

Example 1. Consider a probabilistic personnel database in some university. The interest data is the set of records with respect to "education", "salary" and "pS" of employee as Table 1.

M. Brooks, D. Corbett, and M. Stumptner (Eds.): AI 2001, LNAI 2256, pp. 619–630, 2001.

Table 1. *A probabilistic relation*

EMP#	*Education*	*salary*	*pS*	*EMP#*	*Education*	*salary*	*pS*
3025	*Doctor*	*4100*	*0.8*	*3025*	*Doctor*	*2500*	*0.1*
3025	*Doctor*	*1800*	*0.1*	*6637*	*Doctor*	*3500*	*0.14*
6637	*Doctor*	*2400*	*0.06*	*6637*	*Master*	*3500*	*0.1*
6637	*Master*	*2400*	*0.6*	*6637*	*Master*	*1800*	*0.1*
7741	*Bachelor*	*3500*	*0.1*	*7741*	*Bachelor*	*2400*	*0.1*
7741	*Bachelor*	*1500*	*0.8*				

Let's examine the existing techniques check if some of them can work well on the above table.

1. The first solution (item-based technique) is to identify association rules such as "3025 $\rightarrow$ *Doctor*" and "7741 $\rightarrow$ *Bachelor*".

The above association rules are uninteresting in the probabilistic database. In other words, item-based technique cannot work well on the above table.

To mine such database, we firstly need to partition the domain of *Education* into *Doctor*, *Master*, and *UnderMaster*; and the domain of *Salary* into [3500, $+\infty$), [2100, 3500) and [0, 2100). *Doctor*, *Master*, *UnderMaster*, $[3500, +\infty)$, [2100, 3500) and [0, 2100) are called quantitative items. Secondly, we compute the probabilities of quantitative items in the database. Let X and Y stand for Education and Salary, respectively, $\tau_1, \tau_2, \cdots, \tau_{10}$ be sequentially tuples in Table 1. Then for *EMP#*3025,

$$p(X = Doctor) = \tau_1(pS) + \tau_2(pS) + \tau_3(pS) = 0.8 + 0.1 + 0.1 = 1,$$

$$p(X = Master) = 0, p(X = UnderMaster) = 0, p(Y = [3500, +\infty)) = 0.8,$$

$$p(Y = [2100, 3500)) = 0.1, p(Y = [0, 2100)) = 0.1.$$

2. The second solution (quantitative-item-based technique) is to identify association rules such as "*Education* = *Doctor* $\rightarrow$ *Salary* $\geq$ 3500", *Education* = *Master* $\rightarrow$ *Salary* $\in$ [2100, 3500), and "*Education* = *UnderMaster* $\rightarrow$ *Salary* < 2100", using the techniques proposed in this paper.

Quantitative-item-based technique certainly works better than item-based technique on this table. However, the three rules only express a part of the relationships between attributes "Education" (X) and "Salary" (Y). An ideal approach is advocated in this paper.

3. Our approach (the third solution) applies a conditional probability matrix $M_{Y|X}$ for $X \rightarrow Y$ to fit the probabilistic data. For the data, if they are fitted in a conditional probability matrix $M_{Y|X}$, then the dependency between X and Y can be described by this matrix. A main goal of this paper is to build a model to learn this probabilities in next subsection. Actually, using the algorithm in Section 4 we can acquire a conditional probability matrix $M_{Y|X}$ from the above data as follows.

$$M_{Y|X} = \begin{bmatrix} p_{11}\, p_{12}\, p_{13} \\ p_{21}\, p_{22}\, p_{23} \\ p_{31}\, p_{32}\, p_{33} \end{bmatrix} = \begin{bmatrix} 0.8\; 0.1\; 0.1 \\ 0.1\; 0.8\; 0.1 \\ 0.1\; 0.1\; 0.8 \end{bmatrix}$$

As have seen, dependent rules can perfectly catch the relationship between pairs of multi-values variables and present more challenging than quantitative-item based rules.

The rest of this paper is organized as follows. Section 2 presents some needed concepts. In Section 3, a partitioning is proposed. Section 4 builds a statistical model of mining probabilistic databases using a partition. The experiments are illustrated in Section 5. In the last section, a summary of this paper is presented.

2 Basic Definition

Assume I is a set of items in database D. A subset of a same type of items in I is referred to *quantitative item*.

An *item-based association rule* is a relationship of the form $A \Rightarrow B$, where A and B are itemsets and $A \cap B = \emptyset$. It has both support and confidence greater than or equal to some user specified minimum support (*minsupp*) and minimum confidence (*minconf*) thresholds, respectively.

A *quantitative association rule* is a relationship of the form

$$\langle attribute1, value1\rangle \Rightarrow \langle attribute2, value2\rangle,$$

where $attribute1$ and $attribute2$ are attributes, $value1$ and $value2$ are subsets of the domains of $attribute1$ and $attribute2$ respectively, $\langle attribute1, value1\rangle$ and $\langle attribute2, value2\rangle$ are quantitative items.

A *dependent rule* is a relationship between X and Y of the form $X \rightarrow Y$ with a conditional probability matrix $M_{Y|X}$ [6], where X and Y are variables with valuing in *ranges* $R(X)$ and $R(Y)$ respectively. $x \in R(X)$ is called a *point-value* of X, where x is a quantitative item. And $M_{Y|X}$ is given as $M_{Y|X} \triangleq [p(y_j|x_i)]_{m \times n}$, where, "$\triangleq$" denotes definition symbol. $p(y_j|x_i) = p(Y = y_j|X = x_i)$ are conditional probabilities, $i = 1, 2, \cdots, m, j = 1, 2, \cdots, n$.

The problem of mining dependency rules is to generate all rules $X \rightarrow Y$ that have with both support and $M_{Y|X}$, which support is greater than or equal to some user specified minimum support (minsupp) threshold.

3 Data Partitioning

In data mining, there are two main partitioning data models: knowledge based partitioning model [4] and equi-depth partitioning model [7]. We will propose a so-called "good partition" to generate quantitative items and item variables for a given database, which decomposes the "bad quantitative items" and "bad item variables" and composes the "not-bad quantitative items" and "not–bad item variables".

Generally, a quantitative item doesn't occur in the transactions of a database. To find quantitative association rules from databases, we say that a quantitative item i is contained by a transaction t of a database D if existing at least one element of i occur in t (Note that each quantitative item consists of multiple simpler items). And the support of the quantitative item i is defined as $100 * s\%$ of transactions in D that contain at least one element of i. Or

$$s = |i(t)|/|D|$$

where $i(t) = \{t \text{ in } D|t \text{ contains at least one element of } i\}$.

In this way, we can map quantitative association rules problem into Boolean association rules problem [7]. And some item-based mining techniques and algorithms can also used to identify quantitative association rules.

Quantitative Items. In previous sections, we partition the items in domains of *Education* and *Salary* into $\{Doctor, Master, UnderMaster\}$ and $\{[3500, +\infty), [2100, 3500), [0, 2100)\}$ respectively.

According to different requirements in applications, we can divide them into different sets of quantitative items. For example, we can partition $R(Salary)$ such as $\{[7200, +\infty), [3500, 7200), [2100, 3500), [0, 2100)\}$, $\{[3500, +\infty), [2100, 3500), [0, 2100)\}$. However, a reasonable partition also needs to consider the supports of items and the associated degree with other items. We apply the decomposition and composition for quantitative items to generate good partition.

Clearly, bad quantitative items will not contribute to quantitative association rules. And not-bad quantitative items should also be avoided unless they are required. We shall now present the algorithm to decompose bad quantitative items and compose not-bad quantitative items as follows.

Procedure 1 *DecComposeQI*

begin
Input: *I: set of all items, QI: set of all quantitative items in property,*
Output: *OQI: set of optimized quantitative items;*
(1) **let** $OQI \leftarrow emptyset$; $qset \leftarrow QI$;
for any element q in $qset$ **do**
if $i_1, i_2 \in q$ and they are not associated tolerant **then**
decompose q into two sub-quantitative items q_1 and q_2 such that $q_1 \cup q_2 = q$, $i_1 \in q_1$ and $i_2 \in q_2$,
(2) **for** any two elements q_1 and q_2 in $qset$ **do**
if q_1 and q_2 are not-good quantitative items **then**
compose q_1 and q_2 into a new quantitative item q such that $q = q_1 \cup q_2$ and q is not a bad quantitative item;
(3) **let** $OQI \leftarrow$ all good quantitative items;
output OQI;
end;

Procedure *DecComposeQI* is to generate a set OQI of optimized quantitative items by decomposing "bad quantitative items" and composing (property or associated) tolerant quantitative items.

Item Variables. According to our partitioning model, an attribute can be taken as an item variable. For the above item variables X and Y, X is the set of quantitative items: *Doctor*, *Master* and *UnderMaster* of attribute *Education*, i.e., any element of X is denoted a degree of education; and Y is the set of quantitative items $[3500, +\infty)$, $[2100, 3500)$ and $[0, 2100)$ of attribute *Salary*.

An item variable is the generalization of some quantitative items with a property. For previous examples, $QI = \{q_1, q_2, q_3, q_4, q_5, q_6\}$, we take X and Y as two item variables with domains $R(X) = \{q_1, q_2, q_3\}$ and $R(Y) = \{q_4, q_5, q_6\}$, respectively. And X is the generalization of q_1, q_2 and q_3, Y is the generalization of q_4, q_5 and q_6. Then the sequence of the item variables X and Y is a partition over QI.

As before, bad item variables should not be used to mine dependent rules. And not-bad item variables are also to be avoided unless they are required. We can obtain the decomposition of bad item variables and the composition of not-bad item variables as follows.

Procedure 2 *DecComposeIV*

begin
Input: *OQI: set of all optimized quantitative items, IV: set of all item variables in property;*
Output: *OIV: set of optimized item variables;*
(1) **for** any element X in *vset* **do**
 if $q_1, q_2 \in R(X)$ and they are not associated tolerant **then**
 decompose X into two item variable X_1 and X_2 such that $R(X_1) \cup R(X_2) = R(X)$, $q_1 \in R(X_1)$ and $q_2 \in R(X_2)$;
(2) **for** any two elements X_1 and X_2 in *vset* **do**
 if X_1 and X_2 are not-good item variables **then**
 if X_1 and X_2 are property tolerant and associated tolerant **then**
 compose X_1 and X_2 into a new item variable X such that $R(X) = R(X_1) \cup R(X_2)$ and X is not a bad item variable;
(3) **let** $OIV \leftarrow$ all optimized item variables;
 output OIV;
end;

Procedure *DecComposeIV* is to generate a set OIV of optimized item variables by decomposing "bad item variables" and composing (property or associated) tolerant item variables. This procedure is similar to the procedure *DecComposeQI*.

We now build the algorithm of partitioning model as follows. Let D be a given database, I the set of all items in D.

Procedure 3 *PartitionData*

begin
Input: *D: probabilistic database, I: set of all items in D;*
Output: *OQI: the set of quantitative items, OIV: the set of item variables;*

(1) Generating relative properties, attributes, and constraint conditions for D.
(2) Generating the set QI of all quantitative items by these relative properties, attributes, and constraint conditions, which all quantitative items are formed a partition of I.
(3) Optimizing all the quantitative items into OQI using Procedure 1.
(4) Generating the set IV of all item variables by these relative properties and attributes. This means that each item variable can be viewed as a set of some quantitative items with same property (or attribute) in some sense.
(5) Optimizing all the item variables into OIV using Procedure 2.

end;

Procedure *PartitionData* is to generate a partition on the given database. And obtain the set of optimized quantitative items OQI and the set of optimized item variables OIV.

4 Identifying Dependent Rules

4.1 Preprocess of Data

Generally, probabilistic relations have deterministic keys. That is, each tuple represents a known real entity. The non-key attributes describe the properties of the entities and may be deterministic or stochastic in nature. The Table 1 adopt a 1NF view of probabilistic relations. Its N1NF view is in Table 2.

Table 2. *A probabilistic relation*

EMP#	*Education*	*salary, pS*
3025	*doctor*	*4100, 0.8* *2500, 0.1* *1800, 0.1*
6637	*Doctor, 0.2* *master, 0.8*	*3500, 0.24* *2400, 0.66* *1800, 0.1*
7741	*bachelor*	*3500, 0.1* *2400, 0.1* *1500, 0.8*

In Table 2, $X = (1,0,0)$ and $Y = (0.8,0.1,0.1)$ for $EMP\# = 3025$, $X = (0.2,0.8,0)$ and $Y = (0.24,0.66,0.1)$ for $EMP\# = 6637$, $X = (0,0,1)$ and $Y = (0.1,0.1,0.8)$ for $EMP\# = 7741$.

Though N1NF models provide a framework for describing intuitively the nature of uncertainty data, they pose the usual implementation problems associated with all N1NF relations. Much of previous work on modeling probabilistic data is based on 1NF relations. So, our work in this paper is concentrated on 1NF probabilistic relational model.

For description, the techniques of partitioning quantitative attributes are the same as the above section. And no losing generality, an attribute is taken as an item variable in this section.

$$p(Z = a) = \sum_{\tau(K)=k\wedge\tau(Z)=a} \tau(pS)$$

We now show data preprocess using a procedure as follows.

Procedure 4 *Generatedata*

begin
Input: *D: probabilistic database, γ: threshold values;*
Output: *PS: set of probabilities of interest;*
(1) **call** Partition(D) procedure of partitioning quantitative attributes;
  let $IV \leftarrow$ all item variables;
  let $PS \leftarrow \emptyset$;
(2) **let** $DS \leftarrow \emptyset$,
  for a subset X of set Z of IV **beginfor**
    let $Y \leftarrow Z - X$;
    let $DS \leftarrow DS \cup \{X, Y\}$;
    for each tuple τ in D **beginfor1**
     for each key value $\tau(K) = k$ **beginfor2**
      for each element a in $R(X)$ **do**
       let $p(X = a) \leftarrow \sum_{\tau(K)=k\wedge\tau(X)=a} \tau(pS)$;
      for each element a in $R(Y)$ **do**
       let $p(Y = a) \leftarrow \sum_{\tau(K)=k\wedge\tau(Y)=a} \tau(pS)$;
     endfor2
     if $|X| > 0$ **then**
      let $DS \leftarrow DS \cup \{p(X), p(Y)\}$;
    endfor1
    let $PS \leftarrow PS \cup \{DS\}$;
  endfor
(3) **output** PS set of probability sets;
  endall.
end;

Procedure *Generatedata* is to preprocess the data in a given probabilistic database so as to find all interesting data.

For a given probabilistic database, the preprocess of the database generates a set PS of sets DS of probabilities of item variables.

4.2 Mining Probabilistic Dependencies

In this subsection, we first present a method to calculate conditional probability matrix $M_{X|Y}$ for a possible rule $X \to Y$. Next to estimate the support of the rule.

For a given probabilistic database, X and Y are two item variables. Let $R(X) = \{x_1, x_2, ..., x_n\}$, $R(Y) = \{y_1, y_2, ..., y_m\}$, and $DS = \{(a, b)|a \in S(X), b \in S(Y)\} \in PS$ be a set of k data generated by procedure Generatedata. In order to mine rule of the form $X \to Y$, it needs to determine conditional probability matrix of Y given X: $M_{Y|X}$. The influence of X on Y is the following formula according to Bayesian rule, $P(Y = y_i|X = x) = \sum_k^n p(y_i|x_k) * p(x_k)$, where $x \in R(X)$, $i = 1, 2, \cdots, m$.

In the following, $P(Y = y_i|X = x)$ is denoted by b_i, $p(y_i|x_j)$ is denoted by p_{ji}, where $i = 1, 2, \cdots, m, j = 1, 2, \cdots, n$. Now given $a = (p(x_1) = a_1, p(x_2) = a_2, ..., p(x_n) = a_n) \in S(X)$ as an observation, then b_i can be solved in (2) as $\sum_k^n a_k p_{ki}$, where $i = 1, 2, \cdots, m$.

Intuitively, there is a relation between data a and b in formula (3) if (a, b) is an observation. And p_{ji} are invariant, a_j and b_i are variable factors. Thus, if these properties in (3) are utilized to learn p_{ji} from applications, we can acquire more probabilistic information as possible from the bounded resources.

Our goal is to find the probability p_{ji} from probabilistic databases in this paper. So for DS, the following function is ideally expected for all elements of DS to satisfy:

$$f(p_{1i}, p_{2i}, ..., p_{ni}) = \sum_{t \in DS} (\sum_k^n a_{jk} p_{ki} - b_{ji})^2,$$

and the value of $f(p_{1i}, p_{2i}, ..., p_{ni})$ must be the minimum. Or the above formula can be written as

$$f(p_{1i}, p_{2i}, ..., p_{ni}) = \sum (\sum_k^n a_{jk} p_{ki} - b_{ji})^2.$$

Using the principle of extreme values in mathematical analysis, we can find the minimum by taking the partial derivatives over $f(p_{1i}, p_{2i}, ..., p_{ni})$ with respect to $p_{1i}, p_{2i}, ..., p_{ni}$ we must determine, and then set these derivatives to 0. That is,

$$\begin{cases} \frac{\partial f}{\partial p_{1i}} = 2 \sum (\sum_k^n a_{jk} p_{ki} - b_{ji}) a_{j1} = 0 \\ \frac{\partial f}{\partial p_{1i}} = 2 \sum (\sum_k^n a_{jk} p_{ki} - b_{ji}) a_{j2} = 0 \\ \cdots \\ \frac{\partial f}{\partial p_{1i}} = 2 \sum (\sum_k^n a_{jk} p_{ki} - b_{ji}) a_{jn} = 0 \end{cases}$$

or,

$$\begin{cases} p_{1i}\sum(a_{j1})^2 + p_{2i}\sum(a_{j1}a_{j2}) + \cdots + p_{ni}\sum(a_{j1}a_{jn}) - \sum(a_{j1}b_{ji}) = 0 \\ p_{1i}\sum(a_{j1}a_{j2}) + p_{2i}\sum(a_{j2})^2 + \cdots + p_{ni}\sum(a_{j2}a_{jn}) - \sum(a_{j2}b_{ji}) = 0 \\ \cdots \\ p_{1i}\sum(a_{j1}a_{jn}) + p_{2i}\sum(a_{jn}a_{j2}) + \cdots + p_{ni}\sum(a_{jn})^2 - \sum(a_{jn}b_{ji}) = 0 \end{cases}$$

Let A be the coefficient matrix of this equation group about $p_{1i}, p_{2i}, ..., p_{ni}$. If $d = |A| \neq 0$, then this equation group has the only result, which is

$$p_{1i} = \frac{d_1}{d}, p_{2i} = \frac{d_2}{d}, \cdots, p_{ni} = \frac{d_n}{d},$$

where d_i is the determinant of the matrix of after *ith* rank in A is replaced the constant rank $\sum(a_{j1}b_{ji}), \sum(a_{j2}b_{ji}) \cdots, \sum(a_{jn}b_{ji})$. $i = 1, 2, \cdots, m$.

In the above, p_{ji} represent the probabilities of $Y = y_i$ under the conditional $X = x_j$, $i = 1, 2, \cdots, m; j = 1, 2, \cdots, n$. In order to assure the probability significance level of the probabilities, the results should be:

$$p_{ji} := p_{ji}/(p_{1i} + p_{2i} + \cdots + p_{ni}),$$

where, $i = 1, 2, \cdots, m; j = 1, 2, \cdots, n$.

Another measurement of $X \to Y$ is its support. Because it is a probabilistic dependency rule, we define a metric to check the degree of $M_{Y|X}$ fitting the given fact set. For fact $(a, b) \in DS$, $a = (a_1, a_2, \cdots, a_n) \in S(X)$ and $b = (b_1, b_2, \cdots, b_m) \in S(Y)$, let $b' = (b'_1, b'_2, \cdots, b'_m) = a \cdot M_{Y|X}$, then the fitting error is defined as

$$error(b, b') = |b - b'| = \sum_{i=1}^{m} |b_i - b'_i|.$$

If $error(b, b')$ is less than or equal to some user specified maximum allowance error e, then fact (a, b) support the conditional probability matrix $M_{Y|X}$. Let N be the size of DS the data set of interest, and M the number of data supporting $M_{Y|X}$ in DS. The support of $X \to Y$ is defined as

$$support(X, Y) = M/N$$

If $support(X, Y) \geq minsupp$, $X \to Y$ with $M_{Y|X}$ can be extracted as valid rule.

4.3 Algorithm

We now design the algorithm of the above statistical model.

Algorithm 1 *statisticalm*

Input: *D: probabilistic database, minsupp and e: threshold values;*
Output: $X \rightarrow Y$*: dependent rule,* $M_{Y|X}$*: the conditional probability matrix of* Y *given* X*;*

Begin

Let $DS \leftarrow$ a set of probabilities in D with respect to item variables X and Y;

Calculate $M_{Y|X}$;

For $(a, b) \in DS$ **do**

Statistics M the number of data supporting $M_{Y|X}$ in DS for e;

If $M/|DS| \geq minsupp$ **then**

Output $X \rightarrow Y$ with $M_{Y|X}$ and $support(X, Y)$;

End.

Algorithm *statisticalm* is to generate dependent rules of the form: $X \rightarrow Y$ attached a conditional probability matrix $M_{Y|X}$, from a given probabilistic database D.

The above method can synthesize the probability meanings of all point values of a sample. We now illustrate the use of this algorithm by an example as follows.

Example 2. For a given probabilistic database, X and Y are two item variables. Let $R(X) = \{x_1, x_2\}$, $R(Y) = \{y_1, y_2, y_3\}$, 22 data are generated by procedure Generatedata as follows:

Table 3. *Probabilities of X and Y*

EMP	$p(x_1)$	$p(x_2)$	$p(y_1)$	$p(y_2)$	$p(y_3)$	*EMP*	$p(x_1)$	$p(x_2)$	$p(y_1)$	$p(y_2)$	$p(y_3)$
01	*1*	*0*	*0.5*	*0.3*	*0.2*	*02*	*0*	*1*	*0.1*	*0.6*	*0.3*
03	*0.9*	*0.1*	*0.46*	*0.33*	*0.21*	*04*	*0.1*	*0.9*	*0.14*	*0.57*	*0.29*
05	*0.8*	*0.2*	*0.42*	*0.36*	*0.22*	*06*	*0.2*	*0.8*	*0.18*	*0.54*	*0.28*
07	*0.7*	*0.3*	*0.38*	*0.39*	*0.23*	*08*	*0.3*	*0.7*	*0.22*	*0.51*	*0.27*
09	*0.6*	*0.4*	*0.34*	*0.42*	*0.24*	*10*	*0.4*	*0.6*	*0.26*	*0.48*	*0.26*
11	*0.5*	*0.5*	*0.3*	*0.45*	*0.25*	*12*	*0.95*	*0.05*	*0.48*	*0.315*	*0.205*
13	*0.05*	*0.95*	*0.12*	*0.585*	*0.295*	*14*	*0.85*	*0.15*	*0.44*	*0.345*	*0.215*
15	*0.15*	*0.85*	*0.16*	*0.555*	*0.285*	*16*	*0.75*	*0.25*	*0.4*	*0.375*	*0.225*
17	*0.25*	*0.75*	*0.2*	*0.525*	*0.275*	*18*	*0.65*	*0.35*	*0.36*	*0.405*	*0.235*
19	*0.35*	*0.65*	*0.24*	*0.495*	*0.265*	*20*	*0.55*	*0.45*	*0.32*	*0.435*	*0.245*
21	*0.855*	*0.145*	*0.3*	*0.4*	*0.4*	*22*	*0.654*	*0.346*	*0.4*	*0.2*	*0.4*

We can acquire a lot of probabilistic information for the rule with using the above method from these data as follows.

$$\begin{cases} 8.131241p_{11} + 3.427759p_{21} = 4.3121 \\ 3.427759p_{11} + 7.013241p_{21} = 2.4079 \end{cases}$$

So, we have, $p_{11} = 0.4856369, p_{21} = 0.1059786$.

In the same way, we can obtain, $p_{12} = 0.2793863, p_{22} = 0.595241$; $p_{13} = 0.4059914, p_{23} = 0.2949115$.

In order to assure the probability significance level of the prior probabilities, the results should be:

$$p_{11} = 0.4856369/(0.4856369 + 0.2793863 + 0.4059914) = 0.414715,$$

and $p_{12} = 0.238585, p_{13} = 0.3467; p_{21} = 0.10639, p_{22} = 0.597553, p_{23} = 0.296057$. That is, we acquire a conditional probability matrix $M_{Y|X}$ for the above rule as follows

$$M_{Y|X} = \begin{bmatrix} p_{11} \, p_{12} \, p_{13} \\ p_{21} \, p_{22} \, p_{23} \end{bmatrix} = \begin{bmatrix} 0.414715 \; 0.238585 \;\; 0.3467 \\ 0.10639 \;\; 0.597553 \; 0.296057 \end{bmatrix}$$

If allowance error e is equal to or less than 0.3, then $X \to Y$ with conditional probability matrix $M_{Y|X}$ can be extracted as a valid probabilistic rules, which its support is 1.

5 Experiments

To study the effectiveness of our model, we have performed several experiments. Our server is Oracle 8.0.3, and the algorithm is implemented on Sun SparcServer using Java, and JDBC API is used as the interface between the program and Oracle.

To evaluate our model, we have used a kinds of datasets: relational probabilistic databases, which are randomly generated according to the probabilistic data in the probabilistic databases. Our experimental results demonstrate that the approach in the kinds of datasets is efficient and promising.

The main properties of the data sets are the following. The sizes (*attriN*) of attributes in datasets are in 5 to 15. The numbers (*dsetN*) of data of interest are approximately 100, 1000, 10000, 100000. They are listed as Table 4.

Table 4. *Synthetic data set characteristics*

Data set name	*attriN*	*dsetN*
A5.D100K	*5*	*100*
A5.D100K	*5*	*10000*
A10.D100K	*10*	*100*
A10.D1000K	*10*	*1000*
A10.D10000K	*10*	*10000*
A15.D100000K	*15*	*100000*

To improve statistical model *statisticalm* (Algorithm 1), we have also designed two algorithms *randommodel* (It is called as random search model that performs on a set of instances: random samples) and *partitionm* (It is first to partition the data set into several subsets and then the random search model is applied to these subsets). The experiments are designed to test the effectiveness of our designed algorithms. For the group of data in Table 4, the performances of proposed algorithms are depicted in Figure 1.

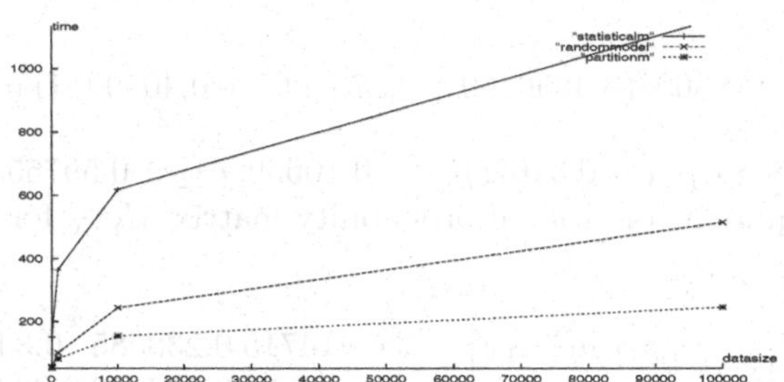

Fig. 1. The running time

In Figure 1, algorithm *partionm* presents the best performance.

6 Conclusion

Today's database systems must handle uncertainties in the data they store. So mining probabilistic databases is necessary to applications. To our knowledge, no work on probabilistic database mining. Researches on association analysis such as [1] and [7] seem quite related to this work. However, previous mining techniques cannot work well on probabilistic databases due to the fact that probabilistic databases are in 1NF. We proposed a new model for discovering useful dependent rules in probabilistic databases in this paper by partitioning. We evaluated the proposed technique, and our experimental results demonstrate that the approach is efficient and promising.

References

1. R. Agrawal, T. Imielinski, and A. Swami, Mining association rules between sets of items in large databases. In: *Proceedings of ACM SIGMOD*, 1993:207-216.
2. R. Cromp and W. Campbell: Data Mining of Multi-dimensional Remotely Sensed Images. In: *Proceedings of CIKM*. 1993: 471-480.
3. D. Dey and S. Sarkar, A probabilistic relational model and algebra, *ACM Trans. on Database Systems*, Vol. 21 3(1996):339-369.
4. J. Han, Y. Cai and N. Cercone, Data-driven discovery of quantitative rules in relational databases. *IEEE TKDE*, Vol. 5, 1(1993):29-40.
5. K. Han, J. Koperski, and N. Stefanovic, GeoMiner: A system prototype for spatial data mining. *SIGMOD Record* Vol. 26, 2(1997): 553-556.
6. J. Pearl, *Probabilistic reasoning in intelligent systems: Networks of plausible inference*. Morgan Kaufmann Publishers, 1988.
7. R. Srikant and R. Agrawal, Mining quantitative association rules in large relational tables. In: *Proceedings of ACM SIGMOD*, 1996: 1-12.

The Complexity of Logic Program Updates

Yan Zhang

University of Western Sydney, Australia
yan@cit.uws.edu.au

Abstract. In the context of logic program updates, a knowledge base, which is presented as a logic program, can be updated in terms of another logic program, i.e. a set of *update rules*. In this paper, we investigate the complexity of logic program updates where conflict resolution on defeasible information is explicitly taken into account in an update. We show that in general the problem of model checking in logic program updates is co-NP-complete, and the corresponding inference problem is Π_2^P-complete. We also characterize particular classes of update specifications where the inference problem has a lower computational complexity. These results confirm that logic program update, even if with the issue of conflict resolution on defeasible information to be presented, is not harder than the principal update tasks.

1 Introduction

In the context of logic program updates, a knowledge base, which is presented as a logic program, can be updated in terms of another logic program, i.e. a set of *update rules*. While the semantics and properties of logic program update have been studied by many researchers recently, e.g. [1,9], its computational complexity still remains unclear when conflict resolution on defeasible information is taken into account in logic program updates. In this paper, we investigate the complexity problem of logic program updates where conflict resolution on defeasible information is explicitly taken into account in our update problems. We show that in general the problem of model checking in logic program updates is co-NP-complete, and the corresponding inference problem is Π_2^P-complete. We also characterize particular classes of update specifications where the inference problem has a lower computational complexity. These results confirm that logic program update, even if with the issue of conflict resolution on defeasible information to be presented, is not harder than the principal update tasks.

The paper is organized as follows. In section 2 we briefly review the prioritized logic program which will be used as a basis for our logic program update formulation. In section 3 we develop a logic program update framework in which both contradiction elimination and conflict resolution are taken into account. In section 4 we analyze the computational complexity of logic program updates in detail, while in section 5 we investigate under what conditions the inference problem in an update can be simplified. Finally, in section 6 we conclude this paper with some remarks.

M. Brooks, D. Corbett, and M. Stumptner (Eds.): AI 2001, LNAI 2256, pp. 631–642, 2001.

2 Prioritized Logic Programs: A Review

In this section we briefly review prioritized logic programs (PLPs) proposed by Zhang & Foo [10]. To specify PLPs, we first introduce the extended logic program and its answer set semantics developed by Gelfond and Lifschitz [7]. A language $\mathcal{L}$ of extended logic programs is determined by its object constants, function constants and predicates constants. *Terms* are built as in the corresponding first order language; *atoms* have the form $P(t_1, \cdots, t_n)$, where t_i $(1 \leq i \leq n)$ is a term and P is a predicate constant of arity n; a *literal* is either an atom $P(t_1, \cdots, t_n)$ or a negative atom $\neg P(t_1, \cdots, t_n)$. A *rule* is an expression of the form:

$$L_0 \leftarrow L_1, \cdots, L_m, notL_{m+1}, \cdots, notL_n, \tag{1}$$

where each L_i $(0 \leq i \leq n)$ is a literal. L_0 is called the *head* of the rule, while $L_1, \cdots, L_m$,*not* $L_{m+1}, \cdots$, *not* L_n is called the *body* of the rule. Obviously, the body of a rule could be empty. A term, atom, literal, or rule is *ground* if no variable occurs in it. An *extended logic program* Π is a collection of rules.

To evaluate an extended logic program, Gelfond and Lifschitz proposed answer set semantics for extended logic programs. Let Π be an extended logic program not containing *not* and *Lit* the set of all ground literals in the language of Π. The *answer set* of Π, denoted as $Ans(\Pi)$, is the smallest subset S of *Lit* such that (i) for any rule $L_0 \leftarrow L_1, \cdots, L_m$ from Π, if $L_1, \cdots, L_m \in S$, then $L_0 \in S$; and (ii) if S contains a pair of complementary literals, then $S = Lit$. Now let Π be an arbitrary extended logic program. For any subset S of *Lit*, let Π^S be the logic program obtained from Π by deleting (i) each rule that has a formula *not* L in its body with $L \in S$, and (ii) all formulas of the form *not* L in the bodies of the remaining rules[1]. We define that S is an *answer set* of Π iff S is an answer set of Π^S. An extended logic program Π is *well defined* if it has a consistent answer set.

The language $\mathcal{L}^P$ of PLPs is a language $\mathcal{L}$ of extended logic programs with the following augments:
- *Names:* $N, N_1, N_2, \cdots$.
- A strict partial ordering $<$ on names.
- A naming function $\mathcal{N}$, which maps a rule to a name.

A PLP $\mathcal{P}$ is a triple $(\Pi, \mathcal{N}, <)$, where Π is an extended logic program, $\mathcal{N}$ is a naming function mapping each rule in Π to a name, and $<$ is a strict partial ordering on names. The partial ordering $<$ in $\mathcal{P}$ plays an essential role in the evaluation of $\mathcal{P}$. We also use $\mathcal{P}(<)$ to denote the set of $<$-relations of $\mathcal{P}$. Intuitively $<$ represents a preference of applying rules during the evaluation of the program. In particular, if $\mathcal{N}(r) < \mathcal{N}(r')$ holds in $\mathcal{P}$, rule r would be preferred to apply over rule r' during the evaluation of $\mathcal{P}$ (i.e. rule r is more preferred than rule r'). Consider the following classical example represented in our formalism:

$\mathcal{P}_1$:
$N_1 : Fly(x) \leftarrow Bird(x),\ not\ \neg Fly(x)$,

[1] We also call Π^S is the Gelfond-Lifschitz transformation of Π in terms of S.

$N_2 : \neg Fly(x) \leftarrow Penguin(x), \, not \, Fly(x)$,
$N_3 : Bird(Tweety) \leftarrow$,
$N_4 : Penguin(Tweety) \leftarrow$,
$N_2 < N_1$.

Obviously, rules N_1 and N_2 conflict with each other as their heads are complementary literals, and applying N_1 will defeat N_2 and *vice versa*. However, as $N_2 < N_1$, we would expect that rule N_2 is preferred to apply first and then defeat rule N_1 so that the desired solution $\neg Fly(Tweety)$ can be derived. In a PLP or an extended logic program, we usually view a rule including variables to be the set of all ground instances of this rule formed from the set of ground literals in the language.

Definition 1. *Let Π be a ground extended logic program and r a rule with the form $L_0 \leftarrow L_1, \cdots, L_m, \, not \, L_{m+1}, \cdots, \, not \, L_n$ (r does not necessarily belong to Π). Rule r is* defeated *by Π iff Π has an answer set and for any answer set S of Π, there exists some $L_i \in S$, where $m + 1 \leq i \leq n$.*

Sometimes, it is also convenient to say that a set S of ground literals *defeats* a rule r if there is some literal L in S and r has a form $L_0 \leftarrow \cdots, notL, \cdots$. Now our idea of evaluating a PLP is as follows. Let $\mathcal{P} = (\Pi, \mathcal{N}, <)$. If there are two rules r and r' in Π and $\mathcal{N}(r) < \mathcal{N}(r')$, r' will be ignored in the evaluation of $\mathcal{P}$, *only if* keeping r in Π and deleting r' from Π will result in a defeat of r', i.e. r' is defeated by $\Pi - \{r'\}$. By eliminating all such potential rules from Π, $\mathcal{P}$ is eventually reduced to an extended logic program in which the partial ordering $<$ has been removed. Our evaluation for $\mathcal{P}$ is then based on this *reduced* extended logic program.

The evaluation of a PLP will be based on its ground form. That is, for any PLP $\mathcal{P} = (\Pi, \mathcal{N}, <)$, we consider its *ground instantiation* $\mathcal{P}' = (\Pi', \mathcal{N}', <')$, where Π', $\mathcal{N}'$ and $<'$ are ground instantiations of Π, $\mathcal{N}$ and $<$ respectively[2]. However, to ensure that ordering $<'$ is well behaved, i.e. $<'$ is also a strict partial ordering and every non-empty subset of Π' has a least element with respect to $<'$, we require that $\mathcal{P} = (\Pi, \mathcal{N}, <)$ be *well formed*: there does not exist a rule r' in Π' that is an instance of two different rules r_1 and r_2 in Π and $\mathcal{N}(r_1) < \mathcal{N}(r_2) \in \mathcal{P}(<)$.

Definition 2. *Let $\mathcal{P} = (\Pi, \mathcal{N}, <)$ be a ground prioritized extended logic program. $\mathcal{P}^<$ is a* reduct *of $\mathcal{P}$ with respect to $<$ if and only if there exists a sequence of sets Π_i ($i = 0, 1, \cdots$) such that:*

1. *$\Pi_0 = \Pi$;*
2. *$\Pi_i = \Pi_{i-1} - \{r_1, r_2, \cdots \mid$ (a) there exists $r \in \Pi_{i-1}$ such that for every j ($j = 1, 2, \cdots$), $\mathcal{N}(r) < \mathcal{N}(r_j) \in \mathcal{P}(<)$ and $r_1, \cdots, r_k$ are defeated by $\Pi_{i-1} - \{r_1, r_2, \cdots\}$, and (b) there does not exist a rule $r' \in \Pi_{i-1}$ such that $N(r_j) < N(r')$ for some j ($j = 1, 2, \cdots$) and r' is defeated by $\Pi_{i-1} - \{r'\}\}$;*

[2] Note that if $\mathcal{P}'$ is a ground instantiation of $\mathcal{P}$, then $\mathcal{N}(r_1) < \mathcal{N}(r_2) \in \mathcal{P}(<)$ implies $\mathcal{N}'(r'_1) <' \mathcal{N}(r'_2) \in \mathcal{P}'(<')$, where r'_1 and r'_2 are ground instances of r_1 and r_2 respectively.

3. $\mathcal{P}^< = \bigcap_{i=0}^{\infty} \Pi_i$.

Definition 3. *Let* $\mathcal{P} = (\Pi, \mathcal{N}, <)$ *be a PLP and Lit the set of all ground literals in the language of* $\mathcal{P}$. *For any subset S of Lit, S is an* answer set *of* $\mathcal{P}$ *iff S is an answer set of some reduct* $\mathcal{P}^<$ *of* $\mathcal{P}$. *A ground literal L is* entailed *from* $\mathcal{P}$, *denoted as* $\mathcal{P} \models L$, *if L belongs to every answer set of* $\mathcal{P}$. $\mathcal{P}$ *is called* well defined *if it has a consistent answer set.*

Using Definitions 2 and 3, it is easy to conclude that $\mathcal{P}_1$ has a unique reduct as follows:

$$\mathcal{P}_1^< = \{\neg Fly(x) \leftarrow Penguin(x), not\ Fly(x),$$
$$Bird(Tweety) \leftarrow, Penguin(Tweety) \leftarrow\},$$

from which we obtain the following answer set of $\mathcal{P}_1$:

$$\{Bird(Tweety), Penguin(Tweety), \neg Fly(Tweety)\}.$$

3 Logic Program Updates

Given a knowledge base which is represented as a logic program (i.e. a finite set of rules), we consider the problem of how to update this knowledge base in terms another logic program (i.e. a set of *update rules*). In our context, since both knowledge base Π_0 and the set of update rules Π_1 are expressed as extended logic programs where rules in Π_0 or Π_1 may contain both classical negation and negation as failure, there are two essential issues to achieve this kind of logic program update: eliminating contradictory rules between Π_0 and Π_1 and solving conflicts among rules in Π_0 and Π_1. That is, if a rule r in Π_0 contradicts some other rule(s) in Π_1, we should remove r from Π_0. But we must be aware that removing r from Π_0 may have effects on other rules. On the other hand, if a defeasible rule r in Π_0 conflicts with another rule r' in Π_1, we should have some way to solve thus conflict. These ideas are elaborated as follows.

Eliminating contradictory rules

To eliminate contradictory rules from Π_0 with respect to Π_1, it cannot be simply to extract a maximal subset Π of Π_0 by requiring $\Pi \cup \Pi_1$ to be well defined. For instance, suppose $\Pi_0 = \{P \leftarrow, R \leftarrow Q\}$ and $\Pi_1 = \{Q \leftarrow P, \neg R \leftarrow Q\}$. Clearly, both $\Pi = \{P \leftarrow\}$ and $\Pi' = \{R \leftarrow P\}$ are maximal subsets of Π_0 such that $\Pi \cup \Pi_1$ and $\Pi' \cup \Pi_1$ are well defined. But intuitively, rule $R \leftarrow Q$ represents a contradictory semantics compared with rule $\neg R \leftarrow Q$ in Π_1, and hence we would like to delete $R \leftarrow Q$ instead of deleting $P \leftarrow$ from Π_0.

To achieve this purpose, we first *update* each answer set S of Π_0 with Π_1, which we call *simple fact update*. The result of this update is a set of ground literals, denoted as S', which has minimal difference from S and satisfies each rule in Π_1. If S' is consistent, we then *extract* a maximal subset $\Pi_{(\Pi_0,\Pi_1)}$ of Π_0 such that S' is *coherent* with $\Pi_{(\Pi_0,\Pi_1)} \cup \Pi_1$, i.e. S' is a subset of an answer set of $\Pi_{(\Pi_0,\Pi_1)} \cup \Pi_1$. Doing this, $\Pi_{(\Pi_0,\Pi_1)}$ is guaranteed to maximally retain rules of Π_0 which are not contradictory to rules of Π_1. The program $\Pi_{(\Pi_0,\Pi_1)}$ is called a *transformed program* from Π_0 with respect to Π_1. If no consistent S' exists, on the other hand, $\Pi_{(\Pi_0,\Pi_1)}$ is simply specified to be any maximal subset of Π_0 such that $\Pi_{(\Pi_0,\Pi_1)} \cup \Pi_1$ is well defined.

Solving conflicts

After transforming Π_0 to $\Pi_{(\Pi_0,\Pi_1)}$, we need to solve possible conflicts between rules in $\Pi_{(\Pi_0,\Pi_1)}$ and Π_1. We call this phase program update. To do so, we specify a prioritized logic program $\mathcal{P}_{(\Pi_0,\Pi_1)} = (\Pi_{(\Pi_0,\Pi_1)} \cup \Pi_1, \mathcal{N}, <)$, where for each rule r in Π_1 and each rule r' in $\Pi_{(\Pi_0,\Pi_1)}$, we specify $\mathcal{N}(r) < \mathcal{N}(r')$. The intuitive idea behind this is that rules in Π_1 should be *more* preferred than rules in $\Pi_{(\Pi_0,\Pi_1)}$ as Π_1 expresses the agent's latest knowledge. Whenever there is a conflict between rules r and r' where $r \in \Pi_1$ and $r' \in \Pi_{(\Pi_0,\Pi_1)}$ respectively, r will override r'. Then, we finally specify the possible resulting program Π_0' after updating Π_0 with Π_1 to be a reduct of $\mathcal{P}_{(\Pi_0,\Pi_1)} = (\Pi_{(\Pi_0,\Pi_1)} \cup \Pi_1, \mathcal{N}, <)$, i.e. $\mathcal{P}^{<}_{(\Pi_0,\Pi_1)}$ (see Definition 3).

Now we give the formal definition for simple fact update. Let Π_0 and Π_1 be two extended logic programs, and S an answer set of Π_0. We specify $\mathcal{L}^P_{new}$ to be a language of PLPs based on Π_0 and Π_1's language $\mathcal{L}$ with one more augment: For each predicate symbol P in $\mathcal{L}$, there is a corresponding predicate symbol $New\text{-}P$ in $\mathcal{L}^P_{new}$ with the same arity of P. To simplifying our presentation, in $\mathcal{L}^P_{new}$ we use notation $New\text{-}L$ to denote the corresponding literal L in $\mathcal{L}$. We use Lit_{new} to denote the set of all ground literals of $\mathcal{L}^P_{new}$. Clearly, $Lit_{new} = Lit \cup \{New\text{-}L \mid L \in Lit\}$.

Definition 4. *Let S be a consistent set of ground literals and Π an extended logic program. The* specification *of* updating *S* with *Π is defined as a PLP of $\mathcal{L}^P_{new}$, denoted as $Update(S,\Pi) = (\Pi^*, \mathcal{N}, <)$, as follows:*

1. *Π^* consists of following rules:*
   Initial fact rules*: for each L in S, there is a rule $L \leftarrow$;*
   Inertia rules*: for each predicate symbol P in $\mathcal{L}$, there are two rules:*
   $New\text{-}P(x) \leftarrow P(x)$, not $\neg New\text{-}P(x)$, and
   $\neg New\text{-}P(x) \leftarrow \neg P(x)$, not $New\text{-}P(x)$,
   Update rules*: for each rule $L_0 \leftarrow L_1, \cdots, L_m$, not $L_{m+1}, \cdots$, not L_n in Π_1, there is a rule $New\text{-}L_0 \leftarrow New\text{-}L_1, \cdots, New\text{-}L_m$, not $New\text{-}L_{m+1}, \cdots$, not $New\text{-}L_n$;*
2. *For any inertia rule r and update rule r', $\mathcal{N}(r) < \mathcal{N}(r')$.*

Definition 5. *(**Simple Fact Update**) A set of ground literals of $\mathcal{L}$, S', is called a* possible result *with respect to the update specification $Update(S,\Pi)$, iff for some answer set S^* of $Update(S,\Pi)$, $S' = \{L \mid New\text{-}L \in S^*\}$.*

The update specification $Update(S,\Pi)$ defined in Definition 4 provides a formal method to derive the possible result of updating S with Π_1. In Particular, inertia rules in Π^* guarantee a minimal change during the update, i.e. any initial fact in S that is not explicitly changed will persist by default. Update rules, on the other hand, specify effects of the update. Since both inertia and update rules may be defeasible[3], possible conflicts may occur between them. Furthermore, from the minimal change principle, initial facts in $Ans(\Pi_0)$ are always preferred to persist during the update whenever there is no explicit violation of update rules. So we specify that inertia rules are more preferred than update rules. Finally, the possible result of this update is derived from answer sets of $Update(S, \Pi)$ as presented in Definition 5.

Lemma 1. *Let $Update(S, \Pi)$ be a well defined update specification as specified in Definition 4. S' is a possible result with respect to $Update(S, \Pi)$ if and only if S' is an answer set of PLP $\mathcal{P} = (\Pi \cup \{L \leftarrow not\overline{L} \mid L \in S\}, \mathcal{N}, <)$, where for each rule $r : L \leftarrow not\overline{L}$ with $L \in S$, and each rule r' in Π, $\mathcal{N}(r) < \mathcal{N}(r')$*[4].

Definition 6. *Let Π_0 and Π_1 be two extended logic programs, S an answer set of Π_0 and $Update(S, \Pi_1)$ as specficied in Definition 4. A subset $\Pi_{(\Pi_0,\Pi_1)}$ of Π_0 is called a* transformed program *from Π_0 with respec to Π_1, iff (1) if $UPdate(S, \Pi)$ has a consistent answer set S', then $\Pi_{(\Pi_0,\Pi_1)}$ is a maximal subset of Π_0 such that S' is coherent with $\Pi_{(\Pi_0,\Pi_1)} \cup \Pi_1$; (2) if $Update(S, \Pi)$ has no consistent answer set, then $\Pi_{(\Pi_0,\Pi_1)}$ is any maximal subset of Π_0 such that $\Pi_{(\Pi_0,\Pi_1)} \cup \Pi_1$ is well defined.*

Definition 7. *(***Program Update***) Let $\Pi_{(\Pi_0,\Pi_1)}$ be defined as in Definition 6. The* specification of updating *Π_0 with Π_1, denoted as P-Update(Π_0, Π_1), is a PLP $(\Pi_{(\Pi_0,\Pi_1)} \cup \Pi_1, \mathcal{N}, <)$, where for each rule r in Π_1 and each rule r' in $\Pi_{(\Pi_0,\Pi_1)}$, $\mathcal{N}(r) < \mathcal{N}(r')$. Π_0' is called a* possible resulting program *after updating Π_0 with Π_1 iff Π_0' is a reduct of $\mathcal{P}_{(\Pi_0,\Pi_1)}$.*

Example 1. Given two extended logic programs $\Pi_0 = \{P \leftarrow, R \leftarrow not\ Q, Q \leftarrow not\ R\}$ and $\Pi_1 = \{\neg P \leftarrow\}$. Consider an update of Π_0 with Π_1. Firstly, to find out the contradictory rule in Π_0 with respect to Π_1, we update every answer set of Π_0 with Π_1. Clearly, Π_0 has two answer sets $\{P, R\}$ and $\{P, Q\}$. Updating these two answer sets with Π_1, we get $\{\neg P, R\}$ and $\{\neg P, Q\}$ respectively. From Definition 7, it is not difficult to conclude that program $\Pi_{(\Pi_0,\Pi_1)} = \{R \leftarrow not\ Q, Q \leftarrow not\ R\}$ is the unique transformed program from Π_0 with respect to Π_1 (i.e. both $\{P, R\}$ and $\{P, Q\}$ are coherent with $\Pi_{(\Pi_0,\Pi_1)} \cup \Pi_1$). Secondly, to solve possible conflicts between rules in $\Pi_{(\Pi_0,\Pi_1)}$ and Π_1, we specify a PLP $\mathcal{P}_{(\Pi_0,\Pi_1)} = (\Pi_{(\Pi_0,\Pi_1)} \cup \Pi_1, \mathcal{N}, <)$ as follows:

$N_1 : R \leftarrow not\ Q,$
$N_2 : Q \leftarrow not\ R,$
$N_3 : \neg P \leftarrow,$
$N_3 < N_1, N_3 < N_2.$

[3] Weak negation *not* may be included in these rules.

[4] $\overline{L}$ stands for the complement of literal L.

Finally, it is concluded from Definition 3 that $\mathcal{P}_{(\Pi_0,\Pi_1)}$ has two reducts $\{\neg P \leftarrow, R \leftarrow not\ Q\}$ and $\{\neg P \leftarrow, Q \leftarrow not\ R\}$, which, as specified in Definition 8, are the two possible resulting programs after updating Π_0 with Π_1. □

4 Complexity of Logic Program Updates

In this section, we address the issue of computational complexity of logic program updates. From previous presentations, it is clear that our update consists of two steps: the simple fact update and program update, where the former is used to remove contradictory rules from the knowledge base and provides a basis for the program update. It is also easy to see that a simple fact update is a special case of program update[5]. For this reason, our complexity analysis will be based on these two phases. In the rest of this section, we assume that all programs are finite propositional programs.

We first introduce necessary notions of the complexity theory, where further descriptions are referred to [5]. The class $P^{\mathcal{C}}$ consists of the problems solvable by a polynomial-time deterministic Truing machine with an oracle for a problem from $\mathcal{C}$, where the class $NP^{\mathcal{C}}$ includes the problems solvable by a nondeterministic Turing machine with an oracle for a problem in $\mathcal{C}$. Let $\mathcal{C}$ be a class of decision problems, by co-$\mathcal{C}$ we mean the class consisting of the complements of the problems in $\mathcal{C}$.

The classes Σ_k^P and Π_k^P of the *polynomial hierarchy* are defined as follows:

$$\Sigma_0^P = \Pi_0^P = P \text{ and}$$
$$\Sigma_k^P = NP^{\Sigma_{k-1}^P},\ \Pi_k^P = \text{co-}\Sigma_k^P \text{ for all } k > 1.$$

It is easy to see that $NP = \Sigma_1^P$, co-$NP = \Pi_1^P$, and $\Sigma_2^P = NP^{NP}$. It is also observed that in general $P \subseteq NP$, $P \subseteq$ co-NP, $NP \subseteq \Sigma_2^P$, and co-$NP \subseteq \Pi_2^P$. Each inclusion relation is usually believed to be proper. A problem A is *complete* for a class $\mathcal{C}$ if $A \in \mathcal{C}$ and for every problem B in $\mathcal{C}$ there is a polynomial transformation of B to A.

4.1 Complexity of Simple Fact Update

Now we consider the simple fact update. Given a consistent set S of ground literals and an extended logic program Π, the update of S with Π is specified by the corresponding update specification $Update(S, \Pi)$ which is a PLP as defined in Definition 5. From Lemma 1, we know that a set S' is a result with respect to $Update(S, \Pi)$ if and only if S' is an answer set of a PLP

$$\mathcal{P} = (\Pi \cup \{L \leftarrow not\overline{L} \mid L \in S\}, \mathcal{N}, <),$$

where for each $r : L \leftarrow not\overline{L}$ with $L \in S$ and each $r' \in \Pi$, $\mathcal{N}(r) < \mathcal{N}(r')$. So we call this $\mathcal{P}$ the *equivalent PLP* of update specification $Update(S, \Pi)$. From this result, it is clear that to evaluate $Update(S, \Pi)$, we only need to compute the answer set of $\mathcal{P}$.

[5] Given S and Π, if we view each literal L in S as a rule $L \leftarrow$, updating S with Π is equivalent to updating Π_S with Π where $\Pi_S = \{L \leftarrow \mid L \in S\}$.

Proposition 1. *Let Π be a well defined program and r a rule. Deciding whether r is defeated by Π is co-NP-complete.*

Now we need to provide a characterization on the answer sets of the particular class of PLPs that are of the form as $\mathcal{P}$ above. Given a PLP $\mathcal{P} = (\Pi_1 \cup \Pi_2, \mathcal{N}, <)$, where for each $<$-relation $\mathcal{N}(r) < \mathcal{N}(r')$ in $\mathcal{P}$, $r \in \Pi_1$ and $r' \in \Pi_2$. Let S be an answer set of $\Pi_1 \cup \Pi_1$. We specify $R^<(S) = (\Phi_1(S), \Phi_2(S))$, where $\Phi_1(S)$ is a subset of Π_1 in which each rule is defeated by S, and $\Phi_2(S)$ is the subset of Π_2 in which each rule is defeated by S.

Definition 8. *Let $\mathcal{P} = (\Pi_1 \cup \Pi_2, \mathcal{N}, <)$ be specified as above, and S and S' two answer sets of $\Pi_1 \cup \Pi_1$. We say S is* more $<$-consistent *with respect to $\mathcal{P}(<)$ than S', denoted as $R^<(S') \sqsubseteq R^<(S)$, if and only if (1) $\Phi_1(S) \subset \Phi_1(S')$ (proper set inclusion); or (2) $\Phi_1(S) = \Phi_1(S')$ and $\Phi_2(S') \subseteq \Phi_2(S)$. S is* maximally $<$-consistent *with respect to $\mathcal{P}(<)$ if there does not exist another S'' such that $R^<(S) \sqsubset R^<(S'')$*[6].

Intuitively, a maximal $<$-consistent answer set of $\Pi_1 \cup \Pi_2$ with respect to $\mathcal{P}(<)$ defeats a minimal number of rules in Π_1 and a maximal number of rules in Π_2. Since for each $\mathcal{N}(r) < \mathcal{N}(r')$ in $\mathcal{P}(<)$, $r \in \Pi_1$ and $r' \in \Pi_2$, this property ensures that S is evaluated by applying rules in Π_1 first, which is consistent with the intuition of $<$-relations specified in $\mathcal{P}(<)$. In general, we have the following result.

Lemma 2. *Let $\mathcal{P} = (\Pi_1 \cup \Pi_2, \mathcal{N}, <)$ be a PLP, where for each $<$-relation $\mathcal{N}(r) < \mathcal{N}(r')$ in $\mathcal{P}$, $r \in \Pi_1$ and $r' \in \Pi_2$. A set of ground literals S is an answer set of $\mathcal{P}$ if S is a maximal $<$-consistent answer set of $\Pi_1 \cup \Pi_2$ with respect to $\mathcal{P}(<)$.*

Theorem 1. *Let $\mathcal{P}$ be the equivalent PLP of an simple fact update specification, and S a set of ground literals. Deciding whether S is an answer set of $\mathcal{P}$ is co-NP-complete.*

Proof. (*Proof Sketch*). Due to a space limit, we only outline our proof idea here. According to our previous description, $\mathcal{P}$ is a PLP of the form $\mathcal{P} = (\Pi \cup \{L \leftarrow not\overline{L} \mid L \in S, \mathcal{N}, <)$, where for each $r : L \leftarrow not\overline{L}$ with $L \in S$ and each $r' \in \Pi$, $\mathcal{N}(r) < \mathcal{N}(r')$. So $\mathcal{P}$ satisfies the condition of Lemma 2. Then the membership is easy to show from Lemma 2. To prove th hardness part, we can reduce the well known NP-complete satisfiability problem to the complement of our problem. In particular, for a given collection of nonempty propositional clauses $\mathcal{C} = \{C_1, \cdots, C_m\}$ on propositional letters $P_1, \cdots, P_n$, we construct a PLP $\mathcal{P} = (\Pi_1 \cup \Pi_2, \mathcal{N}, <)$, where each rule in Π_1 has the form $L \leftarrow not\overline{L}$, and $\mathcal{P}(<)$ is defined to be the set $\mathcal{N}(r) < \mathcal{N}(r')$ for any $r \in \Pi_1$ and $r' \in \Pi_2$, such that an answer set S of $\Pi_1 \cup \Pi_2$ is not maximally $<$-consistent with respect to $\mathcal{P}(<)$ iff $\mathcal{C}$ is satisfiable. Since our construction can be done in polynomial time, this proves co-NP-hardness. □

[6] $R^<(S) \sqsubset R^<(S'')$ means $R^<(S) \sqsubseteq R^<(S'')$ and $R^<(S'') \not\sqsubseteq R^<(S)$.

The following result presents the complexity of inference associated with the simple fact update.

Theorem 2. *Let $\mathcal{P}$ be an arbitrary finite propositional PLP. For a given ground literal L, deciding whether $\mathcal{P} \models L$ is Π_2^P-complete.*

Proof. The membership proof is straightforward. Here we only give the hardness proof. From [4], we know that disjunctive logic program entailment is Π_2^P-hard. This result still holds even if the disjunctive logic program is *head-cycle free*[7]. We will construct a PLP $\mathcal{P}$ from a head-cycle free disjunctive logic program $\mathcal{D}$ such that there exists an one-to-one correspondence between stable models of $\mathcal{D}$ and answer sets of $\mathcal{P}$. Since our construction is in polynomial time, this proves Π_2^P-hardness.

Let $\mathcal{D}$ be a propositional disjunctive normal logic program that involves propositional letters $P_0, \cdots, P_n$. The PLP $\mathcal{P}$ we will construct from $\mathcal{D}$ involves P_i together with $\hat{P}_i$ $(i = 1, \cdots, n)$. Let $\mathcal{P} = (\Pi, \mathcal{N}, <)$. Firstly, we specify Π to consist of the following rules:

(a) For each rule $P_1 \vee \cdots, P_k \leftarrow P_{k+1}, \cdots, P_l, notP_{l+1}, \cdots, notP_m$ in $\mathcal{D}$, we specify k rules in Π as follows:
$P_1 \leftarrow P_{k+1}, \cdots, P_l, notP_{l+1}, \cdots, notP_m, notP_2, \cdots, notP_k,$
$P_2 \leftarrow P_{k+1}, \cdots, P_l, notP_{l+1}, \cdots, notP_m, notP_1, notP_3, \cdots, notP_k,$
$\cdots,$
$P_k \leftarrow P_{k+1}, \cdots, P_l, notP_{l+1}, \cdots, notP_m, notP_1, \cdots, notP_{k-1};$

(b) For each P_i $(i = 1, \cdots, n)$, if P_i does not occur as a head of some rule in Π as specified in Step (a), then rule $\hat{P}_i \leftarrow notP_i$ is included in Π.

Now the $<$-relation in $\mathcal{P}$ is specified as follows:

Let r be a rule in Π specified in Step (a), and r' a rule in Π specified in Step (b), then $\mathcal{N}(r) < \mathcal{N}(r')$.

Now we prove that there is a one-to-one correspondence between $\mathcal{D}$'s stable model and $\mathcal{P}$'s answer set. Firstly, we prove that if S is a stable model of $\mathcal{D}$, then $S' = S \cup \{\hat{P} \mid P \notin S\}$ is an answer set of $\mathcal{P}$. Let $\Pi = \Pi_1 \cup \Pi_2$, where Π_1 includes all rules specified in Step (a) and Π_2 includes all rules specified in Step (b) in the above process.

As there is no propositional letter $\hat{P}$ occurring in Π_1, we can prove that S is a stable model of $\mathcal{D}$ iff S is a stable model of Π_1. Let $\mathcal{D}^S$ be the Gelfond-Lifschitz transformation of $\mathcal{D}$. Clearly, from the stable model definition for disjunctive logic program, S is the minimal model of program $\mathcal{D}^S$, in which no negation as failure sign *not* occurs in the body of each rule. Then for each rule in $\mathcal{D}^S$ of the form $P_1 \vee \cdots \vee P_k \leftarrow P_{k+1}, \cdots, P_l$, if $P_{k+1}, \cdots, P_l$ are in S, then only one of $P_1, \cdots, P_k$ will be in S. Now consider program Π_1^S - the Gelfond-Lifschitz transformation of Π_1 with respect to S. It is observed that for each rule $P_1 \vee \cdots \vee P_k \leftarrow P_{k+1}, \cdots, P_l$ in $\mathcal{D}^S$, if P_i $(1 \leq i \leq k)$ is in S, then there is a rule $P_i \leftarrow P_{k+1}, \cdots, P_l$ in Π_1^S, where $k-1$ rules of the forms

[7] Readers are referred to [2] for the definition of a head-cycle free disjunctive logic program.

$$P_l \leftarrow P_{k+1}, \cdots, P_l, notP_{l+1}, \cdots, notP_m, notP_2, notP_3, \cdots, notP_k,$$
$$\cdots,$$
$$P_{i-1} \leftarrow P_{k+1}, \cdots, P_l, notP_{l+1}, \cdots, notP_m, notP_1, \cdots, notP_{i-2}, notP_i, \cdots, P_k,$$
$$P_{i+1} \leftarrow P_{k+1}, \cdots, P_l, notP_{l+1}, \cdots, notP_m, notP_1, \cdots, notP_i, notP_{i+2}, \cdots, P_k,$$
$$\cdots,$$
$$P_k \leftarrow P_{k+1}, \cdots, P_l, notP_{l+1}, \cdots, notP_m, notP_1, \cdots, notP_{k-1};$$

in Π_1 are eliminated from Π_1^S. This follows that S is the minimal set such that for each rule $P_i \leftarrow P_{k+1}, \cdots, P_l$ in Π_1^S, $P_{k+1}, \cdots, P_l$ in S implies P_i in S. Therefore, S is also a stable model of Π_1. With a similar way, we can prove that if S is a stable model of Π_1, then S is also a stable model of $\mathcal{D}$.

So far, we have showed that S is a stable model of $\mathcal{D}$ iff S is a stable model of Π_1. Then it is easy to see that each reduct of $\mathcal{P}$ has a form $\Pi_1 \cup \Pi_2^*$, where $\Pi_2^* \subseteq \Pi_2$. Clearly, for any rule $\hat{P} \leftarrow notP$ in Π_2 that is eliminated in Π_2^*, P is in every answer set of $\Pi_1 \cup \Pi_2^*$. Furthermore, as $head(\Pi_2^*) \cap body(\Pi_1) = \emptyset$, according to the Generalized Splitting Theorem [11], it concludes that $S \cup \{\hat{P} \mid P \notin S\}$ is an answer set of $\mathcal{P}$.

Similarly, we can also prove that if S is an answer set of $\mathcal{P}$, then $S' = S - \{\hat{P} \mid \hat{P} \in S\}$ is a stable model of $\mathcal{D}$. This shows the one-to-one correspondence between $\mathcal{D}$ and $\mathcal{P}$[8]. So the result holds. □

4.2 Complexity of Program Update

Now we consider the complexity of program update. Given extended logic programs Π_0 and Π_1, updating Π_0 with Π_1 consists of two steps: the first step is to obtain a subset $\Pi_{(\Pi_0,\Pi_1)}$ with respect to some answer set of Π_0, which is to eliminate those contradictory rules from Π_0, and then to specify the update specification $P\text{-}Update(\Pi_0, \Pi_1)$ which is a PLP as defined in Definition 7, which is to solve the conflict between $\Pi_{(\Pi_0,\Pi_1)}$ and Π_1. Hence, computing a resulting program Π_0' after updating Π_0 with Π_1 consists of two components: computing $\Pi_{(\Pi_0,\Pi_1)}$ and computing a reduct of $P\text{-}Update(\Pi_0, \Pi_1)$. We first analyze the computational complexity for the first step - contradiction elimination.

Lemma 3. *Given an extended logic program Π and a set of ground literals S. S is coherent with Π if and only if program $\Pi \cup \{L \leftarrow \mid L \in S\}$ is well defined.*

Theorem 3. *Let S be a consistent set of ground literals and Π a program. Deciding whether S is coherent with Π is NP-complete.*

The following theorem states that the check for contradiction elimination in the first step of a program update is co-NP-complete.

Theorem 4. *Let S be a consistent set of ground literals, Π a program, and Π' a subset of Π. Deciding whether Π' is a maximal subset of Π such that S is coherent with Π' is co-NP-complete.*

---

8 Ben-Eliyahu and Dechter also showed the equivalence between a head-cycle free extended disjunctive logic program and its translation to an extended logic program under the answer set semantics [2]

The following two theorems give the complexity of model checking and inference in program update respectively. It is interesting to note that the inference problem in a program update is eventually not harder than that in a simple fact update as the following theorem states.

Theorem 5. *Let P-Update(Π_0, Π_1) be a logic program update specification. Deciding whether a set of ground literals S is an answer set of some resulting program of P-Update(Π_0, Π_1) is co-NP-complete.*

Theorem 6. *Let P-Update(Π_0, Π_1) be a logic program update specification. Then given a ground literal L, deciding whether L is entailed by every resulting program of P-Update(Π_0, Π_1) is Π_2^P-complete.*

5 Inference with Lower Complexity

In this section, we try to further characterize specific classes of update specifications where the inference problem has a lower computational complexity. We first consider the simple fact update. Let $Update(S, \Pi)$ be an update specification and $\mathcal{P} = (\Pi \cup \{L \leftarrow not\overline{L}\}, \mathcal{N}, <)$ be the equivalence PLP of $Update(S, \Pi)$ as we described in section 4.1. Obviously, if $\mathcal{P}$ has a unique reduct, say Π^*, then for any given ground literal L, the problem of deciding whether $\mathcal{P} \models L$ is reduced to the problem of deciding whether $\Pi^* \models L$. As Π^* is an extended logic program, and we know that the inference problem for extended logic program is co-NP-complete [2], this follows that the inference problem in this specific class of update specifications is lower than the general case. The key idea about this is to extend the notion of *local stratification* of normal logic programs to extended logic programs by treating each negative literal as a new propositional atom [6, 7,11]. Then we have the following result.

Theorem 7. *Let $Update(S, \Pi)$ be a simple fact update specification, and $\mathcal{P} = (\Pi \cup \{L \leftarrow not\overline{L} \mid L \in \mathcal{B}\}, \mathcal{N}, <)$ be the equivalence PLP of $Update(S, \Pi)$. If $S \cap body(\Pi) = \emptyset$ and Π is locally stratified, then for a given ground literal L, deciding whether $\mathcal{P} \models L$ is co-NP-complete.*

The above theorem is achieved by proving a condition of unique reduct: if $S \cap body(\Pi) = \emptyset$ and Π is locally stratified [6], then $\mathcal{P}$ has a unique reduct Π^* [11]. Therefore, deciding whether $\mathcal{P} \models L$ is equivalent to decide whether $\Pi^* \models L$. If we know the unique answer set of Π, we then have the following corollary.

Corollary 1. *Let $Update(S, \Pi)$ be a simple fact update specification. If $S \cap body(\Pi) = \emptyset$ and Π has a unique answer set S^*. Then the resulting knowledge base S' with respect to $Update(S, \Pi)$ can be computed in $\mathcal{O}(|m| \cdot |n|)$ time, where $|m|$ and $|n|$ are cardinalities of sets S and S^* respectively.*

Similarly to the case of simple fact update, we can also characterize a particular class of program update specifications where the inference problem associated to these update problems is reduced to co-NP-complete.

Theorem 8. *Let P-Update*$(\Pi_0, \Pi_1) = (\Pi_{(\Pi_0,\Pi_1)} \cup \Pi_1, \mathcal{N}, <)$ *be a program update specification. If head*$(\Pi_1) \cap$ *body*$(\Pi_0) = \emptyset$ *and* Π_0 *is locally stratified, then for a given ground literal* L*, deciding whether P-Update*$(\Pi_0, \Pi_1) \models L$ *is co-NP-complete.*

6 Conclusions

In this paper, we investigated the semantics of logic program updates under the framework of prioritized logic programs, where priority is introduced to solve conflicts in updates. It turns out that the complexity of logic program updates remains at the same level of the polynomial hierarcy as principal update tasks [8]. It is also interesting to note that although representing a knowledge base as a set of rules adds expressive power in the domain, it actually does not introduce an increase in the complexity. This is because in our framework, a logic program update is specified by two separate steps: simple fact update and program update, and each of these two forms of updates has the same complexity. When a knowledge base is represented as a set of facts, the second step - program update, is identical to the first step and hence becomes unnecessary.

Finally since the focus of this paper is on the complexity of logic program updates, we did not compare our approach with other relevant methods due to a space limit. This part is referred to [11].

References

1. J.J. Alferes, et al, Dynamic logic programming. In *Proceedings of KR-98*, pp 98-109, 1998.
2. R. Ben-Eliyahu and R. Dechter, Propositional semantics for disjunctive logic programs. *Annals of Mathematics and Artificial Intelligence*, **12** (1994) 53-87.
3. G. Brewka and T. Eiter, Preferred answer sets for extended logic programs. *Artificial Intelligence*, **109** (1999) 297-356.
4. T. Eiter and G. Gottlob, On the computational cost of disjunctive logic programming: Propositional case. *Annals of Mathematics and Artificial Intelligence*, **15** (1995) 289-323.
5. M. Garey and D. Johnson, *Computers and Intractability*, Freeman, San Franciso, 1979.
6. M. Gelfond and V. Lifschitz, The stable model semantics for logic programming. In *Proceedings of the Fifth Joint International Conference and Symposium*, pp 1070-1080. MIT Press, 1988.
7. M. Gelfond and V. Lifschitz, Classical negation in logic programs and disjunctive databases. *New Generation Computing*, **9** (1991) 365-386.
8. P. Liberatore, The complexity of belief update. *Artificial Intelligence* **119** (2000) 141-190.
9. T.C. Przymusinski and H. Turner, Update by means of inference rules. In *Proceedings of LPNMR'95*, pp 156-174, 1995.
10. Zhang and N.Y. Foo, Answer sets for prioritized logic programs. In *Proceedings of the 1997 International Logic Programming Symposium (ILPS'97)*, pp 69-83. MIT Press, 1997
11. Y. Zhang, Logic program based update (full version). Manuscript, November, 2000.

Reasoning with Multimedia Information Using Symbolic Projection

Zili Zhang and Chengqi Zhang

School of Computing and Mathematics
Deakin University, Geelong Victoria 3217, Australia
{zili, chengqi}@deakin.edu.au

Abstract. In many multimedia application systems, it is not the final goal to retrieve the relevant multimedia information from different multimedia information sources. Rather, post-processing of the retrieved multimedia information is needed. For example, the retrieved information is used as "known facts". The systems will do some reasoning to obtain further conclusions based on these multimedia form "known facts". We call this reasoning with multimedia information. Most current research work in multimedia information processing is focused on multimedia information retrieval, but post-processing the retrieved information is more or less ignored. This paper explores the way to tackle this problem by using symbolic projection. A case study of reasoning with still image information is presented. Some extensions to symbolic projection–introducing auxiliary pictorial objects in symbolic pictures that need to be processed–are discussed. We expect this paper will stimulate further research on this important but ignored topic.

Keywords: Automated Reasoning, Geometric Reasoning, Spatial Reasoning, Multimedia, Symbolic Projection

1 Introduction

The multimedia revolution started at the beginning of 1990's [11]. Multimedia is virtually revolutionary in many areas such as communications, computing, entertainment, consumer electronics etc. Although there are still many challenging problems remain to be researched and resolved for the further growth of multimedia, with the advent of relatively cheap, large online storage capacities and advances in digital compression, comprehensive sources of text, image, video, and audio etc. multimedia data can be stored and made available for research and applications. Actually, the technical ability to generate volumes of digital multimedia data is becoming increasingly "mainstream" in today's electronic world.

With numerous digital libraries, other large multimedia databases, and multimedia based WWW pages available, sophisticated search or retrieval techniques are required to find relevant information in these large digital data repositories.

M. Brooks, D. Corbett, and M. Stumptner (Eds.): AI 2001, LNAI 2256, pp. 643–654, 2001.

These retrieval techniques should provide not only fewer bits but also the right bits to users.

We notice that to retrieve the right bits from multimedia data repositories is not the final step in many multimedia applications. Further processing of the retrieved multimedia information is needed. In this paper, we call such multimedia information processing post-processing. For example, in our ongoing agent-based financial investment adviser project [1], we need to retrieve stock market information. These data include breaking news in audio or text form that affects stock market, closing price of specific securities (table), security price or moving average chart (see Figure 1), company revenue (pie chart), company profiles etc. In our financial investment advising multi-agent system, different agents are delegated to gather information in different forms. The decision making agents will make financial investment decisions based on their domain knowledge and the retrieved multimedia information. To this end, we come across two problems: How to fuse information in different media forms and how to reason with these multimedia information to obtain new results. These two "how to"s are most important topics in multimedia information post-processing.

With these observations in mind, we proposed that multimedia information processing be divided into three levels–multimedia information storage, retrieval, and post-processing [2]. Currently, most work on multimedia information processing is focused on multimedia information storage and retrieval, especially indexing and content-based access of multimedia information. Post-processing of this information is nearly ignored.

In [2], we identified the concepts of multimedia information post-processing. Two of the important topics in post-processing are fusion of multimedia information and reasoning with multimedia information. In this paper, we will try to deal with some issues in reasoning with multimedia information. The discussions are based on a subtask in our financial investment adviser project.

To give advice about stock buying/selling we need to do some reasoning based on the moving average chart of a specific security as well as many other analyses. There are two main trading rules for moving averages: (1) A buy signal is given when the price moves up and crosses over the moving average from below; (2) A sell signal is given when the price moves down and crosses over the moving average from above. Here, it is more natural and convenient to represent the condition parts of these rules as well as the "known facts" (retrieved moving average charts of some specific securities) by graphics (charts). This is one form of *reasoning with multimedia information*. For this specific problem, it is actually a problem of reasoning with still images. We employ *symbolic projection theory* [3] to do such reasoning. *Symbolic projection* is a theory of spatial relations. This theory is the basis of a conceptual framework for image representation, image structuring and spatial reasoning.

The essential lying in our problem is the matching of two moving average images (charts). Traditional approaches to such problems are measured on the basis of maximum-likelihood or minimum distance criterion. The symbolic description of visual information such as shape or spatial relations is a very difficult task using the traditional approaches. Attempts to describe this information textually can lead to representations that are either too general (refer to the two trading rules) or too complex. Symbolic projection approach is more flexible and efficient [4][5][10]. That is why we turn to symbolic projection theory.

When using symbolic projection to solve our moving average problem, we come across that directly using symbolic projection is not sufficient for our problem. Thus further extensions to symbolic projection are explored. A new concept–introducing benchmark object in symbolic pictures before applying symbolic projections–is developed.

In short, our work in this paper extends the application scope of symbolic projection as well as the theory itself. Furthermore, the problem of reasoning with multimedia information is highlighted.

The rest of the paper is organized as follows. Section 2 presents the problem we want to solve. Using symbolic projection to solve the problem is discussed in Section 3. Section 4 is some discussions. Finally, Section 5 is concluding remarks.

2 Problem Descriptions

When giving some advice to investment in stock market in our financial investment adviser system, the system will use *fundamental analysis, technical analysis* of securities, and other domain knowledge. Fundamental analysis endeavors to determine the fair value of a share. The emphasis of technical analysis is on information generated by the market itself. Technical analysis is an attempt to forecast future prices by studying past prices. Traditionally, this has been done using various types of charts that provide a visual record of past prices. There are four conventional types of charts–the bar chart, the candlestick chart, the point and figure chart, and moving averages. In this paper, we take the processing of moving average charts as an example.

A moving average of past prices can be used as an indicator of a price trend. There are two main trading rules for moving averages:

- A buy signal is given when the price moves up and crosses over the moving average from below.
- A sell signal is given when the price moves down and crosses over the moving average from above.

Based on the trading rules, there are three rules that related to the moving average chart in the knowledge base of decision making agents:

- Rule 1: If the moving average chart of a security is similar to Figure 2 (a), then buy this security;
- Rule 2: If the moving average chart of a security is similar to Figure 2 (b), then sell this security;
- Rule 3: If the moving average chart of a security is similar to Figure 2 (c), then don't buy and sell this security.

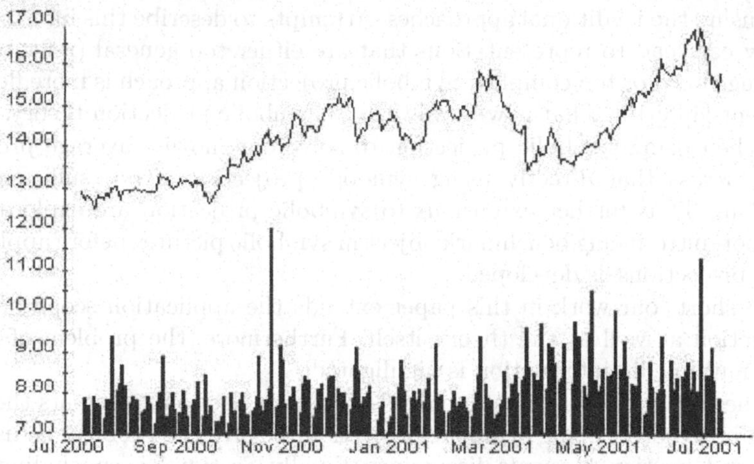

Fig. 1. Example Moving Average Chart

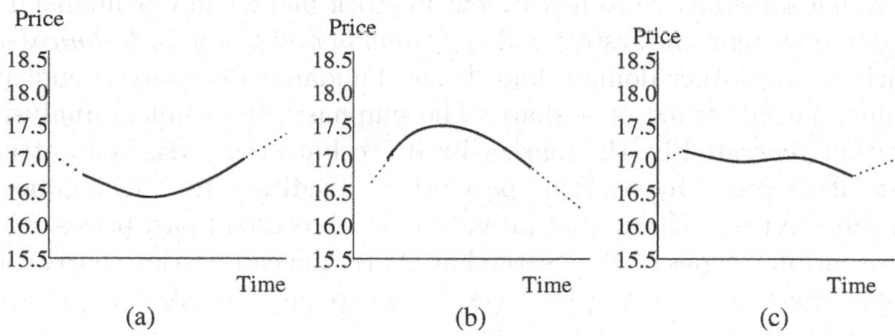

Fig. 2. Moving Averages of Security Price

Here, it is natural to represent the condition parts of these rules directly by graphics (chart). Actually, it is very difficult to represent them in text precisely whereas easy to operate. Now, if we retrieved some web-sites on the Internet and get the moving average chart of a specific security (Figure 3), how can we infer the conclusion using these rules? This is one form of *reasoning with multimedia information*. For this specific problem, it is actually a problem of reasoning with still images.

We employ *symbolic projection theory* to do such reasoning. We represent the moving average chart as $2D$ strings in symbolic projection, and then use $2D$ string matching algorithm to accomplish the reasoning. The details will be discussed in next section.

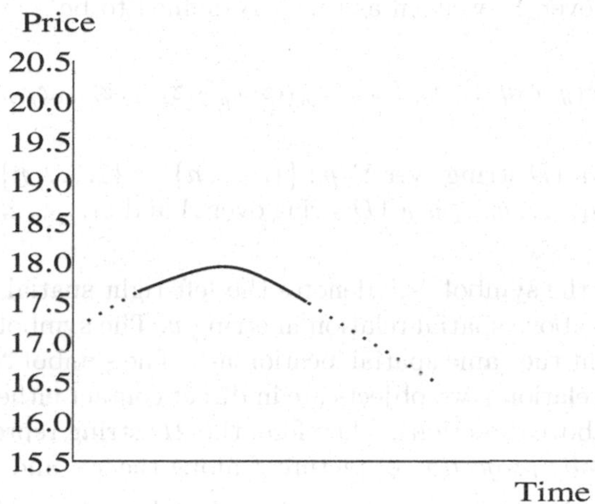

Fig. 3. Retrieved Moving Average of a Specific Security

3 Solving the Problem by Symbolic Projection

The theory of symbolic projection was first developed by Chang and co-workers [4]. It forms the basis of a wide range of image information retrieval algorithms. It also supports pictorial-query-by-picture, so that the user of an image information system can simply draw a picture and use the picture as a query. Many researchers have since extended this original concept, so that there is now rich body of theory as well as empirical results [5][6]. The extended theory of symbolic theory can deal not only with point-like objects, but also objects of any shape and size. Moreover, the theory can deal with not only one symbolic picture, but also multiple symbolic pictures, three-dimensional ($3D$) pictures, a time sequence of pictures, etc.

A symbolic picture is a two dimensional matrix of symbols. Each object of the real image is represented by a symbol located in the centroid of the object. A symbolic picture can have at least two symbolic projections: the x-projection and y-projection. The $x-$ or $y-$projection of a symbolic picture can be constructed by projecting the names of objects in each column of the symbolic picture onto the $x-$ or $y-$axis. A pair of two symbolic projections is called a $2D$ *string*.

3.1 A Brief Introduction of Symbolic Projection

Let Σ be a set of symbols, or the vocabulary. Each symbol might represent a pictorial object, a pixel, etc.

Let A be the set $\{=, <, |\}$, where "=", "<", and "|" are three special symbols not in Σ. These symbols will be used to specify spatial relationships between pictorial objects.

A $1D$ *string* over Σ is any string $x_1x_2 \ldots x_n, n \geq 0$, where the x_i's are in Σ.

A $2D$ *string* over Σ, written as (u, v), is defined to be

$$(x_1 y_1 x_2 y_2 \ldots y_{n-1} x_n, x_{p(1)} z_1 x_{p(2)} z_2 \ldots z_{n-1} x_{p(n)})$$

where $x_1 \ldots x_n$ is a $1D$ string over $\Sigma, p : \{1, \ldots, n\} \rightarrow \{1, \ldots, n\}$ is a permutation over $\{1, \ldots, n\}$, $y_1, \ldots, y_{n-1}$ is a $1D$ string over A and $z_1, \ldots, z_{n-1}$ is a $1D$ string over A.

In the above, the symbol "<" denotes the left-right spatial relation in string u, and the below-above spatial relation in string v. The symbol "=" denotes the spatial relation "at the same spatial location as". The symbol "|" denotes "edge-to-edge" spatial relation (two objects are in direct contact either in the left-right or in the below-above direction). Therefore, the $2D$ string representation can be seen as the *symbolic projection* of picture f along the $x-$ and $y-$axes.

A *symbolic picture* f is a mapping $M \times M \rightarrow W$, where $M = \{1, 2, \ldots, m\}$, and W is the power set of Σ (the set of all subsets of V). The empty set $\{\ \}$ then denotes a null object.

Given f, we can construct the corresponding $2D$ string representation (u, v), and vice versa, such that all left-right and below-above spatial relations among the pictorial objects in Σ are preserved. In [3] (pp. 32-33), a formal algorithm (called **2Dstring**) for constructing $2D$ string (u, v) from f is presented.

$2D$ string representation also provides a simple approach to perform sub-picture matching on $2D$ strings. An algorithm for $2D$ string matching (**2Dmatch**) is given in [3] (pp. 38-40).

With the edge-to-edge operator "|", we can further segment an object into its constituent parts. This is accomplished by introducing cutting lines. A systematic way of drawing the cutting lines is as follows: First, the extremal points are found in both the horizontal and vertical directions. Next, vertical and horizontal cutting lines are drawn through these extremal points. This technique gives a natural segmentation of planar objects into the constituent parts.

With the cutting mechanism, we can also formulate a general representation, encompassing the other representations based upon different operator sets. This consideration leads to the formulation of a generalized $2D$ string system [7].

A *generalized* $2D$ *string system* is a five-tuple $(\Sigma, C, A, \mathbf{e}, \text{``}\langle, \rangle\text{''})$, where Σ is the vocabulary; C is the *cutting mechanism*, which consists of cutting lines at the extremal points of objects; $A = \{<, =, |\}$ is the set of spatial operators; **e** is a special symbol which can represent an area of any size and any shape, called the *empty-space object*; and "$\langle, \rangle$" is a pair of operators which is used to describe local structure.

The cutting mechanism defines how the objects in an image are to be segmented, and also makes it possible for the local operator "$\langle, \rangle$" to be used as a global operator to be inserted into original $2D$ strings.

The spatial operator set A can be extended to contain other spatial relation operators used in different applications. For extension examples, refer to [5][6].

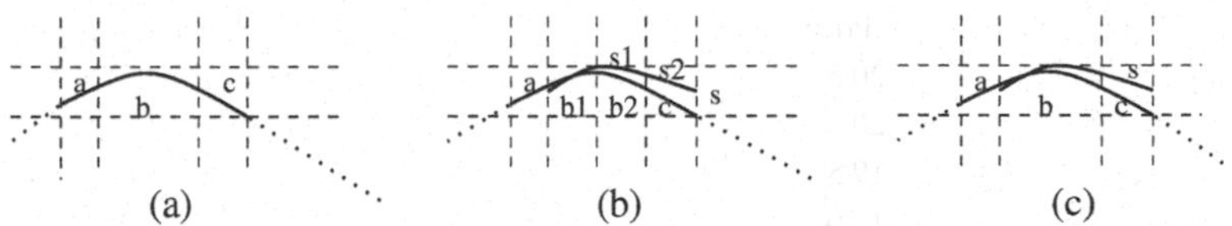

Fig. 4. (a) Moving Average Chart Segmentation Using Cutting Lines; (b) Moving Average With Benchmark Object; (c) Final Moving Average Segmentation With Benchmark Object

3.2 2D String Representation of Moving Average Charts

After we had some basic concepts about symbolic projections, we are now ready to discuss the $2D$ string representation of moving average charts.

Take Figure 2 (b) as an example. The following cutting mechanism C is applied: Choose the upper horizontal extremal point, p, and draw two vertical cutting lines $x = p + \delta$ and $x = p - \delta$. Others remain the same as described in Section 3.1. The segmented moving average chart is shown in Figure 4 (a).

The vocabulary is $\Sigma = \{a, b, c\}$. The $2D$ string representing the picture in Figure 4 (a) is as follows:

$u: a|b|c$, $v: c = a < b$.

Therefore, rule 2 in Section 2 can be expressed as:

Rule 2: If $u: a|b|c$ and $v: c = a < b$ then sell the security.

Similarly, we can obtain the $2D$ string representations of other moving average charts, and rewrite the corresponding rules. We can then employ the $2D$ string matching algorithm or other string matching algorithms to do the reasoning.

3.3 Special Considerations for Our Problem

The above representation does not describe fully the meaning lies in the antecedents of trading rules. For example, in Figure 5, g_1, g_2, and g_3 have different slopes, but their $2D$ representations are the same. This causes one problem: No matter the price trend is indicated by g_1, g_2, or g_3, a sell signal will be given. In practice, when the price drops slightly (indicating by g_3), no sell signal is given.

How can we deal with this problem? This problem occurs due to two reasons. One is the descriptions of trading rules themselves are fuzzy. The other is the insufficient representation of the $2D$ strings. For such a problem, simply extending the spatial operator set A cannot help. One may argue that one generalized symbolic projection–slope projection [3] (Chapter 9) – can be used to solve this problem. But if we remember that no object exists to compare with, we know we still cannot use it directly. What we need is a benchmark picture object that indicates whether the sell or buy signal should be given or not. This is our concept to introduce auxiliary object(s) in symbolic pictures that need to be processed. In our example, we call such an auxiliary picture object *benchmark*

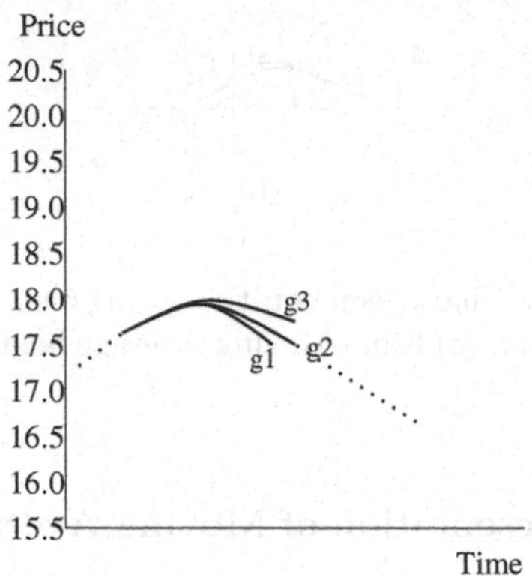

Fig. 5. Moving Average With Different Slopes

picture object. The benchmark picture object can be determined by consulting stock technical analysis experts.

We still take Figure 2 (b) as an example. After introducing the benchmark object, the resulting moving average chart is shown in Figure 4 (b) (the same cutting mechanism used in last subsection is applied, but with one more vertical cutting line through the upper extremal point).

In Figure 4 (b), if the slope of price trend is greater than that of benchmark object s, no sell signal is given. If less than or equal to that of s, a sell signal is generated. The $2D$ string representation corresponding to Figure 4 (b) is as follows:

$u:\ a|b_1|b_2 = s_1|c = s_2,\ v:\ c = a < s_2 = b_2 = b_1 < s_1.$

This $2D$ representation can be further simplified as s_1 is useless for the reasoning, only s_2 can help. In our application, no reconstruction from the $2D$ strings is needed. Thus s_1 can be omitted in the $2D$ representation. We apply exactly the same cutting mechanism as that used in last subsection (see Figure 4 (c)), we obtain the final $2D$ representation for our problem:

$u:\ a|b|c = s,\ v:\ c = a < s = b.$

For rule 2, if the $2D$ string of retrieved price trend is $u:\ a|b|c = s,\ v:\ c = a < s = b$, then a sell signal is given. Otherwise, if the $2D$ string of retrieved price trend is $u:\ a|b|s = c,\ v:\ s = a < c = b$, then no sell signal is given.

With the introduction of benchmark object in the moving average charts, we can exactly represent the meaning in trading rules with $2D$ strings. One more problem remains to be solved: how can we add the benchmark object to a symbolic picture, and automatically construct the $2D$ strings from the corresponding picture?

In our application, the benchmark object is a line segment starting from the extremal point, p. Assume the slope of the benchmark object (line segment) determining by stock technical analysis experts is k. To add the benchmark object is simply drawing a line segment starting from p with slope k. To construct

$2D$ strings from the symbolic picture with added benchmark object, we can still use the **2Dstring** algorithm. The extended **2Dstring** algorithm that can handle the benchmark object problem, **2DstringE**, is outlined below:

Algorithm 2DstringE(*picture*, k, u, v)

/* This algorithm takes symbolic picture *picture* and the slope of benchmark */
/* object k as inputs, k is determined by stock technical analysis experts. */
/* Outputs are the $2D$ string representations (u, v) of *picture*. */
begin
/* object recognition */
recognize objects in the picture;
find the upper or lower extremal point p in *picture*;
/* add benchmark object */
draw a line segment starting from p with slope equal to k;
/* segmentation */
applying cutting mechanism C to *picture*;
find centroid of each object;
find $2D$ string representation using Procedure **2Dstring**
end

4 Discussions

The above discussion is focused on the processing of moving average charts using symbolic projection. In our financial investment application and many other applications, another common used chart form to represent retrieved information is pie chart. For example, when the system gives investment advice to the client, the system may analyze the revenues of the relevant companies or the trading volumes of some promising securities. They are usually represented by pie charts (refer to Figures 6 and 7).

It is more difficult to reason with such kind of pie charts. If we know the boundary lines (see Figure 8) that separate different component parts in the pie chart, the task is relatively easy. Otherwise, we must first determine the boundary lines based on the grey levels of different component parts in the pie chart. After we get the boundary lines in the pie chart, we can convert the real pie chart to a symbolic picture. We then can use symbolic projection theory to process this problem. When using symbolic projection to process pie charts, polar projection and concentric cutting mechanisms must be used [9]. We will discuss the details in another paper.

We successfully solved the problem of reasoning with curve information (still image) by using symbolic projection. Our work presented in this paper indicates that symbolic projection is a very promising methodology to solve the problem of reasoning with still image information. Of course, reasoning with other still image information (other than curve information) is subject to further research.

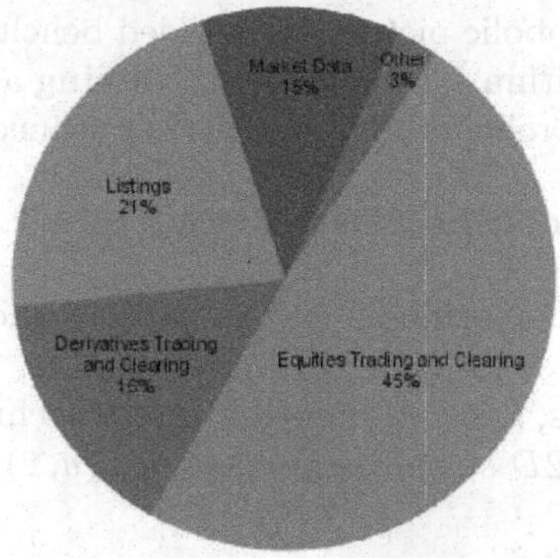

Fig. 6. Revenue of A Company

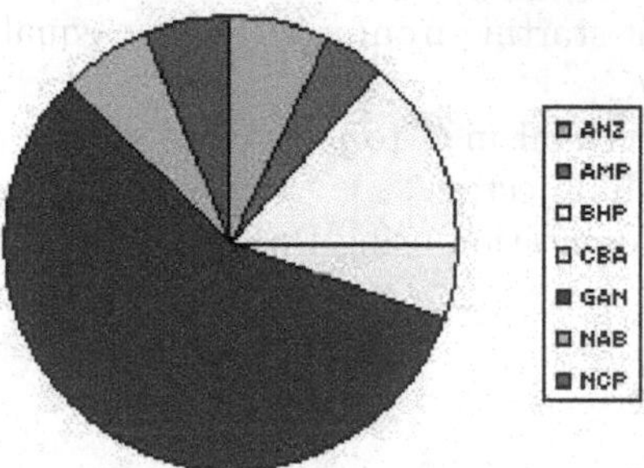

Fig. 7. Trading Volumes of Securities

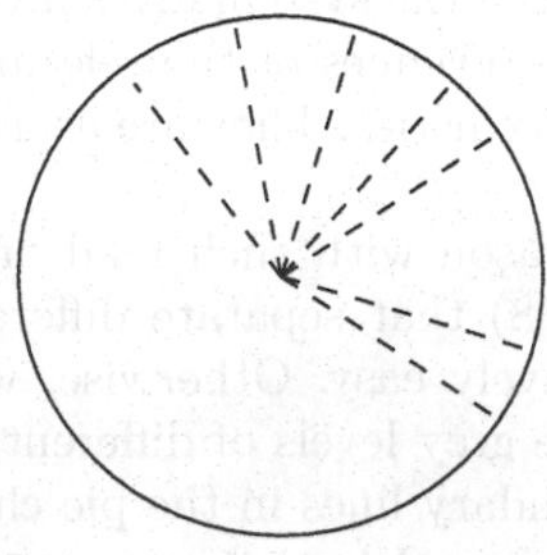

Fig. 8. Boundary lines in Pie Chart

When solving the "reasoning with moving average charts" problem in our application, we introduced the concept of "benchmark objects". By introducing benchmark objects into the moving average charts, we solved the problem effectively. This approach can be generalized and apply to many other problems. For example, one kind of difficult problems, called *dynamic route planning*, can be solved by introducing extra "reference objects" in the symbolic pictures when using symbolic projection theory. This problem can be generally described as follows: A moving object (e.g., a robot) needs to determine its moving direction to an unfamiliar place. In the moving object's memory, there are some reference objects. Once he observes enough reference objects in the environment, he can then decide which direction he will move to. For such kind of problems, we can represent the environment as a symbolic picture. When the moving object sees an object that is identical to one of the reference objects in his memory, we add this object to the symbolic picture as an auxiliary object. After introducing enough auxiliary objects, we can describe the relationships among all the objects in the symbolic picture, furthermore, decide the direction the moving object should forward to. This problem is similar to the problem of determination of the views of a moving object addressed by E. Jungert [12], but much more difficult. Once again, thoroughly solving this problem needs further research.

As mentioned in the introduction section, the problem described in this paper can also be solved using traditional approaches based on maximum-likelihood or minimum distance criterion, or pattern recognition approaches. Those solutions are more time-consuming and complicated.

The theory of symbolic projection was originally developed as a technique for iconic indexing to image databases, and this still is an important application area. Symbolic projection theory also includes other characteristics that made it suitable for various forms of spatial reasoning and in particular for qualitative spatial reasoning. We applied this theory for reasoning with still image information. These two concepts are different whereas have some relations. *Spatial reasoning* is the process of reasoning and making inferences about problems dealing with objects occupying space [8]. The emphasis is on the spatial relationships of objects. The focus of reasoning with multimedia information in general, still image information specific, is on the meaning or knowledge that lies behind the images.

5 Concluding Remarks

We identified that multimedia information consists of three levels – multimedia information storage, retrieval, and post-processing. In post-processing, reasoning with retrieved multimedia information to reach new conclusions is a paramount but relatively ignored topic.

Reasoning with multimedia information includes reasoning with text information, reasoning with image information, reasoning with video information, and reasoning with audio information, etc. There are many techniques for reasoning with text information – this is the task of traditional inference algorithms. There are few to deal with the rest.

This paper proposed to use symbolic projection theory for reasoning with still image information. A case study of reasoning with moving average charts in finance was provided.

When using symbolic projection to solve our problem, a new concept – introducing benchmark object – was developed. This idea can be applied to other difficult problems such as *dynamic route planning.*

There is much work left for reasoning with multimedia information. This paper is a small step in this direction.

References

1. C. Zhang, Z. Zhang, and Y. Li, Multi-Agent Based Financial Investment Adviser: Design and Implementation, *Proceedings of International ICSC Symposium of Multi-Agents and Mobile Agents*, Wollongong, Australia, 2000, 33-43.
2. C. Zhang and Z. Zhang, Post-Processing of Multimedia Information–Concepts, Problems, and Techniques, *Proceedings of ISCA 16th International Conference on Computers and Their Applications*, Seattle, USA, 2001, 318-321.
3. S. K. Chang and E. Jungert, *Symbolic Projection for Image Information Retrieval and Spatial Reasoning*, Academic Press, 1996.
4. S. K. Chang, Q. Y. Shi, and C. W. Yan, Iconic Indexing by 2D Strings, *IEEE Transactions on Pattern Analysis and Machine Intelligence*, Vol. 9, No. 3, 1987, 413-428.
5. S.-Y. Lee and F.-J. Hsu, Spatial Reasoning and Similarity Retrieval of Images Using 2D C-String Knowledge Representation, *Pattern Recognition*, Vol. 25, 1992, 305-318.
6. E. Jungert, Extended Symbolic Projections as a Knowledge Structure for Spatial Reasoning and Planning, in: J. Kittler (ed.), *Pattern Recognition*, Springer, Berlin, 1988, 343-351.
7. S. K. Chang, E. Jungert, and Y. Li, Representation and Retrieval of Symbolic Pictures Using Generalized 2D Strings, *Proceedings of the SPIE Visual Communications and Image Processing Conference*, 1989, 1360-1372.
8. S. Dutta, Qualitative Spatial Reasoning: A Semi-quantitative Approach Using Fuzzy Logic, *Proceedings of Conference on Very Large Spatial Databases*, Santa Barbara, USA, 1989, 345-364.
9. G. Petraglia, M. Sebillo, M. Tucci, and G. Tortora, A Normalized Index for Image Databases, in: S. K. Chang, E. Jungert, and G. Tortora (eds.), *Intelligent Image Database Systems*, World Scientific, Singapore, 1996, 43-70.
10. S. K. Chang, E. Jungert, and G. Tortora (eds.), *Intelligent Image Database Systems*, World Scientific, Singapore, 1996, 1-8.
11. B. Furht, Foreword, in: M. C. Angelides and S. Dustdar (Eds.), *Multimedia Information Systems*, Kluwer Academic Publishers, 1997.
12. E. Jungert, Determination of the Views of a Moving Agent by Means of Symbolic Projection, in: S. K. Chang, E. Jungert, and G. Tortora (eds.), *Intelligent Image Database Systems*, World Scientific, Singapore, 1996, 141-163.

Confidence Relations as a Basis for Uncertainty Modeling, Plausible Reasoning, and Belief Revision

Didier Dubois

IRIT-CNRS,
Université Paul Sabatier,
31062 Toulouse Cedex, France
dubois@irit.fr

Abstract. The aim of this position paper is to outline a unified view of plausible reasoning under incomplete information and belief revision, based on an ordinal representation of uncertainty. The information possessed by an agent is supposed to be made of three items: sure observations, generic knowledge and inferred contingent beliefs. The main notion supporting this approach is the confidence relation, a partial ordering of events which encodes the generic knowledge of an agent. Plausible inference is achieved by conditioning. The paper advocates the similarity between plausible reasoning with confidence relations and probabilistic reasoning. The main difference is that the ordinal approach supports the notion of accepted beliefs forming a deductively closed set, while probability theory is not tailored for it. The framework of confidence relations sheds light on the connections between some approaches to non-monotonic reasoning methods, possibilistic logic and the theory of belief revision. In particular the distinction between revising contingent beliefs in the light of observations and revising the confidence relation is laid bare.

1 Introduction

The aim of this position paper is to present a synthetic view of an approach to plausible reasoning under incomplete information with an ordinal representation of uncertainty. This approach has close connections with various works carried out more or less independently by philosophers like Ernest Adams, David Lewis, in the seventies, and Peter Gärdenfors and colleagues in the eighties, as well as several AI researchers, such as Yoav Shoham, Daniel Lehmann, Judea Pearl, Joe Halpern, Maryanne Williams, and others. Indeed, the issue of an ordinal approach to uncertainty has to do with several important topics of theoretical Artificial Intelligence, such as non-monotonic reasoning, belief revision, conditional logics, and to probabilistic reasoning as well. It seems that the ultimate aim of symbolic AI in plausible reasoning is to perform a counterpart to probabilistic inference without probabilities (Dubois and Prade 1994a).

Suppose an agent who has to reason about the current state of the world. In order to support the above thesis, we claim that the issue of plausible reasoning cannot be properly addressed without assuming that the body of information possessed by the agent contains (at least) three distinct types of items: observations pertaining to the current situation, generic knowledge about similar situations, and beliefs as to the

M. Brooks, D. Corbett, and M. Stumptner (Eds.): AI 2001, LNAI 2256, pp. 655-664, 2001.

features of the current situation. Observations are supposed to be reliable and non conflicting. Beliefs are on the contrary taken for granted, hence brittle. Under this assumption, plausible reasoning precisely consists in inferring beliefs from (contingent) observations, and generic (background) knowledge, valid across situations. This view is classical in probability theory (De Finetti, 1974), and we claim that it also makes sense under a qualitative or an ordinal approach to plausible reasoning

2 From Confidence Relations to Accepted Beliefs

The ordinal approach presupposes that the agent's knowledge is modeled by a relation among events or propositions (built from a language), we call a *confidence relation*. Typically, it is a partial preordering on a set of propositions, that is consistent with classical deduction, expressing that some propositions are generally more plausible than (or at least as plausible as) others. The contingent observations available to the agent form a context according to which the confidence relation is conditioned. Confidence relations include comparative probability relations first introduced by De Finetti (1937) and Koopman (1940), and extensively studied by Savage (1954). All set-functions used in uncertainty modeling (probability measures, possibility measures, belief functions, etc.) generate confidence relations which are complete preorders. The set-functions studied by Friedman and Halpern (1996) under the name of "plausibility measures" generate confidence relations which are partial preorders.

A proposition is called an accepted belief for the agent if it is more plausible (in the sense of the confidence relation) than its negation, in the context of available observations. The term "accepted belief" also means that the agent considers the derived conclusions as valid, until some further observation is obtained that questions them; lastly the agent is allowed to reason with accepted beliefs as if they were true, using classical logic. Hence, by assumption, accepted beliefs form a deductively closed set of propositions. Under this assumption, a confidence relation is called an *acceptance relation* (Dubois and Prade, 1995b; Dubois et al. 1998a).

This logical closure condition for accepted beliefs has a drastic impact on the nature of acceptance relations. Basically it implies that, when a proposition A is more plausible than each of two other ones B and C, where A, B, C are mutually exclusive, considering the disjunction of B and C cannot form a proposition that is more plausible than the most plausible one A. In other words, a notion of negligibility is embedded in the acceptance relation. The closure condition, plus a few other uncontroversial ones (like monotony with respect to set inclusion) are enough to ensure the existence of a representation of the acceptance relation by means of a family of so called "comparative possibility relations" (Dubois et al. 2001). A proposition is then more plausible than another one if and only if the former is more possible than the latter in the sense of all comparative possibility relations in the family.

Comparative possibility relations have been independently introduced by David Lewis (1973) in the seventies, in the framework of modal logics of counterfactuals, and Dubois (1986) in the scope of decision theory. Their numerical counterparts have been introduced by the economist Shackle (1961), the philosopher Cohen (1977), and the systems engineer Zadeh (1978) completely independently of one another. Comparative possibility relations are very simple confidence relations because each of them is completely specified by means of a single complete preordering of elementary events (interpretations, states of nature, possible worlds) distinguishing between normal and less normal worlds. Namely a proposition is more possible than another if the most normal situation where the former is true is more plausible than all situations where the latter is true. The case when the ordering of elementary events is partial is studied by Halpern (1997).

3 Nonmonotonic Reasoning and Default Rules

In practice, the generic knowledge possessed by an agent is often expressed by means of "if then" rules. The condition part of a rule denotes a context (in the above sense: everything the agent has observed in a given situation) and the conclusion is an accepted belief of the agent in this context. Each such rule can thus be modeled as the statement that some proposition is more plausible than another one, and a rule base can be equated to a (partially defined) acceptance relation (or a plausibility measure after Friedman and Halpern, 1996).

Each rule can also be modeled in the framework of a three-valued logic (Dubois and Prade, 1994b). In a given situation, a rule is true or false according to whether its conclusion is true or false, provided that its condition holds in this situation. Otherwise the rule takes the third truth-value which stands for "irrelevant". This is a so-called tri-event introduced by De Finetti (1937). Such generic rules form conditional knowledge bases, and the plausible inference of some proposition consists of syntactically deriving from a rule base a rule whose condition part exactly models the set of available observations, and whose conclusion part is the proposition under concern (Kraus et al, 1991). In the formal framework of acceptance relations, this syntactic inference procedure yields a plausible proposition if and only if this proposition is an accepted belief in the prescribed context, in the sense of the acceptance relation (plausibility measure after Friedman and Halpern, 1996) induced by the rule base

Indeed, under the logical closure condition, the plausible inference relation producing accepted beliefs according to a confidence relation also satisfies all postulates of preferential inference introduced by Kraus et al. (1991) for the purpose of computing what is entailed from a conditional knowledge base (except for the inference from a contradictory context), and conversely these postulates enable the confidence relation to be reconstructed. Similar properties have been laid bare in older conditional logics by Adams (1975), using infinitesimal probabilities, and, of course, Lewis (1973). A rule base also generates a family of comparative possibility relations (" rankings of models " after Lehmann and Magidor, 1992; see Dubois and Prade, 1995a).

If the family of comparative possibility relations reduces to a single one, then the plausible relation satisfies the so-called rational monotony property introduced by Makinson. This feature is characteristic of comparative possibility relations (Benferhat et al., 1997). Plausible inference with a comparative possibility relation meets Shoham (1988)'s view of nonmonotonic inference, as classical inference from the most normal situations in a given context. Plausible inference under a comparative possibility relation can be syntactically managed in possibilistic logic (Dubois et al., 1994; Lang 2000). When an acceptance relation corresponds to a family of more than one comparative possibility relations, there is a principle of information minimization that enables a unique comparative possibility relation in the family to be selected (Dubois and Prade, 1998). It is a most cautious choice ensuring a ranking of elementary events that is as compact as possible. This selection process is at work in Pearl (1990)'s system Z and Lehmahn and Magidor (1992)'s "rational closure", as well the possibilistic handling of default rule bases (Benferhat et al, 1998). Selecting a least informative comparative possibility relation in agreement with an acceptance relation is equivalent to attaching priorities to rules in a conditional knowledge base, the higher priorities being granted to the most specific rules (Pearl, 1990).

4 Plausible Inference versus Probabilistic Reasoning

The originality of the confidence relation approach to plausible inference is that, rather than starting from syntactic objects and intuitive postulates (like Lehmann and colleagues), our starting points are on the one hand the confidence relation that is thought of as a natural tool for describing an agent's uncertain knowledge, and the notion of accepted belief on the other hand. This point of view enables plausible (non-monotonic) reasoning to be cast in the general framework of uncertain reasoning, which includes probabilistic reasoning. The analogy between plausible reasoning with accepted beliefs and probabilistic reasoning is now patent (see also Paris, 1994). In probabilistic reasoning, the confidence relation stems from a probability measure or a family thereof. A set of generic rules is then encoded as a set of conditional probabilities characterizing a family of probability measures. The most popular approach in AI is currently when this family reduces to a single one, and the set of conditional probabilities defines a Bayesian network (Pearl, 1988). When the probabilistic information is incomplete, the selection of a unique probability measure often relies on the principle of maximal entropy. A Bayesian network really represents generic knowledge, like any confidence relation. This network derives either from expert domain knowledge or from statistical data. The selection of a most cautious comparative possibility relation in agreement with an acceptance relation is similar to the selection of a unique probability measure using maximal entropy (Paris, 1994).

Probabilistic inference with a Bayesian network consists in calculating the (statistical) conditional probability of a conclusion, where the conditioning event encodes the available observations (Pearl, 1988). The obtained conditional probability value is interpreted as the degree of belief of the conclusion in the current situation, assuming that this situation is a regular one in the context described by the observations. This procedure is very similar to the derivation of a plausible conclusion by conditioning an acceptance relation, or by deducing a rule from a rule base. The derived rule is valid "generally". Its conclusion is considered as an accepted belief in the current situation assuming that this situation is not an exceptional one in the context described by the observations modeled by the condition part of the derived rule. There is in fact a strong similarity between conditional probability and conditional possibility, and an ordinal form of Bayes rule exists for possibility theory (Dubois and Prade, 1998).

Of course, there are also noticeable differences between probabilistic reasoning and ordinal plausible inference:

i) The latter does not quantify belief;

ii) Plausible reasoning considers the most plausible situations and neglects others, while probability theory performs reasoning in the average.

iii) Lastly, probabilistic reasoning is not compatible with the notion of accepted belief.

Indeed, the conjunction of two highly probable events may fail to be highly probable and may even turn out to be very improbable. However, the arbitrary conjunction of accepted beliefs is still an accepted belief (this is because we assume that the agent considers accepted beliefs as tentatively true). This property of ordinal plausible inference has been criticized by several authors (Kyburg 1988, Poole 1991). It means that ordinal plausible inference suffers from the so-called "lottery paradox" (one can believe that any given player in a one-winner lottery game will lose with arbitrary high probability, all the more so as players are numerous, but one cannot believe that all of them will lose).

Yet, an acceptance relation can also be represented by means of a family of standard probability relations (Benferhat et al., 1999a, Snow, 1999). The corresponding probability measures are very special. They enforce a total ordering of states and are such that the probability of a state is always larger that the sum of the probabilities of less probable states. We call them "big-stepped probabilities". They are in some sense the total opposite of uniformly distributed ones (without expressing pure determinism, though). Indeed, in any context the most likely elementary event in the sense of a big-stepped probability occurs much more often than the disjunction of other elementary events.

We cannot expect to find natural sample spaces equipped with such kinds of empirically observed statistical probability functions. But one may think that for phenomena which have significant regularities, without being purely deterministic (like birds flying!), there may exist at least one partition of the sample space, the elements of which can be ordered via a big-stepped probability, and form a set of conceptually meaningful states for the agent. The existence of probabilities in strict agreement with non-monotonic inference, may also resolve the lottery paradox, that has been proposed as a counterexample to the use of classical deduction on accepted beliefs. Indeed, for big-stepped probabilities (and only for them), the set of probable beliefs $\{A, P(A / C) > 0.5\}$ *remains consistent and deductively closed for any context C.* In the lottery example, it is implicitly assumed that all players have equal chance of winning. The underlying probability is uniform. Hence there is no regularity at all in the lottery game: no particular occurrence is typical and randomness prevails. It is thus unlikely that an agent can come up with a set of consistent default rules about the lottery game.

On the contrary, plausible reasoning based on acceptance relations models an agent's reasoning in front of phenomena which have very regular features (but where exceptional situations may nevertheless occur). We conjecture that domains where a body of default knowledge exists can be statistically modeled by big-stepped probabilities on a meaningful partition of the sample space. If this conjecture is valid, it points out a potential link between non-monotonic reasoning and statistical data, in a knowledge discovery perspective. An open problem along this line is as follows: Given statistical data on a sample space, find the "best" partition(s) of the sample space, on which big-stepped probabilities are induced and meaningful default rules can be extracted (See Benferhat et al. 2001b for preliminary results). The difference between other rule extraction techniques and the one suggested here, is that, in our view, the presence of exceptions is acknowledged in the very definition of symbolic rules for which the proportion of such exceptions is not explicit.

5 Two Kinds of Epistemic Revision

The framework of confidence relations can also account for the AGM revision theory after Alchourron et al (1985), but it somehow questions the idea of Gärdenfors and Makinson (1988) that revision and plausible inference are two sides of the same coin. Indeed, in Gärdenfors revision theory, the agent only possesses a closed set of propositions (a belief set) and receives a sure input that can be understood as a new observation of the (static) world. So, the Gärdenfors revision theory only accounts for the evolution of the beliefs of an agent who makes a new contingent observation.

However, this is only one possible kind of epistemic revision. The distinction between contingent beliefs and generic knowledge forces to consider another meaning of revision: the revision of the generic knowledge, which is not the topic of the AGM theory. It consists of modifying the confidence relation upon arrival of new generic knowledge, for instance when the agent happens to acquire a new default rule on his domain of investigation. Then events that were thought to normally occur are now considered less normal. For instance a medical doctor does not modify his medical knowledge when he gets new test results for a patient. He just revises his beliefs about the patient state. However, a medical doctor may revise his medical knowledge when he reads a specialized book or attends a medicine conference. Several authors like Spohn (1988), Williams (1994), Boutilier and Goldszmidt (1995), Darwiche and Pearl (1997), Dubois and Prade (1997), Benferhat et al.(1999c) have considered tools and principles for generic knowledge revision, although the distinction between the two types of revision is not always so clear from reading these works. Indeed, there is no consensus on a general and systematic approach to that kind of epistemic change in the literature, and the same can be observed for problems of revision of Bayesian networks (which pertain to probability kinematics, see Domotor, 1985).

The AGM revision theory only assumes that a belief set is replaced by another belief set, and it gives minimal rationality constraints relating the prior and the posterior belief sets. Thus doing, it may wrongly suggest that the posterior belief set can indeed be derived from the prior one and the input information only. The confidence relation framework shows that this is not the case. The calculation of the posterior belief set does not use the prior belief set. The posterior belief set is built by means of plausible inference from the generic knowledge encoded in the confidence relation conditioned on the new context formed by all the available observations, including the new one. This is what we called "focusing" in previous publications (Dubois et al., 1998b).

The representation theorem of the AGM theory actually lays bare the existence of an epistemic entrenchment relation (basically the dual of a possibility relation, see Dubois and Prade, 1991) and confirms that the construction of the revised belief set can be expressed by conditioning this particular confidence relation on the input information. This strategy is the same as the one adopted when querying a Bayesian net on the basis of new observations. However, in the AGM theory, the epistemic entrenchment looks like a technical by-product of the formal construction, while we claim that this is the primitive object, and that all the belief sets are derived from it in every context. Concerning the iteration of contingent belief revision, suppose two inputs are obtained in a row. Note that since the inputs are considered as sure observations about a static world, they cannot be contradictory. When the second input arrives, a sound strategy is, in the AGM setting, to revise the original belief set (not the one revised by the first input) by the conjunction of the two inputs. In practice, The case when two observations are inconsistent suggests that, either one of them is wrong, or they do not pertain to the same case.

Some people have claimed that in order to iterate AGM belief revision, one needs to construct not only the new belief set, but also a new epistemic entrenchment relation. In the scope of the revision of contingent beliefs induced by generic knowledge, this is questionable. On the contrary, the same epistemic entrenchment should remain across successive revisions of contingent beliefs caused by new contingent observations. Similarly, in probabilistic reasoning (Pearl, 1988), the same Bayesian network is used when new observations come in. If the epistemic entrenchment must be revised, it means that the input information is a piece of generic knowledge, and such a kind of revision is not the purpose of the AGM theory.

6 Conclusion

To sum up, the framework of confidence relations provides a unified view of non-monotonic and probabilistic reasoning. It also points out the distinction between the revision of contingent beliefs (by focusing the confidence relations on the proper context formed by the observations) and the revision of the confidence relation itself. This distinction is made clear by considering that the information possessed by an agent is made of three items: sure observations, generic knowledge and inferred contingent beliefs. From a computational point of view, plausible inference from a confidence relation can be achieved using a standard theorem-prover in propositional logic, and comes down to a sequence of consistency tests. When the confidence relation takes the form of a unique possibility relation, like in system Z and the like, the problem can be encoded in possibilistic logic, which handles prioritized propositional bases, with a complexity of SAT $*$ $\mathrm{Log}_2 n$ if there are n priority levels (Lang, 2001).

Future lines of research in the ordinal approach to plausible reasoning include the modeling of independence (Dubois et al. 1997, Ben Amor et al. 2000) and the study of graphical models that would be the qualitative counterpart of Bayesian networks (Benferhat et al. 1999b). Some results indicate that possibilistic logic bases, conditional knowledge bases and possibilistic nets have the same expressive power (Benferhat et al., 2001a). However it is no clear which is the most natural framework for knowledge elicitation, and for practical computation. Lastly, by bridging the gap between probability and non-monotonic reasoning, the confidence relation approach paves the way to the data-driven learning of default rules.

Acknowledgements. This paper owes much to Salem Benferhat, Hélène Fargier, Jérome Lang et Henri Prade and reflects our shared concerns and joint past works.

References

E.W. Adams (1975) *The Logic of Conditionals*. Dordrecht: D. Reidel.

C.E.P. Alchourrón, P. Gärdenfors, D. Makinson (1985), On the logic of theory change: Partial meet functions for contraction and revision. *J. of Symbolic Logic*, 50, 510-530.

N. Ben Amor, S. Benferhat, D. Dubois, H. Geffner and H. Prade (2000) Independence in qualitative uncertainty frameworks. *Proc. 7th Int. Conf. on Principles of Knowledge Representation and Reasoning (KR 2000),* Breckenridge, Co, 235-246.

S. Benferhat, D. Dubois, H. Prade (1997) Nonmonotonic reasoning, conditional objects and possibility theory, *Artificial Intelligence*, 92, 259-276

S. Benferhat, D. Dubois, H. Prade (1998) Practical Handling of Exception-tainted rules and independence information in possibilistic logic. *Applied Intelligence*. 9, p. 101-127.

S. Benferhat, D. Dubois, H. Prade (1999a) Possibilistic and standard probabilistic semantics of conditional knowledge. *J. Logic & Computation*, 9, 873-895

S. Benferhat, D. Dubois, L. Garcia, H. Prade (1999b) Directed possibilistic graphs and possibilistic logic. In: *Information, Uncertainty and Fusion*, B. Bouchon-Meunier, R.R. Yager, L. A. Zadeh,.Eds: Kluwer Academic, pp. 365-379.

S. Benferhat, D. Dubois, O. Papini. (1999c) A sequential reversible belief revision method based on polynomials. *Proc 16th Nat Conf. on Artificial Intelligence, (AAAI'99)*, AAAI Press & The MIT Press, 733-738.

S. Benferhat, D. Dubois, S. Kaci (2001a) Bridging logical, comparative and graphical possibilistic representation frameworks, *Sixth European Conf. on Symbolic and Quantitative Approaches to Reasoning with Uncertainty (ECSQARU-2001),* LNAI series, Springer Verlag, Berlin.

S. Benferhat, D. Dubois, S. Lagrue, H. Prade (2001b) Towards learning default rules by identifying big-stepped probabilities. *Joint 9th IFSA World Congress and 20th NAFIPS International Conference*, Vancouver, Ca.

C. Boutilier, M. Goldszmidt M. (1995) Revision by conditionals beliefs. In: *Conditionals: From Philosophy to Computer Sciences* (G. Crocco, L. Fariñas del Cerro, A. Herzig, eds.), Oxford University Press, Oxford, UK

L.J. Cohen (1977) *The Probable and the Provable*. Clarendon Press Oxford.

A. Darwiche, J. Pearl J. (1997) On the logic of iterated belief revision. *Artificial Intelligence*, 89, 1997, 1-29.

B. De Finetti (1937) La prévision, ses lois logiques et ses sources subjectives. *Ann. Inst. Poincaré*, 7, 1-68.

B. De Finetti (1974) *Theory of Probability*, Wiley, New York.

D. Dubois (1986) Belief structures, possibility theory and decomposable confidence measures on finite sets. *Computers and Artificial Intelligence*, 5(5), 403-416..

Z. Domotor (1985) Probability kinematics — Conditional and entropy principles. *Synthese*, 63, 74-115.

D. Dubois, J. Lang, and H. Prade (1994). Possibilistic logic. In D.M. Gabbay et al., editors, *Handbook of Logic in Artificial Intelligence and Logic Programming,* Vol. 3, p. 439-513. Oxford University Press.

D. Dubois, L. Farinas, A. Herzig,H. Prade (1997): Qualitative relevance and independence: A roadmap. *Proc. 15th Int. Joint Conf. on A.I.*, Nagoya, 62-67. Extended version In: *Fuzzy Sets, Logics and Reasoning about Knowledge* (Dubois, D., Prade, H., Klement, E.P., eds.), Kluwer, Academic Publ.,325--359, 1999.

D. Dubois, H. Fargier, H. Prade (1998a) Comparative uncertainty, belief functions and accepted beliefs. *Proc. of the 14th Conf. on Uncertainty in Artificial Intelligence* (G. Cooper, S. Moral, eds.), Madison, WI, Morgan & Kaufmann, San Francisco, CA, 113-120.

D. Dubois, S. Moral and H. Prade.(1998b) Belief change rules in ordinal and numerical uncertainty theories *Handbook of Defeasible Reasoning and Uncertainty Management Systems — Vol3.* Kluwer Academic Publ., Dordrecht, The Netherlands, 311-392.

D. Dubois, H. Fargier, H. Prade (2001) Ordinal and numerical representations of acceptance. In preparation.

D. Dubois, H. Prade (1991) Epistemic entrenchment and possibilistic logic. *Artificial Intelligence*, 50, 223-239.

D. Dubois, H. Prade (1994a): Non-standard theories of uncertainty in knowledge representation and reasoning. *The Knowledge Engineering Review*, 9(4), 399-416.

D. Dubois, H. Prade (1994b) Conditional objects as nonmonotonic consequence relationships, *IEEE Trans. on Systems, Man and Cybernetics*, 24(12), 1724-1740.

D. Dubois, H. Prade (1995a) Conditional objects, possibility theory and default rules. In Conditionals: From Philosophy to Computer Science (G. Crocco, L. Fariñas del Cerro, A. Herzig eds.), Oxford University Press, 311-346.

D. Dubois, H. Prade (1995b), Numerical representations of acceptance. *Proc. of the 11th Conf. on Uncertainty in Artificial Intelligence* (P. Besnard, S. Hanks, eds.), 149-156.

Dubois D., Prade H. (1997) A synthetic view of belief revision with uncertain inputs in the framework of possibility theory. *Int. J. of Approximate Reasoning*, 17(2/3), 295-324.

D. Dubois, H. Prade (1998) Possibility theory: qualitative and quantitative aspects. *Handbook on Defeasible Reasoning and Uncertainty Management Systems* — Vol. 1. Kluwer Academic Publ., Dordrecht, The Netherlands, 169-226

P. Gärdenfors (1988) *Knowledge in Flux*. MIT Press, Cambridge.

N. Friedman, J. Halpern (1996) Plausibility measures and default reasoning. *Proc of the 13th National Conf. on Artificial Intelligence (AAAI'96),* Portland, 1297-1304. To appear in J. Assoc. for Comp. Mach.

J. Halpern (1997) Defining relative likelihood in partially-ordered preferential structures. *J. AI Research*, 7, 1-24

B. O. Koopman (1940) The bases of probabilty. *Bull. Am. Math. Soc.* 46, 763-774.

S. Kraus, D. Lehmann, M. Magidor (1990) Nonmonotonic reasoning, preferential models and cumulative logics. *Artificial Intelligence*, 44, 167-207.

H. E. Kyburg (1988) Knowledge. In: *Uncertainty in Artificial Intelligence* vol 2, J. F. Lemmer and L. N. Kanal eds, Elsevier, 263-272.

J. Lang (2000) Possibilistic logic: complexity and algorithms. *Handbook on Defeasible Reasoning and Uncertainty Management Systems* — Vol. 5. Kluwer Academic Publ., Dordrecht, The Netherlands, 169-226

D. Lehmann, M. Magidor (1992) What does a conditional knowledge base entail? *Artificial Intelligence*, 55(1), 1-60.

D. Lewis (1973) *Counterfactuals*. Basil Blackwell, London.

J. Paris (1994) *The Uncertain Reasoner's Companion*. Cambridge University Press, Cambridge, UK.

D. Makinson and P. Gärdenfors (1991) Relations between the logic of theory change and nonmonotonic reasoning. In : *The Logic of Theory Change* (A. Fürmann, M. Morreau, Eds), LNAI 465, Sprnger Verlag, 185-205

J. Pearl (1988). *Probabilistic Reasoning Intelligent Systems: Networks of Plausible Inference,* Morgan Kaufmann, San Mateo, CA.

J. Pearl (1990) System Z: a natural ordering of defaults with tractable applications to default reasoning. *Proc. of the 3rd Conf. on the Theoretical Aspects of Reasonig About Knowledge (TARK'90),* Morgan and Kaufmann, 121-135.

D. Poole (1991) The effect of knowledge on belief: conditioning, specificity and the lottery paradox in defaut reasoning. *Artificial Intelligence*, 49, 281-307

L.J. Savage (1972) *The Foundations of Statistics*. Dover, New York

G. L. S. Shackle (1961). *Decision, Order and Time in Human Affairs*, (2nd edition), Cambridge University Press, UK.

Y. Shoham (1988). *Reasoning About Change — Time and Causation from the Standpoint of Artificial Intelligence,* The MIT Press, Cambridge, MA.

P. Snow (1999) Diverse confidence levels in a probabilistic semantics for conditional logics. *Artificial Intelligence* 113, 269-279.

W. Spohn (1988) Ordinal conditional functions: A dynamic theory of epistemic states. In W. Harper, and B. Skyrms, editors, *Causation in Decision, Belief Change and Statistics,* pages 105-134.

M.A. Williams (1994) Transmutations of knowledge systems. *Proc. of the 4th Inter. Conf. on Principles of Knowledge Representation and Reasoning (KR'94)* (J. Doyle, E. Sandewall, P. Torasso, eds.), Bonn, Germany, 1994, Morgan & Kaufmann, San Mateo, CA, 619-629.

Zadeh L. A. (1978). Fuzzy sets as a basis for a theory of possibility, *Fuzzy Sets and Systems*, **1**, 3-28.

Author Index

Lecture Notes in Artificial Intelligence (LNAI)

Vol. 2070: L. Monostori, J. Váncza, M. Ali (Eds.), Engineering of Intelligent Systems. Proceedings, 2001. XVIII, 951 pages. 2001.

Vol. 2080: D.W. Aha, I. Watson (Eds.), Case-Based Reasoning Research and Development. Proceedings, 2001. XII, 758 pages. 2001.

Vol. 2083: R. Goré, A. Leitsch, T. Nipkow (Eds.), Automated Reasoning. Proceedings, 2001. XV, 708 pages. 2001.

Vol. 2086: M. Luck, V. Mařík, O. Stěpánková, R. Trappl (Eds.), Multi-Agent Systems and Applications. Proceedings, 2001. X, 437 pages. 2001.

Vol. 2087: G. Kern-Isberner, Conditionals in Nonmonotonic Reasoning and Belief Revision. X, 190 pages. 2001.

Vol. 2099: P. de Groote, G. Morrill, C. Retoré (Eds.), Logical Aspects of Computational Linguistics. Proceedings, 2001. VIII, 311 pages. 2001.

Vol. 2100: R. Küsters, Non-Standard Inferences in Description Logics. X, 250 pages. 2001.

Vol. 2101: S. Quaglini, P. Barahona, S. Andreassen (Eds.), Artificial Intelligence in Medicine. Proceedings, 2001. XIV, 469 pages. 2001.

Vol. 2103: M. Hannebauer, J. Wendler, E. Pagello (Eds.), Balancing Reactivity and Social Deliberation in Multi-Agent Systems. VIII, 237 pages. 2001.

Vol. 2109: M. Bauer, P.J. Gmytrasiewicz, J. Vassileva (Eds.), User Modeling 2001. Proceedings, 2001. XIII, 318 pages. 2001.

Vol. 2111: D. Helmbold, B. Williamson (Eds.), Computational Learning Theory. Proceedings, 2001. IX, 631 pages. 2001.

Vol. 2112: R. Kowalczyk, S.W. Loke, N.E. Reed, G. Williams (Eds.), Advances in Artificial Intelligence. Proceedings, 2000. IX, 363 pages. 2001.

Vol. 2116: V. Akman, P. Bouquet, R. Thomason, R.A. Young (Eds.), Modeling and Using Context. Proceedings, 2001. XII, 472 pages. 2001.

Vol. 2117: M. Beynon, C.L. Nehaniv, K. Dautenhahn (Eds.), Cognitive Technology: Instruments of Mind. Proceedings, 2001. XV, 522 pages. 2001.

Vol. 2120: H.S. Delugach, G. Stumme (Eds.), Conceptual Structures: Broadening the Base. Proceedings, 2001. X, 377 pages. 2001.

Vol. 2123: P. Perner (Ed.), Machine Learning and Data Mining in Pattern Recognition. Proceedings, 2001. XI, 363 pages. 2001.

Vol. 2132: S.-T. Yuan, M. Yokoo (Eds.), Intelligent Agents: Specification, Modeling, and Application. Proceedings, 2001. X, 237 pages. 2001.

Vol. 2143: S. Benferhat, P. Besnard (Eds.), Symbolic and Quantitative Approaches to Reasoning with Uncertainty. Proceedings, 2001. XIV, 818 pages. 2001.

Vol. 2148: A. Nareyek (Ed.), Local Search for Planning and Scheduling. Proceedings, 2000. IX, 171 pages. 2001.

Vol. 2155: H. Bunt, R. J. Beun (Eds.), Cooperative Multimodal Communication. Proceedings, 1998. VIII, 251 pages. 2001.

Vol. 2157: C. Rouveirol, M. Sebag (Eds.), Inductive Logic Programming. Proceedings, 2001. X, 261 pages. 2001.

Vol. 2159: J. Kelemen, P. Sosík (Eds.), Advances in Artificial Life. Proceedings, 2001. XIX, 724 pages. 2001.

Vol. 2166: V. Matoušek, P. Mautner, R. Mouček, K. Taušer (Eds.), Text, Speech and Dialogue. Proceedings, 2001. XIII, 542 pages. 2001.

Vol. 2167: L. De Raedt, P. Flach (Eds.), Machine Learning: ECML 2001. Proceedings, 2001. XVII, 618 pages. 2001.

Vol. 2168: L. De Raedt, A. Siebes (Eds.), Principles of Data Mining and Knowledge Discovery. Proceedings, 2001. XVII, 510 pages. 2001.

Vol. 2173: T. Eiter, W. Faber, M. Truszczynski (Eds.), Logic Programming and Nonmonotonic Reasoning. Proceedings, 2001. XI, 444 pages. 2001.

Vol. 2174: F. Baader, G. Brewka, T. Eiter (Eds.), KI 2001: Advances in Artificial Intelligence. Proceedings, 2001. XIII, 471 pages. 2001.

Vol. 2175: F. Esposito (Ed.), AI*IA 2001: Advances in Artificial Intelligence. Proceedings, 2001. XII, 396 pages. 2001.

Vol. 2182: M. Klusch, F. Zambonelli (Eds.), Cooperative Information Agents V. Proceedings, 2001. XII, 288 pages. 2001.

Vol. 2190: A. de Antonio, R. Aylett, D. Ballin (Eds.), Intelligent Virtual Agents. Proceedings, 2001. VIII, 245 pages. 2001.

Vol. 2198: N. Zhong, Y. Yao, J. Liu, S. Ohsuga (Eds.), Web Intelligence: Research and Development. Proceedings, 2001. XVI, 615 pages. 2001.

Vol. 2225: N. Abe, R. Khardon, T. Zeugmann (Eds.), Algorithmic Learning Theory. Proceedings, 2001. XI, 379 pages. 2001.

Vol. 2226: K.P. Jantke, A. Shinohara (Eds.), Discovery Science. Proceedings, 2001. XII, 494 pages. 2001.

Vol. 2250: R. Nieuwenhuis, A. Voronkov (Eds.), Logic for Programming, Artificial Intelligence, and Reasoning. Proceedings, 2001. XV, 738 pages. 2001.

Vol. 2256: M. Stumptner, D. Corbett, M. Brooks (Eds.), AI 2001: Advances in Artificial Intelligence. Proceedings, 2001. XII, 666 pages. 2001.

Lecture Notes in Computer Science

Vol. 2201: G.D. Abowd, B. Brumitt, S. Shafer (Eds.), Ubicomp 2001: Ubiquitous Computing. Proceedings, 2001. XIII, 372 pages. 2001.

Vol. 2202: A. Restivo, S. Ronchi Della Rocca, L. Roversi (Eds.), Theoretical Computer Science. Proceedings, 2001. XI, 440 pages. 2001.

Vol. 2204: A. Brandstädt, V.B. Le (Eds.), Graph-Theoretic Concepts in Computer Science. Proceedings, 2001. X, 329 pages. 2001.

Vol. 2205: D.R. Montello (Ed.), Spatial Information Theory. Proceedings, 2001. XIV, 503 pages. 2001.

Vol. 2206: B. Reusch (Ed.), Computational Intelligence. Proceedings, 2001. XVII, 1003 pages. 2001.

Vol. 2207: I.W. Marshall, S. Nettles, N. Wakamiya (Eds.), Active Networks. Proceedings, 2001. IX, 165 pages. 2001.

Vol. 2208: W.J. Niessen, M.A. Viergever (Eds.), Medical Image Computing and Computer-Assisted Intervention – MICCAI 2001. Proceedings, 2001. XXXV, 1446 pages. 2001.

Vol. 2209: W. Jonker (Ed.), Databases in Telecommunications II. Proceedings, 2001. VII, 179 pages. 2001.

Vol. 2210: Y. Liu, K. Tanaka, M. Iwata, T. Higuchi, M. Yasunaga (Eds.), Evolvable Systems: From Biology to Hardware. Proceedings, 2001. XI, 341 pages. 2001.

Vol. 2211: T.A. Henzinger, C.M. Kirsch (Eds.), Embedded Software. Proceedings, 2001. IX, 504 pages. 2001.

Vol. 2212: W. Lee, L. Mé, A. Wespi (Eds.), Recent Advances in Intrusion Detection. Proceedings, 2001. X, 205 pages. 2001.

Vol. 2213: M.J. van Sinderen, L.J.M. Nieuwenhuis (Eds.), Protocols for Multimedia Systems. Proceedings, 2001. XII, 239 pages. 2001.

Vol. 2214: O. Boldt, H. Jürgensen (Eds.), Automata Implementation. Proceedings, 1999. VIII, 183 pages. 2001.

Vol. 2215: N. Kobayashi, B.C. Pierce (Eds.), Theoretical Aspects of Computer Software. Proceedings, 2001. XV, 561 pages. 2001.

Vol. 2216: E.S. Al-Shaer, G. Pacifici (Eds.), Management of Multimedia on the Internet. Proceedings, 2001. XIV, 373 pages. 2001.

Vol. 2217: T. Gomi (Ed.), Evolutionary Robotics. Proceedings, 2001. XI, 139 pages. 2001.

Vol. 2218: R. Guerraoui (Ed.), Middleware 2001. Proceedings, 2001. XIII, 395 pages. 2001.

Vol. 2220: C. Johnson (Ed.), Interactive Systems. Proceedings, 2001. XII, 219 pages. 2001.

Vol. 2221: D.G. Feitelson, L. Rudolph (Eds.), Job Scheduling Strategies for Parallel Processing. Proceedings, 2001. VII, 207 pages. 2001.

Vol. 2224: H.S. Kunii, S. Jajodia, A. Sølvberg (Eds.), Conceptual Modeling – ER 2001. Proceedings, 2001. XIX, 614 pages. 2001.

Vol. 2225: N. Abe, R. Khardon, T. Zeugmann (Eds.), Algorithmic Learning Theory. Proceedings, 2001. XI, 379 pages. 2001. (Subseries LNAI).

Vol. 2226: K.P. Jantke, A. Shinohara (Eds.), Discovery Science. Proceedings, 2001. XII, 494 pages. 2001. (Subseries LNAI).

Vol. 2227: S. Boztaş, I.E. Shparlinski (Eds.), Applied Algebra, Algebraic Algorithms and Error-Correcting Codes. Proceedings, 2001. XII, 398 pages. 2001.

Vol. 2229: S. Qing, T. Okamoto, J. Zhou (Eds.), Information and Communications Security. Proceedings, 2001. XIV, 504 pages. 2001.

Vol. 2230: T. Katila, I.E. Magnin, P. Clarysse, J. Montagnat, J. Nenonen (Eds.), Functional Imaging and Modeling of the Heart. Proceedings, 2001. XI, 158 pages. 2001.

Vol. 2232: L. Fiege, G. Mühl, U. Wilhelm (Eds.), Electronic Commerce. Proceedings, 2001. X, 233 pages. 2001.

Vol. 2233: J. Crowcroft, M. Hofmann (Eds.), Networked Group Communication. Proceedings, 2001. X, 205 pages. 2001.

Vol. 2234: L. Pacholski, P. Ružička (Eds.), SOFSEM 2001: Theory and Practice of Informatics. Proceedings, 2001. XI, 347 pages. 2001.

Vol. 2237: P. Codognet (Ed.), Logic Programming. Proceedings, 2001. XI, 365 pages. 2001.

Vol. 2239: T. Walsh (Ed.), Principles and Practice of Constraint Programming – CP 2001. Proceedings, 2001. XIV, 788 pages. 2001.

Vol. 2240: G.P. Picco (Ed.), Mobile Agents. Proceedings, 2001. XIII, 277 pages. 2001.

Vol. 2241: M. Jünger, D. Naddef (Eds.), Computational Combinatorial Optimization. IX, 305 pages. 2001.

Vol. 2242: C.A. Lee (Ed.), Grid Computing – GRID 2001. Proceedings, 2001. XII, 185 pages. 2001.

Vol. 2250: R. Nieuwenhuis, A. Voronkov (Eds.), Logic for Programming, Artificial Intelligence, and Reasoning. Proceedings, 2001. XV, 738 pages. 2001. (Subseries LNAI).

Vol. 2248: C. Boyd (Ed.), Advances in Cryptology – ASIACRYPT 2001. Proceedings, 2001. XI, 603 pages. 2001.

Vol. 2256: M. Stumptner, D. Corbett, M. Brooks (Eds.), AI 2001: Advances in Artificial Intelligence. Proceedings, 2001. XII, 666 pages. 2001. (Subseries LNAI).